PRIVATE LAW
IN THE INTERNATIONAL ARENA

LIBER AMICORUM KURT SIEHR

T.M.C. ASSER INSTITUUT

PRIVATE LAW
IN THE INTERNATIONAL ARENA

From National Conflict Rules Towards
Harmonization and Unification

❖ **LIBER AMICORUM KURT SIEHR** ❖

Edited by

Jürgen Basedow ◆ Isaak Meier ◆ Anton K. Schnyder
Talia Einhorn ◆ Daniel Girsberger

T·M·C·ASSER PRESS

Published by T.M.C.ASSER PRESS,
P.O.Box 16163, 2500 BD The Hague, The Netherlands

Sold and distributed in the U.S.A. and Canada
by Kluwer Law International,
675 Massachusetts Avenue, Cambridge, MA 02139, U.S.A.

In all other countries (except Switzerland) sold and distributed
by Kluwer Law International,
P.O.Box 85889, 2508 CN The Hague, The Netherlands.

Sold and distributed in Switzerland by
Schulthess Juristische Medien AG, Postfach 4438, CH-8022 Zürich
Switzerland, ISBN 3-7255-4096-9

ISBN 90-6704-124-6
© 2000, T.M.C.ASSER PRESS, The Hague, The Netherlands

T.M.C. Asser Instituut – Institute for Private and Public International Law,
International Commercial Arbitration and European Law
Institute Address: R.J. Schimmelpennincklaan 20-22, The Hague, The Netherlands;
P.O. Box 30461, 2500 GL The Hague, The Netherlands; Tel.: (31-70)3420300;
Fax: (31-70)3420359; Website: www.asser.nl
Over thirty years, the T.M.C. Asser Institute has developed into a leading scientific research institute in the field of international law. It covers private international law, public international law, including international humanitarian law, the law of the European Union, the law of international commercial arbitration and increasingly, also, international economic law and the law of international commerce. Conducting scientific research either fundamental or applied, in the aforementioned domains, is the main activity of the Institute. In addition, the Institute organizes congresses and postgraduate courses, undertakes contract-research and operates its own publishing house. Because of its inter-university background, the Institute often cooperates with Dutch law faculties as well as with various national and foreign institutions. The Institute organizes Asser College Europe, a project in cooperation with East and Central European countries whereby research and educational projects are organized and implemented.

Foreword

Ihr naht euch wieder, schwankende Gestalten,
Die Früh sich einst dem trüben Blick gezeigt.
Once more you hover near me, forms and faces
Seen long ago with troubled youthful gaze.

Johann Wolfgang von Goethe,
Faust, Zueignung/ Dedication[*]

This book is a dedication made in deep appreciation, long-standing friendship and affection, to Prof. Dr. iur. KURT SIEHR, a true academic scholar, whose pursuit of knowledge has brought him very close to many people from a whole variety of cultures and backgrounds all over the Globe.

This may seem a paradox. Kurt Siehr is first and foremost a man of books. On the door leading to his office is written "Das Paradies habe ich mir immer als eine Art Bibliothek vorgestellt" (Jorge Luis Borges). He has lived most of his life in his own library among the books that he has collected with the deepest interest and care, every visit to bookshops and antiquarian bookstores at home and abroad adding new, cherished treasures which can do nothing however to quench the thirst. Therefore, Siehr's knowledge seems to be drawn from paper. Even examination questions have often been based on opera libretti, books and occasionally film scripts. Yet, Siehr's insights and understanding for his fellow mankind is current, present not past. "It's in a book", says Alice when accused by Humpty Dumpty of listening at doors and behind trees or down chimneys, or she couldn't have known it.

Siehr's love for books comes from home. "In the beginning was the book". Born in Tilsit, East Prussia on 28 July 1935, Kurt Siehr was raised and fed on books. His

---

[*] Translated by Philip Wayne (Penguin 1949) at p. 29.

J. Basedow et al., eds., Private Law in the International Arena – Liber Amicorum Kurt Siehr
© 2000, T.M.C.Asser Press, The Hague, The Netherlands

father, Dr. Friedrich Carl Alfred Siehr, a lawyer, was a passionate collector of first editions. The volumes of the Brockhaus Encyclopedia were devoured by the Siehr children even before they were strong enough to carry them around. Mrs. Else Siehr's bedtime story reading was a favourite family pastime for them all. The war uprooted the family. In the summer of 1944 the Siehrs had to move first to Munich and then to Hohenems (now in Austria). In 1945 it was necessary to make another move to Hamburg and then again to Maschen (near Lüneburg). Finally, the family settled down in Buxtehude in 1949, a year after Dr. Siehr had started his practice as a lawyer and notary there. Although not much had survived from the original book collection, the Siehr family very soon turned their new home into the "Bookstehude" that it still is to this date.

To the family it was always clear that Kurt Siehr would become a lawyer. He was named after his great uncle, Dr. Kurt Siehr, judge and Senatspräsident in Berlin, well-known in legal circles, author of the second edition of *Freiwillige Gerichtsbarkeit* (Berlin 1930), and deeply loved and appreciated by the family. As soon as Kurt Siehr graduated from high school he started studying law and, at the same time, worked as a student at the Max Planck Institute for Foreign Private and Private International Law in Hamburg, thus acquiring access to the great library. Following his first bar examination in 1960, in recognition of his excellent scholarly achievements, Siehr was awarded a Ford Scholarship to study towards a degree of "Master of Comparative Law" (M.C.L.) at the law faculty of the University of Michigan, Ann Arbor in 1962/63. The young scholar was deeply impressed with the American "case method" used in "lectures" and, no less, with the relationship between the American law professors and their students, all lively described in the letter he wrote together with his colleague Hein Kötz, published in *RabelsZ* 28 (1964) 395.

After his return to Germany, Siehr joined the Max Planck Institute in Hamburg first as a research assistant and later as a research associate, passed his second bar examination in 1967 and completed his doctoral dissertation in 1970 on the effects of the law on children born out of wedlock on private international law and international procedural law. It was at the Max Planck Institute that he had his first opportunity to write, together with his colleague Eike von Hippel, a legal opinion on art and law in the famous case of *Kunstsammlungen zu Weimar* v. *Elicofon* (358 F. Supp. 747), involving two Dürer paintings stolen from the Weimar Art Galleries during the Second World War. These were found later in the apartment of their *bona fide* purchaser, the New York lawyer Edward Elicofon, and eventually returned to Germany, following the lawsuit brought in New York for their recovery.

At the Max Planck Institute the man of books turned out to be not only an ardent reader but also a close and intent listener to music, especially operas, to the sounds of different languages, and, in particular, to people. Kurt Siehr, who diligently worked there day and night, made the Institute a second home to many visitors, whom he would invite to excellent cups of fresh tea, and then use the time to befriend, share and instruct. It was through his eyes that they came to regard the Institute as the Paradise from which one is never expelled for eating from the Tree of Knowledge. For many of those, who considered themselves not only "Kurzbesucher" of the Institute but no less his personal "Kurts-Besucher", Siehr's departure to Zurich in 1991 has left a sense of longing that can hardly be subdued.

One of these visitors, the late Ze'ev Zeltner, Professor of Law at Tel-Aviv University and President of the Israeli District and Appellate Court in Tel Aviv, initiated the life-long bond with Tel-Aviv University. Another visitor, Prof. Dr. Max Keller from the University of Zurich, not only became impressed with Siehr, but also managed to persuade him to join the law faculty there. It was therefore at Zurich that Siehr obtained his Habilitation in 1979. Privatdozent Siehr then became an extraordinary Professor, and finally in 1991 – the academic successor of Max Keller, a truly extraordinary Ordinarius. Many students have had the good fortune to hear his lectures and participate in his seminars in Zurich. The luckiest of them all were, of course, those (more than 100 in number!) who became his doctoral students, and for whom he has been a mentor and a friend, the coach they could not and would not do without, the severe critic who would not hesitate to condemn the student who dares just to play with words instead of conveying the true understanding which results from serious research. "In the beginning was the thought".

The writings of Kurt Siehr not only speak volumes. They read volumes! The reader of this book would be well-advised to turn first to the list of publications of its Jubilar at the very end of this book. The list is not comprehensive as it does not contain works edited by Siehr. Those, though clearly bearing his stamp, are not even mentioned by Siehr among his works. But the reader will find in the list the many subjects that have preoccupied their author and made him deeply appreciated not only in Germany and Switzerland where he has resided and worked, but also carried his name all over Europe, East and West, to the United States, the Far East and the Middle East. Siehr has become a most favoured guest lecturer in places as far apart as Hamburg, Oslo, Tel-Aviv, Rome, Bari, Naples, Dubrovnik, and The Hague, to name just a few. Academics and practitioners alike have drawn numerous answers from this fountain of knowledge. Siehr has taken an active part in law reforms of private international law in many countries. Keller/ Siehr's short introduction to private international law is a masterpiece of clarity and conciseness. Keller/ Siehr's *Allgemeine Lehren des internationalen Privatrechts* is a masterpiece of thoroughness and deep understanding. There are two more books in preparation on the teachings of private international law, clarifying their intricacies and making their very difficult subject-matter a pleasure to study. If we do not mention other writings here it is only for lack of space not merit.

Of special interest and importance are Siehr's contributions in the field of cultural property law. His able mind has brought the treasures of Helen of Troy under the canopy of the teachings of law. As is clearly manifest in his fascinating Hague Lectures, accompanied at the time by colourful slides (published, alas without those illustrations, in the *Recueil des Cours* 1993-VI), this subject requires intimate knowledge of private and public international law, as well as a good understanding of the substantive laws of different countries. Siehr has been the perfect person to master this field, not least because of his passionate love for art and aesthetics combined with his high moral and ethical standards. His chronicles of art and law published twice a year in the *International Journal of Cultural Property* are often the highlight of that publication.

In addition, Siehr has been a member of the German Society of International Law, the Swiss Association of International Law, the International Law Association (Swiss Branch), the International Cultural Property Society, the International Academy of Estate and Trust Law, the Turkish Law Association, the International Association of Judicial Law, the Association of Family Law, the Association of Procedural Law, the German Association of Comparative Law, Groupe européen de droit international privé, German Council of Private International Law, the ILA (International Law Association) Committee on International Civil and Commercial Litigation and the ILA Cultural Heritage Law Committee. Siehr is also a Corresponding Member of UNIDROIT, Rome, and an Honorary Member of the European Law Students Association (ELSA). His membership is an active one. He never fails to come up with new ideas concerning subject-matters deserving further study and then to carry out an appreciable part of the research himself.

This book is dedicated to a rich man. "All that the castle holds within its depths is his already . . . Treasure upon treasure heap in fair array." Kurt Siehr's richness is of the kind that cannot be misappropriated. Quite the contrary! It can – lo, ein Wunder! – be shared ten times more and just keep growing every time it is being further shared.

Yet, we firmly believe that a special gift to make is NOT useless. Therefore, dear Kurt, we give you this modest book with the confidence that you will repay us manifold with your books, articles, legal opinions, and, not least of all, with all those delightful moments that you will continue to share with us in the future.

Jürgen Basedow   Isaak Meier   Anton K. Schnyder

            Talia Einhorn   Daniel Girsberger

Summary Table of Contents

X

XII

Table of Contents

Wilfried Fiedler

Daniel Girsberger

XX

XXII

Jan Kropholler

**Das Haager Kinderschutzübereinkommen von 1996 – Wesentliche Verbesserungen
im Minderjährigenschutz** **379**

Ole Lando

The Principles of European Contract Law and the *lex mercatoria* **391**

Isaak Meier

Franco Mosconi

Rui Manuel Moura Ramos

James A.R. Nafziger

Lennart Pålsson

Hans Michael Riemer

XXXV

Die einfache Gesellschaft oder die Gesellschaft des bürgerlichen Rechts – Aus der Sicht der Rechtsfähigkeit

Tuğrul Ansay[*]

1. EINLEITUNG

A.   Da das neue Millennium schon da ist und der 100. Jahrestag des Bürgerlichen Gesetzbuches bald in Deutschland gefeiert wird, möchte ich in einer Festschrift, die meinem guten alten Freund und Kollegen, dem deutsch/schweizerischen internationalen Juristen KURT SIEHR gewidmet sein wird, eine Institution aus der Entfernung betrachten, die in der Schweiz und in Deutschland sehr ähnlich geregelt wurde, und die Evolutionen des Rechts im Bereich der Rechtsfähigkeit der Personengesellschaften innerhalb des genannten Zeitraums miteinander vergleichen. Es handelt sich um denjenigen Gesellschaftstyp, der in Deutschland die Gesellschaft des bürgerlichen Rechts (GbR, auch BGB-Gesellschaft genannt) und in der Schweiz einfache Gesellschaft (eG) genannt wird. Allgemeine Parallelität in beiden Ländern besteht in der Regelung von mehreren Institutionen, da die 1911 in Kraft getretene Fassung des schweizerischen Bundesgesetzes über das Obligationenrecht (OR) vieles aus dem Anfang des Jahrhunderts stammenden deutschen Bürgerlichen Gesetzbuche (BGB) übernehmen konnte. Im Bereich der Personengesellschaften haben die Vorschriften dieselben Wurzeln.[1]

---

[*] Dr. iur. M.C.L. LL.M., em. Professor an der Universität Ankara/ Hamburg.

[1] Meier-Hayoz/Forstmoser, *Grundriss des schweizerischen Gesellschaftsrechts*, 7. Aufl. (1993) § 6 N. 21; Furrer, *Der gemeinsame Zweck als Grundbegriff und Abgrenzungskriterium im Recht der einfachen Gesellschaft* (Zürich 1996) S. 33. Siehe jedoch Furrer, S. 35 über die Verlustbeteiligung der Gesellschafter nach deutschem Recht.

J. Basedow et al., eds., Private Law in the International Arena – Liber Amicorum Kurt Siehr
© 2000, T.M.C.Asser Press, The Hague, The Netherlands

B. Die Personenvereinigungen werden aus unterschiedlichen Blickwinkeln grup-
piert. Davon können zwei in diesem Aufsatz von Bedeutung sein: Erstens: Zu wirtschaftlichen oder nichtwirtschaftlichen Zwecken gegründete Personenvereinigungen; Zweitens: Personenvereinigungen, die nach ihren Aussenverhältnissen als
juristische Personen oder nicht juristische Personen voneinander unterschieden
werden. Die Vereine, die juristische Personen sind, dürfen in beiden Ländern keine
wirschaftlichen Zwecke verfolgen. Die einfache Gesellschaft bzw. Gesellschaft
des bürgerlichen Rechts ist dagegen keine juristische Person. Beide werden jedoch
für wirtschaftliche oder nicht wirtschaftliche Zwecke gegründet. Nicht zu vergessen sind die Personenvereinigungen, die in der Regel Handelsgewerbe betreiben
aber keine juristischen Personen sind, wie z.B. Kollektivgesellschaften (KolG) in
der Schweiz und offene Handelsgesellschaften (oHG) in Deutschland.
     Der schweizerische Gesetzgeber hat die Personenvereinigungen in zwei Geset-
zen, nämlich im schweizerischen Zivilgesetzbuch (ZGB) und im OR geregelt. Die
Vorschriften über die Vereine, die keine wirschatlichen Zwecke haben sollen, sind
im ZGB zu finden. Dagegen sind die einfachen Gesellschaften und andere Gesell-
schaftsarten, darunter auch die Kollektiv- und Kommanditgesellschaften, Institutionen des OR. Trotz dieser formellen Zersplitterung in zwei Gesetze, sind die
unterscheidenden Linien zwischen dem Verein, der KolG und der eG nicht deutlich. Ein Verein, der nicht für wirschaftliche Zwecke gegründet werden darf, erhält
die juristische Persönlichkeit ohne Eintragung. So wird auch eine einfache Gesellschaft gegründet. Allerdings kann die einfache Gesellschaft auch wirschaftliche
Ziele verfolgen. Das soll in der Regel auch der Zweck einer KolG sein. Sie soll ausserdem im Handelsregister eingetragen werden. Die Eintragung hat jedoch nur eine
deklaratorische Wirkung wenn ein Handelsgewerbe betrieben wird (OR Art. 552
Abs. 2, 553).
     In Deutschland befinden sich die Vorschriften über die Vereine und die GbR im
BGB. Dagegen wurde die oHG im Handelsgesetzbuch (HGB) geregelt. Auch in
Deutschland wird die oHG für den Betrieb eines Handelsgewerbes gegründet und
im Handelsregister eingetragen. In beiden Ländern existieren jedoch Unterschiede
zwischen den einfachen und den sogenannten Handelsgesellschaften, bei denen die
Personen im Vordergrund stehen.

C. Die schweizersiche eG und die deutsche GbR erfüllen ähnliche Funktionen.
Die Vorschriften über die eG bzw. GbR sind auch auf die nicht rechtsfähigen Vereine und KolG bzw. oHG anwendbar.[2] Die Gründung einer eG oder GbR ist einfach.
Beide können ohne schriftliche Vereinbarung gegründet werden. Sie sind sozusagen Gesellschaften für alle Zwecke. Trotz der gesetzlichen Regelung im HGB, daß
die oHG in der Regel für den Betrieb eines Handelsgewerbes gegründet werden

---

[2] Schweiz. ZGB Art. 62, Schweiz. OR Art. 530 Abs. 2, 557 Abs. 2; BGB § 54, HGB § 105 Abs. 2.

soll,[3] trifft man in der Praxis mehrere Gewerbe treibende Gesellschaften des bürgerlichen Rechts. Die neuesten Statistiken zeigen, daß 1998 in Deutschland 36.171 von GbR gegründete Gewerbe neu angemeldet waren.[4] Weil in der Schweiz die einfachen Gesellschaften nicht im Handelsregister einzutragen sind, sind deren Zahlen nicht feststellbar. Über die „ausserordentlich grosse" Bedeutung der eG in der Schweiz gibt es allerdings keinen Zweifel.[5]

KolG und oHG zeigen ebenfalls den zwillingsartigen ähnlichen Rechtstatus. Beide sind keine juristischen Personen. In beiden Ländern wurde ihnen ein bestimmter Grad an Rechtsfähigkeit zuerkannt (OR Art. 562; HGB § 124).

2. DIE EINFACHE GESELLSCHAFT UND DIE GESELLSCHAFT DES BÜRGERLICHEN RECHTS

A. Aus § 705 BGB verstehen wir die GbR als eine Gesellschaft, in der die Gesellschafter untereinander durch den Gesellschaftsvertrag verpflichtet sind, die vereinbarten Beiträge zu leisten und einen gemeinsamen Zweck zu erreichen. Die einfache Gesellschaft wurde im OR als „die vertragsmäßige Verbindung von zwei oder mehreren Personen zur Erreichung eines gemeinsamen Zweckes mit gemeinsamen Kräften oder Mitteln" bezeichnet (OR Art. 530 Abs. 1).

Weder in der Schweiz noch in Deutschland wurden die Vorschriften im OR oder im BGB über die einfachen Gesellschaften oder die Gesellschaften des bürgerlichen Rechts seit dem Inkrafttreten der Gesetze geändert. Allerdings wurde in Deutschland im Jahre 1994 ein neuer Absatz zum § 736 BGB eingefügt. Danach gelten die für die Personenhandelsgesellschaften anwendbaren Regeln des HGB über die Begrenzung der Nachhaftung auch für die GbR.

B. Gesamthandsverhältnisse: In den beiden Ländern wurden die eG und GbR auf dem Gesamthandsverhältnisprinzip aufgebaut. Obwohl der deutsche Gesetzgeber zu der wissenschaftlichen Streitfrage über das Wesen der gesammten Hand nicht Stellung nehmen wollte[6] steht im Gesetz ausdrücklich, daß hier ein Gesammthandsverhältnis bestehe (BGB § 719). Das OR hat ähnlicherweise im Art. 544 Abs. 1 die Gesammthandsverhältnisse als Basis unter den Partnern vorgesehen, allerdings mit dem Ausdruck, daß „dingliche Rechte oder Forderungen, die an die Gesellschaft

---

[3] HGB § 105 Abs. 1.

[4] Angele, „Gewerbeanzeigen 1998", *Wirtschaft u. Statistik* (1999) 359ff., 362.

[5] Meier-Hayoz/Forstmoser (oben N. 1) § 8 N 76; Furrer (oben N. 1) S. 1; siehe auch Portmann, *Die Wahl der Rechtsform als betriebswirtschaftiches Problem für Klein- und Mittelbetriebe* (Zürich 1988) S. 56ff.

[6] *Protokolle der Kommission für die zweite Lesung des Entwurfs des Bürgerlichen Gesetzbuchs,* Bd. 2 (1898) S. 430.

übertragen oder für sie erworben sind, . . . den Gesellschaftern gemeinschaftlich [gehören]".[7]

Über das Gesamthandsverhältnis fehlen im BGB allgemeine Normen. Einige einzelne Institutionen, wie die Erbschaft unter mehreren Erbberechtigten, erhalten jedoch die Form der Gesamthand. In der Schweiz befinden sich allgemeine Regelungen über das Gesamthandseigentum im ZGB, die allerdings nur in bescheidenen drei Artikeln zusammengefasst sind (ZGB Art. 652-654).

Mit dem Gesamthandseigentum wird unter mehreren Personen ein Vermögen gebildet, das rechtlich getrennt behandelt und wegen seiner autonomen Natur in der Lehre Sondervermögen genannt wird.[8] Obwohl das Sondervermögen in beiden Ländern bekannt ist, wurde es als solches im Gesetz nicht besonders geregelt. Als passive Masse von Rechten und Verpflichtungen wird das Sondervermögen als ein Institution des Sachenrechts betrachtet. Sie gewinnt jedoch eine andere Dimension, wenn dieses Vermögen aktiviert wird und durch die Verwaltung von natürlichen oder juristischen Personen in den Rechtsverkehr eintritt. Solche autonomen Vermögen bestehen aber nicht nur wenn ein Gesamthandverhältnis unter mehreren Personen durch einen Vertrag oder durch gesetzlichen Vorschriften zustande kommt (eG; Erbengemeinschaft; Gütergemeinschaft im Familienrecht), sie können nämlich auch ohne zweckgebundenen Personenzusammenschluß existieren. So ist die Konkursmasse in der Schweiz als Sondervermögen betrachtet, dem in der Lehre ein bestimmter Grad an Rechtsfähigkeit anerkannt wurde.[9] Die Konkursmasse ist eine rechtlich autonome, vom Vermögen des Schuldners, Verwalters und der Gläubiger getrennt gehaltenes Sondervermögen.[10] Sie ist zum Abschluss bestimmter Rechtsgeschäfte fähig.[11] Ähnlicherweise erhalten die KolGen und oHGen als Gesammthandgesellschaften nach den gesetzlichen Vorschriften in eine bestimmten Umfang Rechtsfähigkeit. Diese Gesellschaften schliessen Geschäfte unter dem gemeinsamen Namen und die Gesellschafter sind verantwortlich für die unerlaubten Handlungen, die von den Vertretern der Gesellschaft anlässliche der Erfüllung der gesellschaftlichen Geschäfte begangen werden (OR Art. 567 Abs. 3).

---

[7] v. Steiger, „Gesellschaftsrecht, Allgemeiner Teil und Personengesellschaften", in *Schweizerisches Privatrecht* (Hrsg.: Gutzwiller u.a.) (1976) S. 381; Meier-Hayoz/Forstmoser (oben N. 1) § 8 N 13ff.

[8] So, v. Steiger (oben N. 7) S. 381.

[9] Amonn/Gasser, *Grundriss des Schuldbetreibungs- und Konkursrechts*, 6.Aufl. (1997) § 48, S. 390.

[10] Amonn/Gasser (oben N. 9) § 40 I, S. 314.

[11] Für das deutsche Recht Hanisch, *Rechtszuständigkeit der Konkursmasse* (1973) 275ff.

3. SCHEIDEWEG ZWISCHEN EINFACHE GESELLSCHAFTEN UND GESELLSCHAFTEN DES BÜRGERLICHEN RECHTS?

A. Eine im KolG oder oHG gesetzlich ausdrücklich vorgesehene Rechtsfähigkeit, ist für die eG oder GbR nicht selbstverständlich. Vor einigen Dekaden hätte man in deutschen Lehrbüchern über Gesellschaften,[12] genauso wie heute noch in der Schweiz, lesen können, daß eine einfache Gesellschaft keine juristische Person wäre und keine Rechtsfähigkeit hätte. Nach dem Gesamthandsprinzip des germanischen Rechts wurden nur die Gesellschafter als gemeinsamer Rechtsträger angenommen.[13] Diese früher für allgemein richtig gehaltene Ansicht zeigt seit den siebziger Jahren in der deutschen Lehre eine Kursänderung.

B. Die Entwicklung in Deutschland

(1) Basis im BGB

Für den Umstand, daß das BGB für die GbR ein Gesamthandsverhältnis vorgesehen hat, gibt es im BGB mehrere Hinweise. Aus dem Wortlaut verschiedener Vorschriften erhält man ausreichende Anregungen für eine zeitgemässe Auslegung der GbR. So spricht der Randtitel des § 718 vom „Gesellschaftsvermögen" und beschreibt, daß die „Beiträge der Gesellschafter und die durch die Geschäftsführung für die Gesellschaft erworbenen Gegenstände . . . gemeinschaftliches Vermögen der Gesellschaft" (Gesellschaftsvermögen) werden (BGB § 718 Abs. 1). Die Rolle des Gesellschaftsvermögens wurde in mehreren weiteren Bestimmungen zum Ausdruck gebracht (BGB §§ 719, 720, 730, 733, 735, 738 und 739).[14]

Das ursprüngliche Konzept, das im Urtext von § 718 vorgesehen wurde, wurde später zugunsten des Gesamthandsvermögens geändert.[15] In der Kommission wurde verdeutlicht, daß in die Gemeinschaft gelangende Vermögensstücke unmittelbar zu ihrem Zwecke dienstbar gemacht werden, „indem aus ihnen ein selbständiges Gesellschaftsvermögen gebildet wird", da das ganze Gesellschaftsvermögen „zur Deckung der Lasten und Schulden der Gesellschaft gebunden" ist, und daß aus dem Gesellschaftsvermögem „zunächst die Gesellschaftsgläubiger befriedigt" werden[16]. Das Gesellschaftsvermögen ist ein vom Vermögen der einzelnen Gesellschafter getrenntes Vermögen. Damit tritt man in den Bereich des Sondervermögens ein. Das

---

[12] Siehe Lehmann, *Gesellschaftsrecht*, 2.Aufl. (1959) S. 86; auch heute, Sprau, in Palandt, *Bürgerliches Gesetzbuch*, 58. Aufl. (1999) § 705 N 17.

[13] K. Schmidt, *Gesellschaftsrecht*, 3.Aufl. (1997) § 58 IV.

[14] K. Schmidt (oben N. 13) § 59 IV.

[15] *Protokolle der Kommission für die zweite Lesung des Entwurfs des Bürgerlichen Gesetzbuchs*, Bd. 2 (1898) S. 433.

[16] *Protokolle* (oben N. 15) S. 429.

Gesamtvermögen als Sondervermögen übernimmt eine aktive Rolle, wenn es durch die Gesamteigentümer in den Rechtsverkehr eingebracht wird. Das Sondervermögen bleibt also nicht blosses Objekt, sondern erhält den Status eines Rechtssubjekts. Das zweckgewidmete Vermögen wird „gegen Verfügungen einzelner nicht vertretungsbefugter Gesellschafter und gegen den Zugriff von Privatgläubigern" gesichert, und zwar unabhängig von der „jeweiligen personellen Zusammensetzung der Gesamthand".[17]

Darüberhinaus wurde durch die später stattfindenden Änderungen im Gesetz die Eigenständigkeit der Gesellschaft verstärkt. Zuerst wurden mit der Einfügung des zweiten Absatzes ins § 736 BGB die für Personenhandelsgesellschaften geltenden Nachhaftungsregeln sinngemäß für das Ausscheiden eines Gesellschafters aus einer GbR geltend gemacht. Dadurch wurde die GbR dem oHG angenähert.

Mit der Einfügung des § 1059a Abs. 2 ins BGB wurde eine Personengesellschaft, die mit der Fähigkeit ausgestattet ist, Rechte zu erwerben und Verbindlichkeiten einzugehen, einer juristischen Person gleich gestellt.[18]

(2)   In der Lehre

Der Anstoss für eine neue Auslegung des Gesamthandsverhältnisses kommt von Flume, der in seinem jetzt viel zitierten Aufsatz von 1972 über „Gesellschaft und Gesamthand" die These aufstellte, daß die Gruppe der Gesamthand als solche ein Rechtssubjekt sei, ohne juristische Person zu werden (Gruppentheorie).[19] Somit wurde die bis dahin herrschende Meinung, die die GbR als Vermögensmasse ansieht (Vermögenstheorie; Wieacker, Larenz, Zöllner, Stürner) in Frage gestellt und der neuen Generation von Gesellschaftsrechtlern der Weg des Umdenkens geöffnet.

Namhafte Gesellschaftsrechtler der jüngeren Zeit haben die neuen Lehre weiter entwickelt: Ulmer, nach kleineren Beiträgen, zuletzt in seinem Kommentar[20] und K. Schmidt in seinem „Gesellschaftsrecht".[21] Mehrere Juristen haben die neue Lehre verschiedentlich unterstützt.[22] Weil aber die GbR ein Grundtyp der Personenverei-

---

[17] Ulmer, in *Münchener Kommentar zum BGB* (1997) § 718 N 4.

[18] Allerdings herrscht keine Einstimmigkeit in der Lehre, ob mit der „Personengesellschaft" auch die GbR gemeint wird. Dafür: Petzoldt, in *Münchener Kommentar* (1997) § 1059 a N 2. Dagegen: Bassenga, in Palandt, *Bürgerliches Gesetzbuch*, 58. Aufl. (1999) § 1059a N 1, und J. Berndt und K. T. Boin, *Zur Rechtsnatur der Gesellschaft bürgerlichen Rechts*, NJW (1998) S. 2854.

[19] Flume, *Gesellschaft und Gesamthand*, ZHR (1972) S. 177ff.

[20] Ulmer (oben. N. 17) Vor § 705 N 8, § 705 N 127ff.

[21] K. Schmidt (oben. N. 13) § 8, § 58 IV.

[22] Wiedemann, „Zur Selbständigkeit der BGB-Gesellschaft", *FS Kellermann* (1991) S. 529ff.; Wiedemann, „Rechtsverhältnisse der BGB-Gesellschaften zu Dritten", *WM* Sonderbeilage, Nr. 4 zu Nr. 51/52 (1994) 3ff.; Timm, „Die Rechtsfähigkeit der Gesellschaft bürgerlichen Rechts und ihre Haftungsverfassung", *NJW* (1995) 3209ff.; Habersack, „Zur Rechtsnatur der Gesellschaft bürgerlichen

nigungen ist und die Vorschriften des Gesetzes über die GbR auf verschiedene Erscheinungsarten von Personenverbindungen anwendbar sind, wollen Einige in der Lehre die Rechtsfähigkeit nur für die unternehmenstragende GbR befürworten.[23]

Eine noch extremere Ansicht will die GbR mit einer juristischen Person gleichstellen und zwar ohne eine gesetzliche Grundlage.[24]

Das Ende der ernsthaften theoretischen Auseinandersetzungen scheint noch nicht erreicht zu sein. Die Kritiker der Rechtsträgerschaft versuchen durch Gegenargumente die Entwicklung zu stoppen. Zöllner hat die Gruppenlehre mangels praktischen Nutzens grundsätzlich in Frage gestellt.[25] Die Gesetzgebung der neueren Zeit und die Rechtsprechung wurden auch von anderen kritisch unter die Lupe genommen und entsprechend wurde die Rechtsfähigkeit der GbR abgelehnt. Es wird behauptet, daß die neu geregelten Gesellschaftsformen und Gesetzesvorschriften hieran nichts geändert haben.[26]

(3)   Einzelne Fälle und die Rechtsprechung

Der Umfang der Rechtsfähigkeit einer GbR wird auch durch Gerichtsentscheidungen verbreitert. Der Bundesgerichtshof hat für die Durchsetzung der Gruppenlehre verschiedentlich in der Rechtsanwendung grünes Licht gegeben.[27]

Rechts – BAG", *NJW* (1989) 3034, *JuS* (1990) 179ff.; Kindl, „Der Streit um die Rechtsnatur der GbR und seine Auswirkungen auf die Haftung der Gesellschafter für rechtsgeschäftlich begründete Gesellschaftsverbindlichkeiten", *NZG* (1999) 517ff.; Breuninger, *Die BGB-Gesellschaft als Rechtssubjekt im Wirtschaftsverkehr* (1991) S. 34ff. Für eine vollständige Liste siehe Ulmer (oben N. 17) § 705 N. 373.

[23] K. Schmidt, *Gesellschaftsrecht*, § 58 III, 4 und IV; „(Aussen-) Gesellschaft bürgerlichen Rechts mit Gesamthandsvermögen"; Ulmer, „Die Gesamthandgesellschaft – ein noch immer unbekanntes Wesen?" *AcP* (1998) S. 114; Ulmer (oben N. 17) Vor § 705 N 7; Hommelhoff, „Wider das Akzessorietätsdogma in der Gesellschaft bürgerlichen Rechts", *ZIP* (1998) S. 8ff.

[24] Raiser, „Gesamthand und juristische Person im Licht des neuen Umwandlungsrechts", *AcP* (1994) S. 495; Raiser, „Der Begriff der juristischen Person. Eine Neubesinnung", *AcP* (1999) 104ff.; für die Erbengemeinschaft Grunewald, „Die Rechtsfähigkeit der Erbengemeinschaft", *AcP* (1997) S. 305ff.

[25] Zöllner, „Rechtssubjektivität von Personengesellschaften?" *FS Gernhuber* (1995) S. 563ff.

[26] Berndt und Boin, „Zur Rechtsnatur der Gesellschaft bürgerlichen Rechts", *NJW* (1998) S. 2854ff.; ausserdem siehe, Weber-Grellet, „Die Gesamthand – Ein Mysterienspiel", *AcP* (1982) S. 316ff.

[27] BGH, Besch. v. 4.11.1991, *BGHZ* 116, 86, 88 = *NJW* (1992) 499; BGH, Urt. v. 15.7.1997, *NJW* (1997) 2754, 2755; BGH, Urt. v. 2.10.1997, *WM* (1997) 2220f.; BGH, Urt. v. 10.2.1992, *ZIP* (1992) 695, 698; BGH, Urt. v. 8.11.1978, *BGHZ* 72, 267, 271 = *NJW* (1979) 308; BGH, Urt. v. 30.4.1979, *BGHZ* 74, 240f. = *NJW* (1979) 1821; BGH, Urt. v. 15.12.1980, *BGHZ* 79, 374, 377 = *NJW* (1981) 1213; Wackerbarth, „Zur Rechtsscheinhaftung der Gesellschafter bürgerlichen Rechts am Beispiel einer Wechselverpflichtung", *ZGR* (1999) 365ff.

(a) Obwohl im Gesetz nichts davon erwähnt wird, handelt eine GbR in der Praxis unter einem einheitlichen Namen.[28] Die GbR kann also einen gemeinsamen Namen tragen und Geschäfte unter diesem Namen abschliessen. Unter einem einheitichen Namen zu handeln ist nur in bestimmten Fällen ausgeschlossen, wie etwa bei der Grundbucheintragung oder im Prozess, wo die „der Rechtsklarheit dienende und Verwechselung ausschließende Angabe des Rechtsinhabers oder der Partei"[29] im Vordergrund steht. Nach Art. 736 dZPO ist zur Vollstreckung in das Gesamthandsvermögen ein Titel gegen alle Gesellschafter erforderlich.[30]

(b) Der Bundesgerichtshof hat in seiner Entscheidung vom 15.7.1997 die Scheckfähigkeit einer Gesellschaft des bürgerlichen Rechts für zulässig befunden.[31]

(c) In mehreren Entscheidungen hat der Bundesgerichtshof die GbR für fähig beurteilt, sich an einer anderer Gesellschaft zu beteiligen.[32]

(d) Die Gesellschafter einer GbR sollen wie die Gesellschafter einer oHG für die deliktischen Schulden der Gesellschaft haften.[33]

(e) Die GbR kann Aktivprozesse über Gesamtansprüche führen, „mit der Maßgabe, daß unabhängig von der Ausgestaltung der Geschätsführungsbefugnis sämtliche Gesellschafter eine notwendige Streitgenossenschaft bilden".[34] Im weiteren bestimmt die neue Insolvenzordnung, daß die GbR insolvenzfähig ist.[35]

---

[28] Ulmer (oben. N. 17) § 705 N 131; Soergel/Hadding, *Kommentar zum Bürgerlichen Gesetzbuch* (1985) § 705 N 68f.; Kirberger, „Die BGB-Gesellschaft auf dem Weg zur Rechtspersönlichkeit – Eine Zwischenbetrachtung", *FS Leser* (1998) S. 229; für die übertragbare Geschäftsbezeichnung einer GbR siehe OLG Nürnberg, Urt. v. 4.2.1999, *MDR* (1999) 754.

[29] Ulmer (oben. N. 17) § 705 N. 111.

[30] Müther, „Die BGB-Gesellschaft im Zivilprozess", *MDR* 1998, 625ff; siehe jedoch Timm (oben N. 22) S. 3214.

[31] BGH, Urt. v. 15.6.1997, *BGHZ* 136, 254ff. = *BB* (1997) 1861 = *NJW* (1997) 2753 = *JuS* (1998) 83 (Anm. K. Schmidt) = *ZEuP* (1999) 332ff. (Anm. Kieninger).

[32] Zuletzt BGH, Urt. v. 2.10.1997, *MDR* (1998) 55 und vorher BGH, Besch. v. 3.11.1980, *BGHZ* 78, 311 = *NJW* (1981) 682 (GmbH); Grunewald, *Gesellschaftsrecht* (1994) S. 48; Ulmer (oben. N. 17) § 705 N 132. Der Bundesgerichtshof hat die Mitgliedschaft einer GbR in einer Genossenschaft bejaht: BGH, Besch. v. 4.11.1991, *BGHZ* 116, 86 = *NJW* (1992) 499 = *ZIP* (1992) 114; Ulmer, *AcP* (1998) 147.

[33] In Analogie zu BGB § 31; K. Schmidt (oben. N. 13) § 58 V, § 60 II,4 (für die Anwendung HGB § 128 K; Schmidt (oben. N. 13) § 60 III,2); Reiff, *Die Haftungsverfassung nichtrechtsfähiger unternehmenstragender Verbände* (1996) S. 296; Habermeier, „Grundfragen des Gesellschaftsrechts", *JuS* (1998) 871; Ulmer (oben. N. 17) § 714 N 7.

[34] Ulmer (oben. N. 17) § 705 N 132; siehe auch Prütting, „Ist die Gesellschaft bürgerlichen Rechts insolvenzfähig?" *ZIP* 1997, 1725ff.

[35] Ulmer (oben. N. 17) § 705, N 134a; für die Aktivprozessfähigkeit ders., § 705 N 132.

(f) Die Grundbuchfähigkeit einer GbR ist wegen einer eindeutigen Vorschrift fraglich.[36] Ins Grundbuch werden, nach § 47 GBO, die Gesellschafter mit ihrem Namen und dem Zusatz „als Gesellschaft bürgerlichen Rechts" eingetragen. Eine Entscheidung des Höheren Gerichts Düsseldorf nimmt übrigens Grundbuchunfähigkeit einer GbR grundsätzlich dann an, wenn deren Bestand und Zusammensetzung auch nicht anderweitig mit der verlangten Registerpublizität vereinbar ist.[37]

(4) Gesetzgebung

Die neuere Auslegung der gesetzlichen Vorschriften und die Gesetzgebung der neueren Zeit in Deutschland haben die selbständige Existenz der GbR verstärkt bzw. den Umfang der Rechtsfähigkeit verbreitert.

(a) Bedeutungsvoll ist Art. 19 des Grundgesetzes. Absatz 3 dieser Vorschrift sieht eigentlich vor, daß die „Grundrechte auch für inländische juristische Personen" gelten, „soweit sie ihrem Wesen nach auf diese anwendbar" sind. Diese erfasse aber nicht nur die „voll rechtsfähigen juristischen Personen", sondern auch jede von der Rechtsordnung anerkannte und rechtlich verselbständigte Form von Personenzusammenschlüssen, eventuell sogar die GbR.[38]

(b) Neben der schon angesprochenen Änderung im BGB (§ 736 Abs. 2) ist eine weitere gesetzgeberische Neuerung zu erwähnen: Nach der neuen Insolvenzordnung kann nun ein Insolvenzverfahren auch über das Vermögen einer GbR eröffnet werden.[39] Den kleingewerblich tätigen oder ein Vermögen verwaltenden GbR wurde die Eintragung in das Handelsregister ermöglicht.[40]

(5) Die Spiegelung der Gruppenlehre im Rechtsleben scheint noch nicht vollendet zu sein. Auch die Verfolger dieser Lehre der Gesamthandgesellschaft versuchen

---

[36] OLG Düsseldorf v. 5.3.1997, *WM* (1997) 2032 = *JuS* (1997) 946 = *NJW* (1997) 1991 = *ZEuP* (1999) 333ff. (Anm. Kieninger); K. Schmidt, „Personengesellschaft und Grundstücksrecht", *ZIP* (1998) 2ff.; kritisch Grunewald (oben N. 32) S. 48; Timm (oben N. 22) 3214; Soergel/Hadding (oben N. 28) § 718 N 4.
[37] OLG Düsseldorf v. 5.3.1997 (oben N. 36).
[38] Dürig, in Maunz/Dürig/Herzog, *Grundgesetz Kommentar* (1977) Art. 19 Abs. 3, N 8, 29; v. Münch/Hendrichs, *Grundgesetz – Kommentar*, Bd. 1, 3. Aufl. 1985, Art. 19 N 31; Huber, in v. Mangoldt/Klein/Starde, *Grundgesetz I* (1999) Art. 19 N 259.
[39] Insolvenzordnung vom 5.10.1994 (BGBl I 2866), § 11 Abs. 2 Nr. 1, Kirberger (oben N. 28) 237; Cordes, „Die Gesellschaft bürgerlichen Rechts auf dem Weg zur juristischen Person?" *JZ* (1998) 550; für Partnerschftsgesellschaften, PartGG vom 25.7.1994 (BGBl I 177), § 1 Abs. 4, 8 II; ausserdem siehe Umwandlungsgesetz v. 28.10.1994 (BGBl I 3210), §§ 190, 191 und 202; Mülbert, „Die rechtsfähige Personengesellschaft", *AcP* (1999) 199ff.; Raiser, „Gesamthand und juristische Person im Licht des neuen Umwandlungsrechts", *AcP* (1994) 495ff.
[40] HGB § 105 Abs. 2 n.F., BGBl 1998 I 1474ff. Kirberger (oben N. 28) 239.

die Entwicklung selbst-kritisch zu beobachten.[41] Es existieren immer noch einige zerstreute Überbleibsel von Vorschriften, die die völlige Durchsetzung der neuen Lehre verhindern. Die neuere Gesetzgebung und die Praxis der Gerichte haben jedoch schon angedeutet, wie der Weg in der Zukunft aussehen wird.

C.   Einfache Gesellschaft des schweizerischen Rechts

(1)   Der Theorienstreit im deutschen Recht über die Rechtslage der GbR und die Tragweite ihrer Rechtsfähigkeit haben in der Schweiz keinen nennenswerten Anklang gefunden. In der Lehre wird die juristische Persönlichkeit für die eG kategorisch abgelehnt.[42] Ebenfalls ist es fast einstimmige Meinung, daß die eG keine Rechtsfähigkeit besitzt.[43]

In ihrem Ursprung ähnelte die schweizerische einfache Gesellschaft der *societas* des römischen Rechts. Sie war eine formlos begründbare schuldrechtliche Verbindung von Personen zur Verwirklichung eines gemeinsamen Zwecks.[44] Anläßlich der Revison des OR 1911 wurde nach dem deutschen Vorbild das Gesamthandprinzip angenommen und ist die Ausgestaltung des Gesellschaftseigentums als Gesamteigentum in „unzweideutiger Weise" zum Ausdruck gebracht.[45]

Egger findet, daß in den Gemeinschaften zur gesamten Hand das Einzelrecht des Gemeinders zurücktreten muß, damit die Gemeinschaft freier, unabhängiger und aktionsfähiger gestaltet wird. Diese Abwandlung, wie er schreibt, „erfolgt in verschiedenen Graden in einer Stufenfolge". „Die Gemeinschaft erfährt nach bestimmten Richtungen eine E i n h e i t s b e h a n d l u n g, sie wird in diesem Ausmaß j u r i s t i s c h e   P e r s o n".[46] Somit hält er eine Verselbständigung für eine bestimmte rechtliche Beziehungen für möglich.

Als Sachenrechtler sieht Meier-Hayoz bei der Gesamthandsgemeinschaft die einzelnen Gemeinschafter in ihrer Gesamtheit, nicht aber die Gemeinschaft als solche als Rechtsträger; bezüglich der Verfügungsmacht liegt hingegen eine Einheit vor: Nur die Gemeinschaft, nicht auch der Einzelne, kann Rechte ausüben.[47] „Man kann nun nicht einerseits die Einheit bejahen und andererseits die Rechtspersön-

---

[41] Ulmer, *AcP* (1998) 113ff.

[42] Gauch, „Überkommene und andere Gedanken zu Art. 934 OR", *SAG* (1978) 79.

[43] Gauch (oben N. 42) S. 79.

[44] Furrer (oben N. 1) S. 32; v. Steiger (oben N. 7) S. 312; Meier-Hayoz/Forstmoser (oben N. 1) § 6 N 5.

[45] Zitiert in Furrer (oben N. 1) S. 33, N. 150; Nachtrag zur Botschaft (1905) S. 755; siehe auch Siegwart, *Kommentar zum schweizerischen Zivilgestzbuch*, B. 5: Das Obligationenrecht (Zürich 1938) Art. 544 N 8, Art. 531 N 6 u. 7; Meier-Hayoz, Berner, *Kommentar zum ZGB* (1981) Art. 652, N 30; Meier-Hayoz/Forstmoser (oben N. 1) § 6 N 7.

[46] Egger, *Das Personenrecht*, Die juristische Personen, 2. Aufl. (1930) Vorbemerkungen, N 9, Art. 52 N 4.

[47] Meier-Hayoz (oben N. 45) Art. 652 N 13.

lichkeit verneinen".[48] Die Gesamthand ist „nicht eigentumsfähig".[49] Die Gesamthand ist „keine rechtlich verselbständigte, von der Existenz ihrer Teilhaber
weitgehend unabhängige Verbandperson".[50] „Die Verselbständigung des Gesamt-
handvermögens . . . kann durch Gesetz oder Rechtsgeschäft verschieden abgestuft
sein. Eine besonders weitgehende, der Verselbständigung des Vermögens bei einer
juristischen Person sich weitgehend annähernde Sonderexistenz erhält es im Recht
der Kollektiv- und Kommanditgesellschaft".[51] Meier-Hayoz und Forstmoser halten
als Gesellschaftsrechtler sogar Rechtssubjektivität und Rechtsfähigkeit für die Kollektivgesellschaften für unzutreffend. „Sie sind *nicht* juristische Personen, sie *sind
nicht rechtsfähig; sie werden nur in gewissen Bereichen so behandelt, wie wenn sie
es wären*".[52] Bei Meier-Hayoz und Forstmoser kommen bei der eG die Rechts- und
Parteifähigkeit, Handlungs-, Prozess- und Betreibungsfähigkeit nicht in Frage.[53]
Wenn auch ausnahmsweise die eG einen Namen tragen würde, dann sollte dieser
Name neben dem Namen der beteiligten Personen angegeben werden.[54] Trotzdem
halten Meier-Hayoz und Forstmoser es für möglich, daß eine einfache Gesellschaft
Mitglied einer anderen einfachen Gesellschaft wird.[55]

Riemer weist darauf hin, daß im Rechtssystem einige rechtliche „Gebilde" existieren, die in einer Art „Mittelstellung zwischen den natürlichen und juristischen
Personen" ihr eigenes Vermögen haben und obwohl die nicht den Verselbständi-
gungsgrad einer juristischen Person erreicht haben, als einheitliches Rechtssubjekt
auftreten.[56] Gemeint sind die Kollektiv- und Komanditgesellschaften oder Stock-
werkeigentümergemeinschaften. Insbesondere wird aber von Riemer die eG nicht
in diese Gruppe eingegliedert.[57] Er sieht die einfache Gesellschaft nicht als ein „einheitliches Rechtssubjekt bzw. Träger von Rechten und Pflichten".[58] Sie ist nicht
rechtsfähig und damit auch nicht parteifähig in einem Prozess; sie ist auch nicht aktiv oder passiv betreibungsfähig.

Für die Anerkennung einer Rechts- und Handlungsfähigkeit für die einfache Gesellschaft bietet Siegwart kein klares Rezept. In seinem Kommentar fand er auf der
einen Seite den Konzentrationsgrad bei den einfachen Gesellschaften noch nicht so

---

[48] Meier-Hayoz (oben N. 45) Art. 652 N 14.
[49] Meier-Hayoz (oben N. 45) Art. 652 N 17.
[50] Meier-Hayoz (oben N. 45) Art. 652 N 17.
[51] Meier-Hayoz (oben N. 45) Art. 652 N 21; für die einfache Gesellschaft zitiert er Siegwart (oben
N. 45) Art. 544 N 1ff.
[52] Meier-Hayoz/Forstmoser (oben N. 1) § 2 N 45.
[53] Meier-Hayoz/Forstmoser (oben N. 1) § 8 N 13.
[54] Meier-Hayoz (oben N. 45) Art. 652 N 52.
[55] Meier-Hayoz/Forstmoser (oben N. 1) § 8 N 12.
[56] Riemer, *Personenrecht des ZGB* (1995) § 14 N 443; vgl. *BGE* 116 II 651ff., 655 (1950, über
Kol.G).
[57] Riemer (oben N. 56) § 14 N 443.
[58] Riemer (oben N. 56) § 25 N 621.

weit fortgeschritten, um eine juristische Persönlichkeit anzuerkennen. Auf der anderen Seite jedoch schrieb er, daß von Fall zu Fall nach vernünftigen Zweckerwä-
gungn und billigen Interessenabwägungen durch den Gesetzgeber und Richter zu
entscheiden sei, „welche Bedeutung man mehr oder weniger stark verwirklichten
Konzentrationen beimessen will". Er schreibt weiter, daß „schon nach geltendem
Recht . . . bei der einfachen Gesellschaft von einer Art beschränkter Rechsfähigkeit
und Handlungsfähigkeit" gesprochen wird.[59]

In der Lehre ist im weiteren v.Steiger der Meinung, daß die einfache Gesellschaft kein „Gesellschaftsvermögen im Sinne eines Sondervermögens" besitze. Er
meint, daß bei den einfachen Gesellschaften kein Gesellschaftsvermögen wie z.B.
bei Kollektivgesellschaften, wo das Vermögen der Gesellschaftsgläubiger einen
„reservierten Haftungsfonds" darstellt, existiert. Durch die verschiedenen Vorschriften des Gesetzes wird das Gesellschaftsvermögen jedoch als Sondervermögen gegenüber den Privatvermögen der Gesellschafter abgegrenzt.[60] Er weist hin
auf die sprachliche Ausdrucksweise, daß bei der eG das Gesetz vom „Verhältnis der
Gesellschafter gegenüber Dritten" spricht, befaßt sich jedoch bei den Kollektivgesellschaften mit dem „Verhältnis der Gesellschaft zu Dritten".[61] v. Steiger sieht die
einfache Gesellschaft nicht als Rechtssubjekt und daher solle sie weder Rechts-
noch Handlungsfähigkeit genießen. Der einfachen Gesellschaft kommen weder aktive noch passive Partei- und Prozeßfähigkeit zu. Es fehlen auch die aktive und passive Betreibungsfähigkeit.[62]

Trotz dieser Zurückhaltung in der Lehre, deuten einige Entwicklungen einen begrenzten Grad von Rechtsfähigkeit für die einfachen Gesellschaften in der Schweiz
an. Zwar werden nach Art. 543 Abs. 2 des OR die Gesellschafter „im Namen der
Gesellschaft" handeln, es ist aber die allgemeine Ansicht in der Schweiz, daß eine
einfache Gesellschaft keine Firma haben kann.[63] Diese sei faktisch aber nicht rechtlich möglich. Zulässig sei aber die Verwendung einer Kurzbezeichnung, die „nicht
die Eigenschaft einer Firma haben soll und der der Firmenschutz nicht zukommt".[64]
Obwohl die aktive und passive Parteifähigkeit der einfachen Gesellschaft versagt
wird, hält eine weniger formalistische Auffassung die Prozessführung unter einem

---

[59] Siegwart (oben N. 45) Vorb. zu Art. 530-551 N 16.
[60] v. Steiger, „Gesellschaftsrecht, Allgemeiner Teil und Personengesellschaften", in *Schweizeri-sches Privatrecht* (Hrsg.: Gutzwiller u.a.) (1976) Art. 548 OR, S. 381.
[61] Vgl. die Marginalie zu Art. 543ff. OR und die Überschrift zu Art. 562ff. OR; v. Steiger (oben N. 60) S. 528.
[62] v. Steiger (oben N. 60) S. 446ff. Er schreibt aber später, daß die Kollektivgesellschaft in vermö-gensrechtlicher Hinsicht unbeschränkte Rechtsfähigkeit genießt, a.a.O., S. 529ff.; auch Guhl/Merz/Kummer, *Das Schweizerische Obligationenrecht*, 7. Aufl. (1980) sehen keine externe Verselbständi-gung, S. 562, 570.
[63] Meier-Hayoz/Forstmoser (oben N. 1) § 8 N 58.
[64] Meier-Hayoz/Forstmoser (oben N. 1) § 8 N 58 a.

Sammelnamen gelegentlich für möglich.[65] Die Grundstücke können unter einer Sammelbezeichnung unter Angabe, daß es sich um eine einfache Gesellschaft handelt, eingetragen werden.[66]

Das schweizerische Bundesgericht hat die Gläubigergemeinschaft bei Anleihensobligationen (Art. 1157ff. OR) in die Nähe der Kollektivgesellschaften gerückt.[67]

(2)   Im gesetzgeberischen Bereich haben auch in der Schweiz einige Änderungen stattgefunden.

(a)   Der eG ähnlichen Stockwerkeigentümergemeinschaft wurde von der Rechtsordnung ein bestimmtes Mass an Selbständigkeit zuerkannt. Diese Selbständigkeit besteht darin, daß sie nach aussen wie ein eigenes „einheitliches Rechtssubjekt" auftreten kann.[68] Art. 712 l ZGB sieht ausdrücklich Handlungsfähigkeit für solche Gemeinschaften vor.

(b)   Darüber hinaus muß auch auf die in Art. 1156ff. OR geregelte Gläubigergemeinschaft bei Anleihensobligationen hingewiesen werden. Diese Gemeinschaft ist zwar keine juristische Person, sie ist aber nach einer Entscheidung des Bundesgerichts partei- und prozessfähig.[69]

(c)   Ausserdem hat das neue schweizerische IPRG der eG den Status einer Sondereinheit zuerkannt. Nach Art. 150 IPRG werden die Gesellschaften in organisierte und nicht-organisierte Zusammenschlüsse unterteilt. Die organisierte einfache Gesellschaft wird dann dem Gesellschaftsbegriff des IPRG unterstellt, wenn die innere Struktur auch nach aussen sichtbar ist.[70] Somit sind die sogenannten stillen (Innen-) Gesellschaften nicht „Gesellschaften" im Sinne des IPRG.

Die Betrachtung der eG für IPR-Zwecke als Einheit war bereits vor dem Inkrafttreten des IPRG anerkannt.[71]

---

[65]   Siegwart (oben N. 45) Vorb. zu Art. 530-551 N 119.

[66]   Siegwart (oben N. 45) Art. 544 N 12.

[67]   Riemer, *Berner Kommentar, Das Personenrecht* (1993) Systematischer Teil, N 38.

[68]   Riemer (oben N. 68) Syst. Teil, N 37ff.; Bucher, *Berner Kommentar, Das Personenrecht* (1976) Art. 11 N 48f.; Rey, *Schweizerisches Stockwerkeigentum* (1999) S. 60 N 226.

[69]   *BGE* 113 II 28 (23.6.1987); Riemer (oben N. 68) Syst. Teil, N 38; siehe ausserdem, Bucher (oben N. 68) Art. 11 N 43ff., N 80ff. Er findet eine Bedeutungsidentität der Begriffe juristische Persönlichkeit und Rechtsfähigkeit (Art. 11 N 64).

[70]   Vischer, in *IPRG Kommentar* (1993) Art. 150 N 21; Ebenroth/Messer, „Das Gesellschaftsrecht im neuen schweizerischen IPRG", *ZSR* 1989 I, S. 66ff.

[71]   Siegwart (oben N. 45) Vorb. zu Art. 530-551 N 291; W. v. Steiger, „Die einfache Gesellschaften im internationalen Privatrecht", *SchwJb für Internationales Privatrecht* (1957) Bd. 14, S. 17ff., 21.

4.   SCHLUSSBEMERKUNGEN

Seit dem Inkrafttreten des BGB und des schweizerischen OR wurde vieles im wirt-schaftlichen und technischen Leben geändert. In Deutschland haben Lehre und Rechtsprechung, sogar der Gesetzgeber, durch eine neue Lehre der GbR Rechtfä-higkeit in unterschiedlichem Umfang zuerkannt. Angesichts der „weitgehenden materiellen Übereinstimmung zwischen schweizerischen und deutschen Recht" im Bereich der einfachen Gesellschaft legen die schweizerischen Juristen auf die „deutsche Praxis und Lehre als interpretatorisches Hilfsmittel besonders grosses Gewicht".[72] Die kommenden Jahren werden zeigen, ob die deutsche Gruppenlehre auch in der Schweiz Anklang finden wird.

Wenn die Personenvereinigungen, die kaufmännische Gewerbe treiben, ohne Eintragung ins Handelsregister als Kollektivgesellschaft angesehen werden,[73] dann ist das Problem der Rechtsfähigkeit praktisch für diese Gesellschaften gelöst. Auch wenn die Gründer solcher Vereinigungen von einer einfachen Gesellschaft spre-chen, liegt eine Kollektivgesellschaft vor, falls deren wesentlichen Merkmale ver-wirklicht sind.[74] Wie die anderen Kollektivgesellschaften werden auch diese Formen als rechtsfähig angesehen. Bei den Personengesellschaften, die kein kauf-männisches Gewerbe betreiben, erhält die Gemeinschaft ohne Eintragung nicht den Status einer Kollektivgesellschaft. Sie bleiben eine eG und unterstehen deren Recht. Ebenfalls erhält eine Personenvereinigung, die juristische Personen als Mit-glieder hat, nicht den Status einer Kollektivgesellschaft (OR Art. 552 Abs. 1), auch wenn diese Vereinigung ein kaufmännisches Gewerbe betreiben wird. Für diese und weitere andere Arten der eG bleibt das Problem der Rechtsfähigkeit ungelöst. Es wird sich deshalb lohnen, in der Schweiz einen Blick auf die deutsche Gruppen-lehre und deren Entwicklung in der Praxis zu werfen.

SUMMARY
SWISS AND GERMAN PARTNERSHIPS AS SUBJECTS OF RIGHTS

The Swiss and German laws on partnerships are very similar. Having mutually influenced each other, they have reached almost the same solutions. Both systems recognize simple, civil partnerships as well as general, specific partnerships.

Swiss law regulates both kinds of partnerships, albeit in separate provisions, in the Code of Obligations. In Germany they are regulated in the Civil Code and in the Commercial Code, respectively. In both systems the simple, civil partnerships have

[72] Meier-Hayoz, *Berner Kommentar* (1981) Vorb. zu den Art. 646-654 N 51.
[73] OR Art. 553; vgl. Baumbach/Hopt, *Handelsgesetzbuch* (1995) § 105 N 10.
[74] v. Steiger (oben N. 7) S. 478.

no legal personality recognized by the Code. General partnerships, although not having legal personality in the real sense, are yet treated, due to specific legal provisions, as being the subjects of rights. The partnership is thus itself attributed rights which are separate from those of its individual members.

The German scholarly publications and case-law are increasingly recognizing civil partnerships as being subjects of rights. This path, however, has not been followed in Switzerland. It is proposed that Swiss law should closely examine the new trend and treat simple (civil) partnerships as subjects of rights. There are, in fact, indications that such a development is already taking place in Swiss law.

EC Regulations in European Private Law

Jürgen Basedow[*]

1. INTRODUCTION

The traditional instrument of the unification or harmonization of laws in the European Union has been and still is the directive. Under Article 249(3) EC [ex 189 ECT] it is binding, as to the result to be achieved, upon each Member State to which it is addressed, but shall leave to the national authorities the choice of form and method. Directives therefore provide for a two-step process of harmonization, the first on the Community level, the second within the single Member States where national legislation has to be brought into line with the directive. Over many years this peculiar instrument has given rise to a vast body of case law and extensive comments in legal literature.[1]

The other type of Community legislation, i.e., the EC regulation, has not attracted the same attention. Its functions do not appear to raise many doubts: under Article 249(2) EC [ex 189 ECT] a regulation shall have general application and be

---

[*] Prof. Dr.iur. LL.M. (Harvard), Director of the Max Planck Institute for Foreign Private Law and Private International Law, Hamburg.

[1] See e.g. Prechal, *Directives in European Community Law* (Oxford 1995); Brechmann, *Die richtlinienkonforme Auslegung* (München 1994); Lutter, "Die Auslegung angeglichenen Rechts", *JZ* (1992) p. 593; Rodriguez Iglesias/Riechenberg, "Zur richtlinienkonformen Auslegung des nationalen Rechts", in: *Festschrift Everling* vol. II (Baden-Baden 1995) p. 1213; Emmert/Pereira de Azevedo, "L'effet horizontal des directives", *Rev.trim.dr.eur.* (1993) 503; Luttermann, "Die 'mangelhafte' Umsetzung europäischer Richtlinien", *EuZW* (1998) p. 264.

J. Basedow et al., eds., Private Law in the International Arena – Liber Amicorum Kurt Siehr
© 2000, T.M.C.Asser Press, The Hague, The Netherlands

binding in its entirety and directly applicable in all Member States. This is a relatively clear statement. The responsibility for law making is not shared among the
Community and the Member States, but lies entirely with the Community. Potential
conflicts between the Community and the Member States have to be settled before
it comes to the adoption of a regulation; once it is adopted it takes priority over the
national laws of the Member States,[2] and will be applied directly and without the interference of a national legislator by every judge sitting in a Member State. In the
field of private law, however, regulations have not been enacted very often in order
to implement uniform rules. Although their direct effect is much more liable to produce a uniform application which appears particularly necessary in private law matters, Community legislation has preferred the directive so far.[3]

This does not mean, however, that regulations only play a "marginal rôle" in
European private law, as one commentator put it.[4] The following article is meant to
confer an impression of the great variety of private law related regulations in
European Community Law. It will give a survey over these instruments in
accordance with their respective legal bases. Its main purpose is to attract the
attention of legal scholars to a new category of uniform laws which may pose new
problems in the future.

KURT SIEHR to whom these lines are dedicated in long-standing friendship, will
hopefully take some interest in this overview which will refer to many rules situated
at the borderline between the unification of laws and private international law, i.e.,
in an area to which he has devoted so much time and scholarly expertise.

The EC Treaty does not contain a single all-embracing basis for the adoption of
measures concerning private law.[5] Instead, such private law acts form part of the
various policies which the Treaty provides for. Some of these policies are called the
vertical ones and related to particular sectors of the economy; this holds true for
example in the fields of agriculture and transport. By definition these policies are
much narrower in scope than many rules of private law which are meant to govern
commercial relations in different sectors of the economy. Other policies like the
internal market program are tailored in a more comprehensive way, but they will
usually allow for the adoption of regulations only within close limits. As a result of
the survey of private law regulations in the secondary legislation of the European

---

[2] Case 106/77 *Amministrazione delle Finanze dello Stato* v. *Simmenthal SpA (II)*, [1978] *ECR* 629
Recital 17/18; cf. Oppermann, *Europarecht*, 2nd edn. (München 1999) para. 545 at p. 209.
[3] It is significant that the comprehensive volume *Towards a Europen Civil Code* (Hartkamp et al.
eds.) 2nd edn. (Nijmegen 1998) only refers to directives: see Müller-Graff, "EC Directives as a Means
of Private Law Unification", at p. 71.
[4] See Martiny, "Europäisches Privatrecht – greifbar oder unerreichbar?" in: Martiny/Witzleb
(eds.), *Auf dem Wege zu einem Europäischen Zivilgesetzbuch* (Berlin, Heidelberg 1999) pp. 1, 3.
[5] Cf. Schwartz, "Perspektiven der Angleichung des Privatrechts in der Europäischen
Gemeinschaft", *ZEuP* (1994) 559, 570; van Gerven, "Coherence of Community and national laws. Is
there a legal basis for a European Civil Code?" 5 *ERPL* (1997) 465, at p. 466 et seq.

Community we have to expect findings which are far from homogeneous. The following survey will proceed in the order of the respective bases as established by the EC Treaty: agriculture (section 2); judicial co-operation in civil matters (section 3); transport (section 4); competition (section 5); internal market (section 6) and the subsidiary competence under Article 308 EC [ex 235 ECT] (section 7).

2. AGRICULTURE

Under Article 37(2)(3) EC [ex 43 ECT] the Council may in order to implement the common agricultural policy, "make regulations, issue directives or take decisions without prejudice to any recommendations it may also make". This provision is narrow in scope, but gives wide powers to the Community relating to all kinds of Community acts. While it could serve as the legal basis for a regulation of farm tenancy contracts or the sale of live stock the Commission has never endeavored to make such proposals. However, the Community has made a regulation relating to private law under Article 37 EC [ex 43 ECT], i.e., Regulation (EEC) no. 2081/92 of 14 July 1992 on the protection of geographical indications and designations of origin for agricultural products and foodstuffs.[6]

The regulation contains the prerequisites for the protection of geographical indications and designations of origin and provides for the registration of such designations as a necessary pre-condition for their protection. Impairment of the rights protected under the regulation may give rise to injunctions and claims for damages under national law. The validity of Regulation 2081/92 is in dispute; it is contended that it could only be based on Article 37 EC [ex 43 ECT] in so far as it concerns agricultural products and that it should have been based upon Article 94 or 95 EC [ex 100 or 100a ECT] with regard to foodstuffs.[7] The regulation has been applied in several cases which give evidence, however, of the remaining differences between national laws of Member States in the protection of designations of origin.[8]

---

[6] *OJ (EC)* [1992] L 208/1.

[7] See Obergfell, "Der Schutz geographischer Herkunftsangaben in Europa", *ZEuP* (1997) 677, at p. 612; Tilmann, "Grundlage und Reichweite des Schutzes geographischer Herkunftsangaben nach der VO/EWG 2081/92", *GRUR/Int.* (1993) 610, at p. 611 et seq.

[8] Cf. in England *Consorzio del Prosciutto di Parma* v. *Asda Stores Ltd. and Highgrade Foods Ltd.*, [1998] *CMLR* 215 (Ch.) at p. 230 et seq.; in Germany BGH 16.12.1993, *NJW-RR* (1994) 619 = *WiB* (1994) 329 (annotation: Fritzsche); OLG Frankfurt 05.06.1997 *GRUR/Int.* (1991) 751 (annotation: Knaak); in France Cass. Com. 27.02.1996 *Bull. civ.* (1996) IV, p. 48 no. 61; Cass. com. 15.10.1996 *Bull.civ.*(1996) IV, p. 201 no. 231.

3.   JUDICIAL CO-OPERATION IN CIVIL MATTERS

The Treaty of Amsterdam has declared the progressive establishment of an area of freedom, security and justice to be a target of the Community, as stated in Article 61 EC [ex 73i ECT]. In pursuance of that target a new title IV on "Visas/asylum, immigration and other policies related to free movement of persons" comprising Articles 61-69 EC [ex 73i-73q ECT] has been inserted into the EC Treaty. As far as the judicial co-operation in civil matters is concerned, these provisions have transferred the respective policy from the third pillar of the Maastricht Treaty which had not allowed for much progress in this field, into the first pillar, i.e., into the competence of the European Community.[9]

Under Article 61(c) EC [ex 73i ECT] the Council shall adopt measures in the field of judicial co-operation in civil matters as provided for in Article 65 EC [ex 73m ECT]. That provision indicates some areas of private law which may be subject to such measures, i.e., cross-border service of judicial and extra-judicial documents; co-operation and the taking of evidence; the recognition and enforcement of decisions in civil and commercial cases, including extra-judicial cases; the promotion of the compatibility of the rules applicable in the Member States concerning the conflict of laws and jurisdiction; and the elimination of obstacles to the good functioning of civil proceedings, if necessary by the promotion of the compatibility of the rules on civil procedure applicable in the Member States. It is made clear (*"shall include"*) that this list is not exhaustive and the Community may choose other subjects of legislation in the field of judicial co-operation in civil matters as long as they have cross-border implications and in so far as they are necessary for the proper functioning of the internal market.

The precise meaning of this new legal basis is still very much in dispute.[10] It should however be noted that Article 61 empowers the Community to adopt measures of all kind including regulations. The Commission has already made use of its new powers when it presented its proposal for a Council regulation on jurisdiction and the recognition and enforcement of judgements in matrimonial matters and in matters of parental responsibility for joint children.[11] Thereby, the Commission transposes the Convention of 28 May 1998 on the same subject (*"Brussels II"*)

---

[9] Cf. Kohler, "Interrogations sur les sources du droit international privé européen après le traité d'Amsterdam", 88 *Rev.crit.dr.int.pr.* (1999) 1, at p. 6 et seq.; Duff (ed.), *The Treaty of Amsterdam – Text and Commentary* (London 1997) p. 19 et seq.; see also the commentary by Bardenhewer in Lenz (ed.), *EG-Vertrag*, 2nd edn. (Köln 1999) p. 596 et seq. with further references.

[10] See the publications cited in the previous note and, in addition, Basedow, "Die Harmonisierung des Kollisionsrechts nach dem Vertrag von Amsterdam", *EuZW* (1997) p. 609; Besse, "Die justitielle Zusammenarbeit in Zivilsachen nach dem Vertrag von Amsterdam und das EuGVÜ", *ZEuP* (1999) 107, at p. 108 et seq.

[11] *COM* (99) 220 final, recently adopted by the Council, but not yet published in *OJ*.

which was signed by the Member States but has not entered into force yet,[12] into a regulation. According to the Commission the change of form "is warranted by the need to apply strictly defined and harmonized rules to jurisdiction and the recognition and the enforcement of judgements" and by the advantage of a regulation which contains "unconditional provisions that are directly and uniformly applicable in a mandatory way and, by their very nature, require no action by the Member States to transpose them into national law".[13]

Moreover, the Council and the Commission have adopted a common Action Plan on how to implement the provisions of the new title in December 1998.[14] While this Action Plan enumerates various optional measures relating to choice of law and cross-border civil proceedings to be taken within two years or within five years, it also envisages the examination of the possibility "of approximating certain areas of civil law, such as creating uniform private international law applicable to the acquisition in good faith of corporal movables".[15] It is not quite clear whether these intentions refer to uniform conflict rules or to uniform substantive rules; the term private international law would be broad enough to cover both. From the systematic context of the Action Plan, however, the latter solution appears to be more likely, since the harmonization of conflict rules is referred to, in other sections, as an undisputed target and not as the object of further examinations. The more cautious and even timid approach to the approximation of civil law indicates that Commission and Council think of the harmonization of substantive law at this point.

Therefore, it would not appear unlikely that future Community legislation in the field of private law will avail itself to a considerable extent of the new legislative basis under Article 61 EC [ex 73i ECT] and of the form of regulations.

4. Transport

Within the framework of a common transport policy the Community is empowered under Article 71(1) EC [ex 75 ECT] to enact "appropriate provisions". The competence of the Community therefore embraces the adoption of measures of all types including regulations.[16] As can be deduced from the specific reference made in Article 74 EC [ex 78 ECT] to "transport rates and conditions" the Community

---

[12] *OJ (EC)* [1998] C 221/27.

[13] See *COM* (99) 220 final, section 2.2.

[14] Action Plan of the Council and the Commission on how best to implement the Provisions of the Treaty of Amsterdam on an Area of Freedom, Security and Justice, of 03.12.1998, *OJ (EC)* [1999] C 19/1.

[15] Action Plan (supra n. 14) at para. 41(f).

[16] See Mückenhausen in Lenz (supra n. 9) Art. 71 no. 23; Weatherill/Beaumont, *EU Law*, 3rd edn. (London 1999) p. 1063.

competence extends to the making of regulations on the contract of carriage. While the provisions cited above are limited to inland transport by the operation of Article 80(1) EC [ex 84 ECT] the Community also disposes of comprehensive powers and a wide discretion in the choice of the form of its legal acts in sea and air transport under Article 80(2) EC [ex 84 ECT].[17]

(a)   As to *inland transport* the Community has adopted two regulations which deserve attention because of their impact on private law. Both regard the so-called cabotage transport, i.e., transport operations within a Member State by a carrier established in another Member State. The cabotage regulations permit such operations opening the national transport markets for foreign carriers, but they also lay down the conditions under which such operations may be carried out. Regulation no. 3118/93 on road haulage services in cabotage transport[18] contains the following provision in Article 6:

"(1)   The performance of cabotage transport operations shall be subject, save as other-wise provided in Community Regulations, to the laws, regulations and administrative provisions in force in the host Member State in the following areas:

(a)   rates and conditions governing the transport contract . . . "

An analogous provision can be found in Article 3 of Regulation no. 3921/91 on the cabotage transport of goods or passengers by inland waterway:[19]

"The carrying out of cabotage operations shall be subject to the laws, regulations and administrative provisions in force in the host Member State in the following fields, subject to the application of Community rules:

(a)   Rates and conditions governing transport contracts, and chartering and operating procedures . . . "

These provisions are conflict rules of a particular type. They govern the choice of law with regard to the contract of carriage in so far as a conflict between the national

---

[17] Cf. Weatherill/Beaumont (supra n. 16) p. 1063; Frohnmeyer in Grabitz/Hilf (eds.) *Kommentar zur Europäischen Union* (München, looseleaf edn.), Art. 84 paras. 14, 20.

[18] Council Regulation (EEC) No. 3118/93 of 25.10.1993 laying down the conditions under which non-resident carriers may operate national road haulage services within a Member State, *OJ (EC)* [1993] L 279/1.

[19] Council Regulation (EEC) No. 3921/91 of 16.12.1991 laying down the conditions under which non-resident carriers may transport goods or passengers by inland waterway within a Member State, *OJ (EC)* [1991] L 373/1.

laws of different Member States may arise. As pointed out elsewhere, the link between both regulations and the freedom to provide services makes it reasonable to assume that those choice of law rules are only applicable to substantive provisions with a mandatory character,[20] while the conflict of dispositive contract law remains subject to the Rome Convention on the law applicable to contractual obligations.[21] Moreover, the two regulations supersede the Rome Convention only in so far as conflicts between the national laws of different Member States are concerned; with regard to conflicts involving third states, the regulations are inapplicable. By analogy to the conflict of laws in the United States of America, the conflict rules cited above may therefore be addressed to as interstate conflict rules. It is noteworthy that the interstate conflict rules in both EC regulations have been enacted – unlike in the U.S. – at the "federal", i.e., European level.

(b)   In *air transport* the Community has enacted two regulations for the better protection of passengers. By Regulation no. 295/91 common rules for a denied-bording compensation system in scheduled air transport have been established.[22] The common occurrence of overbooking in scheduled air transport has in fact given rise to many passenger complaints. In response to that practice Regulation no. 295/91 grants the passenger certain procedural rights, in particular the choice between reimbursement of the air fare and re-routing, Article 3; in addition, the passenger may claim a minimum compensation from the airline, Article 4. The regulation delineates its own scope of application: it is applicable to all scheduled flights departing from Community airports, Article 1, even if they are bound for third state destinations.[23]

For many years low liability limits fixed by the Warsaw Convention on the

---

[20] Basedow, "Zulässigkeit und Vertragsstatut der Kabotagetransporte", 156 *ZHR* (1992) 413, at p. 424 et seq.; see also Clarke, "Contracts for the Carriage of Goods by Road: Cabotage in the United Kingdom", *J.Bus.L.* (1998) 591, at p. 592 et seq. and Hiblot, "Le cabotage dans les transports routiers en France à compter du 1er juillet 1998", *Gaz. Pal.* (1998) paras. 319-321 p. 38.

[21] Of 19.06.1980 *OJ (EC)* [1980] L 266/1.

[22] Council Regulation (EEC) No. 295/91 of 04.02.1991 establishing common rules for a denied-boarding compensation system in scheduled air transport, *OJ (EC)* [1991] L 36/5; see also the proposed amendments in *OJ (EC)* [1998] C 120/18 (proposal) and in *OJ (EC)* [1998] C 351/7 (amended proposal); cf. Führich, "Entschädigung bei Überbuchung von Linienflügen", *NJW* (1997) 1044; Giemulla, "Überbuchungen bei Luftbeförderungen", *EuZW* (1991) 367; Schmid, "Die Entschädigung von Fluggästen bei Nichtbeförderung wegen Überbuchung", *TranspR* (1991) 128; Basedow/Dolfen in: Dauses (ed.), *Handbuch des EG-Wirtschaftsrechts* (München looseleaf edn. 1993 seq.) para. L 324 et seq.

[23] Cf. LG Frankfurt am Main 29.04.1998 *NJW-RR* (1998) 1589, 1590: flight from Munich to Tunisia by Tunisian air carrier.

international carriage by air of 1929[24] as amended by the Hague Protocol of 1955[25] have raised concern in international civil aviation.[26] Various attempts to adjust those limits to the standards of living in industrialised nations had failed when the Council finally adopted Regulation no. 2027/97 in 1997.[27] With regard to carriers established in the Community this regulation sets aside all financial limits of the liability for damages sustained in the event of death or bodily injury by a passenger in case of accident, Article 3(1)(a). Air carriers established outside the Community which operate to, from or within the Community and intend to restrict their liability contrary to Regulation no. 2027/97, shall expressly and clearly inform the passengers thereof at the time the ticket is purchased, Article 6(3).

Thus, this regulation determines its own scope of application, too, by both personal and geographical criteria. Its particular character catches the eye: with regard to Community carriers it deprives an international treaty of its effects, and it may even provoke outright conflicts with that treaty with regard to third state carriers.[28]

5. COMPETITION

Most regulations which somehow touch upon private law relations have been enacted under Article 83 EC [ex 87 ECT], i.e., in the framework of competition policy. Four different types of regulations have to be separated in this context:

(1) the implementing regulations such as Regulation no. 17/62[29] provide for administrative procedures and sanctions to be inflicted by the European Commission and Member State authorities; they do not deal with private law relations;

---

[24] Convention internationale pour l'unification de certaines règles relatives au transport aérien international, faite à Varsovie le 12.10.1929, *BGBl.* 1933 II, p. 1040.

[25] Protocole, fait à La Haye le 28.09.1955, portant modification de la Convention pour l'unification de certaines règles relatives au transport aérien international signée à Varsovie le 12.10.1929, *BGBl* 1958 II, p. 291.

[26] For a closer account see Basedow, "Haftungshöchstsummen im internationalen Lufttransport: Gold von gestern und Grundrechte von heute", *TranspR* (1988) 353 with many references; Müller-Rostin, "Die Montrealer Protokolle Nr. 1, 2 und 4 sind in Kraft getreten", *TranspR* (1999) 81.

[27] Council Regulation (EC) No. 2027/97 of 09.10.1997 on air carrier liability in the event of accidents, *OJ (EC)* [1997] L 285/1; cf. Silingardi, Reg. CE 2027/97 e[il] nuovo regime di responsabilità del vettore aereo di persone, *Diritto dei trasporti* (1998) 621.

[28] See Ruhwedel, "Verordnung (EG) Nr. 2027/97 des Rates über die Haftung von Luftfahrtunternehmen bei Unfällen vom 09.10.1997", *TranspR* (1998) 13, at pp. 15 et seq.

[29] Regulation no. 17/62: First Regulation Implementing Arts. 85 and 86 of the Treaty, *OJ (EC)* (special Englsh edition) [1959-1962] 87, as last amended by Council Regulation (EC) No. 1216/1999 of 10.06.1999, *OJ (EC)* [1999] L 148/5.

(2) The same is true with regard to Commission regulations dealing with the details of applications, notifications, and hearings provided for in the implementing regulations[30];

(3) A third group of regulations adopted by the Council confers authority on the Commission to grant exemptions for certain categories of agreements under Article 81(3) EC [ex 85 ECT];[31] while these regulations are the indispensable legal basis for the so-called block exemptions they do not alter the private legal relations as such;

(4) The block exemptions adopted by the Commission under the regulations of the third type do in fact have a direct impact on private law. By their enactment the prohibition of cartels under Article 81(1) EC (ex 85 ECT) is declared inapplicable to all agreements covered by the block exemptions; consequently such agreements are not void under Article 81(2) EC [ex 85 ECT].

Block exemptions of this type have become more and more numerous over the years and cannot even be outlined here.[32] Their repercussions are clearly felt in the contractual practices of the sectors concerned, but it should be borne in mind that their direct impact on private law is limited to the question of validity whereas it is up to the pertinent rules of the proper law of the respective contract to decide upon the interpretation and the enforcement of the agreement. While most block exemption regulations define their own scopes of application the significance of such delineations is low. Outside the regulations an individual exemption is still possible.

6.   INTERNAL MARKET

Under Article 95 EC [ex 100 a ECT] the Council shall, for the achievement of the objectives set out in Article 14 EC [ex 7 a ECT], i.e., for the progressive establishment of the internal market, take "the measures for the approximation" of laws of the Member States. Unlike Article 94 EC [ex 100 ECT] which only allows for the adoption of directives, this provision which was inserted by the Single European

---

[30] See e.g. Regulation (EC) No. 3385/94 of the Commission of 21.12.1994 concerning the form, content and the other details of applications and notifications under Regulation No. 17 of the Council, *OJ (EC)* [1994] L 377/28, Regulation No. 99/63/EEC of 25.07.1963 of the Commission on the Hearings Provided for in art. 19(1) and (2) of Council Regulation no. 17, *OJ (EC)* [1963-64] (Special English edition) p. 47.

[31] See e.g. Regulation No. 19/65/EEC of the Council of 02.03.1965 on application of art. 85(3) of the Treaty to certain categories of agreements and concerted practices, *OJ (EC)* [1965-66] (Special English edition) p. 35.

[32] A comprehensive reproduction of the secondary legislation in matters related to competition can be found in Immenga/Mestmäcker (eds.) *EG-Wettbewerbsrecht-Kommentar*, vol. II (München 1997) pp. 2201 et seq. and looseleaf supplement.

Act in 1986 makes it clear that the Community, in order to establish the internal market, may also avail itself of other forms of enactments such as regulations.[33] However, the diplomatic conference at the same time adopted a declaration which suggests that the Commission should couch its legislative proposals in the form of directives by preference where these proposals imply changes of legal provisions in one or more Member States.[34] Although it can be argued that the choice of the legal form should rather depend upon the purposes of Article 95 EC [ex 100 a ECT], i.e., on the requirements of the Internal Market,[35] the Community has effectively made use of its powers to adopt regulations under Article 95 EC [ex 100 a ECT] in rare instances.

One of them is Council Regulation no. 1768/92 concerning the creation of a supplementary protection certificate for medicinal products.[36] This instrument purports to cope with the factual shortening of patent protection for medicinal products which results from the fact that these products, after an application for a patent is filed, have to undergo time-consuming administrative procedures before being admitted to the market. By granting a uniform prolongation of protection for up to five years (Article 13), the Community tries to accomodate to these market conditions and, hereby, to encourage research.[37] A directive was excluded since it would not prevent "the heterogeneous development of national laws leading to further disparities which would be likely to create obstacles to the free movement of medicinal products within the Community and does directly affect the establishment and the functioning of the internal market".[38] Therefore, a regulation appeared to be the most appropriate legal instrument.[39]

The adoption of a regulation in this case can be said to be in line with the above mentioned diplomatic declaration since the act rather created a new instrument instead of requiring the approximation of existing national laws. On the other hand, it may be doubtful whether it still makes sense to limit the Commission's choice concerning the type of legislation after the adoption of the new title IV of the EC Treaty. It should be borne in mind that the measures adopted under Article 65 in the field of judicial co-operation in civil matters must equally serve the proper functioning of the internal market. It is therefore difficult to understand why the Commission should give preference to the instrument of the directive under

---

[33] De Ruyt, *L'acte unique européen*, 2nd edn. (Bruxelles 1989) p. 168; Kapteyn/VerLoren van Themaat, *Inleiding tot het recht van de Europese Gemeenschappen*, 4th edn. (Deventer 1987) p. 309.

[34] *OJ (EC)* [1987] L 169/1.

[35] Langeheine in: Grabitz/Hilf (supra n. 17) Art. 100a para. 45.

[36] Of 18.06.1992, *OJ (EC)* [1992] L 182/1; another example is Regulation (EC) no. 1610/96 of the European Parliament and the Council of 23.07.1996 concerning the creation of a supplementary protection certificate for plant protection products, *OJ (EC)* [1996] L 198/30.

[37] Recitals 2 and 4 of Regulation no. 1768/92 (supra n. 36).

[38] Recital 6 of Regulation no. 1768/92 (supra n. 36).

[39] Recital 7 of Regulation no. 1768/92 (supra n. 36).

Article 95 EC [ex 100 a ECT] while it can freely choose among the various types of acts under Article 65 EC. The Treaty of Amsterdam has indirectly reduced the significance of the diplomatic declaration adopted in 1986.

7. THE SUBSIDIARY COMPETENCE UNDER ARTICLE 308 EC [EX 235 ECT]

At various occasions the Community has made use of its subsidiary competence under Article 308 EC [ex 235 ECT]. This provision empowers the Council to take "the appropriate measures" if action by the Community should prove necessary to attain, in the course of the operation of the common market, one of the objectives of the Community and the Treaty has not provided the necessary powers elsewhere. The Community has not only availed itself of this legal basis for the creation of the European Economic Interest Grouping,[40] a new type of non-profit making company, and the Community trade mark,[41] but also recently for the adoption of Regulation no. 1103/97 on certain provisions relating to the introduction of the euro.[42]

Both former instruments have created new legal institutions which the citizens of the Community may use if they wish to; like in the case of the supplementary protection certificate for medicinal products,[43] the application of the respective regulations is determined by the intention of the private parties. If they have opted for this so-called 16th model and have registered their company as a European Economic Interest Grouping or their trade mark as a Community trade mark all future disputes will be subject to the respective regulations.

Conflict of laws issues will not arise with regard to the outer delineation of their scopes of application, except when there is need to fill gaps in the regulations and recourse must be had to the national law of a Member State to fill them. Both regulations in fact contain conflict rules having that purpose. Under Article 2 of Regula-

---

[40] Council Regulation (EEC) No. 2137/85 of 25.07.1985, *OJ (EC)* [1985] L 199/1; cf. among others Ganske, *Das Recht der Europäischen wirtschaftlichen Interessenvereinigung* (Köln 1988); Santa Maria, *Diritto commerciale comunitario*, 2nd edn. (Milano 1995) pp. 188 et seq.; Werlauff, *Europæisk Selskabsret* (København 1989) pp. 109 et seq.

[41] Council Regulation (EC) No. 40/94 of 20.12.1993 on the Community trade mark, *OJ(EC)* [1994] L 11/1; cf. Hubmann/Götting, *Gewerblicher Rechtsschutz*, 6th edn. (München 1998) p. 408 et seq. and in particular Ingerl, *Die Gemeinschaftsmarke* (Stuttgart 1996); a similar subject is regulated in Council Regulation (EC) no. 2100/94 of 27.07.1994 on Community plant variety rights, OJ(EC) [1994] L 227/1, as amended by Regulation no. 95/2506, *OJ (EC)* [1995] L 258/3.

[42] Council Regulation (EC) no. 1103/97 of 17.06.1997 on certain provisions relating to the introduction of the euro, *OJ(EC)* [1997] L 162/1; see also Council Regulation (EC) no. 974/98 of 03.05.1998 on the introduction of the euro, *OJ (EC)* [1998] L 139/1; cf. Schefold, "Der Einfluß von EG-Währungsrecht auf nationale Zivilrechte", *ZEuP* (1999) p. 271 with many references.

[43] Council Regulation no. 1768/92 (supra n. 36).

tion no. 2137/85 the law applicable to the contract for the formation of the European Economic Interest Grouping and to its internal organisation shall be the internal law of the state in which its official address is situated, as laid down in the contract for the formation of the grouping. Under Article 12 the official address of the Grouping must be situated in the Community, either at its own place of central administration, or where one of the members has its central administration. Therefore, the applicable law under Article 2 is the law of a Member State by necessity.

The same result will usually follow with regard to gaps in the Community trade mark regulation from Article 97(2) of Regulation no. 40/94. Under that provision gaps in the regulation shall be filled by the *lex fori* of the Community trade mark court, including its private international law. Since the gaps of that regulation concern in particular the infringement of a Community trade mark, cf. Article 14(1), the applicable law will almost invariably be the law of a Member State because private international law in this area traditionally refers to the law of the country of protection.[44] Thus, both conflict rules may be referred to as "federal" conflict rules for interstate conflicts as explained earlier;[45] but unlike the conflict rules contained in the cabotage regulations, they are not connected to the enforcement of the Community freedoms, but rather serve the traditional purpose of gap filling in uniform law.

Council Regulation no. 1103/97 on certain provisions relating to the introduction of the euro differs from this pattern. It deals with the main private law issues arising from the substitution of the national currencies by the euro. In Article 3 which is perhaps the most important provision from a contracts perspective it is stated that

> "the introduction of the euro shall not have the effect of altering any term of a legal instrument or of discharging or excusing performance under any legal instrument, nor give a party the right unilaterally to alter or terminate such an instrument. This provision is subject to anything which the parties may have agreed."[46]

Article 3 contains a rule of contract law which is very clearly characterised as dispositive. Regulation no. 1103/97 does not contain, however, any indication as to the scope of application of Article 3. In particular, it is unclear whether this provision is subject to the law of the currency (*lex monetae*) which would mean that Article 3 governs all contractual claims expressed in the currency of a participating

---

[44] Cf. von Hoffmann in: Staudinger, *Kommentar zum Bürgerlichen Gesetzbuch*, Art. 38 nF EGBGB, 12th edn. (Berlin 1992) para. 574 with many references; Kreuzer, "Gutachterliche Stellungnahme zum Referentenentwurf eines Gesetzes zur Ergänzung des Internationalen Privatrechts", in Henrich (ed.), *Vorschläge und Gutachten zur Reform des deutschen internationalen Sachen- und Immaterialgüterrechts* (Tübingen 1991) 37, at pp. 149 et seq.

[45] See the text above, following n. 21.

[46] Council Regulation no. 1103/97 (supra n. 42).

Member State, i.e., expressed in DM, FF, HFL etc., or whether Article 3 should be characterised as a contractual rule forming part of the proper law of the contract. In the latter case Article 3 would be enforced only if the *lex contractus* is the law of a participating Member State, and it could be avoided by an appropriate choice of law by the parties under Article 3 of the Rome Convention.[47] While the dispositive character of Article 3 points to the latter direction,[48] the issue will certainly have to be clarified and decided by the European Court of Justice.

8.   PERSPECTIVES

It is difficult to sum up this survey in a few words. For the area of regulations, it has confirmed the commmon criticism that European private law is characterized by a fragmentary and pointillistic legislation[49] and resembles a world of innumerable islands scattered about the ocean of national law.[50] Indeed, the acts of secondary legislation presented in this paper, are incoherent among themselves and can hardly be said to form part of a consistent policy or of a comprehensive concept of European private law. But our inquiry was not meant to simply corroborate an assessment which has been well known for many years. It rather purports to point to some new issues connected to the use of the regulation as an instrument of secondary legislation.

The new issues are linked to the direct applicability of regulations which entails the necessity to find solutions for two sets of problems: (1) to define the respective scopes of application vis-à-vis the law of Non-Member States by what may be called *outward conflict rules*, and (2) to provide for the filling of their gaps by *inward conflict rules* which refer to the law of a Member State.

As the foregoing report shows, various regulations contain outward conflict rules which employ different connecting factors but the same technic: all of them are unilateral. While they provide for the application of the respective EC regulation they do not deal with the application of corresponding third state legislation. This issue is left to the private international law of the Member States. While the unilateral technic of conflict legislation is appropriate in the field of public law where courts usually exclude the enforcement of foreign law, it can hardly be said to cope with the needs of private law. Here, it might occur that a court is referred by the private international law of the *lex fori*, to the substantive law of a non-Member

---

[47] The Rome Convention on the law applicable to contractual obligations (supra n. 21).

[48] See the extensive discussion by Schefold (supra n. 42) at p. 279 et seq. and at p. 284 et seq.

[49] Cf. Kötz, "Rechtsvereinheitlichung – Nutzen, Kosten, Methoden, Ziele", *RabelsZ* 50 (1986) 1, 5; Ulmer, "Vom deutschen zum europäischen Privatrecht", *JZ* (1992) 1, 6.

[50] Rittner, "Das Gemeinschaftsprivatrecht und die europäische Integration", *JZ* (1995) 849, 851.

State while a Community regulation provides for its own application at the same time.

A second issue which is equally connected with the possibility of applying a foreign law in private law matters concerns the application of Community legislation by courts sitting in non-Member States. Apparently, none of the drafters of the regulations referred to above have thought of the application by third state judges. It should however be borne in mind that there is a basic difference between public law and private law with regard to enforcement. While the application of public law is essentially left within the responsibility of the authorities and the courts of the legislating state, private law is not so much regarded as flowing from the sovereignty of a state, but rather as a response to the needs of private citizens for a framework governing their commercial activities as well as the settlement and solution of disputes. For these private purposes, the application of foreign private law may be more appropriate than that of the *lex fori*, if the case is more closely connected with the foreign jurisdiction than with the forum state. In private law, legislators must therefore always take into account the potential application of their own acts by a foreign court.

A third issue which has become visible is that of gaps in the regulations which have to be filled somehow. While some regulations address this issue by inward or "interstate" conflict rules, referring to the laws of a certain Member State, others do not contain any indication as to how such gaps should be filled. More recent developments in the international arena show that recourse to national law is no longer the only technic which can be applied when it comes to the filling of gaps. The elaboration of general principles in some areas such as contracts[51] has in fact provided for a new technic which may be more appropriate in some instances. This has already been recognised to a limited extent by some EC regulations; for example, Regulation no. 40/94 on Community trade marks makes reference, in the absence of procedural provisions contained in that regulation, to "the principles of procedural law generally recognised in the Member States".[52] Future discussions will have to clarify the bearing of such general principles in other contexts.

A fourth issue which results from the foregoing report concerns the relation between conflict rules, whether inward or outward, contained in the regulations and the general rules of private international law which are in force in the Member States. While this relation is very simple in principle, being characterised by the priority of the regulations, it may give rise to some intricate problems in particular cases, both in Member State and non-Member State courts.

For reasons of space limits the issues described above must be left to future reflection. It should however have become clear that the use of regulations as a

---

[51] Cf. Lando/Beale (eds.), *Principles of European Contract Law* (Dordrecht 1995).
[52] Art. 79 of Regulation no. 40/94 on the Community trade mark (supra n. 41).

legislative instrument which favours the uniform application of European law, also entails some problems which merit a closer look, particularly from the perspective of the conflict of laws.

Englische Anti-suit Injunctions im europäischen Zivilprozessrecht – A Flourishing Species or a Dying Breed?

Stephen V. Berti[*]

I.

1.   Gerichtsbarkeit ist die aus der Gebietshoheit fliessende Befugnis eines jeden Staates, Recht zu sprechen.[1] Internationale Zuständigkeit ist die Zuständigkeit der Gerichte eines Staates in ihrer Gesamtheit.[2] Sie unterscheidet sich von der Gerichtsbarkeit im subjektiven Aspekt der Immunität und bildet neben ihr eine selbständige Prozessvoraussetzung: eine an sich gegebene internationale Zuständigkeit darf nicht ausgeübt werden, wenn die ins Recht gefasste Partei von solcher Gerichtsbarkeit exempt ist. Bezüglich der Grenzen der Ausübung der Gerichtsbarkeit und der Beanspruchung internationaler Zuständigkeit kann dem allgemeinen Völkerrecht Abschliessendes kaum entnommen werden: Nach den Einen bestehen schlicht keine völkerrechtlichen Grenzen;[3] für Andere soll es zwar Mindestanforderungen geben,[4] aber über deren Konkretisierung besteht nicht Einigkeit.[5] So entscheiden die Staaten zunächst aufgrund ihrer Souveränität, für welche Angelegenheiten sie Gerichtsbarkeit ausüben,[6] und beanspruchen bei der Ausgestaltung ihrer internationalen Zuständigkeit „weitgehend freie Hand".[7]

2.   Die Staaten können ihre Gestaltungsfreiheit freiwillig einschränken, indem sie entsprechende völkervertagsrechtliche Verpflichtungen eingehen. Die meisten eu-

---

[*] Dr.iur., Rechtsanwalt in Zürich.
[1] Geimer, *Internationales Zivilprozessrecht*, 3. Aufl. (1997) 120 N 371.
[2] Kropholler, *Handbuch des internationalen Verfahrensrechts*, Bd. I (1982) Kap. III N 4.
[3] Nach Geimer (oben N. 1) 121 N 374 schon deshalb, weil die Reichweite staatlicher Souveränität nicht auf Völkerrecht beruhe, sondern von diesem anerkannt werde.
[4] Kropholler (oben N. 2) 214 N 43 bezeichnet diese als die überwiegende Auffassung.
[5] Überblicke zum Diskussionsstand bei Kropholler (oben N. 2), Kap. III, N 43-46, sowie Geimer (oben N. 1) 120ff., N 373-381.
[6] Habscheid, *Schweizerisches Zivilprozess- und Gerichtsorganisationsrecht*, 2. Aufl. (1990) 72 N 126.
[7] Geimer (oben N. 1) 126 N 383.

J. Basedow et al., eds., Private Law in the International Arena – Liber Amicorum Kurt Siehr
© *2000, T.M.C.Asser Press, The Hague, The Netherlands*

ropäische Staaten einschliesslich der Schweiz haben dies durch Ratifizierung des Brüsseler und/oder des Lugano Übereinkommens getan. Diese Staatsverträge legen die internationale Zuständigkeit der Vertragsstaaten untereinander für den sachlichen Anwendungsbereich des Abkommens mit völkerrechtlicher Verbindlichkeit fest. In einem Vertragsstaat ergangene Entscheidungen werden in den *anderen eo ipso* anerkannt; dabei darf die Zuständigkeit der Gerichte des Ursprungsstaates nur in eng umschriebenen Fällen[8] nachgeprüft werden.[9]

3.   Über die Einhaltung der völkervertragsrechtlichen Verpflichtungen aus dem Brüsseler Übereinkommen wacht der Europäische Gerichtshof. Für das Lugano Übereinkommen fehlt ein entsprechendes, supranationales Gericht. So hört für die Schweiz grundsätzlich die Prüfung der internationalen Zuständigkeit für „Exportentscheidungen" im Inland auf, und für „Importentscheidungen" wird sie im Ausland abgeschlossen. Es entspricht also der Anlage des Lugano Übereinkommens, dass die Schweiz allenfalls konventionswidrige Zuständigkeitsentscheidungen aus dem Ausland hinnehmen muss. Hierbei spielt die Bestimmung des Artikels 21 LugÜ[10] eine zentrale Rolle. Sie lautet:

„[1] Werden bei Gerichten verschiedener Vertragsstaaten Klagen wegen desselben Anspruchs zwischen denselben Parteien anhängig gemacht, so setzt das später angerufene Gericht das Verfahren von Amts wegen aus, bis die Zuständigkeit des zuerst angerufenen Gerichts feststeht.

[2] Sobald die Zuständigkeit des zuerst angerufenen Gerichts feststeht, erklärt sich das später angerufene Gericht zugunsten dieses Gerichts für unzuständig."

---

[8] Nach Artikel 28 Abs. 1 wird eine Entscheidung nicht anerkannt, wenn die Zuständigkeitsvorschriften des 3. [Zuständigkeit für Versicherungssachen], 4. [Zuständigkeit für Verbrauchersachen] oder 5. [ausschliessliche Zuständigkeit] Abschnitts des Titels II verletzt worden sind und wenn ein Fall des Artikels 59 vorliegt [Spezieller staatsvertraglicher Schutz eines Beklagten mit Wohnsitz in einem Drittland vor den – vertragsraumintern verpönten – Zuständigkeiten gemäss Art. 3 Abs. 2]. Weitere Anerkennungsverweigerungsgründe befinden sich in Art. 54b Abs. 3 und Artikel 57 Abs. 4.

[9] Art. 28 Abs. 4 EuGVÜ/LugÜ. Die Vorschriften über die Zuständigkeit gehören nicht zur öffentlichen Ordnung im Sinne des entsprechenden Anerkennungsverweigerungsgrundes des Art. 27 Nr 1 EuGVÜ/LugÜ.

[10] Hingegen schreibt Art. 22 LugÜ vor, dass im Falle nicht identischer, aber verwandter Klagen das später angerufene Gericht die Zuständigkeitsprüfung unter bestimmten Voraussetzungen aussetzen darf (nicht muss).

[11] Dies schliesst aber nicht aus, dass dieses Gericht zuständigkeitsrelevantes Verhalten der Parteien vor später angerufenen Instanzen berücksichtigt. Kommt zum Beispiel das zuerst angerufene Gericht A im Rahmen seiner Zuständigkeitsprüfung zum Schluss, der Beklagte habe sich inzwischen auf das Verfahren vor dem später angerufenen Gericht B eingelassen, so muss das Gericht A diesen Umstand von Amtes wegen berücksichtigen (Artikel 19 und 20) und durch Nichteintretensentscheidung dem Gericht B die Zuständigkeit überlassen.

Bei Anrufung von Gerichten in verschiedenen Vertragstaaten in der gleichen Sache ist es mithin die ausschliessliche *Prärogative* des zuerst angerufenen Gerichtes, darüber zu befinden, ob es nach dem Übereinkommen international zuständig ist.[11] Während dieser Zuständigkeitsprüfung hat das später in der gleichen Sache angerufene Gericht sein Verfahren auszusetzen.

4.   Das Bundesgericht hält hingegen dafür, die Klage sei *„[i]mmerhin [...] in jedem Fall als unzulässig zurückzuweisen, wenn es schon an der internationalen Zuständigkeit fehlt"*[12]. Das widerspricht jedoch dem Wortlaut der Konvention und „übersieht", dass die Voraussetzungen für die internationale Zuständigkeit des zweiten Gerichtes noch während der Zuständigkeitsprüfung des ersten Gerichts erfüllt werden könnten. Fällt nämlich diese Prüfung negativ aus, so steht der Zuständigkeit des zweiten Gerichtes nichts mehr entgegen. Deshalb darf dieses die Klage während der Zuständigkeitsprüfung des erst angerufenen Gerichts *unter keinen Umständen* zurückweisen.[13]

5.   Die Pflicht zur Beachtung ausländischer Rechtshängigkeit (wiewohl auf das europäische Inland beschränkt) war für die meisten EuGVÜ-Vertragsstaaten 1968 eine bedeutende Neuerung.[14] Sie ist notwendige Folge einer geschlossenen Zuständigkeitsordnung, welche mehrere Staaten zu *einem* homogenen Verfahrensgebiet schmieden will. EuGVÜ und LugÜ institutionalisieren gegenseitiges *Vertrauen* der Vertragsstaaten[15] in die Qualität ihrer Rechtsprechung. Sie gehen konsequent von der Ebenbürtigkeit sämtlicher Gerichte des gesamten Vertragsstaatsraumes aus. Die Gerichtspraxis zeigt sich allerdings nicht immer von dieser strukturellen Vertrauensbezeugung beeindruckt. Besonders energisch reagierten englische Gerichte in Fällen, in denen sie ihre internationale Zuständigkeit für zu Unrecht übergangen halten.

Dem soll im folgenden nachgegangen werden. Der Beitrag ist KURT SIEHR zu seinem 65. Geburtstag freundschaftlich-herzlich gewidmet.

II.

6.   Dem Lugano Übereinkommen ging das Brüsseler voraus. Hier wie dort ist das Vereinigte Königreich heute Vertragsstaat. Die Richter am englischen High Court

---

[12] BGE 123 III 414ff., 429 E. 7 a unter Hinweis auf Kropholler (oben N. 2) N 2 vor Art. 21.

[13] Das hatten die Vorinstanzen in dem zu BGE 123 III 414ff. führenden Verfahren denn auch – m.E. konventionskonform – nicht getan.

[14] Schack, *IPRax* (1989) 141 l. Sp.

[15] Kaufmann-Kohler, „L'exécution des décisions étrangères selon la Convention de Lugano", *SJ* (1997) 561ff.

in London erfuhren einen Kulturschock:

"The genesis of the [Brussels] Convention is the jurisprudence of the civil law rather than the common law. Since the original states were all civil law countries, and the United Kingdom played no role in the drafting of the Brussels Convention, this is hardly surprising."[16]

Die englischen Gerichte nehmen besonderen Anstoss, wenn das Zuständigkeitsverhalten einer klagenden Partei zu einer mit der Beklagten abgeschlossenen Zuständigkeitsvereinbarung[17] zugunsten der englischen Gerichte im Widerspruch steht. Sie pflegen dann der (anscheinend) prorogationsuntreuen Partei mit strafbewehrter anti suit-injunction zu befehlen, ihre Prozessführung ausserhalb des vereinbarten Gerichtsstandes zu unterlassen. Auch seit Ratifizierung des EuGVÜ wird diese Tradition fortgesetzt, wie die folgenden drei Fälle zeigen:

7.   Die US-amerikanische *Continental Bank* gewährte 1981 der griechischen *Aeakos Compania Naviera S.A.* und weiteren Gesellschaften ein Darlehen. Der Vertrag enthielt folgende Klausel:

"21.02 Each of the borrowers . . . hereby irrevocably submits to the jurisdiction of the English Courts... ".

Ein Jahr später kamen die Darlehensnehmerinnen ihren Verpflichtungen nicht. Nach fruchtlosen Verhandlungen verklagten sie am 20. November 1990 die Darlehensgeberin vor einem Gericht in Athen auf Schadenersatz. Sie machten geltend, die Bank "exercised its rights under the loan agreement contrary to business morality", und begehrten zudem unter Berufung auf Artikel 919 des griechischen Zivilgesetzbuchs die Feststellung, dass sie frei von aller Verpflichtung aus dem Darlehensverhältnis seien. Am 7. April 1991 ersuchte ihrerseits die verklagte Bank den High

---

[16]   Lord Justice Steyn, in *Continental Bank* v. *Aeakos Compania*, [1994] 1 Lloyd's Rep. 510 r. Sp.

[17]   Gemäss den Artikeln 17 Abs. 1 EuGVÜ/LugÜ, die wortgleich lauten:
    „Haben die Parteien, von denen mindestens eine ihren Wohnsitz in dem Hoheitsgebiet eines Vertragsstaats hat, vereinbart, dass ein Gericht oder die Gerichte eines Vertragsstaats über eine bereits entstandene Rechtsstreitigkeit oder über eine künftige aus einem bestimmten Rechtsverhältnis entspringende Rechtsstreitigkeit entscheiden sollen, so sind dieses Gericht oder die Gerichte dieses Staates ausschliesslich zuständig. Eine solche Gerichtsstandsvereinbarung muss geschlossen werden
    a) schriftlich oder mündlich mit schriftlicher Bestätigung;
    b) in einer form, welche den Gepflogenheiten entspricht, die zwischen den Parteien entstanden sind, oder
    c) im internationalen Handel in einer Form, die einem Handelsbrauch entspricht, den die Parteien kannten oder kennen mussten und den Parteien von Verträgen dieser Art in dem betreffenden Geschäftszweig allgemein kennen und regelmässig beachten."

Court in England um Erlass eines Verbots an die Darlehensnehmer, das Verfahren in Athen weiter zu betreiben. Eine solche *anti-suit injunction* sei gerechtfertigt, weil das Verhalten der Darlehensnehmerinnen gegen eine zwischen den Parteien abgeschlossene ausschliessliche Gerichtsstandsvereinbarung zugunsten der englischen Gerichte verstosse.

8.   Es stand fest, dass das Gericht in Athen das zuerst angerufene im Sinne von Artikel 21 EuGVÜ war. Für den erstinstanzlichen englischen Befehlsrichter Gatehouse J. und den Court of Appeal (Sir Stephen Brown, LJJ Steyn und Kennedy) stand ebenso fest, dass die Parteien eine nach Artikel 17 gültige Gerichtsstandsvereinbarung abgeschlossen hatten. Sie folgerten:

> "If article 17 applies, its provisions take precedence over the provisions of Articles 21 and 22. The structure and logic of the Convention convincingly point to this conclusion."[18]

Das in Athen eingeleitete Verfahren sei eine Verletzung der Gerichtsstandsvereinbarung. Als Abhilfe sei die Zusprechung von Schadenersatz für die erlittenen Umtriebe unzureichend; Rechtsschutzziel könne nur die Realerfüllung der Vereinbarung sein.[19] Für die Darlehensnehmerinnen trug Barbara Dohmann Q.C. vor, Artikel 21 EuGVÜ lasse dem griechischen Gericht zur Klärung der Zuständigkeitsfrage zwingend den Vortritt. Der englische Court of Appeal sah es anders:

> "The consequences that would flow from the adoption of the submission of Miss Dohmann are startling. Art. 21 provides that there shall be a mandatory stay of proceedings in favour of the court first seised, if Courts of different Contracting States are seised of proceedings involving 'the same cause of action'. If Miss Dohmann's submission is correct, it follows that a party will be able to override an exclusive jurisdiction agreement, which is governed by art. 17, by pre-emptively suing in the courts of another Contracting State ... In this way a party who is in breach of the contract will be able to set at naught an exclusive jurisdiction agreement which is the product of the free-will of the parties. The principle of the autonomy of the parties, enshrined in art. 17, cannot countenance such a conclusion."[20]

9.   Die anti-suit injunction wurde so im November 1993 vom Court of Appeal bestätigt. Im Mai 1994 entschied eine andere Zusammensetzung des Court of Appeal (LJJ Neill, Leggatt und Millett) über eine Berufung im Fall *The Angelic Grace*.[21] Es

---

[18] [1994] 1 Lloyd's Rep. 511 l. Sp.
[19] [1994] 1 Lloyd's Rep. 512 l. Sp.
[20] [1994] 1 Lloyd's Rep. 511 l. Sp.
[21] [1995] 1 Lloyd's Rep. 87-97.

ging um England und Italien. Die panamesische Gesellschaft *Aggeliki Charis Compania Maritima S.A.* hatte das Schiff Angelic Grace der italienischen *Pagnan S.p.a.* gechartet. In Chioggia kollidierte die Angelic Grace mit der Clodia, die der *Pagnan S.p.a.* gehörte. Die Charterparty enthielt eine Schiedsklausel mit dem Wortlaut:

> "All disputes from time to time arising out of this contract shall ... be referred to the arbitrament of two arbitrators carrying on business in London... "

Am 15. Januar 1993 verklagte die panamesische Gesellschaft die italienische in London auf Feststellung, dass alle Ansprüche aus der Schiffskollision in Italien unter die Schiedsklausel fielen. Sie ersuchte gleichzeitig um Erlass eines Verbots an die *Pagnan S.p.a.*, Klage in Italien zu erheben. Unbeindruckt verklagte *Pagnan S.p.a.* sie in Venedig am 9. Februar 1993. Der englische Court of Appeal erblickte darin eine nicht hinzunehmende Verletzung der Schiedsvereinbarung. Millett LJ hielt es nicht für angezeigt, das England sich in solchen Fragen Zurückhaltung auferlege:

> "In my judgment, the time has come to lay aside the ritual incantation that [the jurisdiction to grant anti-suit injunctions] is a jurisdiction which should only be exercised sparingly and with great caution. There have been many statements of great authority warning of the danger of giving an appearance of undue interference with the proceedings of a foreign court. Such sensitivity to the feelings of a foreign court has much to commend it where the injunction is sought on the ground of *forum non conveniens* on the general ground that the foreign proceedings are vexatious or oppressive where no breach of contract is involved ... But in my judgment, there is no good reason for diffidence in granting an injunction to restrain foreign proceedings on the clear and simple ground that the defendant has promised not to bring them."[22]

10.   Damit waren immerhin die Empfindlichkeiten ausländischer Gerichte offen angesprochen. Aber der Court of Appeal erblickt einen rechtsrelevanten Unterschied zwischen einem unmittelbaren Befehl an ein ausländisches Gericht und einem Befehl an eine dortige Prozesspartei, der mittelbar genau das gleiche Ergebnis bewirken soll.[23] Sophistisch? Mag sein, aber fortan wussten erstinstanzliche Rich-

---

[22] [1995] 1 Lloyd's Rep. 96 l. Sp.

[23] Kritisch zu dieser Haltung Bell, „Anti-Suit Injunctions in the Brussels Convention", *LQR* (1994) 204-209; Briggs, "Anti-European Teeth for Choice of Court Clauses", *Lloyd's Maritime and Commercial Law Quartely* (1994) 158-163; Briggs (a.a.O. 159) bezeichnet den Entscheid als „bold, attractive, and hopelessly wrong". In den beiden referierten Fällen *Continental Bank* and *Angelic Grace* wurde die Zulassung des Weiterzugs an das House of Lords von letzterem abgelehnt. Die englischen Gerichte hielten eine Vorlage an den EuGH nicht für nötig.

ter, was sie zu tun hatten, wenn um Erlass einer *injunction* ersucht, damit parteiver-
einbarte englische Gerichtsbarkeit richtig zum Zuge komme.

11.   Noch keine Wende zeichnete sich 1997 ab in der Sache *Phillip Alexander
Securities and Futures Ltd. (PASF)* v. *Bamberger and Others.* PASF, eine Gesellschaft mit Sitz in England, hatte von verschiedenen in Deutschland wohnhaften
Personen, deren Eigenschaft als Konsumenten im Sinne von Art. 13 EuGVÜ unbestritten war, Geldanlagen entgegengenommen. Die Verträge enthielten die Abrede,
dass Streitigkeiten einem Schiedsgericht mit Sitz in London zu unterbreiten seien.
Die Konsumenten verklagten PASF vor ihren jeweiligen deutschen Wohnsitzge-
richten auf Ersatz erlittener Verluste. PASF erwirkte vom englischen High Court
gegen einzelne der Konsumenten einstweilige Befehle, die deutschen Verfahren
nicht weiter zu betreiben, und leitete Schiedsverfahren in London an. Ein Gericht in
Düsseldorfer wehrte sich. Es lehnte die Zustellung einer *anti-suit injunction* ab,
denn so etwas würde deutsche Souveränität verletzen:

> „Solche Anordnungen stellen (…) einen Eingriff in die Justizhoheit der Bundesrepublik
> Deutschland dar, weil die deutschen Gerichte ausschliesslich selbst nach den für sie gel-
> tenden Verfahrensgesetzen und nach den bestehenden völkerrechtlichen Verträgen dar-
> über befinden, ob sie für die Entscheidung einer Streitsache zuständig sind oder ob sie die
> Zuständigkeit eines anderen inländischen oder ausländischen Gerichts (auch Schiedsge-
> richts) zu respektieren haben. Auch können ausländische Gerichte keine Weisungen er-
> teilen, ob und in welchem Umfang (…) ein deutsches Gericht in einer bestimmten Sache
> tätig werden kann und darf.“[24]

12.   In der Hauptsache ergingen in England und Deutschland widersprüchliche Urteile bzw. Schiedssprüche. Jedoch hob der englische High Court alle *ex parte* erlas-
sene *anti-suit-injunctions* im Bestätigungsverfahren ab. Er fand, dass die Schiedsvereinbarungen nach englischem Recht ungültig seien.[25] Wären sie aber gültig
gewesen, so – nun kommt die Retourkutsche – hätte das Gericht das Argument, den
deutschen Urteilen seien wegen Verletzung der englischen öffentlichen Ordnung
die Anerkennung zu verweigern, nicht von der Hand gewiesen.[26] Hier stehe nicht

---

[24] OLG Düsseldorf, Beschluss vom 10.1.1996 – 3 VA 11/95, zitiert nach *ZZP* 109 (1996) 222.
[25] Waller J., [1997] I.L.Pr. 102, N 115: "Furthermore, the judgments obtained without notice of any
injunction should be recognised by the English court since, on the views that I have expressed as to the
validity of the arbitration provisions as a manner of English law, there is no argument available to PASF
based on public policy."
Vgl. dagegen, auf gleicher Instanzenebene, aber ohne Erörterung der Frage einer möglichen Ordre
Public-Verletzung Diamond J., in *The Heidberg,* [1994] 2 Lloyd's Rep. 287ff., 301 l. Sp.: "It is in my
judgment beyond doubt that the judgment of a foreign Contracting State on the substance of a dispute,
even if given in breach of a valid arbitration agreement, must be recognised by this court under art. 26."

die Verletzung von Zuständigkeitsvorschriften, sondern der Verstoss einer Partei gegen eine Prozessvereinbarung im Vordergrund.[27]

III.

13. Verträgt sich der *lege artis* auszulegende Wortlaut der Konventionen mit dem Standpunkt der englischen Rechtsprechung? Gehen wir – aus schweizerischer Sicht – vom LugÜ aus. Dieses Übereinkommen

> „ . . . positiviert direkt anwendbare internationale Einheitsnormen, deren Sinn nach den klassischen Auslegungskriterien, aber unter bewusster Berücksichtigung der Besonderheiten einer international vereinheitlichen Ordnung zu ermitteln ist (...) Bei der Auslegung internationaler Einheitsregeln nach den herkömmlichen Kriterien aufgrund des (mehrsprachigen) Wortlauts, der Zielvorgabe und inneren Systematik der harmonisierten Ordnung sowie dem historischen Willen der Abkommensstaaten hat sich das rechtsanwendende Gericht stets bewusst zu sein, dass die eigenen innerstaatlichen Institute und dogmatischen Konstruktionen nicht ohne weiteres den Anschauungen der anderen Abkommensstaaten entsprechen und daher nicht ohne weiteres die Einheitsordnung zugrundeliegen."[28]

14. Vorab ist zu fragen, ob Artikel 21 LugÜ auch zum Zuge komme, wenn eine Gerichtsstandsvereinbarung nach Artikel 17 LugÜ vorliegt. Seinem Wortlaut nach schon: Artikel 21 LugÜ unterscheidet nicht zwischen objektiver und subjektiver Zuständigkeitsanknüpfung, und die Regel, dass das zuerst angerufene Gericht europäische Kompetenz-Kompetenz hat, beansprucht *absolute* Geltung. Dem setzt sich die englische Rechtsprechung entgegen. Wird sie durch die Inanspruchnahme von *Anti-suit*-Zuständigkeit masslos?

Eigentlich schon. Denn so war es nicht gemeint!

---

[26] Waller J, [1997] I.L.Pr. 102, N 121.: "The Court of Appeal in *Continental Bank* and *The Angelic Grace* support the view that the English court is entitled to take the view that contracting parties are to be kept to their bargains. In most instances, since the court of the Member State where the party is being injuncted would take the same view and would be unoffended by the notion that a party should be stopped breaking its agreement, no difficulty will ensue. Instances where the Member State takes a different view will hopefully be rare."

[27] Briggs/Rees, *Civil Jurisdiction and Judgments*, 2. Aufl. (1997), 315 Anm. 45: "It does not infringe the prohibition on applying the test of public policy to the jurisdiction of another contracting state. Rather, it concentrates on the clear breach of contract in seising a court in defiance of the agreement to arbitrate." Gl. Ansicht in bezug auf die grundsätzliche Möglichkeit einer Ordre Public-Prüfung in solchen Fällen Berti, *FS Vogel* (1991) 355.

[28] BGE 123 III 421 E. 4.

15. Die englische Rechtsprechung missachtet das von den Übereinkommen von Brüssel und Lugano gewählte System, wonach das zuerst angerufene Gericht über die Realerfüllung einer mit Artikel 17 konformen Gerichtstandsvereinbarung *souverän* entscheidet. Die Frage, ob eine solche Vereinbarung einen real durchsetzbaren Anspruch auf die Zuständigkeitsausübung des prorogierten Gerichts abgibt, kann nur *konventionsautonom-einheitlich* für alle Vertragsstaaten beantwortet werden.

16. Zwar ist wertungsmässig für die Haltung der englischen Rechtsprechung ein *gewisses* Verständnis aufzubringen. Das Anliegen, den Grundsatz *pacta sunt servanda* durchzusetzen, ist achtenswert. Es wäre ein Leichtes, ihm durch eine Modifikation der Übereinkommen zu entsprechen, etwa durch Einfügung einer Bestimmung, wonach wenn *prima facie* eine ausschliessliche Parteivereinbarung über die Zuständigkeit vorliegt, deren Gültigkeit vorab durch die Gerichte des bezeichneten Vertragsstaates zu prüfen wäre.[29] In der kürzlich erfolgten Teilrevision des Lugano Übereinkommens wurde indessen diesbezüglich nichts unternommen.

17. Die englische Rechtsprechung kann sich zu ihrer Rechtfertigung nicht gut auf den Umstand hinweisen, dass sich der EuGH bislang nicht zur Frage des Verhältnisses zwischen Art. 17 und 21 EuGVÜ erschöpfend geäussert hat, zumal sie – offenbar von der Eindeutigkeit der Rechtslage ausgehend – entsprechende Gelegenheiten für eine Vorlage nicht wahrgenommen hat...

IV.

18. Die englische Rechtsprechung will aber nicht unhöflich, geschweige denn masslos sein. Am 2. April 1998 entschied das House of Lords eine Berufung in der Sache *Airbus Industrie G.I.E.* v. *Patel*. Gegenstand war erneut die Problematik der *anti suit-injunctions* im Kontext der internationalen Zuständigkeit. Der Fall fiel weder unter das Brüsseler noch unter das Lugano Übereinkommen. Europa wurde dennoch im folgenden, bemerkenswerten *obiter dictum* von Lord Goff of Chieveley angesprochen:

"This part of the law is concerned with the resolution of clashes between jurisdictions. Two different approaches to the problem have emerged in the world today, one associated with the civil law jurisdictions of continental Europe, and the other with the common law world. Each is the fruit of a distinctive legal history, and also reflects to some extent cultural differences which are beyond the scope of an opinion such as this.

---

[29] Ähnlich konzipiert – aber für Schiedsvereinbarungen – ist Art. 7 IPRG.

On the contintent of Europe, in the early days of the European Community, the essential need was seen to be to avoid any such clash between Member States of the same community. A system, developed by distinguished scholars, was embodied in the E.C. Judgments Convention (Brussels) 1968, under which jurisdiction is allocated on the basis of well-defined rules. This system achieves its purpose, but at a price. **The price is rigidity, and rigidity can be productive of injustice. The judges of this country, who loyally enforce this system, not only between United Kingdom jurisdictions and the jurisdictions of other Member States, but also as between the three jurisdictions within the United Kingdom itself, have to accept the fact that the practical results are from time to time unwelcome.** This is essentially because the primary purpose of the Convention is to ensure that there shall be no clash between the jurisdictions of Member States of the Community.

In the common law world, the situation is precisely the opposite. There is, so to speak, a jungle of separate, broadly based, jurisdictions all over the world. In England, for example, jurisdiction is founded on the presence of the defendant within the jurisdiction, and in certain specified (but widely drawn) circumstances on a power to serve the defendant with process outside the jurisdiction. But the potential excesses of common law jurisdictions are generally curtailed by the adoption of the principle of *forum non conveniens* – a self-denying ordinance under which the court will stay (or dismiss) proceedings in favour of another clearly more appropriate forum. This principle, which has no application as between states which are parties to the E.C. Judgments Convention, appears to have originated in Scotland (partly, perhaps, because of the exorbitant Scottish jurisdiction founded upon arrestment of the defendant's goods in Scotland) and to have been developed primarily in the United States: but, at least since the acceptance of the principle in England by your Lordships' House in *Spiliada Maritime Corporation* v. *Cansulex Ltd.*, it has become widely accepted throughout the common law world – notably in New Zealand, in Australia, though in a modified form, in Canada, and in India, as is exemplified by the litigation in the present case."[30] [Fettdruck hinzugefügt]

Die Ermahnung zur Vertragstreue als Wink mit dem Zaunpfahl des obersten Gerichts? Die Zukunft wird weisen müssen, ob nun die unteren englischen Instanzen sich fortan an die Prärogative des zuerst angerufenen vertragsstaatlichen Gerichtes halten, wenn auch zähneknirschend, oder ob sie ihren bisherigen methodischen Irrtum aufrechterhalten, um das zu erschleichen, worauf die Übereinkommen keinen Anspruch verleihen: Das Recht, es besser zu wissen als die anderen.

---

[30] [1999] I.L.Pr. 245.

Summary

English Anti-suit Injunctions in European Civil Procedural Law: a Flourishing Species or a Dying Breed?

The Brussels and Lugano Conventions have hitherto proved particularly conducive to forum shopping, and this phenomenon will no doubt continue as long as there are parties who refuse to believe that in Europe all courts are equal. The Conventions contain clear rules regarding the exercise of jurisdiction: the principle laid down in article 21 is that of first come, first served, and any court other than the court first seised shall of its own motion stay proceedings until such time as the jurisdiction of the court first seised is established.

English courts are inclined to disregard this rule in cases where a litigant seises them based on a jurisdiction agreement which *prima facie* conforms to the requirements of article 17 of the Conventions after the opposing party has commenced litigation elsewhere, apparently in the face of the jurisdiction agreement. Is there any room for anti-suit injunctions under the system of the Conventions in such situations?

According to the Continental view examined in this article, and as Lord Goff of Chieveley appeared to accept, albeit *obiter,* in *Airbus Industrie G.I.E.* v. *Patel,* there is no such room. The prerogative of the court first seised to take a jurisdiction agreement in favour of the courts of another country must be respected. Where the Conventions of Brussels and Lugano apply, the anti-suit injunction should not be a flourishing species, but a dying breed.

Altersdiskriminierung im Arbeitsrecht – kollisionsrechtlich betrachtet

Rolf Birk[*]

1.   EINLEITUNG

1.1   Allgemeine Überlegungen

Älterwerden ist zunächst ein individueller Vorgang: Unser Jubilar wird 65 Jahre. Ältere Menschen sind aber auch Teil der Gesellschaft und damit als eigene Gruppe zu identifizieren, seien sie noch selbst im Erwerbsprozess tätig, seien sie bereits aus dem Erwerbsleben ausgeschieden. Die nachfolgenden Ausführungen beschränken sich auf die älteren Menschen, die noch in der Arbeitswelt stehen.

[*] Prof. Dr. Dr. h.c., Direktor des Intituts für Arbeitsrecht und Arbeitsbeziehungen in der Europäischen Gemeinschaft, Trier.

J. Basedow et al., eds., Private Law in the International Arena – Liber Amicorum Kurt Siehr
© 2000, T.M.C.Asser Press, The Hague, The Netherlands

Das Lebensalter eines Arbeitnehmers spielt zwar im allgemeinen im Arbeitsrecht keine besondere Rolle, es ist aber doch häufig Anlass, ihn anders, meist schlechter zu behandeln als jüngere, um ihn etwa wegen angeblicher geringerer Leistungsfähigkeit dlurch solche zu ersetzen, oder um generell aufgrund arbeitsmarktpolitischer Überlegungen der nachwachsenden Generation größere Chancen auf Beschäftigung zu geben. Welche Motive auch im einzelnen dafür ausschlaggebend sein mögen, die Diskriminierung älterer Arbeitnehmer ist ein globales und nicht nur ein amerikanisches, europäisches oder gar deutsches Thema. Freilich, wo internationale (ILO, Europarat) oder europäische (EU) Regelungen bisher fehlen, lässt sich die Antwort nur dem Recht eines einzelnen Staates entnehmen. Dies macht es notwendig, in grenzüberschreitenden Fällen das zuständige und damit anwendbare Recht zu ermitteln. Während die USA hier mit einem relativ umfangreichen Fallmaterial und dessen literarischer Aufbereitung und Diskussion aufwarten können, beschränken sich die deutschen und somit auch die europäischen Bemühungen auf ganz wenige Stimmen. Die Problematik ist in ihrer kollisionsrechtlichen Dimension bislang kaum entdeckt,[1] geschweige eingehender behandelt worden.[2]

Es ist im Rahmen diese Beitrages allerdings nicht möglich, die einzelnen Rechtsordnungen und ihre Behandlung der Altersdiskriminierung im Arbeitsrecht im einzelnen rechtsvergleichend zu untersuchen. Ausgehend von den USA, in denen 1967 der Age Discrimination in Employment Act (ADEA) im Gefolge des Title VII des Civil Rights Act von 1964, der sich mit der Diskriminierung wegen Rasse, Geschlecht, Religion und nationaler Herkunft gefasst, erlassen wurde, hat die Antidiskriminierungsgesetzgebung über die Geschlechtsdiskriminierung hinaus in Australien, Neuseeland und neustens auch in Südafrika breite Bedeutung erlangt und die Diskriminierung wegen des Alters miteinbezogen. Simitisü[3] hat deshalb durchaus recht, wenn er diesen Trend als „denationalizing labour law" charakterisiert. Europa,[3a] insbesondere auch Deutschland, bleibt freilich doch erheblich hinter dieser Entwicklung zurück. In Deutschland gibt es nur vereinzelte Versuche, die Altersdiskriminierung im Arbeitsrecht – und nicht nur da[4] – zu the-

---

[1] Simitis, „Denationalizing Labour Law: The Case of Age Discrimination", 15 *Comp. Lab.L.J.* (1994) 321, 322 N. 7, hat wenigstens auf das Problem hingewiesen.

[2] Mit Ausnahme von Krebber in seiner grundlegenden Schrift *Internationales Privatrecht des Kündigungsschutzes bei Arbeitsverhältnisses* (1997), der die Problematik eingehend aus kündigungsrechtlicher Perspektive beleuchtet.

[3] S. oben N. 1.

[3a] Vgl. jedoch nunmehr Art. 5 des Vorschlages einer Richtlinie des Rates zur Festlegung eines allgemeinen Rahmens für die Verwirklichung der Gleichbehandlung in Beschäftigung und Beruf vom 25. November 1999 (Kom (1999) 546 endg.)

[4] Vgl. Häberle, „Altern und das Alter des Menschen als Verfassungsproblem", in: *Festschrift P. Lerche*, (1993) 177ff.

matisieren[5] und in den internationalen Trend einzufügen.[6]

Eines ist jedenfalls sicher und auch für das Kollisionsrecht von Bedeutung: die Regelungen über und gegen die Altersdiskriminierung im Arbeitsrecht sind im Zusammenhang mit den sonstigen Diskriminierungstatbeständen zu sehen. Ob sie deren kollisionsrechtliches Schicksal teilen, ist eine andere, an dieser Stelle nicht zu beantwortende Frage.

Während in den USA das Recht gegen die Diskriminierung wegen Alters auf zwei Ebenen geregelt ist, nämlich auf der Ebene des Bundes durch den ADEA und der Ebene der Einzelstaaten (z.B. in New York durch das Human Rights Law oder in New Jersey durch das New Jersey Law Against Discrimination (LAD)) fehlt es auf der vergleichbaren Europäischen Ebene an jeglicher Regelung, nur in den einzelnen Mitgliedstaaten der EU finden sich partielle Normen, welche die Altersdiskriminierung in bestimmten Punkten verbieten. Anders als in den USA fehlt ein allgemeines Diskriminierungsverbot im Hinblick auf das Alter. Demgegenüber besitzen etwa ein solches Neuseeland im Human Rights Act von 1993 und Südafrika im Equal Opportunities Act von 1998.

In Deutschland normiert lediglich § 75 Abs. 1 S. 2 BetrVG eine umfassendere, wenn auch wenig klare Pflicht für Arbeitgeber und Betriebsrat, „Arbeitnehmer nicht wegen Überschreitung bestimmter Altersstufen" zu benachteiligen. Ein generelles Diskriminierungsverbot kennt das deutsche Recht zum gegenwärtigen Zeitpunkt nicht. Im Zentrum der Diskussion standen die individual- und kollektivrechtlichen Aspekte der Altersgrenzen, insbesondere die Möglichkeit der „Zwangspensionierung mit 65".[7]

Nur gering ist bisher die Bereitschaft, über die arbeitsmarktpolitische Bedeutung der Pensions- bzw. Ruhestandsgrenze hinaus die Altersdiskriminierung als ein Problem zu sehen,[8] das vor allem den einzelnen älteren Menschen selbst umfassend in seiner Stellung, Beziehung zur Arbeit und seiner Aktivität als Arbeitnehmer betrifft. Das Bedürfnis, aus dem Erwerbsleben auszuscheiden, ist bei dem einzelnen Arbeitnehmer sehr unterschiedlich ausgeprägt. Die gilt auch für seine objektive Leistungsfähigkeit. Dies sieht die Betriebswirtschaftslehre ähnlich, wenn sie die Weiterbeschäftigung pensions – bzw. rentenberechtigter älterer Arbeitnehmer wegen deren Potentials an betriebs – und fachspezifischen Kenntnissen und Erfahrun-

---

[5] Dies gilt vor allem für Simitis (oben N. 1) ders., „Die Altersgrenzen – ein spät entdecktes Problem", *RdA* (1994) 257ff.; ders., „Altersdiskriminierung – die verdrängte Benachteiligung", *NJW* (1994) 1453f. – Vgl. ferner U. Schröder, *Altersbedingte Kündigungen und Altersgrenzen im Individualarbeitsrecht* (1984).

[6] Simitis, (oben N. 1) S. 321ff.; Fenske, *Das Verbot der Altersdiskriminierung im US-amerikanischen Recht* (1998) 272ff., 338ff.

[7] Hanau, „Zwangspensionierung des Arbeitnehmers mit 65?", *RdA* (1976) 24ff.; U. Schröder (oben N. 5) 101ff.

[8] So vor allem Simitis in den zitierten Beiträgen.

gen empfiehlt.[9] Langfristig wird sich Europa und damit auch Deutschland der von den USA eingeleiteten und von einigen anderen Staaten wie Neuseeland und Südafrika fortgeführten Entwicklung zu einem allgemeinen Verbot der Altersdiskriminierung nicht verschließen können. Für die Gleichbehandlung der Geschlechter hat man schon früher diesen Weg beschritten. Das Arbeitsrecht wird so immer stärker auch ein Recht der Nichtdiskriminierung werden; insoweit können wir – horribile dictu – vom amerikanischen Recht lernen.

1.2   Skizze des amerikanischen Rechts

Es ist in diesem Zusammenhang nicht möglich, eine halbwegs verlässliche Bestandsaufnahme des „amerikanischen" Rechts (Bundesrecht: ADEA; Einzelstaaten: z.B. New York Executive Law (Human Rights Law) §§ 296ff.) zu vermitteln. Hierfür besteht an sich auch kein Bedürfnis, da mehrere deutschsprachige, umfangreichere Darstellungen existieren.[10] Ein Rückgriff auf die – sehr umfangreiche – amerikanische Literatur wird freilich bei Einzelproblemen unumgänglich.r[11] Für die kollisionsrechtliche Diskussion ist es freilich unvermeidbar, wenigstens die Anwendungsvoraussetzungen und das wesentliche Instrumentarium des ADEA zu skizzieren, um die Gefahr einer sich verselbständigenden kollisionsrechtlichen Betrachtung zu vermeiden.

Der Age Discrimination in Employment Act (ADEA) wurde 1967 im Gefolge des Title VII des Civil Rights Act von 1964 vom Kongress erlassen[12] und in der Zwischenzeit mehrfach geändert. Der ADEA schützt jeden Arbeitnehmer – und in bestimmtem Umfang Stellenbewerber – über 40 gegenüber dem Arbeitgeber,[13] seinen Vertretern sowie den Arbeitnehmervertretungen, insbesondere also Gewerkschaften, durch ein generelles Diskriminierungsverbot (§ 623), wenn die direkte / unmittelbare (disparate treatment) oder die indirekte / mittelbare (disparate impact) Diskriminierung aufgrund dessen Alters erfolgt ist.

Die Diskriminierung des Arbeitnehmers kann in bestimmten Fällen (z.B. bei sog. BOFQ – bona fide occupational qualification, betrieblicher Altersversorgung, seniority systems[14] und vertraglichem Verzicht) gerechtfertigt sein. Diskriminie-

---

[9] Sadowski, *Pensionierungspolitik* (1977) insbes. S. 104.

[10] Vgl. Hebel, *Age Discrimination in Employment – Das Problem der Diskriminierung älterer Arbeitnehmer im U.S.-amerikanischen Recht* (1992); Fenske, *Das Verbot der Altersdiskriminierung im US-amerikanischen Recht* (1998); ferner Finkin, „The federal law of age discrimination in the USA", *Zeitschr. f. Gerontologie* (1990) 97ff.

[11] Einen guten Überblick gibt Kalet, *Age Discrimination in Employment Law*, 2nd edn. (1990); führend Lindemann/ Grossmann (eds.), *Employment Discrimination Law*, 3rd edn. (1996) Vol. I, 545ff.

[12] 29 United States Code (U.S.C.) §§ 621-634.

[13] Besonderheiten des öffentlichen Dienstes bleiben unberücksichtigt.

[14] Zur Frage der seniority im deutschen Recht Däubler, „Seniorität im Arbeitsrecht", in: *Festschrift A. Gnade* (1992) 95ff.

rende Maßnahmen erstrecken sich zeitlich von der Anbahnung über die Einstellung, und Ausgestaltung bis zur Beendigung des Arbeitsverhältnisses; dem
Gegenstande nach können davon betroffen sein: Stellenanzeigen, Fragen nach dem
Alter, die Ablehnung eines Bewerbers, bei der Einstellung bei der Beförderung,
Herabstufung oder Versetzung, bei der Kündigung durch den Arbeitgeber (discharge) oder der durch ihn veranlassten Kündigung duch den Arbeitnehmer (constructi-
ve discharge).[15] Als Rechtsfolgen einer Verletzung des Diskriminierungsverbotes
kommen in Betracht: Schadensersatz in Geld (z.T. als sog. liquidated damages –
doppelter Schadensersatz), einschließlich des Ersatzes des immateriellen Schadens
– die Einstellung, Beförderung oder Wiedereinstellung durch das Gericht.

Besonders zu beachten ist dabei, dass der ADEA nur Anwendung findet, wenn
der Arbeitgeber mindestens 20 Arbeitnehmer beschäftigt. Im übrigen sind Füh-
rungskräfte vom gesetzlichen Schutz bei der Kündigung ausgenommen, die diese
Position in den letzten beiden Jahren vor der Kündigung eingenommen haben und
mindestens eine jährliche Pension von $ 44,000.- beziehen (§ 631(c)).

Von besonderer Bedeutung ist die Einhaltung des für die Geltendmachung einer
Verletzung des Diskriminierungsverbotes einzuhaltenen Verfahrens, das in zwei
Stufen abläuft. Zunächst findet ein Vorverfahren bei der Equal Employment Op-
portunity Commission (EEOC) statt. Der Arbeitnehmer muss zunächst bei ihr innerhalb von 180 Tagen nach der Verletzung eine Beschwerde einlegen, welcher die
EEOC nachgehen muss; das Vorverfahren kann dann u. U. mit einer Klageerhebung durch die EEOC beendet werden. Frühestens 60 Tage nach Einlegung der Beschwerde darf der Arbeitnehmer selbst Klage erheben. Allerdings schließt die
Erhebung der Klage durch die EEOC eine solche des/der Arbeitnehmer(s) aus. In
Frage kommt auch eine sog. class action; wird Schadensersatz in Geld begehrt, findet das Verfahren vor der Jury statt.

Im übrigen können neben dem ADEA ohne Einschränkung die Altersdiskrimi-
nierungsgesetze der Einzelstaaten angewandt und die in deren Rechten vorgesehenen Verfahren durchgeführt werden. All erdings ist das einzelstaatliche Verfahren
einzustellen, wenn ein Verfahren nach dem ADEA eingeleitet wurde.

2. ALTERSDISKRIMINIERUNG BEI GRENZÜBERSCHREITENDEN
    ARBEITSVERHÄLTNISSEN

Die kollisionsrechtliche Dimension der Problematik ist vor allem in den USA, aber
auch in Deutschland manifest geworden. Und zwar in der Gesetzgebung (USA)
selbst wie auch in der Rechtsprechung (USA, Deutschland). Der amerikanische Se-

---

[15] Vgl. dazu Birk, „Die provozierte Auflösung des Arbeitsverhältnisses", in: *Festschrift W. Zöllner*
(1998) Bd. II, S. 687, 692f.

nat hat im Gefolge der Ablehnung einer extraterritorialen Anwendung des ADEA durch zwei Bundesgerichte[16] 1983 ein besonderes Hearing durch den Unterausschuss „On aging" des Committee on Labor and Human Resources unter dem Thema „Age Discrimination and Overseas Americans, 1983" durchgeführt.[17] Als dessen Ergebnis kann die Änderung des ADEA im Jahre 1984 gelten, durch die in § 623 (h) dessen extraterritoriale Anwendung eingeführt wurde. Sie war später Vorbild für die entsprechende Regelung im Civil Rights Act 1991, in welchem die Diskriminierungstatbestände des Title VII des Civil Rights Act 1964 auf gewisse Auslandssachverhalte für anwendbar erklärt wurden. Eine vergleichbare Norm enthalten Sect. 26 Human Rights Act 1993 von Neuseeland, hinsichtlich der Geschlechtsdiskriminierung sowie Sect. 9 (19) und (20) Sex Discrimination Act 1984 von Australien.

In der Rechtsprechung der USA haben die Gerichte in über 25 Entscheidungen über Sachverhalte mit Auslandselementen geurteilt,[18] über die Zahl der Fälle vor der EEOC konnte nichts genaueres in Erfahrung gebracht werden. Allein vier bezogen sich auf Fälle, in denen in Deutschland der Schwerpunkt lag.[19] Von deutschen

---

[16] *Zahourek* v. *Arthur Young & Co.*, 567 F. Supp. 1453 (D.C. Colorado, 1983), affirmed 750 F. 2d 827 (10th Circuit 1984); *Cleary* v. *United States Lines*, 555 F. Supp. 1251 (D.N.J. 1983), affirmed 728 F. 2d 607 (3rd Circuit 1984); vgl. ferner noch *Thomas* v. *Brown & Root, Inc.*, 745 F. 2d 279 (C.A., 4th Circuit, 1984).

[17] Hearing before the Subcommittee on Aging of the Committee on Labor and Human Resources – Unites States Senate, 89th Congress, First Session on Reviewing certain Provisions of the Age Discrimination and Employment Act (Public-Law 90-202), which affect Americans working abroad, September 23, 1983 – Washington 1984, S. Hrg. 98-558, 48 S.

[18] *Osborne* v. *United Technologies Corp.*, 1977 WL 15422 (D.C. Conn.); *Mas Marques* v. *Digital Equipment Corp. and Digital Equipment GmbH*, 490 F. Supp. 56 (D.C. Mass., 1980); *Cleary* v. *United States Lines, Inc.*, 728 F. 2d 607 (C.A., 3rd circuit, 1984); *Zahourek* v. *Arthur Young & Co.*, 750 F. 2d 827 (C.A., 10th. circuit, 1984); *Thomas* v. *Brown & Root, Inc.*, 745 F. 2d 279 (C.A., 4th circuit, 1984); *Pfeiffer* v. *WM Wrigley Ir. Comp.*, 755 F. 2d 554 (C.A., 7th circuit, 1985); *Wolf* v. *J.I. Case Comp.*, 617 F. Supp. 858 (D.C., Wisc., 1985); *De Yoreo* v. *Bell Helicopter Textron, Inc.*, 785 F. 2d 1282 (C.A., 5th circuit, 1986); *Lopez* v. *Pan Am World Services, Inc.*, 813 F. 2d 1118 (C.A., 11th circuit, 1987); *Helm* v. *South African Airways*, 44 FEP Cases 261 (D.C., S.D. New York, 1987); *MacNamara* v. *Korean Air Lines*, 863 F. 2d 1135 (C.A., 3rd circuit, 1998); *Iwankow* v. *Mobil Corp.*, 541 New York Supp. 2d 428 (N.Y. Supreme Court, 1989); *Akgun* v. *Boing Comp.*, 1990 WL 112609 (D.C., Wash., 1990); *Fortino* v. *Quasar comp.*, 950 F. 2d 389 (C.A., 7th circuit, 1991); *Mochelle* v. *J. Walter, Inc.*, 823 F. Supp. 1302 (D.C., Louis., 1993); *Robinson* v. *Overseas Military Sales Corp.*, 827 F. Supp. 915 (D.C., E.D.N.Y., 1993); *Brownlee* v. *Lear Siegler Management Services Corp.*, 15 F. 3d 976 (C.A., 10th circuit, 1994); Papaila v. *Uniden America Corp.*, 840 F. Supp. 440 (D.C., Texas, 1994); *Mahoney* v. *RFE/RL, Inc.*, 47 F. 3d 447 (C.A., D.C., 1995); *EEOC* v. *Kloster Cruise Ltd.*, 888 F. Supp. 147 (D.C., Florida, 1995); *Rao* v. *Kenya Airways, Ltd.*, 1995 WL 366305 (S.D.N.Y., 1995); *Dewey* v. *PTT Telecom Netherlands*, 68 FEP Cases 1112 (D.C., S.D.N.Y., 1995); *Robins* v. *Max Mara, USA, Inc.*, 914 F. Supp. 1006 (D.C., S.D.N.Y., 1996); *Morelli* v. *Cedel*, 141 F. 3d 39 (C.A., 2d circuit, 1998).

[19] *Osborne* v. *United Technologies Corp.*, 1977 WL 15422 (D.C. Conn.); *Mas Marques* v. *Digital Equipment Corp. and Digital Equipment GmbH*, 490 F. Supp. 56 (D.C. Mass., 1980); *Pfeiffer* v. *WM. Wrigley Jr. Comp.*, 755 F. 2d 554 (C.A., 7th circ. 1985); *G. Mahoney* v. *RFE/RL, Inc.*, 47 F. 3d 447 (D.C. circuit, 1995).

Arbeitsgerichten sind nur zwei Verfahren bekannt geworden. Im ersten lag der Arbeitsort in Deutschland,[20] im zweiten in den USA.[21]

Vom deutschen Kollisionsrecht her stellen sich – vor allem vor dem Hintergrund des ADEA – eine Vielzahl von Fragen, von denen jedoch hier nur einige herausgegriffen werden können. Da weder das internationale Recht (ILO, Europarat) noch das europäische Recht die Altersdiskriminierung im Arbeitsrecht länderübergreifend sachlich einheitlich oder harmonisierend regeln, wird die Problematik nach wie vor dem nationalen Recht zur Regelung trotz aller Globalisierung überantwortet.[22] Welches dieses Recht bei Sachverhalten mit Auslandselementen – dies kann sowohl ein Inlands- wie Auslandssachverhalt sein – ist, entscheidet das deutsche Gericht nach den einschlägigen KollisionsnormenO des Arbeitsrechts, es muss sie zur Entscheidung einem bestimmten nationalen Recht überlassen. Das Problem kann zum echten Dilemma werden, wenn nach der griffigen Formulierung „same boss, different rules"[23] zwei einander widersprechende Verhaltensanforderungen an den Arbeitgeber gerichtet werden, etwa einerseits durch sein „Heimatrecht" und andererseits durch das Recht des Staates, in dem das Arbeitsverhältnis durchgeführt wird.

Im einzelnen sind an kollisionsrechtlichen Fragestellungen bei grenzüberschreitenden Fällen arbeitsrechtlicher Altersdiskriminierung vor allem von Interesse: Welche Kollisionsnorm entscheidet über die Problematik der Altersdiskriminierung? Gilt für diese etwa eine vom Arbeitsvertrags- oder Arbeitsverhältnisstatut unabhängige arbeits- oder gar verfassungsrechtliche Sonderanknüpfung? Welche Einzelfragen stellen sich bei der Anwendung des ADEA[24] bzw. entsprechender einzelstaatlicher Vorschriften oder Normen von anderen Staaten (z.B. von Neuseeland oder Südafrika), etwa nach der „Anerkennung" des ausdrücklichen extraterritorialen Anwendungsanspruchs solcher Gesetze? Wie wirken sich etwa grenzüberschreitende Unternehmensverflechtungen aus?[25]

---

[20] Vgl. die Nachweise der Aktenzeichen bei Simitis (oben N. 1) S. 322 N. 5.

[21] ArbG Bonn, AZ: 5 Ca 2480/87; in diesem Fall war der Verf. als Gutachter tätig.

[22] Auch wenn die Frage selbst eine sachlich internationale bzw. denationale ist: Simitis, (oben N. 1) N. 20.

[23] Barbash, "Same Boss, Different Rules: An Argument für Extraterritorial Extension of Title VII to Protect U.S. Citizens Employment Abroad by U.S. Multinationale Corporations", 30 *Virginia Journal of International Law* (1990) 479ff.

[24] Dazu aus deutscher Sicht grundlegend Krebber, *Internationales Privatrecht des Kündigungsschutzes bei Arbeitsverhältnissen* (1997) S. 160ff., 172ff., 181ff., 261ff., 276ff.

[25] Mit Blick auf die Diskriminierungsverbote bereits Birk, „Die multinationalen Korporationen im internationalen Arbeitsrecht", in: *Berichte der Deutschen Gesellschaft für Völkerrecht* Bd. 18 (1978), S. 263, 300f.

3.   DIE MASSGEBLICHEN KOLLISIONSNORMEN FÜR DIE
     ALTERSDISKRIMINIERUNG IM ARBEITSRECHT

So umfangreich die US-amerikanische Rechtsprechung auch ist, sie hat bislang
stets nur die Frage entschieden, ob das eigene Recht auf Inlandssachverhalte mit
Auslandselementen oder auf Auslandssachverhalte mit Beziehungen zu den USA
angewandt werden kann. Zur Anwendung entsprechender – aus amerikanischer
Sicht – ausländischen Diskriminierungsregeln gibt es hingegen weder in der Rechtsprechung noch in dem recht umfangreichen Schrifttum[26] Aussagen.

Für den deutschen Richter stellt sich die Frage hingegen zuerst, unter welche
Kollisionsnorm die Problematik der arbeitsrechtlichen Altersdiskriminierung sub-
sumierbar ist, zumal es sich ja ersichtlich um keine ausschließliche Frage des
Kündigungsrechts handelt, vielmehr betrifft sie die unterschiedlichsten arbeitsrechtlichen Aspekte. Damit stellt sich zunächst das Problem, ob kollisionsrechtlich
gesehen die Altersdiskriminierung für das ganze Arbeitsverhältnis einheitlich zu
beurteilen ist, oder ob jeweils bei etwaiger besonderer Anknüpfung einzelner Fragen die Diskriminierung lediglich als Annexfrage ihr kollisionsrechtlich folgt. Erst
wenn die zweite Alternative ausgeschlossen werden kann, also einer einheitlichen
Anknüpfung der Altersdiskrimingierung das Wort geredet wird, bedarf es einer
Entscheidung der Frage, ob das Arbeitsverhältnisstatut oder ein davon unabhängi-
ges Recht maßgeblich sein soll.

Bei den Diskriminierungsverboten handelt es sich durchweg um Normen, die
auf die Verfassung rückführbar sind oder sie „ersetzen", wo es entsprechende
Grundrechte – z. B. im Vereinigten Königreich – nicht gibt. Sie partizipieren an den
verfassungsrechtlichen Wertentscheidungen und sind insoweit vom anderen Gesetzesrecht zu unterscheiden. Damit lässt sich zunächst begründen, dass die Diskriminierungsverbote, also auch das Verbot der Altersdiskriminierung oder Teilverbote,
wie etwa das Verbot einer arbeitsrechtlichen „Zwangspensionierung", nicht

---

[26] Ohne Anspruch auf Vollständigkeit seien genannt: Zanar, „Note: Recent Amendments to the
Age Discrimination in Employment Act", 19 *Geo. Wash. J. Int'l L & Econ* (1985) 165 ff.; Street, „Application of U.S. Employment Laws to Transnational Employers in the United States and Abroad",
19 *NYU J. of International Law and Politics* (1987) 357ff.; Zimmerman, „Extraterritorial Application
of Federal Labor Laws: Congress's Flawed Extension of the ADEA", 21 *Cornell Int. L.J.* (1988) 103ff.;
ders., *Extraterritorial Employment Standards of the United States – The Regulation of the Overseas
Workplace* (1992) S. 157 ff.; Equal Employment Opportunity Commission (EEOC), *Policy Guidance:
ADEA/EPA Application to American Firms*, N-915.039 – March 3, 1989 – *EEOC Compliance Manual*
N: 3915; Landerdale, "Age Discrimination – Extraterritorial Application of the Age Discrimination in
Employment Act etc.", 20 *Ga. J. Int'l & Comp. L.* (1990) 207ff.; Cherian, „Transnational Reach of U.S.
Civil Rights Laws: What Left After Aramco?", 42 *Labor L.J.* (1991) 596ff.; Yamakawa, „Territoriality
and Extraterritoriality: Coverage of Fair Employment Laws After EEOC v. Aramco", 17 *N. C. J. Int'l
L. & Com. Reg.* (1992) 71, 88ff.; Krebber (oben N. 24) S. 160ff.; Robertson, „Has the Age Discriminati-
on in Employment Act Remained Effective in the United States as Well as Abroad in an Increasingly
Globalized Economy?", 6 *The Elder Law Journal* (1998) 323ff.

getrennt nach der möglichen Auswirkungssphäre (z.B. Einstellung, Kündigung, betriebliche Altersvieersorgung) einheitlich anzuknüpfen sind. Die zweite Alternative scheidet deshalb aus.

Was ihren räumlichen Anwendungsbereich angeht, sollten sie daher nicht einfach dem Vertragsstatut entnommen werden, auch wenn dieses u. U. ähnliche Normen bereithält. Die Anwendung von Diskriminierungsverboten vom Vertragsstatut und damit auch von der Rechtswahl abhängig zu machen, entspricht nicht der grundrechtsähnlichen Struktur dieser Verbote bzw. Rechte. Dies macht etwa schon z.T. deren Bezeichnung als Civil oder Human Rights (vgl. USA, New York, Neuseeland) deutlich. Die Maßgeblichkeit des Vertragsstatuts ist damit zu verneinen. Die objektive, vertragsstatutunabhängige Anknüpfung (Sonderanknüpfung) der Diskriminierungsverbote folgt den gleichen Regeln wie die Anknüpfung der Grundrechte..[27] Diejenigen Staaten, die ausdrücklich den räumlichen Anwendungsbereich ihrer grundrechtskonkretisierenden Gesetze regeln (USA, New York, Australien, Neuseeland), entziehen sie damit automatisch dem Vertragsstatut. Dass etwa das objektiv bestimmte Vertragsstatut dasselbe Recht beruft, spricht nicht dagegen.

Die Sonderanknüpfung der Diskriminierungsverbote steht danach insoweit sachlich im Einklang mit den erwähnten ausdrücklichen, einseitigen Kollisionsnormen[28] des Auslands. Sie ist auch mit dem EVÜ und EGBGB vereinbar, da diese nicht vorschreiben, wann über die dort geregelten Fälle hinaus eine Frage dem Vertragsstatut unterworfen werden muss. Wäre dies der Fall, so würden in dieser Hinsicht die meisten britischen Arbeitnehmerschutzgesetze dem EVÜ widersprechen. Diese inhaltliche „Aushöhlung" des Vertragsstatuts ist indes zulässig; sie belegt im übrigen die weitgehende Fehlkonstruktion des EVÜ, soweit es sich auf den Arbeitsvertrag bezieht.

Welche Kriterien für die Sonderanknüpfung der Altersdiskriminierung maßgeblich sind, ist bislang offen geblieben. Wir können zunächst nur feststellen, dass es sich um eine allseitige Kollisionsnorm handeln soll und nicht nur um eine einseitige, die das eigene Recht in seinem räumlichen Anwendungsbereich abgrenzen soll. Am naheliegendsten stellt sich die Anknüpfung an den gewöhnlichen Arbeitsort dar, weil ein arbeitsrechtliches Diskriminierungsverbot auf die Dauerbeziehung zwischen Arbeitgeber und Arbeitnehmer bezugeschnitten ist. Diese hat ihren Schwerpunkt am gewöhnlichen Arbeitsort. Wo es einen solchen nicht gibt, tritt an dessen Stelle der Ort, von dem aus der Arbeitseinsatz gesteuert wird; im allgemeinen dürfte dies der tatsächliche Sitz des Arbeitgebers sein. Im Ergebnis deckt sich also die Sonderanknüpfung des Verbotes der Altersdiskriminierung mit dem objek-

---

[27] Aus arbeitsrechtlicher Sicht MünchArb/ Birk (1992) § 19 RdNr. 101ff.
[28] Ob es sich auch um „selbstbeschränkende" Sachnormen handeln kann, mag hier dahinstehen. Vgl. zu dieser Frage Keller/ Siehr, *Allgemeine Lehren des internationalen Privatrechts* (1986), 242ff.

tiven Arbeitsvertragsstatut des Art. 30 Abs. 2 EGBGB bzw. Art. 6 Abs. 2 EVÜ. Es geht jedoch über Art. 34 EGBGB hinaus, da es auch fremdes zwingendes Recht zur Anwendung beruft, das trotz des deutschen Vorbehalts gegen Art. 7 Abs. 1 EVÜ seit jeher im Arbeitsrecht angewandt worden ist.[29] Für die Sonderanknüpfung spricht im übrigen Art. 3 Abs. 1 der Entsende-Richtlinie, der die Diskriminierung wegen des Geschlechts vom Vertragsstatut abkoppelt und dem Recht des Beschäftigungsortes unterwirft.

Regeln die berufenen Rechte den räumlichen Anwendungsbereich selbst, so entstehen dadurch weitere Probleme, auf die erst weiter unten einzugehen ist.

4. DIE ANWENDUNG AUSLÄNDISCHER VORSCHRIFTEN ÜBER DIE ALTERSDISKRIMINIERUNG IM ARBEITSRECHT

Wegen des gegenwärtig noch teilweise bestehenden „Normenmangels" im Recht der Altersdiskriminierung geht es aus praktischer Sicht in erster Linie um die Anwendung ausländischen Rechts durch deutsche Gerichte, vor allem also um die Heranziehung US-amerikanischen Rechts (ADEA, u.U. auch einzelstaatlichen Rechts). Da oben als maßgebliches Anknüpfungskriterium für die arbeitsrechtliche Altersdiskriminierung der gewöhnliche Arbeitsort – und bei wechselndem Arbeitseinsatz der tatsächliche Sitz des Arbeitgebers – herausgearbeitet wurde, empfiehlt es sich die weitere Untersuchung danach vorzunehmen, ob der gewöhnliche Arbeitsort im Ausland oder im Inland liegt.

4.1 Gewöhnlicher Arbeitsort im Ausland

Liegt der gewöhnliche Arbeitsort im Ausland (z.B. in Frankreich, USA, Südafrika, Neuseeland), so verweist unsere ungeschriebene Kollisionsnorm unabhängig vom Statut des Arbeitsvertrages auf dessen Recht der Altersdiskriminierung. Dies kann praktisch zunächst dazu führen, dass das Recht des Arbeitsortes noch über gar kein Recht der Altersdiskriminierung verfügt oder dieses nur rudimentäre Regeln enthält. Andererseits kann das Recht des Arbeitsortes die räumliche Anwendung seiner Vorschriften über die Altersdiskriminierung ausdrücklich und u.U. abweichend von den oben herausgearbeiteten Vorstellellungen regeln. Dieser unterschiedlichen Lage muss bei den nachfolgenden Ausführungen Rechnung getragen werden.

---

[29] S. dazu MünchArb/ Birk, § 19 RdNr. 81-82; Junker, *Internationales Arbeitsrecht im Konzern* (1992) S. 303 ff.; Krebber (oben N. 24) S. 301f.

4.1.1 *Die Anwendung des amerikanischen ADEA durch deutsche Arbeitsgerichte*

(a) Der für ein deutsches Arbeitsgericht, dessen internationale Zuständigkeit hier unterstellt wird, naheliegende Fall ist die Anwendung des amerikanischen ADEA. Liegt der *Arbeitsort in den USA*, so bereitet dies zunächst keine besonderen Probleme. Die deutsche Kollisionsnorm für die Altersdiskriminierung beruft bei amerikanischem Arbeitsort das „amerikanische" Recht zur Anwendung. Dies ist zum einen der ADEA und zum anderen das für den Einzelstaat, in welchem der gewöhnliche Arbeitsort innerhalb der USA liegt (z.B. der Staat New York). Eine Rückverweisung enthält dieses nicht. Es kommt hierbei nicht darauf an, ob ein oder mehrere Sachverhaltselemente tatsächliche oder rechtliche Verbindungen zu Staaten außerhalb der USA besitzen, ob also der Arbeitgeber Ausländer, eine „ausländische" Gesellschaft oder die „amerikanische" Tochtergesellschaft einer ausländischen Muttergesellschaft ist; auch die Nationalität des Arbeitnehmers spielt für die Anknüpfung des ADEA keine Rolle.

Ebensowenig kommt es darauf an, wo das diskriminierende Verhalten – ob außerhalb oder innerhalb der USA – erfolgt ist; im Falle des disparate impact muss lediglich die Auswirkung der Diskriminierung in den USA erfolgen.

Weniger klar erscheint, welche Relevanz den verfahrensrechtlichen Vorschriften des ADEA zukommt, Vorverfahren bei der EEOC und gerichtliches Klageverfahren sind auseinanderzuhalten. Sie müssen in grenzüberschreitenden Fällen jedenfalls dann nicht im gleichen Staat stattfinden, wenne dadurch die Rechtsdurchsetzung selbst nicht ausgeschlossen oder schwer beeinträchtigt wird. Die verfahrensrechtlichen Zuständigkeiten lassen sich dem Grunde nach auf zwei verschiedene Staaten aufteilen.

Da für das Vorverfahren bei der EEOC keine entsprechende inländische Behörde besteht und damit als austauschbare Institution in Frage kommt, bleibt die Möglichkeit der Rechtsdurchsetzung vor einem deutschen Arbeitsgericht davon abhängig, dass bei der für den Arbeitsort zuständigen EEOC durch den betroffenen Arbeitnehmer Beschwerde eingelegt worden ist.[30] Das Vorverfahren ist eine Voraussetzung für die Durchsetzbarkeit des materiellen Anspruchs, es gehört nicht zum Zivilverfahrensrecht und unterliegt deshalb auch nicht der deutschen lex fori, sondern dem ADEA.

Welche prozessualen Instrumente (z.B. Unterlassungsklage) in Frage kommen, entscheidet das deutsche Verfahrensrecht (ArbGG, ZPO) als lex fori. Wenn der ADEA in der Auslegung der amerikanischen Gerichte dem Richter große Freiheit, etwa bei der Frage dert Wiedereinstellung eines wegen Altersdiskriminierung zu Unrecht gekündigten Arbeitnehmers, einräumt, so kann diese auch von einem deutschen Richter wahrgenommen werden, obwohl ihm das deutsche Recht solche

---

[30] Ebenso Krebber (oben N. 24) S. 278f., 345ff.

Handlungsmöglichkeiten bei der Festlegung einer Sanktion nicht einräumt. Andererseits liegt es auf der Hand, dass in Deutschland kein Jury über den Schadensersatzanspruch entscheidet.

Nach dem ADEA ist weiter zu beurteilen, wann der Schwellenwert von 20 Arbeitnehmern erreicht ist, ob etwa hier – amerikanische wie nichtamerikanische – Arbeitnehmer außerhalb der USA desselben Arbeitgebers oder gar desselben Konzerns oder Unternehmensverbundes nach der single-employer-doctrine bzw. der Lehre von den joint employers hinzuzurechnen sind.

(b)   Liegt der *Arbeitsort in einem anderen Staat* als den USA, ist nach deutschem Kollisionsrecht das dortige Recht der Altersdiskriminierung anzuwenden. Gibt es jedoch ein solches nicht, so fragt es sich, ob nicht an dessen Stelle der ADEA tritt, soweit er sich extraterritoriale Wirkung beilegt, was ja § 623(h) in bestimmtem Umfang tut. Hat die fehlende oder weniger weitgehende Regelung des Arbeitsortes die Wirkung, dass die Diskriminierung wegen Alters entweder generell oder teilweise gestattet ist, so stellt sich die weitere Frage, wie dieser Verhaltenskonflikt, in dem sich der Arbeitgeber befindet, gelöst werden kann.

§ 623(h) des ADEA bestimmt, dass das Gesetz auf Sachverhalte außerhalb der USA dann anwendbar sein soll, wenn es sich um diskriminierende Praktiken eines „amerikanischen" Arbeitgebers oder – zur Vermeidung von Umgehungsstrategien – einer von diesem kontrollierten „foreign corporation" handelt; eine solche Kontrolle liegt nach § 623(h)(3) vor bei (a) interrelation of operations, (b) common management, (c) centralized control of labor relations und (d) common ownership or financial control. Ist nach dieser Vorschrift der ADEA demnach auch bei einem Arbeitsort in einem anderen Land (workplace in a foreign country) anwendbar, so entfällt jedoch nach § 623(f)(1) der Vorwurf der rechtswidrigen Altersdiskriminierung, wenn die Befolgung des ADEA „would cause such an employer . . . to violate the laws of the country in which such workplace is located" (sog. foreign laws defense[31]).

Bei der Diskussion der Anwendbarkeit derartiger ausländischer Gesetze, die ihren Anwendungsbereich selbst festlegen – sie kommen relativ häufig im US-amerikanischen und britischen Arbeitsrecht vor – ist bisher kontrovers geblieben, ob diese territoriale Ausdehnung oder Beschränkung ihres Anwendungsbereichs zu beachten und wie sie gegebenenfalls zu begründen wäre.[32] Dass zwingendes Recht eines Drittstaates auch von den deutschen Arbeitsgerichten angewandt werden kann, wurde an anderer Stelle für den tatsächlichen Arbeitsort bereits bejaht; dies sollte indes zumindest auch dann gelten, wenn es sich zwar nicht um zwingendes

---

[31]   Dazu ausführlich Miller, „Note: Re-examining the Role of the Equal Employment Opportunity Commission Regarding Title VII's Foreign Laws Defense", 31 *Geo. Wash. J. Int'l L. & Econ.* (1997-1998) 439ff..

[32]   Ausführlich hierzu Krebber (oben N. 24) S. 301ff.

Recht des tatsächlichen Arbeitsortes handelt, wohl aber ein enger Zusammenhang[33] zwischen dem Drittstaat und dem Sachverhalt, wie hier durch die Zurechnung des Arbeitgebers zu den USA besteht und bei etwaigen Handlungskonflikten das betreffende Recht zurücktritt, wie das ja nach § 623(f)(1) der Fall ist. Die amerikanischen Gerichte legen die Möglichkeit, die foreign law defense zu erheben, verhältnismäßig großzügig aus; so ließen sie etwa in dem deutsch- amerikanischen Fall *Mahoney v. RFE/RL, Inc.*[34] die Berufung auf einen Firmentarifvertrag, der ein automatisches Ausscheiden des Arbeitnehmers mit Vollendung des 65. Lebensjahres dem Diskriminierungsverbot des ADEA in § 623(a) vorgehen.

Wenn demnach ausländisches Recht seinen Anwendungsbereich ausdrücklich selbst festlegt, so beachten wir dies, gleichgültig, ob man in solchen Festlegungen eine „selbstgerechte Sachnorm" oder eine einseitige Kollisionsnorm erblicken will. Die Abgrenzung beider ist ohnehin eher zufällig und nicht stringent zu belegen.[35]

4.1.2 *Die Anwendung des Rechts anderer Staaten*

Die Anwendung des ADEA wurde wegen seiner großen praktischen Bedeutung gesondert untersucht. Die dort gefundenen Ergebnisse lassen sich ceteris paribus auch auf Sachverhalte übertragen, in denen der gewöhnliche Arbeitsort etwa in Australien, Neuseeland, Südafrika oder in Ländern ohne umfassendere Gesetzgebung über die Altersdiskriminierung liegt, wenngleich natürlich in Einzelheiten stets das konkret anzuwendende Recht den Ausschlag gibt. Freilich kann etwa die amerikanische Regelung der foreign laws defense, die sich ja neben dem ADEA auch im Civil Rights Act 1991 findet, durchaus als Vorbild dienen, mögliche Konfliktsituationen zu vermeiden.

4.2 **Gewöhnlicher Arbeitsort im Inland**

Liegt der Arbeitsort in Deutschland, sind nach der oben entwickelten Kollisionsnorm die deutschen Antidiskriminierungsvorschriften zur Anwendung berufen. Das Statut des Arbeitsvertrages entscheidet diese Frage nicht. Das Gleiche sieht im übrigen für die Diskriminierung wegen des Geschlechts auch Art. 3 Abs. 1 Entsende-Richtlinie vor.

Inwieweit auch ausländisches Recht über die Altersdiskriminierung angewandt werden kann, ist eine Frage, die darin mündet, ob daieses selbst den Sachverhalt regelt – wie u.U. der ADEA – und vom deutschen Kollisionsrecht akzeptiert wird. Im Allgemeinen wird man freilich bei Berufung des deutschen Rechts die An-

---

[33] So Krebber (oben N. 24) S. 302.
[34] 47 F. 3d 447 (C.A., D.C. Circuit, 1995).
[35] Vgl. auch Keller/ Siehr (oben N. 28) S. 242.

wendung eines weiteren, ausländischen Rechts als ausgeschlossen ansehen müssen. Die deutsche Kollisionsnorm verweist nun einmal auf das deutsche Sachrecht. Dieses kann nicht einfach sich selbst zugunsten einer anderen Rechtsordnung verdrängen. Es bleibt aber möglich, dass fremdes zwingendes Recht durch deutsches Kollisionsrecht für relevant erklärt wird. Wie wir gesehen haben, ist dies bei allgemeinen Schuldverträgen im EGBGB nicht vorgesehen. Für Arbeitsverhältnisse ist die Lage jedoch gemäß früherer Feststellungen anders zu beurteilen, so dass bei einer entsprechend engen Verbindung des Sachverhalts zu einem anderen Staat, dessen zwingendes Recht – und dazu gehört das Recht gegen Altersdiskriminierung – angewandt werden kann. Im vorliegenden Zusammenhang könnte diese Verbindung etwa dann bejaht werden, wenn Arbeitgeber und Arbeitnehmer Angehörige[36] des betreffenden ausländischen Staates wären. Allerdings wäre ähnlich dem § 623(f)(1) des ADEA eine Voraussetzung, dass ein Handlungskonflikt durch Beachtung der – ungeschriebenen deutschen foreign tlaw defense vermieden werden sollte. Insgesamt gesehen würde damit im wichtigsten Fall, nämlich bei dem ADEA, dessen Anwendung allerdings angesichts seines allgemeinen Diskriminierungsverbots weitgehend leerlaufen, wenn man nicht dem Günstigkeitsprinzip folgen will. Dessen Anwendung muss allerdings schon daran scheitern, dass die Belegschaft am deutschen gewöhn lichen Arbeitsort nicht in unterschiedlich zu behandelnde Gruppen aufgeteilt werden darf, wie § 75 BetrVG belegt, dem insoweit gegenüber der Anwendung ausländischen zwingenden Rechts im konkreten Fall verdrängende Wirkung zukommt.

5.   DIE ANWENDUNG DEUTSCHER VORSCHRIFTEN ÜBER DIE
      ALTERSDISKRIMINIERUNG IM ARBEITSRECHT

Aus den vorangegangenen Ausführungen lässt sich entnehmen, dass deutsche gesetzliche und richterrechtliche Regeln durch deutsche Arbeitsrichter bei gewöhnlichem Arbeitsort im Inland anzuwenden sind. Ob diese Regeln (z.B. § 75 BetrVG) darüber hinaus auf Auslandssachverhalte angewandt werden können, ist nicht pauschal zu beantworten. Wenn eine ausreichende Inlandsbeziehung vorliegt, wird man dies bejahen können. Sie dürfte zumindest dann gegeben sein, wenn der Arbeitnehmer einem inländischen Betrieb zugerechnet werden kann. Das deutsche Recht könnte freilich ein allgemeines Diskriminierungsverbot des ausländischen gewöhnlichen Arbeitsortes nicht aushebeln, falls der betreffende Arbeitnehmer überhaupt noch in diesem Fall einem inländischen Betrieb angehört. Auch hier muss der Gedanke der foreign law defense Platz greifen.

---

[36] Juristische Personen sollten ihren tatsächlichen Sitz im Gebiet der betreffenden Rechtsordnung haben.

6. SCHLUSS

Mein kurzer Rundgang sollte zeigen, dass die Entwicklung des Kollisionsrechts nicht nur vor dem internationalen Arbeitsrecht nicht Halt macht, sondern umgekehrt auch das allgemeine Kollisionsrecht wenigstens als praktisches Beispiel zu beeinflussen in der Lage ist.

Das Kollisionsrecht hat KURT SIEHR viel zu verdanken. Dies gilt auch für das Arbeitskollisionsrecht.[37] Der Verfasser wollte ihm mit diesen Zeilen danken. Für den Jubilar hat dieses Thema freilich allenfalls theoretische, auf keinen Fall praktische Bedeutung, denn wer wollte je auf die Idee kommen, ihn wegen seines Alters zu diskriminieren. Im Gegenteil: Lieber KURT – wir brauchen Dich noch lange, *ad multos annos!*

SUMMARY

AGE DISCRIMINATION IN LABOUR LAW: A PRIVATE INTERNATIONAL LAW PERSPECTIVE

In contrast to the USA there have been only occasional attempts in Germany and in the European Community to deal with age discrimination as a specific topic and thereby contribute to the international debate. Age discrimination has also become a factor to be considered in the legislation of the European Community, as is clearly demonstrated by Article 13 of the ECTreaty in its Amsterdam version. That provision now explicitly refers to age as a relevant criterion of discrimination.

Nevertheless, the choice of law problem relating to national age discriminating provisions must be resolved by the application of the relevant national law. In most cases the national laws have, however, not yet developed their own solutions. German law may at least be orientated towards the American law which has quite a significant number of cases at our disposal. The application of the US ADEA (Age Discrimination in Employment Act) to extraterritorial situations was indeed provoked by some practical incidents and especially by certain decisions of federal courts which denied that the Act should be applied to cases with foreign elements. Therefore, the US legislator introduced § 623 (h) ADEA, which provides that the ADEA would apply also to foreign cases if those concern the discriminating practices of an "American" employer, or, to prevent evasion, also such practices of a "foreign corporation" controlled by American employers, such control being exercised through interrelation of operations, common management, centralized control of labor relations, and common ownership or financial control.

---

[37] Besonders ist auf seinen Beitrag „Billige Flaggen in teuren Häfen", in: *Festschrift F. Vischer* (1983) S. 303ff. zu verweisen.

Is there – according to the terminology of the German choice of law theory – a special connecting factor (*Sonderanknüpfung*) relating to the age discrimination question? In the US, only the application of its own law has been discussed, but not similar provisions of foreign law.

This article supports the use of an independent connecting factor for the rules on age discrimination. The law of the employment contract should not apply. Such a solution is favoured by Article 3 para. 1 of the EC Directive on the Transfer of Workers for the case of gender discrimination. The decisive connecting factor is the place of work, the law of which should prevail over the application of any age discrimination rule of the forum or other national laws.

Unification and Harmonization of Private International Law in Europe

Katharina Boele-Woelki*

1. INTRODUCTION

Private international law is merely private law and is thereby, in principle, national law. As a result of the Treaty of Amsterdam, this description of private international law as a legal field which emanates from days of old will require modification, as far as the Member States of the EU are concerned. In the future, Community private international law will assume a more important position than that of private international law with a national tint. In the years to come, private international law in Europe will, first and foremost, have its origins in European law and only in the second instance will it emanate from national law.

In this contribution we shall briefly dwell on the changed nature of private inter-

---

* Professor of Private International Law and Comparative Law, University of Utrecht.

J. Basedow et al., eds., Private Law in the International Arena – Liber Amicorum Kurt Siehr
© 2000, T.M.C.Asser Press, The Hague, The Netherlands

national law. Which consequences are associated therewith? Is the position of the Hague Conference on Private International Law – which has been in existence for more than 100 years – thereby threatened now that legislation in the field of private international law can be implemented not only by way of treaties between the Member States, but also by the European Commission by means of directives and regulations? How will the Member States of the European Union form their positions in the negotiations concerning a particular convention at the Hague Conference on Private International Law?

2.   ARTICLE 65 EC AS INSERTED BY THE TREATY OF AMSTERDAM

The Amsterdam Treaty of 18 June 1997 entered into force for the 15 Member States on 1 May 1999.[1] The Treaty amends the Treaty on the European Union (Treaty of Maastricht of 7 February 1992)[2] and the three Community Treaties (European Coal and Steel Community (ECSC), European Atomic Energy Community (EAEC) and the European Community (EC)). The amendments primarily concern the Treaty on European Union (TEU) and the EC Treaty.[3] Although the Titles of the TEU are not equivalent, in describing the structure of the Treaty three pillars are generally referred to for which the Union provides the necessary supportive "cover". The First Pillar – also referred to as the Community Pillar – contains the three Communities (ECSC, EAEC and EC). The Second Pillar is concerned with the common foreign and security policy of the Member States while the Third Pillar contains provisions concerning cooperation between the Member States in the area of justice and home affairs. With the Treaty of Amsterdam the judicial cooperation in civil matters, more specifically private international law and procedural law,[4] has been transferred from the Third to the First Pillar. After the entry into force of the Treaty of Amsterdam this Third Pillar is now also called "Provisions concerning police and judicial cooperation in criminal matters".

---

[1] The ratification procedures took place successfully. See the description thereof on a country by country basis by R. Barents, *Het Verdrag van Amsterdam in werking* (Kluwer-Deventer 1999) pp. 19-30.

[2] Entry into force 2 November 1993.

[3] Cf., exhaustively Barents (supra n. 1) pp. 3-11.

[4] Cf., G. Betlem & E.H. Hondius, "Europees privaatrecht na Amsterdam", *Nederlands Juristenblad* (1999) pp. 1137-1147 (1140); I. Tarko, „Ein Europäischer Justizraum: Errungenschaften auf dem Gebiet der justitiellen Zusammenarbeit in Zivilsachen", *Österreichische Juristenzeitung* (1999) pp. 401-407 (403-405); D. Besse, „Die justitielle Zusammenarbeit in Zivilsachen nach dem Vertrag von Amsterdam und das EuGVÜ", *Zeitschrift für Europäisches Privatrecht* (1999) pp. 107-122 (108-117); B. Heß, „Die ‚Europäisierung' des internationalen Zivilprozessrechts durch den Amsterdamer Vertrag – Chancen und Gefahren", *Neue Juristische Wochenschrift* (2000) pp. 23-32.

Whereas the Second and Third Pillars may be qualified as "inter-governmental" because the influence of the Member States directly, or through the Council, is still very strong, in the First Pillar use is made, firstly, of primary law provisions which have direct effect, and, secondly, of secondary law provisions enacted upon the recommendation of the Commission as an independent institution and concerning which the Court of Justice in Luxembourg offers legal protection and legal unity.[5]

The Community authority to legislate in matters concerning cooperation in civil matters having cross-border implications is set out in Articles 65-69 EC. The transfer of Community authority into legislation in the field of private international law will gradually expire according to Article 67 EC. During a transitional period of five years after the entry into force of the Treaty of Amsterdam (this period ending on 1 May 2004), the Council shall act unanimously on a proposal from the Commission, or upon the initiative of a Member State and after consulting the European Parliament. According to a specific procedure, preliminary questions may be sent to the Court of Justice. These questions must be concerned with the interpretation of this Treaty's provisions and the interpretation and the validity of the institutions' actions based on the Title referred to above.[6]

Article 65 EC is embodied in Title IV: visa, asylum, immigration and other policy areas concerning the free movement of persons. This provision reads as follows:

"*Measures* in the field of judicial cooperation in civil matters having *cross-border implications*, to be taken in accordance with Article 67 and *insofar as necessary for the proper functioning of the internal market*, shall include:

(a)   *improving and simplifying*:

– the system for cross-border service of judicial and extrajudicial documents;

– cooperation in the taking of evidence;

– the recognition and enforcement of decisions in civil and commercial cases, including decisions in extrajudicial cases;

(b)   *promoting the compatibility* of the rules applicable in the Member States concerning the conflict of laws and of jurisdiction;

(c) *eliminating obstacles* to the good functioning of civil proceedings, if necessary by promoting the compatibility of the rules on civil procedure applicable in the Member States." [Emphasis added – K. B.-W.].

The formulation of Article 65 EC and the relationship of this provision with Article

---

[5] Cf., Barents (supra n. 1) pp. 7-8.

[6] On the regulation determining the power to pose preliminary questions as amended by the Treaty of Amsterdam cf. Betlem/Hondius (supra n. 4) pp. 1143-1144.

293 EC [ex Article 220] gives rise to many questions.[7]

The first question concerns the legal instrument in question. Article 65 EC uses the notion of "measures". This term is generally employed in the Treaty (see, for example, Article 95 EC)[8] so as to inidicate that diverse legal instruments are possible: binding (regulation, directive) or non-binding (resolution, recommendation) instruments.[9] Based on this provision a treaty cannot be concluded.[10] That it should concern, among other things, *binding* measures may be deduced from Article 68, first paragraph, EC. The term "acts of the institutions" is the collective term for "measures" which are subject to appeal and which may be nullified by the Court of Justice (see Article 230 EC).

Secondly, the weight of the measures varies depending on whether they fall under Article 65 (a), (b) or (c). While (a) speaks of "improving and simplifying", the measures taken under (b) must be concerned with "promoting compatibility", and (c) finally speaks of "eliminating obstacles", once more with the addition "if necessary by promoting the compatibility".

What does a measure based on Article 65 EC look like and when are the criteria satisfied?

The competence to promote the compatibility of regulations excludes harmonising and unifying measures, according to Kohler. These measures, which are limited to "promoting" a certain policy, fall within the category of the least far-reaching competences which European law possesses. This category of measures can only lead to the emergence of soft law as far as the "regulations for collision and jurisdiction disputes" are concerned.[11] This explanation is not completely self-evident, however. Article 65 EC refers to "measures" in the general sense which European law, especially Article 95 EC, attributes to them. Included under measures are not only regulations and directives but also the non-binding decisions, although Article 65 EC does not in fact differentiate between these instruments.

---

[7] On this point see exhaustively and extremely critically Chr. Kohler, « Interrogations sur les sources du droit international privé européen après le traité d'Amsterdam », *Revue critique de droit international privé* (1998) pp. 1-30.

[8] On the scope of this provision, R.H. van Ooik, *De keuze der rechtsgrondslag voor besluiten van de Europese Unie* (diss. Utrecht, Kluwer-Deventer 1999) pp. 73-77.

[9] On the question of which form of harmonisation may be chosen, cf. Van Ooik (supra n. 8) pp. 296-300.

[10] Cf., also F.J.A. van der Velden, "Artikel 65 en het Verdrag van Amsterdam", *Contracteren* (1999) pp. 23-24.

[11] In this sense Kohler, (supra n. 7) pp. 19-21. According to S. Leible, „Kollisionsrechtlicher Verbraucherschutz im EVÜ und in EG-Richtlinien", in: H. Schulte-Nölke & R. Schulze (eds.), *Europäische Rechtsangleichung und nationale Privatrechte* (Baden-Baden, Nomos 1999) pp. 353-392 (387-389), Article 65(b) EC can only be used as a basis for Directives and not for Regulations because the measures which must be taken within the framework of the promotion of compatibility merely look towards harmonisation and not towards unification.

Thirdly, the relationship between Article 65 EC and Article 293 EC [ex Article 220 ECT] is important. In spite of the transfer of powers from the Third to the First Pillar, the latter provision has remained in place.[12] The Member States still have the power to conclude treaties with one another, as is the case with the Convention on the Jurisdiction and Enforcement of Judgments in Civil and Commercial Matters and the Convention on the Law Applicable to Contractual Obligations, whereover the national parliaments have a say in the form of Acts of Approval. Considering the fact that this competence of the Member States under Article 293 has remained in place[13] and that the wording of Article 65 EC can only be termed as vague, Kohler has come to the conclusion that the latter provision does indeed confirm the national authority to determine private international law regulations. According to him, Article 65 EC does not provide the Council with horizontal authority but, rather, with only sectoral powers as regards those fields named in the provision. Kohler regards this provision as having a number of constitutional drawbacks and he concludes, among other things:[14]

"Il est pourtant plus que douteux que, avec ces handicaps, la compétence communautaire prévue à l'article 65 puisse faire évoluer le droit international privé européen de manière substantielle. Le maintien intégral de l'article 220 du traité CE [now Article 293 EC, K. B.-W.] reflète cet état des choses, et l'action intergouvernementale, loin de pouvoir être qualifiée d'anachronique, renaîtra, renforcée, des cendres du troisième pilier, mais sans l'encadrement institutionnel de celui-ci."

A different view is expressed by Barents,[15] a specialist in European law. He submits that Article 293 EC imposes upon the Member States "so far as is necessary" an obligation to negotiate as far as the subjects referred to therein are concerned.[16] According to him, from this wording it follows that treaties between the Member

---

[12] Article 293 EC [ex 220 ECT] reads as follows:
"Member States shall, so far as is necessary, enter into negotiations with each other with a view to securing for the benefit of their nationals:
- the protection of persons and the enjoyment and protection of rights under the same conditions as those accorded by each State to its own nationals;
- the abolition of double taxation within the Community;
- the mutual recognition of companies or firms within the meaning of the second paragraph of Article 48, the retention of legal personality in the event of transfer of their seat from one country to another, and the possibility of mergers between companies or firms governed by the laws of different countries;
- the simplification of formalities governing the reciprocal recognition and enforcement of judgments of courts or tribunals and of arbitration awards."
[13] Betlem/Hondius (supra n. 4) pp. 1137-1147 determine that this important circumstance is not a problem.
[14] Ibid., p. 29.
[15] Ibid., pp. 370-371.
[16] For the text see note 12.

States can only be concluded whenever the EC Treaty does not provide any basis for the necessary measures. Considering the fact that Article 65 EC has introduced a similar legal basis, this provision may be considered as a *lex specialis* compared to Article 293 EC. Article 65 EC also makes use of the phrase "insofar as necessary" and links these words to "for the proper functioning of the internal market". This has as a consequence that the treaties which are concluded between the Member States as a result of the Article 293 EC obligation to negotiate "can now be Communitarised". Barents welcomes this development considering the laborious and lengthy negotiations which are necessary before treaties can be entered into.[17]

In Brussels – as will hereafter be apparent – the Barents' interpretation of Article 65 EC is being followed. In the meantime the Action Plan of the Council and the Commission on how best to implement the provisions of the Treaty of Amsterdam was adopted on 3 December 1998 by the Council (Justice and Home Affairs).[18] This is a concrete plan by which to implement, in a workable system, the changes brought about by the Treaty of Amsterdam in the areas covered by the First Pillar and also by which to be able to designate the necessary priorities. In the following section that part of the plan which is relevant from a private international law perspective will be evaluated while describing the various instruments for its implementation.

3.   European Private International Law: the Current State of Affairs

Having been made subject to the influence of the progressive European integration process, the legal sources of European private international law are now in a transformation phase. A number of conventions are due to be changed, others will be converted into regulations and directives. For the purpose of new legislation use will be made of the Community powers. Changes will gradually occur but the influence of the Member States will remain strong by means of the unanimity rule (and, during the initial period, by means of the Member States' right of initiative).

We must further consider the special position which Denmark, Ireland and the United Kingdom have taken by making reservations to the newly introduced Title IV. For these countries the new private international law legislation which has now emerged, and the legislation that will be transformed by the effect of Article 65 EC

---

[17] In a similar sense, B. von Hoffmann, "The Relevance of European Community Law", in: B. von Hoffmann (ed.), *European Private International Law* (Nijmegen, Ars Aequi Libri 1998) pp. 19-37 (32).

[18] *OJ (EC)* [1999] C 19/1. The relevant passages from a private international law point of view are reproduced in German and English in *IPRax (Praxis des internationalen Privat- und Verfahrensrechts)* (1999) pp. 288-290.

following the entry into force of the Treaty of Amsterdam, will not apply.[19] Apart from the possibility of the opt-in declaration,[20] which may be made by the three countries in question,[21] the possibility exists that the European Union will enter into seperate agreements with Denmark, Ireland and the United Kingdom in order to reach agreement on the Community's private international law legislation.

3.1 Brussels I and the Lugano Convention

The cornerstone of European international procedural law is the Convention on the Jurisdiction and Enforcement of Judgments in Civil and Commercial Matters of 27 September 1968 (hereinafter, Brussels I). This convention has been revised on a number of occasions, most recently by the Accession Convention for Spain and Portugal on 26 May 1989. The (then) six Member States accomplished Brussels I within the framework of Article 220 part 4 EC which was applicable at that time. It is generally accepted that Brussels I, as is the case with the EC Convention on the Law Applicable to Contractual Obligations, can be considered as a multilateral convention between the Member States themselves and that it does not form an integrated element of Community law. As a consequence of Article 65 EC Brussels I in its revised version[22] will be transposed into a regulation.[23] The Convention on the Jurisdiction and Enforcement of Judgments in Civil and Commercial Matters of 16 September 1988 (hereinafter, the Parallel or Lugano Convention), however, will still remain as a convention in its revised version. The variety of sources in the field of international procedural law can only increase. Reduction cannot be expected in this respect.

Now that Brussels I will be embodied in a regulation, there will also be no ex-

---

[19] See the Protocols to the Treaty of Amsterdam concerning the position of the United Kingdom and Ireland, and concerning the position of Denmark (4 and 5). See also Article 69 EC.

[20] Cf., Besse (supra n. 4) pp. 111-112.

[21] For Ireland and the United Kingdom, their participation in a measure which belongs to Title IV EC is simply regulated. They may send a written notification to the Council wherein they declare that they consider themselves to be bound (Article 3 of the Protocol in question). For Denmark it is much more complicated. Article 7 of the relevant Protocol determines that Denmark can notify the other Member States at any time that it no longer wishes to rely on the Protocol in its entirety or as regards a part thereof. Doubt arises as to whether a certain measure can fall within the ambit of the last phrase "a part thereof".

[22] On this cf. Chr. Kohler, „Die Revision des Brüsseler und des Luganer Übereinkommens über die gerichtliche Zuständigkeit und die Vollstreckung gerichtlicher Entscheidungen in Zivil- und Handelssachen", Tagung der Wissenschaftlichen Vereinigung für Internationales Verfahrensrecht (Berlin 1999).

[23] On the reasons for transposition see Besse (supra n. 4) pp. 118-120. On the problem of attuning the Brussels I Regulation with the activities of the Hague Conference within the framework of a world-wide jurisdiction and enforcement convention, cf. Betlem/Hondius (supra n. 4) p. 1143. They advocate an "inverted subsidiarity" because the recognition and enforcement of civil judgments could perhaps be better regulated on a worldwide scale.

planatory memorandum drawn up as is usually the case with international conventions. If an explanation of the provisions of the Brussels I Regulation is necessary, this may be found in the revised Lugano Convention which will contain the same provisions. The explanatory memorandum, which will be written for the latter convention by Professor Fausto Pocar from Italy, may serve as a source of inspiration in explaining the Brussels I Regulation. Who would have ever thought so?

The special position of Denmark,[24] Ireland and the United Kingdom promises additional problems in converting the convention into a regulation because these countries are also signatories to the Lugano Convention. The exclusion of one or more countries from the scope of the Brussels I Regulation could not only create obstacles to the free movement of trade within the internal market, but could also lead to discrimination against the subjects of the countries in question or the persons already residing there. This result, however, is in itself contrary to Article 11 part 1 (c) and (e) EC which corresponds to the prohibition of discrimination.[25] It is only to be hoped that these "special position" countries will, as far as possible, participate simultaneously in measures which safeguard the alignment towards each other and towards the countries for which the Brussels I Regulation will apply without any further decision making on the part of the national Parliaments.

3.2   Rome I

The Convention on the Law applicable to Contractual Obligations of 19 June 1980 (hereinafter, Rome I)[26] is a cornerstone of of European conflicts law.[27] This convention, based on Article 220 EC, will, it is expected, remain as a convention. Whether there are any plans to transpose this convention into a Community act is not yet known. Proposals to make use of the regulation as an *ideale Rechtssetzungsform* for the unification of private international law had already been put forward in German legal literature in 1993. Such proposals are now being specifically propagated with respect to the international law of contracts.[28]

---

[24] According to Barents (supra n. 1) p. 335 "this modest expression alluding to the stubborn refusal on the part of this country, which indeed belongs to the Schengen group, precludes its submission to any Community or Union authority from the very start".

[25] Cf., exhaustively Besse (supra n. 4) p. 121.

[26] After the accession of Spain, Portugal, Finland, Austria and Sweden a consolidated version was published in *OJ (EC)* [1998] C 27/34.

[27] Cf., D. Martiny, „Europäisches Internationales Vertragsrecht – Ausbau und Konsolidierung", *Zeitschrift für Europäisches Privatrecht* (1999) pp. 246-270 (246); A. Junker, „Empfiehlt es sich, Art. 7 EVÜ zu revidieren oder aufgrund der bisherigen Erfahrungen zu präzisieren?" *IPRax* (2000) pp. 65-73 (65).

[28] Cf., Leible (supra n. 11) pp. 387-389, with the literature indicated therein. According to this author, however, Article 65 EC Treaty cannot form the basis for the unification of the international law of contracts by means of a Regulation. He suggests that use should be made in this respect of Art. 308 EC [ex 235 ECT]. Cf., for the scope of this "residual power" van Ooik (supra n. 8) pp. 72-73.

Article 20 Rome I gives priority to Community law. The various directives, for example on unfair contract terms or time-sharing, are mainly concerned with substantive law. Yet, they mostly contain a conflicts rule, on the basis of which the harmonisation effect intended by the Directive must be guaranteed towards non-EU countries. This rule is declared to be a mandatory rule of law when the circumstances have a sufficient connection with a EU Member State. In this way private international law problems which in themselves fall within the scope of Rome I, are kept outside the convention's reach. Concerning the unification effect of Rome I, doubts consequently arise because of the different contents of the implementation acts in the Member States. The unification effect would further suffer from the fact that national legislators do not transpose the directives on time or otherwise convert them incorrectly into national law.[29] In formulating the conflicts provisions the drafters in many cases seem not to have harmonised them with Rome I, which is irritating: for the national legislator it means that the implementation of the Directive in question is not an easy matter; for the court or the lawyer, of course, it is anything but clear.[30] This situation has also been recognized by the drafters of the Action Plan. Within two years a revision of Rome I should be initiated, whereby account will have to be taken of the conflicts provisions in other Community instruments.[31]

3.3 Authentication of Public Documents

The Convention abolishing the legalization of documents in the Member States of the European Communities of 25 May 1987[32] emerged within the framework of European Political Cooperation (EPC). This Convention has not entered into force.[33] This may be explained by the fact that, except for Denmark and Sweden, all the other EU Member States are Contracting Parties to the Hague Authentication Convention of 5 October 1961[34] which is applicable worldwide. Therefore, there does not seem to be any need for any specific regulation between the Member States

---

[29] Cf., exhaustively Martiny (supra n. 26) pp. 249-251.

[30] Cf., Leible (supra n. 11) pp. 367 et seq.; C.A. Joustra, "Europese richtlijnen en internationaal privaatrecht", *Weekblad voor Privaatrecht, Notariaat en Registratie* (1999) no. 6370, pp. 664-670.

[31] Cf., no. 40 (c) of the Action Plan.

[32] *Tractatenblad van het Koninkrijk der Nederlanden* 1987, 166; *Bulletin (EC)* [1987] 124.

[33] Four countries have ratified the Convention: Belgium, Denmark, France and Italy.

[34] Cf., *Hague Conference on Private International Law Collection of Conventions (1951-1996)*, p. 42. This Convention entered into force for Ireland on 9 March 1999. As to the usefulness of the European Authentication Convention there are grave doubts, see H. Duintjer Tebbens, "De Haagse Conferentie, de Europese Gemeenschap en de subsidiariteit", *Nederlands Juristenblad* (1993) pp. 671-672 (672). Alongside this there are currently a few bilateral treaties in force, see J. Pirrung, „Übereinkommen zur justitiellen Zusammenarbeit", in: H. Schulte-Nölke/R. Schulze (eds.), *Europäische Rechtsangleichung und nationale Privatrechte* (Baden-Baden, Nomos 1999), pp. 341-451 (343-344).

of the EU. Nonetheless, there have been proposals to convert the European Authentication Convention into a regulation.[35]

3.4 Recovery of Maintenance

Practically superfluous also seems to be the second Convention which was drafted within the framework of EPC and which did not enter into force.[36] The Convention between Member States of the European Community on the Simplification of Procedures for the Recovery of Maintenance Payments of 6 November 1990 emerged because Ireland was not a Party to the worldwide New York Convention on the Recovery of Maintenance Abroad of 20 June 1956.[37] In the meantime this EU Member State also ratified the UN Convention in November 1995.[38] Also with respect to this Convention there have been proposals to transpose it into a regulation.[39] The European Convention differs from the UN Convention only in that the European regulation concerning the recovery of maintenance applies also to maintenance claims taken over by governmental bodies by way of subrogation.

3.5 Insolvency Proceedings

The third Convention drafted within the framework of EPC has also not fared any better. The Convention deals with – to put it succinctly – the applicability of the universality principle, that is to say with the mutual recognition of insolvency proceedings in other Member States. It has not entered into force because the United Kingdom refuses to accept the non-applicability of the Convention's provisions to Gibraltar. However, Spain is not prepared to allow any amendment to the explanatory report from which the limited territorial field of application is derived.[40] This stalemate would now being relieved, however, by transposing the Convention into a regulation.[41] Doubts may be raised as to whether insolvency law really belongs with measures concerned with the free movement of persons. Is not the recognition of insolvency proceedings really a question of the free movement of

---

[35] Cf. Tarko (supra n. 4) p. 403.

[36] Only Ireland, Italy, Spain and the UK have ratified the Convention.

[37] Cf., 268 *United Nation Treaty Series* 32. Cf., M. Sumampouw, "The EC Convention on the Recovery of Maintenance: Necessity or Excess?", in: M. Sumampouw (ed.), *Law and Reality, Liber amicorum C.A. Voskuil* (Dordrecht/Boston/London, Martinus Nijhoff 1992) pp. 315-336.

[38] Ratification of the Convention was discouraged due to the complexity caused thereby, cf., Pirrung (supra n. 34) pp. 344-345.

[39] Cf., Tarko (supra n. 4) p. 403.

[40] Nos. 300-302 of the explanatory report by Virgos/Schmidt.

[41] See the Initiative of Germany and Finland with an eye on the acceptance of the Council Regulation concerning insolvency proceedings, submitted to the Council on 26 May 1999 (C 221/6), *OJ (EC)* [1999] C 221/8 of 3 August 1999.

companies and services? It cannot be assumed that the United Kingdom will make use of the opportunity to give up its opt-in declaration[42] because the political situation concerning Gibraltar shows no signs of change despite various attempts at mediation. The transformation of the Convention into a regulation will unify the international insolvency law of the other Member States which are, at present, the victims of differences of opinion which the Convention's provisions do not touch upon in any way whatsoever.

3.6 The Service of (Extra-)Judicial Documents

The law concerning the service of documents will also be unified by means of a regulation. The European Service Convention of 26 May 1997[43] has been transposed into the Service-of-Documents-Regulation of 29 March 2000.[44] The Convention emerged, within the framework of judicial cooperation in civil matters as a result of the Treaty of Maastricht,[45] on 26 May 1997,[46] but has not entered into force.[47] Until the end of 1999 it was largely unclear why the Council had first chosen a directive rather than a regulation as a Community instrument by which to address the problem of the service of documents.[48] The service of documents is expressly referred to in Article 65(a) EC. The European Service Regulation will come into force on 1 October 2000 in the Member States which are at the same time parties to the Hague Service Convention of 15 November 1965[49] and had also concluded bilateral agreements between themselves on this matter. The new European legislation is in general considered to be a simplification of the law because direct contacts between the concerned authorities in the various countries will now be made possible ("decentralisation").[50]

3.7 Brussels II (Procedural Divorce Law)

The second Convention to emerge within the framework of judicial cooperation is concerned with international family law. On 28 May 1998 the EU Member States

---

[42] Corresponding Article 3 of the Protocol to the Treaty of Amsterdam.
[43] Cf., Tarko (supra n. 4) pp. 403-404.
[44] COM (2000) 75, 1999/0102 CNS.
[45] Upon the proposal by the Netherlands, supported by Germany. See F.J.A. van der Velden, "Betekening binnen de Europese Unie", in: *Het NIPR geannoteerd* (-'s Gravenhage, T.M.C. Asser Instituut 1996), pp. 158-162.
[46] *Tractatenblad van het Koninkrijk der Nederlanden* 1997, 253; *OJ (EC)* [1997] C 261.
[47] Cf., Pirrung (supra n. 34) pp. 345-347.
[48] Cf., also Betlem/Hondius (supra n. 4) p. 1142.
[49] Cf., *Nederlands Internationaal Privaatrecht* (1999) no. 49.
[50] In this sense Pirrung (supra n. 34) p. 346.

signed Brussels II.[51] This Convention can be compared with Brussels I, by which we
mean the 1968 EC Jurisdiction and Enforcement Convention. It concerns jurisdiction, recognition and enforcement of decisions in the field of the dissolution of marriages and custody after divorce.[52] There has been a proposal to transpose this
Convention into a regulation.[53] The Hague Conventions on the recognition of
divorces and on child protection considerably lose out from a European point of
view. The global regulations of the Hague Conference will be applicable in considerably fewer cases. Family law relations between persons emanating from the EU
Member States[54] will therefore fall under a seperate private international law regime
as far as jurisdiction, recognition and enforcement are concerned.[55]

3.8   Rome II (Non-Contractual Obligations)

The Regulation on the Jurisdiction and Enforcement of Judgments in Civil and
Commercial Matters will, just like its Brussels I counterpart, apply to both contractual and non-contractual obligations.[56] The system of international cooperation in
civil cases will have to be complemented by an instrument whereby not only the
same rules on jurisdiction and recognition will apply in the Member States, but also
the same conflict regulations.[57] The European Group for Private International Law
has made an important first move in this respect by drafting a proposal for a Convention on non-contractual obligations.[58] Once again the question arises whether on
the basis of Article 65(b) EC a regulation on this matter falls under Title IV of the
EC Treaty, namely the free movement of persons. A wide interpretation of this
objective must in any case be provided by exhaustive justification. Finally, there is
still a problem at the national level. In two Member States national legislative

---

[51] Cf., Th. de Boer, "Brussel II: een eerste stap naar een communautair i.p.r.", *Tijdschrift voor Familie- en Jeugdrecht* (1999) 244-250.
[52] Cf., K. Boele-Woelki, "Waarom Brussel II?", *Tijdschrift voor Familie- en Jeugdrecht* (1998) p. 125 and M. Sumampouw, "Parental Responsibility under Brussels II", in: *Liber amicorum Kurt Siehr* p . 729
[53] Cf., the Proposal for a Council Regulation (EC) on jurisdiction and the recognition and enforce-
ment of judgments in matrimonial matters and in matters of parental responsibility for joint children, Doc. 599PC0220.
[54] The problem of the three "special position" countries also emerges here.
[55] Cf., also Pirrung (supra n. 34) pp. 347-350.
[56] Cf., Action Plan no. 40 (b).
[57] The Member States appear to have a great interest in this project. The activities are expected to be completed at the end of 2000. Cf., Tarko (supra n. 4) p. 406.
[58] The French text may be found in *Praxis des internationalen Privat- und Verfahrensrechts* (1999) pp. 286-288 and the English text in *Netherlands International Law Review* (1998) pp. 465-471. Both versions have also been published in M. Fallon, "Proposition pour une convention européenne sur la loi applicable aux obligation non contractuelles", *European Review of Private Law* (1999) pp. 45-68.

activities are unfolding simultaneously with the ongoing discussions in Brussels. In August 1998 the German Government submitted a bill to Parliament on supplementing the private international law provisions in the EGBGB concerning non-contractual obligations[59] and in the Netherlands a bill to regulate conflicts law with regard to obligations arising from wrongful acts (Act regulating the private international law applicable to unlawful acts) was submitted to the Lower House of Parliament in June 1999.[60] In both countries – or so it would certainly appear to me – it must first be awaited to see how the Brussels legislator will regulate these issues.

3.9 Rome III (Conflict Law with Respect to Divorce)

The Action Plan reports that by May 2004 the possibilities for attaining an agreement on regulations which will determine which divorce law is applicable must be investigated on the basis of a thorough study. Brussels II would unify the law of international divorce proceedings. Under this Convention, a number of courts may have the authority to dissolve a marriage, with the resulting risk of "forum shopping".[61] This plan will have important consequences for the Netherlands, for example. A brief look at the conflict regulations concerning divorce which are applicable in the EU Member States reveals that the foreign regulations still deviate from the Dutch approach. A choice of law is not possible in most legal systems and the reality test of the nationality as a connecting factor remains largely a Dutch acquisition. A further-reaching simplification of the matter, namely the application of the *lex fori*, is indeed being advocated with an eye on the planned codification of Dutch private international law.[62] It is to be hoped that these somewhat liberal conflict rules on divorce, which have to be agreed upon between the Member States, may serve as an example.

[59] BR-Drucksache 759/98. Published in *Praxis des internationalen Privat- und Verfahrensrechts* (1998) pp. 513 et seq., with an explanation by R. Wagner, „Der Regierungsentwurf eines Gesetzes zum Internationalen Privatrecht für außervertragliche Schuldverhältnisse und für Sachen", *Praxis des internationalen Privat- und Verfahrensrechts* (1998) pp. 429-437.
[60] Proceedings of the Lower House, 26 608, nos. 1-2. In the Explanatory Memorandum the Brussels activities in this field are not alluded to.
[61] Cf., no. 41 (a) of the Action Plan. Cf., also Pirrung (supra n. 34) p. 349 and Tarko (supra n. 4) p. 407.
[62] Cf., K. Boele-Woelki, „Der favor divortii im niederländischen Scheidungsrecht", in: K. Boele-Woelki *et al* (eds.), *Comparability and Evaluation* (Dordrecht/Boston/London, Martinus Nijhoff 1994) pp. 167-181.

3.10 Brussels III and Rome IV (Law of Matrimonial Property and the Law of Succession)

Two new fields will likewise be taken up within a five-year period. The possibility will be investigated whether legal instruments may be formulated whereby the international jurisdiction, the applicable law and the recognition and enforcement of decisions concerning the law of matrimonial property and the law of succession may be regulated.[63] With regard to procedural law problems, these instruments may be denoted Brussels III and with respect to the conflict regulation aspects one could speak of Rome IV.[64] In the field of matrimonial property law and the law of succession the Hague Conference on Private International Law has to date given rise to two Conventions which have met with little success. The Hague Convention on Matrimonial Property of 14 March 1978 is only applicable to France, Luxembourg and the Netherlands,[65] while the Hague Succession Convention of 1 August 1989 has not yet entered into force. Nevertheless, according to the Action Plan there is an explicit intention to take into account the activities being carried out within this framework by the Hague Conference. Whether this "taking into account" will mean that all EU Member States will ratify both Hague Conventions can only be described as doubtful now that, for example, Germany in no way seems to support these two Conventions. Agreements on the collective ratification of Conventions are not something new, however. Within the framework of judicial cooperation in civil matters, the EU Member States at the beginning of the 1980s all agreed to ratify two Child Abduction Conventions of 1980.[66] This objective was attained in 1999 with the accession of Belgium to the Hague Child Abduction Convention. In this way the worldwide system put in place by the Hague Conference will be implemented and the principle of subsidiarity will be respected.[67] The EU's own private international law regulation is in this way not required. The unification of private international law in the EU Member States will indeed be achieved.

---

[63] No. 41 (b) of the Action Plan.

[64] All the instruments designated as "Brussels" have thus far concerned international jurisdiction and enforcement, while those designated as "Rome" seem to be reserved for conflicts law. The Action Plan itself has also up until now differentiated between Brussels I and II, and Rome I, II and III.

[65] *Nederlands Internationaal Privaatrecht* (1995) no. 49.

[66] This concerns the Hague Child Abduction Convention of 25 October 1980 and the Convention of the Council of Europe on the recognition and enforcement of decisions concerning the custody of children of 20 May 1980.

[67] In a similar sense Pirrung (supra n. 34) pp. 42-43.

4. THE FUTURE ROLE OF THE HAGUE CONFERENCE FOR PRIVATE INTERNATIONAL LAW

The relationship of the Hague Conference with other international organisations which – as described by Duintjer Tebbens – "have the reduction of legal diversity in the world or a part thereof firmly etched on their banners", has never been free of problems.[68] Attuning its work to that of the Council of Europe, the International Commission on Births, Deaths and Marriages, UNCITRAL, UNIDROIT and the EU has, since the Second World War, become a daily ritual for the staff of the Hague Conference's Permanent Bureau. In response to the extension of the Council's powers in the field of judicial cooperation in civil matters in the Maastricht Treaty (Article K.1 sub. 6) Duintjer Tebbens warns of a "new treaty-making power to which the Hague Conference cannot be indifferent".[69] He advocates a healthy subsidiarity, that is to say that regulation by the EC will only be considered after it has become clear, after consultation with the Conference, that a need for such regulation exists and no other way remains open in this respect.[70] The EU Member States, which are all members of the Hague Conference,[71] did not act accordingly in the realisation and ratification of the Treaty of Amsterdam, however. The transfer of judicial cooperation in civil matters from the Third Pillar to the First Pillar will have far-reaching consequences for the Hague Conference. Until now, the delegates from the European countries have had a heavyweight influence on the preparation and negotiation of private international law conventions. In all their diversity they have formed the "hard core" in The Hague. If these countries must henceforth only speak with one voice, then the quality of the Hague legislation would be at issue. Two reasons for concern may here be voiced: firstly, we can only wait and see who exactly will determine the content of the EU standpoint and, secondly, the task of the Dutch State Commission for Private International Law as the administrative body of the Hague Conference will find itself in considerable difficulties if attuning to the EU has to take place beforehand. This all boils down to a loss of influence by the Netherlands, which is after all the Conference's birth-place. The question then arises whether the EU, for reasons of efficiency, should not itself become a member of the Hague Conference. Apart from the discussion on whether the EU indeed satisfies the international legal requirements for the posses-

---

[68] Cf.,

Duintjer Tebbens (supra n. 34) p. 671.

[69] Ibid., p. 672.

[70] Ibid. Cf., also K. Boele-Woelki, Internationaal privatrecht, *Ars Aequi* section 63, pp. 2996-2997.

[71] See the Statute of the Hague Conference on Private International Law, 31 October 1951, *Nederlands Internationaal Privaatrecht* (1999) no. 2.

sion of legal personality,[72] this could give rise to an amendment of the Hague Conference's statute, with the added consequence that the position of the Dutch State Commission for Private International Law would be the subject of discussion. Finally: there is indeed a great need to attune the activities of the EU and the Hague Conference. Rome II (the applicable law in the case of non-contractual obligations) provides an illustrative example. A number of EU Member States are also bound by the Hague Conventions concerning traffic accidents and products liability.[73]

All these views are voiced by apprehensive colleagues who have great concern for the many successful conventions emanating from the Hague Conference. The regional unification of private international law must not lead to the situation where universal unification would become dominated and thereby hampered by the EU. This danger does exist because the EU Member States in this field, which is covered by Article 65 EC, have allowed their own autonomy to slip.

5.   CONCLUDING REMARKS

The ratification of the Treaty of Amsterdam, as far as legislative competence in the field of private international law is concerned, has not given rise to any undue commotion in this respect. In the European literature, too, comparatively little attention has been devoted to the consequences of this treaty for European private international law. It is somewhat astonishing that the radical change with regard to the powers of the European Union concerning legislation in the field of private international law has been received more or less silently. The involvement of experts and politicians has not taken place. National Parliaments and also the European Parliament itself appear to have received little information on the changes in private international law legislation. The consequences cannot be immediately examined and therefore there is still a difference of opinion concerning the interpretation of Article 65 EC. This state of affairs can only be regretted. However, the question is whether the Treaty of Amsterdam would produce negative consequences for private international law? The answer to this question depends largely on the quality of future legislation. If European private international law legislative instruments should prove to be efficient, effective,

---

[72] As confirmed by R.A. Wessel, *The European Union's Foreign and Security Policy, A Legal Institutional Perspective* (diss. Utrecht 1999), pp. 242-318. He concludes the following: "Through the establishment of a new legal person with an international capacity to act, the states created – most probblably unintentionally – a new legal entity, which not only cannot be disregarded by them in their legal practices as members of the Union, but which seems to be as increasingly accepted as such by them as well as by third states" (318).

[73] In this sense also J. Sonnenberger, „Europäisches Internationales Privatrecht im Dienst freien Personenverkehrs", *Recht der internationalen Wirtschaft* (1999) part 4, editorial.

clear and well attuned among themselves as well as to the existing Hague Conference Conventions, then overall acceptance and approval may be expected. However, the non-positive experience thus far with private international law legislation emanating from Brussels does not provide a sound basis for optimism. This does not apply to the conventions which the Member States entered into before the conclusion of the Treaty of Amsterdam, such as Brussels I and Rome I. The legislative competence of the EU Member States has in any case been allowed to slip. A heavy burden rests on the shoulders of the officials in Brussels who in the future will be charged with preparing and agreeing upon private international law legislation.

The Law of the Relations Between Legal Systems: A methodological analysis

Antonio Boggiano[*]

---

[*] Dr. Dr.iur., Professor of Law of the University of Buenos Aires, Judge and former President of the Supreme Court of Argentina.

J. Basedow et al., eds., Private Law in the International Arena – Liber Amicorum Kurt Siehr
© 2000, T.M.C.Asser Press, The Hague, The Netherlands

1.   INTERNATIONAL LAW AND THE LAW OF THE RELATIONS BETWEEN
     LEGAL SYSTEMS

I would like to offer Prof. Dr. KURT SIEHR, University of Zurich, a methodological
study on the law of the relations between the internal legal systems of the subjects of
international law. Not of all kinds of legal systems, therefore. There is a plurality of
legal systems in the juridical universe. Some of those legal systems do not pertain to
a subject of international law. For example, the legal systems of a province, a state,
a region, a *land*, or a canton of federal states are not legal systems of a subject of
international law. There are many legal systems subordinated to a State's legal
system. All of these are not contemplated in this study. Naturally, it includes the
relations between the legal systems of States. It covers also the internal law of
international organizations recognized as subjects of international law. Some
persons may be regarded as subjects of international law but have no internal legal
systems as such. The Catholic Church is a subject of international law with its own
legal system: canon law. Historically, States are not and have not been the only
protagonists or subjects of international law. Furthermore, international law is also
a legal system in itself. Consequently, there are relations between international law
and other legal systems of the subjects of international law, namely the domestic
laws of States.[1]

It is possible to distinguish the relations between the subjects of international law
governed by international law, on the one hand, and the relations between the legal
systems of the subjects of international law, on the other. An additional category is
the relations between international law and the legal systems of the subjects of
international law. The latter relations are governed by the law of the relations
between legal systems.

The general theory of the relations between legal systems has been analyzed in
previous leading studies from which I have drawn much inspiration, although these
sources do not deal with the specific issue of the concrete relations hereby contemplated. Although these studies are on a purely theoretical level, they do cast a great
deal of light on any historical or positive law of the relations between legal systems
and the references here are by no means exhaustive.[2]

---

[1]   I have considered the matter in various previous studies: *Introducción al Derecho Internacional.
Relaciones Exteriores de los Ordenamientos Jurídicos* (Buenos Aires 1995) reviewed by Julio
Oyhanarte, *La Ley* (1995-D) p. 1606 and *La Nación* (25 June 1995) and Rainer Hofmann, in: *Zeitschrift
für Ausländishes Öffenthiches Recht und Völkerrecht* (1995) p. 1246; *Teoría del Derecho
Internacional. Las Relaciones entre los Ordenamientos Jurídicos. Ius Inter Iura* (Buenos Aires 1996)
reviewed by Jayme in: 61 *RabelsZ* (1997) 581, at p. 582 n. 4; *Derecho Internacional y Derecho de las
Relaciones entre los Ordenamientos Jurídicos* (Buenos Aires 1997) and *Derecho Internacinal Público
y Privado y Derecho del Mercosur. En la Jurisprudencia de la Corte Suprema de Justicia de la Nación
Argentina,* 3 vols. (Buenos Aires 1998-1999).
[2]   Santi Romano, *L'Ordinamento Giuridico* (Firenze 1945); Franco Modugno, *Legge-ordinamento*

It has been suggested that public international law arises from the juxtaposition of States, while private international law emanates from the juxtaposition of legal systems.[3] This image is inspiring. Even if in the general theory of law, legal order and legal systems a distinction may be made, I consider these concepts to be analogous for present purposes. Legal systems are the internal State laws, international law and generally the internal laws of any subject of international law. The legal universe is comprised of a juxtaposition of legal systems. The law of the relations between legal systems is that part of the law – we do not claim this part to be a new branch – which attempts to establish a certain order in those relationships, i.e., between the internal legal systems of any subject of international law and between those systems and international law itself.

2.   THE RELATIONS BETWEEN LEGAL SYSTEMS

The relations between legal systems appear from the cases involving different legal systems which transcend one another and provoke the quest for the law or legal system which is applicable to such cases.

Beyond the relations between subjects of international law governed by the *ius inter gentes,* there are relations between legal systems governed by the *ius inter iura*. We can also think in particular of relations between legal systems arising out of the relations between States and persons subject to the jurisdiction of other States; relations between international organizations and persons subject to the jurisdiction of a State; relations between the Catholic Church and persons subject to the jurisdiction of a State; relations between States and persons subject to its own jurisdiction; and relations between persons subject to the jurisdiction of different States.

These relations give rise to the application of international law within the sphere of domestic State legal systems; the application of international law in its own sphere and the application of international law in the legal system of an international organization.

Traditionally, the legal system was almost exclusively the State legal system. Even from the point of view of a State legal system the following questions may arise. Which is the legal system applicable to a relationship which transcends more than one legal system? And, on the other side of the coin: what is the scope of the application of each legal system in order to discover the relations covered and

---

giuridico. *Pluralità degli ordinamenti* (Milano 1985)*;* M.S. Giannini, *Sulla pluralita degli ordenamenti giuridici* (Roma 1950); Cesarini Sforza, "Ordinamenti Giuridici (Pluralita degli)", *Nov. D. I. XII* (1965); N. Bobbio, *Teoria del'ordinamento giuridico*, (Torino 1960).

  [3] *Oppenheim's International Law* by Sir Robert Jennings and Sir Arthur Watts (eds.), 9th edn. (London and New York 1992) Vol. I, pp. 6-7.

governed by it? These are the classic problems of private international law. It would be possible to draw from comparative private international law the principles of coordination of the different legal systems. But what part of the law really governs relations between the legal systems? Do we need this part of the law or is it sufficient to have certain rules in each legal system which deal with such relations between one another? It has been proposed that an external public law could function as international law. The same approach could be expanded to cover all relations between legal systems, considering not only State legal systems but the legal systems of all subjects of international law. This is what I have attempted to do in the studies cited in footnote 1.

Within State legal systems, there are rules relating to international matters, relations or cases in a broad sense. Some legal literature has considered these aspects under the title of *"domestic law for international matters"*[4] or *"external state law"* or *"äusseres Staatsrecht"*. The only title that has become the norm, however, is private international law. It was also possible to distinguish between domestic State law dealing with international matters, cases or relations emanating from international law on the same issues. Thus, criminal international law as internal law and international criminal law as international law; administrative international law as internal law and international administrative law as international law; and constitutional international law as internal law and international constitutional law as international law.

The study of the purely internal aspects of the legal systems must be followed by an analysis of the problems arising from the relations between those legal system with one another. I will hereby restrict the study to the relations between the legal systems of the subjects of international law.

3. METHODOLOGICAL ASPECTS OF THE LAW OF THE RELATIONS BETWEEN LEGAL SYSTEMS

3.1 Unification

One possible form of relationship between two legal systems or a bulk of legal systems is their (partial) unification. Such unification may be achieved by the exercise of competences transferred to a new legal system. In this case the unification is in the form of substitution by what may be called community law. In this case there is no concurrence or need for conflict rules as each legal system has defined or delimited its own scope of application by way of agreement between the legal systems concerned, the community and domestics law. This unification may only be partial

---

[4] Ghirardini, *Il diritto processuale civile internazionale* (Spoleto 1914) p. 5.

of course. But it may also be total as has occured in customs matters when domestic tariffs are substituted by a common tariff. In other cases the unification does not substitute the rules of different legal systems but adds cumulatively some common rules without derogating from the respective domestic rules.

For example, the rules on transport or sales law may be unified without derogating from the rules of the national laws concering domestic sale or transport. In both cases rules establish the scope of the uniform law, by transferring competences to an international organization or by defining the scope of the uniform law with regard to domestic national law.

3.2 Coordination

By way of coordination the substantive rules in force in the legal systems concerned are not modified nor derogated from but are rather organized so that they are of equal ranking.

A legal system is chosen or selected in order to apply the substantive rules of that legal system. It would also be possible to combine a plurality of coordinated self-limitations. The legal systems *conserve* their own substantive rules and the resulting coordination is achieved by the choice or cumulation of effects. Thus, it is possible to choose the law of habitual residence to govern incapacity or to coordinate the effects in social security law having regard to the periodical benefits of the different legal systems under which a worker is subject. The method of selection may also function by according primacy to international law or a community law over and above a national domestic law.

By the method of coordination the coordinated legal systems are not in themselves substantialy modified. They remain unchanged.

On several occasions, a distinction between coordination and harmonization has been attempted. By harmonization the legal systems harmonized conserve their substantive rules but the *purpose* or aim of the domestic substantive rules is determined by another legal system, the applicable community law. The substantive domestic rules must take heed of the community purposes or policies. Authoritative legal literature has referred to this as "approximation" or "*rapprochement des legislations*".[5]

3.3 Harmonization

Harmonization as a method has been considered as ancillary and complementary to substantive unification. The example seems to be that of the EC Community

---

[5] D. Vignes, « Le rapprochement des legislations merite-t-il encore son nom? » in: *L'Europe et le droit: Mèlanges en hommage à Jean Boulouis* (Paris, Dalloz 1991) p. 533.

directives establishing purposes which the European national legal systems have to gradually attain according to the methods of the national laws. There might be different degrees of harmonization or approximation. Nevertheless, there seems to be developing the practice to progressively assimilate directives to substantive direct rules by way of interpreting the directives more as precise rules than as guidelines or even binding directives. The courts of the common legal systems may apply purposeful principles as rules, making new rules as precise as need be in the circumstances. Judge-made law seems to be a really effective method of unification through harmonization.

The recognition of the *equivalence* of different national substantive rules as long as they are basically in line with each other, on the other hand, may be regarded as a more laborious method of harmonization.

3.4   Co-existence and Adaptation

Diverse legal systems may be cumulatively applicable to different aspects of a case, for example, one legal system may be applicable to a succession *mortis causae* and another to the matrimonial property regime of the deceased. In case of conflict of substantive adjustment it would be necessary to find a method of *adaptation* as is known in the field of private international law, be that by way of *selection* and primacy of one legal system or by way of the *creation* of a substantive solution *ad hoc* in the particular case.

Conflicts between Community law and national laws have been solved by giving preference to Community law, but a solution of substantive adaptation may also be attained thereby conserving the co-existence.

3.5   Presumptions as Conflict Rules or Rules of Reference

The presumption that the rules of a national legal system do not have the purpose of conflicting with a rule of international law[6] is indeed, in my view, a conflict rule, analogous to the function of private international law to identity the applicable legal system. This is so because by presuming a lack of intention to contradict a rule of international law, primacy is given, by way of reference or selection, to international law. This presumtion does not apply whenever it is evident that the intention is to derogate from the rule of international law. Except in manifest cases, much discretion is inevitably left to the courts law in this respect.

---

[6] On that practice see *Oppenheim's International Law* (op.cit. n. 3) vol. I, p. 82 n. 1

3.6 Presumptions as Self-limiting Rules

A rule of coordinated self-limitation may be discovered in the presumption whereby the rules of national legal systems on extra-territorial jurisdiction have not been drafted with the intention of applying such rules beyond the territory of the State, at least when they apply to the conduct of foreigners.[7] This presumption is in effect a self-limiting rule of the jurisdiction of States. This presumption is relative and may not even exist when there is a clear extra-territorial application of the national rule.

It is difficult to claim that these presumptions constitute a customary rule of general international law. If such presumptions were to develop and be generally accepted, they should be applied *per se* as international law in the States that apply general international law *per se* as the law of the land. But it seems that we are here only faced with some judge-made national rules in certain States.

3.7 Constitutional Primacy Rules or Conflict Rules

In some national constitutional laws there are rules establishing the relationship between international law and State law. Some of them give priority to general international law over and above State law, e.g., Article 25 German Basic Law, while some give priority to international treaties over domestic legislation, e.g., Article 75 clause 22 Argentine Constitution. These rules may be regarded as choice of law rules referring to the proper applicable law in cases of conflict. Hence, they may be characterized as conflict rules of the law of the relations between legal systems.

Primacy of treaties implies the primacy of the rules of general international law without which international treaties could not have cogency in international law. None the less the primacy of general rules of international law does not necessarily imply the primacy of international treaties. Therefore, in our view Argentine Constitutional law allows the priority of international law as a complete system. The German Constitution only allows priority of general international law over domestic German law.

3.8 The Closest Connection or the Most "Genuine Link"

According to the method of coordination it seems appropriate to choose the legal system most closely connected with the case, affair or legal relationship. In cases which transcend one legal system and are related to various ones, the method of selecting the proper legal system becomes paramount. The legal system which has the most genuine link with the case should govern.

---

[7] Ibid., vol. VI, p. 82 n. 3.

3.9   Diverse Spheres of Competence

The situation is different when facing a rule enacted by a subject of international law within the sphere of its own competence in accordance with its constitution, as occurs with international organizations, especially with those creating a community. If the rule was enacted according to the constitution of the organization, there is no concurrence of rules and therefore no possible conflict. But all in all if a question of exceeding the proper competence of the organization arises, then a problem of the scope of such competence should be decided. Sometimes the implied powers of the organizations are recognized and ultimately the conflict is solved in favour of the law of the legal system of the organization.

3.10   International Obligations Creating Rights upon Individuals

International obligations are created daily with a view to being applied to individuals or to conduct and assets localized in State territories. Here we must not forget the Advisory Opinion of the Permanent Court of International Justice in the *Danzig Railway Service Officials case* whereby the object of an international agreement itself, according to the intention of the parties, may be the adoption of some rules creating rights and obligations upon the individuals which are applicable by national tribunals.[8] It seems that the direct effect of international law upon individuals in the sphere of the national legal system is not at all the exclusive landmark of Community law.

3.11   Primacy of International Law and Foreign Affairs

It would indeed be difficult in practice if States could evade rule-violating international obligations assumed by the same States which can only be respected by the application of international rules to individuals by national courts. This would amount to a mockery as far as the other parties to those agreements were concerned. Nevertheless, the ordinary reception of direct effects accorded by national constitutions in reality amounts to a practical monism which is necessary for coherent foreign affairs. Practical monism means that States cannot reasonably evade international obligations by internal devices and pragmatically such monism may also be explained as "*à la limite une modalité du dualisme*".[9]

In effect, there is an interaction between the legal systems which cannot be regarded as a mere juxtaposition. This interaction must be concretely considered in the relations between the legal systems.

---

[8] (1928) PCIJ Series B N° 15 p. 17.
[9] Combacau and Sur, *Droit International Public*, 2nd edn. (Paris 1995) p. 183.

3.12 The Moral Fundamentals of the Primacy of International Law

No State may pretend to turn a blind eye to the obligations assumed. This moral fundamental principle of the primacy of international law shows all its persuasive force in respect of human rights. In this connection the international law of extradition becomes crucial.[10] Furthermore, all international treaties concerning private international law in a wide sense, including uniform private law, relate to individuals as the subjects of the pertinent rules. The development of international law is demonstrating an increasing detachment from *ius inter gentes* and an increasing attachment to direct effects upon individuals within the national legal systems.

3.13 Cumulative Concurrence

The relations between legal systems may also demonstrate a cumulative application of different legal systems on human rights. Thus, some international treaties on human rights have acquired constitutional hierarchy within the Argentine Constitution (Article 75 clause 22). The application is cumulative with the consequence of *in dubio pro* human rights.

3.14 Unilateral and Multilateral Coordination

The coordination of legal systems is the method *par excellence* of private international law. This coordination may be attempted unilaterally and, oddly enough, multilaterally, which is evidently a more reasonable method. But not only private law has an external effect. Also aspects of constitutional, administrative, and fiscal law, as well as criminal law and, generally, all public law may produce effects or impacts on other foreign legal systems. Traditionally, public law was unilaterally self-limited. At present there is a trend also to coordinate these aspects by agreement between States. Leaving aside Community law, agreements are reached by using a great variety of methods. As a result there is not only a domestic law for international affairs, but there is also the development of international law in the field of the extra-territorial effects of public law.

3.15 The Internationalization of National Court Judgments

In his outstanding study on comparative human rights law, Burgenthal has considered the role of the Privy Council sitting as the Constitutional Court of Jamaica and

---

[10] On human rights and extradition in the Argentine Supreme Court judgments, see my *Derecho Internacional Público y Privado y Derecho del Mercosur en la jurisprudencia de la Corte Suprema de Justicia de la Nación* (Buenos Aires 1998-1999), index of cases on human rights and extradition.

the application of European and American human rights law cumulatively.[11]

Burgenthal highlights the judgment of the Argentine Supreme Court in *Ekmekdjian* v. *Sofovich* (7 July 1992) on the application of the American Convention of Human Rights.[12]

Burgenthal also considers the development of the case law in the United Kingdom and some Scandinavian states according to which judges take international obligations into consideration even if these obligations have not yet been properly incorporated into domestic law, by interpreting the pertinent domestic law in the light of international obligations conventionally assumed by their States.

We can also mention the judgment by the Argentine Supreme Court in the celebrated *Priebke* case (2 November 1995).[13] The extradition of *Priebke* in this case was allowed considering that in the crime of genocide against *iuris gentium* no time limitations could be raised as a defense.

With some time restrictions, the House of Lords has recently applied the Torture Convention allowing universal jurisdiction and denying immunity as the former Head of State to Senator Pinochet.[14]

Both of the last-mentioned judgments may be regarded as applications of *ius cogens* rules of international law in State courts.

3.16 The European Court of Justice and European Citizenship

Nationality as a link between a human person and a State has been considered by the European Court of Justice in the *Micheletti* case.[15] An Argentine national habitually resident in Argentina has acquired Italian nationality by reason of having an Italian parent. The Court applied European law, thereby requiring in fact the suspension of Article 9 of the Spanish Civil Code whereby persons with dual nationality, none of them being Spanish nationality, had to be considered as a national of the State where he or she was habitually resident before entering Spain.

3.17 A Mercosur Court Based on the Benelux Court Model

It has been suggested to constitute a Mercosur Court inspired by the model of the Benelux Court, namely a mixed tribunal to guarantee the uniform application of

---

[11] T. Burgenthal, "International Tribunals and National Courts: The Internationalization of Domestic Adjudication", in: *Fetschrift Rudolf Bernhardt* (1995) 687 at p. 689.

[12] The judgments of the Argentine Supreme Court from 1863 to 1999 are revisited along the chapters and are incorporated in the volumes cited in note 1.

[13] Fallos t. 318 p. 373, 2148, 2226 y 2308 and see also references in note 1.

[14] A study of the *Pinochet* case is forthcoming in Boggiano, *Derecho Internacional 2000,* (Buenos Aires, La Ley 2000).

[15] Case C-369/90, [1992] ECR I-4239.

Mercosur rules. At present the Argentine Supreme Court gives priority to Mercosur and ALALC (Latin American Free Trade Association) laws.[16] But this is not always the case in other Mercosur Member States in practice, where local and foreign investors often use different devices to select the *forum conveniens* for Mercosur law in order to guarantee the benefits of its rules. Even so, the lack of uniformity of Mercosur case law jeopardizes the whole economic integration process of the South American States of Argentine, Brazil, Paraguay and Uruguay.

3.18 The International Court of Justice and State Legal Systems

International law may refer to State legal systems or to the legal systems of other subjects of international law. Thus, to ascertain whether a commercial company had legal personality the International Court of Justice in the *Barcelona Traction Light and Power Co. Ltd.* case[17] considered that international law recognized a commercial company as an institution created by States in a sphere essentially related to its domestic jurisdiction.

Such recognition makes a reference to the pertinent rules of State law or to various State laws essential. Therefore the creation, validity, capacity, function and dissolution of a company or a group of companies in international law is governed by reference to State law including the law of coordination of such State legal systems in that field, that is the so-called private international law. According to the judgment of the Court multinationals or transnationals are governed in *international law* by way of *reference* to the competent State legal systems. This means that international law does not by itself have *substantive rules* on private companies but a *rule of reference* to the proper legal systems concerned, and the laws of the places of incorporation and administration or seat of the company are taken into account as connecting factors for a potential conflict rule of international law.

Human beings may also be regarded as subjects of international law. International law relating to human rights has substantive rules directly applicable to human persons. Nevertheless, a reference to State law may be necessary in order to decide some specific aspect. There may be a cumulative application of both international law and State laws. There may also be a cumulative application of international law to some aspects of human persons and a reference to a relevant State law may govern other aspects. In such cases, the International Court of Justice would, it is likely, have to establish "the genuine link" between the person and a State.

---

[16] *Cafes La Virginia S.A.*, Fallos t. 317, p. 1282 with a separate opinion by the author. See also the full judgment in the books cited in n. 1 Further, see Agustin, "La creciente internalización del derecho y sus efectos", *Rev. La Ley* (1995-D) p. 275; Ekmekdjian, "Un fallo de la Corte Suprema de Justicia de la Nación que apuntala el proceso de integración regional latinoamericana", 160 *Rev. El Derecho* 1995, p. 252.

[17] (1970) ICJ Rep. 3, at para. 33-34.

3.19 Internal Rules with External Effects and External Rules of International Organizations

The internal rules of the legal system of an international organization may have external effects.[18] Concerning external rules, the legal binding force of recommendations has been much discussed.[19] Declarations may influence a legal system. Thus, the Universal Declaration of Human Rights has gained constitutional status in the Argentine Constitution as amended in 1994. Treaties may be negotiated and drafted within international organizations. There may also be some special forms of conventions.[20] The ICAO (International Civil Aviation Organization) "International Standards" and "Recommended Practices" have sometimes been taken into account by the Argentine Supreme Court.[21] The regulations adopted by the WHO (World Health Organization) bind Member States if they do not notify their rejection of a particular rule or reservations to it.[22] Binding decisions upon Member States or individuals may be taken when authorized by the constitution of the international organization. Thus, the resolutions of the Security Council of the United Nations consisting of enforcement measures are binding. The International Court of Justice has established that Article 25 of the Charter is not confined to enforcement decisions.[23] ICAO standards may also be binding on individuals. In the more technical organizations there is a natural binding force of their rules due to practical needs of inescapable cooperation. The problem also arises as to the coordination of the legal systems of international organizations. Serious problems of conflicting policies and actions of international organizations must be coordinated.

3.20 Ascertaining the Solution in a Foreign Legal System

Ir may sometimes not be an easy task to ascertain the precise solution to a problem governed by a law foreign to the authorities of the legal system where the dispute must be decided. We all know the agony that may eventually embarrass a State court when trying to apply foreign law.[24] It is to be hoped that this obsessive entertainment is exceptionally abnormal. It may also be difficult to ascertain some

---

[18] Henry G. Schermers and Niels M. Blokker, *International Institutional Law*, 3rd edn. (The Hague, London, Boston 1999) 747.

[19] Ibid., p. 756 and the literature cited in note 232.

[20] Ibid., pp. 780-2.

[21] *Rodriguez, Jorge*, Fallos t. 320 p. 2851.

[22] WHO, Art. 22.

[23] *Namibia Case*, ICJ Rep. (1971) pp. 52-53.

[24] Jürgen Samtleben, „Der unfähige Guttachter und die ausländishe Rechtpraxis", *NJW* (1992) pp. 3058-3062, on a case where the parties submitted 8 expert opinions, the Bundesgerichtshof suggesting one more.

point of international customary law involving the practice of States. Reasonableness should be the guiding light to avoid a *deni de justice*. At some point, however, comparative legal research must stop. Should the facultative conflict rules doctrine be reconsidered?[25] In the present context it is hardly conceivable to indulge in a facultative escape.

4. INTERNATIONAL LAW AS THE LAW GOVERNING RELATIONS BETWEEN LEGAL SYSTEMS

International law may be re-considered from the standpoint of the relations between legal systems. It has been submitted that international law should not necessarily develop towards centralization. While the international legal system continues to be State-oriented, it becomes progressively more internationally institutionally oriented. The promotion of harmony in the application of rules in order to achieve broader areas of uniformity leads to a comprehensive understanding of the relations of all legal systems concerned. The independence of the international organizations seems to grow *vis-à-vis* Member States. But they seem to be more dependent upon the relations between legal systems. The degree of the hierarchy of the legal systems of international organizations provides for more vertical international law.[26]

Further, there is no constitution for the international legal systems as there is a constitution for the State and the international organizations. Certainly, a *process of constituting* the international community may be traced considering the exercise of the powers of the Security Council.[27] But even in this respect the relations between the United Nations and other international organizations do seem to be relevant (e.g., UN-NATO). The decentralization of the international legal system still allows one to take the view that this system is mainly a law of relations between legal systems. The growing centralization relates to the emerge of partial and functional competences of international organizations. The International Court of Justice reminded us of this doctrine in its opinion of 8 July 1996 on Nuclear Weapons. The United Nations is more of a harmonization *"forum"* than a super State.

Nevertheless, the law of the relations between legal systems transcends international law if this is conceived as a legal system in itself. If international law delimits the competence of States and other subjects of international law, then international law governs the relations between the State legal systems by controlling the extent of their legislative, adjudicatory and enforcement jurisdiction. And the same may be said of the other subjects. The delimitation of the sphere of application of the do-

---

[25] Axel Flessner, „Fakultatives Kollisionsrecht", *RabelsZ* (1970) pp. 547-584.

[26] Schermers and Blokker, op.cit. n. 14, p. 1195.

[27] J. Frowein, "Reaction by Not-Directly Affected States to Breaches of Public International Law", 248 *Recueil des Cours* (1994-IV) at pp. 355-356, 358.

mestic jurisdiction of those subjects imply the definition of which cases fall within the realm of its proper applicable law. So in this respect international law is a law governing the relationships of the domestic legal systems of the subjects of international law. International law is likewise a law between the subjects of international law as there is no World State. The ultimate effectiveness of international law in many contexts depends upon the application of its rules and principles within the legal systems of the subjects of international law, mainly national legal systems. Therefore international law may also be considered as a law of the relations between international law and the legal systems of the subjects of international law. The relations between the legal systems of the subjects of international law may or may not fall within the realm of international law itself. For instance, some rules on the domestic jurisdiction of States may be the object of relations between States' legal systems. But some *limits* to domestic jurisdiction on human rights may be the object of rules of international law. It depends on the way international law evolves.

5.   CROSSING THE THRESHOLD OF THE MILLENNIUM

The increasing inter-relationship between legal systems is the momentum of present international law. Former domestic matters are now of paramount international concern paving the way from the sanctity of national sovereignty to the sanctity of human rights. The isolation of domestic cases and problems under a rigid doctrine of domestic jurisdiction is rapidly turning into problems of inter-related jurisdictions. The NATO intervention in Kosovo would formerly have been considered as an act of aggression. The Serbian crimes in Kosovo and the NATO intervention may give rise to demands for action in presumably analogous situations in China and Tibet, Russia and Chechnya, Turkey and Cyprus, Indonesia and East Timor, India and Kashmir, Israel and Palestine, Britain and Northern Ireland.[28]

To put it in Lord Millet's words in his lucid opinion in the *Pinochet* judgment by the House of Lords: in "the classical theory of international law . . . states were obliged to abstain from interfering in the internal affairs of one another. International law was not concerned with the way in which a sovereign state treated its own nationals in its own territory . . . the way in which a state treated its own citizens within its own borders (has now) become a legitimate concern to the international community".

I submit that this concern must be the object of clear relations between the connected legal systems of States and international organizations, for example UN-NATO or other organizations. International law must develop to meet the concerns

---

[28] See the perceptive article by William Rees-Mogg, "Where's the justice?", *The Times* (29 March 1999) p. 20.

of the international community by way of ascertainable procedures connecting the legal systems involved.

An also brilliant dissenting opinion by Lord Goff of Chieveley in the *Pinochet* case in the House of Lords warned of the possibility that a responsible British Minister might be extradited while on holiday on the grounds of British conduct in Northern Ireland.

International law is changing rather quickly. Comparing the Genocide Convention and the Torture Convention on the crucial issue of the international jurisdiction of national courts, it is hardly understandable that genocide is subject to the jurisdiction of the *loci delicti* and torture to universal jurisdiction. The timing restrictions in the *Pinochet* judgment reflect this state of evolution of international law.

The dignity and value of the human being led to the universality and indivisibility of human rights.[29] These rights relate to all phases of life and all political, social, economic and cultural contexts, including the rights of ethnic groups and minorities to their own existence. The Statute of the International Criminal Court involves the relationship between many legal systems to achieve unification, coordination and cooperation in order to punish genocide, torture and all crimes against humanity

In the evolution from isolation to inter-relation the law of the relations between the legal systems is expected to provide more consensus and certainty for the international community.

---

[29] See, in particular, The Vienna Declaration (25 July 1993) Preamble, 2.

Le contrôle des sentences arbitrales internationales par le juge du siège et par le juge de l'exécution

Gerardo Broggini[*]

1. UNITÉ ET PLURALITÉ DANS LE SYSTÈME SUISSE DU CONTRÔLE DES JUGEMENTS ET DES SENTENCES

Depuis dix ans l'arbitrage international en Suisse est régi par le chapitre 12 de la loi fédérale sur le droit international privé (LDIP). Cet anniversaire nous offre l'occasion de réfléchir sur un aspect des plus discutés, à savoir le contrôle exercé par le juge étatique sur la sentence arbitrale, tel qu'il a été envisagé par le nouveau droit. La LDIP a profondément transformé le droit de l'arbitrage international, en le soustrayant à la procédure cantonale et au Concordat international sur l'arbitrage, qui continue à régir l'arbitrage interne.[1] Comme le chapitre 11 de la loi sur la faillite et

---

[*] Prof. Avv., professeur à l'Università Cattolica di Milano.
[1] Cf. A. Heini/ M. Keller/ K. Siehr/ F. Vischer/ P. Volken, *IPRG-Kommentar* (Zürich 1993) art. 176ss. (*Vischer*); art. 184s. (*Volken*); art. 186ss. (*Heini*); art. 192ss. (*Siehr*); A. Bucher, *Die neue internationale Schiedsgerichtsbarkeit in der Schweiz* (Basel, Frankfurt 1989); P. Lalive/ J.F. Poudret/ C. Reymond, *Le droit de l'arbitrage interne et international en Suisse* (Lausanne 1989); B. Dutoit, *Commentaire de la loi fédérale du 18.12.1987* (Bâle, Francfort 1996) pp. 464ss; Th. Ruede/ R. Hadenfeldt, *Schweizerisches Schiedsgerichtsrecht nach Konkordat und IPRG*, 2ème éd. (Zürich 1993); G. Walter/ W. Bosch/ H. Brönnimann, *Internationale Schiedsgerichtsbarkeit in der Schweiz* (Bern 1991); cf. aussi de G. Walter, « Le rapport sur l'arbitrage international en Suisse », dans le volume édité par P. Gottwald, *Internationale Schiedsgerichtsbarkeit* (Bielefeld 1997), pp. 817ss; P.M. Patocchi/ E. Geisinger, *Code de droit international privé suisse annoté* (Lausanne 1995), pp. 424ss, H. Honsell/ N.P. Vogt/ A.K. Schnyder, *Kommentar zum schweizerischen Privatrecht: Internationales Privatrecht* (Basel, Frankfurt 1996), Einleitung vor Art. 176 (*M. Blessing*), Art. 176 (*F. Ehrat*), Art. 177 (*R. Briner*), Art. 178 (*W. Wenger*), Art. 179 (*W. Peter/ Th.. Legler*), Art. 180 (*W. Peter/ C. Freymond*),

J. Basedow et al., eds., *Private Law in the International Arena – Liber Amicorum Kurt Siehr*
© 2000, T.M.C.Asser Press, The Hague, The Netherlands

le concordat, aussi le chapitre 12 complète de façon très innovative la structure traditionnelle des législations de droit international privé et même est souvent considéré en tant qu'un acte législatif autonome, détaché du reste de la loi et notamment des règles générales et des grands principes qui inspirent le nouveau droit international privé.[2] Néanmoins cette prétendue autonomie ne touche pas aux aspects fondamentaux des règles: l'arbitrage international régi par le chapitre 12 existe – une fois réalisée la condition de l'extranéité – en tant qu'arbitrage international suisse, selon le critère du siège du tribunal arbitral. Sa localisation suisse est déterminante[3] avec la conséquence qu'il est intégré dans l'ordre juridique suisse et notamment respectueux du système des règles de conflit, de procédure et de compétence, élaborées par la LDIP. La règle sur l'arbitrabilité de l'art. 177 utilise la notion de « nature patrimoniale de la cause » dans le même sens que la règle sur l'élection du for selon l'art. 5; la règle du même art. 5 sur la prorogation du for ainsi que celle de l'art. 7 sur le déclinatoire du for en faveur du tribunal arbitral montrent bien que la substitution d'un tribunal avec un autre englobe la fonction arbitrale dans celle des tribunaux ordinaires. En ce sens les deux tribunaux sont « fongibles ».[4] Enfin les voies de recours et les procédures de reconnaissance et d'exécution des décisions étrangères – qu'il s'agisse de jugements ordinaires ou de sentences arbitrales – montrent à l'évidence l'unité de fond du système, malgré les différences des conditions prévues dans les deux cas. Les efforts de compréhension et d'utilisation de la voie ordinaire et de la voie arbitrale, de la part des juristes suisses, conduisent toutefois à des résul-

---

Art. 181 (*N.P. Vogt*), Art. 182 (*M. Schneider*), Art. 183 (*S.V. Berti*), Art. 184 (*M. Schneider*), Art. 185 (*S.V. Berti*), Art. 186 (*W. Wenger*), Art. 187 (*P. Karrer*), Art. 188 s. (*M. Wirth*), Art. 190s. (*S.V. Berti/ A. Schnyder*), Art. 192ss. (*P.M. Patocchi/ C. Jermini*); F. Knoepfler/ Ph. Schweizer, *Droit international privé suisse*, 2ème ed. (Berne 1995) p. 321ss.

[2] L'autonomie du chapitre 12 a été soutenue notamment par P. Lalive dans son introduction au droit de l'arbitrage international en Suisse, et dans le commentaire à l'art. 187, dans Lalive/ Poudret/ Reymond (supra n. 1) pp. 258ss.: « spécificité de l'arbitrage international »; pp. 276ss.: « le chapitre 12 et l'ensemble de la LDIP »; pp. 395ss. Cf. aussi les réflexions de M. Blessing dans son introduction au commentaire du chapitre 12 (supra n. 1) pp. 1350ss. (« Specificity » der internationalen Schiedsgerichtsbarkeit) et particulièrement pp. 1372ss. « Insgesamt darf das 12. Kapitel als schweizerischer Arbitration Act bezeichnet werden, was dessen Eigenständigkeit hervorhebt. Als solcher ist er als stand alone zu verstehen und zu interpretieren ... Cf. aussi P.A. Karrer, « commentaire de l'art. 187 » (loc.cit. n. 1) p. 1604.

[3] Cf. A. Bucher, « Zur Lokalisierung internationaler Schiedsgerichte in der Schweiz », *Festschrift Max Keller* (Zürich 1989) p. 565ss.; ainsi que le commentaire de F. Ehrat à l'art. 176, p. 1416 n. 19 (« Delokalisierte Schiedsverfahren »).

[4] Cf. sur le problème J.M. Vullemien, *Jugement et sentence arbitrale* (Zürich 1990). On connaît bien la conception française de l'arbitrage international dénoué de toute connexion avec l'ordre juridique étatique. Pour ne pas revenir aux ouvrages de J. Robert/ B. Goldman/ R. David, je me limite à citer le *Traité de l'arbitrage commercial international* de Ph. Fouchard/ E. Gaillard/ B. Goldman (Paris 1996) p. 11 ss. (« notion et sources »). Cf. aussi l'introduction de M. Blessing dans le *Kommentar zum schweiz. Privatrecht, Internationales Privatrecht* (supra n. 1) p. 1285ss., ainsi que le rapport général de P. Gottwald dans le volume *Internationale Schiedsgerichtsbarkeit* (supra n. 1) p. 1ss.

tats assez différents, selon qu'on met l'accent sur les aspects unitaires de structure et de fonction, ou sur les distinctions d'après le degré d'autonomie de la procédure utilisée pour atteindre à la décision et pour le contrôle de la même.[5]

Notre examen aboutit à la conviction que l'arbitrage international – ainsi que la *lex arbitri* – s'insère dans le système de la *lex fori*, sans le contredire. Evidemment les différences existent: le juge étatique est soumis au contrôle hiérarchique des tribunaux de deuxième et de troisième degré, en particulier pour ce qui est de la révision au fond du droit applicable, qu'il s'agisse du droit national ou du droit étranger; le contrôle des décisions du tribunal arbitral est limité au « noyau dur » du droit applicable, à savoir l'ordre public. C'est l'ordre public, soit sous l'aspect de la procédure que sous l'aspect du droit matériel qui nous offre le dénominateur commun, entre les dispositions des articles 13 deuxième phrase (« l'application du droit étranger n'est pas exclue du seul fait qu'on attribue à la disposition un caractère de droit public »), 17, 18 et 19 LDIP et de l'art. 190 LDIP à propos de l'annulation de la sentence arbitrale.[6]

D'autre part la comparaison du rôle de la procédure ordinaire et de la procédure arbitrale peut et doit se faire aussi dans la perspective unitaire de la reconnaissance et de l'exécution des décisions étrangères, à savoir des art. 25 ss. LDIP d'une part et des l'art. 194 LDIP de l'autre.

Le premier groupe de règles trouve désormais sont complément majeur dans la

---

[5] Le développement extraordinaire de l'arbitrage commercial international ainsi que l'organisation très étendue des structures d'appui des Chambres de commerce nationales et internationales font croître la conviction de la nature « privée » de la justice rendue par la voie arbitrale. Cf. les considérations récentes de P. Lalive, « Arbitration – the civilized solution? » *Bulletin ASA* (Bâle 1998) p. 483ss.; M. Benedettelli, « L'arbitrato commerciale internazionale tra autonomia privata e coordinamento di sistemi giuridici », *Riv. dir. int. priv. proc.* (1997) p. 899ss.; W. Habscheid, « Die sogenannte Schiedsgerichtsbarkeit der Internationalen Handelskammer », *RIW (Recht der Internationalen. Wirtschaft)* (1998), p. 421ss. A. Briguglio, « Mito e realtà nella denazionalizzazione dell'arbitrato privato », *Riv. dell'arbitrato* (1998) p. 453ss.; P. Gottwald, « International Arbitration. Current Positions and Comparative Trends », *Riv. dell'arbitrato* (1996) p. 211ss. Cf. aussi le rapport général de P. Gottwald dans le volume déjà cité (supra n. 1) *Internationale Schiedsgerichtsbarkeit* (Bielefeld 1997) p. 1ss. Cf. aussi les auteurs cités à la note 1.

[6] Le système étatique reconnaît le rôle de l'autonomie des parties dans le choix entre la juridiction ordinaire, la juridiction d'un autre Etat (*prorogatio fori*) et le tribunal arbitral. Mais le système étatique impose des limites non seulement au choix (arbitrabilité), mais aussi aux résultats objectifs obtenus par les différentes « juridictions » (ordre public). La « spécificité » de l'arbitrage international ne soustrait par cette voie de l'administration de la justice au contrôle étatique. Ce contrôle s'exprime, « en matière internationale » (art. 1 LDIP) aussi à travers l'application des art. 13, 17, 18 et 19 de la loi. Qu'il me soit permis de renvoyer aux arguments développés dans la troisième partie de cet exposé. Quant à l'opinion contraire, j'ai déjà renvoyé à l'introduction de P. Lalive (op. cit. n. 2). Dans la même ligne A. Bucher (supra n. 1) p. 94ss.; F. Knoepfler, « L'art. 19 LDIP est-il adapté à l'arbitrage international? » *Etudes en l'honneur de P. Lalive* (Bâle-Francort 1993) p. 531ss.; P. A. Karrer, « Commentaire de l'art. 187 » (op. cit. n. 1) p. 1619ss. Cf. par exemple à p. 1623: « Damit entfällt eine analoge Anwendung von Art. 18 vollends; eine analoge Anwendung von Art. 19 setzt wesentliche Modifikationen voraus ». A mon avis il ne s'agit pas d'une application par analogie, mais d'une application tout-court.

Convention de Lugano, tandis que l'art. 194 LDIP renvoie simplement à la Convention de New York. Au centre de l'examen nous retrouvons encore la notion de l'ordre public, qu'on définit souvent « atténué », d'après l'art. 27 LDIP, l'art. 27 de la Convention de Lugano et l'art. V, 2 b de la Convention de New York.[7]

Il est de toute évidence que les systèmes nationaux maintiennent une autonomie considérable, en fonction de la présence des codifications nationales du droit privé et de l'organisation nationale des juridictions. L'ordre juridique mondial reste multiculturel et pluraliste. L'effort et le but de l'arbitrage international sont concentrés dans l'atteinte de l'uniformité la plus ample possible des méthodes et des solutions pour réaliser l'unité du droit dans les relations commerciales internationales.

Dans ce domaine, sans nier la localisation nationale des arbitrages, l'épanouissement de l'harmonie internationale trouve sa réalisation à travers des juges privés plus informés des réalités économiques et techniques qui doivent faire l'objet de la décision et à travers des méthodes de procédure plus libres de celles fixées par les systèmes nationaux.

En ce sens les résultats obtenus au niveau mondial par les sentences arbitrales sont plus uniformes de ceux obtenus par la jurisprudence des tribunaux nationaux.

Mais l'unité du système juridique national reste sauvegardée: la tension entre les valeurs de l'unité du système juridique national et les valeurs de l'universalité du droit, finit pour aboutir à la primauté de l'ordre juridique étatique.

Nous voulons concentrer nos réflexions sur le contrôle des sentences arbitrales internationales par le juge du siège et par le juge de l'exécution. Il s'agit d'un aspect important dans le cadre général de l'harmonisation des jugements dans les situations internationales. Nous arrivons à la conclusion que ces deux contrôles s'inspirent des même principes et réfléchissent ainsi l'unité du système.

Les articles de 190 à 194 LDIP prévoient deux interventions distinctes, la première auprès du Tribunal fédéral dans le but de faire annuler la sentence arbitrale rendue en Suisse, le deuxième auprès du tribunal cantonal, compétent d'après la loi fédérale sur la poursuite pour dettes et la faillite (LP) ou d'après l'art. 29 LDIP dans le but de reconnaître et donner exécution à la sentence arbitrale rendue à l'étranger.

Il s'agit de deux procédés distincts, dont l'objet est différent. Mais plus on approfondit la comparaison, plus on est frappé par la structure unitaire des deux procédures, qui acquiert une dimension encore plus marquée, si l'on élargit la comparaison aux solutions adoptées par d'autres pays et notamment à la solution proposée par la loi-type de l'UNCITRAL (CNUDCI) de 1985.[8]

---

[7] Je renvoie à la bibliographie indiquée à la note 1. En ce qui concerne la Convention de New York, cf. aussi le volume publié par l'ASA (Association suisse de l'arbitrage) *The New York Convention of 1958* (ASA Special Series n. 9 1996) et notamment les études de M. Blessing/ J. Werner/ P.M. Patocchi/ J.F. Poudret/ M. Wirth.

[8] Cf. P. Gottwald, *Internationale Schiedsgerichtsbarkeit* (supra n. 1) p. 105: « Die Gründe für die Aufhebung eines inländischen Schiedsspruchs sind danach (im Wesentlichen) dieselben wie die für die

2.   PARALLELISME DU CONTROLE DES SENTENCES ARBITRALES
      INTERNATIONALES

Tandis que la décision du juge suisse, dans les situations internationales, est soumise au contrôle prévue par le procédures cantonales et fédérales, applicables à tous les procès ordinaires suisses et notamment à la révision « au fond » de l'application du droit suisse ou du droit étranger, qui a été retenu applicable, le contrôle de la sentence arbitrale suisse est limité aux hypothèses indiquées à l'art. 190 al. 2 LDIP. Il ne s'agit pas ici de commenter les espèces des différentes lettres de cet article: le législateur a simplifié les conditions prévues à l'art. 34 de la loi-type de la CNUDCI; à côté des vices dans la constitution du tribunal (lettre a), dans la conduction de la procédure (lettre d) et dans la rédaction de la sentence (lettre c) l'art. 190 al. 2 impose le respect de la compétence (al. b) et la compatibilité avec l'ordre public (al. e).[9]

Ainsi nous pouvons saisir la distinction entre l'exigence de respect des conditions fondamentales du « due process »: ordre public procédural d'une part et ordre public matériel de l'autre. Quant au respect de la règle de la compétence, elle peut toucher aux deux: elle touche au fond quand elle s'identifie avec le critère de l'arbitrabilité: l'objet du différend peut ne pas être susceptible d'être réglé par arbitrage (mais le tribunal arbitral a décidé) ou d'être arbitrable (mais le tribunal arbitral a refusé de décider). Nous reviendrons sur ce point.

Le Tribunal fédéral se limite à vérifier les conditions minimales qui permettent d'accepter la sentence arbitrale dans le système suisse; la confiance faite à l'arbitre permet d'exclure un contrôle plus approfondi, notamment en ce qui concerne l'application du droit matériel, qu'il soit suisse ou étranger. Le refus de la révision au fond n'est pas l'expression du manque d'intérêt du système face à la mission de l'arbitre, mais du respect de la volonté des parties qui ont confié la solution du litige à un organe de leur choix.

Et pourtant les limites existent et c'est sur celle de l'ordre public que nous voulons concentrer notre attention. Les subtilités et les fragmentations de la notion d'ordre public sont bien connues à tous les juristes: à commencer de la distinction entre ordre public interne et international, à la notion d'ordre public « transnational » ou « vraiment international », à celle entre ordre public négatif et positif, entre

---

Ablehnung der Vollstreckbarerklärung eines ausländischen Schiedsspruchs ». Cf. aussi Ph. Fouchard/ E. Gaillard/ B. Goldman (supra n. 4) p. 897ss.: « Contrôle étatique de la sentence arbitrale »; quant à la loi-modèle CNUDCI je me permets aussi de renvoyer aux ouvrages de C. Calavros, *Das UNCITRAL-Modellgesetz über die internationale Handelsschiedsgerichtsbarkeit* (Bielefeld 1988) et de G. Husslein-Stich, *Das UNCITRAL-Modellgesetz über die internationale Handelsschiedsgerichtsbarkeit* (Köln, Berlin, Bonn, München 1990).

[9] Je renvoie notamment à l'ouvrage de C. Jermini, *Die Anfechtung der Schiedssprüche im internationalen Privatrecht* (Zürich 1997) en particulier p. 244ss. ainsi qu'au commentaire de l'art. 190 de S.V. Berti/ A.K. Schnyder (supra n. 1).

ordre public procédural et matériel, pour ne pas insister avec la distinction des effets complets et des effets atténués de l'ordre public.

Les distinctions s'expliquent dans le cadre de l'effort de mieux comprendre le contenu de cette notion, fondamentale et vague à la fois (Inhaltserklärung durch Begriftsaufsplitterung).[10]

Mais avant d'entamer l'examen de l'ordre public il y a lieu de comparer le contrôle issu de l'art. 190 al. 2 LDIP avec le contrôle qui découle de l'art. V de la Convention de New York. Les conditions posées par la Convention sont certainement plus nuancées et réfléchissent la situation d'une époque dans laquelle la conformité des sentences arbitrales aux exigences fondamentales de procédure et de fond était certainement inférieure à l'actuelle. Toutefois nous n'avons pas de difficultés majeures dans la comparaison: ce que la Convention impose est aussi le respect de l'ordre public dans la procédure et au fond. Quant à la procédure il s'agit toujours du respect des droit de la défense et du principe du contradictoire, de la composition correcte du tribunal arbitral et de la cohérence entre le contenu de la demande et celui de la sentence. Quant au fond, l'art. V 2 b se réfère expressément à l'ordre public du pays qui est appelé à reconnaître la sentence.

Entre les deux pôles, l'art. V 2 a placé le contrôle de l'arbitrabilité, c.a.d. de la compétence ratione materiae de l'objet du différend. Il n'est pas douteux que cette condition se rapproche au domaine de l'ordre public. Nous pouvons même déduire de l'expérience issue de la comparaison des solutions nationales une règle assez utile: plus on élargit l'arbitrabilité des litiges, plus on élargit le domaine d'intervention de l'ordre public. L'arbitrabilité du droit suisse est très ample, puisqu'elle embrasse toute cause de nature patrimoniale (art. 177 al. 1 LDIP).[11] L'évolution du droit français nous montre d'une façon très efficace cette relation, ayant comme point de départ l'exclusion de l'arbitrage de tout litige « touchant à l'ordre public ».[12] De même la règle italienne qui limite le champ d'application de

---

[10] Ch. Völker, *Zur Dogmatik des ordre public* (Berlin 1998) p. 252. L'auteur consacre un chapitre important au « Sonderproblem Schiedsgerichtsbarkeit » (p. 257ss.) et aboutit à des conclusions auxquelles je me rallie, notamment en ce qui concerne la critique de la fragmentation de la notion unitaire « d'ordre public ». Cf. déjà P. Keller/ K. Siehr, *Allgemeine Lehren des Internationalen Privatrechts* (Zürich 1986) p. 540 s.

[11] Cf. le commentaire et les renvois bibliographiques dans M. Patocchi/ E. Geisinger (op. cit. n. 1) p. 437ss., Adde, le commentaire de l'art. 177 par R. Briner (op. cit. n. 1) p. 1423 ss. En général les auteurs ne mettent pas en relation l'art. 177 avec l'art. 5 LDIP. Cf. toutefois le commentaire de l'art. 5 de M. Hess dans le *Kommentar zum Schweiz. Int. Privatrecht* (op. cit. n. 1) p. 47 n. 50 qui renvoie aussi à H. Reiser, *Gerichtsstandsvereinbarungen nach IPR Gesetz und Lugano-Übereinkommen* (Zürich 1995). Cf. aussi M. Staehelin, *Gerichtsstandsvereinbarungen iminternationalen Handelsverkehr Europas* (Basel 1994) p. 3: « Der Gerichtsstandsvereinbarung wesensverwandt ist die Schiedsgerichtsbarkeitsvereinbarung » ... Les mêmes remarques s'appliquent aussi à la notion de « matière patrimoniale » de l'art. 26 lit. b. et c LDIP. Cf. aussi *C.* Jermini (supra n. 9) p. 182ss.

[12] Ph. Fouchard/ E. Gaillard/ B. Goldman, *Traité de l'arbitrage commercial international* (supra n. 1) p. 328ss., spéc. p. 348ss.

l'arbitrage aux « droits disponibles » (cf. art. 4 ch. 2 loi de réforme du dip), à savoir aux matières qui ne peuvent pas faire l'objet d'une transaction (cf. aussi 806 cpc, 839 cpc) rend évidemment plus restreinte l'intervention de la réserve de l'ordre public.[13] Toutefois le problème plus délicat se pose toujours: il a trait à l'étendue de cette intervention dans l'arbitrage commercial international, qui est certainement une « cause de nature patrimoniale », en présence de « matières patrimoniales sensibles à l'ordre public ».[14]

On finit par élargir l'arbitrabilité à la matière patrimoniale tout court, indépendamment de la présence de dispositions ou de complexes de règles touchant à l'ordre public économique, mais de faire jouer la limite de l'ordre public à l'intérieur de la procédure arbitrale.

Le parallélisme du contrôle de la sentence arbitrale internationale par le juge du siège (annulation éventuelle de la sentence « nationale ») et par le juge de l'exécution (reconnaissance et exécution de la sentence « étrangère ») a été souligné à juste titre par plusieurs auteurs. M. Blessing[15] utilise l'expression « Erwartungssymmetrie », P. Gottwald[16] en comparant les conditions de l'annulation de la sentence arbitrale et de la reconnaissance de la sentence arbitrale selon les art. 34 et 36 de la loi type CNUDCI, arrive à la même conclusion: « Die Gründe für die Aufhebung eines inländischen Schiedsspruchs sind danach (im wesentlichen) dieselben für die Ablehnung der Vollstreckbarerklärung eines ausländischen Schiedsspruchs ». On peut faire les mêmes considérations, en examinant les textes correspondants du droit français (art. 1484-1502-1504 cpc) du droit italien (art. 829-838-839 cpc) et du droit allemand (ZPO § 1059, 1, 2 b, § 1061).[17]

Le parallélisme est particulièrement évident en droit suisse grâce à la disposition de l'art. 192 al. 2 qui impose par voie d'analogie l'application des règles de la Convention de New York (et donc pour ce qui est de l'ordre public, art. V 5b) au contrôle de toute sentence arbitrale internationale, rendue en Suisse, même si les parties ont exclu expressément toute voie de recours.

D'après certains auteurs, cette disposition montre que les causes d'annulation de la sentence arbitrale internationale prononcée en Suisse (art. 190 al. 2 LDIP) seraient plus amples de celles prévues dans la Convention de New York pour la reconnaissance et l'exécution des sentences arbitrales étrangères. Ces dernières

---

[13] Cf. le commentaire de l'art. 4 ch. 2 de R. Luzzatto dans le *Commentario del nuovo diritto internazionale privato* (Padova 1996) p. 33ss.; ainsi que les commentaires des art. 806 et 839 cpc (arbitrage interne et arbitrage international) de M. Briguglio/ E. Fazzalari/ E. Marengo, *La nuova disciplina dell'arbitrato, Commentario* (Milano 1994) p. 3ss. p. 278ss. et de G. Tarzia/ R. Luzzatto/ E.F. Ricci, *Le nuove leggi civili commentate* (Padova 1995) p. 271ss. (L. Fumagalli).

[14] Ph. Fouchard/ E. Gaillard/ B. Goldman (supra n. 4) p. 357.

[15] M. Blessing, Introduction au ch. 12 LDIP, dans le Kommentar (supra n. 1) p. 1388.

[16] P. Gottwald, Introduction au volume (cité supra n. 1) p. 105.

[17] Tous les textes sont publiés dans le volume de P. Gottwald, ibid., p. 161ss.

représenteraient le « minimum » de contrôle qui doit toujours s'imposer.[18] Je ne partage pas cette opinion. A mon avis le législateur suisse a voulu faire état d'une situation particulière, à savoir d'un arbitrage dont le siège a été prévu en Suisse, bien que l'espèce objet du litige n'ait aucun rattachement à la Suisse (ni domicile, ni résidence habituelle, ni établissement en Suisse de deux parties). Il a donc rapproché la sentence arbitrale prononcée en Suisse à une sentence arbitrale étrangère, en la soumettant au même contrôle.

En effet, la loi précise que l'application de la Convention est faite « par analogie »: avec cette expression la loi veut souligner que les règles de la Convention s'appliquent bien que l'arbitrage se soit déroulé en Suisse. Le contrôle n'est pas plus réduit, ou plus ample, mais il a une autre source légale, à savoir la Convention, à cause du rapprochement de l'espèce objet du litige à une procédure arbitrale étrangère à la Suisse.

En ce qui concerne la réserve de l'ordre public, l'application de la Convention par analogie conduit aux mêmes résultats que l'application de la cause de nullité prévue à l'art. 190 al. 2 lett. e (incompatibilité avec l'ordre public).

La solution française rejoint les mêmes résultats: l'art. 1484 garantit le contrôle de la sentence même en cas de renonciation des parties à l'appel. Le contrôle du respect de l'ordre public n'est pas différent selon l'art. 1484, l'art. 1502 et l'art. 1504 cpc.[19]

Enfin le parallélisme du contrôle de la sentence arbitrale par le juge du siège et par le juge de l'exécution ne peut pas empêcher des contrastes et des solutions contradictoires quand les juges ont tendance à amplifier leur pouvoir discrétionnaire dans l'interprétation du texte de la loi, à accroître l'autonomie dans l'exercice de leur fonction, à ne pas tenir compte des systèmes de contrôle des sentences arbitrales dans les structures nationales dans lesquelles elles ont été rendues. L'autonomie conduit aux conflits des solutions nationales, à la « nationalisation de l'arbitrage international ». On affirme couramment le contraire: l'arbitrage international est « délocalisé » et « dénationalisé » du fait que la sentence arbitrale jouit d'une vie autonome et indépendante du tout contrôle judiciaire. Force est bien de rappeler à ce propos les différents arrêts des tribunaux de différents pays, dans les affaires Norsolor, Chromalloy et Hilmarton.

---

[18] Cf. P.M. Patocchi/ C. Jermini, commentaire de l'art. 192 LDIP, dans le Kommentar (cité supra n. 1) p. 1721.

[19] D'après Ph. Fouchard, « International Arbitration en France », dans le volume publié par P. Gottwald, (cité supra n. 1) p. 397: « le droit commun français est beaucoup plus libéral que le droit conventionnel » (le droit de la Convention de New York) au sujet du contrôle de la sentence arbitrale. Toutefois cette affirmation ne concerne pas l'étendue de l'ordre public. Sur le contrôle de la sentence arbitrale internationale dans le droit italien cf. R. Luzzatto, « L'impugnazione del lodo arbitrale internazionale », in: *Collisio legum, Studi per G. Broggini* (Milano 1997) p. 263ss., spec. p. 274s.

Nous ne voulons en aucun cas rediscuter ces aventures judiciaires que *A. Briguglio* a qualifié de « Zibaldone di curiosità ed occasioni di analisi »[20] et que *J.F. Poudret*[21] a bien voulu, encore récemment, approfondir. Nous voulons simplement souligner que la désintégration de la sentence arbitrale du siège de l'arbitrage ou du lieu ou la sentence a été rendue, et de la juridiction de l'Etat saisi du contrôle de la sentence, ne rend pas la sentence arbitrale plus « internationale », mais la rend objet de balancements et de rebondissements et pour finir de solutions contradictoires, qui sont exactement le contraire de l'harmonie internationale.

La même remarque critique doit être soulignée à propos du pouvoir discrétionnaire que prétend le juge américain sur la base du texte anglais de l'introduction à l'art. V 1 et 2 de la Convention de New York: est-ce que l'expression française « la reconnaissance et l'exécution de la sentence ne seront refusées que » contenue dans l'art. V n. 1, est vraiment en contraste avec celle de l'art. V n. 2: « pourront aussi être refusées? » Est-ce que le texte anglais « Recognition of the award may be refused … only if » permet vraiment au juge de décider à sa discrétion sur l'accueil ou le refus de la reconnaissance, une fois constatée la présence des situations énumérées aux lettres a) b) c) e) de l'art. V n. 1 et aux lettres a) b) de l'art. V n. 2 de la Convention? Pour ma part je ne suis pas en mesure d'accepter ces conclusions de la jurisprudence américaine qui contredit les critères classiques de l'interprétation.[22]

3. ORDRE PUBLIC DANS L'ARBITRAGE INTERNATIONAL

Une nouvelle réflexion sur l'ordre public dans l'arbitrage international peut apparaître superflue. Tout a été dit, apparemment, à ce sujet. Et pourtant cette notion est la véritable pierre angulaire – ou si l'on préfère, au contraire, la pierre d'achoppement – du système de contrôle de la sentence arbitrale et de son intégration dans l'ordre juridique étatique. Pierre angulaire, dans la perspective de la garantie d'uniformité du noyau des règles juridiques utilisées dans les sentences arbitrales avec celui des jugements des tribunaux ordinaires d'une part, et dans la perspective de la garantie d'uniformité du noyau des règles juridiques utilisées par les sentences arbitrales rendues dans des pays différents. Pierre d'achoppement, dans la perspective de l'autonomie la plus ample possible des parties qui choisissent la voie arbitrale pour le règlement de leurs controverses, dans la perspective de la désintégration de l'arbitrage commercial international de toute juridiction nationale. En effet, l'ordre public est le symbole de l'autorité, de l'impératif, de la coaction. Pour nous concen-

---

[20] A. Briguglio, *L'arbitrato estero. Il sistema delle convenzioni internazionali* (Padova 1999) p. 50.

[21] J.F. Poudret, « Quelle solution pour en finir avec l'affaire Hilmarton? » *Revue de l'arbitrage* (1998) p. 7ss.

[22] Je me limite à renvoyer aux réflexions de P.M. Patocchi/ G. Jermini, dans le commentaire à l'art. 194 LDIP (cité supra n. 1) p. 1753s. On y trouve les références bibliographiques.

trer sur le phénomène des contrats, l'ordre public a toujours représenté la limite de la liberté des parties: leurs conventions tiennent lieu de loi et doivent être exécutées (art. 1134 ccf), mais la convention n'a aucun effet si la cause est illicite, à savoir prohibée par la loi, contraire aux bonnes moeurs où à l'ordre public (art. 1133). Le droit suisse s'exprime d'une façon analogue, en utilisant aussi la notion d'ordre public (art. 19-20 CO).[23]

L'inspiration du code Napoléon est certainement romaine: la règle « ius publicum privatorum pactis mutari non potest » (Dig. 2, 14, 38) nous emmène directement à l'art. 6 du code civil: « on ne peut déroger, par des conventions particulières, aux lois qui intéressent l'ordre public et les bonnes moeurs ».

Le terme *ius publicum* n'est pas utilisé ici dans le sens de droit public, mais de règles impératives du droit privé (règles d'application nécessaire) qui trouvent leur fondement dans l'intérêt public et qui s'imposent à tous les sujets.

L'intérêt public est l'intérêt de la communauté qui peut s'opposer et prévaloir sur l'intérêt individuel et sur la volonté de l'individu. En ce qui concerne notamment le droit des contrats, la fonction sociale et donc la présence de règles qui s'imposent aux parties est depuis toujours indéniable. *Zweigert* et *Kötz*, ouvrent l'exposé du droit comparé des contrats avec le titre « Freiheit und Zwang im Vertragsrecht ».[24] Liberté et constriction se partagent le terrain. Et *Jacques Ghestin*, dans son Traité de droit civil, expose la formation du contrat en prenant comme point de départ l'autonomie de la volonté, mais en soulignant aussitôt son « déclin » et le rôle de plus en plus important des règles d'ordre public, « la limitation de la liberté contractuelle au nom de l'intérêt de la société ».[25]

Encore une fois le danger consiste dans une vision trop schématique et abstraite des grandes distinctions de l'ordre juridique: droit public et droit privé, droit pénal etc. Au centre de nos refléxions reste l'unum ius, l'unité de l'ordre juridique, la compénétration des différentes positiones iuris, comme les appelaient les romains, à savoir des différentes approches au droit. D'ailleurs cette unité, cette intégration de l'ordre juridique nous la constatons tout particulièrement aujourd'hui, à une époque qui met au centre du système la constitution. La liberté individuelle, les droits fondamentaux de l'individu ne peuvent pas se réaliser en contraste avec l'ordre public, qui acquiert ainsi une dimension constitutionnelle (la « verfassungsmässige Ordnung » dont parle l'art. 3 de la Constitution allemande), qui garde

---

[23] Cf. le commentaire des art. 19 et 10 CO de C. Huguenin, *Kommentar zum Schweiz. Privatrecht, Obligationenrecht I* (Basel 1992) p. 161ss., en particulier p. 169s. Cf. mon étude « Ordine pubblico e norme imperative quali limiti alla libertà contrattuale in diritto svizzero », *Festschrift W. Schönenberger* (Basel 1968) p. 93ss. Cf. aussi A. Guarneri, « Ordine pubblico », *Digesto delle discipline privatistiche, sezione civile* (Torino 1996) vol. XIII, P. 154s.

[24] K. Zweigert/ H. Kötz, *Einführung in die Rechtsvergleichung auf dem Gebiete des Privatrechts*, 3 éd. (Tübingen 1996) p. 314.

[25] J. Ghestin, *Traité de droit civil. La formation du contrat*, 3 éd. (Paris 1993) p. 27ss., spéc. p. 85ss.

une dimension administrative (je pense aux « lois de police » et de sûreté de l'art. 3 du code civil) qui est foncièrement intégré dans le droit privé des contrats (le renvoi est à l'art. 19 CO), au droit intertemporel privé (art. 2 titre final cc)[26] et au droit international privé. Deux éléments sont à mon avis essentiels pour saisir le contenu de la notion d'ordre public, dans sa signification la plus ample possible, telle qu'elle apparaît dans les textes que nous venons de citer: la présence de valeurs éthiques qui inspirent l'Etat constitutionnel et qui s'expriment dans la liberté individuelle et dans la solidarité; la présence de règles de droit positif, tendant à réaliser les intérêts collectifs et publics et par là à limiter la liberté individuelle.

Dans le domaine des relations contractuelles l'ordre public se réfère d'un côté aux valeurs éthiques qui sont à la base du droit des contrats en matière d'autonomie des sujets: obligation de loyauté et de fidélité, interprétation de bonne foi (pacta sunt servanda, bona fides, justice contractuelle), et d'autre côté aux règles de droit positif qui expriment les instruments nécessaires pour réaliser les intérêts publics sur le plan social et économique et qui imposent des limites importantes à la liberté contractuelle.

Je pense notamment à ce qu'on appelle le droit de l'économie. L'unité et l'universalité de la notion d'ordre public n'empêchent pas de reconnaître la pluralité et la localisation de leurs significations spécifiques et historiques, de leurs « sources », comme dit *Jacques Ghestin*.[27]

L'ordre public en droit international privé veut sauvegarder le noyau du droit – le droit absolument applicable, (même si le droit applicable ou le tribunal compétent est celui d'un autre Etat), tandis que l'ordre public en droit intertemporel privé veut imposer le droit nouveau aux rapports juridiques qui sont issus dans un cadre juridique ancien. Le fonctionnement de la règle de l'ordre public suit dans les deux situations la même méthode: écarter une règle juridique en faveur d'une autre, considérée comme indispensable pour la réalisation du droit, tel qu'il est conçu dans un espace déterminé et dans l'actualité.

Quant à l'universalité de la règle de l'ordre public, elle veut d'abord signifier que la méthode de son utilisation est la même partout. Elle veut aussi signifier que le contenu de l'ordre public tend à se généraliser: je pense aux critères de loyauté et de fidélité, à la règle de l'interprétation de bonne foi des contrats, mais je pense aussi aux grands principes du droit de l'économie – ainsi par exemple la garantie de la liberté de concurrence et le contrôle du contenu des contrats en tant qu'instrument de protection de la partie faible – qui tendent à pénétrer dans tous les systèmes juridiques. Néanmoins ces principes universels se concrétisent de façon différente dans les différents Etats. Chaque ordre juridique étatique a son ordre public, bien que le

---

[26] Je me permets de renvoyer au commentaire de l'art. 2 Titre final cc. de M. Vischer, *Kommentar zum Schweiz. Privatrecht, Schweiz. Zivilgesetzbuch II* (Basel 1998) p. 2553ss. Cf. aussi mon commentaire dans *Intertemporales Privatrecht, Schweiz. Privatrecht I* (Bâle 1969).

[27] J. Ghestin, *Traité de droit civil* (cité supra n. 25) p. 90.

contenu tende à devenir universel. Ceci explique le contraste entre les notions d'ordre public interne et d'ordre public international ou transnational: chaque Etat a son ordre public, mais chaque ordre public met de plus en plus en évidence les éléments communs et universels.

Cette double perspective – nationale et internationale – permet de saisir la possibilité pour l'ordre public interne de s'approprier de règles d'ordre public d'un autre Etat pour les imposer dans des situations que le droit interne considère comme « localisées » dans l'autre Etat.

L'approche à l'ordre public dans l'arbitrage international passe nécessairement par l'ordre public en droit international privé. L'encadrement est le même.

Je me rends compte que cette affirmation va soulever des réactions négatives, puisque plusieurs experts de l'arbitrage international soulignent la « spécificité » de cette forme de règlement des controverses jusqu'à exclure l'arbitrage du cercle de l'ordre juridique et de la sphère juridictionnelle étatiques. Cette attitude aboutit à la prétendue <u>autonomie</u> de la notion d'ordre public en matière d'arbitrage international. L'autonomie trouverait ses manifestations les plus évidentes à trois points de vue; <u>premièrement</u> il s'agirait d'un ordre public exclusivement international ou transnational, délié de l'ordre public du siège de l'arbitrage; <u>deuxièmement</u> il s'agirait uniquement d'un ordre public négatif; <u>troisièmement</u> son effet serait toujours atténué.

La conclusion des partisans de la spécificité aboutit à concevoir l'arbitrage international – et notamment l'ordre public dans l'arbitrage international – en tant que structure totalement détachée de celle de l'administration de la justice dans le cadre du droit international privé. Ainsi les principes fondamentaux sur le droit applicable, sanctionnés par les articles 13 à 19 LDIP n'auraient aucune influence pour la compréhension de l'art. 187 LDIP, à savoir sur la règle du droit applicable dans l'arbitrage international et particulièrement pour la compréhension de la notion d'ordre public de l'art. 190 al. 2 e LDIP.

Nous plaidons au contraire en faveur de l'unité de la notion d'ordre public et de la nécessité d'interpréter l'art. 187 LDIP (application du droit qui présente les liens les plus étroits avec la cause) et l'art. 190 al. 2 e LDIP, en tenant compte des principes du droit international privé suisse.

Mais arrêtons nous aux trois affirmations:

A) L'ordre public de l'arbitrage international est un ordre public international, délié de l'ordre public suisse. Cette proposition n'est pas acceptable. Le juge suisse appelé à intervenir soit en tant que Tribunal fédéral en vertu de l'art. 190, soit en tant que juge de la reconnaissance et de l'exécution en vertu des art. 192 al. 2 et 194, est appelé à exprimer un jugement suisse, à concrétiser l'ordre public d'après ses paramètres. Certes, il s'agira d'un « schweizerisches Ordre public in internationalen

Angelegenheiten » comme dit *Marc Blessing*[28], mais l'ordre public qu'exprime le juge suisse est encadré dans le système suisse et dans les valeurs qui sont à la base de ce système. Nous ne pouvons pas affirmer simplement, comme fait *Philippe Schweizer*[29] qu'il s'agit bien « d'un ordre public reflétant les principes juridiques et moraux fondamentaux reconnus dans tous les Etats civilisés » et donc d'un ordre public « plus restreint de l'ordre public international de la Suisse » ou comme dit *Stephen Berti*[30], à propos de l'application des « punitive damages » et donc du droit des Etats Unis dans un arbitrage international ayant son siège en Suisse, que la sentence arbitrale n'est pas incompatible avec l'ordre public de l'art. 190 al. 2 LDIP, parce que celui-ci exprime un standard minimal commun à toutes les nations civilisées et donc aussi aux Etats Unis. Ce qui est permis aux Etats Unis serait « per definitionem » conforme à l'ordre public.

Ce que la notion d'ordre public dans le système suisse veut faire respecter c'est bien l'unité des principes et des valeurs de ce système. Si le juge suisse, dans le cadre de la juridiction ordinaire, affirme que les « punitive damages » sont incompatibles avec l'ordre public, le même juge suisse, dans le cadre du recours ouvert contre la sentence arbitrale rendue en Suisse, ne peut qu'atteindre à la même solution.[31] La sentence arbitrale rendue en Suisse n'est pas une marchandise dont l'exportation est exempte de tout contrôle. L'esprit de l'art. 190 al. 2 LDIP et de l'examen de conformité à l'ordre public ne peut pas faire l'objet de contradictions ou de compromis.

Notre vision unitaire de l'ordre public, tel qu'il doit être appliqué par le juge ordinaire et par le juge du contrôle des sentences arbitrales, « en matière internationale » conduit – nous l'avons déjà dit – à ce que l'arbitre international qui siège en Suisse, utilise les grands principes du droit international privé suisse, applique le droit étranger « même si on attribue à la disposition le caractère de droit public » (art. 13), prenne en considération les lois d'application immédiate suisses, de l'Etat dont le droit est applicable au fond et de l'Etat tiers si la situation visée présente un

---

[28] M. Blessing, Introduction au chapitre 12, dans le Kommentar (cité supra n. 1) p. 1383. « Bei diesem ordre public handelt es sich um den sog. 'Schweizerischen Ordre public in internationalen Angelegenheiten', welcher Begriff enger zu verstehen ist als der interne schweizerische Ordre public ».

[29] Ph. Schweizer, « Commentaire de l'arrêt du T.F. 1ère Cour civile 30.12.1994 », *RSDIE* [1996] p. 550. Cf. aussi Les commentaires à l'arrêt Westland Helicopters du T.F. 1ère Cour Civile 19.04.1994 *RSDIE* [1995] p. 564ss. spéc. p. 572s.; et aux arrêts T.F. 1ère Cour Civile 06.09.1996 *RSDIE* [1998] p. 553ss., spéc. p. 565; T.F. 24.03.1997 *RSDIE* [1998], p. 574ss. spéc. p. 578. Cf. aussi l'arrêt T.F. 1ère Cour Civile 30.12.1994 *Bulletin ASA* (1995) p. 217ss. dont les conclusions (p. 224s.) sont en contradiction évidente avec mes arguments.

[30] S.V. Berti, « Zur Anfechtung eines Schiedsentscheides wegen Unvereinbarkeit mit dem Ordre public nach Art. 190 Abs 2 lit. e IPRG », in: *Rechtskollisionen, Festschrift A. Heini* (Zürich 1995) p. 1ss. spéc. p. 10.

[31] Cf. mon étude « Compatibilità di sentenze statunitensi di condanna al risarcimento di 'punitive damages' con il diritto europeo della responsabilità civile », *Europa e diritto privato* (1999) p. 479ss.

lien étroit avec ce droit (art. 18, 19).[32] La situation la plus évidente est celle de l'application, sous peine de violation de l'ordre public du pays communautaire, du droit de la concurrence communautaire. Un arrêt récent de la Cour de Justice de la Communauté européenne du 1er juin 1999 dans l'affaire *Eco Swiss China Time / Benetton International* confirme ce point de vue.[33] Répondant aux questions préjudicielles posées par le Hoge Raad der Nederlanden, la Cour affirme que l'art. 81 CE [ex article 85 du traité CE] constitue « une disposition fondamentale indispensable pour l'accomplissement des missions confiées à la Communauté pour le fonctionnement, en particulier, du marché intérieur » et que si le juge national doit « faire droit à une demande en annulation d'une sentence arbitrale fondée sur la méconnaissance des règles nationales d'ordre public, elle doit également faire droit à une telle demande fondée sur la méconnaissance de l'interdiction édictée à l'art. 81 par 1 CE ». Cet article peut être considéré comme une disposition d'ordre public, aussi au sens de la Convention de New York. La juridiction nationale doit faire droit à la demande en annulation de la sentence arbitrale contraire à l'art. 81 CE.

B)   La deuxième affirmation, souvent répétée, veut limiter le rôle de l'ordre public dans le contrôle des sentences arbitrales international à l'effet négatif.

Négatif est l'ordre public en ce qu'il se limite à empêcher le fonctionnement normal de la règle de conflit, il protège le système juridique du for, qui est pour ainsi dire réservé (Vorbehaltsklausel). Positif est l'ordre public quand il impose l'application du droit d'un Etat, qu'il s'agisse du système juridique national ou d'un autre système considéré comme « compétent » (plus étroitement lié). Dans les législations modernes de droit international privé, ce deuxième groupe de règles d'ordre public a fini par être qualifiée de façon autonome: « lois d'application immédiate », « Eingriffsnormen ».[34]

---

[32] Sur l'argument cf. M. Maechler/ Erne, Introduction aux art. 13-19 LDIP, dans le Kommentar (cité supra n. 1) p. 109ss.

[33] L'arrêt vient d'être publié dans le *Bulletin ASA* (1999), p. 414ss. L'arrêt du Hoge Road der Nederlanden est publié dans le *Yearbook Commercial Arbitration* vol. XXIII (1998) p. 180ss.

[34] Cf. sur l'argument les publications de A.K. Schnyder, « Pflicht schweiz. Schiedsgerichte zur Prüfung der Anwendbarkeit von Eingriffsnormen, insbes. des EG-Wettbewerbsrechts », *IPRax* (1994) p. 465ss.; Anwendung ausl. Eingriffsnormen durch Schiedsgerichte, 59 *RabelsZ* (1995) p. 293ss.; C. Baudenbacher/ A.K. Schnyder, « Die Bedeutung des EG Kartellrechts für Schweizer. Schiedsgerichte », *Beiheft RDS* 20 (1996) spéc. p. 29ss.; P.A. Karrer, commentaire de l'art. 187 LDIP, Kommentar (cité supra n. 1) p. 1620ss.; cf. aussi le recueil d'études « Objective Arbitrability, Antitrust Disputes, Intellectual Property Disputes », *Bulletin ASA* (1994) (spécial séries n. 6), édité par M. Blessing/ L. Fumagalli, « Mandatory Rules and International Arbitration, an Italian Perspective », *Bulletin ASA* (1998) p. 43ss.; A. Heini, « Wettbewerbsbeschränkungen auf dem EU-Markt vor schweizerischen Schiedsgerichten – zu einem Aufsatz von *Roger Zäch* », in: *Festschrift R. Zäch* (Zürich 1999) p. 317 ss.; et déjà précédemment J. Schiffer, *Normen ausländischen 'öffentlichen' Rechts in internationalen Handelsschiedsverfahren* (Köln, Berlin, Bonn, München 1990).

Toutefois nous savons que l'origine et le fondement des deux groupes de règles sont identiques: toutes les tentatives faites pour distinguer le rôle des principes d'ordre public et des « lois de police » ou d'application immédiate n'aboutissent pas à des résultats satisfaisants. Evidemment le fonctionnement est différent: une fois c'est l'exception qui ne permet pas l'application de la règle, une autre fois c'est la règle qui s'impose et doit être appliquée impérativement.

Tout particulièrement dans l'arrêt rendu le 19 avril 1994 à la suite du recours contre la sentence arbitrale dans l'affaire *Westland Helicopters*, le Tribunal Fédéral a insisté sur la distinction, pour attribuer à l'ordre public selon l'art. 190 al. 2 LDIP uniquement une fonction négative. Je me rallie à la critique très convaincante de *H. Arfazadeh*.[35] Les deux approches sont nécessairement complémentaires. Le juge suisse appelé à appliquer l'art. 190 al. 2 et donc à concrétiser la notion d'ordre public, devra décider si la sentence arbitrale a appliqué les principes et les règles d'ordre public suisse, donc aussi les lois d'application nécessaire (manifestation positive de l'ordre public) et s'il les a violées, en appliquant le droit désigné par la règle de conflits, sans tenir compte de l'ordre public suisse (manifestation négative de l'ordre public).

C   Que faut-il dire à propos de l'effet atténué de l'ordre public en matière d'arbitrage international? Je me suis déjà permis de douter du rôle effectif de cette qualification à propos de l'ordre public dans la reconnaissance des jugements étrangers. L'élément particulier qui qualifie le degré du contrôle du juge de la reconnaissance est plutôt celui de la connection du jugement avec l'ordre juridique de l'Etat du juge, la « Inlandsbeziehung ».[36]

Or le fait de faire reconnaître le jugement étranger en Suisse laisse supposer que le jugement sera exécuté en Suisse: la connection avec la Suisse et donc considérable. Nous ne pouvons pas atténuer le contrôle selon le critère de l'ordre public sur un jugement américain qui condamne une société suisse aux « treble damages », du fait que le jugement a été prononcé aux Etats-Unis.

L'ordre public utilisé par le juge suisse qui contrôle la sentence arbitrale rendue en Suisse et qui probablement n'aura aucune exécution en Suisse (ordre public d'envoi, comme on a défini cette situation) n'offre aucune justification pour être concrétisé d'une façon différente de l'ordre public de la reconnaissance de la sentence arbitrale rendue à l'étranger qui va être exécutée en Suisse, ni de l'ordre pu-

---

[35] H. Arfazadeh, « L'ordre public du fond et l'annulation des sentences arbitrales internationales en Suisse », *RSDIE* (1995) p. 223ss. L'étude est très complète et les arguments sont exposés d'une façon claire et convaincante.
[36] Je renvoie à l'étude (citée supra n. 31).

blic du juge ordinaire en matière internationale. La fonction du juge suisse, son « officium » est toujours le même: garantir le respect des principes d'ordre public et l'unité de l'ordre juridique suisse.[37]

Le Tribunal Fédéral s'est penché à plusieurs reprises, dans ces dernières années, sur le problème, en s'efforçant de définir l'ordre public dans l'arbitrage international. On a même dit que « quant à l'essence et à la nature de l'ordre public visé à l'art. 190 al. 2 les jeux paraissent définitivement faits ».[38] Et bien non: comme le droit intertemporel nous apprend, le droit vivant ne cesse jamais de se transformer: c'est la condition même de la vie, la Wandlung. Le contenu de l'ordre public ne sera jamais définitif.

Je pense notamment à la transformation permanente des instruments étatiques et universels de gestion de l'économie et du commerce international que les arbitres internationaux et les juges appelés à les contrôler ne pourront jamais oublier. Le Tribunal Fédéral devra à nouveau se pencher sur le rôle des lois d'application immédiate, suisses d'abord, mais aussi d'un autre Etat, dont le droit est appelé à régir le rapport contractuel, dans le cadre du contrôle des sentences arbitrales internationales rendues en Suisse. Et les tribunaux cantonaux suisses seront appelés au même effort, dans le cadre de la reconnaissance des sentences arbitrales rendues à l'étranger.

Summary
The Review of International Arbitral Awards by Swiss Courts

This article discusses the control of international arbitral awards by Swiss courts, in the context of both the review of awards rendered by arbitral tribunals having their seat in Switzerland and of the recognition and enforcement of foreign arbitral awards.

The first conclusion is that there is a parallelism in the control exercised by the Swiss judge in the two situations, and thus in the conditions for the annulment of « Swiss » arbitral awards and for the refusal of recognition and enforcement of « foreign » awards.

The main conditions, i.e., arbitrability and public policy, are closely connected.

As regards public policy, the article reaches the conclusion that the unity of the Swiss legal system presupposes a single notion of public policy which must also comprise « positive » public policy (mandatory rules). In international matters subject to international arbitration under the control of the Swiss courts the content

---

[37] En ce sens je ne peux pas partager les arguments et les conclusions de G. Kaufmann-Kohler, « L'ordre public d'envoi ou la notion d'ordre public en matière d'annulation des sentences arbitrales », *RSDIE* (1993) p. 273ss.
[38] Ph. Schweizer, *RSDIE* (1996) p. 550. Il s'agit de l'arrêt Westland Helicopters (supra n. 29).

of public policy is intrinsically identical to that of the public policy to which reference is made in Articles 17, 18 and 19 of the Swiss Private International Law Act.

Aspekte des internationalen Konzernrechts – Eine Fallstudie

Alexander Brunner[*]

*Wenn aber ein Fall eintritt, der in der allgemeinen Bestimmung des
Gesetzes nicht enthalten ist, so ist es, wenn der Gesetzgeber säumig
war, richtig gehandelt, das Versäumte zu verbessern, wie der Gesetzgeber es tun würde, wenn er den Fall vor sich gehabt hätte.*
ARISTOTELES, *Nik.Eth., V.14*

*Kann dem Gesetz keine Vorschrift entnommen werden, so soll der
Richter nach Gewohnheitsrecht und, wo auch ein solches fehlt, nach
der Regel entscheiden, die er als Gesetzgeber aufstellen würde.*
Schweizerisches ZGB 1 Abs. 2

1.   PROLOG – EIN AKTIENRECHTLICHER AUSREISSER

Die vorliegende Arbeit stützt sich auf eine Reihe von Verfahren, deren Beurteilung
den Gerichten ab 1990 oblag und die 1999 einen vorläufigen Abschluss fanden. Es

---

[*] Dr.iur., Oberrichter, Zürich, Lehrbeauftragter an der Universität Zürich.

J. Basedow et al., eds., *Private Law in the International Arena – Liber Amicorum Kurt Siehr*
© 2000, T.M.C.Asser Press, The Hague, The Netherlands

handelt sich dabei insbesondere um Fragen des internationalen Konzernrechts, deren Aktualität ungebrochen ist und angesichts der Globalisierung der wirtschaftlichen Beziehungen noch zunehmen wird. Die Festschrift für meinen verehrten Freund KURT SIEHR erscheint daher als ideales Gefäss, um in Anlehnung an die *aktuelle Praxis*[1] einigen grundlegenden Fragestellungen nachzugehen. Nicht völlig unbeabsichtigt wäre es sodann, wenn die vorliegend zu Tage tretenden Problemlagen den Schweizer Gesetzgeber zum Handeln veranlassen würden. Denn es erscheint vermessen anzunehmen, dass die Rechtsfragen des nationalen und internationalen Konzernrechts auch künftig allein mit den Vernunftgründen des ARISTOTELES[2] begründet werden müssen; oder – um nicht den Gesetzgeber zu bemühen: Handelt es sich bei der hier besprochenen aktuellen Praxis um einen veritablen „aktienrechtlichen Ausreisser", der den Schluss rechtfertigen würde, solches sei einmalig und könne sich in Zukunft nicht wiederholen?

Der Gang der Untersuchung wird eingerahmt durch einen Prolog und einen Epilog, um damit anzuzeigen, dass Handlungen von Verwaltungsräten als Rollenträger in internationalen Konzernen eine gewisse Dramatik entfalten können. Die Gerichte hatten ein transnational operierendes, mit einer einzelnen Person als herrschendem Unternehmer einerseits organisiertes und unter Verwendung einer Kaskade von mehreren Holding-Gesellschaften anderseits strukturiertes Finanz-Konglomerat zu beurteilen, wobei sich Fragen des schweizerischen Kollisionsrechts, des schweizerischen und deutschen Konzernrechts sowie des Rechts eines Off-shore-Gebietes stellten. Dem lag der folgende Sachverhalt[3] zugrunde.

Am 4. September 1991 verfügte der Konkursrichter des Bezirkes Zürich die Konkurseröffnung[4] über den Gemeinschuldner WKR. Dieser hatte in den Jahren zuvor ein Finanz-Konglomerat, den O-Konzern, begründet, mit über hundert ineinander verschachtelten Holding-, Beteiligungs- und Finanzierungs-Gesellschaften, die ihrerseits versuchten, tatsächlich werthaltige Industrie- und Dienstleistungs-Unternehmen an sich zu ziehen. WKR sicherte sich seine Rechtstellung als herrschender Unternehmer mit Mehrheitsbeteiligungen, jedoch ohne Beherrschungs-

---

[1] Der Prozess-Komplex mit fünf nunmehr rechtskräftigen Urteilen (bezeichnet als Urteile A, B.1, B.2, C.1 und C.2), wurde publiziert in *ZR* (Blätter für Zürcherische Rechtsprechung) (1999) Nr. 52 (Volltext). Ausschnitte aus diesen Entscheiden werden unter Hinweis auf die Fundstellen der Urteilspublikation für die vorliegende Abhandlung in einen besonderen systematischen Zusammenhang gebracht und aufgrund neuer Rechtsentwicklungen aktualisiert. Vgl. dazu insb. die Arbeiten des Forum Europaeum Konzernrecht 1992-1999: „Konzernrecht für Europa", *ZGR (Zeitschrift für Unternehmens- und Gesellschaftsrecht)* (1998) 672-772.

[2] Die von Huber vorgeschlagene und vom Gesetzgeber in das Schweizerische Zivilgesetzbuch (SR 210) aufgenommene Grundnorm in Art. 1 ZGB findet sich erstmals bei Aristoteles als rationales Prinzip.

[3] *ZR* (1999) Nr. 52 Sachverhalt.

[4] Privatkonkurs nach Art. 191 SchKG (Bundesgesetz vom 11. April 1889 über Schuldbetreibung und Konkurs; SR 281.1).

verträge zwischen den jeweiligen Ober- und Unter-Gesellschaften, wodurch ein faktischer Konzern[5] entstand. An der Spitze dieses O-Konzerns stand neben der OB-AG die OH-AG, deren Mehrheits-Aktienpaket (sowie weitere Beteiligungen) WKR vom europäischen Kontinent in ein Off-shore-Gebiet verlegte und dem (nach Guernsey-Law errichteten) WKR Trust einverleibte. Vor dem Privatkonkurs des WKR, bei dem Forderungen von über vier Milliarden Schweizer Franken angemeldet wurden, erfolgten Vermögensdispositionen oberer und unterer Konzern-Gesellschaften, deren Rechtmässigkeit in den nachfolgenden Kollokations- und Widerspruchsklagen angefochten wurden. Diesen Rechtsgeschäften war gemeinsam, und hier liegt der Bezug zum internationalen Konzernrecht der vorliegenden Fallstudie, dass es sich zur Hauptsache um eine *transnationale Verschiebung von Vermögenswerten innerhalb des Konzerns* handelte. Einerseits wurden - dies als radikalste Strategie - die Herrschaftsrechte über den gesamten Konzern in einen Off-shore-Trust auf Guernsey Island verlegt.[6] Anderseits wurden Millionen-Darlehen mit Aktien eines übernommenen Schweizer On-shore Industrie-Konzerns abgesichert[7] oder direkt von Unter-Gesellschaften eines übernommenen deutschen On-shore Industrie-Konzerns[8] erhältlich gemacht, worauf die Vermögenswerte schliesslich zu einer in Liquidation stehenden Unter-Gesellschaft flossen, die von Off-shore Zwischen-Gesellschaften gehalten wurde[9], oder einer massiv überschuldeten Off-shore Konzern-Gesellschaft auf Cayman Islands zugingen.[10] oder den Konten von Off-shore Konzern-Gesellschaften auf den Bahamas (mit anschliessender Liquidation) bzw. im Staate Delaware (mit zweifelhafter Bonität des Grundgeschäfts) gutgeschrieben wurden.[11]

Mit Bezug auf den solcherart gegebenen Sachverhalt der vorliegenden Fallstudie dürfen jedoch keine voreiligen Schlüsse gezogen werden. Das transnationale *Cash-Management* innerhalb von internationalen Konzernen gehört in einer globalisierten Welt zu den normalen Fakten des wirtschaftlichen Lebens, zumal die sog. global player heute Bilanzsummen vereinigen, die dem Bruttosozialprodukt (BSP) mittlerer europäischer Staaten entsprechen. Fraglich ist nicht das Cash-Management im internationalen Konzern als Tatsache, sondern der *Machtmissbrauch in den Formen des Rechts*, falls die oberste Konzernleitung – aus welchen Gründen auch immer – sich als Usurpatorin entpuppt. Transnationale Vermögensverschiebungen erscheinen dann in einem anderen Licht, wenn alle relevanten Umstände

---

[5] Vgl. zum faktischen Konzern Maierhofer, *Der faktische Konzern nach geplantem europäischem Recht* (München 1996).
[6] *ZR* (1999) Nr. 52 Sachverhalt A.
[7] Sachverhalt B (oben N. 6).
[8] Sachverhalt C (oben N. 6).
[9] Sachverhalt A (oben N. 6).
[10] Sachverhalt B (oben N. 6).
[11] Sachverhalt C (oben N. 6).

den Schluss nahe legen, die Off-shore Strategie zulasten der Minderheit und der Gläubiger stamme von einem aktienrechtlichen Ausreisser, d.h., einem Raider. Die Wirkungsweise des Raiders[12] wurde im Wirtschaftsalltag durch Übernahmen der Kontrollmacht über Aktiengesellschaften gegen deren Willen, sog. „Unfriendly Takeover" bekannt. Darüber hinaus ist die Wirkungsweise des Raiders geprägt von einer detailliert geplanten, typischen Finanzierungsstrategie, die zur systematischen Aushöhlung gesunder Unternehmen und zur Plünderung derer Liquiditätsreserven führt und damit sämtliche Tätigkeiten des Raiders beherrscht. Der Machtmissbrauch in der Rechtsform des internationalen Konzerns, dies muss nicht weiter betont werden, kann dabei seltsame Gewächse hervorbringen, deren eigenartiges Wuchern kaum mehr zu kontrollieren ist. Zusammengefasst stellen sich daher die Rechtsfragen, welche Normen das materielle, nationale Konzernrecht als Minimalstandard für die Aktionärsminderheit und die Gläubiger[13] enthalten muss (nachfolgend Ziff. 2), welcher Kodex das Verhalten von Verwaltungsräten in Ober- und Unter-Gesellschaften regelt (nachfolgend Ziff. 3), und welche Kautelen das Konzernkollisionsrecht zur Verfügung stellt (nachfolgend Ziff. 4). Abschliessend ist auf einige Aspekte einer künftigen Entwicklung des Konzernrechts[14] einzugehen (nachfolgend Ziff. 5).

2.   GRENZENLOSE KONZERNMACHT ALS FIKTION UND REALITÄT

2.1   Nationale Konstruktion des Konzerns

In Bezug auf das Phänomen privater wirtschaftlicher Macht[15] verlangt die Erfüllung der Aufgaben des Rechts als staatliches Ordnungsprinzip immer wieder nach einer materiellen, wertenden Stellungnahme. Wesentliche Voraussetzungen für die Erfassung von Natur und Tragweite der Aufgabe, private wirtschaftliche Macht zu beschränken, ist es, die mögliche Machtrelevanz von Rechtsnormen aufzudecken.

---

[12] Vgl. dazu ZR (1999) Nr. 52 Urteil B, Erw. 1.2.2, unter Hinweis auf Schluep, „Lauterkeitsrechtliche Aspekte des <Unfriendly Takeover>" in: SAG (Schweizerische Aktiengesellschaft) (3/1988) 89, m.w.H.

[13] Gläubiger von Unter-Gesellschaften internationaler Konzerne sind nicht nur Banken und Anleger, sondern auch Arbeitnehmer dieser Gesellschaften.

[14] Lutter, „Die Harmonisierung des Rechts der Kapitalgesellschaften in Europa", in: Nobel (Hrsg.), Internationales Gesellschaftsrecht (Bern, Stämpfli 1998) 129ff., insb. 150; Thiele, Konzerntatbestand und Vertragskonzern – Faktizitäts- und Vertragsprinzip als gemeinsame Grundlagen einer europäischen Konzernrechtsangleichung (Hamburg, Mauke 1995). Zum schweizerischen Konzernrecht vgl. insb. von Büren, Der Konzern. Rechtliche Aspekte eines wirtschaftlichen Phänomens, SPR VIII/6 (Basel, Helbing & Lichtenhahn 1997).

[15] Vgl. zum folgenden ZR (1999) Nr. 52 Urteil B.1, Erw. 1.1.1ff., insb. unter Hinweis auf Homburger, Recht und private Wirtschaftsmacht (Zürich, Schulthess 1993) 62ff.

Gerade im Bereich der Rechtsform der Aktiengesellschaft als potentieller Macht-träger und hier umso mehr bei Formen von *Unternehmensbeteiligungen und -zu-sammenschlüssen*[16] im Rahmen des Konzerns führt die Ausübung der Privatautono-mie in Richtung auf die Bildung oder die Verstärkung privater wirtschaftlicher Macht. Dadurch, dass der Gesetzgeber die Rechtsform der Aktiengesellschaft unter sehr leicht zu erfüllenden Bedingungen jedermann zur Verfügung stellt sowie da-durch, dass auch die konzernierte Aktiengesellschaft weitestgehend zugelassen ist, wird der Zugang zum Aufbau wirtschaftlicher Machtstellungen unter Verwendung dieser Rechtsform weit und scheinbar grenzenlos geöffnet.

a) Der *schweizerische Gesetzgeber* hat es bisher unterlassen, das Konzern-recht[17] zu kodifizieren. Festzuhalten ist immerhin, dass der Konzern als solcher nicht rechtsfähig ist. Das geltende schweizerische Aktienrecht geht von der Fiktion unabhängiger und nur im eigenen Interesse geführter Gesellschaften aus. Das mass-gebende Abgrenzungskriterium zwischen einer von der Mutter-AG beherrschten Tochter-AG und einer blossen Zweigniederlassung liegt denn auch de lege lata in der *Aufrechterhaltung der rechtlichen Selbständigkeit der Tochtergesellschaft.*[18] Zwar hat der Gesetzgeber[19] mit dem neuen Aktienrecht erstmals die wirtschaftliche Realität des Konzerns ausdrücklich anerkannt. Verschiedene Problemkreise sind indessen ungelöst geblieben und noch immer fehlen über weite Strecken aktien-rechtliche Normen, die dem atypischen Charakter konzernierter Aktiengesellschaf-ten gerecht werden. Das Bestehen von Gesetzeslücken[20] ist heute unbestritten. Rechtsgrundlage für Entscheide im schweizerischen Konzernrecht ist daher Artikel 1 Abs. 2 ZGB, wonach dem Richter bei Fehlen einer gesetzlichen oder gewohn-heitsrechtlichen Bestimmung die Pflicht zukommt, nach der Regel zu entscheiden, die er als Gesetzgeber aufstellen würde. Er hat dabei eine (generell-abstrakte) Regel zu finden, nicht nur einen (individuell-konkreten) Einzelfall zu entscheiden.

Als Konzerne[21] werden Gruppen rechtlich selbständig bleibender, jedoch unter einheitlicher Führung und Geschäftspolitik, „einheitlichem Willen" unterworfener Gesellschaften verstanden. Solche Konzerne werden unter Einsatz verschiedenster

---

[16] Vgl. dazu grundlegend für das schweizerische Recht: Schluep, „Privatrechtliche Probleme der Unternehmenskonzentration und -kooperation", *ZSR* (Zeitschrift für Schweizerisches Recht) (1973 II) 155ff.

[17] Zum folgenden *ZR* (1999) Nr. 52 Urteil B.1, Erw. 1.4.2 unter Hinweis auf Handschin, *Der Kon-zern im geltenden schweizerischen Privatrecht* (Zürich, Schulthess 1994) 22.

[18] BGE 115 Ib 61.

[19] Art. 663e Abs. 1 OR (Obligationenrecht; SR 220).

[20] Vgl. Kritik von Büren, in von Büren/ Hausheer/ Wiegand (Hrsg.), *Grundfragen des neuen Ak-tienrechts* (Bern, Stämpfli 1993) 66; Amstutz, *Konzernorganisationsrecht* (Bern, Stämpfli 1993) 207ff., 211f.; Meier-Hayoz/ Forstmoser, *Grundriss des schweizerischen Gesellschaftsrechts*, 7. Aufl. (Bern, Stämpfli 1993) 445 sowie die Vorschläge gemäss Schlussbericht vom 24. September 1993 der „Groupe de réflexion Gesellschaftsrecht" des EJPD.

[21] *ZR* (1999) Nr. 52 Urteil B.1, Erw. 1.4.1.

Mittel gebildet, so namentlich durch Personalunion in den Führungsspitzen der verschiedenen Gesellschaften. In den der vorliegenden Fall-Studie zugrunde liegenden Sachverhalten konnte der Gemeinschuldner WKR den O-Konzern als *faktischen Konzern*[22] infolge Kapitalmehrheit bilden. Gemäss herrschender Lehre[23] kommt der *Interessenwahrungspflicht*[24] der Einzelgesellschaften im Konzern entscheidende Bedeutung zu: Die Verbindung von Aktiengesellschaften in einem Konzern befreit die Verwaltung nicht von ihrer Pflicht, die Interessen der Tochtergesellschaft auch im Verhältnis zur Mutter-Gesellschaft wahrzunehmen. Die Tochter-Gesellschaft wiederum hat die Geschäfte grundsätzlich im eigenen Interesse und nicht in dem der Unternehmensgruppe zu leiten. In der wirtschaftlichen Faktizität verstärkt sich indessen die Interessensverschmelzung von Mutter- und Tochter-Gesellschaft mit dem Mass der betrieblichen Einordnung der Tochter in den Konzern. Jede Form von Dauerverbindung bringt, wachsend mit deren Intensität, den Gesichtspunkt ins Spiel, dass die Interessenwürdigung sich nicht auf den einzelnen Akt oder die einzelne Angelegenheit beschränken darf, sondern dass die Vorteile aus der Dauerbeziehung als solcher zu berücksichtigen sind. Deshalb kann der einzelne Vorgang für eine Tochter nachteilig sein, lässt sich aber als strategisches Kalkül innerhalb des ganzen Verhältnisses begründen, weil Kompensation erwartet werden kann oder einfach, weil sich das Wohl des übrigen Konzerns wegen der bestehenden Verflechtungen reflexiv auch als Nutzen der Einzelgesellschaft auswirkt. Auch bei vollständiger Beherrschung und Einsetzung der Tochter-Gesellschaft im Dienst des Konzerns kann jedoch nach herrschender Lehre[25] in der Regel beansprucht werden, dass die *Interessen der Tochter gewahrt* werden.

b)   Anders als im schweizerischen Konzernrecht muss sich der Richter im *deutschen Konzernrecht* nicht auf „Ratio"[26] und „Dogma"[27] stützen, da die analoge Aufgabe im deutschen Aktienrecht durch den Gesetzgeber[28] positiv geregelt[29] worden ist. Es handelt sich v.a. um Wertentscheide zur Beurteilung des Verhaltens von Personen im Spannungsfeld zwischen Recht und möglicher Machtausübung im ak-

---

[22] Oben N. 21 unter Hinweis auf Guhl/ Kummer/ Druey, *Das schweizerische Obligationenrecht*, 8. Aufl. (Zürich, Schulthess Verlag 1991) 622f.; Baudenbacher, Vorbem. zu Art. 620 OR N 19, in Honsell/ Vogt/ Watter (Hrsg.), *Kommentar zum Schweizerischen Privatrecht*, 1. Aufl. (Basel, Helbing & Lichtenhahn 1994). Vgl. neuerdings: von Büren (oben N. 14) 28 N 136ff.; Druey/ Vogel, *Das schweizerische Konzernrecht in der Praxis der Gerichte* (Zürich, Schulthess 1999) 5, 29 und 31; Nobel, *Aktienrechtliche Entscheide* (Bern, Stämpfli 1991) 38ff.
[23] Art. 1 Abs. 3 ZGB.
[24] Vgl. zum folgenden *ZR* (1999) Nr. 52 Urteil B.1, Erw. 1.4.3.
[25] Oben N. 24 unter Hinweis auf Druey, „Aufgaben eines Konzernrechts", *ZSR* (1980 II) 305; Meier-Hayoz/ Forstmoser (oben N. 20) 441; ferner Handschin (oben N. 17) 108. Vgl. neuerdings: von Büren, (oben N. 14) 128 N 272ff.
[26] Art. 1 Abs. 2 ZGB.
[27] Art. 1 Abs. 3 ZGB.
[28] Art. 1 Abs. 1 ZGB.
[29] Vgl. dazu *ZR* (1999) Nr. 52 Urteil C.1, Erw. 3.ff.

tienrechtlichen Konzern. Dabei ist daran zu erinnern, dass Machtausübung einerseits durch das Recht begründet (Gebrauch des Rechts), anderseits durch das Recht begrenzt wird (Missbrauch des Rechts). Mit Bezug auf die *Machtausübung durch einen herrschenden Unternehmer* hat daher das deutsche Aktienrecht ausgleichende Regeln[30] geschaffen.

2.2 Globale Konstruktion des Konzerns

Die Aktiengesellschaft als juristische Person ist an und für sich vorerst eine Konstruktion der Rechtswissenschaft und hernach eine Fiktion des nationalen Gesetzgebers, woran Fögen[31] in einer rechtshistorischen Abhandlung erinnert hat. Eine *Fiktion der Fiktion* erscheint daher umso mehr der Konzern als Hyper-Konstruktion juristischer Personen und, in potenzierter Form, der transnational konstruierte globale Konzern; es wäre wohl naiv, wenn die Rechtswissenschaft dieses Faktum nicht im Bewusstsein bewahren würde.

Anderseits zeigt ein philosophischer Exkurs[32], dass *Fiktion Realität* werden kann. Dieser paradoxe Vorgang ist dann möglich, wenn fiktive Vorstellungen auf allgemeiner Akzeptanz beruhen. Man spricht dann von einer gemeinsamen Konstruktion der Wirklichkeit, ein Befund, der für alle Formen menschlicher Gemeinschaft, mithin auch für die staatliche Rechtsordnung, festgehalten werden kann. Das vom nationalen Gesetzgeber geschaffene Recht gilt nicht nur kraft Staatsgewalt, sondern in erster Linie aufgrund der Akzeptanz der Bürger. Insbesondere die Akzeptanz der juristischen Person als Konstruktion und Fiktion des Gesetzgebers[33]

---

[30] Oben N. 29 unter Hinweis auf § 311 AktG in Verbindung mit § 317 AktG mit Literaturauswahl, Emmerich/ Sonnenschein, *Konzernrecht*, 5. Aufl. (München, Beck 1993); Lutter/ Krieger, *Rechte und Pflichten des Aufsichtsrates*, 3. Aufl. (Freiburg im Br., 1993); Flume, *Juristische Person* (Berlin, Springer 1993) § 4 IV; Gessler/ Hefermehler/ Kropff, *Aktiengesetz*; v. Godin/ Wilhelmi, *Kommentar zum Aktiengesetz*, 4. Aufl. (Berlin, de Gruyter 1971); Grossfelder, *Internationales Unternehmesrecht* (Heidelberg, Müller 1986); Handschin (oben N. 17) 10f. (deutsches Recht); Henn, *Handbuch des Aktienrechts* (Heidelberg, Müller 1978); Hüffer, *Aktiengesetz*, Kommentar, 2. Aufl. (München, Beck 1995); Raiser, *Recht der Kapitalgesellschaft*, 2. Aufl. (München, Franz Vahlen 1992); Würdinger, *Aktienrecht und das Recht der verbundenen Unternehmen*, 4. Aufl. (Karlsruhe, Müller 1981). Zur neueren Entwicklung im europäischen Konzernrecht, vgl. Thiele (oben N. 14) sowie Hopt, „Europäisches Konzernrecht?", *EuZW (Europäische Zeitschrift für Wirtschaftsrecht)* (1999) 577.

[31] Fögen, „<Mehr Sein als Schein>? Anmerkungen zur juristischen Person in Theorie und Praxis", *SJZ (Schweizerische Juristen-Zeitung)* (1999) 393ff.; vgl. auch Rausch, „Wieviel Fiktion ist genug?", *FS Meier-Hayoz* (Zürich, Schulthess 1972) 35ff.

[32] Brunner, „Erkenntnistheoretische Grundlagen der Kritik im Bereich des Rechts", in: Schuhmacher (Hrsg.), *Geschlossene Gesellschaft* (Zürich, Rio 1993) 187ff., insb. 205 unter Hinweis auf die Theorie des Konstruktivismus: Luckmann, von Foerster, Watzlawick, u.a.

[33] Die Gesetzesfiktion der rechtlichen Selbständigkeit juristischer Personen ist daher grundsätzlich zu beachten. Der Rückgriff auf die Realität („Durchgriff") ist nur unter dem Vorbehalt des Rechtsmissbrauchs zulässig, vgl. Forstmoser/ Untersander, „Entwicklungen im Gesellschaftsrecht", *SJZ* (1999) 470ff, insb. 474, Ziff. II.

steht und fällt demnach mit dem Vertrauen der Bürger in die Rationalität und Legitimität dieses Rechtsinstitutes, womit auch dessen Entfaltung und Grenzen bestimmt werden.

Bei der globalen Konstruktion von Konzernen in den Formen des Rechts entwickelt sich damit ein Wechselspiel von Fiktion und Realität, das in mehrfacher Hinsicht zu *Illusionen* verleitet. *Einerseits* wird die Konzernmacht als „grenzenlos" im doppelten Sinn beklagt von Bürgern und Regierungen der einzelnen Nationalstaaten, weil sie den Geltungsgrund der Institutionen des Gesellschaftsrechts im staatlich gesetzten Recht und dessen Gestaltbarkeit scheinbar vergessen. *Anderseits* können Konzernleitungen übersehen, dass Unternehmensformen durch eben dieses staatliche Recht geschaffen werden und dass der Ursprung der Konzernmacht in den aktienrechtlichen Formen zu finden ist. *Konzernmacht ist daher auch in transnational konstruierten Konzernen nicht grenzenlos.* Errichtung und Existenz verdankt der Konzern dem Recht des Nationalstaates, der durch Gesetz und völkerrechtliche Abkommen Schranken setzen kann. Sodann stehen die einzelnen Rechtsgeschäfte der Konzernleitungen unter der Bedingung funktionsfähiger Rechtsordnungen der einzelnen Nationalstaaten, d.h., dem rule of law – Prinzip, nicht zuletzt hinsichtlich Aufsicht, Rechtsanwendung und Vollstreckung.

Der transnational strukturierte und operierende Konzern ist deshalb besonders verletzlich, weil er ohne das Vertrauen in die Rechtsförmlichkeit seiner Teile nicht denkbar ist, was für das Innen – und für das Aussenverhältnis zutrifft. Die Fragen des Aussenverhältnisses[34] müssen hier ausgeklammert bleiben. Den Fragen des *Innenverhältnisses* geht die vorliegende Fallstudie nach. Hier kann das berechtigte Vertrauen der Verwaltungsräte von Konzern-Gesellschaften in die Korrektheit und Rechtsförmlichkeit der anderen Teile in ein trojanisches Pferd *umfunktioniert* werden, wenn der internationale Konzern von einem Raider beherrscht wird. Die Tore stehen dann, um bei den Bildern des Dramas zu bleiben, weit offen, was die Stellung der Verteidiger umso hoffnungsloser macht, wenn die Vermögenswerte werthaltiger Konzern-Gesellschaften auf diesem Wege „off the shore" gelangen. So hat der Gemeinschuldner der vorliegenden Fallstudie[35] versucht, die Mehrheitsbeteiligung des Konzerns im Rahmen einer Off-Shore-Strategie in den WKR Trust nach Guernsey-Law zu übertragen und damit scheinbar unsichtbar zu werden. Dies ist ein Verhalten, das zumindest nicht typischerweise mit jenem eines traditionellen (auch transnational operierenden) Konzernführers übereinstimmt und die Frage aufwirft, ob durch die Fiktion auf die Realität zurückgegriffen werden kann und muss. Die entsprechenden Probleme im Innenverhältnis sind dabei eng mit der

---

[34] Vgl. dazu Brechbühl, *Haftung aus erwecktem Konzernvertrauen* (Bern, Stämpfli 1998); Kuzmic, *Haftung aus Konzernvertrauen* (Zürich, Schulthess 1998); Fleischer, „Konzernrechtliche Vertrauenshaftung", *ZHR (Zeitschrift für das gesamte Handels- und Wirtschaftsrecht)* (1999) 461ff.

[35] *ZR* (1999) Nr. 52 Urteil A und Urteil C.1, Erw. 3.2.2.

Rechtstellung der Verwaltungsräte in den Ober- und Unter-Gesellschaften des Konzerns verknüpft.

3.   VERWALTUNGSRÄTE IN TRANSNATIONALEN KONZERNEN

3.1   Perspektiven in Ober-Gesellschaften

a)   Um das Verhältnis zwischen Ober- und Unter-Gesellschaften im Konzern[36] näher auszuleuchten, sind für das schweizerische Recht folgende idealtypische Pflichten festzuhalten: Das geschäftsführende Organ der *beherrschenden Aktiengesellschaft* hat bei der Wahrnehmung seiner Konzernmacht einer eigentlichen *Konzernleitungspflicht*[37] zu genügen. Als Richtlinien für die Beurteilung haben im schweizerischen Recht die – auf das Leitbild eines autonomen Unternehmens zugeschnittenen – Artikel 716a OR und Artikel 717 Abs. 1 OR zu gelten, die dem Verwaltungsrat die Oberleitung der Gesellschaft anvertrauen und ihn dazu anhalten, diese Aufgabe mit aller Sorgfalt und unter Wahrung der Gesellschaftsinteressen in guten Treuen zu erfüllen. Umgekehrt lässt sich die *Abhängigkeit der beherrschten Aktiengesellschaft im Konzernverbund* über verschiedene Mittel begründen.[38] Der Gemeinschuldner der vorliegenden Fallstudie begründete die *Abhängigkeit durch Stimmenmacht*. In den Händen des unternehmerischen Aktionärs ist dies eine Konzernmacht, welche die Beherrschung der Generalversammlung, des obersten Organs der Aktiengesellschaft (Art. 698 Abs. 1 OR), erlaubt. Dadurch wiederum vermittelt sie die Befugnis, einerseits die anderen Organe zu bestellen und anderseits einen entscheidenden Einfluss auf den Statuteninhalt auszuüben (Art. 698 Abs. 2 OR). Insbesondere das Organbestimmungsrecht ermöglicht dem herrschenden Unternehmen, die Geschäftspolitik der abhängigen Gesellschaft faktisch zu kontrollieren: „Der Wink mit der Abberufung dürfte bei den Mitgliedern der Verwaltung zumeist seine Wirkung nicht verfehlen und sie dazu veranlassen, die Geschäfte nach den Anweisungen des Hauptaktionärs zu führen".[39] Damit wird das Recht auf Organbestellung de facto ermöglicht, was wiederum im Grundsatz mit dem Prinzip der eigenverantwortlichen Geschäftsführung der Verwaltung (Art. 717 Abs. 1 OR)

---

[36] Vgl. zum folgenden *ZR* (1999) Nr. 52 Urteil B.1, Erw. 1.4.4. Vgl. nunmehr auch Vogel, *Die Haftung der Muttergesellschaft als materielles faktisches oder kundgegebenes Organ der Tochtergesellschaft*, Diss. St. Gallen (Bern, Paul Haupt 1997); Zweifel, „Die Haftungsverhältnisse im faktischen Konzern infolge Schädigung der abhängigen Gesellschaft durch die herrschende Gesellschaft", *FS Meier-Hayoz* (oben N. 31) 126ff.

[37] Oben N. 36 unter Hinweis auf Amstutz (oben N. 20) 363, 376, 380; vgl. nunmehr überdies: Druey/ Vogel (oben N. 22) 33; von Büren (oben N. 14) 54ff.

[38] Oben N. 36 unter Hinweis auf Amstutz (oben N. 20) 390ff.

[39] Oben N. 36 unter Hinweis auf A. von Planta, *Die Haftung des Hauptaktionärs* (Basel, Helbing & Lichtenhahn 1980) 10.

nicht vereinbar ist. Die Erreichung des Gesellschaftszweckes liegt im Gesellschaftsinteresse und ist zugleich oberste Aufgabe der gesellschaftlichen Organe
(Art. 717 Abs. 1 OR). Stellt nun der statutarische Zweck die Gesellschaft in den
Dienst eines Konzerns, so muss die Verwaltung mit allen ihren zur Verfügung stehenden Mitteln dieses Ziel verfolgen.

Selbst in dieser extremen Ausprägung ist jedoch ihre *Eigenverantwortlichkeit
(Art. 717 Abs. 1 i.V.m. Art. 754 OR) keinesfalls aufgehoben. Das bedeutet, dass sie
weiterhin den regulären Pflichten des Aktienrechts untersteht, dass folglich ihre
formal-juristische Stellung unverändert bleibt.* Die Tochterverwaltung hat in eigener Regie zu entscheiden, wie sie am besten dem Konzern dienlich sein soll. Die ab-
hängige Tochter ist also nicht zur Dienstleistung an die Mutter, sondern zu aktiver
Mithilfe bei der Realisierung des Konzerns verpflichtet. Mutter- und Tochterverwaltung planen und realisieren zusammen – beide aber jeweils in weitgehender
Eigenverantwortlichkeit – die Durchführung des Konzerns.[40] Konzernmacht ist
demnach nicht grenzenlos. Konzernmässige Beeinflussung ist nur insoweit legitim,
wie die damit einhergehenden Benachteiligungen ausgeglichen werden. Nimmt die
Konzernmacht ein Ausmass an, das dem Funktionieren des Systems abträglich ist,
so können die ihretwegen der Tochter-Gesellschaft zugefügten Nachteile unmöglich wettgemacht werden. Die *Grenze der legitimen Konzerngewalt* liegt m.a.W.
da, wo die Tochter-Gesellschaft den Status eines selbständigen Unternehmensträ-
gers verliert, der imstande ist, sein Schicksal aus eigener Kraft zu bewältigen.[41] Verwaltungsräte in Ober-Gesellschaften des Konzerns dürfen diese Grenze demnach
nicht überschreiten.

b)   Auch mit Bezug auf diese Rechtsfrage bestehen im *deutschen Recht*
nicht nur Vernunftgründe, sondern positive Aktienrechtsnormen.[42] Nach deutschem Recht ist auch eine natürliche Person (wie vorliegend der Gemeinschuldner)
durchaus qualifiziert, als sog. *herrschender Unternehmer*[43] aufzutreten. Die Qualifikation einer Person als herrschendes Unternehmen gilt auch dann, wenn der faktische Einfluss als Mehrheitsaktionär auf die Unternehmensleitung des beherrschten
Unternehmens gegeben ist und wenn versucht wird, diesen Einfluss in ein Treu-
handverhältnis zu kleiden[44]. Gemäss dem *Wertentscheid des deutschen Gesetzgebers*[45] ist ein herrschender Unternehmer verpflichtet, die aufgrund seiner
Machtstellung erworbenen Vorteile zurückzuerstatten, wenn das beherrschte Un-

---

[40] Oben N. 36 unter Hinweis auf Amstutz (oben N. 20) 402ff.

[41] Oben N. 36 unter Hinweis auf Amstutz (oben N. 20) 442; F. von Planta, *Der Interessenkonflikt
des Verwaltungsrates der abhängigen Konzerngesellschaft* (Zürich, Schulthess 1988) 153ff.

[42] Vgl. insb. § 117, 311 und 317 sowie § 291 deutsches AktG.

[43] *ZR* (1999) Nr. 52 Urteil C.1, Erw. 3.3.1.a. unter Hinweis auf Schneider, „Die Personengesellschaft als herrschendes Unternehmen im Konzern", *ZHR* (1979) 485-521.

[44] Oben N. 43 unter Hinweis auf Hüffer (oben N. 30) § 15 RN 9 a.E.

[45] *ZR* (1999) Nr. 52 Urteil C.1, Erw. 3.3.1.b.

ternehmen durch ein unvorteilhaftes Geschäft im Rahmen seines Konzerns zu Schaden[46] gekommen ist.

Bei einem Gebilde wie dem globalen O-Konzern der vorliegenden Fallstudie[47] finden sich diese Leitgedanken zum Verhältnis von Mutter- zu Tochter-Gesellschaft innerhalb der Konzernstruktur äusserst unzureichend verwirklicht: Aufgrund der tatsächlich vorherrschenden Machtstrukturen stand einzig die Person des Gemeinschuldners im Zentrum. Zwar wurde eine gesellschaftsrechtliche Konzernstruktur durchaus aufgebaut und benutzt, vom Raider aber als Werkzeug für seine persönlichen Zwecke missbraucht. Er hat die juristische Selbständigkeit der einzelnen Unternehmungseinheiten nie genügend beachtet. Das Cash-Management führte dabei in zwei Richtungen: Einerseits in die oberste Konzern-Gesellschaft und von dort in den Off-shore Trust des Gemeinschuldners, anderseits an die vom Konzernleiter beherrschten Unter-Gesellschaften in verschiedenen Off-shore Gebieten. Welche Sicherheiten bestanden dabei für die beherrschten Gesellschaften und damit für die Gläubiger?

3.2 Perspektiven in Unter-Gesellschaften

a)   Im dramatischen Interessenkonflikt[48] abhängiger Verwaltungsräte, die als Organe der abhängigen Gesellschaft einerseits deren Interessen zu vertreten, gleichzeitig aber die Konzerninteressen wahrzunehmen haben, bietet das geltende *schweizerische Konzernrecht*[49] wiederum keine Handhabe. Der h.L.[50] gemäss dürfen bzw. müssen im Rahmen des Ermessens etwa Weisungen der Ober-Gesellschaft befolgt werden, nicht aber dann, wenn die eigene Gesellschaft dadurch geschädigt würde. Insgesamt wird dieses zentrale, dem Konzern inhärente Problem *vom Gesetzgeber* aber einfach *offen gelassen*. Es wird insbesondere versäumt, die Stellung des Machtbetroffenen durch gesetztes Recht zu stärken. Eine fallweise Lösung des Problems hat demnach durch den Richter in pflichtgemässer Lückenfüllung[51] zu erfolgen. Trotz der unbestrittenen Abhängigkeit unterer Konzern-Gesell-

---

[46]   Oben N. 45 unter Hinweis auf: Luchterhandt, „Leitungsmacht und Verantwortlichkeit im faktischen Konzern", ZHR (1969) 1-60; Emmerich/ Sonnenschein (oben N. 30) 420.

[47]   ZR (1999) Nr. 52 Urteil B.1, Erw. 1.4.5.

[48]   F. von Planta (oben N. 41); Schluep, „Über privatrechtliche Freiheit und Verantwortung des kartellähnlichen Konzerns", FS Meier-Hayoz (oben N. 31) 345ff, insb. 357ff.

[49]   ZR (1999) Nr. 52 Urteil B.1, Erw. 1.4.6. f.

[50]   Oben N. 49 unter Hinweis auf: Meier-Hayoz/ Forstmoser (oben N. 20) 441; Tappolet, *Schranken konzernmässiger Abhängigkeit im schweizerischen Aktienrecht* (Zürich, Schulthess 1973) 76ff.; vgl. nunmehr auch: von Büren (oben N. 14) 125ff. sowie: Zürcher, *Der Gläubigerschutz im schweizerischen Aktienrechtskonzern*, Diss. Zürich (Bern, Stämpfli Verlag 1993) 153ff.; Druey, (oben N. 25) 366ff.

[51]   Oben N. 49 unter Hinweis auf die Kritik bei: von Büren, in von Büren/ Hausheer/ Wiegand (oben N. 20) 59; Homburger (oben N. 15) 67; F. von Planta (oben N. 41) 156.

schaften ist jedoch in einem Wertentscheid nach Artikel 1 Abs. 2 ZGB festzuhalten, dass es objektiv betrachtet in bestimmten Fällen ein *Widerstandsrecht bzw. eine Widerstandspflicht* des „Belehnten" gegenüber dem „Lehensherr", d.h., der Tochter-Gesellschaft gegenüber dem Mutterhaus, der Einzelgesellschaft gegenüber der Konzernleitung gibt. Mindestens insoweit behält als Kriterium und Mass das formelle Gesellschaftsrecht[52] für die Beurteilung der Handlungen der Einzelgesellschaften seine Gültigkeit. In dieser Antinomie zwischen wirtschafts- und machtpolitischer Fremdbestimmung und grundsätzlicher rechtlicher Selbständigkeit der abhängigen Gesellschaft bleibt es jedoch der *Abklärung im Einzelfall* überlassen, ob die eigene Interessenwahrnehmung und damit die Wahrnehmung eines Widerstandsrechts gegen die Ober-Gesellschaft den Organen der Unter-Gesellschaft möglich war. Folgende Entscheid-Kriterien sind dabei massgebend: Ein Verstoss gegen das Gesellschaftsinteresse kann die aktienrechtliche Verantwortlichkeit der handelnden Organe zur Folge haben, da ein Konzernorgan zwar Weisungen entgegenzunehmen, diese jedoch nicht in jedem Fall[53] auszuführen hat. So stellt eine *sachlich unmotivierte Überweisung*, welche ein Verwaltungsrat ausschliesslich auf Weisung der Konzernleitung im Rahmen einer konsolidierten Geschäftsführung tätigt, eine Sorgfaltspflichtverletzung[54] dar. Sodann ist als absolute *Grenze aller gesellschaftlichen Tätigkeit* stets zu beachten, dass Rechtsgeschäfte nichtig sind, sofern sie gegen den *Gesellschaftszweck*[55] verstossen. Bei Aktiengesellschaften besteht der Endzweck in aller Regel im Erzielen von Gewinn.[56] Damit folglich eine Handlung vom Endzweck gedeckt ist, müssen der Gesellschaft unmittelbar oder mittelbar wirtschaftliche Vorteile daraus erwachsen. Im konkreten Fall erfordert die Frage, ob ein Verstoss gegen den Gesellschaftszweck vorliegt, einen Ermessensentscheid. Ausserhalb des Ermessensspielraums liegen Rechtsgeschäfte jedoch stets, wenn sie mit vernünftigen Überlegungen nicht mehr vereinbar sind und zu einem Schaden[57] des Unternehmens führen. Einen Verstoss gegen den Endzweck einer Gesellschaft bilden etwa *unentgeltliche Vermögenszuwendungen*, auch *Liberalitäten* genannt, sowie die faktische Liquidation der Gesellschaft durch freiwillige Veräusserung des Gesellschaftsvermögens.[58] Von Liberalitäten wird ge-

---

[52] Vgl. ebenso nunmehr auch: von Büren (oben N. 14) 125ff.; Druey/ Vogel (oben N. 22) 376ff.

[53] ZR (1999) Nr. 52 Urteil B.1, Erw. 4.2 unter Hinweis auf: Graf, *Verträge zwischen Konzerngesellschaften* (Bern, Stämpfli 1988) 49ff.

[54] Oben N. 53 unter Hinweis auf BGE 108 Ib 37; 110 Ib 132 f. = Pra 1984, 707ff. und OR-Baudenbacher (oben N. 22) zu Art. 620 N 24.

[55] ZR (1999) Nr. 52 Urteil B.1, Erw. 4.2.2.

[56] Oben N. 55 unter Hinweis auf: Forstmoser, *Schweizerisches Aktienrecht*, Bd. I (Zürich, Schulthess 1981) 10 und 63f.; mit Einschränkungen auch gültig für Einzelgesellschaften innerhalb des Konzerns: Graf (oben. N 53) 153f.

[57] Oben N. 55 unter Hinweis auf Schreiber, *Die Zweckbindung bei der Aktiengesellschaft* (Zürich, Iuris 1974) 11.

[58] Oben N. 55 unter Hinweis auf ZK-Bürgi, Art. 698-738 OR; Art. 718 OR N 5; Graf (oben N. 53) 67; Schreiber (oben N. 57) 12.

sprochen, wenn eine Gesellschaft durch die Vornahme von Rechtshandlungen bewusst und ohne wirtschaftliche Notwendigkeit längerfristig auf Gewinn verzichtet oder eine geldwerte Leistung erbringt, die ihr Reinvermögen vermindert, ohne dass der Mittelabgang aus ihrer Sicht geschäftsmässig begründet wäre. Gegen solche unentgeltliche Vermögenszuwendungen haben Verwaltungsräte von Unter-Gesellschaften, insbesondere im Hinblick auf den Gläubigerschutz, Widerstand anzumelden; dieser Wertentscheid gilt umso mehr, wenn der Mittelabfluss in Off-shore Gebiete erfolgt, die bekanntlich erhebliche Probleme im internationalen Vollstreckungsrecht bereiten.

b) Analoge Wertentscheide hat der *deutsche Gesetzgeber* getroffen. Auch bei Geltung der grundsätzlichen Haftung des herrschenden Unternehmers gegenüber dem beherrschten Unternehmen stellt sich die Frage, ob dies auch für solche Entscheide von Organen der Unter-Gesellschaften gelten kann, die in *Missachtung der elementarsten Sorgfaltspflichten einer Unternehmensleitung*[59] erfolgt sind. Stellt der statutarische Zweck die Gesellschaft ausdrücklich in den Dienst eines Konzerns, so muss die Verwaltung zwar mit allen ihr zur Verfügung stehenden Mitteln dieses Ziel verfolgen. Selbst in dieser extremen Ausprägung ist jedoch die *Eigenverantwortlichkeit* der Organe des beherrschten Unternehmens keinesfalls aufgehoben. Dies gilt umso mehr im faktischen Konzern ohne formale Beherrschungsverträge.[60] Das bedeutet, dass der Vorstand der faktisch beherrschten Gesellschaft im Interesse der Minderheitsaktionäre und der Gläubiger weiterhin den regulären Pflichten des Aktienrechts untersteht, dass folglich ihre formal-juristische Stellung unverändert bleibt.

Im bereits erwähnten, schwerwiegenden *Interessenkonflikt abhängiger Verwaltungsräte*, die als Organe der abhängigen Gesellschaft einerseits deren Interessen zu vertreten, gleichzeitig aber den Ansinnen der Konzernführung Rechnung zu tragen haben, bietet das geltende deutsche Aktienrecht eine klare Handhabe. Auch wenn jedoch die grundsätzliche Abhängigkeit von Personen in Organstellungen in Tochter-Gesellschaften des Konzerns feststeht, ist festzuhalten, dass es auch im deutschen Recht ein *Widerstandsrecht bzw. eine Widerstandspflicht*[61] der Tochter-Gesellschaft gegenüber dem Mutterhaus, der Einzelgesellschaft gegenüber der Konzernleitung gibt. Insoweit behält das formelle Gesellschaftsrecht für die Beurteilung der Handlungen der Einzelgesellschaften und ihrer Organe auch im deutschen Konzernrecht seine Gültigkeit.

---

[59] ZR (1999) Nr. 52 Urteil C.1, Erw. 3.3.2.
[60] Oben N. 59 unter Hinweis auf § 291 AktG und Hüffer (oben N. 30) § 76 RN 19.
[61] Oben N. 59 unter Hinweis auf Luchterhandt, „Leitungsmacht und Verantwortlichkeit im faktischen Konzern", *ZHR* (1969) 1-60; insb. 51: „*Pflicht zum Widerstand*"; vgl. dazu, selbst bei Vorliegen eines Beherrschungsvertrags, Ballerstedt, „Schranken der Weisungsbefugnis aufgrund eines Beherrschungsvertrags", *ZHR* (1973) 388ff.; Clemm, „Die Grenzen der Weisungsbefolgungspflicht des Vorstands der beherrschten AG bei bestehendem Beherrschungsvertrag", *ZHR* (1977) 197-208.

4.   KONZERNKOLLISIONSRECHT

4.1   **Internationales Zivilprozessrecht**

Der Inhalt des anzuwendenden ausländischen Rechts ist *von Amtes wegen* festzustellen, was sich im schweizerischen Kollisionsrecht aus Artikel 16 des Bundesgesetzes über das Internationale Privatrecht (IPRG; SR 291) ergibt.[62] Diese Norm hält zwar fest, dass bei vermögensrechtlichen Ansprüchen der Nachweis den Parteien überbunden werden kann. Von dieser Möglichkeit sollten die Gerichte jedoch zurückhaltend Gebrauch machen, vor allem dann, wenn es sich um ausländisches Recht von Staaten des europäischen Binnenmarktes handelt. Dieser Grundsatz sollte vor allem im beschleunigten Verfahren[63] in der Vollstreckung gelten. Das hindert ein Gericht selbstverständlich nicht, die Mitwirkung der Parteien beim Nachweis ausländischen Rechts in Anspruch zu nehmen. Die Überprüfung der richtigen Anwendung des ausländischen Rechts kann in vermögensrechtlichen, berufungsfähigen Verfahren jedoch nicht durch das Bundesgericht[64] erfolgen. Wie vorstehende Ausführungen zeigten, hatte das Gericht den transnationalen Sachverhalt der vorliegenden Fallstudie nach ausländischem materiellem Recht zu beurteilen. Neben den konzernrechtlichen Fragen nach *deutschem Aktienrecht* gehörten dazu insbesondere auch das *Trustrecht von Guernsey Island.*[65]

a)   Die Kanalinsel Guernsey gehört als „dependency" zum British Empire, jedoch nicht zu Grossbritannien. Guernsey hat – wie Jersey – eine eigenständige Rechtsordnung. Gerade im Trustrecht kommt indessen der englischen Rechtsprechung, die sich seit dem Mittelalter entwickelt hat, auf den Channel Islands entscheidende Bedeutung zu. Besonders zu beachten ist zudem die Rechtsentwicklung in Jersey, welche ähnlich wie jene Guernsey's verlaufen ist. Sowohl Jersey als auch Guernsey haben das Trustrecht kodifiziert.[66] In Guernsey war 1991 sodann der Fall des Kamel Abdel Rahman – Trust entschieden worden. In Anwendung dieser Rechtsprechung[67] bzw. mangels Trustabsicht und wegen Scheingeschäfts musste in der Folge der WKR Trust ungültig[68] erklärt werden.

---

[62] *ZR* (1999) Nr. 52 Urteile A und C.1.

[63] Vgl. zu diesem Verfahren: Brunner/ Houlmann/ Reuter, *Kollokations- und Widerspruchsverfahren nach SchKG* (Bern, Stämpfli 1994).

[64] Mächler-Erne, Anhang: Aufhebung und Änderung des geltenden Bundesrechts, N 12, in: Honsell/Vogt/Schnyder (Hrsg.), *Kommentar zum Schweizerischen Privatrecht, Internationales Privatrecht* (Basel, Helbing & Lichtenhahn 1995); vgl. auch *ZR* (1996) Nr. 2 sowie BGE 119 II 93.

[65] *ZR* (1999) Nr. 52 Urteil A.

[66] Jersey: Trusts (Jersey) Law 1984; Guernsey: Trusts (Guernsey) Law, 1989.

[67] Eingehend *ZR* (1999) Nr. 52 Urteil A, Erw. 2.2.2.

[68] Oben N. 67, Erw. 2.2.3.

b)   Das schweizerische internationale Konzern- bzw. Gesellschaftsrecht führte wie bereits erwähnt, auch zur Anwendung[69] des deutschen Konzernrechts von Amtes wegen im Fall[70] des im Konkursverfahren des Gemeinschuldners klagenden deutschen Industrie-Konzerns HA-AG.

4.2   Internationales Privatrecht

a)   Mit Bezug auf die kollisionsrechtliche Beurteilung[71] des vom Gemeinschuldner errichteten Off-shore-Trusts, womit der Zugriff der Gläubiger auf das Haftungssubstrat des transnationalen Konzerns erschwert werden sollte, ergab sich nach schweizerischem Recht folgendes: Gemäss Artikel 154 Abs. 1 IPRG unterstehen Gesellschaften dem Recht des Staates, nach dessen Vorschriften sie organisiert sind, wenn sie die darin vorgeschriebenen Publizitäts- oder Registrierungsvorschriften dieses Rechts erfüllen oder, falls solche Vorschriften nicht bestehen, wenn sie sich nach dem Recht dieses Staates organisiert haben. Mit dieser Bestimmung bekennt sich das schweizerische IPRG zur *Inkorporationstheorie*.[72] Nach dem Wortlaut der Trusturkunde wurde der „WKR Trust" gemäss den Gesetzen von Guernsey begründet und das Recht von Guernsey als anwendbares Recht bezeichnet. Das Recht von Guernsey sieht keine speziellen Publizitäts- oder Registrierungsvorschriften für die Begründung eines einfachen Trusts vor[73]. Da der „WKR Trust" gemäss Trusturkunde nach dem Recht Guernseys organisiert wurde, war auf diesen das *Recht von Guernsey* anwendbar.[74]

Bei der Errichtung eines Trusts[75] erfolgt eine *Eigentumsübertragung vom Settlor auf den Trustee*[76]. Der Trustee erwirbt „legal ownership" am Trustvermögen. Er hat das Eigentum für einen Begünstigten („beneficiary") zu halten. Dieser erwirbt am selben Vermögen „equitable ownership". Diese Eigentumsspaltung ist das Kennzeichen des Trusts. Das *Trustvermögen wird unter die Kontrolle des Trustee* gebracht. Ihm obliegt es, das Trustvermögen zu verwalten und darüber zu verfügen. Die Gründungsurkunde kann als Verfassung des Trusts betrachtet werden. Der Settlor hat bei ihrer Gestaltung grosse Freiheit; er kann ein rechtliches Gebilde nach seinen Wünschen und Vorstellungen schaffen. Als Grenzen dieser Gestaltungsfrei-

---

[69] *ZR* (1999) Nr. 52 Urteil C.2; die Anwendung des deutschen Aktienrechts wurde durch das Zürcher Kassationsgericht überprüft, da eine Berufung an das Bundesgericht in diesem Punkt nicht möglich war.
[70] *ZR* (1999) Nr. 52 Urteil C.1.
[71] *ZR* (1999) Nr. 52 Urteil A, Erw. 2.1.2.
[72] BGE 112 II 494ff., insb. 500f.
[73] Art. 6. (1) Trusts (Guernsey) Law, 1989.
[74] Art. 154 Abs. 1 IPRG.
[75] Vgl. dazu neuerdings Mosimann, *Der angelsächsische Trust und die liechtensteinische Treuhänderschaft unter besonderer Berücksichtigung des wirtschaftlich Begünstigten* (Zürich 1999).
[76] *ZR* (1999) Nr. 52 Urteil A, Erw. 2.2.

heit wirken erst die Verletzung der Moral, d.h., der „public policy", was grundsätzlich dem kontinentalen ordre public entspricht, sowie die Missachtung von Gesetzesbestimmungen. Wenn ein an sich gültiger Trust gegen diese Grundsätze verstösst, ist er rechtlich nicht durchsetzbar.[77]

Bei der *Beurteilung der Gültigkeit des WKR Trusts* war demnach zu prüfen, ob die in der Trusturkunde niedergelegten wesentlichen Bestimmungen über dessen Gestaltung mit den Grundsätzen des Trustrechts vereinbar waren und, ob bei Errichtung und Führung des Trusts die erforderliche Trustabsicht des Settlors vorhanden war. Als Ergebnis dieser Beurteilung musste die Ungültigkeit des „WKR Trusts" festgestellt werden, nachdem der Gemeinschuldner zahlreiche Übergriffe und Verstösse gegen die Grundsätze des Trustrechts von Guernsey Island zu vertreten hatte. Die Gläubiger erhielten damit (zumindest theoretisch) Zugriff auf das Haftungssubstrat des transnationalen Konzerns im Off-shore Gebiet.

b)   Die weitere kollisionsrechtliche Rechtsfrage nach dem anwendbaren Recht auf *Ansprüche wegen Einflussnahme als herrschender Unternehmer* ist im schweizerischen Recht[78] zufolge Fehlens eines Konzernrechts gesetzlich nicht geregelt[79]. Demgegenüber kennt das deutsche Recht wie dargelegt eine eingehende Konzerngesetzgebung im Aktienrecht, das insbesondere die Rechte des beherrschten Unternehmens schützen soll. Es geht insbesondere um den Schutz der Minderheitsaktionäre und der Gläubiger einer im Inland gemäss nationalem (deutschem) Recht inkorporierten Aktiengesellschaft. In systematischer *Berücksichtigung* von Artikel 19 IPRG war dementsprechend auf das Beherrschungsverhältnis jenes Recht anzuwenden, das *zum Schutz der allein dem nationalen Recht unterworfenen Minderheitsaktionäre und Gläubiger* geschaffen wurde und das zur Erreichung dieses Gesetzeszwecks auch *transnationale Wirkung entfalten* soll.[80]

Unterstehen somit das herrschende Unternehmen und das beherrschte Unternehmen gemäss deren Gesellschaftsstatuten verschiedenen nationalen Rechtsordnungen, so ist das Recht der abhängigen Gesellschaft anwendbar, da einer abhängigen (nationalen) Aktiengesellschaft der Schutzstandard auch im transnationalen Verhältnis[81] erhalten bleiben soll. Anders entscheiden hiesse, die vom nationalen Gesetzgeber getroffenen Wertentscheide zwecks Begrenzung wirtschaftlicher Macht bezüglich transnationaler Konzerne faktisch aufzuheben bzw. zu umgehen, d.h., es

---

[77] Oben N. 76 unter Hinweis auf Baker/ Langan, *Snell's Principles of Equity*, 28th edn. (London, Sweet and Maxwell 1982) 91.

[78] Vischer, „Das internationale Gesellschaftsrecht der Schweiz", in: Nobel (oben N. 14) 27ff., insb. 35f.

[79] ZR (1999) Nr. 52 Urteil C.1, Erw. 2.1.2 unter Hinweis auf A. von Planta, Art. 150 N 6, in: *Kommentar zum Schweizerischen Privatrecht, Internationales Privatrecht* (oben N. 64).

[80] Oben N. 79 unter Hinweis auf Mächler-Erne, Art. 19 N 14, in: *Kommentar zum Schweizerischen Privatrecht, Internationales Privatrecht* (oben N. 64).

[81] Immenga/ Klocke, „Konzernkollisionsrecht", *ZSR* (1973 I) 27ff., insb. 46ff.

gingen die ausgleichenden Bemühungen des Rechts der souveränen Staaten[82] durch quasi-souveräne Entscheide internationaler Konzerne ins Leere. Für konkrete Haftungsfälle ist damit die vorgenannte Fiktion der Fiktion eines transnationalen Konzerns zumindest teilweise in die Realität zurückzuführen. Im Sinne von Artikel 1 Abs. 2 ZGB gilt damit folgende *kollisionsrechtliche Grundregel: Für die Beurteilung des Verhältnisses zwischen herrschendem und beherrschtem Unternehmen ist das Schutzrecht am Sitz des beherrschten Unternehmens anwendbar.*[83] Das massgebliche Schutzrecht erstreckt sich dabei insbesondere auf die Rechte der Unternehmensleitung,[84] der Minderheitsaktionäre[85] und der Gläubiger[86] des beherrschten Unternehmens gegenüber dem herrschenden Unternehmen. Es handelt sich um eine vollkommen zweiseitige Kollisionsnorm in dem Sinne, dass sich ein beherrschtes Unternehmen stets auf das an seinem Sitz geltende Schutzrecht berufen kann, unabhängig davon, welche transnationalen Rechtsverhältnisse eines internationalen Konzerns vorliegen. Für Schweizer Unternehmen in einem Beherrschungsverhältnis gilt damit Schweizer Recht und dessen tiefer Schutzstandard, eine Feststellung im übrigen, die den Gesetzgeber zum Handeln auffordert.

4.3   Internationales Vollstreckungsrecht

In einem der Verfahren[87] der vorliegenden Fallstudie machte die beklagte Konkursmasse geltend, die positive Kollokationsklage der klagenden Konzern-Gesellschaft dürfe nicht geschützt werden, andernfalls der Gemeinschuldner als Eigentümer der Aktien der Zwischen- und Mutter-Gesellschaften der Klägerin im Ergebnis vom Haftungssubstrat der Konkursmasse profitieren könne. Zur Begründung wurde u.a.

---

[82] Zu denken ist insb. an die revidierten Aktienrechtsnormen zum Schutz der Minderheitsaktionäre (vgl. dazu Bratschi, *Die Stellung des freien Aktionärs im Konzern* [Bern, Stämpfli 1996] 43ff.) und vor unfreundlichen Übernahmen sowie an das *Aufsichtsrecht* im Bereich der Finanzdienstleistungen und des Anlegerschutzes. Vgl. bereits Mestmäcker, „Multinationale Unternehmen im nationalen und internationalen Wirtschaftsrecht", in: Sternenberger (Hrsg.), *Recht und Macht in Politik und Wirtschaft* (Zürich, Schulthess 1976) 109-135.

[83] ZR (1999) Nr. 52 Urteil C.1; vgl. ebenso: von Büren (oben N. 14) 412ff, insb. 414 N 19 unter Hinweis auf Vischer, N 25 der Vorbemerkungen zu IPRG 150-165, in: Heini/ Keller/ Siehr/Vischer/ Volken (Hrsg.) *Kommentar zum IPRG* (Zürich, Schulthess 1993). Vgl. sodann: Immenga, „Internationales Konzernrecht – deutsche Perspektiven", in: Nobel (oben N. 14) 117ff., insb. 122ff.; Rohr, *Der Konzern im IPR unter besonderer Berücksichtigung des Schutzes der Minderheitsaktionäre und Gläubiger*, Diss. Freiburg (Zürich, Schulthess 1983); Plüss, „Zur Rechtsstellung des <Konzernführers>" *FS Forstmoser* (Zürich, Schulthess 1993) 147ff., insb. 150.

[84] F. von Planta (oben N. 41).

[85] Bratschi (oben N. 82); Zweifel (oben N. 36).

[86] Zürcher (oben N. 50).

[87] ZR (1999) Nr. 52 Urteil A.

ein aktienrechtlicher Durchgriff[88] im internationalen Privatrecht postuliert. Nach Feststellung der Ungültigkeit des Trusts auf Guernsey Island zeigte sich denn auch in der Folge, dass das *Vermögen* der Klägerin über die Zwischen-Gesellschaften des Konzerns[89] im Eigentum des Gemeinschuldners stand. Solche Konstellationen sind im Vollstreckungsrecht keineswegs selten, weshalb sie stets als Möglichkeit einer schuldnerischen Strategie[90] in Betracht zu ziehen sind. *Verfahrensrechtlich* wurde daher geltend gemacht, die klägerische Forderung sei eine Forderung des Gemeinschuldners gegen sich selbst und könne als solche wegen wirtschaftlicher Identität von Gläubigerin und Gemeinschuldner in der laufenden Vollstreckung keine Berücksichtigung finden. *Konzernrechtlich* wurde argumentiert, diese rechtsmissbräuchliche Wirkung rechtfertige einen Durchgriff und es müsse die rechtliche Selbständigkeit der Klägerin und ihrer Mutter-Gesellschaften unbeachtet bleiben.

a) Bei einer solchen Sachlage stellt sich die Frage nach der *Qualifikation der Durchgriffsproblematik*[91] im internationalen Privatrecht. Die schweizerische Lehre und Praxis fasst den Durchgriff überwiegend als Qualifikationsproblem im Sinne von Artikel 2 ZGB auf. Die ausnahmsweise Nichtbeachtung der rechtlichen Selbständigkeit juristischer Personen als Umkehr von der Fiktion zur Realität kann dementsprechend nur unter den Gesichtspunkten des Prinzips von Treu und Glauben und des Rechtsmissbrauchverbots erfolgen. Als fundamentale Grundsätze der Rechtsordnung gehören sie zweifellos zum *positiven ordre public im Sinne von Artikel 18 IPRG*. Die Qualifikation von Artikel 2 ZGB als loi d'application immédiate[92] lässt sich insbesondere auch insofern rechtfertigen, als die Rechtsfragen der Vollstreckung einen starken Binnenbezug aufweisen. Der transnationale konzernrechtliche Durchgriff in der Vollstreckung ist daher *nach schweizerischem Recht* zu beurteilen.

b) Ein direkter aktienrechtlicher Durchgriff durch den Schleier der Konzernstruktur wurde in der Folge jedoch materiellrechtlich verneint,[93] auch wenn die *wirtschaftliche Betrachtungsweise* einen anderen Schluss hätte nahe legen können. Ein Grund für die Beachtung der rechtlichen Selbständigkeit der juristischen Person lag darin, dass *nach* der Konkurseröffnung über den Gemeinschuldner Drittin-

---

[88] Vgl. zum Durchgriff im Konzernrecht, Pedrazzini, *Gesellschaftsrechtliche Entscheide* (Bern, Stämpfli Verlag 1998) 156ff. unter Hinweis auf BGE 113 II 31 = Pra 1987 Nr. 174; Behrens, „Der Durchgriff über die Grenze", *RabelsZ* (1982) 308ff.

[89] *ZR* (1999) Nr. 52 Urteil A., Erw. 2.2.3.c am Ende.

[90] Zum *„Oktopus-Effekt" in der Vollstreckung* als transnationale Strategie künftiger Schuldner, vgl. Brunner, „Gläubigerschutz im internationalen Konkursrecht", *AJP (Aktuelle Juristische Praxis)* (1/1995) 3ff., insb. Ziff. III.1.3.

[91] Zum folgenden *ZR* (1999) Nr. 52 Urteil A, Erw. 3.

[92] Zur Kritik dieser Rechtskonstruktion, vgl. Siehr, „« False Conflicts », « lois d'application immédiate » und andere « Neuentdeckungen » im IPR", *FS Drobnig* (Tübingen, Mohr Siebeck 1998) 443ff.

[93] *ZR* (1999) Nr. 52 Urteil A., Erw. 3.2. und 3.3.

teressen an der Klägerin nicht ausgeschlossen[94] werden konnten. Die positive Kollokationsklage drang indessen gleichwohl nicht durch, da der Gemeinschuldner als herrschender Unternehmer des Konzerns ein in der Höhe ständig variierendes persönliches Darlehen von rund acht Millionen Franken während Jahren bei der Klägerin – einer Bank mit Sitz in Genf – ohne schriftliche Unterlagen „stehen" gelassen hatte. Dies verstiess gegen den Liquidationszweck der Klägerin, da die Aufsicht, d.h., die Eidgenössische Bankenkommission (EBK), dieser bereits zehn Jahre zuvor die Banklizenz entzogen hatte, mit der Auflage, umgehend die Liquidation der Gesellschaft einzuleiten. Die Liquidation wurde jedoch nicht vollzogen; vielmehr wurde die Klägerin vom herrschenden Unternehmer faktisch als „Kontoposten" des O-Konzerns verwendet.[95]

c) Eine Eventualbegründung[96] zur Frage des Rechtsmissbrauchs kam jedoch zum Schluss, dass die Beziehung einer juristischen Person zur ihren (indirekten) Aktionären nicht alleine unter dem Gesichtspunkt des direkten Durchgriffs gewürdigt werden kann. Der Rechtsschutz kann allgemein und einer juristischen Person im besonderen selbst bei Beachtung ihrer Selbständigkeit verweigert werden, wenn dessen Gewährung zu einem offensichtlich stossenden Ergebnis führen würde. Dies ist insbesondere dann der Fall, wenn die faktische Machtstellung einerseits und die normative Rechtstellung anderseits in einem offenbaren Missverhältnis stehen und das in Frage stehende Rechtsverhältnis im Übermass beherrscht.[97] Artikel 2 ZGB in seiner ganzen Tragweite und in der Gesamtheit seiner Anwendungsfälle verpflichtet den Richter, das Ergebnis einzelner Erwägungen im Hinblick auf die Gesamtheit der dargelegten Umstände zu würdigen. *Rechtsmissbrauch im Zusammenhang mit juristischen Personen* konkretisiert sich nicht allein im Anwendungsfall des direkten Durchgriffs. Es sind vielmehr *weitere Fälle*[98] denkbar, in welchen der Rechtsschutz zu verweigern ist, ohne dass ein Durchgriff vorgenommen werden müsste oder könnte.[99] Die rechtliche *Möglichkeit transnationaler Konzernstrukturen als Gesetzesfiktion* darf nicht soweit gehen, dass ein Schuldner als vormaliger herrschender Unternehmer eines Konzerns *in Realität gegen sich selbst* zum Nachteil der Gläubiger Forderungen geltend machen könnte.

---

[94] Oben N. 93, Erw. 3.2.3; dies insb. im Zeitpunkt des Urteils (vgl. § 188 Zürcher ZPO).
[95] Oben N. 93, Erw. 4 (Zusammenfassung).
[96] Oben N. 93, Erw. 5.
[97] Oben N. 93 unter Hinweis auf Homburger (oben N. 15) 33-35.
[98] Vgl. zur Rechtsprechung insb. Druey/ Vogel (oben N. 22) 59ff.
[99] Vgl. zu den allgemeinen Grundsätzen: Zeller, *Treu und Glauben und Rechtsmissbrauchsverbot* (Zürich, Schulthess 1981) 313ff.

5.   EPILOG – NACHSEHEN UND VORSEHEN

Die verschiedenen Instrumente des materiellen und internationalen Konzernrechts konnten nicht verhindern, dass die Gläubiger im Konkurs über den vormals herrschenden Unternehmer sowie im Verfahren betreffend Nachlassliquidation der Ober-Gesellschaften des Konzerns in wirtschaftlicher Hinsicht das *Nachsehen* haben. Als Epilog zur verschachtelten transnationalen Struktur, zu den Finanzstrategien und Beziehungen mit kreditgebenden Banken im Aussenverhältnis sowie zu den gegenseitigen Abhängigkeiten und Geldflüssen im Innenverhältnis des Konzerns bietet die griechische Mythologie denn auch die Geschichte des König Midas an; offensichtlich sind die geschädigten Gläubiger ebenso wie die abhängigen Verwaltungsräte davon ausgegangen, dass alles zu Gold werde, was der Gemeinschuldner anfasse.[100] Die erst durch den Richter auf *Missbrauchstatbestände* aufgrund von Artikel 2 Abs. 2 ZGB reagierende Rechtsordnung erfasst damit eine extreme private wirtschaftliche Machtausübung, wie sie in der vorliegenden Fallstudie zu Aspekten des internationalen Konzernrechts aufgezeigt wurden, in jedem Fall erst retrospektiv und damit zu spät[101]. Darlehen und Geldflüsse, die im transnationalen Finanzkonglomerat versickerten, sind zum grossen Teil verloren.

Vorsehen sollten sich daher nicht nur künftige Gläubiger, sondern auch der Gesetzgeber, wenn Lehren aus dem dargelegten aktienrechtlichen Ausreisser gezogen werden sollen. Der säumige Gesetzgeber könnte dabei auf die Arbeiten des FORUM EUROPAEUM KONZERNRECHT[102] zurückgreifen, um das Richterrecht[103] von Artikel 1 ZGB durch das demokratisch breiter abgestützte Gesetzesrecht zu ersetzen. Im vorliegenden Zusammenhang interessiert dabei vor allem das Kapitel „Geschäftsleiterpflichten in der Krise (wrongful trading)", das dem englischen Recht nachgebildet ist. Zutreffend wird – wie auch die vorliegende Fallstudie zeigt – festgestellt,[104] dass das Recht vielfach zu spät mit gesteigerten Pflichten des herrschenden Unternehmers eingreift, d.h. erst im Konkurs einer unteren Konzern-Gesellschaft. In solchen Gesellschaften muss der Zeitpunkt für die Pflichtenverschärfung nach vorne verschoben werden, wenn das herrschende Unternehmen auf

---

[100] *ZR* (1999) Nr. 52 Urteil B.1, Erw. 1.4.5 unter Hinweis auf den Sachwalterbericht der Revisionsgesellschaft über die OH-AG in Nachlassstundung vom 2. Oktober 1991; zit. in *NZZ (Neue Zürcher Zeitung)* vom 12. Oktober 1991.

[101] *ZR* (1999) Nr. 52 Urteil B.1, Erw. 1.1.1.

[102] An den Arbeiten im Forum Europaeum Konzernrecht beteiligten sich aus der Schweiz: Jean-Nicolas Druey, Universität St.Gallen, Peter Nobel, Universität St. Gallen, und Frank Vischer, Universität Basel; vgl. zum Schlussbericht: „Konzernrecht für Europa" (oben N. 1).

[103] Druey (oben N. 25) 273ff., insb. 360f., begrüsst eine richterliche Rechtsfortbildung des Konzernrechts, jedenfalls solange der Gesetzgeber säumig bleibt.

[104] Druey (oben N. 102) 771 Ziff. (23).

das beherrschte Unternehmen Einfluss genommen hat. Das Forum Europaeum Konzernrecht schlägt daher folgende Richtlinienregelung vor:[105]

(1) „Sobald in einer nachgeordneten Gruppengesellschaft keine vernünftige Aussicht mehr besteht, deren Auflösung aus ihren eigenen Kräften zu vermeiden (Kriseneintritt), ist die Muttergesellschaft verpflichtet, unverzüglich entweder die durchgreifende Sanierung der Gruppengesellschaft oder ihre geordnete Liquidation zu betreiben. ...‟

(3) „Handelt die Muttergesellschaft ihrer Verpflichtung nach Abs. 1 zuwider, so haftet sie der Gruppengesellschaft in deren Liquidation oder Konkurs für den Ausgleich des Verlustes, den die Gesamtheit ihrer Gläubiger durch die Fehlbehandlung der Mutter erlitten hat. Dabei wird vermutet, dass die Mutter den Kriseneintritt in der Gruppengesellschaft kannte oder hätte erkennen können. . . . ‟

Die Beachtung und Durchsetzung dieser Grundsätze für das herrschende Unternehmen einerseits sowie die gesetzlich zu verankernden Widerstandsrechte und -pflichten abhängiger Verwaltungsräte beherrschter Unternehmen anderseits könnten den Zeitpunkt der Krisenbewältigung im *Innenverhältnis des Konzerns* früher eintreten lassen und damit zumindest die Vergrösserung von Verlusten für die Gläubiger vermeiden helfen.

SUMMARY
ASPECTS OF INTERNATIONAL CORPORATE GROUP LAW – A CASE STUDY

The case study at issue is based on a series of court proceedings in Switzerland, which began in 1990 and found an ended in 1999. In september 1991 the bankrupt "WKR" was declared insolvent with debts of more than four billion Swiss francs. In the 1980s it constructed a corporate group with some hundred companies and holding companies interlocked in the financial trade. The corporate group attracted industrial companies with assets of intrinsic value. The bankrupt company ensured its control of the attracted companies without however entering clear controlling contracts. Two holding companies ("OB Ltd." and "OH Ltd.") headed the corporate group. The controlling interest and other supplemental assets had been removed from the Continent to an offshore trust on Guernsey Island. The bankrupt company broke the trust, giving detailed instructions to the trustee. Furthermore, the person controlling the international corporate group induced the board of directors of the controlled companies to shift offshore real assets within the international corporate group (Bahamas, Cayman, Delaware). Consequently, the creditors of the corporate

---

[105] Druey (oben N. 102) Ziff. (24).

group and the shareholders of the controlled industrial companies lost their investment. In the several ensuing international bankruptcy cases the courts had to analyse the legal questions of conflict of laws of corporate groups according to Swiss law, German law and the law of Guernsey. This case study discusses the judgements and seeks to provide answers regarding the protection of the interest of controlled companies operating in a globalized economic sphere.

Jewish Divorce in the International Arena

Talia Einhorn*

1. THE PROBLEM IN A NUTSHELL

Jewish law, like other religious laws, commands universal application to all Jews. Had all states chosen religious law to apply to marriage and divorce, limping marriages and divorces would have been restricted to persons who are regarded as belonging to several religions (decided from the point of view of that religion), or to none. This would have also been the case had all persons, regardless of the civil law

---

* Dr. iur. (Hamburg), Professor of Law, T.M.C. Asser Institute, The Hague/ Concordia International University Estonia, Tallinn.

J. Basedow et al., eds., Private Law in the International Arena – Liber Amicorum Kurt Siehr
© 2000, T.M.C.Asser Press, The Hague, The Netherlands

applicable to such matters, adhered to religious laws. However, as long as some states, e.g., Israel, apply religious law to personal status, whereas others apply civil law, limping personal status poses a very real problem.[1] Such conflicts befall also Jews who regard themselves bound not only by the civil laws of their state of habitual residence, but also, by autonomous choice, by Jewish law precepts.

The modern, relatively free movement of persons in the international arena has created an urgent need for harmonization of personal status under civil and religious laws. A Jewish couple, married and domiciled in Israel, may move to a country which recognizes only civil divorces. Following an irretrievable marriage breakdown, one spouse sues for divorce and has the marriage dissolved by the civil court. Civil divorce is not recognized by Jewish law. Should the wife return to Israel she would remain *agunah*, i.e., anchored or chained to her husband until a Jewish divorce is effected. Any children that she may have as a result of her relations with another Jewish man would be considered *mamzerim*, bastards according to Jewish law, unable to marry a Jew, unless the intended spouse is a *mamzer* too, or a proselyte.

I shall first explain the Jewish law rules regarding divorce and their application in Israel. An analysis will follow of the response of Jewish law to the problems of limping personal status. Although it is in the first place the responsibility of the rabbinical authorities to help the members of their religious community, it is arguable that Western Civilization, by separating State from Religion, has deprived religious authorities of the power they had previously to deal with such situations.[2] Indeed, the civil courts of many states found ways to mitigate the suffering of chained spouses, mostly wives but occasionally some husbands. Some states have even responded with helpful legislation.

The extensive comparative research of KURT SIEHR, to whom this article is dedicated with deep appreciation, gratitude and long-standing friendship, instructs me that, "[h]ere we have to answer the question of why the law of different countries should be compared. Of course, this can be done for the sake of curiosity and for a drive to know more about foreign countries. But is this almost ethnological

---

[1] Cases from Western jurisdictions, involving Jews moving between Israel and the Diaspora, prove that this is by no means a theoretical problem: *In the Marriage of Shulsinger*, 2 *Fam LR* (1977) 611, 13 Australian LR (1976-77) 537 (Australia); *Schwebel* v. *Ungar* 42 DLR (2d) 622 (1963) (Ont., Canada); *Berkovitz* v. *Grinberg* [1996] 1 FCR 586 (England); *Maples (formerly Melamud)* v. *Maples* [1987] 3 All ER 188 (England); *Dame Benheim* c. *Zerbib* (TGI de la Seine, 22.6.1967), 58 *Rev.crit.d.i.p.* 474 (1969) (France); OLG Koblenz 2.2.1994, *FamRZ* (1994) 434 (Germany); BayObLG 29.8.1985, *IPRax* (1986) 180 (Germany); OLG Köln 19.3.1973, *MDR* (1973) 768 (Germany); HCJ 301/63 *Streit* v. *Israel Chief Rabbi* 18(1) PD 598 (Israel); CA (Civil Appeal) 191/51 *Skornik* v. *Skornik* 8 PD 141 (Israel); *Shapiro* v. *Shapiro* (14.9.1981) 442 NYS 2d 928 (NY, USA); *Nardi* v. *Segal* (27.12.1967) 234 N.E. 2d 805 (Ill., USA).

[2] Rabbinical courts could impose a *herem*, excommunication, which totally isolated the offender. The threat alone often sufficed to induce the recalcitrant husband to deliver the *get*.

approach an end in itself? The answer has to be denied because the ultimate aim of comparative law is a very practical and secular one: How should problems be solved by the legislature, by courts and by scholars in their laboratory of legal research? To solve these problems comparative law is used as a *method* . . . [B]y studying the developments one can decide whether to follow the same or to choose a different solution . . . As has been remarked by Rudolph von Jhering: 'Nobody will get from distant lands what he has at home in equal or better quality, but only a fool will decline China-bark because it did not grow on his own cabbage field'".[3]

2.   JEWISH LAW: THE IMPORTANCE OF GETTING THE GET

Marriage, under Jewish law, is a contract initiated and terminated by the parties involved. The marriage contract is recorded in the *ketubbah*, stating the date of marriage, the names of bridegroom, bride and witnesses, and that the bridegroom says to the bride, "Be thou my wife in accordance with the law of Moses and Israel and I will work, honor, support and maintain thee in accordance with the practices of Jewish husbands". . .

Jewish divorce is effected by the husband delivering his wife a *get* (bill of divorce, twelve lines written in a fixed form mandated by Jewish law). Personal attendance is not required. The spouses may appoint agents to give and accept the *get*. The *Beth-Din* (BD, rabbinical court) only ensures that Jewish law is observed. The spouses do not profess any faith. No reference is made to God neither in the *get* nor during its delivery. It is customary that, after its delivery, the wife gives the *get* to the BD, which gives her a document stating that she has been divorced according to law. The BD then tears the *get* to avoid subsequent claims that it was not legal and files it away. For Reform Jews a civil divorce is sufficient. But if the divorced spouse would later on wish to marry an Orthodox or a Conservative Jew he or she would still require a religious divorce.

A rabbinical enactment, *herem de-Rabbenu Gershom,* issued by Rabbi Gershom b. Judah (known as Rabbenu Gershom the Light of the Diaspora) in the 11th Century, banned the husband from divorcing his wife against her will.[4] Consent has always been a proper ground for divorce. Each spouse may also demand divorce upon justified grounds (e.g., adultery or bad conduct). Yet, even when justified grounds

---

[3] Kurt Siehr, "Review of Rabello (ed.), *Essays on European Law and Israel* (1996)", 36 *Netherlands International Law Review* (1999) 122, 124. See the citation of v. Jhering, here translated by Kurt Siehr, in v. Jhering, *Geist des Römischen Rechts auf den verschiedenen Stufen seiner Entwicklung,* vol. 1, 7th/8th ed. (Leipzig 1924): "Niemand wird von der Ferne holen, was er daheim ebensogut oder besser hat, aber nur ein Narr wird die Chinarinde aus dem Grunde zurückweisen, weil sie nicht auf seinem Krautacker gewachsen ist."

[4] Cf., Scherschewsky, "Divorce", *Encyclopaedia Judaica*, vol. 6, 122-135.

exist for demanding divorce, the BD's judgment does not by itself dissolve the marriage. The BD's role is to help enforce rights that already exist. The couple remains married until a *get* is delivered, an act to which they must both agree. Although the delivery of the *get* is ordinarily a voluntary act, and a *get* given by the husband under duress or coercion is invalid *(get me'useh)*, a certain degree of compulsion is acceptable if e.g., the husband has abandoned his wife, and refuses to cohabit with her and support her according to the terms of the marriage contract.

The wife is "sanctified" to her husband and a purported second marriage would have severe results. She would forever be forbidden to both men and they must give her a *get*.[5] Even if one of them dies she continues to be forbidden to the survivor. It does not matter if the bigamous marriage was intended or inadvertent (e.g., if the wife, mistakenly, thought that her first husband had died). The offspring of the relation between a married Jewish woman and a Jewish man who is not her husband, is a bastard, *mamzer* who cannot marry a Jew, unless the intended spouse is a *mamzer* or a proselyte. The punishment of the offspring is not confined to the first generation but applies also to all their descendants to the tenth generation (Deut. 23:3). The problem of the 'mamzer' is all the more striking, since Jewish law does not otherwise distinguish between children born in and out of wedlock. No child is "illegitimate". All children have the right to maintenance, succession etc. irrespective of the circumstances of his or her birth.

The husband's position is very different. His second marriage is permitted under Biblical law, and is dissolved only by death or divorce. Another rabbinical enactment, *herem de-Rabbenu Gershom*, prohibits men from marrying a second wife. But should the husband, the enactment notwithstanding, marry a second wife, this marriage would be valid, and his children would enjoy all rights of legitimate children. Unlike the prohibition on divorcing a wife against her will which applied in all Jewish communities, the *herem* forbidding bigamy only applied where *Ashkenazi* Jews formed the majority of the community, polygamy being forbidden also by the dominant religion, Christianity. The *herem* did not extend to *Sephardi* Jews.

In addition, the husband may be released from the prohibition on bigamy under special circumstances. A BD may grant him permission to marry a second wife if the first becomes insane and cannot be divorced because of her incapacity to consent. Permission may also be granted if the wife disappears, or refuses to accept a *get* despite the BD's order that she do so, e.g., in the case of a prohibited marriage; the wife's adultery; or when the couple have been married for ten years and have no children. Following the BD's decision to exempt the husband from the *herem*, the matter is referred to 100 rabbis for approval, and, if approved, the permit *(heter me'ah rabbanim)* becomes effective.

---

[5] Cf., Scherschewsky, "Bigamy", *Encyclopaedia Judaica*, vol. 4, 985-990.

The wife will never be permitted to remarry. Even if the husband disappears and his abode is unknown, she remains *agunah*, unless she can prove his death.

3. THE APPLICATION OF JEWISH LAW IN ISRAEL

Israeli law applies personal law to matters of marriage and divorce. For Israeli citizens or residents this is their religious law, for non-resident foreigners – the law of their nationality. Israeli law followed in essence the model set by the British Mandate, which in turn modeled itself, with modifications, on Ottoman law.[6] When Israel was established (1948), the Jewish secular majority expected that jurisdiction in matters of marriage and divorce would be vested in the civil courts.[7] The Muslim minority was first to oppose, arguing that, as a large majority they had willingly granted Jews exclusive jurisdiction of the rabbinical courts in matters of personal status. By depriving them of their vested religious privileges the Jews would render evil for good! The Orthodox parties, the rabbinical establishment, and the various Christian Churches, joined in insisting that they retain the jurisdiction they had enjoyed previously. The Provisional Government could not withstand the concerted pressure. For Jews this resulted with the *status quo*, i.e., Jewish religious laws and customs were to apply as, and to the extent that, they prevailed in Palestine. Hence the hegemony, under Israeli law, of the Orthodox (rather than the Conservative or Reform) movement over marriage, divorce and other personal matters submitted to religious jurisdiction.

4. A MAJOR DIFFICULTY: THE LACK OF HIERARCHY IN JEWISH LAW

To appreciate the difficulty Jewish law has in developing solutions to problems, it is essential to understand the nature of the *halakhah*, being the product of the efforts of many generations of scholars without any legislative institution empowered to enact a systematic code of laws. Since the middle of the 11th Century, there has been no single spiritual center whose decisions were considered authoritative for the whole Jewish world. To date, there is no code that combines all the rules in a way which eliminates the need to have recourse to other sources. Therefore, on many matters there is no settled *halakhah* at all.

In the 16th Century the *halakhah* was codified in the *Shulchan 'Arukh*, a

---

[6] Vitta, *The Conflict of Laws in Matters of Personal Status in Palestine* (Tel-Aviv, Bursi 1947) 1-25; Goadby, *International and Inter-religious Private Law in Palestine* (Jerusalem, Hamadpis 1926) 113 ff.

[7] Haim Cohn, "Religious Freedom and Religious Coercion in the State of Israel", in: *Israel among the Nations* (A.E. Kellermann, K. Siehr, T. Einhorn (eds.), The Hague, Kluwer 1998) 79, 94.

codification which was finally accepted in the 17th Century by world Jewry following the incorporation of later authoritative commentaries into its final structure.[8] Yet, even the *Shulchan 'Arukh* has never been considered binding law, although later authorities would depart from its rulings only with reluctance. This has made it, together with the many commentaries written on it, the starting point for every inquiry into Jewish law. But to render a decision in Jewish law, one must also consult the Talmudic commentaries, the *novellae* ("additions" to the commentaries on the Talmud), and the *responsa* literature (all of which recorded rulings and decisions rendered by the *halakhic* authorities in the post-Talmudic era in response to questions submitted in writing), as well as the enactments and customs that followed the code.

This process is further complicated by the existence of conflicting opinions among the authorities that made the decisions. The Chief Rabbinate in Israel does not command global authority.[9] Not even all of Israel's Orthodox religious public recognize the exclusive *halakhic* authority of the Chief Rabbinate. Different approaches are taken by the leaders of Conservative and Reform Judaism. In the United States the latter movements represent the majority of the Jewish Communities. In Israel, on the other hand, they bear little weight.

5. HALAKHIC SOLUTIONS TO THE PROBLEM

The plight of the *agunah* has been one of the most agonizing challenges confronting Jewish law throughout the generations.[10] Although no scholar can provide one solution acceptable to Jews worldwide, Jewish authorities have handed down numerous decisions and written commentaries suggesting a variety of plausible solutions demonstrating that the *halakhah* is, in principle, capable of meeting the challenge.[11] The following is an inexhaustive list:

5.1 Extending the Grounds Justifying Women's Claims for Divorce

A woman may sue for a divorce under Jewish law if certain objective criteria justify her claim, e.g., the husband contracting a loathsome disease, abandonment, infidel-

---

    [8] Elon, *Jewish Law: History, Sources, Principles*, vol. 3, (Philadelphia, The Jewish Publication Society 1994) 1417-1422.

    [9] England, *Jewish Law in Ancient and Modern Israel (Selected Essays)* (New Jersey, Ktav 1971) 168, 184.

    [10] Gordis, *The Dynamics of Judaism* (Bloomington, Indiana University 1990), 156 ff.

    [11] Modern comprehensive studies of the sources are e.g., Breitowitz, *Between Civil and Religious Law: The Plight of the Agunah in American Society* (Westport, Connecticut, Greenwood 1993); Antelman, *The Great Aguna Debate* (Providence RI, 1997).

ity, abuse. But rabbinical authorities are divided whether a woman may require a divorce just because the husband is repulsive to her *(ma'is 'alai)*. The answer depends on the interpretation of the talmudic statement that, if a woman claims that her husband is repulsive to her, she is not forced to have sexual relations with him.[12] Under one interpretation, the husband is obliged to set her free. Another interpretation regards this as a mere relaxation of her duties towards her husband, which does not compel him to divorce her. Maimonides held that a BD should force the husband to divorce her immediately because she is not a captive woman who must have sexual relations with one whom she hates. Another great scholar of the same era, Rabbenu Tam, argued that such an attitude was improper and undermined family stability.[13] Both the *Shulchan 'Aruch* (codified for *Sephardi* Jews) and the Rema (Rabbi Moshe Issarlis, who adapted the Code for *Ashkenazi* Jews) adopt the interpretation offered by Rabbenu Tam.

In the post-talmudic era, the *geonim* (leaders of the major Babylonian academies of Jewish learning for several centuries, following the redaction of the Talmud, up to the 11th Century) enacted the *dina de'metivta*, enactment of the Academy, that a husband could be forced to give his wife a *get*, if she claimed that irreconcilable differences made it impossible for her to cohabit with him. The stated purpose of the enactment was to prevent Jewish women from turning to gentiles to coerce their husbands to give them a *get*, or from converting into Islam, since, under Islamic law, a converted woman could obtain an immediate divorce from her husband who refused to convert.[14] The enactment was widely relied upon throughout the Jewish communities in Europe, Palestine and North Africa for almost 500 years, yet fell out of use since the 12th Century, having been considered an emergency measure enacted for a particular period of need.[15]

Modern Orthodox authorities have proposed to re-institute the view of Maimonides or the *takkanah* of the *geonim,* so far however with very limited success.[16]

---

[12] T.B., ketubbot 63b.

[13] Maimonides (Spain, Egypt, 1135-1204), *Mishneh Torah*, hilkhot ishut 14:8; Rabbenu Tam (France, 1100-1171), *Tosafot to T.B.*, ketubbot 63b

[14] According to a responsum of Rav Natronai Gaon, head of the Sura academy in the middle of the 9th Century, *Otzar ha'geonim* 8, p. 189.

[15] Cf. the authories cited by Breitowitz (op.cit. n. 11) 51-52.

[16] Falk, *The Divorce Action by the Wife in Jewish Law* (Jerusalem, Institute for Legislative Research and Comparative Law, 1973) (Heb.), 40-48; Haut, *Divorce in Jewish Law and Life* (New York, Sepher-Hermon 1983) 49, 96-97; cf. also Halperin-Kaddari, "'tav le-meitav tan du milemeitav armelo': Women's Perpetual Marital Preference and their Construction as 'others' in Jewish Law" in: Helpern, Safrai (eds.), Jewish Legal Writings by Women, Vol. 2 (Jerusalem, Urim 2000) (forthcoming).

5.2   The Conditional *ketubbah*

This solution makes the *halakhic* marriage subject to a condition that, if a civil divorce is granted and the husband fails to give the wife a *get* within a stated period, the marriage is annulled retroactively. The annulment has no effect on the status of the children, since, unless born out of an adulterous relationship, there is no problem of illegitimacy. Such a condition could be inserted in a prenuptial agreement. The proposal has been rejected by most Orthodox rabbis on the grounds that subsequent cohabitation constituted a waiver of the condition.

In 1954 the Rabbinical Assembly of America (Conservative) implemented an enactment, proposed by Saul Lieberman, which incorporated into the *ketubbah* a clause providing that the bride and the bridegroom "agree to recognize the Beth Din of the Rabbinical Assembly and the Jewish Theological Seminar of America . . . as having authority . . . to summon either party at the request of the other in order to enable the party so requesting to live in accordance with the law of Jewish marriage. . .". The BD may impose such terms of compensation as it may see fit for failure to respond to its summons or carry out its decision.[17]

5.3   Rabbinical Annulment

The Talmud offers a remedy in extreme cases, e.g. where a woman receives the *get* from an agent appointed by her husband, unaware of the fact that the husband had, prior to its delivery, revoked the appointment.[18] To prevent the harsh results accruing to the wife, the Talmud uses the concept that all Jews who marry do so under the conditions laid down by the rabbis and the rabbis may therefore annul the marriage.[19] The woman is considered to have never been married at all. This concept is based on the statement made by the husband, during the marriage ceremony, that the wife is betrothed to him in accordance with the law of Moses and Israel. If the marriage is deemed improper according to rabbinical law, the rabbis may annul it. Following the instatement of civil divorce in France (1884), French Chief Rabbi Michel Weill, proposed to empower a rabbinical court to annul marriages dissolved by civil courts. The proposal was not approved by most Orthodox rabbis.

A similar result is reached by annulling the marriage on the grounds of mistake, *mekach ta'ut*. Had the wife known that the husband she had married would abuse her, evade his matrimonial duties and refuse to give her a *get*, she would never have married him. There was therefore no informed consent. In our times this construction has been used by Rabbi Moshe Feinstein and by Rabbi Emanuel Rackman. The

---

[17] Friedman, "Ketubbah: conservative and reform", *Encyclopaedia Judaica*, vol. 10, 929-930.
[18] T.B. gittin 33a; yevamot 90b.
[19] T.B. gittin 33a; bava batra 48b; Yevamot 110a.

latter, Chancellor of the Israeli Orthodox Bar-Ilan University, has established a BD in the US, which has set free hundreds of women, some of them having remarried since.[20] Not all Orthodox rabbis recognize this annulment and that includes the Israeli Chief Rabbinate.[21]

5.4 *Get zikkui* (a *get* that benefits)

This *get* is an application of the *halakhic* general principle that one can do certain *mitztvot*, religious duties (commonly taken to mean good deeds) for others for their benefit. Since it is a *mitzvah* for the husband to give his wife a *get* if circumstances call for it, the BD may do the *mitzvah* for him.[22] The requisite conditions: Husband refuses to give a *get*, despite a BD decision to that effect; 18 months have elapsed since the husband abandoned his wife of his free will; the BD has given him notice of 60 days that, unless he delivers the *get*, the BD would do that instead. Rabbi Antelman has established a BD that applies this method, and has even delivered such bills of divorce to Israeli women at the premises of the US Embassy in Israel. Although not recognizing such divorces, the Israeli Rabbinate then used its powers to make these recalcitrant husbands deliver a *get*.[23]

5.5 Out of (religious) Wedlock Relationships, or Finding Fault with the Marriage

Another solution is to avoid altogether the religious marriage ceremony.[24] This solution would only remedy the situation for couples who do not consider themselves bound to have a proper Jewish marriage. A similar solution applies where the parties purported to have a proper Jewish marriage ceremony, yet failed to comply with any of its requirements. It suffices that one of the witnesses is not competent, according to Jewish law, for the marriage to be considered null and void. *Halakhic* authorities agree that, even if a man and woman married in a

---

[20] *Igrot Moshe*, EH: 179-180; Rackman, *Modern Halakha for Our Time,* (Hoboken, New Jersey, Ktav 1995) 68-72; Susan Aranoff, "A Response to the Beth Din of America" (1999) (unpublished manuscript); Rackman and Aranoff, "Making The Case For Agunot", *The Jewish Week* 9.10.1998.

[21] Cf., Shochetman, "Annulment of Marriage – A Possible Way of Solving the Problem of Refusal to Provide a Get?" 20 *Shenaton Ha-Mishpat Ha-'ivri* (1995-1997) 349 (Heb.).

[22] Antelman, *The Great Aguna Debate*, (Providence RI, 1997), 47-48; Id., *To Release Those Awaiting a Divorce* (Tel-Aviv, Golan 1994) (Heb.).

[23] Antelman, *To Release Those Awaiting a Divorce*, op.cit. n. 22, p. 345; cf. *infra* para. 8.

[24] Silberg, "Civil Marriage would enable the Solution of the *Mamzeruth* Problem", in *The Writings of Moshe Silberg*, (Jerusalem, Magnes 1998) (Heb.), 239; Shifmann, *Civil Marriage in Israel: the Case for Reform,* (Jerusalem, Jerusalem Institute for Legal Studies 1995) (Heb.).

ceremonial manner believing in good faith that their marriage was valid, such a marriage would be considered null under Jewish law and there is no need for a *get* to dissolve it.[25]

6.   THE RESPONSE OF CIVIL COURTS IN WESTERN CIVILIZATION COUNTRIES

6.1   The Constitutional Challenge

The separation of State and Church is enshrined in the constitutions of Western States. The recalcitrant husband often explains that to do so would encroach on his freedom of religion. An overwhelming number of courts in the US, Australia, the Netherlands, and England have rejected such allegations. The courts have accepted that the *get* procedure is a release document devoid of religious connotation. "The entry of an order compelling defendant to secure a *get* would have the clear secular purpose of completing the dissolution of the marriage. Its primary effect neither advances nor inhibits religion since it does not require husband to participate in a religious ceremony or to do acts contrary to his religious beliefs. Nor would the order be excessive entanglement with religion".[26] The *get* procedure is not more religious than the marriage ceremony sanctioned by the legislature. It promotes free exercise by encouraging Jewish divorcées to remarry, establish a home and raise a family within their chosen faith.[27] It mostly turned out that the refusal was an issue of monetary gain ("akin to extortion"[28]). Dislike for Orthodox Judaism is not a protected religious belief.[29]

The NY Supreme Court held that ordering the specific performance of the husband's undertaking in the conservative *ketubbah* to submit to the BD, requires

---

[25] In an old English case, the secular judge went himself into the intricacies of Jewish law requirements, annulling the marriage, while providing a lively account of its faults: one of the witnesses "had profaned the Sabbath, by riding in coaches, and snuffing lighted candles, stirring the fire, and eating forbidden meats; acts trifling to us, perhaps . . . but not so according to the rites and ordinances of the Jewish religion." He has been seen repeatedly, over ten years, do these acts and, when reproved, replied that he was no Jew, considering himself bound only to the exterior observances of the religion: *Goldsmid* v. *Bromer* (17.12.1798), per Sir William Scott, 161 ER 568, 570 (1 Hag. Con. 324); Cf. also *Lindo* v. *Belisario* (5.6.1795), 161 ER 530-546 (1 Hag. Con. 216).

[26] *Minkin* v. *Minkin* (22.7.1981), N.J. Super. Ch., 434 A. 2d 665, 668. Thus it was found to satisfy the three prongs of the *Lemon* test for determining whether an act violates the Establishment Clause of the First Amendment (so-called after *Lemon* v. *Kurtzman*, 411 US 192 (1973)).

[27] *Feuerman* v. *Feuerman* (1.8.1984), Mich CircCt OaklandCty, 10 FLR 1576.

[28] *Burns* v. *Burns* (4.12.1987), 538 A. 2d 438 (N.J.Superior Ch. 1987).

[29] *Goldman* v. *Goldman* (30.3.1990), 554 N.E. 2d 1016 (Ill.App. 1 Dist. 1990).

only the application of neutral principles of contract law, without reference to any religious principle.[30]

The Family Court of Australia interpreted the Commonwealth Constitution narrowly, holding that it only prohibited courts from discriminating against any person for holding any religious beliefs or exercising his religion.[31]

In a landmark decision the Dutch Hoge Raad held that civil courts should be reluctant to intervene in religious matter or religious law.[32] However, the husband owes a civil duty to cooperate with his wife in the matter of the *get* before the BD. By ordering him to discharge this duty the court does not tread on the territory of the religious authorities. The question of the right to obtain the *get* will be dealt with by the BD, and the civil court just provides the power that the BD lacks to make the husband live up to his civil law obligation.

The French courts have not directly ordered husbands to cooperate before the BD, since that would violate their freedom of conscience. They have however regarded the husband's objection to deliver the *get* a civil delict, irrespective of his motivation.[33] In 1982, a Jewish French citizen applied to the European Court of Human Rights, complaining that his freedom of conscience and religion guaranteed under Article 9, para. 1 of the Convention, had been infringed by a French Court order to compensate his wife for not delivering a *get*. The Commission of the Council of Europe rejected the claim as being manifestly unfounded,[34] noting that the applicant did not allege that, in delivering the *get* he would be obliged to act against his conscience, since it is an act by which divorce is regularly established under Jewish law, and since "it appears from the Court of Appeal's judgment of 16 January 1981 that under Hebrew law it is customary to hand over the letter of repudiation after the civil divorce has been pronounced, and that no man with

---

[30] *Avitzur* v. *Avitzur*, 446 NE 2d (NY 1983) 136, 29 ALR4th 736, 740 (1983) (in line with *Presbytarian Church* v. *Hull Church*, 393 US 440 (1969) and *Jones* v. *Wolf*, 443 US 595 (1979)); Similarly, a Delaware family court ordered the husband to perform an obligation he had undertaken in a settlement of ancillary matters to cooperate with the wife in allowing her to obtain a *get*, *Scholl* v. *Scholl*, Del.Fam.Ct., 621 A.2d 808 (1992); cf. also *Waxstein* v. *Waxstein* (28.7.1976), 395 NYS 2d 877 (1976), aff'd 394 NYS 2d 253 (2d Dept. 1977), in which the Court further held that husband's statement that the ceremony before the Rabbinate takes from two to two and one-half hours "is not worthy of discussion. That is not much out of a lifetime, especially if it will bring peace of mind and conscience to one whom the defendant must at one time have loved".

[31] *In the Marriage of Shulsinger* (supra n. 1) 540-541. The Court added that "[i]t is contrary to all notions of justice to allow a possibility that the husband would obtain a civil divorce in Australia yet refuse to free his wife, and to say that the court can do nothing".

[32] Hoge Raad (22.1.1982), NJ 1982 Nr. 489, p. 1692.

[33] The *Darienté* Case, Cass.-req. (28.2.1976) S. 1877.1.27; *Gasman* c. *Dame Kulbokas*, Civ. 2e, (13.12.1972) D. 1973, 493; *Attar* c. *Obadia*, Bull. Arrêts Cour Cass. Ch. Civ. 1985, 76, N° 113; Cass. civ. 2e (21.11.1990) Recueil Dalloz Sirey 1991, 434.

[34] Application N° 10180/82 *D.* v. *France*, European Commission of Human Rights, Decisions and Reports, N° 35-39 (February 1984) 199, 202.

genuine religious convictions would contemplate delaying the remittance of this letter to his ex-wife".

The German Appellate Court in Köln declined to enforce the wife's undertaking in a divorce settlement, "to make the necessary declarations before the Rabbinate in Köln".[35] The wife claimed that she had performed her obligation by making a hand-written declaration. The husband explained that none of them had been familiar with the *get* procedure when they entered the settlement, but asked the Court to order the wife to cooperate before the BD. The Court of First Instance decided that the wife had discharged her contractual duty. The Appellate Court stated its (with respect, mistaken) understanding that the wife must appear in person before a BD and take part in a religious ceremony. Ordering her to do so would violate her right of free exercise under Article 4, para. 2 of the German Basic Law. The Court acknowledged that parties may undertake obligations restricting their basic free-doms, but in this case they have not done so. According to the Court, compensation for non-fulfilment might have been a possible remedy. It may be wondered if the Court would have reached the same conclusion had it been aware that the wife is not required to participate in the ceremony but may appoint an agent instead, or if the obligation undertaken had been correctly drafted.

The hypothetical apostate husband, who not only changed his mind and decided not to deliver a *get*, but also changed his beliefs, has not yet surfaced in real life case reports.[36]

6.2   Causes of Action

6.2.1 *Contracts*

In some cases the Orthodox *ketubbah* itself was regarded as a binding contract between husband and wife. On its face it contains language of consideration and mutual promises, and is enforceable if it is not unconscionable to do so and if the performance to be compelled is not contrary to public policy.[37] An agreement is against public policy if it is injurious to the interest of the public, contravenes some established interest of society, violates some public statute, is against good morals,

---

[35] OLG Köln (19.3.1973), MDR 1973, 768; The Reichsgericht has rendered null and void an under-taking in a divorce settlement to deliver a *get*: RG 16.2.1904, RGZ 57, 250; see discussion by Remien, *Rechtsverwircklichung durch Zwangsgeld* (Tübingen, Mohr 1992) 169-170; OLG Köln mentions that it might have reached a different decision had Israeli law applied. Cf., *Shapiro* v. *Shapiro* (supra n. 1) where the NY Supreme Court recognized, under the principle of comity, an Israeli decree directing husband to deliver his wife a *get*.

[36] This has been pointed out by Meislin, "Pursuit of the Wife's Right to a 'get' in United States and Canadian Courts", 4 *The Jewish Law Annual* (1981) 250, 259.

[37] E.g., *Minkin* v. *Minkin* (supra n. 26); *Burns* v. *Burns*, 538 A.2d 438 (N.J.Super.Ch. 1987); *Goldman* (supra n. 29) at 1021.

tends to interfere with the public welfare or safety, or, as it is sometimes put, it is at war with the interests of society and is in conflict with public morals. The *ketubbah* is not contrary to public policy. The Appellate Court of Illinois held that the *ketubbah* text "be thou my wife according to the law of Moses and Israel" meant that Orthodox Jewish law would govern the status and validity of the marriage.[38] Therefore, if the marriage were to be dissolved a *get* had to be given according to Orthodox precepts of Jewish law. In *Avitzur* v. *Avitzur* the obligation of the man undertaken in a Conservative *ketubbah* was upheld by the NY Supreme Court. However, a civil court may not convene a rabbinical tribunal, if the parties have undertaken to appoint one but could not reach agreement.[39] The Arizona Court of Appeals considered the ordinary Orthodox *ketubbah* too vague to be interpreted as including an obligation to deliver a *get*.[40] It is submitted that the result may have been different had it been a Conservative *ketubbah*.

In contrast, English courts have regarded ante-nuptial agreements as contrary to public policy, for undermining the concept of marriage as a life-long union, and therefore unenforceable.[41] But such agreements could still have evidential weight if the terms of the agreement are relevant to subsequent divorce proceedings before the court. Furthermore, some aspects of those agreements may be enforceable. In one case the parties entered before their wedding an ante-nuptial agreement, in contemplation of and conditional upon their marriage. It included a clause that, in the event of any matrimonial dispute they will both attend the London BD when requested to do so and that they will comply with the instructions of the BD, which would resolve their disputes in accordance with *halakhah* under the Arbitration Acts in accordance with the BD's procedural rules. The Court held that the agreement was meant to regulate the parties' affairs in the event of divorce, and therefore the public policy argument applied.

In another line of cases the contractual obligation was included in separation settlements.[42] The NY Supreme Court rejected a husband's claim that the undertaking was contrary to public policy, holding that not all agreements conditioned on divorce are illegal. In another case, that Court granted specific performance of a separation agreement which provided that, prior to the wife vacating the premises, the parties should obtain a *get*.[43] The Delaware Family Court

---

[38] *Goldman* (supra n. 29) at 1019; cf. also *Stern* v. *Stern* (The Supreme Court, King's County, NY), decided 26.7.1979, brought in 4 *The Jewish Law Annual* (1981) 272, where the court enforced the *ketubbah*, and ordered the husband, who had alleged infidelity on the part of the wife, to give his wife a *get*, on the grounds that, under the laws of Moses and Israel referred to in the *ketubbah*, the mere allegation by the husband of an act of adultery obligated him to give her a *get*.

[39] *Pal* v. *Pal* (17.6.1974), 356 NYS 2d 672.

[40] *Victor* v. *Victor*, 866 P.2d 899 (Ariz.App.Div. 1 1993).

[41] *N.* v. *N.* [1999] 2 FCR 583; [1999] 2 FLR 745.

[42] *Koeppel* v. *Koeppel*, 138 NYS 2d 366 (1954, Sup).

[43] *Waxstein* (supra n. 30).

ordered a husband to properly cooperate and deliver an Orthodox *get* rather than the Conservative one he was willing to deliver.[44]

Although it has been stated that an oppressive misuse of the religious veto power by a spouse subjects the economic bargain which follows between them to review and potential revision, and that a divorce settlement tainted by duress is void, not merely voidable, civil courts have been reluctant to review the agreements.[45] The NY Supreme Court reasoned that, absent a showing of fraud, mistake, duress or overreaching, property settlements in divorce proceedings will not be disturbed by the court; there is a strict surveillance of all transactions between married persons, and the courts have thrown their cloak of protection about separation agreements and made it their business to see to it that they are arrived at fairly and equitably. However, the Court held that the wife did not freely and voluntarily enter into a separation agreement allegedly produced through rabbinical arbitration.[46] The Court was presented with evidence that the procedure did not properly protect the wife, who was compelled to sign the settlement under the threat of becoming forever chained to her husband.

6.2.2 *Torts*

Under Dutch law, the denial of the delivery of the *get* is regarded as a breach of a duty of care that a husband owes his wife. Such behaviour is unlawful and amounts to a civil delict.[47] The Dutch courts have not hesitated to remedy this situation (as one might expect in case of harassment) by ordering the husband to cooperate with a rabbinical tribunal in giving the *get*.

The French courts also regard the refusal to deliver or accept the *get* as a civil delict, either on the grounds of *faute* (fault), or on the grounds of *abus de droit* (abuse of right), or *abus de liberté* (abuse of freedom).[48] They do not order the recalcitrant spouse to give or accept the *get*, and even do not order him to appear before a BD, since that would be an impermissible treading on his freedom of conscience. However, the denial of the *get* constitutes a civil delict *per se*, irrespective of the spouse's motives.[49] As such, the suffering spouse should be compensated. In recent years the amount of compensation has become quite substantial. In one case, after the husband had paid FF 80,000 imposed as compensation in 1992, the wife sued

---

[44] *Scholl* (supra n. 30).

[45] *Perl* v. *Perl*, 512 NYS 2d 372 (A.D. 1 Dept. 1987).

[46] *Golding* v. *Golding*, 581 NYS 2d 4 (A.D. 1 Dept. 1992).

[47] Hoge Raad, (22.1.1982), NJ 1982 Nr. 489, p. 1692; Rechtbank Middelburg (28.5.1986), NIPR 1986, 413; President Rechtbank Haarlem (17.2.1989), NIPR 1989, 227.

[48] Civ. 2e, 13.12.1972, D. 1973, 493; Trib.civ.Seine. 1re, 22.2.1957, Gaz.Pal. 1957.2. 246; Civ. 2e, 21.4.1982, Gaz.Pal. 1983.2.590; Civ. 2e, 21.11.1990, D. 1991, 434; cf. Gaudemet-Tallon, "La Désunion du couple en droit international privé", 226 *Rec.d.Cours* (1991) 9, 248-251.

[49] 2e, 21.11.1990, D. 1991, 434.

him again in 1995, claiming that the compensation only covered her damages prior to the 1992 decision. The husband argued that this was a *chose jugée* (*res judicata*). The court upheld the wife's claim and imposed an additional sum of FF 130,000 for the period 1992-1995. An appeal was dismissed.[50]

The NY Supreme Court held that the husband's refusal to deliver a *get* unless his wife agreed to a property settlement giving him virtually all of their property does not subject him to liability in tort.[51] The Court reasoned that such liability required proof of intention, which would entangle the court in exploring the sincerity of any spouse who refused to furnish a *get*, upon religious grounds in whole or in part. The separation of Church and State requires that the courts should not resolve controversies in a manner requiring consideration of religious doctrine. It has been argued that American law is amenable to recognizing a tort if severe emotional distress is caused, intentionally or recklessly, by extreme and outrageous conduct.[52]

6.2.3 *Matrimonial Law*

We have already mentioned separation and divorce settlements in which an obligation has been inserted to deliver and accept a *get*, or to cooperate before a BD in obtaining one. The courts have also used other means to "encourage" the recalcitrant spouse to cooperate.

An Australian Family Court used its general ancillary power in matrimonial causes to order a recalcitrant wife to appear before a BD. The Court considered it its duty to ensure that appropriate orders regarding the dissolution of that marriage are made fully effective not only in theory but also in fact.[53]

The English Court of Appeal ordered that the husband pay his wife a lump sum of £ 30000, payable in two instalments, £ 25000 within 14 days and the balance of £ 5000 three months later, if by that time he has not delivered a *get*.[54] A similar result has been reached by the Full Court of the Family Court of Australia.[55] The Court ordered that the husband pay his wife a lump sum maintenance of $ 4000 within three months. That sum would be reduced to $ 2000 if the husband were to deliver a *get*. The Court reasoned that "the husband has it within his power to prevent the wife from remarrying and gaining the benefit of additional financial support which might come to her from marriage. Because of this it is proper . . . for a larger sum to be ordered as maintenance if the wife is denied the opportunity of marriage".

---

[50] Arrêt n° 54-1 (14.11.1996), Cour d'appel de Versailles (unreported).

[51] *Perl* (supra n. 45).

[52] Breitowitz (op.cit. n. 11) 239-249, relying on the Restatement of Torts, 2d, § 46.

[53] *In the marriage of Gwiazda*, unreported (23.2.1982), cited by Strum, "Jewish Divorce: What can the Civil Courts Do?" 7 *Australian Journal of Family Law* (1993) 225, 245-247.

[54] *Brett* v. *Brett* [1969] 1 All ER 1007.

[55] *Steinmatz* and *Steinmatz* (No 2), (1981) 6 Fam LR 554; [1981] FLC 91-079.

Another remedy has been the withholding of the civil divorce until the *get* has been delivered. This has been done by the Australian Court *in re Shulsinger*.[56] The wife, an Israeli citizen and resident, would have been unable to remarry in Israel. Since it was the husband who had applied for the civil divorce, this was an effective remedy. A similar result was reached by the English Family Court.[57]

In other cases courts refrained from entertaining claims brought by recalcitrant spouses. This could affect applications for additional contact with children,[58] or decisions regarding the equitable distribution of the parties' assets,[59] or making payment of support and alimony conditional upon the wife's accepting the *get*.[60]

6.3 Contempt of Court

Where a spouse has been ordered to deliver, or accept, a *get*, or appear before a BD that would supervise the *get*, the American, English, Australian and Dutch courts have determined that, unless that party has made reasonable efforts to comply with the court's order within so many days, he or she would be subject to substantial sanctions for being in contempt of court. A US court decided that powers of enforcement under contempt proceedings do not include imprisonment. The husband could purge his contempt by paying fines or by complying with the stipulation.[61]

6.4 Legislative Responses

The NY Domestic Relations Law (DRL) § 253 requires, since 1983, plaintiffs in divorce or annulment actions, whose marriage was solemnized by a clergyman, to include in their file a statement to the effect that they have or shall, prior to the entry of final judgment, remove any barriers to the defendant's remarriage. Although phrased in neutral terms, its stated purpose was to help Jewish spouses obtain the *get*. Courts have relied on this provision to direct the recalcitrant spouse to cooperate in the delivery of the *get*, on pain of contempt and the withholding of economic relief or the civil divorce.[62] DRL § 236:B 5(h) (inserted in 1992) requires the court to consider, where appropriate, the effect that a barrier to remarriage would have on

---

[56] *In re Shulsinger* (supra n. 1).

[57] *W. v. W.* (decree absolute), [1998] 2 FCR 304.

[58] *N. v. N.* (supra n. 41): the court may decline to hear the recalcitrant husband's application for contact with his child, provided that did not prejudice the child's welfare. Similarly, *Frey v. Frey*, Family Court of Australia (22.2.1984), unreported, brought by New, 6 *Jewish Law Annual* (1983), 210.

[59] *Friedenberg v. Friedenberg*, 523 NYS2d 578 (A.D.2 Dept. 1988); *Schwartz v. Schwartz*, 583 NYS2d 726 (Supp. 1992).

[60] *Rubin v. Rubin*, 348 NYS 2d 61, per Judge Gertenstein.

[61] *Margulies v. Margulies*, 344 NYS 2d 482, appeal dismissed 352 NYS 2d 447.

[62] *Friedenberg* (supra n. 59); *Schwartz* (supra n. 59). If the statement is incorrect this may lead to criminal proceedings: cf. *Kalika v. Stern*, 911 F.Supp. 594 (EDNY 1995).

the statutory factors, enumerated in § 236:B 5 (d) (1)-(13), on equitable distribution of marital property.

Article 2(4) of the Canadian Divorce Act requires (since 1990) both spouses to file, in divorce proceedings, affidavits that they have, or shall, remove all barriers to religious remarriage. The court may dismiss applications and strike out other pleadings and affidavits made by a spouse who does not comply with this provision. The Ontario Family Law Act requires such an affidavit to be submitted by any party to an application regarding family property, questions of title between spouses, or support. The court may dismiss the proceeding, or strike out the defence, of a party who fails to comply.

When Article 9 of the English Family Law Act 1996, or, alternatively, the Divorce (Religious Mariages) Bill (which reiterates the principle of Article 9), comes into force, it will empower the courts, before making a divorce order, to direct spouses married in a religious ceremony to declare that they have taken all necessary steps to dissolve the marriage in accordance with the usages applicable to such marriages.

7.   DISPELLING THE FEAR OF GET ME'USEH

Civil courts have been cautioned on occasion that, if they direct the husband to fulfil his undertaking to deliver the *get*, this would render the *get* void, due to the Jewish law rule requiring that the husband give the *get* out of his free will, which seemingly excludes recourse to regular law enforcement measures.[63] Nevertheless, Jewish scholars found ways to authorize the BD to compel the husband to give the *get*. The Talmud takes the view that enforcement proceedings, such as fines, imprisonment, and corporal punishment, apply also to *get*-orders.[64] According to Maimonides, the husband really wants to follow the decision of the BD and is just prevented from doing so by evil inclination. Therefore, so goes the fiction, the court applies coercion not to overcome the husband's free will, but rather to remove the impediment that prevents him from exercising it.

In Israel the courts have been given powers to incarcerate recalcitrant husbands.[65] This was not always very effective. In one case the husband preferred to

---

[63] Cf. *N*. v. *N*. (supra n. 41) at 751: "the courts have also, of course, been aware that a get obtained by compulsion is invalid in Jewish law, and, according to Professor Freeman, the rabbinical authorities now regard a get obtained in circumstances as those prevailing in *Brett v. Brett* as coerced and thus invalid". This is indeed the view taken by e.g., Breitowitz (op.cit. n. 11), and Freeman, "Law, Religion and the State: The Get Revisited", in *Families Across Frontiers* (Lowe and Douglas (eds.)) (The Hague, Martinus Nijhoff 1996), 361, 366.

[64] T.B. gittin 88b.

[65] Art. 6, Jurisdiction of Rabbinical Courts (Marriages and Divorces) Law, *Sefer Ha-Chukkim* 134.

sit in jail till the end of his days.[66] Besides, courts were reluctant to order imprisonment. On 2.3.1995 the *Knesset* enacted the Rabbinical Courts (Compliance with Divorce Judgments) (Temporary Provision) Law, 5755-1995,[67] empowering BDs to impose sanctions on husbands who refuse to divorce their wives despite a rabbinical judgment ordering them to do so. These include a prohibition of foreign travel; suspension of a driver's license; prohibition to engage in an occupation that requires licensing or is regulated by law; denial of the right to open or to operate a bank account etc. These means do not help if the husband is absent or in jail, or if the wife has failed to obtain a rabbinical judgment ordering a divorce. The effectiveness of the law depends on the availability to the wife of grounds justifying her claim for divorce, and the extent to which the BD makes use of its powers.[68]

The Talmud validates the use of coercion by non-Jewish courts only to enforce rabbinical court (BD) decisions.[69] There are conflicting authorities as to the validity of a ruling of a non-Jewish court decision directly requiring the husband to execute a *get*.[70] According to Maimonides, if non-Jews enforce a *get* which the husband is in fact obliged to give under Jewish law but no BD has yet ordered, such a *get* is not Biblically invalid, and therefore of no possible effect, but only invalid by reason of rabbinical enactment.[71] It is therefore open to change by a later, different rabbinical enactment. It has been submitted that the procedural requirement of a prior BD ruling was a later rabbinical device to discourage violent self-help.[72] Rabbi Isaac Herzog, the late Chief Rabbi of Israel, suggested that as soon as there are justified grounds for divorce, then even if the coercion was improper and tortious, the *get* thereby secured would still be valid.[73]

Orthodox Rabbis, when called to testify in US Courts, conceded that "although giving of 'get' is ordinarily voluntary act on part of husband, certain degree of

---

[66] *Attorney General v. Yichiah and Ora Avraham*, 22 (1) PD 29. At that point Mr. Avraham had already served five years in prison, the A.G. wished to set him free, but the courts dismissed that application, holding that he should remain in jail until he delivered the *get*.

[67] *Sefer Ha-Chukkim* 1507.

[68] According to Dr. Ruth Halprin-Kaddari of Bar-Ilan University, the so-called 1995 Sanctions Law has done relatively little to help *agunot*, since it is rarely employed: see Chabin, "*Agunot* Problem Greater in Israel", *The Jewish Week*, July 2, 1999. However, after Rabbi Antelman's BD had delivered a *get zikkui* to three chained women, the Israeli BD jailed one of the recalcitrant husbands. Thereafter all three delivered the *get* out of "free" will: cf., Antelman (op.cit. n. 23).

[69] TB gittin 88b.

[70] Cf., Bet Shmu'el, E.H. 134:8 (15), validating such a decision, with R. Meir Ha'levi Abulafia, cited in Tur E.H. gittin 134, invalidating it.

[71] Cf., Maimonides, *Mishneh Torah*, hilkhot gerushin 2:20; regarding the distinction between a Biblically invalid get and one that is invalid only by reason of a rabbinical enactment see ibid., 2:7.

[72] Breitowitz (op.cit. n. 11) at p. 39.

[73] *Otzar ha-poskim* 2, comments by Rabbi Herzog, pp. 11-12; cf. also Rabbi Basri, "A Divorce Given under Coercion (get me'useh)", 16-17 *Shenaton Ha-mishpat Ha-'ivri* (1991) 535 (Heb.).

compulsion was acceptable under circumstances where husband abandoned wife and refused to cohabit with her and support her according to terms of marriage contract".[74] After all, the Rabbinical courts are aware of the grave results of a decision avoiding a *get*. Once given, if accompanied by a waiver signed by the recalcitrant husband, the *get* will not any more be investigated if it was indeed given of his free will.[75]

8. CONCLUSIONS

Jewish law owes its resilience throughout the generations to its responsiveness to changing circumstances. The *halakhah* can cope with modernity and meet its challenges.[76] The response of most of Jewish Orthodoxy has been less than adequate, and this is especially true of Israel, where no Jew can even choose to exercise freedom from religion.

This comparative study demonstrates that, despite the separation of State from Church in Western countries, there is a range of causes of action and remedies available to the civil legislature and the civil courts to help chained women in getting the *get*. It also dispels the fear that a *get* given following such intervention would be void under Jewish law. It is submitted that such intervention reflects on the solutions offered by the Jewish rabbinical authorities, and that, in fact, the solutions are linked and each has an impact on the other. Even in the absence of civil divorce in Israel, the Knesset and the Israeli civil courts should avail themselves of solutions used in other jurisdictions to encourage recalcitrant spouses to cooperate in obtaining the *get*.

---

[74] *Goldman* (supra n. 29). cf., decision of the Dutch Supreme Court, NJ 1982 Nr. 489: Based upon the opinion of an Orthodox Rabbi, the Court concluded that the husband's free will would eventually be assumed in the spirit of the teachings of Maimonides, and that, in any case, it seems that the husband will willingly grant the *get* once the Court orders him to cooperate before the BD.

[75] Cf. the opinion given by Rabbi Ezra Basri to an American Tribunal, *get me'useh*, 16/17 *Shenaton Ha-Mishpat Ha-'ivri* 1990/91 535. In that case a recalcitrant husband claimed that he had eventually delivered the get (and also signed a letter stating that he has waivered any claims that may invalidate the get) subsequent to being imprisoned and threatened by hoodlums. Yet, Rabbi Basri validated the get; cf. also Zemer, "Purifying mamzerim", 10 *The Jewish Law Annual* (1992) 99, regarding the refraining of US Orthodox rabbis from investigating the validity of the *get*.

[76] Rackman (op.cit. n. 20) 63ff.

Towards Internationally Mandatory Directives for Consumer Contracts?

Marc Fallon[*] and Stéphanie Francq[**]

This article focuses on the development of internationally mandatory rules contained in Community acts in the field of civil and commercial matters.[1] It is submitted that the use of special 'applicability' rules in a directive is a technique which may create difficulties when implementing them into national law.

The analysis is concerned with 'applicability' rules only. The adoption of choice of laws rules in the strict sense, meaning a rule which designates a legal system as a

---

[*] Professor of Law, Université catholique de Louvain (Belgium).

[**] Junior Fellow, Fonds National de la Recherche Scientifique (Belgium).

[1] The question of the influence of Community law on private international law, on the double point of view of the compatibility of national rules with the free movement provisions of the EC Treaty and of the powers of the Community to enact civil law rules, is outside the scope of this study. Today, numerous articles cover the interaction between both Community law and the law of conflict of laws. See the references cited by M. Fallon, "Les conflits de lois et de juridictions dans un espace économique intégré – L'expérience des Communautés européennes", 253 *Recueil des cours* (1995) 9-

J. Basedow et al., eds., Private Law in the International Arena – Liber Amicorum Kurt Siehr
© 2000, T.M.C.Asser Press, The Hague, The Netherlands

whole[2] is not addressed. An applicability rule – in French a *règle particulière d'applicabilité* – aims only at defining the spatial scope of a set of substantive rules, the mandatory character of which requests them to be applied irrespective of the law designated by the choice of law rule. More precisely, following the functional approach of the so called *lois de police* (*lois d'application nécessaire, lois d'application immédiate*), such mandatory rules demand their application if the law normally applicable does not reach the substantive result they want to achieve. It is well known that internationally mandatory rules in the field of civil and commercial matters tend to offer a minimal protection to private parties. Thus they follow a substantive policy. Other internationally mandatory rules tend to promote the general good as well in the field of penal or public law. Article 7 of the Rome Convention of 19 June 1980 on the law applicable to contractual obligations is an attempt to give effect to both categories of rules. This contribution will only consider rules of the first type.

Community law nowadays offers a large set of mandatory rules in the field of civil and commercial matters. Most concern the law of contracts and intellectual property. Some affect the law of torts. The strongest efforts are focused on consumer protection. In addition, a large variety of techniques are used in practice to determine the international scope of uniform rules. For this reason, the ambit of this study will be limited to this set of Community acts.

The acts at stake are more frequently directives than regulations. In the field of consumer law, regulations were adopted only in relation to transport. Indeed, these acts were adopted on the basis of Article 84 ECT [now Article 80 EC], in the framework of a common policy submitted to the exclusive powers of the Community. This may explain why the Community did not want national implementation laws to intervene. Regulations were also adopted in the framework of the implementation of the internal market, in the field of intellectual property, in order to create a new legal institution in addition to national ones.[3] As it will be stated later, the

---

281, and more recently: P. von Wilmowsky, "EG-Vertrag und kollisionsrechtliche Rechts-wahlfreiheit", 62 *RabelsZ* (1998) 1-37. More scarcely, some papers focus on the question of the method of fixing the international applicability of secondary law. See for example: A. Bonomi, *Le norme imperative nel diritto internazionale privato* (Zürich, Schulthess 1998) at 120ff; S. Knöfel, "EC legislation on conflict of laws. Interactions and incompatibilities between conflicts rules", 47 *International and Comparative Law Quarterly* (1998) 439-445; J. Meeusen, "Directive 94/45 concernant les comités d'entreprise européens: aspects de droit international privé", in: *Comités d'entreprise européens* (M. Rigaux & F. Dorssemont (eds.)) (Antwerp, Intersentia 1999) 237-271; P.-C. Müller-Graf, "EC Directives as a Means of Private Law Unification", in: *Towards a European Civil Code* (Hartkamp et al (eds.)) 2nd edn. (Nijmegen, Ars Aequi 1998) 71-89.

2   The phenomenon of formally Community choice of law rules still appears to be marginal. See, in the field of insurance contracts, Directive 88/357 of 22 June 1988, *OJ(EC)* [1988] L 172/1, and Directive 90/619 of 8 November 1990, *OJ(EC)* [1990] L 330/50.

3   E.g., Regulation 40/94 of 20 December 1993 on the Community trade mark, *OJ(EC)* [1994] L 11/1.

choice of the type of act is important from the point of view of the international scope of uniform rules.

With regard to their content, these acts approximate internal substantive laws of the Member States on specific issues concerning a contractual relation. This means that the implementing legislation thereof tends to make itself a substitute for internal law, however for some aspects only. E.g., for distance contracts, Directive 97/7 of 20 May 1997[4] regulates the information due to the consumer before concluding the contract and gives a right of withdrawal, without considering other contractual issues. These acts normally do not contain choice of law rules, and the substantive rules are applicable to both international and internal situations. In this respect, they differ from, e.g., the Rome Convention on the one hand and the Vienna Convention of 11 April 1980 on the international sale of goods on the other. However, choice of law rules were adopted in the field of insurance contracts and, presumably, some directives on substantive law could contain isolated choice of law rules, as may be the case of the directive concerning cultural goods.[5]

The question arises whether such rules may be characterized as mandatory provisions, and whether their application depends on Article 7 of the Rome Convention.

The answer to the first question is affirmative, since the intention of the Community legislator is to fix a certain level of protection for the consumer in respect of two of his main policies, namely the free movement of goods and of services. In other words, since the regime of free movement allows the State to provide, to some extent, for the territorial application of protective rules in an indistinct way to national goods or services as well as to foreign ones, the Community is interested in securing equivalent levels of protection in the Member States in order to minimize a possible obstacle to trade. Thus, it is often because the national measures at stake are internationally mandatory that the Community enacts uniform private law rules.

Answering the second question is more difficult. Of course, implementing provisions, being part of national law, are covered by Article 7 of the Rome Convention – and by article 5 for consumer contracts as well – provided they are "mandatory" in the sense of these Articles. The question is rather whether the international applicability of such provisions relates to an autonomous process, independent of any recourse to the above mentioned Articles. Hypothetically, the answer could depend on the methods used by a directive to determine its scope of application.

In fact, these methods are diverse (Section 1) and some of them create difficult implementation problems (Section 2) so that a large debate should occur today

---

[4] *OJ(EC)* [1997] L 144/19.
[5] Directive 93/7 of 15 March 1993, *OJ(EC)* [1993] L 74/74, Art. 12 stating that "ownership of the cultural good after return shall be governed by the law of the requesting Member State".

about the choice of the most appropriate tools for the approximation of national private international laws (Section 3).

1.   WHICH METHODS TO DETERMINE THE INTERNATIONAL SCOPE OF COMMUNITY RULES?

The Community used, up to now, several methods in order to determine the international applicability of secondary substantive rules. Apparently, five methods were used. A single act may use several methods, or contain several applicability rules, depending on the content of the substantive rules at stake.[6]

1.1   No Applicability Rule?

The first generation of directives does not contain any applicability rule. This is the case for acts adopted in the eighties, e.g., Directive 85/374 on product liability of 25 July 1985.[7] It establishes a complete regime of product liability similar to the one provided for by national law.

According to this technique, the spatial scope of the concerned substantive rules is fixed by national private international law rules. Actually, the Community substantive rules, by means of the implementation process, are merely integrated into internal law. Thus, they become part of internal law and their own applicability depends on the applicability of internal law.

Practically speaking, when a French court has to deal with a product liability case, it will first of all determine which law is applicable, using the French choice of law rules. France ratified the Hague Convention of 5 October 1973. If a consumer, residing in France, was injured in the United States by a product acquired in Belgium and produced in the United States by an American firm, American law will be applicable under the Convention (Art. 4, b). However, if the product was produced in Belgium, Belgian law would apply (Art. 4, c). Belgian law encompasses the provisions adopted in order to implement the Directive.

This method does not create special problems from the point of view of private international law. But from the perspective of Community law, it leaves it to national law to determine the scope of Community rules. This means that in some Member States situations affecting the internal market could be governed by the law of a third State, or could escape the application of any implementing provision.[8] The

---

[6] For a comment in this sense of Directive 94/45 of 22 September 1994, *OJ(EC)* [1994] L 254/64, see J. Meeusen (supra n. 1).

[7] *OJ(EC)* [1985] L 210/29.

[8] This may be the case when the implementing law introduces a restrictive applicability rule not contained in the directive itself. See below, with respect to consumer credit.

question arises whether such a result would constitute an infringement of Community law in the sense of Article 226 EC [ex Article 169 ECT].

1.2 Rigid Applicability Rule?

Some directives contain a special provision fixing their international scope. This is the case in the field of travel contracts and timeshare.

Directive 90/314 of 13 June 1990 on package travel, package holidays and package tours[9] approximates the laws relating to "packages sold or offered for sale in the territory of the Community" (Art. 1). Directive 94/47 of 26 October 1994 on the protection of purchasers in respect of certain aspects of contracts relating to the purchase of the right to use immovable properties on a timeshare basis[10] obliges the Member States to "take the measures necessary to ensure that, whatever the law applicable may be, the purchaser is not deprived of the protection afforded by this Directive, if the immovable property concerned is situated within the territory of a Member State" (Art. 9).

In both cases, there is a special applicability rule determining which situations fall into the scope of the afforded protection. Both use a rigid connecting factor, of a territorial nature. In the case of package travel, the first factor apparently relates to the conclusion of the contract. It then adds another factor, relating to the terms under which the offer was made. Thus, the substantive rules may apply in two alternative cases, when the conclusion takes place on the territory of the Community or when an offer was made in the Community even though the conclusion occurred abroad. Such an alternative rule is well known in the theory of the *lois de police*: it guarantees an effective application of mandatory provisions in every case affecting the policy at stake.

In the case of timeshare, the Community legislator preferred a single factor, namely the location of the immovable, to one relating to the conclusion of the contract.

In doing so, the Community ensures a uniform scope of applicability to a minimal protection afforded to the consumer. Contrary to the former method, the international applicability of national implementation rules does not depend on the content of national choice of law rules. From the point of view of national law, the applicability rules of the above mentioned directives are supposed to play the same role as national applicability rules affecting internationally mandatory rules. From the point of view of Community law, it remains uncertain why both factors were chosen. From an internal market perspective, directives on the approximation of laws should cover – at least – the scope of the rules of primary law on the free move-

---

[9] *OJ(EC)* [1990] L 158/59.
[10] *OJ(EC)* [1994] L 280/83.

ment, which means, in the field of services, an application to every provider established in a Member State. The scope of the Timeshare Directive, it is submitted, does not correspond to the scope of the EC treaty. It could be that a timeshare contract concluded between a Belgian consumer and a German undertaking regarding an immovable located in Switzerland, falls under the EC Treaty but not under the Directive. Conversely, a contract concluded with respect to an immovable located in Spain between a US firm and a US consumer – or even a Belgian consumer – would fall within the scope of the Directive but not of the EC Treaty.

The implementation of this method does not raise, as will be seen, any special difficulty other than the reference to "the territory of the Community". The relation between national implementation rules and the Rome Convention of 19 June 1980 might as well turn out to be tricky.

1.3   The "Close Connection" Test versus Party Autonomy?

Since 1993, the use of the "close connection" test seems to have become a landmark in the field of consumer law. This method has been inaugurated in Directive 13/93 of 5 April 1993 on unfair terms in consumer contracts.[11] Under Article 6, paragraph 1 of which proclaims the mandatory character of the substantive rules by providing that an unfair term shall not be binding on the consumer, the State is obliged to take the necessary measures "to ensure that the consumer does not lose the protection granted by this Directive by virtue of the choice of the law of a non-Member country as the law applicable to the contract if the latter has a close connection with the territory of the Member States" (Art. 6, para. 2). The same provision was adopted in Directive 7/97 of 20 May 1997 on the protection of consumers in respect of distance contracts[12] (Art. 12, para. 2). This text states that the close connection should exist "with the territory of one or more Member States". The same concept is used in Directive 44/1999 of 25 May 1999 on certain aspects of the sale of consumer goods and associated guarantees[13] (Art. 7, para. 2).

Surprisingly, the above cited provisions only cover the case where the parties chose the law of a third State to be the applicable law. In other words, the rule does not cover the case where no choice was made by the parties. Which rule is then to be applied by the court in the latter case? Apparently, it will have to use national conflicts rules of the forum. The reason for such a limitation on the parties' autonomy is unclear, at least for directives not restricted to the issue of unfair terms.

A comparison between acts concerning sales methods shows an evolution. Indeed, Directive 85/577 of 20 December 1985 protecting the consumer in respect

---

[11] *OJ(EC)* [1993] L 95/29.
[12] *OJ(EC)* [1997] L 144/19.
[13] *OJ(EC)* [1999] L 171/12.

of contracts negotiated away from business premises[14] does not contain any applicability rule at all, so that this act belongs to the first generation. It is difficult to say why the Community decided to add an applicability rule in 1993. The reason could be found in the entry into force in 1991 of the Rome Convention of 19 June 1980. This event seems, at first sight, to have brought about the major contextual difference between the eighties and the nineties. If this is true, the introduction of special applicability rules would be the reaction to the provisions of the Convention. As will be seen in Section 2, the latter contains special provisions on the law applicable to consumer protection.

The method of the close connection test not only creates problems regarding the reference to "the territory of Member States". As the implementing laws demonstrate, it has also provoked a serious misunderstanding concerning the term "close connection". This will be further explained in Section 2.

1.4 Towards a Close Connection Test plus a Rigid Rule?

A fourth method was used by a draft Directive concerning the distance marketing of consumer financial services.[15] Under Article 11, paragraph 3, "[c]onsumers may not be deprived of the protection granted by this Directive where the law governing the contract is that of a third country if the consumer is resident on the territory of a Member State and the contract has a close link with the Community".

This rule combines the second and the third methods, by using a rule of a conditional character. Two conditions have to be fulfilled for the material provisions to be applied. Not only must the contract have a "close connection" with the Community, but furthermore the consumer must reside in the Community. In other words, the draft Directive seems to favor the method of a rigid rule, but expresses the view that the residence of the consumer does not provide sufficient connection.[16] Compared with the second method, the policy is far more restrictive for the consumer, since the Package Travel Directive applied as soon as one of some connecting factors has been met, whether the offer was made within or outside the Community.

Another difference from the third method results from the hypothesis underlying the rule. The third method covers only one option concerning the choice of law made by the parties, whereas the fourth method extends to every case involving a choice of law. In fact, limiting the hypothesis to a choice by the parties only makes sense in the context of unfair terms, since the choice itself may be considered an unfair term. This consideration is not at issue does not apply in the other directives

---

[14] *OJ(EC)* [1985] L 372/31.
[15] *OJ(EC)* [1998] C 385/10.
[16] This could be in response to some interpretations of the "close connection" concept: see section 2.2 below.

concerning distance contracts and guarantees.

One could wonder whether the fourth method used for financial services is coherent from the point of view of a distance selling policy, once the Community has enacted a different provision for the general directive on distance selling. It is unclear why financial services should be governed by an applicability rule different from the one prevailing for other distance contracts. In other words, the content of applicability rules should be consistent in all directives.

The draft Directive on financial services raises yet another problem concerning the issue of international applicability. The above cited provision concerns mandatory rules contained in the national implementing law, but the Directive itself seems to contain its own applicability rule, since its Article 2, concerning definitions, refers to "institutions" covered by several directives on access to the internal market – such institutions being presumably understood as those covered by Article 49 EC [ex Art. 59 ECT] – and defines the consumer as "any natural person resident in the territory of the Community". Thus, the act apparently concerns only parties established in the Community, while the applicability rule of the mandatory provisions seems to concern a consumer resident in the Community even if the other party is established outside the Community. Furthermore, while the Directive seems to apply once the parties are established in the Community, the provision on mandatory rules still requires a "close link" with the Community.

One may submit that inserting two sets of applicability rules in a directive – one for the act itself and the other for the national implementing rules – is not an appropriate technique since it creates a risk of provisions which are either redundant or contradictory. Thus the two provisions can only be read as a single but cumulative applicability rule to be adopted by the implementing law. The amended proposal for a Directive on financial services fortunately simplifies the definition of the "institutions" and the "consumer" affected by the Directive, keeping only Article 11, paragraph 3 as an applicability rule.[17]

1.5   **Back to the Past?**

Eventually, the Community has tried another way, which is a step back towards the first method. The Directive on certain aspects of electronic commerce in the internal market[18] establishes principles of access to the market, liability of professional persons and some issues concerning the contract (admissibility, information to the consumer prior to the conclusion, moment of the conclusion). It specifies that it "does not establish additional rules on private international law"

---

[17] COM 385 (1999) final (23 July 1999).

[18] Several versions of the draft were elaborated, namely a proposal published in the *OJ(EC)* [1999] C 30, an amended proposal of September 1999, COM 427 (1999) final, and a common position of 28 February 2000 (*OJ(EC)*) [2000] C 128/32). Directive no. 2000/31 was adopted on 8 June 2000 (OJ(EC) [2000] L 178).

(Art. 1, para. 4). Furthermore, each Member State has to ensure that "the information society services provided by a service provider established on its territory comply with the national provisions applicable in the Member State" (Art. 3, para. 1). This duty covers the provisions concerning access to the market, torts as well as contractual obligations[19]. Nevertheless, the provision enacting this duty (Art. 3) does not apply, among others, to "contractual obligations concerning consumer contracts" (Annex to the Directive).

That part of Article 3 referring to the national provisions applicable in the State of establishment, uses a single rigid factor, pertaining to the territory of the implementing State. Two observations may be made. Firstly, the territory referred to is not that of the Community but rather that of a given State. Thus, the reference to an area points to a national area, not to a Community area. In fact, this feature is common to other directives concerning the field of the information society, so that one may assume that the difference could be attributed to the Commission Directorate which prepared the text. Secondly, the factor chosen corresponds to the factor used by the primary law in order to fix the scope of the free movement regime: it is the freedom to provide services for the undertaking which is at stake,[20] and, indeed, as to its content, the Directive aims at protecting the provider rather than the consumer as to liability. Furthermore, by submitting the provider to the law of his place of establishment, the Directive tends to imply that only the law of origin has to be applied, without any exception made for the protection of the consumer: this is clearly meant by para. 2 of Article 3, stating that "[m]ember States may not, for reasons falling within this Directive's coordinated field, restrict the freedom to provide information society services from another Member State". This "internal market clause" may be seen as a strict formulation of the Community mutual recognition principle.

In any case, the provision, being an applicability rule, contains a rule of private international law, notwithstanding the terms of Article 1, para. 4, of the Directive. Thus, this part of Article 3 of the Directive does not amount to a step backward.

This Directive is also interesting from the point of view of applicability methods,

---

[19] The now outdated version of September 2000 added that this duty would cover contracts "only in so far as the law of the Member State applies by virtue of its rules of private international law". This provision means that, in an individual case, the court would have to apply its national choice of law rules – the 1980 Rome Convention rules – : hence, the law of the implementing State, when applicable by virtue of the choice of law rule of the forum, would be applied only if the service provider is established in that state. Such limitation may be seen as a cumulative applicability rule requiring, for a law to be applied, two connecting elements. One is provided for by the multilateral choice of law rule of the forum and the other can be found in the directive itself (Art. 3, para. 1, i.e., the place of establishment of the provider). This second element is of a unilateral nature as it must be located on the forum's territory.
[20] Thus, the Directive uses Articles 47 EC [ex Art. 57 ECT] and 55 EC [ex Art. 66 ECT], along with the general provisions of Article 95 EC [ex Art. 100a ECT] as a legal basis.

as far as consumer contracts are concerned. By excluding these contracts from the scope of Article 3, paragraph 1, it means that, in this subject matter, determining the spatial scope of application of the mandatory rules at stake is left entirely to the private international law rules of the forum. In other words, Article 5 of the 1980 Rome Convention is still to be used and may designate the law of a third State, even if the service provider is established in the Community.

This method of leaving it to the national conflict rules to determine the law applicable to consumer contracts, is similar to the one described above as the first method used in the past. Still, it seems somewhat questionable in regard of both the inner coherence of the Directive and the consumer policy of the Community in general, as the Community has been using the previous methods in this field.

As far as consumer policy is concerned, the Directive ends up establishing two distinct sets of conflict rules. The first one covers electronic consumer contracts, which fall within the scope of the Directive as to substance. The applicable law however is chosen according to Article 5 of the Rome Convention, which only protects the passive consumer. The second set of conflict rules covers all non electronic consumer contracts. These may fall within the scope of the distance contracts Directive which contains its own applicability rules. The existence of a dual regime of conflict of laws appears contradictory since electronic consumer contracts are often distance contracts.

As far as the inner coherence of the Directive is concerned, it leaves it to the States to choose the applicable law by means of their own conflict rules. The States are likely to designate the law of the consumer (Article 5 of the Rome Convention). However, from the perspective of the establishment of the internal market, the so-called "internal market clause" (see Article 3, paragraph 2 of the Directive) forbids States to restrict the freedom to provide services on issues falling within the Directive's coordinated field – i.e., issues on information requirement, commercial communications, conclusion of the contract and liability of intermediaries – which might imply the obligation to apply the law of the provider's place of establishment. Indeed, under the regime of free movement established by the EC Treaty itself,[21] the host State has a duty of so called "mutual recognition" of the laws of other Member States, when equivalent. The law of the State of origin of a product or service does not have to be identical, but merely equivalent, in law or in fact, and this equivalence might result from a directive approximating Member States' laws. Hence, a national rule purporting to regulate a foreign product or service, when this product or service already complies with the law of its country of origin which is equivalent to the law of the host country, would be a forbidden obstacle to trade.[22]

---

[21] In general, see M. Fallon, *Droit matériel général des Communautés européennes* (Louvain-la-Neuve, Paris, Academia-Bruylant, LGDJ 1997) pp. 135 and 166-167.

[22] The Directive itself allows major derogations from the internal market clause provided that the national measure is necessary for one of the reasons pertaining to the general good cited by the text and

2.   WHICH IMPLEMENTATION FORMULA FOR APPLICABILITY RULES?

It is well known that directives are not applicable as such to individual cases. They have to be implemented by the State, so that national rules are applied by the court. This feature of the directives is significant in private international law, at least as far as the substantive rules at stake fix their international scope directly.

The implementation of several directives in the field of consumer protection led to difficulties related to private international law. An example of these can be found in the disparity of national laws resulting from the implementation of the landmark 93/13 Directive concerning unfair terms.[23]

2.1   Reference to the Territory of the Community?

When referring to the territory of the Community – or to the territory of "a" Member State as well – a directive makes it almost impossible for the State to implement it correctly.

Of course, such reference makes sense from the perspective of Community law. After all, a directive is a norm of an autonomous legal system and, like every legal system, Community law has to fix its own spatial scope. Thus, it seems normal for a directive to determine its scope by means of a reference to the frontiers of its own legal system. The method is not different from the one used by a national internationally mandatory rule or *loi de police*. When fixing its international scope by means of a special applicability rule, it could not do otherwise than fix its scope unilaterally by a reference to the frontiers of the State enacting the rule.

In fact, as long as a directive is not deemed to be applied formally but to be implemented into national law, the "applicability rule" provided for by a directive should only concern the application of the national rule of law. Therefore referring in a directive to the territory of the Community is presumptuous. The method used by the Directive on electronic commerce referring to the territory of one, discrete State is easier to implement. Indeed, when considering the implementation of several directives referring to the territory of the Community or of a Member State, the

---

is proportionate to the achievement of this objective (see Art. 3, para. 4), but the effect of this provision seems to be limited to a "safeguard clause" in the sense of Art. 95, para. 10 EC, permitting provisional measures in individual emergency cases. The link between the internal market clause and the application of the law of the service provider's place of establishment appears quite clearly in Article 4 of Directive 93/1999 of 13 December 1999 on electronic signatures (*OJ(EC)* [2000] L 13/12). The meaning of the obligation to apply the law of origin still deserves further developments in the light of the EC Treaty.

[23] See M. Fallon, "La loi applicable aux clauses abusives après la transposition de la directive n° 93/13", *Rev. eur. dr. cons.* (1996) 3-27; P. de Vareilles-Sommières, "Un droit international privé européen?" in: de Vareilles-Sommières (ed.), *Le droit privé européen* (Paris, Economica 1998) 136-147.

common trend is to refer to the territory of the implementing State itself.

This may lead to implementations focused on the applicability of the law of the forum, no account being taken of the law of other Member States. This tendency may materialize in various ways.

A first trend is to cover exclusively situations connected to the forum, so that the implementation says nothing about cases affecting other Member States. It then leaves open the question whether the applicability rule inserted into the implementation law may be used in a multilateral way or whether the court has to examine the general conflict of laws rules of the forum. This method of implementation must be considered as unsatisfactory because of its partial character, which could even justify an action against the State before the Court of Justice. Thus, the German law[24] implementing the Unfair Terms Directive provides for the application of German law when the case has a close connection with Germany, without saying anything about cases having a close connection with France. It must be added that the same phenomenon occurred with the implementation of a real choice of law rule, in the field of insurance contracts. This rule was also formulated in a unilateral way, so that the implementing State could consider, at first sight, that it was sufficient to translate it in a unilateral way into national law.[25]

Another trend is to extend significantly the application of the forum's law. Indeed, some implementation laws typically state that, once the situation has a close connection with "a" Member State, they will apply. For example, the German law[26] implementing the Timeshare Directive states that it applies when the immovable is located on the territory of a Member State: a German court will apply German law to a contract between a Belgian consumer and a French undertaking about an immovable located in Spain. The French implementation[27] seems more elegant, since it states that the applicable law is the law of the place of the immovable, while French law is applied on a subsidiary basis, only in the absence of implementation provisions in the law of the foreign State.

The French method used for timeshare contracts suggests that a correct implementation of a unilateral applicability rule consists in building up a real choice of law rule, designating the law applicable to the case on a neutral basis, be it the national law or a foreign law. Furthermore, such rules should designate the law of a Member State only, not the law of a third State. In other words, Community applicability rules pave the way to an "intra-Community choice of law system", somewhat like the "interstate choice of law" rules in the United States. Such a rule uses a

[24] Law of 19 July 1996, BGBl. 1996, I, 1013.
[25] This has been the case, for example, in Belgium (arrêté royal of 22 February 1991, *Moniteur*, 11 April 1991, later corrected into a multilateral rule by the arrêté royal of 8 January 1993, *Moniteur*, 9 February 1993).
[26] Law of 20 December 1996, BGBl. 1996 I, p. 2154.
[27] Law n° 98-566 of 8 July 1998, JO(RF) 9 July 1998, p. 10486.

condition pertaining to the subject matter of the choice of law rule, by designating the law of a Member State or being applied only to a case connected with a Member State. It also requires a subsidiary rule providing for the choice of the law for all cases not covered by the special rule. Compared with the United States, such a distinction, it is true, appears to be rather formal, but it is uncertain whether it requires, as to its content, two distinct sets of rules. The United States' experience shows that the distinction between international and interstate conflict rules does not necessarily require the existence of two really distinct sets of rules and it may suffice to have the distinction drawn in a formal way.

In order to facilitate uniform implementation, it would perhaps be more appropriate to formulate multilateral rules in the directive itself. Thus, in the case of the Timeshare Directive, the rule could have provided as follows: "[t]he consumer may not be deprived of the protection afforded to him by the law of that Member State on the territory of which the immovable is located".

2.2   Reference to a Close Connection?

The third and fourth methods quoted in Section 1 determine the applicability of the substantive protection rules by means of a "close connection" test. At first sight, this method does not seem to create any problem of interpretation. Indeed, as the practice in national law suggests, the concept corresponds to a flexible approach rather than to a rigid rule, leaving it to the court itself to appreciate with which State the case is most closely connected after having taken all circumstances in to account. By nature, the concept cannot be reduced to a fixed localization criterion. Admittedly, it would be difficult to reach predictability of the results thus obtained. However, it is conceivable that such a rule could be combined with the advantages of a rigid rule, as the Rome Convention suggests, by accompanying the close connection test with a presumption in favor of the habitual residence of the debtor having to effect the characteristic performance.

The central question raised by the directives at stake concerns the intention of the authors of the close connection provision.

Under one interpretation, it could be assumed that the provision leaves it to the implementing State to determine the concept by means of a rigid rule. Such interpretation reflects the nature of a directive, for it binds only as to the result to be achieved and leaves it to the Member States to choose the best way for achieving it. Thus, regarding the Unfair Terms Directive, the "close connection" term was translated as meaning, in France, a reference to the residence of the consumer, provided that either an offer was made in that State, or the contract was concluded or performed in that State. The residence alone is not considered sufficient to form a "close connection". Such a connection is rather established by using any element leading to the conclusion of the contract. In Germany, the rule refers also to connecting factors concerning the residence of the consumer and elements of the contract, but such elements are understood in a stricter way, covering only an offer or an advertisement: it is well-known that such a scheme is copied from Article 5 of the Rome Convention. The difference is that the German law seems to consider the factors used as an indication of a close connection, without excluding the possibility for the court to refer to other circumstances of the case.[28] The French implementation provides only a rigid rule. It is inspired by the Rome Convention without copying it: the French applicability rule is less restrictive than Article 5, for it ensures the protection of the consumer as soon as any element of the contract – offer, conclusion or performance alternatively – is located in the State of the consumer, without requiring that the consumer accepts in that State an offer made in that State.

The German implementation fundamentally expresses the view that the "close connection" exists when the law applicable to the case by virtue of the choice of law rule of the forum is the law of a Member State.[29] This result is reached in the case of the Unfair Terms Directive by using the same rule as the one governing consumer contracts by virtue of the Rome Convention. Other implementation laws reached the same result in another way, by enacting simply that the protection is due when the law applicable to the contract would be the law of a country which is a Member of the European Economic Area. This Nordic model[30] was followed by Belgium.[31]

Under an alternative interpretation, the "close connection" provision can be understood as a provision having direct effect, intended to be applied by the court in an individual case, leaving it to the court itself – and not to the implementation law – to appreciate the appropriate connection, taking into consideration the circumstances of the case. This method prevailed in the framework of the Unfair Terms Directive, in the United Kingdom,[32] in Italy,[33] and in Portugal.[34] It may be argued that, presumably, it corresponds to the real intention of the authors of the Community provision. Indeed, the "close connection" provision obviously uses the same terms as Article 7 of the Rome Convention. It is worth noting that the terms refer, in both cases, to "a" close connection. By contrast, the close connection test used by Article 4 of the Rome Convention uses the terms "most closely connected". In other words, while Article 4 is constructed as a choice of law rule, able to designate "the" law applicable to the case, Article 7 only provides a condition to give effect to "a" national

---

[28] Indeed, the text reads as follows: "Ein enger Zusammenhang ist insbesondere anzunehmen, wenn (…)".

[29] In this sense more generally, see E. Jayme and Ch. Kohler, "L'interaction des règles de conflit contenues dans le droit dérivé de la Communauté européenne et des conventions de Bruxelles et de Rome", 84 *Rev. crit. dr. int. pr.* (1995) 1-40.

[30] Swedish law n° 1512 of 15 December 1994, § 13; Danish law n° 1098 of 21 December 1994, § 38d.

[31] Law of 7 December 1998 (*Moniteur*, 23 December 1998), Art. 4, § 2.

[32] Unfair Terms in Consumer Contracts Regulations 1994, Section 7.

[33] Law n° 52 of 6 February 1996 (*Gazz. Uffic.*, 10 February 1996), Art. 25.

[34] Law n° 220/95 of 31 January 1995 (*Diario da Republica*, 31 August 1995).

mandatory set of rules. Two remarks must be made in this respect. First, Article 7 does not replace a choice of law rule. It only adds a possibility to consider other substantive rules than the ones contained in the law otherwise applicable. Thus, it does not eliminate the necessity for the forum to maintain a choice of law rule, this rule being for instance Article 5 of the Rome Convention. Secondly, the "close connection" test of Article 7 is not sufficient to designate the substantive mandatory rules at stake. Another condition is that those rules must be applied "under the law of the latter country". This means that the court has to consider any applicability rule contained in the law the application of which is at stake.

Transposed to the Community directives under discussion, this reasoning leads to the conclusion that an interpretation of the "close connection" in the light of Article 7 of the Rome Convention gives an *effet utile* to the special applicability rule. If the intention had been to refer only to cases where the law of a Member State was applicable to the contract, the insertion of such a rule would have been redundant. A waiver of the choice of law made by the parties, intervening whenever the law of a Member State is applicable to the contract in the absence of a choice made by the parties, would have been sufficient. On the contrary, rather than reflect the strict provisions of the Rome Convention relating to consumer contracts, the intention has probably been to counter them. Thus, the directives improve the protection provided by the Rome Convention by adding to the case of doorstep selling – which constitutes the core of Article 5 of the Rome Convention – the protection of a more active consumer as well.

In any case, Community directives in the field of contractual obligations cannot and should not be understood without taking into account the basic provisions of the Rome Convention.

2.3 Which Constraints about Minimum Protection Rules?

The need for a Member State to reconcile secondary Community law with the Rome Convention is also apparent in the "minimum protection" concept. It will be shown that this perspective could necessitate the review of the policy underlying the content of both sets of rules.

In the field of consumer law, the approximation of laws tends to provide a common minimum protection for the consumer, without prejudice to more protective national rules. This concept raises some questions, concerning the scope of the international application of national mandatory provisions.

A first question is whether the implementing State may extend the protection of a directive to cases falling outside the international applicability thereof. For instance, when the Timeshare Directive provides that the protection is due when the immovable is located in the Community, does it exclude the possibility that a national timeshare law would extend to consumer contracts concerning immovables located outside the Community? French law made an attempt in such direction, by covering a consumer residing in a Member State under circumstances similar to the ones covered by Article 5 of the Rome Convention. By doing so, France considered that "timeshare contracts" were outside the scope of Article 5, and therefore it was necessary to enact a special provision to ensure similar protection. This mode of legislating raises some difficulties. As an international treaty, the Rome Convention prevails over national law, when such law goes beyond what is necessary for the implementation of Community law.[35] Thus, one has to ascertain whether the Rome Convention permits the enactment by a State of special applicability rules distinct from the uniform choice of law rules. If timeshare contracts are outside the scope of Article 5, and therefore fall within the scope of the general provisions of Article 3 and Article 4, paragraph 3 (presumption in favor of the law of the place of the immovable), contracting States still have the choice of introducing *lois de police* in the sense of Article 7. The national applicability rule could then appear as a way of defining a proper "close connection" in the sense of paragraph 1. On the contrary, if timeshare contracts are covered, as it appears to be,[36] by Article 5, the possibility of enacting diverging applicability rules on the basis of Article 7 runs the risk of depriving Article 5 of any *effet utile*. Actually, the interaction of Articles 5 and 7 still remains controversial.

A second question concerns the choice left to the national legislator to enact a special applicability rule where the directive has not done so, and to interpret the intention of the Community legislator regarding situations not covered by the directive.[37] For instance, in the field of consumer credit, a directive[38] was enacted without providing any applicability rule, so that, as was stated in Section 1 (under method one), the Community legislator seems to have left it to the Member States to decide the applicability of the protection rules. The Belgian legislator provided for the protection of consumers placed under circumstances similar to those covered by Article 5 of the Rome Convention (the passive consumer), adding the case where both parties reside in Belgium. What about a credit contract between a Belgian bank and a Luxembourg consumer when the consumer is not a passive one? On first impression, the Belgian special protective rules should not apply. A Belgian court, applying Article 4 of the Rome Convention, would designate the application of the law of the bank, the latter being the debtor having to effect the characteristic performance. The case falling outside the scope of the law of 12 June 1991, only the general provisions of Belgian law on contracts should apply. Another interpretation

---

[35] Indeed, insofar as national law provisions implement Community law they take precedence over the Rome Convention (Art. 20).

[36] Indeed, these contracts contain a complex set of services accompanying the mere use of an immovable. In this sense concerning the interpretation of Directive 85/577 see Court of Justice, case C-423/97 *Travel Vac.* v. *Antelm Sanchis* [1999] ECR I-2195 (22 April 1999).

[37] On this issue see A. Bonomi (supra n. 1) at p. 125.

[38] Directive 87/102 of 22 December 1986, *OJ(EC)* [1987] L 42/48.

could be that the intention of the legislator was to cover a "minimal scope" only, without excluding other cases *per se*. Thus Belgian law should apply as a whole by virtue of the multilateral choice of law rule. Still, such a result would be surprising, because the applicability rule reproduces – partly at least – Article 5 of the Rome Convention, and in the case at issue this Convention does not foresee that protection be afforded to the consumer. But it is also right to state that, if the Belgian mandatory rules are not applied in that case, the consumer will not benefit from any national law implementing the Directive, a result which would be contrary to Community law.[39] In other words, any Community directive should be considered as containing an implicit applicability rule, extending the scope of the substantive rules, at least, to every situation coming within the scope of the EC Treaty provisions on free movement. Such conclusion, admittedly, is irreconcilable with a submission that a directive containing substantive rules of private law should not contain specific applicability rules, leaving it to choice of law rules to determine which law is to be applied.

These questions suggest not only that using a special applicability rule in a national statute implementing a Community directive could be a dangerous process in respect of Community law, but also that the way of ascertaining the content of applicability rules proper to determine the scope of the protection in relation to the "European Area" is a hard task. In the near future more attention should be paid to two elements: on the one hand, the way the EC Treaty defines the limits of its provisions on free movement, and, on the other hand, the discrepancies between the Rome Convention and secondary law revealing the need for some revision of the former.

3. WHICH TOOLS FOR THE ENACTMENT OF PRIVATE COMMUNITY LAW?

The experience of secondary Community law in the field of conflict of laws is not yet really conclusive. Until now, only unilateral rules were used, mainly in the sense of a specific applicability rule. In one case, for insurance contracts, the Community used a choice of law technique while limiting the scope of the conflict rules to intra-Community cases. By contrast, the Rome Convention, which is linked with the European Union and anticipated an intergovernmental co-operation in civil matters in the sense of Article K of the EU Treaty *avant la lettre*, contains a set of rules of a classical type. These are "savignyan" multilateral – i.e. of a universal character in the sense of Article 2 of this Convention – choice of law rules.

---

[39] Answer of the Commission to question n° 1562/97 of 6 May 1997, concerning consumer credit – protection of non-residents by Belgian legislation, *OJ(EC)* [1997] C 391/98; *Riv. dir. int. pr. proc.* (1998) 1003.

There have been difficulties not only with respect to the technique of implementation of the Community conflicts provisions into national law, but also with respect to the content of these provisions once read in the light of the Rome Convention. Questions arise regarding the interpretation as well as the appropriateness of some connecting factors in regard of both the effectiveness of the protection policy at stake and the proper delimitation of the scope of application of primary law on free movement of goods and services. Yet another question arises concerning the influence of the latter on the content of the choice of law rules: does it imply a preference for the application of the law of origin or of the law of the State where the product or the service is furnished?

Presumably, an answer to the latter question would facilitate answers to the others. In the meantime, some observations may be made regarding the techniques available to the Community, with special regard paid to the new provisions introduced by the Treaty of Amsterdam.

3.1   New Community Enacting Powers?

Upon the entry into force of the Treaty of Amsterdam the Community received new powers in the field of private international law. Within a period of five years starting in May 1999, the Council is to take measures in order to ensure free movement of persons in the sense of Article 14 EC [ex Art. 7a ECT], in the field of judicial co-operation in civil and commercial matters (Art. 61). These measures tend, among others, to promote "the compatibility of the rules applicable in the Member States concerning the conflict of laws and of jurisdiction" (Art. 65, b). Whatever the precise meaning of this provision might be, namely the significance of the term "compatibility" and of the reference to the issue of the movement of persons,[40] it is the first time the Community is given express powers in the field of conflicts of laws. As a matter of fact, in the past, other provisions already provided such a legal basis. These are still in force. Thus, the general provisions of Articles 94 EC [ex Art. 100 ECT] and 95 EC [ex Art. 100a ECT] provide for the approximation of laws affecting the establishment or the functioning of the internal market. In this respect, as long as a provision of civil or commercial law is likely to create an obstacle to intra-Community trade, as some judgements of the Court of Justice already show,[41]

---

[40] On this issue, see Ch. Kohler, "Interrogations sur les sources du droit international privé européen après le traité d'Amsterdam", *Rev. crit. dr. int. pr.* (1999) 1-30.

[41] *Per se*, the disparity of national legislations in the field of private law may create an obstacle to free movement, since the definition of an obstacle to trade does not depend on the nature – private, penal, public – of the rule of law at stake. This was stated by the Court of justice, mainly, about the law of civil procedure, namely the *cautio judicatum solvi* (e.g. case C-20/92 *Hubbard* v. *Hamburger* [1993] ECR I-3777), the law of guarantees in sale contracts (case C-339/89 *Alsthom Atlantique* v. Sulzer [1991] ECR I-107) or the law applicable to employment contracts (case C-214/94 *Boukhalfa* v. *Germany* [1996] ECR I-2253).

the adoption of a directive or a regulation is allowed. On this basis, the Community enacted a directive on product liability.[42] As stated earlier in this contribution, some of these acts already contain international applicability rules. Another special legal basis is embodied in Article 47 EC [ex Art. 57 ECT] concerning services and was used in the sector of insurance contracts to justify the adoption of choice of law rules. However, this early practice concerns rules of private international law incidental to the approximation of substantive rules. This is the case, not only regarding special applicability rules *per se*, but also for the choice of law rules in the field of insurance contracts. Indeed, these latter rules constitute only one aspect of a service provider's access to the market, together with other provisions organizing the granting of a license and the administrative control of undertakings. In any case, the power to enact independent choice of law rules does exist, if one accepts that, either the principle of subsidiarity requires to limit as far as possible any infringement of national identity and therefore supports the approximation of choice of law rules rather than of substantive rules, or, that a conflict rule, as such, is able to create an obstacle to interstate trade.[43]

Thus, there is room for a "private Community law", which could be created by means of directives or regulations. Furthermore, the Community will be tempted to use its new powers in order to accelerate the process. Thus, in the field of conflicts of jurisdictions, a revision of the Brussels Convention of 27 September 1968 is contemplated which could lead to a regulation instead of a new Convention. The same could occur regarding the law applicable to non contractual obligations. Eventually, if the planned revision of the Rome Convention of 19 June 1980[44] ever takes place, the new provisions would be adopted by a Community act.

3.2 Regulation versus Directive

The question then arises whether the Community should adopt regulations instead of directives, and choice of law rules instead of substantive rules combined with applicability rules. The experience of international consumer contracts, at least, gives some guidance.

Initially, one may assume that the answers would differ depending on whether

---

[42] Supra n. 7.

[43] As far as we know, the Court of Justice had the opportunity to deal explicitly with this problem in one case only, concerning the free movement of persons. See the *Boukhalfa* judgment (supra n. 41). Cf. case C-35/97 *Commission* v. *France* [1998] ECR I-5325, criticizing an applicability rule limiting the benefit of a social advantage to workers residing in France; case C-336/96 *Gilly* v. *Directeur des Services Fiscaux* [1998] ECR I-2793, admitting as a commonly accepted rule the use of nationality as a connecting factor in the field of tax law, and determining that, in the subject matter at stake, the obstacle to free movement was not due to the choice of the connecting factor itself but to the content of the applicable substantive tax law.

[44] Action Plan of the Council and the Commission of 3 Dec. 1998, *OJ(EC)* [1999] C. 19/1.

one adopts the point of view of the Community or that of the Member State. On the one hand, a regulation containing uniform substantive rules covering a legal field as a whole is more efficient from the point of view of Community law. On the other hand, Member States favor the tool of the directive, especially in the field of civil law.[45]

Indeed, regulations have direct applicability; they enter into force at the date fixed by their publication in the Official Journal, and apply directly to cases brought by individuals. Furthermore, the approximation of substantive law creates a legal area corresponding to the economic area of the internal market where undertakings may compete under common conditions.

Where the Community legislator aims at the coherence of the community legal order, each Member State is responsible for the coherence of its own legal system. The method of the directive was enhanced by the authors of the Treaty as a subtle tool allowing the States to achieve this goal. At their origin, directives are similar to classical conventions since they must be introduced formally into the national legal systems after being adopted unanimously, yet they are original because they are open to adaptation to the peculiarities of national law. In a perhaps paradoxical way, this may be seen as a feature of the approximation of laws in an integrated area: treaties often add new rules to the national ones, superimposing uniform rules for international cases on the national legal system without affecting the national rules applicable to internal cases.[46] By doing so, treaties build up a "super law" and exacerbate the gap between national and uniform law. On the contrary, the directive, by its content, tends to reduce or eliminate legal discrepancies between internal and international – intra-Community – cases. Not only does the directive allow the State to insert smoothly external rules and preserve the coherence – substantial as well as formal – of its legal system. It also tends to create rules which are common to international and internal cases.

In this sense, a directive is superior to a regulation. The latter is quite revolutionary as far as the method of approximation is concerned. Indeed, once adopted, nowadays maybe by a majority vote, it assumes a life of its own: from a formal point of view, a regulation contains merely Community rules and must be applied without recourse to national law other than the intervention of the court. In other words, a regulation may appear to be external to the national system, far more so than a treaty.

These considerations could play a role in the approximation process of private international law. We do not consider, in the context of this report, the appropriate-

---

[45] Interestingly enough, after the principle of subsidiarity was introduced in Art. 5 EC [ex Art. 3b ECT], the Commission (*Rev. trim. dr. eur.* (1997) 728, at 738) was of the opinion that, when there is a choice of adopting a directive or a regulation (e.g. Art. 95 EC referring to "measures", which covers any type of act), the technique of the directive should be preferred for its compatibility with this principle.

[46] E.g., treaties concerning transport and sale.

ness of a unification of substantive law rather than that of rules on the conflict of laws.

3.3 Regulations for the Approximation of Private Law?

First of all, attention must be paid to the fact that the legal field under consideration pertains to private law rather than economic law. The Community experience with the approximation of legislations largely concerns economic law, i.e. provisions of a rather regulatory character on the access to the market and the exercise of a professional activity, as well as regarding the composition and presentation of a product: such aspects of the legal treatment of social activities are traditionally covered in Member States by sectorial regulations, enacted product by product, service by service. By contrast, private law – be it substantive or conflict of laws rules – is traditionally part of a large set of concepts, general principles, built up along decades through precedents or comprehensive codification.

Thus, it appears that a directive should be preferred to a regulation as a method of approximation of private law, especially when the covered field is a narrow one. Of course, from a purely formal point of view, the enactment of Community rules covering the substantive law of contracts as a whole, or conflict of laws in civil matters as a whole, by way of a regulation, should be acceptable for Continental Member States at least. A regulation is also acceptable as far as it covers intra-Community situations, excluding purely internal situations. For the internal situations, national law should remain unaffected. For example, a regulation rather than a directive was appropriate in order to establish a Community trademark regime,[47] distinct from national trademarks.

Transposing this reasoning to private international law implies that a regulation is proper to enact, for example, common rules on jurisdiction and the enforcement of judgments similar to the Brussels Convention. Indeed such provisions supplement corresponding national rules without replacing them. They are applicable to "Community litigations" only, i. e. when – roughly speaking – the defendant is domiciled in a Member State or when the judgment was pronounced in a Member State. Thus, the conflict of laws rules can be enacted by regulations as long as their scope is limited to "Community cases".

The same could be said for the approximation of substantive rules in a narrow field when the scope thereof is limited to the territory of the Community by means of a special applicability rule, at least where the substantive rules do not replace the internal ones but concern interstate cases only. Where such rules replace internal law, a regulation may be problematic when the court, by virtue of its choice of law

---

[47] Regulation 40/94 of 20 December 1993, *OJ(EC)* [1994] L 11/1.

rules, has to apply the law of another Member State to a case falling outside the spatial scope of the regulation.

3.4   Directives for the Approximation of Conflicts of Laws?

Turning now to the enactment of Community multilateral choice of law rules, similar, for instance, to the Rome Convention of 19 June 1980 on the Law Applicable to Contractual Obligations, we may assume that a directive is appropriate as a tool for the approximation of laws if such rules would replace the corresponding national ones. This method would seem more transparent and acceptable to national authorities of Member States which usually regulate private law by means of codification – e.g., a "Code civil".

Common conflicts rules could constitute the major mean of approximation of private law. They could also serve as a complementary method, accompanying the approximation of substantive law. For instance, when the Community legislator intends to approximate substantive rules concerning consumer protection, he may adopt such rules without any special applicability rules and add uniform choice of law rules as a supplement.

Does enacting a directive rather than a regulation necessarily mean a step backward for the Community? We agree with P.-C. Müller-Graf[48] in so far that "private law mainly consists of very precise rules", that "detailed rules nearly inevitably become part of the result to be achieved", and that "directives for the approximation of private law contain closely knit provisions" which "may then partially approach the linguistic structure of regulations". The need for precise provisions is far greater in the field of private law than in the field of economic law because the risk of discrepancies is greater. Indeed, by saying that private law consists of "precise" rules, we mean that their content must be precise enough to address specific cases. The formulation of the rule however may be – or even must be – open, because a private law rule, in the Continental tradition, is a concise provision of an abstract character proper to cover a large set of individual and diverse cases.

But does this mean, as the above mentioned author contends, that, necessarily, "legislation by directives implies a certain danger of discharging the directive-issuing institutions of their responsibility to define coherent and applicable rules"? One must admit that the provision eventually applicable in the individual case is a national one. Yet this does not imply, as this author states, that "the wording of a directive can be wider than is useful for the result to be achieved". Of course, there is a risk of Community institutions sacrificing, for political reasons, a precise wording for the achievement of a partial or minimal approximation. But this does not *per se* exclude the possibility of a precise wording. The Directive on Product

---

[48] P.-C. Müller-Graf (supra n. 1) 71-89, especially at p. 81.

Liability for instance was formulated in such a precise way, each term being the result of a long discussion, that any divergent version in national law could amount to an infringement of Community law.[49] It is worth noting that the wording of the Directive is largely inspired by and very close to the text of an international treaty, the Convention of the Council of Europe of 27 January 1977. This text – had it entered into force – would have been directly applicable in individual cases after ratification by the State.

In any case, even at the risk that the wording of a directive may not be precise enough or might allow discrepancies among the respective national implementing laws, national courts are under duty to interpret national law, as far as possible, in conformity with the directive, the interpretation of which remains under the control of the Court of Justice.[50] Doing so, Community law provides for a subtle mechanism proper to guarantee the uniformity of the rules despite their possible adaptation to the peculiarities of each national legal system.

After all, rules of conflict, too, tend to coordinate distinct national systems without altering their inner coherence.

4. CONCLUSION

The analysis of Community practice in the field of consumer law shows a trend of complementing substantive mandatory rules with special applicability rules. Several methods are used in this respect.

The analysis of the implementation of these provisions reveals an intrinsic difficulty in translating specific applicability rules into national law. This is partially due to factors external to private international law. First, a clear definition of the international scope of "primary" Community law on free movement is still lacking despite the fact that this constitutes the framework for the enactment of "secondary" law. Secondly, it is uncertain which legal instrument is the most appropriate for the approximation of private law, be it substantive law or private international law.

Community practice in the field of consumer law shows the need of overruling Article 5 of the Rome Convention. However, the Community legislator, rather than launch a revision of the Convention, has until now favored a step by step approach, using specific unilateral applicability rules to accompany uniform substantive rules. Thereby he followed the well known model of the internationally mandatory provision or *loi de police*. However, at this stage, one may submit that when directives are adopted instead of regulations, the technique of special multilateral

---

[49] About Directive 85/374 on product liability, a claim against the United Kingdom concerning the implementation of the risk development provision was rejected by the Court of Justice: case C-300/95 *Commission* v. *UK* [1997] ECR I-2649.
[50] Case C-106/89 *Marleasing* [1990] ECR I-4135.

choice of law rules – even if limited to the designation of the law of a Member State – is preferable to a unilateral applicability rule referring to the territory of the Community.

This thesis still needs to be tested in fields other than consumer protection, namely the law of intellectual property, company law or labor law.

The Uncitral Draft Convention on Assignment in Receivables Financing: Critical Remarks on Some Specific Issues

Franco Ferrari[*]

1. INTRODUCTION

In one of his very many publications, Professor SIEHR pointed out that the unification of international contract law can be divided into basically two periods:

---

[*] Legal officer, United Nations Office of Legal affairs, International Trade Law Branch. The views expressed in this paper are the personal views of the author and do not necessarily reflect those of the United Nations.

J. Basedow et al., eds., Private Law in the International Arena – Liber Amicorum Kurt Siehr
© 2000, T.M.C.Asser Press, The Hague, The Netherlands

one which relates to the unification of the law of those contracts, such as transport contracts and the contract for the sale of goods, which are universally accepted and the unification of which did therefore not pose too many problems,[1] and a more recent one in which efforts were being made to unify the so-called "innominate contracts".[2] These two periods had one thing in common: they focused mainly on the unification of specific contracts. Since 1988 – when Professor SIEHR wrote those remarks[3] – this has changed. Unification efforts are actually under way which go beyond the unification of specific contracts. This paper will focus on one of these efforts: the Uncitral efforts to unify the law relating to the assignment of receivables which after several years of preparatory work by the Working Group on International Contract Practices resulted most recently in a Draft Convention on Assignment in Receivables Financing[4] submitted to the Commission at its session held in New York, 12 June to 7 July 2000.

Given the limited space allocated to this paper, I will be able to focus only on a few issues raised by the elaboration of the Draft Convention, such as its sphere of application, the general provisions as well as its provision on the conflict of conventions. The reasons I picked these issues relate to the need to put these unification efforts into a perspective which, although the starting point of any unification effort, seems to have been forgotten: the need to create *one* uniform law. The elaboration of new international uniform law conventions which are not co-ordinated among themselves and/or with already existing instruments merely leads to a multiplication of the sources of law and, thus, to a result contrary to that aimed at by trying to elaborate those very same uniform law conventions. In this respect, it is not sufficient, however, to complain about the lack of an overall unification plan.[5] This is why this paper will merely discuss issues dealt with by the Draft Convention which are also dealt with by other international uniform law conventions, thus trying to emphasize the need if not of an overall unification plan, at least that of a uniform method in approaching specific problems and of the use uniform concepts.

---

[1] K. Siehr, "Unificazione internazionale del diritto dei contratt innominati", *Dir. comm. int.* (1988) 83 at p. 85.

[2] Siehr (loc. cit. supra n. 1) at p. 85.

[3] See also K. Siehr, "Internationale Rechtsvereinheitlichung in Innominatverträgen", in: P. Tercier et al. (eds.), *Festschrift für Schluep* (Zurich, Schulthess 1988), pp. 25ff.

[4] This paper is based upon the Draft Convention on Assignment in Receivables Financing (herein-after: Draft Convention) in its version of 2 November 1999, published as annex I to the Report of the Working Group on International Contract Practices on the Work of Its Thirty-First Session (Vienna, 11-22 October 1999) (hereinafter: Report), published in document A/CN.9/466; this document can be found on the internet: www.uncitral.org

[5] For a sinilar affirmation, see J. Kropholler, *Internationales Einheitsrecht. Allgemeine Lehren* (Tübigen, Mohr 1975) p. 167.

2.   THE STRUCTURE OF THE DRAFT CONVENTION

Before focusing on some specific provisions of the Draft Convention, it may be useful to spend some words on its structure which mirrors that of several international uniform law conventions, such as the Vienna Sales Convention and the 1988 Unidroit Conventions on International Factoring and International Financial Leasing: the substantive law provisions are preceded by a Preamble and a chapter containing both provisions defining the Draft Convention's sphere of application and "general provisions". Like in other international uniform commercial law conventions, the Draft Convention's substantive law provisions are succeeded by Final Provisions dealing basically with public international law issues, such as that of the Draft Convention's entry into force, the concept of Contracting State, the Draft Convention's relationship with other conventions, etc. The Draft Convention is, however, innovative in as far as it contains – at least in the version to be discussed in this paper – a chapter, chapter V, exclusively dealing with private international law issues, which is not common for substantive law conventions and which has led to much criticism by some members of the Working Group.[6] Whether this chapter will be retained is doubtful; one can only hope that it will be deleted, above all because according to the Draft Convention's current version the aforementioned chapter would be applicable – unless a specific reservation was declared[7] – in a Contracting State independently of whether the Draft Convention's territorial requirements are met.[8] As evidenced by the Report, some delegations shared this criticism and stated that "from a legislative point of view it would not be appropriate to attempt, in essence, to prepare a mini private international law convention within a substantive law convention."[9]

Overall, however, the structure of the Draft Convention is modeled after a structure which has proved to be generally accepted and which should therefore be taken into account when drafting future conventions as well. The Draft Convention does, however, not only correspond in respect of its structure (with the aforementioned exception relating to chapter V) to the most recent international uniform commercial law conventions. It is also similar in nature, since like these

---

[6]   See A/CN.9/466, p. 38ff.

[7]   See the following note.

[8]   See Art. 1(3): "The provisons of chapter V apply to assignments of international receivables and to international assignments of receivables as defined in this chapter independently of paragraphs (1) and (2) of this article. However, those provisions do not apply if a State makes a declaration under Article 37."

[9]   See A/CN.9/466, p. 39.

conventions, it does constitute a self-executing treaty,[10] i.e., a convention "where legal rules arising from the convention are open for immediate application by the national judge and all living persons in a Contracting State are entitled to assert their rights or demand fulfillment of another person's duty by referring directly to the legal rules of the treaty",[11] without there being a need for a further legislative act by the national legislator.[12] The self-executing nature of a convention – such as the Draft Convention – has the obvious advantage to highlight – instead of conceal – the convention's international origin.[13]

3.   THE PREAMBLE

The provisions of the Draft Convention are preceded by a Preamble. If one compares this Preamble with that of other international uniform commercial law conventions, one will notice that they are not dissimilar. Indeed, the Draft Convention's Preamble does not only reaffirm – like that of other conventions[14] – the "conviction that international trade on the basis of equality and mutual benefit is an important element in the promotion of friendly relations among the States",[15] but it also reaffirms the goal behind the elaboration of any international uniform commercial law convention, i.e., the promotion of international trade by reducing legal uncertainties.[16] The fact that the Draft Convention has the same goal as any other international uniform commercial law convention is without any doubt helpful in (and paramount to) trying to create *one* uniform commercial law. One must, however, point out that "the [mere] adoption of uniform rules"[17] is – contrary to what the

---

[10] It has often been pointed out that both the Vienna Sales Convention and the Unidroit Convention on International Factoring constitute self-executing treaties; see, e.g., Ferrari, *Il factoring internazionale* (Padova, Cedam 1999) p. 12 (referring to the Unidroit Convention on International Factoring); Ch. Häusler, *Das Unidroit Übereinkommen über internationales Factoring (Ottawa 1988) unter besonderer Berücksichtigung seiner Anwendbarkeit* (Frankfurt a. M., Peter Lang 1998) p. 89 (referring to the Unidroit Convention on International Factoring); P. Volken, "The Vienna Convention: Scope, Interpretation and Gap-Filling", in: P. Sarcevic and P. Volken (eds.), *International Sale of Goods. Dubrovnik Lectures* (New York/Rome, Oceana 1986) 19 at pp. 21-22 (in respect of the Vienna Sales Convention); *Filanto s.p.a.* v. *Chilewich Int'l Corp.*, 789 F.Supp. 1129 (S.D.N.Y. 1992) (in respect of the Vienna Sales Convention).

[11] P. Volken, "Das Wiener Übereinkommen über den internationalen Warenkauf; Anwendungsvoraussetzungen und Anwendungsbereich", in: P. Schechtriem (ed.), *Einheitliches Kaufrecht und nationales Obligationenrecht* (Baden-Baden, Nomos 1987) 81 at p. 83.

[12] See Kropholler (op. cit. n. 5) at p. 101.

[13] See Kropholler (op. cit. n. 5) at p. 102.

[14] See Preamble of the Vienna Sales Convention.

[15] Preamble(1) of the Draft Convention.

[16] Preamble(2) and (3) of the Draft Convention.

[17] Preamble(4) of the Draft Convention.

drafters seem to believe – not sufficient to lead to this result.[18] It is common knowledge that mere "textual uniformity of the law (...) is insufficient."[19] The preamble should reflect this.

4. THE INTERNATIONAL SPHERE OF APPLICATION

Not unlike other international uniform commercial law conventions, the Draft Convention does define its own substantive, international, territorial and temporal sphere of application. The corresponding provisions are to be found basically in chapter I, i.e., at the beginning of the text.[20] This does not, however, preclude some concepts which are relevant to the determination of the Draft Convention's sphere of application from being dealt with in other chapters. In this respect, it suffices to point out that the definition of Contracting State, which is without any doubt a concept relevant to the Draft Convention's sphere of application, is to be found, not unlike in other international uniform commercial law conventions,[21] in the chapter devoted to the final provision.[22] The same is to be said in respect of the provision dealing with the Draft Convention's temporal sphere of application, which is also dealt with in that chapter.[23]

As far as the international sphere of application of the Draft Convention is concerned, one notices that it exclusively covers international situations. For very many years, the drafters of international uniform commercial law conventions have been directing their efforts to merely cover situations which can somehow be defined as "international".[24] Most recently, however, this trend has been criticized on the occasion of the discussion of some international uniform commercial law conventions. Some authors claim that international situations raise the same problems as purely domestic ones.[25] Although this may be true, one has to consider that the restriction of the unification efforts to international situations has the advantage of not impacting on the domestic law and, thus, the solutions characterizing a particular

---

[18] See also Preamble(2) of the Unidroit Convention on International Factoring.

[19] L.M. Ryan, "The Convention on Contracts for the International Sale of Goods. Divergent Interpretations", 4 *Tulane J. Int'l & Comp. L.* (1995) 99 at p. 101 (referring to the Vienna Sales Convention).

[20] See Kropholler (op. cit. n. 5) at p. 189, stating that the fact that putting the provisons defining a convention's sphere of application at the beginning of the convention is a systematically correct way to proceed.

[21] See Article 99 of the Vienna Sales Convention; Article 14 fo the Unidroit Convention on International Factoring.

[22] See Article 43(1) and (2) of the Draft Convention.

[23] See Article 43(3) of the Draft Convention.

[24] In this respect, cf. B. Lemhöfer, "Die Beschränkung der Rechtsvereinheitlichung auf internationale Sachverhalte", 25 *RabelsZ* (1960) pp. 401ff.

[25] See A. Rosett, "Critical Reflections on the United Nations Convention on Contracts for the International Sale of Goods", 45 *Ohio St. L. J.* (1984) 265 at p. 269.

legal system which, therefore, will not be altered.[26] Consequently, countries with a particular legal, economic and political system will not be prevented from bringing into force the results of these unification efforts which otherwise would be unacceptable.

5. THE INTERNATIONAL SPHERE OF APPLICATION: THE ASSIGNMENT OF INTERNATIONAL RECEIVABLES IN GENERAL

While the limitation of the Unictral efforts to international situations cannot surprise, the same is not true in respect of the definition of "internationality" contained in the Draft Convention. According to the draft the internationality criterion is met (and the need to determine the Draft Convention's applicability is triggered) where either the assignment relates to international receivables or the receivables are assigned internationally.[27]

The latter criterion to determine internationality corresponds to that provided for in the Unidroit Convention on International Factoring, since this convention also defines internationality on the basis of the internationality of the receivables.[28] In view of the creation of *one* uniform commercial law, the use of one and the same definition in more than one convention is to be appreciated, since this avoids the need for the interpreter to keep in mind and examine as many different definitions as there are conventions: this would indeed be detrimental to the certainty of law at which all unification efforts aim.

6. THE INTERNATIONAL SPHERE OF APPLICATION: CRITICAL REMARKS ON THE ASSIGNMENT OF INTERNATIONAL RECEIVABLES

The identity between the aforementioned Draft Convention's definition of internationality and that of the Unidroit Convention on International Factoring is a rather recent achievement. Indeed, while the Factoring Convention's internationality is exclusively based upon the parties to the underlying contract (debtor and as-

---

[26] For this statement, see Kropholler (op. cit. n. 5) at p. 168.
[27] See Article 1(1)(a) of the Draft Convention: "(1) This Convention applies to: (a) assignments of international receivables and to international assignments of receivables as defined in this chapter, if, at the time of the conclusion of the contract of assignment, the assignor is located in a Contracting State."
[28] See also B. A. Diehl-Leistner, *Internationales Factoring* (Munich, Beck 1992) pp. 126-127; F. Ferrari, "Der internationale Anwendungsbereich des Ottawa-Übereinkommens von 1988 über internationales Factoring", *RIW (Recht der Internationalen Wirtschaft)* (1996) at pp. 183-184.
[29] For this see also F. Ferrari, "La sphère internationale d'application de la Convention d'Ottawa de 1988 sur l'affacturage international", *Rev. dr. aff. int.* (1999) 895 at p. 898-899; Häusler (op. cit. n. 10)

signor) having their place of business in different countries,[29] the definition of the Draft Convention's internationality had not always been dependent on where the debtor and the assignor had their place of business. Indeed, according to an earlier version of the Draft Convention, the location to be taken into account was not as much the place of business of a party, but rather the place of the party's "central administration".[30] After a lengthy discussion during the Working Group's last meeting,[31] the reference to the "central administration" was fortunately deleted – although not totally – in favor of a reference to the "place of business".[32] Recourse to new concepts, such as that of "central administration", is to be avoided where possible, since it would only create more uncertainty.

In the light of what has just been said, it appears that the definition of internationality of the receivables provided for in the Draft Convention is identical to that to be found in the Factoring Convention. Although this is true where the parties involved have only one place of business, it is not true where one party has multiple places of business. Indeed, whereas the Factoring Convention solves the problem of identifying the relevant place of business by referring to "the place of business which has the closest relationship to the relevant contract and its performance",[33] the Draft Convention refers – where the party having multiple places of business is either the assignor or the assignee – to the "place where its central administration is exercised".[34] The introduction of this rule is to be criticized not only for its introducing a concept not provided for in the international uniform contract law conventions to come into force most recently and for which a more appropriate substitute exists, but also for its deviation from rules which are widely accepted.[35]

---

at pp. 282ff.

[30] See Article 5(k) of the Draft Convention's version of 30 March 1999, to be found in document A/CN.9/456: "(k) For the purposes of articles 1 and 3: (i) the assignor is located in the State in which it has that place of business which has the closest relationship to the assignment; (ii) the assignee is located in the State in which it has that place of business which has the closest relationship to the assignment; (iii) the debtor located in the State in which it has that place of business which has the closest relationship to the original contract; (iv) in the absence of proof to the contrary, *the place of central administration of a party is presumed to be the place of business* which has the closest relationship to the relevant contract. If a party does not have a place of business, reference is to be made to its habitual residence; (v) several assignors or assignees are located at the place in which their authorized agent or trustee is located." [emphasis added]

[31] See document A/CN.9/466, p. 8f.

[32] Article 6(i) of the Draft Convention.

[33] Article 2(2) of the Factoring Convention.

[34] Article 5(i)(ii) of the Factoring Convention.

[35] See, apart from the provision referred to in note 33, Article 10 of the Vienna Sales Convention.

7.   INTERNATIONALITY, BULK ASSIGNMENTS AND FUTURE RECEIVABLES

As far as the internationality is concerned which is based upon the parties to the underlying contract having their place of business in different countries, one must
point out that it can cause some problems, as in the case where a bulk assignment is
made and where the assigned receivables are in part domestic ones, in part international ones.[36] Where, for instance, the creditor assigns the receivables to a party
which has its place of business in the same State as the creditor, the internationality
de quo can lead to the application of both the Draft Convention as well as domestic
law, although only one (bulk) assignment has been made to one and the same
assignee. The disadvantages resulting from this are apparent.

As far as the assignment of future receivables is concerned, the problem is somewhat different: where a creditor assigns future receivables to a party having its place
of business in the same State as the assignor, at the time of the assignment one does
not necessarily know which rules govern the assignment, domestic ones or those of
the Draft Convention.[37] The answer to this question will, indeed, depend upon
whether the receivables will be regarded as international or domestic ones, i.e.,
whether at the time of the conclusion of the original contract the debtor will have its
place of business in a State different from that in which the assignor has its place of
business.

8.   THE INTERNATIONAL SPHERE OF APPLICATION: THE INTERNATIONAL ASSIGNMENT OF RECEIVABLES

Whereas the Factoring Convention's concept of internationality depends solely on
the parties to the original contract having their place of business in different States,[38]
under the Draft Convention said concept is not the only one to be relevant for its
applicability.[39] As mentioned already, the Draft Convention may also be applicable

---

[36] For a similar criticism, referred, however, to the internationality requirement provided for by the
Factoring Convention, see Ferrari (op. cit. n. 10) at pp. 59ff.

[37] This is due to fact that under the Draft Convention it is not necessary, unlike under some
domestic laws, to identify the debtor at the time of the assignment, as long as the receivables "can, (...)
at the time of the conclusion of the original contract, be identified as receivables to which the
assignment relates." Article 9(1)(b).

[38] See, apart from the authors quoted in n. 28, R. Monaco, "La convenzione internazionale per i
contratti di factoring", *Bancaria* (1989) 11 at p. 13; E. Rebmann, "Das Unidroit Übereinkommen über
das internationle Factoring (Ottawa 1988)", 53 *RabelsZ* (1989) 599 at p. 605.

[39] S.V. Bazinas, "Die Arbeit von Uncitral im Bereich der Forderungsabtretung zur Kredit-
finanzierung", in: W. Hadding and U.H. Schneider (eds.), *Die Forderungsabtretung, insebosndere zur
Kreditsicherung, in ausländischen Rechtsordnungen* (Berlin, Duncker & Humblot 1999) 99 at p. 106.

where the assignor and the debtor have their place of business in one and the same State, as long as the assignment is international, i.e., as long as the assignee's place of business[40] is – at the time of the assignment – located in a different State.[41] Consequently, where a bulk assignment is made by an assignor located in a State different from that in which the assignee has its place of business, the assignment as such can be subject to the rules of the Draft Convention, independently of whether the receivables are international or domestic. In respect of the assignment of future receivables as well, the internationality *de quo* does not cause the problems which can arise from the internationality criterion based upon the debtor and the assignor having their place of business in different States. Indeed, for the Draft Convention's applicability it is irrelevant whether the future receivables will be domestic or international ones, since one of the alternatively listed internatonality requirement is met without any doubt at the time of the assignment if the assignor has its place of business in a State different form that in which the assignee has its place of business.

The only question which comes to one's mind at this point is that of whether such a broad definition of internationality (i.e., that resulting from the two internationality criteria) is appropriate. Is it appropriate, in other words, to merely exclude the domestic assignment of domestic receivables from the Draft Convention's international sphere of application? When considering this question one should not forget that the Draft Convention does not contain, unlike the Vienna Sales Convention,[42] any provision which protects the parties reliance upon the domestic setting of the transaction.[43]

9. FURTHER REQUIREMENTS FOR THE DRAFT CONVENTION'S APPLICABILITY: GENERAL REMARKS

In order for the Draft Convention to apply, it is not sufficient that the internationality requirement be met. Like many recent international uniform commer-

---

[40] Not unlike under other international uniform commercial law conventions (see, e.g., Article 1(3) of the Vienna Sales Convention), the citizenship of the parties involved is irrelevant for the purpose of determining the internationality.

[41] See Article 3 of the Draft Convention: "A receivable is international if, at the time of the conclusion of the original contract, the assignor and the debtor are located in different States. An assignment is international if, at the time of the conclusion of the contract of assignment, the assignor and the assignee are located in different States."

[42] See Article 1(2) of the Vienna Sales Convention.

[43] Note that neither does the Factoring Convention contain a provision which protects the parties' reliance upon the domestic setting of the (factoring) transaction; for this, see Ferrari (op. cit. n. 10) at 66.

cial law conventions, unlike, however, the 1964 Hague Uniform Sales Laws,[44] the Draft Convention requires that there be a link with at least one Contracting State. The fact that a further requirement is needed to trigger the Draft Convention's applicability is to be considered positive not only from a substantial point of view, but also from a methodological one, since a uniform methodology is paramount to the creation of *one* uniform law.

As far as that link is concerned, it can either be a "territorial" one, such as the one provided for in Art. 1(1)(a) of the Vienna Sales Convention, which requires that the parties to the sales contract have their place of business in (different) Contracting States, or a legal one, such as the one provided for in Art. 1(1)(b) of the Vienna Sales Convention to name just the most famous example,[45] by virtue of which the convention is also applicable where the rules of private international law lead to the law of a Contracting State.

Unlike the Factoring Convention[46] which – given the subject matter – is without any doubt very closely related to the Draft Convention, the latter does not rely upon a "legal" criterion of the aforementioned kind for its application. The Draft Convention does not contain any provision anymore which can lead to its applicability even where the "territorial" requirement is not met.[47] Why this criterion has not been retained is not easily understood. In my opinion, the arguments put forward by some delegations that "the level of uncertainty resulting from the reference to the rules of private international law was unacceptable" and that "the scope of the Draft Convention (...) was so broad that no further extension by reference to any rule of private international law was needed",[48] should not have led to the deletion of the private international law criterion of applicability. This

---

[44] It has often been pointed out that the 1964 Hague Sales Laws were applicable without any other requirement having to be met (at least where the forum State had not declared any reservation); see, e.g., F. Ferrari, *International Sale of Goods* (Basle/Brussels 1999) pp. 32ff.

[45] Very many papers have been written on the issues arising from Art. 1(1)(b); see, among others, K. Siehr, "Der internationale Anwendungsbereich des UN-Kaufrechts", 52 *RabelsZ* (1988) pp. 587ff.; Ch. Bernasconi, "The Personal and Territorial Scope of the Vienna Convention on Contracts for the International Sale of Goods (Article 1)", *NILR (Netherlands International Law Review)* (1999) pp. 137ff.; F. Ferrari, "CISG Art. 1(1)(b) and Related Matters: Brief Remarks on the Occasion of a Recent Dutch Court Decision", *NIPR (Nederlands Internationaal Privaatrecht)* (1995) pp. 317ff.; H. Pünder, "Das Einheitliche UN-Kaufrecht –Anwendung kraft kollisionsrechtlicher Verweisung nach Art. 1 Abs. 1 lit. b UN-Kaufrech'", *RIW* (1990) pp. 869ff.

[46] See Article 2(1)(b) of the Unidroit Convention on International Factoring.

[47] See, however, Article 1(1) of the Draft Convention's version discussed during the meeting Working Group's 27th session (Vienna, 20-31 October 1997), reprinted in document A/CN.9/445: "(1) This Convention applies to assignments of international receivables and to international assignments of receivables as defined in this Chapter: (a) if, at the time of the assignment, the assignor and the assignee have their places fo business in a Contracting State; or (b) if the rules of private international law lead to the application of the law of a Contracting State."

[48] Report of the Working Group on International Contract Practices on the Work of Its Twenty-Seventh Session (Vienna, 20-31 October 1997), published in document A/CN.9/445, p. 34.

does not mean, however, that the deletion was not justifiable. Indeed, since a chapter containing private international law rules was to be included (chapter V), the retention of the private international law criterion of applicability would have resulted in problems of co-ordination which had to be avoided at all costs.

10.   THE TERRITORIAL REQUIREMENT OF APPLICATION

In order for the Draft Convention to apply, a territorial requirement in addition to the internationality requirement must be met: the assignor (and, unlike in earlier drafts,[49] only the assignor)[50] must – at the time of the conclusion of the assignment[51] – have its place of business (or, where the assignor has more than one place of business, the place where its central administration is exercised) in a Contracting State.[52] If one compares this "territorial" requirement with that provided for in the Factoring Convention which requires that all the parties involved have their place of business in a Contracting State (debtor, assignor and assignee),[53] it becomes apparent that the Draft Convention's "territorial" scope is broader than that of the Factoring Convention. In my opinion, this broad scope is justified on the grounds that the Draft Convention is applicable exclusively on the basis of the aforementioned territorial criterion of applicability (whereas, for instance, the Factoring Convention is also applicable where the rules of private international lead as regards both the underlying contract and the factoring contract to the law of a Contracting State).

As far as the definition of Contracting State is concerned, the Draft Convention follows established practice and requires – apart from the deposit of an instrument of ratification, acceptance, approval or accession – the expiration of a specific period of time (six months) following the end of the month in which the deposit occurred.[54]

The temporal sphere of application is governed by Article 43(3) according to which the Draft Convention applies only to those assignments made on or after the date when the Convention enters into force in respect of the Contracting State referred to in Article 1(1).

---

[49]   See former Article 1 (supra n. 47).

[50]   Note, however, that where the assignor assigns domestic receivables internationally or where he assigns international receivables domestically, at least two parties involved in the transaction are located in a Contracting State. Only where international receivables are assigned internationally is it possible that only the assignor is located in a Contracting State.

[51]   For the purposes of the Convention's applicability it is irrelevant whether the assignor transfers its place of business after the assignment.

[52]   See Article 1 (supra n. 27).

[53]   See Article 2(1)(a) of the Factoring Convention.

[54]   See Article 43(1) and (2) of the Draft Convention.

11.   THE SPHERE OF APPLICATION RATIONE MATERIAE

As far as the substantive sphere of application is concerned, it must be pointed out that the Draft Convention defines "assignment". This is to be appreciated, since the lack of a definition could induce the interpreters to resort to a domestic definition, although this would run counter Article 8(1) which states, not unlike provisions in most recent international uniform commercial law conventions,[55] that "in the interpretation of this Convention, regard is to be had to its international character and to the need to promote uniformity in its application and the observance of good faith in international trade."

The more concepts are defined in an international uniform commercial law convention, the less probable it is that interpreters have recourse to domestic definitions.

Article 2(a) defines the assignment as the "transfer by agreement from one person ('assignor') to another person ('assignee') of the assignor's contractual right to payment of a monetary sum ('receivable') from a third person ('debtor'). The creation of rights in receivables as security for indebtedness or other obligation is deemed to be a transfer."

Article 2(a) does, however, not only define "assignment", it also defines "receivables". This definition appears to be broader than that found in the Factoring Convention according to which "receivables" (the assignment of which may be covered by the Factoring Convention) are merely those arising from contracts for the sale of goods and for the supply of services.[56] Although this is true, i.e., although the Draft Convention's definition of "receivables" includes *any contractual right* to payment of a monetary sum, even where it does arise from contracts other than those for the sale of goods or the supply of services, one must emphasize that where the "receivable" is a receivable other than a "trade receivable" (defined as "a receivable arising under an original contract for the sale of goods or the provision of services other than financial services"),[57] some of the Draft Convention's provisions will not be applicable to that assignment.

Not unlike the Factoring Convention, the Draft Convention provides for some exclusions from its sphere of application.[58] One of these appears – at least at first

---

[55] See Article 7(1) of the Vienna Sales Convention; Article 4(1) of the Unidroit Convention on International Factoring; Article 6(1) of the Unidroit Convention on International Financial Leasing.

[56] See Ferrari (op. cit. n. 10) p. 46ff.

[57] See Article 6(l) of the Draft Convention.

[58] See Article 4 of the Draft Convention: "(1) This Convention does not apply to assignment: (a) made to an individual for his or her personal, family or household purposes; (b) to the extent made by delivery of a negotiable instrument, with any necessary endorsement; (c) made as part of the sale, or change in the ownership or the legal status, of the business out of which the assigned receivables arose. (2) This Convention does not apply to assignments listed in a declaration made under article 39 by the State in which the assignor is located, or with respect to the provisions of this Convention which deal

sight – to be very similar to the one provided for by the Factoring Convention which excludes[59] from its sphere of application international factoring contracts regarding receivables arising from contracts for the sale of goods bought exclusively for personal, family or household use.[60] If one looks closer, however, one can notice that the Draft Convention's exclusion does not exclude the assignment of consumer receivables from its sphere of application, but rather the assignment made for consumer purposes.[61] Although it results from the Report that the delegates were aware that their exclusion differed from that of the Factoring Convention,[62] they did not offer a valid justification for departing from the type of exclusion provided for in the Factoring Convention.

12. GENERAL PROVISIONS: PARTY AUTONOMY AND EXCLUSION OF THE DRAFT CONVENTION

As mentioned in the introduction, this paper also discusses some of the issues linked to the Draft Convention's general provisions (Articles 6-8).

Like many other international uniform commercial law conventions,[63] the Draft Convention contains a provision dealing with its exclusion, according to which "the assignor, the assignee and the debtor may derogate from or vary by agreement provisions of this Convention relating to their respective rights and obligations. Such an agreement does not affect the rights of any person who is not a party to the agreement."[64] Unlike, however, the provisions of other international uniform commercial law conventions, such as Article 3 of the Factoring Convention which – on the contrary – only admits an exclusion *in toto*,[65] Article 7 of the Draft Convention does not allow for the exclusion of the Draft Convention as a whole. Unfortunately, the Draft Convention does not specify the form the exclusion must take: can it be made implicitly or does it have to be made explicitly? It would be helpful if the Commission were to deal with this issue, albeit briefly, when examining the Draft Convention as

---

with the rights and obligations of the debtor, by the State in which the debtor is located."

[59] See Article 1(2)(a)) of the Unidroit Convention on International Factoring.

[60] For comments regarding the provision referred to the previous note, see Ferrari (op. cit. n. 10) at 48ff.; Häusler (op. cit. n. 10) p. 278ff.

[61] Note that the consumer purpose must lie with the assignee.

[62] See document A/CN.9/466, p. 17.

[63] See Article 6 of the Vienna Sales Convention; Article 3 of the Unidroit Convention on International Factoring.

[64] Article 7 of the Draft Convention.

[65] For similar statements with respect to Article 3 of the Unidroit Convention on International Factoring, see L. J. Kitsaras, *Das Unidroit-Übereinkommen über das internationale Factoring vom 28.5.1988 (Ottawa) aus der Sicht des deutschen und griechischen Rechts* (Athens, Sakkoulas 1994) pp. 50-51.

a whole. This would help to avoid the problems of interpretation encountered under the Vienna Sales Convention, in respect of which some authors[66] and courts[67] claim that the Convention can be excluded implicitly, whereas other authors[68] and courts[69] claim that the exclusion can only be made expressly.

13.   GENERAL PROVISIONS: THE INTERPRETATION OF THE DRAFT CONVENTION

The Draft Convention's chapter containing the "general provisions" also deals with the issue of the Draft Convention's interpretation. In this respect, one notices that the text of Article 8(1) of the Draft Convention is identical to that of Article 7(1) of the Vienna Sales Convention. If one takes into account the need to create *one* international uniform commercial law through a uniform methodology and, where possible, a body of uniform concepts, then that very same fact appears to be positive. However, a closer look allows one to wonder whether there are only upsides to this. Thus, one must wonder why the drafters did not, from the start of the drafting efforts, model Article 8(1) along the lines of Articles 4(1) of the Factoring Convention and 6(1) of the Leasing Convention which (affirmatively) solve a problem which under Article 7(1) of the Vienna Sales Convention has led to a dispute among legal writers, that of whether the Preamble is to be taken into account in interpreting the Convention. Indeed, these conventions expressly state that in their interpretation "regard is [also] to be had to its objects and purpose as set forth in the preamble", a statement unfortunately not to be found in either the Draft Convention nor the Vienna Sales Convention.

The fact that the drafters (until very recently) literally copied Article 7(1) of the Vienna Sales Convention can be criticized for another reason as well: it means not to take into account the results to which the discussion of Article 7(1) of the Vienna Sales Convention has led. In this respect it suffices to recall that various authors have pointed out that despite the obligation to have regard to the international char-

---

[66] See B. Audit, *La vente internationale* (Paris, L.G.D.J. 1990) p. 38; K. Bell, "The Sphere of Application of the Vienna Convention on Contracts for the International Sale of Goods", 8 *Pace Int'l l. Rev.* (1996) 237 at p. 255; B. Czerwenka, *Rechtsanwendungsprobleme im internationalen Kaufrecht* (Berlin, Duncker & Humblot 1987) p. 170.

[67] See LG München, May 29, 1995, Unilex; OLG Celle, May 24, 1995, Unilex.

[68] See I.I. Dore and J.I. Defranco, "A Comparison of the Non-Substantive Provisions of the UNCITRAL Convention on the International Sale of Goods and the Uniform Commercial Code", 23 *Harv. Int'l L. J.* (1982) 49 at p. 53; c.?? D. Klepper, "The Convention for the International Sale of Goods: A Practical Guide for the State of Maryland and Its Trade Community", 15 *Maryland J. Int'l L. & Trade* (1991) 235 at p. 238.

[69] See LG Landshut, April 5, 1995, Unilex (stating that the parties are only allowed to exclude the Vienna Sales Convention expressly); *Orbisphere Corp.* v. *United States*, 726 F.Supp. 1344 (1990) (stating the same).

acter of the Convention and the need to promote uniformity in its application, which basically results in the "autonomous" interpretation of the Convention,[70] not all concepts can be interpreted autonomously.[71] The concept of "party to a contract", for instance, is not an "autonomous" one; indeed, who is "party to a contract" depends on the law applicable by virtue of the private international law rules of the forum.[72] Would it not be better if the drafters were to insert some wording to show that the obligation to interpret the Draft Convention "autonomously" is not absolute and, maybe, even pointed out which concepts are not to be interpreted "autonomously"?

The drafters should also avoid another dispute arisen in connection with Article 7(1) of the Vienna Sales Convention: that of the value to attribute to foreign court decisions and arbitral awards. If the drafters were to expressly state that these decisions can only have persuasive value, as they should,[73] no legal writer could even think of asking for the creation of a "supranational *stare decisis*" as was done by one author when discussing the Vienna Sales Convention.[74]

14. GAP-FILLING AND GENERAL PRINCIPLES: GENERAL REMARKS

Not unlike any other international uniform commercial law convention,[75] the Draft Convention does not constitute an exhaustive body of rules. In other words, the Draft Convention does not deal with all the issues which can arise in connection with assignments falling under its sphere of application. That the drafters of the Draft Convention were aware of this, can easily be derived from the adoption of Article 8(2) which lays down a rule on gap-filling. According to this rule – which is to be found in many recent international commercial law conventions[76] – "questions concerning matters governed by this Convention which are not expressly settled in it are to be settled in conformity with the general principles on which it is based or,

---

[70] For papers discussing the Vienna Sales Convention's autonomous interpretation, see, among many others, F. Diedrich, "Maintaining Uniformity in International Uniform Law via Autonomous Interpretation: Software Contracts and the CISG", 8 *Pace Int'l L. Rev.* (1996) pp. 303ff.

[71] For this, see Ferrari, "CISG Case Law:A New Challenge for Interpreters?", *J. L. & Com.* (1998) pp. 245ff.

[72] See Ferrari (op. cit. n. 10) at pp. 66f. (with respect to the Unidroit Convention on International Factoring).

[73] For similar statements, referred, however, either the Vienna Sales Convention or to the Unidroit Convention on International Factoring, see Enderlein/ Maskow, *International Sales Law* (New York, Transnational 1992) p. 56; Ferrari (op. cit. n. 10) at p. 115; Ea. Kramer, "Uniforme Interpretation von Einheitsrecht – mit besonderer Berücksichtigung von Art. 7 UNKR", *JBl.* (1996) p. 146.

[74] L. Dimatteo, "The CISG and the Presumption of enforceability: Unintended Contractual Liability in International Business Dealings", *Yale J. Int'l L.* (1997) p. 113.

[75] For a similar conclusion, see Kropholler (op. cit. n. 5) at p. 170.

[76] See Articles 7(2) of the Vienna Sales Convention, 4(2) of the Unidroit Convention on International Factoring, 6(2) of the Unidroit Convention on International Financial Leasing.

in the absence of such principles, in conformity with the law applicable by virtue of the rules of private international law."

The fact that the drafters have inserted a rule on gap-filling which is to be found in other conventions as well is *per se* positive, in that it promotes the creation of a uniform methodology which is necessary in order to create *one* uniform law. In the case at hand, one has, however, to consider the downside of the drafters copying a rule which is generally embedded in a different context, i.e., a context of substantive law. Unlike most other international uniform commercial law conventions, the Draft Convention contains a chapter exclusively dealing with private international law issues to which the aforementioned rule on gap-filling necessarily extends as well, unless the drafters were to insert wording to the contrary. One has to wonder whether the drafters are aware of that. Do they really want to oblige the interpreters to identify general principles of private international law upon which the Draft Convention is based?

The most practical problem posed by Article 8(2) is, however, a different one: that of identifying the general principles upon which the Draft Convention is based.

15.   GAP-FILLING AND GENERAL PRINCIPLES: SPECIFIC GENERAL PRINCIPLES

Since according to many legal writers the principle of "party autonomy" is a general principle which inspires many international uniform commercial law conventions,[77] one may be led into believing that it is one upon which the Draft Convention is based, too. In my opinion, this view is not tenable. The parties' not being allowed to exclude the Draft Convention *in toto*,[78] does not allow one to consider the principle of "party autonomy" as one of the principles upon which the Draft Convention is based.

One of the "true" general principles of the Draft Convention – but this is also true as far as the Factoring Convention is concerned[79] – is that of the *favor cessionis*. This

---

[77] See, in respect of the Vienna Sales Convention, M. Karollus, *UN-Kaufrecht* (Vienna, Springer 1991) pp. 16f.; P. Schlechtriem, *Internationales UN-Kaufrecht* (Tübingen, Mohr 1996) p. 33; with respect to the Unidroit Convention on International Financial Leasing, see F. Ferrari, "General Principles and International Uniform Commercial Law Conventions: A Study of the 1980 Vienna Sales Convention and the 1988 Unidroit Conventions", *Uniform L. Rev.* (1997) 451 at p. 468; A. Schermi, "Il leasing finanziario e la convenzione internazionale di Ottawa del 28 maggio 1988", *Giust. civ.* (1994) 725 at p. 727; in respect of the Unidroit Convention on International Factoring, see C. Gargiulo and E. Giancoli, "La cessione del redito sotto la lente Unidroit", *Commercio internazionale* (1993) 1296 at p. 1303; contra, see Ferrari (op. cit. n. 10) at p. 127 (denying that the Factoring Convention is based upon the principle of "party autonomy").

[78] See supra the text accompanying n. 65.

[79] See Ferrari (op. cit. n. 10) at p. 128.

can easily be derived from Article 9, the provision according to which an assignment is effective whether it relates to "existing or future, one or more, receivables" or "parts of, or undivided interests in, receivables". The *favor cessionis* principle also results from the provision which states that "an assignment of a receivable is effective notwithstanding any agreement between the initial or any subsequent assignor and the debtor or any subsequent assignee, limiting in any way the assignor's right to assign its receivables."[80]

Another general principle is that according to which the assignment cannot put the debtor in a position which is worse than that in which he would have been if the assignment had not taken place. This principle is clearly expressed in Article 17(1) according to which "an assignment does not, without the consent of the debtor, affect the rights and obligations of the debtor, including the payment terms contained in the original contract." This principle can also be evinced from Article 20, which expressly provides in case of a claim by the assignee for the debtor's possibility to raise against the assignee all defenses or right of set-off arising from the original contract of which the debtor could avail itself if such claim were made by the assignor.

The space allocated to this paper does not allow me to exhaustively list the general principles underlying the Draft Convention. It just allows me to point out that where an internal gap cannot be filled by having recourse to one of the general principles, one has – as *ultima ratio* – to resort to the domestic law to which the rules of private international law lead. Since, however, the Draft Convention contains a chapter of private international law, one must wonder which private international law is to be taken into account in identifying that domestic law, the domestic one or that laid down by the Draft Convention (or maybe both)? The deletion of chapter V would solve this as well as many other problems.

16.   CONFLICT OF CONVENTIONS

Since the number of international uniform commercial law conventions grows constantly, conflicts of conventions become inevitable. The drafters of the most recent conventions are very well aware of this problem.[81] This is why it is not surprising that the Draft Convention as well contains a conflict of conventions rule in respect of which it is worth pointing out that it has undergone several changes. While it had been initially based upon the Draft Convention's giving precedence to other international agreements, the rule was later modified to state that the Draft

---

[80]   Article 11(1).

[81]   See Article 90 of th Vienna Sales Convention; Article 15 of the Unidroit Convention on International Factoring; Article 17 of the Unidroit Convention on International Financial Leasing.

Convention "prevails over any international convention or other multilateral or bilateral agreement which has been or may be entered into by a Contracting State and which contains provisions concerning matters governed by this Convention."[82] Fortunately, on the occasion of the last meeting of the Working Group, the drafters gave up this aggressive approach and adopted the original one which is more in line with established practice.[83] Thus, the Draft Convention "does not prevail over any international agreement which has already been or may be entered into and which contains provisions concerning the matters governed by"[84] the Draft Convention. Consequently, as noted by the drafters themselves, the Draft Convention will not prevail over the Factoring Convention, for instance, the latter being the more specific one.[85]

What has just been said shows – like most of the earlier remarks – that the more unification efforts will be undertaken, the more one must try to coordinate them. In the long run, uncoordinated unification efforts cannot be helpful to anybody.

---

[82] Article 33 of the Draft Convention's version discussed at the last meeting of the Working Group.
[83] See document A/Cn.9/466, p. 51.
[84] Article 36 of the Draft Convention.
[85] See document A/CN.9/466, p. 51.

Die Alliierte (Londoner) Erklärung vom 5.1.1943: Inhalt, Auslegung und Rechtsnatur in der Diskussion der Nachkriegsjahre

Wilfried Fiedler[*]

Am 5.1.1943 ist in London von „den großen Fünf", den britischen Dominien und den Exilregierungen der von Deutschland besetzten Länder folgende Erklärung herausgegeben worden:[1]

Inter-Allied Declaration

Against Acts of Dispossession Committed in Territories Under Enemy Occupation or Control January 5, 1943

---

[*] Prof. Dr. iur., Professor für Staatsrecht, Verwaltungsrecht und Völkerrecht an der Universität des Saarlandes, Leiter des Seminars für Völkerrecht und der Forschungsstelle "Internationaler Kulturgüterschutz".

[1] Erklärung mit amtlicher Übersetzung aus G. Schmoller/ H. Maier/ A. Tobler, *Handbuch des Besatzungsrechts* (Tübingen 1957) § 52, S. 5f. Vgl. auch den Text in: W. Fiedler (Hrsg.), *Internationaler Kulturgüterschutz und deutsche Frage* (Berlin 1991) S. 282f. Herrn Gerichtsreferendar Alexander Schupp möchte ich für wichtige Vorarbeiten zu diesem Beitrag danken.

J. Basedow et al., eds., Private Law in the International Arena – Liber Amicorum Kurt Siehr
© 2000, T.M.C.Asser Press, The Hague, The Netherlands

Declaration

The Union of South Africa, the United States of America, Australia, Belgium, Canada, China, the Czechoslovak Republic, the United Kingdom of Great Britain and Northern Ireland, the Union of Soviet Socialist Republics, Greece, India, Luxembourg, the Netherlands, New Zealand, Norway, Poland, Yugoslavia, and the French National Committee;

Hereby issue a formal warning in all concerned, and in particular to persons in neutral countries, that they intend to do their utmost to defeat the methods of dispossession practiced by the governments with which they are at war against the countries and peoples who have been so wantonly assaulted and despoiled.

Accordingly, the governments making this declaration and the French National Committee reserve all their rights to declare invalid any transfers of, or dealings with, property, rights and interests of any description whatsoever which are, or have been, situated in the territories which have come under the occupation or control, direct or indirect, of the governments with which they are at war or which belong or have belonged, to persons, including juridical persons, resident in such territories. This warning applies whether such transfers or dealings have taken the form of open looting or plunder, or of transactions apparently legal in form, even when they purport to be voluntarily effected.

The governments making this declaration and the French National Committee solemnly record their solidarity in this matter.

London, January 5th, 1943

Alliierte Erklärung

über die in den vom Feinde besetzten oder unter seiner Kontrolle stehenden Gebieten begangenen Enteignungshandlungen vom 5. Januar 1943

Die Regierungen der Süd-Afrikanischen Union, der Vereinigten Staaten von Amerika, Australiens, Belgiens, Canadas, Chinas, der Tschechoslowakischen Republik, des Vereinigten Königreichs von Großbritannien und Nordirland, Griechenlands, Indiens, Luxemburgs, der Niederlande, Neu-Zeelands, Norwegens, Polens, der Union der Sozialistischen Sowjet-Republiken, Jugoslawiens und der Französische Nationalausschuß:

Warnen hiermit ausdrücklich sämtliche in Frage kommenden Personen und insbesondere diejenigen, die in neutralen Ländern wohnhaft sind, daß sie mit allen Mitteln danach streben werden, die Enteignungsmethoden zu vereiteln, die von den Regierungen, mit de-

nen sie in Feindseligkeiten begriffen sind, den schimpflich angegriffenen und beraubten Nationen und Völkern gegenüber gebraucht werden.

Infolgedessen behalten sich die diese Erklärung abgebenden Regierungen und der Französische Nationalausschuß das Recht vor, jede Übertragung und Veräußerung von Eigentum, Guthaben, Rechten und Anrechten, welcher Natur sie auch seien, für nichtig zu erklären, die sich in den von den Regierungen, mit denen sie in Feindseligkeiten begriffen sind, besetzten oder mittelbar oder unmittelbar kontrollierten Gebieten befinden oder befunden haben, oder die im Besitz von den in den betreffenden Gebieten wohnhaften Personen (einschließlich der juristischen Personen) sind oder gewesen sind. Die gegenwärtige Warnung gilt auch, wenn solche Übertragungen oder Veräußerungen unter der Form eines offensichtlichen Raubes oder scheinbar gesetzmäßiger Geschäfte vorgenommen worden sind, und selbst, falls es angegeben wird, daß die besagten Übertragungen oder Veräußerungen ohne jeden Zwang getätigt worden sind.

Die diese Erklärung abgebenden Regierungen und der Französische Nationalausschuß stellen ihre Solidarität in dieser Frage ausdrücklich fest.

London, den 5. Januar 1943

Bedeutung erlangte diese Erklärung im besonderen Maße in den Nachkriegsjahren, in denen sie als Grundlage für die Restitutionen in Deutschland sowie den anderen im Krieg mit Deutschland verbündeten Staaten („Achsenmächte") diente. Ihre Bedeutung über die Nachkriegsjahre hinaus läßt sich insbesondere auf die umstrittene Praxis der alliierten Besatzungsmächte bei der Durchführung der Restitutionen in Deutschland[2] zurückführen, welche bis heute und aller Wahrscheinlichkeit nach auch in der Zukunft eigentumsrechtliche Fragen aufwirft und aufwerfen wird.[3] Sowohl für das Privatrecht als auch für das Völkerrecht wirft die Erklärung erhebliche Fragen auf, die zugleich für die breiten Arbeitsgebiete von KURT SIEHR kennzeichnend sind.

Im folgenden soll unter besonderer Berücksichtigung der Rechtsliteratur in den un-

---

[2] Für die US-Zone vgl. H. Weber, *Die völkerrechtlichen Restitutionen*, Diss. München (1949) S. 84ff.

[3] So wurden im Pariser Louvre erst kürzlich acht Gemälde entdeckt, die seit dem Ende des zweiten Weltkrieges auf der Verlustliste des „Von-der-Heydt-Museums" in Wuppertal stehen. Die Gemälde wurden während des Krieges vom damaligen Direktor des Museums in französischen Galerien und Privatsammlungen erworben, nach dem Kriege aber von der französischen Besatzungsmacht beschlagnahmt und nach Paris gebracht. Das Herausgabeverlangen des „Von-der-Heydt-Museums" wurde von französischer Seite mit der Begründung abgelehnt, die Bilder seien aufgrund der Londoner Erklärung rechtmäßig eingezogen worden und des weiteren bestehe der Verdacht, daß die Verkäufe damals unter Druck zustandegekommen seien. (Quelle: *Art*, Das Kunstmagazin, Ausgabe Nr. 3, März 1998)

mittelbaren Nachkriegsjahren[4] versucht werden zu analysieren, was im Einzelnen die „Londoner Erklärung" regelt und welche Rechtsverbindlichkeit ihrem Inhalt zukommt. Schwerpunkt der Untersuchung wird die Frage sein, wieweit der private Geschäftsverkehr außerhalb staatlicher Betätigung in den von Deutschland und seinen Verbündeten besetzten Gebieten von der Erklärung betroffen war – und rechtlich sein konnte.

1.   BEGRIFF DER RESTITUTION

Das aus dem lateinischen „restituere" stammende Wort „Restitution" bedeutet soviel wie „Wiederherstellung" und fand Eingang in das Völkerrecht im Laufe des 19. Jahrhunderts, als sich im Völkerkriegsrecht der Grundsatz der Unverletzlichkeit feindlichen Privateigentums entwickelte.[5]

Dieser Grundsatz wurde in der Haager Landkriegsordnung (HLKO) vom 18.10.1907 (vgl. insbesondere die Art. 46 f. sowie Art. 53 HLKO) kodifiziert, vor allem aber in den verschiedenen Friedens- und Waffenstillstandsverträgen, beginnend mit dem „Pariser Frieden" von 1814 bis hin zum „Versailler Vertrag" von 1919,[6] der auch (und vor allem) staatliches Eigentum umfaßte.

In einem Versuch, einen allgemeinen und unspezifischen Tatbestand der Restitution aus diesen Verträgen (die sehr viel weitergehend als die HLKO sind) zu entnehmen, kann Restitution beschrieben werden als die Rückgabe von Gegenständen in natura, welche eine Kriegspartei während des Krieges aus dem Hoheitsgebiet der anderen Kriegspartei *unter ganz bestimmten Umständen* entfernt hatte und welche nach Beendigung eines Krieges auf dem Hoheitsgebiet der einen Kriegspartei noch feststellbar sind.[7] Diesen „ganz bestimmten Umständen" der einzelnen Friedensverträge ist gemeinsam, daß bis zum Ende des 2. Weltkrieges offenbar nur einseitige Wegnahmehandlungen („enlever", „saisir" oder „sequestrer") als restitutionspflichtige Akte angesehen wurden.[8]

Die Londoner Erklärung hingegen umfaßt dem Wortlaut nach auch vertragliches Handeln („dealings", „transactions apparently legal in form").

Dem trägt auch die bereits angesprochene Praxis der Besatzungsmächte Rechnung, die – unter Berufung auf die Londoner Erklärung, welche als offizielle Handlungs- und Rechtsgrundlage jedoch erst in der Kontrollratsdirektive vom

---

[4] Unter weitestgehendem Verzicht auf spätere Literatur

[5] Dazu eingehend schon H. Weber (oben N. 2) S. 13ff.; allgemein W. Fiedler, „Zur Entwicklung des Völkergewohnheitsrechts im Bereich des internationalen Kulturgüterschutzes", in: *Festschrift Doehring* (Berlin 1989) S. 199ff.

[6] Vgl. H. Weber (oben N. 2) S. 15ff.; zum Text vgl. statt anderer W. Fiedler (oben N. 1) S. 250ff.

[7] Vgl. H. Weber (oben N. 2) S. 28; G. Schmoller/ H. Maier/ A. Tobler (oben N. 1) S. 3.

[8] H. Weber (oben N. 2) S. 35ff., 38

21.1.1946[9] genannt wird – sehr umfangreich auch vertraglich erworbene Güter in das Ursprungsland zurückführten.[10]

Diese Praxis stieß auf einhellige Ablehnung in der deutschen Rechtsliteratur der Nachkriegsjahre. Während einige anhand der Londoner Erklärung sowie der Militärgesetzgebung versuchten, die Ungesetzlichkeit des Vorgehens der Besatzungsmächte nachzuweisen,[11] verwarfen andere, ohne sich zunächst mit der genannten Gesetzgebung auseinanderzusetzen, bereits die völkerrechtliche Legitimation zu einem solchen Vorgehen.[12]

Für eine rechtliche Bewertung der Nachkriegsgeschehnisse in Bezug auf Restitutionsfragen bedarf es indes der Beachtung beider Blickwinkel. Dies schon alleine deshalb, weil jeder dieser beiden für sich zu kurz greift: Wer nur die Sichtweise des Völkerrechts, wie es zu Vorkriegszeiten anerkannt wurde, ohne Beachtung der Inhalte Alliierter Erklärungen berücksichtigt, übersieht den Einfluß, den diese auf das Völkerrecht gehabt haben mögen. Auf der anderen Seite mag die Analyse alliierter Vorschriften die zu jener Zeit sachlich hilfreichere Methode gewesen sein, Rechtsverletzungen zu begegnen oder vorzubeugen. Für eine umfassende rechtliche Würdigung der Gesamtumstände reicht sie freilich ebenfalls nicht aus. Es geht folglich zunächst darum, den Regelungsgehalt der Londoner Erklärung zu ermitteln und dann zu überprüfen, in welchem Verhältnis sie zum geltenden Völkerrecht steht.

2.   DER REGELUNGSGEHALT DER LONDONER ERKLÄRUNG

Inhaltlich gliedert sich die Londoner Erklärung in zwei rechtlich bedeutsame Teile auf. Absatz 2 enthält eine Warnung, gerichtet insbesondere an Bewohner neutraler Staaten, daß die Erklärenden die Enteignungsmethoden der Regierungen der Achsenmächte zunichte zu machen anstreben.

In Absatz 3 wird der Vorbehalt ausgesprochen, jede Übertragung von Eigentum und sonstigen Rechtspositionen für nichtig zu erklären, die in den besetzten Gebieten vorgenommen wurde.

Hinsichtlich der nach dem 2. Weltkrieg in Deutschland durchgeführten Restitutionen stehen insbesondere zwei Fragen im Vordergrund:

1.   Gilt der Vorbehalt, alle Übertragungen für nichtig zu erklären, *absolut* oder nur innerhalb der in Absatz 3 Satz 2 genannten Beschränkungen, d.h. nur hinsicht-

---

[9] Abgedruckt in G. Schmoller/ H. Maier/ A. Tobler (oben N. 23).

[10] Vgl. auch G. Schmoller/ H. Maier/ A. Tobler, ibid., S. 9ff.

[11] So insbesondere E. Kaufmann, „Die völkerrechtlichen Grundlagen und Grenzen der Restitution", *AöR* 75 (36 N.F.) (1949) S. 1ff.

[12] Vgl. E. Langen/E. Sauer, *Die Restitution im internationalen Recht* (Düsseldorf 1949); H. Weber (oben N. 2).

lich „scheinbar gesetzmäßiger Geschäfte", bei welchen nur *behauptet* wird, sie seien ohne jeden Zwang zustande gekommen?

2. Berührt der Vorbehalt der Nichtigkeitserklärung den gutgläubigen Erwerb von aus den besetzten Gebieten stammenden Objekten?

2.1 Reichweite des Nichtigkeitserklärungsvorbehalts

Zunächst erscheint der Inhalt der Londoner Erklärung widersprüchlich. Während in Absatz 2 davon die Rede ist, die *Enteignungsmethoden* der Regierungen der Achsenmächte zunichte zu machen („to defeat the methods of dispossession"), wird in Absatz 3 *demgemäß* („accordingly") der Vorbehalt erklärt, *jede Übertragung und Veräußerung von Eigentum (...) für nichtig zu erklären* („to declare invalid any transfers of, or dealings with, property"). Diese Warnung, Enteignungsmethoden vereiteln zu wollen, einerseits und die Aussage, „demgemäß" auch sonstige Übertragungsakte für nichtig erklären zu können andererseits, erscheint nicht recht kohärent. *Eugen Langen* und *Ernst Sauer* kommen daher zu dem Schluß, daß „[w]ollte man diese Erklärung als materielles Völkerrecht behandeln, so wäre sie schon wegen eines inneren Widerspruches hierzu schlecht geeignet."[13]

In der Tat war das Vorgehen der Alliierten in der Restitutionsfrage eher von Widersprüchen geprägt, als von klaren Vorgaben. So belegen Statistiken[14] und Aussagen des amerikanischen Militärgouverneurs General *Clay*[15] daß zunächst alles, was aus den ehemals besetzten Gebieten stammte, eingezogen und zurückgeführt wurde, ohne daß sich die deutschen Besitzer zu den Erwerbsumständen äußern konnten. So berichtet *Hans Weber*, daß bis zum November 1947 in der amerikanischen Besatzungszone sogar jenes Gut für restitutionspflichtig erachtet wurde, das Deutsche in das besetzte Gebiet hinein- und später wieder herausgebracht hatten.[16] Erst Ende 1947 wurde Deutschen die Möglichkeit eingeräumt, sich zum Restitutionsbegehren ausländischer Regierungen zu äußern.[17] Angesichts der Regelung im bereits angesprochenen Kontrollratsabkommen vom Januar und März 1946, daß „die Frage der Rückerstattung von Eigentum, das von den Deutschen aus den alliierten Ländern entfernt (*removed*) wurde, [...] in allen Fällen unter dem Gesichtspunkt (*in the light of*) der Erklärung vom 5. Januar 1943 geprüft werden [muß]",[18] läßt dieses un-

---

[13] E. Langen/E. Sauer, ibid., S. 5

[14] Z.B. hinsichtlich der amerikanischen Restitutionspolitik von H. Weber (oben N. 2) S. 84ff.

[15] L.D. Clay, *Entscheidung in Deutschland* (Frankfurt a.M. 1950) S. 341ff.

[16] H. Weber (oben N. 2) S. 86.

[17] H. Dabelstein, „Restitutionen und Rechtsmangelhaftung", *Der Betriebs-Berater* (1949) S. 22, 23; H. Weber (oben N. 2) S. 86ff.

[18] Quellen: E. Kaufmann (oben N. 11) S. 1ff., 4; W. Wilmanns, *Restitutionen* (Hamburg 1947) S. 17; G. Schmoller/ H. Maier/ A. Tobler (oben N. 1) S. 23 (Anlage I).

einheitliche Vorgehen den Schluß zu, daß eine von Anfang an verbindliche Auslegung der Erklärung seitens der Alliierten nicht existierte.[19]

Unklar war insbesondere die Frage, ob die Erklärung tatsächlich alle Übertragungen in den besetzten Ländern unter den Vorbehalt der Nichtigkeitserklärung
stellt, wie der Eingangssatz des Abs. 3 („to declare invalid any transfers") sugge-
riert, oder nur das unter Zwang Erworbene, worauf der letzte Satz des Abs. 3
(„transactions apparently legal in form, even when they purport to be voluntarily effected") hindeutet.

In der zeitgenössischen Literatur wurde die erste der beiden Auslegungsmög-
lichkeiten ganz überwiegend abgelehnt.[20] Der Amerikaner *L.H. Woolsey* schrieb
schon 1943, daß „[t]he warning apparently contemplates singling out the dealings
which are illegal or which are directly or indirectly the result of undue military pressure and compulsion".[21]

Unter den Nachkriegsautoren vermutet lediglich *Hans Dabelstein* hinter dem
Vorbehalt, jede Übertragung von Vermögensgegenständen für nichtig zu erklären
„den alten anglo-amerikanischen Grundsatz, der jedes ‚trading with the enemy'
verbietet".[22] Diese Auffassung erscheint indes kaum haltbar, betrachtet man die Ur-
teilsbegründung im Nürnberger IG-Farben-Prozeß vom 29./30.7.48 durch das Militärgericht VI der USA.[23] Gerade hinsichtlich der Frage, ob Rechtsgeschäfte von
Deutschen in den besetzten Gebieten als wirksam zu betrachten sind, stellt es klar,
daß das Völkerrecht es nicht verbietet, Handel in besetzten Gebieten zu betreiben.
Wörtlich heißt es (in der Übersetzung): „Vergeblich suchen wir in den Haager Bestimmungen eine Vorschrift, welche die weitgehende Auffassung rechtfertigen
würde, daß private Bürger des Landes, das die militärische Besetzung durchführt,
auch dann nicht das Recht haben, in besetzten Gebieten Verträge über Vermögenswerte abzuschließen, wenn die Einwilligung des Inhabers tatsächlich freiwillig gegeben wird".[24] Die Londoner Erklärung wird in sofern nicht als hierzu im
Widerspruch stehend eingestuft.

Hans Weber[25] führt hinsichtlich des oben angeführten „inneren Widerspruchs"
zwischen Abs. 2 und Abs. 3 aus: „Hier werden also scheinbar Gegenstände für

---

[19] W. Wilmanns, ibid., S. 19, deutet an, daß Klarheit hinsichtlich der Restitutionsvoraussetzungen
möglicherweise nicht einmal gewollt war.

[20] Es wird überwiegend ganz selbstverständlich von der zweiten Auslegungsmöglichkeit ausge-
gangen. Vgl. E. Kaufmann (oben N. 11) S. 4ff; G. Schmoller/ H. Maier/ A. Tobler (oben N. 1) S. 6; A.
Arndt, Anmerkung zu OLG Hamburg vom 3.2.48, *Süddeutsche Juristenzeitung* (1948) Sp. 323ff., 324.
Eingehender dagegen H. Weber (oben N. 2) S. 37f.

[21] L.H. Woolsey, „The Forced Transfer of Property in Enemy Occupied Territories", 37 *AJIL*
(1943) S. 282ff., 283.

[22] H. Dabelstein (oben N. 17) S. 22.

[23] Zitiert nach E. Langen/ E. Sauer (oben N. 12) S. 12 und 20.

[24] Auch wiedergegeben in G. Schmoller/ H. Maier/ A. Tobler (oben N. 1) S. 17.

[25] Oben N. 2, S. 37f.

künftige Restitutionen vorgesehen, die ohne jeden Zwang in den besetzten Gebieten erworben worden waren. Doch ist dies nur scheinbar der Fall. Denn die Londoner Erklärung richtet sich doch gegen die Enteignungshandlungen der
Achsenmächte in den besetzten Gebieten. Im 1. Abs. (gemeint ist der 2. Abs., der
Verf.) erklären die Alliierten, daß sie mit allen Mitteln danach streben werden, die
Enteignungsmethoden der Achsenmächte zu vereiteln. Der 2. Abs. (gemeint ist der
3. Abs., der Verf.) ist nichts anderes als ein Vorbehalt, der gegebenenfalls es ermöglichen soll, jede Enteignungshandlung zu erfassen, selbst wenn sie sich unter einem
scheinbar gesetzmäßigen Geschäft verbirgt und selbst, wenn die Ausrede gebraucht
wird, daß die betreffende Übertragung oder Veräußerung ohne jeden Zwang getätigt worden ist." Ferner verweist er auf die Formulierung in der Londoner Erklärung
„...und selbst, falls es angegeben wird, daß die besagten Übertragungen oder Veräußerungen ohne jeden Zwang getätigt worden sind", in der es eben nicht heißt:
„...und selbst, wenn die besagte Übertragung ohne jeden Zwang getätigt worden
ist". In der Tat erscheint Abs. 3 Satz 2 der Londoner Erklärung sinnlos, sofern er
nicht als Einschränkung des Satzes 1 gewertet wird.

Schließlich wird für diese Auslegung Art. 75 des als „Modellvertrag" angesehe-
nen[26] Italienischen Friedensvertrages herangezogen, nach dem Italien die Prinzipien der Londoner Erklärung akzeptiert (Ziff. 1).[27] In Ziff. 2 heißt es: „The
obligation to make restitution applies to all identifiable property at present in Italy
which was removed by force and duress...". Nach *Weber* kann diese Definition restitutionspflichtiger Akte in Ziff. 2 („unter Anwendung von Gewalt und Zwang entfernt") zugleich als eine Art Legaldefinition der „Enteignungshandlungen"
(„dispossessions") der Londoner Erklärung angesehen werden.[28]

Weiter gab es in den Nachkriegsjahren Unstimmigkeiten, wie der Begriff „looting"
(Raub) auszulegen sei. *W. G. Downey*[29] berichtet von Restitutionsansprüchen verschiedener Regierungen (u.a. Ungarns, Polens, Jugoslawiens, Belgiens und Norwegens) hinsichtlich von Gegenständen der Militärausrüstung. Sie betrachteten alles
von den deutschen Streitkräften beschlagnahmte Eigentum als „looted" i.S.d. Londoner Erklärung. Diese Einschätzung beachtete aber nicht hinreichend die im
Kriegsrecht seit 1907 geltende HLKO, welche in Art. 53 Abs. 1 regelt, welche Gegenstände *legal* beschlagnahmt werden können. Diese unterliegen auch nicht einer
späteren Restititutionspflicht.[30] *Downey* führt hierzu aus: „However, in these and similar cases, because of the Declaration of London, it was necessary to establish that

---

[26] W. Wilmanns (oben N. 18) S. 7.
[27] Vgl. zum Text W. Wilmanns, ibid., S. 7 f.
[28] H. Weber (oben N. 2) S. 39.
[29] W. G. Downey, „Captured Enemy Property: Booty of War and Seized Enemy Property", 44 *AJIL*
(1950) S. 488ff., 503
[30] Vgl. H. Weber (oben N. 2) S. 61ff.

such captured enemy property had not been ‚looted‘ by the German forces".[31] Die auf diese Weise beschlagnahmten Gegenstände fallen folglich auch nicht unter den Nichtigkeitserklärungsvorbehalt.

2.2   Gutgläubiger Erwerb

In den Verhandlungen, die der Londoner Erklärung vorausgingen, wurde auch die Frage des guten Glaubens angesprochen. Speziell mit Bezug auf Deutschland wurde die Rückgabe des von den besetzten Gebieten stammenden Eigentums gefordert, „selbst wenn es der letzte deutsche Besitzer durch klipp und klare Zahlung erworben hatte".[32] Diese Forderung findet sich etwas verborgen in der Londoner Erklärung wieder, wenn von Übertragungen von Eigentum u.a. die Rede ist, welches sich in den besetzten Gebieten *befunden hat* („. . . or have been situated in the territories which have come under the occupation or control . . . "). Der Nichtigkeitserklärungsvorbehalt betrifft also auch den gutgläubigen Erwerb von Eigentum, welches unter den oben genannten Umständen erlangt wurde.

3.   RECHTSNATUR DER ERKLÄRUNG

Der Frage, welche Rechtsnatur der Londoner Erklärung zukommt oder welche sie beansprucht, wird in den Kommentaren zur Restitutionsfrage in Deutschland nur geringe Beachtung geschenkt.

Dies mag daran liegen, daß sie nicht auf eine direkte Rechtsfolge gerichtet ist. Stellvertretend für die insoweit in der Literatur bestehende Einigkeit sei *L.H. Woolsey* zitiert, der befindet: „However, it goes not further than to reserve the right to declare such dealings invalid".[33] Es handelt sich damit lediglich um eine Vorankündigung späterer Forderungen auf Restitutionen.[34] Von dem Vorbehalt, die in Absatz 3 der Londoner Erklärung genannten Übertragungen für nichtig zu erklären, haben die Alliierten auch nach Beendigung des Krieges keinen Gebrauch gemacht. Es wäre ohnehin äußerst fraglich gewesen, welche Bedeutung eine Erklärung der 17 Erklärungsparteien für das innerstaatliche Zivilrecht der eigenen und auch fremder Länder zugekommen wäre.[35] Nach *L. H. Woolsey*[36] sind nur die legitimen Regierungen der einzelnen besetzten Staaten dazu berechtigt, Rechtsgeschäfte für nichtig zu erklären. Diese Autorität sei bei den Parteien der Erklärung

---

[31] W. G. Downey (oben N. 29).
[32] Zitiert nach H. Weber (oben N. 2) S. 40.
[33] L.H. Woolsey (oben N. 21) S. 282.
[34] G. Schmoller/ H. Maier/ A. Tobler (oben N. 1) S. 6.
[35] W. Wilmanns (oben N. 18) S. 6.
[36] L. H. Woolsey (oben N. 21) S. 282.

aber überwiegend zweifelhaft.

Man mag fragen, warum nicht schlicht erklärt wurde, daß nach der Niederwerfung der Achsenmächte alles mit Gewalt und Zwang fortgenommene Eigentum zurückverlangt werde. *Werner Wilmanns*[37] zufolge erklärt sich dies „aus der besonderen Rechtslage, die hinsichtlich des in neutralen Ländern befindlichen fortgenommenen Eigentums vorauszusehen war. Gegenüber den neutralen Ländern konnten die Erklärenden nicht erwarten, völkerrechtliche Rechte des Siegers oder etwaiger Friedensverträge geltend zu machen. Ihnen gegenüber können nur Ansprüche durchdringen, die auf das ursprüngliche privatrechtliche Eigentum der Geschädigten gegründet sind." Möglicherweise war es die zweifelhafte Rechtsverbindlichkeit, welche die Alliierten von der Nichtigkeitserklärung Abstand nehmen ließ.

Die Rolle der Londoner Erklärung in der Restitutionsfrage ist vor allem daher schwierig in rechtliche Begriffe zu kleiden, weil sie nicht, wie in Italien, Bestandteil eines Friedensvertrags wurde. Daß sie aber auch in Deutschland für höchst bedeutend gehalten wurde, ergab sich bereits aus ihrer Erwähnung in nahezu jeder Abhandlung zum Thema Restitutionen. Eine rechtliche Zuordnung wird indes zumeist vermieden. *Erich Kaufmann* bezeichnet sie rechtlich neutral als „Ausgangspunkt" der alliierten Restitutionspolitik,[38] enthält sich weiter aber jeder rechtlichen Zuordnung. *G. Schmoller/ H. Maier/ A. Tobler* immerhin gestehen ihr deklaratorischen Charakter zu,[39] ohne diese Einschätzung allerdings näher zu begründen.

Anders verhält es sich in der US-Amerikanischen Literatur. *W. G. Downey*[40] beschreibt deutlich das Verhältnis des geschriebenen und ungeschriebenen Völkerrechts zur Londoner Erklärung, indem er ausführt: „Certainly it would not be maintained on any legal ground that the Declaration of London invalidated or rendered inoperative the unwritten rules of the international law of war or the written rules contained in the Hague and Geneva Conventions." Ähnlich auch *Jacob Robinson*:[41] „Moreover, [the Declaration] does not attempt to fill out the existing gaps in international law".

Es konnte somit die Feststellung als konsensfähig erachtet werden, daß die Londoner Erklärung bestehendes Völkerrecht nicht abändert. Es fragt sich somit, mit welcher Berechtigung sie „Ausgangspunkt" der Restitutionen in Deutschland wurde. Das Militärgericht VI der USA führt im erwähnten Nürnberger IG-Farben-Prozeß dazu aus: „Zwar stellt die interalliierte Erklärung kein Gesetz dar und hätte nicht mit rückwirkender Kraft ausgestattet werden können (...); es ergibt sich aber

---

[37] W. Wilmanns (oben N. 18) S. 7.
[38] E. Kaufmann (oben N. 11) S. 2; *ders.*, *Deutschlands Rechtslage unter der Besatzung* (Stuttgart 1948) S. 64.
[39] G. Schmoller/ H. Maier/ A. Tobler (oben N. 1) S. 6f.
[40] W. G. Downey (oben N. 29) S. 502f.
[41] J. Robinson, „Transfer of Property in Enemy Occupied Territory", 39 *AJIL* (1945) S. 216ff., 229.

aus der Erklärung, daß Verletzungen der in der Erklärung genannten Rechte von den Signatarmächten als Handlungen angesehen werden, die einen Verstoß gegen das bestehende Völkerrecht darstellen".[42]

Setzt somit die Londoner Erklärung kein Völkerrecht und ist insofern nur deklaratorischer Natur, so geht ihre rechtliche Bedeutung doch so weit, wie sie Völkerrecht *enthält*.

4. DER VÖLKERRECHTSGEHALT DER LONDONER ERKLÄRUNG

Der Inhalt der Londoner Erklärung könnte unproblematisch Grundlage von Rückforderungen gegenüber deutschen Erwerbern von Gegenständen (Immobilien seien hier ausgeklammert) in den im Krieg besetzten Gebieten gewesen sein, wenn ein völkerrechtlicher Restitutionstatbestand dies vorgesehen hätte.

Völkerrechtlich anerkannt sind weithin die Normen der HLKO, welche jedoch nur einen Teilbereich der durch die Londoner Erklärung umfaßten Tatbestände abdeckt. Als eindeutige Restitutionsvorschrift kann lediglich Art. 53 Abs. 2 HLKO (Rückgabepflicht von beschlagnahmten Kriegsmitteln, die im Privateigentum standen) genannt werden. Gleiches muß aber „*a majore ad minus*" auch für Verletzungen des Art. 46 HLKO (i.V.m. Art. 3 HLKO) gelten, so daß auch hier Restitution verlangt werden kann. Abgedeckt sind hierbei die Handlungen der zur bewaffneten Macht einer Kriegspartei gehörenden Personen (Art. 3 HLKO). Für die Frage, in welchen Fällen Art. 46 HLKO als verletzt anzusehen ist, liegen in der Londoner Erklärung in Reaktion auf das Vorgehen von Angehörigen der deutschen Streitkräfte (inkl. des Verwaltungspersonals)[43] bedenkenswerte Ansätze für dessen „Neu"-Auslegung. Diese könnte dazu führen, daß auch formell rechtsgeschäftliches Handeln unter den Tatbestand der „Einziehung" bzw. der „Nichtachtung" fremden Privateigentums in Art. 46 HLKO fallen kann. Es ist aber weder auf Seiten der Alliierten noch der deutschen Literatur hinsichtlich Restitutionsfragen jemals dieser Möglichkeit nachgegangen worden.[44] Ausgegangen wird durchweg von der Existenz eines allgemeinen völkerrechtlich anerkannten Restitutionstatbestands. Für die vorliegende Untersuchung ist der möglicherweise aus der HLKO abzuleitende Restitutionsbegriff aber nicht von übergeordneter Bedeutung, da die HLKO Handlungen von Privatpersonen, um die es hier in der Hauptsache gehen soll, ohnehin nicht erfaßt.

Die Begründung eines über die HLKO hinausgehenden ungeschriebenen, d.h.

---

[42] Zitiert nach E. Langen/ E. Sauer (oben N. 12) S. 12.

[43] Eine umfassende Darstellung findet sich bei J. Robinson (oben N. 41) S. 216ff.

[44] Eine Tendenz hierzu läßt sich den Ausführungen von A. Arndt (oben N. 20) Sp. 323 entnehmen, demzufolge sich die (völkerrechtlichen) Restitutionen aus der modernen Beschränkung des Besatzungsrechts, wie sie in der HLKO kodifiziert ist, ergeben.

„völkergewohnheitsrechtlichen" Tatbestands gestaltet sich jedoch äußerst schwierig. Ist den vorliegenden Friedensverträgen noch ein gewisser Konsens, also eine
für die Entstehung von Gewohnheitsrecht erforderliche gleichbleibende Übung,
hinsichtlich der Restitutionsvoraussetzungen zu entnehmen, so wird dagegen weit
weniger einfach die notwendige allgemeine Rechtsüberzeugung, eine *opinio juris
vel necessitatis* nachzuweisen sein. Denn auch wenn Friedensverträge einfache völkerrechtliche Verträge darstellen, die als solche unbestritten bei entsprechend
gleichartigen Vertragsbestimmungen zu allgemein geltendem Völkerrecht erstar-
ken können, so darf nicht übersehen werden, daß es sich bei diesen Verträgen um
die Vorlage von Bedingungen der Sieger an die Besiegten im Krieg handelte, die
letztere unter Zwang annehmen mußten. Dementsprechend wird auf Seiten der Besiegten kaum von einer Rechtsüberzeugung hinsichtlich der Vertragsinhalte gesprochen werden können, zumal Restitutionen zumeist nur von ihrer Seite geleistet
werden mußten.[45] Aus diesen Überlegungen wird gefolgert werden müssen, daß ein
auf Gewohnheitsrecht oder auf allgemeiner Rechtsüberzeugung basierender völkerrechtlicher Restitutionstatbestand außerhalb der HLKO hinaus nicht existiert[46] –
oder zumindest zur Zeit der alliierten Besatzung noch nicht existierte. Bestärkt wird
diese Auffassung durch die Tatsache, daß das Thema „Restitution" im hier behandelten Sinne in den Völkerrechtslehrbüchern der heutigen Zeit nahezu nicht vorkommt. Immerhin, in einem kurzen Absatz und in Übereinstimmung mit der hier
vertretenen Auffassung, schreibt *D.W. Greig*: „It is doubtful whether there is any
right to restitution under customary international law except perhaps in relation to
territory (...) it is probably more correct to say that an international tribunal has no
power to *decree* restitution unless that power is expressly granted by agreement between the parties, either for the purposes of a particular case, or generally."[47]

Man mag darüber spekulieren, warum nicht auch mit Deutschland, wie es in der
Nachkriegsliteratur im Sinne der Rechtssicherheit erhofft – oder gar erwartet –
wurde,[48] ein Friedensvertrag nach dem Vorbild Italiens geschlossen wurde, der jeden Zweifel an der Rechtsgrundlage alliierten Handelns hätte beseitigen können. In
einem solchen Vertrag hätte angesichts der Erwerbspraktiken besonders von Deutschen in den besetzten Gebieten[49] ein gegenüber den bisherigen Friedensverträgen
sehr viel weitreichenderer Restitutionstatbestand niedergelegt werden können. Die
Suche nach einer völkerrechtlich akzeptablen Rechtsgrundlage für die Vielzahl der
in Deutschland gerade bei Privatpersonen restituierten Güter wird durch die Abwe-
senheit eines Friedensvertrags jedenfalls nicht erleichtert.

---

[45] Auf diesen Umstand verweist H. Weber (oben N. 2) S. 45f.
[46] So auch H. Weber, ibid., S. 45f.
[47] D.W. Greig, *International Law*, 2nd edn. (London 1976) S. 606.
[48] Vgl. W. Wilmanns (oben N. 18) S. 8.
[49] Eindrucksvoll hierzu J. Robinson (oben N. 41) S. 219ff.

5.   DIE LONDONER ERKLÄRUNG UND INTERNATIONALES PRIVATRECHT

5.1   Anwendbarkeit des IPR in Restitutionsfragen

Kann ein völkerrechtlicher Restitutionstatbestand außerhalb der HLKO nicht fest-gestellt werden, so ist damit freilich noch nichts über die völkerrechtliche Zulässig-keit der in der Londoner Erklärung aufgestellten Tatbestände gesagt. Auch wenn keine über die HLKO hinausgehende Restitutionsregelung feststellbar ist, ver-bleibt, da die Frage der Rückgabe von Eigentum zivilrechtlichen Charakters ist, der Rückgriff auf das Internationale Privatrecht. Hiernach kommen die zivilrechtlichen Regelungen des Staates, von dessen Boden der Gegenstand entfernt wurde, zur An-wendung. Maßgebliches Recht ist entsprechend der Resolution 7 der Londoner In-ternational Law Conference 1943 „the law of the occupied country as applied by the reconstituted authorities after the liberation of the country".[50]

So kann es als gesichert angesehen werden, daß Drohung, Gewalt und Zwang im Zivilrecht der besetzten Staaten einen privatrechtlich gültigen Titel nicht entstehen ließen, so daß das Fortbestehen des Eigentums zu einem Herausgabeanspruch ge-genüber dem Erwerber führte. Gleiches sieht die Londoner Erklärung vor: Wenn von „Übertragungen oder Veräußerungen unter der Form (...) scheinbar gesetzmä-ßiger Geschäfte (...), und selbst, falls es angegeben wird, daß die besagten Übertra-gungen oder Veräußerungen ohne jeden Zwang getätigt worden sind" die Rede ist, so kann dies nur bedeuten, daß tatsächlich eben doch Zwang ausgeübt wurde.[51] Freilich handelt es sich bei Herausgabeansprüchen, die auf internationales Privat-recht gestützt sind, nicht um völkerrechtliche Restitutionen im Sinne der HLKO oder des angeführten Völkervertragsrechts. Für die Rechtmäßigkeit der angekün-digten oder vorgenommenen Rückführungen von aus dem besetzten Gebiet erwor-benen Gegenständen spielt es indes keine Rolle, wie diese bezeichnet wurden. Entscheidend ist nur das Bestehen eines Anspruchs auf der Seite, die von den Rück-führungen profitierte.

Die Einbeziehung der in der Londoner Erklärung benannten „Schein-Rechtsge-schäfte" in den von den Alliierten und Teilen der deutschen Literatur als selbstver-ständlich angenommenen völkerrechtlichen Restitutionstatbestand[52] fand in Deutschland – bei aller Kritik an der schließlichen Praxis – weitgehend Zustim-mung. Nach den Worten von *Adolf Arndt*[53] ist „[d]ie Anwendung von Gewalt oder Zwang (...) nach dem gegenwärtigen Völkerrecht nicht nur dahin zu verstehen, daß es sich um Wegnahme unter Anwendung von physischer Kraft handeln muß, viel-mehr wird im modernen Kriege auch der mittelbare Zwang als ausreichend angese-

---

[50] Zitiert nach E. Langen/ E. Sauer (oben N. 12) S. 20.
[51] Vgl. auch H. Weber (oben N. 2) S. 37f.
[52] Für die deutsche Lit. vgl. nur G. Schmoller/ H. Maier/ A. Tobler (oben N. 1) S. 17ff.
[53] A. Arndt (oben N. 20) Sp. 324.

hen werden müssen. Die neue Auslegung des Begriffs Zwang war der Sinn der
Londoner Erklärung der Alliierten vom 5. l. 43, die das Völkerrecht einseitig weder
abändern konnte noch wollte, sondern den Vorbehalt zum Ausdruck brachte, daß
die Alliierten solche Handlungen für nichtig erklären würden, bei denen ‚Enteignungsmethoden' zu Anwendung gekommen sind. Damit ist gesagt, daß es für die
Auslegung des völkerrechtlichen Begriffs Zwang nicht auf die Form sondern allein
auf die Sache ankommt, mithin als zwangsweise Entfernung eines Gegenstandes
aus dem besetzten Gebiet auch die Besitzergreifung unter dem Schein eines Vertrages angesehen werden kann". Nach Auffassung von *Langen* und *Sauer*[54] berücksichtigt die Deklaration von 1943 „zum erstenmal im Völkerrecht die neue
Entwicklung, wonach die Regierungen gelernt haben, unter der Maske privatwirt-
schaftlicher und privatrechtlicher Maßnahmen Krieg zu führen. Infolgedessen wird
die private Rechtssphäre damit belastet, derartige maskierte Räuber zu kennzeich-
nen und aus ihrem Gebiete zu verweisen. Hierbei muß, um das höhere Gut eines
friedlichen und gesicherten privaten Eigentums zu erhalten, notfalls mit Schärfe
vorgegangen werden."

5.2   Annahme von Gewalt oder Zwang – Beweislastfragen

So sehr jedoch Einigkeit über das Grundprinzip der Restitution i.S.d. Londoner Erklärung besteht, so unterschiedlich sind die Meinungen darüber, wer die Umstände,
unter denen der Erwerb einer Sache in den besetzten Gebieten zustande kam, zu beweisen hat. Ihrem Wortlaut nach („und selbst, falls es angegeben wird . . . ") enthält
die Londoner Erklärung eine gewisse Vermutung gegen die Annahme freiwilliger
Übertragungen.[55] Die Praxis der Besatzungsmächte in dieser Hinsicht ist weitgehend dokumentiert[56] und soll hier nur kurz zusammengefaßt werden.

1.   Im Regelfall wurde das Vorliegen von Gewalt und Zwang hinsichtlich des Erwerbs des aus den besetzten Gebieten stammenden Gegenstandes unterstellt. Der
deutsche Erwerber mußte beweisen (wenn überhaupt der Beweisantritt zugelassen
wurde), daß der Erwerb ohne Druckmittel zustandegekommen ist (Umkehr der Beweislast). Darüberhinaus wurden sog. „Compulsory Lists" aufgestellt, in denen Firmen im besetzten Gebiet aufgeführt waren, deren sämtliche Lieferungen ohne Zulässigkeit eines Gegenbeweises als erzwungen angesehen wurden sowie umgekehrt
deutsche Firmen, deren Bezüge ohne weiteres als Raubgut gelten sollten.[57]

---

[54] E. Langen/ E. Sauer (oben N. 12) S. 28.
[55] Hierauf weisen mit Recht E. Langen/ E. Sauer, ibid., S. 14, hin.
[56] Ausführlich in G. Schmoller/ H. Maier/ A. Tobler (oben N. 1) S. 9ff.
[57] E. Langen/ E. Sauer(oben N. 12) S. 15; G. Schmoller/ H. Maier/ A. Tobler (oben N. 1) S. 10 be-
richten davon, daß diese Listen später wieder abgeschafft wurden.

2. Es wurden Tatbestände aufgeführt, bei denen ausnahmsweise keine Restitutionspflicht angenommen wurde. Wichtigste Ausnahme war der Fall, daß der Gegenstand aufgrund „normaler Handelsbeziehungen" erworben wurde (Handelsbeziehungen schon vor der Besatzungszeit).[58]

Insbesondere in der Frage, wer die Beweislast in Restitutionsfragen zu tragen hatte, wurde das Vorgehen der Alliierten scharf kritisiert.[59] In der Tat wird es kaum ein Zivilrecht der Welt – erst recht keine völkerrechtliche Bestimmung – geben, in der der Erwerber einer Sache beweisen muß, daß er sie ohne Gewalt oder Zwang erworben hat. Man wird daher mit einiger Berechtigung sagen können, daß die in Punkt eins genannten Grundsätze nicht mit denen des internationalen Privatrechts übereinstimmen. Auf rechtliche Bedenken stößt auch Punkt zwei. Die Bedingung des Bestehens einer Handelsbeziehung schon vor der Besatzungszeit läuft praktisch auf die Erklärung des Handelsverbots der Besatzungsmacht auf dem besetzten Gebiet hinaus. Einen solchen Grundsatz jedoch „suchte", wie oben zitiert, das Militärgericht VI der USA[60] „vergeblich".

Allerdings, und auch dies wird von deutscher Seite zugestanden, ist die Frage von Gewalt und Zwang in einem „totalen" Wirtschaftskrieg, wie es der Zweite Weltkrieg war,[61] mit dem „normalen" bürgerlichen Recht des betroffenen Staats möglicherweise nicht zufriedenstellend zu lösen.[62] Denn, anders als in Friedenszeiten, mag die Grundannahme, ein Rechtsgeschäft sei ohne die Verwendung von Gewalt oder Zwang zustandegekommen, im Hinblick auf die Methoden deutscher „Handel Treibenden", wegen derer die Alliierten sich schließlich zu einer Einhalt gebietenden Erklärung genötigt sahen, nicht so ohne weiteres angemessen sein. Aus diesem Blickwinkel betrachtet, könnte in der regelmäßigen Annahme von Gewalt oder Zwang bei Rechtsgeschäften von Deutschen im besetzten Gebiet lediglich eine an die Rechtswirklichkeit angepasste und damit gerechtfertigte Neubewertung der Beweislast für die Zeit der Besetzung gesehen werden. In der Tendenz wird eine solche „angepasste Neubewertung" auch in der deutschen Literatur nicht grundsätzlich abgelehnt. *Langen* und *Sauer*, welche eindeutig das internationale Privatrecht als maßgebend für Restitutionsfragen ansehen, schreiben: „uns scheint, daß man zum Schutze der Bewohner eines besetzten Gebietes weitergehen und in bestimmten Fällen mit einer Vermutung für Zwang arbeiten muß".[63] Nach ihrer Meinung sollte aber der Beweis, daß der Erwerb zu einem gerechten

---

[58] Zu den weiteren Ausnahmen vgl. G. Schmoller/ H. Maier/ A. Tobler, ibid., S. 10.

[59] G. Schmoller/ H. Maier/ A. Tobler, ibid., S. 17ff.

[60] Zitiert nach E. Langen/ E. Sauer, ibid., S. 12 und 20; s. oben unter 2 a.

[61] Es sei noch einmal auf die Darstellung deutschen Vorgehens in den besetzten Staaten bei J. Robinson (oben N. 41) hingewiesen.

[62] Zu dieser Einschätzung tendieren E. Langen/ E. Sauer (oben N. 12) S. 21.

[63] E. Langen/ E. Sauer, ibid., S. 21.

Preis erfolgte, die Beweislast wieder umkehren.[64] Auch *Wilmanns* ist der Auffassung, daß gegen ein Vorgehen im Sinne des italienischen Friedensvertrags, nach dem die Pflicht der Identifizierung beim Anspruch stellenden Staat und der Beweis der Rechtmäßigkeit des Rechtsgeschäfts auf Seiten Italiens liegt, „im Grundsatz wohl noch Einwände formeller, nicht aber materieller Gerechtigkeit geltend gemacht werden" könnten.[65] Es ist jedoch zu fragen, ob eine generelle Beweislastumkehr für jedes Rechtsgeschäft eines jeden Deutschen in den besetzten Gebieten nicht weit an der Rechtswirklichkeit, wegen derer sie ja eingeführt wurde, vorbei geht. Sollte dies der Fall sein, so fehlte dieser ohnehin rechtlich ungesicherten Abänderung des zivilrechtlichen Grundsatzes, daß derjenige, der einen Anspruch geltend macht, auch die für ihn günstigen Umstände beweisen muß, jede Grundlage.

Einzugehen ist daher auf die einzelnen Begründungen der Alliierten für die Beweislastumkehr. Basis für diese Umkehr der Beweislast war die Behauptung eines ständigen „kollektiven Zwanges" der Bewohner in den besetzten Gebieten, für den allerdings unterschiedliche Ursachen genannt wurden.[66]

Kollektiver Zwang sei anzunehmen, weil

1. die Präsenz und das Auftreten deutschen Militärs einen solchen Druck auf die Bevölkerung ausgeübt hätten, daß Geschäfte mit Deutschen grundsätzlich als unter Zwang abgeschlossen angesehen werden müßten.
2. sich der wirtschaftliche Zustand des besetzten Gebietes infolge der Besatzung rapide verschlechterte.
3. die Geschäfte aufgrund der Besatzung mit abgewertetem Geld getätigt wurden.

Insbesondere die in Punkt zwei und drei vorgebrachten Begründungen wurden in der deutschen Literatur einhellig abgelehnt.

Wirtschaftliche Schäden und Währungsschäden seien solche Schäden, die dem Staat als ganzes zugefügt würden und für die er bei Abwicklung der Kriegsschäden Schadensersatz in Form von Reparationszahlungen verlangen könnte. Würde eine Zwangslage des einzelnen aufgrund solcher Umstände anerkannt werden, würde jedes Rechtsgeschäft im besetzten Gebiet als Zwangsgeschäft angesehen werden müssen, was schließlich zu einer Lahmlegung jedes Rechtsverkehrs führen würde.[67]

Weber[68] beleuchtet diese Frage in Auslegung der Begriffe „Gewalt" und „Zwang" in einem Rechtsgeschäft. Danach muß Zwang oder Gewalt in einem

---

[64] E. Langen/ E. Sauer, ibid., S. 22, berufen sich hierbei auf ein von Mezger (*Französisches Rückerstattungsrecht* (1948) S. 35) mitgeteiltes Urteil des Appellationsgerichts Paris vom 7. 12. 46.

[65] W. Wilmanns (oben N. 18) S. 16.

[66] Zusammenstellung aus G. Schmoller/ H. Maier/ A. Tobler (oben N. 1) S. 18; A. Arndt (oben N. 20) Sp. 325; E. Kaufmann, *Deutschlands Rechtslage unter der Besatzung* (1948) S. 72f.

[67] vgl. insbesondere A. Arndt (oben N. 20) Sp. 325.

[68] S. 100.

Rechtsgeschäft zumindest mit demjenigen in Verbindung stehen, mit dem das Rechtsgeschäft geschlossen wurde. Der Verkäufer selbst muß fürchten, daß ihm, wenn er das Rechtsgeschäft nicht tätigt, ein Übel zugefügt wird, das mit dem Käufer in Verbindung steht, so daß er nicht frei wählen kann, ob er den Vertrag schließen will oder nicht.

Sollen die Begriffe „Gewalt" und „Zwang" nicht sinnentleert und als bloße Schlagworte für nahezu selbstverständlich mit dem Krieg einhergehende Schwächung von Wirtschaft und Währung verwendet werden (für die schließlich Reparationen zu leisten sind), so geht an der Auslegung Webers kaum ein Weg vorbei. Wirtschafts- und Währungsschäden sind keine tauglichen Anhaltspunkte für das Vorliegen von Zwang in privaten Rechtsgeschäften. Der Oberste Gerichtshof von Manila hatte in einem Urteil vom 9.4.48[69] festgestellt, daß die in Zusammenhang mit einer Besetzung eintretende Verschlechterung der Währung keinen Einfluß auf die Gültigkeit von Verträgen hat, bei denen mit Geld in verschlechterter Währung bezahlt wurde.

Weniger leicht von der Hand zu weisen ist indes Punkt eins der Alliierten Begründung des Kollektivzwangs. Denn es erscheint durchaus vorstellbar, daß deutsche Käufer auf die Verkäufer im besetzten Land einen Druck dahingehend ausübten, daß letztere fürchten mußten, bei Nichtverkauf Repressalien seitens der Besatzungsmacht ausgesetzt zu sein, so daß Käufer und Zwang in einem unmittelbaren Zusammenhang stehen. Dies gilt insbesondere für Angehörige von Volksgruppen, die wegen ihrer Rasse oder Nationalität Verfolgungen ausgesetzt waren (wie beispielsweise Juden und Polen), was auch in der deutschen Literatur Anerkennung findet.[70] Zweifelhaft erscheint aber, ob gleiches so allgemein etwa auch für Holländer oder Franzosen gelten kann. Dennoch war es nach Aussage des vielzitierten Militärgouverneurs *Clay*[71] gerade Frankreich, welches die generelle Rückgabe aller Gegenstände forderte, die aus den seinerzeit besetzten Gebieten nach Deutschland verbracht wurden, auch soweit sie nicht gewaltsam oder unter Druck entfernt worden waren. Solches Vorgehen steht jedoch klar in Widerspruch zu Art. 46 HLKO. Denn ist davon auszugehen, daß der Handel in besetzten Gebieten nicht grundsätzlich verboten war (s.o.), so hatte der deutsche Käufer, sofern er nicht Zwang auf den Verkäufer ausübte, Eigentum an dem gekauften Gegenstand erworben. Die Rückforderung stellt folglich einen rechtswidrigen Eingriff in Privateigentum dar.

Wie sich daraus ersehen läßt, bedarf die Frage, ob eine Umkehr der Beweislast zumindest aus Gründen der materiellen Gerechtigkeit angemessen erscheint, einer differenzierten Betrachtung. Es ist zweifelhaft genug, ob sich privatrechtliche Grundsätze wie der der Beweislast bei Änderung der Gesamtumstände zwangsläu-

---

[69] *NJW* (1951) S. 125.
[70] Vgl. nur A. Arndt (oben N. 20) Sp. 324f.
[71] Ibid., S. 341.

fig mit verändern. Möchte man dies annehmen, so muß jedenfalls gesichert sein, daß die Änderung der Rechtsgrundsätze auch in jedem Fall gerechtfertigt ist. Gerade hier aber mangelt es bei der allgemeinen Umkehr der Beweislast. Es kann eben nicht so ohne weiteres angenommen werden, daß Erwerbungen deutscher Privatleute in Holland, Frankreich oder gar Italien[72] unter Zwang vorgenommen wurden. Hier scheint eine Umkehr der Beweislast unangemessen und damit unrechtmäßig.

Es kann hier nicht darum gehen, in jedem Einzelfall deutscher Erwerbungen zu entscheiden, wer nun die Beweislast zu tragen hat. Selbstverständlich gab es auch Fälle in den eben aufgeführten Ländern, in denen von privater oder öffentlicher Seite direkt oder indirekt Druck ausgeübt wurde. Auch steht außer Zweifel, daß der Schutz der Eigentumsinteressen der Angehörigen der überfallenen Staaten ein rechtlich nicht zu beanstandendes Motiv für die Handlungen der Alliierten Besatzungsmächte nach dem Zweiten Weltkrieg darstellt. Dennoch sind gewisse rechtliche Rahmenbedingungen auch hierbei zu beachten, soll nicht uneingeschränktes „Siegerrecht"[73] neues Unrecht schaffen. Die gerechte Verteilung der Beweislast stellt eine solche Rahmenbedingung dar.

Ob die Londoner Erklärung einer differenzierten Beweislastregelung im angeführten Sinne entgegensteht, ist trotz der Tendenz zur generellen Umkehr der Beweislast nicht zweifelsfrei zu beantworten. Der Wortlaut   „Die gegenwärtige Warnung gilt auch, wenn solche Übertragungen oder Veräußerungen unter der Form eines offensichtlichen Raubes oder scheinbar gesetzmäßiger Geschäfte vorgenommen worden sind, und selbst, falls es angegeben wird, daß die besagten Übertragungen oder Veräußerungen ohne jeden Zwang getätigt worden sind" kann auch dahingehend verstanden werden, daß nur die Fälle einer Beweislastumkehr unterliegen sollten, in denen „Scheingeschäfte" anzunehmen waren. Eine derartige Regelung entspräche den oben dargestellten Prinzipien im vollen Umfange.

5.3   Gutgläubiger Erwerb

Der Frage, ob gutgläubiger Erwerb an Gegenständen, die unter Gewalt oder Zwang aus dem besetzten Gebiet entfernt wurden, möglich ist, wird in der deutschen Nachkriegsliteratur kaum Beachtung geschenkt. Umstritten war vielmehr, ob der gutgläubige Erwerber für den Fall, daß die erworbene Sache von den Besatzungsbehörden restituiert wurde, Ansprüche gegen den Veräußerer wegen Rechtsmangels hat.[74] Dies mag an der Selbstverständlichkeit liegen, mit der die Alliierten alle aus

---

[72] Ludwig Engstler, *Die territoriale Bindung von Kulturgütern im Rahmen des Völkerrechts* (Köln 1964) S. 151f. berichtet von der Restitution eines Gemäldes, das 1941 in dem damals verbündeten Italien – also bar jeglicher Besatzung – vom Deutschen Reich gekauft wurde, nachdem es zuvor auf verschiedenen Kunstauktionen keinen Käufer gefunden hatte.

[73] Oder „Recht des Stärkeren", wie es vielfach hieß; vgl. W. Wilmanns (oben N. 18) S. 16.

[74] Vgl. OLG Hamburg, *SJZ* (1948) Sp. 320ff.; A. Arndt (oben N. 20) Sp. 324; G. Schmoller/ H. Maier/ A. Tobler (oben N. 1) S. 22f. m.w.N.

ihrer Sicht unrechtmäßig aus den ehemals besetzten Gebieten entfernten Güter unabhängig von den Erwerbsumständen des letzten Besitzers einzogen. Praktisch relevant, weil vor deutschen Gerichten verhandelbar, war folglich nur noch die Frage der Rückgriffsansprüche gegen den Vorbesitzer.

Dennoch gibt es auch vereinzelte Stellungnahmen zum gutgläubigen Erwerb selbst, soweit es sich um völkerrechtliche Restitutionsansprüche handelt. Hier vertreten *Arndt* und *Weber* die Ansicht, daß gutgläubiger Erwerb restitutionspflichtiger Gegenstände nicht möglich ist. *Weber* begründet dies mit dem Schutzzweck der Normen der HLKO sowie dem Primat des Völkerrechts über das nationale Recht,[75] *Arndt* aus dem Gedanken heraus, „daß die kriegerische Besetzung (occupatio bellica) (...) nicht dauernde Rechtsänderungen bewirken kann, sondern alle ihre Folgen lediglich vorübergehender Art sind".[76] Er verweist schließlich auf die im Grundsatz gleichlautende Bestimmung in den verschiedenen Friedensverträgen, u.a. mit Italien (Art. 75) und Rumänien (Art. 23), in denen unter Zwang oder Gewalt entfernte Gegenstände unabhängig von späteren Transaktionen als rückgabepflichtig erachtet werden.[77]

Ob gleiches auch für Herausgabeansprüche nach dem internationalen Privatrecht gilt, scheint indes zweifelhaft. Konsequenterweise müßte man annehmen, daß sich die Frage des gutgläubigen Erwerbs nach dem Recht des Veräußerungsorts richtet, d.h. gutgläubiger Erwerb grundsätzlich möglich ist. Dagegen bestimmt die bereits angesprochene Resolution 7 der Londoner International Law Conference sinngemäß, daß an Sachen, welche von Angehörigen einer Besatzungsmacht nach dem Recht des besetzten Staates unrechtmäßig erworben wurden, auch nicht gutgläubig Eigentum erworben werden kann.[78] Ob diese Regelung völkerrechtlich bindend ist, soll offen bleiben. Jedenfalls dient auch sie, ähnlich wie die partielle Umkehr der Beweislast im oben dargestellten Sinne, den Grundsätzen materieller Gerechtigkeit, d.h. dem anerkennenswerten Schutzbedürfnis der vielzähligen Opfer von Zwangsgeschäften.

6. SCHLUSSFOLGERUNGEN

Die Londoner Erklärung der Alliierten vom 5.1.1943 hat in Rechtskreisen mehr Verwirrung denn Klarheit gestiftet. Die Vielfältigkeit ihrer Interpretationsmöglichkeiten spiegelt sich deutlich in den Widersprüchlichkeiten der alliierten Besatzungspolitik, angefangen mit mißverständlicher, in nahezu jeder Zone unterschiedlicher Gesetzgebung, welche abermals eine Reihe unterschiedlichster

---

[75] H. Weber (oben N. 2) S. 55ff.
[76] A. Arndt (oben N. 20) Sp. 323.
[77] Textauszug aus dem ital. Friedensvertrag bei A. Arndt, ibid., Sp. 323f.
[78] Vgl. Originaltext bei E. Langen/ E. Sauer (oben N. 12) S. 20.

Interpretationen nach sich zog, bis hin zur uneinheitlichen Restitutionspraxis, wieder. Der deutsche Rechtsliteratur wiederum, angetreten, um Licht ins rechtliche Dunkel alliierter Verhaltensweisen zu bringen, gelingt es nicht, die Londoner Erklärung in bestehende Rechtskategorien einzuordnen. So bleibt die Begründung eines völkerrechtlichen Restitutionstatbestands, soweit geschehen, eher diffus belegt und kommt über die bloße Behauptung kaum hinaus. Es scheint so, als diene die Formel „völkerrechtlich allgemein anerkannt" nur zur Überdeckung dieser Begründungsschwierigkeiten. Nur selten klingt an, daß es sich bei der Frage nach Restitutionen in Deutschland nach dem Zweiten Weltkrieg um einen völkerrechtlichen Präzedenzfall handelt. Restitutionen waren bisher vom Sieger dem Besiegten vertraglich auferlegt worden. Zuvor waren es (außerhalb von Eroberungen) meist die im Krieg siegreichen Staaten, die die Frage der Wiedergutmachung selbst in die Hand nahmen, zumal mit dem Anspruch, hierbei Völkerrecht zu verwirklichen.

In einer Frage besteht, abseits von allen sonstigen rechtlichen und begrifflichen Unklarheiten, innerhalb der deutschen Literatur Einigkeit: Es gibt keinerlei rechtliche Grundlage, weder im Völker- noch im Privatrecht, für die Annahme, daß in den besetzten Gebieten erstandene Güter unabhängig von ihren Erwerbsumständen in jedem Fall zurückgegeben werden müßten. Solches sieht auch keine alliierte Vorschrift, auch nicht die Londoner Erklärung vor. Vorgelegen haben muß vielmehr eine Besitzentziehung unter Zwangseinwirkung (Drohung oder Gewalt).

Darüberhinaus ist, wie dargelegt, mit der Umkehr der Beweislast zulasten des deutschen Erwerbers sehr vorsichtig umzugehen. Denn eine derartige Umkehr entspricht weder völkerrechtlichen noch zivilrechtlichen Grundsätzen und ist lediglich unter dem Aspekt materieller Gerechtigkeit in bestimmten Fällen als zulässig zu erachten.

Die Grundsätze der Londoner Erklärung widersprechen dem nicht. Aus heutiger Sichtweise und im Hinblick insbesondere auf die mit den ehemals mit dem Deutschen Reich im Krieg verbündeten Staaten geschlossenen Friedensverträge, erscheint die Erklärung mehr ein Memorandum darüber, was die Alliierten im Falle des Sieges zu tun beabsichtigten, als ein völkerrechtlich wirksames Rechtsdokument zu sein. Es wird ernsthaft auch keine Staatengemeinschaft verlangen können, ein von ihr einseitig formuliertes Rechtsdokument sei unmittelbar als geltendes Völkerrecht zu behandeln, es sei denn, es enthielte bereits bestehendes Völkerrecht.

Es gilt zum Schluß festzuhalten, daß die Frage der Restitutionen zu keinem Zeitpunkt bisher Eingang in eine zufriedenstellende rechtswissenschaftliche Debatte gefunden hat. So bleiben bis heute aktuelle Fragen über das rechtliche Schicksal erheblicher aus Deutschland ausgeführter Vermögenswerte nach wie vor unbeachtet. Die vorliegenden Überlegungen sollen ein kleiner Beitrag zur Lösung der nach wie vor offenen Fragen sein.

SUMMARY

THE ALLIED (LONDON) DECLARATION OF JANUARY 5, 1943: CONTENT, INTERPRETATION AND LEGAL NATURE IN THE POST-WAR DISCUSSION

The article examines the signification of the London Declaration of 1943 for private transactions in countries occupied by Germany or her Allies and tries to answer the question wether the London Declaration is in harmony with the relevant principles of public international law and of private law.

The public international law institute of restitution which has its basis in the Hague Rules of Land Warfare and the practice of States as expressed in a number of peace treaties presupposes a unilateral act of the occupying power (sequestration, seizure, confiscation), whereas the London Declaration also includes private dealings based on private law ruled contracts. Of particular importance in this respect is the reservation made in article 3 of the London Declaration to declare invalid any transfer of property or other rights situated in the occupied territories. Here, two questions arise: is this reservation absolute or does it concern only transactions apparently legal in form, but in truth based on force or duress, and does it further exclude *bona fide* acquisition of objects originating in the occupied countries?

With regard to the first question, the allied practice in occupied Germany had changed. Whereas in the first time the obligation of restitution concerned all objects coming from occupied territories, the restitution was finally restricted to objects acquired under force or duress. Only this restricted use of the principle of restitution was in accordance with the text of the London Declaration and public international law principles as expressed in State practice. Moreover, Art. 53 of the Hague Rules considers legally confiscated objects not as „loot" that has to be restituted.

Considering the second question the author remarks that the London Declaration also excludes bona fide acquisition of objects originating in the occupied countries.

The legal nature of the London Declaration and its signification in public international law are unsettled. In any case it has only declaratory character and didn't change public international law principles. Inasmuch as it embraces dealings of private persons, it is not supported by customary public international law. Moreover, a peace treaty with Germany does not exist.

Apart public international law the London Declaration has also significance for the title of property in private law. This question is regulated by „the law of the occupied country as applied by the reconstituted authorities after the liberation of the country" (Resolution 7 of the London International Law Conference 1943). Force or duress exclude in the private law of the occupied countries the acquisition of property. The problem was the evidence of force or duress and the burden of proof.

Regularly, the presumption of force or duress took place amd the burden of proof was reversed. The counter-evidence required the existence of „normal commercial relations" before the outbreak of the war. This was a very controversial point of the Allied practice of restitution in Germany. The arguments pro and contra a reversion of the burden of proof are discussed in the article. The author concludes that the presumption was certainly justified in the case of jews, but that it could not be generalized for all cases of transactions.

The author agrees nevertheless with the exclusion of *bona fide* acquisition which he considers necessary for the protection of the victims of transactions under force or duress.

The article concludes with sceptical remarks about the legal signification and the content of the London Declaration which could finally not satisfactorily clarify the question of restitution.

Erfolg mit dem Erfolgsort bei Vermögensdelikten?

Daniel Girsberger[*]

1.   PROBLEM

Der Siegeszug der „Auflockerung" des Deliktsstatuts der vergangenen Jahrzehnte hat die sogenannten „reinen" Vermögensdelikte wie Betrug, Haftung für falsche Auskunft, Veruntreuung und ungetreue Geschäftsführung noch nicht erreicht im Gegensatz etwa zur Haftung für Verkehrsunfälle, Produktehaftpflicht, zum Wettbewerbs-, Umwelt- und Immissionenrecht.

Der Grundsatz, dass grenzüberschreitende Vermögensdelikte nicht nur nach dem Recht des Handlungsortes zu beurteilen sind, sondern zusätzlich oder stattdessen nach einem weiteren Recht, ist nach wie vor in vielen civil- und common law-Rechtsordnungen anerkannt.[1] Neben dem Handlungsort im Vordergrund steht der Ort, an dem der „Erfolg"[2] der schädigenden Handlung oder Unterlassung eingetre-

---

[*] PD Dr. iur., Rechtsanwalt, LL.M., Privatdozent an der Universität Zürich.

[1] Rechtsvergleichende Übersichten s. Werner Lorenz, „Die allgemeine Grundregel betreffend das auf die ausservertragliche Schadenshaftung anzuwendende Recht", in: Ernst von Caemmerer (Hrsg.), *Vorschläge und Gutachten zur Reform des deutschen internationalen Privatrechts der ausservertraglichen Schuldverhältnisse* (Tübingen 1983) 97, 99ff.; Gerhard Hohloch, *Das Deliktsstatut – Grundlagen und Grundlinien des internationalen Deliktsrechts* (Frankfurt a.M. 1984) 103ff.

[2] Zur nicht gerade glücklichen Bezeichnung als „Erfolgsort" s. Christian von Bar, *Internationales Privatrecht*, Band II (München 1991) Rdnr. 663.

J. Basedow et al., eds., Private Law in the International Arena – Liber Amicorum Kurt Siehr
© 2000, T.M.C.Asser Press, The Hague, The Netherlands

ten ist, falls er sich – bei sog. „Distanzdelikten" – vom Handlungsort unterscheidet.[3]

Mit Bezug auf „reine" Vermögensdelikte wird der Erfolgsort nach wie vor überhaupt nicht oder nur ungenau definiert.[4] Der internationalen Lehre und Praxis fällt es schwer, für Vermögensdelikte den massgeblichen Erfolgsort zu umschreiben, und es werden mit diesem oder ähnlichen Begriffen die verschiedensten Auffassungen verbunden.[5] Die einen bemerken resignierend, die Definition müsse dem Richter im konkreten Fall überlassen werden;[6] andere versuchen, Fallgruppen zu bilden[7] nach dem Deliktstyp (Auskunfts- und Betrugsdelikte; übrige Vermögensdelikte[8]), nach der Art der Haftung (Verschulden- oder Kausalhaftung, Vorsatz- und Fahrlässigkeitsdelikte[9]) oder nach weiteren Kriterien (z.B. ob der in Frage stehende Deliktstatbestand „kompensatorischer" oder „admonitorischer" Natur sei[10]).

Ein Beispiel für eine *gesetzliche Anknüpfung* primär an den Erfolgsort gibt das schweizerische IPRG von 1987, dessen Entstehung der Jubilar als kritischer Beobachter mitverfolgt und – durch konstruktive Kritik – mitgestaltet hat[11], und dessen

---

[3] Demgegenüber hat in den Vereinigten Staaten seit den fünfziger Jahren die sog. „Krise" des IPR zu verschiedenen neuen Ansätzen geführt, die sich in der vielfältigen Rechtsprechung der einzelstaatlichen und der „federal" Gerichte niedergeschlagen haben, vgl. dazu z.B. Luther McDougal III, „Toward the Increased Use of Interstate and International Policies in Choice-of-Law Analysis in Tort Cases under the Second Restatement and Leflar's Choice-Influencing Considerations", 70 *Tulane L.Rev.* (1996) 2465ff.; Symeon C. Symeonides, „Choice of Law in the American Courts in 1993 (and in the Six Previous Years)", 42 *Am.J. Comp.L.* (1994) 599ff.

[4] Einen Versuch zur Umschreibung macht einzig das englische Gesetz von 1995 betreffend das Kollisionsrecht für Deliktsobligationen: Private International Law (Miscellaneous Provisions) Act 1995 (ch. 42), abgedruckt z.B. bei Jason Chuah, *Statutes & Conventions on Private International Law* (London 1998) 290-293, dazu unten bei N. 45.

[5] Zum Ganzen eingehend Hohloch (oben N. 1) 111ff.; Lorenz (oben N. 1) 101ff. Günther Beitzke, „Auslandswettbewerb unter Inländern", *JuS* (1966) 139ff., 141, stellt fest, dass die Rechtsvergleichung zu keinem hilfreichen Ergebnis für die Bestimmung des Tatorts führe.

[6] Vgl. z.B. Georges A. Droz, „Regards sur le droit international privé comparé, Cours général de droit international privé", *Recueil des Cours* (1991 IV) 286.

[7] Übersicht bei Lorenz (oben N. 1) 108ff.; *Beitzke*, JuS (1966) (oben N. 5) 141.

[8] Dazu eingehend Jan von Hein, *Das Günstigkeitsprinzip im Internationalen Deliktsrecht* (Tübingen 1999) § 7, 350ff.

[9] Vgl. Ernst Rabel, *The Conflict of Laws*, Vol. II (Ann Arbor / Chicago 1947) 328ff.

[10] Dazu Albert A. Ehrenzweig, „Der Tatort im amerikanischen Kollisionsrecht der ausservertraglichen Schadenersatzansprüche", in: Hans Dölle/ Max Rheinstein/ Konrad Zweigert (Hrsg.), *Festschrift E. Rabel* (Tübingen 1954) 655-683, 657f.; Max Keller/Kurt Siehr, *Allgemeine Lehren des internationalen Privatrechts* (Zürich 1986) § 27 III e), S. 360. Ähnlich Frank Vischer/ Andreas von Planta, *Internationales Privatrecht*, 2. Aufl. (Basel & Frankfurt a.M. 1982) 199, 202f., die aber ausschliesslich auf den Handlungs- und nicht den Erfolgsort abstellen wollen, wenn nicht die Risikoverteilung im Vordergrund steht, sondern ein „besonders missbilligtes Verhalten des Schadensverursachers erforderlich ist", wie etwa bei Ehrverletzung, Betrug, Ehebruch und Tötung, soweit sie nicht im Zusammenhang mit einem kompensatorischen Tatbestand stehen.

[11] Vgl. statt vieler Publikationen Keller/Siehr (oben N. 10) 356ff., 359ff. (zum Erfolgsort); Kurt Siehr, „Internationales Recht der Produkthaftung", in: Anton K. Schnyder / Helmut Heiss / Bernhard

Entwicklung er seit dem Inkrafttreten kritisch analysiert.[12] Im November 1998 hatte das schweizerische Bundesgericht erstmals Gelegenheit, sich zur IPRG-Anknüpfung an den Erfolgsort zu äussern.[13] Das Bundesgericht bekannte zwar ebenfalls nicht abschliessend Farbe, machte aber einige wichtige Hinweise. Ich will anhand des vom Bundesgericht beurteilten Sachverhaltes einzelne Aspekte des Erfolgsortes bei reinen Vermögensdelikten näher beleuchten.

2.   SACHVERHALT UND AUSGANGSLAGE

Der Beklagte, Verwaltungsrat einer liechtensteinischen AG mit Wohnsitz in Monaco, wurde von mehreren Personen, die mit einer Ausnahme alle Wohnsitz in Deutschland hatten, aus unerlaubter Handlung in Anspruch genommen. Die Kläger hatten einer Bank mit Sitz auf den karibischen St. Vincent & Grenadines im Vertrauen auf hohe Renditeversprechen grössere Geldbeträge überlassen, offenbar zum Teil durch Einzahlung auf schweizerische Konten der Bank, zum Teil durch Einzahlung oder Übergabe von Barbeträgen in Liechtenstein. Die liechtensteinische AG, deren Verwaltungsrat der Beklagte war, war im fraglichen Zeitpunkt an der Bank beteiligt. Unklar aufgrund des vom Bundesgericht geschilderten Sachverhalts ist, ob der Beklagte selber die Renditeversprechen abgab oder wenigstens von solchen Versprechen wusste, ob und wie er auf die Angelegenheiten der Bank Einfluss nehmen konnte oder tatsächlich nahm, und – im gleichen Zusammenhang – ob die liechtensteinische AG Mehrheits- oder sogar Alleinaktionärin der Bank war. Nach dem Konkurs der liechtensteinischen AG und später der Bank belangten die Kläger den liechtensteinischen Verwaltungsrat in der Schweiz,[14] gestützt auf unerlaubte Handlung. Welche Art von unerlaubter Handlung oder Unterlassung des Beklagten die Kläger vor dem St. Galler Gericht geltend machten, geht aus dem Urteil nicht hervor. Denkbar sind die folgenden Anspruchsgrundlagen:

a)   Mittäter- oder Gehilfenschaft des Beklagten zum Anlagebetrug;
b)   Haftung aus falscher Auskunft oder Unterlassung von Informationspflichten

---

Rudisch (Hrsg.), *Internationales Verbraucherschutzrecht* (Tübingen 1995) 111-129; ders., *Grenzüberschreitender Umweltschutz*, 45 *RabesZ* (1981) 377-398.

[12] Vgl. nur die jährlichen Zusammenfassungen in der Schweiz. Juristenzeitung, z.B. 93 *SJZ* (1996) 66-69.

[13] BG, 2.11.1998, BGE 125 III 103ff.

[14] Zuständig war der Richter am schweizerischen Arrestort. Näheres s. Daniel Girsberger, „Erfolgsort bei grenzüberschreitenden Vermögensdelikten", *AJP* (2000) 117-120, 117.

als Organ der mit der karibischen Bank eng verbundenen liechtensteinischen AG[15];
c)   Veruntreuung (falls es sich um die der Karibik-Bank anvertrauten Gelder gehandelt hätte).

Vom Bundesgericht war einzig die Frage des auf den Deliktsanspruch anwendbaren Rechts zu lösen. Bei der Vorinstanz wollten die Kläger ihr deutsches Wohnsitzrecht angewandt haben mit der Begründung, dort sei der deliktische Erfolg, die Schädigung ihres Vermögens eingetreten. Die Vorinstanz beurteilte den Anspruch demgegenüber wie schon die erste Instanz nach liechtensteinischem Recht mit der Begründung, der massgebende Handlungsort befinde sich in Liechtenstein. Erfolgsort sei in Fällen wie diesem, in dem „Investoren einem im Ausland befindlichen und eine Geschäftstätigkeit dort ausübenden Institut Gelder übergeben", nicht der Wohnsitz des geschädigten Investoren, sondern der „Ort, von dem aus die Anlagen auch getätigt wurden". Dass die Anlagen von Deutschland aus getätigt worden seien, hätten die Kläger nicht nachgewiesen, obwohl sie die Beweislast treffe. Dieser letzteren Feststellung folgte das Bundesgericht Es berief sich auf seine beschränkte Kognition mit Bezug auf tatsächliche Feststellungen und liess deshalb offen, wo sich der Erfolgsort im konkreten Fall befunden hätte.

3.   MASSGEBENDE KOLLISIONSNORM FÜR REINE VERMÖGENSDELIKTE

3.1   Primäre Anknüpfung an den Erfolgsort bei Distanzdelikten

Mit der Einführung des IPRG wurde in der Schweiz die zuvor angewandte traditionelle „Tatortregel" aufgegeben. Früher konnte der Geschädigte wählen, ob sein Anspruch nach dem Recht am Handlungs- oder am Erfolgsort zu beurteilen sei.[16] Heu-

---

[15] Aufgrund der Schilderung des Bundesgerichts unklar bleibt, ob und in welchem Verhältnis zum Deliktstatbestand auch aktienrechtliche Verantwortlichkeit in Betracht fiel. Diese wäre nach schweizerischem Recht nach dem Gesellschaftsstatut zu beurteilen gewesen, vgl. Art. 155 lit. g IPRG, dazu Anton Heini/ Max Keller/ Kurt Siehr/ Frank Vischer/ Paul Volken (Hrsg.), *IPRG Kommentar* (zitiert: *IPRG-Bearbeiter)* (Zürich 1993) Art. 155 N 27; Hans-Jürgen Sonnenberger, in: von Caemmerer (oben N. 1) 466ff.

[16] Vgl. zuletzt BGE 113 II 476ff., 479 E. 3a.; BG, 15.6.1917, BGE 43 II 309ff., 315f.; BG, 11.5.1950, BGE 76 II 110ff., 112; Vischer/ von Planta (oben N. 10) 201. W.Nachw. s. Frank Vischer, „Das Deliktsrecht des IPR-Gesetzes", in: Ivo Schwander (Hrsg.), *Beiträge zum neuen IPR des Sachen-, Schuld- und Gesellschaftsrechts, Festschrift für Rudolf Moser* (Zürich 1987) 119ff., 120 Anm. 4. Die Anknüpfung an den Erfolgsort war im Vorfeld des IPR-Gesetzes allerdings bis zuletzt umstritten, vgl. Wilhelm Schönenberger/ Peter Jäggi, in: (*Zürcher) Kommentar zum schweizerischen Zivilgesetzbuch, Das Obligationenrecht,* Teilband V/1a, Allgemeine Einleitung, 3. Aufl. (Zürich 1973) Rdnr. 336. W.Nachw. s. Ralf Busch, *Die Ubiquitätsregel im internationalen Deliktsrecht unter besonderer Berücksichtigung des schweizerischen IPRG* (Pfaffenweiler 1996) 40ff., 45ff. Zur Anknüpfung an den Erfolgsort bei Vermögensdelikten durch Lehre und Praxis in Deutschland vgl. OLG München,

te ist in der Schweiz bei Distanzdelikten ausschliesslich - und ohne einseitige Wahlmöglichkeit - das Recht des Erfolgsortes anzuwenden, allerdings nur, wenn der Schädiger mit dem Eintritt des Erfolges an diesem Ort rechnen musste (Art. 133 Abs. 2 a.E. IPRG). Diese Anknüpfung wird als subsidiär angesehen gegenüber den Spezialanknüpfungen für Strassenverkehrsunfälle, Produktehaftung, Wettbewerbsverletzungen, Umweltschäden, Immissionen.[17] Sie tritt ausserdem zurück gegenüber der akzessorischen Anknüpfung an ein „vorbestehendes Rechtsverhältnis" (Art. 133 Abs. 3)[18] und gegenüber dem Recht des gemeinsamen Aufenthalts der Parteien (Art. 133 Abs. 1).

Die schweizerische Regel ist von *Ernst Rabel*[19] und neueren U.S.-amerikanischen Tendenzen[20] beeinflusst. Danach soll primär den Interessen des Geschädigten Rechnung getragen werden, und zwar durch Bevorzugung des Erfolgsorts im Gegensatz zum Handlungsort als dem Umfeld des Schädigers,[21] jedoch nur soweit dieser Erfolgsort für den Schädiger vorhersehbar ist.[22] Dadurch wird bewusst von der traditionellen Tatortregel abgewichen, die noch heute in verschiedenen Rechtsordnungen bestimmend ist. Etwa der deutsche IPR-Gesetzgeber hat jüngst die Tatort-

---

31.10.1984, WM 1985, 189ff., 191 (missbräuchliche Inanspruchnahme einer Bankgarantie); OLG München, 22.3.1974, WM 1974, 583ff., 585 (unrichtige Auskunft). W.H. s. von Bar (oben N. 2) Rdnr. 665; Busch, ibid., 75ff.

[17] Art. 134-139 IPRG.

[18] Auf die Frage der *akzessorischen Anknüpfung* geht das Bundesgericht nicht ein. Je nachdem, wie die Vorwürfe der Kläger lauteten, wäre eine solche Anknüpfung zu prüfen gewesen, vgl. Girsberger (oben N. 14) 117f.

[19] Rabel (oben N. 9) 323ff.

[20] Vgl. z.B. McDougal (oben N. 3) 2465ff.; Symeonides (oben N. 3) 599ff.

[21] Vgl. namentlich Vischer/von Planta (N. 10), 201f. Zur Geschichte der schweizerischen Rechtsnorm vgl. Busch (oben N. 16) 40ff. Zur Bedeutung des Erfolgsortes vgl. Verena Trutmann, „Das neue Bundesgesetz über das internationale Privatrecht in der praktischen Anwendung: Deliktsrecht", *Basler Juristische Mitteilungen* (1989) 293-305, 299; dies., *Das internationale Recht der Deliktsobligationen* (Basel 1973) 6ff., 92ff. Frau Trutmann war Mitglied der massgebenden Experten-Subkommission. Allgemein zur Interessenabwägung zwischen der Anknüpfung an den Handlungsort einerseits und den Erfolgsort anderseits Gerhard Kegel, *Internationales Privatrecht*, 7. Aufl. (München 1995) § 18 IV a), S. 535f.

[22] Zum Kriterium der Vorhersehbarkeit eingehend von Hein (oben N. 8) 181-221. Ähnliche Regeln wie in der Schweiz (primäre Anknüpfung an den – vorhersehbaren – Erfolgsort) gelten neben einzelnen anglo-amerikanischen Rechtsordnungen etwa in Portugal (Art. 45 Abs. 2 Código Civil) und Peru (Art. 2097 Abs. 2 peruanischer Código Civil). Weitere rechtsvergleichende Hinweise s. Busch (oben N. 16) 51; von Hein (oben N. 8) 182f.; Hohloch (oben N. 1) 112ff.; Lorenz (oben N. 1) 114ff.; Bernd von Hoffmann, in: *J. v. Staudingers Kommentar zum Bürgerlichen Gesetzbuch, Einführungsgesetz zum Bürgerlichen Gesetzbuch*, Teil 2 b: *Internationales Schuldrecht I*, 13. Aufl. (Berlin 1998) Art. 38 Rdnr. 43.

regel mit Wahlrecht des Geschädigten – trotz z.T. heftiger Kritik — im revidierten EGBGB festgeschrieben.[23]

In unserem Ausgangsfall sagte das Bundesgericht zur Auslegung des Begriffs „Erfolgsort" in Art. 133 Abs. 1 IPRG folgendes:

1)   *Erfolgsort sei der Ort, wo das geschützte Rechtsgut verletzt wurde. Davon zu unterscheiden sei der Schadensort als der „Platz, an dem weiterer Schaden eintritt" (E. 2 b)aa). Fallen Schadensort und Erfolgsort auseinander, sei einzig letzterer massgebend und damit nicht der Wohnsitz des Geschädigten (E. 2b)bb).*
2)   *Massgeblich sei, wo die erste, unmittelbare Einwirkung auf das durch den Tatbestand einer Deliktsnorm geschütze Rechtsgut stattgefunden habe (E.2b)aa).*
3)   *Die Beweislast für einen vom Handlungsort abweichenden Erfolgsort liege beim Kläger (E. 3).*

3.2   Definition des „Erfolgsorts"

Das schweizerische IPRG enthält keine Definition des „Erfolgsorts" zum Zwecke der Anknüpfung von Vermögensdelikten. Es ist aber unbestritten, dass mit dem *Erfolgsort der Ort der Rechtsgutverletzung* gemeint ist.[24] Mit einer solchen Definition wird allerdings bloss ein unbestimmter Rechtsbegriff durch einen anderen ersetzt. Genauer sind Umschreibungen wie die des Bundesgerichts im vorliegenden Fall, wonach als Erfolgsort ausschliesslich derjenige Ort zu betrachten sei, *„wo das haftungsbegründende Ereignis den unmittelbar Betroffenen geschädigt hat".*[25] Aufgrund dieser Definition wird versucht, den massgebenden Erfolgsort gegenüber dem Ort des Schadenseintritts abzugrenzen; nur der *Ort der unmittelbaren Schädigung* wird als massgebender Erfolgsort akzeptiert.[26] Diese Abgrenzung hilft aller-

---

[23] Vgl. Art. 40 Abs. 1 des seit dem 1. Juni 1999 geltenden Gesetzes zum Internationalen Privatrecht für ausservertragliche Schuldverhältnisse und für Sachen vom 21. Mai 1999, BGBl. 1999 I Nr. 26, S. 1026 = *IPRax* (1999) 285. Dazu Rolf Wagner, „Zum Inkrafttreten des Gesetzes zum Internationalen Privatrecht für ausservertragliche Schuldverhältnisse und für Sachen", *IPRax* (1999) 210-212. Kritisch zum Referentenentwurf von 1993 Bernd von Hoffmann, „Internationales Haftungsrecht im Referentenentwurf des BJM vom 1.12.1993", *IPRax* (1996) 4f.

[24] So bereits BGE 113 II 476ff., 479; IPRG-Heini (oben N. 15) Art. 133 N 10; Schönenberger/ Jäggi (oben N. 16) Rdnr. 336; Vischer/ von Planta (oben N. 10) 199, 201f.; Lorenz (oben N. 1) 108f.; Jan Kropholler, *Internationales Privatrecht*, 3. Aufl. (Tübingen 1997) 457ff. W.Nachw. s. Busch (oben N. 16) 75ff.; von Hein (oben N. 8) 307 Anm. 9.

[25] Das Bundesgericht verweist auf Jan Kropholler, *Internationales Privatrecht*, 2. Aufl. (Tübingen 1994) 442, der aber einräumt, dass die alternative Anknüpfung an Handlungs- und Erfolgsort eine Verlegenheitslösung ist und die schweizerische Lösung als die bessere bezeichnet, weil „im modernen Haftungsrecht der Rechtsgüterschutz gegenüber dem Handlungsunrecht im Vordergrund steht" (ibid., 444).

[26] Karl Kreuzer, in: *Münchener Kommentar zum BGB*, Band 10, EGBGB, 3. Aufl. (München 1998) Art. 38 Rdnr. 48, m.w.Nachw. in Anm. 138-141; Kegel (oben N. 21) § 18 IV a), S.540. Differenzierend

dings nicht weiter, wo der Schaden massgebliches Tatbestandsmerkmal des in Frage stehenden Delikts ist oder wenigstens nach einer der in Frage stehenden Rechtsordnungen wäre.[27]

Auch nach der Rechtsprechung des EuGH zur internationalen Zuständigkeit in Zivil- und Handelssachen im Gefolge des „leading case" *Bier*,[28] namentlich in den Fällen *Dumez*[29] und *Marinari*[30] ist der Ort, an dem sich eine Vermögensschädigung auswirkt, nicht als Erfolgsort i.S. von Art. 5 Abs. 3 Brüsseler / Lugano-Übereinkommen zu berücksichtigen. Damit soll einerseits sichergestellt werden, dass eine enge Verbindung besteht zwischen dem Streitgegenstand und dem Gericht, das ihn beurteilt.[31] Andererseits soll verhindert werden, dass der Wohnsitzgerichtsstand zugunsten eines Klägergerichtsstands ausgehöhlt und ein *Forum shopping* ermöglicht wird.[32] Ähnliche Analysen zum Zweck der Vermeidung von „schwachen" Gerichtsständen finden sich auch in der nationalen Rechtsprechung von Gerichten, die nicht an die Besonderheiten des europäischen Zuständigkeitssystems gebunden sind.[33]

Busch (oben N. 16) 75ff.

[27] IPRG-Heini (oben N. 15) Art. 133 N 10. Zur Frage, inwieweit auf die nationale Regelung abzustellen ist um festzustellen, ob der Schadenseintritt zum Tatbestand der Rechtsgutverletzung gehört, vgl. Busch (oben N. 16) 77ff.; Alexander Lüderitz, in: Soergel (Hrsg.), *Bürgerliches Gesetzbuch mit Einführungsgesetz und Nebengesetzen*, Bd. 10, EGBGB, 12. Aufl. (Stuttgart/ Berlin/ Köln) Art. 12 Rdnr. 11.

[28] EuGH 30.11.1976 – 21/76 *Handelskwkerij G.J. Bier BV* v. *Mines de potasse d'Alsace SA*, Slg. 1976, 1735.

[29] EuGH 11.1.1990 – C-220/88 *Dumez France SA et al. / Hessische Landesbank et al.*, Slg. 1990, I-49.

[30] EuGH 9.9.1995 – C-364/93 *Antonio Marinari / Lloyds Bank plc and Zubaidi Trading Company*, Slg. 1995, I-2719.

[31] *Marinari* (oben N. 30) Rdnr. 10, 20; *Dumez* (oben N. 29) Rdnr. 17. Dadurch werden *forum non conveniens* Elemente im europäischen IZPR bejaht, vgl. Adrian Briggs, „Urteilsanm. zu Marinari", *Lloyd's Maritime and Commercial Law Quarterly* (1996) 27 Anm. 6, 29.

[32] *Dumez* (oben N. 29) Rdnr. 16-20; Volker Holl, „Urteilsanmerkung zu Marinari", *EuZW* (1995) 765, 767. W.Nachw. vgl. Jan Kropholler, *Europäisches Zivilprozessrecht*, 6. Aufl. (1998) Art. 5 Rdnr. 67.

[33] Vgl. *Metall- und Rohstoff AG* v. *Donaldson Lufkin & Jenrette Inc. et al.*, [1988] All. E.R. 116 = [1988] 3 W.L.R. 548 (Q.B.): Klägerin war eine schweizerische Gesellschaft in Zug, die über das Broker-Unternehmen A.M.L. an der Londoner Metallbörse handelte. Der leitende Aluminiumhändler der Klägerin betrieb mit Unterstützung von Angestellten von A.M.L. betrügerischen Handel. Davon wussten sowohl leitende Organe der A.M.L. als auch von deren Mutter- und Holdinggesellschaften in den U.S.A. Als A.M.L. insolvent wurde, klagten die Geschädigten gegen die U.S.-amerikanischen Mutter- und Holdinggesellschaften auf Schadenersatz, unter anderem gestützt auf „conspiracy" und Verleitung zum Vertragsbruch. Das englische Gericht beurteilte die Frage aufgrund der erweiterten Zustellungs- und Zuständigkeitsvorschriften, die ihrerseits ihren Anlass in der Rechtsprechung des EuGH zu Art. 5 Nr. 3 des Brüsseler/ Lugano-Übereinkommens haben, dazu Hans-Jürgen Ahrens, „Die internationale Deliktszuständigkeit im englischen Recht", *IPRax* (1990) 128-133. Danach soll es nunmehr ausreichen, wenn entweder der Schaden im Bereich der inländischen Gerichtsbarkeit eingetreten ist oder auf einer Handlung innerhalb dieser Rechtsordnung beruht. Der Schaden sei zwar an in verschiedenen

Für den Bereich des *anwendbaren Rechts* sind die Kriterien des internationalen Zuständigkeitsrechts nicht ausschlaggebend. [34] Es fragt sich dennoch, ob es sich auch beim anwendbaren Recht rechtfertigt, den Ort, an dem der Schaden eintritt – und der in der Regel mit dem (Wohn-) Sitz des Geschädigten zusammenfällt[35] – für alle Vermögensdelikte ohne weiteres abzulehnen. [36] Das Verweisungsrecht im engeren Sinne folgt zwar grundsätzlich eigenen Anknüpfungsprinzipien. [37] Wo jedoch – wie beim internationalen Deliktsrecht – unterschiedliche Prinzipien konkurrieren und keines besonders dominiert, kann eine einheitliche Auslegung des Anknüpfungsgegenstands „Erfolgsort" für die Zwecke der internationalen Zuständigkeit und des anwendbaren Recht zur Vermeidung eines *forum shopping* wünschbar sein. [38] Gleichzeitig könnte sich aus der Weiterentwicklung der Praxis des EuGH, dem die nationalen Gerichte folgen, ein autonomer Begriff des „*Erfolgsorts*" auch für das Verweisungsrecht im engeren Sinne ergeben.

Nicht für eine Analogie geeignet ist demgegenüber das Strafrecht, wo andere Anknüpfungsgesichtspunkte zu beachten sind:[39] Im Strafrecht steht – im Gegensatz

---

Staaten eingetreten, unter anderem am Hauptsitz der Klägerin in Zug und in London, wo die Beklagten widerrechtlich Vermögen der Klägerin mit Beschlag belegt bzw. „gestohlen" hätten. Für die Frage der Zuständigkeit käme aber einzig London in Frage, weil dort der unmittelbare Schaden eingetreten sei und die Gefahr paralleler Prozesse an diesem Ort und am Ort der mittelbaren Schadens in der Schweiz vermieden werden müsse. Ähnlich argumentierte das australische Gericht in *Voth* v. *Manildra Flour Mills Pty Ltd.* (1990) 171 C.L.R. 538, 568-571, wo ein Gleichlauf von Forum und Ius als wünschbare Regel formuliert und deshalb vom ordentlichen Gerichtsstand des Erfolgsorts als *forum non conveniens* abgewichen wurde. Zum Ganzen Peter Nygh, „Transnational Fraud", in: Campbell McLachlan/ Peter Nygh (Hrsg.), *Transnational Tort Litigation: Jurisdictional Principles* (Oxford 1996) 83-104, 96ff.

[34] Von Bar (oben N. 2) Rdnr. 655.

[35] Die Unterscheidung zwischen Ort des Schadenseintritts und Wohnsitz wurde im Fall *Marinari* (oben N. 30) auch von der deutschen Bundesregierung unterstrichen, die den Schadenseintritt aufgrund der in Frage kommenden nationalen Normen ermitteln wollte, *Marinari* (oben N. 30) Rdnr. 17. Zum Ganzen Busch (oben N. 16) 77ff.; von Hein (oben N. 8) 306ff.

[36] Eine Anknüpfung an diesen Ort nahm die französische Cour de Cassation im Jahre 1984 vor, vgl. Cass.civ., 8.2.1983, *Clunet* 1984, 123-125 (fahrlässige Mitwirkung einer französischen Bank beim Verkauf von gestohlenen Aktien an der spanischen Börse). Handlungs-, Erfolgsort und lex fori waren identisch, vgl. Gérard Légier, Urteilsanm., *Clunet* 1984, 125ff., 131, 133.

[37] Vgl. Busch (N. 16), 79ff. und die Rechtsprechung des BGH, welche eine Anknüpfung an den Ort des Schadenseintritts nur dann ausdrücklich ausscheidet, „wenn der Eintritt des Schadens nicht zum Tatbestand der Rechtsgutsverletzung gehört", BGH, 20.12.1963, BGHZ 40, 391, 395 = *NJW* (1964) 969ff. (unlauterer Wettbewerb). W.Nachw. s. Busch (oben N. 16) 77ff.; von Hein (oben N. 8) 306ff.

[38] Robert Umbricht, in: Heinrich Honsell/ Nedim Peter Vogt/ Anton K. Schnyder (Hrsg.), *Kommentar zum Schweizerischen Privatrecht, Internationales Privatrecht* (Basel/ Frankfurt a.M. 1996) Art. 133 N 7; zur wünschbaren Parallelität zwischen Brüsseler/Lugano Übereinkommen und dem englischen Act (oben N. 4) vgl. Jonathan Harris, „Choice of Law in Tort", 6 *The Modern Law Review* (1998) 33-55, 41ff., m.w.Nachw.

[39] Vgl. Ursula Cassani, *La Protection pénale du patrimoine*, Lausanne 1988, 41ff., 48ff. Zum strafrechtlichen Erfolgsortbegriff in Deutschland vgl. z.B. OLG Frankfurt, 12.12.1988, *NJW* (1989) I 675 (Tatbestand der Untreue).

zum Zivilrecht – nicht primär der Vermögensausgleich im Vordergrund, sondern Prävention und Bestrafung. Eine Analogie zum strafrechtlichen Definition des Erfolgsorts ist deshalb abzulehnen.[40] Das führt zu den folgenden Alternativen:

1) Die kollisionsrechtlich *einfachste Lösung* bestünde darin, als Erfolgsort den *Ort der Vermögenszentrale des Geschädigten*, also bei juristischen Personen und Gesellschaften im Zweifel die geschädigte *Niederlassung* und bei natürlichen Personen den *Wohnsitz oder gewöhnlichen Aufenthalt* anzusehen.[41] A priori auf die Vermögenszentrale abzustellen, würde jedoch den Intentionen des Gesetzgebers widersprechen, selbst wenn er nicht – wie der englische – ausdrücklich ein anderes Anknüpfungsmerkmal gewählt hat.[42] Das bedeutet jedoch nicht umgekehrt, dass der Wohnsitz für Vermögensdelikte mit dem Erfolgsort im Einzelfall nicht zusammenfallen könnte.[43]

2) Als Alternative zum Wohnsitz kommt zunächst der *Lageort der geschädigten Vermögenswerte* als Erfolgsort in Frage. Er entspricht der in *Deutschland* vertretenen Auffassung[44] und findet sich als Anknüpfungspunkt ausdrücklich im *englischen* Gesetz von 1995 betreffend das Kollisionsrecht für Deliktsobligationen:[45]

---

[40] Vgl. zum schweizerischen Recht Bundesgericht, 2.11.1998, BGE 125 III 103ff., 105 E. 2a; Frank Vischer/ Paul Volken, *Bundesgesetz über das internationale Privatrecht (IPR-Gesetz), Gesetzesentwurf und Begleitbericht*, Schweizer Studien zum internationalen Recht, Band 12 (Zürich 1978) 147; Frank Vischer/ Paul Volken (Hrsg.), *Bundesgesetz über das Internationale Privatrecht (IPR-Gesetz), Schlussbericht der Expertenkommission zum Gesetzesentwurf*, Schweizer Studien zum internationalen Recht, Band 13 (Zürich 1979) 236 b); Jean-Louis Delachaux, *Die Anknüpfung der Obligationen aus Delikt und Quasidelikt im Internationalen Privatrecht*, Diss. Zürich (1960) 165f., 179; Schönenberger/Jäggi (oben N. 16) Rdnr. 335, S. 123. Das schweizerische Bundesgericht vor Inkrafttreten des IPRG und das deutsche Reichsgericht hatten demgegenüber die kollisionsrechtliche lex loci delicti-Regel vor allem mit der Notwendigkeit einer Analogie zum strafrechtlichen Ubiquitätsprinzip begründet. Zum schweizerischen Recht vgl. Bundesgericht, 11.5.1950, BGE 76 II 110ff., 112, wonach es einen „unerträglichen Widerspruch" bedeuten würde, wenn man ein Distanzdelikt „bezüglich der Strafbarkeit als an beiden Orten, bezüglich der Verpflichtung zu Schadenersatz als nur an einem Ort begangen betrachten und dementsprechend international verschiedenem Recht unterstellen müsste." W.Nachw. s. Delachaux, ibid., 167 Anm. 110. Zum deutschen IPR vgl. Lorenz (oben N. 1) 113.

[41] So z.B. Lorenz (N. 1), 110ff.; Staudinger-von Hoffmann (N. 22), Art. 38 Rdnr. 498. Kritik s. von Hein (oben N. 8) 344 Nr. 3, 349ff.

[42] Vgl. zur Frage der Zuständigkeit Reinhold Geimer, „Anmerkung zur Marinari-Entscheidung" (oben N. 30) 50 *JZ* (1995) 1108: „Es gibt keine „money pocket rule" nach dem Motto: <the damage was suffered in my pocket>; Hans-Jürgen Ahrens (oben N. 33) 132, je m.w.Nachw.

[43] Dazu eingehend von Hein (oben N. 8) 349ff.; 375f.; 362f. (für Betrugsfälle).

[44] BGH, 28.2.1989, *WM* (1989) 1047, 1049 = *IPRspr.* 1989, Nr. 184 (Anlagebetrug). W.Nachw. s. von Hein (oben N. 8) 344f. Nr. 2. Eine vermittelnde Ansicht vertritt von Bar (oben N. 2) Rdnr. 665 für Auskunfts- und Täuschungsdelikte (nur sofern der Schädiger mit der Herrschaft dieses Rechts rechnen konnte).

[45] Private International Law (Miscellaneous Provisions) Act 1995 (ch. 42) abgedruckt z.B. bei Jason Chuah, *Statutes & Conventions on Private International Law* (London 1998) 290-293.

„The general rule is that the applicable law is the law of the country in which the events constituting the tort or delict in question occur. (2) Where elements of those events occur in different countries, the applicable law under the general rule is to be taken as being – (b) for a cause of action in respect of damage to property, *the law of the country where the property was when it was damaged.*"[46]

Die Schwäche des Lageorts als des Erfolgsortes besteht darin, dass er völlig zufällig sein kann.[47] Dieser Schwäche trägt die schweizerische Regel in Art. 133 Abs. 2 IPRG allerdings genügend Rechnung, weil sie überhaupt nur auf den Erfolgsort abstellt, wenn er für den Schädiger erkennbar war. Aber auch sonst ist der Anknüpfungspunkt vor allem bei immateriellen Vermögenswerten wie Forderungen und Immaterialgüterrechten schwach, weil man von einem eigentlichen „Situs" nicht sprechen kann und deshalb von einer Fiktion der „Belegenheit" ausgehen muss.[48] Die Anknüpfung an den Lageort wird zusätzlich erschwert, wenn der Geschädigte Vermögen in mehreren Rechtsordnungen besitzt und entweder mehrere dieser Vermögensteile gleichzeitig betroffen sind oder nicht klar bestimmt werden kann, welcher Vermögensteil durch das behauptete Delikt angegriffen worden ist.[49] Hätten etwa die Kläger in unserem Ausgangsfall gleichzeitig über verschiedene Konten an ihrem deutschen Wohnsitz, in der Schweiz und in Liechtenstein verfügt, so würde sich die Frage stellen, ob und in welchem Umfang alle drei oder nur einzelne dieser Rechtsordnungen anzuwenden wären.[50]

3)   Als Erfolgsort für Vermögensdelikte liesse sich auch der Ort ansehen, *an dem die vermögensschädigende Verfügung getroffen wird.*[51] Dieser Ort kann, muss aber nicht immer mit dem Lageort der „geschädigten" Vermögenswerte übereinstimmen. Eine Anknüpfung an den Ort der Vermögensdisposition hat etwa die deutsche Rechtsprechung für Auskunfts- und Täuschungsdelikte vertreten, allerdings bisher

---

[46] Hervorhebung durch Verfasser. Kritisch wegen der zu allgemeinen Formulierung der Kollisionsnormen zum insoweit identischen Vorentwurf P.B. Carter, „Choice of Law in Tort and Delict", 107 *Law Quarterly Rev.* (1991) 412ff.; Harris (oben N. 38) 55, je m.w.Nachw.

[47] Lorenz (oben N. 1) 112; Staudinger-von Hoffmann (oben N. 22) Art. 38 Rdnr. 498; von Hein (oben N. 8) 348.

[48] Aus diesem Grund lehnt *Leo Raape* die Anknüpfung an den Erfolgsort überhaupt ab: „Wo ist eigentlich der Ort des Vermögens, wo folglich der Ort der Vermögensbeschädigung? Ist er überall da, wo sich Vermögensstücke befinden, oder da, wo der Wohnsitz des Vermögenssubjekts ist, gemäss dem Satz res ossibus haerent?" in: *Staudinger* (oben N. 22) 9. Aufl., Art. 12, S. 203; vgl. auch Leo Raape, *Internationales Privatrecht*, 4. Aufl. (Berlin/Frankfurt 1955) 536ff. Dazu von Hein (oben N. 8) 348, m.w.Nachw. in Anm. 30.

[49] So Lorenz (oben N. 1) 112; von Hein (oben N. 8) 347 bei Anm. 28.

[50] Vgl. die Kritik an der Lösung des Restatement First von Albert A. Ehrenzweig, „The Place of Acting in Intentional Torts: The Law and Reason versus the Restatement", 36 *Minn. L.Rev.* (1951) 1; ders., *FS Rabel* (oben N. 10) 656f. W.Nachw. s. Busch (oben N. 16) 85f.

[51] Vgl. die Nachw. bei von Hein (oben N. 8) 344ff. Nr. 4.

nur in Fällen, wo der Ort der Vermögensverfügung mit dem Ort der Vermögenszentrale des Geschädigten zusammenfiel.[52] Dieselbe Auffassung hatten in unserem Ausgangsfall die Vorinstanzen im Kanton St. Gallen, obwohl hier unklar war, ob der Ort der Vermögensverfügung mit der Vermögenszentrale des Geschädigten zusammenfiel.[53] Stellt man auf den Ort der Vermögensverfügung ab, so muss man sich ausserdem entscheiden, wo er zu lokalisieren ist: Wo verfügt der Geschädigte über ein Konto, wenn er in Deutschland wohnt und über das Internet[54] oder aus einer – möglicherweise im nachhinein nicht mehr lokalisierbaren – Telefonzelle auf der Durchreise seine Bank instruiert, das Geld auf ein liechtensteinisches Konto des Schädigers oder eines Dritten zu überweisen, das auf den Namen einer karibischen Bank lautet?[55] Eine solche Unsicherheit über den Ort der Vermögensdisposition hatte gerade im Ausgangsfall dazu geführt, dass auf die Anknüpfung an den Erfolgsort – mangels Beweises des Orts der Vermögensdisposition durch die Geschädigten – ganz verzichtet wurde (dazu unten III.).

4)   Die Zufälligkeit des Ortes der Vermögendisposition spricht dagegen, dass er auch dann massgebend sein soll, wenn er nicht mit dem Lageort der Vermögenswerte zusammenfällt, über die verfügt wird.[56] Fallen diese beiden Anknüpfungspunkte dagegen zusammen, so ergibt dies eine genügend starke Anknüpfung, wenn der Schädiger mit dem Erfolg in diesem Staat rechnen musste.[57] Das ist immer der Fall, wenn der Schädiger selbst über die Vermögenswerte verfügt und sie dadurch schädigt. In den anderen Fällen, d.h. bei Auskunfts- und Täuschungsdelikten, sollte auf den Ort der Vermögensdisposition, der nicht mit dem Lageort des geschädigten Vermögenswerts übereinstimmt, nur dann abgestellt werden, wenn er mit dem Ort des Vermögenszentrums des Geschädigten zusammenfällt.[58] Das ist bei natürlichen

---

[52] Vgl. die Nachweise bei Staudinger-von Hoffmann (oben N. 22) Art. 38 Rdnr. 498f.; von Hein (oben N. 8) 344ff.

[53] Vgl. Bundesgericht, 2.11.1998, BGE 125 III 103ff. E. 3a, unter Berufung auf Delachaux (oben N. 40) 181, der sich seinerseits anlehnt an Rabel (N. 9), 326, und den Kommentar zum *Restatement First.* In BGE 113 II 476ff., 479 (Haftung aus mangelnder Aufklärung über vormundschaftliche Beschränkung der Handlungsfähigkeit) fiel der südafrikanische Lageort des Vermögens mit dem Wohnsitz der Geschädigten zusammen.

[54] Vgl. zum Erfolgsort im Internet David Rosenthal, „Das auf unerlaubte Handlungen im Internet anwendbare Recht am Beispiel des Schweizer IPR", *AJP* (1997) 1340-1350, 1345.

[55] Ähnlich das Beispiel bei Staudinger-von Hoffmann (oben N. 22) Art. 38 Rdnr. 498; dazu von Hein (oben N. 8) 357f.

[56] Ähnlich Staudinger-von Hoffmann (oben N. 22) Art. 38 Rdnr. 498f. Ebenso mit Bezug auf die Zuständigkeit BGH, 24.9.1986, *NJW* (1987) 592ff., 594 = *IPRax* (1988) 159ff. (selbst wenn Zahlungsort und Sitz der Geschädigten zusammenfallen).

[57] Abweichend von Hein (oben N. 8) 360ff., der analog zum Vertragsrecht an den Sitz des Geschädigten als den Ort der charakteristischen Leistung anknüpfen will.

[58] So im Ergebnis wohl betreffend Zuständigkeit BGH, 28.2.1989, *WM* (1989) 1047ff., 1049 = *IPRspr.* 1989, Nr. 184. Abweichend von Hein (oben N. 8) 350ff., der zumindest bei Veruntreuung („Untreue") akzessorisch anknüpfen will.

Personen der Wohnsitz, bei Gesellschaften und juristischen Personen der Sitz oder die Niederlassung, die – für den Schädiger erkennbar - die Vermögensdisposition vornimmt. In diesem Fall – und nur in diesem – ist die Anknüpfung im Deliktsrecht der Anknüpfung an den Lageort des geschädigten Vermögens vorzuziehen.

3.3   Anknüpfungszeitpunkt

Sofern nicht an das Vermögenszentrum, sondern an den Lageort des Vermögens oder den Ort der Vermögensdisposition angeknüpft wird, entstehen zusätzliche Unsicherheiten bei der Frage des Anknüpfungs*zeitpunktes*: Möglich sind eine kumulative, alternative oder ausschliessliche Berufung des Rechts am Ort der „ersten", der „relevanten" oder der „letzten" Rechtsgutsverletzung.[59]

Wenn verhindert werden soll, dass der Geschädigte bloss dadurch einen Vorteil erlangt oder benachteiligt wird, dass entweder das betroffene Vermögen ohne direkten Zusammenhang mit dem Delikt seinen Lageort ändert oder die Vermögensdisposition mehrstufig oder zeitlich gestreckt erfolgt, muss man sich für einen der möglichen Zeitpunkte entscheiden. Am naheliegendsten ist die „erste" Beeinträchtigung des Rechtsgutes.[60] Diese Auffassung ist für Vermögensdelikte – trotz der irreführenden Terminologie – vergleichbar, wenn auch nicht identisch, mit der in den Vereinigten Staaten verbreiteten „last event"- Rule,[61] denn mit „last event" ist nicht die letzte Vermögensbeeinträchtigung gemeint, sondern das letzte für die Erfüllung des Deliktstatbestands notwendige Element.[62]

Welches ist nun diese „erste" Beeinträchtigung? Im Ausgangsfall ging es offensichtlich um ein Delikt, durch das die Kläger zu einer Vermögensdisposition veranlasst wurden (Anlagebetrug, falsche oder unterlassene Auskunft). Im Prozess war umstritten, ob die Geschädigten Geld von Konten an ihrem Wohnsitz abgehoben und auf ein schweizerisches oder liechtensteinisches Konto der Karibik-Bank überwiesen hatten, oder ob sie das Geld in Liechtenstein einbezahlt oder sogar bar über-

---

[59] Zum schweizerischen IPR-Gesetzesentwurf Günther Beitzke, „Das Deliktsrecht im schweizerischen IPR-Entwurf", 35 *Schweiz. Jahrbuch für internationales Recht* (1979), 93-93-114, 110 bei Anm. 37. Rechtsvergleichend Busch (oben N. 16) 75ff.

[60] Eingehend Busch (oben N. 16) 81f.; von Hein (oben N. 8) 307ff., 311ff., je m.w.Nachw. Für das schweizerische Recht Beitzke (oben N. 59) 110 bei Anm. 37. Es gehe dabei um ein allgemeines Problem des internationalen Deliktsrechts, nicht bloss um ein schweizerisches Problem.

[61] Dazu Ehrenzweig, *FS Rabel* (oben N. 10) 663-665, 670, ablehnend gegenüber ihrer Begründung durch Beale im *Restatement First* (American Law Institute (Hrsg.), *Restatement of the Law, Conflict of Laws* (St. Paul, Minn. 1934) § 377 N 4).

[62] Vgl. Rabel, *The Conflict of Laws*, II (oben N. 9) 323: „A tort is localized at the precise place in which it is completed by „harm" to a person or tangible thing, or, in a broader term, by „injury" inflicted on a protected interest. More closely, it is the first invasion of the interests that counts.... Damage may develop from there on in various ways." (Hervorhebung durch mich.) Vgl. dazu Delachaux (oben N. 40) 164.

geben hatten. Die Vorinstanzen waren davon ausgegangen, dass sich der Erfolgsort am Ort der Einzahlung befunden hätte, also in Liechtenstein, wenn die Kläger, wie offenbar der Beklagte behauptete, das Geld in Liechtenstein einbezahlt hätten, oder in der Schweiz, wenn sie die Gelder an die Karibik-Bank auf deren schweizerisches Postcheck-Konto einbezahlt hätten.[63]

Vorausgesetzt, massgebender Anknüpfungspunkt sei der Lageort des Vermögens, der mit dem Ort der Vermögensdisposition übereinstimmt, lautet die für den Anknüpfungszeitpunkt relevante Frage also: Auf welchen Zeitpunkt ist abzustellen, auf denjenigen in der juristischen Sekunde, in dem das Vermögen in den Herrschaftsbereich des Schädigers (oder eines vom Schädiger bezeichneten Dritten) verschoben wird (Einzahlung), oder auf den Zeitpunkt, in dem der Geschädigte erstmals auf das Vermögen greift, um eine solche Verfügung vorzunehmen? Im ersten Fall wäre massgebend der Zeitpunkt der behaupteten Einzahlung in Liechtenstein oder auf die schweizerischen Postcheckkonten, im zweiten Fall der Zeitpunkt, in dem das Geld abgehoben wurde, um die Verfügung (Einzahlung oder Überweisung) vorzunehmen. Die schweizerischen Vorinstanzen schienen der ersten Lösung den Vorzug zu geben, ohne sich im konkreten Fall dazu äussern zu wollen.

Meines Erachtens zeigt gerade die Konstellation in unserem Ausgangsfall, dass es *falsch wäre, auf den Zeitpunkt der Einzahlung* durch den Geschädigten (in Liechtenstein oder der Schweiz) abzustellen anstatt auf den wohl dauerhafteren Zeitpunkt der Vermögensverfügung zum Zwecke der Überweisung oder Einzahlung. In diesem Zeitpunkt lag das Vermögen wohl noch am deutschen Wohnsitz der Kläger. Vorzug verdient in jedem Fall eine Lösung, bei der es auf die Zufälligkeiten der Vermögensdisposition nicht ankommt:[64] Es kann kollisionsrechtlich nicht massgebend sein, ob der Geschädigte seine Bank mit einer direkten Überweisung auf das Konto einer karibischen Bank beauftragt, sei das Konto nun in Liechtenstein, in der Schweiz oder in der Karibik, oder ob er einen Zwischenschritt vornimmt, indem er das Geld abhebt, um es nach Liechtenstein mitzunehmen und dort in bar einzuzahlen.[65]

Es ist also abzustellen auf den *Zeitpunkt der ersten relevanten Disposition mit dem äusserlich erkennbaren Ziel der Vermögensverschiebung zum Schädiger (oder einem vom Schädiger bezeichneten Dritten).* Dieser Zeitpunkt ist weniger zufällig als derjenige der Einzahlung oder Überweisung.

Dieser Anknüpfungszeitpunkt ist verallgemeinerungsfähig sowohl für Fälle, in denen die Geschädigten ihre Dispositionen aufgrund der deliktischen Handlung oder Unterlassung des Schädigers selber vornehmen (Fälle von Betrug und Schädi-

---

[63] Bundesgericht, 2.11.1998, BGE 125 III 103ff., E. 3b.
[64] Ebenso von Hein (oben N. 8) 313, 357ff. (für Betrugsfälle).
[65] So im Ergebnis (allerdings für die Frage der Zuständigkeit) auch BGH, 23.6.1964, *NJW* (1964) 2012f., 2012.

gung infolge falscher Auskunft), als auch für die übrigen Vermögensdelikte, bei denen nicht der Geschädigte selbst die Verschiebung veranlasst, sondern der Schädiger.[66] In diesen letzteren Fällen ist die Bestimmung des Anknüpfungszeitpunktes in der Regel einfacher, weil er mit dem Zeitpunkt der Handlung (oder der Unterlassung) des Schädigers zusammenfällt. Massgebend ist der Lageort des betroffenen Vermögens in diesem Zeitpunkt. Hätten die Geschädigten dem liechtensteinischen Verwaltungsrat also eine Veruntreuung oder ein ähnliches Delikt vorgeworfen, so wäre der Erfolgsort, sofern er vom Handlungsort überhaupt abgewichen wäre, einfach zu bestimmen gewesen.[67]

3.4   Beweislast

Nach der Auffassung der St. Galler Gerichte in unserem Anschauungsfall, die vom schweizerischen Bundesgericht bestätigt wurde, trägt der Geschädigte die Beweislast für einen *vom Handlungsort abweichenden Erfolgsort*. Diese Auffassung hat, wenn sie richtig ist, zur Folge, dass immer dann an den Handlungsort anzuknüpfen ist, wenn der Geschädigte nicht zu beweisen vermag, wo er im massgebenden Zeitpunkt über das geschädigte Vermögen verfügt hat oder wo es belegen war. Eine ähnliche Regelung hat neuerdings der deutsche Gesetzgeber für das revidierte EGBGB getroffen: Danach hat der Geschädigte zwar die Wahl zwischen dem Recht am Erfolgsort und dem Recht am Handlungsort. Trifft er sie jedoch nicht rechtzeitig, so gilt ohne weiteres das Recht am Handlungsort.[68]

Die Anknüpfung an den Erfolgsort dient primär dem Geschädigten.[69] Aber der Schutz des Geschädigten ist nicht das einzig massgebende Motiv; von Bedeutung ist ebenfalls die Voraussehbarkeit für beide Parteien.[70] Ausserdem ist die Anknüpfung an den Erfolgsort vom schweizerischen Gesetzgeber – im Gegensatz zum deutschen – bewusst nicht als Recht des Klägers ausgestaltet worden, sondern von

---

[66] Im Ausgangsfall verweist das Bundesgericht für solche Fälle auf Literaturstimmen, für die der Ort des „*Sitzes des konkret verletzten Vermögenswertes*", mangels eines konkreten Vermögenswertes, der „*Sitz des Hauptvermögens*" massgebend ist. Diese Anknüpfung entspricht einer weit verbreiteten Auffassung, vgl. die Nachw. bei Busch (oben N. 16) 87 Anm. 397.

[67] Wäre *Metall- und Rohstoff AG* v. *Donaldson Lufkin & Jenrette Inc.* (oben N. 33) unter der Herrschaft des neuen englischen Gesetzes zu beurteilen gewesen, so wäre als Regel massgebend der Lageort des Vermögens zum Zeitpunkt der „Wegnahme" durch ungerechtfertigte Aneignung („Beschlagnahme") gewesen, also englisches Recht..

[68] Art. 40 Abs. 1 des seit dem 1. Juni 1999 geltenden Gesetzes zum Internationalen Privatrecht für ausservertragliche Schuldverhältnisse und für Sachen vom 21. Mai 1999, BGBl. 1999 I Nr. 26, S. 1026, wonach der Geschädigte bis zu einem gewissen Zeitpunkt erklären muss, dass er das Recht am Erfolgsort angewendet haben will. Mangels einer solchen Erklärung gilt das Recht des Handlungsorts, Art. 40 Abs. 1 Satz 2 und 3.

[69] Vgl. Kegel (oben N. 21) 535f., 540f.

[70] Vischer/ Volken, *Begleitbericht* (oben N. 40) 147; *Schlussbericht* (oben N. 40) 236 (Vermeidung einer „unfair surprise").

Amtes wegen vorzunehmen. Ein „fakultatives Kollisionsrecht"[71] kennt das schweizerische IPR-Gesetz nicht.[72] Daraus folgt: Wo der kollisionsrechtliche Schutz des Geschädigten wie etwa nach neuem deutschen Recht durch das Günstigkeitsprinzip sichergestellt ist, mag eine Regel gerechtfertigt sein, die es dem Geschädigten überlässt, das für ihn günstigere Recht anzurufen.[73] Wo die alternative Anknüpfung jedoch – wie in der Schweiz – zum Zweck eines besseren Interessensausgleichs zwischen Schädiger und Geschädigten fallen gelassen wurde, ist von einer solchen Beweisvorschrift zulasten des Klägers abzusehen. Dasselbe gilt für den Beweis der Vorhersehbarkeit des Erfolgsorts, um Manipulationen des Schädigers oder des Geschädigten zu vermeiden.[74]

4. ZUSAMMENFASSUNG

1. Für die Bestimmung des anwendbaren Rechts ist die Definition des Erfolgsorts nicht notwendigerweise dieselbe wie für die Bestimmung der Zuständigkeit im IZPR, da den Anknüpfungen teilweise unterschiedliche Zwecke zugrunde liegen. Eine möglichst einheitliche Qualifikation ist jedoch im Interesse der Vermeidung eines *forum shopping* anzustreben, wenn nicht gewichtige kollisionsrechtliche Gesichtspunkte dagegen sprechen.

2. Erfolgsort ist bei reinen Vermögendelikten der Ort, an dem die Vermögensdisposition vorgenommen wird, wenn er mit dem Lageort des Vermögens zusammenfällt. Andernfalls ist zu unterscheiden, ob ein Auskunfts- oder Täuschungsdelikt in Frage steht oder ein Delikt, bei dem der Schädiger selbst über das Vermögen verfügt. Bei letzterem ist massgebend der Lageort des Vermögens, über das verfügt wird, beim ersten das Vermögenszentrum des Geschädigten, in der Regel also der (Wohn-) Sitz oder die Niederlassung.

3. Anknüpfungszeitpunkt ist der *Zeitpunkt der ersten relevanten Disposition mit dem äusserlich erkennbaren Ziel der Vermögensverschiebung zum Schädiger.* Die-

---

[71] Axel Flessner, *Fakultatives Kollisionsrecht*, 34 *RabelsZ* (1970) 547-584.
[72] Die Beweislast nach ZGB 8 bezieht sich auf Tatsachen, aus denen der Kläger ein Recht ableiten will, und nicht auf die tatsächlichen Grundlagen einer Kollisionsnorm. Richtigerweise hätte also das Bundesgericht die Sache zur Ermittlung des massgebenden Erfolgsorts zurückweisen müssen, selbst wenn es am Ort, an dem über das Vermögen disponiert wurde, als Anknüpfungsmerkmal hätte festhalten wollen. Für eine gemeinsame Rechtswahl, die im Prozess möglich gewesen wäre (Art. 132 IPRG), hätte zumindest eine übereinstimmende Willensbekundung dargetan werden müssen.
[73] Vgl. Kreuzer (oben N. 26) Art. 38 Rdnr. 35ff. Kritisch sogar gegenüber der deutschen Regel Staudinger-von Hoffmann (oben N. 22) 4f.
[74] Vgl. Ivo Schwander, *Einführung in das internationale Privatrecht, 2. Band: Besonderer Teil* (St. Gallen 1997) Rdnr. 657; Beitzke (oben N. 59) 110f.

ser Zeitpunkt ist weniger zufällig als derjenige der Einzahlung oder Überweisung. Er ist nicht von der Art des Delikts abhängig.[75]

4.   Die Beweislast dafür, wo sich der kollisionsrechtliche Erfolgsort befindet, kann dem Geschädigten nur auferlegt werden, wo – wie in Deutschland – das Günstigkeitsprinzip gilt. Wenn dagegen – wie in der Schweiz – der Erfolgsort das ausschliessliche (primäre) Anknüpfungsmerkmal ist, ist der Erfolgsort von Amtes wegen zu ermitteln.

5.   Die aus dem schweizerischen Anschauungsfall gewonnenen Erkenntnisse für die Definition des Erfolgsorts bei Vermögensdelikten sind verallgemeinerungsfähig. Sie lassen sich auch auf allgemeiner formulierte Kollisionsregeln anwenden, etwa auf das neue englische oder deutsche Recht. Sie haben den Vorteil, dass sie im Rahmen der zunehmenden Vereinheitlichung des Zuständigkeitsrechts einerseits und des anwendbaren Rechts anderseits zu einem autonomen Begriff des Erfolgsortes nicht nur für das IZPR, sondern auch für da IPR führen könnten, der den Idealen des Kollisionsrechts etwas näher käme,[76] namentlich der internationalen Entscheidungsharmonie und einer Vermeidung des *forum shopping*, einem Ziel, das der Jubilar, dem dieser Beitrag gewidmet ist, seit Jahrzehnten predigt.

SUMMARY
RELEVANCE OF THE PLACE OF IMPACT IN TORTS / DELICTS AFFECTING PROPERTY

An analysis of recent cases in Switzerland and elsewhere shows that it is still difficult to determine the *locus delicti* in the context of mere financial damage or loss of property. The following conclusions, however, may be drawn:

1.   The definition of the place of impact (*Erfolgsort*) is not necessarily the same for determining the applicable law and the place of jurisdiction, because the connecting factors are based in part on different underlying purposes. However, in

---

[75] Nicht massgebend ist also, ob es sich um eine Tätigkeits- oder Unterlassungs-, ein Tätigkeits- oder Erfolgsdelikt, eine Kausal- (Gefährdungs- oder Geschäftsherren-) oder Verschuldenshaftung handelt.

[76] Der Vorschlag des „*Groupe européen de droit international privé*" einer europäischen Konvention über das auf ausservertragliche Obligationen anwendbare Recht vom 25.-27. September 1998 (abgedruckt in der französischen Fassung in *IPRax* (1999) 286-288) geht nicht einmal soweit, dass er bei Distanzdelikten eine Anknüpfung an den Erfolgsort vorsieht. Er enthält bloss Vermutungen, wo die engste Verbindung sich befindet. Falls Handlungs- und Erfolgsort (der nicht weiter definiert wird) sich im gleichen Land befinden, wird vermutet, dass sich dort die engste Verbindung befinde, Art. 3(3) des

order to avoid forum shopping, a unified characterization of that place should be attempted, unless important conflict-of-law aspects mandate otherwise.

2.   The place of impact in cases of financial damage to property is the place where the property is disposed of, provided that it is identical with the location of the property. If they are not identical, one must distinguish between situations of misinformation or fraud on the one hand, and situations where the tortfeasor himself misappropriates the property on the other. In these latter situations, the *locus delicti* is at the place where the misappropriated property is located. In the former situations, it is where the main assets of the injured person are located, i.e., usually her domicile or residence.

3.   From the temporal point of view, the relevant time of connection is the time when the specific property is first disposed of with the intention to pay or transfer it to the tortfeasor. This moment of time is less arbitrary than the mostly accidental time of payment or transfer. In addition, it is not dependent upon the type of tortious act committed.

4.   The burden of proof to determine the *locus delicti* should be discharged by the injured person only where she can chose between the place of impact (*Erfolgsort*) and the *lex delicti comissi* (*Handlungsort*) (as is the case in Germany). If, however, the place of impact is the exclusive, or primary, connecting factor (as is the case in Switzerland), the *locus delicti* must be determined *ex officio*.

5.   These rules, which have been developed on the basis of Swiss law, may also be adapted to other jurisdictions such as the recently revised German law. They may lead to an autonomous and unified definition of the place of impact for the purpose of determining both the applicable law and the forum having jurisdiction. This would promote international harmony and prevent *forum shopping*, a goal which has been vigorously supported by KURT SIEHR, to whom this article is dedicated.

On Comity, Reciprocity, and Public Policy in U.S. and German Judgments Recognition Practice

Peter Hay[*]

I.

Various policies affect the readiness to recognize a judgment of another state. *Comity* recognizes the interdependence of legal systems and favors recognition. *Reciprocity* and the *ordre public* exception emphasize local concerns and may disfavor or block recognition. The following comments trace these policies in American law. They also consider briefly how U.S. judgments fare in Germany under these policies and the European aversion against a double exequatur.

American judgments recognition-practice traditionally distinguishes between judgments of sister states (interstate recognition) and those of foreign countries (international judgment recognition). There are two reasons. The "*Full Faith and Credit*" command of the Federal Constitution[1] applies only to sister state, and not to international judgments. The same is true of the "merger doctrine" of the common law. It holds that a judgment merges the underlying cause of action: only the judgment exists, nothing else remains that could be subject to examination.[2] As a result, a judgment for money (unlike the underlying cause of action, which is now removed from examination) cannot offend public policy[3] – "money is money". Even absent a Constitutional mandate, the merger doctrine, combined with common law notions of *res judicata*, would assure interstate recognition in many cases over a public policy defense.

A foreign country (international) judgment, in contrast, does not merge the underlying cause of action.[4] The claim may be sued upon anew or may serve as a basis for an examination of the foreign judgment itself. It has been suggested that the non-merger approach is justified, even necessary, because of differences in the

[*] L.Q.C. Lamar Professor of Law, Emory University, Atlanta (USA) and Professor of Law, Technische Universität Dresden (Germany).
[1] U.S. Constitution Art. IV, Sec. 1.
[2] See Scoles/Hay/Borchers/Symeonides, *Conflict of Laws* §§ 24.1, 24.3 (3d ed. 2000).
[3] See *Fauntleroy* v. *Lum*, 210 U.S. 230, 28 S.Ct. 641, 52 L.Ed. 1039 (1908).
[4] Scoles/Hay/Borchers/Symeonides (supra n. 2) at § 24.3.

J. Basedow et al., eds., Private Law in the International Arena – Liber Amicorum Kurt Siehr
© 2000, T.M.C. Asser Press, The Hague, The Netherlands

res judicata effect legal systems attribute to judgments.[5] More importantly, the Full Faith and Credit mandate does not apply to international judgments. As a result, the recognition of foreign country judgments therefore is not automatic in the United States. In the absence of a constitutional mandate, applicable recognition treaties with foreign nations[6], or federal statutory resolution, the recognition of foreign judgments is thus a matter for the law of the several states.[7]

State practice could track the (constitutionally mandated) interstate recognition practice also with respect to international judgments. Over thirty states do, in the form of the Uniform Recognition of Foreign Country-Money Judgments Act.[8]

---

[5] See, e.g., Smit, "International Res Judicata and Collateral Estoppel in the United States," 9 *U.C.L.A. L. Rev.* 44 (1962). For criticism, see Scoles/Hay/Borchers/Symeonides (supra n. 2) at § 24.3. The suggestion leaves unexplained why even English judgments (i.e., judgments from legal systems rooted in the common law) also do not seem to fall within the merger rule. For further discussion, see infra at nn. 30 et seq.

[6] An attempt to fashion a recognition treaty (with the United Kingdom) failed. See Hay/Walker, "The Proposed Recognition-of-Judgments Convention Between the United States and the United Kingdom," 11 *Tex. Int'l L. J.* 421 (1976); Hay/Walker, "Le projet anglo-americain de Convention sur la reconnaissance des decisions et la Convention Communautaire," [1977] *Cahiers de droit europeen* 3; Adler, "If We Build It, Will They Come? The Need for a Multilateral Convention on the Recognition and Enforcement of Civil Monetary Judgments," 26 *Law & Pol'y Int. Bus.* 79, 91-94 (1994). On United States perspectives with respect to current efforts for a multilateral convention under the auspices of the Hague Conference, see the contributions of Juenger and Weintraub in: "Symposium," 24 *Brook. J. Int'l L.* 111 and 167 (1998), respectively; von Mehren, "Recognition and Enforcement of Foreign Judgments: A New Approach for the Hague Conference?", 57 *Law & Contemp. Probs.* 271 (1994); Schack, "Perspektiven eines weltweiten Anerkennungs- und Vollstreckungsabkommens," 1 *Zeitschrift für Europäisches Privatrecht* 306 (1993); Schack, "Entscheidungszuständigkeiten in einem weltweiten Gerichtsstands- und Vollstreckungsübereinkommen", 6 *Zeitschrift für Europäisches Privatrecht* 931 (1998).

[7] In its decision in *Hilton* v. *Guyot*, 159 U.S. 113, 16 S.Ct. 139, 40 L.Ed. 95 (1895), the U.S. Supreme Court discussed the preconditions for the recognition of foreign judgments in the United States. The decision, in large part *obiter dictum* (see *Johnston* v. *Compagnie Generale Transatlantique*, 242 N.Y. 381, 152 N.E. 121 (1926)), preceded the determination in *Erie R.R. Co.* v. *Tompkins*, 304 U.S. 64, 58 S.Ct. 817, 82 L.Ed. 1188 (1938), that federal courts lack subject matter jurisdiction to fashion federal common law in areas in which Congress does not possess delegated legislative competence under federal Constitution. *Erie* was extended to conflicts law in *Klaxon* v. *Stentor Electric Mfg. Co.*, 313 U.S. 487, 61 S.Ct. 1020, 85 L.Ed. 1477 (1941). It is therefore generally thought that *Hilton* no longer binds the states and that foreign-country judgment recognition is therefore a matter of state law. Scoles/Hay/Borchers/Symeonides (supra n. 2) at § 24.6. Today, there is no doubt federal lawmaking authority with respect to private international subject matters. The Hague Convention the Law Applicable to Decedents' Estates (not yet in force) and the ongoing work on a multilateral Hague Judgments Convention (supra n. 6) are examples. Nevertheless, it remains true that the Supreme Court will not take the lead in fashioning federal law, but will defer to the legislature. Scoles/Hay/Borchers/Symeonides (supra n. 2) at § 3.49. Until Congress has legislated or the President has ratified a treaty with the advice and consent of the Senate, judgment recognition remains committed to state law.

[8] Interstate judgment recognition is constitutionally mandated and does not allow for individual state variation. (*But see* the continued uncertainty about the interstate effect of collateral estoppel: Hay/Weintraub/Borchers, *Conflict of Laws* 241-42 (11th ed. 2000)). In international practice, in contrast, variation is permissible and will no doubt occur. With respect to the Uniform Act, an example is the addition of a reciprocity requirement by Colorado, Georgia, Idaho, Massachusetts, Ohio and Texas. See

Other states recognize and enforce foreign judgments on the basis of decisional law,[9] with the Hilton decision's adaptation of "comity" to American use[10] as the starting point. However, a handful of states require, by addition to the uniform act or by separate statute, that reciprocity for the recognition of forum state decisions be assured in the law of the rendering country.[11] And some decisions, given the inapplicability of the merger doctrine, look behind the foreign judgment to examine the compatibility of the claim, of the law applied, and of the result with the public policy of the forum.

The notion of "comity", when recognition is not mandated by statute, and the deviations from interstate recognition practice in the form of reciprocity requirements or an examination of the foreign judgment for possible violation of the public policy of the forum form the subject of the brief comments that follow.

II.

"Comity" has its linguistic origins in the Justinian Digests.[12] The concept became central to Huber's theory and those following the Dutch school. It gained currency as the bridge between territorial sovereignty and the openness to extraterritorial concerns openness required for the effective and efficient operation of rules of law and of legal systems.[13]

In Continental Europe in which the *communis opinio doctorum* was a major source of law in the sixteenth and seventeenth centuries,[14] "comity" gained universal acceptance. It was a superlaw notion, not national in origin as today's international uniform laws (e.g. treaties like the Vienna Sales Convention), but international in character. Huber seems to have seen the roots of comity in international law,[15] though he notes at the same time that, without it, "nothing could be

---

Hay et al., supra this n., at 214. See also infra n. 11.

[9] An early example is New York. See the *Johnston* decision (supra n. 7).

[10] See Nadelmann, "Introduction" to Yntema, "The Comity Doctrine," 65 *Mich. L. Rev.* 1 (1966).

[11] See supra n. 8. In addition, Georgia, Idaho, and New Hampshire require reciprocity (the last of these, only with respect to Canadian judgments). The Colorado provision (Col. Rev. Stat. Ann. § 13-62-102 (1)) renders that state's adoption of the Uniform Act meaningless. It defines "foreign state" as a "governmental unit [that] has entered into a reciprocal agreement with the United States recognizing any judgment of a court of record of the United States ... ." To date, there are no such agreements.

[12] Yntema (supra n. 10) at 23.

[13] Juenger, *Choice of Law and Multistate Justice* 20 et seq (1993).

[14] H. Berman, "Religious Dimensions of the Western Legal Tradition," in: Petersen & Pater (eds.), *The Contentious Triangle – Church, State, and University: Festschrift G.H. Williams* 281, 289 (LI Sixteenth Century Essays & Studies 1999).

[15] Juenger (supra n. 13) at 21.

more inconvenient to commerce and to international usage than that transactions valid by the law of one place should be rendered of no effect elsewhere . . .".[16] The same reasons of convenience, even necessity, lead to the formulation of today's superlaw, the *lex mercatoria*.[17] Except for the Vienna Sales Convention, it also is not "given," but it "grows," receiving authority through practice and official recognition, for instance by its application in arbitration.[18]

Huber's thoughts on comity were quoted in American decisions since 1788,[19] they received emphatic support from Story in his great work,[20] and the latter in turn influenced Dicey in England, Savigny in Germany, as well as French doctrine.[21] The U.S. Supreme Court, speaking through Justice Story, spoke of "the law ... of the commercial world".[22] In occasional later decisions, the Court regards the Constitution's Full Faith and Credit Clause to be the direct (positive law) source of the requirement to give extraterritorial effect to the law of another state of the Union.[23] American federalism indeed suggests that deference to sister state law – in whatever circumstances are deemed to be appropriate – should track the required recognition of sister state judgments under the Full Faith and Credit Clause.[24] However, the U.S. Supreme Court has not drawn this parallel. Instead, subject to only outer Constitutional limits,[25] the states are free to go their own ways in choice of law, with the resulting and well-known divergence in approaches.[26]

Uniformity thus exists only with respect to interstate judgment recognition. The *Restatement (Second) of Conflict of Laws* (§ 103) contemplates an exception to the Constitution's recognition-requirement whenever recognition "would involve an

---

[16] See the English translation of Huber in Lorenzen, *Selected Articles on the Conflict of Laws* 162, 164-65 (1947).

[17] See H. Berman & Dasser, "The New Law Merchant and the Old: Sources, Content, and Legitimacy," in: Carbonneau (ed.), *Lex Mercatoria and Arbitration* 53 (rev. ed. 1998); U. Stein, *Lex Mercatoria – Realität und Theorie* (1995). See also Trakman, *The Law Merchant: The Evolution of Commercial Law* (1983).

[18] See Juenger, "The Need for a Comparative Approach to Choice-of-Law Problems," 73 *Tulane L. Rev.* 1309, 1330-31 (1999).

[19] *Camp* v. *Lockwood*, 1 U.S. (1 Dall.) 393, 398, 1 L.Ed. 192 (Phila. County, Pa., C.P. 1788), cited according to Nadelmann (supra n. 10) at 2.

[20] J. Story, *Commentaries on the Conflict of Laws, Foreign and Domestic* § 35, at p. 34 (1834).

[21] Scoles/Hay/Borchers/Symeonides (supra n. 2) § 2.4 (p.12), with references.

[22] *Swift* v. *Tyson*, 41 U.S. (16 Pet.) 1, 19 (1842). *Swift* was overruled by the decision in *Erie*, for the reasons discussed in n. 7, supra.

[23] See *Order of United Commercial Travelers* v. *Wolfe*, 331 U.S. 586, 67 S.Ct. 1355, 91 L.Ed. 1687 (1947) (membership rights in fraternal benefit society governed by the law under which it was established); *CTS Corp.* v. *Dynamics Corp. of America*, 481 U.S. 69, 107 S.Ct. 1637, 95 L.Ed.2d 67 (1987) (law of state of incorporation governs corporations internal affairs).

[24] Hay, "Full Faith and Credit and Federalism in Choice of Law," 34 *Mercer L. Rev.* 709 (1983).

[25] Scoles/Hay/Borchers/Symeonides (supra n. 2) at §§ 3.20-3.35; Hay, "Judicial Jurisdiction and Choice of Law: Constitutional Limitations," 59 *Colo. L. Rev.* 9 (1988).

[26] See Scoles/Hay/Borchers/Symeonides (supra n. 2) chapters 2 (approaches), 17 (tort), 18 (contract).

improper interference with important interests of the [recognizing state]." The few decisions invoking Section 103, however, can all be explained on other grounds.[27] For interstate recognition practice of money judgments, the conclusion must be that the merger doctrine, noted initially, prevents relitigation of the claim; that comity for the recognition of another state's judgments is positive law of constitutional rank (the Full Faith and Credit Clause); and that there is therefore no room for considerations of reciprocity. The matter may be different when the judgment is not for money or declaratory of rights, but orders acts or forebearance.[28] Here, the applicability of the merger doctrine is at best debatable, and it is here that Sec. 103 of the Second Restatement states a truism: what the first state decrees may well be unacceptable to the second. It may violate the second state's public policy.

III.

No Full Faith and Credit requirement exists with respect to foreign-country ("international") judgments. The several states are as free to go their separate ways, the same as they may domestically with respect to choice of law. Perhaps they are even freer in this area because it is difficult to imagine whatever other, outer constitutional limits might apply to a refusal to accord recognition.

The generally assumed inapplicability of the merger doctrine to international judgments exacerbates the problem (making second suits theoretically possible or facilitating *révision au fond*[29]).[30] Why notions of merger should not apply to inter-

---

[27] See, e.g., *Thompson* v. *Thompson*, 645 S.W.2d 79 (Mo. App. 1982), in which the court granted additional support although the law of the state, under which support had been awarded, provided that the obligation ceases when the child attains the age of eighteen. As in *Elkind* v. *Byck*, 68 Cal. 2d 453, 67 Cal. Rptr. 404, 439 P.2d 316 (1968), to which the Missouri court also makes reference, the result can be reached without reliance on § 103 by construing the scope of the early award, i.e. its res judicata effect. See further Reynolds, "The Iron Law of Full Faith and Credit," 53 *Maryland L.Rev.* 412, 436-49 (1994); Scoles/Hay/Borchers/Symeonides (supra n. 2) § 24.21.

[28] "The Court has never placed equity decrees outside the full faith and credit domain. Equity decrees for the payment of money have long been considered equivalent to judgments at law entitled to nationwide recognition.... Orders commanding action or inaction have been denied enforcement in a sister State when they purported to accomplish an official act within the exclusive province of that other State or interfered with litigation over which the ordering State had no authority. Thus, a sister State's decree concerning land ownership in another State has been held ineffective [also referring to antisuit injunctions]." *Baker* v. *General Motors Corp.*, 522 U.S. 222, 235, 118 S.Ct. 657, 664, 139 L.Ed.2d 580, 593 (1998). This is a useful statement but does not provide a "bright line." Moreover, it is obiter dictum. The reason why the Missouri court was not required to honor the Michigan decree was that the parties sought to be precluded had not been before the Michigan court. *Id.* at 522 U.S. 222, 239 n. 12, 118 S.Ct. 657, 668 n. 12, 139 L.Ed.2d 580, 596 n. 12.

[29] For a recent example, see the decision discussed at n. 55 infra.

[30] *The Restatement (Second) of Conflict of Laws* § 95 (c)(1) preserves the plaintiff's option to sue anew on the original claim.

national judgments – incidentally – is not entirely clear or, to put it differently, the case against merger has not been made convincingly. Defenders of non-merger point to differences in foreign rules of res judicata[31] and the difficulty of ascertaining them.[32] In addition, non-merger is said to protect the judgment creditor against currency devaluation.[33] The Uniform Foreign Money Claims Act[34] now deals with monetary losses due to devaluation, introduction of new money, or default in payment.[35] Beyond that, it is difficult to see why the judgment debtor should bear the risk of daily fluctuations in monetary value any more than in the domestic context. The other argument – the difficulty in ascertaining differing rules of foreign law – hardly addresses a problem unique to res judicata. In contrast, practical reasons (apart from the theoretical construct of "merger") speak against multiple litigation, resulting in multiple titles[36] with respect to the same claim.

But non-merger is not the only potential obstacle to recognition: even a judgment merging the claim could be refused recognition for any number of reasons, including lack of jurisdiction or of reciprocity or violation of public policy.

In view of these potential hurdles, it is rather remarkable how recognition-friendly American courts are. Story's propagation of comity and the Supreme Court's reliance on the concept in *Hilton*[37] resulted in a recognition practice for international judgments that virtually tracks the interstate practice. States requiring reciprocity remain few, and even they do not deny recognition on this basis.

This development has parallels in Canada. In 1990, the Supreme Court of Canada "rejected the nineteenth-century common law's reluctance to recognize and enforce foreign judgments"[38] and for reasons of comity and the needs of a federal system such as Canada's adopted a "full faith and credit" requirement.[39] The

---

[31] See Millar, "The Premises of the Judgment as Res Judicata in Continental and Anglo-American Law", 39 *Mich. L. Rev.* 1 (1940). See also Smit (supra n. 5).

[32] So, originally, Nussbaum, *Principles of Private International Law* 245-46 (1943).

[33] Ehrenzweig/Jayme, *Private International Law*, Vol. 2 61 (1973).

[34] See Hay/Weintraub/Borchers, *Conflict of Laws* 745 (11th ed. 2000); Hay, "Fremdwährungsansprüche und -urteile nach dem US-amerikanischen Uniform Act," [1995] Recht der Internationalen Wirtschaft 113.

[35] Hay (supra n. 34) at 117.

[36] Compare the view of the European Court of Justice in Case 42/76 *Wolf v. Cox. BV*, [1976] ECR 1759, at para. 13.15: "... to accept the duplication of main actions ... might result in the creditor's possessing two orders for enforcement on the basis of the same debt." The Court held (at p. 1768) that "the provisions of the [Brussels] Convention ... prevent a party who has obtained a judgment in his favour in a Contracting State ... from making application to a court in [another contracting] State for a judgment against the other party in the same terms as the judgment delivered in the first State."

[37] Supra n. 7.

[38] Tetley, "Current Developments in Canadian Private International Law", 78 *Can. B. Rev.* 152, 186 (1999).

[39] *Morguard Investments Ltd.* v. *De Savoye*, [1990] 3 S.C.R. 1077.

Ontario Court of Appeal applied this decision in 1996 to recognize the decision of an American federal court in Michigan, and the Canadian Supreme Court dismissed leave to appeal.[40]

This leaves the usual catalog of possible defenses – from lack of jurisdiction of the rendering court, to lack of opportunity to be heard, to violation of public policy. They are reflected in the case law[41] as well as in the Uniform Foreign Money-Judgments Recognition Act.[42]

In view of the far reading jurisdiction U.S. courts claim for themselves,[43] even a "mirror image" requirement should ordinarily lead to the conclusion that the foreign court had jurisdiction.[44] Assuming no other procedural problems with the foreign proceeding and in the absence of a reciprocity requirement, one should think that foreign money judgments would then ordinarily be entitled to (virtually automatic) recognition. *Révision au fond*, the review of the foreign judgment for its legal (substantive or conflicts) correctness (or both) is no longer part of judgment-recognition practice in most legal systems.[45]

However, the matter is not quite this simple in the context of American recognition of international judgments: at this point problems arising from lack of merger, from concerns for the local *ordre public*, and the temptations of *révision au fond* intersect.

In the American interstate context, the question does not arise. The money judgment merges the claim. The present claim (for recognition and enforcement of the first court's judgment) is for money and money judgments do not offend public policy.[46] Since the underlying claim is "gone", the question cannot arise (and invite

---

[40] *United States of America* v. *Ivey*, (1996) 93 O.A.C. 152, leave to appeal dismissed [1996] S.C.C.A. No. 582.

[41] Scoles/Hay/Borchers/Symeonides (supra n. 2) §§ 24.41 et seq.

[42] 13 U.L.A. 261 (Master ed. 1986 and Supps.). For discussion, see Scoles/Hay/Borchers/Symeonides (supra n. 2) § 24.36. For a decision dealing with the interrelation of this Act and the (interstate) Uniform Foreign Judgments Recognition Act, see infra at n. 68.

[43] Scoles/Hay/Borchers/Symeonides (supra n. 2), chapters 5-10. See also Juenger, "A Hague Judgments Convention?", 24 *Brook. J. Int'l L.* 111 (1998).

[44] Scoles/Hay/Borchers/Symeonides (supra n. 2), § 24.42; Hay, "International versus Interstate Conflicts Law in the United States," 35 *Rabels Zeitschrift* 429, 450 n. 101 (1971).

[45] See *Treinies* v. *Sunshine Mining Co.*, 308 U.S. 66, 60 S.Ct. 44, 84 L.Ed. 85 (1939) (decision of a court with proper jurisdiction not subject to collateral review for correctness of result reached). See, similarly, § 722 (1) German ZPO; Art. 29 Brussels Convention.

[46] Supra n. 3. In the interstate context, an award of excessive punitive damages may violate due process and may therefore be subject to reversal upon appeal. See *BMW of North America* v. *Gore*, 517 U.S. 559, 116 S.Ct. 1589, 134 L.Ed.2d 809 (1996). However, even a possible violation of due process ripens into res judicata and is not subject to review collaterally. *Treinies* (supra n. 45). In international practice, German courts consider punitive damages to violate German public policy. English courts do not seem find such awards violative of English public policy. Dicey & Morris, 1 *The Conflict of Laws* 526 (13th ed. by Collins et al., 2000). For further comments on public policy and *révision au fond*, see infra at nn. 53 et seq.

a possible *révision au fond*) whether the forum would have decided the matter differently had it been pending there.

Lack of merger, in the international context, makes both kinds of review possible.

All legal systems will ultimately deny recognition when the foreign judgment violates the forum's *ordre public*. Some stress by express statutory provision[47] the exceptional nature of this defense. But even quite generally, there is consensus that the defense should be invoked with restraint.[48]

But there is the temptation to question the foreign decision. It is indeed a fine line between the appropriate review of a foreign decision for its compliance with the local *ordre public* and an inappropriate *révision au fond*.

Measuring foreign law by one's own standards (including the decision whether foreign law should apply at all) is not unusual in choice of law. This phenomenon is very much part of all modern American approaches to choice of law.[49] It begins to be part of contemporaneous European conflicts law as well. A good example is the new (1999) Art. 40(3), no. 1 of the German Conflicts Statute (EGBGB) which apparently makes German notions of "appropriate" ("*angemessen*") compensation the test for the use of the damage law or practice of the otherwise applicable law.[50] The forum's view of all sorts of other things obviously also is outcome determinative, for instance, whether a transaction has a close connection or perhaps an even "closer" connection to this or that legal system.[51]

---

[47] E.g., § 328 (1) No. 4 German ZPO.

[48] See, e.g., Dicey & Morris (supra n. 46) at 525.

[49] Compare also Juenger (supra n. 18) at 1328 et seq.

[50] "Claims that are governed by the law of another state may not be entertained to the extent that they 1. go substantially beyond that which is required for appropriate compensation of the injured person ... " (author's translation). The original proposal referred to "damages" rather than "compensation" and lacked the word "appropriate". The change was to assure that immaterial harm is covered and that damages for pain and suffering may be awarded at levels higher customary under German law ("appropriate"), subject to some upper limit ("substantially" higher). For the original proposal, see Germany, Bundestags Drucksache 14/343 at 4 and 12 (1999), for the modification, ibid., at 20 and 22. The official comment to the original proposal states that the limitation ("substantially" higher) serves the same purpose as the *ordre public*-exception of Art. 6 EGBGB, in that the result must be incompatible with the basic values of German law (ibid., at 12). The analogy does not fit. Art. 6 requires a violation of German law or German legal values. A sum of money cannot do that. It may be grossly inappropriate and the court may therefore decide not to award compensation at that level. Such a threshold, however, is lower than that of Art. 6. For further comment see Hay, "From Rule-Orientation to 'Approach' in German Conflicts Law. The Effect of the 1986 and 1999 Codifications," 47 *Am.J.Comp.L.* 633 (1999).

[51] See Art. 28 (1) German EGBGB (= Art. 4(1) Rome Convention on the Law Applicable to Contractual Obligations) – "closest connection," to be determined on the basis of the presumptions in paragraphs 2-4, and paragraph 5, exceptionally permitting displacement of the otherwise applicable law by an (even) more closely connected law. See also Art. 41 German EGBG, permitting displacement of the otherwise applicable law in tort by an even "more closely connected" law.

Does any of this carry over into judgment recognition? It does, albeit less obviously and is hardly ever as express as it is in choice of law.

The forum court makes evaluative determinations. For judgment recognition, for instance, jurisdiction of the rendering court is a prerequisite everywhere. Such jurisdiction may be based on objective facts (e.g., submission, forum selection clause, location of the property in litigation, etc.) but also upon such findings ("judgment-calls" in American parlance) as to whether there was a "real and substantial connection" between the action and the rendering court, as in recent Canadian case law.[52]

The new German conflicts provision just mentioned introduces a weighing that, in choice of law, seems to adopt a lower threshold for the rejection of foreign law than does the general *ordre public* provision for choice of law (Art. 6 EGBGB) or its counterpart for judgment recognition (sec. 328 I no. 4 ZPO). In judgment recognition, perhaps as the result of the express prohibition of *révision au fond* in sec. 723(1) ZPO, the focus is on the *ordre public*. All that this means, however, is that the threshold may be higher.

In its 1992 decision involving the recognition of an American judgment awarding compensatory damages, damages for pain and suffering, as well as punitive damages, the German Supreme Court had no difficulty with the two extremes: recognition of compensatory damages, non-recognition of punitive damages.[53] The weighing that occurred concerned damages for pain and suffering. The Court of Appeals had thought them to be excessive. The Supreme Court disagreed: by living and having acted in the United States, the defendant should expect to be judged by the standards of his (American) community, and by the standards of that community, the award was not excessive.

One might ask why the same line of thought does not support the recognition of awards of punitive damages? Or, to turn the problem around: could not a very large award of damages for pain and suffering simply be characterized as "punitive" and be denied on that ground? Art. 40(3), no. 2 of the German conflicts statute, as amended in 1999, is the analogy in choice of law[54]. In short, evaluations take place in judgment recognition as in choice of law. There is not, there cannot be, a "bright line" separating the (appropriate) *ordre public* defense from the proscribed, or at least undesirable, *révision au fond*.

---

[52] *Morguard* (supra n. 39); *Ivey* (supra n. 40); *Mutual Trust Co.* v. *St-Cyr*, [1996] R.D.J. 623 (C.A.), leave to appeal denied, [1997] S.C.C.A. No. 65; Tetley (supra n. 38) at 196.

[53] BGH, Judgment of June 4, 1992, BGHZ 118, 312; [1992] *Wertpapiermitteilungen* 1451. See Hay, "The Recognition and Enforcement of American Money-Judgments in Germany," 40 *Am.J.Comp.L.* 1001 (1992). Although case law is scant, it is possible that Swiss courts may take a more differentiated approach, attempting to assess whether factors additional or of greater importance than punishment may underlie the American award. See Piantino, "Switzerland's Treatment of U.S. Money Judgments," 46 *Am.J.Comp.L.* 181, 190-92 (1998).

[54] Supra n. 50.

Given the inapplicability of the merger doctrine to international judgments, the above trends now also appear in American practice. Thus, a 1995 decision held an English judgment in a libel action not to be entitled to recognition and enforcement on constitutional and public policy grounds: the court considered the English standards underlying the judgment to violate the forum's public policy and to deprive the debtor of his rights under the First and Fourth Amendments to the Federal Constitution.[55]

The judgment was for money. In an interstate context, it would not have been reviewable, as discussed previously. English notions of *res judicata* closely resemble those of American law: the claim may not be relitigated,[56] the law applied will not be reviewed, in short: the foreign determination is conclusive.[57] For these reasons, public policy is no defense to the recognition of a foreign money judgment.[58] Under English law, foreign judgments, like domestic judgments, can produce collateral estoppel effects,[59] a matter that is still somewhat uncertain in the United States.[60]

The American exclusion of foreign country money judgments from the notion of merger therefore may lead to some sort of review. That review may be styled as one for public policy reasons. Yet its effect is the same as a *révision au fond*: how would the forum decide the (non-merged) claim if it were pending before it? Was the foreign court's approach appropriate as a matter of (forum) conflicts (or substantive) law?

IV.

Public policy also underlies the general European refusal to recognize a judgment that, in turn, recognized a third court's judgment (double exequatur): "*exequatur sur exequatur ne vaut*," so the title of *Kegel*'s well-known contribution.[61] Various reasons have been advanced for why this should be so: that the recognition judgment (the second judgment) is territorially limited, that it did not decide

---

[55] *Matusevitch* v. *Telnikoff*, 877 F.Supp. 1 (D.D.C. 1995). The court referred to public policy exception in Maryland's version of the Uniform Money-Judgment Recognition Act (Md.Code Ann., Cts. & Jud. Proc. § 10-704(b)(2) and to two provisions of the federal Constitution: the First Amendment, guaranteeing freedom of expression, and the Fourth Amendment, prohibiting unreasonable searches and seizures. See also *Bachchan* v. *India Abroad Publications Inc.*, 154 Misc.2d 228, 585 N.Y.S.2d 661 (1992).

[56] Dicey & Morris (supra n. 46) at 514.

[57] Ibid., at pp. 512 et seq.

[58] Compare ibid., at pp. 525-531.

[59] Ibid., at 514, citing *Carl Zeiss Stiftung* v. *Rayner & Keeler Ltd. (No. 2)*, [1967] 1 A.C. 853; *The Sennar (No.2)*, [1985] 1 W.L.R. 490 (H.L.).

[60] Hay/Weintraub/Borchers (supra n. 8) at 516.

[61] In: *Festschrift für Müller-Freienfels* 377 (1986).

substantive issues, and so forth.[62] None of these ultimately convinces.[63] Instead, the concern is rather that the requirements of the forum's practice might be circumvented. Examples: a foreign judgment not entitled to recognition for lack of reciprocity might become effective by means of recognition by a country with which reciprocity is assured (or in the European Union, where recognition is mandated, full-faith-and-credit style); application for a German exequatur of an English exequatur of an American judgment awarding punitive damages, arguably recognizable in England but not – directly – in Germany.[64]

The defensive posture of European literature and case law does not convince entirely. Perhaps differentiation between exequatur decrees issued by courts from within and without the European Union (= Brussels Convention) is indicated. Within a "federal" structure, there is little room for the non-recognition of "sister-state" (to borrow the American phrase) money judgments on public policy grounds (despite Art. 27 No. 1, Brussels Convention).[65] If this is so, it should make no difference whether the foreign decree reduces to judgment a claim arising – say – under English substantive law or whether it recognizes and decrees enforcement in favor of an American judgment. Prevailing opinion, however, is otherwise.

In the United States, judgments do not merge. For inconsistent judgments, however, the result is the same because the last judgment in time is entitled to Full Faith and Credit.[66] For *consistent* (sequential) judgments, the inapplicability of the (claim) merger-rule to judgments means that *both* judgments may claim recognition, even if the second merely grants recognition to the first (thereby perhaps lengthening limitation periods). The national policy of "Full Faith and Credit" is stronger than particularistic definitions of an *ordre public*.[67]

---

[62] The literature is collected in Borges, *Das Doppelexequatur von Schiedssprüchen* 355, 357 (1997).

[63] Ibid., at 358-377. With respect to German law, Borges ultimately joins the opponents of the double *exequatur* on the basis of a theological interpretation of § 328 German ZPO: a restrictive construction is required to preserve the effectiveness of the bases on which recognition of a foreign judgment may be denied. *Id.* at 435. This is a public policy argument. See text immediately following.

[64] See supra nn. 46, 53.

[65] The provision, originally intended to operate "only in exceptional circumstances" . . . , by the Convention's own terms (Art. 28(3)), does not permit a review of the rendering court's jurisdiction. Beyond this, there remains little scope for its application, at least with respect to money judgments. See also text following n. 69.

[66] *Treinies* (supra n. 45).

[67] When a foreign-country judgment has been recognized in one state of the Union, the latter's decree in turn is entitled to recognition under Full Faith and Credit in other states (for foreign judgments – sister-state and foreign-country – registered under Uniform Acts, see text at n. 68 infra). This may even be so when the foreign decree would not have been entitled to recognition directly in the present forum. For example: only five states and the Virgin Islands recognize Haitian and Dominican Republic divorces (granted bilaterally on application, with no residence requirements). If one of these states subsequently recognizes such a divorce, the recognition arguably "domesticates" the divorce (e.g., enabling parties to remarry) even in states where the divorce would not have been recognized directly. See Hay/Weintraub/Borchers (supra n. 8) at 878.

But there are departures here as well, "cracks" in the established system. Thus, a Texas court held that, while it might enforce a Canadian judgment under the Uniform Foreign Money-Judgment Recognition Act, it would not register a Louisiana decree under the (interstate) Uniform Enforcement of Foreign Judgments Act that had recognized the Canadian judgment. To grant the relief, so the court, would have the effect of giving the foreign-country judgment full faith and credit recognition "through the back door."[68]

To be sure, the issue arose under uniform acts – state laws (the interstate version merely providing an alternative and simplified procedure for interstate recognition and enforcement) and did not raise the *constitutional* Full Faith and Credit problem. The decision, however, echoes the general European concern: to remain the master of one's own recognition practice.

V.

Res judicata and judgment recognition protect party expectations. At the same time, they also promote what, in 1599, Lord Coke said to be the goal of all law: "rest and quietness"[69] within the legal system. The latter may be the single state or it may be a number of legal system united into a greater whole. These are the federated legal systems of the United States and of the Europe of the Brussels Convention. It is not surprising that they should show remarkable similarities. At the same time, and in view of the rather parallel needs for effective legal integration, each could adopt successful features of the other. Thus, the public policy defense (Art. 27 No. 1 Brussels Convention) seems dispensable for money judgments, and Arts. 21-22 (on *lis pendens*) might provide more effective ways for dealing with parallel litigation in the United States than now exist.[70]

---

[68] *Reading & Bates Construction Co.* v. *Baker Energy Resources Corp.*, 976 S.W.2d 702 (Tex.App. 1998). The question has also arisen in purely interstate practice: does a judgment of one state, registered in another state under the (interstate) Uniform Recognition of Foreign Judgments Act, become a judgment of the second state and, as such, in turn be entitled to recognition under the Uniform Act? The court in *Tanner* v. *Hancock*, 5 Kan.App.2d 558, 619 P.2d 1177 (1980), gave a negative answer: "Registration ... may not be deemed to create a judgment conferring more benefits upon the judgment creditor ... than the original ... judgment." (ibid. at 1182). The effect of the decision is a definition by the second (or third) state of what constitutes a "judgment" of another state. Under the Uniform Acts, in issue in *Tanner*, states are free to construe their own law; they may not undertake such a unilateral definition when the command of the Full Faith and Credit Clause applies.

[69] *Ferrer's Case*, VI Coke 7, 77 E.R. 263 (K.B. 1599).

[70] In contrast to the *lis pendens* rules of many legal systems, American law does not provide for deference to the pendency of litigation in another forum. While the Full Faith and Credit Clause does refer to "judicial proceedings" and not to (final) judgments, as Justice Jackson noted in his concurrence in *Barber* v. *Barber*, 323 U.S. 77, 65 S.Ct. 137, 89 L.Ed. 82 (1944), only final judgments are generally

There is no less need internationally for "rest and quietness" and party protection. For lack of a superlaw, comity is invoked to internationalize the intrasystem harmony. Its success will be mixed so long as national public policy not only defends against unacceptable results but pursues decidedly national interests. Reciprocity requirements do not bring litigation to an end, they do not protect parties, but instead seek to implement national goals on the backs of the parties.[71] *Révision au fond* introduces forum-centered approaches to choice of law into judgment recognition. Broad assertions of jurisdiction, favoring local plaintiffs, will produce unacceptable judgments under mirror-image rules: the national public policy of one state meets with that of another.

Agreement on more well-defined, more limited bases of jurisdiction will lessen the effect of divergent approaches to choice of law and, theoretically, reduce the perceived need to intervene for public policy reasons, whether by means of the *ordre public* exception itself or more indirectly through a *révision au fond*. It will require express agreement on standards and on possible future directions. A "common law" of comity alone is unlikely to achieve Lord Coke's formulated goal internationally.

---

deemed to be covered by the constitutional command. (Modifiable support orders are generally recognized as a matter of *state practice*. Scoles/Hay/Borchers/Symeonides (supra n. 2) § 15.34.) As a result parallel litigation – the "race to judgment" – remains possible. Antisuit injunctions are the result; they in turn are not entitled to recognition, principally because they do not address the merits of the litigation. *Id.* at § 24.21 and *Baker*, supra n. 28. In federal practice, courts will defer (suspend their own proceedings) in favor to the action "first filed". Here, the problem may be decide whether the action "first filed" is a genuine suit or a preemptive strike. Hay/Weintraub/Borchers, *Conflict of Laws* 184 (11th ed. 2000). Again, the matter turns into a review of another court's proceedings.

[71] See also Juenger, "Private International Law and the German Legislature", in: Kübler, Scherer, Treeck, *The International Lawyer – Freundesgabe für Döser* 623, 625 (1999).

Das neue deutsche IPR für ausservertragliche Schuldverhältnisse und für Sachen von 1999 im Vergleich mit dem schweizerischen IPRG

Anton Heini[*]

Während der Hauptharst des deutschen IPRG schon 1986 in Kraft getreten ist, hat sich der deutsche Gesetzgeber reichlich Zeit genommen für die Regelung der im Titel genannten Materien. Es erscheint reizvoll, die schweizerischen den neuen deutschen Regeln einander gegenüberzustellen. Hinsichtlich der ausservertraglichen Schuldverhältnisse beschränke ich mich auf die unerlaubten Handlungen.

1.   UNERLAUBTE HANDLUNGEN

1.1 Hier fällt zunächst ein unterschiedlicher "approach" auf. Zwar enthält das schweizerische IPRG in Art. 133 –ähnlich Art. 40 des deutschen Gesetzes –eine allgemeine Anknüpfungsregel, legt aber das Schwergewicht auf einzelne Tatbestände (Art. 134-139), nämlich Strassenverkehrsunfälle, Produktemängel, unlauterer Wettbewerb, Wettbewerbsbehinderung, Immissionen und Persönlichkeitsverletzung.

Der **schweizerische** Gesetzgeber liess sich dabei von der Überlegung leiten, „einerseits die <statistisch> im Vordergrund stehenden Fallgruppen in relativ aussagekräftige Typenregeln zu kleiden . . . , andererseits den <Restbereich> in einer

---

[*]   Dr. iur., em. Professor der Universität Zürich.

J. Basedow et al., eds., Private Law in the International Arena – Liber Amicorum Kurt Siehr
© 2000, T.M.C.Asser Press, The Hague, The Netherlands

Subsidiärregel aufzufangen".[1] Demgegenüber begnügt sich die **deutsche** Lösung mit einer allgemeinen Bestimmung (Art. 40), ergänzt durch eine Ausweichklausel (Art. 41) und die Zulässigkeit der Rechtswahl (Art. 42 –Gesetzestexte s. Anhang).

1.2 Was vorab die **Rechtswahl** betrifft, schränkt Deutschland die wählbaren Rechtsordnungen nicht ein. Dies im Gegensatz zum schweizerischen IPRG (Art. 132), welches nur die Wahl des Rechts am Gerichtsort, mithin des schweizerischen Rechts zulässt. Eine solche „Zwerg"-Autonomie erscheint verunglückt. Im (schweizerischen) Gesetzgebungsverfahren wurde u.a. argumentiert, der Wahlmöglichkeit werde über das Akzessorietätsprinzip wie auch im Rahmen einiger Einzeltatbestände genügend Rechnung getragen. Nicht zuletzt befürchtete man, Versicherungsgesellschaften könnten – aufgrund der *action directe* – dem Geschädigten eine ungünstige Rechtswahl aufdrängen. Die deutsche Lösung ist indessen vorzuziehen. Sie berücksichtigt zurecht, dass es sich hier stets um privat-(schuld)rechtliche Ansprüche handelt, über welche die Parteien frei verfügen können.[2] Beide Gesetze lassen aber eine Rechtswahl erst nach Eintritt des schädigenden Ereignisses zu.

1.3. Den beiden allgemeinen Regeln der Art. 40 und 41 des deutschen Gesetzes entspricht auf schweizerischer Seite –wenigstens teilweise –diejenige des Art. 133.

1.3.1   Grosses Gewicht hat der **schweizerische** Gesetzgeber der **akzessorischen Anknüpfung** beigemessen, welche in Abs. 3 des Art. 133 wie folgt formuliert ist:

> „Wird durch eine unerlaubte Handlung ein zwischen Schädiger und Geschädigtem bestehendes Rechtsverhältnis verletzt, so unterstehen Ansprüche aus unerlaubter Handlung, ungeachtet der Absätze 1 und 2, dem Recht, dem das vorbestehende Rechtsverhältnis unterstellt ist."

Der Weg zu dieser offenkundigen Verwirklichung des kollisionsrechtlichen Vertrauensprinzipes wurde bekanntlich frühzeitig gewiesen, so etwa von *Neuhaus* schon 1951,[3] *Beitzke* 1965,[4] *Cavers* 1965[5] und vor allem *Kropholler* 1969.[6]

---

[1] Heini, in: Anton Heini/ Max Keller/ Kurt Siehr/ Frank Vischer/ Paul Volken (Hrsg.), *IPRG Kommentar* (Zürich 1993) vor Art. 132-142 N. 3.

[2] Vgl. in diesem Sinne schon Kropholler, „Ein Anknüpfungssystem für das Deliktstatut", 33 *RabelsZ* (1969) 601 S. 640-641.

[3] P.-H. Neuhaus, 16 *RabelsZ* (1951) 651, S. 655.

[4] G. Beitzke, „Les obligations délictuelle en droit international privé", *Recueil des Cours* (1965 – II) 67, S. 107ff.

[5] D. Cavers, *The Choice-of-Law Process* (Ann Arbor, University of Michigan 1965) S. 166ff.

[6] Kropholler (oben N. 2) S. 625ff.

Während nun die schweizerische Fassung eine akzessorische Anknüpfung nur dann zulässt, wenn das Delikt **in Verletzung** des vorbestehenden **Rechtsverhältnisses** begangen wurde, geht der deutsche Gesetzgeber weit über die schweizerische Lösung hinaus: in Abs. 2 Ziff. 1 der Ausweichklausel des Art. 41 („Wesentlich engere Verbindung") heisst es:

(2) Eine wesentlich engere Verbindung kann sich insbesondere ergeben
1. aus einer besonderen rechtlichen oder tatsächlichen Beziehung zwischen den Beteiligten im Zusammenhang mit dem Schuldverhältnis ...

Es genügt also schon eine tatsächliche Beziehung zwischen den Beteiligten und der blosse „Zusammenhang mit dem Schuldenverhältnis". Diese Lösung gibt dem deutschen Richter ein grosses Manövrierfeld, und es wird sich weisen, ob die primäre lex loci delicti-Regel des Art. 40 in der Praxis nicht zu einem Schrumpfdasein verkümmern wird.

1.3.2 In der **allgemeinen Norm** der beiden Gesetze – Art. 133 Abs. 2 CH, Art. 40 D – wird primär auf den Handlungsort abgestellt. Aber bei den **Distanzdelikten** trennen sich die Wege. Deutschland bleibt der "alten" Ubiquitätsregel insofern treu, als der Verletzte anstelle des Rechtes des Handlungsortes dasjenige des Erfolgsortes wählen kann. Demgegenüber hat der schweizerische Gesetzgeber die früher auch in der Schweiz praktizierte Ubiquitätsregel(bzw. das Wahlrecht des Geschädigten) in der Subsidiärregel abgeschafft und sich bei Distanzdelikten für den Vorrang des Rechtes des Erfolgsortes entschieden; dies allerdings mit dem Zusatz, "wenn der Schädiger mit dem Eintritt des Erfolges in diesem Staat rechnen musste". Immerhin kennt das schweizerische Gesetz ein solches Wahlrecht im konkreten Tatbestand der Grundstückimmissionen (Art. 138), während hinsichtlich „Produktemängel" (Art. 135) und „Persönlichkeitsverletzung" (Art. 139) auf diese Tatbestände spezifisch zugeschnittene Rechtswahlmöglichkeiten statuiert werden.
Beide Gesetze enthalten keine nähere Umschreibung des **Erfolgsortes**; das wäre auch kaum möglich. Schwierigkeiten bereitet dessen Bestimmung insbesondere in den Fällen der **Vermögensschädigung**.[7] Will man sich hier auf verlässlichem Boden bewegen, so sollte man im Zweifel den Erfolgsort am Wohnsitz bzw. Sitz des Geschädigten lokalisieren.[8] Andernfalls verstrickt man sich in schwer überwindbare Schwierigkeiten, wie ein neuer Entscheid des schweizerischen Bundesgerichtes (I. Zivilabteilung) demonstriert.[9] Das Gericht hatte eine Anknüpfung an den Wohnsitz des Geschädigten abgelehnt und in mühsamen Windungen nach dem "Standort

---

[7] Vgl. etwa K. Kiethe, „Internationale Tatortzuständigkeit bei unerlaubter Handlung –die Problematik des Vermögensschadens", *NJW* (1994) S. 222ff.
[8] Vgl. auch Kropholler, *Internationales Privatrecht*, 3. Aufl. (Tübingen 1997) S. 458 oben.
[9] BGE 125 III 103 (1999).

[sc. des Vermögens] im Moment der unerlaubten Handlung" als Erfolgsort gesucht
(S. 107). Interessanterweise hat der Kassationshof des Bundesgerichtes ein Jahr zuvor in einer Strafsache entschieden, bei einer Schädigung des Vermögens durch
eine Veruntreuungs- oder Betrugshandlung im Ausland sei der Erfolg am schweizerischen Sitz der geschädigten AG eingetreten.[10]

1.4 Wiederum generell geregelt ist im deutschen Gesetz, Art. 40 Abs. 3 Ziff. 1 und
2, eine **lex americana**, d.h. die Unzulässigkeit von Ansprüchen, „die dem Recht eines anderen Staates unterliegen" . . . „soweit sie 1. wesentlich weitergehen als zur
angemessenen Entschädigung des Verletzten erforderlich, 2. offensichtlich anderen Zwecken als einer angemessenen Entschädigung des Verletzten dienen". . .
Eine ähnliche Barriere hat auch der schweizerische Gesetzgeber vorgesehen, jedoch nicht generell, sondern in den konkreten Tatbeständen der Produktehaftung
(Art. 135 Abs. 3) und der Wettbewerbsbehinderung (Art. 137 Abs. 2). Indessen gilt
als Messlatte, was „nach schweizerischem Recht zuzusprechen" wäre. Mit dem
Wörtchen „wesentlich" (weiter) erscheint die deutsche Formulierung in der erwähnten Ziff. 1. etwas vorsichtiger bzw. flexibler als die heimatschützerisch gefärbte schweizerische Fassung. Doch befolgen beide Gesetze das lobenswerte Ziel,
den exorbitanten amerikanischen *punitive damages* einen Riegel zu stossen; im
Grunde handelt es sich um konkretisierte ordre public-Regeln. Es ist überhaupt
höchste Zeit, dass die europäischen Länder der amerikanischen Rechtsunkultur
Grenzen setzen.[11]

1.5 Im Unterschied zum schweizerischen Recht (Art. 142) enthält das deutsche
Gesetz keine **Qualifikationsnorm**, d.h. eine Bestimmung, die den Geltungsbereich
des auf die unerlaubte Handlung anwendbaren Rechts umschreibt. Die schweizerische Norm erscheint recht hilfreich, wird durch sie doch u.a. klargestellt, dass die
Frage nach dem Kreis der haftpflichtigen Personen (z.B. juristische Person, Geschäftsherr) ebenfalls vom Deliktsstatut beantwortet wird. Als nützlich erweist sich
m.E. auch der Hinweis in Art. 142 Abs. 2, wonach die „Sichterheits- und Verhaltensvorschriften am Ort der Handlung . . . zu berücksichtigen" seien – für den deutschen Gesetzgeber offenbar eine Selbstverständlichkeit.[12]

---

[10] BGE 124 IV 241 (1998).
[11] Vgl. die beissende Analyse von Heinrich Honsell, „Amerikanische Rechtskultur", in: Peter
Forstmoser, Hans Caspar von der Crone, Rolf H. Weber, Dieter Zobl (Hrsg.), *Der Einfluss des europäischen Rechts auf die Schweiz, Festschrift Roger Zäch* (Zürich 1999) S. 39ff.
[12] R. Wagner, „Der Regierungsentwurf eines Gesetzes zum Internationalen Privatrecht für ausservertragliche Schuldverhältnisse und für Sachen", *IPRax* (1998) S. 429ff., S. 434. Die (schweizerische)
Botschaft zum IPRG vom 10. Nov. 1982 bezeichnet diese Regel ebenfalls als selbstverständlich, vgl.
Nr. 284.4 a.E.; ebenso der Bericht zur österreichischen Regierungsvorlage, s. bei Köhler/ Gürtler, *Internationales Privatrecht* (1979) S. 138. Betreffend ausländische Gesetze und internat. Übereinkommen s. Heini (oben N. 1) Art. 142 N 16.

2.   SACHENRECHT

2.1   Auch das Sachenrecht wird in Deutschland mit nur drei Rechtsanwendungs-
normen geregelt (Art. 43-45 – Gesetzestexte s. Anhang), während der schweizerische Gesetzgeber deren neun erlassen hat. Im Unterschied zum deutschen enthält
das **schweizerische IPR-Gesetz spezifische Bestimmungen** über Sachen im Tran-
sit (Art. 101), den Eigentumsvorbehalt (Art. 102 Abs. 2 und 3, Art. 103), die
Rechtswahl (Art. 104), die Verpfändung von Forderungen, Wertpapieren und anderen Rechten (Art. 105), sowie Warenpapiere (Art. 106).

Eine spezifische Norm kennt das **deutsche** Gesetz hinsichtlich der **Grundstückimmissionen**; diesbezüglich stimmen die Regelungen beider Rechtsordnungen
im Ergebnis überein: Art. 99 des schweizerischen IPRG –die Bestimmung steht
ebenfalls im Sachenrecht –verweist auf die Regeln über unerlaubte Handlungen,
wo sich eine eigene Norm über Grundstückimmissionen findet (Art. 138); das deutsche Gesetz enthält in Art. 44 eine ähnliche Verweisung, allerdings auf die Grundnorm des Art. 40 Abs. 1.

Eine besondere Anknüpfungsregel findet sich im **deutschen** Gesetz sodann hinsichtlich der **Transportmittel** (Art. 45): bei Luftfahrzeugen wird auf die Staatsangehörigkeit abgestellt, bei Wasserfahrzeugen auf das Recht des Registerstaates, bei
Schienenfahrzeugen auf das Recht des Staates der Zulassung. Diese Materie ist
vielfach Gegenstand von Staatsverträgen, die i.d.R. vorgehen. In der Praxis eine
wichtige Rolle spielen bei den genannten Transportmitteln die **gesetzlichen Sicherungsrechte**. Nach Art. 45 Abs. 2 des **deutschen** Gesetzes unterliegen sie dem
Recht, „das auf die zu sichernde Forderung anzuwenden ist", also nicht, wie vielfach vertreten, dem Ortsrecht.[13] Dieses kommt allerdings für die Rangfolge zur Anwendung (Art. 45 Abs. 2 letzter Satz). Das **schweizerische** IPRG begnügt sich in
Art. 107 mit einem Vorbehalt „anderer Gesetze" über dingliche Rechte an Transportmitteln. Diese Bestimmung lässt der Lückenfüllung einen breiten Raum. Aber
auch die deutsche Norm erfasst nicht alle Transportmittel. In der Regel wird man
hier auf die Grundnorm der *lex rei sitae* zurückgreifen, wie dies v.a. für die Kraft-
fahrzeuge vertreten wird.[14]

2.2   Im „harten Kern" – der **Herrschaft der lex rei sitae als Grundnorm** – stimmen beide Gesetze überein (D: Art. 43, CH: Art. 100 und 102). Den Grundsatz, dass
ein in einem ersten Staat entstandenes Sachenrecht bei Verschiebung der Sache in
einen zweiten Staat nur nach den (materiellen) Regeln des letzteren ausgeübt werden kann, bringen die beiden Gesetze mit unterschiedlichen Formulierungen zum
Ausdruck: nach Art. 43 Abs. 2 des deutschen Gesetzes können die in einem Staat

---

[13] Vgl. hiezu Staudinger/ Stoll, 13. Bearbeitung, Rdz. 407; *Heini*, IPRG-Kommentar Art. 107 N. 8.
[14] So z.B. von Staudinger/ Stoll ibid., Rdz. 411.

entstandenen Rechte **nicht im Widerspruch** zur neuen *lex rei sitae* ausgeübt werden; nach der schweizerischen Fassung unterstehen gemäss Art. 100 Abs. 2 „Inhalt
und Ausübung dinglicher Rechte . . . dem Recht am Ort der gelegenen Sache". Die
deutsche Formulierung betont – wie mir scheint – eher die Abwehrstellung der neu-
en Rechtsordnung, stellt dafür aber m.E. klar, dass es sich dabei nicht um einen Anwendungsfall des ordre public handelt, wie gelegentlich behauptet worden ist. Die
schweizerische Fassung legt überdies nahe, dass die im Erwerbsland entstandene
Rechtsposition derjenigen der neuen Sachenrechtsordnung anzupassen ist.[15] Beide
Gesetze sehen sodann vor, dass im Ausland geschaffene Tatbestandselemente, die
dort noch nicht zu einem Sachenrechtserwerb geführt haben, der inländischen lex
rei sitae zugerechnet werden (D: Art. 43 Abs. 3, CH: Art. 102 Abs. 1).

2.3 Auffällig ist, dass die **Rechtswahl** ins **deutsche** Gesetz nicht aufgenommen
wurde; dies obwohl ein erster Sachkenner wie Hans *Stoll* sich seit Jahren vehement
für die Parteiautonomie im Mobiliarsachenrecht eingesetzt hat (vgl. etwa *Staudin-
ger/Stoll*, 13. Bearbeitung, Rdz. 285 ff.). Zur Begründung wird geltend gemacht,
die Rechtswahl würde den numerus clausus der Sachenrechte durchbrechen und
das von den Parteien gewählte Recht sei für Dritte nicht erkennbar.[16] Das **schweizerische** Gesetz lässt in Art. 104 zwar eine Rechtswahl zu, degradiert sie aber zur Be-
deutungslosigkeit; denn nach Abs. 2 kann sie Dritten nicht entgegengehalten werden.[17]

3.   DIE AUSWEICHKLAUSELN

Besonderes Interesse erweckt das **deutsche** Gesetz mit seinen **Ausweichklauseln**
der Art. 41 bei den unerlaubten Handlungen und Art. 46 im Sachenrecht, jeweils
überschrieben mit "Wesentlich engere Verbindung". Danach kann ganz generell
von dem nach den Art. 40 Abs. 1 und 2 bzw. 43-45 massgebenden Recht abgewichen werden.

3.1 Das **schweizerische** IPRG hält in Art. 15 eine für das **ganze** Gesetz geltende
Ausnahmeklausel bereit. Gegenüber den deutschen Fassungen ist sie indessen sehr
zurückhaltend formuliert.[18] Dass es sich dabei um eine eng begrenzte Ausnahme

---

[15] So aber auch R. Wagner, S. 435.
[16] R. Wagner, ibid.
[17] Siehe auch die Kritik Stoll (oben N. 13) Rdz. 285.
[18] Art. 15:
    1   Das Recht, auf das dieses Gesetz verweist, ist ausnahmsweise nicht anwendbar, wenn nach
       den gesamten Umständen offensichtlich ist, dass der Sachverhalt mit diesem Recht in nur gerin-
       gem, mit einem anderen Recht in viel engerem Zusammenhang steht.

handelt, hat das schweizerische Bundesgericht unmissverständlich zum Ausdruck gebracht: „Cette disposition est une règle d'exception, partant d'application stricte".[19] Stimmen aus dem Schrifttum sind dabei nicht zu hören, die versuchen, ihnen nicht passende Lösungen mit Art. 15 zu korrigieren. Solchen Ausweichklauseln liegt gewiss das Anliegen zugrunde, dasjenige Recht zur Anwendung zu berufen, mit denen die Parteien rechnen dürfen und müssen (kollisionsrechtliches Vertrauensprinzip).[20] Diesem Grundsatz hat das schweizerische Gesetz durch seine detaillierten Regeln weitgehend Rechnung getragen, sodass für eine Ausweichung nach Art. 15 sehr wenig Platz bleibt.

3.2   Ganz anders das **deutsche** Gesetz. Hier genügt für die Abweichung von dem durch die Kollisionsnormen an sich berufenen Recht bereits "eine wesentlich engere Verbindung" mit dem Recht eines andern Staates. Bei **unerlaubten Handlungen** ist die Gefahr eines "Dammbruches" allerdings dadurch gemindert, dass bei Ausübung des Wahlrechts durch den Verletzten (Art. 40 Abs. 1) sowie bei der lex communis (Abs. 2) die Ausweichklausel nicht zum Zuge kommen dürfte. Sodann erhält diese Klausel mit der – wenn auch etwas vagen – Umschreibung des Akzessorietätsprinzipes eine gewisse Präzisierung.

Demgegenüber ist die Ausweichklausel im **Sachenrecht** (Art. 46) sehr offen formuliert, was die Rechtssicherheit gewiss nicht fördern dürfte.

3.3   Schliesslich fragt sich, wie die genannten Ausweichklauseln sich zum **Renvoi** verhalten. Das **schweizerische** IPRG ist Renvoi-feindlich; ein Renvoi kommt gemäss ausdrücklicher Anordnung des Art. 14 nur zum Zuge, wo das Gesetz ihn vorsieht. Das trifft weder für die unerlaubten Handlungen noch für das Sachenrecht zu. Allerdings fehlt es nicht an Stimmen, die in das schweizerische internationale Sachenrecht einen Renvoi hineinlesen. So vertritt z.B. unser Jubilar die Meinung, ob nach Art. 102 Abs. 2 IPRG ein Eigentumsvorbehalt an einer importierten Sache im Ausland „gültig begründet" worden sei, lasse sich nur auf Grund des gesamten Rechts des Erwerbsstatuts beantworten.[21] Diese Auffassung hat viel für sich, scheitert aber m.E. am klaren Willen des schweizerischen Gesetzgebers, wonach – abgesehen von den wenigen in Art. 14 genannten Fällen – die Verweisungen des IPRG als Sachnormverweisungen zu gelten haben.[22]

Im **deutschen** Recht dürfte die Grundregel der Gesamtverweisung, Art. 4, so-

---

2   Diese Bestimmung ist nicht anwendbar, wenn eine Rechtswahl vorliegt.

[19] BGE 121 III S. 247.

[20] Vom schweiz. Bundesgericht schon 1885 formuliert, BGE 11, S. 364.

[21] Siehr, „Renvoi und wohlerworbene Rechte" in: Isaak Meier und Kurt Siehr (Hrsg.), *Rechtskollisionen, Festschrift Anton Heini* (Zürich 1995) 419.

[22] Vgl. z.B. Dutoit, *Droit international privé suisse, Commentaire de la loi fédérale du 18 décembre 1987*, 2e éd. (Basel und Frankfurt a.M. 1997) Art. 14 N. 1.

wohl im Delikts- wie im Sachenrecht Anwendung finden.[23] Ausgeschlossen ist sie aber bei Ausübung des Wahlrechts des Verletzten bzw. der Parteien wie auch der lex communis (Deliktsrecht), sowie in Fällen, wo auf die Ausweichklausel gegriffen wird (Delikts- und Sachenrecht). In all diesen Fällen wäre ein Renvoi zweckwidrig (Art. 4 Abs. 1 und 2 des deutschen IPRG).[24]

4.   FAZIT

Gewiss wird man bei beiden Gesetzeswerken einen Grundkonsens feststellen, nicht zuletzt das Bemühen, dasjenige Recht zur Anwendung zu berufen, mit dem die Beteiligten rechnen dürfen und müssen. **Deutschland** begnügt sich mit wenigen aber allgemein abstrakten Normen kombiniert mit Ausweichklauseln. Da bleibt vieles der Rechtsprechung und der Schreibfreudigkeit der deutschen Gelehrten überlassen. Das **schweizerische** IPRG ist in den beiden Materien erheblich detaillierter und erscheint mir deshalb –man verzeihe mir die Parteilichkeit –benutzerfreundlicher.

---

[23]Vgl. z.B. Staudinger/ Stoll, 13. Bearb., Rdz. 134 für das Sachenrecht.
[24]Vgl. Kreuzer, *Münch.Komm.*, 3. Aufl., Art. 38 Rd.Nr. 26.

Artikel 40
Unerlaubte Handlung

(1) Ansprüche aus unerlaubter Handlung unterliegen dem Recht des Staates, in dem der Ersatzpflichtige gehandelt hat. Der Verletzte kann verlangen, dass anstelle dieses Rechts das Recht des Staates angewandt wird, in dem der Erfolg eingetreten ist. Das Bestimmungsrecht kann nur im ersten Rechtszug bis zum Ende des frühen ersten Termins oder dem Ende des schriftlichen Vorverfahrens ausgeübt werden.

(2) Hatten der Ersatzpflichtige und der Verletzte zur Zeit des Haftungsereignisses ihren gewöhnlichen Aufenthalt in demselben Staat, so ist das Recht dieses Staates anzuwenden. Handelt es sich um Gesellschaften, Vereine oder juristische Personen, so steht dem gewöhnlichen Aufenthalt der Ort gleich, an dem sich die Hauptverwaltung oder, wenn eine Niederlassung beteiligt ist, an dem sich diese befindet.

(3) Ansprüche, die dem Recht eines anderen Staates unterliegen, können nicht geltend gemacht werden, soweit sie

1. wesentlich weiter gehen als zur angemessenen Entschädigung des Verletzten erforderlich,

2. offensichtlich anderen Zwecken als einer angemessenen Entschädigung des Verletzten dienen oder

3. haftungsrechtlichen Regelungen eines für die Bundesrepublik Deutschland verbindlichen Übereinkommens widersprechen.

4. Der Verletzte kann seinen Anspruch unmittelbar gegen einen Versicherer des Ersatzpflichtigen geltend machen, wenn das auf die unerlaubte Handlung anzuwendende Recht oder das Recht, dem der Versicherungsvertrag unterliegt, dies vorsieht.

Artikel 41
Wesentlich engere Verbindung

(1) Besteht mit dem Recht eines Staates eine wesentlich engere Verbindung als mit dem Recht, das nach den Artikeln 38 bis 40 Abs. 2 massgebend wäre, so ist jenes Recht anzuwenden.

(2) Eine wesentlich engere Verbindung kann sich insbesondere ergeben

1. aus einer besonderen rechtlichen oder tatsächlichen Beziehung zwischen den Beteiligten im Zusammenhang mit dem Schuldverhältnis oder

2. in den Fällen des Artikels 38 Abs. 2 und 3 und des Artikels 39 aus dem gewöhnlichen Aufenthalt der Beteiligten in demselben Staat im Zeitpunkt des rechtserheblichen Geschehens; Artikel 40 Abs. 2 Satz 2 gilt entsprechend.

Artikel 42
Rechtswahl
Nach Eintritt des Ereignisses, durch das ein ausservertragliches Schuldverhältnis entstanden ist, können die Parteien das Recht wählen, dem es interliegen soll. Rechte Dritter bleiben unberührt.

Sachenrecht

Artikel 43
Rechte an einer Sache
(1) Rechte an einer Sache unterliegen dem Recht des Staates, in dem sich die Sache befindet.

(2) Gelangt eine Sache, an der Rechte begründet sind, in einen anderen Staat, so können diese Rechte nicht im Widerspruch zu der Rechtsordnung dieses Staates ausgeübt werden.

(3) Ist ein Recht an einer Sache, die in das Inland gelangt, nicht schon vorher erworben worden, so sind für einen solchen Erwerb im Inland Vorgänge in einem anderen Staat wie inländische zu berücksichtigen.

Artikel 44
Grundstücksimmissionen
Für Ansprüche aus beeinträchtigenden Einwirkungen, die von einem Grundstück ausgehen, gilt Art. 40 Abs. 1 entsprechend.

Artikel 45
Transportmittel
(1) Rechte an Luft-, Wasser- und Schienenfahrzeugen unterliegen dem Recht des Herkunftsstaats. Das ist

    1.bei Luftfahrzeugen der Staat ihrer Staatszugehörigkeit,
    2.bei Wasserfahrzeugen der Staat der Registereintragung, sonst des Heimathafens oder des Heimatortes,
    3.bei Schienenfahrzeugen der Staat der Zulassung.

(2) Die Entstehung gesetzlicher Sicherungsrechte an diesen Fahrzeugen unterliegt dem Recht, das auf die zu sichernde Forderung anzuwenden ist. Für die Rangfolge mehrerer Sicherungsrechte gilt Artikel 43 Abs. 1.

Artikel 46
Wesentlich engere Verbindung
Besteht mit dem Recht eines Staates eine wesentlich engere Verbindung als mit dem Recht, das nach den Artikeln 43 bis 45 massgebend wäre, so ist jenes Recht anzuwenden."

SUMMARY

THE 1999 GERMAN PIL OF NON-CONTRACTUAL OBLIGATIONS AND PROPERTY COMPARED WITH THE SWISS PILA

The German and the Swiss conflict rules on torts and property converge on one essential policy: they try to find solutions which the parties must or may expect. However, the two legislations differ to a certain extent in the method chosen to achieve that goal.

1.   With respect to the provisions on <u>torts</u>, both legislations no longer stick exclusively to the old traditional *lex loci delicti* rule. Yet, the German legislator still has a predilection for abstract provisions, whereas the Swiss code contains a number of rules dealing with specific torts such as product liability, unfair competition, antitrust, cross-border environmental disturbances, and defamation through mass media. The German legislator, on the other hand, has opened the door widely to flexible approaches through a broadly framed escape clause (article 41). Most welcome in both legislations is the barricade erected against excessive punitive damages of US origin: whereas the Swiss code has express provisions of this kind only in its rules on unfair competition and antitrust practices, the German legislator has enacted – fortunately I would like to say – a general rule dismissing claims which go beyond a justified compensation.

2.   Concerning the law of <u>property</u>, both the German and the Swiss rules confirm the basic principle of *lex rei sitae*. However, the German legislator, in its endeavour to secure flexibility, allows deviations from this principle by way of a non-specified escape provision (article 46) which in my opinion jeopardizes legal certainty. The Swiss legislator attempted to reach flexibility by providing a number of different rules for specific situations, such as reservation of title, pledges of rights, negotiable instruments and the like.

Vorsorgeleistungen in internationalen Scheidungen

Monique Jametti Greiner[*]

1. FRAGESTELLUNG

Das neue schweizerische Scheidungsrecht normiert mit den Art. 122ff. ZGB erst-mals ausdrücklich, was mit Anwartschaften aus der beruflichen Vorsorge im Schei-dungsfall geschehen soll. Das schweizerische materielle Recht unterscheidet je nachdem, ob ein Vorsorgefall bereits eingetreten ist oder nicht. Vor Eintritt eines Vorsorgefalles geht das Gesetz von einer grundsätzlich hälftigen Teilung der An-sprüche nach dem Bundesgesetz über die Freizügigkeit vom 17. Dezember 1993[1] aus (Art. 122 Abs. 1 ZGB), wobei jeweils nur der Differenzbetrag zu teilen ist, wenn beiden Ehegatten gegenseitig Ansprüche zustehen (Art. 122 Abs. 2 ZGB). Diese Vorsorgeleistungen sind der Dispositionsfreiheit grundsätzlich entzogen; die Ehegatten verfügen nur insoweit über eine beschränkte Gestaltungsmöglichkeit, als eine entsprechende Alters- und Invalidenvorsorge auf andere Weise gewährleistet

---

[*] Dr. iur., Fürsprecherin, Bundesamt für Justiz, Bern.
[1] SR 831.42.

J. Basedow et al., eds., Private Law in the International Arena – Liber Amicorum Kurt Siehr
© 2000, T.M.C.Asser Press, The Hague, The Netherlands

ist (Art. 123 Abs. 1 ZGB).[2] Bei Vorliegen besonderer Umstände kann das Gericht die Teilung der Austrittsleistungen ganz oder teilweise verweigern, wenn aufgrund der güterrechtlichen Auseinandersetzung oder der sonstigen wirtschaftlichen Verhältnisse ein Zusprechen solcher Leistungen offensichtlich unbillig erscheint (Art. 123 Abs. 2 ZGB). Ist ein Vorsorgefall bereits eingetreten, oder können Ansprüche aus der beruflichen Vorsorge, die während der Dauer der Ehe erworben worden sind, nicht geteilt werden, so ist eine angemessene Entschädigung zu leisten (Art. 124 Abs. 1 ZGB). Vorliegend stellt sich die Frage, wie solche Vorsorgeleistungen im internationalen Verhältnis zu behandeln sind.

Das IPRG regelt die Frage der Zuständigkeit und des anwendbaren Rechts hinsichtlich internationaler Scheidungen abschliessend, wobei es sich nicht darüber ausspricht, wann ein internationales Verhältnis vorliegt. In der Doktrin werden denn auch unterschiedliche Auffassungen vertreten. Nach der vorherrschenden Meinung soll das IPRG immer massgebend sein, wenn ein plurinationaler Sachverhalt vorliegt, i.e. wenn die einzelnen Tatbestandselemente nach offensichtlicher Prüfung Bezugspunkte zu mehr als einer nationalen Rechtsordnung aufweisen.[3] Etwas enger umschrieben soll es ausreichen, dass nicht alle Anknüpfungspunkte in der Schweiz belegen sind, wobei hier nicht nur die Regeln für die internationale Zuständigkeit, sondern ebenso sehr die Vorschriften zum anwendbaren Recht zu berücksichtigen sind.[4],[5] Nach einer Minderheitsmeinung ist für jede sich stellende Frage –sei es jene nach der Zuständigkeit oder nach dem anwendbaren Recht[6] – ohne Rücksicht auf die übrigen Bereiche unabhängig festzulegen, wann ein internationales Verhältnis vorliegt.[7],[8]

---

[2] Ein Verzicht auf die Teilung der Vorsorgeleistungen wird nicht leicht angenommen werden; nach Art. 141 Abs. 3 ZGB hat das Gericht bei Vorliegen einer Vereinbarung von Amtes wegen zu prüfen, ob der verzichtende Ehegatte über eine ausreichende Alters- und Invalidenvorsorge verfügt.

[3] So Bucher, *Droit international privé suisse*, tome I/1, *partie générale – conflits de juridictions* (Basel und Frankfurt a.M. 1998) N 18; Schwander, „Zum Gegenstand des Internationalen Privatrechts", in: *FS Pedrazzini* (Bern 1990) 360; für eine Prüfung im Einzelfall: Keller/ Siehr, *Allgemeine Lehren des internationalen Privatrechts* (Zürich 1986) 254ff.

[4] Vgl. auch Dutoit, *Droit international privé suisse, Commentaire de la loi fédérale du 18 décembre 1987*, 2e éd. (Basel und Frankfurt a.M. 1997) N 2 f ad art. 1.

[5] Im vorliegenden Fall würde sowohl in der etwas weiteren Umschreibung als auch in der Beschränkung auf die Anknüpfungspunkte jedenfalls alle Scheidungen von ausländischen oder schweizerisch-ausländischen Ehegatten in der Schweiz angesprochen sowie Scheidungen, bei denen die Ehegatten oder einer von ihnen – ungeachtet der Staatsangehörigkeit – den Wohnsitz im Ausland haben.

[6] Bei der Frage nach der Anerkennung und Vollstreckung einer ausländischen Entscheidung ist allein die Herkunft der Entscheidung für die Anwendbarkeit des IPRG ausschlaggebend – ungeachtet, ob die Entscheidung in einem rein nationalen Sachverhalt ergangen ist oder ob die beurteilte Sachlage ein internationales Element aufgewiesen hat.

[7] Stoffel, „Le rapport juridique international", in: *Conflits et harmonisation, Mélanges en l'honneur d'Alfred von Overbeck* (Fribourg 1990) 450.

[8] Die Meinung entspricht nicht der publizierten bundesgerichtlichen Rechtsprechung, die sich allerdings nur am Rande mit dem Konzept des internationalen Verhältnisses auseinandergesetzt hat; vgl.

In allen Fällen, in denen die Zuständigkeit des schweizerischen Scheidungsge-
richts auf dem IPRG beruht, wird daher die vorliegende Fragestellung relevant sein.
Dies wird zutreffen, wenn einer der Ehegatten (auch) eine ausländische Staatsangehörigkeit hat oder wenn einer der beiden im Ausland lebt. Nach der herrschenden
Auslegung der Frage, was unter einem internationalen Verhältnis zu verstehen ist,
ist sodann das anzuwendende Recht seinerseits regelmässig dem IPRG zu entnehmen, wenn die Zuständigkeit der schweizerischen Gerichte durch die Art. 59 oder
60 IPRG beantwortet wird.[9]

Zuzüglich zu diesen Fällen bleiben aber sodann noch jene Konstellationen zu
berücksichtigen, in welchen die scheidungsrelevanten Umstände auf einen reinen
Inlandfall hinweisen -beide Ehegatten sind Schweizer Bürger und haben ihren
Wohnsitz in der Schweiz-, aber die Vorsorgeeinrichtung selbst im Ausland belegen
ist, weil beispielsweise ein Ehegatte im Ausland einer Erwerbstätigkeit nachgegangen und auch dort einer Vorsorgeeinrichtung angegliedert ist.[10] Ebenfalls wird die
Konstellation Fragen aufwerfen, bei welcher ein Scheidungsverfahren im Ausland
stattfindet und der eine oder beide Ehegatten Ansprüche gegenüber einer Vorsorgeeinrichtung in der Schweiz haben. Das IPRG enthält für diese Konstellationen keine eigenständige Regelung.

2. DIE INTERNATIONALE SCHEIDUNG UND VORSORGELEISTUNGEN

2.1 Zuständigkeit

Das IPRG bestimmt, unter welchen Voraussetzungen ein schweizerisches Gericht
ein Scheidungsbegehren im internationalen Verhältnis an die Hand nehmen muss.[11]
Nach dem System des Gesetzes umfasst die Scheidungszuständigkeit auch die Zuständigkeit zur Regelung der Nebenfolgen, wobei nirgends festgehalten wird, was

---

etwa BGE 119 II 167ff, 118 II 468ff und 83ff.

[9] Die dem IZPR zugehörigen internationalen (und örtlichen) Zuständigkeitsbestimmungen sind im
Gegensatz zu den eigentlichen Kollisionsregeln strikte unilateral ausgerichtet, indem ein Staat nur einseitig festlegen kann, unter welchen Voraussetzungen seine Gerichte und Behörden in einem internationalen Sachverhalt einen Fall annehmen müssen. Diesfalls wird sich dann das anzuwendende Recht
regelmässig nach dem IPRG zu richten haben.

[10] Das Bundesgesetz (BG) vom 25.6.1982 über die berufliche Alters-, Hinterlassenen- und Invalidenvorsorge (SR 831.40) gilt nur für Personen, die bei der AHV versichert sind (Art. 5 BVG). Das BG
vom 20.12.1946 über die Alters- und Hinterlassenenversicherung (AHVG), das grundsätzlich auf alle
Personen mit Wohnsitz in der Schweiz anwendbar ist (Art. 1 Abs. 1), sieht seinerseits die Möglichkeit
einer Nichtversicherung vor für Personen, die einer ausländischen staatlichen Alters- und Hinterlassenenversicherung angehören, sofern der Einbezug in die Versicherung für sie eine nicht zumutbare Dop-
pelbelastung bedeuten würde.

[11] Hinsichtlich der direkten Zuständigkeit existieren keine bi- oder multilateralen Übereinkommen, die dem IPRG vorgehen würden.

darunter fällt. Im Gegensatz zum anwendbaren Recht enthält indessen das IPRG keine zuständigkeitsrechtlichen Sonderanknüpfungen für spezifische Aspekte der Scheidung, sodass sämtliche Folgen, die als Wechsel des Status eintreten, erfasst sind. Das scheint auch auf die Vorsorgeleistungen zuzutreffen. Für gewisse Nebenfolgen ist gegebenenfalls[12] das Lugano-Übereinkommen vom 16. September 1988 über die gerichtliche Zuständigkeit und die Vollstreckung gerichtlicher Entscheidungen[13] zu berücksichtigen, da dieser Staatsvertrag als Gegenausnahme zu dem nicht erfassten Personen- und Familienrecht (Art. 1 Abs. 2 Ziff. 1 LugÜ) die Zuständigkeit für Unterhaltssachen[14] und die Vollstreckung der entsprechenden Unterhaltsentscheidungen abdeckt (vgl. Art. 5 Ziff. 2 und Art. 25 LugÜ). Es wird noch zu prüfen sein, inwiefern Vorsorgeleistungen nach Art. 122ff. ZGB unter das LugÜ fallen.

2.2   Anwendbares Recht

Das zuständige schweizerische Scheidungsgericht wird die Scheidung als Statusfrage regeln und sich zu allen Nebenfolgen äussern müssen. Das auf das Scheidungsverfahren anwendbare Recht gilt dabei grundsätzlich auch für die Scheidungsfolgen. Das Gericht wird auf die Scheidung grundsätzlich schweizerisches Recht anwenden (Art. 61 Abs. 1 IPRG). Als einziger Staatsvertrag in diesem Bereich ist der bilaterale Niederlassungsvertrag mit dem Kaiserreich Persien vom 25. April 1934[15] zu berücksichtigen, wonach die Scheidung dem Heimatrecht der beteiligten Parteien[16] untersteht.

In besonderen Fällen kann ausländisches Scheidungsrecht zum Zuge kommen, wenn beide Ehegatten dieselbe ausländische Staatsangehörigkeit besitzen und wenn einer der Ehegatten im Ausland und der andere in der Schweiz wohnhaft ist (Art. 61 Abs. 2 IPRG). Ein allfälliger Renvoi des ausländischen auf das schweizerische Recht ist dabei zu berücksichtigen.[17] Anstelle des ausländischen kann sodann

---

[12]   Soweit der Beklagte seinen Wohnsitz in einem Vertragsstaat hat. Vertragsstaaten sind Belgien, Dänemark, Deutschland, Finnland, Frankreich, Griechenland, Irland, Island, Italien, Luxemburg, die Niederlande, Norwegen, Österreich, Polen, Portugal, Schweden, Schweiz, Spanien und das Vereinigte Königreich (Stand: 1. Februar 2000). Das Vereinigte Königreich hat eine Ausdehnungserklärung für Gibraltar abgegeben, deren Zulässigkeit jedoch von Spanien bestritten worden ist.

[13]   LugÜ; SR 0.275.11.

[14]   Gaudemet-Tallon, *Les conventions de Bruxelles et de Lugano*, 2e éd. (Paris 1996) 24f.; Geimer/ Schütze, *Europäisches Zivilverfahrensrecht, Kommentar zum EuGVÜ und zum Lugano-Übereinkommen* (München 1997) Art. 1 N 64.

[15]   SR 0.142.114.362.

[16]   Handelt es sich bei der einen Partei um eine Person mit Doppelbürgerrecht oder trifft dies gar auf beide Ehegatten zu, so ist der Staatsvertrag nicht anwendbar und es gilt die allgemeine IPRG-Regelung; vgl. auch Dutoit/ Knoepfler/ Lalive/ Mercier, *Droit international privé suisse*, tome III (Bern 1982) 169.

[17]   Vgl. Art. 14 IPRG; Siehr, in: Honsell/ Vogt/ Schnyder, *Kommentar zum schweizerischen Privat-*

auf das schweizerische Recht zurückgegriffen werden, wenn jenes ausserordentlich strenge Bedingungen an die Scheidung oder Trennung stellt (Art. 61 Abs. 3 IPRG).[18] Ausnahmsweise kann das schweizerische – sei es als primär anwendbares Recht im Sinne von Art. 61 Abs. 1 IPRG oder als sekundär zum Zuge kommende Rechtsordnung im Rahmen von Art. 61 Abs. 3 IPRG – oder das gemeinsame Heimatrecht beiseite geschoben werden, wenn nach den gesamten Umständen offensichtlich ist, dass der Sachverhalt mit dem an sich massgebenden Scheidungsstatut einen nur geringen, mit einer anderen Rechtsordnung jedoch einen viel engeren Zusammenhang aufweist (Art. 15 Abs. 1 IPRG).[19]

Wie bereits erwähnt, umfasst das Scheidungsstatut die Scheidung als Statusfrage sowie die als Nebenfolgen der Scheidung qualifizierten Rechtsansprüche. Diese folgen dem letztlich für massgeblich erklärten materiellen Recht. Wird ausländisches Recht auf die Scheidung angewandt, so gilt dies auch für die Nebenfolgen. Dasselbe trifft für den Fall zu, dass zufolge des Renvoi anstelle des ausländischen das schweizerische Recht zum Zuge kommt oder dann, wenn die Ausweichklausel des Art. 15 IPRG angewandt wird. Jedoch sind regelmässig die besonderen Bestimmungen über den Namen, die Unterhaltspflicht der Ehegatten, das eheliche Güterrecht, die Wirkungen des Kindesverhältnisses und den Minderjährigenschutz vorbehalten (Art. 63 Abs. 2 IPRG).

Zu klären gilt, wie die Vorsorgeleistungen qualifiziert werden – ob sie zu den unterhaltsrecht-lichen Ansprüchen zu zählen sind (vgl. unten 3.1), ob sie unter das Güterrecht fallen (vgl. 3.2), ob sie den Regeln folgen, die die Vorsorgeeinrichtung beherrschen (Vorsorgestatut, vgl. unten 3.3) oder ob für sie als Nebenfolgen das Scheidungsstatut massgebend bleibt (vgl. 4).

2.3 Die Anerkennung ausländischer Scheidungen mit Vorsorgeleistungen

Eine im Ausland ausgesprochene Scheidung wird nach Massgabe der allgemeinen Voraussetzungen der Art. 25ff. IPRG sowie der besonderen Vorschriften bezüglich der indirekten Zuständigkeit nach Art. 65 IPRG anerkannt. Dabei reicht es nach herrschender Ansicht aus, wenn die Scheidung in irgend einem Verfahren stattgefunden bzw. ein öffentliches Organ massgeblich mitgewirkt hat.[20] Die indirekte Zuständigkeit ist nach Art. 65 Abs. 1 IPRG gegeben, wenn die Entscheidung im Staat

---

recht, Internationales Privatrecht (zitiert: IPR-Bearbeiter) (Basel 1995) Art. 61 N 16.

[18] Das setzt allerdings voraus, dass einer der Ehegatten das Schweizer Bürgerrecht besitzt oder sich seit mindestens zwei Jahren in der Schweiz aufgehalten hat.

[19] Für einen Anwendungsfall von Art. 15 IPRG vgl. BGE 118 II 79ff. Vgl. auch BGE 121 II 246ff, wo die Berufung auf die Ausnahmeklausel abgelehnt wurde.

[20] Botschaft des Bundesrates zum BG über das internationale Privatrecht, BBl 1983, 361 (IPRG-Botschaft). Das ist im Rahmen der Scheidungsurteile von grosser Bedeutung, sehen doch zahlreiche ausländische Rechtsordnungen Scheidungen vor, bei denen die Mitwirkung einer Behörde (wenn überhaupt) sich auf minimale Aufgaben beschränkt, vgl. BGE 122 II 344, 348.

des Wohnsitzes, des gewöhnlichen Aufenthaltes oder der Staatsangehörigkeit eines Ehegatten ergangen ist oder in einem dieser Staaten anerkannt wird.[21] Allerdings enthält Art. 65 Abs. 2 IPRG einige Einschränkungen, die immer dann Platz greifen, wenn die Entscheidung nicht auf einer gemeinsamen Heimatzuständigkeit beruht hat.[22] Alternativ kann eine Anerkennung erfolgen, wenn sich der Beklagte der Zuständigkeit des ausländischen Gerichts vorbehaltlos unterworfen hatte oder wenn er in der Folge mit der Anerkennung der Entscheidung in der Schweiz einverstanden ist.[23]

Soweit eine Scheidung aus einem Vertragsstaat[24] des Haager Übereinkommens vom 1. Juni 1970 über die Anerkennung von Ehescheidungen und Ehetrennungen[25] stammt, ist dieses zu beachten. Der Staatsvertrag verfolgt das Günstigkeitsprinzip[26] (vgl. Art. 17) und lässt somit zu, dass für die Anerkennung einer Ehescheidung aus einem Vertragsstaat das möglicherweise günstigere nationale Recht zur Anwendung gelangt.[27] Der Staatsvertrag äussert sich nicht zu den Nebenfolgen.

Die Anerkennung des Statusverhältnisses ist nicht zwingend Voraussetzung dafür, dass das ausländische Urteil bezüglich der Nebenfolgen anerkannt werden kann. Vielmehr sind auf Nebenfolgen dieselben Vorschriften anzuwenden, wie sie für die Scheidung gelten. Das gilt insbesondere für die Vorschriften zur indirekten Zuständigkeit nach Art. 65 IPRG.[28] Denkbar ist also, dass Nebenfolgen als aner-

---

[21] Bei letzterem handelt es sich nicht mehr um eine Bestimmung der indirekten Zuständigkeit, sondern im Grunde um eine kollisionsrechtliche Anerkennung, da es genügt, dass die Ehescheidung in einem dieser drei Staaten anerkannt wird. Das führt dazu, dass eine Entscheidung als anerkennbar gilt, wenn sie in einem Staat ausgefällt worden ist, zu dem weder der eine noch der andere Ehegatte einen auch nur minimalen Bezug aufweist, solange die Entscheidung beispielsweise im Aufenthaltsstaat des einen Ehegatten anerkannt wird.

[22] Demnach wird eine ausländische Ehescheidung oder Trennung in der Schweiz nur anerkannt, wenn im Zeitpunkt der Klageeinleitung wenigstens ein Ehegatte im erkennenden Staat wohnhaft war oder sich dort für gewöhnlich aufgehalten hat und der Beklagte seinen Wohnsitz nicht in der Schweiz hatte (Art. 65 Abs. 2 lit. a IPRG).

[23] Die Kautelen von Art. 65 Abs. 2 IPRG wollen verhindern, dass sich ein in der Schweiz wohnhafter Ehegatte einen Ehescheidungsakt entgegenhalten lassen muss, der in einem ausländischen Staat erlassen worden ist, dessen Staatsangehörigkeit er nicht besitzt. War hingegen einer der Ehegatten im Ausland wohnhaft und erging die Scheidung an seinem Wohnsitz, so verdient der beklagte Ehegatte diesen besonderen Schutz nicht - genauso wenig natürlich, wie wenn er ausdrücklich oder implizit darauf verzichtet hat.

[24] Ägypten, Australien, Dänemark, Finnland, Hong Kong, Italien, Luxemburg, Niederlande (einschliesslich Aruba), Norwegen, Polen, Portugal, Schweden, Schweiz, Slowakei, Tschechien, Vereinigtes Königreich (einschliesslich Guernsey, Jersey, Insel Man, Gibraltar, Bermudas) und Zypern (Stand 1. Februar 2000).

[25] SR 0.211.212.3.

[26] Vgl. hierzu Siehr, „Günstigkeits- und Garantieprinzip", in: *Recht und Rechtsdurchsetzung. FS Walder* (Zürich 1994) 409ff.

[27] Je nach Konstellation empfiehlt sich daher das Abstellen auf die Konvention oder ein Beizug von Art. 65 IPRG.

[28] Bucher, *Droit international privé suisse, tome II, Personnes, Famille, Successions* (Basel und

kennbar und vollstreckbar erscheinen, obwohl die ausländische Scheidung als solche nicht anerkannt werden kann. Diesfalls liegt eine Teilaner-kennung vor. Für den Fall, dass Vorsorgeleistungen nicht als Nebenfolgen der Scheidung qualifiziert werden, sondern als Ansprüche unterhalts- oder güterrechtlicher Natur oder als Ansprüche sui generis, die dem Vorsorgestatut unterstehen, so gelten neben den allgemeinen Bestimmungen der Art. 25ff. IPRG die entsprechenden unterhalts- bzw. güterrechtlichen Vorschriften des 3. Kapitels des IPRG, im letzteren Fall allein die Art. 25ff. IPRG.

Vorbehalten bleiben indessen staatsvertragliche Regelungen, wie sie multilateral im Unterhaltsbereich bestehen.[29]

Verschiedene bilaterale Anerkennungs- und Vollstreckungsübereinkommen finden ebenfalls auf Nebenfolgen von Scheidungen oder Trennungen Anwendung, lassen aber günstigere Bestimmungen des nationalen Rechts zu.[30]

3.   DIE QUALIFIKATION VON VORSORGELEISTUNGEN

Mit den IPR-Verweisungsnormen wird festgehalten, welche Anknüpfungsregel zur Bestimmung des anwendbaren Rechts beigezogen werden muss. Die in den Verweisungs-normen verwendeten Rechtsbegriffe decken sich nicht notwendigerweise mit jenen des nationalen Sachrechts, sondern gehen oft über deren Bedeutung hinaus um zu verhindern, dass gewisse Sachverhalte nicht erfasst würden. Entsprechend sind die Verweisungsnormen im allgemeinen weit auszulegen.[31]

Nach dem neuen schweizerischen Scheidungsrecht sind Vorsorgeleistungen als eine spezifisch scheidungsrechtliche Folge aufzufassen. So führt denn schon die Botschaft des Bundesrats aus, dass der Vorsorgeausgleich weder unterhaltsrechtlich noch güterrechtlich zu qualifizieren sei – unterhaltsrechtlich nicht, weil er sich nicht an den Bedürfnissen des Berechtigten orientiere und güterrechtlich nicht, weil der Anspruch nicht während, sondern eben erst bei Auflösung der Ehe entstehe.[32]

Frankfurt a.M. 1991) N 586.

[29] LugÜ, vgl. Fn 13 sowie Haager Übereinkommen vom 2. Oktober 1973 über die Anerkennung und Vollstreckung von Unterhaltsentscheidungen, SR 0.211.213.02.

[30] Es betrifft dies die bilateralen Verträge mit Spanien vom 19.11.1896 (SR 0.176.193.321), mit Belgien vom 29.4.1959 (SR 0.276.191.721), mit Österreich vom 16.12.1960 (SR 0.276.191.632) sowie mit dem Fürstentum Liechtenstein vom 25.4.1968 (SR 0.276.195.141), mit Italien vom 3.1.1933 (SR 0.276. 194.541); mit Schweden vom 15.1.1936 (SR 0.276.197.141) mit der Slowakei und mit Tschechien vom 21.12.1926 (SR 0.276.197.411), vgl. hierzu Dutoit/ Knoepfler/ Lalive/ Mercier (oben N. 16).

[31] Vgl. Keller/ Siehr (oben N. 3) 442ff.

[32] Botschaft des Bundesrates über die Änderung des Schweizerischen Zivilgesetzbuches (Personenstand, Eheschliessung, Scheidung, Kindesrecht, Verwandtenunterstützungspflicht, Heimstätten, Vormundschaft und Ehevermittlung, Botschaft zum Scheidungsrecht) BBl 1996, 100.

Die Konzeption der güterstands- und verschuldensunabhängigen Vorsorgeregelung erfuhr in der Folge während der parlamentarischen Beratungen keine Modifikationen. Insbesondere wurde die Idee einer güterstandsabhängigen Vorsorgeleistung bereits in der vorberatenden Kommission abgelehnt.[33]

3.1 Qualifikation als unterhaltsrechtliche Ansprüche?

3.1.1 *nach den Haager Unterhaltsübereinkommen*

Für die unterhaltsrechtlichen Ansprüche unter Ehegatten verweist das IPRG auf das Haager Übereinkommen vom 2. Oktober 1973 über das auf die Unterhaltspflichten anzuwendende Recht[34] (Art. 49 IPRG). Es handelt sich dabei um einen deklaratorischen Hinweis, da dieser Staatsvertrag ohne Rücksicht auf die Gegenseitigkeit Anwendung findet (erga omnes). Für den Begriff des Unterhalts zwischen Ehegatten verweist das schweizerische Kollisionsrecht auf die multilaterale Konvention. Diese deckt alle Ansprüche ab, die sich aus Beziehungen der Familie, der Verwandtschaft, Ehe oder Schwägerschaft ergeben, einschliesslich der Unterhaltspflicht gegenüber einem nichtehelichen Kind (Art. 1). Für Ehegatten gelten während der Dauer der Ehe und während eines allfälligen Verfahrens auf Eheauflösung die allgemeinen Anknüpfungsregeln.[35] Nach ausgesprochener Scheidung oder Trennung wird nach Art. 8 das Statut perpetuiert, welches für die Auflösung oder Ungültigerklärung der Ehe massgebend war (Scheidungsstatut).

Das Übereinkommen will sämtliche unterhaltsrechtlichen Beziehungen zwischen Ehegatten und geschiedenen Ehegatten regeln, ohne darauf abzustellen, ob diese Ansprüche rein unterhaltsrechtlichen, kompensatorischen oder einen gemischten Charakter aufweisen.[36] Auch ist es irrelevant, ob die Unterhaltsleistung in einer Kapitalabfindung oder in Rentenform ausbezahlt wird. Im Interesse einer staatsvertragskonformen Auslegung müsste sodann der Unterhaltsbegriff so weit wie möglich ausgelegt werden, sodass darunter auch Vorsorgeleistungen fallen sollten.

Der Unterhaltsbegriff im klassischen Sinne setzt indessen voraus, dass die Bedürfnisse des Berechtigten wie die wirtschaftlichen Verhältnisse des Unterhaltsverpflichteten gleichermassen berücksichtigt werden. Die Konvention geht sogar so

---

[33] Sutter/ Freiburghaus, *Kommentar zum neuen Scheidungsrecht* (Zürich 1999) N 7 ad Vorb. zu Art. 122-124/141-142.

[34] SR 0.211.213.01.

[35] Vgl. Art. 4-6, wonach in erster Linie das am jeweiligen gewöhnlichen Aufenthalt der unterhaltsberechtigten Person geltende Recht anwendbar ist, erstsubsidiär das gemeinsame Heimatrecht und in weiterer subsidiärer Anknüpfung die *lex fori*.

[36] Verwilghen, „Rapport explicatif", *Conférence de La Haye de droit international privé, Actes et Documents de la douzième session, Bd IV, Obligations alimentaires* (Den Haag 1975) 459.

weit, dass sie diese Voraussetzungen für massgeblich erklärt, selbst wenn das anzuwendende Recht etwas anderes bestimmen sollte (Art. 11 Abs. 2). Ist die Festsetzung des Unterhalts tatsächlich an der Bedürftigkeit des Berechtigten zu messen, so wird es auch bei einer grosszügigen Konzeption der Bedürfnisse des Unterhaltsgläubigers ausserordentlich schwierig, Vorsorgeleistungen noch als Unterhalt zu qualifizieren. Immerhin basiert der Vorsorgeausgleich auf der Idee des Ausgleichs für die Rollenteilung, wie sie während der Ehedauer gelebt worden ist.[37] Solche Kompensationsüberlegungen sind indessen mit traditionellen unterhaltsrechtlichen Belangen nicht mehr vereinbar. Diese Überlegungen führen zum Schluss, dass Vorsorgeleistungen vom Übereinkommen wohl nicht erfasst sind.[38],[39]

Würde der Staatsvertrag trotzdem als massgeblich erachtet, so wäre ungeachtet des Zeitablaufs und ohne Rücksicht auf allfällige Wohnsitzwechsel der betreffenden Parteien ausschliesslich das materielle Recht anwendbar, welches tatsächlich auf die Scheidung angewandt worden ist. Für in der Schweiz ausgesprochene Scheidungen bedeutet dies in der Regel die Massgeblichkeit schweizerischen Rechts, wenn nicht das gemeinsame ausländische Heimatrecht zum Zuge kommt.[40]

3.1.2 *nach dem Lugano-Übereinkommen*

Dem Unterhaltskläger steht im Verhältnis zum Lugano-Ausland der allgemeine Gerichtsstand nach Art. 2 am Wohnsitz des Beklagten oder alternativ der besondere Gerichtsstand am Wohnsitz oder am gewöhnlichen Aufenthalt des Unterhaltsberechtigten sowie, unter Einschränkungen, der Gerichtsstand eines hängigen Verfahrens über den Personenstand zur Verfügung (Art. 5 Ziff. 2).[41] Diese sogenannte Verbundszuständigkeit steht nicht zur Auswahl, wenn das forum ausschliesslich

---

[37] Sollen Familienarbeit und entlöhnte Tätigkeit tatsächlich als gleichwertig betrachtet werden, so wird jener Ehegatte, der wegen der Familienarbeit keine (genügende) Altersvorsorge aufbauen konnte, im Scheidungsfall auf Ausgleichszahlungen zählen dürfen.

[38] Vgl. auch Jayme, „Wandel des Unterhaltsbegriffs und Staatsverträge im internationalen Privatrecht", in: *FS von Overbeck* (Fribourg 1990) 529ff. A.A. Bucher, tome II (oben N. 28) N 556ff.

[39] Soweit ersichtlich hat sich das Bundesgericht zu dieser Frage nie äussern müssen. Die Rechtsprechungsübersicht des Asser Instituts zu den Haager Konventionen (*Les nouvelles conventions de La Haye, leur application par les juges nationaux*, herausgegeben von Sumampouw, Den Haag 1976/1980/1984/1994/1996) weist in den fünf bislang erschienen Bänden auf einen Entscheid der Cour d'appel de Luxembourg vom 1. April 1987 hin (Bd. IV, 1994, 54ff.). Das luxemburgische Gericht hatte die Anwendung des Haager Unterhaltsübereinkommens auf die prestation compensatoire des französischen Rechts abgelehnt.

[40] Wurde dieses wegen ausserordentlich strenger Bedingungen zugunsten des schweizerischen Rechts beiseite geschoben, so ist unter Art. 8 Unterhaltsstatutübereinkommen das effektiv angewendete Recht massgebend. Dasselbe gilt an sich auch bei Massgeblichkeit der Ausweichklausel von Art. 15 IPRG. Beim nachehelichen Unterhalt gilt indessen anstelle von Art. 15 IPRG als Korrektiv Art. 11 des Unterhaltsstatutübereinkommens, IPR-Siehr (oben N. 17) Art. 49 N 10; vgl. auch BGE 123 III 1 und die kritischen Bemerkungen hierzu von Bucher in *SZIER* (1998) 279f.

auf der Staatsangehörigkeit nur der einen Partei beruht.[42]

Die Unterhaltsleistungen sind staatsvertragsautonom auszulegen.[43] In bislang vier Entscheidungen[44] hat sich der EuGH nach einer vorsichtigen Abgrenzung zum Güterrecht[45] wohl im Interesse einer staatsvertraglich möglichst weitgehenden Umfassung der Zivil- und Handelssache für eine weite Interpretation des Unterhalts ausgesprochen.[46] Dabei hat der EuGH darauf hingewiesen, dass die prestation compensatoire des französischen Rechts sich nach den Bedürfnissen und den Mitteln richteten und daher zum Unterhalt gehörten.[47]

Aus den Begründungen des EuGH ist keine verlässliche Prognose darüber zu gewinnen, ob die Vorsorgeleistungen des schweizerischen Rechts unter den Unterhaltsbegriff des LugÜ fallen oder nicht. Für eine möglichst umfassende Interpretation der Unterhaltsansprüche und somit für eine Abdeckung der Vorsorgeleistungen spricht aus teleologischer Hinsicht, dass sich nur so eine einheitliche Rechtsprechung in den Vertragsstaaten wird entwickeln können. Dem stehen Bedenken gegenüber, dass die prestation compensatoire eine Abwägung der wirtschaftlichen Lage der Ehegatten erheischt, während dies bei den Vorsorgeleistungen des schweizerischen Rechts gerade nicht zutrifft.[48] Daher liegt es wohl näher, Vorsorgeleistungen wegen ihres starken Bezugs zur Scheidung nicht unter das LugÜ zu subsumieren. Der Kläger würde somit hinsichtlich der Zuständigkeit auf das IPRG verwiesen. Auf die Frage des anwendbaren Rechts hat diese Problematik

---

[41] Dies entspricht im Ergebnis nur teilweise der Lösung des IPRG (Art. 63 Abs. 1 i.V.m. Art. 59 IPRG), welche nach wie vor gegenüber den Staaten, die dem Lugano-Übereinkommen nicht angehören, massgebend ist.

[42] Aus der Sicht des schweizerischen Rechts bedeutet dies, dass der Heimatgerichtsstand gegenüber Lugano-Vertragsstaaten nur dann unbedenklich ist, wenn beide Ehegatten das Schweizer Bürgerrecht besitzen.

[43] Geimer/ Schütze (oben N. 14) Art. 5 N 114.

[44] De Cavel I, Rs. 143/78, Slg. 1979, 1055; de Cavel II, Rs. 120/79, Slg. 1980, 731; W.v. H., Rs. 25/81, Slg. 1982, 1189; van den Boogard v. Laumen, Rs. 220/95, Slg. 1997, I 1176; zum Begriff des Unterhaltsberechtigten vgl. sodann Farrell v. Long, Rs. 295/95, Slg. 1997, I-1683.

[45] De Cavel I sowie W. v. H., ibid.

[46] De Cavel II Nr. 5: „Ferner betreffen die Ausgleichsleistungen, die in Artikel 270ff. Code civil geregelt sind . . . finanzielle Verpflichtungen zwischen den früheren Ehegatten nach der Scheidung, welche sich nach den beiderseitigen Mitteln und Bedürfnissen bestimmen; sie haben ebenfalls den Charakter von Unterhaltsleistungen. . . "

[47] Vgl Hausmann, „Der Unterhaltsbegriff in Staatsverträgen des internationalen Privat- und Verfahrensrechts", IPRax (1990) S. 382ff., der sich spezifisch mit der prestation compensatoire des französischen Rechts auseinandersetzt.

[48] Auch Vorsorgeleistungen werden nicht losgelöst von allen bedarfs- und leistungsbezogenen Überlegungen zugesprochen und sind gerade unter wirtschaftlichen Aspekten einer beschränkten Dispositionsfreiheit der Ehegatten zugänglich. Allerdings ist es mehr als nur ein gradueller Unterschied, ob sich die Ansprüche wie bei der prestation compensatoire regelmässig nach einer Bedarfs- und Leistungsprüfung richten oder ob dieser Prüfungsmassstab gegebenenfalls als Korrektiv für eine gesetzlich vorgesehene strikte hälftige Teilung angewandt wird.

keinen Einfluss. Hingegen würde die Anerkennung und Vollstreckung von Entscheidungen über Vorsorgeleistungen innerhalb der Vertragsstaaten des LugÜ erheblich erleichtert, wenn Vorsorgeleistungen als Unterhalt nach Art. 5 Ziff. 2 LugÜ qualifiziert würden, während es nach der hier vertretenen gegenteiligen Meinung auf das jeweilige nationale Recht ankommt, ob die Entscheidung anerkannt und vollstreckt wird.

3.2   Qualifikation als güterrechtliche Ansprüche?

Das eheliche Güterrecht umfasst die Gesamtheit der Normen, denen das Vermögen der Ehegatten um der Ehe willen unterstehen.[49] Anknüpfungsbegriff ist demnach die Rechtsstellung der Ehegatten mit Bezug auf die ehelichen Vermögenswerte.[50] Vorsorgeleistungen könnten mit der Rechtsstellung der betroffenen Personen an den auf die Ehe bezogenen Vermögenswerten in Verbindung gebracht werden. Diese ist aber höchstens indirekter Natur, da der Aufbau der Altersvorsorge während des aktiven Erwerbslebens das verfügbare Einkommen schmälert. Zudem werden Vorsorgeleistungen gerade und nur im Hinblick auf die Auflösung der Ehe geschuldet.

Vorsorgeleistungen und güterrechtliche Ansprüche unterscheiden sich insoweit, als letztere als Konsequenz der gelebten Ehe erscheinen, währenddem eine Ausgleichszahlung gegebenenfalls geschuldet wird, weil die Ehe noch zu Lebzeiten der Ehegatten aufgelöst wird. Das spricht gegen eine Unterstellung der Vorsorgeleistungen unter das Güterstatut. Ein weiteres Argument gegen eine güterrechtliche Qualifikation ist auch die Dispositionsfreiheit der Parteien.[51] Würden Vorsorgeleistungen güterrechtlich zu qualifizieren sein, so könnten die Ehegatten Bestand und Umfang solcher Ansprüche bewusst wählen –ein Umstand, der dem Sinn und Zweck der Kompensationszahlungen wenig gerecht wird. Schliesslich ist zu beachten, dass der Vorsorgeausgleich nur dann beseitigt werden kann, wenn die Altersvorsorge der an sich anspruchsberechtigten Person anderweitig sichergestellt ist.[52]

---

[49] IPRG-Botschaft (oben N. 20) 347.

[50] Heini im Kommentar zum IPRG, N 1 vor Art. 51-58.

[51] Die Rechtswahl nach Art. 52 IPRG ist ohne weiteres auch noch während des laufenden Scheidungsverfahrens möglich: Zur Wahl stehen das Wohnsitzrecht oder das Recht des Heimatstaates eines Ehegatten, wobei für letzteres jedes Heimatrecht (und nicht nur die effektive Staatsangehörigkeit) herbeigezogen werden kann. Die allfällige Rechtswahl gilt dabei nach der hier vertretenen Auffassung stets für das gesamte Güterrecht, Jametti Greiner/ Geiser, *Zeitschrift des Bernischen Juristenvereins* (1991) 1, 15; a.A. IPR-Siehr (oben N. 17) Art. 52 IPRG N 9, der eine Teilrechtswahl zugunsten des Rechts am Lageort eines Grundstückes zulässt.

[52] Sei es, dass sich ein hälftiger Ausgleich nicht lohnt, dass der Ehegatte ohnehin bereits eine ausreichende Altersvorsorge besitzt oder dass die Vorsorgeleistung sich angesichts besonderer Umstände gar negativ auswirkt, vgl. Vetterli/ Keel, „Die Aufteilung der beruflichen Vorsorge in der Scheidung", *AJP* (1999) 1618.

All diese Hinweise lassen es als wenig überzeugend erscheinen, Vorsorgeleistungen aus schweizerischer Sicht als zum Güterrecht gehörend zu betrachten. Besonders kritisch erscheint die Qualifikation von Vorsorgeleistungen als güterrechtliche Ansprüche, wenn man die Entstehungsgeschichte der Art. 122ff. ZGB heranzieht.[53] Die Vorstellung einer güterstandsabhängigen Ausgleichung von Vorsorgeansprüchen im nationalen Sachrecht ist bekanntlich explizit abgelehnt worden. Gründe, weshalb sie in gegenläufiger Tendenz im internationalen Verhältnis unter das Güterrechtsstatut fallen sollten, bestehen keine.[54]

3.3 Qualifikation als Ansprüche, die dem Vorsorgestatut unterstehen?

Die Bestimmungen des neuen Scheidungsrechts weisen auf Freizügigkeitseinrichtungen hin, die dem BG über die Freizügigkeit vom 17. Dezember 1993[55] unterstehen. Auch werden die technischen Anordnungen zur Berechnung der Vorsorgeleistungen im Freizügigkeitsgesetz und nicht im ZGB abgehandelt. Den Vorsorgeeinrichtungen kommt bei der Berechnung der Leistungen eine Informationspflicht und ein Mitbestimmungsrecht zu.[56] Können sich die Ehegatten zusammen mit der betreffenden Vorsorgeeinrichtung auf eine Aufteilung der Ansprüche einigen, so wird die Vereinbarung der Ehegatten[57] vom Scheidungsgericht genehmigt. Fehlt es an der Vereinbarung oder der Zustimmung der Vorsorgeeinrichtung, so kann das Scheidungsgericht nur über die prozentuale Aufteilung der Austrittsleistung entscheiden und hat die Streitsache an das nach Art. 73 des BG vom 25. Juni 1982 über die berufliche Alters-, Hinterlassenen- und Invalidenvorsorge (BVG) bezeichnete Gericht weiterzuleiten.[58]

Diese Bestimmungen über Freizügigkeitsleistungen sind vom Wortlaut her auf Einrichtungen in der Schweiz ausgerichtet. Aber dies bedeutet wohl kaum, dass die Art. 122ff. ZGB nur dann als relevant zu betrachten wären, wenn in einem Scheidungsfall Einrichtungen der beruflichen Vorsorge mit Sitz in der Schweiz betroffen

---

[53] Sutter/ Freiburghaus (oben N. 33) N 7 ad Vorb. zu Art. 122-124/141-142 sowie Geiser, „Berufliche Vorsorge im neuen Scheidungsrecht", in: Hausheer (Hrsg.), *Vom alten zum neuen Scheidungsrecht* (Bern 1999) 63.

[54] Auch rechtsvergleichend spricht angesichts der vielfältigen Regelungen wenig für eine zwingende Qualifikation der Vorsorgeleistungen als zum Güterstatut gehörend. Neben Rechtsordnungen, welche Vorsorgeleistungen oder Anwartschaften auf Altersrenten güterrechtlich qualifizieren, sind auch unterhalts-, scheidungs- oder sozialversicherungsrechtliche Lösungen anzutreffen; vgl. für einen Überblick Jayme, „Die Lösungsansätze im internationalen Vergleich", 289ff., in: Zacher (Hrsg), *Der Versorgungsausgleich im internationalen Vergleich und in der zwischenstaatlichen Praxis* (Berlin 1985) S. 289ff.

[55] SR 831.42.

[56] Vetterli/ Keel (oben N. 52) 1624.

[57] Die beteiligten Vorsorgeeinrichtungen müssen die Durchführbarkeit der von den Ehegatten ins Auge gefassten Teilungsvorschläge bestätigen.

[58] Vetterli/ Keel (oben N. 52) 1625.

sind. Die Konsequenzen einer derart engen Auslegung wären offensichtlich unbillig: So würden die Scheidungsfolgen von Ehe-paaren in vergleichbaren Situationen je nach Belegenheit der Vorsorgeeinrichtung unter-schiedlich aussehen, indem im einen Fall Kompensationszahlungen zu leisten wären, im anderen jedoch nicht, wenn die Vorsorgeeinrichtung sich im Ausland befindet. Darüber-hinaus könnten Leistungen nach den Art. 122ff. ZGB auszugleichen sein, obwohl ein ausländisches Scheidungsstatut massgebend ist und ungeachtet, ob dieses dem Vorsorge-aspekt anderweitig Rechnung trägt. Das dürfte dem Sinn und Zweck der Bestimmungen über die Vorsorgeleistungen nicht gerecht werden. Vielmehr ist davon auszugehen, dass der Gesetzgeber die Altersvorsorge und die damit im Zusammenhang stehenden Anwart-schaften im Scheidungsfall generell ausgleichen wollte.

Zu prüfen bleibt indessen, ob sich die Vorsorgeleistungen nach jenem Recht richten sollten, das die Vorsorgeeinrichtung beherrscht (Vorsorgestatut). Diese Auffassung wird zumeist damit begründet, dass beim Erlass des IPRG dieses Problem noch gar nicht gesehen wurde, so dass heute von einer echten Gesetzeslücke auszugehen sei; einzig ein Abstellen auf das Vorsorgestatut könne sicherstellen, dass ein Anspruch des geschiedenen Ehegatten gegenüber der Vorsorgeeinrichtung nur und nur in jenem Umfang gutgeheissen werde, den das Recht, das die Vorsorge-einrichtung beherrscht, zulasse.[59] Insofern spricht für diese Lösung die innere Kohärenz. Sie kann jedoch zu willkürlichen Resultaten führen, indem Vorsorgeleistungen geteilt werden, obwohl möglicherweise das Scheidungsstatut den ehe-auflösungsbedingten Nachteilen bereits anderweitig Rechnung getragen hat. Umgekehrt würden scheidungswillige Ehegatten mit Wohnsitz in der Schweiz den Art. 122ff. ZGB regel-mässig entgehen, soweit sie einer ausländischen Vorsorge-einrichtung angeschlossen sind. Die Anknüpfung an das Vorsorgestatut vermag sodann auch aus der Systematik des IPRG nicht zu überzeugen. Die Teilung der Austrittsleistungen der beruflichen Vorsorge im Sinne von Art. 122 ZGB sind typische Nebenfolgen der Scheidung und müssen daher konsequenterweise auch der generellen Anknüpfungsregel von Art. 63 Abs. 2 IPRG unterstehen; ein Abrücken hätte einer ausdrücklichen Sonderanknüpfung bedurft. Den Schwierigkeiten, die sich in internationalen Verhältnissen und mit Blick auf ausländische Vorsorgeeinrichtungen ergeben können, hat der Gesetzgeber mit der flexiblen Lösung von Art. 124 ZGB zu begeg-nen versucht: Die „anderen Gründe", die einer Teilung entgegenstehen, können sich auch und gerade auf ausländische Vorsorgeträger beziehen.[60]

---

[59] Geiser (oben N. 53) 67f., Bucher, tome II (oben N. 28) N 564; Schwander, *AJP* (1999) 1651.

[60] Vgl. Botschaft zum Scheidungsrecht (oben N. 32) 106: „Ein Ehegatte kann z.B. einer ausländischen Vorsorgeeinrichtung angeschlossen sein, und das massgebliche ausländische Recht kennt keine Aufteilungsmöglichkeit. . . "

4.   KONSEQUENZEN EINER ANKNÜPFUNG AN DAS SCHEIDUNGSSTATUT

Ansprüche gegenüber einer Vorsorgeeinrichtung werden nach dem Scheidungssta-tut behandelt. Soweit das Scheidungsverfahren in der Schweiz stattfindet, ergeben sich hierzu folgende Konstellationen:

– Untersteht die Scheidung dem schweizerischen Recht und befindet sich die Vorsor-geeinrichtung in der Schweiz, so gelten die Art. 122ff. ZGB ohne weite-res.

– Dasselbe gilt für den Fall, dass das schweizerische Recht mittels Renvoi oder gestützt auf Art. 15 IPRG zum Zuge kommt.

– Untersteht die Scheidung schweizerischem Recht und befindet sich die Vorsorgeein-richtung im Ausland, so steht das schweizerische Scheidungsgericht vor dem Problem, über Anwartschaften oder Ansprüche entscheiden zu müssen, über deren Umfang es möglicherweise keine verlässlichen Angaben erhält. Aber auch wenn das Gericht eine Berechnung vornehmen kann und die Teilung der Vor-sorgeguthaben verfügt, wird das schweizerische Urteil wegen mangelnder Voll-streckbarkeit möglicherweise ins Leere weisen.[61] Dies trifft auch dann zu, wenn nur die grundsätzliche Teilung der Vorsor-geguthaben ausgesprochen, die Berechnun-gen und Modalitäten jedoch vollumfänglich den Gerichten am Ort der Vorsorgeein-richtung überlassen wird, weil keinerlei Gewähr dafür besteht, dass sich die ausländische Vorsorgeeinrichtung nach den Vorgaben des schweizerischen Schei-dungsurteils richtet bzw. richten kann. Denkbar ist dieser Lösungs-ansatz dann, wenn die Scheidungsparteien mit der Vorsorgeeinrichtung eine entspre-chende Vereinbarung haben treffen können, auf die dann im schweizerischen Schei-dungs-urteil Bezug genommen werden kann. Eine Sistierung des schweizerischen Schei-dungsverfahrens, bis über das Schicksal der ausländischen Vorsorgeguthaben entschieden wird, kann nur in jenen Fällen in Betracht gezogen werden, in welchen am Ort der Vorsorgeeinrichtung ein Gerichtsstand und ein entsprechendes Verfah-ren überhaupt zur Verfügung steht. Ist dies der Fall, so besteht sodann keinerlei Ge-währ darüber, dass das ausländische Gericht von einer grundsätzlich hälftigen Teilung ausgeht. Das wird sich in der Schweiz wegen des Verbots der révision au

---

[61] Eine Kalkulierung der Ansprüche ohne Beizug der betreffenden Vorsorgeeinrichtung dürfte fak-tisch wohl unmöglich sein, vgl auch Schwander, *AJP* (1999) 1651. Aber sogar wenn dies bewerkstel-ligt werden könnte, wären die Parteien jedenfalls auf die Vollstreckung des Urteils im betreffenden auslän-dischen Staat angewiesen. Die Vollstreckung ihrerseits dürfte unmöglich sein, wenn die Vor-sorgeein-richtung dem ausländischen öffentlichen Recht untersteht; sie könnte auch höchst problema-tisch sein, wenn die Vorsorgeeinrichtung in ihrer Vereinbarung mit dem Berechtigten eine Teilung der Guthaben nicht zulässt. Grundsätzlich könnte sie wohl nur dann erfolgen, wenn die (private) Vorsorge-einrichtung eine solche Flexibilität zulässt und das schweizerische Scheidungsurteil oder gegebenen-falls auch nur einzelne Nebenfolgen im Ausland anerkannt würden.

fond auch nicht nachprüfen lassen. Ohnehin könnte je nach Konstellation eine Anerkennung der ausländischen (Teil-)Entscheidung in der Schweiz an den Vorgaben
des Art. 65 Abs. 2 IPRG scheitern.[62] Dieselben Bedenken bezüglich der fehlenden
indirekten Zuständigkeit bestehen auch gegenüber einer Zuweisung dieser Nebenfolge in ein separates Verfahren. Letztlich wird sich eine praktikable Lösung nur
treffen lassen, wenn die Parteien zu einer einvernehmlichen Regelung Hand bieten.
Der Hinweis auf die Möglichkeit, nach Art. 124 Abs. 1 ZGB eine angemessene Entschädigung auszusprechen, weil sich die Anwartschaften und Ansprüche im Ausland nicht feststellen lassen, könnte eine Einigung der Parteien in dieser Hinsicht
fördern.

– Untersteht die Scheidung ausländischem Recht und befindet sich die
Vorsorge-einrichtung in der Schweiz, so wird sich dem ausländischen Scheidungsstatut entnehmen müssen, nach welchen Gesichtspunkten mit solchen Ansprüchen
zu verfahren ist. Schweigt sich das ausländische Recht dazu aus bzw. unterwirft es
Anwartschaften und Ansprüche gegenüber einer Vorsorgeeinrichtung nicht einem
Umverteilungsmechanismus, so wird das schweizerische Scheidungsgericht diese
Haltung respektieren müssen. Ein generelles Abstellen auf Art. 15 IPRG nur für
diesen Aspekt der Scheidungsnebenfolge ist nicht tunlich; es widerspräche auch
dem Grundkonzept der Einheit des Scheidungsstatuts.

– Untersteht die Scheidung ausländischem Recht und befindet sich die
Vorsorge-einrichtung in einem Drittstaat, so können sich dieselben grundsätzlichen
Schwierigkeiten ergeben, wie sie für eine Scheidung nach schweizerischem Recht
dargelegt worden sind.

Ist ein Scheidungsverfahren im Ausland hängig oder bereits ausgesprochen und befindet sich eine Vorsorgeeinrichtung in der Schweiz, so können folgende Fälle unterschieden werden:

– Das ausländische Scheidungsurteil äussert sich zu den Vorsorgeleistungen und weist die schweizerische Einrichtung an, eine Teilung oder eine Gutschrift
vorzunehmen. Ob das ausländische Urteil anerkannt werden kann, richtet sich nach
den Art. 25ff. und 65 IPRG.

– Das ausländische Scheidungsurteil trägt dem Umstand, dass einer der
Ehegatten gegenüber einer schweizerischen Vorsorgeeinrichtung Ansprüche hat,
anderweitig Rechnung. So könnte beispielsweise der Anspruchsberechtigte verpflichtet werden, dem anderen Ehegatten eine angemessene Entschädigung auszu-
richten oder ihm Vermö-genswerte zu übereignen oder ihm eine Rente

---

[62] Wenn der Anspruchsberechtigte im Ausland als Kläger auftritt, der Beklagte sich das Ergebnis
des ausländischen Verfahrens nicht entgegenhalten lassen will und beide dieselbe Staatsangehörigkeit
haben.

auszuzahlen. Eine solche Haltung müsste allerdings im Dispositiv des Urteils ersichtlich sein, da sie sich andernfalls nur aus einer verbotenen révision au fond heraus ergeben könnte.

– Das ausländische Scheidungsgericht berücksichtigt die Vorsorgeansprüche nicht. Damit stellt sich die Frage, ob der andere Ehegatte in der Schweiz auf eine hälftige Teilung der Anwartschaften oder Ansprüche klagen kann und welcher Gerichtsstand ihm hier zur Verfügung steht. Mit der Qualifikation der Vorsorgeleistungen als Nebenfolge der Scheidung wird ein solches Begehren nur an die Hand genommen werden können, wenn sich aus dem ausländischen Scheidungsurteil selbst ergibt, dass es die Neben-folgen nicht oder nicht vollumfänglich geregelt hat; der Gerichtsstand hierfür bestimmt sich nach Art. 64 Abs. 1 IPRG. Der Umstand allein, dass der Ehegatte gegenüber einer Vorsorgeeinrichtung in der Schweiz Anwartschaften oder Ansprüche hat, berechtigt den anderen Ehegatten nicht automatisch zu einer hälftigen Teilung.

SUMMARY
PENSION PLAN CLAIMS AND SWISS PRIVATE INTERNATIONAL LAW IN
DIVORCE CASES

Switzerland's amended divorce act contains new provisions on how departure payments of compulsory occupational pension plans have to be allocated to each of the divorcing spouses. In the event that the couple divorces before an insured event has occurred, each of the spouses is entitled to half of the payment the other spouse is entitled to. After an insured event has occurred, sharing is no longer possible and thus the spouse receiving occupational pension plan payments is required to pay an appropriate indemnification to the other spouse.

In transnational cases, the question arises which law should apply to the question of how to deal with occupational pension plan claims in divorces. Due to the absence of a specific conflict of law rule in the Swiss Private International Law Act (PIL) various national laws may apply as the proper law: The law applicable to the maintenance obligations, to the matrimonial property regime, to the pension fund or the law applicable to the divorce might be taken to decide the question. A closer look reveals that the proper law of the divorce is the law most appropriate to decide how to allocate departure payments of occupational pension plans to the divorcing spouses; allocation of departure payments is a side-effect of the divorce which aims at compensating losses suffered as a result of the divorce. Neither the proper law of maintenance obligations determined pursuant to the Hague Convention of 2 October 1973 on the Law Applicable to Maintenance Obligations nor the one of the matrimonial property regime appears to be appropriate. Maintenance obligations require a correlation to be made between a person's need of means to cover living costs and his or her financial capacity which would not be appropriate with departure payments; the matrimonial property regime is one of the consequences of the marriage itself whereas allocation of departure payments is a consequence of the divorce only. Finally, application of the proper law of the occupational pension fund leads to dissatisfactory results in cases in which it requires sharing of departure payments whereas the proper law of the divorce also provides for sufficient compensation of losses suffered through the divorce as well as in other cases.

Application of the proper law of the divorce to departure payments leads to the following notable consequences:

– In the event that the divorce is subject to Swiss law and the pension fund is abroad, the foreign pension fund could well disregard the Swiss judgement. The fact that the Swiss court may fix an appropriate indemnification (Art. 124 para. 1 CC) might make the parties to settle the matter insofar as the claims abroad cannot be determined.

– Should a Swiss court under the PIL-Act have to apply a foreign law which does not deal with, or provide for reallocation of any kind of, Swiss departure payments, it is not justifiable to exceptionally apply Swiss law pursuant to Art. 15 PIL to the allocation of departure payments is concerned.

If a foreign judgement does not have regard in any manner to departure payments of a Swiss pension fund the other spouse may only bring an action for sharing in Switzerland if the foreign judgement does not exhaustively deal with the side-effects of the divorce; in this case, the court having competent jurisdiction is determined pursuant to Art. 64 para. 1 PIL. The simple fact that one spouse has claims for departure payments against a Swiss pension fund does, though, not in itself entitle the other to sharing in equal parts pursuant to Art. 122 ss. CC.

Antonio Canova und die Nationalisierung der Kunst

Erik Jayme[*]

1.   EINFÜHRUNG

Der Jubilar hat das Verdienst, den neuen Wissenschaftszweig des Kunstrechts mit aus der Taufe gehoben zu haben. Er war einer der ersten, der sich mit Akribie und interdisplizinärem Verständnis den Auswirkungen des Kulturgüterschutzes auf das Privatrecht widmete.[1] Bei den häufig grenzüberschreitenden Sachverhalten wurde vor allem deutlich, daß hier Völkerrecht und Internationales Privatrecht eng miteinander verflochten sind. Hinzu trat die Rechtsvereinheitlichung.[2] Das Kunsthandelsrecht wurde ein zentrales Forschungsgebiet von KURT SIEHR.[3] Besonders bedeutsam ist aber in diesem Zusammenhang auch das Europarecht, dem sich Siehr immer

---

[*] Prof. Dr. iur. Dr. h.c., Professor und Direktor des Instituts für ausländisches und internationales Privat- und Wirtschaftsrecht, Universität Heidelberg, Präsident des Institut de Droit International.

Der Beitrag enthält eine Erweiterte Fassung eines unveröffentlichten Vortrags, welchen der Verfasser am 2. März 1999 auf dem Studientag „Das Museum – Neue Tendenzen um 1800" der Bibliotheca Hertziana in Rom gehalten hat.

[1] Kurt Siehr, „Kunstraub und das internationale Recht", *Schweizerische Juristen-Zeitung* (1981) 189ff., 207ff.

[2] Vgl. Kurt Siehr, „Vereinheitlichung des Mobiliarsachenrechts in Europa, insbesondere im Hinblick auf Kulturgüter", 59 *RabelsZ* (1995) 454ff.

[3] Vgl. hierzu Kurt Siehr, „Handel mit Kulturgütern in der Europäischen Union und in der Schweiz", in *Aspekte des Wirtschaftsrechts – Festgabe zum Schweizerischen Juristentag* (Zürich, Schulthess 1994) 353ff.

J. Basedow et al., eds., Private Law in the International Arena – Liber Amicorum Kurt Siehr
© 2000, *T.M.C.Asser Press, The Hague, The Netherlands*

wieder gewidmet hat.[4] Artikel 36 des EG-Vertrags spricht vom „Schutz des nationalen Kulturguts von künstlerischem, geschichtlichem oder archäologischen
Wert". Die Vorschrift geht also davon aus, daß es „nationale" Kunstwerke gibt. Ungelöst ist die Frage der Maßstäbe, nach denen die Zurechnung eines Kunstwerks zu
einer Nation erfolgen soll.[5]

Der Schutz der Kulturgüter durch den Staat und die Staatengemeinschaft hat
zwei geistige Wurzeln. Die erste ist die Idee des „nationalen" Kunstwerks, dessen
Abwanderung in das Ausland verhindert werden soll und das, wenn es geraubt wur-
de, zurückzuführen ist. Die zweite betrifft den Denkmalschutz als öffentliche Auf-
gabe. Antonio Canova hat zu beiden Ideen Grundlegendes beigetragen. Hinzu tritt,
daß er selbst „nationale" Kunstwerke schuf, welche das Streben nach nationaler
Einheit verkörperten. Sie wurden zu sinnstiftenden Zeugnissen der kulturellen
Identität Italiens. Schließlich hat Canova Bedeutung für die Nationalisierung der
Kunstgeschichte als historischer Wissenschaft. Seine Gespräche mit Napoleon im
Jahre 1810 sowie seine Heidelberger Äußerungen beim Besuch der Sammlung der
Gebrüder Boisserée zeigen ihn als einen sensiblen Kenner nationaler Eigenheiten.
Schließlich hat Canova den Gedanken eines nationalen Museums auf vielfältige
Weise gefördert.[6]

Im Vordergrund der folgenden Betrachtungen steht die Bedeutung Canovas für
die Nationalisierung der Kunst. Eine solche Studie ist zugleich einem Kenner der
Kunstgeschichte[7] in herzlicher Verbundenheit und Dankbarkeit für viele gemeinsame Kulturerlebnisse gewidmet.

2.   NATIONALES KULTURGUT UND EXPORTVERBOTE

Papst Pius VII erließ am 1.10.1802 durch den Kardinal Giuseppe Doria Pamphilj
ein Edikt.[8] Das Gesetz enthält in § 2 die Ernennung von Antonio Canova zum Gene-
ralbeauftragten für die Schönen Künste (ispettore generale di tutte le belle arti). In
den §§ 3 und 4 findet sich ein Exportverbot von Antiken und Gemälden: „De vetita
extractione ab urbe rerum ad pulchras artes spectantium".

---

    [4] Vgl. Kurt Siehr, „Handel mit Kulturgütern in der EWG", *NJW* (1993) 2206ff.
    [5] Vgl. hierzu Erik Jayme, *Kunstwerk und Nation – Zuordnungsprobleme im internationalen Kul-
turgüterschutz* (Heidelberg, Carl Winter 1991).
    [6] Zu denken ist hier vor allem an das neu eingerichtete Museo Chiaramonti; zu der geschickten
Kunstpolitik Canovas vgl. in diesem Zusammenhang Massimiliano Pavan, „I Musei Vaticani, il Canova ed il governo napoleonico (1809 –1814)", in *Studi in onore di Elena Bassi* (Ateneo Veneto 1998)
145ff.
    [7] Vgl. z.B. Kurt Siehr, „Ist ein Caracci ein schlechter Poussin? – Zum Irrtum beim Kauf von Kunst-
werken", in: *Festschrift Hanisch* (Köln, Carl Heymanns 1994) 247ff.
    [8] Bullarii Romani Continuatio Summorum Pontificium, Tomus Septimus Pars I, Pius VII. (Prati,
1850) 562ff.

Das Gesetz enthält in den beiden ersten Paragraphen – wie heute eine EG-Richt-linie – einen narrativen Teil, in dem die Erwägungsgründe mitgeteilt werden, wel-che zu dem Gesetz geführt haben. Es geht um die „celebrità di questa metropoli, ed anche dello stato". Die Schönen Künste erscheinen als „uno dei pregi più singolari, che distingue da tutte le altre questa città". Dann folgt ein Hinweis auf den Verlust derjenigen Werke „che le vicende dei tempi ci hanno involate". Gemeint sind die von Napoleon nach dem Vertrag von Tolentino nach Paris verbrachten römischen Kunstwerke. Schließlich werden in § 4 die Kulturgüter unterschieden in solche, de-ren Ausfuhr niemals gestattet wird und solche, deren Export nach entsprechender Prüfung erlaubt werden darf.

Das Gesetz dürfte auf einen Entwurf von Antonio Canova zurückgehen.[9] Es fand später Eingang in den von ihm inspirierten Freskenzyklus in den Lunetten des Mu-seo Chiaramonti; eine Lünette zeigt, wie Engel das Gesetz vom Papst erhalten, um es in die Welt zu tragen[10]: „veteris artium monumentis servandis comparandisque data lex", lautet die Unterschrift unter dem Fresko. Hier liegen zugleich die Anfän-ge der bisher kaum erforschten Kunstrechts-Ikonographie, d.h. der Darstellung kunstrechtlich bedeutsamer Vorgänge mit den Mitteln der Bildenden Künste.

In nuce ist in dem Gesetz ein bis auf den heutigen Tag gültiges Schema aufge-stellt. Für die Erhaltung der Kunst sorgt der Staat. Die Kunstwerke dürfen den Staat nicht verlassen. Canova wird zu ihrem Hüter bestellt. Von der Nation ist 1802 noch nicht die Rede. Die Identifikation des Kirchenstaates mit der klassischen Antike hat aber eine lange Geschichte. Die ersten römischen Museumsbauten, in denen die Antiken aufgestellt wurden, zeigen bereits, daß die Päpste an die Tradition der rö-mischen Kaiser anknüpfen wollten.[11] Erst durch Canova tritt aber die Nation und zwar Italien in den Vordergrund.

3.   Canova als Schöpfer „nationaler" Kunstwerke

Zwei Werke von Antonio Canova sind es vor allen, welche dem nationalen Gedan-ken Ausdruck gaben, die „trauernde Italia" auf dem Alfieri-Grabmal in Santa Croce in Florenz und die „Venere italica", in der Galleria Palatina im Palazzo Pitti. Beide Werke hängen miteinander zusammen.

Die „trauernde Italia" trägt die Mauerkrone mit Türmen. Das entspricht der klas-sischen Ikonographie, wie sie für die Allegorie der Italia in der „Iconologia" von

---

[9] Vgl. Melchior Missirini, *Della vita di Antonio Canova* (Prato 1824) 164.

[10] Diesen Hinweis verdanke ich Gesprächen mit Yvonne Gräfin zu Dohna im Museo Chiaramonti sowie einem Vortrag der Autorin, „Canova und die Nazarener", in der Bibliotheca Hertziana am 1. März 1999 in Rom.

[11] Vgl. hierzu Gian Paolo Consoli, *Il Museo Pio-Clementino – La scena dell'antico in Vaticano* (Modena 1996).

Cesare Ripa 1603 beschrieben ist:

„una bellissima donna vestita di un abito sontuoso e ricco con un manto sopra, seduta su un globo coronata di torri e di mura. . . ".[12]

Antonio Canova belebte mit der „Italia turrita" zugleich eine antike Figur, wie sie als „Italia" schon von Statuen in Agrigent bekannt war.[13] Die Anspielung auf die Antike verknüpfte Größe und Ruhm der römischen Glanzzeit mit dem neuen, aufkeimenden italienischen Nationalgefühl. Hinzu trat eine verborgene Kampfansage an den Mißbrauch der „Italia turrita" in der Staatsikonographie im napoleonischen Italien, vor allem in der cisalpinischen Republik. Dort erscheint das besiegte Italien – etwa im Bild „La riconoscenza" von Giuseppe Bossi, heute im Istituto Lombardo in Mailand – in demütig-dankbarer Haltung und senkt das Haupt mit der Mauerkrone vor Napoleon.

Vittorio Alfieri war am 8.10.1803 gestorben. Die Gräfin von Albany, die Geliebte des Dichters, nahm die Verhandlungen mit Canova auf. Das Alfieri-Grab in Santa Croce in Florenz wurde das erste Werk eines nicht-toskanischen Künstlers, das in dieser Kirche aufgestellt wurde. Es galt dem aus Asti in Piemont stammenden Schriftsteller, dessen Werke das Ideal der Freiheit beschworen hatten. Alfieri war der Dichter der unerlösten Nation.

Die trauernde Italia wurde auch sofort als nationales Kunstwerk begriffen. Die Gräfin Isabella Teotochi Albrizzi veröffentlichte 1809 in Florenz ein Buch über die Werke Canovas.[14] Die Kirche Santa Croce in Florenz wird darin – in Anspielung auf die „Sepolcri" von Ugo Foscolo[15] – zum „sublime Monumento dell'Italiana gloria".[16] Zu der Statue der „trauernden Italia" schreibt die Autorin:

„vi pose una donna colossale, turrita, nobilissima nell'aspetto, d'ampie e regali vesti riccamente coperta, e piangente. Essa è l'Italia, che piange il suo figlio. . . "[17]

Diese Beschreibung mündet in politisch-romantische Exklamationen:

[12] Zitiert nach dem Ausstellungskatalog *Caravaggio e i suoi – Percorsi caravaggeschi in Palazzo Barberini* (Claudio Strinati e Rosella Vodret (Hrsg.)) (Electa 1999) 128, aus der Erläuterung zu Valentin de Boulogne, Allegoria d'Italia.

[13] Ilaria Porciani, in: Soldani/ Turi (Hrsg.), *Fare gli italiani*, Band I, *La nascita dello Stato nazionale* (Il mulino 1997) 400f. Der Verf. dankt Herrn Professor Aldo Mazzacane, Rom, für diesen Hinweis.

[14] Opere di Scultura e di plastica di Antonio Canova descritte da Isabella Albrizzi nata Teotochi (Firenze 1809).

[15] Es ist überliefert, daß Canova, während er an der Statue arbeitete, sich die „sepolcri" von Ugo Foscolo vorlesen ließ, vgl. Porciani (oben N. 13) 401.

[16] Oben N. 15, 78.

[17] Oben N. 15, 77.

„Deh! possano questi preziosi, e alla patria si cari nomi di Alfieri e di Canova riuniti per sempre, e dal tempo distruttore rispettati, sostenere, ed attestare alla più tarda posteriorità la gloria e lo splendore d'Italia."[18]

In zeitlichem Zusammenhang mit dem Alfieri-Grabmal steht die „Venere italica". Die ersten Überlegungen zu diesem Schlüsselwerk der „nationalen" Kunst liegen sogar noch früher.[19]

Im Dezember 1802 ist Canova auf der Durchreise in Florenz, der Hauptstadt des 1801 von Napoleons Gnaden gegründeten Königreichs Etrurien. Der König dieses Staates, Ludwig von Bourbon-Parma, bittet den Künstler, einen Ersatz für die am 11. September 1802 von Napoleon aus Florenz weggeführte „Venus von Medici" zu schaffen. Giovanni degli Alessandri[20] – Präsident der Fiorentina Accademia delle Belle Arti und so etwas wie der Kunstberater des Königs – führt die Feder und dankt Canova in einem Schreiben vom Februar 1803 für die Übernahme des Auftrags „ a decor della Patria".[21] Es ist dies der Moment, in dem der Staat zur Nation transzendiert. Italien wird sichtbar.[22]

In früheren Zeiten war die Kunst durchaus auch als Ruhmesblatt einer Nation betrachtet worden[23], bei Canova aber ist die Kunst selbst der Träger der Nation.

4.   DIE RESTITUTION DER VON NAPOLEON GERAUBTEN KUNSTWERKE

Canova war der Sonderbotschafter des Papstes, als im Herbst 1815 die Siegermächte über die Rückführung der von Napoleon geraubten Kunstwerke entschieden.[24]Zu den Argumenten Canovas, welche schließlich der Restitution zum Durchbruch verhalfen, gehörte auch der Gedanke, daß Kunstwerke eine Heimat haben.[25] Nach der Rückkehr der Kunstwerke bittet Canova den Cardinal Consalvi um einen Brief an den Baron Wilhelm von Humboldt, in dem der Verpflichtung Ausdruck gegeben werden soll

---

[18] Ibid.

[19] Vgl. hierzu und zum folgenden Mazzocca, „Venere italica", in Ausstellungskatalog, Antonio Canova (Venedig 1992) 282.

[20] Zu Giovanni degli Alessandri vgl. Leonardo Ginori Lisci, *The Palazzi of Florence – Their History and Art*, Band 2 (Florenz 1985) 551ff., 554.

[21] F(ernando) M(azzocca) (oben N. 19).

[22] F(ernando) M(azzocca), ibid.: „Impresa dunque che assumeva subito una forte connotazione patriottica, poi accentuata dalla titolazione della statua. . . ".

[23] Vgl. z.B. Edouard Pommier, „Poussin et la gloire de l'École française de la création de l'Académie royale de peinture et de sculpture à la Révolution", 53 *Zeitschrift für Schweizerische Archäologie und Kunstgeschichte* (1996) 267ff.

[24] Katherine Eustace, „Questa Scabrosa Missione"– Canova in Paris and London 1815, in: *Ausstellungskatalog, Antonio Canova – Ideal Heads* (Ashmolean Museum Oxford 1997) 9ff.

[25] Vgl. Erik Jayme (oben N. 5) 20.

„che gliene avranno le arti, Italia e Roma".[26]

Roma und Italien erscheinen hier nicht als Gegensatz sondern in einer natürlichen Verbindung.

Es ergibt sich die interessante Frage, wie das Italien in Canovas Gedankenwelt in politischer Hinsicht verstanden werden soll. Es ist kaum anzunehmen, daß Canova damals an eine Einigung Italiens durch den König von Sardinien-Piemont dachte, wie sie 1860 erfolgte. Zwar sprach für die piemontesische Herrscherfamilie ihre italienische Abstammung; hieraus entwickelte aber erst König Carlo Alberto, der 1831 den Thron bestieg, die italienische Nationalmonarchie als politisches Programm seines Hauses, was sich auch in der Ikonographie seiner Kunstaufträge niederschlug.[27] Canovas „Italia turrita" läßt eher an eine Republik der Kommunen denken. Die Verbindung zwischen Rom und Italien zeigt aber auch die Möglichkeit einer Einigung Italiens unter der weltlichen Herrschaft des Papstes. Es war dies eines der in Italien kurze Zeit später diskutierten Grundmuster für eine politische Einigung, wie sie etwa Carl Mittermaier in seinem Buch „Italienische Zustände" darstellte.[28] Diese Auffassung wurde z.B. von Gioberti vertreten. Mittermaier schrieb:"Der Verfasser erwartet das Heil für Italien, das in einer geistigen Einheit wirken und dadurch mächtig werden soll, von einer politischen Conföderation der italienischen Staaten unter der ordnenden und leitenden Autorität des Papstes."[29] Denkbar war aber auch eine römische Republik als Zentrum Italiens.[30]

Ein Echo dieser Gedanken findet sich im Finale des 2. Akts von Richard Wagners 1842 uraufgeführten Oper „Rienzi – der letzte der Tribunen", als Rienzi den Gesandten zuruft:

„Im Namen Roms nehmt vollen Dank!
Nie ende Neid den schönen Bund!
(in wachsender Begeisterung.)
Ja Gott, der Wunder schuf durch mich,
verlangt, nicht jetzt schon stillzustehn:-
so wißt, nicht Rom allein sei frei; nein ganz Italien sei frei!
Heil dem ital'schen Bunde!"

---

[26] Vgl. zum ganzen Erik Jayme, „Antonio Canova und das nationale Kunstwerk – Zur Ideengeschichte des europäischen Kulturgüterschutzes", in Jayme (Hrsg.), *Nationales Kunstwerk und Internationales Privatrecht, Gesammelte Schriften,* Band 1 (1999) 11.

[27] Vgl. Susanne von Falkenhausen, „Monumentalgemälde: Politik mit Bildern – ,Risorgimento' in der Kunst", in *Forschung – Mitteilungen der DFG (Deutschen Forschungsgemeinschaft)* 2/92, 16ff.

[28] C.J.A. Mittermaier, *Italienische Zustände 1844* (Neudruck herausgegeben von Jayme, Heidelberg, Manutius 1988) 57ff.

[29] Mittermaier, ibid., 58.

[30] Vgl. G.M. Trevelyan, *Garibaldi's Defence of the Roman Republic 1848-9* (London 1988).

Hier zeigen sich zugleich die Parallelen zur deutschen Einigungsbewegung.

5.   DIE NATIONALISIERUNG DER KUNSTBETRACHTUNG

Es gibt kaum ein Thema, das die Kunstbetrachtung des wiedervereinigten Deutschland so beschäftigt, wie das der „Deutschen Kunst".[31] Die Nationalisierung der Kunstbetrachtung läßt sich mit auf Antonio Canova zurückführen.

Im Dezember 1815 besuchte Antonio Canova auf der Durchreise von London kommend Heidelberg.[32] Dieser Besuch erneuerte die Freundschaft mit dem Prorektor der Universität, Friedrich Wilken, die sich in Paris bei den Verhandlungen über die Rückführung der Kunstwerke bewährt hatte.[33] Canova und Wilken besuchten die Kunstsammlung der Brüder Boisserée. In Briefen an verschiedene Empfänger berichtet Sulpiz Boisserée über die Äußerungen Canovas vor der spätmittelalterlichen Bildern. In einem Brief an Goethe vom 9.1.1816 lesen wir:[34]

„Die Bemerkung nämlich, daß die altdeutschen Maler immer ganz vollkommen wußten, was sie machen wollten, und so gerade auf ihren Zweck losgingen, machte Canova vorzüglich beim Eyck. Er meine damit, sagte er, die größere Neigung zum Wahren und Natürlichen, die sich im Gegensatze gegen die alten Italiener, von Anfang her bei allen altdeutschen Malern zeige."

Weitere Betrachtungen Canovas betreffen zusätzliche Unterschiede zwischen der deutschen und der italienischen Malerei auf. Hier zeigen sich Anfänge einer nach nationalen Schulen differenzierenden Kunstgeschichte.

6.   NATIONALE KUNSTWERKE IM RECHT: DIE REZEPTIONSTHEORIE

Betrachtet man die Ideengeschichte des nationalen Kunstwerks und ihren Niederschlag in den verschiedenen Rechtsnormen[35], so sollte für die Qualifikation und Zu-

---

[31] Vgl. z.B. Sebastian Preuss, „Deutsche Kunst" *Berliner Zeitung* 11. Mai 1999, 11.

[32] Vgl. hierzu Erik Jayme, *Antonio Canova (1757 - 1822) als Künstler und Diplomat – Zur Rückkehr von Teilen der Bibliotheca Palatina nach Heidelberg in den Jahren 1815 und 1816* (Heidelberg 1994) 4ff.

[33] Vgl. Friedrick Wilken, *Geschichte der Bildung, Beraubung und Vernichtung der alten Heidelbergischen Büchersammlungen nebst einem beschreibenden Verzeichnis der im Jahr 1816 von Papst Pius VII. der Universität zurückgegebenen Handschriften, und einigen Schriftproben* (Heidelberg 1817) 241-242, der über Canova schreibt: „ . . . der berühmte Künster, ein Mann von dem edelsten Sinne und allgemein anerkannter Billigkeit und Liberalität . . . "

[34] Sulpiz Boisserée, *Briefwechsel, Tagebücher*, Band 2 (Göttingen 1970; facsimiledruck der 1. Aufl. von 1862) 98

[35] Vgl. neuestens das Gesetz zum Schutz deutschen Kulturgutes gegen Abwanderung (Neufassung), BGBl. 1999 I, 1755.

weisung der kulturelle Zusammenhang des Kunstwerks mit einem Land den Ausschlag gaben. Maßgebend sollte die Rezeption des Kunstwerks sein, weniger die
Nationalität des Künstlers.

Konflikte lassen sich auch so kaum vermeiden. Mit der zunehmenden Internationalisierung der Kunst bleibt zu hoffen, daß sich mit der fortlaufenden Rezeption die
Konflikte abschwächen. Es bleiben dann nur noch wenig wirklich „nationale"
Kunstwerke übrig, die einen absoluten Schutz genießen. Zu diesen Kunstwerken
gehören sicher einige Werke von Antonio Canova, wie die „trauernde Italia" und
die „Venere italica" in Florenz.

SUMMARY
ANTONIO CANOVA AND THE NATIONALIZATION OF ART

Under modern laws „national" art treasures are protected against exportation. The
question remains how the „nationality" of an art object is to be determined. The
„nationalization" of art can be traced back to the sculptor Antonio Canova (1757
–1822). The artist served the Pope as diplomat in 1815 at the Paris conference on
the restitution of the art objects taken away from Italy by Napoleon. Canova
advanced the argument that art objects have a home country where they belong to,
and persuaded the other participants of the conference to allow the return of theses
objects to Rome and other parts of Italy. In addition, two of his sculptures have
become the symbols of the Italian nation, the statue of Italy at the tomb of Alfieri,
and the „Venere italica", both in Florence. Historically speaking it is the cultural
link between an art object and a given nation which determines the „nationality" of
works of art.

The Problem with Private International Law

Friedrich K. Juenger[*]

1. THE CRUX OF THE PROBLEM

A glance at the abundant literature, case law and legislative activity in the field of private international law might suggest that it is a vibrant discipline chock full of new and exciting developments. In fact, one should expect as much in light of the fact that more transactions than ever cross state lines. By virtue of the unprecedented mobility of our times, conflict of laws problems arise with ever-increasing frequency; in this era of "globalization," to use that clichéd term, the effects of broken promises, defective goods, traffic accidents and marital squabbles are no longer

---

[*] Edward L. Barrett, Jr., Professor of Law, University of California at Davis.

J. Basedow et al., eds., Private Law in the International Arena – Liber Amicorum Kurt Siehr
© 2000, T.M.C.Asser Press, The Hague, The Netherlands

confined to the territory of one particular state or nation. Jurisdictional, choice-of-law and recognition problems are daily fare. This is true especially within regional organizations such as the European Community, a supranational entity with quasi-federal features akin to those of the old "conflicts paradise,"[1] the United States of America, whose states serve as "legal laboratories"[2] for the testing of new approaches. Given its practical importance, one should hope that private international ought to have been sufficiently perfected to cope with these challenges.

Alas, looking at the practice of courts, the handiwork of legislatures and the voluminous literature, it is clear that the discipline has not attained the desirable maturity and solid doctrinal grounding necessary to alleviate the legal hazards that threaten interstate and international transactions. This is true, especially, as regards private international in the narrow sense, that is the field of choice of law. While rules on jurisdiction and judgments recognition also leave much to be desired, the most problematic are those that attempt to determine what law governs interstate or international transactions. After eight centuries of scholarship, which has produced an enormous wealth of literature, this question still awaits satisfactory answers. Outstanding jurists such as Bartolus, Story, Savigny and Mancini – not to mention renowned scholars of more recent vintage – have wrestled with it, but their efforts have yet to yield a *communis opinio doctorum*. Legislative and judicial solutions vary greatly, attorneys and judges (if they do not simply overlook choice-of-law problems or deliberately disregard them) rarely find the pertinent rules and approaches satisfactory. Indeed, dissatisfaction with the conventional wisdom is so great that the United States has witnessed what has been called a conflicts "revolution."[3] What, then, is wrong with private international law?

The quick answer would be: "quite a few things." But there is a fundamental malaise. Contrary to what the term "private international law" suggests, neither its rules nor the rules to which they refer are of an international or supranational nature.[4] Rather, choice-of-law approaches, much as they diverge from one another, have one thing in common: they attempt to resolve problems that transcend territorial boundaries by recourse to domestic laws. Any of these laws are supposedly equally appropriate to deal with the task of governing interstate and international

---

[1] Kurt G. Siehr, "Domestic Relations in Europe: European Equivalents to American Evolutions", 30 *Am. J. Comp. L.* 37, 69 (1982) (using that term to refer to European family law conflicts).

[2] *New State Ice Co.* v. *Liebmann*, 285 U.S. 262, 311 (1932) (Brandeis, J., dissenting).

[3] *Babcock* v. *Jackson*, 191 N.E.2d 279, 286 (1963) (Voorhis, J., dissenting). This term has subsequently become part of American conflicts parlance. See, e.g., Hans Baade, "Counter-Revolution or Alliance for Progress? Reflections on Reading Cavers, The Choice of Law Process", 46 *Tex. L. Rev.* 141, 143 (1967); Albert E. Ehrenzweig, "A Counter-Revolution in Conflicts Law: From Beale to Cavers", 80 *Harv. L. Rev.* 377 (1966). Concerning this reorientation see infra n. 35-66 and accompanying text.

[4] "*Krebsschaden des IPR: es ist staatliches Recht*." Gerhard Kegel, *Internationales Privatrecht* 12 (7th ed. 1995).

relationships, notwithstanding the fact that their quality varies greatly. But domestic laws are usually made with domestic exigencies in mind; legislators are not necessarily imbued with an urbane, cosmopolitan spirit, nor should one blame them for having their constituents' interests uppermost in mind. Submitting international transactions to a disparate array of domestic laws is akin to fashioning a silk purse out of a sow's ear, as the adage goes. To accomplish this daunting feat, two principal methods have been used: the first looks at the substantive rules that "conflict" to determine which of them ought to apply, the second allocates a transaction that straddles territorial boundaries to one state or the other.

Both of these methods have been used by legislatures, courts and scholars. The first of them, the so-called "unilateralist" approach,[5] focuses on the spatial reach of substantive rules and asks "does this rule of decision claim application to the facts at hand?" For instance, if the issue arises whether a contract between a French and an English corporation lacks an appropriate basis, the judge might ponder whether the French concept of *cause* or the English doctrine of consideration should control. Alternatively, the court asks "is this an English or a French contract?" In other words, instead of looking at the potentially pertinent rules of decision, the "multilateral" (or "bilateral") method lets the resolution of the issue of validity depend on whether the contract "belongs" to the French or the English legal system. The views on which of these approaches is preferable have differed in the past, and they still differ today. But whichever may be the prevailing orthodoxy at a given time, neither of them is satisfactory because both lead to the application of domestic laws that may be ill-equipped to deal with interstate and international transactions.

2. FROM UNILATERALISM TO MULTILATERALISM

2.1 The Statutists

By posing the question whether or not a particular city state's *statutum* governs a given transaction, the medieval scholars who first pondered choice-of-law problems[6] hit upon the unilateralist method. Thus the "statutists" addressed the *quaestio anglica* (*i.e.* whether the inheritance of Italian immovables by an Englishman is subject to the English rule of primogeniture) by asking whether or not the English "statute" is real or personal in nature. Put differently, they speculated about whether the rule of primogeniture deals with property (and therefore could not reach Italian

---

[5] On the distinction between the unilateral and multilateral methodologies see Friedrich K. Juenger, *Choice of Law and Multistate Justice* 13 (1993).

[6] Although they taught Roman law, which they believed to be of universal purport, the glossators also paid attention to the scope of the *statuta* of the city states in which the were teaching. See Juenger, ibid., at 11-12.

immovables) or the person (in which case it would apply to the English heir). As one might expect, dividing rules of law into "real" and "personal" ones proved to be highly unsatisfactory, if only because – as Beale noted – "every law has both a territorial and a personal application;"[7] it reigns within the state and, at the same time, binds the state's subjects. It is, therefore, hardly surprising that the statutists could never agree upon the criteria that control the classification of particular rules of decision as personal or real.

The problematic nature of this distinction finds a vivid illustration in Bartolus' discussion of the *quaestio Anglica*.[8] Taking the position that the wording of a rule determines its classification, Bartolus argued that if the English rule of primogeniture were to provide "the firstborn shall succeed," it should be classified as personal, but if it were to read "the possession of deceased persons shall pass to the firstborn," it would be real. This ludicrous attempt to cast a common law principle in statutory terms, and then to derive legal conclusions from its fictitious wording, earned Bartolus much mockery from later writers. The efforts of other statutists, however, proved to be no more convincing, so that the fundamental question concerning which laws should be considered personal (and could therefore operate extraterritorially) and which ought to be characterized as real (and therefore apply only within the state) remained forever unresolved. Nor did it help that scholars later invented the new category of "mixed" statutes. As has been noted about these vain classificatory attempts, "it is truly amazing how professors sweat when drawing these distinctions."[9]

2.2 The Multilateralist "Revolution"

Given its obvious defects, the statutists' unilateralist methodology was destined to be challenged. In the United States it was rejected early on by the Louisiana Supreme Court in the landmark decision of *Saul* v. *His Creditors*[10] and by Joseph Story.[11] In Europe, first Wächter[12] and then Savigny[13] denounced the statutist learning, which Savigny replaced with a multilateral approach. While multilateral

---

[7] 3 Joseph H. Beale, The Conflict of Laws 1929 (1935). He added: "and where a conflict arises, it is because one sovereign wishes to apply his own law to a juridical relation arising on his territory, while another wishes to throw around his own subject, who is one of the parties to the relation, the protection of his personal law." Ibid.

[8] See Juenger (supra n. 5) at 14.

[9] Johannes Nicolaus Hert, quoted in Max Gutzwiller, *Geschichte des Internationalprivartechts* 201-02 (1977).

[10] 5 Mart. (n.s.) 569 (La. 1827).

[11] See Joseph Story, *Commentries on the Conflict of Laws* 15-24 (1834).

[12] See Carl Georg von Wächter, "Über die Collision der Privatrechtsgesetze verschiedener Staaten" (part 2), 24 *Archiv für die civilistische Praxis* 161, 270-311 (1842).

[13] See 1 Friedrich Carl von Savigny, *System des heutigen Römischen Rechts* 3, 121-26 (1849).

choice-of-law rules were not entirely new (the glossators had already recognized such precepts as *locus regit actum*), he gave it the aura of a scientific system. Savigny maintained that it was the task of private international law to determine the "seat" of legal relationships.[14] To make them sit, that is to allocate such relationships as property, obligations or domestic relations to a particular legal system, he relied on choice-of-law rules that link these categories by means of "connecting factors" to a particular legal system. Thus issues concerning property would be governed by the law of the situs, obligations by the law of the place where they are to be performed, and domestic relations by the law of the parties' domicile.

For his classificatory method Savigny offered a seemingly convincing rationale: noting that the jurisdictional bases of different states frequently overlap, he justified his "seat" principle by arguing that it would be unjust to let the applicable law be determined by the plaintiff's choice among available fora.[15] He believed that linking each legal relationships with a particular state or nation by means of a fixed connecting factor could eradicate this evil by assuring a uniform result irrespective of where a dispute is litigated. In other words, multilateralism seeks to discourage forum shopping by promoting what is nowadays called "decisional harmony."[16] That ideal is dear to the heart of multilateralists to this day; indeed it has been said, somewhat extravagantly, that Savigny "*a fait jaillir la lumière de la vérité au sein d'une quasi-obscurité,*" which "*éclaire tout le droit international privé contemporain,*"[17] and brought about a "Copernican revolution" in the conflict of laws.[18]

3. THE DEFECTS OF MULTILATERALISM

3.1 Decisional Disharmony

Savigny's prestige assured his methodology widespread acceptance, even though his methodology could not possibly attain its stated objective. First of all, the notion that by guaranteeing identical results in any forum the plaintiff might choose, multilateralism might dissuade plaintiff from forum shopping, is misguided. Forum shoppers do not necessarily seek the application of a favorable substantive law;

---

[14] "[F]or each legal relationship that jurisdiction must be determined to which that legal relationship, according to its peculiar nature, belongs or is subjected (wherein it has its seat)." Savigny, ibid. at 108; see also ibid., at 120, 200.

[15] Ibid., at 129.

[16] See, e.g., Pierre Mayer, *Droit international privé* 56 (5th ed. 1994) ("*harmonie des decisions*"); Max Keller & Kurt Siehr, *Allgemeine Lehren des internationalen Privatrechts* 57 (1986) ("*Entscheidungsharmonie*").

[17] Mayer, ibid. at 54.

[18] Ibid.; Paul Heinrich Neuhaus, *Die Grundbegriffe des Internationalen Privatrechts* 94 (2d ed. 1976).

they frequently shop for procedural advantages. To mention but one example: victims injured in Europa by defective products are generally well advised to sue in the United States. The reason is usually not the more favorable American products liability law.[19] Rather, products plaintiffs can more readily afford to litigate in the United States because American attorneys are willing to take personal injury cases on a contingent fee basis. In consequence, the victims do not have to pay counsel to bring an action, nor are they required to reimburse the defendant's attorney fees should they lose. Beyond that, litigating in the United States is attractive because American juries grant verdicts that far exceed the amounts that can be recovered in a European court.[20]

Multilateral rules do not, therefore, spell the end of forum shopping. Nor can they guarantee that the same substantive rules will indeed be applied irrespective of where a particular transaction is litigated. To attain the goal of "decisional harmony" would require each and every state to adopt identical choice-of-law rules, which was indeed what Savigny had optimistically predicted.[21] But private international law, its name notwithstanding, is domestic law, and one cannot possibly expect all jurisdictions of this world to live up to the German jurist's prediction. To mention only the most striking example of the vast disparities that exist:[22] as a result of Mancini's successful advocacy, many civil law countries rely on citizenship to link a person with a state, whereas common law jurisdictions use the connecting factor of domicile (which Savigny had preferred). Moreover, there are substantial variations in the way that different legal systems organize their domestic laws. For instance, while some protect surviving spouses by means of matrimonial property

---

[19] By virtue of Council Directive 85/374 of 25 July 1985 on the Approximation of the Laws, Regulations and Administrative Provisions of the Member States Concerning Liability for Defective Products, the pertinent rules in the member states of the European Community are, on their face, quite as favorable (*OJ* [1985] L 210/29).

[20] To quote Lord Denning's famous statements:

"As a moth is drawn to the light, so is a litigant drawn to the United States. If he can only get his case into their courts, he stands to win a fortune. At no cost to himself, and at no risk of having to pay anything to the other side. The lawyers there will conduct the case on 'spec' as we say, or on a 'contingency fee' as they say . . . The courts of the United States have no such costs deterrent as we have. There is also in the United States a right to trial by jury. These are prone to award fabulous damages . . . The plaintiff holds all the cards."

Smith Kline & French Laboratories, Ltd. v. *Bloch*, [1983] 2 All E.R. 72, 74 (C.A.).

[21] "Unless the . . . evolution of the law is disturbed by unforeseen external circumstances, it can be expected that it will ultimately lead to a completely identical treatment of our teachings in all countries." Savigny (supra n. 13) at 114.

[22] There are many others. For instance, most civil law countries follow the principle of universal succession, whereas common law jurisdictions distinguish between the distribution of movables, to which they apply the law of decedents' last domicile, and the descent of immovables, which is governed by the *lex situs*. Apart from such patent differences, there are subtler ones, such as variant definitions of domicile or the *lex loci delicti commissi* (place of acting versus place of injury).

regimes, others use domestic relations or succession rules to that end.[23] Such discrepancies, which already existed during Savigny's times,[24] have not diminished. If anything, they have been exacerbated as shown by recent European private international law codifications, not two of which are alike.

3.2 Multilateralism's Self-Inflicted Problems

Not only does the conflict of conflict of laws rules assure that Savigny's ideal of decisional harmony will never be attained, but differences in classification and connecting factors have created puzzling new problems to boot. For example, if a married couple from a state that protects the surviving spouse by means of inheritance rights retires in a community property state, the survivor may be left without protection because no assets may have been acquired in the retirement state and the change of domicile eliminates the inheritance rights the former domicile provided.[25] Whereas differences in classification create the conundrum known as "qualification" or "characterization," variations in connecting factors prompt the dreaded "*renvoi*." Assume that a national of a country that follows the domiciliary principle moves to one that uses citizenship as the connecting factor in determining the law applicable to the succession to movables.[26] If that person dies leaving personal property in both jurisdictions, not only will their choice-of-law rules produce different results but the courts of each nation are required to apply the law of the other country. Even if these courts choose to take into account the choice-of-law rules of the jurisdiction to which the forum's choice-of-law rule refers, there is still no guarantee that both courts will in fact reach identical results.

Thus, the seeming simplicity of the multilateral approach is deceptive. Put to the test, that methodology fails to produce the promised decisional harmony and introduces intractable new difficulties.[27] Accordingly, as was true of the statutists' unilateralist approach, which imposed the impossible task of classifying rules of decision, multilateralism poses questions for which there are no satisfactory answers. Just as there never was a consensus on which statutes are personal and which are real, courts and scholars will never agree on how to deal with *renvoi* and

---

[23] See Juenger (supra n. 5) at 71.

[24] See Savigny (supra n. 13) at 98-99 (noting the French Civil Code's reliance on the national law principle), 336-37 (characterization of surviving spouse's property rights) .

[25] See Juenger (supra n. 5) at 72.

[26] Cf., *In re Annesley*, (1926) Ch. 692.

[27] An American unilateralist, after criticizing multilateralism's "metaphysical apparatus," noted that it creates "problems that did not exist before." Brainerd Currie, *Selected Essays on the Conflict of Laws* 180 (1963).

characterization.[28] As a glance at the grab bag of implausible "solutions" to the artificial problems engendered by a misguided approach assembled in the "General Part" of the conflict of laws shows, multilateralism's design defects are beyond repair. Worse yet, there is the problem of substantial justice. Choice-of-law rules that single-mindedly pursue the elusive goal of "decisional harmony" pay insufficient attention to the quality of conflicting rules. To prevent intolerable results, multilateralists were forced to resort to a desperate corrective, the public policy exception, about which Lorenzen said that it "ought to have been a warning that there was something the matter with the reasoning upon which the rules to which it is the exception were supposed to be based."[29]

3.3   The Problem of Justice

The need for the public policy reservation demonstrates that the intellectual efforts multilateralism's complex apparatus demands are not compensated by the results it yields in practical application. With regrettable frequency, traditional choice-of-law rules produce unsatisfactory decisions because mechanical precepts whose hard and fast connecting factors indiscriminately invoke foreign law must inevitably produce hardship. For instance, once the world became motorized, the *lex loci delicti commissi* rule brought before domestic courts many foreign tort rules that were sure to offend the forum judiciary's sense of justice.[30] Similarly, once people no longer simply stayed at home, domestic relations choice-of-law rules of the classical type are prone to import noxious foreign rules of decision, especially in those legal systems that have adopted the national law principle.[31]

Hard and fast as it is, citizenship offers an ideal connecting factor from the multilateralists' perspective. A person's nationality can usually be ascertained more readily than his domicile; it is more resistant to change; it has fewer shades of meaning; and it cannot be as readily manipulated. Accordingly, that connecting factor is more likely to promote the desired "decisional harmony" than the domiciliary nexus.[32] But, by the same token, the national law principle burdens foreign nation-

---

[28] Nor are characterization and *renvoi* the only self-inflicted difficulties of the multilateral approach. The incompatibility of institutions found in foreign legal systems with domestic ones provoke the legerdemain called "adaptation;" realization that the traditional categories used to classify legal relationships are overly broad have prompted legal scholars to wrestle with the phenomenon known as the "incidental question;" and the parties' manipulation of connecting factors spawned much writing about "fraud on the law."

[29] Ernest G. Lorenzen, Selected Articles on the Conflict of Laws 13-14 (1947).

[30] See infra n. 35-41 and accompanying text.

[31] In contrast, the soft connecting factor of domicile can be readily manipulated. See Juenger (supra n. 5) at 176.

[32] For which reason the national law principle has been called the "gold standard" of private international law. Neuhaus (supra n. 18) at 209.

als, who usually occupy the social ladder's lower rungs, with intricate conflicts and foreign law problems.[33] In consequence, cases to which aliens are parties impede the efficient administration of justice by adding delays and costs to the litigation of run-of-the-mill domestic relations disputes. Worse yet, the *lex patriae* is prone to import foreign law that may fall so far below the forum's standards of decency as to offend constitutional tenets. In Germany, for instance, the obsession with decisional harmony combined with the dysfunctional national law principle first prompted large-scale evasion by German divorcees, who were precluded from marrying aliens from countries that did not recognize German divorces, and then the Constitutional Court's intervention.[34]

4. THE AMERICAN "CONFLICTS REVOLUTION"

4.1 The Demise of the First Conflicts Restatement

In the United States the multilateral approach's propensity to import noxious foreign rules of decision provoked a complete reorientation of American tort choice of law. Most of the cases that triggered this sea change dealt with automotive accidents,[35] others involved airplane crashes.[36] Until the nineteen-sixties and seventies, more than half of the American states barred recovery by injured passengers from the driver, either by virtue of so called "guest statutes" or because of the intra-family immunity doctrine. Also, quite a few states imposed arbitrary statutory monetary limits on liability for wrongful death, some of which were ridiculously low.[37] Judges in states that had never adopted such substandard rules, or had reformed their domestic tort law, began to balk at applying unreformed sister-state law, which – given the American public's mobility – the authoritative

---

[33] See Axel Flessner, Interessenjurisprudenz im internationalen Privatrecht 32-34 (1990).

[34] See Juenger, "The German Constitutional Court and the Conflict of Laws", 20 *Am. J. Comp. L.* 290 (1972).

[35] That problem is not unique to the United States. In France, the *Cour de cassation*'s steadfast insistence on the *lex loci delicti commissi* rule frequently barred or severely limited recovery, which prompted lower courts to use various and sundry devices designed to neutralize the rule, especially in cases where French parties were injured abroad. See 1 Henri Batiffol & Paul Lagarde, *Droit international Privé* 237-39 (7th ed. 1983). The traffic accident problem was alleviated by France's ratification of the 1971 Hague Convention on the Law Applicable to Traffic Accidents, which provides for a number of exceptions to the rigid *lex loci delicti commissi* rule and invokes French law with greater frequency.

[36] See, e.g., *Kilberg v. Northeast Airlines*, 172 N.E.2d 526 (N.Y. 1961); *Griffith v. United Airlines*, 203 A.2d 796 (1964); cf. *Van Dusen v. Barrack*, 376 U.S. 612 (1964).

[37] See cases cited in preceding note (Massachusetts wrongful death statute limiting recovery to a maximum of $ 15,000).

First Conflicts Restatement's[38] *lex loci delicti commissi* rule imported *en masse*.

To ward off such foreign *statuta odiosa*, especially in cases involving out-of-state accidents of forum residents, American judges resorted to various and sundry escape devices. While paying lip service to the *lex loci delicti commissi* rule, they avoided its brunt by resorting to the "General Part" of conflicts law.[39] Thus they characterized foreign tort rules as "procedural,"[40] invoked the *renvoi* doctrine[41] or wielded the heavy club of public policy[42] to block undesirable foreign tort rules. Inevitably, large-scale resort to such maneuvers undermined the credibility of the rule the courts purported to apply. At the same time American conflicts scholars, under the influence of the legal realist school, had become disenchanted with the hard and fast rules compelled by precedent and the First Restatement. In addition, the Restatement's authority was undercut, shortly after its publication, by the United States Supreme Court. While the highest American court originally embraced the multilateral approach, it later retreated from this position, granting state courts and legislatures a substantial measure of freedom in dealing with choice-of-law problems.[43]

The Supreme Court's stance emboldened judges to experiment with different choice-of-law approaches, prompting what has since been called a "conflicts revolution."[44] Eschewing the pretense of relying on fine-spun escape devices, the New York Court of Appeals, in *Babcock* v. *Jackson*,[45] decided to abandon the *lex loci delicti commissi* rule. Many other highest state courts followed suit, and the place-of-the-accident rule now only prevails in a minority of American jurisdictions.[46] Yet, while the unsatisfactory nature of the First Restatement's choice-of-law rule was widely recognized, those who believed in the need for a changed choice-of-law approach could not agree on what exactly should take its place. Two principal substitutes emerged: (1) a "soft" multilateralism that would replace hard and fast connecting factors with flexible formula, and (2) a return to the unilateralist approach.

---

[38] *Restatement of Conflict of Laws* (1934).

[39] See Juenger (supra n. 5) at 96.

[40] See, e.g., *Grant* v. *McAuliffe*, 264 P.2d 944 (Cal. 1953); *Kilberg* v. *Northeast Airlines*, 172 N.E.2d 526 (N.Y. 1961).

[41] See *Haumschild* v. *Continental Cas. Co.*, 95 N.W.2d 814, 821 (Wis. 1959) (concurring opinion); cf. *University of Chicago* v. *Dater*, 270 N.W. 175 (Mich. 1936) (contract choice of law).

[42] See *Kilberg* v. *Northeast Airlines*, 172 N.E.2d 526 (N.Y. 1961).

[43] See *Pacific Employers Ins. Co.* v. *Industrial Accident Commission*, 306 U.S. 493 (1939); *Alaska Packers Ass'n* v. *Industrial Commission*, 294 U.S. 532 (1935); see also *Carroll* v. *Lanza*, 349 U.S. 145 (1955).

[44] See supra n. 3.

[45] 240 N.E.2d 279 (N.Y. 1963).

[46] For a recent lineup of the various rules and approaches to tort choice of law see Symeon C. Symeonides, "Choice of Law in the American Courts in 1997", 46 *Am. J. Comp. L.* 233, 266-73 (1998).

4.2   Soft Multilateralism

The First Restatement's deficiencies had first become apparent in contract choice of law. The *lex loci contractus* rule, which, according to its Reporter Beale, followed with ineluctable logic from the vested rights theory he espoused,[47] had several obvious defects (as did Savigny's *lex loci solutionis*).[48] For this reason, most legal systems opted for what British courts call the "proper law" approach, *i.e.* the principle of party autonomy or, in the absence of a choice-of-law clause, application of the law that has the "closest connection" with the contract.[49] But while the U.S. Supreme Court originally took a similar stance,[50] under the spell of Beale's teachings most American states adopted the dysfunctional *lex loci contractus* rule (which some apply to this day[51]). Since the mid-century, however, when, in *Auten* v. *Auten*,[52] the New York Court of Appeals opted for the open-ended "most significant contacts" formula, American courts began to align themselves with the practice in other nations.

In an article published in an American law review, an English conflicts scholar contended that this flexible connecting factor need not be limited to contract choice of law and advocated the adoption of a "proper law of torts."[53] Nine years after it decided *Auten* v. *Auten,* the New York Court of Appeals followed this suggestion and embraced the "most significant contacts" test in the landmark tort choice-of-law case *Babcock* v. *Jackson.*[54] In a slightly modified form, this formula became a key element of the Second Conflicts Restatement, where it parades under the name of "most significant relationship."[55] Ostensibly, the adoption of a flexible in lieu of a rigid connecting factor still preserves the multilateral approach. But in reality it undercuts the very thrust of multilateralism: because different courts are bound to interpret this impressionistic phrase in different ways, it is antithetical to the ideal of "decisional harmony." This may explain why Savigny took pains to characterize his

---

[47] "The question whether a contract is valid . . . can on general principles be determined by no other law than that which applies to the acts, that is by the law of the place of contracting . . . If . . . the law of the place where the contract is made annexes no legal obligation to it, there is no other law which has the power to do so."

2 Joseph H. Beale, *A Treatise on the Conflict of Laws* 1288 (1935).

[48] See Juenger (supra n. 5) at 53-54.

[49] See ibid., at 55-58.

[50] See *Pritchard* v. *Norton*, 106 U.S. 124 (1882), which let choice of law turn on the parties' "presumed intent." This fictive subjective component was subsequently objectified to become the "closest connection." See Juenger (supra n. 5) at 57.

[51] See Symeonides (supra n. 46) at 251-53, 266.

[52] 124 N.E.2d 99 (N.Y. 1954).

[53] See J. H. C. Morris, "The Proper Law of a Tort", 64 *Harv. L. rev.* 881 (1951).

[54] 191 N.E.2d 279 (N.Y. 1963).

[55] See, e.g., *Restatement (Second) of Conflict of Laws* §§ 145 (torts), 188 (contracts).

notion of the "seat" of legal relationships – to which the proper law approach is indebted[56] – as a mere "formal principle," which must be given substance by less open-ended connecting factors.

4.3 Interest Analysis

In addition to the most-significant-contacts test, *Babcock* v. *Jackson* contained an ingredient that is entirely at odds with the multilateralists' philosophy. Judge Fuld's opinion in that case also referred to state "interests" and "concerns," which are catchphrases of the "governmental interest analysis" developed by Brainerd Currie.[57] This approach, which a majority of American conflicts writers favor, attempts to resolve choice-of-law problems by an analysis of the concerns Currie believed states have in effectuating the policies underlying their laws. Since it focuses on the reach of substantive rules rather than on the "seat" of legal relationships, this methodology amounts to a return to the unilateralist approach the statutists had invented. Currie's version of interest analysis, however, largely avoids the difficulty of classifying substantive rules as either personal or real. Proceeding from the assumption that governments are interested not so much in what happens within their territories than in the well-being of their subjects, Currie's methodology relied almost entirely on the personal nexus.[58]

The idea that – to speak in statutist terms – all statutes are personal does not, however, avoid all of the problems inherent in the unilateralist approach. If the parties to a transaction hale from different states, reliance on their personal law can cause either an overlap (*cumul*) or a legal void (*lacune*) of norms.[59] To cope with this difficulty, Currie advocated application of the *lex fori* whenever his method produced what he called a "true conflict" or an "unprovided for" case.[60] Accordingly, interest analysis invokes the *lex fori* in practically all cases, so that it amounts to little more than a complex pretext for not applying foreign law.[61] Nor is parochialism the only flaw of interest analysis. Because it requires each issue posed by a multistate case to be analyzed separately, norms from different states may have to be applied to the same transaction. This is apt to produce the phenomenon called *dépeçage*, an admixture of norms from different states that may bear no resemblance to the law that prevails in any one of them.[62] Such an amalgamation

---

[56] See Juenger (supra n. 5) at 57.

[57] See generally Currie (supra n. 27).

[58] See Juenger (supra n. 5) at 100-01.

[59] See ibid., at 138.

[60] See ibid., at 137.

[61] Not without reason, Currie has been accused of harboring a "nihilist view of conflicts law in the traditional sense." Eugene F. Scoles & Peter Hay, Conflict of Laws 16 (2d ed. 1992).

[62] See Juenger (supra n. 5) at 76, 138-39.

may well make sense, because the law applied to an international transaction need not necessarily conform to any particular domestic law, but it flies in the face of a methodology designed that is designed to effectuate the interests of "sovereigns."[63] As is apparent, unilateralism is no less prone to creating artificial problems than the multilateral approach.[64]

4.4   The "Conflicts Revolution's" Consequences

Since *Babcock* v. *Jackson*, a majority of American states have rejected the *lex loci delicti commissi* rule to adopt one or the other of the various approaches proffered by scholars. In consequence, tort choice of law in the United States has – as domestic and foreign observers have noted – become chaotic and confused.[65] Yet, the decisions American courts nowadays reach in tort choice-of-law cases are usually more satisfactory than those of the bygone era, so that the level of interstate and international justice has been enhanced.[66] The reasons are obvious. The flexibility judges enjoy by virtue of such formulae as the "most significant relationship" allows them first to determine the law they wish to apply and then to find arguments bolstering the assertion that this law has the closest connection. In this fashion they can avoid the foreign *statuta odiosa* that the classical First Restatement invoked with deplorable regularity. Similarly, because tort actions are usually brought in jurisdictions whose law is favorable to the plaintiff, the homing trend inherent in interest analysis eliminates rules of decision that unreasonably bar or diminish the victim's recovery. Thus, while the American conflict of laws may lie in shambles, the First Restatement's demise improved the quality of decisions in interstate and international tort cases, which poses the fundamental question: might we not be better off without private international law?

4.5   Echoes Abroad

Conflicts scholars who start from the premise that all substantive laws are created equal must, of necessity, tolerate untoward results in interstate and international cases. To sugarcoat the iniquities that inevitably follow from the pursuit of "decisional harmony," they have invented the term "conflicts justice."[67] That turn of

---

[63] Which is why Currie and other interest analysts felt uncomfortable about *dépeçage*. See Juenger, ibid., at 139.

[64] For which, as noted earlier, Currie had criticized the multilateralists (supra n. 27). An even more fundamental difficulty with his approach is that no one has ever been able to demonstrate that governments do indeed have an interest in effectuating the policies underlying their private law rules.

[65] See Juenger (supra n. 5) at 121-28.

[66] See ibid., at 146-49.

[67] See Kegel (supra n. 4) at 106-08.

phrase suggests that private international law, unlike all other law, it is not concerned with the results of its application; justice is done as long as the law applied has the closest connection with the case at hand. Yet even those who believe in "conflicts justice" cannot be entirely oblivious to outcomes.[68] To avoid wholly unacceptable results, they can of course rely on the public policy reservation. That escape device is, however, rather blunt and it rubs with the fundamental assumption that all laws are created equal. Looking for subtler ways to reach palatable decisions in international cases, scholars, courts and legislatures have experimented with expedients similar to those that have surfaced during the American "conflicts revolution."

By now, soft connecting factors and a dash of unilateralism have also become fashionable outside the United States.[69] Thus both the Rome Convention on the Law Applicable to Contractual Obligations and the draft Convention on the Law Applicable to Non-Contractual Obligations ("Rome II") use the "closest connection" test[70] as well as the unilateralist notion of "*lois de police*."[71] To be sure, interest analysis has found few takers outside the United States and the sporadic recognition of *lois de police* hardly spells a return to statutism. Yet, it is remarkable that unilateralism, which not too long ago seemed to be dead and buried on account of Savigny's "Copernican revolution," is now experiencing a renaissance.[72] Conversely, some American conflicts writers have attempted to combine the unilateralist approach with multilateral elements.[73] Thus, the two incompatible approaches now live in uneasy coexistence; in fact, "methodological pluralism"[74] – a tacit recognition of the traditional methodologies' deficiencies – may well be the hallmark of today's private international law. But is eclecticism the only possible cure for what ails private international law?

---

[68] See ibid., at 116-18.

[69] See Siehr (supra n. 1) at 40-46, 55-57, 71.

[70] See Rome Convention art. 4; draft Convention arts. 3 and 4.

[71] See Rome Convention art. 7; draft Convention art. 9 ("mandatory rules").

[72] See Pierre Gothot, "Le renouveau de la tendance unilatéraliste en droit international privé" (parts 1-3), 60 *Rev. crit. d.i.p.* 1, 209, 415 (1971). Savigny himself had referred to a species of *lois de police* when he spoke of "strictly positive laws." See Savigny (supra n. 13) at 33-37. Moreover, he apparently considered unilateralism and multilateralism as but two sides of the same coin, ibid., at 1-3, 10-11.

[73] See, e.g., David F. Cavers, *The Choice of Law Process* 108-24 (1965); Arthur Taylor von Mehren & Donald Theodore Trautman, *The Law of Multistate Problems* 76-79 (1965); Baxter, "Choice of Law and the Federal System", 16 *Stan. L. Rev.* 1 (1963).

[74] A term coined by Henri Batiffol, "Le pluralisme des méthodes en droit international privé", 139 *Rec. des Cours* 71 (1973-II).

5.   WHERE DO WE GO FROM HERE?

5.1   Uniform Choice-of-Law Rules

To return to the beginning of this paper: the basic problem with traditional private international law is that it relies on domestic rules to resolve problems that are inter-national in nature.[75] It therefore invokes rules of decision that are frequently not at-tuned to the exigencies of international commerce. In addition, private international rules, themselves being domestic in nature, differ from one state to the next, which – as has been pointed out[76] – dooms the hoped-for decisional harmony. To be sure, the latter problem can be cured: seizing upon a suggestion Savigny had made,[77] Mancini (who had less reason to be optimistic about the universal adoption of his national law principle), advocated international conventions as a means of harmo-nizing choice-of-law rules. By alleviating disparities in national legislation and case law, conventions can indeed avoid some of the embarrassments of the "General Part," such as characterization and *renvoi*, and thereby ensure a greater measure of uniformity. Yet, even an overarching treaty framework leaves open the possibility of conflicting interpretations, especially of such vague connecting factors as the "closest connection."

Thus, unless a central court is empowered to issue binding interpretations of its provisions, even a choice-of-law convention cannot guarantee uniformity. Worse yet, unless it contains a fairly broad public policy reservation, such an instrument cannot resolve the fundamental problem of dysfunctional national rules of decision. The original Hague Conventions in the field of family law stand as a warning exam-ple of how the focus on "decisional harmony," especially when combined with the national law principle, can work havoc with human relationships.[78] Preventing mar-riages and divorces, and, in the spectacular *Boll* case,[79] frustrating the welfare and protection of a molested child, they cogently illustrate the dangers of a single-minded pursuit of uniformity. The fact that it took quite some time to denounce

---

[75] Reliance on domestic law to resolve multistate problems creates the further difficulty of judges having to apply foreign law. Multilateralists and unilateralists alike assume that any court is able to ap-ply whatever foreign rules of decision their approaches may invoke. Few judges, however, are comfort-able dealing with any law other than their own and if they do rely on foreign law experts, the margin of error in decisionmaking inevitably increases. And who is to pay the experts' fees? What if the parties are impecunious? From the point of view of an efficacious administration of justice, how can one jus-tify (especially in disputes of minor significance) having judges jump the hurdles first of complex choice-of-law issues and then of knotty foreign law problems?

[76] See supra n. 21-24 and accompanying text.

[77] See Savigny (supra n. 13) at 114-15.

[78] See Friedrich K. Juenger, "The National Law Principle", in: *Mélanges Fritz Sturm* ?? (1999).

[79] See Application of the Convention of 1902 Governing the Guardianship of Infants (*Swed.* v. *Neth.*), 1958 I.C.J. 55 (Judgment of Nov. 28).

them demonstrates a further difficulty: because amendments of choice-of-law conventions require the consent of all signatories, they cannot be readily adapted to changed circumstances.

In the future, choice-of-law rules in the European Community may take the form of council regulations because the Treaty of Amsterdam confers authority upon the Community's institutions to legislate in this area with supranational effect. Such regulations would unify choice of law more effectively than a mere convention because, by virtue of article 177 of the Rome Treaty, the Court of Justice would become be the ultimate arbiter concerning their interpretation. One may, however, well doubt the benefits of such action by the Community. To lay down supranational choice-of-law rules means, in effect, that the Community embarks on a policy to preserve disparate national laws that may impede the traffic between member states. Even if such a commitment to "subsidiarity" would make sense, inflicting on an already overburdened tribunal the additional task of divining the meaning of such weasel words as "closely connected" hardly serves the interest of an efficient administration of justice. More importantly, supranationalizing it will not cure the Rome Convention's shortcomings[80] and the European authorities' earlier dabbling with choice-of-law rules in several directives has prompted mixed reactions.[81] As noted earlier, for a while the U.S. Supreme Court toyed with constitutionalizing choice-of-law rules.[82] The decisions it rendered during those bygone days stand as a warning against federalizing the conflict of laws.[83]

5.2   Uniform Substantive Law

Choice-of-law rules tell a judge whether, for example, issues arising from a dispute relating to a contract between an Italian and a German firm are governed by German or Italian law. But an agreement that straddles national frontiers clearly is not truly German or Italian; it is an international transaction. To submit it to one national legal system or another may not be entirely satisfactory; the parties' interests would probably be better protected by applying a law conceived with international realities in mind. Recognizing the need for an international law of contracts, many

---

[80] See Friedrich K. Juenger, "Two European Conflicts Conventions", 28 *Victoria U. Wellington L. Rev.* 527, 535-42 (1998). Nor does Rome II inspire greater confidence. That draft convention, for example, fails to include the commonsensical alternative reference rule developed in German practice. See infra n. 97 and accompanying text.

[81] Compare Erik Jayme & Christian Kohler, "L'interaction des règles de conflict contenues dans le droit dérivé de la Communauté européenne et des conventions de Bruxelles et de Rome", 84 *Rev. crit. d.i.p.* 1 (1995), *with* Bernd von Hoffmann, "Richtlinien der Europäischen Gemeinschaft und Internationales Privatrecht", 36 *ZfRV* 45 (1995).

[82] See supra n. 43 and accompanying text.

[83] See, e.g., *New York Life Ins. Co.* v. *Dodge*, 246 U.S. 357 (1918); *Slater* v. *Mexican Nat'l R.R. Co.*, 194 U.S. 120 (1904).

nations have ratified the Vienna Convention on the International Sale of Goods. Unification does not, however, necessarily require a convention, uniform statutes may be sufficient for the purpose.[84] In fact, it may not even require legislation: the UNIDROIT Principles of International Commercial Contracts, a private restate-ment,[85] can serve that need.

The desirability of an overarching *lex mercatoria*, as it once existed,[86] was recog-nized by such noted jurists such as the Dutch scholar Daniël Josephus Jitta, the Uru-guayan Quintín Alfonsín and the Frenchman Berthold Goldman. The great French comparativist René David, denouncing those whom he characterized as "conflictualists,"[87] scathingly observed that

> the lawyers' idea which aspires to submit international trade, in every case, to one or more national systems of law is nothing but bluff. The practical men have very largely freed themselves from it, by mean of standard contracts and arbitration, and states will be abandoning neither sovereignty nor prerogatives if they open their eyes to reality and lend themselves to the reconstruction of international law.[88]

The quest for such a law has become more pressing since new realities have emerged that are at odds with those that spawned the traditional choice-of-law ap-proaches. Take, for instance, the Internet, whose "transnational nature confounds the conventional law of territorial jurisdiction and national borders."[89] Are not "[t]raditional notions of jurisdiction . . . outdated in a world divided not into nations, states, and provinces but networks, domains and hosts"?[90]

5.3   Alternative Choice-of-Law Approaches

The unification of substantive law of course obviates the need for choice-of-law rules. Outside the field of commercial law, however, the prospects of unification – even within a regional organization such as the European Community – are less than promising. While it may therefore seem that only the merchant class can bene-

---

[84] As shown by the example of the American federal system, where the Uniform Commercial Code offers a substantial measure of uniformity.

[85] See generally Michael Joachim Bonell, *An International Restatement of Contract Law* (2d ed. 1997).

[86] See *Swift* v. *Tyson*, 41 U.S. (16 Pet.) 1, 19 (1842) (Story, J.).

[87] René David, "The International Unification of Private Law", in: 2 *International Encyclopedia of Comparative Law* Chapter 5, at 25 (1969).

[88] Ibid., at 212.

[89] Jane C. Ginsburg, "The Private International Law of Copyright in an Era of Technological Change", 273 *Rec. des Cours* 239, 383 (1998).

[90] Matthew R. Burnstein, "Conflicts on the Net: Choice of Law in Transnational Cyberspace", 29 *Vand. J. Transnat'l L.* 75, 81 (1996).

fit from a universal law, commercial cases suggest that other fields as well could profit from possible alternatives to the simple-minded traditional choice-of-law methods. As noted earlier, in contract cases courts found better ways to deal with the choice-of-law problem than to either allocate contracts to a legal system by means of hard and fast connecting factors or speculating about the reach of rules of decision.[91] Emulating the substantive policy of freedom of contract, judges – undaunted by the academicians' scruples[92] – have embraced the principles of party autonomy, which allows the parties to an agreement to select the law that is most suitable to their transaction. Obviously, this solution is at loggerheads with the traditional approaches, which rely on objective connecting factors rather than the parties' subjective intent, but it does work well in practical application.

Although party autonomy usually still leads to the application of national law, some legal systems happen to be better adapted to the exigencies of international commerce than others. English maritime law, for example, approximates the standards one would expect from truly international norms. Moreover, the principle of freedom of contract permits the parties to stipulate out of obsolete or misguided national rules of decision. If they should, however, be unable to agree on any national legal system, the parties can submit their agreement to the *lex mercatoria* or the UNIDROIT Principles of International Commercial Contracts. While some legal writers (and presumably the Rome Convention) take the position that individuals and enterprises are limited to the choice of a positive law,[93] such a paternalistic view is at odds with the very principle of freedom of contract. In any event, as a practical matter it presents no serious obstacle because party autonomy also has a procedural aspect: the contracting parties are free to designate the forum; and if courts cannot be expected to respect their choice, arbitrators certainly will.

The principle of party autonomy illustrates that there are choice-of-law methods beyond the traditional unilateral or multilateral approaches. That principle need not be confined to contract choice of law; in fact, it has been used in such areas as marital property and succession.[94] Nor is party autonomy the only choice-of-law principle that can ensure palatable results in transnational cases. Result-oriented alternative reference rules, for instance, are not exactly new to private international law.[95] According to authority dating back to the Middle Ages, multistate contracts need comply only with the formalities that prevail at either the place of performance

---

[91] See supra n. 47-52 and accompanying text.

[92] See Juenger (supra n. 5) at 54-55.

[93] See Paul Lagarde, "Le nouveau droit international privé des contrats après l'entrée en vigueur de la Convention de Rome du 19 juin 1980", 80 *Rev. crit. d.i.p.* 287, 300-01 (1991).

[94] See Keller & Siehr (supra n. 16) at 374-75. Article 8 of the European draft Convention on the Law Applicable to Non-Contractual Obligations would allow the parties to choose the applicable law by means of an agreement entered into after the obligation arises.

[95] See Juenger (supra n. 5) at 178.

or the place of execution. This rule validates agreements that may violate one or the other of the many pesky form requirements that abound on the international scene, such as common law statutes of frauds or the pertinent form requirements found in French-inspired civil codes. Alternative reference rules have also been applied to save contracts from potential substantive invalidity caused by the motley array of American usury statutes.[96]

Again, alternative reference need not be limited to contracts. More than a century ago, the German *Reichsgericht* developed a choice-of-law rule for long-distance torts, which assured the victim the benefit of the more favorable law prevailing at either the place of acting or the place of injury.[97] An extraordinarily broad alternative reference rule is found in the Hague Convention on the Law Applicable to Wills, which invokes the rules of a variety of legal systems to safeguard testamentary dispositions against the international risk of formal invalidity. Rules of this nature are designed to effectuate a substantive policy, such as the validity of contracts or other legal transactions or the protection of tort victims. In this fashion they promote what German writers have called the "substantification"[98] of private international law. Such a substantive law approach shows how the conflicts technique can be used to further the unification of law, which is the only effective way to assure true "decisional harmony." This kind of uniformity is superior to that which multilateralists pursue because it not only guarantees similar results irrespective of the place of adjudication but also a higher level of substantive justice.

Although it relies on domestic legal norms, the alternative reference technique – a variant of the multilateral approach – uses them not as *the* applicable law but as mere raw material for fashioning transnational rules. Similar to the principle of party autonomy, this technique helps neutralize *statuta odiosa* that burden international intercourse. Its salutary effect can be enhanced by borrowing from unilateralism the notion that each specific issue of an international dispute requires separate analysis: by avoiding *all* potentially applicable *statuta odiosa, dépeçage*[99] can thus offer tailor-made solutions to international disputes. In this fashion, the conflict of laws can play a role akin to that of the general principles of law of civilized nations in article 38 of the Statute of the International Court of Justice, namely

---

[96] Observing this judicial practice, Ehrenzweig (who, however, believed that validating usurious contracts made little sense) derived from it a more general rule of validation. See Albert E. Ehrenzweig, *A Treatise on the Conflict of Laws* 464-85 (1963).

[97] See 72 RGZ 41 (1909); 23 RGZ 305 (1888). While the European draft Convention on the Law Applicable to Non-Contractual Obligations eschews this rule (see supra n. 80) article 40(1), second sentence, of the Introductory Act to the German Civil Code, as amended by the recent Act on the Private International Law Concerning Non-Contractual Obligations and Property, allows the injured party to the law of the place of injury instead of the place of acting, which normally applies.

[98] "*Materialisierung*" is the term coined by Paul Heinrich Neuhaus, "Neue Wege im europäischen Internationalen Privatrecht?", 35 *RabelsZ* 401, 407-10 (1971).

[99] See supra n. 62-63 and accompanying text.

to serve as a source for the creation of an international law. Private international law can thus help overcome the legal isolationism the emergence of modern nation states has prompted, especially in the civil law orbit, where codification destroyed the cohesion the *ius commune* once provided and the common law still does provide. Now that these two great legal cultures are peacefully united in the European Union – an endeavor inspired by the need to take Europe beyond the confines of the nation state – it would seem appropriate to create, for the united states of Europe, a common law comparable to that which prevails in the United States of America.

6.   In Conclusion

By now the defects of the two principal approaches to dealing with interstate and international transactions ought to be painfully apparent. Since exclusive reliance on national law cannot satisfactorily resolve international problems, the quest for the touchstone has been in vain. In the foreseeable future, private international law will continue to produce disappointing results when applied to real-life problems because recent cases, statutes and conventions have done little to reform private international law. Yet, bad decisions in multistate cases, which may have been bearable in more sedentary times, will become less tolerable as long as the volume of international transactions keeps increasing. Why, then, do we cling to the conventional wisdom, the idea that national law must govern international transactions and that all national laws are of equal value? Among the reasons that come to mind there are, first and foremost, the force of habit and the hesitation to deviate from the trodden path. Commenting on the mixed reaction of lawyers and academics to Lord Denning, the late great innovator, a New Zealand judge wrote:

> There is in this paradox between the seemingly genuine admiration for the man and his work and the complacency with which these practitioners then adhere to their orthodoxy, an observable feeling of superiority. It is better, it seems, to belong to the priesthood and conform to its rituals than to carry the cross for justice and relevance in the law.[100]

The priesthood and rituals of private international law are especially prone to discourage unorthodox behavior for their mastery requires novices to make a hefty investment. Moreover, these rituals are less open to challenge on grounds of common sense and reason because they attract speculative minds, whose fascination with this arcane specialty "entails the danger of losing the solid footing of concrete facts and recognized values."[101] This danger also threatens courts and legislatures, who

---

[100] E. W. Thomas, "Lord Denning 1899-1999", (1999) *New Zealand L. J.* 92, 93 (April).
[101] Neuhaus (supra n. 18) at 3.

usually defer to scholars in pursuing the elusive benefits traditional private international law promises to offer. As the recent wave of widely divergent private international law codifications shows, their misguided quest for "decisional harmony" has the perverse effect of further balkanizing private international law. Should we not instead seek to enhance the quality of transnational dispute resolution? Or shall we be forever saddled with methodologies that leave those who expect "to achieve results in multistate cases that are as satisfying in terms of standards of justice and of party acceptability as those reached in purely domestic cases . . . doomed to disappointment"?[102]

---

[102] Arthur Taylor von Mehren, "Choice of Law and the Problem of Justice", 41 *Law and Contemp. Probs.* 27, 42 (Spring 1977).

Distribution Proceedings and Relationships among Creditors in a Comparative Perspective

Konstantinos D. Kerameus[*]

1.   INTRODUCTION

When it comes to an auction of a debtor's assets which have been levied, the proceeds, although they might cover the claim of the enforcing creditor, will very often prove to be insufficient in order to meet the claims of all the creditors. In most cases, the attachment and auction of the debtor's movables or immovables imply a financial situation in which the debtor's assets overall are insufficient to cover his liabilities or, in other words, in which his insolvency has become patently obvious through a sequence of fruitless levies. Such a situation is referred to in France as *de-*

* Dr. iur., Dres.h.c., Professor of Civil Procedure, Athens University School of Law; President, International Academy of Comparative Law. This essay was written while working on the chapter on "Enforcement Proceedings" for the International Encyclopedia of Comparative Law. In preparing the chapter, I have enjoyed the valuable aid of two regional reports by Prof. Stalev (Sofia) and Prof. Vescovi (Montevideo), on European Socialist and Latin American law, respectively.

J. Basedow et al., eds., Private Law in the International Arena – Liber Amicorum Kurt Siehr
© 2000, T.M.C.Asser Press, The Hague, The Netherlands

confiture but does not yet at this point lead to collective enforcement or bankruptcy proceedings.[1]

In material terms, however, the difference may not be so great. In the first place, it often depends on the creditor's decision whether to individually enforce rather than to request the commencement of bankruptcy proceedings, all other conditions having been complied with. Secondly, in some systems bankruptcy proceedings may only be commenced against merchants and commercial entities, so that a non-commercial person, no matter how deeply insolvent he may have become, is only subject to individual enforcement. In such systems, mostly the Romanic ones, there is no complete two-pronged execution mechanism according to the degree of insolvency.

These observations indicate that, in some significant respects, the economic background of debtors subject to individual enforcement or bankruptcy may not be so dissimilar. Hence also the question whether the well-known bankruptcy principle of the equal treatment of creditors may be applicable even in individual enforcement. In fact, some systems, and here again mostly the Romanic ones, do adopt such equal treatment by denying any substantive preference to the creditor who has taken the initiative to enforce. By contrast, other systems adhere to an execution-extended principle of *iura vigilantibus scripta sunt*[2] and either reserve a preferential position for the enforcing creditor or place creditors into groups which are determined by time. In between, all imaginable variations are possible. Part of the difference in approach may indeed be attributed to structural features, e.g., the one just indicated with regard to the admissibility of bankruptcy proceedings against all debtors, commercial and non-commercial alike. A large part of the differences, however, can be attributed to nothing more than arbitrariness. As has been pointed out, "[a]ll priority systems are arbitrary; none can avoid unfairness".[3] Because of this mixture of structural divergence and arbitrary decisions, modern systems of distributing auction proceeds have become increasingly complex.[4]

2.   FRENCH LAW: THE BASICS AND ENFORCEMENT CONCERNING MOVABLES

Even French law, which is generally considered as the outstanding exponent of the equal treatment of creditors, regardless of who is pursuing enforcement, calls for

---

[1] Carbonnier, *Droit civil IV : Droit des obligations*, 16th ed. (Paris 1992) no. 369 at p. 656.

[2] *Iura vigilantibus succurrunt, tarde venientibus ossa*; see Carbonnier, ibid., no. 369b p. 655.

[3] Goode, "The Right to Trace and its Impact in Commercial Transactions", 92 *LQR* (1976) 360-401, 528-568, at p. 568.

[4] See Karlen, *Civil Litigation* (Indianapolis, New York and Charlottesville 1978) 110.

several distinctions and qualifications.[5] In the first place, not only is the successive garnishment of a debtor's claim subject to a special first-in-time rule, but namely the highly relevant division between movables and immovables in France has an important impact on distribution proceedings as well. In fact, the two parts of these proceedings, depending on whether movables or immovables have been sold at public auction, have disjunctively become the object of major legislative reforms over the centuries. Thus, a law of 21 May 1858 replaced Articles 749-779 of the Code of Civil Procedure determining distribution with regard to immovables. A more recent global replacement of the reformed text has not yet entered into force,[6] presumably awaiting the large-scale reform of execution on immovables in general. By contrast, distribution proceedings with regard to movables are now governed by the new rules on enforcement which have been in force since 1 January 1993.[7] In addition to this coexistence of different legislative regimes, even with respect to movables ancient French law recognized the priority of the creditor pursuing enforcement.[8]

In modern times, however, Article 2093 of the Civil Code, after proclaiming that the debtor's assets are his creditors' common security,[9] establishes the rule that the proceeds are distributed among them by contribution unless there are legitimate grounds for priority among the creditors.[10] "Distribution by contribution" is a technical French term implying that the totality of the claims cannot be met by the auction proceeds which have then to be apportioned so that each creditor contributes to the general loss in proportion to his claim.[11] Therefore, execution concerning movables is qualified as bankruptcy in miniature,[12] and no priority is granted to the creditor who has proceeded to enforce.[13] The proportional payment of all concurring claims requires, of course, that the respective creditors have intervened by filing

---

[5] Cf. already Fragistas, *Das Präventionsprinzip in der Zwangsvollstreckung auf rechtsvergleichender Grundlage dargestellt* (Mannheim 1931) 32.

[6] Decree no. 67-167 of 1 March 1967, particularly Art. 25.

[7] Law no. 91-650 of 9 July 1991 [henceforward referred to as: Law], in particular Art. 38, 97; Decree no. 92-755 of 31 July 1992 [henceforward referred to as: Decree], in particular Art. 283-293.

[8] See Fragistas (supra n. 5) 34 with n. 2; cf. Pothier, "Traité de la procédure civile" in: Bugnet (ed.), *Oeuvres de Pothier X* (Paris 1848) no. 513; Josserand, *Précis élémentaire des voies d'exécution*, 3rd ed. (Paris 1925) no. 32 at p. 38 with n. 1.

[9] See Kerameus, *Geldvollstreckungsarten in vergleichender Betrachtung. Festschrift für Albrecht Zeuner* (Tübingen 1994) 389-390.

[10] Like the ones enumerated in Art. 2101, 2102 CC for movables, and Art. 2103-2105 for immovables.

[11] See Carbonnier (supra n. 1) no. 369 p. 656; Vincent and Prévault, *Voies d'exécution et procédures de distribution*, 18th ed. (Paris 1995) no. 495 p. 336 and n. 1, no. 561, who also point to the synonymous expression *au marc le franc*: one franc against one mark which was a unit of weight for gold.

[12] See Fragistas (supra n. 5) 37, 39.

[13] Vincent and Prévault (supra n. 11) no. 260; Id., *Voies d'exécution*, ed. 9 (Mémento Dalloz, Paris 1994) 49 sub II; Fragistas (supra n. 5) 34 at n. 2.

their opposition[14] to the creditor pursuing enforcement for himself. Such opposition has to be made use of before the verification of the assets levied upon[15] and may take three forms:[16] (a) joining in the levy (*adjonction à la première saisie*), whereby the auction will be pursued by the first creditor[17] only; (b) extension of the first levy to other assets (*extension de la première saisie*),[18] which in principle is not affected by the nullity of the first levy;[19] or (c) subrogation in pursuing the enforcement (*subrogation dans les poursuites*).[20]

All these creditors, enforcing and opposing alike, including the ones who have already imposed a preserving attachment in the form of a provisional measure (*saisie conservatoire*),[21] have to be taken into account in drafting, within a month after the auction, the distribution plan (*projet de répartition*).[22] Before the reform of the law of execution all creditors having intervened within a month of the auction date were entitled to participate in the distribution,[23] so that these creditors constituted a first group whose claims would be satisfied first, while later participants were relegated to whatever proceeds might be left over.[24] The legislative reform has granted to all creditors, even to those who have not intervened in time, equal standing to challenge the distribution plan.[25] Nevertheless, the sparse French legal literature maintains that these latecomers are, under the new law as well, limited to the remainder of the proceeds, if any.[26]

3.   FRENCH LAW ON IMMOVABLES

Such a system of bankruptcy-like equal treatment of creditors is restricted to execution concerning movables only. Both in execution concerning immovables and in garnishment, although by virtue of different techniques, French law introduces a sequence for the satisfaction of claims, basically in terms of the time at which the re-

---

[14] Law Art. 50 para. 2.

[15] Law Art. 54; Decree art. 90 sent. 2, 118 para. 2. The new law seems to emulate the system prevailing before the Code of Civil Procedure of 1806 insofar as it allows opposition before the auction; see Vincent and Prévault (supra n. 11) no. 216 p. 161.

[16] See Vincent and Prévault (supra n. 11) no. 260-263.

[17] Law Art. 50 para. 2; Decree Art. 119, in particular para. 3.

[18] Decree Art. 120-122.

[19] Decree Art. 125. See Vincent and Prévault (supra n. 11) no. 262.

[20] Decree Art. 123.

[21] Law Art. 74-76; Decree Art. 220-233, in particular 232-233.

[22] Law Art. 54; Decree Art. 284, 285.

[23] Old CCProc. Art. 656-660; see Vincent and Prévault (supra n. 11) no. 609, 615 with n. 11.

[24] Fragistas (supra n. 5) 34-36.

[25] Decree Art. 286, 288; see Vincent and Prévault (supra n. 11) no. 564-565 p. 383.

[26] Gilles Taormina, *Le nouveau droit des procédures d'exécution et de distribution: Droit et patrimoine*, t. 3 (Paris 1993) 68-73, at p. 70.

spective creditor became active in executing his claim. With regard to immovables, distribution takes the form of the *ordre,* i.e., a classification of the creditors enjoying a special privilege as regards the immovable property or a mortgage.[27] Obviously, no distribution proceedings whatsoever follow if there is only one creditor, and distribution proceeds through contribution rather than through the *ordre* if there are no privileged creditors making a claim on the immovable property.[28] While the priority of privileged creditors reflects the very nature of enforcement preferences and is also valid with regard to movables,[29] with regard to immovables the most important privilege, namely the judicial mortgage (*hypothèque judiciaire*), may be recorded in favor of any creditor whose claim has been established by any judgment, including a default or a provisional judgment; arbitral awards and foreign judgments declared enforceable in France produce the same effect.[30]

Thus, here, the equal treatment of creditors is qualified, or affected, by imposing a real right on the immovable rather than by the imposition of a levy. Such imposition is allowed on any immovable owned by the debtor, even one which has already been levied, up to the time at which the ownership of the immovable passes to the highest bidder.[31] For the rest, distribution through the *ordre* may be conventional (*ordre consensuel*), which is an ordinary contract without any judicial intervention,[32] or amicable (*ordre amiable*), which is proposed by the particular judge dealing with distribution proceedings[33] and has to be accepted by all the creditors.[34] If the attempt at an amicable classification fails, the judge draws up a provisional classification which, on opposition, is reviewed and made final by the multi-member court of first instance (*ordre judiciaire*).[35]

4. FRENCH LAW ON GARNISHMENT

With regard to garnishment, several garnishors of the same debtor's claim against the garnishee are basically paid out in sequence depending on the time when the

---

[27] See the detailed presentations by Vincent and Prévault (supra n. 11) no. 498-555 and Donnier, *Voies d'exécution et procédures de distribution,* 2nd ed. (Paris 1990) no. 1249-1380.

[28] Vincent and Prévault (supra n. 11) no. 495, 2°, no. 498 p. 341 with n. 1; Donnier (supra n. 27) no. 1251, 1255-1257; cf. Cour Paris 28 Oct. 1994, D.S. (1995) 347, 348, annotation Prévault .

[29] See CC Art. 2093 (text at supra n. 10).

[30] CC Art. 2123 para. 1, 2; see Fragistas (supra n. 5) 43-44 and n. 4-6.

[31] See CC Art. 2123 para. 3; Fragistas (supra n. 5) 33 sub 3, 43-44.

[32] Vincent and Prévault (supra n. 11) no. 503.

[33] CCProc. (old) Art. 749: *juge aux ordres*; see Vincent and Prévault (supra n. 11) no. 496, 4°, 516, 2°; Donnier (supra n. 27) no. 1245, 1281-1286.

[34] CCProc. (old) Art. 750, 751; see Vincent and Prévault (supra n. 11) no. 509, 515, 516.

[35] CCProc. (old) Art. 756, 758, 761, 762, 764, 765; see Vincent and Prévault (supra n. 11) no. 529-534; Donnier (supra n. 27) no. 1337-1354. With respect to conflicts see Remery, "L'ordre entre créanciers et la distribution par contribution en droit international privé", Gaz. Pal. 1989.II.D.654.

garnishors lodged their claim. Under the old Code of Civil Procedure, since garnishment required nothing more than documentary evidence of the garnishor's claim against the debtor, a judicial confirmation of garnishment was necessary.[36] At the time of confirmation and by its very nature the garnished claim, if a monetary one, was presumed to have been assigned to the garnishor;[37] such assignment was no longer affected by any ulterior garnishments.[38] In substance, the same rules have been adopted by the new law dealing with garnishment which is now called *saisie-attribution*.[39]

However, since garnishment now requires an enforceable instrument,[40] the judicial confirmation has been eliminated, and priority is granted to the garnishor from the time of service on the garnishee.[41] Exceptions are admitted as far as garnishments served on the same day[42] or garnishments of wages[43] are concerned, in which cases the principle of equal treatment again becomes applicable. Other than these exceptions, the principle of priority in favor of the first garnishor has again been clearly established[44] after a vehement legislative and doctrinal debate.[45] Since, however, the previous law was not substantially different, the resulting discord should be attributed to the declaration of the priority principle *in conjunction with the abolition of judicial confirmation* rather than to the priority of the first garnishor as such.

In any event, French law in both instances – execution concerning immovables and the garnishment of money claims – departs in fact (in the first case) or in law (in the second case) from the principle of equal treatment through the means of substantive rather than procedural law: by allowing any judgment to function as a title to mortgages and by construing garnishment as an immediate and automatic assignment of the claim. Such techniques might have made the introduced exceptions to the principle of *par condicio creditorum* more palatable since they refer to legitimate substantive evaluations[46] rather than to traditional procedural axioms.

---

[36] CCProc. (old) Art. 557, 563, 568, 579.

[37] Cass.civ. 15 Jan. 1923, D.P. 1925.1.183; Cass.civ. 2me 5 Dec. 1984, Gaz. Pal.1985 Som. 141, annotation Véron.

[38] Cass.req. 14 Fev. 1899, D.P. 1899.1.227; Cass.civ. 6 July 1899, D.P. 1900.1.483-485. Cf. Fragistas (supra n. 5) 40-41.

[39] Law Art. 42-43.

[40] Law Art. 42; See Vincent and Prévault (supra n. 11) no. 143 para. 1, 1°, no. 151 sub 7, 4°.

[41] Law Art. 43 para. 1, 2.

[42] Law Art. 43 para. 3.

[43] Labor Code (Law no. 73-4 of 2 Jan. 1973) Art. L. 145-7, introduced by Law no. 91-650 of 9 July 1991 Art. 49; see Taormina (supra n. 26) 73.

[44] The same principle is also extended to preserving the garnishment of a monetary claim in the form of a provisional measure; within its set amount, such a garnishment does not allow a second one to be made: Law Art. 75 para. 1-2; see Vincent and Prévault (supra n. 11) no. 311.

[45] Vincent and Prévault, ibid., no. 145 pp. 108-109 and the references at n. 2.

[46] Already mentioned in CC Art. 2093 (text at supra n. 10).

5.   OTHER ROMANIC LEGAL SYSTEMS

Other Romanic systems basically follow the same principles as French law. Thus, in Italy all creditors, even without an enforceable instrument or a mature claim,[47] may join in the proceedings[48] and share proportionally in the distribution of proceeds.[49] While only secured creditors have priority in the distribution of proceeds,[50] such priority is also granted to a judgment creditor insofar as he records a mortgage based on this judgment.[51] In general, the similarity to the distribution of bankruptcy proceeds is salient.[52] Priorities, to the extent that they are provided for, usually pass the test of constitutionality.[53] Belgian law also knows the distinction between distribution through the *ordre*[54] and distribution through contribution,[55] and adheres to the principle of the equal treatment of creditors.[56] Therefore, both the collective aspects of the levy[57] and the increased publicity of the latter[58] are stressed as methods of securing distribution by contribution in the widest possible terms. Similarly, in the Netherlands the principle of treating creditors equally is adhered to, subject to the exception of certain privileges[59] and the priority granted to mortgagees and pledgees.[60]

Finally, this issue became controversial during the elaboration of the new Japanese Civil Execution Law.[61] The old Code of Civil Procedure (1890), although strongly influenced by the German ZPO of 1877, deliberately followed, with regard

---

[47] CCProc. Art. 563 para. 1.

[48] CCProc. Art. 499.

[49] CC art. 2741 para. 1. See Cappelletti and Perillo, *Civil Procedure in Italy* (The Hague 1965) 327.

[50] CC Art. 2741 para. 2.

[51] CC Art. 2808 para. 1, 2818-2820.

[52] See Proto Pisani, *Lezioni di diritto processuale civile*, ed. 2 (Naples 1996) 803-804; cf. Zanzucchi-Vocino, *Diritto processuale III: Del processo di esecuzione*, ed. 5 (Milan 1964) 70-74, with historical and comparative remarks.

[53] Cf., e.g., Corte Cost. no. 25 of 15 Febr. 1984, *Foro it.* 1984, I, col. 1803-1813, annotation Tucci; id., "Il diritto dei privilegi di fronte al principio di uguaglianza costituzionale", ibid., col. 647-655.

[54] Judicial Code Art. 1639-1654.

[55] Ibid., Art. 1627-1638.

[56] De Leval, *Traité des saisies (règles générales)* (Liège 1988) no. 105 p. 208 at n. 837.

[57] De Leval, ibid., no. 105-118, in particular no. 105-108.

[58] See Krings, *Les saisies conservatoires et les voies d'exécution*, Faculté de Droit de l'Université de Liège, Étude du projet de Code judiciaire (Liège and The Hague 1966) 139-140; JudC Art. 1627 para. 2 allows the bailiff to invite even "all third parties pretending to be creditors" to present their claims with supporting documents.

[59] Both the old CC Art. 1185, 1195 (as well as some tax statutes) and the new CC Book 3 Art. 277 para.1, 283-289.

[60] See Koopmans, *International Encyclopedia of Comparative Law I: National Reports*, N-19 sub 7; now new CC Art. 278 para. 1.

[61] Law no. 4 (1979): *Minzi Shikkō Hō*, effective on 1 Oct. 1980.

to the equal satisfaction of creditors, the French Civil Code.[62] When drafting the new law on enforcement, some voices regretted the resulting delay and complication in connection with the equality principle in distribution and would have preferred to have it replaced by the more expeditious priority principle following the German pattern.[63] In the end, the new law again adopted the equality principle; some restrictions were, however, introduced with regard to the time-limits for presenting claims for satisfaction from the auction proceeds.[64]

6. SOCIALIST LEGAL SYSTEMS

In general, these systems follow the pattern of Romanic countries, however with some deviations.[65] Creditors other than the enforcing one, if they are equipped with an enforceable instrument, may on their application join in in the enforcement.[66] Besides, some specified creditors are presumed to join in *ex lege*, e.g., the creditor with a lien on the attached property, or the one in whose favor a preserving levy or garnishment has been imposed on the attached property as a security for his claim;[67] in Bulgaria such a creditor is even the State in order to recover taxes.[68] The joinder can be effectuated until the distribution plan is announced. As a rule, the joined creditor has the same rights in the enforcement proceedings as the creditor who has initiated them;[69] only in the former German Democratic Republic was the latter allowed priority in the satisfaction of his claim.[70] The distribution plan is prepared by the enforcement officer, in the former Czechoslovakia by the court, while in the former

[62] Nakamura, *Einführung in das japanische Zivilprozessrecht: Die japanische ZPO in deutscher Sprache* (transl. by H. Nakamura and B. Huber, Cologne 1978) 1, 22, 23.
[63] Hattori and Henderson, *Civil Procedure in Japan* (New York 1985) §11-4; Mikazuki, *Kyōsei shikkō ni okeru byōdō-shugi no seisei* (Origins of the principle of equality in compulsory execution): *Saibanhō no shomondai* 3 (1970) 201-294.
[64] Art. 49, 51, 87, 140, 165. See Hattori and Henderson (supra n. 63) § 11-4; Iseki and Higashi, *Civil Execution* in: Kitagawa (ed.), *Doing Business in Japan* VII (New York 1989) XIV 6-26, 6-35, 6-36, 6-41.
[65] See, in general, Dobrzanski, Lisiewski, Resich and Siedlecki, *Kodeks postepowania cywilnego, Komentarz II* (Warsaw 1969) 1311-1330; Wengerek, *Sadowe postepowanie egzekucyjne w sprawach cywilnych*, 2nd ed. (Warsaw 1978) 220-224; Stalev, *Bulgarsko grazhdansko protsessualno pravo*, 3rd ed. (Sofia 1979) 634-639; Nemeth, *Die aktuelle Entwicklung des Rechts der Zwangsvollstreckung in Ungarn* (Budapest 1983) 31-32.
[66] Ger. East ZPO § 105, 125; Czech. CCProc. § 316, 317; Polon. CCProc. Art. 1030, 1035; Bulg. CCProc. Art. 350; RSFSR CCProc. Art. 417.
[67] Bulg. CCProc. Art. 354; Polon. CCProc. Art. 1030, 1035.
[68] Bulg. CCProc. Art. 353.
[69] Cf. Bulg. CCProc. Art. 351.
[70] Ger. East ZPO § 105 para. 2, § 125 para. 1 with the qualification that several levies on the same day are satisfied in proportion to their amount.

RSFSR it had to be confirmed by the court.[71] That country also offered a typical example of the distribution order including the following privileged claims:[72]

A. For alimony, wages, copyright, personal injuries, after which came claims for social security.

B. For taxes and other payments in favor of the Treasury.

C. Of State credit institutions from credit transactions not secured by a lien.

D. Of Socialist organizations not secured by a lien.

E. All other claims.

Secured claims, if advanced by State credit institutions, come between the first and second order, otherwise between the second and third order.[73] Creditors belonging to the same order are satisfied in proportion to their amount.[74]

7.   IBERIAN AND LATIN AMERICAN SYSTEMS

Under both the Iberian and Latin American systems, distribution issues seem neither to have met with extensive legislative treatment nor to have become particularly relevant in practice. In general, both Spanish[75] and Portuguese[76] law deny to the enforcing creditor any real lien on the thing levied upon but they do grant him a right of priority in the distribution of the proceeds. In the legal literature, this priority right is cursorily qualified as an "exclusively temporary" one which "does not alter the nature" of the enforcing creditor's claim,[77] but the obvious meaning of such a qualification is that priority only pertains to the distribution, without requiring or allowing a lien on the thing attached as such.

A similar priority has been adopted by several Latin American systems,[78] including Argentina,[79] and this recently found global expression in the Ibero-American Model Code. Under its Article 327.2, the auction proceeds are distributed in the following way: (1) judicial costs and expenses; (2) auction expenses and the enforcing creditor's legal expenses; (3) the enforcing creditor's claim, subject to the existence

---

[71] CCProc. Art. 427.

[72] Ibid., Art. 419-424.

[73] Ibid., Art. 424.

[74] Czech. CCProc. § 332 para. 2; Bulg. CCProc. Art. 355.

[75] Ramos Méndez, *Derecho procesal civil*, 5th ed. (Barcelona 1992) II Ch. 71.1 d p. 1049, cf. also Ch. 72 V 4 pp. 1093-1094.

[76] Dos Reis, *Processo de execucaõ* 3rd ed. (Coimbra reprint 1985) II 106 sub a; cf., in general, Luis Gonçalves, "Privilégios creditórios. Evolução historica. Regime. Sua inserção no tráfico creditício", 67 *Bol. Fac. Coimbra* (1991) 29-46.

[77] Ramos Méndez (supra n. 75) II Ch. 71.1 d p. 1049.

[78] *Vescovi Report* 26.

[79] Rodríquez, *Tratado de la ejecución* (Buenos Aires 1984) I 138ff.

of preferred claims; (4) claims of other enforcing creditors in the order of their registration; (5) the remainder goes to the debtor. No explanation is offered in the statement of reasons for this particular order of distribution.[80] It should be added,
however, that if the proceeds are insufficient to meet all the claims then bankruptcy
proceedings are often resorted to,[81] which in some countries is made easier due to
the possible bankruptcy of non-commercial persons as well.[82]

8.   THE GERMAN AND AUSTRIAN PRIORITY PRINCIPLE

German law is generally considered as a system which, rather than introducing the
equal treatment of all creditors in case of enforcement against their common debtor,
determines their satisfaction according to the point in time at which each one
attached the particular asset of the debtor. Hence its qualification as a priority
princi-ple[83] or system: *prior tempore potior iure*. Technically, the principle has
been established by determining[84] that the creditor acquires a lien on the attached
items by means of the actual attachment; this lien secures for the creditor in relation
to other creditors the same rights as a pledge acquired by contract, including
preferential treatment in the case of bankruptcy; finally, since further attachments
are not prevented, a lien based on an earlier attachment has precedence over those
based on a later one.

To be sure, the legislative concept of the levy as a creation of a lien is not
regarded as an indispensable element of the system since the main practical
consequence of the lien here is the preference granted to the enforcing creditor

---

[80] *El codigo procesal civil modelo para Iberoamerica. Texto del anteproyecto* (ed. by the Instituto Iberoamericano de Derecho Procesal, Montevideo 1988) p. 82.

[81] Cf. *Vescovi Report* 26.

[82] As in Brazil: CCProc. Art. 748ff., in particular Art. 786; See H.-J. Henckel, *Zivilprozess und Justizalternativen in Brasilien. Recht, Rechtspraxis, Rechtstatsachen – Versuch einer Beschreibung* (Frankfurt a.M.) 105; cf. Barbosa Moreira, "Brazilian Civil Procedure: An Overview", in: Dolinger and Rosenn (eds.), *A Panorama of Brazilian Law* (University of Miami 1992) 183, 199 the text following the reference to n. 111.

[83] In the past the principle was called in German *Präventionsprinzip*, which implied that subsequently enforcing creditors were prevented from being satisfied as long as a previous creditor was not; cf. Fragistas (supra n. 5) 7, 80; today still Blomeyer, *Zivilprozessrecht. Vollstreckungsverfahren* (Berlin, Heidelberg and New York 1975) 328-330. Nowadays the term *Prioritätsprinzip* seems to be equally used, highlighting the time element that is inherent in the principle; cf. Baur and Stürner, *Zwangsvollstreckungs-, Konkurs- und Vergleichsrecht*, 12th ed. (Heidelberg 1995) no. 6.37-6.43, 27.16; Jauernig, *Zwangsvollstreckungs- und Insolvenzrecht* (Munich 1996) §16 IV; also Rosenberg, Gaul and Schilken, *Zwangsvollstreckungsrecht*, 11th ed. (Munich 1997) §50 III 3 e, §59 I; Stein, Jonas and Münzberg, *Kommentar zur Zivilprozessordnung* VI, 21st ed. (Tübingen 1995) 804 no. 38; Bruns and Peters, *Zwangsvollstreckungsrecht. Eine systematische Darstellung*, 3rd ed. (Munich 1987) 128-129, 219.

[84] ZPO § 804. See Blomeyer (supra n. 83) 173-177; Rosenberg, Gaul and Schilken (supra n. 83) §50 III p. 586-597; Stein, Jonas and Münzberg (supra n. 83) §804 no. 38, 39.

during the distribution of proceeds, and such preference could also have been immediately granted without resorting to the form of the lien.[85] Nevertheless, this form has been part of German law for well over a century and, although it was introduced in 1877 in contrast to most older German legal systems,[86] it has by now been deeply enshrined in German legal thinking up to the point where it is often viewed as self-explanatory or obvious. An older leading author wrote that "the entire further enforcement is described as the realization of the lien created through the attachment".[87]

For the distribution of proceeds, German law thus abides by the sequence of attachments. It arranges such priority as a consequence of a private law lien on the thing attached, and it establishes this lien by means of a public law act which is the attachment itself. Amidst the indicated private and public law points of reference a whole range of theories have been put forward concerning the qualification of the lien.[88] In general, the lien is construed as a right which is accessory to the main claim and dependent both upon it and upon the debtor's ownership of the object attached; however, such conditions determining the validity and the consequences of the lien can only be challenged within the time-limits and the other constraints provided by the law of enforcement.[89]

In Germany itself the priority principle came under attack from two points of view. First, the 1931 reform project of the Code of Civil Procedure attempted, following the Swiss pattern,[90] to reduce the relevance of the time element by assigning all creditors attaching the same thing within ten days to a particular group. While all the creditors within that group would be equally satisfied, the priority principle would only apply among the groups, so that the random factor would be limited to group-borderlines.[91] The project never reached fruition, however, and the post-World War II attempts at reform never seemed to touch upon this subject again. The second criticism was rather *de lege lata* and maintained that the priority principle does not conform to constitutional equality.[92] This notion was not generally shared

---

[85] See Stein, Jonas and Münzberg (supra n. 83) §804 no. 1 with n. 3; Fragistas (supra n. 5) 7 with n. 18. Cf., however, Gilliéron, *Poursuite pour dettes, faillite et concordat* (Lausanne 1988) 29 sub b.

[86] Stein, Jonas and Münzberg (supra n. 83) §804 no. 1 with n. 1.

[87] Goldschmidt, *Zivilprozessrecht*, 2nd ed. (Berlin 1932) §94, 1.

[88] See Blomeyer (supra n. 83) 173-177; Rosenberg, Gaul and Schilken (supra n. 83) §50 III 3 a-c, pp. 586-595; Baur and Stürner (supra n. 83) no. 27.7-27.15; Stein, Jonas and Münzberg (supra n. 83) §804 no. 1a-5; Jauernig (supra n. 83) §16 III p. 70-75; Bruns and Peters (supra n. 83) §20 III pp. 124-132.

[89] Blomeyer (supra n. 83) 176-177; Rosenberg, Gaul and Schilken (supra n. 83) §50 III 3 b pp. 591-594; Baur and Stürner (supra n. 83) no. 27.12, 27.13; Stein, Jonas and Münzberg (supra n. 83) §804 no. 4 n. 15; Jauernig (supra n. 83) §16 III C 1 pp. 72-73; Bruns and Peters (supra n. 83) §20 III 2 d, e at pp. 129-131.

[90] See the text at infra section 9.

[91] See Jauernig (supra n. 83) §16 IV p. 76.

[92] Schlosser, "Vollstreckungsrechtliches Prioritätsprinzip und verfassungsrechtlicher Gleichheitssatz", 97 ZZP (1984) 121-138.

either,[93] partly because of the fact that the priority principle is deeply established and partly because it is often considered in connection with private law autonomy.[94]

The priority principle is also followed in the two other types of enforcement concerning the debtor's assets, namely enforcement as regards immovables and garnishment, although here the comparative interest is considerably reduced since these types of enforcement are governed by priority-oriented rules even under the otherwise egalitarian Romanic legal systems.[95] As far as immovables are concerned, real rights established before the attachment are to be satisfied first; the enforcing creditor has precedence over subsequently created real rights; among several enforcing creditors the time when attachment is made is decisive.[96] With regard to garnishment, claims are treated like movables: the garnishor acquires a lien on the claim garnished; additional garnishment of the same claim by other creditors is allowed, but the time at which each creditor has made use of the garnishment determines the precedence,[97] although the lien on the claim only matures (*Pfandreife*) after judicial confirmation of the garnishment.[98]

Austrian law equally adheres to the priority principle and offers no significant deviations from German law with respect to the distribution of the auction proceeds or the compulsory administration proceeds.[99]

9.   SWISS LAW

By contrast, Swiss law, as has already been indicated,[100] chose a middle of the road solution. While each canton has its own Code of Civil Procedure, including rules on enforcement as well, exceptionally with regard to the enforcement of money claims there has been in effect, for over a century now, a Federal Act on the enforcement and bankruptcy proceedings of 11 April 1889 (SchKG).[101] The conflict between the

---

[93] See the extensive response by Stürner, "Prinzipien der Einzelzwangsvollstreckung", 99 *ZZP* (1986) 291, 322-329.

[94] See Rosenberg, Gaul and Schilken (supra n. 83) §5 VI 4 e at pp. 52-53; Jauernig (supra n. 83) §16 IV p. 75; Blomeyer (supra n. 83) §70 II: "alertness of the first enforcing creditor".

[95] See supra sections 3 and 4.

[96] *Gesetz über die Zwangsversteigerung und die Zwangsverwaltung* of 24 March 1897 (hereinafter referred to as ZVG) 10, 11. See Rosenberg, Gaul and Schilken (supra n. 83) §67; Jauernig (supra n. 83) §22 IV 4; Blomeyer (supra n. 83) §83.

[97] Blomeyer (supra n. 83) 229-233; Rosenberg, Gaul and Schilken (supra n. 83) §55 I 3 a at pp. 649-650; Jauernig (supra n. 83) §19 V 5, 7; Stein, Jonas and Münzberg (supra n. 83) §829 no. 124.

[98] Blomeyer (supra n. 83) §55 III.

[99] See Rechberger and Simotta, *Exekutionsverfahren* (Vienna 1992) no. 439, in particular sub e, g, 546, 569-576, 641 sub 3, 661, 665-667.

[100] See text at supra n. 90.

[101] *Bundesgesetz über Schuldbetreibung und Konkurs* of 11 April 1889 (henceforward referred to as SchKG) Art. 8.

individual collection of money judgments with priority recognized to the enforcing creditor, on the one hand, and bankruptcy proceedings for the administration of insolvent estates subject to the equal treatment of all creditors, on the other, occupied the legal debate in Switzerland during the 1870's and 1880's and finally led to the compromise solution adopted by the SchKG in 1889.[102]

The compromise consists of determining groups of creditors:[103] while the groups are classified in relation to time and thus obey the priority principle, within each group all creditors are treated equally. Each group includes all the creditors who have requested attachment within thirty days after the first attachment; for some privileged creditors, such as spouses and children, this period is extended to forty days.[104] An item already attached can be re-attached, however not for the benefit of the creditors belonging to a previous group since the following groups will receive nothing anyway unless all the previous groups have been fully satisfied.[105] Within each group and depending on the total amount of registered claims, the Enforcement Office is allowed to proceed to a supplementary levy (*Ergänzungspfändung*) in an attempt to meet all the claims.[106]

This group system has been qualified as "one of the most original creations of the law".[107] By considerably reducing the incentive for the creditors to catch the first attachment, it brought about a certain moderate solution which seems to comply with Swiss mentality, and to avoid giving rise to disputed issues or decisions of the Federal Tribunal.[108] Nevertheless critical voices have also been heard, particularly with regard to the accommodation of diverging interests within each group.[109]

10. ENGLISH LAW

English law, while it has no general principle under which the auction proceeds are to be distributed, nevertheless adopts, as a matter of obvious precedence in time, the rule that if several writs are delivered to the sheriff by different judgment creditors for execution against the same judgment debtor, he must execute them in the correct

---

[102] A good description of the legislative history is offered by Fritzsche and Walder, *Schuldbetreibung und Konkurs nach schweizerischem Recht*, 3rd ed., I (Zurich 1984) §2 pp. 12-21, §27 no. 1. On this particular issue see Fragistas (supra n. 5) 59-62; cf. Röhrig, *Prioritäts- oder Ausgleichsprinzip in der Zwangsvollstreckung (mit besonderer Berücksichtigung des schweizerischen Rechts)* (thesis Leipzig 1933).

[103] SchKG Art. 100, 101.

[104] Ibid., Art. 101. See Fritzsche and Walder (supra n. 102) §27 no. 12-30.

[105] SchKG Art. 100 para. 3. See BGE 61 III 85; Fritzsche and Walder (supra n. 102) §27 no. 8.

[106] Fritzsche and Walder (supra n. 102) §27 no. 6.

[107] Ibid., §27 no. 1.

[108] Ibid., §27 no. 1 p. 390, no. 31 p. 401.

[109] Cf. ibid., §27 no. 31 p. 402, §32 no. 13-23 on drafting and challenging the distribution plan (*Kollokationsplan*).

order, according to the day and hour at which each was delivered to him.[110] If, however, the sheriff interchanges writs and first executes the later one, the purchaser ob-
tains good title and the money must be handed to the creditor whose writ was executed.[111] Finally, if several writs have to be executed against the same debtor, the
sheriff need not make separate seizures, but one seizure inures for the benefit of all
in order of priority.[112] Based on such cases, modern doctrine admits that if the debtor's assets are not sufficient to meet all his debts, the several creditors are treated
on a first-come, first-served basis.[113] If, however, administration orders have been
granted, then the several creditors are paid *pari passu*.[114] In any event, the costs of
execution enjoy first priority, so "that the process of execution should be regarded
as more important than the process of satisfying the judgment creditor and producing for him the fruits of execution".[115]

Characteristically, this system is described in England as a system of equal treatment. The Payne Report[116] maintains that "[u]nder the present system of enforcement each judgment creditor ranks equally with the others irrespective of the origin
and nature of his debt". Equality is here perceived in the fact that each creditor "pursues his own course", retains for his own benefit whatever proceeds he may recover
as a result of his own enforcement process and, conversely, "no particular judgment
creditor has any claim to any proceeds recovered by another judgment creditor".[117]
In fact, it is a "disjointed"[118] rather than an equal system of enforcement, whereby it
is assumed that all further qualifications, such as "equal" or "preferential" treatment
of creditors, require an integrated machinery of enforcement[119] like the one suggested by the Payne Committee.

Within this integrated system the above Committee basically submitted three
proposals: First, they assessed the need for the priority of debts, since "the character
or origin of the debt should not be lost in the judgment".[120] Second, they would, although not completely satisfied with the present system of priorities recognized in

---

[110] *Guest* v. *Cowbridge Rly Co* (1868) LR 6 Eq. 619. See Halsbury, *The Laws of England*, 4th ed.
XVII (London 1976) sub Execution para. 439 n. 1.

[111] *Rybot* v. *Peckham* (1778) 1 Term Rep. 731 n; *Payne* v. *Drewe* (1804) 4 East 523. See Halsbury
(supra n. 110) sub Execution para. 439 n. 7.

[112] *Re Henderson, ex parte Shaw* (1884) W.N. 60 (C.A.); *Re Hille India Rubber (no. 2)* (1897)
W.N. 20. See Halsbury (supra n. 110) sub Execution para. 439 n. 10.

[113] Nash, *Civil Procedure. Cases and Text* (Sydney 1976) 424; White, *The Adminisration of Justice*, 2nd ed. (Oxford 1991) 215-216; Black, *Enforcement of a Judgment*, 8th ed. (London 1992) 55.

[114] Jacob, *The Enforcement of Judgment Debts* (London 1982) 297; White (supra n. 113) 215-216.

[115] Jacob (supra n. 114) 291.

[116] *Report of the Committee on the Enforcement of Judgment Debts* (Cmnd. 3909 London 1969;
hereinafter *the Payne Report*), para. 1109.

[117] Ibid.

[118] Ibid., para. 1110.

[119] Ibid., para. 1109, 1110, 1111(c), 1112, 1137(1).

[120] Ibid., para. 1112, 1137(1).

bankruptcy, introduce them to the new enforcement system as well, because otherwise creditors might resort to bankruptcy in order to obtain preferential treatment which they could not have in individual enforcement.[121] And third, as among non-preferential creditors, it has been proposed to allow them a share in moneys received after each has made his application for enforcement.[122] Conversely, no judgment creditor will share in the moneys received before he has made his application.[123] The result of such a rule would be a rush towards enforcement,[124] but such a rush in fact already exists under present English law.[125] The Payne Committee regarded this as "an inevitable result of a fair shares system".[126] In fact, it is a particular "group system", classifying all the creditors according to the day on which they applied for enforcement.[127] But it is, in contrast to the Swiss system of thirty-day creditor groups,[128] very much an open-ended system in that all the applicant creditors share in the benefit of all future payments into the Enforcement Office, but to none made before this. Interestingly, even preferential creditors should follow the same rule by enjoying priority as regards the moneys only to be received from that time onwards.[129]

11. AMERICAN LAW

In the United States[130] the availability of, and the consequences from, a judgment lien govern most issues of distribution. In most jurisdictions a judgment creates a lien on the real estate of the judgment debtor in the county where it is docketed or recorded;[131] in Louisiana money judgments create judicial mortgages[132] following the French example.[133] Both the judgment lien and the judicial mortgage also extend to subsequently acquired real property.[134] The lien comes into existence at the moment when the judgment is docketed: "It is the docketing of the judgment that crea-

---

[121] Ibid., para. 1117, 1118, 1137(2).

[122] Ibid., para. 1133.

[123] Ibid.

[124] Ibid.

[125] See text at supra n. 110, 111.

[126] *Payne Report*, para. 1133.

[127] Ibid., para. 1134, 1137(11).

[128] See text at supra n. 103-105.

[129] *Payne Report* para. 1126, 1137(9); see also para. 1128, 1137(10).

[130] The following account is based on Riesenfeld, *Cases and Materials on Creditors' Remedies and Debtors' Protection*, 4th ed. (St. Paul, Minn. 1987) at pp. 89-91, 120-123, 149-151, 154-155, 168-172.

[131] Ibid., 89.

[132] La. CC Art. 3299, 3300, 3302-3306, 3330.

[133] See text at supra n. 30, 31.

[134] See, in particular, *Zink* v. *James River Nat. Bank*, 58 N.D. 1, 224 N.W. 901 (Supreme Court of N.D., 1929); Riesenfeld (supra n. 130) 120-123.

tes the lien; not the issuance of, or levy under, an execution. The execution is the remedy for the enforcement of the lien, but does not create the lien".[135] Senior liens
enjoy priority over junior ones. Subsequently acquired property automatically becomes subject to an existing judicial lien at the moment of acquisition; if, therefore,
several judgments against the same defendant have been docketed, they create liens
on subsequently acquired property at the same time, i.e., the time of acquisition, and
enjoy equal ranking in this respect.[136]

With regard to movables, the lien is created by either the delivery of a writ of execution to the sheriff or, in a growing number of jurisdictions, by the actual levy
rather than by the judgment itself.[137] Here again the lien equally extends to chattels
which are acquired by the judgment debtor after the delivery of the writ and prior to
its return date.[138] Article 9 of the Uniform Commercial Code protects creditors who
acquire a lien on the collateral by judicial process after the attachment of a security
interest and prior to its perfection.[139] However, applicable state law still determines
at what time the crucial lien is acquired (delivery of the writ, or the actual levy).[140,141]

12.   COMPARATIVE CONCLUSION

The problem of how the auction proceeds are to be distributed among several creditors has on a few occasions been dealt with from a comparative viewpoint, mainly
with regard to the juxtaposition "equal treatment of creditors" versus "priority in
terms of time".[142] Indeed this is one of the two issues within the whole area of enforcement proceedings that have so far aroused the interest of comparatists, the other
one being the methods of enforcing non-money judgments.[143] Particularly the pro-

---

[135] *Zink* v. *James River Nat. Bank*, ibid.

[136] Ibid.

[137] Riesenfeld (supra n. 130) 149-150. By way of exception, only in three states (Alabama, Georgia
and Mississippi) the governing statutes provide that a *judgment* creates a lien upon the debtor's chattels:
Riesenfeld (supra n. 130) 150-151 with n. 44-48.

[138] Ibid., 154 note 2.

[139] UCC §9-301(1)b, (3).

[140] See text at supra n. 137.

[141] See Riesenfeld (supra n. 130) 171-172.

[142] See Fragistas (supra n. 5) *passim*, in particular 67-84; Association des procéduralistes grecs
(ed.), *Rapports et procès-verbaux du IV Congrès International d'Athènes pour la procédure civile du
mois de septembre 1967* (Athens 1972) 343-432 (reports by Liebmann, de Miguel, Derrida, Devis
Echandia, Fasching, Kuru, Larsson and H. Smit), 554-607 (general discussion); cf. also Behr,
*Wertverfolgung. Rechtsvergleichende Überlegungen zur Abgrenzung kollidierender Gläubiger-
interessen* (Frankfurt a.M. 1986), however mostly in connection to bankruptcy, e.g., 67-110, 348-358,
591-615.

[143] See Jacobsson and Jacob (eds.), *Trends in the Enforcement of Non-money Judgments and Or-*

blem of distribution has been regarded as an important field of conflict between collective and individual aspects in the realization of private claims.

Nowadays the relevance and impact of the subject seem to have been reduced on two counts: first, part of the problem has to be attributed to a kind of legal semantics. We have seen[144] that the present English system is qualified as a system of equal treatment of creditors, although elsewhere it would be considered as a pure system of preference accorded to the first enforcing creditor. The reason for this dissonance lies in understanding equality: in England it implies equality of opportunity, on the European Continent it means a *pro rata* distribution of actual proceeds. Second, the *pro rata* distribution among all the creditors, even under the Romanic systems which have always been the traditional supporters of this principle, only in fact applies to the execution as regards movables.[145] By contrast, the execution concerning immovables and garnishment both introduce, although by means of different techniques, a sequence of satisfaction, basically in terms of time. Since garnishment covers by far the largest number of enforcement cases,[146] the relevance of execution as regards movables has been accordingly diminished. Therefore, the field in which the opposite systems actually conflict now has a considerably reduced impact, as compared to the past, within the whole area of enforcement. It should perhaps be added that an attempt at reviving the old controversy by subjecting it to constitutional standards of equality has apparently failed.[147] It is for the ordinary legislature, exempt from constitutional constraints, to opt for the one solution or the other.

This choice, no matter how free it may be, depends, as the review of the various legal families has shown, on certain parameters. Three such parameters deserve special mention from an organizational, technical and systematic point of view. *Organizationally*, any attempt to introduce either the *pro rata* satisfaction of several creditors or the consideration of preferences requires an integrated system of enforcement. If each creditor disparately pursues his own course without a central channeling of such individual endeavors, the very framework for any evaluation of conflicting creditors' claims is missing, and the solution would necessarily be to leave each creditor to retain for himself the fruits of his own application. English law, both in its present shape and in the recommendations by the Payne Committee,[148] proves this statement. On the other hand, systems which allow several credi-

---

ders. The First International Colloquium on the Law of Civil Procedure (June 1985) (Faculty of Law, University of Lund; Deventer 1988); Remien, *Rechtsverwirklichung durch Zwangsgeld* (Tübingen 1994); Scholtz, *Naturalexekution in skandinavischen Rechten* (Berlin 1995).

[144] See text at supra n. 116-119.

[145] The characteristic situation under French law is described supra sub 3 and 4.

[146] Blomeyer (supra n. 83) §56 I at p. 245; Jauernig (supra n. 83) §19 IX; Rechberger and Simotta (supra n. 99) no. 567 p. 307; Lindblom, "Procedure" in: Strömholm (ed.), *An Introduction to Swedish Law* I (Deventer 1981) 95-132, 130; Jacob (supra n. 114) 294.

[147] See, for German law, the text at supra n. 92-94.

[148] Cf. White (supra n. 113) 218.

tors consecutively to levy the same assets of a common debtor and which, contemporaneously, grant priority by the sequence of levies resort to the *technical* instrument of establishing a lien on the asset levied upon for the creditor's benefit rather than to depend uniquely on the course of time. Both German and American law, no matter how different they may be in other respects, demonstrate that a kind of automatic right *in rem* usually goes hand in hand with the preferential treatment of the first enforcing creditor: time alone is not regarded as a sufficient ground for granting priority to the creditors depending on the sequence of their levies.

Finally, the organizational point of view mentioned earlier leads to a convergent *systematic* one. The degree of *systematic* integration required for any mutual collation of several creditors' claims culminates in bankruptcy proceedings or, for that matter, in an administration order. To the extent that these insolvency mechanisms apply to everyone, merchant and non-merchant alike, the respective legal system may well adopt the priority principle in individual enforcement;[149] in such a case, every creditor, regardless of the commercial qualification of the debtor, may request his bankruptcy and, thus, at the end of the day will allow the principle of *par condicio creditorum* to prevail. Conversely, if only merchants are subject to bankruptcy, it is hardly possible for the respective legal system not to allow, at least as far as non-commercial debtors are concerned, all creditors to announce their claims and to expect *pro rata* satisfaction.[150] In such systems the equal treatment of creditors is but a functional equivalent of the missing availability of declaring non-commercial debtors bankrupt.

---

[149] Cf. Rosenberg, Gaul and Schilken (supra n. 83) 5 VI 4 e p. 53 text at note 117.
[150] See Vincent and Prévault (supra n. 11) no. 260.

La Convention de Rome du 19 juin 1980 sur la loi applicable aux obligations contractuelles – Vingt ans après

Catherine Kessedjian[*]

N'ayant pas le talent d'Alexandre Dumas, nous n'allons pas faire revivre pour nos lecteurs la saga de la Convention de Rome durant les vingt années qui nous séparent de son adoption. Nous avons une ambition plus limitée. Mais le choix du sujet nous a été dicté par la personnalité du collègue et ami pour lequel ces lignes sont écrites. Européen, enseignant dans une université hors de l'Europe communautaire, citoyen du monde, KURT SIEHR a toujours fait preuve de curiosité intellectuelle et d'un éclectisme puisant à des sources multiples. C'est pourquoi, nous avons pensé lui offrir une brève analyse du sort de la Convention de Rome sur la loi applicable aux obligations contractuelles, non seulement devant les tribunaux nationaux mais aussi devant des tribunaux arbitraux, ce dernier aspect étant le plus étonnant puisque les arbitres du commerce international sont normalement libres de déterminer la loi applicable au contrat ayant donné lieu au différend qu'ils ont à arbitrer. Mais avant de voir comment la Convention a été reçue en jurisprudence, nous nous attacherons à montrer qu'elle a été complétée, voire même remplacée, par certaines directives européennes, bouleversant ainsi parfois la hiérarchie des normes avant que d'être

---

[*] Professeur des Universités, en détachement auprès de la Conférence de La Haye de droit international privé. Les idées exprimées dans cet article sont celles de l'auteur et ne représentent pas celles de l'organisation pour laquelle elle travaille.

J. Basedow et al., eds., Private Law in the International Arena – Liber Amicorum Kurt Siehr
© *2000, T.M.C.Asser Press, The Hague, The Netherlands*

purement et simplement transformée en règlement en raison de l'entrée en vigueur du Traité d'Amsterdam, modifiant le Traité instituant la Communauté européenne.

1. LA CONVENTION DE ROME ET SA PLACE DANS LES NORMES EUROPÉENNES DE DROIT INTERNATIONAL PRIVÉ

A l'origine, la Convention devait porter à la fois sur les obligations contractuelles et non contractuelles.[1] Sa négociation n'avait pourtant pas été prévue par les pères fondateurs de la Communauté économique européenne comme en atteste le silence gardé par l'ancien article 220 du Traité de Rome[2] qui ne prévoyait une harmonisation que pour les jugements et les sentences arbitrales.[3] C'est pourquoi, l'unification du droit international privé avait commencé par les jugements avec ce qui devait devenir la Convention de Bruxelles du 27 septembre 1968. Mais, tout comme les négociateurs s'étaient rendus compte très rapidement qu'une convention sur les jugements ne pourrait donner pleinement satisfaction sans une unification des règles de compétence juridictionnelle directe, ils convinrent également que la Convention de Bruxelles devait être complétée par une autre convention portant sur les conflits de lois. C'était d'autant plus important que la Convention de Bruxelles prévoyait des fors concurrents, notamment en son article 5, donnant ainsi la possibilité aux plaideurs, si les règles de conflit de lois n'étaient pas harmonisées, de se livrer à un *forum shopping* peu souhaitable, leur permettant de choisir le tribunal non en fonction de sa commodité et de sa pertinence pour une saine et bonne administration de la justice, mais en vue du résultat substantiel escompté compte tenu de la règle de conflit de lois que le juge saisi appliquerait. Un résultat similaire pouvait être atteint avec l'application de l'article 17 permettant de valider les clauses d'élection de for, selon certaines conditions énoncées au texte.

Mais la Convention de Rome n'a jamais eu l'ambition de régler de manière complète tout le domaine des obligations contractuelles. Tout d'abord, elle exclut cer-

---

[1] Voir, notamment, l'article de Jacques Foyer, « L'avant-projet de Convention CEE sur la loi applicable aux obligations contractuelles et noncontractuelles » , *J.D.I.* (1976) p. 555. Le Groupe européen de droit international privé, auquel le dédicataire et l'auteur de ces lignes appartiennent tous deux, a relancé l'idée d'une convention sur la loi applicable aux obligations non contractuelles. On peut consulter le texte de ce projet avec une présentation de Marc Fallon et un commentaire dans la *Revue belge de droit international* (1997) p. 682.

[2] Devenu l'article 293 en raison de la nouvelle numérotation rendue nécessaire par le Traité d'Amsterdam, la substance du texte est restée inchangée. La subsistance de l'article 293 avec l'article 65 nouveau pose des difficultés d'interprétation épineux, analysés avec finesse par Christian Kohler « Interrogations et sources du droit international privé européen après le traité d'Amsterdam » , *Rev. crit. Dr. int. pr.* (1999) p. 1.

[3] On sait qu'en raison de l'existence des conventions de New York de 1958 (à laquelle tous les Etats membres de l'Union européennes sont parties) et de Genève de 1961, les Etats membres ont renoncé, à juste raison, à la préparation d'une convention européenne en la matière.

taines matières de son champ d'application substantiel. Il en va ainsi, notamment des contrats d'assurance. L'article 1 § 3 est ainsi libellé : « Les dispositions de la présente Convention ne s'appliquent pas aux contrats d'assurance qui couvrent des risques situés sur les territoires des Etats membres de la Communauté économique européenne. Pour déterminer si un risque est situé sur l'un de ces territoires, le juge applique sa loi interne ». C'est pourquoi, les directives en matière d'assurances proposent des règles de conflit de lois.[4] De surcroît, la Convention a prévu la primauté du droit européen dérivé dans des domaines spécialisés.[5] Mais, loin de seulement compléter les dispositions de la Convention, certaines normes de droit dérivé ont modifié, parfois sensiblement, les solutions admises par la Convention, rendant extrêmement confuses la hiérarchie des normes européennes en la matière.[6] La confusion est à son comble avec l'entrée en vigueur du Traité d'Amsterdam qui laisse subsister deux textes, semble-t-il incompatibles, ce à quoi nous consacrerons brièvement une seconde section.[7]

1.1 Les règles de conflit de lois contenues dans des directives

Avant de proposer quelques remarques sur le contenu des règles de conflit de lois insérées dans les directives choisies à titre d'exemple, nous voudrions réfléchir quelques instants sur la méthode utilisée et l'efficacité que représente la directive comme instrument d'unification des règles de conflit de lois. La terminologie que nous venons d'utiliser montre combien, en matière de conflits de lois, il est important de parler d'unification plutôt que d'harmonisation. En effet, la règle de conflit

---

[4] Nous nous bornerons à faire référence brièvement aux directives de deuxième et troisième génération sur les assurances non vie. On désigne par là les directives portant sur les risques autres que l'assurance vie.

[5] L'article 20 est ainsi libellé : « La présente convention ne préjuge pas l'application des dispositions qui, dans des matières particulières, règlent les conflits de lois en matière d'obligations contractuelles et qui sont ou seront contenues dans les actes émanant des institutions des Communautés européennes ou dans les législations nationales harmonisées en exécution de ces actes. »

[6] Nous nous contenterons de prendre l'exemple des contrats entre un professionnel et un consommateur.

[7] La Convention réserve également la possibilité pour les Etats membres de demeurer ou devenir partie à d'autres conventions internationales (article 21). C'est ainsi que les Etats qui avaient ratifié la Convention de La Haye du 15 juin 1955 sur la loi applicable aux ventes à caractère international d'objets mobiliers corporels, ou celle du 14 mars 1978 sur la loi applicable aux contrats d'intermédiaires et à la représentation, sont demeurés parties à ces conventions. Seule la Belgique a jugé approprié de dénoncer la Convention de 1955 au motif que la Convention de Rome est suffisante pour les contrats de vente internationale de marchandises, sans qu'il soit besoin d'une convention spéciale. Quant aux Pays-Bas et au Portugal, c'est après l'entrée en vigueur de la Convention de Rome, qu'ils ont au contraire décidé de ratifier la Convention de 1978 à laquelle ils n'étaient pas encore partie. Ce choix a été dicté par le fait que, sans la Convention de 1978, la Convention de Rome aurait dû être appliquée à ces contrats. Or, ses solutions modifiaient à certains égards celles admises par la jurisprudence pour les contrats d'agence si bien que les solutions de la Convention de 1978 ont semblé plus appropriées à cette matière spécialisée.

de lois est, avant tout, une règle de méthode. Certes, depuis l'époque de Savigny à laquelle il est de tradition de faire remonter la règle de conflit classique, les règles de conflit ont évolué. Elles peuvent intégrer des objectifs substantiels de telle manière qu'elles perdent une partie de leur qualité intrinsèque. Il n'en demeure pas moins que, même si elles sont « mâtinées de substance », les règles de conflit de lois demeurent des règles de méthode destinées à faire vivre ensemble des systèmes de solution différents, voire contradictoires. C'est la raison pour laquelle nous pensons que seule une unification des règles de conflit de lois peut être faite au niveau international ou régional, l'harmonisation n'étant pas suffisante.

Or, la directive est avant tout une règle d'harmonisation. Elle fixe des cadres, des principes, des structures minimales, au sein desquels les Etats demeurent libres de créer des normes d'adaptation. C'est d'ailleurs la raison pour laquelle, les directives ne sont pas d'application directe et doivent être transposées en droit interne par les Etats membres de l'Union. A cet égard, les directives jouent un peu le rôle des lois modèles dans le contexte des Etats fédéraux ou dans le contexte d'harmonisation internationale du droit privé. Certes, nous n'ignorons pas que, depuis l'origine, les directives ont subi de profonds changements. Elles sont devenues de plus en plus précises, laissant de moins en moins de liberté aux Etats de se départir des solutions préconisées. Cette évolution a également entraîné une autre conséquence induite par la Cour de Justice des Communautés européennes : lorsque leurs dispositions sont suffisamment précises, les directives ont un effet direct en ce sens, notamment, que les juges nationaux doivent appliquer leur droit national en fonction des directives même si celles-ci ne sont pas encore transposées (à condition que la date limite de transposition soit dépassée) ou ont été mal transposées.[8]

Compte tenu de ce qui précède, nous sommes d'avis que pour qu'une règle de conflit de lois contenue dans une directive soit efficace et atteigne son but, il faut qu'elle soit complète et précise et qu'elle soit transposée sans modification dans les droits nationaux des Etats membres. Or, nous allons le voir, c'est loin d'être le cas.

La directive de 1988 sur l'assurance non vie[9] comporte un article 7 entièrement consacré à une règle de conflit de lois extrêmement complexe dont nous ne pourrons donner ici qu'un aperçu tant le système mis en place est difficile à comprendre.[10] Elle montre d'abord que les Etats membres ne sont pas parvenus à s'entendre sur le sort à réserver à l'autonomie de la volonté dans le cadre du contrat d'assurance. Comme dans beaucoup de matières (droit des sociétés, par exemple), les Etats européens se divisent selon un éventail et une gradation progressive entre ceux qui n'acceptent pas la liberté contractuelle (dont la France fait partie) et ceux

---

[8] Nous ne pouvons pas, dans le cadre de cette brève contribution, approfondir les conditions et les effets de cette évolution. Le lecteur voudra bien nous pardonner de rester à ce niveau de généralité.

[9] *JO(CE)* [1988] L 172/1 (4 juillet 1988).

[10] Une thèse a récemment été consacrée au conflits de lois en matière d'assurance. Cf. Nicolas Auclair (Thèse, Paris I, 1999) (monographiée).

qui, au contraire, sont très libéraux (c'est le cas, avant tout de l'Irlande et du Royaume-Uni). Compte tenu de cette divergence, la règle de conflit laisse aux Etats membres à trois reprises (article 7 § 1 a) et d), et § 3) une marge de manœuvre pour admettre ou non l'autonomie de la volonté. Les transpositions nationales montrent l'immense complexité des solutions retenues. Quand le droit néerlandais renvoie purement et simplement à la Convention, l'Italie réserve ses propres dispositions impératives, l'Autriche, le Portugal et l'Allemagne admettent l'autonomie de la vo-lonté sauf cas limitativement énumérés et la France procède comme à l'accoutumée par une rédaction unilatérale. Il en résulte qu'un même contrat pourra faire l'objet de solutions différentes selon que le litige qui en est issu sera soumis à l'un ou l'autre des juges des Etats membres. C'était pourtant exactement ce que l'on avait cherché à éviter.

En matière de protection des consommateurs, nous prendrons l'exemple de deux directives, celle concernant les clauses abusives dans les contrats conclus avec les consommateurs[11] et celle concernant la protection des consommateurs en matière de contrats à distance.[12] A étudier les dispositions nationales de transposition, on se rend compte que chaque Etat ajoute certaines précisions ou même modifie la règle de telle manière qu'elle ne correspond plus à celle de la directive. Or, si chaque Etat modifie la règle de conflit de lois, il ne peut plus y avoir de coordination des systè-mes de manière harmonieuse. En ce qui concerne la directive 93/13/CEE, l'Alle-magne, par exemple, rend la disposition applicable quelle que soit la loi étrangère désignée[13] alors que le Danemark précise qu'il faut que le droit étranger applicable

---

[11] Directive 93/13/CEE du Conseil du 5 avril 1993, *(JO)CE* [1993] L 95/29 (21 avril 1993) dont l'article 6 est ainsi rédigé :

« 1. Les Etats membres prévoient que les clauses abusives figurant dans un contrat conclu avec un consommateur par un professionnel ne lient pas les consommateurs, dans les conditions fixées par leurs droits nationaux, et que le contrat restera contraignant pour les parties selon les mêmes termes, s'il peut subsister sans les clauses abusives.

2. Les Etats membres prennent les mesures nécessaires pour que le consommateur ne soit pas privé de la protection accordée par la présente directive du fait du choix du droit d'un pays tiers comme droit applicable au contrat, lorsque le contrat présente un lien étroit avec le territoire des Etats membres. »

[12] Directive 97/7/CE du Parlement européen et du Conseil, du 20 mai 1997, *JO(CE)* L 144/19 (4 juin 1997). L'article 12 de cette directive dispose :

« 1. Le consommateur ne peut renoncer aux droits qui lui sont conférés en vertu de la transposition en droit national de la présente directive.

2. Les Etats membres prennent les mesures nécessaires pour que le consommateur ne soit pas privé de la protection accordée par la présente directive du fait du choix du droit d'un pays tiers comme droit applicable au contrat, lorsque le contrat présente un lien étroit avec le territoire d'un ou de plusieurs des Etats membres. »

[13] § 12 de la loi sur les clauses générales d'affaires, telle que modifiée par la loi du 19 juillet 1996 (BGBl. 1996 I, p. 1013). Cette disposition devrait être remplacée par une disposition générale à insérer dans la loi introductive au Code civil (EGBGB) après l'article 29 qui correspond à l'article 5 de la Con-vention de Rome.

soit celui d'un Etat tiers par rapport à l'Espace économique européen[14] et que la France se contente de dire que la loi doit être celle d'un Etat situé en dehors de l'Union européenne.[15] Selon que le contrat soumis au droit norvégien sera soumis à un juge allemand, danois ou français, les solutions pourraient donc différer, malgré l'effort qui a été fait d'uniformiser. Ce défaut a été perçu par le législateur allemand qui, dans une proposition de disposition générale, a suivi la voie montrée par le Danemark.[16]

D'autres différences peuvent être notées avec des conséquences tout aussi dommageables. Certains Etats ont défini, chacun pour lui-même, ce qu'il faut entendre par « lien étroit » au sens de la directive. Pour l'Allemagne, le lien étroit existe, notamment, « lorsque le contrat a été conclu suite à une offre publique, une publicité publique ou une activité commerciale similaire exercée dans un Etat membre de l'Union européenne ou dans un autre Etat contractant de l'accord sur l'Espace économique européen et que l'autre partie contractante a, au moment où elle déclare vouloir conclure le contrat, son domicile ou sa résidence habituelle dans un Etat membre de l'Union européenne ou dans un autre Etat contractant de l'accord sur l'Espace économique européen ». Pour la Grèce, en revanche, le lien étroit n'existe que si le contrat est conclu ou exécuté en Grèce.[17]

Nous pourrions multiplier les exemples. Toutefois, il nous semble patent que la méthode utilisée n'est pas la bonne même si, comme nous l'avons dit plus haut, les lois nationales doivent être appliquées à la lumière des objectifs et des dispositions de la directive. C'est pourquoi, quitte à sortir du cadre de la convention internationale, la méthode du règlement est bien préférable à celle de la directive.

1.2   La transformation de la Convention de Rome en un Règlement

En raison de l'entrée en vigueur du Traité instituant les Communautés européennes tel que révisé par le Traité d'Amsterdam, une proposition a été faite de transformer la Convention de Rome en un règlement. C'est ce que, dans le jargon de l'Europe communautaire, nous appelons le « reformatage ». Indépendamment des controverses que cette nouvelle formule a suscitée,[18] force est de reconnaître que l'intégra-

---

[14] Loi n°1098 du 21 décembre 1994 modifiant la loi sur les contrats, texte inséré à la suite de l'article 38.

[15] Loi n°95-96 du 1er février 1995 concernant les clauses abusives et la présentation des contrats et régissant diverses activités d'ordre économique et commercial (JO(RF) du 2 février 1995, p. 1755), disposition insérée à l'article L.135-1 du code de la consommation.

[16] Voir ci-dessus note 13.

[17] Loi n°2251 du 16 novembre 1994 sur la protection des consommateurs (JO, partie A, fasc 191 du 16 novembre 1994).

[18] Cf. Notamment l'article de Christian Kohler cité ci-dessus note 2 et, plus récemment, H. Gaudemet-Tallon, « Droit privé et droit communautaire : quelques réflexions », *Revue du Marché commun et de l'Union européenne* (2000) n°437, p. 228.

tion européenne appelle une plus forte uniformité du droit privé au sein de l'espace intégré. Il en va du bon fonctionnement du marché intérieur. Cela permet également d'éviter certaines distorsions de concurrence qui pourraient naître, notamment, des niveaux de protection contractuelle différents accordés selon les Etats. Certes, dans cette perspective, les règles de droit international privé ne participent que dans une faible mesure au fonctionnement économique. Mais même si elles demeurent à la marge, elles ne doivent pas être ignorées, notamment, vis-à-vis des Etats tiers par rapport au territoire unifié considéré. C'est pourquoi, il nous apparaît souhaitable que les règles de conflit de lois soient unifiées par le biais d'un règlement.

De surcroît, alors que les Etats membres n'ont pas pris les mesures nécessaires pour permettre l'entrée en vigueur du protocole additionnel à la Convention de Rome permettant la saisine de la Cour de Justice des Communautés européennes pour des questions préjudicielles, le règlement permettra de faire entrer les règles de conflit de lois directement dans le cadre du droit communautaire et entraîner automatiquement la compétence de la Cour de Justice à cet égard. En applaudissant ce nouveau développement permettant une meilleure interprétation uniforme, nous n'ignorons pas que les juges de la Cour n'ont pas forcément la formation nécessaire ni le goût pour appliquer avec aisance des textes de droit privé, parfois complexes et très techniques. Mais nous ne doutons pas que l'adaptation que cette évolution va leur demander saura les stimuler compte tenu des grandes compétences qui sont les leurs, notamment dans le domaine du droit économique.

Mais loin de devoir se limiter à la seule Convention de Rome, nous nous interrogeons sur le point de savoir s'il ne conviendrait pas de prendre avantage de cette opportunité pour consolider les règles de conflit de lois existant dans les directives et les intégrer dans un seul instrument. Nous voyons deux grands avantages à une telle manière de procéder. Tout d'abord, l'inconvénient de la méthode de la directive, tel qu'illustré ci-dessus par les distorsions de transposition dans les Etats membres, serait supprimé pour parvenir à une véritable unification des règles de conflit de lois dans le cadre européen. Par ailleurs, en procédant à cette consolidation, il apparaîtra certainement des redondances inutiles, des divergences entre les règles des directives et celles de la Convention elle-même qui pourront ainsi être éliminées. Leur application concrète n'en sera que facilitée. De plus, il sera possible d'adapter les règles que nous connaissons aujourd'hui aux besoins de l'évolution des techniques de conclusion et d'exécution des contrats par voie électronique. A cet égard, nous n'innovons pas puisque cette possible adaptation des règles européennes de conflit de lois figure dans le plan d'action du Conseil et de la Commission du 3 décembre 1998,[19] même si des questions restent encore en suspens sur le contenu exact de cette révision et la base juridique sur laquelle elle est fondée.

---

[19] *JO(CE)* [1999] C 19 (23 janvier 1999).

2.   LA CONVENTION DE ROME ET SA RÉCEPTION PAR LA JURISPRUDENCE

Dans les développements qui suivent, il nous a paru intéressant de ne pas limiter nos commentaires à la seule jurisprudence des tribunaux nationaux mais de voir également si la Convention avait eu une influence sur la pratique arbitrale.

2.1 **La jurisprudence des tribunaux nationaux**

Fin octobre 1998, le service de recherche et documentation de la Cour de Justice des Communautés européennes avait répertorié 381 décisions publiées émanant des tribunaux des Etats parties. La répartition par Etat révèle que la très grande majorité de cette jurisprudence émane de l'Allemagne et des Pays-Bas[20] alors qu'il n'y en a aucune émanant de l'Autriche, de l'Espagne, de la Finlande, de l'Irlande ou de la Suède.[21]

L'analyse succincte de cette jurisprudence révèle que, de toutes les dispositions de la Convention, c'est l'article 4 qui fait l'objet du plus grand nombre de décisions. En revanche, l'article 5 n'est presque jamais en question. Cela ne veut pas dire, cependant, que ce texte ne pose aucune difficulté. Les décisions publiées, en effet, sont rarement celles de tribunaux de première instance. Or, il est peu fréquent que des litiges de consommation fassent l'objet d'une procédure longue incluant un appel ou, plus encore, une cassation. La vision que l'on peut avoir de ce contentieux n'est donc pas significative et devrait, pour être parlante, faire l'objet d'une étude empirique de terrain.

A cet égard, une décision récente de la Cour de cassation doit être mentionnée ici.[22] Il s'agissait de savoir si la loi française sur le crédit à la consommation du 10 janvier 1978, en tant que norme impérative, était encore d'application en présence des solutions prévues par la Convention de Rome en ses articles 5 et 7. Précisons immédiatement que l'opération en cause dans cette décision avait eu lieu avant l'entrée en vigueur de la Convention de Rome. Or, la Cour d'appel avait appliqué ces dispositions, faisant par là même une application anticipée de la Convention, ce que censure la Cour de cassation. Comme le montre la note du Professeur Lagarde, la Cour de cassation qualifie de loi de police la loi française sur le crédit à la consommation du 10 janvier 1978 sans égard à ses objectifs de protection ni au rat-

---

[20] 305 au total, dont 132 pour l'Allemagne et 173 pour les Pays Bas.

[21] Pour l'Autriche, la Finlande et la Suède, cela s'expliquerait par la récente acccession de ces pays à la Convention (Voir *JO(CE)* [1997] C 15/2 (15 janvier 1997)). En revanche, pour l'Espagne et l'Irlande, l'explication est plus difficile à trouver. Pour l'Espagne, voir A. Borras Rodriguez, « La applicacion en espagna del convenio de Roma de 19 de Junio de 1980 sobre ley applicable a las obligaciones contractuales » , *Anales de la Academia Matritense del Notariado,* tomo XXXIV (Madrid 1995) p. 267.

[22] Civ. 1, 19 octobre 1999, *Rev. crit. Dr. int. pr.* (2000) p. 29, note P. Lagarde.

tachement du contrat en cause avec l'ordre juridique français. Pour la Cour, il semble suffire que les emprunteurs aient été résidents français sans se préoccuper du fait que c'était eux qui avaient choisi de contracter le prêt à l'étranger. Toutefois, cette solution serait sans doute différente si la Cour avait eu à appliquer la Convention de Rome. En effet, elle devrait alors trancher la question du rapport entre ses articles 5 et 7, à supposer le premier inapplicable. Si, pour continuer avec l'exemple de la loi française de 1978, celle-ci n'était pas applicable du fait des conditions exigées par l'article 5, pourrait-elle l'être au titre de l'article 7? Aucune réponse claire ne peut être tirée de l'arrêt du 19 octobre 1999 puisque la Cour évite de répondre et se réfugie derrière l'application dans le temps de la Convention. Dans sa note, M. Lagarde suggère, mais avec prudence, que la loi de 1978 ne pourrait pas être qualifiée de loi de police, au moins dans son ensemble, afin de voir son application « sauvée » par l'article 7 de la Convention de Rome. Il est fort possible que ce soit la prochaine étape admise par la Cour. Mais il faudra attendre une confirmation plus claire. Dans une telle hypothèse, on ne pourrait que constater une diminution de la protection du consommateur français du fait du droit européen.[23]

Il ne nous est pas possible, dans le cadre limité de cette contribution, de passer en revue tous les autres aspects de la Convention de Rome telle qu'appliquée par les tribunaux nationaux et nous nous proposons de nous tourner maintenant vers la réception de ce texte par les arbitres du commerce international.

2.2 La réception de la Convention de Rome par les arbitres du commerce international[24]

Dans le livre qu'il dédie à ses soixante années d'expérience en matière d'arbitrage du commerce international,[25] Pieter Sanders consacre seulement onze pages à la question de la loi applicable au fond du litige qu'il intitule, selon la terminologie ac-

---

[23] Cette conclusion est contestée par M. Lagarde. Toutefois, il est permis de se demander si la protection du consommateur, telle que nous l'avons connue dans la seconde moitié du vingtième siècle, ne subit pas des attaques de plus en plus pertinentes et ne doit pas être revue, notamment au regard de la nouvelle économie électronique.

[24] Nous n'abordons ici que la loi applicable au fond du litige puisque la Convention de Rome exclut de son champ d'application la convention d'arbitrage (article 1 § 2). Toutefois, il est admis par certains auteurs que les règles posées par la Convention, notamment en son article 9 sur la forme des actes, pourraient servir de modèle compte tenu du caractère moderne de la solution proposée. Voir à cet égard, Fouchard, Gaillard, Goldman, *Traité de l'arbitrage commercial international* (Paris 1996) p. 382 n°603. Ces auteurs font la même remarque pour la cession de la convention d'arbitrage par rapport à la solution de l'article 12 de la Convention de Rome (cf. p. 434, n°696).

[25] Pieter Sanders, *Quo Vadis Arbitration? – Sixty years of arbitration practice* (Kluwer Law International 1999).

ceptée aujourd'hui « Rules applicable to the merits » .[26] L'auteur part de la loi modèle CNUDCI sur l'arbitrage[27] et signale, en la critiquant, la différence de
traitement que ce texte fait de la question, selon qu'est visé le choix effectué par les
parties ou, en l'absence de choix, le rôle des arbitres dans la détermination du droit
applicable. Dans ce dernier cas, en effet, l'article 28 § 2 de la loi modèle précise que
le tribunal arbitral doit appliquer la loi désignée par la règle de conflit de lois qu'il
juge applicable.[28] Or, la question se pose de savoir, (question à laquelle la loi modèle ne répond pas, non plus que les divers règlements d'arbitrage) où le tribunal arbitral va-t-il chercher la règle de conflit de lois qui va lui permettre de déterminer la
loi qu'il appliquera à la substance du litige qu'il doit trancher.

Dans un article déjà ancien, Pierre Lalive faisait le point sur les différentes règles
de conflit de lois qui pourraient être appliquées par le tribunal arbitral.[29] Loin de
vouloir reprendre cette hypothèse de travail sur laquelle tout a été dit et mieux que
nous ne pourrions le faire, il nous est apparu intéressant de voir comment les arbitres du commerce international avaient utilisé la Convention de Rome pour justifier
leur choix d'une loi applicable. Mais avant de ce faire, il convient de dire deux mots
du statut des conventions internationales de droit privé devant les arbitres.

La plupart des systèmes admettent que les arbitres du commerce international,
contrairement aux juges, n'ont pas de for[30] et que le lieu de l'arbitrage, même s'il a
été choisi par les parties, correspond essentiellement à une fiction juridique permettant de déterminer avec facilité le système de recours dans lequel la sentence sera
insérée et, si nécessaire, les règles de procédure par défaut qui pourraient être utilisées par le tribunal arbitral. N'ayant pas de for, donc pas d'Etat au nom duquel il va
rendre justice, l'arbitre du commerce international ne serait donc lié, a priori, par
aucune convention internationale.[31] Cela est vrai pour les conventions de droit ma-

---

[26] Pendant longtemps, les règlements d'arbitrage ou les lois internes traitant de l'arbitrage parlaient
de « loi applicable » alors que, désormais, à l'instar du droit français de l'arbitrage, il convient de parler
de « règles applicables » . Ce changement de terminologie démontre un changement profond d'attitude
vis-à-vis du droit applicable puisque les arbitres pourront éventuellement se satisfaire de l'application
de règles puisées en dehors des lois nationales éventuellement applicables, la recherche de cette dernière n'étant plus systématiquement nécessaire à la bonne administration de l'instance arbitrale.

[27] Loi type du 21 juin 1985.

[28] La même disposition se retrouvait dans le règlement d'arbitrage de la CCI applicable à compter
du 1er janvier 1988 (article 13.3) mais a été modifiée par le nouveau règlement en vigueur depuis le 1er
janvier 1998 (article 17) qui ne vise que les règles de droit. Les règlements de la LCIA et de l'AAA visent les deux expressions « laws or rules of law » .

[29] Pierre Lalive, « Les règles de conflit de lois appliquées au fond du litige par l'arbitre international
siégeant en Suisse » , *Rev. arb.* (1976) 155. Cette liste d'options n'a pas changé depuis.

[30] Cette constatation a notamment été faite par le Parlement européen dans une résolution sur la
promotion du recours à l'arbitrage pour la résolution des conflits d'ordre juridique, *JO(CE)* [1994] C 59
(25 juillet 1994).

[31] Dans ce sens, voir par exemple, Pierre Mayer, « L'application par l'arbitre des conventions internationales de droit privé » , *Mélanges en l'honneur d'Yvon Loussouarn* (Dalloz 1994) p. 275.

tériel telle la Convention de Vienne de 1980 sur la vente internationale de marchandises. Cela devrait l'être *a fortiori* pour la Convention de Rome qui ne dicte aucune règle matérielle mais présente une méthode de raisonnement pour parvenir à déterminer la loi applicable au litige.

Toutefois, les sentences arbitrales ne sont pas rares qui font référence à la Convention de Rome. Certaines d'entre elles le font même avant l'entrée en vigueur de ce texte et alors même que les différentes lois en conflit ne sont pas des lois des Etats parties à la Convention ou que le tribunal arbitral ne siège pas dans un Etat partie ou qui a vocation à le devenir.[32] Cette application « anticipée »[33] confirmerait s'il en était besoin que le principe directeur qui préside à l'application d'une convention par les arbitres relève exclusivement de leur volonté.[34] Toutefois, cette attitude n'est pas spécifique aux arbitres car certains juges nationaux européens ont également fait une application anticipée des solutions de la Convention de Rome.[35]

Si l'on examine de plus près le raisonnement des arbitres, on se rend compte que ceux-ci voient dans la Convention de Rome, comme dans la Convention de La Haye de 1955 en matière de loi applicable au contrat de vente internationale de marchandises, une règle internationalement acceptée. C'est le cas par exemple de la sentence rendue sous l'égide de la CCI dans l'affaire 6360,[36] dans laquelle les arbitres s'expriment ainsi : « [il s'agit de] règles de droit international privé généralement acceptées contenues dans le Traité CEE de Rome du 19 juin 1980 (articles 3 et 4) lequel est aussi appliqué par anticipation sur sa ratification formelle par les juridictions néerlandaises » .

En revanche, certains arbitres prennent le soin de citer la Convention de Rome (comme d'autres conventions de conflit de lois[37]) seulement à titre de *ratio decidendi* après un raisonnement de droit international privé comparé montrant que la loi qu'ils décident d'appliquer serait de toute manière celle désignée par les règles conventionnelles.[38]

Une question vient immédiatement à l'esprit concernant l'application anticipée.

---

[32] La Convention de Rome est une convention régionale fermée puisque seuls les Etats appartenant à la Communauté européenne sont aptes à en devenir membres.

[33] Cette expression n'est pas vraiment exacte en l'occurrence puisque pour l'arbitre la convention n'est jamais obligatoire. Il ne peut donc, à proprement parler s'agir d'application anticipée. Toutefois, elle montre que l'arbitre a appliqué la convention à une époque où celle-ci n'était pas en vigueur et n'était donc pas obligatoire même pour les juges des Etats parties.

[34] En ce sens, Pierre Mayer (supra n. 31) à la p. 289.

[35] Cf. notamment en Allemagne, aux Pays-Bas et en France. Mais pour une décision récente ayant refusé une telle application anticipée (voir supra n. 22).

[36] Sentence rendue en 1989, *Bulletin CCI* (décembre 1990) vol. 1, n°2, p. 24.

[37] Notamment, la Convention de La Haye du 15 juin 1955 sur la loi applicable aux ventes à caractère international d'objets mobiliers corporels.

[38] Sentence rendue en 1985 sous l'égide de la CCI, affaire n°4996, *J.D.I.* (1986) 1131. Même raisonnement dans la sentence rendue en 1982 dans l'affaire 2730, *J.D.I.* (1984) 914 et 9 *Yearbook ICCA* (1984) 118 (sous une référence semble-t-il erronée 2930).

Elle est particulièrement importante, nous semble-t-il, en matière contractuelle puisque la prévision des parties (ou leur attente légitime) demeure le principe d'interprétation communément admis, conséquence de l'autonomie de la volonté qui leur est reconnue. Or, notamment dans l'affaire 4996, le contrat avait été signé le 1er septembre 1981. Peut-on (doit-on ?) estimer que les parties ont dû prendre en considération les solutions prévues dans le texte de la Convention alors que celle-ci n'avait été adoptée que depuis quelques mois et qu'il faudrait attendre encore dix années pour son entrée en vigueur ?

* _ * _ *

Les efforts d'unification des règles de conflit de lois entrepris avec l'adoption de la Convention de Rome de 1980 ont été en partie annihilés du fait de l'absence d'interprétation uniforme et de l'intervention postérieure de directives laissant une certaine liberté aux Etats membres, liberté peu propice à faciliter la vie des citoyens compte tenu de la nature particulière des normes de droit international privé. Il est donc à espérer que les institutions communautaires n'attendront pas dix années supplémentaires pour proposer un règlement consolidé permettant d'unifier réellement les règles de conflit de lois en matière contractuelle. L'entrée en vigueur du Traité (révisé après Amsterdam) instituant la Communauté européenne constitue l'occasion à ne pas manquer.

Summary
The Rome Convention of 19 June 1980 on the Law Applicable to Contractual Obligations – Twenty Years After

Twenty years after its adoption, the Rome Convention on the Law Applicable to Contractual Obligations is the center of renewed interest due to the entry into force of the revised Treaty instituting the European Community according to the Treaty of Amsterdam. This contribution shows briefly that it would not be satisfactory to use directives, previously considered preferable, for introducing new conflict of laws rules to either complete or amend the Convention. In contrast, regulations would be appropriate to consolidate all the existing rules and put an end to the divergent implementations of the rules by Member States. In the second part, the author gives a few examples of application of the Convention both by judges of Member States and by international arbitrators.

Internationaler Unterlassungsrechtsschutz zwischen materiellem Recht und Prozeßrecht

Harald Koch[*]

1. UNTERLASSUNGSKLAGEN IM DIENSTE POLITISCHER STRATEGIEN

„Government by injunction" – Regieren durch Unterlassungsgebote – wurde der amerikanischen Justiz in den 30er Jahren vorgeworfen. Gemeint war damit der ge-

---

[*] Universitätsprofessor und Richter am Oberlandesgericht Rostock.

J. Basedow et al., eds., Private Law in the International Arena – Liber Amicorum Kurt Siehr
© 2000, T.M.C.Asser Press, The Hague, The Netherlands

werkschaftsfeindliche Kurs der Bundesgerichte, die in einer großen Zahl von Fällen Arbeitskampfmaßnahmen mit Hilfe vorbeugenden (meist einstweiligen) Rechtsschutzes untersagten[1] und damit erheblich in die Arbeits- und Wirtschaftspolitik eingriffen. – Unterlassungsbegehren werden also zum Politikum, wenn sie als Instrumente sozial-, wirtschafts- oder allgemeinpolitischer Strategien eingesetzt und vor allem im Wege des einstweiligen Rechtsschutzes verfolgt werden. Die besondere, mit den Konzepten der subjektiven Rechtskraft nur unvollkommen zu erfassende Breitenwirkung des Unterlassungsurteils, auf die noch zurückzukommen ist, läßt gerade diese Rechtsschutzform als besonders geeignet erscheinen, für überindividuelle Gruppen-, bisweilen auch für öffentliche Interessen zu streiten und damit die traditionelle Funktionsbeschränkung des Zivilprozesses auf den Indidividualrechtsschutz zu erweitern.[2] Gleichzeitig macht das historische Beispiel aus der Zeit vor F. D. Roosevelts „New Deal" deutlich, wie wichtig geeigneter Rechtsschutz und seine Formen für die Verwirklichung bestimmter materieller Ziele sein kann.

2.   GRENZÜBERSCHREITENDE UNTERLASSUNGSKLAGEN:
      ANWENDUNGSFELDER UND ÜBERBLICK ÜBER RECHTSPROBLEME

Der enge Zusammenhang zwischen materiellem Recht und Prozeßrecht wirft besonders bei grenzüberschreitenden Unterlassungsbegehren eine Reihe von Problemen auf, die in neuerer Zeit zu erheblicher Aktualität geführt haben, aber bisher erst vereinzelt als Problem dieses Rechtsschutz-Ziels identifiziert wurden.

Die *Bedeutung*, die solche internationalen Unterlassungsklagen in einigen *Rechtsgebieten* erlangt haben, reflektiert die immer intensivere grenzüberschreitende Betätigung vieler Unternehmen, deren dadurch gestiegenes Rechtsverletzungspotential entsprechende Abwehrreaktionen hervorruft.[3] Besonders auffällig ist dies etwa im Medienrecht, wo unzutreffende Berichterstattung in mehreren Ländern

---

[1] Berühmt ist die empirische Untersuchung von Frankfurter und Green, *The Labor Injunction* (1930). Vgl. dazu Piehler, *Einstweiliger Rechtsschutz und materielles Recht* (1980) 158ff.

[2] Vgl. dazu Carrington/ Babcock, *Civil Procedure*, 4th ed. (1992) Ch. 11; Koch, *Prozeßführung im öffentlichen Interesse* (1983).

[3] Im Folgenden beschränkt sich der Verfasser auf Unterlassungsbegehren im materiellen Recht, behandelt also nicht die ausschließlich prozeßrechtlich induzierten Unterlassungsklagen wie etwa die „Mareva injunction" des englischen Rechts: Diese gewährt einen unserem dinglichen Arrest entsprechenden Rechtsschutz, vgl. dazu Schack, *Internationales Zivilverfahrensrecht*, 2. Aufl. (1996) Rn. 427 (ausführliche Nw.: Rn. 411); Koch, „Neuere Probleme der internationalen Zwangsvollstreckung einschließlich des einstweiligen Rechtsschutzes", in: Schlosser (Hrsg.), *Materielles Recht und Verfahrensrecht und die Auswirkungen der Unterscheidung im Recht der internationalen Zwangsvollstreckung* (1992) 171, 193 und 257; Grunert, *Die „worldwide" Mareva Injunction* (1998).

veröffentlicht und vertrieben wird und daher zu grenzüberschreitenden Unterlassungsklagen führt.[4] Die (drohende) Verletzung gewerblicher Schutzrechte findet nicht selten gezielt im Ausland statt, um die grenzüberschreitende Rechtsverfolgung zu erschweren.[5] Umweltbeeinträchtigungen machen in Gestalt von toxischen oder radioaktiven Immissionen keinen Halt an nationalen Grenzen und werden daher immer wieder negatorisch bekämpft.[6] Verstärktes internationales Marketing von Waren und Dienstleistungen auf neuen Vertriebswegen ruft Verbraucherorganisationen und Behörden auf den Plan, die mit Hilfe von Unterlassungsrechtsbehelfen die Verbraucher vor rechtswidrigen Praktiken zu schützen versuchen.

Die Kommission der Europäischen Gemeinschaft hat bereits 1993 in ihrem Grünbuch „Zugang der Verbraucher zum Recht und Beilegung von Rechtsstreitigkeiten der Verbraucher im Binnenmarkt"[7] den „freien Verkehr der Unterlassungsklagen" in Europa gefordert und damit wiederum das plastische Bild von frei zirkulierenden Rechtsakten gebraucht, deren grenzüberschreitende Anerkennung nicht durch prohibitive, nationale Anforderungen behindert werden dürfe.[8] Auf der Grundlage von Art. 100 a EGV (a. F.) wurde 1998 sodann nach kontroverser Diskussion über Rechtsgrundlage und Erforderlichkeit die Unterlassungsklage-Richtlinie verabschiedet,[9] die die Mitgliedsstaaten verpflichtet, bis Ende 2000 bestimmten „qualifizierten Einrichtungen" die Unterlassungsklagebefugnis zum Schutze der im Anhang aufgelisteten Verbraucherinteressen zu übertragen.

Die besonderen Probleme grenzüberschreitender Unterlassungsklagen, um die es in diesem Beitrag geht, sind einfachen Leistungsbegehren unbekannt. Das hängt einmal mit der unklaren Einordnung des Unterlassungsrechtsschutzes in das materielle Recht oder Prozeßrecht zusammen und erfordert damit eine Klärung der für das anzuwendende Recht maßgeblichen Anknüpfungsgesichtspunkte. Zum anderen ist die Rechtsdurchsetzung „zweiter Stufe" – nämlich die Vollstreckung – im Falle von Unterlassungsurteilen unmittelbar nicht möglich, sondern kann nur durch mittelbare Sanktionen erfolgen. Diese sehen im Lande des Unterlassungsgläubi-

---

[4] Vgl. z.B. BGH *NJW* (1996) 1128 (Caroline von Monaco); Schack, „Rechtsschutz gegen grenzüberschreitende Persönlichkeitsverletzungen durch Rundfunksendungen", in: *Das Persönlichkeitsrecht im Spannungsfeld zwischen Informationsauftrag und Menschenwürde* (1989) 113; ders., „Die grenzüberschreitende Verletzung allgemeiner und Urheberpersönlichkeitsrechte", *UFITA* 108 (1988) 51; Hohloch, „Neue Medien und Individualrechtsschutz", *ZUM* (1986) 165.

[5] S. Literaturnachweise bei Soergel/ Kegel, *BGB Bd. 10: Einführungsgesetz*, 12. Aufl. (1996) Art. 12 Anh. 6; Behr, „Internationale Tatort-Zuständigkeit für vorbeugende Unterlassungsklagen bei Wettbewerbsverstößen", *GRUR Int.* (1992) 604.

[6] Dazu Siehr, „Grenzüberschreitender Umweltschutz, Europäische Erfahrungen mit einem weltweiten Problem", 45 *RabelsZ* (1981) 377; U. Wolf, *Deliktsstatut und internationales Umweltrecht* (1995); Deutsche Gesellschaft für Völkerrecht (Hrsg.), *Umweltschutz im Völkerrecht und Kollisionsrecht* (Berichte der DGVR 32, 1992) 336.

[7] KOM (93) 576 end., S. 87ff.; dazu etwa Reich, *Europäisches Verbraucherrecht*, 3. Aufl. (1996) 508.

gers vielfach ganz anders aus als im Lande des Schuldners. Auf beiden Rechtsan-
wendungsebenen ergeben sich also komplexe Folgefragen aus der Internationalität
des Sachverhalts, die auch den Ruf nach Harmonisierung lauter werden lassen.

3. NEGATORISCHER RECHTSSCHUTZ IN EUROPA (ÜBERBLICK)

Ein kurzer Überblick soll uns zunächst jene Unterschiede des negatorischen
Rechtsschutzes in den europäischen Nachbarländern vor Augen führen.

3.1 Am Auffälligsten sind die Unterschiede im Umfang richterlichen Ermessens
bei der Gewährung negatorischer Rechtsbehelfe. Da das angelsächsische *Common
Law* ursprünglich als Reaktion auf Rechtsverletzungen nur Ansprüche auf Schadensersatz (damages) gewährte, bedurfte es der Intervention der Krone „in equity"
(und später des dafür zuständigen equity-Gerichts, der Court of Chancery), um negatorischen, auch vorbeugenden Rechtsschutz in Form der „injunction" zuzulassen. Die „injunction" war also – wie für die equity-Rechtsprechung charakteristisch
– ursprünglich ein nur subsidiär zu erlangender Notbehelf.[10] Das equity-Verfahren
zeichnete sich sodann aber durch die große Flexibilität in den Rechtsfolgen und allgemein durch das richterliche Ermessen aus, das mit unserem Konzept eines subjektiven Rechts (Anspruchs) kaum verträglich ist.[11]
  Aus der equity-Genese ergibt sich ferner der von vornherein deutliche prozessual geprägte Charakter dieses Rechtsbehelfs, der immerhin bis zur Fusion der Ge-
richtsbarkeiten 1875 (Judicature Acts) nur in einer anderen als der „ordentlichen"
Gerichtsbarkeit zu erlangen war. Noch heute werden equity-Rechtsbehelfe in den
USA prozessual anders als „suits at common law" behandelt: Sie werden nicht vor
einer „civil jury" verhandelt.[12]

---

[8] Ähnlich schon die Begründung des Brüsseler Gerichtsstands- und Vollstreckungsübereinkom-
mens (EuGVÜ 1968), dessen Rechtsgrundlage der programmatische Artikel 220 EWGV (a.F.) auch
die Freizügigkeit der Gerichtsentscheidungen forderte, vgl. dazu *Hdb. IZVR* (Basedow), Bd. I (1982)
Kap. II Rn. 5.
[9] Richtlinie 98/27, *Abl.(EG)* [1998] L 166/51. Zur Entstehungsgeschichte Meyer, *WM* (1998)
1507; Hopt/ Baetge, in: Basedow/ Hopt/ Kötz/ Baetge, *Die Bündelung gleichgerichteter Interessen im
Prozeß – Verbandsklage und Gruppenklage –* (1998) 11, 30; Koch, „Die Verbandsklage in Europa",
ZZP (2000)(im Erscheinen).
[10] Kötz, „Vorbeugender Rechtsschutz im Zivilrecht – Eine rechtsvergleichende Skizze", *AcP* 174
(1974) 145, 154.
[11] Dazu Spry, *The Principles of Equitable Remedies*, 4th ed. (1990) 4; Stoll, in: *Int. Enc. Comp. L.
XI/2 (Torts: Consequences of Liability)*, Ch. 8, 184, 189.
[12] Im VII. Zusatzartikel zur US Constitution findet sich die Garantie des Jury Trial nur für „all suits
at common law".

3.2 Im *französischen Recht* sucht man zunächst vergeblich nach einer eigenen Klageart der Unterlassungsklage: Im Prozeßrecht wird nach traditionellem Muster unterschieden zwischen „actions personelles" und „actions réelles" und zwischen „actions pétitoires" und „actions possessoires".[13] Allerdings wird die Möglichkeit negatorischen Rechtsschutzes aus dem allgemeinen Deliktsrecht hergeleitet, nämlich aus dem Grundsatz der Naturalrestitution, wonach dem Richter die Befugnis zu sehr weit verstandener Wiederherstellung und Anordnung von Maßnahmen zur Verhinderung künftiger Schädigungen und Beeinträchtigungen zusteht.[14] Wenn die Herleitung des Unterlassungsrechtsschutzes aus allgemeinem Deliktsrecht auch bedeutet, daß der volle Tatbestand des Art. 1382 Code civil einschließlich rechtswidrig-schuldhaften Verhaltens erfüllt sein muß, so zeigt sich doch in der Praxis, daß der Unterschied zum deutschen Recht – das negatorischen Rechtsschutz auch ohne Rücksicht auf Verschulden gewährt – so groß nicht ist, da die Verschuldensanforderungen sehr niedrig sind.[15]

3.3 Für *Italien* gilt prima facie eine ähnliche Gesetzeslage wie in Deutschland: Art. 7 – 9, 10, 949 Abs. 2, 1079 Codice civile enthalten ausdrückliche Unterlassungsgebote für den Fall der Verletzung bestimmter absoluter Rechte. Allerdings hat die italienische Rechtsprechung diesen Rechtsschutz nicht über die bereits erfolgte Rechtsverletzung hinaus vorverlegt, geschweige denn andere Rechtsgüter in den Schutz mit einbezogen.[16] Gelegentlich versuchen allerdings die Gerichte mit vorsichtiger Analogie, vor allem im Bereich des einstweiligen Rechtsschutzes gemäss Art. 700 der Zivilprozeßordnung, eine „azione inibitoria" auch dort zuzulassen, wo der Unterlassungsanspruch nicht gesetzlich geregelt ist, insbesondere dann, wenn anderenfalls ein irreparabler Nachteil für den Betroffenen drohte.[17]

3.4 Das neue *niederländische* Burgerlijk Wetboek[18] enthält in seinem bemerkenswerten Buch 3 („Allgemeines Vermögensrecht") im Titel 11 („Ansprüche") eine ganz allgemeine und damit umfassende Regelung auch von Unterlassungsansprüchen: Art. 296 Abs. 1 bestimmt, daß derjenige, der zum Tun oder Unterlassen verpflichtet ist, dazu durch den Richter auf Klage des Berechtigten verurteilt werden

---

[13] Perrot, *Institutions judiciaire*, 4.éd. (1992) nos. 500ff.; Vincent/Guinchard, *La justice et ses institutions*, 3. éd. (1991) nos. 795ff.

[14] Ghestin/ Viney, *Traité de droit civil – Les obligations, La responsabilité: effets* (1988) no. 10; Calais-Auloy, „Les actions en cessation exercées dans l'intérêt des consommateurs (droit français, droit communautaire)", in: *Liber amicorum N. Reich* (1997) 789; auch Kötz, *AcP* 174 (1974) 145, 158ff. sowie Stoll, *Int. Enc. Comp. L.* (oben N. 11) Ch. 8-182.

[15] Kötz (oben N. 14) S. 162ff.

[16] Stoll, *Int. Enc. Comp. L.* (oben N. 11) Ch. 8-181.

[17] Busnelli, „Landesbericht Italien", in: von Bar (Hrsg.), *Deliktsrecht in Europa* (1994) 50f.

[18] Vgl. die zweisprachige Ausgabe *Niederländ. Bürgerl. Gesetzbuch* (Nieper und Westerdijk (hrsg.)) (1995).

kann. Auch das im Allgemeinen Schuldrecht geregelte Deliktsrecht (Buch 6 Titel 3) geht von der Möglichkeit negatorischen Rechtsschutzes aus, wenn es in Art. 168 Abs. 1 heißt, eine Klage auf Unterlassung rechtswidrigen Verhaltens könne mit der Begründung abgewiesen werden, dieses sei aus Gründen schwerwiegender gesellschaftlicher Interessen zu dulden.[19]

3.5 Die Unterlassungsklage ist auch in der *österreichischen* ZPO nicht gesondert geregelt, sondern wird als materiellrechtlich begründete Rechtsschutzform (verschuldensunabhängiger Unterlassungsanspruch) verstanden, mit der weitere oder unmittelbar drohende Rechtsverletzungen abgewendet werden sollen.[20] Überwiegend wird die Wiederholungsgefahr zwar als erforderlich angesehen, nicht aber als Prozeßvoraussetzung behandelt; die erstmals drohende Rechtsverletzung soll zwar eine besondere Form des Rechtsschutzbedürfnisses darstellen, deren Fehlen aber nicht zur Unzulässigkeit der Klage führt.[21]

3.6 Im *schweizerischen* Obligationenrecht ist der Unterlassungsanspruch vor allem zum Schutze absoluter Rechte anerkannt, da nur der negatorische Schutz die Ausschlußbefugnis des Rechtsträgers gewährleisten könne.[22] Dem entspricht die Zulassung einer Unterlassungsklage in den kantonalen Prozeßrechten, die allerdings nur bei Vorliegen eines Rechtsschutzbedürfnisses (unmittelbares Drohen einer widerrechtlichen Handlung) möglich sein soll; freilich stellt das Bundesgericht an den Nachweis dieses Rechtsschutzinteresses keine allzu hohen Anforderungen.[23] Auch im schweizerischen Recht wird der Unterlassungsanspruch (im Unterschied zum Rechtsschutzbedürfnis) als Frage des materiellen Rechts bezeichnet.[24]

4.   INTERNATIONALE ZUSTÄNDIGKEIT FÜR UNTERLASSUNGSKLAGEN

Ebensowenig wie für andere Leistungs-, Feststellungs- oder Gestaltungsklagen gibt es besondere Zuständigkeitsvorschriften für Unterlassungsklagen. Vielmehr richtet sich die internationale Zuständigkeit nach allgemeinen Regeln. Neben dem Beklagtenwohnsitz (§§ 12 ff. ZPO, Art. 2 EuGVÜ) kennen autonomes und europäi-

---

[19] Vgl. zu dieser Duldungspflicht Fokkema/ Hartkamp, „Law of Obligations", in: Chorus et al., *Introduction to Dutch Law*, 2nd ed. (1993) 93, 105.

[20] Böhm, *Unterlassungsanspruch und Unterlassungsklage* (1979); Jelinek, „Das ‚Klagerecht' auf Unterlassung", *ÖBl.* (1974) 125; Fasching, *Lehrbuch des österreichischen Zivilprozeßrechts*, 2. Aufl. (1990) Rn. 1069ff.

[21] OGH *ÖJZ* (1978) 205 sowie die Vorigen; a. A. Ballon, *Einführung in das österreichische Zivilprozeßrecht*, 5. Aufl. (1995) Rn. 188: Prozeßvoraussetzung!

[22] Bucher, *Schweizerisches Obligationenrecht, Allgemeiner Teil*, 2. Aufl. (1988) § 4 III 1 (S. 32).

[23] Vgl. Merz, „Obligationenrecht", in: *Schweizerisches Privatrecht*, Bd. VI/1 (1984) 256.

[24] Vgl. Guldener, *Schweizierisches Zivilprozeßrecht*, 3. Aufl. (1979) 206.

sches Zuständigkeitsrecht eine Reihe besonderer Gerichtsstände, die für Unterlassungsklagen von Bedeutung sein können. Wird das Begehren auf einen gesetzlichen Unterlassungsanspruch gestützt – wie im Falle von Verletzungen des Persönlichkeits-, Wettbewerbs-, Verbraucher- oder Umweltrechts[25] –, so kommen i.d.R. Deliktsgerichtsstände in Betracht (§ 32 ZPO, Art. 5 Nr. 3 EuGVÜ), bei Verletzung vertraglicher Unterlassungspflichten auch Zuständigkeiten des Vertragsrechts. Insoweit haben wir es bei Unterlassungsklagen also nicht mit Zuständigkeitsregeln zu tun, die für diese Rechtsschutzform spezifisch wären.

5. UNTERLASSUNGSANSPRUCH UND UNTERLASSUNGSKLAGE: ANKNÜPFUNG AN DAS FORUM ODER DEN ANSPRUCHSGRUND?

Die enge Verknüpfung von Anspruch und Klagerecht im Falle der Unterlassungsklage wirft zunächst die Frage nach der Anknüpfung auf: Nach welchem Recht sind die Klagbarkeit, die Zulässigkeit und prozessualen Voraussetzungen der Unterlassungsklage zu beurteilen?

Die damit zunächst gestellte Qualifikationsfrage wird zwar grundsätzlich aus der Sicht der *lex fori* beantwortet. Das hieße in einem Prozeß vor deutschen Gerichten die nach unserem Verständnis prozessualen Voraussetzungen dem deutschen Recht zu unterstellen, dagegen den materiellen Unterlassungsanspruch selbst aber nach der *lex causae* anzuknüpfen. Allerdings wird mit dem strikten Vorgehen nach der *lex fori* der beschriebene, enge Zusammenhang zwischen materiellem Recht und Prozeßrecht verkannt, so daß insoweit eine funktionale Qualifikation zu einleuchtenderen Ergebnissen führt: Klagbarkeit und andere, besondere Zulässigkeitsvoraussetzungen einer Unterlassungsklage sollten als „Zubehör des materiellen Rechts behandelt" werden,[26] da der funktionelle Zusammenhang zum materiellen Recht unübersehbar ist.

Geht es also etwa um das *Rechtsschutzbedürfnis* für eine Klage auf Unterlassung geschäftsschädigender Äußerungen oder von Schutzrechtsverletzungen, so ist dieses nach dem in der Sache anzuwendenden Recht zu beurteilen: Dieses entscheidet über ein ggf. besonderes Erfordernis für Unterlassungsklagen, mit dem sich Gerichte vor überflüssiger Inanspruchnahme schützen wollen – etwa weil die *lex causae* in einer Unterwerfungserklärung den Wegfall des Rechtsschutzbedürfnisses erblickt oder den Kläger auf Schadensersatz verweist und den Rechtsschutz nach der Maxi-

---

[25] Nw. oben N. 4–6 sowie Pastor/ Ahrens(-Bähr), *Der Wettbewerbsprozeß*, 4. Aufl. (1999) Kap. 22 Rn. 33; Schack, „Das internationale Prozeßrecht in umweltrechtlichen Streitigkeiten", in: *Ber. DGVR* 32 (1992) 315; Pfeiffer, „Der Umweltgerichtsstand als zuständigkeitsrechtlicher Störfall", *ZZP* 106 (1993) 159; w. Nw. zum Verbraucherrecht bei Schack, *IZVR*[2] Rn. 278 und Geimer/ Schütze, *Europäisches Zivilverfahrensrecht* (1997) Art. 13 EuGVÜ Rn. 21.

[26] Kropholler, *Internationales Privatrecht*, 3. Aufl. (1997) § 17 I (S. 113).

me „Dulde und Liquidiere" organisiert.[27]

Ob für die Zulässigkeit der Unterlassungsklage eine *Wiederholungsgefahr* vorauszusetzen ist, hängt davon ab, ob es sich dabei um ein prozessuales Erfordernis handelt oder um einen Bestandteil des materiellen Anspruchs. Diese (von *Medicus* als „praktisch bedeutungslos" bezeichnete)[28] Frage gewinnt im internationalen Zivilprozeß also beträchtliche Bedeutung. Wenn in der Lehre gelegentlich die Unterlassungsklage als rein prozessuales Institut, also als besonderer Klagetypus ohne materielle Anspruchsgrundlage angesehen wird,[29] so können damit zwar die Schwierigkeiten der subjektiven Zuordnung von Unterlassungsansprüchen vermieden werden (dazu unter 6). Aber schon die gesetzlichen Regelungen (z. B. §§ 12, 862, 1004 BGB, 37 Abs. 2 HGB, 1, 3 UWG, 15 Abs. 4 MarkenG) gehen von einem materiellen Unterlassungsanspruch aus, und nur diese „materiellrechtliche Rechtslage"[30] vermag die Entwicklung des negatorischen Rechtsschutzes über die im Gesetz geregelten Unterlassungsansprüche hinaus zu erklären.[31] Damit ist auch die Wiederholungs- bzw. (im Falle der vorbeugenden Unterlassungsklage) die Erstbegehungsgefahr im deutschen Recht als Voraussetzung des gesetzlichen Unterlassungsanspruchs, also als Bestandteil des materiellen Rechts anzusehen und scharf vom prozessrechtlichen Rechtsschutzinteresse zu trennen.[32] Fehlt die Wiederholungsgefahr, ist eine Unterlassungsklage dann als unbegründet abzuweisen, wenn das in der Sache anzuwendende Recht sie (ebenso wie das deutsche Recht) zu den materiellen Voraussetzungen zählt. Allgemeiner: Im Falle internationaler Unterlassungsklagen ist eine möglicherweise vorausgesetzte Wiederholungsgefahr nach demjenigen Sachrecht zu beurteilen, das auf den Unterlassungsanspruch anzuwenden ist.

Im Falle *vertraglich* vereinbarter Unterlassungsansprüche, von denen bisher nicht die Rede war, kann dies anders sein: Dort kann sich aus der Vereinbarung ergeben, daß eine Wiederholungsgefahr nicht erforderlich ist, um den Anspruch zu verfolgen. In einem solchen Falle kann jedoch einer Unterlassungsklage nach deutschem Recht das fehlende Rechtsschutzbedürfnis entgegengehalten werden, wenn es keinen Anlaß für die Befürchtung gibt, der Schuldner werde seine Unterlas-

---

[27] Zum Rechtsschutzbedürfnis bei Unterlassungsklagen im deutschen Recht Stein/ Jonas/ Schumann, *ZPO*, 21. Aufl. (1996) Vor § 253 Rn. 11ff.; HansOLG *GRUR* (1974) 108; Melullis, *Handbuch des Wettbewerbsprozesses*, 2. Aufl. (1995) Rn. 274ff., Oppermann, *Unterlassungsanspruch und materielle Gerechtigkeit im Wettbewerbsprozeß* (1993) 53ff.

[28] *MünchKomm/BGB*, 3. Aufl. (1996) § 1004 Rn. 82.

[29] So in Deutschland etwa Esser/Weyers, *Schuldrecht*, Bd. 2, 7. Aufl. (1991) § 62 IV.

[30] Zeuner, „Gedanken zur Unterlassungs- und negativen Feststellungsklage", in: *FS Dölle*, Bd. I (1963) 295, 307.

[31] Dazu Fikentscher, *Schuldrecht*, 9. Aufl. (1997) Rn. 1359ff.

[32] Dazu Stein/ Jonas/ Schumann, *ZPO²¹*, Vor § 253 Rn. 11; Oppermann, Unterlassungsanspruch (oben N. 27) 133.

sungspflicht verletzen.[33] Für die Qualifikation bedeutet dies, daß diese Frage vor deutschen Gerichten prozeßrechtlich einzuordnen. und folglich unabhängig vom materiellen Vertragsstatut nach der deutschen *lex fori* zu beurteilen ist.

6. KLAGEBEFUGNIS

Eingangs war bereits von der Eigenart von Unterlassungsansprüchen die Rede, welche in ihrer undeutlichen subjektiven Zuordnung darin besteht, daß sie als Abwehransprüche keinen eigentlichen Begünstigten haben. Die Unterlassungsklage ist mehr auf Unterbindung rechtswidrigen Verhaltens als auf den Schutz eines bestimmten Verletzten gerichtet, so daß es viel leichter fällt, von einer Unterlassungs*pflicht* des Beklagten zu sprechen als von einem Unterlassungs*anspruch* des Klägers.[34] Diese Verengung des Blicks auf den Rechtsverletzer bringt zugleich eine diffusere prozessuale Attribution der Rechtsdurchsetzungsbefugnis mit sich: Wer soll berechtigt sein, den Unterlassungsanspruch gerichtlich geltend zu machen? Die herkömmliche, enge Beschränkung der Klagebefugnis, allgemeiner: der Prozeßführungsbefugnis auf Rechtsinhaber soll die Gerichte vor ihrer unkontrollierten Inanspruchnahme durch den „quivis ex populo" schützen und dient damit neben der Prozeßökonomie auch der Funktionsgerechtigkeit der dritten Gewalt.[35] Rechtsinhaber im Falle der Unterlassungsklage ist der Inhaber des Unterlassungsanspruchs, der dem (potentiell) Verletzten zusteht. Damit scheint aus der Sicht des deutschen Rechts festzustehen, daß die in der Prozeßführungsbefugnis steckende Vorfrage nach der materiellen Berechtigung auch kollisionsrechtlich nach dem jeweils maßgeblichen (Sach-)Recht anzuknüpfen ist.[36]

6.1 Prozeßstandschaft zwischen *lex causae* und *lex fori*

Schon die Frage nach der Prozeßstandschaft Rechtsfremder indessen – die das eigentliche Problem der Prozeßführungsbefugnis erst aufwirft – läßt an der Selbstverständlichkeit ihrer materiellrechtlichen Qualifikation Zweifel aufkommen, weil das dafür maßgebliche Charakteristikum der materiellen Rechtsinhaberschaft dort fehlt. Auch begegnen uns Prozeßführungsbefugnisse in in- und ausländischen Rechten, deren Gründe lediglich in prozessualen Erwägungen zu finden sind. Dies

---

[33] Stein/ Jonas/ Schumann, ibid., § 259 Rn. 9.

[34] Zeuner in: *FS Dölle* (oben N. 30) S. 304; vgl auch Henckel, „Vorbeugender Rechtsschutz in Zivilsachen", *AcP* 174 (1974) 97, 124; Piehler, *Einstweiliger Rechtsschutz und materielles Recht* (oben N. 1) 219.

[35] Allgemein dazu Koch, *Prozeßführung im öffentlichen Interesse* (1983) 99ff., 269.

[36] So für die Prozeßführungbefugnis allgemein Geimer, *Internationales Zivilprozeßrecht*, 3. Aufl. (1997) Rn. 326 und 2235ff.

gilt etwa für die Prozeßstandschaft des Rechtsnachfolgers in § 265 Abs. 2 ZPO oder für die „action oblique" des französischen Rechts, die aus Gründen der Praktikabiltität und der Einordnung in das System von Gesamt- und Einzelvollstreckung prozeßrechtlich zu qualifizieren sind.[37] Die Prozeßführungsbefugnis läßt sich mithin nicht grundsätzlich nach der *lex causae* anknüpfen, sondern unterliegt bei verfahrensrechtlicher Begründung auch der *lex fori*.

Für individuelle Unterlassungsklagen bedeutet dies zunächst, daß die Sachbefugnis (Aktivlegitimation) bei Grundstücksbeeinträchtigungen der *lex rei sitae*, im Falle von Delikten und Wettbewerbshandlungen dem Recht des Tat- oder Marktortes oder der *lex protectionis* bei Schutzrechtsverletzungen unterliegt. Geht es hingegen um die Übertragung von Klagbefugnissen auf Verbände – wie etwa im deutschen Recht nach § 13 UWG oder § 13 AGBG – oder öffentliche Repräsentanten – wie etwa den Director General of Fair Trading in England[38] – so handelt es sich dabei nicht um Rechtsinhaber, die mit der Unterlassungsklage auf die Verletzung ihrer Rechte reagieren, sondern um Kontrollkompetenzen, die dem Verband (oder dem Director) im Interesse wirkungsvoller Rechtsdurchsetzung verliehen sind.

6.2   Individuelle Unterlassungsklagen

Nur die „echten" verfahrensrechtlichen Grundlagen der Unterlassungsklage sind nach der *lex fori* zu beurteilen. Am Beispiel des Wettbewerbsrechts sei dies näher erläutert: Im Falle einer individuellen Untersagungsverfügung steht die Klagebefugnis dem Antragssteller zunächst als unmittelbar Verletztem (materiellem Rechtsinhaber) zu. Das deutsche, schweizerische und österreichische Wettbewerbsrecht gehen darüber noch hinaus, wenn sie dem Konkurrenten eine „typisierte Betroffenheit" attestieren: Nach § 13 Abs. 2 Nr. 1 dt. UWG (§ 9 schweiz. UWG, § 14 öst. UWG) muß der Wettbewerber keine konkrete Verletzung seiner subjektiven Rechte geltend machen, sondern kann sich auf die abstrakte Störung (wesentliche Beeinträchtigung) des Wettbewerbs um Waren oder Dienstleistungen auf demselben Markt berufen, an dem auch der Verfügungskläger teilnimmt.[39] Bei grenzüberschreitenden Sachverhalten steht mithin diese „abstrakte" Klagebefugnis auch den Konkurrenten zu, wenn das Recht des Marktortes dies vorsieht.

---

[37] Dazu Schack, *Internationales Zivilverfahrensrecht*, 2. Aufl. (1996) Rn. 552, 555.

[38] Vgl. dazu Ellger, in: Basedow/ Hopt/ Kötz/ Baetge, *Bündelung gleichgerichteter Interessen* (oben N. 9) 103, 123ff.

[39] Vgl. zu den Voraussetzungen des § 13 II Nr. 1 UWG im einzelnen Emmerich, *Das Recht des unlauteren Wettbewerbs*, 5. Aufl. (1998) § 22.3; Baumbach/ Hefermehl, *Wettbewerbsrecht*, 20. Aufl. (1998) UWG § 13 Rn. 11ff.; *Großkomm UWG/ Erdmann* (1992) § 13 Rn. 15ff.; Pastor/ Ahrens (Jestaedt), *Wettbewerbsprozeß* (oben N. 25) Kap. 23 Rn. 9ff.; Häsemeyer, *AcP* 188 (1998) 140, 155ff.; zum österreichischen Recht vgl. Koppensteiner, *Wettbewerbsrecht, Bd. 2: Unlauterer Wettbewerb*, 2. Aufl. (1987) § 15 I 5 (S. 281ff.).

6.3   Verbandsklagen

Noch einen Schritt weiter in der Loslösung der Klagebefugnis von der materiellen Rechtsinhaberschaft gehen die Rechtsordnungen, die den *Verbänden* oder *öffentlichen Stellen* die Prozeßinitiative zur Kontrolle (Untersagung) wettbewerbs- oder sonst rechtswidrigen Verhaltens zugestehen.[40] Erkennt man allerdings solchen Einrichtungen <u>eigene</u> Unterlassungsansprüche zu, wie dies in Deutschland im Wettbewerbsrecht überwiegend noch geschieht, dann stellt sich hier keine Frage nach einer besonderen Prozeßführungsbefugnis, da diese mit der Sachlegitimation grundsätzlich einhergeht: Wir hätten es dann von vornherein nicht mit der Prozeßführung durch Rechtsfremde zu tun[41]. Dieser Auffassung ist jedoch entgegenzuhalten, daß damit der Unterschied zwischen echter Eigenbetroffenheit und abgeleiteter Rechtsinhaberstellung vernachlässigt, zudem auch nicht konsequent beachtet wird: Denn auch nach h.M. soll die Klagebefugnis bzw. Gläubigerstellung von Verbänden ein Zulässigkeitsproblem sein.[42] Deshalb wird in der Literatur mit Recht zunehmend von einer echten Prozeßführungsbefugnis des Verbandes gesprochen, deren Ableitung allerdings noch unterschiedlich begründet wird.[43]

Im deutschen IPR werden solche Prozeßführungsbefugnisse folgerichtig prozessual eingeordnet und daher nach der lex fori beurteilt: Jede Prozeßordnung entscheide nach eigenen Maßstäben, ob Popular- oder Verbandsklagen zugelassen seien.[44] Angesichts unterschiedlicher Herleitung von Prozeßführungsermächtigungen, die auf materiell- oder prozessrechtlicher Grundlage beruhen können (o. vor 6.1), ist jedoch auch im Falle von Verbandsklagen eine Differenzierung erforderlich. Freilich ist erneut daran zu erinnern, daß damit die Anerkennung eines mate-

---

[40] Rechtsvergleichend (aus Anlaß der in der Unterlassungsklage-Richtlinie vorgesehenen Betrauung „qualifizierter Einrichtungen" mit kollektiven Klagebefugnissen) s. Basedow/ Hopt/ Kötz/ Baetge, *Die Bündelung gleichgerichteter Interessen im Prozeß* (oben N. 9); Koch, *ZZP* (2000) (im Erscheinen).

[41] So wohl die Rspr., vgl. BGH *NJW* (1970) 243; Baumbach/ Hefermehl, *Wettbewerbsrecht*[20], UWG § 13 Rn. 5; *GroßKomm UWG/ Erdmann* (oben N. 39) § 13 Rn. 18; Rosenberg/ Schwab/ Gottwald, *Zivilprozeßrecht*, 15. Aufl. (1993) § 47.2 (S. 244); Gerlach in: *MünchKomm/BGB*, 3. Aufl. (1993) § 13 AGBG Rn. 50ff.

[42] Die Vorigen; aus der Rspr.: BGH *NJW* (1990) 3149 (Beachtung von Zweifeln von Amts wegen auch noch in der Revisionsinstanz). Krit. *Ahrens*, Die internationale Verbandsklage in Wettbewerbssachen, *WRP* (1994) 649.

[43] Von der Wahrnehmung eines „materiell-rechtlichen Kollektivanspruchs der betroffenen Verbrauchergruppe" entspricht Gilles, *ZZP* 98 (1985) 1, 10; einen Unterlassungsanspruch des Staates nimmt Marotzke, *ZZP* 98 (1985) 160, 196 an; Hadding, *JZ* (1970) 305, Lindacher in: *MünchKomm/ ZPO* (1992), vor § 50 Rn. 73, Leipold, in: Gilles, *Effektivität des Rechtsschutzes* (1983) 57, 65, 79; Häsemeyer, *AcP* 188 (1988) 140, 156f.; E. Schmidt, *NJW* (1989) 1192 und H. Koch, *KritV* (1989) 323, 329 gehen von einem vom materiellrechtlichen Anspruch unabhängigen Prozeßführungsrecht im öffentlichen bzw. Sozialschutzinteresse aus.

[44] Schack, *IZVR*[2] Rn. 556; ders., *Ber. d. DGVR* 32 (1992) (oben N. 6) 337; Geimer, *IZPR*[3] Rn. 341.

riell-rechtlichen Unterlassungsanspruchs einhergeht.[45] Dementsprechend
entscheidet auch die lex causae darüber, welche Ansprüche der Verband oder die
sonst „qualifizierte Einrichtung" soll geltend machen können, wogegen die lex fori
über die formellen Voraussetzungen der Klagebefugnis befindet: Partei- und Prozeßfähigkeit, evtl. Mindestmitgliederzahl, Satzungsaufgaben und ihre tatsächliche
Wahrnehmung etc.[46]

7.   EINSTWEILIGER RECHTSSCHUTZ DURCH UNTERLASSUNGSKLAGEN

Da Unterlassungsklagen zur Vermeidung künftiger Rechtsverletzungen dienen,
nehmen sie vielfach die Form von Eilverfahren an. Denn in der ganz überwiegenden Mehrzahl der Fälle besteht die für das besondere Präventionsbedürfnis erforderliche Wiederholungsgefahr gerade in der unmittelbar bevorstehenden (erneu-
ten) Rechtsverletzung. Welche Auswirkungen haben die oben dargelegten
Zuordnungen der Unterlassungsklage zum materiellen Recht bzw. Verfahrensrecht
für den einstweiligen Rechtsschutz?

7.1   Materiellrechtliche Grundlagen

Daß und in welcher Weise *materiellrechtliche Zielvorstellungen* den Erlaß einstweiliger Rechtsschutzmaßnahmen beeinflussen, ist schon mehrfach ausführlich
untersucht worden.[47] Die materielle Rechtsgrundlage einstweiligen Rechtsschutzes
in Gestalt des Arrest- bzw. Verfügungsanspruchs (§§ 916, 936 ZPO) ist nach dem
in der Sache maßgeblichen Recht zu beurteilen, während die formellen Voraussetzungen für den Erlaß einer einstweiligen Maßnahme (Verfügungsgrund) und ihre
Gestalt sich nach der lex fori richten müssen.[48] Daß eine einstweilige Verfügung –
wie in aller Regel – auf Unterlassung gerichtet ist,[49] ändert am anwendbaren Recht
nichts.

---

[45]   Zum Streit darüber s. Ahrens, *WRP* (1994) 649, 656.

[46]   So auch Ahrens, *WRP* (1994) 649, 656, der allerdings lex fori und lex causae in der Weise kumu-
lieren will, daß beide die Verbandsklage akzeptieren müssen; Koch, *Verbraucherprozeßrecht* (1990)
116f.; ders., Art. „Verbandsklage" in: *Lexikon des Rechts Gr. 17/1750* (1995) 8ff.; ders., „Europäische
Verbandsklage", in: *FS Fenge* (1996) 85, 90.

[47]   Vgl. vor allem Piehler (oben N. 1) zum Wettbewerbs-, Arbeitskampf- und Patentrecht in
Deutschland und in den USA; zum Zusammenhang von materiellem und Prozeßrecht in dogmatischer
Hinsicht vgl. Minnerop, *Materielles Recht und einstweiliger Rechtsschutz* (1973).

[48]   Geimer, *IZPR³* Rn. 1984.

[49]   Im englischen Sprachgebrauch wird oft nur verkürzt von „injunction" gesprochen, wenn eine
„preliminary, interlocutory injunction" gemeint ist.

7.2 Prozessuale Voraussetzungen

Zweifelhaft ist allerdings, ob die lex fori auch für besondere *prozessuale Voraussetzungen* der einstweiligen Verfügung, wie das deutsche Recht sie in § 25 UWG und das österreichische in § 24 UWG kennt, gilt.

Danach kann eine einstweilige Untersagungsverfügung im Wettbewerbsrecht auch dann erlassen werden, wenn die Voraussetzungen der §§ 935, 940 ZPO (§ 381 oest. EO) an sich nicht vorliegen, d.h., wenn es an einem Verfügungsgrund fehlt; die Dringlichkeit wird also vermutet.[50] Gesetzliche Vermutungen werden dem materiellen Recht zugeordnet, selbst wenn sie widerleglich sind, und daher nach der lex causae beurteilt.[51] Das wird aus Art. 32 Abs. 3 S. 1 EGBGB (= Art. 14 I Röm. EuVÜ 1980) gefolgert, der die gesetzlichen Vermutungen wie Sachnormen behandelt (und sie daher nicht von dem Vertragsstatut trennen will).

Diese Begründung trifft nicht zu für prozessuale Vermutungen, die keinen direkten Bezug zum materiellen Recht haben.[52] Von § 25 UWG läßt sich allerdings gerade nicht sagen, die Vorschrift habe keinen direkten Bezug zum materiellen Recht. Nicht nur ihre ratio ist allein wettbewerbsrechtlich zu erklären – unabhängig von der dogmatischen Einordnung der Dringlichkeitsvermutung als Prozeßvoraussetzung oder Bestandteil der Begründetheit.[53] Denn die einstweilige Verfügung soll in Wettbewerbssachen deshalb erleichtert werden, weil sie infolge schnellwirkender und kurzlebiger Wettbewerbsmaßnahmen dort im hohen Maße geeignet ist, eine endgültige Regelung des Streits herbeizuführen; eine Verweisung auf spätere Schadensersatzsanktionen könnte einen Verstoß kaum wirksam korrigieren. Darüber hinaus zeigt die genaue Betrachtung des § 25 UWG, daß dort nicht auf eine prozessuale Voraussetzung des allgemeinen einstweiligen Rechtsschutzes verzichtet wird. Vielmehr entfällt lediglich die Notwendigkeit, die Dringlichkeit vorzutragen und glaubhaft zu machen. Dies aber ist Ausdruck einer besonderen wettbewerbspolitischen und damit materiellen Wertung, nämlich der Gewährleistung der Lauterkeit des Wettbewerbs als seiner grundlegenden Funktionsbedingung. Damit soll der Wettbewerb als Institution und nicht in erster Linie der einzelne, konkret verletzte Wettbewerber oder Verbraucher geschützt werden.[54] Ob die Dringlichkeit wie in § 25 UWG vermutet wird oder nachzuweisen ist, ist deshalb keine nach der

---

[50] Emmerich, *Das Recht des unlauteren Wettbewerbs*[5], § 26.2 (S. 374ff.); Pastor/ Ahrens(-Traub), *Der Wettbewerbsprozeß* (oben N. 25) Kap 49 Rn. 19 f.; Koppensteiner, *Wettbewerbsrecht*[2], § 16 I 3 (S. 305).
[51] Grundlegend Coester-Waltjen, *Internationales Beweisrecht* (1983) 309, 319; Geimer, *IZPR*[3] Rn. 2284; Schack, *IZVR*[2], Rn. 465, 466.
[52] Die amtliche Begründung zu Art. 32 III 1 EGBGB, BT-Dr. 10/504, 82; vgl. auch Coester-Waltjen, ibid., Rn. 329; Geimer, *IZPR*[3] Rn. 2288.
[53] Nw. zu beiden Positionen bei Baumbach/ Hefermehl, *UWG* § 25 Rn. 9.
[54] Vgl. zu dieser Deutung mit rechtsvergleichender Begründung namentlich Piehler, *Einstweiliger Rechtsschutz und materielles Recht* (oben N. 1) 217ff.

lex fori zu beurteilende Prozeßvoraussetzung, sondern unterliegt der lex causae, in Wettbewerbssachen also der Marktortregel.

7.3 Europäisches Zivilprozeßrecht

Im *europäischen Zivilprozeßrecht* gelten gegenüber dem autonomen IZPR keine Sonderregeln: Insbesondere enthält das EuGVÜ entgegen dem ersten Anschein auch keine eigenen Zuständigkeitsregeln für einstweilige Rechtsschutzanträge. Denn Art. 24 stellt lediglich den sonst geltenden Vorrang der einheitlichen europäischen Zuständigkeitsordnung zugunsten der zusätzlichen Eilgerichtsstände des nationalen IZPR zurück, ohne damit allerdings die „normalen" Hauptsache-Gerichtsstände des Übereinkommens zu versperren.[55] Eine einstweilige Unterlassungsverfügung kann in Deutschland daher gem. §§ 937 i.V.m. 32 ZPO bzw. Art. 5 Nr. 3 EuGVÜ am Tatort-Gerichtsstand erwirkt werden.

Die nach Art. 3 EuGVÜ ausgeschlossenen, exorbitanten Gerichtsstände bleiben im einstweiligen Rechtsschutz allerdings zugänglich.[56] Für den negatorischen Rechtsschutz kann dies etwa bedeuten, daß die bloße Zustellung einer „injunction" in England an einen durchreisenden Deutschen nach englischem Recht zuständigkeitsbegründend wirkt[57] – was nach Art. 24 hinzunehmen ist. Eine darauf ergehende englische Entscheidung ist hierzulande auch anzuerkennen, obwohl die Zuständigkeit aus autonomem englischen Recht hergeleitet wurde.[58]

8. MATERIELLE RECHTSKRAFT GRENZÜBERSCHREITENDER UNTERLASSUNGSURTEILE UND IHRE ANERKENNUNG

Die Frage nach den grenzüberschreitenden materiellen Rechtskraftwirkungen eines Unterlassungsurteils stellt sich insbesondere im Falle der Mehrfachverfolgung:

---

[55] S. etwa OLG Frankfurt/M., *RIW* (1980) 799; Kropholler, *Europäisches Zivilprozeßrecht*, 6. Aufl. (1998) Art. 24 Rn. 6; Schack, *IZVR*[2] Rn. 424; Koch, „Neuere Probleme der internationalen Zwangsvollstreckung einschließlich des einstweiligen Rechtsschutzes", in: Schlosser (Hrsg.), *Materielles Recht und Prozeßrecht*. . . (1992) 183, 197f. – a. A. Schlosser, *EuGVÜ* (1996) Art. 24 Rn.1, der die Zuständigkeitsregeln des Übk. für einstweilige Maßnahmen ganz ausschließen will.

[56] So die h.M., Schack, *IZVR*[2] Rn. 424 m. w. Nw.; Geimer/ Schütze, *Europäisches Zivilverfahrensrecht* (oben N. 24) Art. 24 Rn. 1; Koch, „Neuere Probleme", ibid., 171, 182f. – differenzierend Kropholler, *EuZPR*, ibid., Art. 24 Rn. 8ff.

[57] Zu dieser „transient jurisdiction" oder „presence rule" vgl. Koch, „Grenzüberschreitendet einstweiliger Rechtsschutz", in: Heldrich/ Kono (Hrsg.), *Herausforderungen des internationalen Zivilverfahrensrechts* (1994) 85, 88f.

[58] Art. 26 EuGVÜ, keine Zuständigkeitsnachprüfung: Art. 28 III; dazu Kropholler, *EuZPR* Art. 28 Rn. 1; nur im Falle einer schlechterdings nicht hinnehmbaren exorbitanten Zuständigkeit soll ein Rückgriff auf die ordre public-Sperre möglich sein: Schlosser, *EuGVÜ* Artt. 27–29 Rn. 30.

Steht einer Unterlassungsklage in Deutschland ein Urteil in der Schweiz zum selben Streitgegenstand (oder über eine Vorfrage) entgegen? Umgekehrt: Ist ein hiesiges Unterlassungsurteil ein Hindernis für ein zweites Verfahren im Ausland?

8.1 Anerkennung von Rechtskraftwirkungen

Genauere Betrachtung zeigt, daß es sich dabei um ein *Anerkennungsproblem* handelt: Ist das schweizerische Urteil hierzulande anzuerkennen, dann kommt ein Folgeverfahren nicht in Betracht.[59] An dieser Stelle kann nicht näher auf die Anerkennungsfragen eingegangen, sondern soll nur auf das bei *Unterlassungsklagen* zugespitzt auftretende Problem der genauen Bestimmung des Streitgegenstandes hingewiesen werden. Soweit dieser durch Antrag und Sachverhalt charakterisiert wird, bedarf es beim Unterlassungsbegehren zwar einer genauen Beschreibung des inkriminierten Verhaltens (Bestimmtheitsgebot), damit der Beklagte weiß, um welchen Handlungsspielraum er kämpfen und welche Pflichten er (im Falle eines Urteils) einhalten muß.[60] Das bringt jedoch das Risiko mit sich, daß der Beklagte durch nur geringfügige Abänderung des verbotenen Verhaltens (der ehrverletzenden Darstellung, der Werbebehauptungen) das Urteilsverbot unterlaufen und damit auch seine Vollstreckung verhindern kann. Daher stellt die deutsche Rechtsprechung im Interesse wirkungsvollen Rechtsschutzes bei der *Auslegung* eines Unterlassungstenors darauf ab, welches Verhalten des Beklagten den rechtlichen Kern des klägerischen Vorwurfs ausmachte und damit verboten werden sollte (sog. Kerntheorie).[61] Von diesen für den innerstaatlichen negatorischen Rechtsschutz entwickelten Grundsätzen kann zunächst bei grenzüberschreitenden Verfahren ebenfalls ausgegangen werden, insbesondere soweit sie die objektiven Rechtskraftgrenzen großzügiger ziehen als bei anderen Leistungsklagen. Wenn Anerkennung ausländischer Urteile bedeutet, daß ihre Wirkungen (in den Grenzen des hier Zulässigen) auf das Inland erstreckt werden,[62] dann dürfte dies angesichts der vergleichsweise strengen deutschen Rechtskraftlehre[63] i.d.R. zur problemlosen Anerkennung führen. Dies gilt erst recht im *europäischen* Zivilprozeß: Nach Art. 26 EuGVÜ werden Entschei-

---

[59] Allg. dazu schon Riezler, *Internationales Zivilprozeßrecht* (1948) 520ff.; Schack, *IZVR*[2] Rn. 887; *AK-ZPO/Koch* (1987) § 328 Rn. 11ff.; Geimer, *IZPR*[3] Rn. 2801, 2808 (auch zur streitige Frage, ob der Rechtskrafteinwand bei ausländischem Urteil zur Unzulässigkeit führt oder nur zur materiellen Bindung des Zweitgerichts).

[60] Vgl. etwa Pastor/Ahrens, *Der Wettbewerbsprozeß* (oben N. 25) Kap.40 Rn. 6.

[61] Baumbach/ Hefermehl, *Wettbewerbsrecht*[20], UWG Einl. Rn. 485 m. w. Nw.; Pastor/ Ahrens, *Wettbewerbsprozeß* Kap. 40 Rn. 9.

[62] Grundlegend dazu Martiny, in: *Hdb. IZVR* Bd. III/1 (1984) Rn. 362 ff.; *AK-ZPO/Koch*, § 328 Rn. 14ff.

[63] Zeuner, „Rechtsvergleichende Bemerkungen zur objektiven Begrenzung der Rechtskraft im Zivilprozeß", in: *FS Zweigert* (1981) 603 (krit.); Schack, *IZVR*[2] Rn. 913 m. vgl. Hinweisen.

dungen aus Vertragsstaaten ohne Sachprüfung und inzidenter (Absatz 1) anerkannt;
die Anerkennung erfaßt vor allem die materielle Rechtskraft.[64]

8.2 Einwand ausländischer Rechtshängigkeit

Am Deutlichsten tritt die im Vergleich zum innerstaatlichen Streitgegenstandsbegriff großzügigere Regelung des internationalen Anerkennungsrechts zutage, wenn die *Rechtshängigkeit* eines (Unterlassungs-)Verfahrens im anderen Land eingewendet wird: Nach autonomem deutschen IZPR ist für den Rechtshängigkeitseinwand eine Anerkennungs*prognose* erforderlich, in dessen Rahmen naturgemäß nicht alle Voraussetzungen des § 328 I ZPO überprüft werden können (eben weil sie noch nicht alle feststehen, wie z.b. die ordre public-Verträglichkeit des Ergebnisses der Anerkennung einer ausländischen Entscheidung, § 328 I Nr. 4 ZPO).[65] Im Unterschied zum autonomen deutschen Recht ist das *europäische* Zivilprozeßrecht in der Beachtung ausländischer Rechtshängigkeit unter mehreren Gesichtspunkten noch großzügiger (aus der Perspektive des *späteren* Klägers strenger!): Es kommt nach Art. 21 EuGVÜ weder auf die Anerkennungsprognose an, noch ist Identität des Streitgegenstandes erforderlich. Der Begriff „desselben Anspruchs", der in Art. 21 Voraussetzung für den wirksamen Rechtshängigkeitseinwand ist, wird vom EuGH vertragsautonom und sehr viel weiter als der des deutschen Streitgegenstandsbegriffs[66] verstanden; er soll lediglich verhindern, daß im „Kernpunkt" identische Verfahren parallel betrieben werden können.[67] Dies steht im Einklang mit der in Art. 22 für nicht identische, aber im Sachzusammenhang stehende Verfahren vorgesehenen Aussetzungsmöglichkeit.

Für den negatorischen Rechtsschutz stellt die Praxis zu Art. 21 zwar eine nicht unbeträchtliche Einschränkung des Klägers dar, da er durch die (scheinbare) Großzügigkeit in der Beachtung ausländischer Rechtshängigkeit gehindert ist, jede auch nur im Kernpunkt gleichartige (wenn auch anders tenorierte) Sache erneut vor Gericht zu bringen.[68] Im Interesse größerer internationaler Entscheidungsharmonie, der Freizügigkeit (i.S.v. Anerkennungsfreundlichkeit) von Justizakten und letztlich auch der Prozeßökonomie ist diese Tendenz der europäischen Rechtsprechung aber zu billigen.

---

[64] Statt Vieler: Schlosser, *EuGVÜ* Art. 26. Rn. 3.

[65] Allg. dazu Geimer, *IZPR³* Rn. 2688ff.; Keller/ Siehr, *Allgemeine Lehren des IPR* (1986) 595.

[66] Schack, *IZVR²* Rn. 761ff.; Geimer, *IZPR³* Rn. 2693ff.; Geimer/ Schütze, *EuZVR* (oben N. 25) Art. 21 Rn. 28ff.

[67] EuGH Rs. 144/86 – *Gubisch ./. Palumbo* -, Slg. 1987, 4861= *NJW* (1989) 665 = *IPRax* (1989) 157 (Schack, 139) und Rs. C-406/92 – *Ship Tatry ./. Ship Maciej Rataj* – , Slg. 1994 I 5439 =*JZ* (1995) 616 (Huber 603) = *IPRax* (1996) 108 (Schack 80).

[68] So die Kritik bei Gottwald, *MüKo-ZPO* (1992) Bd. III, Art. 21 GVÜ Rn. 4; M. Wolf, in: *FS Schwab* (1990) 561; Leipold, *GS Arens* (1993) 227.

8.3   Antisuit injunctions

Ein besonderes Problem internationalen Unterlassungs-Rechtsschutzes hat uns die anglo-amerikanische Praxis der *„antisuit injunctions"* beschert: Damit kann dem Beklagten untersagt werden, einen Prozeß in gleicher Sache im Ausland zu führen bzw. fortzuführen.[69] Da es sich dabei – anders als bei den bisher behandelten, auf materiellrechtlich relevantes Verhalten zielenden Unterlassungsbegehren – um ausschließlich prozeßrechtliche Strategien handelt, soll es bei zwei kurzen Hinweisen sein Bewenden haben: Zum einen hängt die Wirkung ausländischer Prozeßführungsverbote von den Sanktionen ab, die an Verstöße geknüpft werden, und damit von ihrer grenzüberschreitenden Vollstreckbarkeit (dazu unten 9). Die Beachtung einer ausländischen „antisuit injunction" als Prozeßhindernis für das inländische Verfahren kommt jedenfalls mangels Identität des Streitgegenstandes nicht in Betracht. Zum anderen sind den kontinentaleuropäischen Rechten solche (gesetzlichen) Prozeßführungsverbote deshalb fremd, weil die Inanspruchnahme staatlicher Gerichte – selbst wenn sie unzuständig sind! – als solche allenfalls in Ausnahmefällen rechtswidrig sein kann: Der Justizgewährungsanspruch schließt die unmittelbar prozeßhindernde Wirkung von Prozeßführungsverboten i.d.R. aus.

9.   GRENZÜBERSCHREITENDE VOLLSTRECKUNG VON UNTERLASSUNGSURTEILEN

Die Rechtsverwirklichung von Unterlassungsansprüchen über die Grenze hinweg in Gestalt der Zwangsvollstreckung wirft eine Reihe von Problemen auf, die vor allem mit der territorialen Begrenzung von Hoheitsbefugnissen sowie der Durchsetzung von Beugemitteln in Form von Zwangs- oder Ordnungsgeldern zusammenhängen: Wie sollen Zwangsvollstreckungsmaßnahmen außerhalb des Gerichtsstaates vollzogen werden? Können ausländische Zwangsgeldentscheidungen auch dann hierzulande vollstreckt werden, wenn sie dem Gläubiger statt dem Fiskus zugute kommen? Erleichtert das System des europäischen Zivilprozeßrechts die grenzüberschreitende Vollstreckung von Unterlassungsurteilen?
   Da ich solchen Fragen bereits in anderem Zusammenhang nachgegangen bin und sie auch von anderen ausführlicher erörtert worden sind,[70] sollen hier einige zu-

---

[69] Dazu statt Vieler Schack, *IZVR*[2] Rn. 770ff. (ausf. Nw. Rn 769); Koch, „Neuere Probleme" (oben N. 55) 490ff. – Zu Prozeßführungsverboten im deutschen Recht vgl. J. Schröder, in: *FS Kegel* (1987) 523 und Kurth, *Inländischer Rechtsschutz gegen Verfahren vor ausländischen Gerichten* (1989).

[70] Vgl. Remien, *Rechtverwirklichung durch Zwangsgeld* (1992) 299ff.; Stutz, *Die internationale Handlungs- und Unterlassungsvollstreckung unter dem EuGVÜ* (Diss. Konstanz 1992); Treibmann, *Die Vollstreckung von Handlungen und Unterlassungen im europäischen Zivilrechtsverkehr* (1994); Koch, „Neuere Probleme" (oben N. 55) 195ff.

sammenfassende Stichworte genügen.

Die mit der Anordnung von Beugemaßnahmen zur Auslandsvollstreckung von Unterlassungstiteln verbundenen Souveränitätsbedenken erweisen sich nicht als stichhaltig. Denn weder die Zustellung eines gerichtlichen Unterlassungsgebotes, noch die darin oft enthaltene Androhung von Zwangsmitteln stellen für sich bereits einen Eingriff in die Souveränität des Adressatenstaates dar. Denn solche Maßnahmen bedürfen noch der nach dem Recht und mit den Ordnungsmitteln des Vollstreckungsstaates ablaufenden Vollziehung (ggf. mit den dortigen Hoheitsmitteln). D.h.. die Vollstreckung selbst unterliegt immer dem Recht des Vollstreckungsstaates (lex fori executionis), dessen Vollstreckungsorgane auch die ausschließliche Zuständigkeit dafür haben (s. auch Art. 16 Nr. 5 EuGVÜ).

Am Beispiel des französischen Zwangsgeldes (astreinte) sei gezeigt, wie sich auch die in Europa unterschiedlichen Formen der Durchsetzung von Unterlassungsurteilen grenzüberschreitend vollziehen lassen:

Spricht ein französisches Gericht im Zusammenhang mit einem Unterlassungsurteil eine „astreinte" aus, so stellt dies zunächst lediglich eine Eventualverurteilung dar, d.h., das zunächst angeordnete Zwangsgeld ist erst dann zu zahlen, wenn dem Unterlassungsurteil zuwider gehandelt und die Höhe der „astreinte" sodann gerichtlich festgesetzt wird (liquidation).[71] Mit der ersten Eventualanordnung der „astreinte" wird also der Ausschließlichkeitsanspruch ausländischer Vollstreckungszuständigkeit (Art. 16 Nr. 5 EuGVÜ) noch nicht in Frage gestellt. Erst die spätere Zwangsgeldfestsetzung (liquidation) im Urteilsstaat stellt einen gemäss Art. 43 anerkennungsfähigen Vollstreckungstitel dar, der im Vollstreckungsstaat mit dessen Mitteln und durch seine Organe durchgesetzt wird.[72]

Zwar stellten die Zwangsgelder in Frankreich und in den Benelux-Staaten (astreinte, dwangsom), die ursprünglich als Kompensation gedacht waren und daher dem Gläubiger zufließen, das Modell für die Regelung in Art. 43 EuGVÜ dar. Doch müssen auch die Zwangs- und Ordnungsgelder des deutschen, österreichischen oder englischen Rechts (contempt fines), die an den Fiskus gehen, als im Ausland anerkennungsfähige Entscheidungen gelten, die dort freilich u.U. anzupassen sind: Wird bei Verstoß des französischen Schuldners gegen ein deutsches Unterlassungsurteil hier ein Ordnungsgeld gegen ihn gemäss § 890 ZPO verhängt und soll diese Entscheidung in Frankreich exequiert werden, so ist der deutsche Titel dort in eine (gläubigerbegünstigende) „astreinte" umzuformulieren, da er nur mit dortigen Vollstreckungsmitteln durchgesetzt werden kann.[73]

---

[71] Art. 33ff. d. Ges. Nr. 91-650 vom 9.7.1991 zur Reform des Zwangsvollstreckungsrechts, *JO* [1991] 9228. Ausführlich zum gleichlautenden Vorgänger-Gesetz von 1972, Remien (oben N. 70) 42ff.

[72] Remien, ibid., 324ff.; Schlosser, *EuGVÜ* Art. 43 Rn. 4; Koch, „Neuere Probleme" (oben N. 55) 198ff.

[73] Koch, „Neuere Probleme" (oben N. 55) 200; skeptisch zwar, i.E. aber ebenso Schack, *IZVR2* Rn.

Andere Vorschläge gehen dahin, Zwangs- oder Ordnungsgeldentscheidungen zugunsten des Staates als Gläubiger nach Art. 43 EuGVÜ anerkennen und vollstrecken zu lassen.[74]

Die gegen das Exequatur staatsnütziger Ordnungsgelder vorgebrachten Bedenken rühren her aus ihrem angeblichen öffentlichrechtlichen, gar strafrechtlichen Charakter und aus den Zweifeln an ihrer Eigenschaft als Sachentscheidung.[75] Selbst wenn solche Bedenken letztlich nicht zu überzeugen vermögen, kann ihnen unter dem Blickwinkel praktisch aussichtsreicher Rechtsdurchsetzung doch dadurch pragmatisch Rechnung getragen werden, daß nicht erst die Ordnungsgeldentscheidung, sondern schon das Hauptsacheurteil im Vollstreckungsstaat zur Anerkennung gebracht und mit den dortigen Mitteln vollstreckt wird.[76]

Geht es umgekehrt um ein französisches Unterlassungsurteil, das mit einer astreinte-Festsetzung (liquidation) gegen einen deutschen Beklagten versehen ist, so soll dies ohne weiteres in Deutschland und anderen Vertragsstaaten vollstreckt werden können.[77] Im Interesse der Gleichbehandlung vertragsstaatlicher Unterlassungsurteile auch in der Vollstreckungsphase spricht deshalb viel dafür, den grenzüberschreitenden Zugang zu dieser Phase mit der oben vertretenen Anpassungslösung allen Urteilen aus Vertragsstaaten zu ermöglichen.

Summary

INTERNATIONAL INJUNCTIONS BETWEEN SUBSTANTIVE AND PROCEDURAL LAW

Injunctive relief across the border becomes more and more frequent in fields like media and industrial property law, unfair competition, environmental and consumer law. The EU Council Directive 98/27 – although restricted to collective consumer remedies – asks for European harmonization in one of the fields where injunctions are common.

The article tries to identify "injunctions" as a specific form of relief raising special problems in international litigation: first, the question of substantive or procedural qualification is of relevance for the conflicts rule (*lex fori, lex causae*). Substantive law aspects like the plaintiff's proving an imminent injury have to be connected to the *lex causae*, whereas truly procedural aspects like the court's

---

977 m.w.Nw.; abl. Remien (oben N. 70) 310, 323. Ablehnend allerdings auch TGI Paris, *Rev.crit.* (1980) 782; dazu krit. Geimer/ Schütze, *EuZVR* (oben N. 25) Art. 31 Rn. 92.

[74] Remien, ibid., 320; Stürner, *FS Henckel* (1995) 809, 870; Schlosser, *EuGVÜ* Art. 43 Rn. 8.

[75] Geimer/ Schütze, *EuzVR* (oben N. 25) Art. 43 Rn. 2; w.Nw. bei Remien, ibid., 309/310 u. 317ff.

[76] Daß dieser Weg umständlicher und teurer als der über Art. 43 sein soll (so Remien, ibid., 321) leuchtet nicht ein: Er führt ebenfalls über Artt. 31 ff., zu denen Art. 43 nur eine Qualifikation enthält.

[77] Schlosser, *EuGVÜ* Art. 43 Rn. 4; Remien, ibid., 320.

jurisdiction or former standing requirements are governed by the *lex fori*. Preliminary (interlocutory) injunctions in German law are granted only if the plaintiff shows urgency and a substantive law basis for his suit; thus, both prerequisites can be governed by different legal systems. Anti-suit injunctions are unknown in German law.

As injunctions can be enforced only under the threat of penalties, their cross border enforcement is difficult, even if European procedural law reigns. Different enforcement systems (like the French *astreinte*, the German *Ordnungsgeld* and the English contempt fines) should be approximated in transborder litigation, as otherwise the necessary sanctions for illegal conduct are running idle.

Das Verhältnis zwischen dem engsten Zusammenhang und der charakteristischen Leistung (Art. 117 Abs. 1 und 2 IPRG) – dargestellt anhand ausgewählter Innominatverträge

Jolanta Kren Kostkiewicz[*]

1.   ZUR ANKNÜPFUNG IM ALLGEMEINEN

Die Anknüpfung von Rechtsfragen im internationalen Personen-, Familien- und Erbrecht bezieht sich in der Regel auf natürliche Personen (das Kind, der Erblasser, die Ehepartner). Dabei geht es hauptsächlich um die Frage, ob an den gewöhnlichen Aufenthalt, den Wohnsitz oder die Staatsangehörigkeit dieser Personen angeknüpft werden soll. Im Sachenrecht bestimmt regelmässig der Lageort der Sache das an-

---

[*] o. Professorin an der Universität Bern.

J. Basedow et al., eds., Private Law in the International Arena – Liber Amicorum Kurt Siehr
© 2000, T.M.C.Asser Press, The Hague, The Netherlands

wendbare Recht. Im Bereich der grenzüberschreitenden Schuldverträge stellt sich die Frage nach dem anwendbaren Recht komplizierter.

2. ZUR ANKNÜPFUNG VON SCHULDVERTRÄGEN IM BESONDEREN

Bei den meisten Schuldverträgen – ausser einseitig belastenden Verträgen oder solchen, in denen eine Partei im positiven Recht als besonders schützenswert gilt – kann nicht a priori nur auf Anknüpfungsverhältnisse, die sich in der Person einer Vertragspartei verwirklichen, abgestellt werden. Vielmehr ist grundsätzlich von der Gleichstellung der Vertragsparteien auszugehen, was von vorneherein die Anknüpfung an den Wohnsitz oder Sitz einer Partei ausschliesst. Die Obligationen und die Rechtsverhältnisse, aus denen Schuldverträge entstehen, sind nämlich geistige Entitäten, die äusserlich nicht wahrnehmbar sind; sie bieten deshalb wenig Bodenhaftung für einen Anknüpfungspunkt des IPR. Ausnahmen sind der Ort, wo der Vertrag geschlossen wird, und der Ort, wo er erfüllt werden soll. Wie die Geschichte des IPR zeigt, sind dies aber ebenfalls wenig tragfähige Pfeiler für eine Anknüpfung.[1]

Das moderne IPR geht im Grundsatz von einem einheitlichen Vertragsstatut aus, einer einzigen anwendbaren Rechtsordnung vom Beginn bis zum Ende des Vertrages, das lediglich von einigen wenigen Sonderanknüpfungen durchbrochen wird.[2] Im IPR wird somit die Anknüpfung grundsätzlich nicht nach der Streitfrage (Konsens, Willensmangel, richtige Erfüllung, positive Vertragsverletzung usw.) differenziert.

Das am 1. Januar 1989 in Kraft getretene IPR-Gesetz legt in Art. 116 für die Frage nach dem auf Schuldverträge anwendbaren Rechts zunächst den Vorrang einer Rechtswahl fest.

Die Art. 118 bis 122 IPRG stellen mit Bezug auf einzelne Vertragstypen besondere Regeln hinsichtlich des anwendbaren Rechts auf. Es handelt sich um Mobiliar- und Immobiliarkaufverträge, Konsumentenverträge, Arbeitsverträge und Verträge über Immaterialgüterrechte, und zwar zunächst um die Zulässigkeit einer Rechtswahl und sodann um das bei Fehlen einer Rechtswahl anzuwendende Recht.

Für die nicht ausdrücklich genannten Schuldverträge gilt der Vorrang der Rechtswahl unbeschränkt (Art. 116 IPRG). Falls die Parteien keine Rechtswahl treffen, kommt das mit der Generalklausel des Art. 117 IPRG zu bestimmende Recht zur Anwendung, das Recht, mit dem der Vertrag am engsten zusammenhängt bzw. das Recht, dem die charakteristische Leistung „angehört".

---

[1] Vgl. statt vieler Adolf F. Schnitzer, *Handbuch des Internationalen Privatrechts*, Bd. I, 4. Aufl. (Basel 1957) 52ff., Bd. II, 4. Aufl. (Basel 1958) 619ff.

[2] Z.B. Art. 123 oder Art. 124 IPRG.

3.   PROBLEMSTELLUNG

Die Beziehung zwischen dem „engsten Zusammenhang" nach Art. 117 Abs. 1 IPRG einerseits und dem Prinzip der „charakteristischen Leistung" nach Art. 117 Abs. 2 IPRG andererseits wirft zwei methodologische Fragen auf, auf die nachfolgend kurz eingegangen wird.[3]

Die *erste Frage* bezieht sich auf die Rangordnung zwischen „engstem Zusammenhang" und „charakteristischer Leistung": bildet der „engste Zusammenhang" nach Art. 117 Abs. 1 den methodologischen Ausgangspunkt, d.h. ist zunächst individualisierend im einzelnen Schuldvertrag – nach welchem Kriterium auch immer – ein engster Zusammenhang zu einer bestimmten nationalen Rechtsordnung zu suchen? Ist weiter, wie in der Lehre vorgeschlagen wird,[4] erst dann, wenn ein solcher engster Zusammenhang in Auslegung des einzelnen Vertrages nicht erkennbar ist, auf Absatz 2 derselben Bestimmung zurückzugreifen? Oder ist, im Gegenteil, von der „Vermutung" auszugehen, der engste Zusammenhang werde, wie es in Absatz 2 heisst, durch die charakteristische Leistung vermittelt? Ist in diesem Falle nur subsidiär nach einem engsten Zusammenhang zu suchen, wenn die Anknüpfung aufgrund der charakteristischen Leistung versagt, etwa weil der Vertrag gar keine charakteristische Leistung aufweist oder die Anknüpfung nach Absatz 2 zu einer unbefriedigenden Lösung führt? Letzteres entspricht der zur Zeit herrschenden Auffassung, wonach Absatz 2 als Grundsatz, Absatz 1 als Ausnahme zu gelten hat.[5]

Eine *zweite Frage* stellt sich nach der Abgrenzung zwischen den beiden Anknüpfungspunkten des „engsten Zusammenhangs" und der „Vermutung aufgrund

---

[3] Diese Probleme sind in der schweizerischen Lehre nach wie vor kontrovers. Eine einheitliche Meinung hat sich auch im Ausland in der Auslegung der inhaltlich dem Art. 117 Abs. 1 und 2 IPRG im Grundsatz entsprechenden Bestimmung des Europäischen Übereinkommens über das auf vertragliche Schuldverhältnisse anzuwendende Recht (EVÜ, Römer Übereinkommen) vom 19.6.1980 (Abl.EG Nr.L 266/6 vom 9.10.1980) nicht durchgesetzt. Dies ist wohl auf das späte Inkrafttreten des Übereinkommens – erst am 1. April 1991 – zurückzuführen, bzw. auf den Umstand, dass es vorher in mehreren Staaten als nationales IPR angewendet worden war. Im folgenden wird auf rechtsvergleichende Hinweise verzichtet, vor allem auch deswegen, weil die Schweiz dem Übereinkommen nicht angehört und das schweizerische IPRG teilweise von Formulierungen des Übereinkommens abweicht und, was vor allem entscheidend ist, einer anderen Systematik und somit nicht notwendigerweise derselben Reihenfolge der methodologischen Schritte folgt; zu den ausführlichen rechtsvergleichenden Hinweisen vgl. aber Frank Vischer/ Lucius Huber/ David Oser, *Internationales Vertragsrecht*, 2. Aufl. (Bern 2000) Rdnr. 216ff.

[4] Anton Heini, „Vertrauensprinzip und Individualanknüpfung im internationalen Vertragsrecht", in: *Festschrift Frank Vischer* (Zürich 1983) 149ff.

[5] So z.B.: Marc Amstutz/ Nedim Peter Vogt/ Markus Wang, *IPRG–Kommentar* (Basel 1996) Art. 117 N 12, zu Art. 117; Max Keller/ Jolanta Kren Kostkiewicz, in: *IPRG–Kommentar* (Anton Heini/ Max Keller/ Kurt Siehr/ Frank Vischer/ Paul Volken (Hrsg.)) (Zürich 1993) Art. 117 N 43; Ivo Schwander, „Internationales Vertragsschuldrecht – Direkte Zuständigkeit und objektive Anknüpfung", in: *Festschrift Rudolf Moser* (Zürich 1987) 79ff., insb. 87; vgl. auch Vischer/ Huber/ Oser (oben N. 3) Rdnr. 258ff.

der charakteristischen Leistung". In welchem inhaltlichen Zusammenhang stehen die beiden Begriffe? Ist der erste Begriff eine Generalklausel, welcher durch den zweiten eine bestimmte Auslegungsrichtung erhält? Was heisst „vermutet" in Art. 117 Abs. 2? Was versteht man unter „engstem Zusammenhang", was unter „charakteristischer Leistung"? Welches Anknüpfungsverhältnis besteht zwischen Absatz 1 und Absatz 2? Ist dabei der systematische Zusammenhang mit Art. 117 Absatz 3 zu beachten, indem Absatz 2 sich hauptsächlich auf die in Absatz 3 aufgezählten Vertragstypen bezieht, während Absatz 1 die übrigen Vertragstypen und insbesondere die Innominatverträge erfasst?

Aus diesen Problemkreisen folgen dann konkrete Auslegungsfragen: unter welchen Voraussetzungen muss oder darf der Richter von den Anknüpfungsergebnissen abweichen? Wieweit darf die Beachtung der Individualität oder Atypizität eines einzelnen Vertrages gehen? Welche Rolle spielt es dabei, ob eine Vereinbarung einem Vertragstypus entspricht oder ein Innominatvertrag ist?

4.   Zur Anknüpfung von Innominatverträgen im allgemeinen

Im folgenden wird diesen beiden Fragen anhand von Innominatverträgen nachgegangen. Dies rechtfertigt sich unter mehreren Gesichtspunkten:

–   Es gibt Innominatverträge mit oder ohne charakteristische Leistung, während gesetzliche Vertragstypen meistens eine „charakteristische" Leistung haben.

–   Innominatverträge weisen andererseits eine breite Spanne auf, von zusammengesetzten Verträgen (z.B. Franchising-Systeme oder Generalunternehmervertrag), die gesetzliche Vertragstypen zusammenfügen, über gemischte Verträge aus Nominat- oder Innominatverträgen (z.B. Pensionsvertrag) bis zu Verträgen sui generis (z.B. Alleinvertriebsvertrag oder Franchisingvertrag), die sich in der Praxis einem richterrechtlich typisierten Standardvertrag nähern, bis hin zu höchst individuell ausgearbeiteten oder atypischen Verträgen.[6]

---

[6] Aus der umfangreichen Literatur über die Anknüpfung von Innominatverträgen vgl. nebst den in den Fussnoten zitierten Werken u.a.: Rolf Bär, „Das internationale Privatrecht (Kollisionsrecht) des Immaterialgüterrechts und des Wettbewerbsrechts", in: *Schweizerisches Immaterialgüter- und Wettbewerbsrecht*, Band 1/I (Basel 1995) 87ff.; Hans-Rudolf Bener, *La fusion des sociétés anonymes en droit international privé* (Diss. Genf 1967); Balthasar Bessenich, *Die grenzüberschreitende Fusion nach den Bestimmungen des IPRG und des OR* (Diss. Basel 1991); Marco Dragic, *Die IPR-Anknüpfung der Schuldverträge – Vergleich zwischen dem jugoslawischen und dem schweizerischen Recht* (Diss. St. Gallen 1996); Dirk Gunst, *Die charakteristische Leistung. Zur funktionellen Anknüpfung im Internationalen Vertragsrecht Deutschlands, der Schweiz und der Europäischen Gemeinschaft* (Diss. Konstanz 1994); Martin Hiestand, *Die Anknüpfung internationaler Lizenzverträge* (Frankfurt am Main 1993); Lucius Huber, *Das Joint-Venture im internationalen Privatrecht* (Diss. Basel 1992); Christian

Ergründet man die Konsequenzen der Anwendung von Art. 117 Abs. 1 und 2 IPRG auf diese ganze Spannweite von Innominatverträgen, bestehen bessere Aussichten, das Verhältnis zwischen Absatz 1 und Absatz 2 zu erhellen, als wenn man von allgemein rechtspolitischen Überlegungen oder der Entstehungsgeschichte des Art. 117 ausgeht.[7]

5.   RANGORDNUNG ZWISCHEN „ENGSTEM ZUSAMMENHANG" UND „CHARAKTERISTISCHER LEISTUNG"

Gemäss Systematik des IPR-Gesetzes sind zunächst die besonderen Kollisionsregeln von Art. 118 bis 122 IPRG zu konsultieren. Ihnen gemeinsam ist, dass sie durch ihren Gegenstand bestimmt sind, d.h. ihre Abgrenzung erfolgt aufgrund einer Einordnung ratione materiae: Mobiliar- oder Immobiliarkauf, Arbeitsvertrag, Vertrag über Immaterialgüterrechte. Einzig der Konsumentenvertrag beruht auf einer Mischung aus ratione materiae und ratione personae.

Bei diesen speziellen Regeln ist nicht nach einer charakteristischen Leistung zu fragen, auch wenn eine solche an sich ohne weiteres feststellbar wäre (Leistung des Verkäufers, des Anbieters, des Arbeitnehmers, des am Immaterialgut Berechtigten). Die Frage eines engeren oder engsten Zusammenhangs könnte sich hier höchstens im Rahmen der Ausnahmeklausel von Art. 15 Abs. 1 IPRG stellen; Art. 117 Abs. 1 IPRG ist hier nicht anwendbar.[8]

Im Rahmen dieser speziellen Kollisionsregeln bewegt sich etwa der Innominatvertrag des Leasing[9]: betrifft der Leasing-Gegenstand ein Konsumgut, kann der Leasingvertrag unter Art. 120 IPRG fallen, mit der Folge, dass eine Rechtswahl nicht zulässig ist, sondern ausschliesslich dem Recht am gewöhnlichen Aufenthalt des Konsumenten untersteht. Immobiliar-Leasing ist nach Art. 119 IPRG zu beurteilen. Mobiliar-Leasing kann, wenn es sich um ein solches mit faktischem (wirt-

---

Alexander Meyer, *Der Alleinvertrieb: Typus, vertragsrechtliche Probleme und Qualifikation im IPR* (St. Gallen 1990); Frank Vischer, *Die kollisionsrechtlichen Regeln der Anknüpfung bei internationalen Verträgen* (Bern 1962); ders., „Methodologische Fragen bei der objektiven Anknüpfung im internationalen Vertragsrecht", *SJIR* (1957) 43ff.; Christoph Wildhaber, *Franchising im internationalen Privatrecht: unter besonderer Berücksichtigung des schweizerischen Schuldrechts und mit Hinweisen auf die Vertragsgestaltung namentlich unter IPR-Gesichtspunkten* (Diss. St. Gallen 1991); Charles Wyniger, *Vom Alleinverkaufsvertrag, insbesondere im internationalen Privatrecht der Schweiz* (Diss. Bern 1963); Urs Zenhäusern, *Der internationale Lizenzvertrag* (Diss. Freiburg 1991).

[7] Die bisherige Diskussion hat nämlich gezeigt, dass die vorgeschlagenen Auslegungsvarianten wohl zu Ergebnissen, zu Meinungen, zu Stellungnahmen geführt haben, nicht aber zu einem in sich geschlossenen Konzept.

[8] So auch Ivo Schwander, *Einführung in das internationale Privatrecht, Zweiter Band: Besonderer Teil* (St. Gallen 1997) Rdnr. 545; a. M. Keller/ Kren Kostkiewicz (oben N. 5) Art. 117 N 42.

[9] Zum Leasingvertrag im internationalen Privatrecht grundlegend Daniel Gisrsberger, *Grenzüberschreitendes Finanzierungsleasing* (Zürich 1997).

schaftlichem) Kaufzwang handelt, ohne dass die speziellen Voraussetzungen des Konsumentenvertrags erfüllt sind, dem Haager Übereinkommen von 1955[10] oder eventuell Art. 117 Abs. 3 lit. a, in den übrigen Fällen Art. 117 Abs. 3 lit. b IPRG unterstellt sein.

Ebenfalls kommt es bei einer zulässigen und gültig getroffenen Rechtswahl weder auf eine charakteristische Leistung noch auf den engeren oder engsten Zusammenhang an (Art. 116 und Art. 15 Abs. 2 IPRG).

Die charakteristische Leistung wird in der Regel jedoch relevant sein im Rahmen der in Art. 117 Abs. 3 IPRG genannten Vertragstypen wie Veräusserungsverträge, Gebrauchsüberlassungsverträge, Dienstleistungsverträge, Verwahrungsverträge, Garantie- und Bürgschaftsverträge.

Diese Aufzählung in Art. 117 Abs. 3 IPRG wird in der Lehre allgemein als illustrativ angesehen.[11] Sie leuchtet wie selbstverständlich ein, in dem sie nur Beispiele gibt und der Definition in Absatz 2 normativ nichts hinzufügt. Genau genommen liegen sogar einfache Zirkelschlüsse vor:

Dienstleistungsverträge sind Verträge mit Dienstleistungen als Gegenstand und deshalb gilt die Dienstleistung als die „charakteristische", die vertragstypische Leistung. Verwahrungsverträge sind Verträge, die mit der Leistung des Verwahrers charakterisiert werden, weshalb im Regelfall die Leistung des Verwahrers als charakteristische Leistung zu gelten hat.

Normativ lässt sich somit Art. 117 Abs. 3 IPRG – abgesehen von dessen Erläuterungsfunktion – eigentlich nur entnehmen, dass die hier aufgezählten Arten von Verträgen zumeist Vertragstypen sind, bei denen eine charakteristische Leistung überhaupt feststellbar ist. Dies ist aber nicht zwingend. Es gibt z.B. im Dienstleistungsbereich Innominatverträge ohne eigentliche charakteristische Leistung, so der Franchising-Vertrag, bei welchem sowohl die Leistung des Franchise-Gebers (der das Konzept zur Verfügung stellt) als auch diejenige des Franchise-Nehmers (der am Ort erfüllt, die wesentliche Investition im Rahmen des einzelnen Vertrages erbringt usw.) Dienstleistungen sind, aber keine der beiden Dienstleistungen allein gibt dem Vertrag sein Gepräge.

An einem weiteren Beispiel lässt sich zudem belegen, dass nicht einmal die in Art. 117 Abs. 3 IPRG aufgeführten Kategorien auf einem konsequent durchführbaren Unterscheidungsmerkmal beruhen: wie schon die Botschaft zum IPR-Gesetz erwähnt,[12] ist für den Alleinvertriebsvertrag das Auftrags- bzw. Dienstleistungselement das entscheidende[13] und nicht das Veräusserungselement.

---

[10] Art. 118 Abs. 1 IPRG; Übereinkommen betreffend das auf internationale Kaufverträge über bewegliche körperliche Sachen anzuwendende Recht vom 15. 6 1955, SR 0.221.211.4.

[11] Vgl. u.a.: Schwander (oben N. 8) Rdnr. 503ff.; Vischer/ Huber/ Oser (oben N. 3) Rdnr. 218ff.

[12] Nr. 282.23 unter Hinweis auf BGE 100 II 450; vgl. auch BGE 124 III 188ff.

[13] Vgl. BGE 124 III 192 E. 4b/bb.

Mit Art. 117 Abs. 2 IPRG wechselt im Gegensatz zu den Art. 118 ff. (und auch zu den in Art. 117 Abs. 3 genannten Vertragskategorien) der Vergleichsmassstab. Art. 117 Abs. 2 IPRG hat nicht mehr den Gegenstand der vertraglichen Leistungen – Veräusserung, Überlassung, Dienstleistung, Verwahrung, vertragliches Einstehenmüssen, Kauf von Mobilien oder Immobilien, Konsumgütererwerb, Arbeitsleistung, Nutzung von Immaterialgütern – als Abgrenzungskriterium im Auge. Es geht vielmehr um diejenigen Vertragstypen oder individuell ausgehandelten, gesetzlich geregelten oder Innominatverträge, welche überhaupt eine charakteristische Leistung haben.

Methodisch ergibt sich nun daraus, wie dies die herrschende Lehre[14] annimmt, ein Vorrang der Anknüpfung an die charakteristische Leistung vor derjenigen an den engsten Zusammenhang.[15] Einen engeren oder engsten Zusammenhang kann es bei allen Arten von Verträgen geben, nicht hingegen eine charakteristische Leistung. Art. 117 Abs. 2 hat einen spezielleren Inhalt; es ist daher in erster Linie danach zu fragen, ob dem vorgelegten Schuldvertrag eine charakteristische Leistung zugrunde liegt.

6. INHALTLICHE ABGRENZUNG ZWISCHEN DER ANKNÜPFUNG AN DEN „ENGSTEN ZUSAMMENHANG" UND DER ANKNÜPFUNG AN DIE „CHARAKTERISTISCHE LEISTUNG"

Auch hier ist methodisch so vorzugehen, dass zuerst die „charakteristische Leistung" als der engere Begriff zu definieren ist.

6.1 Zum Wesen der „charakteristischen Leistung"

6.1.1 *Funktion der „charakteristischen Leistung"*

Die Anknüpfung aufgrund der charakteristischen Leistung ist keine Leerformel bzw. kein blosses Bild wie jene an den „engsten Zusammenhang", den „Schwerpunkt" oder „Sitz" des Lebensverhältnisses. Sie ist vielmehr ein heuristisches Prinzip, es weist den Weg. Es soll nicht der Schuldvertrag in allen Einzelheiten a posteriori betrachtet werden, sondern es soll – wenn ein Vertragstyp vorliegt – a priori nach der einen Leistung gefragt werden, welche dem Vertragstyp das Gepräge gibt. Das Prinzip der charakteristischen Leistung reduziert damit die Betrachtung des Vertrages, indem vorerst nicht alle individuellen Besonderheiten abgewogen werden, sondern sich der Blick darauf konzentriert, welches die dem Vertragstyp eige-

---

[14] Vgl. statt vieler Schwander (oben N. 8) Rdnr. 506.
[15] Siehe oben N. 4.

ne charakteristische Leistung ist, und wo somit im Normalfall der Schwerpunkt liegt.[16]

Damit wird klar, worin die Vorteile des Prinzips der charakteristischen Leistung liegen: hier findet der Gedanke der Vertragstypen aus dem materiellen Schuldrecht im IPR seine Entsprechung. Es wird an ein relativ leicht feststellbares, meist klares Kriterium angeknüpft, womit man dem Bedürfnis des internationalen Handels nach Vorhersehbarkeit des anwendbaren Rechts entgegenkommt; und es wird zugleich an die Leistung derjenigen Vertragspartei angeknüpft, welche die für das Wirtschafts- und Sozialleben relevante Funktion ausübt.[17]

Damit wird aber auch klar, dass die Formulierung von Art. 117 Abs. 2 IPRG *„es wird vermutet, der engste Zusammenhang bestehe mit dem Staat, in dem die Partei, welche die charakteristische Leistung erbringt (...)"* keine Vermutung im Sinne der Rechtsterminologie ist. Es liegt kein Schluss vom Bekannten auf Unbekanntes vor, sondern ein Grundsatz, eine Richtlinie, eine brauchbare Methode. Damit wird gesagt, dass die charakteristische Leistung nicht immer die stärkste Beziehung darstellt.

Die charakteristische Leistung ist ein relativ starres Kriterium, das dem Vertragstyp das Gepräge gibt und ihn gegen andere Vertragstypen abgrenzt. Sie wird abstrakt und a priori bestimmt: hat man es mit einem Werkvertrag zu tun, kann nur die Leistung des Unternehmers die charakteristische sein; auf seine Leistung ist das Vertragsprogramm ausgerichtet. Ob der Besteller des Werkes nebst der Zahlung des Werklohnes noch andere Leistungen erbringt, etwa das Material liefert, oder ob weitere individuelle Abmachungen einbezogen sind, ändert nichts daran, dass nur die Leistung des Unternehmers als charakteristische Leistung in Frage kommt.[18]

Dies zeigt, dass die Rechtsfindung bei der Bestimmung der charakteristischen Leistung relativ kurz greift und – im Interesse der Vorhersehbarkeit des anwendbaren Rechts – auch kurz greifen soll. Die Fragestellung wird bewusst vereinfacht und eingeschränkt. Sobald man aufgrund individueller Merkmale des einzelnen Vertrages weiter differenziert, verlässt man das nicht immer leicht feststellbare, aber objektive Kriterium des Charakteristischen eines Vertragstypus.

Das Kriterium der charakteristischen Leistung ist daher nicht weiter entwicklungsfähig. Lehre und Rechtsprechung können zwar im Verlaufe der Zeit die Auf-

---

[16] Schnitzer (oben N. 1) Bd. I, 52-54, Bd. II, 639-643.

[17] Adolf F. Schnitzer, „Die funktionelle Anknüpfung im internationalen Vertragsrecht", *Festschrift Schönenberger* (Fribourg 1968) 387ff., 396ff.

[18] Als einfache Hilfsregel wurde dabei in der Lehre formuliert, dass bei Austauschverträgen die charakteristische Leistung regelmässig diejenige sei, die nicht in Geld besteht; wo sich, wie beim Devisentausch – zwei Geldsummen – oder wie beim Briefmarkentausch – zwei Sachleistungen – gegenüberstehen, wird danach gefragt, welches diejenige Vertragsleistung ist, deretwegen der Vertrag überhaupt abgeschlossen wird; vgl. u.a.: Amstutz/ Vogt/ Wang (oben N. 5) Art. 117 N 26; Keller/ Kren Kostkiewicz (oben N. 5) Art. 117 N 28.

fassungen, was das einem Vertragstyp Wesentliche sei, ändern; aber das Kriterium des „Charakteristischen" der einen oder anderen Leistung bleibt unverändert.[19]

6.1.2 Verknüpfungen der „charakteristischen Leistung"

Die Rigidität und die Selbstbeschränkung des Kriteriums der charakteristischen Leistung ist in den letzten Jahren in einem Teil der Lehre und der Rechtsprechung m.E. zu wenig beachtet worden.[20] Leider wurde auch nicht weiter diskutiert, mit welchem anderen Kriterium die charakterisische Leistung verknüpft werden soll. Vor Inkrafttreten des IPR-Gesetzes war in der Bundesgerichtspraxis bald vom Wohnsitz, bald vom gewöhnlichen Aufenthalt, bald von der Niederlassung des Er- bringers der charakteristischen Leistung die Rede.[21] Art. 117 Abs. 2 IPRG bestimmt nunmehr ausdrücklich, dass es auf den gewöhnlichen Aufenthalt des Erbringers der charakteristischen Leistung ankommt, oder, wenn der Vertrag aufgrund einer be- ruflichen oder gewerblichen Tätigkeit geschlossen worden ist, auf die gewerbliche Niederlassung.[22]

Diese Verknüpfung wirft zwei Fragen auf: kommt es *erstens* auf die Aufent- halts- oder Niederlassungsverhältnisse im Zeitpunkt des Vertragsschlusses, der Vertragsabwicklung oder gar erst der Klage an? M.E. sind es die Verhältnisse im Zeitpunkt des Vertragsschlusses, es sei denn, es wäre beiden Parteien bewusst, dass die Aufenthalts- oder Niederlassungsverhältnisse sich demnächst ändern bzw. viel- leicht gerade auch wegen der Vertragserfüllung ändern werden (z.B. zwecks Erfül- lung eines Dienstleistungsvertrages). In einem solchen Fall kann auf die vorhersehbaren Verhältnisse im Zeitpunkt des Beginns der Vertragserfüllung abge- stellt werden. Weitere Änderungen in den Verhältnissen sollten jedoch nicht beach- tet werden; die Parteien müssen sich schon in der Phase der Vertragsabwicklung auf die Anwendbarkeit eines bestimmten Rechts verlassen können.[23]

Die *zweite* Frage ist: kann – nachdem die charakteristische Leistung festgestellt worden ist – allenfalls das Anknüpfungskriterium des gewöhnlichen Aufenthaltes

---

[19] Es wäre auch falsch, das klare Kriterium der charakteristischen Leistung mit dem materiell- rechtlichen Postulat des Schutzes der schwächeren Vertragspartei zu verbinden. Sozialpolitische Erwä- gungen sind entweder im materiellen Recht oder im IPR in Form einer speziellen Kollisionsregel zu be- rücksichtigen, wie dies auch in Art. 120 IPRG (Konsumentenvertrag) geschehen ist, oder aber über Eingriffsnormen (Art. 18 und 19 IPRG). Dass etwa, um den Konsumenten oder den Mieter zu schützen, deren Geldzahlungen als charakteristische Leistung anzusehen seien, lässt sich nicht behaupten.

[20] Damit sind zwar nicht immer die Ergebnisse, zu denen man gelangt war, als falsch anzusehen, wohl aber die dabei angewandte Methode der Rechtsfindung. In diesem Zusammenhang ist aber auf Schwander (oben N. 8) Rdnr. 506ff. sowie auf das zum Zeitpunkt der Drucklegung dieses Beitrages er- schienene Werk von Vischer/ Huber/Oser (oben N. 3) hinzuweisen. Die letzten Autoren setzen sich eingehend mit dem Prinzip der charakteristischen Leistung auseinander.

[21] So beispielsweise: BGE 101 II 83ff., 118 II 348ff., 119 II 173ff.

[22] Also das Advokaturbureau, die Arztpraxis, der Sitz oder die Niederlassung der Bank.

[23] So auch Schwander (oben N. 8) Rdnr. 501.

oder der Niederlassung des Erbringers der charakteristischen Leistung korrigiert werden? Das IPRG lässt im Rahmen der Ausnahmeklausel Art. 15 Abs. 1 Korrekturen zu, wenn ein Anknüpfungskriterium nicht überzeugt. Solche Änderungen können in mancherlei Hinsicht praktikabel und naheliegend sein.

Die charakteristische Leistung ist mit der (einen) vertraglichen Leistung identisch. Wäre es dann nicht sachgerecht, an den Ort ihrer Erfüllung anzuknüpfen, und nicht an den gewöhnlichen Aufenthalt oder die Niederlassung ihres Schuldners? Wenn man einst die Lösung Savignys, nämlich die Anknüpfung an den Erfüllungsort, verlassen hatte,[24] so gerade deswegen, weil dies bei synallagmatischen Verträgen zur Spaltung der anwendbaren Rechte – z.B. Lieferort und Zahlungsort beim Kaufvertrag – geführt hatte. Folgt man aber dem Prinzip der charakteristischen Leistung, entfällt dieser Haupteinwand gegen die Anknüpfung an den Erfüllungsort, weil eben nur noch der eine Erfüllungsort der charakteristischen Leistung in Frage kommt.[25]

Zwei der speziellen Kollisionsregeln folgen bereits diesem Prinzip: nach Art. 119 IPRG kann bei Verträgen über Grundstücke oder deren Gebrauch die Erfüllung der charakteristischen Leistung nur am Ort der gelegenen Sache erfolgen. Dasselbe gilt für Art. 121 Abs. 1 IPRG; hier wird die Erfüllung der charakteristischen Leistung an den gewöhnlichen Arbeitsort geknüpft.

Aber auch bei manchen Innominatverträgen, bei denen eine charakteristische Leistung feststellbar ist, befriedigt die Anknüpfung an den gewöhnlichen Aufenthalt ihres Erbringers weniger als die Anknüpfung an den Erfüllungsort. Zu erinnern ist an die längst nicht entschiedene Kontroverse um den Franchising-Vertrag. Einige Autoren vertreten die Meinung, dass der Franchise-Geber die charakteristische Leistung erbringt[26]: er lässt rechtlich geschützte Immaterialgüter nutzen, stellt Know-how und ein betriebswirtschaftliches Konzept zur Verfügung und übernimmt oft Schulungspflichten. Dieses Paket stellt die charakteristische Leistung dar.

Andere Autoren betonen die Leistungen des Franchise-Nehmers, seinen Einsatz und seine Umsetzung des Pakets, teilweise auch seine wirtschaftliche Abhängigkeit und wollen daher an seine Niederlassung bzw. seinen gewöhnlichen Aufenthaltsort anknüpfen.[27]

---

[24] Vgl. u.a. Keller/ Kren Kostkiewicz (oben N. 5) Art. 117 N 2ff.

[25] So bereits für ausnahmsweise Anknüpfung an den Erfüllungsort bei Innominatverträgen Ivo Schwander, „Die Behandlung von Innominatverträgen im internationalen Privatrecht", in: *Innominatverträge, Festgabe zum 60. Geburtstag von Walter R. Schluep* (Peter Fostmoser et al. (Hrsg.)) (Zürich 1988) 509.

[26] So u.a.: Frank Vischer, „Haftung des Kreditkartenunternehmens gegenüber dem Vertragsunternehmen: Überlegungen zu einigen materiell- und kollisionsrechtlichen Aspekten des Kreditkartenfranchising", in: *Festgabe Walter R.. Schluep*, ibid., 517; vgl. auch Vischer/ Huber/ Oser (oben N. 3) Rdnr. 671ff.

[27] So u.a.: Amstutz/ Vogt/ Wang (oben N. 5) Art. 117 N 62; Schwander (oben N. 25) 510.

All diese Argumente laufen m.E. auf eine Entstellung des Begriffes der charakteristischen Leistung hinaus. Weil aber die charakteristische Leistung wesensgemäss aufgrund des geschlossenen Vertrags nur an einem andern Ort erbracht werden kann als dem Sitz des Franchise-Gebers – er will ja andernorts expandieren – und andererseits der Franchise-Nehmer sie auch nur dort nutzen kann, darf es auch nur auf diesen Erfüllungsort ankommen.

Dieses Beispiel zeigt, dass keineswegs das Prinzip der charakteristischen Leistung zu hinterfragen ist, sondern dass vielmehr die Verknüpfung der charakteristischen Leistung mit dem Anknüpfungskriterium des gewöhnlichen Aufenthalts bzw. der Niederlassung ihres Erbringers problematisch sein kann. Dort wo das ganze Vertragsprogramm auf die Erfüllung der charakteristischen Leistung an einem bestimmten Ort hinausläuft, sollte an deren Erfüllungsort angeknüpft werden.[28] Das ist m.E. de lege ferenda auch für den Werkvertrag zu fordern, wenn das Werk an einem bestimmten Ort zu erstellen ist.

Entsprechendes kann auch für eine Reihe von Innominatverträgen postuliert werden, deren charakteristische Leistung in einem bestimmten Staat, in einem bestimmten Markt zu erbringen ist, wie Alleinvertriebsverträge, Exklusivverträge (auch im Sinne der Verpflichtung zur Nichtbearbeitung des Marktes), Kartellvereinbarungen, aber auch Stimmbindungsverträge und andere gesellschaftsbezogene Innominatverträge, die auf ein Verhalten am Sitz oder gegenüber den Organen der Gesellschaft ausgerichtet sind. Dasselbe gilt für Automatenaufstellungs- und Tankstellenverträge, Gast- und Spitalaufnahme-Verträge.[29]

Im geltenden IPRG sind solche Korrekturen – Anknüpfung an den Erfüllungsort der charakteristischen Leistung – m.E. für Schuldverträge, die nicht unter Art. 117 IPRG fallen, nach Art. 15 Abs. 1 möglich. Im Rahmen von Art. 117 IPRG nimmt hingegen Absatz 1 diese Funktion als Korrekturbehelf wahr. Der engere Zusammenhang wird dann nicht durch die Lokalisierung des Erbringers der charakteristischen Leistung, sondern unmittelbar durch den Erfüllungsort dieser Leistung hergestellt.[30]

6.2 Zum Wesen des „engsten Zusammenhanges"

6.2.1 *Funktion des „engsten Zusammenhanges"*

Welche Funktion kommt dem Prinzip des engsten Zusammenhanges nach Art. 117 Abs. 1 IPRG zu?

---

[28] Für die Anknüpfung am Erfüllungsort der charakteristischen Leistung auch Yvo Schwander, Bemerkungen zum BGE 124 III 188ff, in: *SZIER* (1999) 515ff.; ders. (oben N. 8) Rdnr. 502.

[29] Vgl. hierzu auch Schwander (oben N. 8) Rdnr. 509.

[30] Vgl. hierzu auch Schwander (oben N. 8) Rdnr. 507.

Die herrschende Lehre[31] ist sich darin einig, dass diese Bestimmung zwei Funktionen wahrnimmt:

– im Verhältnis zu Absatz 2 (Prinzip der charakteristischen Leistung) eine Korrekturfunktion ähnlich der Ausnahmeklausel des Art. 15 Abs. 1 IPRG;[32]

– überall, wo Absatz 2 zu keinem Ergebnis führt, insbesondere wo eine charakteristische Leistung nicht feststellbar ist, wird der Schuldvertrag unmittelbar gestützt auf das Prinzip des engsten Zusammenhangs angeknüpft.[33]

Zur ersten Funktion: die Anknüpfung nach dem Grundsatz der charakteristischen Leistung kann zu einem kollisionsrechtlich nicht überzeugenden Ergebnis führen. Mit den Worten des Art. 15 Abs. 1 IPRG gewinnt der Richter die Überzeugung, dass *„nach den gesamten Umständen offensichtlich ist, dass der Sachverhalt mit diesem Recht in nur geringem, mit einem anderen Recht jedoch in viel engerem Zusammenhang steht"*. Dann muss der Richter diejenige Rechtsordnung anwenden, zu welcher die engste Beziehung besteht. Wie bei Art. 15 Abs. 1 kommen etwa folgende Fallgruppen in Betracht: Parteierwartungen und akzessorische Anknüpfungen zur Herstellung oder Beachtung eines zeitlichen, räumlichen oder sachlichen Konnexes. Im Bereich der Schuldverträge ist insbesondere an wirtschaftlich zusammengehörige, rechtlich aber selbständige Verträge, die innerlich aufeinander bezogen sind, zu denken. Hier stellt sich die Frage der Unterwerfung der verschiedenen Verträge unter ein einheitliches Vertragsstatut.[34] Auch eine Korrektur im gegenteiligen Sinn ist denkbar, z.B. Abspaltung einer Teilfrage im Sinne einer richterrechtlichen Sonderanknüpfung, wenn sie derart eng mit einem anderen Sachgebiet, etwa dem Sachen- oder Immaterialgüterrecht zusammenhängt, dass es von Vorteil ist, die Modalitäten dieser vertraglichen Leistung dem Sachstatut bzw. dem Immaterialgüterstatut zu unterstellen.[35]

Im Rahmen der *ersten Funktion* des Art. 117 Abs. 1 IPRG spielt aber wiederum der Anknüpfungsgrundsatz aufgrund der charakteristischen Leistung eine Rolle, nämlich diejenige des Vergleichsmassstabes.[36] Damit gestützt auf Art. 117 Abs. 1 ein anderes Recht anwendbar werden kann, bedarf es eines Vergleiches: nur ein

---

[31] Vgl. statt vieler Schwander (oben N. 8) Rdnr. 506ff.

[32] Wie eben ausgeführt, in Fällen, in denen die Anknüpfung an den gewöhnlichen Aufenthalt oder die Niederlassung des Erbringers der charakteristischen Leistung zu einem unbefriedigenden Ergebnis führt; vgl. auch Schwander (oben N. 8) Rdnr. 507.

[33] Schwander (oben N. 8) Rdnr. 509.

[34] Schwander (oben N. 8) Rdnr. 508.

[35] Eine solche Abspaltung sieht – im Gegensatz zum schweizerischen IPRG, das vom Grundsatz eines einheitlichen Vertragsstatuts ausgeht – Art. 4 Abs. 1 zweiter Satz des erwähnten EG-Übereinkommens (oben N. 3) ausdrücklich vor; vgl. auch Schwander (oben N. 8) Rdnr. 508f.

[36] So bereits Schwander (oben N. 8) Rdnr. 506; ders., (oben N. 25) 508 Anm. 25.

Anknüpfungspunkt, der kollisionsrechtlich deutlich besser überzeugt als die Anknüpfung aufgrund der charakteristischen Leistung, kann als „engerer" oder „engster" Zusammenhang vorgehen.[37]

Zur *zweitgenannten Funktion*: wenn eine charakteristische Leistung nicht feststellbar ist, bleibt nichts anderes übrig, als das auf den betreffenden Schuldvertrag anwendbare Recht direkt nach dem „inhaltlosen" Grundsatz des engsten Zusammenhanges zu bestimmen.[38]

6.2.2 Situationen für eine direkte Anknüpfung an den „engsten Zusammenhang"

Bei welchen Schuldverträgen kann der Anknüpfungspunkt des engsten Zusammenhanges direkt angewendet werden:

– bei Verträgen *ohne* ausgeprägte charakteristische Leistung, so z.B. bei aussergerichtlichen Vergleichen, mit denen beide Parteien Kompromisse eingehen;[39]
– bei Verträgen mit zwei oder mehreren charakteristischen Leistungen, was bei gesetzlich geregelten Vertragstypen nicht zutrifft, wohl aber z.B. bei zusammengesetzten Verträgen, welche zwei Vertragstypen umfassen oder Innominatverträge, mit denen Dienstleistungen und Sachleistungen ausgetauscht werden;
– bei höchst individuell ausgehandelten Verträgen mit einer Vielzahl von Verästelungen gegenseitiger Rechte und Pflichten, z.B. bei einem Zusammenarbeitsvertrag.[40]

Das letztgenannte Beispiel ist besonders geeignet, um die Methode der Rechtsfindung im Rahmen des Art. 117 Abs. 1 IPRG (engster Zusammenhang) zu veranschaulichen.

Angenommen, die Unternehmen A und B beschliessen eine längerfristige Zusammenarbeit auf verschiedenen Ebenen: Forschung, Produktion, Marketing. Eine charakteristische Leistung wird nicht auszumachen sein; eine Organisation der Zusammenarbeit im Sinne einer einfachen Gesellschaft ist auch nicht gegeben (Art. 150 Abs. 2 IPRG). Dann kann nur versucht werden, a posteriori alle einzelnen Gesichtspunkte der vereinbarten Rechte und Pflichten zu betrachten und kollisionsrechtlich zu bewerten.

---

[37] So wenn die Anknüpfung an den gewöhnlichen Aufenthalt des Erbringers der charakteristischen Leistung zu unbefriedigenden Resultaten führt, oder wenn die charakteristische Leistung umstritten ist.

[38] Der hier nichts anderes bedeutet als der „Sitz des Lebensverhältnisses", wie ihn Savigny verstanden hatte.

[39] Vgl. hierzu bereits Schwander (oben N. 25) 511.

[40] Vgl. auch Aufzählung bei Schwander (oben N. 25) 508.

Dabei spielen folgende Gesichtspunkte eine Rolle:

–   Ist der Vertrag ein Rahmenvertrag oder ein einzelner Vertrag, welcher mit anderen gleichgeordneten Verträgen zusammenhängt?

–   Was hat der Vertrag zum Gegenstand: Mobilien oder Immobilien, Immaterialgüterrechte, Marktordnungsrecht (Exklusivklauseln, Kartelle), Gesellschaftsrecht?

–   Wird die richtige Erfüllung des Vertrages derart weitgehend von dieser anderen Sachmaterie bzw. dort zu beachtenden zwingenden Normen (Art. 18 und 19 IPRG) beherrscht, dass eine Anknüpfung an eine andere Rechtsordnung als diejenige der Sachmaterie oder der zwingenden Normen gar nicht durchsetzbar wäre?

Dementsprechend kann es beim vorliegenden Zusammenarbeitsvertrag dazu kommen, dass – mangels einer Rechtswahl – der Richter eventuell Spaltungen des anwendbaren Rechts vornehmen muss. Zum Beispiel wird er die Gültigkeit oder Nichtigkeit der Gebietsaufteilungsabsprachen nach dem Markt- bzw. Auswirkungsprinzip beurteilen, Fragen der gemeinsamen Forschung nach dem Recht am Ort des Forschungszentrums, Fragen der Produktion nach dem Recht am Produktionsort, Fragen der Verbindlichkeit des Rahmenvertrages kumulativ nach den beiden Rechtsordnungen der Sitze beider Gesellschaften.

Je individueller der Schuldvertrag gegenseitige Verästelungen von Rechten und Pflichten der Parteien ausgestaltet hat, ohne dass eine charakteristische Leistung ersichtlich ist, desto mehr ist man auf eine nachträgliche Sicht angewiesen. Das Kriterium der Rechtssicherheit tritt dann hinter dasjenige der Sachgerechtigkeit zurück, denn die Parteien haben selber ein sorgfältig ausgehandeltes Spinnennetz gewoben, in dem sie sich jetzt befinden und worin sie ausharren müssen, bis das Gericht nach Gesichtspunkten entschieden hat, welche – dem individuellen Vertragswerk angepasst – von beiden Seiten als fair empfunden werden.

Eigentlich sollte man von Parteien, die ein sehr individuelles, atypisches Vertragsverhältnis erarbeiten, erwarten können, dass sie auch eine Rechtswahl treffen. Wenn sie dies nicht getan haben, so ist konsequenterweise auch nach dem Hintergrund der Unterlassung zu forschen.

Haben die Parteien keine Rechtswahl getroffen, weil sie z.B. absolutes Vertrauen in die Gegenpartei hatten oder weil sie insgeheim von gewissen Erwartungen hinsichtlich des anwendbaren Rechts ausgegangen waren oder weil sie sich – we-

---

[41]   Dieses zuletzt dargestellte methodische Vorgehen im Rahmen des Art. 117 Abs. 1 IPRG unterscheidet sich damit radikal von demjenigen nach Art. 116 (wonach der subjektive Rechtsanwendungswille der Parteien unbeachtlich ist, wenn er nicht in einer nach Art. 116 zulässigen und gültigen Rechtswahl zum Ausdruck kommt) und demjenigen nach Art. 117 Abs. 2 und 3 IPRG (charakteristische Leistung).

gen der Komplexität der Materie – gar nicht auf eine einzige Rechtsordnung hätten einigen können, so hat das Gericht von Amtes wegen abzuklären, welche Umstände zum Verzicht auf eine Rechtswahlklausel geführt haben.

Wenn eine Absicht oder eine tatsächliche Parteierwartung nicht ersichtlich sind, ist gegebenenfalls ähnlich vorzugehen wie bei einer Vertragslückenfüllung, d.h. es können im Rahmen dieser nachträglichen, individuellen Anknüpfung atypischer Verträge auch subjektive Faktoren der Parteien berücksichtigt werden. Dabei muss nicht analogieweise auf Anknüpfungen zurückgegriffen werden, die im Gesetzesrecht vorkommen, sondern es kann in diesem Rahmen auch auf den hypothetischen Vertragswillen „vernünftiger" Parteien oder auf das in einer Handelsbranche Übliche abgestellt werden.[41]

Die Bestimmung der charakteristischen Leistung im Sinne des Art. 117 Abs. 2 IPRG ist eine reine Rechtsfrage. Die Gerichte haben daher die Analyse und Subsumtion des vorgelegten Vertrages von Amtes wegen in eigener rechtlicher Würdigung vorzunehmen. Den Parteien ist es natürlich unbenommen, zu dieser Rechtsfindung beizutragen. Sie müssen sich jedoch damit abfinden, dass das Gericht die charakteristische Leistung einigermassen schematisch, a priori und ohne Detailwürdigung von individuellen Besonderheiten des Vertrages festlegt.

Anders verhält es sich im Rahmen der Bestimmung des engsten Zusammenhanges nach Art. 117 Abs. 1 IPRG. Zwar ist die Bestimmung des engsten Zusammenhangs ebenfalls eine Rechtsfrage; sie setzt aber eine intensive Auseinandersetzung mit dem ganzen Vertragswerk vom Beginn bis zum Ende, in allen Stadien und unter Berücksichtigung aller Umstände, und damit auch eine rechtliche Würdigung aller für die Auslegung relevanten Tatsachen voraus. Auch wenn in diesem Zusammenhang nicht von Behauptungs- und Beweislasten gesprochen werden kann, weil nach Art. 16 IPRG die Bestimmung des anwendbaren Rechts dem Richter als Amtspflicht obliegt, ist die Konsequenz der Untätigkeit einer Partei im Prozess hinsichtlich dieser Tatsachen eine ähnliche wie bei Behauptungs- oder Beweislasten, denen eine Partei nicht genügen konnte.

7. ZUSAMMENFASSUNG

Was die Rangordnung zwischen „engstem Zusammenhang" und „charakteristischer Leistung" betrifft, kann zusammenfassend folgendes gesagt werden:

(1) Auszugehen ist von den speziellen Kollisionsregeln Art. 118 bis 122 IPRG. Sind sie anwendbar, aber führen sie zu einem unbefriedigenden Ergebnis, so ist nach einem engeren oder engsten Zusammenhang im Rahmen der Ausnahmeklausel von Art. 15 Abs. 1 IPRG zu fragen.

(2) Finden die Art. 118 bis 122 IPRG keine Anwendung, so ist im Rahmen des Art.

117 Abs. 2 IPRG als erster Schritt nach einer charakteristischen Leistung zu fragen. (3) Danach ist zu prüfen, ob die Anknüpfung an den gewöhnlichen Aufenthalt oder Sitz des Erbringers der charakteristischen Leistung zu einem befriedigenden Ergebnis führt.

(4) Ist dies nicht der Fall, muss im Rahmen von Art. 117 Abs. 1 IPRG nach einem anderen Anknüpfungskriterium für die charakteristische Leistung, insbesondere nach dem „Erfüllungsort" gefragt werden.

(5) Ist eine charakteristische Leistung nicht feststellbar, so ist direkt im Rahmen von Art. 117 Abs. 1 IPRG nach einem „engsten" Zusammenhang zu fragen.

Für die Frage nach der inhaltlichen Abgrenzung zwischen den Anknüpfungspunkten „engster Zusammenhang" und „Vermutung aufgrund der charakteristischen Leistung" gilt :

(1) Der Begriff des „engsten Zusammenhanges" in Art. 117 Abs. 1 IPRG ist ein inhaltsloser Grundsatz, der durch verschiedene Anknüpfungskriterien bestimmt werden kann: Parteierwartungen, akzessorische Anknüpfungen zur Herstellung eines zeitlichen, räumlichen oder sachlichen Konnexes, innerer Zusammenhang der einzelnen Teile zusammengesetzter Verträge, Eingriffsnormen.

(2) Der Begriff der „charakteristischen Leistung" ist ein engeres, leicht bestimmbares Kriterium, das dem Vertragstyp das Wesenseigene, das Charakteristikum verleiht und im Sinne eines methodischen Prinzips den Vorgehensweg weist.

(3) Die Vermutung als Anknüpfungsgrundsatz aufgrund der charakteristischen Leistung erfüllt die Rolle des Vergleichsmassstabes, in dem Sinne, dass nur ein Anknüpfungsgesichtspunkt, der kollisionsrechtlich deutlich besser überzeugt als die Anknüpfung aufgrund der charakteristischen Leistung als „engerer" oder „engster" Zusammenhang (Art. 117 Abs. 1 IPRG) vorgehen kann.

(4) Der Begriff des „engsten Zusammenhanges" erfüllt zwei Funktionen:
(a)   im Verhältnis zu Absatz 2 (Prinzip der charakteristischen Leistung) eine Korrekturfunktion ähnlich der Ausnahmeklausel des Art. 15 Abs. 1 IPRG;
(b) überall, wo Absatz 2 zu keinem Ergebnis führt, ist er ein unmittelbarer Anknüpfungspunkt, insbesondere wenn eine charakteristische Leistung nicht feststellbar ist.

(5) Art. 117 Abs. 2 IPRG erfasst alle Verträge (somit auch Innominatverträge), die eine charakteristische Leistung aufweisen.

(6) Nach Art. 117 Abs. 1 IPRG sind Verträge anzuknüpfen:
(a) ohne ausgeprägte charakteristische Leistung, so z.B. aussergerichtliche Vergleiche, mit denen beide Parteien Kompromisse eingehen;
(b) mit zwei oder mehreren charakteristischen Leistungen, z.B. zusammengesetzte Verträge, welche zwei Vertragstypen umfassen oder Innominatverträge, mit denen Dienstleistungen und Sachleistungen ausgetauscht werden;
(c) höchst individuell ausgehandelte Verträge mit einer Vielzahl von Verästelungen gegenseitiger Rechte und Pflichten, z.B. ein Zusammenarbeitsvertrag.

SUMMARY
THE RELATIONSHIP BETWEEN THE "CLOSEST CONNECTION" AND THE "CHARACTERISTIC PERFORMANCE" – THE CASE OF SOME INNOMINATE CONTRACTS –

As far as the hierarchy between the "closest connection" and the "characteristic performance" is concerned, the following statements are to be recapitulated:
1. In order to determine the law governing a contract, the conflict rules of article 118 to 122 Swiss PIL Act (PILA) have to be consulted. In case they are applicable, their application would still raise a difficult legal issue – the closer or closest connection has to be determined within the framework of the exception clause of article 15 section 1 PILA.
2. If none of the articles 118 to 122 PILA are applicable, the characteristic performance has to be determined in a first step within the framework of article 117 section 2 PILA.
3. In a second step, a reference to the customary residence or business location of the party having to perform the characteristic obligation has to be examined for its adequacy.
4. If the latter must be declined, another *point de rattachement* has to be looked for in the application of article 117 section 1 PILA, which is in particular the place of performance of the contract.
5. If it is impossible to ascertain the characteristic performance, the "closest" connection has to be determined in direct application of article 117 section 1 PILA.

The distinguishing features between the *points de rattachement* of the "closest connection" and the "presumption on the basis of the characteristic performance" can be outlined as follows:
1. The term "closest connection" in article 117 section 1 PILA is an empty principle, which can be determined by different means of a *point de rattachement*: expectation of the parties, ascertaining the applicable law by the law governing the main contractual relation in order to establish temporal, spatial or material

connection, coherence of the individual parts of composed contracts, *lois d'application immédiate*.

2.   The term "characteristic performance" is a more restricted, easily determinable criterion, which lends the characteristic traits to an individual contract and in the sense of a methodical principle shows the way to proceed.

3.   The *point de rattachement* of the presumption on the basis of the characteristic performance serves as a comparative standard in so far as only a criterion of *rattachement* which is clearly more persuasive in the conflict of laws than the *point de rattachement* of the characteristic performance may take precedence as the "closer" or "closest" connection in the sense of article 117 section 1 PILA.

4.   The concept of the "closest connection" has two different functions:

a.   In relation to section 2 (principle of the characteristic performance) it serves as a corrective similar to the exception clause of article 15 section 1 PILA;

b.   whenever section 2 does not lead to a legal issue, it is meant to be a direct *point de rattachement*, in particular when there is no characteristic performance ascertainable.

5.   Article 117 section 2 PILA includes all kinds of contracts (i.e. also innominate contracts), in which a characteristic performance can be found.

6.   The following contracts are to be subsumed under article 117 section 1 PILA:

a.   Contracts without any particular characteristic performance, e.g. extra-judicial arrangements based on compromises of both parties;

b.   contracts with two or more characteristic performances, e.g. composed contracts including two different types of contract or innominate contracts providing for the exchange of services and payments in kind;

c.   most individually arranged contracts with a high complexity of mutual rights and liabilities, e.g. co-operation agreements.

Das Haager Kinderschutzübereinkommen von 1996 – Wesentliche Verbesserungen im Minderjährigenschutz

Jan Kropholler[*]

In einem Beitrag zu Ehren von KURT SIEHR liegt es nahe, mit dem Haager Minderjährigenschutz einen Themenkreis aufzugreifen, der uns beide über Jahrzehnte wiederholt beschäftigt hat. Zunächst haben wir um eine praktikable Auslegung des Haager Minderjährigenschutzabkommens (MSA) von 1961[1] gerungen, dessen Verständnis vor allem aufgrund des dort verankerten unklaren Kompromisses zwi-

---

[*] Referent am Max-Planck-Institut für ausländisches und internationales Privatrecht, Professor an der Universität Hamburg.
[1] Übereinkommen über die Zuständigkeit der Behörden und das anzuwendende Recht auf dem Gebiet des Schutzes von Minderjährigen vom 5.10.1961, BGBl. 1971 II 219.

J. Basedow et al., eds., Private Law in the International Arena – Liber Amicorum Kurt Siehr
© 2000, T.M.C.Asser Press, The Hague, The Netherlands

schen Staatsangehörigkeits- und Aufenthaltsprinzip große Schwierigkeiten bereitet.[2] Nachdem die Revision dieses Abkommens als Gegenstand der 18. Session der
Haager Konferenz beschlossen war, haben wir uns beide über die anzustrebenden
Inhalte Gedanken gemacht.[3] KURT SIEHR hat sodann als Mitglied der deutschen
Delegation im Haag an der Ausarbeitung der revidierten Fassung in Gestalt des
neuen Kinderschutzübereinkommens (KSÜ)[4] vom 19.10.1996 mitgewirkt und über
dieses Übereinkommen auch bereits ausführlich berichtet.[5]

Ziel meiner Ausführungen soll es nicht sein, das neue Übereinkommen, das mit
seinen 63 Artikeln viel detaillierter und ausführlicher geworden ist als sein Vorläu-
fer, im einzelnen zu würdigen. Vielmehr sollen nur die wichtigsten Vorzüge des
KSÜ von 1996 herausgearbeitet werden, denen entsprechende Schwächen des
MSA von 1961 gegenüberstehen.[6] Im einzelnen sind folgende fünf wesentliche
Verbesserungen auszumachen: der klare Primat der internationalen Zuständigkeit
am gewöhnlichen Aufenthalt des Kindes (dazu sogleich unter 1); die Abstimmung
mit dem Haager Kindesentführungsübereinkommen von 1980 (unter 2); die un-
zweideutige Einbeziehung der kraft Gesetzes bestehenden elterlichen Verantwortung in den Anwendungsbereich des Übereinkommens und ihre Unterstellung unter
das Aufenthaltsrecht des Kindes (unter 3); die vertragsautonome Festlegung der
Anerkennungs- und Vollstreckungsvoraussetzungen (unter 4); und schließlich die
Schaffung eines institutionellen und sachlichen Rahmens für eine wirksame internationale Behördenzusammenarbeit (unter 5).

---

[2] Vgl. MünchKomm-*Siehr*, 3. Aufl., Bd. 10 (1998) Anh. I zu Art. 19 EGBGB und *Staudinger-Kropholler*, 13. Aufl. (1994) Vorbem. zu Art. 19 EGBGB Rz. 16 ff., jeweils m.w.Nachw.

[3] Siehe *Kropholler*, Gedanken zur Reform des Haager Minderjährigenschutzabkommens, RabelsZ 58 (1994), 1; *Siehr*, Die Rechtslage der Minderjährigen im internationalen Recht und die Entwicklung in diesem Bereich – Zur Revision des Haager Minderjährigenschutzabkommens, FamRZ 1996, 1047. Siehe ferner etwa *Boelck*, Reformüberlegungen zum Haager Minderjährigenschutzabkommen von 1961 (1994); *Oberloskamp*, Reformüberlegungen zum Haager Minderjährigenschutzabkommen von 1961, FamRZ 1996, 918; *Sturm*, Stellungnahme zum Vorentwurf eines Übereinkommens über den Schutz von Kindern, IPRax 1997, 10.

[4] Der volle Titel lautet: Übereinkommen über die Zuständigkeit, das anzuwendende Recht, die Anerkennung, Vollstreckung und Zusammenarbeit auf dem Gebiet der elterlichen Verantwortung und der Maßnahmen zum Schutz von Kindern. Deutscher Text RabelsZ 62 (1998), 502 ff.

[5] *Siehr*, Das neue Haager Übereinkommen von 1996 über den Schutz von Kindern, RabelsZ 62 (1998), 464; siehe ferner etwa *Picone*, Riv.dir.int.priv.proc. 32 (1996), 705 ff.; *Bucher*, SZIER 1997, 67 ff.; *Lagarde*, Rev.crit. 86 (1997), 217 ff.; *van Iterson*, Uniform Law Review 1997, 474 ff.; *Pirrung*, Festschrift Rolland (1999), 277 ff.; *Roth/Döring*, Familie und Recht 1999, 195 ff.

[6] Vgl. zu letzteren auch *Siehr* (vorige Note), 467.

1. INTERNATIONALE ZUSTÄNDIGKEIT

1.1 **MSA von 1961**

Das MSA von 1961 stellt in seinem Art. 1 zwar die Aufenthaltszuständigkeit für Schutzmaßnahmen mit Recht an die Spitze, aber nur vorbehaltlich der Bestimmungen der Artt. 3 und 4. Diese beiden Vorbehalte zugunsten des Heimatrechts bzw. der Heimatzuständigkeit haben sich in der Praxis als höchst problematisch und wenig sachgerecht erwiesen.

a)   Gemäß Art. 3 MSA ist ein „Gewaltverhältnis", das nach dem Heimatrecht des Kindes kraft Gesetzes besteht, wie z.B. die elterliche Sorge, in allen Vertragsstaaten anzuerkennen. Was es bedeuten soll, daß dieser Art. 3 in der Zuständigkeitsnorm des Art. 1 MSA vorbehalten bleibt, war von vornherein unklar, und der Vorbehalt hat Anlaß zu einem langen Theorienstreit gegeben. Am sinnvollsten erscheint die sog. Anerkennungstheorie, die besagt, daß die nach Art. 1 zuständigen Aufenthaltsgerichte ein ex-lege-Gewaltverhältnis bei ihren Maßnahmen zwar anerkennen und beachten müssen, daß sie dadurch in ihrer Zuständigkeit aber grundsätzlich nicht beschränkt sind.[7] Demgegenüber bevorzugt die deutsche Rechtsprechung überwiegend die sog. Heimatrechtstheorie, die dem Art. 3 eine Schranke für die Aufenthaltszuständigkeit dann entnimmt, wenn das Heimatrecht des Kindes im konkreten Fall keine Maßnahme vorsieht.[8] Diese durch die Unklarheit des MSA ausgelöste Rechtsprechung, die darauf hinausläuft, daß die Aufenthaltsgerichte vor einem Eingreifen in ein gesetzliches Gewaltverhältnis erst prüfen müssen, ob das ausländische Heimatrecht des Kindes einen solchen Eingriff in der jeweiligen Situation zuläßt, bietet angesichts der Zielsetzung des MSA keine befriedigende Lösung; denn den Aufenthaltsgerichten sollte ein einfaches und schnelles Eingreifen nach ihrem eigenen Recht (Art. 2 MSA) möglich sein.[9]

b)   Nach Art. 4 MSA, der im Rahmen der Aufenthaltszuständigkeit des Art. 1 ebenfalls vorbehalten ist, können die Heimatbehörden eingreifen, wenn sie der Auffassung sind, „daß das Wohl des Minderjährigen es erfordert", und nachdem sie die Aufenthaltsbehörden verständigt haben. Die Aufenthaltskompetenz ist dann grundsätzlich ausgeschlossen. Gemäß Art. 4 IV MSA treten die im Heimatstaat getroffenen Maßnahmen an die Stelle derjenigen der Aufenthaltsbehörde und genießen also Vorrang. Gemäß Art. 8 MSA schließt Art. 4 es aber nicht aus, daß die Aufenthaltsbehörden bei ernstlicher Gefährdung des Minderjährigen tätig werden.

In der gerichtlichen Praxis wurde von der Heimatzuständigkeit mit Recht ver-

---

[7] In diesem Sinne etwa MünchKomm-*Siehr* (oben N. 2) Rz. 117 ff. und *Staudinger-Kropholler* (oben N. 2) Rz. 162 ff., jeweils m.w.Nachw.

[8] Siehe insbesondere BGH 11.4.1984, NJW 1984, 2761 = IPRax 1985, 40, 23 Aufsatz *Jayme* = IPRspr. 1984 Nr. 81.

[9] MünchKomm-*Siehr* (oben N. 2) Rz. 116; *Staudinger-Kropholler* (oben N. 2) Rz. 200 ff.

hältnismäßig selten Gebrauch gemacht, da die fernen Heimatbehörden die Erfordernisse des Kindeswohls in der Regel schlechter beurteilen können als die Behörden an seinem gewöhnlichen Aufenthalt.[10] Das MSA gibt den Heimatbehörden also eine zu starke Stellung.

c)   Insgesamt hat sich der im MSA verankerte Kompromiß zwischen Aufenthalts- und Staatsangehörigkeitsprinzip, der namentlich im Vorbehalt der Artt. 3 und 4 im Rahmen der Aufenthaltszuständigkeit zum Ausdruck kommt, also nicht bewährt.

1.2   KSÜ von 1996

Im KSÜ wird ein Kompromiß zwischen Aufenthalts- und Staatsangehörigkeitsprinzip nicht mehr angestrebt, sondern die Aufenthaltszuständigkeit eindeutig bevorzugt. Dadurch ist die Zuständigkeitsregelung einfacher und sachnäher.

Die Behörden des Vertragsstaates, in dem das Kind seinen gewöhnlichen Aufenthalt hat, sind nach Art. 5 I grundsätzlich uneingeschränkt zuständig, Maßnahmen zum Schutz der Person des Kindes oder seines Vermögens zu treffen. Diese primäre Zuständigkeitszuweisung an die Aufenthaltsbehörden ist gerechtfertigt; denn die Aufenthaltsbehörden sind dem Kind räumlich nahe; sie können seine Lage und seine Bedürfnisse daher regelmäßig gut beurteilen, schnell eingreifen und die getroffenen Maßnahmen vor Ort auch verhältnismäßig leicht vollziehen und überwachen.

Ein dem Art. 1 MSA vergleichbarer Vorbehalt zugunsten der ex-lege-Gewaltverhältnisse besteht nicht; letztere sind im KSÜ im übrigen auch dem Aufenthaltsrecht und nicht mehr dem Heimatrecht zu entnehmen (siehe unter 3). Eine konkurrierende Zuständigkeit der Heimatbehörden findet sich ebenfalls nicht mehr. Vielmehr können die Heimatbehörden als solche nur noch ausnahmsweise und im Einvernehmen mit den Aufenthaltsbehörden tätig werden. Dabei kann die Initiative entweder von der Aufenthalts- oder von der Heimatbehörde ausgehen. Zum einen kann die Aufenthaltsbehörde gemäß Art. 8 KSÜ die Heimatbehörde ersuchen, die Zuständigkeit ausnahmsweise zu übernehmen; die Heimatbehörde wird dem Folge leisten, wenn sie der Auffassung ist, daß es dem Wohl des Kindes dient (Art. 8 IV). Zum anderen kann die Heimatbehörde, wenn sie sich im Einzelfall für besser geeignet hält, das Wohl des Kindes zu beurteilen, die Aufenthaltsbehörde um eine entsprechende Zuständigkeit ersuchen (Art. 9 I); die Heimatbehörde darf die beantragte Zuständigkeit ausüben, wenn die Aufenthaltsbehörde den Antrag angenommen hat (Art. 9 II). Die gleichen Möglichkeiten einer einvernehmlichen Zuständigkeitsübernahme bestehen gemäß Art. 8 II KSÜ auch für die Behörden in

---

[10] Bisweilen wurde die Heimatzuständigkeit auch entgegen den Zielen des MSA in Anspruch genommen, so wenn bei doppelter Staatsangehörigkeit des Kindes die ineffektive benutzt wurde, um eine Entscheidung der Aufenthaltsbehörde umzustoßen; siehe Cass. 16.12.1986, Rev.crit. 76 (1987), 401 krit. Anm. *Lagarde*.

anderen Vertragsstaaten, etwa im Staat der Vermögensbelegenheit oder der Ehescheidung.

In der Befreiung der Aufenthaltszuständigkeit vom Ballast der in Art. 1 MSA enthaltenen Einschränkungen liegt einer der wesentlichen Vorzüge des KSÜ.

2.   KINDESENTFÜHRUNG

Die Fälle der Kindesentführung, in denen ein Elternteil gegen den Willen des anderen sorgeberechtigten Elternteils das Kind ins Ausland entführt oder es dort nach einem Besuch zurückhält, münden oft in einen erbitterten, mitunter auch von der Öffentlichkeit beachteten Kampf der Eltern vor den Gerichten. Eine befriedigende Lösung dieses Konfliktes, die regelmäßig in einer raschen Rückführung des Kindes besteht, ist besonders wichtig.

2.1   MSA von 1961

Das MSA von 1961 enthält keine besondere Norm über die Kindesentführung. Der Grund für diese gravierende Lücke besteht darin, daß man sich seinerzeit im Haag über die Formulierung einer entsprechenden Vorschrift noch nicht einigen konnte.

Bescheidene Ansätze zu einer Lösung können im Rahmen des MSA nur mittels einer teleologischen Auslegung des Begriffs gewöhnlicher Aufenthalt gefunden werden. Ein neuer gewöhnlicher Aufenthalt im Zufluchtsstaat darf nicht sogleich bejaht werden, so daß die Behörden im Herkunftsstaat gemäß Art. 1 MSA zunächst zuständig bleiben.[11] Ist es jedoch durch Zeitablauf zu einer sozialen Eingliederung des Kindes im Zufluchtsstaat gekommen, so kommt die Rechtspraxis nicht umhin, die Begründung eines neuen gewöhnlichen Aufenthalts anzunehmen, so daß über die elterliche Sorge für das entführte Kind (neu) entschieden werden kann.[12] Das MSA bietet gegenüber einem Entführer, der die Zeit für sich arbeiten läßt, also keine ausreichende Handhabe.[13]

2.2   KSÜ von 1996

Das KSÜ regelt die internationale Zuständigkeit bei Kindesentführungen ausdrücklich in einer gesonderten Bestimmung (Art. 7 KSÜ). Das Haager Kindesentfüh-

---

[11] Vgl. etwa MünchKomm-*Siehr* (oben N. 2) Rz. 30 ff.; *Staudinger-Kropholler* (oben N. 2) Rz. 406 f.

[12] So etwa BGH 29.10.1980, BGHZ 78, 293 = FamRZ 1981, 135, 536 Anm. *Schlosshauer-Selbach* = IPRspr. 1980 Nr. 94.

[13] *Boelck* (oben N. 3), 41 f.

rungsübereinkommen (KEntfÜ) vom 25.10.1980[14] wird durch das KSÜ gemäß seinem Art. 50 grundsätzlich unberührt gelassen. Das Anliegen, die schnelle
Rückführung des entführten Kindes staatsvertraglich zu fördern, bleibt also primär
Aufgabe des Kindesentführungsübereinkommens. Das KSÜ mußte lediglich eine
auf dieses spezielle Übereinkommen abgestimmte, aber auch für dessen Nichtver-
tragsstaaten geltende Regelung über eine gewisse Zuständigkeitsfortdauer am Her-
kunftsort bereitstellen, um möglichst zu verhindern, daß der Entführer aus seinem
widerrechtlichen Handeln den Vorteil einer Zuständigkeitsveränderung zu seinen
Gunsten zieht.[15] Dies ist in Art. 7 KSÜ geschehen.

Nach Art. 7 I KSÜ bleiben bei „widerrechtlichem Verbringen oder Zurückhalten
des Kindes" die Aufenthaltsbehörden so lange zuständig, bis das Kind einen neuen
gewöhnlichen Aufenthalt erlangt hat und der Sorgeberechtigte dem Verbringen
oder Zurückhalten zugestimmt hat (Anlehnung an Art. 13 I lit. a KEntfÜ). Statt des
letztgenannten Erfordernisses genügt es für eine Zuständigkeitsveränderung auch,
daß das Kind sich im Zufluchtsstaat mindestens ein Jahr aufgehalten hat, nachdem
der Sorgeberechtigte seinen Aufenthaltsort kannte oder hätte kennen müssen, kein
während dieses Zeitraums gestellter Rückgabeantrag mehr anhängig ist und das
Kind sich in seinem neuen Umfeld eingelebt hat (Art. 7 I lit. b KSÜ in Anlehnung
an Art. 12 KEntfÜ). Die Regelung harmoniert mit Art. 16 KEntfÜ, wonach eine
Sorgerechtsentscheidung im Zufluchtsstaat erst ergehen darf, wenn entschieden ist,
daß das Kind nicht zurückzugeben ist, oder wenn kein Rückgabebegehren anhängig
gemacht wurde.

Anders als das MSA nimmt sich das KSÜ der brisanten Problematik der Kindesentführung also ausdrücklich an und fördert ihre Lösung in Abstimmung mit dem
KEntfÜ. Der Begriff des „widerrechtlichen Verbringens oder Zurückhaltens des
Kindes" konnte aus dem KEntfÜ übernommen und ebenso wie dort definiert werden.[16] Daß der gewöhnliche Aufenthalt des Kindes auch als Folge einer Entführung
wechseln kann, erkennt Art. 7 I KSÜ implizit an. Die Vorschrift läßt die Entscheidung über die Zuständigkeit aber mit Recht nicht allein von der Interpretation des
Begriffs „gewöhnlicher Aufenthalt" abhängen; vielmehr stellt sie für einen Zustän-
digkeitswechsel – in Anlehnung an das KEntfÜ – weitere, klar umrissene Bedingungen auf. Dies alles bedeutet einen deutlichen Fortschritt gegenüber dem
insoweit völlig unzureichenden MSA.

---

[14] BGBl. 1990 II 207.
[15] Vgl. dazu im einzelnen Bericht *Lagarde*, Actes et documents de la Dix-huitième session 1996,
Bd. 2 (Den Haag 1998), 556 ff. Nrn. 46 ff.
[16] Die Definition in Art. 7 II KSÜ stimmt wörtlich mit Art. 3 KEntfÜ überein.

3.   ELTERLICHE VERANTWORTUNG

Dem Minderjährigenschutz dienen nicht nur gerichtliche Maßnahmen, sondern auch kraft Gesetzes bestehende Schutzverhältnisse wie die elterliche Sorge. Will man den internationalen Minderjährigenschutz durch ein Übereinkommen möglichst umfassend regeln, muß die gesetzliche elterliche Verantwortung deshalb einbezogen und das auf sie anwendbare Recht festgelegt werden.

3.1   MSA von 1961

Das MSA von 1961 ist auch in dieser Frage nicht geglückt. Maßgebend ist Art. 3 MSA, der von einem nach dem Heimatrecht kraft Gesetzes bestehenden „Gewaltverhältnis" spricht und damit vor allem die elterliche Sorge meint. Die Reichweite der Bestimmung, die allen Vertragsstaaten vorschreibt, ein solches Gewaltverhältnis „anzuerkennen", ist nicht nur im Rahmen der Zuständigkeitsnorm des Art. 1 unklar (vgl. oben 1.1 a); vielmehr ist auch die kollisionsrechtliche Tragweite des Art. 3 MSA nicht eindeutig zu erkennen. Ist Art. 3 MSA nur dann zu beachten, wenn die Voraussetzungen einer Schutzmaßnahme zu prüfen sind, oder auch in jeder anderen Situation? Kommt der Vorschrift also eine selbständige kollisionsrechtliche Bedeutung zu?

Die Frage ist umstritten und wird in den Vertragsstaaten nicht einheitlich beantwortet.[17] Zu einem sinnvollen Minderjährigenschutzsystem, wie es das MSA bieten will, fügen sich seine Bestimmungen am ehesten zusammen, wenn man die kraft Gesetzes bestehenden „Gewaltverhältnisse" als eigenen Regelungsgegenstand des Abkommens betrachtet.[18] In Deutschland entscheiden der Bundesgerichtshof und die überwiegende Praxis freilich anders; danach soll es außerhalb der Anordnung von Schutzmaßnahmen nicht auf Art. 3 MSA ankommen, sondern bei den Regeln des autonomen deutschen Kollisionsrechts bleiben.[19]

Eindeutig, aber nicht überzeugend geregelt ist durch Art. 3 MSA, daß für die kraft Gesetzes bestehenden Gewaltverhältnisse auf das Heimatrecht des Kindes und nicht – wie für Schutzmaßnahmen (vgl. Art. 2 MSA) – auf das Recht an seinem gewöhnlichen Aufenthalt abzustellen ist. Die unterschiedliche Anknüpfung vermag sachlich nicht zu überzeugen und schafft Anpassungsprobleme. Die Notwendigkeit, das ausländische Heimatrecht zu ermitteln, erschwert überdies die Rechtsanwendung.[20]

---

[17] Näher etwa *Boelck* (oben N. 3), 74 ff.

[18] MünchKomm-*Siehr* (oben N. 2) Rz. 158 und *Staudinger-Kropholler* (oben N. 2) Rz. 280. Ebenso namentlich die herrschende Meinung in Frankreich.

[19] BGH 2.5.1990, BGHZ 111, 199 = IPRax 1991, 254, 231 Aufsatz *Sturm* = IPRspr. 1990 Nr. 143 m.w.Nachw.

[20] Siehe zu diesen und anderen Nachteilen im einzelnen *Boelck* (oben N. 3), 93 ff.

3.2 KSÜ von 1996

Das KSÜ von 1996 vermeidet diese Nachteile. Es nennt in Art. 1 I lit. c als eines seiner Ziele, „das auf die elterliche Verantwortung anzuwendende Recht zu bestimmen", und auch der Titel des Übereinkommens spricht die elterliche Verantwortung neben den Maßnahmen zum Schutz von Kindern ausdrücklich an.[21] Es besteht somit kein Zweifel, daß die Festlegung des auf die elterliche Verantwortung anzuwendenden Rechts einen eigenständigen Regelungsgegenstand des KSÜ bildet. Die Verfasser des KSÜ sahen also ein hinreichend starkes Regelungsbedürfnis für eine einheitliche Kollisionsnorm über die elterliche Verantwortung.[22]

Die in Art. 16 I KSÜ enthaltene Kollisionsnorm unterwirft die Zuweisung oder das Erlöschen der elterlichen Verantwortung kraft Gesetzes – anders als Art. 3 MSA – dem Recht am gewöhnlichen Aufenthalt des Kindes. Dies steht im Einklang damit, daß die für Schutzmaßnahmen nach Art. 5 I KSÜ zuständige Aufenthaltsbehörde gemäß Art. 15 I ihr eigenes Recht, also ebenfalls das Aufenthaltsrecht, anwendet. Der Einklang vereinfacht die Rechtsanwendung im internationalen Kinderschutz erheblich und ist auch sachlich gerechtfertigt; denn das Aufenthaltsrecht als das Recht der Umwelt, in die das Kind integriert ist, erscheint am ehesten berufen, für seinen Schutz zu sorgen, gleichgültig ob es sich um eine Maßnahme oder um das kraft Gesetzes bestehende Schutzverhältnis der elterlichen Sorge handelt.

Der Art. 16 I ist eindeutig als Kollisionsnorm formuliert („bestimmt sich") – im Unterschied zu Art. 3 MSA („wird anerkannt"). Auch darin liegt eine Rechtsverbesserung. Die durch die Berufung des Aufenthaltsrechts neu entstandene Frage, wie sich ein Aufenthaltswechsel des Kindes auf die elterliche Verantwortung auswirkt, ist in Art. 16 III, IV und Art. 17 KSÜ ausdrücklich beantwortet.

4. ANERKENNUNG UND VOLLSTRECKUNG

4.1 MSA von 1961

Die Anerkennung und Vollstreckung von Schutzmaßnahmen ist im MSA von 1961 in einem einzigen Artikel (Art. 7 MSA) nur unvollständig und unzureichend geregelt.

Nach Art. 7 Satz 1 MSA sind alle Vertragsstaaten zur Anerkennung der Maßnahmen verpflichtet, welche die nach dem Übereinkommen zuständigen Behörden getroffen haben. Neben dem Fehlen einer Zuständigkeit aufgrund des Übereinkom-

---

[21] Vgl. den vollen Titel oben in N. 4.
[22] Meine insoweit in RabelsZ 58 (1994), 9 f. geäußerten Zweifel haben sich erfreulicherweise nicht bestätigt; vgl. Bericht *Lagarde* (oben N. 15), 576 Nr. 94.

mens bildet der ordre public (Art. 16 MSA) die einzige Anerkennungsschranke. Die Bestimmung des Art. 7 Satz 1 enthält hinsichtlich der von ihr erfaßten Maßnahmen einige Unklarheiten, und der Verzicht auf die Nennung einzelner Anerkennungshindernisse, wie die Verletzung des rechtlichen Gehörs, führt zu einer Überfrachtung des ordre public.[23]

Zur Vollstreckung von Schutzmaßnahmen verpflichtet das MSA nicht. In Art. 7 Satz 2 MSA wird vielmehr für die Anerkennung und Vollstreckung auf das innerstaatliche Recht des Vollstreckungsstaates verwiesen. Damit vollzieht sich nicht nur die Vollstreckung außerhalb des MSA, sondern Art. 7 Satz 2 entzieht dem Abkommen im Falle einer notwendigen Vollstreckung auch die Anerkennung der Schutzmaßnahme. Dies bedeutet, daß vom Vollstreckungsgericht auch eine „révision au fond" durchgeführt werden kann. Das Fehlen einer Regelung über die Vollstreckung von Schutzmaßnahmen aus anderen Vertragsstaaten beeinträchtigt die Wirksamkeit des MSA und stellt damit eine empfindliche Lücke innerhalb seines Anwendungsbereichs dar.

4.2 KSÜ von 1996

Das KSÜ von 1996 widmet der Anerkennung und Vollstreckung ein eigenes Kapitel und regelt diesen wichtigen Bereich also ausführlich (Artt. 23-28). Es unterscheidet dabei deutlich zwischen Anerkennung (Art. 23), Vollstreckbarerklärung (Art. 26) und Vollstreckung (Art. 28). Eine „révision au fond" ist grundsätzlich ausgeschlossen (Art. 27).

Die Gründe, aus denen eine Anerkennung versagt werden kann, zählt Art. 23 II KSÜ erschöpfend auf und hält damit Anschluß an den internationalen Standard, wie er beispielsweise auch in Art. 27 EuGVÜ Ausdruck findet. Insbesondere sind die relevanten Fälle fehlenden rechtlichen Gehörs ausdrücklich genannt (Art. 23 II litt. b und c KSÜ). Die Anerkennung erfolgt grundsätzlich kraft Gesetzes (Art. 23 I KSÜ), jedoch kann auch eine gesonderte Entscheidung beantragt werden (Art. 24 KSÜ).

Die Vollstreckung einer Schutzmaßnahme in einem anderen Vertragsstaat setzt voraus, daß sie dort für vollstreckbar erklärt oder registriert wurde; die Vollstreckbarerklärung oder die Registrierung darf nur aus einem der in Art. 23 II KSÜ vorgesehenen Gründe versagt werden (Art. 26 III KSÜ). Damit sind die Voraussetzungen der Vollstreckung konventionsimmanent festgelegt. Allein die Ausgestaltung des Verfahrens der Vollstreckbarerklärung oder Registrierung bleibt dem nationalen Recht der Vertragsstaaten überlassen.

Die für vollstreckbar erklärten fremden Schutzmaßnahmen werden wie inländische Schutzmaßnahmen vollstreckt (Art. 28 Satz 1 KSÜ). Das Vollstreckungsver-

---

[23] Näher *Kropholler*, RabelsZ 58 (1994), 14 f.; *Boelck* (oben N. 3), 119 ff.

fahren richtet sich nach der lex fori, wobei das Kindeswohl zu berücksichtigen ist (Art. 28 Satz 2 KSÜ).

Mit dieser Regelung ist die im MSA für die Vollstreckung von Schutzmaßnahmen bestehende Lücke geschlossen. Die für die Anerkennung und Vollstreckung im KSÜ aufgestellten einheitlichen Regeln dürften weithin konsensfähig sein.

5.   BEHÖRDENZUSAMMENARBEIT

Für einen wirksamen Minderjährigenschutz auf internationaler Ebene ist wesentlich, daß die Behörden in den beteiligten Vertragsstaaten mit den notwendigen Informationen über die Lage des Kindes versorgt werden und daß sie möglichst reibungslos zusammenarbeiten.

5.1   **MSA von 1961**

Das MSA von 1961 hat den Nutzen der Behördenzusammenarbeit bereits erkannt und sie in verschiedenen Formen vorgesehen: In Artt. 4 I und 5 II MSA wird vor der Anordnung einer Schutzmaßnahme im Heimatstaat oder im neuen Aufenthaltsstaat die vorherige Verständigung der Aufenthaltsbehörde bzw. der bisherigen Aufenthaltsbehörde verlangt. Nach Art. 10 MSA ist vor dem Erlaß jeder Schutzmaßnahme ein Meinungsaustausch mit den Behörden derjenigen Vertragsstaaten zu pflegen, deren Entscheidungen noch wirksam sind. Schließlich verpflichtet Art. 11 MSA alle Behörden, die aufgrund des Übereinkommens Maßnahmen bereits getroffen haben, dies unverzüglich den Heimatbehörden und gegebenenfalls den Aufenthaltsbehörden mitzuteilen.

Nach Art. 11 II MSA bezeichnet jeder Vertragsstaat die mitteilungspflichtigen und empfangsberechtigten Behörden. In einigen Vertragsstaaten sind dies die Gerichte und Behörden, die auch die Schutzmaßnahmen treffen; so hat Deutschland die für die Maßnahmen zuständigen Gerichte und Jugendämter benannt. Andere Vertragsstaaten, wie die Niederlande und die Schweiz, lassen die Zusammenarbeit über ihr Justizministerium laufen.[24]

In der Praxis hat der im MSA vorgesehene Behördenverkehr allerdings kaum stattgefunden. Dieses Manko wird zum einen mit den sprachlichen Problemen erklärt, denen die Behörden gegenüberstehen, zum anderen mit der Schwierigkeit, die nach dem MSA zuständige Stelle im Ausland zu ermitteln und zu erreichen.[25]

---

[24] Siehe im einzelnen die Übersicht in MünchKomm-*Siehr* (oben N. 2) Rz. 365 ff.
[25] Siehe etwa *Boelck* (oben N. 3), 114 m.w.Nachw.

5.2   KSÜ von 1996

Das KSÜ von 1996 hat aus diesem Fehlschlag die Lehren gezogen, indem es die organisatorisch-technische Gestaltung der Zusammenarbeit vereinfacht, die Möglichkeiten der grenzüberschreitenden Information und Hilfe erheblich ausgebaut[26] und das Sprachenproblem geregelt hat.

Um die Durchführung der Zusammenarbeit zu erleichtern, sieht Art. 29 KSÜ die Einrichtung einer Zentralen Behörde in jedem Vertragsstaat vor, an die sich die Behörden der anderen Vertragsstaaten wenden können und der die allgemeine Aufgabe zur Zusammenarbeit und zur Erteilung von Auskünften obliegt (Art. 30 KSÜ). Das KSÜ folgt damit der Regelung in Artt. 6, 7 I KEntfÜ, die sich bewährt hat und die deshalb auch bereits in andere Übereinkommen übernommen wurde.[27]

Neben den allgemeinen Aufgaben der Zentralen Behörde (Artt. 30, 31 KSÜ) sind die Aufgaben beim Ergreifen von Maßnahmen (Artt. 32-34 KSÜ) und die Hilfe bei der Durchführung von Maßnahmen, insbesondere beim Umgangsrecht, detailliert festgelegt (Art. 35 KSÜ).[28]

Das Sprachenproblem ist in Art. 54 KSÜ geregelt – wiederum in Übereinstimmung mit dem KEntfÜ (dort Art. 24). Eine Mitteilung an die Zentrale Behörde oder eine andere Behörde eines Vertragsstaates wird in der Originalsprache des Absenders zugesandt. Sie muß aber von einer Übersetzung in die Amtssprache des Empfängers, notfalls von einer Übersetzung ins Englische oder Französische, begleitet sein.

Insgesamt berechtigen die positiven Erfahrungen mit der Behördenzusammenarbeit im Rahmen des KEntfÜ zu der Hoffnung, daß die ähnlich normierte Zusammenarbeit im KSÜ ebenfalls erfolgreich verlaufen kann.

6.   AUSBLICK

Das KSÜ bringt – wie gezeigt wurde – in den fünf genannten Kernbereichen eine ganz wesentliche Rechtsverbesserung. Daneben enthält es gegenüber dem MSA eine Reihe weiterer Verbesserungen in Einzelfragen, auf die hier nicht näher eingegangen werden kann. Genannt seien etwa: die genaue und konkrete Eingrenzung des sachlichen und persönlichen Anwendungsbereichs des Übereinkommens (Artt. 1-4); die Einräumung einer Scheidungszuständigkeit nur unter engen Voraussetzungen (Art. 10); die Regelung der doppelten Rechtshängigkeit (Art. 13); die Bestimmung des anwendbaren Rechts für jede auf das Übereinkommen gestützte

---

[26]   Vgl. Bericht *Lagarde* (oben N. 15), 588 ff. Nrn. 136 ff.
[27]   Siehe etwa *Pirrung*, RabelsZ 57 (1993), 135 f.
[28]   Einen näheren Überblick über die verschiedenen Aufgaben gibt *Siehr*, RabelsZ 62 (1998), 496 f.

Maßnahme in Verbindung mit einer Ausweichklausel (Art. 15 I, II).

Das KSÜ ist trotz seiner bedeutenden Vorzüge bislang nicht in Kraft getreten.[29] Aber die im Haag erreichten Verbesserungen rechtfertigen seine Ratifikation. Mit ihr sollte nicht gezögert werden.

SUMMARY
THE 1961 HAGUE CONVENTION ON THE PROTECTION OF CHILDREN – A
SUBSTANTIAL IMPROVEMENT IN THE PROTECTION OF MINORS

In comparison with the 1961 Convention on the Protection of Minors, the new 1996 Hague Convention on the Protection of Children includes five major improvements: first, the clear and unambiguous acceptance of the child's habitual residence as the primary basis for jurisdiction; second, a better harmonization with the 1980 Hague Convention on the Abduction of Children; third, the explicit inclusion of parental responsibility arising by operation of law into the scope of the Convention and its determination by the law of the State of the habitual residence of the child; fourth, the autonomous stipulation of the conditions for the recognition and enforcement of measures; and finally the creation of an institutional and substantive framework for an effective international co-operation between State authorities. These improvements as set out in more detail in this paper justify the ratification of the new Hague Convention.

---

[29] Bis zum 1.1. 2000 hatte nur Monaco ratifiziert.

The Principles of European Contract Law and the *lex mercatoria*

Ole Lando[*]

1. INTRODUCTION

In 1974 KURT SIEHR, Bernd von Hoffmann and I organised an international colloquium in Copenhagen on what was then the European Preliminary Draft Convention on the Law Applicable to Contractual and Non Contractual Obligations. Together we edited a book containing the acts and documents of that colloquium.[1] The preliminary draft convention was later to become the Rome Convention on the Law Applicable to Contractual Obligations. Our collaboration was harmonious and rewarding, I believe, for all of us. Von Hoffmann and I learned to appreciate KURT SIEHR's qualities a as an eminent collaborator and a scholar.

---

[*] Professor of Law (emeritus), Copenhagen Business School/ Chairman of the Commission on European Contract Law.

[1] *European Private Law of Obligations*, (Ole Lando, Bernd von Hoffmann and Kurt Siehr (eds.)), *Materialien zum ausländischen und internationale Privatrecht 23* (Tübingen 1975).

J. Basedow et al., eds., Private Law in the International Arena – Liber Amicorum Kurt Siehr
© 2000, T.M.C.Asser Press, The Hague, The Netherlands

Things have changed since then. By the beginning of the third millennium Europe is undergoing big changes. The European Union has brought about an economic, cultural and legal integration. So far, this integration is only a halfway house, but it has proved to be a self-increasing process. The trade in Europe and the international trade is expanding. and soon, if not already now, more services are traded than goods. The peoples of Europe are wealthier than ever before in history. They travel more and communicate more. The computer and the internet have introduced new contractual techniques, which have opened up new markets. The increasing trade and communication have generated a need for a unification of the law of contracts.

The background of this paper is the author's work in the Commission on European Contract Law which is preparing the *Principles of European Contract Law.*[2] It brings some thoughts about a future unified or harmonised contract law in Europe. It is submitted that such a unification is both needed and feasible, and that a European contract law may be brought about by legislation and may become part of the *lex mercatoria.* Emphasis is laid on this latter aspect.

2.   WHY UNIFY THE EUROPEAN CONTRACT LAW?

Why should contract law be unified and why should it be europeanised? To europeanise is to unify or harmonise European law. The term Europe covers those countries which are or will become members of the European Union.

Many of the reasons for and against a unification of contract law are valid both for Europe and for the world. However, the eurpeanisation is in some respects to be treated separately because the Union has brought its members close together and now has the institutions and the tools for a further harmonisation of their laws.

The Union of today is an economic community. Its purpose is the free flow of goods, persons, services and capital. The idea is that the more freely and abundantly these can move across the frontiers the wealthier and happier we will get. It should therefore be made easier to conclude contracts and to calculate contract risks.

Anyone doing business abroad knows that some of his contracts with foreign partners will be governed by a foreign law. The unknown laws of the foreign countries is one of his risks. They are often difficult for him and his local lawyer to get to know and to understand. They make him feel insecure, and may keep him away from foreign markets. This is an impediment to world trade. In Europe the existing variety of contract laws is a non-tariff barrier to the inter-union trade. It is the aim of

---

[2] See Lando & Beale (eds.), *Principles of European Contract Law, Part 1: Performance, Nonperformance and Remedies* (Deventer 1995) on the Commission on European Contract Law .

the Union to do away with restrictions of trade within the Communities, and therefore the differences of law which restrict this trade should be abolished.

2.1   Can We Not Contend Ourselves with the Existing Eurpeanisation?

In the last decades there have been important developments of what may be called the EU contract law. Most important is perhaps the Directive on Unfair Terms in Consumer Contracts.[3] In addition the EEC has issued several other directives providing protection of the consumer as a contracting party.[4] Some of the directives on labour relations provide rules for the protection of the employee. Furthermore, the EEC has established a law of competition which provides restrictions of the parties' contractual freedom by laying down which contract terms are permissible and which are not. The Directive of 18 Dec 1986 on the Self-employed Agent contains mandatory rules most of which protect the agent.[5]

The Union legislation mentioned above has provided some eurpeanisation of the contract law. However, it is only a fragmentary harmonisation. It is not well co-ordinated, and, since the national laws of contract are different, it causes problems when it is to be adjusted to the various national laws.[6] There is no uniform European law of contract to support these specific measures.

2.2   The Rome Convention

The rapidly increasing commerce in the European Union have made the countries of the European Communities provide uniform choice of laws rules with respect to contracts. The Rome Convention of 19 June 1980 on the Law Applicable to Contractual Obligations is now in force in all the Member countries. However, for many lawyers choice of law rules are *terra incognita*, and will entail the application of foreign law. To ascertain and apply foreign law is often a cumbersome operation. For these reasons many lawyers shy away from the conflict of laws. The law of the forum country is then applied to the detriment of the foreign party. It is therefore preferable to unify the substantive law rules and thereby prevent conflict of laws cases from arising.

---

[3] Directive 93/13 of 5 April 1993, *OJ(EC)* L [1993] 95/29.

[4] See Directives on Doorstep Sales (85/577, 20 Dec. 1985, *OJ(EC)* [1985] L 372/31), Consumer Credit (87/102, 22 Dec. 1986, *OJ(EC)* [1987] L 42/48), Package Tours (90/314, 13 June 1990 *OJ(EC)* [1990] L 314/59), Time Share Agreements (94/47, 26 Oct. 1994, *OJ(EC)* [1994] L 280/83), Distant Sales (97/7, 20 May 1997, *OJ(EC)* [1997] L 144/9),and on certain aspects of the Sale of Consumer Goods and Associated Guarantees (99/44, 25 May 1999, *OJ(EC)* [1999] L 171/12).

[5] Directive 86/653, 18 Dec. 1986, *OJ(EC)* [1986] L 382/17.

[6] See R.. Zimmermann, "Civil Code and Civil Law", 1 *Columbia Journal of European Law* (1994/95) 63, 73 and H. Kötz, Rechtsvereinheitlichung, Nutzen, Kosten, Methoden"., 50 *Rabels Zeitschrif für ausländisches und internationales Privatrectt* (1986) 3.

3.   IS THE EURPEANISATION OF THE CONTRACT LAW FEASIBLE? CAN
      THE 15 OR MORE STATES AGREE ON A UNIFIED CONTRACT LAW?

3.1   Differences and Similarities

European lawyers are divided by different legal methods and rules and by different
legal languages. The greatest divergence is between the legal method and language
of the civil law countries of the European Continent and the common law countries
of the British Isles. But there are also considerable differences between the legal
systems of the Continent.

In spite of differences in the social, political and intellectual history of the various countries, and in spite of the fact that the law makers, be they legislators or
courts, have pursued their policies through very different legal techniques, we see
that the legal values are basically the same. This, it is submitted, has several causes.

One is the common roots of the laws of Europe. Everywhere there has been the
impact of the Christian ethics, the great European moralists, and in modern times
the democratic institutions and the unified and harmonised laws of the European
Union. At present there is already a European Law and it is growing. It has already
and will also continue to establish a considerable uniformity of legal thinking.

Another factor is the similarity of economic and social conditions in the
countries of the Union, the market economy of the industrial states. In these
societies the legal problems that arise are similar and so are the answers which
economic consideration give to the problems. The agents of the market need safety
and foreseeability. They wish to have rules which make the conclusion of contracts
swift and inexpensive, and at the same time they need a measure of flexibility.

Ideas regarding the contents of such rules have alway travelled from one country
to another. From early times the legislators have borrowed from foreign sources, and
nowadays they do so to an increasing extent. Modern media makes it easy for political ideas to gain ground. When, for instance, mass production and mass consump-
tion make some leading nations legislate in order to protect the consumer this idea
spreads all over the world. This has also added and will add to the common core.

3.2   The European *Homo Judicans*

A third factor is the environment of the judges which has produced a common
ideology and behaviour. This environment creates a peculiar species of mankind,
the case-deciding man *(homo judicans)*. Most of the guardians of our law and
justice have grown up in well-to-do bourgeois homes with moral traditions. In
school and at the university the judge *in spe* was a good and relatively virtuous
student with strong ties to his home. He was often a right-winger.[7] His life in court

---

[7] See for what was then West-Germany W. Kaupen, *Die Hüter von Recht und Ordnung. Die soziale*

has maintained his bourgeois attitude, and has confirmed his conservative response to life, which promotes scepticism towards new ideas and trends. The judges in the higher courts are elderly gentlemen or ladies, and elderly people tend to be even more conservative than young people.

Lawyers who have read foreign court decisions have often discovered that the foreign courts have come to a result which is similar to the one his own courts had arrived at in a similar situation, and this in spite of the fact that the foreign courts have applied rules that are different from those governing in his own country. The Court of Justice of the European Communities has judges from all the Member Countries and some of these Judges have told me about a similar experience. There is often agreement about the outcome of a case although the reasons for the decision vary considerably. The common attitudes to legal problems is also found among academic lawyers. This was the experience of the members of. the UNIDROIT Working Group which drafted the *Principles of International Commercial Contracts* and of the *Commission on European Contract Law*. During the discussions and when preparing the meetings they would consider how the courts of their own country have or would have reacted to the problems discussed. They often found that the courts would reach the same results, especially when they tried to illustrate the problems with decided or imaginary cases.

3.3   The Resistance to Change

However, one must realise that today many, if not most, lawyers in Europe do not wish contract law to be europeanised. Some still adhere to the ideas of the great German writer *Friedrich Karl von Savigny* who considered the national law as part of the nation's cultural heritage. It reflects the spirit of the people. The law of a nation is based on its entire past. It must develop, but the historical roots are innate in the people and should not be cut off.[8] What is true for the lawyers of one state may be false for the lawyers of another state. The truth about contract law, they argue, is not the same for a Swede as for an Italian, for an Englishman or for a German.

To introduce a new contract law in Europe will admittedly cost sweat, tears, and money. And many lawyers will hate to see all that which they themselves have learned and practised disappear and no less hate to have to learn a new contract law instead.

No doubt the emotional wish to preserve the peculiar character of each of our

---

Herkunft, Erziehung und Ausbildung der deutschen Juristen, 2. Aufl. (1971) and Ralf Darendorf, *The education of an Elite. Law Faculties and German Upper Class, Transactions of the 5th World Congress of Sociology* (Louvain 1964) 259-274.

[8] See von Savigny, *Vom Beruf unsrer Zeit für Gesetzgebung und Rechtswissenschaft* (Heidelberg 1814) reprinted in: Hattenhauer, *Thibaut und Savigny, Ihre programmatischen Schriften* (München 1973) 95ff.

national laws will prove to be a serious political obstacle, but it is one which must be overcome if the European Union is to function satisfactorily. Contract law and commercial law are not folklore. Who today mourns in Paris *"les coutumes de Paris"* which governed in Paris before the Great Revolution, and in Prussia – *"das allgemeine Landrecht für die preussischen Staaten"* which was the code for Prussia until the year 1900?

4.   THE EUROPEAN EFFORTS AT HARMONISATION

The Commission on European Contract Law and the Study Group on a European Civil Code:

It was these considerations which led to the efforts at unifying the law. In 1982 the Commission on European Contract Law began to establish Principles of European Contract Law (hereinafter called PECL). It has drafted articles which, like the American Restatements, are supplemented with comments explaining the operation of the articles. In these comments there are illustrations, ultra short cases which show how the rules are to operate in practice, and notes which disclose the sources of the rules.

With a few exceptions the members of the Commission of European Contract Law have been academics, but many of the academics are also practising lawyers. The Members have not been representatives of specific political or governmental interests, and they have all pursued the same objective, to draft the most appropriate contract rules for Europe.

Similarly to other parts of the world, Europe is undergoing a rapid change of both legal technique and legal values. The Commission has therefore endeavoured to draft broad principles which leave a certain latitude for the court's discretion. The Principles should be interpreted and developed in accordance with their purposes; a strict and narrow interpretation should be avoided.

Part 1 of the Principles dealing with performance, non-performance and remedies was published in 1995.[9] In 1992 the Second Commission on European Contract Law began to work on the formation, validity, interpretation and contents of contracts and on the authority of an agent to bind his principal. The Second Commission held its last meeting in May 1996, and Part 2 of the Principles which includes a revised version of the Principles of Part 1 was published in 1999.[10] In 1997 the Third Commission began to prepare rules which are common to contracts, torts and unjust

---

[9] Lando & Beale (eds.) (supra n. 2).
[10] See Ole Lando and Hugh Beale (eds.), *Principles of European Contract Law – Parts 1 and 2* (The Hague 1999).

enrichment, such as plurality of creditors and debtors, assignment of debts and claims, set-off, and prescription.

In 1989 and again in 1994 the European Parliament passed Resolutions requesting a start to be made on the necessary preparatory work on drawing up a European Code of Private Law.[11] In the preamble to the 1989 Resolution it is mentioned that "unification can be carried out in branches of private law which are highly important for the development of a Single Market, such as contract law . . . "

The proposal to draft a code has been supported by some governments in the Union. Thanks to a grant from the German and Dutch governments a Study Group on a European Civil Code is now in operation in Germany and the Netherlands to establish Principles of European Law governing certain specific contracts, extra-contractual obligations and non possessory security interests in moveables.

5.   THE LEX MERCATORIA

5.1   The Genesis of the *lex mercatoria*. Its Sources

The main purpose of the Principles is to serve as a first draft of a part of a European Civil Code. However, it may take time before they are enacted in the entire Union. Until then and even afterwards, as well as in transactions between parties in the Union and outside of the Union and between parties outside of the Union, the Principles may also be applied as part of the *lex mercatoria*. Article 1:101(3)(a) PECL provides: "These Principles may be applied when the parties have agreed that their contract is to be governed by "general principles of law, the *lex mercatoria* or the like".[12]

In modern times the *lex mercatoria* emerged from cases where the arbitration clauses had empowered the arbitrators not to follow the strict rules of law and to decide their case *ex aequo et bono*, or as they say in French to decide as "*amiables compositeurs*". Arbitrators who were entrusted with this task often felt that, although they were not bound to apply the strict rules of a legal system, their award should nevertheless be based on grounds of principle.

Since about the mid-fifties the theory on the *lex mercatoria* has been developed by English[13] and French[14] authors who could show that the concept was already ac-

---

[11]   See Resolutions of 1989 *OJ(EC)* [1989] C 158/401 and of 1994: *OJ(EC)* [1994] C 205/518.

[12]   A court or arbitral tribunal applying the *lex mercatoria* which chooses the PECL to govern issues covered by the Principles, may let the *lex mercatoria* replace national law in issues not covered by the PECL.

[13]   See on Schmitthoff's theory on the new law merchant, Filip de Ly, *International Business Law and Lex Mercatoria* (Amsterdam, North-Holland 1992) at p. 209f.

[14]   On the theories of Goldmann and Kahn see Filip de Ly, ibid., at p 210ff.

cepted in international business circles and applied by arbitral tribunals. One of its main fields of operation was contracts governed by international usages and practices. The international reinsurance treaty was an example of such contracts.

Insurance companies from all over the world cover their great risks by way of re-insurance. In Europe the dominant market is the English, but the German and the Swiss markets are also important. The international character of the re-insurance trade has influenced the rules of law governing the reinsurance treaties. They are dominated by the usages and practices of the big European centres.[15] For this reason the governments of most European countries have abstained from legislating on re-insurance. Thus, when in the twenties the Nordic countries enacted a Uniform Insurance Contract Act they decided to exclude re-insurance from the scope of the Act. In the *Travaux préparatoires* to the Act this was explained by the fact that these "issues are of a typically international character, and as the modern foreign laws on insurance contracts have not embarked upon them the time does not seem ripe to do it with us either".[16]

Before 1985 the *lex mercatoria* was an upstart.[17] Its many adversaries rejected it, invoking grounds of principle. The main arguments against the application of the *lex mercatoria* were first, that no state authority has given binding force to its rules, and, second, that it is a diffuse and fragmented body of law without much substance; it gives the parties no certainty as to what will be the outcome of a dispute between them. It is arbitrary and therefore unsupportable. The trade, and especially the international trade, needs certainty and foreseeability. The *lex mercatoria* consists of undefined and indefinable standards described as a *lex* of unknown origin. The outcome of cases decided by application of the *lex mercatoria* is mere lottery.[18]

---

[15] See Thomas Wilhelmsson, *Om reassurandörs ersättningsskyldighet vid skadesförsäkring* (Stockholm 1976) at pp. 23 and 32-33.

[16] See Swedish Proposition 1927 no. 11:1 pp. 350-352, and *SOU* 1925: 21 p. 66. An example of an award based on considerations of principle is an award of 23 December 1922 in a case between a Finnish and a Danish insurance company. Relying on what seems to have been an "equity clause" in the re-insurance contract the three Danish arbitrators chose to treat a negligent misrepresentation by the Finnish reinsured party regarding the risks involved in the same way as it was to be treated under § 9 of the Nordic Draft Insurance Contract Bill which for such cases provided for a reduction of the indemnity to be paid by the re-insurer. The arbitrators found the reduction principle of the Bill, although not in conformity with what was then "the strict rules of law", to be "in accordance with justice and equity". See arbitral award of 23 December 1922 reported in *Samling af Domme. Kendelser og Responsa vedrørende Forsikringsforhold* (Court decisions, awards and opinions regarding insurance) published by *Assurandør-Societetet i København* (the Society of Insurers in Copenhagen) (1925) 78.

[17] See Lando, "The *lex mercatoria* in international commercial arbitration", 34 *International and Comparative Law Quarterly* (1985) 747, and Carbonneau (ed.), *The lex mercatoria and arbitration* (New York 1990). Among the contributors to this work who are adversaries of the *lex mercatoria* are F.A. Mann, Georges Delaume, and Keith Highet, and among the supporters Berthold Goldman, who was one of the "inventors" of the modern *lex mercatoria*, and furthermore Andreas F. Lowenfeld and Friedrich Juenger.

[18] See F.A. Mann in: Carbonneau, ibid., at pp. XIXff.

As for the first argument we must refer to the fact that the arbitrators' application of the *lex mercatoria* has been endorsed by several legislators and courts, even though it is a "state-less" law. In 1985 the *lex mercatoria* was made respectable by the UNCITRAL: see section 5.2 below.

Regarding the second argument, the diffuse and fragmented character of the *lex mercatoria*, it must be pointed out that it is not undefined and indefinable. The *lex mercatoria* consists of the international customs and usages of the international trade, the rules which have been drafted for this purpose, and the rules which are common to most of the States engaged in international trade or to the States connected with the dispute. The arbitrator may, but need not, apply these rules. When he cannot find such common rules or when he does not find them suitable to the case he will "apply" the rules which appear to him to be the most appropriate and equitable. This judicial process is partly an application of rules and partly a selective and creative process.

In the last decades new elements have been added to the substance of the *lex mercatoria*.[19] Among them is the Convention on Contracts for the International Sale of Goods (CISG) which entered into force on January 1, 1989, and which in 1999 had been adopted by more than 50 countries. Its rules may now be regarded as part of the common core of the legal systems.[20] Other important new elements of the *lex mercatoria* are the UNIDROIT Principles of International Commercial Contracts (hereinafter the UNIDROIT Principles) and the Principles of European Contract Law. (PECL).

Another source is the *International Encyclopedia of Comparative Law* which is published by the *Max Planck Institute for Foreign Private and Private International Law* in Hamburg. The Encyclopedia brings a comparative survey of the laws of the world on subjects within civil law, commercial law and the law of civil procedure. Several volumes of this work deal with contracts.[21] It brings the existing common core if any, the typical solutions of the legal systems, and often also the authors' views on what in their opinion is the "better law".

There have also been important developments of the EU contract law. The Community legislation mentioned in section 3 has provided a certain eurpeanisation of the contract law in the Member States. It is somewhat fragmented and uncoordinated, but it is there. Furthermore, the EEC and the European Union have promoted

---

[19] See Lando, "The *lex mercatoria* in international commercial arbitration", 34 *International and Comparative Law Quarterly* (1985) 747, 752-755.

[20] See Bernard Audit, "The Vienna Sales Convention and the *lex mercatoria*", in: Carbonneau (supra n. 17) at p.139.

[21] The *International Encyclopaedia of Comparative Law* is published in instalments and is not yet completed. Several chapters on contract matters have been published in Volume VII on *Contracts in General*, VIII on *Specific Contracts*, IX on *Commercial Transactions and Institutions*, XII on *Law of Transport* and XV on *Labour Law*.

the establishment of an international *régime* of academic lawyers whose platform is no longer their own country but Europe and the world, and whose writings and debates will influence the future law. In addition to the already existing international and European law reviews several new ones have emerged in the 1990s.[22] Noteworthy in this respect is also the planned work in two volumes by *Flessner & Kötz European Contract Law* of which the first volume has appeared.[23] It treats the contract law in general in Europe. Its aim is to establish the common core of the European laws, to suggest common solutions where the laws are different and thereby to satisfy the needs of a European contract law.

It must be admitted that the *lex mercatoria* will never reach the level of the copious and well-organised national legal systems. But even they are not so perfect as many lawyers claim them to be. As will be shown in section 5.3 below the national laws are incomplete and not always well equipped to regulate international contracts in a changing world.

5.2   *Lex mercatoria* before Arbitral Tribunals

Art 28 (l) of the *United Nations (UNCITRAL) Model Law on International Commercial Arbitration l985*[24] provides:

> "The arbitral tribunal shall decide the dispute in accordance with *the rules of law* as are chosen by the parties" (emphasis added).

The term *rules of law* implies that the parties may choose the *lex mercatoria* to govern their contract. The model law has been adopted by Australia, Canada, Egypt, Germany, Hong- Kong, Hungary, India, Mexico, New Zealand, Russian Federation, Ukraine, Scotland and 15 other countries, and by 8 of the United States.[25] The Italian, French, and Dutch codes of civil procedure have similar provisions. They even allow the arbitrators to apply the *lex mercatoria* when the

---

[22]   E.g., *European Review of Private Law* (Kluwer, Belgium 1993-), *Uniform Law Review* (Unidroit, Rome 1996-), *Maastricht Journal of European Comparative Law* (Bruylant ,Belgium 1994-) and *European Journal of Law Reform* (Kluwer, Netherlands 1998-)

[23]   Kötz, *European Contract Law*, Vol. I (Oxford 1997).

[24]   Adopted by the United Nations Commission on International Trade Law (UNCITRAL) on June 21 1985, reprinted in Mustill & Boyd, *The Law and Practice of Commercial Arbitration in England*, 2nd ed. (London 1989) at p. 730.

[25]   See Pieter Sanders, "Unity and Diversity in Adoption of the Model Law", 11 *Arbitration International* (1995) 1. and UNCITRAL. Status of the Conventions and Model Laws, updated 9 October 1998 .The other countries were Bahrain, Bermuda, Bulgaria, Cyprus, Guatemala, Iran, Kenya. Lithuania, Malta, Nigeria, Oman, Peru, Singapore, Sri Lanka and Tunisia. The 8 American States were California, Connecticut, Florida, Georgia, North Carolina, Ohio, Oregon and Texas.

parties have not chosen it.[26] Section 46(1) (b) of the English *Arbitration Act 1996* provides that "if the parties so agree the arbitral tribunal shall decide the dispute in accordance with such other considerations (than the law) as are agreed between them or determined by the tribunal". In the explanatory notes to the Bill of July 1995, made by a Departmental Advisory Committee on Arbitration,[27] it was said that the section corresponds to art 28 of the Model Law.[28]

Furthermore, the Austrian Supreme Court has upheld an arbitral award made in Vienna where the arbitrators had applied the *lex mercatoria* to the case even though the parties had not agreed upon its application. The Court held that by applying the *lex mercatoria* the arbitrators had not exceeded their mandate.[29] Without much discussion the Norwegian Supreme Court has given "full legal effect " to an ICC arbitral award which had been decided under the *lex mercatoria*.[30]

It is now widely held that arbitrators deciding international commercial disputes may apply the *lex mercatoria*. The fact that laws, conventions and court decisions recognise the application of non-national rules of law has persuaded most lawyers that the *lex mercatoria* has come to stay.

It remains, however, a question as to what extent the *lex mercatoria* should replace national law. Some will, in principle, let it operate as a legal body of its own, whereas others would rather apply it only when the applicable national law gives no answer or no reasonable answer.

Those authors who will only call on the *lex mercatoria* when the applicable national law gives no answer or no reasonable answer will apply it as a supplement and a corrigendum. Furthermore, in their opinion, the arbitrator should not act as a social engineer when he cannot find any answer in the *lex mercatoria*. He then has to apply the rules of the law applicable to the contract. The arbitrator may only replace the rules of the law applicable to the contract by the rules that may reasonably be claimed to exist as part of the *lex mercatoria*.

Under the theory which lets the *lex mercatoria* replace national law no national legal system governs the contract. When the arbitrator cannot find existing rules in the *lex mercatoria*, or when he does not find them suitable for the dispute in question he will "apply" the rules which appear to him to be the most appropriate and equitable. This does not mean that national rules of law are completely out of the picture. The arbitrator must give effect to rules of the forum or another law

---

[26] See art 1496 of the French Code of Civil Procedure, art 1054 of the Dutch Code of Civil Procedure, and art 834 of the Italian Code of Civil Procedure.

[27] Department of Trade and Industry, Consultative paper on an Arbitration Bill, July 1995. Section 1, and Section 2: Draft Clauses of an Arbitration Bill, July 1995.

[28] Consultative paper, ibid., at p 38.

[29] Austrian Supreme Court 18.Nov.1982, *RIW* (1983) 868

[30] See Justice, later Chief Justice, Carsten Smith's majority opinion in Judgement of 5 December 1987, *NRt* (1987) 1449 at p. 1456.

closely connected with the issue which are directly applicable or which are rules of public policy.

It is submitted that this solution is the most appropriate. It is possible to provide greater consistency and harmony in adjudication if an open system of rules such as the *lex mercatoria* is allowed to govern the contract than the one that would emerge if one were to try and shake a cocktail of the rigid rules of national law and the open rules of *the lex mercatoria*. Therefore, unless the parties have agreed otherwise, the *lex mercatoria* should replace national law.

In international cases it has one great advantage. When the *lex mercatoria* is applied, and those who are involved in the proceedings – parties, counsels and arbitrators – are from different countries, all plead and argue on an equal footing: nobody has the advantage of having the case pleaded and decided by his own law, and nobody has the handicap of seeing it governed by a foreign law.

It is much in dispute whether arbitrators should be permitted to apply the *lex mercatoria* when *the parties have not chosen it*. The French, Italian and Dutch laws of civil procedure allow the arbitrators to do so. English law and most of the laws which have incorporated the UNCITRAL Model Law seem to permit the arbitrators to apply non-national rules of law only when the parties have chosen them as applicable to the substance of the dispute.

5.3   May Courts Apply the *lex mercatoria*?

It is the general opinion that under the Rome Convention on the Law Applicable to Contractual Obligations the courts must apply national law even though the parties should have chosen the *lex mercatoria*.[31]

However, even if the courts consider the *lex mercatoria* to be too diffuse and reject it on that ground, they will probably have to give effect to the parties' choice of the UNIDROIT Principles or the PECL as an *incorporation*. The contract will then be governed by a national legal system. The Principles will apply to the extent that their rules do not violate mandatory rules of that system. In addition, the courts will have to give effect to those rule of the forum or another law closely connected with the issue which are directly applicable to the issue or which are rules of public policy.

The Dutch professor *Katharina Boele-Woelki* has proposed that in a future amendment to article 3 (1) of the Rome Convention it should be provided that the parties be permitted to choose the *Unidroit Principles of International Commercial Contracts* or *the Principles of European Contract Law* not merely as an incorpora-

---

[31] Lagarde says in *Revue critique de droit international privé* (1991) 300: "*La Convention de Rome s'est placé dans la perspective d'un choix par les parties d'une loi étatique*".

tion but as the rules of law governing the contract.[32] Professor *Boele-Woelki* seems to be of the opinion that the parties should be permitted to combine their choice of the Principles with the choice of other elements of *the lex mercatoria* to govern those issues in contract which are not covered by the Principles.[33]

This would mean that parties to an international commercial contract would have their contract governed by the Principles, be it the UNIDROIT Principles or the PECL, by the usages and practices of international trade, by the common core of the legal systems or of those systems to which the contract is connected and by other sources which make out the *lex mercatoria*. Those would replace the national law as the law governing the contract. However, as was mentioned above, courts and arbitrators must observe the public policy of the forum country and in some cases also the directly applicable rules of another country closely connected with the contract.

Many of the arguments in favour of applying the *lex mercatoria* to international arbitration may also apply to the court's adjudication of international disputes.

Parties who go to court and have their dispute governed by a national law will often have the benefit of more foreseeability but must expect more rigidity. Parties who choose the *lex mercatoria* must be prepared to have a more open and flexible system governing their dispute. The judge who applies the *lex mercatoria* will act as a social engineer more than the judge who applies national law.

However, national law also has white spots. No legal system provides a predictable answer to any legal issue, and every system provide rules which the courts do not find appropriate for the situation at hand. In such situations judges sometimes substitute the rules of law by their concept of what they believe to be expedient, fair and just. This is sometimes necessary, especially since many legal systems carry with them ancient relics of a dead past.

Under the present rapid change of legal technique and legal values, contracts and other relationships can only be governed by rules which leave a certain latitude for the court's discretion. National rules must also be developed taking into account the changed situations. Many judges make themselves guilty of "double-speak" when they deny that they now and then strain the rules of their codes and precedence. If by the law of a country one understands what the courts do in fact, the national legal system is more pluralistic than many lawyers would like to admit. Applying the *lex mercatoria* is not something to which most judges will be unaccustomed.

Furthermore, state courts have accepted that arbitrators apply a non-national legal system. Why should the courts not be permitted to do so themselves? The experienced judges of those courts which frequently deal with international commercial cases are at least as suitable to apply the *lex mercatoria* as are the arbitrators. It seems therefore that if the parties so decide state courts dealing with

---

[32] See K. Boele-Woelki, *Principles en IPR* (Utrecht 1995); Id., "Principles and Private International Law", *Uniform Law Review* (1996) 652ff.

[33] K. Boele-Woelki, *Uniform Law Review*, ibid., at p 664f.

international cases should be authorised to apply the *lex mercatoria* to replace national law. The common legal tradition, and the common social and economic background will often guide the European judge in the same direction as his brethren in other countries, and this is a safeguard against the application of "undefined and indefinable standards" which the antagonists of the *lex mercatoria* fear.

Unusual Bedfellows – Renvoi and Foreign Characterization Joined Together

Kurt Lipstein[*]

1.   BASIC PREMISES

For the purpose of the present investigation it may be useful to set out the premises on which it is based.[1]

Renvoi can arise when the choice of law rule of the forum employs one connecting factor to the operative facts[2] of the forum's choice of law rule in order to determine the applicable law, while the choice of law rule of the law referred to employs a different connecting factor to its operative facts. Any different characterization of the latter has been taken into account when the function of the rule of foreign law pleaded by a party has been analysed in order to determine which conflicts rule of the forum operates (see *infra*). The forum recovers the power to apply its own do-

---

[*] Q.C., Ph.D., LL.D., Dr.iur.h.c., Emeritus Professor of Law and Fellow of Clare College in the University of Cambridge.

[1] Lipstein, *International Encyclopedia of Comparative Law*, Vol. III Ch. 23, nos. 1-21 (in course of publication).

[2] The term "operative facts" indicates that part of a choice of law rule which represents a category of typical legal situations, such as contract, tort, succession. The term is used for want of a better expression. See Rabel, *Conflict of Laws*, 2nd edn. (1958) Vol. I, 47. For other terms see Neuhaus, *Die Grundbegriffe des internationales Privatrechts*, 2. Aufl. (1976) 103, 126; Rigaux, *La théorie des qualifications en droit international privé* (1956) p.244.

J. Basedow et al., eds., Private Law in the International Arena – Liber Amicorum Kurt Siehr
© 2000, T.M.C.Asser Press, The Hague, The Netherlands

mestic law but need not do so.

Characterization affects the interpretation of the operative facts of the forum's choice of law rules in the light of a claim or a defence formulated and pleaded in accordance with some system of laws, foreign or local. It is a preliminary process which determines which operative facts among two or more choice of law rules of the forum are involved leading to the application of a particular system of law to the issue in question.

2.   CONSEQUENCES

Renvoi determines the ultimate choice of the relevant connecting factor attached to a single category of operative facts embodied in the choice of law rule both of the *lex fori* and of the law referred to.

Characterization results in the selection of one of several operative facts, forming part respectively of two or more choice of law rules of the forum after an analysis of the function of the legal provision pleaded by the party or parties coupled with a broad interpretation of the operative facts in issue. Once this process has been concluded the appropriate choice of law rule has been ascertained and proof of foreign law can begin.

Thus, at most, the choice of law process in the forum may comprise first a characterization of the claim or defence resulting in the choice of the appropriate choice of law rule of the forum leading to a reference to a particular legal system. Subsequently the application of the legal system so found may end in a reference back, if the forum accepts the substitution of its own connecting factor by another referred to, if foreign.

In the normal type of case, once characterization by the forum of the claim or defence has taken place by analysing the function of the law pleaded coupled with a broad interpretation of the operative facts of the forum's choice of law rule, a secondary characterization according to the law found to be applicable is not called for. The reason given by this writer is that, as shown above, the function of the rule pleaded by the party has already been taken into account during the process of selecting the applicable law. A repetition of this exercise fails in its purpose for it only represents an invitation to the forum to reconsider – now in the light of the law found to be applicable – the selection of the appropriate choice of law rule reached already in the light of the law pleaded by the parties.[3] This may, or may not, be the law found to be applicable at the conclusion of this process.

---

[3] Lipstein (supra n.1) no. 50.

3.   MOVABLES, IMMOVABLES; UNITARY OR SEPARATE TREATMENT

Complications can arise, however, on two levels when the question before the court involves property.[4]

Firstly, in some countries the notion of property is a unitary one, in others (common law countries) it distinguishes between interests in land (realty) and other interests (personalty) which latter notion includes not only interests in tangibles but also in intangibles (choses in action).

Secondly, independently of this division of substantive legal interests, the choice of law rules in some countries (mainly but not exclusively common law countries) distinguish between movables and immovables and between interests in either of them.

4.   EFFECT UPON CONNECTING FACTOR AND OPERATIVE FACTS

This distinction between reliance on the factual nature of immovables and movables on the one hand and interests in immovables and movables on the other hand has been little noticed in the practice and in literature.[5] This is not surprising since in the relevant choice of law rules, such as "succession to immovables is governed by the *lex situs*", "matrimonial property relations between spouses are governed by their personal law if the property is movable and by the *lex situs*, if immovable", the inclusion of a reference to immovables and movables serves a dual purpose.

Firstly, taken alone they form part of the operative facts and thus represent a *legal category* of *rights* (or *interests*) in *immovable* or *movable property*. They cover the legal claims or defences relating to property. The notion has a legal connotation. As in all operative facts it signifies rights or interests in immovables or movables.[6]

---

[4] Jayme, "Qualifikationsverweisung im internationalen Privatrecht", 17 *Zeitschrift für Rechtsvergleichung* (1976) 93-107.

[5] Dicey and Morris, *Conflict of Laws*, 9th edn. (1973) Rule 77; (12th edn. (1993)) Rule 113 cited by Jayme, supra, at pp. 93, 98, 101, 104, but see 95 (now 13th edn. (2000) rule 111). The English practice suggests it to a certain extent; as regards the legal interests in the object:

Chatfield v. *Berchtold* (1872) L.R. 7 Ch. App. 192, 193; *Re Fitzgerald* [1904] Ch. 573, 588, 589; *Re Cutcliffe* [1940] 565, 571; *Re Ritchie* [1942] 3 D.L.R. 330, 335; *Re O'Neill* (1922) N.Z.L.R. 468, 474; *Hacque* v. *Hacque* (1964-1965) 114 C.L.R. 98, 106, 119-120, 125, 135.

As regards the factual nature of the object:

Freke v. *Lord Carbery* (1873) L.R. 16 Eq. 461, 467; *Duncan* v. *Lawson* (1889) 41 Ch. D. 394; *Re Hoyles* [1911] 1 Ch. 179; *Hacque* v. *Hacque* (supra) 107-109; *Macdonald* v. *Macdonald* (1932) S.C. (H.L.) 79, 84, 85, 88.

Confusing: *Freke* v. *Lord-Carbery* (supra) 466; *Hacque* v. *Hacque* (supra) 98, 105-106; 109, 123, 133, 134, 136.

The account given by Rabel, *Conflict of Laws*, Vol. IV (1958) 15ff is inconclusive; see also Niboyet, *Traité de droit international privé* III (1944) no.967; IV (1947) nos. 1153, 1190.

Secondly, at the same time, read in conjunction with the reference to the *lex situs* it *represents a fact* and displays some of the characteristics of a connecting factor.

The quandary is now clear. Possessing the characteristics of both parts of a choice of law rule the terms immovables and movables may become subject to two different processes of characterization according as their character as a legal interest or as a connecting factor is in question. As shown above, the practice of the courts shows little appreciation of this difference.[7]

5.   AS A CONNECTING FACTOR

The combination of a reference to the factual character of immovables or movables with a reference to the *lex situs* results in a connecting factor of a mixed nature. It is therefore not easy to call in aid directly the test which serves to interpret connecting factors, namely the domestic law of the forum and not that of the *situs*. The present dispute as to whether the *lex fori* or the *lex situs*[8] must determine the factual nature of the object bears out this distinction.

---

[6] The following are interests in immovables: Rentcharges, *Re Berchtold* (1872) 7 App. Cas. 193, 199; Mortgages, *Re Hoyles* [1911] 1 Ch. 179, 187; *Hacque* v. *Hacque* (supra n. 5) 114 C.L.R. 88, 100ff.; *Re Ritchie* [1942] 3 D.L.R. 330, but see to the contrary the cases cited by Dicey and Morris, *Conflict of Laws*, 13th edn. (2000), esp. *Re O'Neill* [1922] N.Z.L.R. 468; Leaseholds: *Freke* v. *Lord Carbery* (1873) L.R. 16 Eq. 461, 466; *Duncan* v. *Lawson* (1889) 41 Ch. D. 394, 398; Debenture Stock: *Re Cutcliffe* [1940] Ch. 565, 571; Scots Heritable Bonds: *Re Fitzgerald* [1904] 1 Ch. 573, 588, 589.

[7] See supra n.5.

[8] *Lex fori* Kahn, Abhandlungen zum internationalen Privatrecht I 73, 491, 494: Niboyet, Traité III (supra n. 5) no. 957; Lehmann, *Juriscl. dr. int.* VIII Fasc. 531 (1988); Staudinger(-Hausmann), *Kommentar zum Bürgerlichen Gesetzbuch mit Einführungsgesetz und Nebengesetzen: Einführungs- gesetz zum Bürgerlichen Gesetzbuch*, 13th edn. (1996) art.3-6; art. 4 no.65-69; Staudinger(-Dörner) same, 13th edn., (1996), art. 25, 26; art. 25 nos. 477-487; Staudinger (-Firsching), same, 12th edn. (1984) art.24-28 a.F. 5, 6 n.F., 12th edn. (1991) no.226ff. preceding art.24-25; Soergel Siebert (-Kegel), nos. 75, 562 preceding art.7, no.92 preceding art. 24; art. 27 no. 36.

France: Cass. civ. 28 July 1862 S.1862.1.988; Cass. req. 15 July 1885, S.1886.1.285; Cass. civ. 22 June 1955, D. 1956 J. 73, J.C.P. 1955 II 8928, Clunet 1955, 728, T.I.J. Seine 12 Jan. 1966, Rev. crit. d.i.p. 1967, 120, note Loussouarn 125 ff, J.C.P. 1968 II 15266, Germany: R.G. 5 July 1934, R.G.Z. 145, 85, 86.

With Exceptions: Cass. plén 15 April 1988, *Rev. crit. d.i.p.* (1989) 100 (note: Droz); Clunet 1989, 86 (note: Kahn); D.S. 1988 J. 325 (note: Malaurie); J.C.P. 1988. II. 21066 (note: Barbieri) on appeal from Montpellier 18 Dec. 1984, *Rev. crit. d.i.p.* (1985) 559 (note: Batiffol); D.S. 1985 210 (note: Maury); J.C.P. 1988 II 21066; Paris 21 Sept. 1995, Clunet 1996, 683.

Lex situs:Austrian P.I.L. para. 31(2); Louisiana Code (1991) art. 353; Quebec, C.C. (1986) art. 3078; Bartin Clunet 1897, 225, 249, 250, 253; Principes de droit international privé I (1930) para. 888, p. 236; Lerebours-Pigeonnière (-Loussouarn), *Droit international privé*, 7th edn. (1959) no. 361 p. 423(d); Batiffol and Lagarde, *Droit international privé* I, 8th edn. (1993) no. 288 p. 489; Batiffol, *Rev. crit. d.i.p.* (1985) 563; Cass. civ. 5 April 1887, S.1889.1.387; Trib. civ. Seine 14 March 1894, Clunet 1894, 815; T.I.G. Seine 12 Jan. 1966 (supra); Jayme (supra n. 4) at pp. 93, 98.

In principle the *lex fori* must determine the meaning of any connecting factor, for the *lex fori* determines in what circumstances a legal system is to be applied. On the other hand, reliance on the *lex situs* is supported by considerations of effectiveness in the realm of property. This consideration must clearly prevail when legal interests in immovables or movables are in issue. It is, however, doubtful when it comes to interpret the connecting factor which relies on the nature of a movable or an immovable. Little difficulty exists where the object is land, a fact recognized equally by the *lex fori* and the *lex situs*. Accessories such as *immeubles par destination* (chickens on the land) create difficulties, but it would seem that even then the *lex fori* rather than the *lex situs* (if different) must be called in aid for only the factual aspects of the asset are in issue.

6. AS A LEGAL INTEREST

It is different when the legal interest in the asset must be determined. Here the question as to whether the claim or defence is based on an interest in a movable or immovable must follow the usual pattern. The claim presented in the light of some legal systems and the operative facts of the choice of law rule of the forum must be interpreted in terms of each other in order to decide whether a legal interest in an immovable or a movable is involved.

7. CONFLICTS SITUATIONS

The problems discussed here do not, however, present themselves always in the same form when a conflicts rule distinguishes between immovables and movables and applies different laws to them respectively.

In the first place, their solution is simple when the conflict rules of the *lex fori* themselves incorporate the division between immovables and movables and the interests in them. The question whether an immovable or a movable is in issue will be solved in the usual way by relying on the *lex fori*. The function of the legal provision pleaded by a party, examined in the light of the operative facts of the *lex fori* interpreted broadly will show whether the claim or defence falls within the ambit of the forum's conflict rule on immovables or movables as understood by the latter.

In the second place, when the choice of law involves a court and parties which are both subject to a common law system which distinguishes between realty and personalty and therefore do not differ from each other, the English Court of Appeal held in 1910[9] that it is unnecessary to have recourse to private international law and

---

[9] *Re Hoyles* [1911] 1 Ch. 179.

to determine whether an interest in a movable or an immovable is involved. In terms of modern parlance, the conflict is a false one. This solution has not found universal approval. Not only the domestic rules of the two legal systems may differ in details. It also remains unclear whether the law applied in the end is that of the forum or of foreign law. On the answer to this question may depend whether an appeal is possible, because the *lex fori* is being applied or foreign law in which case no appeal is possible.

This leaves the situation where the forum has a unitary rule of private international law (e.g. succession is governed by the *lex patriae*, matrimonial property relations are governed by the law of the parties' domicile) while the foreign law referred to contains a conflict rule which is binary and distinguishes between immovables and movables as connecting factors and between interest in immovables and movables as operative facts governed respectively by the *lex situs* or the personal law of the parties. If the forum accepts a reference back and the claim concerns land situated in the country of the forum, the problems discussed above become reality.

8.   THE PROBLEM IN PRACTICE

Such was the case which faced the Landgericht in Wiesbaden (Germany).[10]

An American domiciled in Indiana, while serving with the Army in Germany, married a German woman: separation of goods applied. During the marriage the wife acquired valuable land in Germany. In the course of a divorce the husband, basing his claim on German law which provided for a division between the spouses of the increase of their respective fortunes during marriage (*Zugewinngemein-schaft*), brought an action in Germany.

The German court applied its choice of law rule concerning matrimonial property which referred to the personal law of the husband, which turned out to be Indiana. According to Indiana law movable matrimonial property was governed by the law of the husband's domicile, Indiana, and immovable property by the *lex situs*, Germany. The German court accepted the reference back and held that the *lex situs* determined whether an object was an immovable or a movable. It then found that according to German law the claim concerned an interest in a movable being in the nature of an economic rather than of a proprietary kind. Thus the personal law of the husband, Indiana law applied, which ignored a claim of the kind allowed by German law.

---

[10] L.G. Wiesbaden 30 March 1973, I.P. Rspr. 1973 no. 46; *Fam. R.Z.* (1973) 657; Jayme (supra n. 4) at p. 94.

If the principles developed above are applied, a critical examination of the decision of the court in Wiesbaden must start from two questions:

(i)   Is land in Germany subject to a *Zugewinngemeinschaft* an immovable?
(ii) Is the right in a *Zugewinngemeinschaft* consisting exclusively of land an interest in an immovable?

For the forum, which was the court in Wiesbaden, the first question to be decided according to the *lex fori*, which also happened to be the *lex situs*, was therefore whether land constituted the connecting factor (see *supra* para. 4). In fact, the Court disregarded this aspect and faced immediately the second, which was whether the interest in issue concerned an immovable or a movable. For the purpose of characterizing the interest in issue, the German court held that it was more economic than proprietary in nature and was therefore an interest in a movable. This characterization was unnecessary at this stage, since it was clear that, for the purpose of the German conflict rule, the claim concerned matrimonial property and that the personal, i.e. Indiana, law applied. In short, the German court anticipated without good reason a characterization according to Indiana law, the applicable law, including its conflict rules which distinguishes in matters of matrimonial property whether the claim in issue concerns an interest in a movable or an immovable.

Since German law was prepared to accept the reference back by Indiana law, it now became necessary to determine firstly, what was the connecting factor of the Indiana conflicts rule which distinguished between immovables and movables? Secondly, since unlike in normal cases of a reference back, where only the connecting factor changes but not the operative facts, another question arose. Was the interest represented by the *Zugewinngemeinschaft* consisting exclusively in land in Germany an interest in an immovable or a movable, having regard to the Indiana conflicts rule that immovable matrimonial property is governed by the *lex situs* and movable property by the *lex domicilii*.

As regards the first question, it was suggested above (para. 4) that the *lex fori* determines the connecting factor. In a case of a reference back this must be the foreign law referred to, i.e. in the present case the law of Indiana. It was also suggested above (para. 4) that this is a question of fact. Thus the proceedings concerned land in Germany. The second question should have been whether the interest in a *Zugewinngemeinschaft* consisting exclusively of land in Germany is an interest in an immovable or a movable. The court in Wiesbaden answered it by characterizing it according to German law. In fact the problem was one of characterization according to Indiana law in order to decide whether the choice of law rule concerning immovable or movable of Indiana conflict of laws applied. In a German court this should have been one of proof of foreign law. The answer would have depended upon whether according to Indiana law a *Zugewinngemeinschaft* creates a community of goods in the combined increase in the value of the separate fortunes of husband and wife brought into the marriage irrespective of the movable or immovable nature of the assets, not unlike a partnership. If so, the interest therein of a spouse is not an interest in an immovable. If this were accepted, the Indiana choice of law rule on matrimonial property relations concerning movables (which term includes choses in action such as rights in a partnership) would apply. This points to the law of the domicile of the parties (Indiana). The answer to this question is, however, disputed. It must depend upon whether the economic or the proprietary character of the interest is regarded as predominant by Indiana law. Whatever the answer, this is not an instance of *secondary characterization*. It is a second, additional characterization.

9.   CONCLUSIONS

To sum up: the conclusion reached here and the conclusion reached by the court of Wiesbaden may lead to the same result, but not necessarily. According to the method set out here,

(a)   the German court characterizes the claim as affecting matrimonial property and refers to the national law of the parties – found to be Indiana law;

(b)   the Indiana court finds that land is concerned and applies its rule that matrimonial property relations concerning immovables are governed by the *lex situs*;

(c)   the Indiana court characterizes the claim arising out of a *Zugewinngemeinschaft* in German land;

(d)   according as the Indiana court finds the economic interest to predominate over the proprietary one, its characterization of the claim will result in the application of Indiana or of German law.

The situation is unique. It occurs only if the choice of law rule of the forum is unitary and the choice of law rule of the law referred to is binary, distinguishing between immovables and movables and interests in them respectively.

Private International Law of the Republic of China: Past, Present and the Future

Herbert Han-Pao Ma[*]

This article is written primarily to introduce the current conflicts rules of the Republic of China on Taiwan (ROC), entitled the "Law Governing the Application of Laws to Civil Matters Involving Foreign Elements". Promulgated in 1953, these rules are based on the old Statute Governing the Application of Laws of 1918. However, the new Law of 1953 differs from the old Statute both in substance and in form. It also contains a number of provisions, which are unique in many respects, thus making the 1953 legislation an interesting subject of study.

Any study of the private international law of Republic of China has to rely heavily, if not completely, on her codified conflicts rules. This is so because, for a considerable period of time before and after the enactment of the Statute of 1918,

---

[*] Law Foundation Professor of Law, National Taiwan University; former Grand Justice, Judicial Yuan, Republic of China.

J. Basedow et al., eds., Private Law in the International Arena – Liber Amicorum Kurt Siehr
© 2000, T.M.C.Asser Press, The Hague, The Netherlands

owing to diplomatic reasons, conflicts cases in China were either nonexistent or negligible. And as soon as diplomatic circumstances allowed an increase of conflicts cases, the internal political situation in China was such as to make such an increase difficult or impossible. As a result, the two sets of rules of 1918 and 1953 became the major source of private international law of the Republic of China. For this reason, before discussing the 1953 rules themselves, it seems necessary to make some preliminary remarks on two matters: first, the historical background against which the old conflicts rules of 1918 were first enacted; second, the circumstances that made the legislation of the current rules imperative.

1.   HISTORICAL BACKGROUND OF THE STATUTE OF 1918

China began her relations with foreign countries in the most unpleasant manner. During the late period of the Ch'ing Dynasty in the middle of the nineteenth century her gates were forced open to Western powers wishing to trade with her. This was followed by a series of unequal treaties, which China had to sign under duress.[1] On the basis of these treaties, foreign countries were granted consular jurisdiction and various other forms of extra-territorial concessions, which had direct impact on the development of Chinese conflicts. For instance, the scope of consular jurisdiction as defined in the treaties signed with major Western powers was approximately as follows:

(1)   Civil and criminal cases between foreigners of the same nationality were to be handled by the consul of the country of nationality;

(2)   Disputes between people of a country with which China had treaty relations and people of a third country were excluded from the jurisdiction of Chinese officials (in fact, such disputes were handled by the consul of the country to which the defendant belonged);

(3)   A civil or a criminal case between a Chinese and a foreigner was to be tried by the consul of the country to which the defendant belonged, in accordance with the law of that country. The case was to be tried by Chinese officials in accordance with Chinese law if the defendant was Chinese. But in the latter case, the foreign consul retained "the right to observe the trial" or "the right to a joint trial". In observing a trial, the foreign consul could not only dispute the proceedings but also insist on applying the law of his country. The right to a joint trial, which originated in those for-

---

[1] Chien Tai, *The Causes and Abolition of Unequal Treaties with China* (Taipei, National War College 1961) pp. 63-68.

eign settlements generally known as "concessions" in the big port cities, was at first limited to cases between Chinese and foreigners. Later it was extended to cases involving Chinese only. In some of these big city concessions another form of extraterritoriality existed, that is a formal foreign court composed of foreign judges conducting circuit sessions.[2]

From 1843 to 1918, almost all the countries having commercial intercourse with China in those days exercised consular jurisdiction or some form of extraterritoriality as described above. Nationals of countries that had not concluded treaties with China could always avail themselves of the protection of the consul of a country having consular jurisdiction in China. Therefore, it is no exaggeration to say that almost all foreigners then within Chinese territory were beyond the jurisdiction of Chinese courts and Chinese law.[3]

Since China began negotiating the recovery of her judicial sovereignty, the first encouraging response from major Western powers came in 1902 and 1903, when Britain and the United States agreed that they would give up extraterritoriality if China made such reforms in her law and legal system that would satisfactorily meet Western standards.[4] Henceforth, the efforts on the part of China under the Ch'ing Dynasty were focussed in this direction. These efforts were continued and accelerated after the establishment of the Republic in 1912.

As far as legislation is concerned, the European codified system existing in Germany, France, Switzerland etc., was followed. Although most of the important laws – civil, criminal, commercial as well as administrative – were not promulgated until after 1929, the first set of conflicts rules, the Statute Governing the Application of Laws, was formally promulgated as early as 1918 by the Peking Government under the warlords. These rules were not enacted primarily to meet urgent actual demands, but rather to convince foreign countries of China's determination to recover her judicial sovereignty, conflicts cases in the early years being at best very few in number.

Following China's unification after the overthrow of the warlords, a National Government was set up in Nanking in 1927. The conflicts rules in the Statute of 1918 remained in force.[5] But, it was not until after China fought side by side with Britain and the United States in winning the Second World War that in 1943 Britain and the United States led the way in formally abolishing all unequal treaties imposed on China.

---

[2] Ibid.
[3] Chien Tai (op. cit. n. 1) pp. 19-21.
[4] Art. 12, Sino-British Treaty of Commerce, Sept. 5, 1902; Art. 15, Sino-American Treaty of Commerce, Oct. 18, 1903.
[5] Hsieh Chengmin (ed.), *Legislative History of the Republic of China* (Shanghai, Cheng-Chung Book Store 1948) p. 242.

The fact that, for a hundred years, most foreigners within Chinese territory were beyond the reach of Chinese courts and Chinese law, interfered severely with the development of the private international law of China. For one thing, since the very foreign nationals who conducted most transactions in China, or with Chinese, were those protected by consular jurisdiction, China was denied a major source of conflicts cases.

In the wake of the Second World War, when China emerged victorious on equal terms with Western powers, it seemed that circumstances would guarantee a bright future for this branch of law. But, within a few years' time, the Chinese Communists overran the country and the National Government was forced to move its seat to the island province of Taiwan.

In summary, the history of modern China has been such as to offer insufficient opportunity for the application of her rules of conflict of laws. As a result, conflicts cases lacked variety in terms of both the foreign elements involved and the nature of the cases. This state of affairs, which stifles theoretical interest, is believed to have contributed to the long-standing lack of experts and treatises relating to this branch of law.

2. NECESSITY OF NEW LAW

The Statute of 1918 remained in force after the National Government of the Republic of China had moved to Taiwan in 1949. Geographical limitations alone, not to mention other unfavorable factors in the first few years, would no doubt have prevented any increase in the application of conflicts rules. However, perhaps for the first time in all these unstable decades the authorities concerned were given the opportunity to study and reflect on the rules created some 30 years ago. As a result, the Statute of 1918 was found no longer viable in many respects.

As it was strongly felt that new legislation was needed, the Ministry of Justice started preparing a draft in 1952. The new Law was finally passed by the Legislative Yuan in 1953. Compared with the old Statute, the new Law has introduced many changes both in structure and in content, including changes in some basic principles. I shall point out these changes when discussing the new Law itself hereunder. Suffice it to say here that the new Law was a timely piece of Legislation. As a matter of fact, a year or two after its enactment the ROC government, in order to accelerate economic growth in Taiwan, initiated positive steps for promoting foreign investments – chiefly in the form of introducing a series of new investment laws.[6]

---

[6] Notably, the Statute for Encouragement of Investment (1960); the Enforcement Rules of the Statute for Encouragement of Investment (1961); the Statute for Investment by Foreign Nationals (1954, amended 1959); and the Statute for Investment by Overseas Chinese (1955).

Gradually an ever-increasing number of foreign individuals and corporations began to set up business connections on this island. While most of the credit for this should be given to the investment laws, it is beyond doubt that the new rules on conflict of laws have also contributed to Taiwan's economic developments.

3.   LAW GOVERNING THE APPLICATION OF LAWS TO CIVIL MATTERS INVOLVING FOREIGN ELEMENTS

3.1   The Structure

In the first place it is noteworthy that the new Law of 1953 like the old Statute of 1918 is an independent statutory enactment dealing exclusively with conflict of laws problems and related matters. However, the two sets of rules differ from each other considerably in structure. The old Statute with its 27 articles is divided into 7 chapters each bearing a title. Hence, Chapter I General Provisions (Arts. 1-4); Chapter II Law Concerning Persons (Arts. 5-8); Chapter III Law Concerning Family (Arts. 9-19); Chapter IV Law Concerning Succession (Arts. 20-21); Chapter V Law Concerning Property (Arts. 22-25); Chapter VI Law Concerning Forms of Juristic Acts (Article 26); Chapter VII Supplementary Provisions (Article 27).

Such an arrangement may be criticized from two aspects. On the one hand, to group 27 articles under as many as 7 entitled chapters with several chapters containing only one or two articles does not seem appropriate from the standpoint of classification. Moreover, the four articles under the first chapter deal respectively with (1) the exceptions to the application of foreign law, (2) multiple nationality, statelessness, lack of a unitary system of law, (3) the recognition of foreign juristic persons and (4) *renvoi*. All these provisions are more in the nature of exceptions to the question of application of laws than principles of it. Therefore, to place these articles in the first chapter and entitle it "General Provisions" is obviously unsatisfactory.

In answer to these defects, the new Law has been drafted in a completely different form. Primarily modeled after the pattern of Japanese and German legislation, the new Law has 31 articles. The first 24 articles form the main part of the Law, and are arranged in the same order as the several Books of the Chinese Civil Code, without chapters or sections. Thus, the first 5 articles deal with matters contained in the first Book of Civil Code, entitled "General Principles" (Articles 1-2, persons; Article 3, interdiction; Article 4, declaration of death; Article 5, the forms of juristic acts). Articles 6-9 deal with Obligations, which are the subject-matter of the second Book of the Civil Code. Article 10 deals with the contents of the third Book of the Civil Code, entitled Rights over Things. Articles 11-21 deal with Family, which corresponds to the fourth Book of the Civil Code and Arts. 22-24 deal with succession, corresponding to the fifth Book of the Civil Code. The various other related matters are provided in the last 7 articles of the Law. Thus, Article 25 concerns the exceptions to the application of foreign law; Article 26, multiple nationality; Article 27, statelessness; Article 28, lack of a unitary system of law; Article 29, *renvoi*; Article 30, absence of provisions in the law; Article 31, date of promulgation.[7]

While the structure of national conflicts rules are not of necessity logically dependent on that of domestic law[8], it is nevertheless a great convenience to lawyers, judges and other administrators of law that such rules use the same terms as used in domestic private law and adopt an order of arrangement corresponding to that used in the Civil Code.

3.2 The Name

Since the positive conflicts rules of China, old and new, take the shape of an independent statutory enactment, it became necessary for each enactment to have a name of its own. The old name "Statute Governing the Application of Laws", taken over from Japan, is misleading in that it gives the impression that the Statute governs the application of laws in all matters. The present name "Law Governing the Application of Laws to Civil Matters Involving Foreign Elements" is an obvious improvement on the old one in at least two respects. First, it is made clear that, as a set of rules primarily concerned with the applicable law, the new Law only governs matters involving foreign elements. Second, such matters are limited to those, which are civil in nature.[9]

While this name may not have covered the whole nature and function of this branch of law, it has come close to it.

3.3 Legislative Policy

The guiding policies for the new legislation are twofold: (1) respect for the rights and interests of foreigners, (2) protection of the interests of nationals and maintenance of public order and *boni mores*.[10]

The second policy calls for some elaboration because quite a number of provisions, which were not in the old Statute, have been enacted on the basis of this policy. The following instances may serve as illustrations: (1) when an alien is interdicted in accordance with Article 3, para. 1, the effect of such an interdiction is

---

[7] Explanations of the Draft of the Law Governing the Application of Laws to Civil Matters Involving Foreign Elements (hereinafter cited as "Explanations"), documents Related to Bills of the first Legislative Yuan, Yuan Tsun Tze No. 98, government Bill No. 55, 1952.

[8] Rabel, *The Conflict of Laws: A Comparative Study*, 2nd edn. (Ann Arbor, Michigan 1958) Vol. 1, Ch. 2: Structure of Conflicts Rules, pp. 47 et seq.

[9] Explanations.

[10] Ibid.

governed by ROC law (Article 3, para. 2). (2) If the spouse, or a lineal relative by blood, of a missing alien is a ROC national and has domicile or residence within the Republic of China, such an alien may, upon application of his spouse or lineal relative by blood, be declared dead under ROC law, not being subject to the restrictions specified in Article 4, para. 1 (Article 4, para. 2). (3) If one of the parties to a marriage is a national of ROC, and the marriage is celebrated within the Republic of China, the form of celebration is governed by ROC law. (Article 11, para. 2). (4) When a woman, who is the wife of an alien, has not lost her ROC nationality and has domicile or residence within the Republic of China, or when an alien who is the *chui-fu*[11] of a national of ROC, the effects of such a marriage are decided by ROC law rather than by the national law of the husband (Article 12). (5) If either of the spouses is a national of ROC, the grounds for divorce are governed by ROC law (Article 14, proviso). (6) In the case of a woman who is the wife of an alien and who has not lost her ROC nationality, or in the case of an alien who is the *chui-fu* of a national of ROC, the effects of his or her divorce are governed by ROC law rather than by the national law of the husband (Article 15, para. 2). (7) When the father has lost his ROC nationality and the mother and child remain nationals of ROC, the legal relations between parents and child are governed by ROC law rather than the national law of the father (Article 19, proviso). (8) When, under ROC law, a national of ROC is an heir, he may succeed to the deceased's property, which is in the Republic of China (Article 22, proviso).

It is clear that an emphasis on the protection of internal public and private interests results in an expansion of the application of domestic law or *lex fori*. However, an increase in the application of ROC law does not necessarily endanger the interests of foreigners, because when ROC law applies, it applies to nationals of ROC and foreigners equally. Except for certain specific limitations,[12] foreigners have the same rights and duties as nationals of ROC.

The reasons for adopting such legislative policy may be summarized as follows:

First, the new Law was enacted some ten years after China retrieved her long-lost judicial sovereignty. The memory that, for almost a century, cases involving foreign elements within Chinese territory had to be subject to foreign jurisdiction and foreign law, is still vivid in the mind of every Chinese lawmaker. If the new legislation should savor of nationalism and an emphasis on *lex fori*, it is not completely without justification. This also marks the difference in policy between the new Law

---

[11] A *Chui-fu*, like an adopted husband, is a man who is married into the family of his wife. He prefixes to his surname that of the wife and his children assume the surname of the mother. See Arts. 1000, 1002, 1059 of the Book of Family, Civil Code.

[12] The restrictions on foreigners set forth in Mining Law, Land Law, Maritime Law, Civil Aviation Law, Company Law, etc., have either been relaxed or completely removed as a result of the national policy for promoting foreign investment. See for instance Arts. 18, 19 of Statute for Investment by Foreign Nationals.

and the old Statute, which was, to a great extent, created to impress and appease the foreign powers then having consular jurisdiction in China.

Secondly, the framers of the new Law used several European legislations[13] as models, among which the Introductory Law to the German Civil Code of 1986 was a significant one. Most of the conflicts rules contained in this part of German law, which are so-called unilateral or one-sided rules, aim at the protection of German nationals and limit themselves to cases in which the application of German law is required.[14] It is beyond doubt that the new Chinese law has been much influenced by these German rules.

It must, nevertheless, be stressed that the strong nationalistic tendency shown in certain provisions of the new Law does not impair progressiveness. This is evidenced by the important principles adopted by the new legislation, which we shall presently deal with.

3.4 **Important Principles**

The following principles, adopted by the Law of 1953, are not only in conformity with the standards of civilized countries in those years, but are also advanced in certain aspects.

3.4.1 *Lex partiae*

Following the models of most civil law countries, the ROC legislation of 1953, like the old Statute of 1918, adopts the principle of nationality in determining an individual's personal law. The sphere of application of the law is quite broad. Thus, "[t]he disposing capacity of a person is determined by his national law" (Article 1, para.1); "The requisites for the conclusion of a marriage are determined respectively by the national law of each party" (Article 11, para.1); "The effects of marriage are determined by the national law of the husband" (Article 12, para.1); "A divorce may be obtained, if the fact is considered to be a ground for divorce both under the national law of the husband and the ROC law at the time when an action is instituted thereof" (Article 14); "The effects of divorce are determined by the national law of the husband" (Article 15, para.1); "The legitimacy of a child is determined by the national law of the husband of its mother at the time of the birth of the child. If the marital relationship has already ceased to exist before the birth of the child, the national law of the husband of its mother at the time when the marital relationship becomes non-existent shall apply" (Article 16); "The requisites for the rec-

---

[13] They were the laws of Germany, France and Italy. The Japanese Law of 1898 was another important model.

[14] Leo Raape, *Internationales Privatrecht*, 5. Neubearbeites Aufl., pp. 34-35 (1961); Rabel, (op. cit. n. 8) Vol. 1, p. 29.

ognition of a child born out of wedlock are determined respectively by the national law of the person who makes the recognition and the one who is being recognized at the time when such recognition is made. The effects of recognition are determined by the national law of the person who makes the recognition" (Article 17, para. 1-2); "The establishment and termination of adoption are determined respectively by the national law of the adopter and the adopted person. The effects of adoption are determined by the national law of the adopter" (Article 18); "The legal relations between parents and child are determined by the national law of the father" (Article 19); "The establishment of a guardianship is determined by the national law of the ward" (Article 10); "The obligation of support is determined by the national law of the person who is obliged to furnish support" (Article 21); "Succession is determined by the national law of the deceased at the time of his death" (Article 22); "The requisites for the establishment and the effects of a will are determined by the national law of the testator at the time of establishing the will. The revocation of a will is determined by the national law of the testator at the time of revoking the will" (Article 24, para. 1-2).

A full-fledged adoption of the nationality principle as a test for personal law makes it necessary to establish certain supplementary rules. On the one hand, the nationality principle causes difficulties in its application to persons who have more than one nationality. On the other hand, it cannot be applied at all to persons who are not nationals of any country.[15]

The 1953 Law provides in detail for both types of cases. According to Article 26, "[w]hen the national law of the party concerned shall be applied under this law and the party concerned has two or more nationalities acquired at different times, the national law of the party concerned shall be determined by the nationality last acquired by him; if the nationalities were acquired simultaneously, the law of the country which is closest in relationship with the party concerned shall apply; provided that if the party concerned is to be considered as a national of the Republic of China, the law of the Republic of China shall apply". Article 27 provides: "When the national law of the party concerned shall be applied under this Law and the party concerned is stateless, the law of his domicile shall apply. When his domicile is unknown, the law of the place of his residence shall apply. If the party concerned has two or more domiciles, the Law of that domicile which is closest in relationship shall apply. If he has a domicile within the Republic of China, the law of the Republic of China shall apply. The provision in the preceding paragraph shall apply *mutatis mutandis* if the party concerned has two or more residences. If his residence is unknown, the law of the place of his actual presence shall apply."

Furthermore, in cases where the law of the country to which the party concerned belongs is split into territorially different systems, nationality alone is insufficient

---

[15] Rabel (op. cit. n. 8), at p. 131.

for ascertaining the applicable law. A secondary rule becomes necessary.[16] In this context, the 1953 Law provides that "the law of the domicile within the person's national country shall apply. If the person's domicile within his national country is unknown, the law of the capital of his national country shall apply." (Article 28)

3.4.2 *Lex rei sitae*

In conformity with a general principle, Article 10 of the 1953 Law provides that rights over things are governed by *lex rei sitae* or the law of the place where the things are situated. This law applies to movables as well as immovables. It governs the creation, modification or termination of rights over them, but also the formalities of transactions creating, modifying or terminating such rights. However, real rights in a vessel or in an aircraft are governed by the law of the country to which the vessel or the aircraft belongs. The law is the law of the flag in the case of a vessel, and the law of the place of registration in the case of an aircraft (Article 10, para. 4). Article 10 further provides that with respect to rights over things, the object of which is another right, e.g., mining or fishing right, the law of the place where such another right is created shall apply. This is so because such a right, unlike ordinary real rights the object of which is a thing, does not have a clear *lex situs*. It is necessary to determine the applicable law by certain standards.[17] The 1953 Law deems the place where the right is created as closest in relationship with the right. Whether a right may be the object of the real right is therefore best determined by the law of such a place. Should there be any change in the law of the place where a thing is situated, the acquisition and loss of the right over such a thing shall be governed by the *lex rei sitae* at the time when the fact giving cause for such acquisition and loss is complete (para. 3). This applies in particular to ownership based on acquisitive prescription (usurpation), or where the loss of a real right is founded on acquiescence during a long period. In such cases, the decisive law is the law of the *situs* under which the set of facts still incomplete at a former *situs* has been brought to a close.

3.4.3 *Locus regit actum*

The significance of the maxim *locus regit actum* had long been reduced to the problem of form.[18] In other words, whatever law may govern a juridical act, the law of the place where it is made determines whether any formalities are obliging, and if so, which are required. This is the principle followed by the old Statute of 1918. However, the majority of modern enactments adopt the principle only as an op-

---

[16] Ibid., at p. 136.
[17] Explanations.
[18] Friedrich Carl von Savigny, *Systeme des heutigen Römischen Rechts* (Berlin 1849) Vol. 8, § 382, pp. 359 et seq.

tional rule, and the ROC Law of 1953 is no exception. Using German law as a model[19], its Article 5 provides that the form of a legal transaction is determined by the law applicable to such an act. But the same article also allows the form to be governed by the law of the place where the legal transaction is done (para. 1). In other words, the *lex causae* is considered as governing primarily. But, if its formal requirements are not fulfilled, validity is saved by compliance with the local law. As to the form of a legal transaction disposing rights over things, it is still the *lex rei sitae* that governs (Article 5, para. 2).

However, *locus regit actum* has been accorded exclusive compulsory force with respect to the form of a legal transaction exercising or preserving the rights over bills and notes (Article 5, para. 3). This is in agreement with a generally accepted principle that the form of an act contained in a bill or note is subject to the *lex loci actus*, that is the law of the place where this act is done.[20]

3.4.4 *Party autonomy*

Article 6 of the 1953 Law provides that, "[i]n the case of a legal transaction creating an obligation, the law applicable to the requisites for establishing such an act and the effect of the act is determined by the intention of the parties to the act." (para. 1). This provision applies to unilateral legal transactions (*einseitige Rechtsgeschäfte*) such as wills and gifts, as well as bilateral legal transactions (*zweiseitige Rechsgeschäfte*) such as contracts.[21] However, since unilateral transactions are less common, it may be said that the significance of Article 6 is in emphasizing that the law applicable to contracts is determined by the intention of the parties, thus reflecting the principle of party autonomy. As far as the wording of the above provision is concerned, where the intention of the parties is known, party autonomy is recognized without reservation. Legislative policy also seems to support this interpretation.[22] When, however, the intention of the parties is unknown, elaborate rules are provided for the determination of the applicable law. First of all, in cases when both parties are of the same nationality their common national law shall apply. If they are of different nationalities, the *lex loci actus* shall apply. If the act was done at different places, that place whence the notice of offer was issued shall be deemed as the place of the act. If the other party did not know the place whence the notice of offer was issued at the time when the offer was accepted, the place of the offer's domicile shall be deemed as the place of the act. If the place of the act mentioned above spans over two or more countries, or if it does not belong to any country, the *lex loci solutionis* shall apply.

[19] Art. 11 of the old Introductory Law to the German Civil Code.
[20] Rabel (op. cit. n. 8) Vol. 4, p. 158.
[21] Explanations.

Now, although there have been many international contract cases coming before the courts since the enforcement of the new Law, it remains to be seen how well Chinese judges can apply these rules to cases where the parties' intention is not known, in order to do justice to the individual contract. By way of suggestion, the present writer has elsewhere[23] pointed out that in most legal systems recognizing party autonomy, "intention" covers both express and tacit intention.[24] Therefore, when express intention is lacking, tacit intention of the parties should first be ascertained, before regarding such intention as unknown. In finding out the tacit intention, all objective facts of the individual contract should be taken into consideration to see if any of these facts point to a country with which the contract has the most real connection, or, if most of the facts all point to one locality. If and when these objective facts fail to reveal such a place, then the fixed standards in the law become imperative. It is submitted that such an approach will not only do justice to the individual contract, but will also best effect the legislative policy which is based on an unconditional recognition of party autonomy.

3.4.5 *Principles governing other "obligatory relations"*

Among other sources of obligation recognized by the ROC civil law,[25] the 1953 conflict rules provide for torts, *negotiorum gestio* and unjust enrichment. The principle generally adopted for torts is that the *lex loci delicti commissi* governs.[26] This is accepted by the ROC rules (Article 9, para. 1). However, Wächter and Savigny advanced the opinion that tort rules of the various municipal laws were of such an ethical and imperative nature that no country would ever apply the tort rule of another country, especially when it does not consider the act unlawful. Hence, tort problems should always be governed by the law of the forum. This thesis, formed in close relationship with ideas current in penal law, has influenced the law and courts of many countries.[27] As a result, the ROC rules limit the tort liability arising under the law of the place of wrong to the standard of the *lex fori* (Article 9, para. 1, and proviso). Article 9 further provides that "claims for compensation or for taking other measures arising from a wrongful act, shall be limited to those acceptable by

---

[22] Ibid.

[23] Ma Han-Pao, "General Principles of Conflict of Laws", 12th edn. (Taipei 1997) Ch. 8, pp. 140-148.

[24] Hessel E. Yntema, "'Autonomy' in Choice of Law", 1 *American Journal of Comparative Law* (1952) 341, at p. 345 n. 14.

[25] The Book of Obligations of the Civil Law lists as sources of obligations: contract, conferring of mandate, *negotiorum gestio* (management without a mandate), unjust enrichment and torts (Ch. 1, sec. 1).

[26] Rabel (op. cit. n. 8) Vol. 2, p. 235.

[27] Ibid., at p. 237.

the law of the Republic of China" (Article 9, para. 2). This means that local law is applied when determining the existence of liability as well as the measure of damages. But, unlike German law,[28] the ROC rules – that a claim for tort must be actionable under the law of the forum – result in the protection of every defendant, rather than nationals of ROC alone.

An obligation arising from *negotiorum gestio*, unjust enrichment or any other legal fact is governed according to Article 8 of the 1953 law, by the law of the place where the act occurred. To illustrate this point, if a person voluntarily does work or spends money for the preservation of another person's property, his right to recover his expenses is determined according to the law of the country where the gestor acted.

3.4.6 *Renvoi*

The controversy on *renvoi* is one of the most famous disputes in conflicts law. At present, although *renvoi* is prescribed by statutory provisions in many countries and practiced by the courts of many other countries, the codes of a few other countries have rejected it.[29] And even those countries which adopt or practice *renvoi*, vary greatly in the form and extent of doing so.

In this matter, the ROC Law of 1953 is unique. It adopts the *renvoi* doctrine in its widest possible form, i.e., remission, transmission and a third form which either allows *renvoi* to be extended beyond transmission to a third foreign law, or allows a reference back to ROC law from the second foreign law. Such provisions are a step forward as compared with the old Statute, which recognized only remission. While the practical value of these provisions remains to be tested, they should provide an additional pillar in support of the doctrine.

3.4.7 *Ordre public*

In certain cases, foreign law normally applicable is excluded for special reasons. Such exceptional non-application occurs particularly when the application would lead to a result inconsistent with some fundamental principle of the law of the forum. The conceptions employed for achieving this purpose vary from country to country. In general, the conception of *ordre public* is representative of European countries and "public policy" is the term for Common Law countries.[30]

---

[28] Art. 12 of the Introductory Law to the German Civil Code, first replaced by Art. 38 of the new rules of private international law of 1986, and recently amended in 1999 (German Federal OJ I p. 1026).

[29] E.g., Art. 32 of the Civil Code of Greece, Art. 31 of the Civil Code of Iraq. The Benelux Convention rejects renvoi in practice under its Art. 1. On the other hand, Italy has accepted *renvoi* under Art. 13 of its 1995 PIL Reform.

[30] Martin Wolff, *Privat International Law*, 2nd edn. (Oxford 1950) p. 176, n. 4.

The ROC conflicts rules provide that a foreign law is to be excluded, if its provisions are in contravention to the *ordre public* or *boni mores* of the Republic of China. Like the statutory provisions of most other countries, the ROC rules are simple and vague. The legislator defined *ordre public* as "the concrete expression of the spirit on which the nation was founded and the basic 'national policies' and *boni mores*, . . . the ethical conceptions of the people".[31] Being too broad to be properly grasped these definitions are of little help, and much depends on their wise application by the judges in particular cases.

When a foreign law is excluded, its place is, as a rule, filled by the *lex fori*.[32] While the ROC law makes no provision to that effect, it is generally so understood. Furthermore, this substitution should be restricted as far as possible. If the foreign law normally applicable contains a provision A which is unobjectionable, but which is subject to an exception B, and if B is contrary to ROC *ordre public* or *boni mores*, the exclusion of B does not entail the application of ROC law, but that of the foreign provision A.[33]

4.   CONCLUSION

The current Republic of China conflicts rules of 1953, entitled the "Law Governing the Application of Laws to Civil Matters Involving Foreign Elements", are primarily based on the old Statute of 1918. However, they differ from the latter in both form and substance to no small extent. As far as the contents are concerned, first of all, it takes on a strong tincture of nationalism. In many matters of personal law, where a national of the Republic of China is involved, ROC law invariably applies. Such a turn of affairs may be ascribed to the fact that the 1953 Law was the first such enactment after China recovered her judicial sovereignty lost for almost a century. An extension of the application of ROC law to ROC nationals is easily understandable. Secondly, many provisions in the old Statute have been either enlarged or modified, notably those concerning *renvoi* and form of legal transactions. Thirdly, great care has been given to rules for the filling of gaps. Aside from certain specific provisions such as Arts. 7, 23,[34] an independent rule was added, which serves to cover whatever may still be left out. Article 30 reads as follows: "In civil matters involving foreign elements, if no provision in this law is applicable, the provisions in other laws shall

---

[31] Explanations.
[32] Wolff (op. cit. n. 30) p. 183.
[33] Explanations.
[34] Art. 7 provides "With respect to effect of a transfer of an obligatory right upon a third party, the law applicable to the creation and effect of the original obligatory right shall apply". Art. 23 provides "In the case of death of an alien who left property within the Republic of China and the property under his national law is to be inherited by nobody, it shall be dealt with according to Chinese law."

apply. If other laws have no such provision, the general principles of law shall be followed."

Therefore, the ROC conflicts rules of 1953 are, generally speaking, more elaborate and detailed than the 1918 Statute. The principles and doctrines adopted therein are partly based on general acceptance, partly advanced by modern theoreticians. Set against its historical background, an emphasis on the internal public and private interests with its ensuing expansion of *lex fori* is understandable. However, it is not easy to evaluate conflicts rules just on reading them. They have to be tried in the fire of litigation. As far as the Republic of China is concerned, the question remains as it always has been, that conflicts cases are comparatively few or of such a nature as to provide few opportunities for the application of the more elaborate rules. As a result, the practical value of the Law of 1953 has yet by and large to be proven. Furthermore, recent developments in this branch of law in many countries have also provided strong reasons for the revision of the 1953 conflicts rules. In fact, the Judicial Yuan, the highest judicial organ of the Republic of China, has recently formed a special committee for revising the 1953 conflicts rules.[35] The Committee is still in its initial stage of collecting materials and deliberating guidelines. At present, it can be said that the revision will affect most of the current rules and the number of articles will be largely increased. The principle of equality of the sexes, the doctrine of "the most significant relationship" and the concept of "habitual residence" as adopted by European legislations[36] are some of the issues that will receive special attention.

Finally, it may be mentioned that a new legislation was promulgated by the Republic of China on Taiwan in September 1992, dealing partly with civil matters between the peoples on Taiwan and Mainland China.[37] Though it is based on principles of conflict of laws, its usefulness remains to be seen.

---

[35] Committee on Revision of Law Governing the Application of Laws to Civil Matters involving Foreign Elements was formed by the Judicial Yuan in October 1998, of which Grand Justice Liu Te-cheng of Judicial Yuan and the present writer were made co-chairmen.

[36] See in particular, the new Swiss legislation of 1987.

[37] Statute Governing Relations between Peoples in the Taiwan Area and The Mainland Area.

Der Regreßanspruch des Letztverkäufers nach der Richtlinie über den Verbrauchsgüterkauf

Ulrich Magnus[*]

1. EINFÜHRUNG

Die „Richtlinie 1999/44/EG zu bestimmten Aspekten des Verbrauchsgüterkaufs und der Garantien für Verbrauchsgüter"[1] – am 7. Juli 1999 in Kraft getreten und bis zum 1.1.2002 von den Mitgliedstaaten umzusetzen – beschäftigt sich in erster Linie mit den Rechten, die Verbraucher als Käufer gegenüber professionellen Verkäufern bei der Lieferung mangelhafter Verbrauchsgüter haben. Dabei regelt die Richtlinie nur jene Verbraucherrechte, die den Minderwert der gelieferten Ware, ihren eigentlichen Mangelunwert und damit das Äquivalenzinteresse des Verbrauchers ausgleichen sollen. In der Harmonisierung dieser Rechtsbehelfe für eine Kernmate-

---

[*] Dr.iur., Professor an der Universität Hamburg, Richter am Hanseatischen Oberlandesgricht Hamburg.
[1] *ABl(EG)* L [1999] 171/12 (7.7.1999) = *NJW* (1999) 2421ff.

J. Basedow et al., eds., Private Law in the International Arena – Liber Amicorum Kurt Siehr
© 2000, T.M.C.Asser Press, The Hague, The Netherlands

rie des Zivilrechts liegt der für das europäische Privatrecht bedeutsame Effekt der Richtlinie.[2] Dagegen steht der Ausgleich für Schäden, die mangelhafte Waren an anderen Gütern kaufender Verbraucher anrichten, außerhalb der Neuregelung.[3]

Allerdings greift die Richtlinie über das Verhältnis Endkäufer – Endverkäufer in einem Punkt doch hinaus. Ausdrücklich räumt Art. 4 RL[4] dem Letztverkäufer ein Regreßrecht gegen seine Vormänner in der Veräußerungskette – u.U. bis zurück zum Hersteller – ein. Damit nimmt die Richtlinie auch die – regelmäßig professionelle, handelsrechtliche – Vertragsbeziehung zwischen dem Letztverkäufer und seinem Lieferanten und darüber hinaus die gesamte Absatzkette in den Blick. Viel, nämlich die Bestimmung des Haftenden, das „entsprechende Vorgehen und die Modalitäten" will sie insoweit allerdings wieder dem innerstaatlichen Recht überlassen (Art. 4 S. 2 RL).

Der genaue Regelungsgehalt des Art. 4 RL ist wenig klar.[5] In den bisherigen Erörterungen zur Richtlinie und ihren Vorentwürfen hat die Vorschrift meist nur am Rande Beachtung gefunden.[6] Da mit der Regreßmöglichkeit das wichtige „Scharnier" zwischen Verbraucherkauf und Handelskauf angesprochen wird, verdient die Vorschrift aber durchaus Aufmerksamkeit.[7] Im folgenden soll der genaue Gehalt des Art. 4 RL deshalb näher untersucht werden.

Gewidmet sind diese Zeilen dem europäischen Gelehrten und guten Freund KURT SIEHR, der sich mit dem Kaufrecht sowohl unter internationalrechtlichen[8] als

---

[2] Vgl. insbesondere Reich, *NJW* (1999) 2397, 2398.

[3] Vgl. Begründung zum RL-Vorschlag von 1996 KOM (95) 520 endg., S. 7: „von dem Vorschlag keineswegs berührt wird also die Frage der Haftung für etwaige direkte oder indirekte durch das fehlerhafte Produkt entstandene Schäden."

[4] Der Text lautet: Art. 4. Rückgriffsrechte. Haftet der Letztverkäufer dem Verbraucher aufgrund einer Vertragswidrigkeit infolge eines Handelns oder Unterlassens des Herstellers, eines früheren Verkäufers innerhalb derselben Vertragskette oder einer anderen Zwischenperson, so kann der Letztverkäufer den oder die Haftenden innerhalb der Vertragskette in Regreß nehmen. Das innerstaatliche Recht bestimmt den oder die Haftenden, den oder die der Letztverkäufer in Regreß nehmen kann, sowie das entsprechende Vorgehen und die Modalitäten.

[5] Ebenso Medicus, *ZIP* (1996) 1925, 1928; auch Kircher, *ZRP* (1997) 290, 294: „schafft also mehr Widersprüche als er beseitigt"; Micklitz, *EuZW* (1997) 229, 233, kritisiert die „dogmatische Enge des Regelungsansatzes".

[6] Nur knappe oder keine Hinweise etwa bei Antenbrink/Schneider *VuR* (1996) 367, 370; Hondius, *ZeuP* (1997) 130, 136; Junker, *DZWir* (1997) 271; Micklitz, *EuZW* (1997) 229, 233; Schlechtriem, *JZ* (1997) 441; Staudenmayer, *NJW* (1999) 2393, 2396. Etwas ausführlicher aber Ehmann/Rust, *JZ* (1999) 853, 862f.; Kircher, *ZRP* (1997) 290, 294; Medicus, *ZIP* (1996) 1925, 1928f.; Reich, *NJW* (1999) 2397, 2399; Schmidt-Ränsch, *ZIP* (1998) 849, 850; ders., *ZeuP* (1999) 294, 298f.

[7] Staudenmayer, *NJW* (1999) 2396 sieht Art. 4 RL zwar als „eher harmlos" an, weist aber zu Recht darauf hin, daß die Vorschrift „in der Umsetzung große Bedeutung für das Handelsrecht entwickeln" kann.

[8] Siehr, „Der internationale Anwendungsbereich des UN-Kaufrechts", *RabelsZ* 52 (1988) 587ff.; Siehr, in: Honsell (Hrsg.), *Kommentar zum UN-Kaufrecht* (1996) Art. 1-6, 89-101 und VertragsG

auch materiellrechtlichen Aspekten[9] eingehend beschäftigt und zur Lösung seiner Probleme beigetragen hat.

2.   ZWECK DES ART. 4 RL

2.1   Schutz des Letztverkäufers vor ungerechtfertigten Lasten

Der Zweck des Art. 4 RL ist recht klar: Die Vorschrift will erreichen, daß der Letztverkäufer, der dem Endkäufer wegen der Mängel der Ware haftet, nicht auf dieser Haftung sitzen bleiben soll, wenn den Warenmangel andere Glieder der Veräußerungskette zu verantworten haben. Die Begründung zum Richtlinienvorschlag von 1996 hatte deshalb ausgeführt:

„In der Regel sind die einzelstaatlichen Rechtsvorschriften, die auf Kaufgeschäfte zwischen Gewerbetreibende anwendbar sind, weniger streng als die Bestimmungen für Kaufabschlüsse zwischen einem Gewerbetreibenden und einem Verbraucher. So nehmen Verkäufer beispielsweise häufig in ihre Verträge Haftungsausschlußklauseln hinsichtlich der gesetzlichen Garantie auf. Solche Klauseln sind übrigens im gemeinschaftsrechtlichen Sinne zulässig, da die Richtlinie 93/13/EWG über mißbräuchliche Vertragsklauseln lediglich für ‚Verträge zwischen Gewerbetreibenden und Verbrauchern‘ gilt.

Dies kann allerdings dazu führen, daß der Letztverkäufer unberechtigterweise die gesamte Verantwortung für Sachmängel übernehmen muß, die letzten Endes auf eine Handlung oder Unterlassung eines Dritten zurückzuführen sind. Dies trifft beispielsweise zu bei Herstellungsmängeln, bei Mängeln, die auf unsachgemäßen Gebrauch durch eine vorausgegangene Zwischenperson zurückzuführen sind oder sogar bei Konformitätsmängeln aufgrund der in Artikel 2 Absatz 2 Buchstabe d) aufgeführten Aussagen.

Obgleich es in dem Richtlinienvorschlag um den Letztverkauf von Verbrauchsgütern geht, erweist es sich als erforderlich, darin einen Rückgriffsanspruch des Letztverkäufers gegen die haftbaren Personen vorzusehen, auf die er die durch die Mängel, die diesen zuzuschreiben sind, verursachten Kosten abwälzen können muß. Die Modalitäten für die Inanspruchnahme des Rückgriffsanspruchs werden durch innerstaatliches Recht geregelt."[10]

Im geltenden Richtlinientext gibt Erwägungsgrund 9 diese Intention des Richtliniengebers ebenfalls – freilich etwas abgeschwächt – wieder:

---

[9] Keller/Siehr, *Kaufrecht*, 3. Aufl. (Zürich 1995).
[10] Vgl. KOM (95) 520 endg. v. 18.6.1996 S. 15.

„(9) Der Verkäufer muß dem Verbraucher gegenüber unmittelbar für die Vertragsmäßigkeit der Güter haften. Dieser klassische Grundsatz ist in den Rechtsvorschriften der Mitgliedstaaten verankert. Der Verkäufer muß allerdings nach Maßgabe des innerstaatlichen
Rechts den Hersteller, einen früheren Verkäufer innerhalb derselben Vertragskette oder
eine andere Zwischenperson in Regreß nehmen können, es sei denn, daß er auf dieses
Recht verzichtet hat. Diese Richtlinie berührt nicht den Grundsatz der Vertragsfreiheit in
den Beziehungen zwischen dem Verkäufer, dem Hersteller, einem früheren Verkäufer
oder einer anderen Zwischenperson. die einzelstaatlichen Rechtsvorschriften bestimmen, gegen wen und wie der Verkäufer Regreß nehmen kann."

Der Richtliniengeber hält damit den Letztverkäufer in gewissem Umfang für ebenso schutzbedürftig wie einen Endverbraucher. In früheren Entwicklungsstadien der
Richtlinie ist die Regelung denn auch zusätzlich mit positiven Auswirkungen für
ganz kleine sowie für kleine und mittlere Unternehmen (KMU) begründet worden.[11]Hondius hat deshalb in diesem Zusammenhang nicht zu Unrecht von einer
„Art, unterdrückte Mittelständler'-Forderung" gesprochen.[12]

2.2   Schutz nur des Letztverkäufers?

Allzu überzeugend ist dieses Argument des Mittelstandsschutzes allerdings nicht;
denn vielfach treten nicht kleine oder mittlere Unternehmen, sondern Großunter-
nehmen, etwa Absatzketten als Letztverkäufer auf. Daß sie gegenüber ihren Vor-
männern in der Stufenfolge von Warenherstellung und -absatz besonders schutzbedürftig seien, wird sich kaum sagen lassen. Problematisch ist weiter auch, daß die
Richtlinie nur dem Letztverkäufer ein Regreßrecht zubilligt.[13] Denn damit ver-
schiebt sie ggfs. die Belastung mit der gesamten Haftung nur auf die vorgelagerte
Absatzstufe. Dort ist diese Haftung indessen ebenso unberechtigt wie auf der letzten Absatzstufe angesiedelt, wenn in der Absatzkette vorangehende Personen für
den Warenmangel verantwortlich sind. Unterschiedliche Regreßrechte für die einzelnen Absatzglieder schreibt die Richtlinie andererseits nicht ausdrücklich vor.
Bei der Umsetzung wird deshalb nicht nur dem Letztverkäufer, sondern auch vorangehenden Zwischenverkäufern ein gleiches Rückgriffsrecht einzuräumen sein.
    Allerdings nimmt die Richtlinie den Schutz des Zwischenhandels nicht so ernst,
daß sie das Rückgriffsrecht für unabdingbar erklärt. Erwägungsgrund 9 der Richtlinie stellt vielmehr unzweideutig klar, daß das Regreßrecht des Letztverkäufers
nicht zwingend ist. Denn den Grundsatz der Vertragsfreiheit und damit die Möglichkeit, das Regreßrecht vertraglich auszuschließen, schränkt die Richtlinie in keiner Weise ein.[14] Ein Gebot, jeden oder jedenfalls den AGB-mäßigen Ausschluß des

---

[11] Vgl. Begründung zum Richtlinien-Vorschlag von 1996, KOM (95) 520 endg., S. 26 und 29.
[12] Hondius, *ZeuP* (1997) 136.
[13] Kritisch deshalb auch Ehmann/Rust, *JZ* (1999) 862.

Regreßrechts zwischen Kaufleuten für unzulässig zu erklären,[15] läßt sich aus der Richtlinie daher nicht ableiten.

2.3 Verhältnis zu bestehenden Kaufrechtsbehelfen

Wenn zwar auch die Stoßrichtung des Regreßrechts klar ist, so ist doch sein Verhältnis zu den vorhandenen Kaufrechtsbehelfen bei Lieferung schlechter Ware wenig deutlich. Dem Richtliniengeber war natürlich bekannt, daß die europäischen Kaufrechte auch einem professionellen Käufer, dem mangelhafte Ware geliefert wird, durchaus Gewährleistungsansprüche gegen seinen professionellen Verkäufer einräumen. Die ädilizischen, verschuldensunabhängigen Rechtsbehelfe der Wandlung und Minderung gelten überall auf dem europäischen Festland; Schadenersatz und Vertragsaufhebung sind im Common Law vorgesehen und setzen ebenfalls kein Verschulden voraus.[16] Das einheitliche UN-Kaufrecht, das in zwölf der fünfzehn EU-Staaten gilt, sieht alle diese Behelfe vor und gewährt Nacherfüllung, Minderung und Schadensersatz und – eingeschränkt – Vertragsaufhebung.[17] Liefert ein Zwischenhändler mangelhafte Ware, dann haftet er dem Letztverkäufer dafür also in aller Regel; er muß den Warenmangel nicht einmal verursacht haben. Der Verkauf schlechter Ware ist hinreichender Grund für seine Garantiehaftung.

2.4 Ausgleich für Haftungsinkongruenz

Welchen Zweck kann dann ein zusätzlicher Regreßanspruch des Letztverkäufers haben? Daß der Regreßanspruch zusätzlich wirken und die bereits bestehenden Kaufrechtsbehelfe nicht verdrängen soll, erscheint selbstverständlich. Denn es ist weder ersichtlich noch zu unterstellen, daß die Richtlinie, die dem Verbraucherschutz verschrieben ist, solche Kaufgewährleistungsansprüche zwischen Kaufleuten beschneiden will, die nach nationalem Kaufrecht oder nach dem CISG derzeit bestehen. Der Regreßanspruch des Art. 4 RL soll vielmehr ersichtlich zu diesen bestehenden Behelfen hinzutreten. Die Regreßregelung der Richtlinie macht damit nur dann Sinn, wenn sich eine Inkongruenz zwischen der Haftung des Letztverkäufers gegenüber seinen Käufern, wie sie die Richtlinie jetzt vorschreibt, und den möglichen Ansprüchen ergibt, die der Letztverkäufer gegen Vormänner nach der-

---

[14] Vgl. Erwägungsgrund 9: „Diese Richtlinie berührt nicht den Grundsatz der Vertragsfreiheit in den Beziehungen zwischen dem Verkäufer, dem Hersteller, einem früheren Verkäufer oder einer anderen Zwischenperson."

[15] So aber – rechtspolitisch motiviert – Ehmann/Rust, *JZ* (1999) 863.

[16] Vgl. insbes. Basedow, *Die Reform des deutschen Kaufrechts* (Köln 1988), von Westphalen (Hrsg.), *Handbuch des Kaufvertragsrechts in den EG-Staaten einschließlich Österreich, Schweiz und UN-Kaufrecht* (Köln 1992).

[17] Vgl. Art. 46ff. CISG.

zeitigem nationalen Recht oder CISG geltend machen kann. In dem Ausgleich einer
solchen möglichen Haftungsinkongruenz liegt daher der eigentliche Sinn des Regreßrechts.

2.5   Mögliche Haftungsinkongruenzen

Eine Inkongruenz zwischen der Haftung des Letztverkäufers für schlechte Ware
und seinen eigenen Anspruchsmöglichkeiten gegenüber Vorleuten kann in mehrfacher Hinsicht auftreten:

–   Sie kann zum einen daraus folgen, daß die Vorleute des Letztverkäufers dessen
    mögliche Gewährleistungsansprüche wirksam abbedingen. Diese Abdingbarkeit
    will die Richtlinie allerdings gerade nicht einschränken, wie Erwägungsgrund 9 der
    Richtlinie deutlich hervorhebt.[18] Eine hieraus folgende Haftungsinkongruenz wird
    daher hingenommen. Auf sie bezieht sich der Regreßanspruch der Richtlinie des-
    halb nicht.

–   Eine Haftungsinkongruenz kann ferner daraus folgen, daß die Verjährungs-
    fristen für Verbraucheransprüche länger sind als jene für die Mangelgewährlei-
    stungsansprüche des Letztverkäufers. Der Letztverkäufer muß dann seinen Abneh-
    mern länger haften, als er seinerseits seine Lieferanten in Anspruch nehmen kann.
    Die Richtlinie schafft oder verstärkt diese Haftungsinkongruenz überall dort deut-
    lich, wo bisher kürzere kaufrechtliche Verjährungsfristen gelten als die Zweijahres-
    frist des Art. 5 (1) RL, wie etwa im deutschen, griechischen, italienischen oder ös-
    terreichischen Recht.[19] Ob die Richtlinie auch diese Inkongruenz ausgleichen will,
    ist zweifelhaft.[20] Problematisch ist die Antwort deshalb, weil einige europäische
    Rechte – wie das deutsche und österreichische (§§ 377, 378) HGB, der italienische
    Codice civile (Art. 1495, 1511), insbesondere aber auch das UN-Kaufrecht[21] – für
    Sachmängelansprüche des professionellen Käufers eine rasche Mängelrüge for-
    dern, deren Versäumung Gewährleistungsansprüche gänzlich oder überwiegend
    entfallen läßt. Bei Fehlern, die bei ordnungsgemäßer Untersuchung erkennbar wa-
    ren und nicht gerügt wurden, verliert der professionelle Käufer schon nach kurzer
    Zeit und nicht erst nach Ablauf der Verjährungsfrist seine Ansprüche, muß aber
    selbst noch bis zu deren Ende haften. Dem Institut der kaufmännischen Mängelrüge
    ist also eine bestimmte Haftungsinkongruenz immanent.

    Bezweckt Art. 4 RL das zu ändern? Soll dem Letztverkäufer nach der Richtlinie
auch dann ein Regreßanspruch zustehen, wenn er die ordnungsgemäße Mängelrüge
versäumt hat? M.E. ist diese Frage zu verneinen. Es ist nicht erkennbar noch zu unterstellen, daß die Richtlinie einen so weitreichenden Eingriff in nationale Handels-

---

[18] Vgl. oben N. 15.
[19] Vgl. sechs Monate: § 477 BGB, § 933 Abs. 1 ABGB; ein Jahr: Art. 1495 Abs. 3 Codice civile.
[20] Wohl dafür Reich, *NJW* (1999) 2402f.
[21] Vgl. Art. 38, 39 CISG.

rechte und auch in das CISG vornehmen und die kaufmännische Mängelrüge praktisch beseitigen wollte. Ein solches Ergebnis würde aber erreicht, wenn der Letztverkäufer trotz versäumter Mängelrüge Regreß nehmen könnte. Die Regelung des CISG (Art. 38, 39) zu diesem Punkt würde gänzlich ausgehebelt und die insoweit erreichte Rechtsvereinheitlichung für Europa wieder aufgelöst. Die Mangelrüge hat für den professionellen Kauf auch ihren guten Sinn. In richtigen Maßen gehandhabt, führt sie zu rascher und praktischer Klärung über die Rechtsfolgen eines Liefergeschäfts. Aus diesem Grund hat das Einheitskaufrecht sie übernommen. Auch die Richtlinie selbst erlaubt es den Mitgliedstaaten, für Verbraucherkäufe eine Rügeobliegenheit einzuführen (Art. 5 Abs. 2 RL). Es wäre widersprüchlich und unverständlich, wenn die Richtlinie eine Rügeobliegenheit für den Verbraucherkauf zuließe, sie aber für Handelskäufe beseitigen wollte. Damit bleibt es aber zwangsläufig bei einer Haftungsinkongruenz, soweit erkennbare Sachmängel der Ware betroffen sind. Art. 4 RL intendiert nicht, diese Inkongruenz auszugleichen.

Anders dürfte die Intention der Vorschrift aber für Fälle verborgener Fehler zu beurteilen sein. In diesen Fällen führt eine versäumte Untersuchung noch nicht zum Verlust der Gewährleistungsrechte. Vielmehr können Fehler – rasch nach Entdeckung – innerhalb der gesamten Verjährungsfrist gerügt werden. Unterschiedliche Verjährungsfristen für Verbraucher- und Handelskäufe belasten hier allein den Letztverkäufer, der seinem Abnehmer zwei Jahre lang haftet, aber jedenfalls nach deutschem Recht längstens sechs Monate eigene Ansprüche hat. Diese Haftungsinkongruenz will Art. 4 RL gerade beheben. Dieser Intention ist m.E. das Richtliniengebot zu entnehmen, daß die Verjährungsfristen für Handelskäufe jenen für Verbraucherkäufe gesetzlich anzupassen sind.[22] Auch rechtspolitisch ist eine Gewährleistungslücke, wie sie gegenwärtig bei Versäumung der Rüge bis zum Ablauf der sechsmonatigen Verjährungsfrist akzeptiert wird, nur bei erkennbaren Fehlern hinnehmbar. Denn dann kann eine ordnungsgemäße, rechtzeitige Untersuchung den Fehler aufdecken; der professionelle Käufer kann Ansprüche rechtzeitig geltend machen. Bei verborgenen Fehlern erscheint es dagegen untragbar, daß die Haftung des Letztverkäufers auf zwei Jahre ausgedehnt wird, seine eigenen Gewährleistungsrechte aber nach sechs Monaten verjähren. Eine generelle Anhebung der kaufrechtlichen Verjährungsfrist auf zwei Jahre entspricht auch der Zweijahresfrist des Art. 39 CISG, nach deren Ablauf Sachmängelbehelfe ausgeschlossen sind. Vielfach wird eine „Garantiezeit" von zwei Jahren auch heute schon – etwa für Neuwagenkäufe – freiwillig eingeräumt. Bedenkt man ferner, daß das UN-Übereinkommen über die Verjährung beim internationalen Warenkauf von 1974[23] eine unabdingbare vierjährige Verjährungsfrist vorsieht,[24] dann stellt sich eine generelle

---

[22] Ebenso Schmidt-Ränsch, *ZeuP* (1999) 298f.

[23] Text in: Staudinger (-Magnus), *Wiener UN-Kaufrecht (CISG)* (Bearbeitung 1999) Anh. II; die Bundesrepublik hat das Übk bisher nicht ratifiziert.

[24] Art. 8 i.V.m. Art. 22 des Verjährungs-Übk.

Frist von zwei Jahren für die Verjährung kaufrechtlicher Sachmängelansprüche als maßvoll dar.

– Als weitere Haftungsinkongruenz, die die Richtlinie auffangen will, bleibt ferner der Fall, daß der Begriff der Vertragsmäßigkeit der Richtlinie weiter reicht als der Sachmängelbegriff der jeweiligen nationalen oder der einheitsrechtlichen Regelung, die für den Handelskauf gilt. Die Definition der Vertragsmäßigkeit in Art. 2 RL entstammt freilich im wesentlichen dem CISG (Art. 35). Im Interesse möglichster Deckungsgleichheit sollten Art. 2 RL und Art. 35 CISG auch im gleichen Sinn verstanden und interpretiert werden. Vergleicht man beide Definitionen im einzelnen, dann scheint die Fehlerdefinition des CISG teilweise etwas weiter, teilweise weniger weit als jene der Richtlinie zu reichen. Denn nach Art. 35 Abs. 2 lit. b CISG muß die Ware sich für solche bestimmten Zwecke eignen, die der Käufer dem Verkäufer zur Kenntnis gebracht hat, soweit der Käufer auf eine überlegene Sachkunde des Verkäufers vertrauen durfte. Nach Art. 2 Abs. 2 lit. b RL muß der Verkäufer dagegen der Eignung für den bestimmten Zweck zugestimmt haben. Andererseits sieht Art. 2 Abs. 2 lit. d RL eine Verkäuferhaftung für die Qualität und Leistungen vor, „die bei Gütern der gleichen Art üblich sind und die der Verbraucher vernünftigerweise erwarten kann, wenn die Beschaffenheit des Gutes und gegebenenfalls die insbesondere in der Werbung oder bei der Etikettierung gemachten öffentlichen Äußerungen des Verkäufers, des Herstellers oder dessen Vertreters über die konkreten Eigenschaften des Gutes in Betracht gezogen werden". Eine gleiche Formulierung fehlt in Art. 35 CISG. Eine Haftung für öffentliche Werbeaussagen über „konkrete" Eigenschaften der Ware wird sich aus Art. 35 Abs. 2 CISG nur schwer ableiten lassen. Freilich darf auch Art. 2 Abs. 2 lit. d RL nicht mißverstanden werden. Er sieht keine generelle Haftung für öffentliche Werbeaussagen, sondern eine Haftung für öffentlich angegebene „konkrete" Eigenschaften der Ware vor. Beispiele hierfür sind etwa Angaben über den Kraftstoffverbrauch eines Kfz, über eine bestimmte software-Kompatibilität oder ähnliche Eigenschaftsangaben über die Ware.[25] Ein höherer als der öffentlich angepriesene Kraftstoffverbrauch wird aber auch unter dem CISG als Vertragswidrigkeit anzusehen sein.[26] Im Ergebnis dürfte und sollte daher regelmäßig Deckungsgleichheit zwischen dem Begriff der Vertragswidrigkeit nach Art. 2 RL und nach Art. 35 CISG bestehen.

Im wesentlichen besteht, wie Schmidt-Ränsch nachgewiesen hat, aber auch Deckungsgleichheit zwischen Art. 2 RL und dem Fehlerbegriff des deutschen unvereinheitlichten Rechts.[27] Zwischen den Sachmängelbegriff der Richtlinie und jenen des CISG, aber auch des deutschen BGB-Kaufrechts paßt deshalb wohl kaum das berühmte Blatt Papier. Allenfalls in seltenen Randfällen mag es zu Diskrepan-

---

[25] Ebenso Schmidt-Ränsch, *ZIP* (1998) 851.

[26] Jedenfalls der heimlich veränderte Kilometerstand und das falsch ausgepreiste Alter eines Kfz sind als Fehler i.S.d. Art. 35 CISG angesehen worden: OLG Köln 21.5.1996, CLOUT Nr. 168.

[27] Schmidt-Ränsch, *ZIP* (1998) 850f.

zen kommen. Ferner mag diese Diskrepanz in einigen anderen EU-Staaten etwas größer zu sein.

– Schließlich kann sich eine Haftungsinkongruenz aus einer für Verbraucher und Letztverkäufer unterschiedlichen Beweislastregelung ergeben. Wer die Vertragswidrigkeit und die Kausalität für Art. 4 RL zu beweisen hat, regelt die Richtlinie nicht. Insoweit gilt das im übrigen anwendbare Landesrecht, das ganz regelmäßig dem Anspruchssteller die Darlegungs- und Beweislast auferlegt. Beweiserleichterungen, wie sie Art. 2 Abs. 4 und insbesondere Art. 5 Abs. 3 RL dem Verbraucher gegenüber dem Letztverkäufer einräumen, sieht die Richtlinie im Verhältnis des Letztverkäufers zu möglichen Regreßschuldnern nicht vor. Damit wird häufiger die Situation entstehen, daß der Letztverkäufer dem Verbraucher haftet, seinerseits einen Regreßanspruch gegen den Vormann aber nicht nachweisen kann. Das Richtlinienziel läßt sich hier nur dadurch erreichen, daß die Beweislastregeln der Richtlinie auch für den Handelskauf eingeführt werden.

Zusammengenommen ergibt sich eine Haftungsinkongruenz, die der Regreßanspruch des Art. 4 RL beheben soll, bei verborgenen Fehlern und vielleicht in seltenen Randfällen, in denen der Begriff der Vertragswidrigkeit der Richtlinie und der herkömmliche Fehlerbegriff des BGB sich nicht vollständig decken. Für diese Fälle verpflichtet die Richtlinie, einen eigenen Anspruch des Letztverkäufers einzuräumen. Daß der Richtliniengeber die Schaffung eines solchen Anspruchs intendierte, folgt auch deutlich aus der Begründung zum Richtlinienentwurf von 1996, in der es zum Regreßrecht heißt: Daher „erweist es sich als erforderlich, darin einen Rückgriffsanspruch des Letztverkäufers gegen die haftbaren Personen vorzusehen . . . “[28]

Da Art. 4 S. 2 RL die Einzelheiten des Regreßanspruchs – Person des oder der Haftenden, Verfahren und Modalitäten – allerdings dem innerstaatlichen Recht überläßt, ergibt sich aus der Richtlinie nur das Gebot für die Mitgliedstaaten, „daß ein irgendwie gearteter Rückgriff des haftenden Letztverkäufers bestehen muß“.[29] Die Vorgaben der Richtlinie für die Ausgestaltung dieses zusätzlichen Rückgriffsrechts sind freilich gering und auch nicht ganz klar.[30] Ferner ist die Grenze zwischen der Begründung des Regreßanspruchs und seinen Modalitäten nicht gerade einfach zu ziehen.[31] Dennoch enthält Art. 4 RL gewisse Vorgaben, denen das Rückgriffsrecht jedenfalls genügen muß.

---

[28] KOM (95) 520 eng. v. 18.6.1996, S. 15. Darauf, daß ein Anspruch begründet werden sollte, hat schon Medicus *ZIP* (1996) 1928 hingewiesen.

[29] Staudenmayer, *NJW* (1999) 2396 (Staudenmayer war der für diese Richtlinie zuständige Kommissionsbeamte); ebenso Schmidt-Ränsch, *ZIP* (1998) 850: „Es wird lediglich bestimmt, daß es überhaupt einen Rückgriff geben muß.“

[30] Ebenso Staudenmayer, Schmidt-Ränsch jeweils aaO.

[31] So mit Recht bereits Medicus, *ZIP* (1996) 1928.

3. Vorgaben

3.1 Haftung des Letztverkäufers aufgrund einer Vertragswidrigkeit

Zunächst setzt das Regreßrecht voraus, daß der Letztverkäufer seinem Endabnehmer, dem Verbraucher, aufgrund einer Vertragswidrigkeit haftet. Auch wenn diese Haftungsvoraussetzung mehr oder minder als selbstverständlich erscheint, wirft sie die Frage auf, ob mit „Haftung" eine abstrakt bestehende Verantwortlichkeit des Letztverkäufers für Vertragswidrigkeiten gemeint ist oder ob der Regreßanspruch voraussetzt, daß der Letztverkäufer dem Verbraucher tatsächlich Ausgleich leisten mußte. ME spricht der Wortlaut recht deutlich für letztere Auslegung. Denn Art. 4 S. 1 RL verlangt, daß der Letztverkäufer „haftet"; dann darf er „Regreß nehmen". Das setzt aber wohl eine eigene, tatsächlich realisierte Einstandspflicht des Letztverkäufers voraus. Nur einen realen Haftungsschaden soll der Letztverkäufer zurückwälzen können. Für die Rückwälzung eines lediglich möglichen Haftungsrisikos besteht kein überzeugender Grund.

Damit verpflichtet die Richtlinie nur dann dazu, einen eigenständigen Regreßanspruch einzuführen, der über die ohnehin bestehenden Gewährleistungsrechte hinausgeht, wenn der Letztverkäufer von seinem Abnehmer konkret – und berechtigterweise – wegen einer Vertragswidrigkeit in Anspruch genommen wird. Daß eine solche Regelung aber nicht bei erkennbaren Fehlern Platz greifen kann, wurde schon oben unter II.5. ausgeführt. Denn sie darf nciht das Institut der kaufmännischen Mängelrüge unterlaufen. Infrage kommt ein Regreßanspruch also nur bei verborgenen Vertragswidrigkeiten.

3.2 Verantwortlichkeit vorangehender Glieder der Absatzkette

Das Regreßrecht nach Art. 4 RL setzt weiter voraus, daß der Letztverkäufer dem Endverkäufer „aufgrund einer Vertragswidrigkeit infolge eines Handelns oder Unterlassens des Herstellers, eines früheren Verkäufers innerhalb derselben Vertragskette oder einer anderen Zwischenperson" haftbar ist. Dem Wortlauf wird zu entnehmen sein, daß das Verhalten des Vormannes die Vertragswidrigkeit der Ware verursacht haben muß, um das Regreßrecht auszulösen. Folgt man diesem Wortlaut, dann hat das die folgenden Konsequenzen: Auf der Stufe des Zwischenhandels würde ein Rückgriffsanspruch des Letztverkäufers gegen den vorangehenden Verkäufer nur dann einzuräumen sein, wenn die Vertragswidrigkeit auf ein Verhalten des Vorverkäufers zurückzuführen ist. Bei reiner Zwischenveräußerung verursacht der Zwischenverkäufer die Vertragswidrigkeit aber regelmäßig nicht. Bei wortgetreuem Verständnis des Art. 4 RL ist ein Rückgriffsanspruch des Letztverkäufers gegen den Zwischenverkäufer damit für den Regelfall abzulehnen und etwa nur zu gewähren, wenn der Zwischenverkäufer die Vertragswidrigkeit tatsächlich verursacht hat – z.B. durch zu lange oder unsachgemäße Lagerung, Behandlung etc. Da dem Letztverkäufer freilich stets seine „normalen" Kaufgewährleistungsansprüche gegen seinen Verkäufer verbleiben, ist dieses Ergebnis auch nicht zu beanstanden.

Daß Zwischenhändler oder dritte „Zwischenpersonen" eine Vertragswidrigkeit der Ware verursacht haben, für die der Letztverkäufer dem Endabnehmer haftet, nach Handelskaufrecht aber keinen eigenen Gewährleistungsanspruch gegen den Zwischenhändler oder Dritten hat, dürfte als Fallgestaltung so selten sein, daß eine eigenständige Regreßregelung sich wohl in den meisten nationalen Rechten und jedenfalls im deutschen Recht erübrigt. Die Richtlinie verlangt hier nur, daß der nationale Gesetzgeber im Handelskaufrecht den gleichen Begriff der Vertragswidrigkeit verwendet, wie ihn die Richtlinie in Art. 2 definiert. Bei Deckungsgleichheit beider Begriffe ist der Richtlinien-Forderung nach einem Regreßanspruch des Letztverkäufers deshalb in diesem Punkt Genüge getan.

3.3 Regreßanspruch gegen den Hersteller

Etwas problematischer ist allerdings der häufigere Fall, daß der Hersteller die Vertragswidrigkeit der Ware iSd Art. 4 RL verursacht hat. Hier stellt sich die Frage, ob die Richtlinie dazu zwingt, in den Rechtsordnungen einen direkten Regreßanspruch gegen den Hersteller einzuführen, in denen man einen solchen Anspruch – insbesondere in Gestalt der action directe des französischen Rechts – bisher nicht kennt.

Häufig wird den Letztverkäufer keine unmittelbare Vertragsbeziehung mit dem Hersteller verbinden. Kaufrechtliche Gewährleistungsansprüche kann er dann nicht geltend machen, auch wenn er selbst dem Endabnehmer haftet. Zu beachten ist aber, daß der Letztverkäufer – jedenfalls bei der vorgeschlagenen Deckungsgleichheit der Vertragswidrigkeitsbegriffe im Verbraucher- und Handelskaufrecht – Gewährleistungsansprüche gegen seinen unmittelbaren Vormann hat. Denn auch eine vom Hersteller verursachte Vertragswidrigkeit bleibt eine Vertragswidrigkeit, für die dem Letztverkäufer die üblichen Kaufrechtsbehelfe gegen seinen Verkäufer zustehen. Da die Richtlinie es dem nationalen Recht überläßt, „den oder die Haftenden (zu bestimmen), den oder die der Letztverkäufer in Regreß nehmen kann", braucht neben der kaufrechtlichen Haftung des unmittelbaren Vormannes keine weitere Haftung – zusätzlich des Herstellers – vorgesehen zu werden. Zwar läßt die Richtlinie das zu; in der Logik des Regreßanspruchs liegt auch eine Rückwälzung der Haftung zum eigentlich Verantwortlichen, der bei mangelhafter Produktplanung, Fabrikation oder Anleitung der Hersteller ist. Doch verlangt die Richtlinie nicht zwingend einen Regreßanspruch des Letztverkäufers gegen den Hersteller.

3.4 Zwang zur Einführung eines eigenen Regreßanspruches?

Folgt man der Forderung, die Verjährungsfrist für den Verbraucher- und Handelskauf einheitlich auf zwei Jahre festzulegen, die Beweislastregeln der Richtlinie auf den Handelskauf zu erstrecken, wird ferner für den Handels- und den Verbraucherkauf derselbe Fehlerbegriff verwendet, dann werden Inkongruenzen zwischen der Haftung des Letztverkäufers und seinen eigenen Gewährleistungsansprüchen ganz weitgehend vermieden. Der Intention des Regreßrechts des Art. 4 RL ist dann Rechnung getragen. Ob die Vorschrift darüber hinaus auch der Form nach verlangt, einen selbständigen Regreßanspruch einzuführen, ist zweifelhaft und m.E. zu verneinen. Richtlinien geben Ziele vor, lassen aber den nationalen Rechten die Form und die Mittel der Umsetzung frei (Art. 249 EGV). Wenn die genannten Forderungen im Rahmen der Änderung des Kaufrechts verwirklicht werden, sind die Richtlinienvorgaben für ein Regreßrecht des Letztverkäufers erfüllt. Denn innerhalb des allgemeinen Gewährleistungsrechts erhält er, was ihm Art. 4 RL gewähren will.

4.   ZUSAMMENFASSUNG UND BEWERTUNG

Für die Umsetzung des Art. 4 RL in das deutsche Recht ist erforderlich, aber auch ausreichend:

1.   Eine Angleichung der Verjährungsfrist für Handelskäufe an die Zweijahresfrist der Richtlinie;
2.   Eine Übernahme der Beweislastregelung der Richtlinie auch für Handelskäufe.

Eine formelle Übernahme des Begriffs der Vertragswidrigkeit der Richtlinie in das Handelskaufrecht ist dagegen nicht erforderlich, da der Begriff mit jenem des CISG weitgehend identisch ist und damit gesetzlich bereits für das (internationale) Handelskaufrecht gilt. Trotzdem ist eine förmliche Übernahme in das Handelskaufrecht aus Gründen der Klarheit wünschenswert.

    Die vorgeschlagenen Regeln sollten nicht zwischen Letztverkäufern und anderen professionellen Verkäufern differenzieren, um nicht ungerechtfertigte Unterschiede zwischen Absatzstufen einzuführen.

    Die Richtlinie erfordert es ferner nicht, einen außervertraglichen Direktanspruch des Letztverkäufers gegen den Hersteller vorzusehen, auch wenn ein solcher Anspruch als praktikabel und nach der Intention des Richtliniengebers wohl wünschenswert erscheint.

    Insgesamt hat die unscheinbare Vorschrift des Art. 4 RL eine beachtliche Sprengwirkung für das Handelsrecht. Sie führt für den wichtigen Bereich des Handelskaufs zu einer erheblichen Angleichung zwischen Verbraucher- und Handelskauf und gibt der Auffassung Nahrung, die die Berechtigung für ein eigenständiges Handelsrecht eher bezweifelt.

SUMMARY
THE REGRESSIVE CLAIM OF THE FINAL SELLER UNDER THE DIRECTIVE ON
THE SALE OF CONSUMER GOODS

1. Introduction

The Directive 1999/44 EC on certain aspects of the sale of consumer goods and associated guarantees of May, 25th 1999 is mainly concerned with the buying consumer's remedies – except damages – against his professional seller for the sale of non-conforming goods.

However, in Article 4 the Directive addresses also the relationship between the final seller and his suppliers: "Where the final seller is liable to the consumer because of a lack of conformity resulting from an act or omission by the producer, a previous seller in the same chain of contracts or any other intermediary, the final seller shall be entitled to pursue remedies against the person or persons liable in the contractual chain. The person or persons liable against whom the final seller may pursue remedies, together with the relevant actions and conditions of exercise, shall be determined by national law". The precise scope of application of this provision is far from clear. But since the final seller's right of redress constitutes the connecting link between consumer sales and merchants' sales, Article 4 deserves serious attention.

2. Goal of Article 4

2.1 Protection of the final seller

The broad goal of Article 4 is rather clear. The final seller should not, at the end of the day, be burdened with the extended liability under the Directive when other members of the same chain of contracts are responsible for the non-conformity of the sold goods. Therefore, the last seller shall have a right of redress against a previous seller or the producer or even other persons who have caused the non-conformity.

2.2 Protection of the final seller only?

Article 4 provides that the final seller exclusively must be granted a right of redress. It does not regulate whether other members of the same contract chain when made liable by their preceding buyer should also be given such a right. It is this author's opinion that the maxim of equality demands equal treatment of all members of a chain of supply contracts. On the other hand, the reasoning in consideration 9 of the Directive shows that any right of redress can be excluded by agreement. Freedom of contract among commercial sellers and buyers thus remains intact.

2.3 Relationship with remedies under existing sales laws

It seems clear that Article 4 does not intend to abolish existing remedies of final sellers against their sellers when national or international sales laws (e.g. the CISG) provide such remedies.

2.4 Compensation for incongruent liability

The underlying reason and real goal of Article 4 then seems to be the compensation of the final seller for a possible incongruent liability established under the Directive as compared with the present existing – national or international – sales law.

2.5 Possible inconsistencies in liability

– A discrepancy between the final seller's own liability and his right to claim redress occurs when his redress claim is excluded by contractual agreement with his seller. However, the Directive accepts such inconsistency because it admits freedom of contract.

– A further possible inconsistency is due to the fact that some European laws and especially the CISG recognize a duty to examine the goods and to give notice of defects within short or reasonable time. If the final seller fails to fulfill this duty he loses all remedies. It is argued here that the Directive does not intend to change this existing law, but that in case of latent defects, which could not be detected by reasonable examination, it provides redress even if prescribed periods of limitation which are shorter than two years have lapsed. The Directive therefore requires to introduce at least the two years' limitation period also to redress claims of final sellers. This is also in line with the CISG (art. 39 para. 2)

– Further discrepancies between the final seller's liability and his own right of redress may appear where the definitions of conformity or the rules on burden of proof under the Directive and national law or CISG differ. In the author's opinion Article 4 is designed to protect the final seller also in these cases. The Directive therefore requires the adaptation of national law in these respects – where necessary – to the standard of the Directive.

Altogether, national laws are required to introduce a right of redress of the final seller – and of previous sellers – where the mentioned discrepancies exist. Although the Directive leaves much to the national law regarding how to deal with the particularities of the right to redress, Article 4 states some basic requirements.

3. Requirements

3.1 Liability of the final seller because of non-conformity

Even though the requirements of liability for non-conformity are pretty much self-evident, it must nevertheless be stressed that Article 4 presupposes actual, not potential liability of the final seller. When the consumer does not exert his remedy the final seller also cannot claim redress.

3.2 Liability of previous sellers in the contracts chain

Article 4 further presupposes that the non-conformity resulted "from an act or omission by the producer, a previous seller in the same chain of contracts or any other intermediary". Literal interpretation restricts the right of redress then to cases where previous sellers have caused the non-conformity of the goods through their conduct. Since the "normal" remedies (price reduction, termination etc.) of final sellers towards their sellers are not abolished by Article 4 and do not presuppose any specific conduct on the part of the seller, this requirement adds nothing to existing law.

3.3 Right of redress against producer

Article 4 seems to require a final seller's right of redress also against the producer. But since any non-conformity caused by the conduct of the producer remains a non-conformity for which the seller prior to the final seller is liable, the Directive allows but does not compel the introduction of an *action directe* against the producer.

3.4 Need to introduce an independent right of redress in Germany

It is argued that all that is required from German law under Article 4 is to introduce a two years' limitation period both for consumer and commercial sales, to extend the rules of the Directive on the burden of proof to commercial sales, and apply the same definition of non-conformity of goods to consumer and commercial sales.

4. Summary

Article 4 of the Directive leads to an approximation of consumer and commercial sales and nourishes doubts whether and to what extent special rules and in particular a specific Commercial Code today are still necessary or justified.

Chapter 11 im Vergleich mit dem schweizerischen Nachlassverfahren

Isaak Meier[*]

---

[*] Dr.iur., o. Prof. an der Universität Zürich.
Erweiterte Fassung des Vortrages des Verfassers vom 26.6.1999 am Europainstitut der Universität Zürich im Rahmen des Nachdiplomstudiums für Internationales Wirtschaftsrecht.

J. Basedow et al., eds., Private Law in the International Arena – Liber Amicorum Kurt Siehr
© 2000, T.M.C.Asser Press, The Hague, The Netherlands

1. ALLGEMEINES ZUM AMERIKANISCHEN KONKURS- UND
    SANIERUNGSRECHT[1]

1.1 Rechtsgrundlagen

1.1.1 *US Bankruptcy Code und Nebengesetze*

Die Einzelzwangsvollstreckung ist im state law, d.h. im gliedstaatlichen Recht, geregelt und weist grosse Unterschiede auf.[2] Das Vorgehen zur Verwertung eines beweglichen Pfandes ergibt sich allerdings aus dem Uniform Commercial Code
(UCC).

Demgegenüber besteht für „bankruptcy law“, zu dem die Amerikaner nicht nur
das Konkursrecht im engeren Sinne, sondern auch das Sanierungsrecht zählen,
schon seit 1787, d.h. seit Schaffung der Verfassung, eine Kompetenz des Bundes.
Der heute geltende Bankruptcy Code (BC) mit zahlreichen Teilrevisionen datiert
von 1979 (Title 11 U.S. Code). Ergänzende Bestimmungen zum Konkurs- und Sanierungsrecht ergeben sich aus dem 18. Titel (Konkursdelikte) und 28. Titel des
U.S. Code (Wahl und Organisation von Konkursgericht und United States Trustee).
Für verfahrensrechtliche Fragen bei Streitigkeiten aus Konkurs- und Sanierungs-

---

[1] Literaturauswahl: Michael J. Herbert, *Understanding Bankruptcy* (Legal Text Series, Matthew
Bender 1995); Douglas G. Baird, *The Elements of Bankruptcy* (Westbury, New York 1993); George
M. Treister/ J. Ronald Trost/ Leon S. Forman/ Kenneth N. Klee, *Fundamentals of Bankruptcy Law,*
ALI/ABA, 4. Aufl. (Philadelphia 1995); Elizabeth Warren, *Business Bankruptcy* (Federal Judical Cen-
ter, Washington 1993); siehe auch den Überblick über das amerikanische Sanierungsrecht bei Daniel
Hunkeler, *Das Nachlassverfahren nach revidiertem SchKG* (Diss. Freiburg 1996) S. 83ff. und mit Her-
vorhebung der Schwächen vom Verfahren nach chapter 11 im Vergleich zum neuen deutschen Insolvenzrecht Reinhard Bork, „Der Insolvenzplan“,109 ZZP (1996) S. 481ff.

[2] Vgl. hierzu Isaak Meier/ Peter Zweifel/ Christoph Zabarowski/ Ingrid Jent-Sørensen, *Lohnpfän-*
dung – Optimales Existenzminimum und Neuanfang? (Zürich 1999) S. 74.

recht kommen sodann die vom Supreme Court erlassenen Federal Rules of Bankruptcy Procedure zur Anwendung (vgl. 28 U.S.C.A. § 2075).[3] Von den Nebenerlassen, die für die Durchsetzung von Geldforderungen von Bedeutung sind, seien hier schliesslich erwähnt: Der Fair Debt Collection Practices Act von 1994 (15 U.S.C.A. §§ 1692ff.), der sich gegen missbräuchliche Praktiken bei der aussergerichtlichen Geltendmachung von Forderungen richtet, und der Fair Credit Reporting Act von 1995 (15 U.S.C.A. §§ 1681 i ff.), der sich mit der Registrierung und Weitergabe von Daten betreffend die Kreditwürdigkeit von Konsumenten befasst.

1.1.2 *Rechtsprechung*

Wie es dem amerikanischen Rechts- und Gerichtssystem entspricht, bedeutet die bundesrechtliche Natur des Konkursrechtes, dass dies auch ausschliesslich von Bundesbehörden gehandhabt wird. Für das Konkursrecht existiert eine eigene Gerichtsbarkeit, mit den Bankruptcy Courts bzw. District Courts als erstinstanzliche Gerichte[4] und den Courts of Appeals als Rechtsmittelinstanzen. Entscheide der Courts of Appeals können an den Supreme Court weitergezogen werden.

Trotz der – mit kontinentaleuropäischem Recht vergleichbaren – Kodifizierung des Konkursrechts sind Gerichtsentscheide fast wichtiger als der Gesetzestext.

1.2 Formen von Konkurs- und Sanierungsverfahren für Business und Consumer Fälle

Der BC sieht im Wesentlichen drei Verfahrensformen vor, die man allgemein nach ihrem Regelungsort im Gesetz zu nennen pflegt. Es sind dies die Verfahren nach chapter 7, chapter 11 und chapter 13. Das chapter 7 ist ein Liquidationsverfahren und entspricht unserem Konkursverfahren nach Art. 293ff. SchKG. Das chapter 11 ist ein Nachlass- und Sanierungsverfahren. Das Verfahren nach chapter 13 ist schliesslich ein besonderes Schuldenbereinigungsverfahren für Private.[5]

Für Unternehmen (corporation, sole proprietorship, partnership) stehen die Verfahren nach chapter 11 und 7 im Vordergrund. Privatpersonen wählen vor allem zwischen chapter 7 und 13.

Nachfolgend werde ich mich ausschliesslich mit dem Verfahren nach chapter 11 befassen.

---

[3] Treister et al (oben N. 1) § 1.05 (a).

[4] Zum komplizierten Verhältnis der Bankruptcy Courts zu den District Courts siehe Herbert (oben N. 1) § 5.04; Treister et al (oben N. 1) § 2.01.

[5] Eingehend hierzu Meier/ Zweifel/ Zaborowski/ Jent-Sørensen (oben N. 2) S. 76ff.

1.3   Grundideen des amerikanischen Konkurs- und Sanierungsrechts

Das amerikanische Konkursrecht ist für Unternehmen und noch ausgeprägter für
Privatpersonen extrem schuldnerfreundlich. Dahinter stehen vor allem zwei
Grundgedanken:

Gewährung eines neuen Starts (fresh start): Das Konkursrecht will Unternehmen und Privatpersonen, wenn sie wirtschaftlich gescheitert sind, insbesondere
durch Erlass oder Reduktion der Schulden eine neue Chance gegeben. Damit soll
jedermann – zum Wohl der ganzen Gesellschaft – ermuntert werden, finanzielle
und wirtschaftliche Risiken einzugehen.[6]

Erhaltung von Unternehmen zum Schutz von Arbeitnehmern und anderen betroffenen Personen und Gemeinschaften: Durch das grosszügige Sanierungsrecht
sollen insolvente und/oder überschuldete, jedoch überlebensfähige Unternehmen
wenn immer möglich gerettet werden. Damit sollen vor allem die Arbeitnehmer
und andere Personen, wie etwa Lieferanten, geschützt werden. Dieses Anliegen ist
in den USA besonders wichtig, da dort bekanntlich nur ein beschränkter Sozial-
schutz besteht. Durch die Verhinderung des Konkurses eines Unternehmens
können sodann nicht nur andere Firmen, sondern oft auch ganze Lebensgemein-
schaften erhalten werden. So kann etwa die Sanierung eines Warenhandels bewirken, dass die anderen kleineren Geschäfte eines Shopping-Centers und damit das
Lebenszentrum einer ländlichen Gemeinschaft bestehen bleibt.[7]

2.   ATTRAKTIVITÄT VON CHAPTER 11: DICHTUNG UND WAHRHEIT

2.1   Alltäglichkeit der Einleitung eines Verfahrens nach chapter 11

Das Verfahren nach chapter 11 weist ohne Zweifel weltweit den grössten Bekannt-
heitsgrad auf. Zusammen mit den class actions, punitive damages, civil jury und
contingent fee gehört es zum medienwirksamen „Gruselkabinett" des amerikanischen Rechts. In der NZZ vom 15.10.98 heisst es etwa, die „Pittsburgh Penguins",
ein berühmter Club der National Hockey League, habe „unter dem berühmt-be-
rüchtigten chapter 11 um Nachlasstundung nachgesucht."[8]

Das chapter 11 hat in der amerikanischen Wirtschaft in der Tat einen wichtigen
Stellenwert. Zahlreiche namhafte Unternehmen haben schon zu diesem Verfahren
Zuflucht genommen oder nehmen müssen. Erwähnt seien nur als Beispiele: Ver-

---

[6] Warren (oben N. 1) S. 13; Herbert (oben N. 1) § 1.01 (B).
[7] Zum Community-Ansatz in den neueren Theorien des amerikanischen Konkursrechts insbesondere Karen Gross, *Failure and Forgiveness, Rebalancing the Bankruptcy System* (New Haven/ London
1997) S. 193ff.
[8] *NZZ* 1998 Nr. 239, S. 59.

schiedene Fluggesellschaften, grosse Warenhausketten, unzählige Shopping Malls und eine lange Liste von Unternehmen, die wegen horrenden Summen aus Produktehaftpflicht keinen anderen Ausweg als die Anrufung des chapter 11 sahen. Die Wichtigsten sind: Mehr als 15 Asbest Produzenten, Dow Corning Corp., ein Gemeinschaftsunternehmen von Dow Chemical und Corning, das Brustimplantate herstellt,[9] A.H. Robins, welche auf Verhütungsmittel spezialisiert ist und Flugzeuhersteller wie Piper Aircraft und Fairchild Aircraft.

Alle diese Fälle lassen den Einruck entstehen, dass ein Verfahren nach chapter 11 nicht weiter „ehrenrührig" ist und offenbar zu den normalen Handlungsvarianten eines Unternehmens gehört.

Nachfolgend soll versucht werden, der Attraktivität des chapter 11 auf die Spur zu kommen. Vorerst muss allerdings die praktische Bedeutung des chapter 11 relativiert werden.

2.2   Relativierung der praktischen Bedeutung von chapter 11 durch Vergleich mit der Verbreitung des schweizerischen Nachlassverfahrens

Das schweizerische Nachlassverfahrensrecht hat nur ein geringe praktische Bedeutung. Die Firmen, die in den letzten 10 Jahren mit einem Nachlassverfahren gerettet worden sind, können vermutlich an wenigen Händen abgezählt werden.[10] In den seltenen Fällen, in denen ein Nachlassvertrag zustande kommt, funktioniert er meist als Form der Liquidation, die dem Schuldner gegenüber dem normalen Konkurs gewisse Vorteile bringt. Man würde deshalb annehmen, dass das attraktive Chapter 11 gemessen an der Zahl der Einwohner viel häufiger vorkommt als das schweizerische Nachlassverfahren. Dies ist jedoch, wie die nachfolgende Tabelle zeigt, nicht der Fall. Die Anzahl der bewilligten Sanierungspläne bewegt sich in ähnlichen Grössenordnungen wie die Anzahl der bewilligten Nachlassverträge in der Schweiz.

---

[9] Vgl. zu diesem Fall etwa *NZZ* vom 26.8.97, Nr. 196, S. 23.

[10] In gleichem Sinne lautet die Einschätzung der im Rahmen der SchKG-Revision 1997 eingesetzten Expertengruppe „Sanierungsrecht". Revision SchKG, Kommission des Nationalrates, *Bericht der Expertengruppe Sanierungsrecht zu ihrem Entwurf vom 14. September 1992*, S. 6. (unveröffentlicht; zu beziehen beim Bundesamt für Justiz). Untersuchungen über die Anzahl der Unternehmen, die durch die Einleitung eines Nachlassverfahrens gerettet worden sind, existieren nach Kenntnis des Verfassers nicht.

Chapter 11	Anzahl pro 1Mio Einwohner (260 Mio)	Nachlass-verträge	Anzahl pro 1Mio Einwohner (7 Mio)
1995	12,904 (Einleitung des Verfahrens)	50 (d.h. ca. 17 Plan-bewilligungen)[11]	147	21

Die Feststellung, dass man die Bedeutung von extremen Erscheinungsformen des amerikanischen Rechts überschätzt, ist übrigens in ähnlicher Form auch schon für die punitive damages gemacht worden.[12]

Trotz der eher geringen Zahl von Verfahren nach chapter 11 ist (wohl) unbestreitbar, dass dieses Verfahren bedeutend wirksamer als unser Nachlassverfahren ist. Zwar sind durchschnittlich nur 20 % der Verfahren erfolgreich. Bei den erfolgreichen Verfahren sind jedoch die grossen Unternehmen mit börsenkottierten Aktien (publicly held companies) weit übervertreten. Nach einer Schätzung besteht für diese Gesellschaften eine Erfolgschance von ca. 95 %.[13]

3.   GRUNDZÜGE DES VERFAHRENS NACH CHAPTER 11

3.1   **Organe**

Nachfolgend sind die Akteure im Verfahren nach chapter 11 vorzustellen:

DIP = Debtor in possession:

Eine Besonderheit des amerikanischen Sanierungsverfahrens besteht darin, dass kein Sachwalter ernannt wird, sondern dass vielmehr der Schuldner bzw. seine Organe und Manager das Unternehmen selber weiterführen und ebenso auch sämtliche administrativen Aufgaben des Sanierungsverfahrens wahrnehmen. Das Gesetz spricht dabei vom *debtor in possession* (z.B. 11 U.S.C. § 1107, 1203). Allgemein üblich ist die Kurzbezeichnung *DIP*. Die Selbstverwaltung des Schuldners steht allerdings unter der relativ strengen Aufsicht und Kontrolle von folgenden Personen

---

[11] Die Zahl der bewilligten Nachlassverfahren wird in der Statistik nicht ausgewiesen. Man schätzt, dass nach 1986 etwa 25 bis 30 % der Sanierungspläne die Zustimmung des Gerichtes gefunden haben.

[12] Vg. Felix Dasser, „Punitive damages: Vom ‚fremden Fötzel‘ zum ‚Miteidgenoss‘?", 96 *SJZ* (2000) S. 103f.

[13] Zu diesen Schätzungen siehe Warren (oben N. 1) S. 31; Lynn LoPucki & William Whitford, „Venue Choice", *Wis. L. Rev.* (1991) 11, 41; Lynn LoPucki, „The Debtor in Full Control – Systems Failure under Chapter 11 of the Bankruptcy Code", 57 *Am. Bankr. L.J.* (1983) 99, 109.

und Organen: Anwalt des Schuldners, Gläubigerausschuss (comitee of creditors) und United States Trustee (hierzu sogleich später).

Anwalt des Schuldners:

Die Durchführung eines Verfahrens nach chapter 11 ist ohne Einschaltung eines spezialisierten Anwalts nicht möglich. Mit der Bestimmung des Anwalts wählt der Schuldner quasi seinen eigenen Aufseher (vgl. 11 U.S.C. § 327). Der Anwalt handelt nicht im Interesse der Organe und Manager des Unternehmens. Vielmehr ist er eine Art Treuhänder des Unternehmens.[14]

Allgemein kann gesagt werden, dass das gesamte amerikanische Konkursrecht von einer hoch spezialisierten und sehr gut ausgebildeten Anwaltsschaft getragen wird. Dieser wird allerdings auch nachgesagt, dass sie das Konkursverfahren enorm verteuert. In zutreffender Weise drückt dies Herbert wie folgt aus: „There is a perception – not entirely without basis in fact – that complex bankruptcies are nothing but cash cows for bankruptcy professionals".[15]

Case Trustee:

Der DIP ist zwar die Regel. Wenn der Schuldner zum DIP unfähig ist oder betrügerische Handlungen unternommen hat, kann ausnahmsweise ein Sachwalter (case trustee) ernannt werden (11 U.S.C. § 1104 (a)).

United States Trustee:

Jedem Konkursgericht ist ein United States Trustee zugeordnet. Seine Hauptaufgabe ist die mehr formelle Kontrolle der Geschäftsführung des DIP (Kontrolle von Buchführung und Zahlungen etc.; vgl. 11 U.S.C. § 586 (a) (3)). Daneben hat er auch wenige administrative Aufgaben in den einzelnen Verfahren: So leitet er die am Anfang des Verfahrens stattfindende Versammlung zur ersten Information der Gläubiger (meeting of creditors; 11 U.S.C. § 341 (a)). Im weiteren setzt er den oder die Gläubigerausschüsse ein (comitees of creditors; 11 U.S.C. 1102).

Creditors Comitee:

Ein vor allem in grösseren Fällen bedeutsames Organ ist der Gläubigerausschuss, in

---

[14] Siehe die treffende Schilderung dieser Situation von Lynn LoPucki, „The Debtor's Lawyer as a Trojan Horse", in: Warren/ Westbrook, *The Law of Debtors and Creditors, Text, Cases and Problems*, 3. Aufl. (Boston 1986) S. 780ff.

[15] Siehe Herbert (oben N. 1) § 20.01.

dem in der Regel die sieben grössten Gläubiger Einsitz nehmen.[16] Seine Aufgaben sind Überwachung des Schuldners und Einflussnahme auf seine Geschäftsführung (11 U.S.C. § 1103). Er kann als Nebenintervenient in Aktiv- und Passivprozessen der Masse teilnehmen und muss vom Gericht vor allen Entscheiden angehört werden (11 U.S.C. § 1109). Meist ist er auch der wichtigste Ort für die Aushandlung des Nachlassvertrages mit dem Schuldner. Bei sehr unterschiedlich gelagerten Interessen der Gläubiger können auch mehrere Gläubigerausschüsse eingesetzt werden (z.B. besonderer Ausschuss für Gläubiger einer mass tort – class action gegen den Schuldner).

Bankruptcy Courts:

Den Konkursgerichten obliegt nicht nur Prüfung und Genehmigung des Sanierungsplans und die Fällung von Zwischenentscheiden, wie etwa die Aufhebung der Stundung zugunsten eines Pfandgläubigers oder die Zustimmung zur Veräusserung von Vermögenswerten, sondern auch weitgehend die Beurteilung aller Klagen, die in Zusammenhang mit dem Sanierungsverfahren stehen. Hierzu gehören insbesondere Klagen betreffend die Zulassung von Forderungen, Aussonderungsklagen etc.

3.2   Ablauf des Verfahrens und Inhalt des Sanierungsplans

3.2.1 *Einleitung des Verfahrens durch den Schuldner und ausnahmsweise durch die Gläubiger*

Das Sanierungsverfahren nach chapter 11 wird regelmässig durch den Schuldner eingeleitet (voluntary cases; vgl. 11 U.S.C. § 301). Theoretisch können jedoch drei Gläubiger die Eröffnung eines Verfahrens beantragen (11 U.S.C. § 303 (b)). Mit Einleitung des Verfahrens tritt „automatisch" die Nachlassstundung ein, ohne dass dies einer an bestimmte Voraussetzungen geknüpfte Bewilligung bedarf (automatic stay; siehe hierzu 3.3.1).

3.2.2 *Aufgaben und Verfahrensschritte*

In einem Verfahren nach chapter 11 sind vom Schuldner als DIP (siehe oben 3.1.) und anderen Personen und Organen drei unterschiedliche Aufgaben wahrzunehmen: Weiterführung des Geschäftsbetriebes, Administration des Sanierungsverfahrens, Ausarbeitung des Sanierungsplans und „Umwerbung" (soliciting) der Gläubiger für die Zustimmung zum Plan.

---

[16] Herbert, ibid., § 17.04.

Weiterführung des Geschäftsbetriebes durch den Schuldner:

Der Geschäftsbetrieb wird, wie schon gesagt, durch den Schuldner bzw. seine Manager weitergeführt. Die Tätigkeit dieser Personen ist allerdings auf Handlungen beschränkt, die der normale Geschäftsbetrieb mit sich bringt (ordinary courses of business, vgl. 11 U.S.C. § 363 (a)). Für andere Handlungen, wie Verkauf von Geschäftsteilen etc., ist die Zustimmung des Konkursgerichtes notwendig (11 U.S.C. § 363 (a)).[17] Eine besondere richterliche Erlaubnis ist auch für den Gebrauch von flüssigen Mitteln (Geld oder geldwerten Mitteln; sog. „cash collateral"; 11 U.S.C. § 363) notwendig. Die Bereitschaft von Dritten, mit dem Schuldner neue Verpflichtungen einzugehen, wird dadurch massgeblich erleichtert, dass diese zu Massaschulden werden (Schulden mit sog. „superpriority"; 11 U.S.C. § 364).

Administration des Verfahrens:

Die Administration des Sanierungsverfahrens erfolgt durch den Schuldner als DIP bzw. seine Vertreter, soweit hierfür nicht ausnahmsweise andere Organe und Amtsstellen zuständig sind. Diese Handlungen umfassen vor allem:
– Einberufung und Durchführung einer Gläubigerversammlung als Information für die Gläubiger;
– Bildung von Gläubigerausschüssen durch den United States Trustee;
– Feststellung der Aktiven;
– Feststellung der Passiven;
– Durchführung und Erledigung von sanierungsrechtlichen Streitigkeiten aller Art (Aussonderungsklagen, Admassierungsklagen, Kollokationsklagen, Verfahren zur Aufhebung der Nachlassstundung zugunsten von gesicherten Gläubiger etc.).

Arbeiten in Zusammenhang mit dem Sanierungsplan:

Wichtige Aufgabe des Schuldner und seiner Vertreter ist schliesslich auch die Ausarbeitung des Sanierungsplans und sein „Verkauf" gegenüber den Gläubigern. Dabei gilt, dass der Schuldner in den ersten 120 Tagen seit Eintritt der Nachlassstundung das ausschliessliche Recht hat, einen Sanierungsplan vorzuschlagen (11 U.S.C. § 1122 (c)). Falls der Schuldner diese Frist nicht einhält oder der rechtzeitig vorgelegte Plan nicht innert 180 Tagen seit Eintritt der Nachlassstundung bewilligt wird, haben auch die Gläubiger die Möglichkeit, einen Sanierungsplan zu entwerfen (11 U.S.C. § 1121 (c)). In der Praxis machen allerdings die Gläubiger von dieser Möglichkeit kaum Gebrauch. Anzumerken ist schliesslich, dass das Konkursge-

---

[17] Herbert, ibid., 9.03 (C) (1).

richt die genannten Fristen aus zureichenden Gründen ohne zeitliche Schranke verlängern kann (11 U.S.C. § 1121 (d)).

3.2.3 *Inhalt des Sanierungsplans*

Der Sanierungsplan weist typischerweise (unter anderem) folgenden Inhalt auf:

1.   Angaben über Umfang von Erlass und/oder Stundung der Forderungen; statt Bezahlung einer Dividende kommt allenfalls auch Übergabe von Anteilen am Unternehmen in Frage. Die Auszahlung der Dividende muss dabei grundsätzlich nicht sichergestellt werden. Als Besonderheit des amerikanischen Rechts ist sodann hervorzuheben, dass die Gläubiger nicht absolut, sondern nur innerhalb der Gruppe gleich behandelt werden müssen (hierzu 3.3.5).
2.   Angaben darüber, welche Verträge vom Schuldner akzeptiert, zurückgewiesen oder auf einen Dritten übertragen werden (hierzu 3.3.2).
3.   Darlegung, wie das Unternehmen saniert und wie der Plan erfüllt werden soll. Hierzu gehört etwa die Bezeichnung der Vermögenswerte oder Teile des Unternehmens, die verkauft oder liquidiert werden sollen.
4.   Regelung der Verfahrenskosten.

3.3   Wichtige Einzelfragen

3.3.1 *Stundung (automatic stay): Voraussetzungen, Wirkungen und Zeitdauer*

Wie schon gesagt, muss die Stundung nicht bewilligt werden. Vielmehr tritt sie automatisch ein (11 U.S.C. § 362). Der Schuldner erhält damit alle Rechte und Pflichten eines DIP. Den Gläubigern ist es nunmehr verboten, auf eigene Faust gegen den Schuldner ausserrechtliche und rechtliche Schritte einzuleiten (11 U.S.C. § 362 (a)). Handlungen, die dieses Verbot missachten, sind nicht nur ungültig, sondern unterstehen auch den strengen Strafandrohungen des contempt of court.[18]

Die Stundung kennt grundsätzlich keine zeitlichen Schranken. Eine Zeitvorgabe besteht lediglich für das Exlusivrecht des Schuldners, einen Sanierungsplan vorzuschlagen. Nach Ablauf der oben genannten Fristen (3.2.1) können zusätzlich auch die Gläubiger einen Sanierungsplan entwerfen. Falls weder Gläubiger noch Schuldner einen Plan vorlegen, kann die Nachlassstundung über Jahre andauern.[19]

---

[18] Treister et al (oben N. 1) § 5.01 (c)
[19] Vgl. Herbert (oben N. 1) § 17.11 (A). Dies wird in den rechtsvergleichenden Untersuchungen allgemein als eine Schwäche des amerikanischen Sanierungsrechts betrachtet; Reinhard Bork, „Der Insolvenzplan", 109 *ZZP* (1996) S. 482.

3.3.2 *Eingriff in Verträge*

Im Anhang eines chapter 11-Plans muss der Schuldner auch angeben, welche Verträge er erfüllen (assume), nicht erfüllen (reject) oder auf einen Dritten übertragen will (assign).[20] Entscheidet sich der Schuldner für die Erfüllung des Vertrags, wird die vom Schuldner zu erbringende Leistung zur Massaverbindlichkeit, die im Rahmen des Plans umfassend erfüllt werden muss. War der Schuldner mit Vertragsleistungen im Rückstand, kann auch dies durch „adequate assurance" geheilt werden (11 U.S.C. § 365 (b) (1)). Vertragsbestimmungen, wonach ein Vertrag bei Konkurseröffnung und/oder Insolvenz als aufgelöst gilt oder vom Dritten aufgelöst werden kann, werden dabei als nichtig betrachtet (11 U.S.C. § 363 (l)). Im Falle einer Nichterfüllung des Vertrags wird die (Schadenersatz-) Forderung des Gläubigers zur ungesicherten Forderung, die meist nur zu einem Bruchteil befriedigt wird. Für Mietverträge gilt die Besonderheit, dass Schadenersatz lediglich im Umfang von höchstens einer Jahresmiete oder 15 % des gesamten, bis zur Vertragsbeendigung geschuldeten Mietzinses verlangt werden kann (11 U.S.C. § 502 (b) (6)). Die Übertragung auf einen Dritten ist schliesslich eine Form der Verwertung von Aktiven des Schuldners. Zur Erleichterung der Abtretung und damit der Versilberung des fraglichen Rechts erklärt das Zwangsvollstreckungsrecht gewisse Vertragsklauseln zur Einschränkung der Abtretung für ungültig (vgl. 11 U.S.C. § 365 (f) (1)).

Konkret bedeutet diese Möglichkeit des Eingriffs in bestehende Verträge etwa, dass der Schuldner einen langfristigen Mietvertrag zum Dahinfallen bringen kann. Der Vermieter muss sich dann für den Schadenersatz mit einer Konkursdividende im genannten Umfang begnügen.

3.3.3 *Eingriff in Sicherungsrechte*

Wesentliche Besonderheiten des amerikanischen Konkursrechts sind auch die Instrumente und Bestimmungen, die dem Schuldner ermöglichen, verpfändete Vermögenswerte zu erhalten. Diese Regelungen sind in den USA besonders bedeutsam, da die Schuldner meist einen Grossteil ihrer beweglichen und unbeweglichen Vermögenswerte verpfändet haben. Das amerikanische Recht kennt sowohl das besitzlose, als auch das lediglich der Gattung nach umschriebene Pfand an beweglichen Sachen.[21]

Der Schuldner hat insbesondere die Möglichkeit, das Pfand auszulösen, indem er dem Pfandgläubiger im Rahmen des Sanierungsplans nicht den Forderungsbe-

---

[20] Für die Annahme eines Vertrags ist die Zustimmung des Gerichtes erforderlich. Henry J. Sommer, *Consumer Bankruptcy Law and Practice*, 5. Aufl. (Boston 1996) § 12.9.2. N 256.

[21] Näheres hierzu etwa bei William H. Lawrence/ William H. Henning/ R.Wilson Freyermuth, *Understanding Secured Transactions* (Legal Text Series, Matthew Bender 1997).

trag, sondern nur den Schätzwert des Pfandes zahlt. Der nicht gedeckte Teil der Pfandforderung wird wie eine gewöhnliche ungesicherte Forderung behandelt (vgl. 11 U.S.C. 1129 (b) (2)). Der Schuldner braucht sodann den Schätzwert nicht bereits mit Bewilligung des Planes zu bezahlen. Vielmehr kann er die Zahlung auch während der Plandauer in Raten leisten.[22]

Eine interessante und praktisch bedeutsame Einrichtung zugunsten der gesicherten Gläubiger ist die Möglichkeit dieser Gläubiger, im Einzelfall die richterliche Aufhebung der Nachlassstundung zu erlangen, und damit die Pfandverwertung zu ermöglichen, falls der Schuldner nicht für einen allfälligen Wertzerfall ausreichende Sicherheit leisten kann (11 U.S.C. § 362 (d); adequate protection).

3.3.4 *Rückgängigmachung von Rechtshandlungen zur Sicherstellung der Gleichbehandlung von Gläubigern*

Der Schuldner kann und muss als DIP auch alle paulianisch anfechtbaren Rechtshandlungen als ungültig erklären (11 U.S.C. § 548; fraudulent transfers and obligations). Eine stark erleichterte Anfechtung gilt dabei für Rechtshandlungen, die in den letzten 90 Tagen vor Konkursantrag vorgenommen worden sind (11 U.S.C. § 547; preferences). Schliesslich können ausnahmsweise auch gesetzliche Pfandrechte als ungültig erklärt werden (11 U.S.C. § 545; avoidance of statutory liens).

3.3.5 *Einteilung der Gläubiger in privilegierte und nicht privilegierte Gläubiger und Bildung von Gläubigergruppen*

Die Gläubiger sind zum einen in privilegierte und nicht privilegierte Gläubiger unterteilt. Zum anderen können sie verschiedenen Gruppen mit gleich gelagerten Interessen angehören.

Die privilegierten Gläubiger entsprechen unseren privilegierten Klassen nach Art. 219 SchKG. Im amerikanischen Recht werden 9 Prioritäten unterschieden (11 U.S.C. § 507). Die erste Priorität haben die Massakosten (administrative expenses). Zu den privilegierten Gläubigern zählt in weitem Umfange auch der Fiskus (11 U.S.C. § 507 (a) (8)), soweit diesem nicht sogar ein gesetzliches Pfandrecht zusteht.[23] Für alle gilt grundsätzlich, dass der Sanierungsplan nur bewilligt werden kann, wenn diese vollumfänglich auf einmal oder wenigstens in Raten bezahlt werden.

Die (privilegierten und nicht privilegierten) Gläubiger können vom Schuldner in verschiedene Gruppen mit gleichgelagerten Interessen (classes) eingeteilt und als-

---

[22] David G. Epstein, *Bankruptcy and other Debtor Creditor Laws*, 5. Aufl. (St. Paul, Minnesota 1995) S. 266ff. und die dort angeführten Beispiele.
[23] Treister et al (oben N. 1) § 6.04 Ziff. 8.

dann bei der Verteilung auch unterschiedlich behandelt werden (11 U.S.C. § 1122). Denkbar ist etwa die Bildung einer Gruppe bestehend aus einem oder mehreren Grossgläubigern mit einer kleinen Dividende und einer Gruppe von Kleingläubigern, deren Forderungen ganz oder zu einem hohen Prozentsatz bezahlt werden (11 U.S.C. § 1122 (h)). Falls am Konkurs eine Masse von Gläubigern aus Produktehaftpflicht (mass tort creditors) beteiligt sind, werden diese regelmässig in einer besonderen Gläubigergruppe zusammengefasst. Gläubiger mit unterschiedlicher Priorität gehören grundsätzlich in getrennte Klassen. Jeder gesicherte Gläubiger bildet (grundsätzlich) eine eigene Klasse.[24]

Subordinierte Forderungen (subordinated claims): Die Forderungen, die hinter die ordentlichen nicht privilegierten Forderungen zurückzustehen haben, können einerseits durch Rangrücktrittserklärungen im Rahmen eines Vertrages begründet werden (11 U.S.C. § 510 (a)). Andererseits können Forderung auf Antrag des DIP durch das Konkursgericht in diese Klasse eingeteilt werden, wenn dies wie häufig bei Darlehen von Gesellschafter als angemessen erscheint (11 U.S.C. § 510 (c); sog. „equitable subordination").

3.3.6 Stellung von Einzelunternehmer und Personen, die Anteile an der Gesellschaft innehaben oder Mitglieder von ihr sind (equity holder)

Eine interessante Besonderheit des amerikanischen Konkursrechts ist die Behandlung der Inhaber und Eigentümer des sanierungsbedürftigen Unternehmens (equity holder). Als Grundsatz gilt, dass diese Personen erst etwas erhalten, wenn sämtliche ungesicherten und gesicherten Gläubiger voll befriedigt sind.

Als Folge dieser sog. „absolute priority rule" verlieren die Eigner grundsätzlich ihre Stellung! Die Anteile am Unternehmen bzw. seine Aktiven gehen auf die Gläubiger über oder werden von Dritten erworben.[25] Die Eigner haben allerdings die Möglichkeit im Unternehmen zu verbleiben, wenn die Mehrheit der Gläubiger dem zustimmt oder sie dem Unternehmen neue Mittel zufügen und damit eine richterliche Bewilligung des Sanierungsplans entgegen dem Willen der Gläubigermehrheit möglich ist (hierzu sogleich näheres unter g).[26]

3.3.7 Voraussetzungen für die Bewilligung des Sanierungsplans; cramdown

Ein Sanierungsplan kann auf zwei Arten zustande kommen:

---

[24] Vgl. Treister et al, ibid., § 9.03 (c).
[25] Vgl. Herbert (oben N. 1) § 17.05.
[26] Vgl. hierzu auch Lynn M. LoPucki/ William C. Whiteford, „Bargaining over Equity's Share in the Bankruptcy Reorganization of Large, Publicly Held Companies", 139 *U.Pa.L.Rev.* 125.

1. Variante: Vorliegen gewisser Grundvoraussetzungen und Zustimmung aller Gläubigergruppen zum Plan:

Ein Sanierungsplan kann zunächst bewilligt werden, wenn folgende Voraussetzungen gegeben sind:

Grundvoraussetzungen für die Bewilligung des Plans:

- Die Gläubiger dürfen nicht schlechter gestellt werden, als wenn das Unternehmen in einem Verfahren nach chapter 7 liquidiert worden wäre (11 U.S.C. § 1129 (a) (7); sog. „best interest test");
- Der Plan muss die volle Bezahlung der privilegierten Gläubiger vorsehen (11 U.S.C. § 1129 (a) (9)). Die Bezahlung muss jedoch nicht bereits bei der Bewilligung des Plans erfolgen oder sichergestellt werden. Vielmehr genügt es, wenn die Bezahlung während der Dauer des Plans erfolgt.
- Der Plan muss schliesslich auch gegenüber den nicht privilegierten Gläubigern als erfüllbar erscheinen (11 U.S.C. § 1129 (a) (11); sog. „feasibility"). Wie die hohe Rate der Verfahren, die später nicht erfüllt werden, zeigt, werden dabei an diese Voraussetzung in der Praxis keine hohen Anforderungen gestellt.[27]

Gutheissung des Plans durch alle Gläubigergruppen:

Zusätzliche Voraussetzung bei dieser 1. Variante ist, dass sämtliche Gläubigergruppen dem Plan zustimmen (11 U.S.C. § 1129 (a) (8)). Innerhalb der Gläubigergruppen muss dabei die Mehrheit der Forderungen (nicht Gläubiger!), die zusammen mindestens 2/3 der Forderungssumme einer Gruppe ausmachen, für den Plan stimmen (11 U.S.C. § 1126). Gläubigergruppen, die voll befriedigt werden, gelten dabei zum Vornherein als zustimmende Gruppen.

2. Möglichkeit: Richterliche Bewilligung des Plans entgegen dem Willen der Mehrheit der Gläubiger (sog. „cramdown"):

Eine wichtige Besonderheit des amerikanischen Konkursrechts besteht darin, dass ein Sanierungsplan letztlich gegen den Willen der Mehrheit der Gläubiger bewilligt werden kann (11 U.S.C. § 1129 (b))! Ein solches cramdown, wie dieser Vorgang allgemein bezeichnet wird, verlangt folgende Voraussetzungen:

- Erfüllung der eben genannten Grundvoraussetzungen.
- Zustimmung lediglich einer Gläubigergruppe (11 U.S.C. § 1129 (a) (10))!

---

[27] Herbert (oben N. 1) § 17.15 (C).

– Einhaltung der sog. „absolute priority rule" als zusätzliche Voraussetzung (vgl. 11 U.S.C. § 1129 (b)):[28] Das bedeutet, dass die Prioritätsregel (keine Befriedigung von nachgehenden Forderungen, falls die vorgehenden Forderungen nicht voll bezahlt werden) in jedem Fall eingehalten werden muss. So dürfen insbesondere die bisherigen Eigner grundsätzlich nichts – auch nicht in Form von Anteilen am Unternehmen – behalten, falls nicht alle vorgehenden Gläubiger voll gedeckt werden. Anderes gilt nach der Rechtsprechung nur, wenn die Eigner in massgeblichem Umfang neue Mittel einschiessen (sog. „new value exception to the absolute priority rule").[29]

3.3.8 *Mass tort liability und chapter 11*

Wie bereits eingangs erwähnt wurde, sehen sich viele Unternehmen, die von Opfern von fehlerhaften Produkten für horrende Summen belangt werden, gezwungen, ein Verfahren nach chapter 11 einzuleiten. Es lässt sich somit sagen: Das extrem opfer – bzw. Gläubigerfreundliche amerikanische Haftpflichtrecht wird durch das extrem schuldnerfreundliche Konkursrecht auf das gesunde Mass reduziert.[30]

4. DIE 10 FUNDAMENTALSTEN UNTERSCHIEDE DES VERFAHRENS NACH CHAPTER II ZUM SCHWEIZERISCHEN NACHLASSVERFAHRENSRECHT

4.1 Kurzcharakterisierung des schweizerischen Nachlassverfahrens[31]

Beim Nachlassvertrag nach Art. 293ff. SchKG handelt es sich um ein Verfahren zur Erlangung eines Zwangsvergleichs, der der Zustimmung einer qualifizierten Mehrheit der Gläubiger bedarf und nach Bewilligung durch das Nachlassgericht auch für die nicht zustimmenden Gläubiger verbindlich ist. Inhalt des Zwangsvergleichs können insbesondere Teilerlass und/oder Stundung der Forderungen (Art. 314

---

[28] Diese Regel wird aus der in dieser Bestimmung umschriebenen Voraussetzung hergeleitet, der Plan müsse „fair and equitable" sein. Treister et al (oben N. 1) § 9.04 (f) (2).

[29] Herbert (oben N. 1) § 17.15 (4) und die dort zitierten Entscheide; Warren (oben N. 1) S. 234ff.

[30] Zu den besonderen Problemen, die sich bei Massenklagen aus Produktehaftpflicht stellen siehe Herbert, ibid., § 22.02.

[31] Literaturauswahl zum Nachlassvertrag nach revidiertem Recht: Hunkeler; Dominik Gasser, „Das neue Sanierungsverfahren", 57 *BlSchK* (1993) S. 201ff.; derselbe, „Nachlassverfahren, Insolvenzerklärung und Feststellung neuen Vermögens nach revidiertem SchKG", 132 *ZBJV* (1996) S. 1ff.; Christoph Stäubli, „Konkursaufschub/Nachlassvertrag/Einvernehmliche private Schuldenbereinigung", 115 *ZSR NF* (1996-I) S. 138ff.; Alexander Vollmer, *Basler Kommentar* (Basel 1998) Art. 293 – 304 SchKG; Hans Ulrich Hardmeier, Basler Kommentar (Basel 1998) Art. 305 – 313 SchKG; Jürg Guggisberg, *Basler Kommentar* (Basel 1998) Art. 314 – 316 SchKG; A. Winkelmann/ L. Lévy/ V. Jeanneret/ O. Merkt/ F. Birchler, *Basler Kommentar* (Basel 1998) Art. 317 – 332 SchKG.

SchKG) oder Abtretung eines Vermögensteils an die Gläubiger (Art. 317ff. SchKG) sein. Voraussetzung für die Bewilligung durch das Nachlassgericht ist (unter anderem) Bezahlung oder Sicherstellung der privilegierten Gläubiger und der Nachlassdividende (Art. 306 Abs. 2 Ziff. 2 SchKG). Das Verfahren unterteilt sich in die Phase der Nachlassstundung, das Verfahren zur Bewilligung des Nachlassvertrages durch das Gericht und allenfalls der Erfüllung des Nachlassvertrages. Während der Dauer der Nachlassstundung steht der Schuldner unter der relativ strengen Kontrolle des Sachwalters (insb. Art. 295 und 298 SchKG).

4.2   Die 10 wichtigsten Unterschiede

Nachfolgend sollen die 10 wichtigsten Unterschiede des Nachlassverfahrensrechts nach Art. 293ff. SchKG zum Sanierungsverfahren nach chapter 11, wie dies oben unter C dargestellt worden ist, aufgezeigt werden.

1.   Stundung: Die Nachlassstundung nach Art. 293 SchKG wird nur auf ein eingehend begründetes Gesuch hin bewilligt, während dem der automatic stay des amerikanischen Sanierungsrecht, wie schon sein Name sagt, automatisch eintritt. Die Nachlassstundung kann sodann maximal auf 24 Monate verlängert werden (Art. 295 Abs. 4 SchKG). Der automatic stay kennt demgegenüber grundsätzlich keine zeitlichen Schranken.

2.   Stellung des Schuldners: Der amerikanische Schuldner führt grundsätzlich als DIP die Geschäfte in eigener Regie weiter. Im schweizerischen Recht steht demgegenüber der Schuldner unter der Kontrolle eines gerichtlich bestellten Sachwalters (insb. Art. 295 und 298 SchKG).

3.   Inhalt des Plans: Betreffend den Inhalt des Sanierungsplans ist als praktisch wesentlicher Unterschied hervorzuheben, dass die privilegierten Forderungen und die Nachlassdividende im schweizerischen Recht bei Bewilligung des Vertrages bezahlt oder hinlänglich sichergestellt werden müssen (Art. 306 Abs. 2 Ziff. 2 SchKG).[32] Demgegenüber hat der amerikanische Schuldner grundsätzlich lediglich darzulegen, dass die Bezahlung dieser Forderungen über die Plandauer als machbar (feasible) erscheint .

4.   Rückgängigmachung von Handlungen zum Nachteil der Gläubiger: Im schweizerischen Recht kommt eine Rückgangigmachung von Handlungen zum Nachteil der Gläubiger lediglich beim Nachlassvertrag mit Vermögensabtretung,

---

[32] Obwohl das Gesetz nur von „hinlänglicher" Sicherstellung spricht, wird in der Praxis stets eine umfassende Sicherstellung verlangt. Hardmeier, ibid., Rz 22 zu Art. 306 SchKG.

nicht jedoch beim Stundung- oder Prozentvergleich in Frage (Art. 331 Abs. 1 SchKG). Das amerikanische Recht lässt demgegenüber eine Anfechtung in allen Formen von Sanierungsplänen zu.

5. Eingriff in Vertragsrechte: Das schweizerische Recht kennt die Möglichkeit des Schuldners bzw. des Konkursverwalters, sich über die Erfüllung oder Nichterfüllung eines Vertrages auszusprechen lediglich im Konkurs-, d.h. im Liquidierungsverfahren (Art. 211 SchKG). Im Sanierungsverfahren ist dies jedoch, anders als im amerikanischen Recht, nicht möglich.[33]

6. Gesicherte Gläubiger: Das Nachlassverfahren nach SchKG lässt dingliche Rechte – abgesehen vom Aufschub der Pfandverwertung (vgl. Art. 297 Abs. 1 und Art. 306a SchKG) – völlig unangetastet. Im US-Recht müssen sich die gesicherten Gläubiger demgegenüber gewisse Einschränkungen, insbesondere die Spaltung der Forderung in einen gesicherten und einen ungesicherten Teil, gefallen lassen. Dafür haben sie anders als im schweizerischen Recht ausnahmsweise die Möglichkeit, die Aufhebung der Nachlassstundung für ein Sicherungsrecht zu erlangen.

7. Bildung von Gläubigergruppen: Im schweizerischen Recht bilden grundsätzlich alle ungesicherten Gläubiger eine Gläubigergruppe. Eine Ungleichbehandlung von Gläubigern wird nur ganz ausnahmsweise zugelassen.[34] Für das amerikanische Recht ist es demgegenüber typisch, dass die Gläubiger in Gruppen von gleichgelagerten Interessen eingeteilt und alsdann auch unterschiedlich behandelt werden.

8. Bewilligung des Plans: Eine Sanierungsplan nach chapter 11 kann entgegen dem Willen der Gläubigermehrheit bewilligt werden (sog. „cramdown"). Im schweizerischen Recht muss demgegenüber die Mehrheit der Gläubiger nach Art. 305 SchKG in jedem Fall zustimmen.

9. Spezialisierungsgrad von Richter und Anwaltschaft: Das amerikanische Sanierungsrecht ist getragen von einer hoch spezialisierten Richter- und Anwaltschaft. In der Schweiz findet sich demgegenüber eine gewisse Spezialisierung von Anwalt- und Richterschaft lediglich in grossen Kantonen bzw. Gerichtsbezirken. So werden etwa Nachlassgesuche am Bezirksgericht Zürich, dem grössten Gericht

---

[33] Im Rahmen der SchKG-Revision wurden eine Übernahme von Art. 211 SchKG in das Nachlassverfahrensrecht geprüft. Schliesslich wurde diese jedoch mit folgender Begründung verworfen: „Derartige Normen wären . . . nicht nur dogmatisch schwer zu rechtfertigen, sie würden auch allzu sehr in die Rechtsverhältnisse des Schuldners mit Dritten eingreifen, was nur für den Fall der Generalexekution durch Konkurs gerechtfertigt ist . . .". Bericht Sanierungsrecht, S. 13.

[34] Hans Fritzsche/ Hans Ulrich Walder, *Schuldbetreibung und Konkurs nach schweizerischem Recht*, Bd. II (Zürich 1993) S. 630.

in der Schweiz, stets von der gleichen Richterperson, die ausschliesslich für Nach-
lass- und Konkurssachen zuständig ist, behandelt. In den meisten Teilen der
Schweiz gehört demgegenüber das Nachlassverfahrensrecht zu den unzähligen
Rechtsgebieten, mit denen sich ein Gerichtspräsident mit umfassender sachlicher
Zuständigkeit in Zivil- und Strafsachen bzw. ein Anwalt mit allgemeiner Praxis be-
fasst.

10. Imageverlust: In Amerika hält sich der Imageverlust eines Unternehmens, das
sich in einem chapter 11-Verfahren befindet, offenbar in Grenzen. In der Schweiz
wird demgegenüber von den Gläubigern die Einleitung eines Nachlassverfahrens
weitgehend einer Konkurseröffnung gleichgestellt.

5.   ZUR FRAGE DER REVISIONSBEDÜRFTIGKEIT DES REVIDIERTEN
      NACHLASSVERFAHRENSRECHTS

Bei der am 1.1.1997 in Kraft getretenen Totalrevision des SchKG war man sich bewusst, dass das Nachlassverfahrensrecht eigentlich der umfassenden Überarbeitung bedürfte.[35] Wörtlich heisst es hierzu im Bericht zum Sanierungsrecht: „Die
Schaffung eines eigentlichen Sanierungsrechts für notleidende Unternehmen mit
weitreichenden Eingriffen in die Gläubigerrechte nach amerikanischem Vorbild
wäre allenfalls wünschenswert, ist aber ohne breiter angelegte Studie, verbunden
mit einem Vernehmlassungsverfahren, in kurzer Zeit nicht zu verwirklichen. . .“[36]
Entsprechend beschränkte man sich auf wenige punktuelle Änderungen. Hiervon
sind die praktisch bedeutsamsten: Verlängerung der Nachlassstundung, Herabset-
zung des erforderlichen Quorums für die Zustimmung zum Nachlassvertrag und
Ermöglichung des Verkaufs von Grundstücken und Unternehmensteilen bereits
während der Nachlassstundung.[37] Schon jetzt steht fest, dass das Nachlassverfahrensrecht trotz dieser begrüssenswerten Änderungen wohl kaum grössere Verbrei-
tung erfahren wird.[38] Hierzu wäre vielmehr eine tiefgreifende Umgestaltung not-

---

[35] Zu dieser Überzeugung kam man allerdings erst bei der Beratung des Entwurfes des Bundesrates
in der Kommission des Nationalrates. Veranlasst durch einen Antrag von Nationalrat Couchepin, dem
heutigen Bundesrat, setzte das Bundesamt für Justiz nachträglich eine Expertengruppe für das Sanierungsrecht ein (Bericht Sanierungsrecht, S. 1). In der Botschaft des Bundesrates zum SchKG von 1991
hatte es noch optimistisch geheissen, dass Nachlassverfahrensrecht sei ein „durchaus" modernes Sanierungsrecht, „worum im Ausland noch gerungen wird." (S. 9).

[36] Bericht Sanierungsrecht S. 13.

[37] Siehe hierzu die oben in Fussnote 31 zitierte Literatur.

[38] In den ersten drei Jahren seit Inkrafttreten des neuen Rechts haben die Bewilligungen von Nach-
lassverträgen nicht wesentlich zugenommen. Die entsprechenden Zahlen lauten: 131 (1998), 113
(1997) gegenüber durchschnittlich 144 von 1992 bis 1996.

wendig gewesen, wie sie im obigen Zitat der Expertengruppe zum Sanierungsrecht angesprochen wird.

Diese kurzen rechtsvergleichenden Ausführungen zum amerikanischen Sanierungsrecht zeigen, in welche Richtung eine solch tiefgreifende Revision gehen könnte. In Betracht fallen dabei vor allem folgende Instrumente: Lockerung des Erfordernisses, die Nachlassdividende sicherzustellen, Aufnahme von Art. 211 SchKG in das Sanierungsrecht und Möglichkeit der Rückgängigmachung von anfechtbaren Handlungen in allen Formen des Nachlassvertrages. Ein wesentlicher Beitrag zur Effizienzsteigerung des Nachlassverfahrensrecht könnte m.E. auch durch die Schaffung von interkantonalen bzw. überregionalen Spezialgerichten geleistet werden.

Summary
Chapter II and the Swiss Reorganization Procedure – Comparative Perspectives

This article compares the reorganisation of business enterprises according to chapter 11 U.S. Bankruptcy Code with the Swiss reorganisation procedure (the so called "Nachlassverfahren"). It answers the question why the American procedure, unlike its Swiss counterpart, is such a powerful tool for business enterprises in financial distress. The author reaches the conclusion that the reason for this difference is not only because American law is much more debtor-friendly. An additional crucial factor is the application in practice of the American Bankruptcy Law by highly qualified and specialised judges and lawyers. By contrast, in Switzerland specialised judges and lawyers are mainly to be found in urban areas of the larger cantons, whereas in other parts of Switzerland the reorganisation procedure is usually handled by judges and lawyers who have no special training in this field.

A Few Questions on the Matter of International Uniformity of Solutions and Nationality as a Connecting Factor

Franco Mosconi[*]

1.   INTRODUCTION

I would like here to return to the matter of equality of treatment of the *lex fori* and the applicable foreign law and to the matter of international uniformity – or harmonization of solutions – with regard to the conflict rules autonomously laid down by the national legislators. I shall then conclude with a question as to the relevance of nationality as a connecting factor in current times.

These are, of course, recurring and central issues of private international law, but my comments will be kept to a minimum, in harmony with the teaching of my mentor who wrote as follows when he was still quite young: "Il Diritto Internazionale Privato, richiedendo per sua natura il contemperamento di esigenze diverse, lo sviluppo equilibrato di principi non contrastanti in linea di massima e quindi

---

[*] Professor of International Law, University of Pavia and Catholic University of Milan.

J. Basedow et al., eds., Private Law in the International Arena – Liber Amicorum Kurt Siehr
© 2000, T.M.C.Asser Press, The Hague, The Netherlands

combinabili ma contraddittori se integralmente applicati, è veramente, per dirla col Pillet, « una scienza di sacrifici' ».[1]

2. RESOLUTIONS OF THE INSTITUT DE DROIT INTERNATIONAL

2.1 The Siena Session, 1952

I shall essentially refer to some important resolutions of the Institut de droit international, commencing from the somewhat concise resolution which finally saw the light of day, after a rather laborious gestation period, at the 1952 session in Siena and which bears the title: "The influence of Demographic Conditions on the Settlement of Conflict of Laws".[2] Starting from the consideration that "the influence of demographic conditions on private international law – like that of political factors – should be kept within certain limits", the resolution then addresses the legislators affirming two principles:

> "1. The rules of private international law should not, for demographic reasons, make use of connecting factors (*points de rattachement*) which give rise to a difference between the spheres of application of national and foreign legislation.
> 2. The rules of private international law should, generally speaking, use criteria which are capable of internationalization, i.e., which lend themselves, in particular, to adoption in international conventions, thus avoiding the danger of conflicting solutions of a given case in different countries."

This subject, chosen by the Bureau and entrusted to José de Yanguas Messía, Professor of Private International Law at the University of Madrid, gave rise to no few uncertainties. Such uncertainties were based on the verification of the different lines of approach contained in the private international law rules of immigration as opposed to emigration States, it having been discovered, albeit not without exceptions, that the former tended to be in favour of using domicile as the principal connecting factor whereas the latter were inclined to give preference to nationality.[3]

---

[1] R. de Nova, *L'estinzione delle obbligazioni convenzionali nel diritto internazionale privato* (Pavia 1930) p. 77: "As by nature Private International Law calls for the tempering of different needs, the balanced development of principles which, generally speaking, do not conflict and are therefore compatible but contradictory if applied in full, so that it is really, to use the words of Pillet, « a science of sacrifices »"; the reference is to A. Pillet, *Principes de droit international privé* (Paris 1903) p. 326.

[2] Institut de droit international, 44 *Annuaire* (1952-II) p. 477; point 1 of the Siena resolution is referred to by W. Wengler, "The General Principles of Private International Law", 104 *Recueil des Cours* (1961-III) pp. 273-465, on p. 368.

[3] Institut de droit international, 44 *Annuaire* (1952-II) p.409.

However, instead of focusing on the traditional dichotomy, the attention of the Rapporteur de Yanguas Messía concentrated on and resulted in a criticism of those about-turns – from that of nationality to that of domicile – due to the influence of demographic factors rather than to the "motifs traditionnels que nous sommes habitués à entendre: identification du domicile avec le milieu social où l'individu développe sa vie juridique, facilité des transactions et de l'accès aux tribunaux". "Le territorialisme né des conditions démographiques" – the rapporteur also writes – "laisse à l'écart le patrimoine juridique de la personne et fixe le centre de gravité de sa doctrine dans les conditions sociales et politiques changeantes, dont l'étranger domicilié subit les conséquences sur son propre statut personnel, mais dont on veut sauver le national à l'étranger en réclamant pour lui le respect – difficile, ainsi, à obtenir – de sa loi d'origine".[4]

Among the remarks made during the final stage of the work, those of Valladão and Perassi would seem to me to be worthy of special mention, but for different reasons. For Haroldo Valladão, Professor of Private International Law at the University of Brazil and the Catholic University of Rio de Janeiro, " . . .le droit international privé est une science foncièrement juridique, multiséculaire, ayant des règles et des préceptes déjà établis; son but est de protéger la personnalité humaine dans son expansion dans l'espace en défendant la justice et l'équité. Il ne peut donc être régi par des facteurs de nature exclusivement politique et d'un caractère purement transitoire, comme une législation fluctuante et occasionnelle dans le genre de celle adoptée pour les tarifs douaniers ou pour les contingents et permis d'importation et d'exportation. Telle serait la destinée du droit international privé si ses règles finissaient par dépendre des mouvements migratoires révélés périodiquement dans chaque pays par les statistiques." Valladão therefore admits that demographic factors may at most have a merely secondary effect and one that is subordinate to factors of a juridical nature, provided that such an effect be "limitée aux matières régies dans presque tous les pays par les principes de la nationalité ou du domicile, c'est-à-dire seulement à la matière du statut".[5]

The observations of Tomaso Perassi, Professor of International Law at the University of Rome, concern the resolution's preamble. It had been proposed that it should be worded to the effect that the influence of the demographic factors, just as that of other factors of a political nature, "ne devrait pas dépasser des limites juridiques qu'il faut respecter". In a concise but incisive comment Perassi criticizes the expression *limites juridiques*: "Si l'on entend par là se référer à des limites découlant du droit international public, l'Institut prendrait position d'une façon

---

[4] Institut de droit international, 43 *Annuaire* (1950-I) p. 475ff.; as far as de Yanguas Messía is concerned, "la préoccupation démographique peut être plus efficacement servie par des procédés autre que celui de règlement territorialiste des conflits de lois: dosage en nombre et, surtout, en origine des immigrants pour mieux assurer leur assimilation; facilités et encouragements pour l'accès à la nationalité...".

[5] Institut de droit international, 44 *Annuaire* (1952) p. 414 and p. 415.

incidente sur la question de savoir si le droit international public comporte des limites à la liberté de chaque Etat d'adopter ses propres règles de droit international privé. On ne saurait, d'autre part, préciser ces limites, comme on l'a suggéré, par référence aux principes fondamentaux de droit international privé, l'existence de ces principes, en tant que principes juridiques, ne pouvant être catégoriquement affirmée".[6]

For my part, I would only underscore the following. In point 2 the Siena Resolution, by suggesting the use of criteria which are capable of being internationalized, explicitly refers to connecting factors that can be used in international treaties. In essence, therefore, the suggestion that States should conclude international treaties, thereby regulating the matter, is implied in the resolution adopted by the Institut in Siena.

2.2   The Santiago de Compostela Session, 1990

Many years later, at the Santiago de Compostela session in 1990, the Institut stated that it "deems it useful to elaborate and supplement" the Siena resolution and to adopt a far broader and more complex new resolution entitled "Equality of treatment of the law of the forum and foreign law".[7]

Of the numerous affirmations on which the preamble bases such a new stance, the most significant one would appear to me to be the one according to which "international harmonization is one of the objectives that States are to pursue in establishing and implementing choice of law rules" as well as the one according to which "the adoption of bilateral choice of law rules tends usually to favour this

---

[6] Institut de droit international, 44 *Annuaire* (1952-II) p. 421. For some comments with regard to the *vexata quaestio* of the (public) international law/foundations of private international law see F. Mosconi, "Exceptions to the Operation of Choice of Law Rules", 217 *Recueil des Cours* (1989-V) pp. 9-214, on p. 19ff. Recently, see Ch.G. Weeramantry, "Private International Law and Public International Law", *Riv.dir.int.priv.proc.* (1998) pp. 313-324, in the speech, that he delivered in his capacity as Deputy President of the International Court of Justice, to the European Group for Private International Law on the occasion of the latter's visit to the Palais de la Paix, in The Hague, *Weeramantry* observes that: "there seems to be a need now for greater interaction between these two disciplines which at one stage were considered to be separate bodies of learning. They are slowly moving closer together and interacting and intersecting more frequently under the influence of irresistible global forces" (p. 313).

[7] Institut de droit international, 63 *Annuaire* (1990-II) p. 333ff. This is a subject which has been extensively addressed by E. Vitta, "Cours général de droit international privé", 162 *Recueil des Cours* (1979-I) pp. 9-243, especially p. 45ff. (his previous writings on the matter are also mentioned in the bibliography). After having maintained that "[l]es origines du principe d'égalité se trouvent dans les théories de P. S. Mancini" (p. 45), Vitta – preceding the Institut – so concludes: "Or nous estimons que, quel que soit le futur du principe de nationalité dans les conflits de lois (et son importance y est ancore bien grande), le principe d'égalité, tel qu'il ressort du système mancinien, continuera à jouer un rôle de premier plan dans les conflits de lois. En effet il s'agit d'un principe à prendre en considération non seulement pour apprécier les systèmes ayant à leur base la nationalité, mais aussi bien les systèmes fondés sur le domicile ou n'importe quel autre rattachement" (p. 49).

objective", while it is assumed that "it is contrary to a balanced and open-minded regulation of international relations to regard the law of the forum as superior in nature to foreign law".

Among the recommendations which the States should follow "unless their essential interests require otherwise", the most interesting here would appear to be the following: "(a) adopt choice of law rules based on connecting factors which lead to the application of foreign law under the same conditions as lead to the application of the law of the forum; and consequently, (b) refrain from adopting choice of law rules which broaden the scope of the application of the law of the forum as against that of foreign law; and, in particular, exclude such rules whenever their application would result in discrimination between parties based on factors under which one of them is personally connected to the state of the forum such as *nationality* or *religion*".[8]

The impression that one gains from such a resolution and from the reports prepared by Pierre Gannagé, Professor at the University of Beirut, is that, despite a certain caution expressed in the preamble (" . . .international harmonization is one of the objectives"), the Institut nevertheless continued to consider the conflictual method as the main and preferable method of co-ordination between the different legal systems[9] and international harmony as the primary objective of such co-ordination.

---

[8] Institut de droit international, 63 *Annuaire* (1990-II) p. 333ff. (emphasis added). Seeing religion placed alongside the traditional connecting factor of nationality gives one an idea of the concerns that led to the resolution of the Institut in 1990. As to letter (b), a precise example of a solution to be avoided can be inferred from Article 310 of the French Civil Code "qui dans le domaine du divorce, pour fixer le domaine de la loi française, se fonde aussi sur un double rattachement, nationalité et domicile, de manière à appliquer celle-ci aux français domiciliés à l'étranger comme aux étrangers domiciliés en France". Along these lines see the draft report by Pierre Gannagé, in Institut de droit international, 63 *Annuaire* (1989-I) p. 219. It may be of interest to note that this solution was taken into consideration by P. Picone, *I metodi di coordinamento tra ordinamenti nel progetto di riforma del diritto internazionale privato italiano,* now also in the volume, *La Riforma italiana del diritto internazionale privato* (Padua 1998) pp. 3-53, on pp. 12-13, as a possible amendment of the experts' draft in view of the interest which Italian law has in governing family relationships concerning foreigners who may be resident in Italy. In fact, the solution of Article 310 of the French Civil Code may well appear to be lacking in elegance, but it is probably also practical and by no means pointless. Nevertheless, as will be stated next in the text, the Institut seems to have difficulty in admitting that the respective legislator of private international law should be guided by considerations relating to the social reality and legal characteristics of his own legal system.

[9] See the draft report by Gannagé, in Institut de droit international, 63 *Annuaire* (1989-I) p. 205ff., on p. 215: "Méthode objective qui consacre l'application de la loi avec laquelle cette situation présente les liens les plus significatifs ... Le bilatéralisme a en effet pour conséquence de fonder la désignation de la loi applicable essentiellement sur l'analyse des matières et des situations juridiques qui conduit le législateur ou le juge à choisir l'élément de rattachement le plus significatif, le plus approprié. Et cet élément pourra indiquer la loi étrangère, comme la loi du for". The highlighting of an important aspect is, however, lacking: is the most significant connecting factor the one considered to be such by the individual legislator (based on his own point of view) or does the principle mean that there are significant connecting factors (by necessity as far as all the legislators are concerned) or should the evaluation attempt to be absolute?

In actual fact, in all private international law systems one can find both rules which are aimed at making national legal systems more conducive and open to foreign legal systems as well as rules which are opposed to this aim and permit each national system to withdraw into its own shell. It is a complex phenomenon which involves both the legislator (or a general rule that can be inferred from legal precedents) and the judiciary[10] and harmony between the two levels does not necessarily exist, given that open-oriented written rules of Private International Law may well be construed to the contrary by forum-orientated court decisions, whereas legislation demonstrating little inclination towards internationalism may well be construed by an open-minded judiciary.

3.   INTERNATIONAL UNIFORMITY AS A NON-ABSOLUTE VALUE

3.1   **A Value which Co-exists with Other Values**

As the Institut almost reluctantly admits, there seems to be nothing reprehensible about the fact that a legislator may, intentionally, decide to retain, with respect to the search for international uniformity of solutions, considerations linked to social reality and to the legal system in which and with regard to which they operate.[11]

It does not seem possible to give any absolute value to the search for international harmonization upon which the legislator should base his statutes,[12] even at the cost of sacrificing other values (and at the same time acknowledging the lack of neutrality incumbent in choice of law rules) such as, for example the observance of equal dignity of spouses or other family-related principles, the protection of the weaker party, the protection of the safety (reliability) of a commercial or financial

---

[10] Cf. F. Mosconi, "Lex fori v. lex causae", *Riv.dir.int.priv.proc.* (1990) pp. 813-820.

[11] Because of its inconsistency, the choice made by the Italian legislator with regard to *renvoi* is even more baffling, inasmuch as he would seem to seek uniformity of solutions by means of Article 13.1 (a) which permits transmission (*renvoi au second degré*), while appearing to waive it (in most cases) under (b) which, resorting to an inevitable expedient, brings about the interruption of the inextricable circle, accepting remission (*renvoi au premier degré*). For the sake of patriotism it must, however, be said that inconsistency in the matter of *renvoi* is also common to a number of foreign legislations. Cf. the draft report by Gannagé (supra n. 9) p. 234: "Il va de soi que l'égalité recherchée sera compromise par les legislations qui admettent seulement le renvoi à la loi du for et rejettent le renvoi à une loi étrangère. Une pareille attitude sera accueillie avec d'autant plus de réserves que le renvoi à la loi tierce, lorsque cette loi accepte sa compétence, réalise l'harmonie des solutions, effet que ne produit pas le renvoi à la loi du for".

[12] G. Barile would seem instead to attribute an absolute value to the principle of international harmonization of solutions, "Diritto internazionale privato", 12 *Enc. Dir.* (1964) pp. 1035-1055 (while admitting that the construction of positive law must be confined "nei limiti permessi dalla rigidità più o meno pronunciata delle regole vigenti").

market, but also the more general principle of predictability.[13,14] If it is true, as is usually stated, that it is a disadvantage for individuals when a particular case that affects them is treated in a discordant way under the different legal systems to which it
is linked, it is certainly a no less serious disadvantage for individuals not to be able
to make any forecast as to the way in which a certain case will be assessed by each
of the countries with which it is connected and only to know that each of them will
pursue (in its own way in the absence of international conventions) the necessary
harmonization. In other words, is it indeed possible to exclude that it is of any use
for individuals to be able to foresee, with reasonable accuracy, that in State A their
case will be assessed in a certain way (by means of the application of a particular
law) while in State B, possibly, in some other way (by means of the application of a
different law)? It would seem to me that the answer to this question can only be in
the negative: the strong interest of the individual in being aware of the predictability
of the case does exist and I believe that for balancing this factor with respect to the
interest that he or she also has in the uniformity of solutions certain comments by
Wilhelm Wengler concerning the problem of continuous balancing are indeed en-
lightening: "En vertu du principe général de politique léglislative, valable pour tout
le domaine du droit et en particulier pour le droit international privé, les sujets de
droit, avant de si livrer à des actes ou des omissions susceptibles de leur valoir par la
suite des sanctions juridiques en raison d'une sentence judiciaire, devraient avoir la
plus grande certitude sur le droit que le juge va leur appliquer par la suite. . . En tout
cas les justiciables ont plus intérêt à connaître avec certitude le droit applicable
ultérieurement dans un Etat du for qu'à savoir que le juge est prêt à appliquer le
droit qui selon lui est déterminé par la somme la plus importante des éléments de

---

[13] Cf. H. Batiffol, "Les intérêts de droit international privé", in: *Festschrift für G. Kegel* (Frankfurt
a M. 1977) p. 11ff.

[14] The predictability is directly and strictly connected with the certainty of the law or rather it is an
essential aspect thereof (cf. M. Corsale, "Certezza del diritto 1) Profili teorici", 6 *Enciclopedia
giuridica* (1988) p. 1: " . . .dal punto di vista del singolo utente, essa [la certezza del diritto] si traduce in
ultima analisi nella prevedibilità delle consequenze giuridiche della propria azione"). As such it is a
value in each branch of the law and can neither be disregarded nor underestimated in private international law: cf. W. Wengler, "L'évolution moderne du droit international privé et la prévisibilité du droit
applicable", *Revue critique* (1990) pp. 657-674, on pp. 659-660: ". . .ni [la] science [juridique] ni la pratique n'ont guère compris pendant des siècles qu'en fin de compte les sujets du droit privé sont
gravement lésés lorsqu'il ne sont pas à même de prévoir avec la plus grande sécurité possible le droit
que le tribunal compétent va appliquer par l'intermédiaire du rattachement considéré par lui comme
déterminant". For interesting considerations see also P. Hay, "Flexibility versus Predictability and Uniformity in Choice of Law: Reflections on Current European and United States Conflicts Law", *Recueil
des Cours* (1991-I) pp. 9-280, who examines "the goals and objectives of private international law from
the perspective of the tension between predictability and flexibility created by different approaches to
judicial jurisdiction and to choice of law in Europe and in the United States" (Hay uses the term "uniformity" to express the notions of certainty and predictability – with reference to all rules, not only conflict
rules – rather than to express the notion of international harmonization of solutions: see especially pp.
291-292).

rattachement".[15]

Perhaps, even more than the need to guarantee the predictability of the solution, in Private International Law one speaks more frequently of the need for the expectations of the individual(s) concerned to be taken into account in deciding a case. In itself this may simply be another way of expressing the same need for predictability,[16] but it often seems fair to say that that need is required in order to extend judicial discretion and not, instead, to limit it, at the cost therefore of predictability.[17]

Moreover, the observation that the uniformity of solutions cannot prevail over the omnipresent limits of public policy as well as over the mandatory rules of the forum leads one to think that the search for international uniformity of solutions cannot be considered as an absolute value. Here I mean that the search for international uniformity of solutions cannot prevail over the need to preserve the internal consistency of the law of the forum[18] – or rather of the individual legal system – as far as the two components thereof are concerned (substantive law and conflict rules), and also because only the latter need corresponds to the objective interest of an integrated social community in the form of the State, but which – leaving aside the internationalistic fervour of certain statements (Valladão) – is not yet to be found at the international level.[19]

The result outlined above, or in other words the affirmation that the search for international uniformity of solutions cannot be seen as an absolute value that can be imposed upon the legislator, gives rise to a substantial consequence with regard to

---

[15] Wengler (supra n. 14) p. 668. It would seem to me that Wengler's reasoning is even more convincing (also in the light of considerations which will be outlined in the text immediately below) with regard to the principle of international uniformity of solutions rather than with regard to the specific purpose of Wengler's criticism.

[16] This point of view is shared by Wengler (supra n. 14) p. 657ff. who, also using rather suggestive images, carries out a discerning review of a series of legislative and court decision approaches and solutions which, for the most part, broaden the margins of judicial discretion, but jeopardise the possibility of knowing *ex ante* under which law a given case is destined to be determined.

[17] It may be of interest to note that the *Restatement (Second), Conflict of Laws* (1971) Section 6.2, includes in the list of factors of relevance for the purposes of the determination of the applicable law both "the protection of justified expectations" (letter *d*) and, collectively, under a single separate letter (*f*) "certainty, predictability and uniformity of result"; cf. Hay, loc.cit.n.14, especially pp. 371-374. As to certain special aspects see P.E. Nygh, "The Reasonable Expectations of the Parties as a Guide to the Choice of Law in Contract and in Tort", 251 *Recueil des Cours* (1995) pp. 269-400.

[18] Cf. Wengler (supra n. 2) p. 373: "In the present state of private international law it cannot be expected that a state would sacrifice such a strong governmental interest [to apply a certain rule of the *lex fori*] for the sake of the international uniformity of decisions"; and previously by the same author, "Die allgemeinen Rechtsgründsätze und ihre Kollisionen", *Zeit. für öffentliches Recht* (1943-1944) pp. 473-509 (also in *Revue critique* (1952) pp. 595-622, and (1953) pp. 37-60).

[19] It must, however, be noted that there are signs of a possible evolution: for example, as far as criminal law is concerned, under its Statute the International Criminal Court will have jurisdiction over "the most serious crimes of concern to the international community as a whole" (Article 2.1); one must also consider the recently emerged tendency to affirm that as far as certain criminal cases are concerned, the criminal jurisdiction of the individual States is universal.

the interpretation and construction of conflict rules by academic commentators/ scholars and the courts, in the sense that the interpreter may not disregard the intention of the legislator – when it is sufficiently clear – simply because it does not serve the purpose of (alleged) uniform solutions.[20]

3.2 Identifying the Legal Systems with Respect to which Uniformity is Pursued

At this point I must highlight another consideration which concerns the very concept of international harmonization. Harmonization, absolute international uniformity, in space and in time, is not even conceivable in theory.[21] It is, therefore, for the

---

[20] Wengler (supra n. 14) pp. 660-661, after having observed that most of the legislative codifications of private international law "présentent davantage de lacunes que de dispositions positives", writes: "Mais personne ne prétendra sérieusement que le juge national devrait se refuser à observer les directives législatives existantes relatives au droit applicable parce que l'élément de rattachement donné par le législateur n'est pas le 'bon'". These words, in my opinion, may be appropriately "Italianized" and interpreted as an authoritative warning against the risk of the resurfacing of the temptation, which has been witnessed in the past with regard to previously existing conflict rules, to supplement a particular rule or even to amend it by means of solutions deemed to be "better" than those laid down by the legislator. For a well-known example, one may consider the fervour with which Rolando Quadri affirmed his own singular opinions, disregarding "l'obbiezione . . . fondata sulla formulazione letterale delle norme italiane di d.i. privato" contained in the general provisions of the Italian Civil Code of 1942 and, in particular, with regard to "art. 30 disp. prel. che dà soluzione negativa al problema del rinvio". Article 30, so Quadri continues, "presuppone, per poter essere vitale, che il sistema abbia veramente il senso che fu ad esso attribuito dagli autori dell'art. 30. In altri termini l'art. 30, invece che condizionare il senso delle altre norme, è condizionato dalla *esattezza* dell'*opinione* che circa il sistema (articolo 30 dedotto) avevano i suoi autori. Poiché tale opinione, in base a quanto precede [i.e., according to Quadri himself] è erronea, così l'art. 30, mancando il presupposto del suo funzionamento, *vale come non scritto*" (R. Quadri, *Lezioni di diritto internazionale privato,* 5th ed. (Naples 1969) pp. 295-297; the first two emphases are in the text, while the others have been added).

[21] Cf. Wengler (supra n. 2) p. 365, who proposes "the principle of the 'minimum of conflicting decisions', because it cannot be expected that absolute uniformity of decisions will be reached, and because there might be other principles which sometimes require that reliance be placed on an allocation factor, though one may be sure that other states will not do so" (emphasis added). See also E. Vitta, *Diritto internazionale privato,* vol. I (Turin 1972) p. 30, footnote 42 " . . .i sistemi ispirati a tendenze universalistiche possono raggiungere in pratica soluzioni uniformi solo relativamente agli Stati i quali adottino norme di conflitto simili alle loro. Verrà invece meno l'uniformità nei confronti di quegli altri Stati le cui norme siano ispirate da moventi nazionalistici (oppure che perseguano ideali universalistici battendo strade diverse dalle loro)"; Hay (supra n. 14) p. 338: "Multilaterism that is also universal – in which all conflicts law, world-wide, is in harmony and in which international 'harmony of decision' thus prevail in every case – is a 'romantic utopia'" (W. Müller-Freienfels is quoted here, "Über nationales Ziel und nationale Kodifikation internationalen Privatrechts heute", in: *Festschrift für Frank Vischer* (Zurich 1983) p. 223-255). E. Jayme, "Identité culturelle et intégration: Le droit international privé postmoderne", 251 *Recueil des Cours* (1995) pp. 9-268, at p. 89, after having affirmed that "l'harmonie des décisions constitue l'objectif central du droit international privé. . . ", continues as follows: "On a critiqué ce but en objectant que l'harmonie des décisions ne peut pas, en réalité être atteinte. Il est vrai qu'il serait irréel d'y aspirer dans la totalité des cas. A mon avis, il est tout de même bon de décrire une utopie malgré l'existence d'obstacles à sa réalisation".

purposes of harmonization that one recognizes – or takes for granted – that only a particular legal system or the few foreign legal systems which, at a given point in time, appear to be competent in concurrence – and at the same time are in competition – with that of the forum, are to be taken into consideration.[22]

It is not easy, however, to establish which legal system or systems are to be considered competent for the purpose of pursuing uniformity. The one that is considered as such – i.e., competent – by the majority of the other legal systems? The one that considers itself as such? The one that is considered as such by the legal system of the forum? The inadequacy of the first solution clearly emerges from the difficulty and the relativism inherent in the statistical investigation that it entails. But not even the second prospect appears immune from criticism and doubts when one simply considers the by no means remote possibility that more than one foreign legal system may consider itself to be competent. If, therefore, one wishes to avoid far from satisfactory majority solutions (such as: international harmonization can be attained by means of the solution which satisfies the majority of the legal systems which consider themselves to be competent), then one may only overcome this difficulty by resorting to the third solution which, moreover, is actually the one within the scope of which the desire for international harmonization more or less explicitly falls. Which foreign legal system or systems are to be considered for the purposes of the search for uniformity, for harmony, can be determined from the legal system of the forum – albeit, in order to avoid a one-way mirror effect, not from a specific conflict rule but from its private international law system as a whole.[23]

This amounts to relativizing the principle of international uniformity to a considerable extent, especially as the relativization concerns both the time when the conflict rule was laid down by the legislator and the time when it is actually applied.[24]

At this level the individual judge experiences the same pressures which, as I have already said, can be perceived on the part of the legislator in terms of being more conducive and open to other legal systems or, alternatively, looking inwardly

---

[22] One often speaks of the legal systems concerned and of the laws present, but it is, obviously, a matter of vague expressions, which in themselves are inadequate for the purposes of furnishing a basis for precise and concrete reasoning.

[23] The conceptual operation referred to is of the kind made by R. de Nova, "Quando un contratto è 'internazionale'?", *Riv.dir.int.priv.proc.* (1978) pp. 665-680 (and, under the title "Wann ist ein Vertrag 'international'?", in: *Konflikt und Ordnung. Festschrift für Murad Ferid* (Munich 1978) pp. 307-323). It must also be underlined that, as it is a matter of family relationships, the various connecting factors should apply not only to each of the persons involved in the relationship itself but also – in order to avoid any antinomies – to the persons involved in relationships connected with the former (for instance, marriage and filiation: both the spouses and each of the children): which gives rise to an extension of the area of harmonization to be pursued and to increased difficulties which have to be overcome.

[24] Cf. G. Kegel, "Paternal Home and Dream House – Traditional Conflict of Law and the American Reformers", *AJCL* (1979) p. 615ff.

(to safeguard internal consistency) to the legal system of the forum. For the judge too, the search for international harmonization does not rank as an absolute value.

It is perhaps worthwhile adding that these considerations only apply in the case of conflict rules autonomously laid down by the national legislator. Uniform conflict rules, or in other words those laid down by means of international conventions or measures adopted by international organizations (such as Community regulations and directives), are established with a view to achieving uniformity and naturally it is from this standpoint that they should be interpreted and applied, as it is authoritatively pointed out in the Italian law of 1995: "The interpretation of [international] conventions shall take into account their international character as well as the need for uniform application" (Article 2, paragraph 2).[25]

4.   THE CONFLICT BETWEEN NATIONALITY AND DOMICILE AS CONNECTING FACTORS

It should also be noted that the problem of international harmonization has traditionally been much debated with regard to the use of nationality as a connecting factor as opposed to that of domicile: a conflict which is based on reasons of a demographic nature[26] which certainly cannot be convincingly argued one way or the other.

At the 1987 Cairo session the Institut de droit international devoted an analytical resolution to "The duality of the nationality principle and the domicile principle in private international law", in which it recognized that such dualism "remains an important problem of private international law".[27] The recommendation addressed to the States is to permit the testator, on the one hand, and spouses, on the other, to

---

[25] An English translation of Law No. 218 of 31 May 1995 is given in 35 *International Legal Materials* (1996) p. 760. Not even conventional conflict rules are, moreover, in themselves immune from the divergence of the interpretative processes, the main causes of which are "The specific features of national legal traditions, the tendency of the judges to use the legal categories most familiar to them, variations in the different language versions, the different techniques for transposing a convention into the national legal systems": A. Tizzano, *Report on the Protocols on the Interpretation of the Law applicable to Contractual Obligations, Signed in Brussels on 19 December 1988, OJ(EC)* [1980] C 219 of 3 September 1980.

[26] For an extensive review see the final Yanguas Messía report, Institut de droit international, 43 *Annuaire* (1950-I) p. 461ff. Also the Loussouarn report on *La dualité des principes de nationalité et de domicile en droit international privé* (in: Institut de droit international, 62 *Annuaire* (1987-I) p. 295ff., especially pp. 328-329 and 334 and 338 – which will be covered in the text below – devotes special attention to the importance of demographic factors in determining the said duality and emphasizes the fact that the increasing complexity of migratory phenomena renders the drawing up of satisfactory proposals more difficult with regard to the private international law aspects.

[27] Institut de droit international, 62 *Annuaire* (1987-II) p. 290ff.; cf. A.E. von Overbeck, "Renvoi in the Institute of International Law", *AJCL* (1963) p. 439.

choose to subject his or her succession or, respectively, their marriage either to the law of nationality or to the law of domicile and, similarly, in matters of matrimonial property regimes, States should allow spouses to select either the law of nationality or the law of domicile of either of them. In cases of conflict between personal laws, the Resolution recommends that "(a) States whose rules of conflicts of law give effect to the law of the nationality should apply the law of the common domicile when persons involved in the legal relationship in question are of different nationalities, and there is no good reason to prefer the law of one or other nationality; (b) States whose rules of conflicts of law give effect to the law of the domicile should apply the law of the common nationality when the persons involved in the legal relationship in question do not have a common domicile, and there is no good reason to prefer the law of one or other domicile."

In these recommendations one can hear the echo of an attempt that was made many years ago by The Hague Conference on Private International Law, but which ultimately proved to be a dismal failure. I am referring to the Hague Convention of 15 June 1955 to regulate the conflicts between the national law and the law of domicile, which only obtained two ratifications and died an early death. It established that account should be taken of the *renvoi* made by national law to the law of the domicile, thereby obliging the contracting States to give (a certain) preference to domicile as a connecting factor, which was to be understood, moreover, according to the definition offered by the convention itself, as meaning the habitual place of residence.[28] It would, however, be arbitrary to confine the problem of international harmonization to the settlement of the conflict between *lex patriae* and *lex domicilii*; other connecting factors can, in fact, be envisaged and used.

In particular, Articles 29 and 31 of the Italian law of 1995, in concurrence with the connecting factor of the common nationality of the spouses, as well as Article 39, in concurrence with the connecting factors of common nationality and common domicile of the adopters, use the (new) connecting factor of the main location of matrimonial life, a criterion which constitutes the transposition and specification of

---

[28] With regard to this agreement, see R. de Nova, "Accettabilità della Convenzione dell'Aja sul rinvio", *Scritti di diritto internazionale privato* (Padua 1977) pp. 106-115 (also in *Studi in onore di G.M. De Francesco*, vol. I (Milan 1957) pp. 173-181), who, after having noted that, in fact, as a result of the conflict between *lex patriae* and *lex domicilii* "è sorto il problema, che tanta confusione ha gettato nella teoria e nella prassi del diritto internazionale privato moderno", observed that "sarebbe una specie di riparazione se il rinvio dovesse operare . . . come rimedio (sia pure parziale) agli inconvenienti che derivano dalla pluralità dei sistemi vigenti di diritto internazionale privato!" (pp. 110-111). With regard to the 1955 Convention see, among others, E. Rabel, "Suggestions for a Convention on Renvoi", *Int. Law Quarterly* (1951) pp. 402-411, and in *Gesammelte Aufsätze,* vol. II (Tübingen 1965) pp. 439-447; G. Sauser-Hall, "La septième session de la Conférence de d.i.p. de La Haye (9-31 octobre 1951)", *Annuaire suisse de dr.int.* (1951) pp. 113-124; Ph. Francescakis, "La Convention de La Haye de 1955 pour régler les conflits entre la loi nationale et la loi du domicile", *Travaux du comité français de droit international privé 1958/59* (Paris 1960) pp. 151-169.

the closest connecting factor.[29] Harmonization should, therefore, certainly be sought in that direction as well, while bearing in mind the complication deriving from the rather wide margin of discretion[30] with which each judge will determine the place where a given matrimonial or family relationship is to be deemed as being mainly located.

5.   THE CURRENT ROLE OF NATIONALITY AS A CONNECTING FACTOR IN THE SEARCH FOR INTERNATIONAL UNIFORMITY OF SOLUTIONS

Here, even though many national legislators, including the Italian legislator, continue to remain loyal to the role of nationality as a connecting factor (at least in principle), it is perhaps worthwhile asking oneself whether nationality is indeed a connecting factor which really meets the realities of the present day and whether – in essence – it is the same connecting factor which was theorized and "imposed" by Pasquale Stanislao Mancini in the mid-19th century.

In this respect, it may be of interest to refer to a work that appeared some seventy years ago in Dutch and was translated around forty years ago into Italian, neither of which languages are widely used today. I am referring to a booklet published in 1929 by Roenald Duco Kollewijn[31] which was prompted by two events that had recently occurred – the divorce of the Ferrari (or De Ferrari) couple in France[32] and the denunciation by Switzerland, with effect from 1 June 1929, of the Hague Convention of 12 June 1902 concerning divorce[33] – in order to criticize certain excessive interpretations of the principle of nationality.

As far as the Dutch scholar was concerned, "married women have always been a source of embarrassment in private international law. Especially since they have been intent on gaining an equal footing under the law with respect to men". In actual fact – he observes – "the connecting factor of nationality is of no use when the con-

---

[29] The closest connecting factor had, on the other hand, already been used in other private international law systems and is used in the Italian law (Article 19, paragraph 2) to supplement the connecting factor of nationality in relation to persons in possession of more than one foreign nationality.

[30] See in this regard the critical comments by Wengler (supra n. 14) p. 662ff.

[31] R.D. Kollewijn, *Ontaarding van het nationaliteitsbeginsel in het moderne internationaal privaatrecht,* Weltevreden (1929) and in Italian under the title "Degenerazione del principio di nationalità nel diritto internazionale privato moderno", *Diritto internazionale* (1959) pp. 508-525 (also in ISPI, *Antologia di diritto internazionale privato* (Milan 1964) pp. 77-96). R. De Nova, to whom we owe the translation, stated that he thereby wished to "far conoscere in Italia una critica, ancora attuale, di concezioni, norme e valutazioni giudiziali legate alla 'scuola manciniana' del diritto internazionale privato". The two passages quoted in the text are respectively to be found on p. 520 and p. 524 of the Italian translation, on which the English translation is based.

[32] Now in B. Ancel and Y. Lequette, Grands arrêts de la jurisprudence française de droit international privé, 3rd ed. (Paris 1998) p. 91.

[33] Cf. comment in *Journ.Dr.Int.* (1929) p. 813.

tending parties are of different nationality". In this case, "the factor of the relation-ship that is the same as far as both the husband and the wife are concerned and is capable of determining the law to be applied is their domicile. The law of the coun-try where they live their married life must also govern their marriage".[34] The follow-ing are the arguments submitted: "cases where the husband and wife are not of the same nationality are becoming more and more numerous; cases where they do not have a common domicile, even at the beginning of their marriage, will always re-main *occasioni malsane*. It is not feared that, in accepting the connecting factor of domicile in such cases, marriage law will find itself based upon weak founda-tions . . . It will never be easy to take up permanent residence with wife and children in another country ... the unilateral change of residence by will of one of the spouses only will not be able to exert any influence with regard to the law to be applied".[35]

But Kollewijn also suggested that in order to adequately resolve at least one of the various aspects of the private international law problem concerning marriage the States should "eliminate the difficulty at its very roots" and harmonize their own laws on the matter of granting nationality, accepting under a convention "the rule that a woman who gets married in her own country to a foreigner does not acquire her husband's nationality against her own will, if she continues to live with her hus-band in her own country".[36]

I certainly do not intend to resume here the comparison of the respective advan-tages and disadvantages of nationality and domicile (or the habitual residence) as connecting factors. I would, instead, like to express some doubts as to the lasting relevance of nationality as a connecting factor to the present day, given that the na-ture of the link thereby expressed has changed.

It is, in fact, relevant that the reasons furnished by Mancini, in the middle of the 19th century, to explain the choice of giving preference to nationality concerned the fact that the factors on which the identity of a person was based and established co-incided with those which established nationality and dependent upon which citizen-ship was granted.[37]

---

[34] In this passage, at least in De Nova's Italian translation thereof, it would seem by no means ardu-ous to note the heralding of the prevailing location of matrimonial life as the connecting factor.

[35] Kollewijn, *Degenerazione* (supra n. 31) p. 524.

[36] Kollewijn, *Degenerazione* (supra n. 31) p. 523. In actual fact the relative homogeneity that is to be found (and which was also to be found in the past) in national laws concerning nationality does not in itself imply direct advantages for the purposes of private international law.

[37] Cf. Kollewijn, *Degenerazione* (supra n. 31) p. 508, which cites a passage by F. Laurent, *Droit civil international,* vol. III (Brussels-Paris 1880) p. 176: "Si les nations sont de Dieu, et si leur indépendance doit être reconnue comme un droit divin, il en est de même des lois qui régissent les personnes, membres de la nation; elles sont l'expression de leurs sentiments et des leurs idées; elles doivent donc les suivre partout, comme le sang qui coule dans leurs veines. Ainsi statut personnel ou national, et nationalité, sont un seul et même principe; la personnalité du statut découle de la nationalité".

It is also relevant that Mancini laid down the general provisions of the Italian Civil Code of 1865 and drafted his report to the Institut[38] in the middle of a long era throughout which (even) in transnational families the nationality of the entire household was that of the man at the head thereof: save for certain exceptions, children acquired the nationality of their father only and women, through their marriage, not only acquired the nationality of their husband, but they in all cases also lost – as Kollewijn laments – their own original nationality.

Nowadays, on the contrary, it is by no means unusual that the various members of a family have different nationalities, or have in common two or even more nationalities. Situations of dual or multiple nationality, which were the exception and the ending of which was encouraged – if not imposed – under the laws in force,[39] are now the rule for transnational families and indeed tend to be very much on the increase.[40] Tendentially, in fact, each spouse transmits to the other – albeit not entirely automatically – his or her own nationality (often more than one) and the children acquire and retain the nationality (often the nationalities) of each parent.

Various recent codifications of private international law, in addressing this situation, contemplate, by means of specific rules, the possibility that nationality should be taken as a connecting factor in relation to actual cases in which the person in question has more than one nationality. The solution usually adopted consists of giving precedence to the nationality of the forum or, failing this, to the one among the nationalities possessed that is granted by the State to which the person is most closely connected.[41] Obviously, this is an asymmetric solution which, on the one hand, favours the formal aspect (and disregards the recommendations of the Santiago de Compostela Resolution adopted by the Institut du droit international) and, on the other, provides the judge called upon to assess how close the connection

---

[38] The Italian text originally published in *Il Filangieri,* vol. I (1876) pp. 625-683, is reproduced in *Diritto Internazionale* (1959) pp. 267-397 and in the ISPI volume (supra n. 31) pp. 43-76. The French version was published in the *Journal du droit international privé* (1874) pp. 221-239 and 285-304, and in the *Revue de droit international et de législation comparée* (1875) pp. 329-363. As to the polyhedric personality and multiform activity of the Neapolitan jurist and politician, suffice it to refer to the writings of R. De Nova, "Pasquale Stanislao Mancini", the Institut de droit international's *Livre du centenaire 1873-1973: évolution et perspective du droit international* (Basle 1973) pp. 3-10, and of E. Jayme, *P.S. Mancini Internationales Privatrecht zwischen Risorgimento und praktischer Jurisprudenz* (Edelsback 1980) (Italian translation by A. Ruini (Padua 1988)).

[39] Also along these lines, the European Convention on the Reduction of Cases of Multiple Nationality and Military Obligations in Cases of Multiple Nationality (Strasbourg 6/5/1963, ETS No. 43).

[40] Cf. among others, A.M. Del Vecchio, "Problematiche derivanti dal vincolo di cittadinanza a livello internazionale (con particolare riferimento alla cittadinanza originaria 'iure soli' e 'iure sanguinis')", *Riv.int.dir.uomo* (1998) p. 669-693, especially p. 682ff. and p. 693. See also the European Convention on Nationality (Strasbourg 6/11/1997, ETS No. 166, not yet in force), which is very different from the one referred to in the preceding footnote.

[41] See, for example, Article 19, paragraph 2 – as well as Article 29, paragraph 2 – of the Italian Law of 1995. Cf. the Loussouarn Report (supra n. 26) p. 325, but also the critical remark by Wengler (supra n. 14) p. 665.

actually is with a wider margin of discretionary powers.

It would therefore seem to me that the connecting factor of nationality has, over the course of time, lost a great deal of its original weight as a strong connecting factor and the degree of indelibility with which it was perceived by Mancini and recognised by scholars and legislators of private international law and that this loss – indeed, this weakening – also jeopardizes its ability to perform the decisive role traditionally attributed to it in the search for international uniformity of solutions.

Succession et coexistence d'approches et de procédés au fil du temps: l'adoption en droit international privé portugais

Rui Manuel Moura Ramos[*]

1. INTRODUCTION

Le droit international privé portugais présente, en matière d'adoption, au cours de notre siècle, un tableau de solutions très contrasté où on trouve certaines des approches méthodologiques qui ont marqué l'évolution récente de cette discipline. Il a été d'abord proposé, à un moment où cette institution était inconnue du système portugais de droit privé,[1] de traiter certains des problèmes qu'elle soulevait dans les situa-

---

[*] Professeur de droit international privé à la Faculté de droit de l'Université de Coimbra; Membre de l'Institut de Droit International. Juge au Tribunal de Première Instance des Communautés Européennes.

[1] En effet, le premier Code civil portugais (1867) avait écarté l'institut de l'adoption qui était cependant connu de l'ancien droit portugais. C'est le Code de 1966 qui a renoué avec la tradition juridique interrompue en 1867, en le rétablissant, bien que sous une inspiration et téléologie différentes. Sur l'évolution de l'institut de l'adoption au Portugal, voir notamment Almeida Costa, «Adopção», in «Temas de História do Direito. III) Instituições», 44 *Boletim da Faculdade de Direito da Universidade de Coimbra* (1968) pp. 271-276, Rabindranath Capelo de Sousa, *A adopção. Constituição da relação adoptiva* (Coimbra 1972) A. Meneres Barbosa, «A nova disciplina do instituto da adopção no Código Civil Português», in : *Reforma do Código Civil* (Lisboa 1981), pp. 221 et seq., F. Pereira Coelho, «Por-

J. Basedow et al., eds., Private Law in the International Arena – Liber Amicorum Kurt Siehr
© 2000, T.M.C.Asser Press, The Hague, The Netherlands

tions plurilocalisées dans le cadre de la condition des étrangers. Cette approche dépassée, elle a été remplacée par le recours à la méthode conflictuelle, une règle bilatérale à structure complexe et avec un rattachement cumulatif à caractère matériel ayant été consacrée par le Code civil de 1966.[2] Si cette règle a survécu jusqu'à présent[3] malgré l'évolution des données de droit privé qui d'une certaine façon justi-

---

tugal» in : «L'Adoption dans les principales législations européennes I. – Droit interne», 33 *Revue internationale de droit comparé* (1985) pp. 671-686 et Almiro Rodrigues, «O novo regime jurídico da adopção», 14 *Revista do Ministério Público* (1993) pp. 79-97.

[2] Voir les articles 60 et 61 du Code civil, dont nous reproduisons le libellé.

Article 60 (Filiation adoptive)

La loi applicable à l'établissement de la filiation adoptive est la loi personnelle de l'adoptant; si, toutefois, l'adoption est réalisée par deux époux ou si l'adopté est l'enfant du conjoint de l'adoptant, la loi compétente est la loi nationale commune des époux; à défaut, la loi de leur résidence habituelle commune; à défaut, la loi personnelle du mari.

Les rapports entre adoptant et adopté et entre celui-ci et sa famille d'origine sont soumis à la loi personnelle de l'adoptant; toutefois, au cas prévu par la seconde partie de l'alinéa précédent, est applicable la disposition de l'article 57.

Si la loi compétente pour régir les rapports entre le futur adopté et ses parents ne connaît pas l'institution de l'adoption, ou ne l'admet pas quant à ceux qui se trouvent dans la situation familiale du futur adopté, l'adoption n'est pas permise.

Article 61 (Conditions spéciales de la légitimation, de la reconnaissance ou de l'adoption)

1. Si la loi personnelle du futur légitimé, reconnu ou adopté exige le consentement de celui-ci en tant que condition pour l'établissement du rapport de légitimation, filiation naturelle ou adoptive, cette exigence sera respectée.

2. Sera également respectée l'exigence de consentement d'un tiers à qui l'intéressé se trouve rattaché par un quelconque rapport juridique de nature familiale ou de tutelle si elle découle de la loi régissant ce rapport.

[3] Avec la seule modification (déterminée par le principe constitutionnel de l'égalité des conjoints) introduite par la révision du Code civil entreprise en 1977 par le Décret-loi n 496/77, du 25 septembre 1977. Après cette réforme, la rédaction des dispositions en question est la suivante: Article 60 (Filiation adoptive)

Sous réserve de la disposition de l'alinéa suivant, la loi applicable à l'établissement de la filiation adoptive est la loi personnelle de l'adoptant.

Si l'adoption est réalisée par deux époux ou si l'adopté est l'enfant du conjoint de l'adoptant, la loi compétente est la loi nationale commune des époux et, à défaut, la loi de leur résidence habituelle commune; à défaut, on appliquera la loi du pays avec lequel la vie familiale des adoptants présente les liens les plus étroits.

Les rapports entre l'adoptant et l'adopté et entre celui-ci et sa famille d'origine, sont soumis à la loi personnelle de l'adoptant; dans le cas prévu à l'alinéa précédent, on appliquera la disposition de l'article 57.

Si la loi compétente pour régir les rapports entre le futur adopté et ses parents ne connaît pas l'institution de l'adoption, ou ne l'admet pas quant à ceux qui se trouvent dans la situation familiale du futur adopté, l'adoption n'est pas permise.

Article 61 (Conditions spéciales de la légitimation, de la reconnaissance ou de l'adoption)

1. Si la loi personnelle du futur reconnu ou adopté exige le consentement de celui-ci en tant que condition pour l'établissement du rapport de filiation, cette exigence sera respectée.

2. Sera également respectée l'exigence de consentement d'un tiers à qui l'intéressé se trouve rattaché

fiaient son contenu,[4] elle s'accompagne désormais[5] de normes de droit international privé matériel qui, dans le sillage de celles contenues à la Convention de la Haye du 29 mai 1993 sur la protection des enfants et la coopération en matière d'adoption internationale,[6] essaient de faire face à certains problèmes nouveaux qui se sont posés dans les situations internationales d'adoption.

On peut dire ainsi que la réglementation de cette institution, sur le plan du droit international privé, au Portugal, témoigne d'une façon incontestable de l'évolution méthodologique de cette branche du droit et du lien profond entretenu entre cette évolution, les objectifs que ses règles se sont assignés et les problèmes sociaux auxquels elles ont dû faire face.

Son étude présente donc, à notre avis, un intérêt indéniable. Nous présenterons donc l'essor et le bilan de ces transformations, qui suivent d'une certaine façon la

---

par un quelconque rapport juridique de nature familiale ou de tutelle si elle découle de la loi régissant ce rapport.

Pour le sens et la portée de cette réforme, voir Moura Ramos, «Portugal – Droit de la famille – Dispositions intéressant le droit international privé», 67 *Rev. crit. dr. internat. privé* (1978) pp. 598 et seq., Ferrer Correia, «A reforma do Código Civil e o direito internacional privado», 283 *Boletim do Ministério da Justiça* (février 1979) pp. 19 et seq., Almeno de Sá, «A revisão do Código Civil e a Constituição», 3 *Revista de Direito e Economia* (1977) pp. 425 et seq., pp. 443 à 445 et Baptista Machado, *Lições de Direito Internacional Privado*, 2ième éd. (Coimbra, Almedina 1982) pp. 404 et seq., pp. 422-426.

[4] Nous avons souligné à la note précédente que le seul changement apporté par la réforme du système conflictuel opérée par la révision (de 1977) du Code civil était dû à l'introduction du principe (constitutionnel) de l'égalité des conjoints *(Gleichberechtigung)*. En outre, il faut souligner que cette révision s'est caractérisée, dans le domaine du droit interne, par un profond remaniement de la législation régissant l'adoption plénière, dans le sens de donner une plus large ouverture à l'institution : voir Pereira Coelho (supra n. 1) p. 671. Remaniement qui, à deux reprises (1993 et 1998), a été poursuivi, dans le même sens, par la législation subséquente (Décrets-lois n s 185/93, du 22 mai 1993, et 120/98, du 8 mai 1998).

Ces modifications dans le droit matériel de l'adoption ne sont d'ailleurs pas spécifiques à l'ordre juridique portugais, présentant au contraire un caractère général. Pour la ligne générale qui les soutient, voir Erik Jayme, «L'adozione internazionale. Tendenze e riforme», 18 *Rivista di Diritto Civile* (1984) pp. 545-558.

[5] À la suite de l'entrée en vigueur des Décrets-lois n s 185/93 et 120/98, cités à la note précédente.

[6] Qui est en vigueur depuis le 1er mai 1995 et qui a recueilli jusqu'à présent (16 juillet 1999) la ratification (26) ou l'adhésion (9) de 35 Etats, ayant encore été signée (bien que non ratifiée) par 12 autres. Le Portugal ne fait cependant pas partie de ce nombre.

On doit aussi signaler, dans le cadre interaméricain, la Convention sur les conflits de lois en matière d'adoption de mineurs, signée à La Paz, le 24 mai 1984, et la Convention interaméricaine sur le trafic international de mineurs, approuvée à la CIDIP-V (Mexico-1994). Sur ces instruments, voir respectivement Carlos E. Boucault, « A Convenção interamericana sobre conflito de leis em matéria de adopção) CIDIP-III) e seu reflexo no direito brasileiro» in : Paulo Borba Casella et Nadia de Araújo (coordenadores), *Integração Jurídica Interamericana. As Convenções interamericanas de Direito Internacional Privado (CIDIP) e o direito brasileiro* (São Paulo, Editora LTR 1998) pp. 499-513 et Carlos Alberto de Salles, «Tráfico internacional de Menores: Problemas e soluções da Convenção Interamericana», ibid., pp. 564-580.

ligne générale qui est évoquée par le présent ouvrage dans le développement de la réglementation des relations de droit privé dans la scène internationale.

2. REFUS DE RECONNAISSANCE DE L'INSTITUTION: LE RECOURS À LA CONDITION DES ETRANGERS ET À LA NOTION D'ORDRE PUBLIC

La méconnaissance de l'institution de l'adoption, par l'ordre juridique portugais, pendant la période qui s'est écoulée entre 1867 et 1966 ne pouvait ne pas avoir des conséquences sur le droit international privé. Étant inconnue, l'adoption ne pouvait pas être créée dans des situations juridiques internes et aussi dans les situations internationales pour lesquelles la loi portugaise eût été compétente. L'adoption ayant toujours été considérée comme une institution appartenant au statut personnel, et ce dernier étant réglé, d'après le droit portugais,[7] par la loi nationale, il en résultait que l'adoption ne pouvait être permise au Portugal aux nationaux portugais.[8]

On pouvait se demander en revanche si la constitution d'une relation d'adoption serait admise, au Portugal, pour les étrangers nationaux de pays où l'adoption était connue. Les relations de famille étant réglées, en droit international privé portugais, par la loi nationale,[9] on aurait pu en effet songer à admettre une telle solution. Mais la doctrine portugaise se prononçait, à ce propos, dans un sens contraire. M. Machado Vilela,[10] notamment, invoquait deux arguments. D'après le premier, tiré du droit de la condition des étrangers, ceux-ci ne pourraient pas avoir au Portugal des droits non reconnus aux portugais. Or les portugais, on l'a déjà dit, n'avaient pas, à ce moment-là, le droit d'adopter.[11] D'autre part, les cas d'application dans l'État du for d'une institution qui y est inconnue ne constitueraient pas des hypothèses de conflits de lois mais de conflits d'institutions, et dans ces situations on ne devrait pas, selon l'auteur, reconnaître dans un pays une institution juridique qui ne serait pas

---

[7] Voir dans ce sens l'arrêt de la Cour Suprême portugaise du 2 octobre 1956, 60 *Boletim do Ministério da Justiça* (novembre 1956) pp. 512-519: l'état, la capacité et les relations de famille et de succession sont réglés par la loi nationale.

[8] Il n'y a pas de décisions de jurisprudence consacrant directement cette hypothèse, mais elle découle logiquement des conclusions de certains arrêts. Ainsi, la Cour d'appel de Lisbonne, dans un arrêt du 16 novembre 1955 (in *Jurisprudência das Relações*, 1955, pp. 955-958), a déclaré que «l'adoption, réglée par les Ordenações Filipinas, n'est plus une catégorie juridique au Portugal depuis que l'actuel Code civil (celui de 1867) a été publié».

[9] Voir, au-delà de l'arrêt de la Cour Suprême cité à la note 7, Machado Vilela, *Tratado Elementar (Teórico e Prático) de Direito Internacional Privado*, v. I (Coimbra, Coimbra Editora Limitada 1922) p. 441, Isabel de Magalhães Collaço, *Direito Internacional Privado*, v. III (Lisboa 1963) p. 87 et Ferrer Correia, *Lições de Direito Internacional Privado*, v. II (Universidade de Coimbra 1963) pp. 620-623.

[10] Ibid., v. II, p. 652.

[11] Voir la décision citée à la n. 8.

[12] Voir, dans le même sens, la position prise par la Cour de révision judiciaire de Monaco dans un

admise par sa propre loi. La jurisprudence a consacré la même solution, bien qu'en faisant appel à un fondement distinct: celui de l'ordre public.[12] Ainsi, la Cour d'appel de Lisbonne[13] a dit à l'époque que «l'institution de l'adoption n'est pas admise dans notre pays parce qu'elle est contraire aux principes fondamentaux de notre droit de la famille et, dans cette mesure, elle ne peut être pratiquée au Portugal par les étrangers, de même que ses effets ne peuvent pas être reconnus».

La même position restrictive a été prise par la jurisprudence à l'égard des adoptions réalisées par des citoyens portugais à l'étranger, dans des pays connaissant l'institution de l'adoption. Ainsi, la Cour Suprême a déclaré que l'adoption faite au Brésil par un citoyen portugais, au temps où le Code civil de 1867 était en vigueur, ne produisait pas d'effets au Portugal.[14] Et la Cour n'a même pas fait référence à l'argument tiré du fait que la loi compétente (la loi portugaise, en l'occurrence) n'admettant pas l'adoption,[15] celle-ci ne pouvait en conséquence être reconnue. On a dit, tout simplement, qu'il s'agissait d'un acte juridique inexistant.[16]

Enfin, la jurisprudence portugaise a aussi refusé la reconnaissance des adoptions faites à l'étranger par des citoyens qui étaient ressortissants de pays dont la loi nationale prévoyait cette institution. Dans deux arrêts différents, la Cour d'appel de Lisbonne a invoqué l'argument tiré de la condition des étrangers, d'après lequel les étrangers ne peuvent pas avoir au Portugal des droits non reconnus aux citoyens portugais.[17] Et la Cour Suprême, dans une décision déjà citée, a appliqué la même solution par le biais de l'exception d'ordre public.[18] Cette position, qui s'appuyait

---

arrêt du 6 mai 1965 in 54 *Rev. crit. dr. internat. privé* (1965) pp. 708 et seq., avec la note de Francescakis. Pour une utilisation beaucoup plus nuancée de l'ordre public dans ce cas, et l'examen du problème sur le plan de la qualification, Pierre Bourel, «Adoption», *Jurisclasseur de Droit International*, Fasc. 548-B, n 113-119 et au Portugal, Nuno Ascensão e Silva, *A constituição da adopção de menores nas relações privadas internacionais: alguns aspectos (polic.)* (Coimbra 1995) vol. I, pp. 80-81.

[13] Dans un arrêt du 7 décembre 1956 (in *Jurisprudência das Relações,* 1956, pp. 1013-1015). La solution est approuvée, même si avec certaines nuances dans sa motivation, par Ferrer Correia, «O princípio da autonomia do direito internacional privado no sistema jurídico português», 12 *Revista de Direito e Economia* (1986) pp. 3-37, p. 13, note 17.

[14] Voir l'arrêt du 8 avril 1969 [in 186 *Boletim do Ministério da Justiça* (mai 1969) pp. 230-235]. Dans la doctrine on invoquait, pour fonder le même résultat, le défaut d'autorités ayant compétence pour l'établissement d'un tel lien. Voir Isabel Magalhães Collaço, «Sobre o esboço de convenção acerca da 'Adopção internacional de crianças', emanado da Conferência da Haia de Direito Internacional Privado», 16 *Revista da Faculdade de Direito da Universidade de Lisboa* (1963) pp. 207-271, p. 233 et Ferrer Correia, cité à la n. précédente.

[15] Position qui, au contraire, était prônée par un des juges dans son opinion dissidente, ibid., pp. 233-234.

[16] Sur le plan du fonctionnement des règles de conflit, la solution, telle qu'elle est présentée à l'opinion dissidente citée à la note précédente, doit certainement être approuvée.

[17] Arrêts du 7 décembre 1956 (voir supra n. 13) et du 16 novembre 1955 (voir supra n. 8). Dans cette dernière décision, on fait aussi appel à l'idée d'ordre public.

[18] Voir l'arrêt cité supra à la n. 13.

sur les enseignements de M. Machado Vilela[19] et sur un avis de la *Procuradoria da República*,[20] était néanmoins fortement critiquée par d'autres auteurs.[21]

3.   La prise en compte de l'adoption par le systeme portugais de
      conflits de lois

Dans la décennie précédant l'entrée en vigueur du Code civil de 1966, la doctrine portugaise[22] soutenait déjà ouvertement la thèse d'après laquelle les questions d'adoption internationale[23] devraient être résolues dans le cadre du système de conflits de lois. À cet effet, et malgré l'absence d'équivalent dans le système interne du for, l'adoption (comme toute autre institution étrangère méconnue *in foro domestico*) devrait pouvoir être reconduite à une des catégories de rattachement du système conflictuel du for dont les concepts désignatifs seraient donc interprétés d'une façon autonome à l'égard de leurs homologues utilisés par les dispositions de droit matériel.[24]

Avec le nouveau Code civil, cependant, la difficulté additionnelle qu'une telle approche pouvait soulever est disparue. En effet, en accueillant l'institut de l'adoption, quoique d'une façon timide, le législateur de 1966 ouvrait la porte à la prévision expresse d'une règle de conflit spécifique en matière d'adoption.

Cette règle[25] faisait référence à la loi personnelle[26] de l'adoptant, tout en prévoyant néanmoins, pour le cas où l'adoption serait réalisée par deux époux et pour les cas où l'adopté serait l'enfant du conjoint de l'adoptant, la compétence de la loi des effets du mariage: la loi nationale commune des époux, à défaut la loi de leur résidence habituelle commune, à défaut la loi personnelle du mari.[27] Suite à la réforme (de 1977) du Code civil, toutefois, la référence à la loi nationale du mari a été rem-

---

[19] Ferrer Correia (supra n. 10).

[20] Avis n 75/55, du 12 janvier 1956, 56 *Boletim do Ministério da Justiça*, pp. 222 et seq.

[21] Dans ce sens, voir Ferrer Correia, *Lições de Direito Internacional Privado* (supra n. 9) pp. 190 et seq., Isabel Magalhães Collaço, *Direito Internacional Privado* (supra n. 7) pp. 82-83, Taborda Ferreira, *Sistema do Direito Internacional Privado segundo a Lei e a Jurisprudência*, (Lisboa, Atica 1957) pp. 83-84 et Baptista Machado, «Problemas na aplicação do direito estrangeiro) Adaptação e substituição», 36 *Boletim da Faculdade de Direito da Universidade de Coimbra* (1960) pp. 326-351, pp. 343 et seq. L'orientation de ces auteurs avait été accueillie dans un arrêt de la Cour Suprême du 15 mai 1934 qui est cependant demeuré isolé – voir pour cet arrêt et pour la note critique de Barbosa Magalhães, 48 *Gazeta da Relação de Lisboa*, pp. 342 et seq.

[22] Voir les auteurs et les ouvrages cités à la note précédente.

[23] Comme de toute autre institution inconnue du droit matériel du for.

[24] Pour la démonstration de cette thèse, à l'égard des données du droit portugais, voir Ferrer Correia, «O princípio da autonomia do direito internacional privado no sistema jurídico português» (supra n. 13) pp. 14 et seq.

[25] L'article 60, n 1 du Code civil. Pour son libellé (voir supra n. 2).

[26] D'après le Code civil (article 31, n 1) cette loi était la loi nationale.

[27] Voir l'article 52 du même Code.

placée, pour remplir les exigences constitutionnelles[28] de la *Gleichberechtigung*, par celle de la loi présentant avec la vie familiale des adoptants les liens les plus étroits.

Cependant, il est aussi prévu[29] que si la loi compétente pour régir les rapports entre le futur adopté et ses parents ne connaît pas l'institut de l'adoption ou ne l'admet pas quant à ceux qui se trouvent dans la situation familiale du futur adopté, l'adoption n'est pas permise.

En outre, toujours en matière de constitution de l'adoption,[30] l'article 61 impose aussi le respect de l'exigence du consentement soit de l'adopté soit d'un tiers à qui l'intéressé se trouve rattaché par un quelconque rapport juridique de nature familiale ou de tutelle si, respectivement, la loi personnelle du futur adopté ou la loi régissant ce rapport juridique de nature familiale ou de tutelle l'exige.

La situation apparaît donc comme assez restrictive, pour ce qui est de la constitution de l'adoption. On exige à ce propos la concrétisation d'un rattachement multiple à nature cumulative à caractère limité, qui requiert au delà de l'accord entre la loi de l'adoptant[31] et celle qui régit les rapports entre le futur adopté et sa famille d'origine,[32] le respect de certains consentements au cas où ils seraient exigés par d'autres lois.

---

[28] Voir les ouvrages cités supra à la n. 3. Et, en général sur les rapports entre la Constitution et les règles de conflit, dans la doctrine portugaise, Moura Ramos, *Direito Internacional Privado e Constituição. Introdução a uma análise das suas relações* (Coimbra, Coimbra Editora 1979) et, dernièrement Marques dos Santos, «Constituição e direito internacional privado. O estranho caso do artigo 51. , n 3 do Código Civil», in : Jorge Miranda (organizador), *Perspectivas Constitucionais. Nos 20 anos da Constituição de 1976*, v. III (Coimbra, Coimbra Editora 1998) pp. 367-390.

En droit espagnol, les mêmes exigences ont amené (avec la loi 21/1987 du 11 novembre) à la consécration de la compétence de la loi personnelle (nationale) de l'enfant. Sur la réforme entreprise par cette loi, voir Nuria Bouza Vidal, *Comentarios a les reformas del Código Civil. Desde la Ley 21/1987, del 11 de noviembre, a la Ley 30/1991, del 20 de diciembre* (coordinador : Rodrigo Bercovitz Rodriguez-Cano), Tecnos p. 15 et seg.

[29] Au n 3 de l'article 60, devenu, après la réforme de 1977, le n 4 du même article.

[30] Pour ce qui concerne les effets de l'adoption (rapports entre adoptant et adopté et entre celui-ci et sa famille d'origine) l'article 60, n 2 (devenu 60, n 3 en 1977) prévoyait la compétence de la loi personnelle de l'adoptant. Cependant, pour le cas où l'adoption serait réalisée par deux époux ou l'adopté serait l'enfant du conjoint de l'adoptant, la compétence reviendrait à la loi nationale commune des adoptants, à défaut à la loi de leur résidence habituelle commune et, à défaut, à la loi personnelle de l'adopté (avant 1977, il s'agissait de la loi personnelle du père). La solution est différente de celle de la récente loi italienne (loi n 218 du 31 mai 1995) qui, en cas de défaut de résidence habituelle commune, fait référence à la loi de l'État avec laquelle la vie matrimoniale présente les liens les plus étroits.

Pour les solutions du droit italien avant cette réforme, voir Angelo Davi, *L'adozione nel diritto internazionale privato italiano* (Milano, Giuffrè 1981) et «La nouvelle réglementation italienne de l'adoption internationale», 73 *Rev. crit. dr. internat. privé* (1984) pp. 173-178.

[31] Ou la loi des effets du mariage, dans le cas où l'adoption est faite par un couple marié ou se rapporte à l'enfant du conjoint de l'adoptant.

[32] L'accord de cette loi est limité puisqu'on exige simplement qu'elle connaisse l'institution de l'adoption et qu'elle l'admet quant à ceux qui se trouvent dans la situation familiale du futur adopté.

La première condition semble trouver son fondement dans le besoin accru de stabilité des relations d'adoption, qui aurait mené le législateur à essayer d'éviter au
maximum la constitution de situations boiteuses *(hinkende Adoptionen; limping
adoptions)* ou génératrices de conflits de prétentions.[33] Elles se présenteraient toujours que l'adoption risquerait de ne pas être reconnue dans le pays d'origine de
l'adopté, ou, plus précisément, dans celui dont la loi régirait les rapports entre celui-
ci et sa famille d'origine. L'exigence au préalable de l'accord de cette loi pour la
constitution de l'adoption vise donc à empêcher la naissance de tout conflit de prétentions qui pourrait se présenter par la suite. Et il semble que c'est le même objectif
qui est poursuivi par la deuxième condition, une fois que l'exigence des consentements (celui de l'adopté et celui de la personne se trouvant rattaché à ce dernier par
une relation quelconque à caractère familiale ou de tutelle) n'est pas posée en elle-
même mais seulement dans la mesure où elle serait consacrée par une loi donnée.[34]
D'autre part, et contrairement à ce qui arrive avec certains systèmes,[35] cette exigence ne peut pas être contournée par l'application de la *lex fori.*[36]

C'est ce souci de la stabilité du rapport de droit à constituer, qui présente un net
caractère substantiel, qui explique les solutions en question, et non le souhait de
mieux localiser le rapport.[37] D'autre part, le résultat, clairement restrictif à l'égard
de l'adoption internationale, s'accommodait très bien des solutions de droit matériel prévues en 1966, où les conditions requises pour l'établissement du rapport
adoptif étaient trop sévères.[38] Cependant, il a été maintenu sans aucune modification lorsque le droit matériel a été remanié, en 1977, dans le sens d'une plus large
ouverture à l'institution adoptive. Ce qui fait plutôt penser à une indépendance des

---

[33] Voir dans ce sens Moura Ramos, «Portugal», in «L'adoption dans les principales législations européennes. II. Droit international privé», 33 *Revue internationale de droit comparé* (1985), pp. 845-
864, pp. 853-855 et Ascensão e Silva, *A constituição da adopção de menores nas relações privadas internacionais: alguns aspectos* (supra n. 12) v. II, pp. 358-373.

[34] Ce qui fait penser qu'on veut surtout éviter qu'on puisse se fonder sur une telle loi pour, plus tard,
et étant donné l'absence de consentement, mettre en question la constitution du rapport d'adoption.

[35] Voir l'article 23 de l'EGBGB allemand tel qu'il est resté après la loi du 25 juillet 1986 (rappelons
que la modification que cette règle a subi avec la réforme du 16 décembre 1997 n'a pas touché la solution y contenue à propos de l'adoption), qui permet la constitution de l'adoption quand l'intérêt du mineur (das Wohl des Kinders) l'exige, et l'article 38 de la nouvelle loi italienne de droit international
privée (cit. supra, note 30) qui commande l'application du droit italien toujours qu'il est demandé à un
juge italien l'adoption d'un mineur lui donnant le statut d'enfant légitime. Sur la méthode de l'application généralisée de la lex fori que ces solutions entérinent voir dernièrement Paolo Picone, *La riforma
italiana del diritto internazionale privato* (Padova, Cedam 1998) pp. 471 et seq.

[36] Ce qui peut évidemment aboutir à un certain favor adotionis. Pour d'autres voies d'obtenir le
même résultat, voir Ascensão e Silva, *A constituição da adopção de menores nas relações privadas internacionais* (supra n. 12) v. I, pp. 133 et seq.

[37] Voir Moura Ramos, *Da lei aplicável ao contrato de trabalho internacional* (Coimbra, Almedina
1990) p. 248, note 356.

[38] Dans ce sens Moura Ramos, «L'adoption internationale», 37-38 *Documentação e Direito Comparado* (1989) pp. 5-32, note 71 et Pereira Coelho (supra n. 1) p. 671.

objectifs servis par le droit de conflits et par le droit matériel ou, au moins, à la coexistence de ces objectifs, malgré son apparente contradiction.

4.   L'ESSOR DES REGLES DE DROIT INTERNATIONAL PRIVE MATERIEL

L'évolution du droit matériel de l'adoption s'est cependant poursuit. À deux reprises, en 1993 et en 1998,[39] le législateur portugais s'est occupé de l'adoption. Toujours dans le but de renforcer cette institution, considérée de plus en plus comme une forme de protection de remplacement aux enfants temporairement ou définitivement privés de son milieu familial.[40] S'il n'a pas touché aux solutions conflictuelles du Code civil décrites ci-avant, il a néanmoins créé des règles de droit international privé matériel.[41] Ces règles s'adressent à deux situations différentes, celle du placement à l'étranger de mineurs résidant au Portugal en vue de son adoption[42] et celle de l'adoption, par des résidants au Portugal, de mineurs résidant à l'étranger,[43] et doivent être comprises à la lumière des modifications introduites au même moment dans le droit matériel.[44] Nous envisagerons par la suite ces deux types de situations.

4.1   Le placement à l'étranger de mineurs résidant au Portugal en vue de son adoption

Dans ces hypothèses, le changement le plus important a été celui qui a fait dépendre le placement à l'étranger de mineurs résidant au Portugal en vue de son adoption d'une décision judiciaire préalable portant sur la confiance du mineur (article 15, n 1, devenu 14, n 1, avec le Décret-loi n 121/98, du Décret-loi n 185/93). Cette décision, à laquelle sont applicables, *mutatis mutandis*, les normes qui règlent le même institut dans l'ordre interne,[45] est cependant subordonnée au jeu d'un principe de

---

[39] Voir supra n. 4, in fine.

[40] Dans le sillage de l'orientation accueillie à l'article 20 de la Convention des Nations Unies sur les droits de l'enfant, du 20 novembre 1989.

[41] Voir les articles 15 à 27 du Décret-loi n 185/93 qui, après le Décret-loi n 120/98 (article 3) sont devenus les articles 14 à 27.

[42] Articles 15 à 24 (devenus 14 à 22 avec le Décret-loi n 120/98) du Décret-loi n 185/93.

[43] Articles 25 à 27 (devenus 23 à 27 avec le Décret-loi n 120/98) du Décret-loi n 185/93.

[44] Ces modifications se rapportent surtout à la création d'un nouveau institut (le placement du mineur en vue de l'adoption) et à des changements concernant les conditions de l'adoption, les consentements exigés, le caractère secret de la procédure et des personnes des parents biologiques et adoptifs et les changements apportés au nom de l'adopté à la suite de l'adoption.
Pour le rappel des idées directrices de ces modifications, voir Almiro Rodrigues (supra n. 1).

[45] L'article 1978 du Code civil et les articles 166 et 167 de l'Organisation Tutélaire des Mineurs (voir le n 2 de la disposition citée dans le texte).

subsidiarité,[46] le placement d'un mineur en vue de son adoption à l'étranger n'étant permis que si l'adoption au Portugal n'apparait pas viable (article 16, n 1, devenu 15, n 1, du Décret-loi n 185/93[47,48]).

En outre, cette décision judiciaire ne pourra intervenir que si les consentements exigés par le droit portugais ont été prêtés,[49] les services compétentes de l'État de la résidence des candidats à devenir adoptants ont reconnu leur idonéité et estimé possible dans ce pays l'adoption du mineur en question et une période de stage est prévue aux fins d'apprécier la convenance de l'établissement du lien d'adoption. Il faut aussi qu'il apparait que l'adoption envisagée présente des avantages réels pour le futur adopté, se fonde en des motifs légitimes et qu'il semble raisonnable de supposer qu'elle amènera à l'établissement entre l'adoptant et le futur adopté d'un lien semblable à celui de la filiation (article 17, devenu 16, du Décret-loi n 185/93).

La loi portugaise s'insère donc dans la tendance, suivie par beaucoup des États d'où proviennent habituellement les enfants à adopter,[50] et légitimée par la Convention de la Haye,[51] qui entoure de précautions particulières l'adoption internationale,

---

[46] Principe que, bien que dans une formulation plus nuancée, apparait en tant qu'orientation générale dans l'article 4, alinéa b) de la Convention de la Haye du 29 mai 1993, qui dispose que «les adoptions visées par la Convention ne peuvent avoir lieu que si les autorités compétentes de l'État d'origine (...) ont constaté, après avoir dûment examiné les possibilités de placement de l'enfant dans son État d'origine, qu'une adoption internationale répond à l'intérêt supérieur de l'enfant»

[47] D'après le numéro 2 de cette disposition, on considère viable l'adoption au Portugal toujours que, «au moment de la demande de confiance judiciaire, il y a des candidats résidant au pays dont la prétention semble présenter des possibilités d'avoir du succès en temps utile pour le mineur»

[48] La règle n'est néanmoins d'application si le mineur a la nationalité du candidat à adoptant, s'il est l'enfant de son conjoint ou si l'intérêt du mineur conseille l'adoption à l'étranger (n 3 de l'article cité au texte).

[49] Sauf si leur dispense est permise par ce droit.

[50] Voir par exemple, et dans une version plus radicale, le droit brésilien, où la loi n 8.069, du 13 juillet 1990 (Statut de l'Enfant et de l'Adolescent) considère, dans son article 31, le placement familial d'un enfant dans une famille de remplacement étrangère une mesure exceptionnelle, qui n'est admissible que dans la modalité de l'adoption et interdit dans son article 51, § 4, la sortie du futur adopté du territoire national avant la consommation de l'adoption.

Sur la réponse entreprise par cette loi à cet égard et ses précédents, voir Vera Maria Barreira Jatahy, «A adoção internacional: o direito comparado e as normes estatutárias» in : Tânia da Silva Pereira (coordenação), *Estatuto da criança e do adolescente: lei 8.069/90: «estudos socio-jurídicos»* (Rio de Janeiro, Renovar 1992) pp. 183-205, António Chaves, *Adoção internacional e o Tráfico de Crianças* (São Paulo, Editora da Universidade de São Paulo 1994), Sônia Maria Monteiro, *Aspectos novos da adoção* (Rio de Janeiro, Forense, spécialement 1997) pp. 51-60. Et pour le rôle joué en droit brésilien par les conventions internationales dans cette matière, voir Carlos E. Boucault, «A convenção interamericana sobre conflito de leis em matéria de adoção) CIDIP-III) e seu reflexo no direito brasileiro» (supra n. 6) et Georgette Nacarato Nazo, «Adoção internacional: valor e importância das convenções internacionais vigentes no Brasil», 92 *Revista da Faculdade de Direito da Universidade de São Paulo* (1997) pp. 301-319.

[51] D'après son article 28, en effet, «la Convention ne déroge pas aux lois de l'État d'origine (État contractant où réside habituellement un enfant, au sens de l'article 2) qui requièrent que l'adoption d'un enfant résidant habituellement dans cet État doit avoir lieu dans cet État ou qui interdisent le placement

dans le but de garantir qu'elle ait lieu «dans l'intérêt supérieur de l'enfant et le respect de ses droits fondamentaux, ainsi que pour prévenir l'enlèvement, la vente ou la traite d'enfants».[52]

Parmi ces précautions, le droit portugais établit aussi un mécanisme de coopération entre les différentes autorités étatiques, s'inspirant également à cet égard dans les solutions consacrées par cette Convention. D'après ce mécanisme, les candidats à adoptants devront faire parvenir sa volonté d'adopter à l'autorité centrale portugaise par l'intermédiaire des services compétents de l'État de sa résidence ou d'autres entités agréées (article 18, devenu 17, n 1, du Décret-loi n 185/93). Cette volonté, qui doit être accompagnée de la preuve de l'existence des conditions auxquelles la loi subordonne le placement du mineur à l'étranger, fera l'objet d'une première appréciation de la part de l'autorité centrale portugaise dans un délai de dix jours (article 17, n 2 du Décret-loi n 185/93 dans sa rédaction actuelle). Au cas où elle est acceptée,[53] cette autorité examinera la viabilité concrète de l'adoption envisagée ensemble avec l'organisme de sécurité sociale de l'aire de la résidence du mineur, eu égard au profil des candidats et aux caractéristiques de l'enfant (article 18 du même Décret-loi).

Le rapport élaboré à ce sujet par les services de sécurité sociale,[54] sera communiqué à l'entité ayant présentée la prétention et, au cas où sa conclusion soit favorable à la viabilité de l'adoption, au Ministère Public, pour que la confiance judiciaire soit requise (article 19 du Décret-loi cité).[55]

Il est encore prévu que l'autorité centrale portugaise fera le suivi de la situation en rapport avec l'autorité centrale ou autre entité compétente de l'État de la résidence des candidats à adoptants, en transmettant les informations reçues à l'organisme de sécurité sociale et au tribunal ayant décidé la confiance judiciaire du mineur. Au cas où le suivi effectuée permet de conclure que la situation ne correspond pas à l'intérêt du mineur, on envisagera les mesures nécessaires de protection du mineur, en mettant en oeuvre un projet de vie alternatif qui soit à même de sauvegarder cet intérêt (article 20 du même décret-loi). Une fois une adoption décrétée à l'étranger, l'autorité centrale devra faire parvenir au tribunal ayant décidé la confiance judiciaire du mineur une copie de cette décision, dont la reconnaissance (s'agissant d'un mineur ayant la nationalité portugaise) devra être requise par le Mi-

---

de l'enfant dans l'État d'accueil ou son déplacement vers cet État avant l'adoption».

[52] Voir la quatrième considerandum de la Convention de la Haye de 1993.

[53] L'autorité centrale peut aussi la rejeter ou inviter le requérant à la compléter ou perfectionner. Mais elle devra toujours informer de sa décision l'entité qui lui avait communiqué la prétention.

[54] Ce rapport contiendra notamment l'identité du mineur, l'appréciation de la possibilité de l'adoption, la caractérisation du milieu social et de l'évolution personnelle et familiale du mineur, son passé médical et celui de sa famille.

[55] L'autorité centrale portugaise et l'entité étrangère ayant présentée la prétention du candidat à adoptant qui a été estimée viable feront le nécessaire à l'obtention des permis de sortie de l'État d'origine et d'entrée et de séjour dans l'État d'accueil.

nistère Public[56] si elle ne l'a pas été par les adoptants dans les trois mois suivant le moment où elle a acquis force de chose jugée. Enfin, dans toute la procédure de reconnaissance le secret de l'identité sera préservé (articles 21 et 22).

Pour l'essentiel, les nouvelles dispositions entourent donc de grandes précautions la sortie d'un enfant du territoire portugais en vue d'une adoption à l'étranger, en assujetant à des lourdes conditions l'octroi de la décision judiciaire de confiance du mineur, devenue désormais nécessaire. Elles essayent également d'organiser, entre les autorités portugaises (par l'intermédiaire de l'autorité centrale) et les entités compétentes de l'État de la résidence des candidats à l'adoption, une coopération qui concernera soit la période précédant la décision sur la confiance du mineur, soit le suivi de la situation (au cas où une telle confiance fût accordée) jusqu'au prononcé d'une décision d'adoption à l'étranger. L'inspiration du dispositif établi par la Convention de La Haye à cet égard peut être aisément reconnue.

4.2   L'adoption, par des résidents au Portugal, de mineurs résidant à l'étranger

Pour cette deuxième situation, le législateur portugais envisage des solutions qui, bien que parallèles à celles prévues pour la précédente, présentent une plus grande simplicité. En effet, il n'est plus maintenant question d'entourer de précautions la sortie d'enfants à l'étranger, et la portée de la réforme s'est donc limitée à la mise en oeuvre des mécanismes de coopération entre autorités inspirés dans les règles conventionnelles adoptées à La Haye.

Il est d'abord prévu que les personnes résidant habituellement au Portugal qui veulent adopter un mineur résidant à l'étranger devront présenter sa candidature à l'organisme de sécurité sociale de l'aire de sa résidence. Celui-ci étudiera alors une telle prétention dans le but d'établir l'aptitude du requérant pour l'adoption internationale[57] (article 23 du Décret-loi n 185/93 dans sa dernière rédaction). Au cas où une telle aptitude se voit reconnue, la candidature sera transmise, par l'intermédiaire de l'autorité centrale portugaise, aux services compétents ou aux entités agréées de l'État de la résidence du futur adopté.

Les autorités portugaises (l'autorité centrale et l'organisme de sécurité sociale) analyseront alors la viabilité de l'adoption envisagée, eu égard au profil du candidat et au rapport sur la situation du mineur établi par l'entité compétente de l'État de sa résidence. Au cas où elles arrivent à une conclusion positive à cet égard, ce résultat sera communiqué aux entités compétentes de l'État de la résidence du mineur et la

---

[56] Qui recevra à cet égard de l'autorité centrale tous les éléments nécessaires.

[57] On appliquera à ce propos (article 23, n 2) les règles prévues pour les adoptions internes. On doit mentionner à cet égard que, d'après l'article 7 du décret-loi en question, un recours devant le tribunal compétent en matière de droit familial est prévu contre les décisions rejetant les candidatures présentées.

procédure amenant à confier le mineur au candidat à adoptant devra être dé-clenchée.[58]

Une fois la confiance octroyée et la période de pré-adoption entamée, l'orga-nisme de sécurité sociale de l'aire de résidence du candidat à adoptant fera le suivi de la situation du mineur en informant, par l'intermédiaire de l'autorité centrale, les entités compétentes de l'État de la résidence du mineur.[59] Si à la fin de la période de pré-adoption l'enquête menée par l'organisme de sécurité sociale est favorable à l'adoption celle-ci pourra être requise, la décision finale devant alors être commu-niquée par l'intermédiaire de l'autorité centrale à l'entité compétente de l'État de la résidence du mineur.

5.   CONCLUSION

L'évolution précédemment décrite montre comment le droit international privé portugais, après avoir regardé le problème de l'adoption internationale comme une question relevant de la condition des étrangers, s'est confié après à la seule méthode des conflits de lois, pour se rallier plus tard au groupe de ceux qui considèrent né-cessaire le recours à des règles de droit international privé matériel. Si la première démarche était condamnée à l'échec et avait été écartée même avant la modification législative du droit matériel (celle de 1966) qui a amené à la réintroduction de l'ins-titut de l'adoption dans cet ordre juridique, la façon dont la deuxième a été concré-tisée a bientôt révélée son absence de syntonie avec la politique législative (la *policy)* suivie en droit interne à propos de la filiation adoptive. En effet, le rattache-ment cumulatif adopté, s'il était la conséquence d'une préoccupation avec la stabili-té des rapports d'adoption,[60] ne constituait pas moins un lourd entrave à sa constitution sur le plan international. Cela étant, il entrait en contradiction avec le développement du droit matériel qui favorisait toujours plus la constitution de l'adoption. Le législateur n'a cependant pas essayé de résoudre cette contradiction au niveau du droit conflictuel, en laissant en vigueur une solution qui, bien que ré-pondant à des préoccupations compréhensibles, présente une certaine rigidité.

---

[58] Il faut, à ce propos, que l'autorité centrale portugaise et l'entité compétente de l'État de la rési-dence du mineur s'occupent, respectivement, de l'obtention du permis d'entrée et de séjour du mineur au Portugal et de celui de sa sortie de son État d'origine.

[59] Si, pendant le suivi de la situation dans cette période, il s'avère que la situation ne correspond pas à l'intérêt du mineur, on prendra les mesures nécessaires à sa protection en mettant en oeuvre un projet de vie alternatif qui sauvegarde un tel intérêt.

[60] Un but qui pourrait également être atteint par d'autres voies, notamment par l'adoption de la mé-thode de la référence à l'ordre juridique compétent. Sur la supériorité de cette méthode à cet égard, voir surtout Paolo Picone, *Ordinamento competente e diritto internazionale privato* (Padova, Cedam 1986) et, dernièrement, Id., *La reforma italiana del diritto internazionale privato* (Padova, Cedam 1998) pp. 20 et seq.

Ce caractère est encore mis en évidence par l'introduction de règles de droit international privé matériel, par lesquelles on a essayé de renforcer les procédures utilisées dans les adoptions internationales, dans le but d'assurer le respect de l'intérêt supérieur de l'enfant et de ses droits fondamentaux, dans le sillage des objectifs poursuivis par la Convention de la Haye du 29 mai 1993.[61] Certes, les dispositions en question ne s'appliquent pas à toutes les adoptions internationales, mais seulement à celles qui impliquent un déplacement du mineur,[62] soit la sortie du Portugal (pays où il réside) pour l'État de la résidence des adoptants, soit l'entrée au Portugal d'un enfant domiciliée à l'étranger pour être adopté ici par des adoptants résidant dans cet État.[63] Et, dans cette situation, l'interférence des nouvelles dispositions matérielles avec le système conflictuel semble ne pas avoir lieu que dans cette dernière hypothèse, la seule où dans la pensée du législateur, l'adoption est prononcée au Portugal et où partant, les règles de conflit portugaises sont d'application.

Dans la première situation prévue, celle de la sortie du Portugal d'un enfant qui y avait sa résidence pour être adopté à l'étranger par des personnes y résidant, la loi se limite à entourer une telle sortie du pays de précautions particulières[64] et à essayer d'assurer un suivi de la situation de l'enfant pendant toute la période précédant l'adoption. L'objectif semble tout à fait justifiable, mais on voit mal comment la coopération internationale nécessaire à cet effet peut être instituée unilatéralement par un dispositif de droit étatique.[65]

Par contre, dans le deuxième groupe de situations, celui où des mineurs résident à l'étranger seraient adoptés (au Portugal) par des personnes qui ont sa résidence dans cet État, l'application des nouvelles dispositions aura lieu parallèlement à la mise en oeuvre des règles de conflit du for. Le risque d'une collision est cependant écarté, vu que le mécanisme prévu ne s'applique que pendant la période précédant l'adoption (articles 23 à 26 du Décret-loi n 185/93 dans sa rédaction actuelle) et une fois que celle-ci ait été prononcée (article 27 du même Décret-loi), c'est-à-dire en amont et en aval de l'application des règles de conflit. Mais il demeure tout de

---

[61] Voir le quatrième considerandum de son préambule.

[62] Dans les autres situations d'adoption internationale (par exemple, adoption au Portugal d'un enfant capverdien par un couple belge, tous les intéressés étant domiciliés au Portugal) il ne faudra que prendre en compte les règles de conflit du Code civil. Ce qui amène à conclure que, dans une hypothèse comme celle que nous venons d'envisager, le droit interne portugais pourra bien ne pas être pris en considération: la loi compétente pour l'adoption serait dans ce cas la loi belge et le rattachement cumulatif de l'article 60, n 4 n'exigeait pas que l'accord de la loi capverdienne. De même, si un enfant portugais résidant au Cap-vert devrait être adopté par un couple belge résidant en Belgique, la loi portugaise ne serait également appliquée, sauf si les règles de conflits de l'État où l'adoption serait prononcée estimeraient compétente la loi nationale de l'adopté.

[63] Le champ d'application matériel de ces règles coïncide donc avec celui des dispositions de la Convention de la Haye de 1993, tel qu'il est énoncé à l'article 2 de cet instrument conventionnel.

[64] Notamment, l'existence d'une décision judiciaire préalable de confiance du mineur.

[65] Rappelons que l'institutionnalisation d'une telle coopération au niveau multilatéral a été l'un des objectifs de la Convention de la Haye de 1993.

même vrai que la coopération entre les autorités qui est supposée par ces disposi-tions ne semble non plus pouvoir être organisée que par un instrument de droit conventionnel.

La création des règles de droit international privé matériel à caractère interne pour les situations d'adoption à rattachement multiple ne constitue donc une alter-native à la ratification d'une convention comme celle de la Haye du 29 mai 1993 qui organise précisément la coopération internationale des autorités dans cette matière, vu le manque de caractère obligatoire, à l'égard des autres États, des mécanismes qu'on essaie de cette façon de mettre en oeuvre.

Si, au contraire, on emprunte cette autre voie, il faudrait alors considérer si la so-lution conflictuelle en vigueur, qui a été pensée pour un contexte différent,[66] demeu-rerait adéquate dans une conjoncture nouvelle où la coopération internationale serait établie.[67] On devrait alors décider si, la politique législative étant favorable au développement de l'adoption et une fois l'intérêt supérieur du mineur et le respect de ses droits fondamentaux assurés par le mécanisme de coopération cité, le ratta-chement cumulatif demeure encore la solution la plus adéquate. Question à laquelle on peut douter que la réponse doive nécessairement être positive. Il est vrai que, même si le but de la règle actuelle aura été épuisé par le respect des conditions pro-cédurales de l'adoption internationale prévues dans la Convention de la Haye de 1993, aux cas où elle sera applicable, la prévention de la création de situations juri-diques boiteuses demeure nécessaire dans les cas où cet instrument ne pourra pas être pris en considération. Mais il n'est pas certain qu'une application distributive des systèmes juridiques de l'adoptant et de l'adopté, qui serait toujours moins nui-sible à la constitution de l'adoption internationale, ne soit à même d'assurer un tel résultat. Ou qu'il ne puisse pas être poursuivi également, et important moins de li-mitations à la constitution d'une adoption internationale, dans le cadre de la mé-thode de la référence à l'ordre juridique compétent.[68]

SUMMARY
THE EVOLUTION OF THE PORTUGUESE PRIVATE INTERNATIONAL LAW ON ADOPTION

In this article, the author considers the evolution of the Portuguese private inter-national law on adoption. At first, Portuguese law had to deal with this matter only

---

[66] Où le droit interne réservait à l'adoption une portée réduite, ce qui permettrait de mieux com-prendre la solution restrictive adoptée au niveau du droit de conflits.

[67] Par la Convention de la Haye, par tout autre instrument multilatéral ayant le même but ou par un faisceau d'instruments à caractère bilatéral.

[68] Voir aussi, à ce propos, Ascensão e Silva, *A constituição da adopção de menores nas relações privadas internacionais: alguns aspectos* (supra n. 12) v. II, pp. 358-373.

in the context of aliens, since adoption was unknown in Portuguese domestic law. Afterwards, the Portuguese legal system has chosen a conflict-of-laws approach. In this framework, in order to prevent the creation of limping adoptions, a cumulative connection was chosen, requiring that reference be made to the personal laws of both persons involved and that the adoption be recognised under both. This approach had therefore a restrictive effect on the formation of adoption relationships. Later, substantive rules were enacted with respect to either the foster placement of minors resident in Portugal following an adoption abroad or an adoption by Portuguese residents of minors residing in foreign countries. Even if the aims set by these rules deserve approval in general, it is submitted that the provisions are ill-fit to contribute to the necessary co-operation between the different state authorities involved in inter-country adoptions. International instruments are the only appropriate way to achieve this goal. Furthermore, it is submitted that the gap between, on the one hand, the internal policy which is favourable to adoption, and the restrictive position taken on the international level, on the other, would lead to an eventual conflict. Different methods are suggested to limit the scope for such conflicts.

Towards a More Collaborative Regime of Transnational Cultural Property Law

James A.R. Nafziger[*]

1. INTRODUCTION

Cultural property law, as KURT SIEHR has ably demonstrated,[1] transcends both national and jurisprudential boundaries. Rules of private law operate within a limited framework of public law that is increasingly transnational. The trend in the development of this body of law, though slow, is toward harmonization or unification of such troublesome rules of municipal law as those of the bona fide purchaser, formalities for valid transfer of title, and statutes of limitations.[2] Over time, private international law, equipped with general rules of jurisdiction, choice of law and enforcement of foreign judgments, will help stabilize expectations concerning the outcome of dispute resolution within the constraints of public law.

---

[*] Thomas B. Stoel Professor of Law, Willamette University College of Law, Salem, Oregon, USA.

[1] See, e.g., Kurt Siehr, "International Art Trade and The Law," 243 *Recueil des Cours* 9 (1993-VI) [hereinafter International Art Trade]; Kurt Siehr, "The Protection of Cultural Property: The 1995 UNIDROIT Convention and the EEC Instruments of 1992/93 Compared," 3 *Uniform L. Rev./Revue de Droit Uniforme* 671 (1998) [hereinafter The Protection of Cultural Property]; Kurt Siehr, "Vereinheitlichung des Mobiliarsachenrechts in Europa, insbesondere im Hinblick auf Kulturgüter," 59 *Rabels Zeitschrift* 454 (1995).

[2] But see Lyndel V. Prott, "Problems of Private International Law for the Protection of the Cultural Heritage," 217 *Recueil des Cours* 215, 277 (1989-V) ("The prospect of achieving a harmonization of these rules is not good.").

J. Basedow et al., eds., Private Law in the International Arena – Liber Amicorum Kurt Siehr
© 2000, T.M.C.Asser Press, The Hague, The Netherlands

Despite this favorable forecast, however, some basic premises of the emerging regime should be reconsidered, if not reformed.

When we use the term "cultural property," we are typically referring to a legal category that extends beyond "property" in a strict sense. The term "cultural heritage" may be more accurate.[3] Moreover, even when we are referring to property in a strict sense, the cultural element often renders the normal rules of property inapposite. Thus, the development of cultural property law in the international arena continues to be handicapped by the description of cultural heritage as "property." As a result, such entrenched rules as the *lex rei sitae* inhibit the growth of concepts, such as that of a *res extra commercium*,[4] that are better suited to the cultural heritage.

The adversarial model for resolving general property disputes is also a handicap. Great emphasis is placed on exclusive rights of ownership and the elaboration of rules for the return or restitution of stolen or illegally exported property. Clearly, such rules are essential, as increasing adjudication of ownership, return and restitution claims attest. Conversely, the absence of detailed rules inhibits resolution of cultural property disputes, as the impasse in German-Russian negotiations over return of World War II-related material suggests.

It is unclear, however, whether an adversarial process and either-or rules provide an appropriate foundation for protecting and properly allocating the cultural heritage of humankind. It may be advisable, instead, to put greater emphasis on the concept of commonality, the principle of sharing, and the technique of open, well-informed collaboration.

One is reminded of the parable of the two sisters, each of whom wants a single orange. How should it be allocated? One solution would be to award the orange to the sister with the greater "rights" to the orange, if that can be determined. That is the strictly adversarial approach that often characterizes the formal resolution of cultural property disputes today. A second solution would be to award half of the orange to each of the sisters, an appealing compromise until it becomes apparent that one sister wants the orange only to eat its pulp whereas the other wants only the orange peel for cooking. Thus, although compromises may often be preferable to either/or solutions, they typically fail to take contending interests, as opposed to stated positions, into account. A third, better-informed allocation of the disputed orange would be to encourage the sisters to express their respective interests in the orange and then to work out a mutually productive, more-than-zero-sum solution to

---

[3] In her Hague lectures, Lyndel Prott clarified the distinctive features of cultural heritage, including such examples as rituals, ceremonies, oral histories, and contextual information, all of which are difficult if not impossible to classify as "property." Prott (supra n. 2) at 307-309.

[4] See Kurt Siehr, Kulturgüter als *res extra commercium* in internationalen Rechtsverkehr," in: *Lebendiges Recht–Von den Sumerern bis zur Gegenwart. Festschrift für Reinhold Trinker* 703 (Heidelberg, Verlag Recht und Wirtschaft 1995).

a dispute (For example, one sister can have the pulp, which is all she wants, whereas the other can have the peel, which is all she wants).

Process issues of this sort are important in the development of a body of private international law capable of fashioning multi-jurisdictional solutions and maximizing the satisfaction of contending interests in disputes involving cultural property. Process is also an important issue for public international law as it seeks to overcome the reluctance of potential participants and to pour content into the often hollow language of international cooperation.

2. THE FRAMEWORK OF PUBLIC INTERNATIONAL LAW

It was only in the last quarter century of the past millennium that the global community acted with any real deliberation to construct a comprehensive regime of law for regulating and protecting the cultural heritage of humankind. The only earlier multilateral agreements of any significance were the Roerich Pact (1935)[5] and the Hague Convention (1954)[6] to protect cultural property in time of armed conflict. The on-going project to establish a more comprehensive regime has relied heavily on the leadership of intergovernmental and international nongovernmental organizations with the cooperation of national governments and private institutions.

The emerging legal regime has five components. One is the identification, rescue and protection of heritage. Two examples of this component are the UNESCO Convention Concerning the Protection of the World Cultural and Natural Heritage (1972)[7] and the Council of Europe's Convention on the Protection of the Archaeological Heritage (1992).[8] A second component includes measures to deter and respond to illegal trafficking in cultural material. The salient example is the UNESCO Convention on the Means of Prohibiting and Preventing the Illicit Import, Export and Transfer of Ownership of Cultural Property (1970).[9] A third component of international rules seeks to provide for cooperation in the restitution and return of objects. The most important instruments are the 1970 UNESCO Convention and the UNIDROIT Convention on the Return of Stolen or Illegally Exported Cultural Ob-

---

[5] Treaty on the Protection of Artistic and Scientific Institutions and Historic Monuments, Apr. 15, 1935, 167 *LNTS* 289.

[6] Convention for the Protection of Cultural Property in the Event of Armed Conflict, May 14, 1954, 249 *UNTS* 240.

[7] Convention Concerning the Protection of the World Cultural and Natural Heritage, *done* Nov. 23, 1972, 1037 *UNTS* 151.

[8] Eur. T.S. No. 143 (1992).

[9] Convention on the Means of Prohibiting and Preventing Illicit Import, Export and Transfer of Ownership of Cultural Property, *adopted* Nov. 14, 1970, 96 Stat. 2350, 823 U.N.T.S. 231 [hereinafter 1970 UNESCO Convention].

jects (1995).[10] A fourth component, more informally organized by UNESCO and satellite organizations, includes programs of professional and public education, improvement of national antiquities legislation, promotion of equitable change, and facilitation of international cooperation. The fifth and weakest component of the emerging regime includes various processes for resolving disputes arising out of implementation of the law. This component relies on scattered provisions in regional and international instruments but mostly on litigation in national courts and intergovernmental judicial cooperation. Finally, it should be noted that some normative instruments include multiple components, for example, the 1970 UNESCO Convention and the International Law Association (Buenos Aires)/ UNESCO Draft Convention on the Protection of the Underwater Cultural Heritage (1994, 1999).[11]

Overall, the international regime of cultural property law has been only marginally effective. That is partly because it is still quite new, partly because of a lack of funding to assist countries in protecting their heritage from pillage and other threats, and partly for other reasons including the failure of European countries with substantial art markets to support more than regional measures to protect cultural heritage. The normative structure and vocabulary of the law may itself be partly to blame, too. The dominant theme of international cooperation in regulating cultural heritage, often expressed in binary sets of terms, relates to trafficking in cultural material and return of it to rightful ownership. The legal model is adversarial. The evolving vocabulary of international cooperation to regulate heritage therefore relies heavily on binary classifications or dichotomies: for example, art exporting/ art importing countries (sometimes expressed as art rich/art poor countries or source nations/market nations); common heritage/national patrimony (and its sib-

---

[10] Final Act of the Diplomatic Conference for the Adoption of the Draft UNIDROIT Convention on the International Return of Stolen or Illegally Exported Cultural Objects, June 24, 1995, 34 I.L.M. 1322 (1995) [hereinafter UNIDROIT Convention].

[11] See Buenos Aires Draft Convention on the Protection of the Underwater Cultural Heritage, in ILA Report of the Sixty-Sixth Conference 432 (1994) [hereinafter Report]. A summary of the Working Session on the Draft Convention at the ILA Conference appears in id. at 448. For the Report, Draft Convention, Selected Bibliography, and article-by-article Commentaries, see Patrick O'Keefe & James A.R. Nafziger, "The Draft Convention on the Protection of the Underwater Cultural Heritage," 25 *Ocean Dev. & Int'l L.* 391 (1994) and 26 *Ocean Dev. & Int'l L.* 193 (1995) (Update) [hereinafter Update]. The convention is reprinted in 6 *Int'l J. Cultural Prop.* 119 (1997). The International Law Association's Buenos Aires Draft Convention has served as a basis for drafting a UNESCO Convention. Draft Convention on the Protection of the Underwater Cultural Heritage, UNESCO Doc. CLT-96/CONF. 202/5 Rev. (April 1999) [hereinafter UNESCO Draft Convention]; UNESCO Doc. CLT-96/Conf. 202/5 (Rev. 2) (July 1999) [hereinafter Revised UNESCO Draft Convention]; Preparatory work within UNESCO includes the Preliminary Study on the Advisability of Preparing an International Instrument for the Protection of the Underwater Cultural Heritage, UNESCO Doc. 28C/39 (Oct. 4, 1995); the Feasibility Study for the Drafting of a New Instrument for the Protection of the Underwater Cultural Heritage, UNESCO Doc. 146 EX/27 (Mar. 23, 1995); Anastasia Strati, "Draft Convention on the Protection of Underwater Cultural Heritage, A Commentary," UNESCO Doc. CLT-99/WS/8 (April 1999).

lings, cultural internationalism/cultural nationalism); national retention/free trade in heritage; underwater salvage/protection of the underwater heritage; property interests/heritage interests; the generic terms claims/counter-claims; and so on. Classifications of this sort are, of course, normal if not essential as analytical constructs in developing any system of law and governance, just as such classifications are normal in the moral development of individuals and societies. But a thoroughly binary vision is myopic.

3.   THE INTERNATIONAL LAW ASSOCIATION'S PROJECT

In order to move the regime of cultural property law beyond a more or less adversarial model, the Committee on Cultural Heritage Law of the International Law Association (ILA) prepared a Report on Heritage Law Creation which was "directed toward the development of a broader organizational framework that would incorporate principles of sharing the common cultural heritage and encouraging better public access to its educational benefits."[12] The Committee's Report, which focuses on the work of both nongovernmental and intergovernmental organizations, was adopted by the ILA at its Sixty-Sixth Conference in 1998.[13]

In its 1996 mandate to the Committee, the International Law Association (ILA) had noted "persistent weaknesses in the conventional mechanisms"[14] for international cooperation to protect cultural property and their failure to resolve tensions between claims for the return of cultural material and market-based defenses to retain such material. The adversarial system was not working very well. The ILA resolution also observed that "there is a growing interest in developing alternative schemes for avoiding or resolving these tensions through a greater orientation toward sharing of cultural heritage and enhanced access to it."[15] The ILA therefore requested the Committee to develop a set of recommendations designed to advance consideration and understanding of a broader regime of international cooperation that would overcome the limitations of binary classifications or dichotomies. In carrying out this assignment, the Committee acknowledged that such classifications or dichotomies are fundamental, even inescapable. It was acknowledged that they must be taken fully into account in developing a stronger regime of international cooperation. The Committee therefore set about not to replace but to transcend the time-worn labels by starting down a new path toward a "more collaborative and eclectic approach to developing international cultural heritage law."[16]

---

[12] "Heritage Law Creation–Second Report," in International Law Association, *Report of the Sixty-Eighth Conference* 219 (1998) [hereinafter ILA Report].

[13] ILA Report, ibid. at 18, 720.

[14] Ibid. at 218.

[15] Ibid.

[16] Ibid. at 219.

4.   LIMITATIONS OF A RULE-ORIENTATION

In responding to a number of problems, including environmental degradation, the international legal system has relied increasingly on broad framework agreements within which the details of cooperation are left to be worked out in a prescribed process of rule-making, implementation, and dispute resolution. The conventional law to protect and regulate the cultural heritage does not conform to this trend, however. To the contrary, the regime is fundamentally rule-oriented and the rules are subject to conflicting interpretations. The 1998 ILA Report highlighted a related problem that merits serious attention: the lack of a process for consultation and collaboration in interpreting and applying rules and norms. This deficiency is particularly troublesome because of the semantic and normative confusion within and among the various instruments that constitute the regime.[17]

Take, for example, the chapter in the UNIDROIT Convention that provides for return of illegally exported cultural objects. The UNIDROIT Convention as a whole represents a major advancement by harmonizing and unifying national laws. It provides a detailed framework for international restitution of stolen objects and return of illegally exported objects. The Convention also provides a new vocabulary for international cooperation in the sphere of cultural property. Unfortunately, some of the vocabulary of the conventional rules is subject to widely varying interpretation. For example, the core provision, Article 5, lists four "interests" in cultural objects any one of which, if "significantly impair[ed],"[18] may require a court of a state party to order return of an object to a requesting state. The list of interests is subject to divergent interpretations. One might note, for example, the stipulated interest in "the preservation of information of, for example, a scientific or historical character."[19] Would this support requests for return of poorly maintained colonial material from developing countries to Spain, France and other former imperial powers? Would it support claims, in the interest of enhancing historical "integrity" of a complex object, for the return to a country of origin of cultural material that

---

[17] Kurt Siehr has noted this problem in the wake of a proliferation of new international instruments during the last decade of the past millennium. See Siehr, "The Protection of Cultural Property"(supra n. 1).

[18] UNIDROIT Convention (supra n. 10) Art. 5. Article 5(3), ibid., reads as follows:
The court or other competent authority of the State addressed shall order the return of an illegally exported cultural object if the requesting State establishes that the removal of the object from its territory significantly impairs one or more of the following interests:
(a)   the physical preservation of the object or of its context;
(b)   the integrity of a complex object;
(c)   the preservation of information of, for example, a scientific
or historical character;
(d)   the traditional or ritual use of the object by a tribal or
indigenous community, [sic]
or establishes that the object is of significant cultural importance for the requesting State.

[19] Ibid., Art. 5(3)(c).

forms only a portion separated from a larger oeuvre? (An example would be one panel from a triptych that has been unhinged and divided into separate panels, each of which has been transported outside the triptych's country of origin.)

More generally, Article 5's list of specific interests is followed by a catchall category for objects of "significant cultural importance for the requesting State."[20] In determining whether an object would fall within this catchall provision, it should be noted, first, that an item can easily be of "significant cultural importance" for more than one state, including the requested state. Which state gets the object in that case? It must also be noted that the UNIDROIT negotiators deliberately lowered the threshold language from "outstanding" to "significant" cultural importance. The result of that unfortunate change in itself may be to open up a pandora's box of questionable claims.

In interpreting whether the cultural importance of a particular object may be "significant," the travaux of the UNIDROIT negotiating conference offer some guidance.[21] Several delegations argued that a claim for return of an object in itself indicated sufficient importance of the object to deny review by foreign authorities of that presumption. Art-importing countries responded that "importance" was not self-defining: a requesting state would have to prove its case to the authorities of the requested state. The UNIDROIT negotiating conference struck a compromise by holding open the possibility that foreign authorities could make their own determination of an object's "importance" within the reasonable limits of that term. To an extent, these limits are more precisely defined by reference to an Annex to the UNIDROIT Convention that lists categories of objects as in the 1970 UNESCO Convention. Arguably, some of the language in this listing limits the discretion of the requested state to question the importance of an object to a requesting state. For example, qualifying language in the Annex (e.g., "rare," "more than one hundred years old") would seem to clarify significance and thereby discourage extravagant claims to objects of little importance. Such limiting language is, however, helpful but not definitive in resolving issues of significance.

The 1970 UNESCO Convention on illegal trafficking provides an alternative litmus of "cultural significance," as follows:

> Official registration of the object by a national service, in an inventory of protected property whose export would constitute an appreciable impoverishment of the national cultural heritage, shall constitute prima facie evidence that the object is of outstanding cultural significance to the requesting state. Other evidence shall include, but not be limited to, published scholarship, scholarly testimony, and previous decisions of the competent authority of the State addressed.[22]

---

[20] Ibid., Art. 5(3).

[21] See, e.g., UNIDROIT Committee of Governmental Experts on the International Protection of Cultural Property, Report of the Second Session, Study LXX–Doc. 30, June 1992, at 26.

[22] 1970 UNESCO Convention (supra n. 9) Art. 5.

Unfortunately, however, this more precise language was not transplanted into the UNIDROIT Convention. Confusion may therefore arise, regardless of whether a state is party to both agreements or only one of them. Ultimately, of course, words are only words. The UNIDROIT framework for return of objects must therefore rely less on constructions of conventional language than the good faith and good will of state parties.

Even when there is no quarrel about the significance of a cultural object, it is questionable whether cultural material necessarily should be subject to *mandatory* return on the request of the country of origin, as the "shall order" language in Article 5(3) of the UNIDROIT Convention indicates. Take, for example, two objects of the greatest cultural importance to the United States, one from its early history as an English colony and the other from its contemporary culture. Powhatan's Mantle, from the early seventeenth century, consists of four deer skins sewn together with sinew thread and decorated with shells forming human and animal figures. The garment, or possibly wall hanging, is associated with a North American tribal chief who was the father of the legendary Pocohantas. The mantle has been described as "perhaps the most important North American Indian relic to survive anywhere."[23] The contemporary object, created in 1952, is "Blue Poles," by Jackson Pollock, who has been described as America's greatest painter and is certainly one of the most innovative and celebrated artists of the twentieth century.[24] "Blue Poles" is the last, and perhaps the finest, of Pollock's monumental abstract paintings.

Both of these items are, however, in foreign collections. Powhatan's Mantle is the most famous exhibit in the Tradescent Collection that has formed a core of the Ashmolean Museum at England's Oxford University ever since the museum opened its doors in 1683. "Blue Poles" reposes in the National Gallery of Australia in Canberra. Although Powhatan's Mantle certainly is as much a part of the English imperial heritage as it is the American colonial heritage, Pollock's masterpiece has nothing directly to do with the Australian heritage except as his work may have inspired that country's artists. Instead, the painting has everything to do with Native American elements, Thomas Hart Benton and the twentieth-century muralist traditions of the United States and Mexico, the tastes of American heiress Peggy Guggenheim, and the eccentricities of the New York art scene and American society.[25]

It is hard to imagine two more significant parts of the United States cultural heritage, both of them located abroad. Even so, there has been no serious claim for a permanent "return" of the objects to the United States, nor should there be. Whenever possible, cultural objects ought to be shared internationally as part of a com-

---

[23] Ashmolean Museum (Oxford University), The Tradescent Room 4 (no date).
[24] See The Museum of Modern Art (New York), Jackson Pollock, November 1, 1998–February 2, 1999, at 1, 4 [hereinafter Jackson Pollock].
[25] Jackson Pollock, ibid., at 2-3.

mon heritage of humankind, so long as their countries of origin have a representative collection of kindred heritage. (The lack of any statutory basis under United States law for claiming return of the two objects is, of course, material to the merits of the claim, but even when national laws support a claim for such objects or prohibit their export, international criteria are needed to strike a balance between the values of patrimonial retention and international dispersion of objects.)

5.   THE ALTERNATIVE OF A MORE COLLABORATIVE REGIME

A more collaborative approach toward the protection and allocation of cultural heritage would entail a shift in the legal model of binary classifications and adversarial processes. The new model would in no way entail a rejection of the need for rules. It would simply recognize their limitations and, in applying them, reduce the reliance placed on a construction of them in an essentially adversarial process. The agenda for developing cultural heritage law would therefore give greater priority to information exchange, consultation, consensus-building, and sharing of material. The development of new rules would still be important, but no longer predominant.

No multilateral instruments provide in any detail for a collaborative process to facilitate sharing and redistribution of heritage. On the other hand, numerous private and bilateral governmental agreements provide for sharing, exchanges and collaborative activity.

National legislation also provides models of consensus and collaboration-building. One example is the Native American Graves Protection and Repatriation Act (NAGPRA)[26] of the United States. This extraordinarily important legislation requires the repatriation of human remains and a range of specified categories of cultural items from museums and federal agencies to Native American and Native Hawaiian groups and, in the instance of human remains, to lineal descendants. NAGPRA therefore establishes a binary framework of claim and response to serve the interests of native cultures, but its provisions establish a much broader agenda of cooperation. In less than a decade, NAGPRA has set in motion a pattern of consultation and collaboration among native groups, museums, and federal agencies. In addressing repatriation issues, the required communications and negotiations, though often heated and protracted, have generally led to mutual agreements rather than formal dispute resolution.[27]

---

[26] 25 U.S.C. §§ 3001-13 (1994).

[27] See James A.R. Nafziger & Rebecca Dobkins, "The Native American Graves Protection and Repatriation Act In Its First Decade," 8 *Int'l J. Cultural Prop.* 77, 82-83, 96 (1999). For empirical descriptions of the process at work, see id. at 83; James A.R. Nafziger, "The New Fiduciary Duty of United States Museums to Repatriate Cultural Heritage: The Oregon Experience," *U. Brit. Colum. L. Rev.* 37, 42 (Spec. Issue 1995).

An international regime should likewise rely more on consultation and collaboration in giving effect to requirements for the restitution and return of cultural heritage.[28] Potential adversaries should be encouraged to work out their differences in a mutually satisfactory manner. This may not be possible in all cases, but it should be encouraged.

6.   SOME SPECIFIC STEPS

A first step toward a more collaborative framework of regulation would be to implement Recommendation C in the 1998 ILA Report on Heritage Law Creation.[29] It provides as follows:

> In order to inhibit illegal removal and trafficking in cultural heritage and to support the core values of education and globalism, the legal regime must put greater emphasis on sharing and enhanced circulation of cultural heritage.

For example, more resources should be put into loans and exchanges. Traveling exhibitions may involve costs and risks that will understandably inhibit their frequency, but they provide an excellent alternative to controversial acquisitions of objects that so often generate issues of retention and return.

The 1998 ILA Report recommended to UNESCO that it take a second set of steps by adopting guidelines to encourage systematic publication of archaeological and artistic discoveries and analyses, especially on CD-ROM and other electronic media, and by encouraging states, particularly through UNESCO consultations, to adopt cooperative, rather than unrealistically restrictive, legislation. The ILA presented this proposal as a promising alternative to an over-reliance on principles of retention and return as one technique for managing the international flow of cultural property.

In fostering collaboration as a preferred mode of implementation and dispute resolution, a third step would be to develop some kind of multi-value framework to

---

[28] See Roger W. Mastalir, "A Proposal for Protecting the 'Cultural' and 'Property' Aspects of Cultural Property Under International Law," 16 *Fordham Int'l L.J.* 1033, 1067-68 (1992-1993) (suggesting that dispute resolution procedures in NAGPRA (supra n. 21) could provide a model for international application).

[29] ILA Report (supra n. 12) at 233. The ILA Report suggested that three factors would encourage such cooperation: (1) agreement on international criteria to define the genuine (outstanding) significance of objects; (2) the provision of substantial financial assistance, perhaps within the UNESCO structure, for economically poor but "art-rich" countries and cultures, to protect their most important heritage, to permit them to retain some objects otherwise available for export, and to help them more adequately resolve disputes involving heritage claims; and (3) support for expanded programs of loans and exchanges of objects on either a short-term or long-term basis.

shape agreements for sharing and redistribution of objects. Such a framework might help overcome some of the semantic problems in Article 5 of the UNIDROIT Convention. A starting point might be to develop a consensus on a set of underlying values, such as the following:[30]

1. Scientific examination and preservation of surrounding archaeological-historical evidence or context, particularly of the original sites;
2. Identification of the objects with their original geographical-historical milieu on the territory of the requesting state;
3. Preservation of the objects in a manner that is well-suited to enrich the national conscience, foster community pride, educate the public, and enhance scholarship;
4. Visibility and accessibility of the objects to scientists and the general public;
5. Protection and display of the objects under satisfactory circumstances; and
6. Deterrence of production of forgeries.

A fourth step would be to develop a less adversarial process of dispute resolution. Clearly the current, more or less adversarial system for resolving cultural property disputes is unsatisfactory. Instead, it should be better appreciated that in such disputes, the range of implicated interests is apt to be especially broad. If so, then greater recourse to mediation might offer a promising alternative to litigation. A skillful mediator would develop an extensive inventory of those interests. The advantage of doing so would be to increase the probability that parties to a dispute, each attributing different values and priorities to the implicated interests, would "trade one off against the other for 'mutual gain.'"[31]

For example,[32] difficult issues of ownership, long-standing adverse possession and repose, good faith purchase, and the like arise in very different contexts. The context can help define a mediated solution, on a case-by-case basis. The dispute between the Norton Simon Museum and the Government of India over an Indian bronze sculpture of Shiva was resolved when the museum agreed to recognize India's entitlement to the sculpture in return for a ten-year loan of it to the museum. A mirror-image solution confirmed the entitlement of the Cleveland Museum to a Poussin painting in return to an extended loan of the work to the claimant museum, the Louvre. A more collaborative and eclectic approach, moving beyond binary classifications and black-letter injunctions, will require a framework agreement. To achieve a greater measure of uniformity among states, it might be advisable to begin

---

[30] See generally James A.R. Nafziger, "The New International Legal Framework for the Return, Restitution or Forfeiture of Cultural Property," 15 *N.Y.U. J. Int'l L. & Pol.* 789, 807 (1983).

[31] Alan Scott Rau, "Mediation in Art-Related Disputes," in: *Resolution Methods For Art-Related Disputes* 153, 160 (Quentin Byrne-Sutton & Fabienne Geisinger-Mariéthoz (eds.)) (Zurich, Schulthess 1999).

[32] Professor Rau has made a "partial list" of some fifteen types of art-related interests that could be traded off against each other for mutual gain. What follows in the text is his first example. Rau (supra n. 31) at 160-61.

this project by formulating a set of principles for consultation and collaboration that national authorities could adopt.

7.   RESTRUCTURING OF THE UNESCO PROCESS

UNESCO, working with nongovernmental organizations (NGOs), would be the most obvious center for developing, providing, and promoting a more collaborative regime. It would be advisable, however, first to address persistent problems in the rule-making and decision-making mechanisms of this organization. In 1996 the ILA's First Report on Heritage Law Creation[33] identified a number of procedural problems in UNESCO's drafting of international instruments, centering on the qualifications of conference delegates and the role of experts.[34] The 1998 (Second) ILA Report examines these deficiencies in the processes of law-creation by UNESCO, UNIDROIT and other intergovernmental organizations while expressing uncertainty about the specific role of NGOs in creating and developing the law. UNESCO, in particular, is highly politicized and often polarized. As a result, it may be handicapped in providing unbiased direction, undertaking effective conflict management, and guiding member states toward common goals.

In view of these organizational issues within UNESCO, the 1998 ILA Report made two recommendations.[35] The first of these began by noting that very little research and publication have been directed to the pivotal role of NGOs in the creation and development of international cultural heritage law and that even less is known about the deliberative processes of NGOs acting on their own or in their association with IGOs. The report therefore requested UNESCO to study and disseminate information about the alternative processes by which NGOs help develop international cultural heritage law.

The report's second recommendation for restructuring UNESCO's treaty and rule-making process proceeded from an observation that the political process for reviewing draft conventions within IGOs is often haphazard and procedurally unsatisfactory. The report recommended, therefore, that UNESCO undertake more systematic review and prioritization of agenda for the development of cultural heritage law. The report also recommended that UNESCO and other IGOs invite national delegations to submit their official positions on a draft instrument prior to a drafting conference. The underlying assumption is that this would concentrate the attention of governmental bureaucracies in advance of a drafting conference and encourage better preparations and formulation of arguments for the conference.

---

[33] "Heritage Law Creation–First Report," in International Law Association, Report of the Sixty-Seventh Conference 327 (1996).

[34] Ibid. at 330.

[35] ILA Report (supra n. 12) at 233-34.

Opening position statements would remain an essential part of the negotiating process.

The 1998 ILA Report recommended, further, that IGOs consider the formation of non-political, expert study groups, which would continue their role throughout the process of drafting an instrument and that study group members be encouraged to attend the drafting conference. The study groups would therefore serve as on-going drafting bodies that could be on call to improve the integrity of the text. They would also be available to draft amendments to preliminary drafts, thereby helping ensure that such amendments would conform to the original criteria on which the drafts were based.[36] Finally, the report recommended that IGOs consider the merits of revising the leadership at reviewing conferences to include three Chairpersons, two of whom would chair each session, one in seniority to the other, supported by the Secretary-General or other senior administrative officer of the convening organization.

8.   CONCLUSION

This essay has suggested several steps toward a less adversarial, more collaborative regime of transnational cultural property law. Taking the steps implies an openness to new ideas and to a spirit of compromise that public law by itself cannot ensure.[37] Implementation of international conventions, for example, too often relies on political posturing. KURT SIEHR's Hague lectures concluded with the observation, however, that "[c]onventions are just a small-scale device to support cultural protection at home...it would be a remarkable step forward if all States could agree that every nation is only the trustee of a common cultural heritage and that it does not matter where treasures of such a heritage are located provided that they are well protected and accessible to the public."[38] This is a lofty goal, but one worth pursuing. Debate will continue about such issues as the rights of return and restitution of cultural material to national patrimonies. A more collaborative regime based on the values of protection and sharing of heritage offers the best possibility, however, for reconciling national and global interests.

---

[36] Of course, this concept might be impaired when a Conference is primarily convoked to adopt amendments for political reasons. However, the original expert study group could alert the Conference to the effect of the proposed changes on the overall concept of the convention and to internal inconsistencies in a draft.

[37] Lyndel Prott concluded her Hague lectures by observing that "[i]t is only by imaginative legal thinking that we can attempt to meet the challenges of the future in a world which changes rapidly and in which threats to valued parts of our inheritance can develop far more quickly than settled law can be stretched to accommodate." Prott (supra n. 2) at 316.

[38] Siehr, International Art Trade (supra n. 1) at 279.

Forum Non Conveniens and *Lis Alibi Pendens*: the Australian Experience

Peter Nygh[*]

Increasing mobility and widening bases of jurisdiction have offered plaintiffs a wide choice of possible fora. As this article will show, the phenomenon is not new, but its incidence has increased greatly in recent decades. The mechanism whereby common law courts in the United Kingdom, the United States and Australia have sought to deal with the most blatant examples of "forum shopping" is through the notion of *forum non conveniens*. This institution is unknown to civil lawyers who regard it with considerable distrust. They prefer to rely on the mechanism of *lis alibi pendens* with an automatic priority to the proceedings first commenced. Although the term *lis alibi pendens* is known to common lawyers, at least in Anglo-Commonwealth jurisdictions, it has traditionally borne a quite different meaning there. This paper seeks to trace the development of the notions of *forum non conveniens* and *lis alibi pendens* in the common law jurisdictions and will illustrate the differences which have sprung up between Australia and the other common law jurisdictions.

[*] LL.D. (Syd.), S.J.D. (Mich.) , Adjunct Professor, University of New South Wales, Sydney, Australia.

J. Basedow et al., eds., Private Law in the International Arena – Liber Amicorum Kurt Siehr
© 2000, T.M.C.Asser Press, The Hague, The Netherlands

1. THE ENGLISH ORIGINS

The basis for the relevant law in England and Australia was the law of England as it developed in the 19th and early 20th centuries. Ultimately, the law in each country was proclaimed by the same judges either sitting as the Judicial Committee of the House of Lords within the United Kingdom or as the Judicial Committee of the Privy Council for the remainder of the British Empire. The knowledge that English (and some Scottish) judges would have the final say, incalculated a deference in colonial judges for their counterparts in the mother country, even if those counterparts had not reached the august heights of the Law Lords.

The fact that the United Kingdom was a multi-jurisdictional State with English, Scottish and Irish subdivisions and in turn presided over a huge Empire with over 100 individual colonial units, meant that the problems of parallel litigation and the use of inappropriate *fora* arose at an early stage of the development of private international law. The first stirrings came as early as 1799.[1] By the time *Bushby* v. *Munday*[2] was decided in 1821 the principles appear to have been well established.

Although the term *lis alibi pendens* has been used by English jurists to describe the phenomenon of parallel litigation, it should not be confused with the civil law doctrine of the same name. There never was any suggestion that the first *lis* should have precedence. Indeed in *Bushby* v. *Munday* it was the first action brought in Scotland that was restrained in favour of the second English suit. Nor was it ever suggested that having two actions pending simultaneously between the same parties in respect of the same subject matter was necessarily a bad thing. As Scrutton L.J. said in *Cohen* v. *Rothfield*: "It is not prima facie vexatious for the same plaintiff to commence two actions relating to the same subject-matter, one in England and one abroad. . . ."[3] The bringing of a double action only becomes vexatious if there is nothing which can be gained by them over and above what might be gained in local proceedings.[4]

The basis upon which English courts intervened in the 19th century to deal with vexatious parallel litigation was the inherent power of the English courts to "prevent its own processes being used to bring about injustice".[5] That power was not confined to international litigation or even to the *lis pendens* situation. It could be exercised in respect of purely domestic litigation where the proceedings, even if in-

---

[1] *Wharton* v. *May* (1799) 31 E.R. 454 (5 Ves. Jun 27, 71).

[2] (1821) 56 E.R. 908 (5 Madd. 297).

[3] (1919) 1 K.B. 410 at 414.

[4] *Peruvian Guano Co.* v. *Bockwoldt* (1883) 23 Ch. D. 225 at 234; *Bank of Tokyo Ltd* v. *Karoon* [1987] A.C. 45 at 60 per Goff L.J.

[5] *CSR Ltd* v. *Cigna Insurance Australia Ltd* (1997) 189 CLR 345 at 391 per Dawson, Toohey, Gaudron, McHugh, Gummow and Kirby JJ.

stituted singly, are so utterly absurd that they cannot possibly succeed.[6] As Bowen L.J. said in *McHenry* v. *Lewis*, the court's power rests on "the general principle that the court can and will interfere whenever there is vexation and oppression to prevent the administration of justice being perverted for an unjust end."[7] His Lordship declined to define what was meant by "vexation and oppression" and more than a hundred years later we are not much further advanced.[8] However, in its original formulation it involved an element of malice on the part of the plaintiff who brought the action solely to "vex and annoy" the defendant without any legitimate advantage to himself or herself. It was not enough that the defendant was placed at a disadvantage. The underlying notion, as exemplified by the words of Bowen L.J. cited above, was an abuse of the legal system on the part of the plaintiff. Once it could be shown that the plaintiff, if sent away, would lose a legitimate advantage given to him or her by the procedures of the forum, the plea of vexation and oppression was defeated, notwithstanding the fact that the plaintiff might also have selected the forum because it was inconvenient to the defendant. A "legitimate juridical advantage" to the plaintiff could consist of: the possibility of an earlier trial, greater scope for discovery of evidence, the possibility of recovering more in damages and costs, different forms of relief, a better opportunity of enforcing the judgment and, above all, a longer limitation period.[9]

There was, however, a countervailing principle with which modern civil lawyers can more readily identify. That is the principle that the plaintiff should not be refused his or her choice of forum. It was expressed by Scott L.J. in *St Pierre* v. *South American Stores (Gath & Chaves) Ltd* in almost constitutional terms: "The right of access to the King's court must not be lightly refused".[10] It could only be refused if the defendant could establish that the plaintiff's action was vexatious or oppressive. Since this was seen as an abuse of the judicial system, it was hardly an exception to the right of access. No right entitles one to abuse it. The result was that until 1974, when the House of Lords adopted a broader definition of "vexation and oppression" in *The Atlantic Star*,[11] the plaintiff's access to an English court was hardly ever refused even where the dispute had little to do with England.[12]

---

[6] See, *Peruvian Guano Co.* v. *Bockwoldt* (1883) 23 Ch. D. 225 at 230 per Jessel M.R.

[7] (1882) 22 Ch. D. 397 at 408.

[8] In *Oceanic Sun Line Special Shipping Co. Inc* v. *Fay* (1988) 165 CLR 197 at 247 Deane J. in the High Court of Australia defined "vexatious" as: "productive of serious and unjustified trouble and harassment", and "oppressive" as "seriously and unfairly burdensome, prejudicial or damaging". All of this is in the eye of the beholder.

[9] See, for instance, *Keeton* v. *Hustler Magazine, Inc.* 465 US 770 (1984) at 779 where the US Supreme Court said that a plaintiff is entitled to make "a successful search for a State with a lengthy statute of limitations".

[10] [1936] 1 K.B. 382 at 398.

[11] [1974] A.C. 436.

[12] As in *Maharanee of Baroda* v. *Wildenstein* [1972] 1 Q.B. 282.

However, in England at least, the "right to access to the King's court" applied only where the court's jurisdiction was based on the unwritten common law, that is, the service of the defendant within the jurisdiction. Service out of the jurisdiction was authorised by statute and was viewed by English courts as discretionary. In such a case the plaintiff's right to access was not absolute but had to be balanced against that of the foreign defendant.[13] As late as 1984, the statutory extra-territorial jurisdiction of English courts was described by Lord Diplock as "exorbitant" per se.[14] There was a lingering suggestion that the defendant in such a case was brought before the English court in defiance of international principles of territorial jurisdiction.

In Australia the position was different from that in England, even before 1974. There most judges at first instance failed to draw a distinction between jurisdiction based on common law principles and jurisdiction based on statute. In each case the plaintiff was prima facie entitled to have the jurisdiction exercised unless vexation or oppression could be established by the defendant.[15] The right of the plaintiff to access to the court of his or her choice was therefore formulated by Deane J. on a much broader basis in *Oceanic Sun Line Special Shipping Co. Inc* v. *Fay* as: "A party who has regularly invoked the jurisdiction of a competent court has a prima facie right to insist upon its exercise and to have his claim heard and determined."[16] It is a matter of debate whether the Australian position was the result of Australian judges failing to recognise the subtleties of the English approach or of a deliberate policy which saw no logical distinction between jurisdiction conferred by the common law and by statute. However, the essential similarity of both kinds of jurisdiction was formally acknowledged by the High Court of Australia in *Voth* v. *Manildra Flour Mills Pty Ltd*.[17]

As we shall see, the Australian difference was important in the development of the doctrine of *forum non conveniens* in Australia. Australian judges were not used to "balancing" the interests of plaintiffs and defendants. The primary issue was: is the court chosen by the plaintiff competent to entertain the action? Once that was established, it was difficult to dislodge the plaintiff's claim to consideration. It mattered not that the jurisdiction claimed by the plaintiff could be seen from a foreign perspective as exorbitant. Indeed, in *Oceanic Sun Line Shipping Co. Inc* v. *Fay*[18] the jurisdiction exercised by the Supreme Court of New South Wales was clearly exor-

---

[13]   *Rosler* v. *Hilbery* [1925] Ch. 250 at 259 per Pollock M.R.

[14]   See, *Amin Rasheed Shipping Corp.* v. *Kuwait Insurance Co.* [1984] A.C. 50 at 65-6.

[15]   See, *Cope Allman (Australia) Ltd* v. *Celermajer* (1968) 11 FLR 488; *Lyndsay Edmonds and Associates Pty Ltd* v. *Quest Sales Pty Ltd* (1979) 60 FLR 349 at 353 per Helsham C.J. in Eq.

[16]   (1988) 165 CLR 197 at 241 (Brennan, Deane and Gaudron JJ.; Wilson and Toohey JJ. dissenting).

[17]   (1990) 171 CLR 538 at 554 per Mason C.J., Deane, Dawson and Gaudron JJ.

[18]   See, supra n. 16.

bitant. It was based on continuing pain and discomfort suffered by the plaintiff within the jurisdiction following injuries received in an accident in Greece.

In both England and Australia the means whereby the court could prevent vexation and oppression were the same. The court could stay the action before it, either temporarily or through a so-called "permanent" stay,[19] or it could issue an injunction addressed to the defendant restraining the defendant from pursuing an action abroad. Initially both remedies were based on the same notion of vexation and oppression. However, the first-named remedy developed in England into the notion of *forum non conveniens*. The last-named remedy became known as the anti-suit injunction. This paper is only concerned with the former.

2. THE ENGLISH ACCEPTANCE OF FORUM NON CONVENIENS

It has often been said that the notion of *forum non conveniens* is an importation into English law from Scotland. In one sense this is true. In 1987 in *Spiliada Maritime Corp.* v. *Cansulex Ltd*[20] the House of Lords on appeal from England formally adopted as part of English law the definition of the principle given by Lord Kinnear in the 1892 Scottish decision of *Sim* v. *Robinow* where his Lordship said after re-iterating the traditional presumption that the plaintiff is entitled to select the forum:

> . . . the plea can never be sustained unless the court is satisfied that there is some other tribunal, having competent jurisdiction, in which the case may be tried more suitably for the interests of all the parties and for the ends of justice.[21]

It is of the essence of the *Spiliada* test that there be "a clearly more appropriate forum" which Lord Goff of Chieveley defined in that case as the forum "with which the action has the most real and substantial connection".[22] This forum, in principle, should have jurisdiction over the defendant and the subject matter of the dispute, although, as we shall see, it is not essential that it will actually determine the matter on the merits. This place, sometimes referred to as the "natural forum", is to be identified not merely by reference to so-called "convenience factors", such as the residence of the parties and their witnesses, but also with reference to factors such as the applicable law. It is for the defendant to establish that such an alternative forum exists.

The procedural "legitimate juridical advantages" of the plaintiff remain relevant,

---

[19] The reference is to "so-called", because in principle a stay can always be discharged. A dismissal is truly permanent, but Commonwealth courts have always preferred the stay.

[20] [1987] 1 A.C. 460 at 474 per Lord Goff of Chieveley.

[21] [1892] 19 R. 665 at 668.

[22] [1987] 1 A.C. 460 at 477-8.

but can be offset by the other considerations. Thus, the prospect of greater financial recovery within the forum seised is no longer to be seen as of crucial importance and the relevance of the barring of the action in the foreign forum will depend on whether the plaintiff bore responsibility for the delay and whether the defendant could and did waive its rights under the foreign limitation statute. [23] Judicial chauvinistic comparisons between local and foreign procedures such as the famous words of the late Lord Denning that the plaintiff who goes forum shopping in England will find it a good place to shop in "both for the quality of the goods, and the speed of the service",[24] are now frowned upon.

Finally, Lord Goff in *Spiliada* formulated a "fail-safe" mechanism to guard against injustice. Even if the defendant could establish the existence of a clearly more appropriate forum at the first stage of the test, the plaintiff could defeat the granting of a permanent stay by showing at the second stage of the test that he or she would not receive justice there.[25] This is somewhat comparable to the notion of "denial of justice" which may permit a civil law court to assume jurisdiction, although it must be stressed that in its English version it affirms, rather than founds, jurisdiction. Thus, it is reasonable to assume that an Iraqi plaintiff will not, following the Gulf War, obtain justice before a Kuwaiti court, or, at the very least, that this jurisdiction will not be available to him because in all likelihood he will not be allowed to enter it.[26] More controversial is the proposition accepted by the majority of the House of Lords in *Connelly* v. *R.T.Z. Corp. Plc*[27] that the denial of legal aid in the more appropriate forum can amount to a denial of justice if the "case calls for highly professional representation, by both lawyers and scientific experts".[28]

However, as has been pointed out above, even before 1987 English courts had exercised a discretion whether or not to assume jurisdiction over a foreign resident. As early as 1885 it was said that an English court "must consider seriously whether it would be a convenient forum to try the rights and obligations of a foreigner, who, at common law, owes no allegiance or obedience to the court."[29] This can be described as the *"forum conveniens* test" whereby the court has to decide whether England is a convenient forum to try the action, although in practice it was applied negatively, rather than positively. The application of this test on occasion led to a refusal to assume statutory jurisdiction where the connection between the forum and the alleged wrong was slight and the matter could be more effectively dealt with

[23] [1987] 1 A.C. 460 at 482-4 per Lord Goff of Chieveley.
[24] *The Atlantic Star* [1973] 1 Q.B. 364 at 382.
[25] *Connelly* v. *R.T.Z. Corp. Plc* [1998] A.C. 854 at 871-2 per Lord Goff of Chieveley.
[26] *Mohammed* v. *Bank of Kuwait and the Middle East* [1996] 1 WLR 1483.
[27] [1998] A.C. 854.
[28] Ibid. at 874 per Lord Goff of Chieveley. But see the criticism of this proposition by Lord Hoffmann in his dissenting speech at 876.
[29] Per Pearson L.J. in *Societé Générale de Paris* v. *Dreyfus Bros.* (1885) 29 Ch. D. 239 at 242-3.

by a foreign court.[30] Thus the notion of a "convenient forum" was known to English law at least 100 years before the decision in *Spiliada*. One could argue therefore that all *Spiliada* did was to equalise the rules in relation to both common law and statutory jurisdiction. It supplanted the hitherto accepted notion of vexation and oppression in relation to the exercise of common law jurisdiction. Even the notion of "denial of justice" is not new: as early as 1937 did an English court refuse to refer a German Jewish plaintiff to the mercies of a Nazi court.[31]

3. THE DEVELOPMENT OF FORUM NON CONVENIENS IN THE UNITED STATES

The common law in the United States shares the same basic roots as that in England and Australia. It is therefore not surprising that the present law of *forum non conveniens* in the United States started from the same inherent power of the courts to stay or dismiss an action "when a plaintiff chooses a forum not solely in search of justice but to 'vex, harass, or oppress' the defendant".[32] As in England, this power would originally have been seen as a very limited qualification on the right of the plaintiff to select the forum.

However, as in England, that power came to be exercised not only in situations where the inconvenience was maliciously inflicted upon the defendant, but also where that inconvenience flowed from objective factors. The accepted formula is that stated by Professor Weintraub as follows:

> Under the doctrine of *forum non conveniens*, a court may decline to exercise its jurisdiction if the court finds that it is a "seriously inconvenient" forum and that the interests of the parties and of the public will be best served by remitting the plaintiff to another, more convenient, forum that is available to him.[33]

As can be seen, there are several points of coincidence with the English version, despite the difference in formula. As in England, the US version looks for another more convenient forum that is "available", that is to say, is one that will have jurisdiction over the defendant. Unlike the English test, however, the US formula also requires a finding that the forum originally chosen by the plaintiff is "seriously inconvenient". In theory, at least, an English court may stay an action even if the English forum is "appropriate" as long as it is satisfied that the other potential forum is

---

[30] *Kroch* v. *Rossell et Cie* [1937] 1 All E.R. 725; *Rosler* v. *Hilbery* [1925] Ch. 250.
[31] *Oppenheimer* v. *Louis Rosenthal & Co. A.G.* [1937] 1 All E.R. 23.
[32] See, Del Luca and Zaphiriou, United States Report, in Fawcett (ed.), *Declining Jurisdiction in Private International Law* (Oxford, OUP 1995) at p. 402.
[33] Weintraub, *Commentary on the Conflict of Laws*, 3rd edn. (Foundation Press 1986) at p. 213.

"clearly more appropriate". In practice, a finding that another forum is "clearly more appropriate" will in most cases involve a finding that the English forum is inconvenient.[34] As in England, the inconvenient US forum does not transmit the case to the more appropriate forum directly, but dismisses the action (with or without conditions) and leaves the plaintiff to approach the other forum.[35]

The major difference is the reference in the US formula to "the interests of the public" in addition to that of the parties. The English formula refers to "the interests of justice", but this is a question of justice to the parties, especially to the plaintiff. As we have seen, its application can lead to a foreign plaintiff gaining access to an English court even though it is not the "natural forum". Under the US test, at least on the federal level, the public interest may require the dismissal of a foreign plaintiff's claim even if this might lead to injustice to that plaintiff.[36] The foreign plaintiff is therefore deprived of the benefit of the starting presumption that he or she is entitled to select the forum.

Prior to the decision in *Spiliada* the issue of public interest consideration was raised in England briefly. In *Rockware Glass Ltd* v. *MacShannon*[37] a Scots worker employed in a Scots factory owned by a company incorporated in England brought an action in England in respect of an injury received at work in Scotland. Apparently it was the policy of the union to which he belonged which was also headquartered in England, to encourage its members to bring the actions they financed before English courts. The House of Lords unanimously held the action brought in England to be oppressive and vexatious because of the absence of any real link other than the incorporation of the defendant with England. But Lord Diplock suggested that an "element of public policy" was involved to avoid any unnecessary diversion of resources from English courts. The other Law Lords reaffirmed that the only relevant question was that of justice in the individual case. This clearly remains the English position.

The starting point for the doctrine of *forum non conveniens* in the United States is the 1947 decision of the Supreme Court in *Gulf Oil Corp.* v. *Gilbert*.[38] That case did not involve an international element; the choice of forum lay between the federal district court in New York and a state court in Virginia. However, the Supreme Court upheld the action of the district court in dismissing the suit on the basis that it was *forum non conveniens*. In coming to that conclusion the Supreme

---

[34] See, for instance, *Cleveland Museum of Art* v. *Capricorn Art* [1990] 2 Lloyd's Rep. 166, and *Re Harrods (Buenos Aires) Ltd (No.2)* [1991] 4 All ER 348.

[35] In rare cases this can lead to multiple refusals, see *Muduroglu* v. *TC Ziraat Bankasi* [1986] QB 1225 where the English court declined to hear an action by a Turkish Cypriot plaintiff against a Turkish bank, followed by a refusal (albeit on constitutional grounds) to hear the same action by the German BGH in BGH, 2 July 1991, BGHZ 115, 90; IPRax (1992) 160 No. 25.

[36] Del Luca and Zaphiriou (supra n. 32) at p. 406.

[37] [1978] A.C. 795.

[38] 330 US 501 (1947).

Court listed as relevant both private and public factors. The private factors are those which are also considered by English courts, such as the convenience of the place chosen for trial for the hearing of the dispute, including procedural advantages and disadvantages to the parties. The public factors, on the other hand, view the dispute and the parties from the court's perspective. Some of these might also be relevant in an English court, such as the applicability of foreign law. But others are more directly oriented to the needs of the court seised, such as court congestion. The lastnamed was developed by the same court in *Piper Aircraft Co. v. Reyno*[39] where the plaintiff was foreign. Although the defendant was a US corporation and was sued in a forum about which it could hardly complain, the incident which gave rise to the claim had occurred in Scotland where the plaintiffs were also resident. Because of the foreign character of the plaintiff, the presumption in favour of the plaintiff's choice of forum was held to be entitled to less deference. Consequently the action was dismissed not so much because of any inconvenience to the defendant, but by reason of the inconvenience to the court.

4.   DISMISSAL OF PROCEEDINGS IN AUSTRALIA

4.1   The Single Forum Situation

As we have seen, the Australian courts did not accept that there was a distinction be-tween common law and statutory jurisdiction. The prima facie right of the plaintiff to access to the court legitimately chosen by him or her applied to both categories subject to the same objection where the defendant could establish vexation or op-pression. This objection was not regarded as an exception to the plaintiff's right of choice since the presence of vexation or oppression deprived the plaintiff's choice of legitimacy. Consequently, the introduction of the *forum non conveniens* doctrine constituted a much greater innovation to the Australian judicial system. It is there-fore in retrospect not surprising that the High Court of Australia rejected the Anglo-Scots version of *forum non conveniens*.

The formal rejection came in *Oceanic Sun Line Shipping Co. Inc. v. Fay*[40] where a majority of the High Court refused to follow the House of Lords in *Spiliada*. How-ever, the reasoning in that case is unsatisfactory on several grounds. In the first place, the majority of the High Court was narrow (three out of five justices sitting) and the reasoning of the majority was not unanimous. Brennan J. rejected *Spiliada* because he wanted to adhere to the law as it was established in England prior to

---

[39]   454 U.S. 235 (1981). See also, *In re Union Carbide Corp Gas Plant Disaster at Bhopal, India*, in December 1984 809 F.2d 195 (2nd Cir. 1987).

[40]   See, supra n. 16.

1974, namely that the court should only decline jurisdiction when its process was being abused through a malicious or frivolous vexation or oppression of the defendant by the plaintiff.[41] Deane and Gaudron JJ. appeared willing to accept that oppression and vexation need not be malicious. As Deane J. put it: ". . . the onus lies on the defendant to satisfy the local court in which the particular proceedings have been instituted that it is so inappropriate a forum that their continuation would be oppressive and vexatious to him."[42] His Honour defined vexatious as "productive of serious and unjustified trouble and harassment" and oppressive as "seriously and unfairly burdensome, prejudicial or damaging".[43] This, in contrast to the earlier law, can be described as "objective vexation and oppression" where the state of mind of the plaintiff is not relevant. It is the effect of the proceedings on the defendant that must be looked at. This test is in fact similar to the position reached by the House of Lords in 1974 in *The Atlantic Star*.[44] Although it may be technically correct to say that Australia has not accepted the principle of *forum non conveniens*, it has in practice adopted a technique for dismissing actions brought in an inappropriate forum.

Another defect in the reasoning of the High Court in *Fay* was the omission of any reference to the fact that the defendant had been served out of the jurisdiction in a procedure that at that time required prior leave to proceed. The question of whether that leave should or should not have been granted was not raised before the High Court. Nor was any consideration given to the fact that the tort complained of had taken place entirely in Greece. It was clear, however, that by reason of a contractual agreement, the plaintiff's right of recovery in a Greek court would have been limited to US $ 5000, a figure which was totally inadequate having regard to the injury he had suffered. It was therefore a hard case inviting the making of bad law.

It became necessary for the High Court to reconsider the matter in *Voth* v. *Manildra Flour Mills Pty Ltd.*[45] This time six justices sat and made a serious effort to achieve consensus. The result was an agreed statement of the law on the part of five justices.[46] Furthermore, the Court did address the question of service out of the jurisdiction and did have regard to the fact that the tort complained of had been wholly committed outside the forum. The result was an affirmation of the "objective oppression and vexation test" which in the event resulted in the Australian forum being held to be *non conveniens*.

---

41 Ibid., 233.
42 Ibid., at 247.
43 *Ibid.*
44 [1974] A.C. 436.
45 (1990) 171 CLR 538.
46 A joint opinion was delivered by Mason CJ, Deane, Dawson and Gaudron JJ. Brennan J. delivered a concurring judgment on the law, but dissented on the outcome. Toohey J. dissented on the law, but concurred in the result.

The High Court rejected the traditional "subjective malice" test largely because nobody in the common law world believes in it anymore. Ironically, it rejected the *Spiliada* "clearly more appropriate forum" test because there was no general common law acceptance of it.[47] The United States approach was seen as different from the English test because it took account of public interest factors. The majority of the High Court therefore decided to reject both the current United States and English approaches. The result is the Australian inquiry into whether the Australian forum seised is "clearly inappropriate". It is fair to say that an important consideration in adopting this approach was the fear on the part of the majority of too much flexibility and resultant uncertainty.

The majority saw a positive benefit in a test which concentrated only on the appropriateness of the forum seised. There would be no need to inquire whether another forum was more appropriate and make invidious comparisons between them. Indeed, one could envisage a situation where there was no other forum available and yet the Australian forum was "clearly inappropriate". This would also render superfluous the application of the second stage inquiry, as suggested by Lord Goff in *Spiliada*, whether the plaintiff would obtain justice in the foreign forum.[48]

In reality, of course, the existence of an alternative forum is relevant and this is made clear in the subsequent decision of the High Court in *Henry* v. *Henry*,[49] a case which will be considered later under the *lis alibi pendens* heading. In that case proceedings were pending in both Monaco and Australia between the same parties concerning the same subject matter: their marital relationship and their matrimonial property rights. The relationship between the marriage and Australia was slight; the spouses had lived their entire married life in Europe where the husband had made his fortune. Only the husband had Australian nationality and domicile. The husband believed that Australian law would be more favourable to him, the wife put her faith in French and German law. She filed in Monaco, their last matrimonial residence; he briefly returned to Australia to start proceedings there.

Only Brennan C.J. maintained the line that the existence of the proceedings abroad were irrelevant. He agreed that the Australian forum was "clearly inappropriate" for lack of substantial connection. The question whether the husband could obtain relief in Monaco or not was to him immaterial. The majority of the High Court, however, did compare the competing *fora* and decided, in effect, that the foreign forum was "more appropriate", not merely because of its greater connection with the marriage but also because the decision of the Monégasque court would be

---

[47] Even though it is part of the law of New Zealand: *Club Mediterranée NZ* v. *Wendell* [1989] 1 NZLR 216; Canada: *Amchem Products Inc.* v. *British Columbia* (1993) 102 DLR (4th) 96 at 119 per Sopinka J., and a number of other smaller Commonwealth countries, see: Cheshire and North, *Private International Law*, 13th edn. (Butterworths 1999) at p. 335.

[48] (1990) 171 CLR 538 at 559 per Mason CJ, Deane, Dawson and Gaudron JJ.

[49] (1996) 185 CLR 571.

entitled to recognition. Had they decided that the court in Monaco was not available to the husband or that its judgment would not have been enforceable in Australia or elsewhere, it is clear that the majority of the High Court would have permitted the husband to proceed with the action in Australia despite the tenuous link between Australia and the subject matter of the dispute. It is therefore submitted that under the Australian test an Australian forum will not be held to be "clearly inappropriate" unless there is in fact a more appropriate forum in existence which is available to the plaintiff, even though it may not be more convenient to him or her. This is somewhat similar to the double test found in the United States.

However, a forum may be "appropriate" even though another forum is "clearly more appropriate". This is illustrated by the decision of the House of Lords in *Connelly* v. *R.T.Z. Corp. Plc.* In that case the plaintiff, who was Scottish, brought suit in England against two English companies in respect of injuries he had suffered in Namibia where he had been employed by a local subsidiary of the defendants. All relevant events had taken place in Namibia and it was conceded that the Namibian forum would have been "more appropriate". Nevertheless, as Lord Goff of Chieveley pointed out, England "was an appropriate jurisdiction in which to serve proceedings on them".[50] The defendants were resident in that country and the plaintiff did not have to rely on an assumed and exorbitant jurisdiction.

Under the Australian test, if the jurisdiction is "appropriate", it cannot by definition be "clearly inappropriate". A somewhat similar situation arose before the New South Wales Court of Appeal in *Goliath Portland Cement* v. *Bengtell.*[51] The plaintiff had suffered injuries due to his employment in Tasmania at a factory owned by a Tasmanian company. His action in that State was barred by the local statute of limitations. He brought action in New South Wales, where the relevant period of limitations was open-ended, against his former employer which maintained a registered office in that State and against a New South Wales company as co-defendants. There was no doubt that Tasmania was the "natural forum", but by reason of the "residence" of both companies in New South Wales, it could not be said that that State was "a clearly inappropriate forum". Furthermore, under the law of Tasmania he could no longer obtain relief which the court found had not been due to any fault on his part. Hence the Court of Appeal refused to stay the action on the ground of *forum non conveniens*. The decision illustrates both the sufficiency of local residence as well as the need for the availability to the plaintiff of another forum.

In *Voth* v. *Manildra Flour Mills Pty Ltd*[52] the action was brought by an Australian plaintiff against a defendant in respect of a negligent misrepresentation made to the US subsidiary of the plaintiff by its local accountant. As a result the plaintiff

---

[50] [1998] A.C. 868 at 873.
[51] [1994] 33 NSWLR 414.

parent company paid more Australian tax than necessary. The majority of the High Court found that the tort was committed entirely within the United States. Consequently, the only basis for jurisdiction of the Australian court was the consequential harm suffered by the plaintiff in Australia. This was seen by the majority of the High Court as too slight a connection with Australia for Australia to qualify as an appropriate forum. The action was stayed on the ground of *forum non conveniens*. Although the plaintiff was statute barred in the US forum, the defendant had undertaken to waive his rights. The lack of entitlement by the plaintiff to costs under the US system was not seen by the court as of sufficient importance. Thus, an alternative forum was available to the plaintiff even if not as advantageous to the plaintiff as the Australian forum.

On the basis of those decisions it is possible to put forward a proposition when an Australian forum will be found to be clearly inappropriate. It will only be so when there is no substantial connection between Australia and the defendant or the subject matter of the dispute. The fact that there is a greater connection with a foreign forum is not sufficient to disqualify the Australian forum. As we have seen, if the defendant resides within the jurisdiction, the Australian forum cannot be described as "clearly inappropriate", even if a more appropriate forum exists and is available. Likewise, if the subject matter of the dispute, be it a marital relationship or a tort, has even partial links with the jurisdiction, there is a sufficient connection although purely economic consequential loss will not be enough. Finally, the Australian forum, however tenuous the connection, is unlikely to be characterised as "clearly inappropriate" if there is no alternative forum available to the plaintiff where he or she can litigate the substance of his or her claims. However, the mere fact that the plaintiff will recover less in that alternative forum does not necessarily render it "unavailable".

Unlike the United States, the Australian practice does not discriminate against foreign plaintiffs. In *James Hardie & Co. Ltd* v. *Grigor* [53] the plaintiff, a resident and citizen of New Zealand, sued an Australian company in respect of injuries suffered as the result of using the defendant's products in New Zealand. The tort was wholly committed in New Zealand. The plaintiff had apparently been advised that he would recover more in Australia than in New Zealand. The defendant sought to argue that the action should be stayed on public interest grounds to avoid a flooding of the Australian court system by foreign plaintiffs. The New South Wales Court of Appeal, while expressing sympathy for that view, considered itself bound by the rejection of the United States model by the High Court in *Voth* v. *Manildra Flour Mills Pty Ltd*. The High Court refused to grant leave to appeal as it considered the law on this point to be clear.

---

[52] (1990) 171 CLR 538.
[53] Unreported, New South Wales Court of Appeal, 18 June 1998.

4.2   The *Lis Alibi Pendens* Situation

As has been stated earlier, the common law did not know of *lis alibi pendens* as a situation to which particular rules were applicable. The existence of a *lis alibi pendens* did not even give rise to a presumption that such a situation was undesirable. At most, the term described a factual situation.

In *Henry* v. *Henry*, which, as we have seen, did involve a *lis alibi pendens* situation, the majority of the High Court, while pointing out that under the traditional pre-*Voth* test the bringing of similar actions in different countries had not been regarded as prima facie vexatious or oppressive, "the problems which arise if the identical issue or the same controversy is to be litigated in different countries which have jurisdiction with respect to the matter are such . . . that, prima facie, the continuation of one or the other should be seen as vexatious or oppressive within the *Voth* sense of the words".[54] It must be remembered that this was not a case of a plaintiff instituting similar actions in different *fora*, but the classical situation of each side choosing his and her favourite forum.

This represents quite a change from the traditional common law approach outlined above. It is true that the High Court did not embrace any automatic priority role, although it did list the question of priority amongst the factors to be considered and did indeed stay the later Australian proceedings in favour of the earlier Monégasque proceedings. The relevance of the statement is its recognition that the *lis alibi pendens* creates a situation to which somewhat different rules apply than in the case of a single action. As will be remembered, in the latter case one starts off with the presumption that the plaintiff is entitled to choose the forum. In the *lis alibi pendens* situation one of the parties must be deprived of that advantage, although the Court does not say which party this should be. Whether this is a sensible distinction or whether it is simply an invitation to create a parallel litigation situation, can be argued about.

4.3   The Related Actions Situation

The situation in *Henry* v. *Henry* was a textbook example of *lis alibi pendens*: the same parties were litigating in different countries over the same subject – the division of considerable assets acquired during the course of the marriage. In *CSR Ltd* v. *Cigna Australia Ltd*[55] the parties and the subject matter of the litigation were not identical. The Australian litigation included claims which were not before the United States court and in the United States proceedings a claim for treble damages under the Sherman Anti-Trust Act was made against one of the parties which had

---

[54]   (1996) 185 CLR 571 at 591.
[55]   (1997) 189 CLR 345.

not been made in the Australian proceedings and, even if it had been made there, was not one which an Australian court could grant. However, the factual sub-stratum of the two actions was the same: all actions arose out of a dispute between an Australian company and its insurers in respect of the same risk. It was therefore a case of "related actions" within the meaning of Article 22 of the Brussels Convention.

The situation was resolved in a manner somewhat analogous to Article 22 of the Brussels Convention by asking whether all claims could be brought before the US court which had been first seised. The High Court noted that all claims made in the Australian proceedings could be brought by way of counterclaim in the US proceedings. However, the claim for damages for breach of the Sherman Act could not be brought before an Australian court. Since the defendant to that claim was a US corporation, any resulting judgment could be enforced against it in that country. Hence the Australian proceedings added nothing and should be stayed. Although the Australian forum per se was not "clearly inappropriate" because the defendant in the Australian proceedings was an Australian corporation and some of the claims had arisen in Australia, the overall effect made it oppressive and vexatious to allow the Australian proceedings to continue.

We see therefore another step on the road to a different test to be applied when there is parallel litigation in existence. Whereas the existence of *lites pendentes* in *Henry* v. *Henry* raised a presumption that one of them was "clearly inappropriate", in the *CSR* case the test of "clearly inappropriate" was abandoned in favour of the inquiry which forum could best deal with all the issues between the parties. Once the United States was identified as that forum, the Australian proceedings became oppressive and vexatious even though the Australian forum could not have been described as "clearly inappropriate", if it had been a single forum.

5. CONCLUSION

The Australian experience differs quite markedly from that in England and the United States. In relation to single forum situations, the Australian courts are much more reluctant than English courts to stay or dismiss an action regularly brought in an Australian court. To prevent a stay or dismissal it is sufficient that the Australian forum have sufficient connections with the defendant or the subject matter of the litigation to be "appropriate", even though another forum may have much closer connections. Even if the Australian forum were to be "inappropriate", it is arguable that an Australian court would assume jurisdiction if no other forum was available. Unlike US courts, however, the Australian courts do not discriminate against foreign plaintiffs.

In relation to parallel litigation, the Australian High Court has struck out on its own path. Alone among common law jurisdictions it has developed specific rules for *lis alibi pendens* and related actions. In contrast to civil law jurisdictions there is no principle of the priority of the court first seised as such, although in each of the relevant decisions this was in fact the end result. But, in contrast to the traditions of the common law, there is an acknowledgment that parallel litigation is undesirable whether the parallelism is exact or consists of differing but related actions. In the case of a *lis alibi pendens* there is an inquiry into the more appropriate forum with priority having a deciding influence if things are otherwise in balance. In relation to related actions, the High Court favours an inquiry as to where the various claims can best be consolidated. It is clear that this differentiation between the three situations is the result of the reluctance of the High Court to be too flexible in relation to single forum situations. The principle that only the appropriateness of the Australian forum can be in issue, is no solution in parallel litigation situations.

Freedom of Movement of Spouses and Registered Partners in the European Union

Hans Ulrich Jessurun d'Oliveira[*]

1. INTRODUCTION

In this article I wish to address some issues concerning the relationship between Community Law (Union Law) and developments on the municipal level of the Member States in the field of family law. Examples to illustrate the ways in which both legal orders are interwoven in this area will be taken from some rather spectacular developments in the Netherlands. Not only has the Netherlands introduced the institution of the registered partnership as from 1 January 1998, but it has even more recently introduced a bill to make the institution of marriage available to same-sex partners. Questions to be examined in this contribution will be:

(a) how do Community instruments deal with the family member known as a "spouse" in cases concerning the freedom of movement and in employment cases and EU staff regulations?;
(b) does private international law play a role in defining the categories of persons mentioned in secondary legislation who are entitled to install themselves with and to accompany a worker who is a national of one Member State and who is employed in the territory of another Member State?;

---

[*] Professor emeritus, University of Amsterdam/ European University Institute (Florence).

J. Basedow et al., eds., Private Law in the International Arena – Liber Amicorum Kurt Siehr
© 2000, T.M.C.Asser Press, The Hague, The Netherlands

(c) are the proposals to adapt EU legislation to modern social developments adequate to deal with these new developments concerning registered partnerships and same-sex marriages?

The European Court of Justice has repeatedly dealt with the question of which persons should be considered as "spouses" under Article 10 Regulation 1612/68. It is an important question, as one of the fundamental freedoms of the EC, the freedom of movement, is involved. Furthermore, human rights and fundamental freedoms in the sense of the ECHR, especially protecting the right to respect for private and family life (Art. 8) play their pervasive role. The EU has pledged to respect these rights as general principles of Community law. The exclusion of persons from the definition of "spouse" in Regulation 1612/68 and similar secondary legislation will, in practice, amount to a barrier to the freedom of movement of the person in question.

Workers and self-employed persons are the most conspicuous, but other categories of nationals of Member States are involved as well: pensioners, students, employees of the EU and others. If they are not allowed to be accompanied by their partner then obviously their willingness to avail themselves of the freedom of movement guaranteed by the Treaty will be severely reduced.

2.   THE EXCLUSION OF NON-MARRIED PARTNERS FROM THE FREEDOM OF MOVEMENT

It is now an undeniable fact that Denmark, Sweden and the Netherlands (Finland soon to follow) as well as Spain (at least in the regions of Catalonia and Aragon), all Member States of the European Union, have introduced the institution of the registered partnership, and that Iceland and Norway as EFTA Member States have done the same. Furthermore, a number of other EU Member States are developing or have been putting into place legislation concerning unmarried couples and other forms of cohabitation outside marriage: Belgium (statutory cohabitation), France (the PACS), Spain, Portugal and Germany. This raises questions about the status of registered partners and other cohabitees in European Union law. These issues are important primarily in the context of the freedom of movement as one of the fundamental freedoms of the EC, and furthermore in the context of staff regulations.[1] In the background, human rights and fundamental freedoms also play their role, as the Union pledges to respect them as general principles of Community law. The ECHR

---

[1] See H.U. Jessurun d'Oliveira, "Lesbians and Gays and the Freedom of Movement of Persons", in: Waaldijk and Clapham (eds.), *Homosexuality: A European Community Issue* (Nijhoff, The Hague 1993) pp. 291-316; Kees Waaldijk, "Free Movement of Same-Sex Partners", 3 *Maastricht Journal of European and Comparative Law* (1996) pp. 271-284.

and the constitutional traditions common to the Member States will guide the Union in delineating the contours of these human rights and fundamental freedoms.[2]

2.1 Unmarried Partners are not Spouses

Regulations and directives which shape the freedom of movement of persons as guaranteed in primary Community law such as Article 39 EC [ex Article 48 ECT] allow a certain category of persons the right to install themselves with the person whose freedom of movement derives from primary Community law.[3]

An important example is to be found in the aforementioned Regulation 1612/68, Art. 10 of which reads as follows:

"1. The following shall, irrespective of their nationality, have the right to install themselves with a worker who is a national of one Member State and who is employed in the territory of another Member State:

(a) his spouse and their descendants who are under the age of 21 years or are dependents (...);

2. Member States shall facilitate the admission of any member of the family not coming within the provisions of paragraph 1 if dependent on the worker referred to above or living under his roof in the country from whence he came."

Are registered partnerships (with a third country national) to be considered as being analogous to the "spouses" in Article 10 of this Regulation or, in other words, is the "spouse" to be construed as including registered partners? If this last question is to be answered in the negative, then are they at least covered by S. 2 ("any member of the family not coming within the provisions of para. 1")? The first issue was addressed in the well-known *Reed* case,[4] in which two opposite-sex British nationals living in a stable non-marital relationship wanted to settle in the Netherlands. They both looked for a job, but only the man succeeded in finding one, and that was the reason why his partner applied for the dependent status under Article 10 Regulation 1612/68.

The Court held in 1986:

"In the absence of any indication of a general social development which would justify a broad construction, and in the absence of any indication to the contrary in the regulations, it must be held that the term 'spouse' in Art. 10 of the Regulation refers to a marital relationship only."

---

[2] Art. 6 Treaty on European Union.
[3] See generally J. Handoll, *Free Movement of Persons in the EU* (Wiley 1995).
[4] Case 59/85 [1986] ECR 1286, at p. 1300.

It is indeed understood that the concept of "spouse" in this regulation is an autonomous Community concept, which is liable to be interpreted in a dynamic way, but such dynamics are, according to the court, dependent on "a general social development", not only the situation in one Member State. It is clear that the court at the time did not think it wise to come up with an extensive interpretation in this sensitive area, and this sensitivity in the Member States is only heightened when it comes to same-sex partnerships. While not explicitly stating that social and cultural developments have to be demonstrated in each and every Member State, the Court would expect a broad majority in order to bind a minority of States which shy away from accepting same-sex relationships or non-marital relationships in general. It may be useful to contrast this decision with the reasoning in *Diatta*,[5] which concerned a married couple who no longer lived under the same roof, the Senegalese wife intending to divorce her French husband. The Court considered that:

> "[17] Having regard to its context and the objectives which it pursues, that provision (Art. 10 Reg. 1612/68 – d'O) cannot be interpreted restrictively."

The ECJ took the formal view that, as long as the marriage had not been terminated by a competent authority, and even if the spouses no longer lived together, the partners in this empty shell nevertheless counted as "spouses" and were thus eligible for dependent residence rights. The consequence of *Reed* and *Diatta* is that the ECJ has retained marriage as a formal condition for being treated as a "spouse" under Community law, but that this condition may be devoid of any substance: not only all kinds of arrangements involving living apart together seem to be allowed, but also marriages of which the existence only continues for the convenience of the advantages of Community law. If one confronts the excerpts just quoted from the judgments in *Reed* and *Diatta*, we see paradoxically that both broad and restrictive interpretations of the word "spouse" are out of the question if the context, social and otherwise, does not dramatically depend thereon. The Court has also repeatedly held that as a fundamental freedom is involved, interpretation should be as broad as possible.

2.2   The Company of a Non-Married Partner May Be a "Social Advantage"

As it is, the Court in *Reed* refused to assimilate a stable partner with a "spouse", but it nevertheless found a back door to allow her in: Article 7(2) of Regulation 1612/68 afforded the opportunity to declare that the right of the worker to be accompanied by his partner was to be construed as a "social advantage" mentioned in that

---

[5] Case 267/83 *Diatta* v. *Land Berlin* [1985] ECR 574.

provision, which the foreign worker shall enjoy on an equal footing with national workers. Because the Netherlands allows Dutch nationals to "import" their partners under certain conditions, the same right has to be granted to workers from other Member States, according to the court. The equality principle or, in other words, the prohibition on discrimination against the nationals of other Member States, is the key issue here. If a Member State does not allow its own nationals to "import" their (third country national) partner into the country, other Member State nationals are not allowed to do so either under Article 7(2) Regulation 1612/68. It is remarkable to see that the exercise of human rights is considered as a social advantage, available to some, but not to others.[6]

3.   REGISTERED PARTNERS ARE NOT SPOUSES EITHER

Has anything changed in the meantime? In a recent case concerning staff regulations the status of a registered partnership was directly at issue for the first time: *D. v. Council.*[7] D, a Swedish national, was a staff member of the Council, and requested that his civil status as a registered partner be assimilated with being "married" under Annex VII of the Statute (Staff Regulations), as it would be under Swedish law according to an affidavit delivered by the Swedish administration. Sweden appeared as party in the proceedings. This request was refused by the Court of First Instance; granting it would have implied the obligation for the Council to pay family allowances (*allocation de foyer*). The Court of First Instance took a cautious stance and started out by explaining that the statutory provisions (Art. 1(2)(a) of Annex VII to the Statute) contained Community law notions of "marriage" and "spouse" and were exclusively related to marriage in the traditional sense of the term.[8] As the meaning of the terms was clear, the Council as the employer was not obliged to resort to the law of the Member States in order to detect this meaning. And it pursued:

> "28. En tout état de cause, la Cour européenne des droits de l'homme interprète l'article 12 de la Convention en ce sens qu'il ne vise que le "mariage traditionnel entre deux personnes de sexe biologique différent."

---

[6] In case C-356/98 *Kaba* v. *Secretary of State* (11 April 2000), the equality principle was watered down on the basis of the assumption that there may exist objective differences between home nationals and nationals of other Member States.

[7] Case T-264/97 *D. and Sweden* v. *Council* (Court of First Instance, 28 January 1999), [1999] ECR-SC II-1. Case C-122/99 *D.* v. *Council* and Case C-125/99 *Sweden* v. *Council* are pending appeal before the ECJ. In case T-102/99 *Van Hamme* the Court of First Instance persisted in its denial of regarding registered partners as coming within the concept of "spouse".

[8] It referred in this respect to T-65/92 *Arauxo-Dumay* v. *Commission* [1993] ECR II-597, para. 28.

Il s'ensuit que, ainsi qu'il a été récemment jugé par la Cour de Justice, en l'état actuel du droit au sein de la Communauté, les relations stables entre deux personnes du même sexe ne sont pas assimilées aux relations entre personnes mariées (arrêt de la Cour du 7 février 1998, *Grant*, C 249/96, Rec. p. I-621, points 34 et 35)."

The reference to the *Grant* case was, however, in itself not sufficient. In that case the employer refused to pay travel allowances for a same-sex partner in a stable relationship, not being a registered partnership. That is why the Court of First Instance added:

"29. Dans ces conditions, un employeur n'est pas tenu d'attacher à la situation d'une personne entretenant, comme le requérant, une relation stable avec un partenaire de même sexe, même ayant fait l'objet d'un enregistrement officiel par une administration nationale, les effets découlant de l'état civil d'une personne engagée dans les liens du mariage traditionnel (arrêt *Grant*, précitée, point 35) (emphasis added – d'O.)."

This, I submit, is not what was said in *Grant*. The case at hand is different from the *Grant* case precisely in its being concerned with a registered partnership, which in municipal law is assimilated to marriage. Furthermore, such a registered partnership is recognized in a number of other EC countries as being equal to marriage. This makes a great difference when compared with *Grant*, because stable non-married, non-registered couples are less likely to be considered on the same footing as married couples in their home country and abroad. The Court of First Instance has therefore lost the opportunity to distinguish *Grant* and to engage in a more dynamic approach in the stronger case of registered partnerships.

Mention must be made of a slight legislative development, which was noticed by the Court but could not play a role as it was enacted after the material events: Regulation 781/98 of 7 April 1998, amending the Staff Regulations (...) in respect of equal treatment.[9] This Regulation inserted a new Article 1a in the Staff Regulations of officials of the European Communities which reads as follows:

"1. Officials shall be entitled to equal treatment under these Staff Regulations without reference, direct or indirect, to race, political, philosophical or religious beliefs, sex or sexual orientation, without prejudice to the relevant provisions requiring a specific marital status." (...) (emphasis added – d'O)

This provision leaves the situation pretty much unchanged, except for the new and explicit mention of sexual orientation as a forbidden ground for discrimination. This is given with one hand, but with the other most of it is taken back by the *pro-*

---

[9] Council Regulation 781/98 of 7 April 1998, *OJ* [1998] L 113/4-5.

viso that provisions requiring a (!) specific marital status will prevail. The Court in the instant case added that the Council had inserted in the minutes of the Council a declaration in which it "invited the Commission to proceed to necessary research concerning (...) the recognition of the situations of registered partnerships and to submit, on the basis of this research, appropriate proposals in these areas."

4.   Is There a Conflicts of Law Problem Lurking behind the Community Concept of "Spouses"? And What about Same-Sex Marriages?

It is remarkable that neither the ECJ nor the Court of First Instance have ever addressed the general question whether the marital relationship, which forms the basis for the exercise of the right to be accompanied by a partner, is subject to considerations of private international law. It is, in other words, not clear whether, according to Community law, the marital relationship is to be considered as an autonomous concept of Community law (as yet imperfectly defined) or as a concept which first has to undergo the scrutiny of the conflicts of law rules prevailing in the Member State in which Community rights are invoked.

(a)   Most Member States have rules on the celebration and recognition of marriages in international cases. These rules define in which cases marriages celebrated in other countries will be recognized and to what extent. Some marriages, although undoubtedly falling under the category of marriage will not, or only in certain respects, be recognized elsewhere. Polygamous marriages are a case in point. As most Member States of the EU do not allow their nationals to enter into a polygamous marriage, and at least will not recognize such a marriage, the problem will only seldom arise on the EC level. The example demonstrates, however, that "marital relationship" as the foundation of the concept of "spouse" for Community law purposes, is problematic, and has only been superficially dealt with by the ECJ.

Some EC Member States have ratified the Hague Convention on Celebration and Recognition of the Validity of Marriages (1978).[10] This Convention excludes "informal marriages" from its recognition regime (Art. 8), but not – at least not explicitly – polygamous marriages. Various provisions allow contracting States to refuse to recognize the validity of a marriage on certain grounds (Arts. 11, 14). Central to the chapter on recognition is the provision that "a marriage validly entered into under the law of the state of celebration (...) shall be considered as such in all Contracting States(...)" (Art. 9).

The first chapter on the celebration of marriages contains no definition of

---

[10] The Netherlands and Luxembourg as from 1 May 1991.

marriage, in accordance with a standing tradition of the Hague Conference not to stir up problems in the wrong place. Thus, the concept of marriage in the Convention includes incestuous marriages, polygamous marriages, child marriages, and even same-sex marriages, as is evident from various indications in the preparatory documents.[11] This broad definition of marriage is compensated by a provision containing the usual public policy exception (Art. 5), necessary in a universal convention, even if it scored only three ratifications.

Interesting questions will arise if the Dutch Bill, allowing same-sex partners to marry, will become law.[12] In the first place one may wonder whether existing conventions concerning marriage will be able to absorb the Dutch same-sex marriage. This question I would answer affirmatively, albeit with exceptions. This positive answer does not preclude, however, the use of public policy arguments to withhold recognition in other contracting States. The second question deals with Community law and could be posed as follows: does Community law, using the terms "spouse" or "marriage", include same-sex marriages? This question can also be answered in the affirmative. According to the consistent case-law of the ECJ where fundamental freedoms are involved the interpretation should be broad. Furthermore, its case-law has up until now systematically excluded categories of relationship other than marriages from the concept of "spouse", but it has included, substantially speaking, even the most tenuous marriages by accepting marriages all but dissolved and marriages devoid of any content, which have only been kept alive only for Community law purposes. It would take some courage to exclude marriages, validly entered into in one of the Member States, from the blessings of the fundamental freedom of movement and establishment. A deviation would imply that the strictly formal view on marriage which the Court has maintained would be exchanged for a piercing of the veil of marriage approach. This last perspective has been reserved for so-called "sham marriages" which Member States are entitled to combat.[13] This last proviso in *Surinder Singh*[14] suggests that it is up to the Member States to define, according to their law and including private international law, a valid marriage, also for Community law purposes.

(b) There are inconveniences related to the freedom of the Member States to define what a marriage is for Community law and other purposes. In the first place,

---

[11] See *Actes et Documents de la treizième session 4 au 23 octobre 1976* (1978) T. III, pp. 9, 41, 116, 162, 293.

[12] As the Bill has been introduced on the repeatedly expressed wish of Parliament, it is very likely that the Act will be passed during the course of this year (2000). The latest document on Bill 26.672 is the Nota naar aanleiding van het Verslag, nr. 5 dated 3 May 2000.

[13] Cf. d'Oliveira, "The Artifact of 'Sham Marriages'", 1 *Yearbook of Private International Law* (1999) pp. 49-84, referring, among other things, to case 370/90 *Surinder Singh* [1992] ECR I-4265.

[14] See the previous note.

there is a certain diversity leading to inequality. A person, validly married in the Netherlands, can be denied the status of a spouse in Germany, if Germany does not recognize marriages between same-sex partners or because it considers a marriage, notwithstanding its celebration in the Netherlands, as a sham marriage. There is even a certain interest in non-recognition of foreign marriages by host States because this would reduce the number of persons availing themselves of the right to freedom of movement or establishment. These considerations have led to an autonomous definition by the Community of the concept of worker and other kindred concepts of persons entitled to Community rights. Similarly, there is an argument to deal likewise with the concept of marriage and to develop a Community concept of this institution. One thing is clear: the courts have become rather cautious in this area.[15] They are inclined to leave the definition of "spouse" and "marital relationship" to the Community legislative bodies.

5.   AWKWARD AMENDMENTS EXPANDING THE CATEGORY OF FAMILY MEMBERS

The Court of First Instance concluded that it was up to the Council as the Community legislator to change the legal situation concerning family allowances (as this is not up to the courts). In line with the above-mentioned Council Regulation 781/98, in 1998 the Commission came up with a proposal for a European Parliament and Council Regulation to amend Regulation 1612/68 and Directive 68/360[16] in order to adapt these instruments to "the new socio-economic and political conditions of the Community", and to incorporate the principles of ECJ case-law. Other directives are involved as well, both in the area of freedom of movement and staff regulations. It repeats the prohibition of discrimination on the grounds of sexual orientation as an obstacle to the freedom of movement.

Article 10 of Regulation 1612/68 is to be amended in the proposal in order to allow not only spouses to install themselves with a worker in another Member State, but also:

"any person corresponding to a spouse under the legislation of the host Member State".

---

[15] In his case-note on C-337/97 *Meeusen* ([1999] ECR I-3289), Mortelmans, in *Ars Aequi* (1999) pp. 838-848, suggests that the Court has the task of clarifying how broad or narrow the concept of spouse is: the "classical" spouse, the partners in a living-apart-together arrangement, a homosexual couple, etc. That *Reed* (supra n. 4) gives a lead towards a broad construction of the concept of "spouse" has been remarked upon, but given *Grant* (case C-249/96 *Grant* v. *South-West Trains Ltd.* [1998] I-621) and *D and Sweden* v. *Council* (supra n. 7) I am not convinced that the Courts will go beyond formal marriages.

[16] COM. 394 (1998) fin. A previous attempt by the Commission to revise both instruments, introduced in 1989, met its Waterloo in 1992 when the Council raised insurmountable objections.

This addition is nothing more than the consecration of the principle expressed by the Court in *Reed*.[17] This is acknowledged in the Explanatory Memorandum:[18]

"This possibility which merely reflects sociological developments in certain Member States, has already been recognized in the case-law and constitutes only an application of the principle of equal treatment. This provision does not oblige Member States to recognize unmarried couples and will be applied only in cases where such recognition has been decided by the legislator."

There is a major shift compared with *Reed*, however, in that the Court in that case refused to bring unmarried couples within the ambit of Article 10, and brought them under Article 7 by broadening the concept of "social advantages" in that provision. The proposal includes them under Article 10, but the right under Article 10 is conditional upon acceptance by the host State. I "*reed*" the new Article 10 as implying that host Member States which under their – written – rules of private international law recognize, for example, registered partnerships entered into in another Member State, including the effects attached to that status according to the *lex loci celebrationis*, are obliged to allow the registered partner of the worker to settle in their territory with the Union citizen.

This is very much a halfway house. Although presumably equality of treatment is attained by allowing workers from other Member States to bring along their quasi-spouse in the same way as the host country will normally allow its own nationals to bring their quasi-spouse into the country, nevertheless a differential treatment will still exist as some Member States will admit (registered) partners while others will refuse the same partner. In this respect one must conclude that, if the Commission indeed had the intention to incorporate *Reed* into the Regulation, it would have been more appropriate to do this in Article 7, as this article guarantees equal treatment in a number of aspects to workers possessing the nationality of the Member State involved. In the Explanatory Memorandum equal treatment is referred to as the legal basis of the provision concerning non-marital partners, but the conclusion that the provision should find its place in Article 7 rather than in Article 10 has not been drawn. The structure of the regulation is disturbed, however, if the partner involved is covered by Article 10 and not by Article 7, although the recognition by the host State legislation is crucial.

Article 7, in turn, is to be amended as well. Especially Article 7(2) is expanded where it originally only spoke of "social and tax advantages". It now reads:

---

[17] Case C 59/85 *Reed* (supra n. 4).
[18] At p. 12. The emphasis on legislative recognition is remarkable. Other sources of domestic law are ignored by Community law. Case law, for example, seems to be irrelevant!

"A worker who is a national of a Member State shall enjoy the same financial, fiscal, social, cultural and other advantages of national workers."

One may well ask whether the "social advantage" of being accompanied by one's companion can still be covered by Article 7(2), as in *Reed*, or whether a worker may in the future only rely on the new Article 10.[19]

As for the Parliament, mention must be made of a Resolution dated 17 September 1998 on equal rights for gays and lesbians in the EC,[20] which endows the EC with a special responsibility to ensure equal treatment for all citizens, irrespective of their sexual orientation, within the framework of its activities and areas of responsibility, and the EP calls on the Commission to present, among other things, a draft recommendation on equal rights for lesbians and homosexuals. This recommendation should seek to end "the barring of lesbians and homosexual couples from marriage or from an equivalent legal framework, and should guarantee the full rights and benefits of marriage, allowing the registrations of partnerships".

At an earlier stage, on the occasion of the previous Commission proposal[21] to amend Article 10 Regulation 1612/68, the EP proposed to include within the right to install themselves:

"the persons with whom the worker lives in a *de facto* union recognized as such for administrative and legal purposes, whether in the Member State of origin or the host state, and their dependent offspring."

This was not accepted by the Commission under the current decision structure.[22] This goes to show that the task of bringing secondary legislation on the freedom of movement up to date is cumbersome and it meets with strong cultural and ideological resistance. Both institutions, the Court and the Commission, hide behind one another: the Court indicates that the legislator is the prime mover, and the Commission merely incorporates the case-law of the court, without daring to go beyond it. What will emerge from the latest proposals is not very clear. Some take a dim view of the activities of the EU in this field, as registered partnerships are in some Member States either hotly debated or are a complete taboo.[23] Others, in a more theoretical perspective, have given pessimistic forecasts as well.[24]

---

[19] The Explanatory Memorandum is silent on the subject, and does not mention *Reed* (supra n. 4) as one of the Court's decisions to be reflected in the amendment to Art. 7, although the Court included the right to be accompanied by one's partner under Art. 7 and not under Art. 10.

[20] *OJ* [1998] C 313/186.

[21] COM 815 (88) fin.

[22] Cf. d'Oliveira, supra n. 1 at p. 308.

[23] R. Barents, *Het Verdrag van Amsterdam in werking* (Deventer 1999) p. 154. The author proposes looking for solutions within the ambit of Art. 6a, a possibility hinted at in *Grant* (para. 48) as well.

ILPA describes the present situation concerning the implementation of the freedom of movement generally as follows:[25]

"The Commission's mid-1998 proposals for changes to Regulation 1612/68 and Directive 68/360 are moving slowly. The Austrian and German Presidencies made no effort to begin negotiations on these proposals, doubtless because they are wholly opposed to them. The outgoing EP gave the proposals a first reading in May, suggesting only minor technical amendments. By doing so, the plenary turned down some very liberal amendments regarding family members that were proposed in committee. However, since the EP at least backs the Commission's text, it may be prepared to fight the Council in the 'co-decision' procedure if the Council weakens this when the Council adopts a Common Position. As noted below, it is not clear whether the Finnish Presidency is prepared to begin talks on this proposal; it may be that it will have to await the following Presidency for attention, as Portugal likely greets the proposal with more enthusiasm. But then, with a more conservative EP just elected, it is less likely that the Council will have a fight on its hands if it does approve a fairly modest Common Position."

In a recent policy document,[26] the Dutch Government assessed the situation rather gloomily:

"Neither Germany nor Finland have tabled the proposals. It is as yet unknown whether the Portuguese will put the proposals on the agenda. The little eagerness to table these proposals is possibly inspired by the negative stand of a considerable number of countries during the preparatory negotiations on the level of the Commision. Germany, the United Kingdom, France and Belgium, amongst others, have problems with the extension of the categories of persons entitled to family reunification."

In the meantime France has introduced its PACS and Belgium its statutory cohabitation. Germany is preparing legislation in the same field. Therefore the balance

---

[24] David Bradley, "Convergence in Family Law: Mirrors, Transplants and Political Economy", 6 *Maastricht Journal of European and Comparative Law* (1999) pp. 127 et seq.: "The lengthy project in France for the introduction of the Pacte Civil de Solidarité (PACS) indicates contrary to predictions in the transplants thesis construction of a unitary legal system in this area of private law will not be entirely trouble-free." (at p. 132).

[25] ILPA (Immigration Law Practicioners' Association), European Update: June 1999, p. 11. See also Kees Waaldijk, "Towards Equality in the Freedom of Movement of Persons", in: Mark S. Bell (ed.), *Sexual Orientation and the European Union after Amsterdam*, ILGA (forthcoming in English, French, German and Spanish) Ch. 4.

[26] Tweede Kamer, 1998-1999, 22.112 no. 126, p. 9 dated 31 August 1999. It should be added that the Netherlands expressed its (strong) reservations as well, although it agreed to the proposal to add non-marital partners as it had, in its municipal law, already placed registered partners on an equal footing with spouses.

may be shifting towards expanding the categories of persons allowed to follow Member State nationals who avail themselves of Community rights and freedoms. The prospects are, in other words, less gloomy than they have been for the last decade. Although no Member State is applauding the prospect of Community law forcing them to accept a growing number of non-active persons, partly third country nationals, there are nevertheless countervailing arguments. In the first place, unemployment is decreasing, and, second, as the number of countries in which the registered partnership and similar affilations have been instituted increases, their interest in having these partners acknowledged in the Community grows. Furthermore, the mobility of workers in the EU is rather limited: less than 2% of the European population of working age consists of nationals of one Member State working in another. I submit that the full recognition by the European Community and its Member States of registered partnerships and the like for the purposes of the exercise of Community rights and freedoms is urgently needed.[27]

On the one hand, the exercise of freedom of movement is clearly hampered by the existing situation which denies registered partners the right to install themselves with their partner in another Member State. The Commission's proposals lower this barrier somewhat, but they create new unequal treatment. Registered partners, of which one is a worker or self-employed, may be allowed to take his/her partner to Member State A, but not to Member State B:

> "A Dutch worker will be deterred from moving to the UK if he or she cannot bring his long-term same-sex non-Community national partner; equally a British national will be deterred from transferring his or her place of work back from the Netherlands to the UK if this means separation because the British are not required to issue the partner the same residence permit as the Dutch have."[28]

This situation boils down to a Europe with different speeds, and, seen from a territorial point of view, a checkered freedom of movement which has to jump over countries not allowing registered partners in.

On the other hand, the phrase "any person corresponding to a spouse under the legislation of the host state" does not take into account the dynamics and structure of private international law prevailing in the Member States.

As has been shown, the recognition of marriages depends primarily on their

---

[27] Many contributors to the discussion which took place at the Conference in 1991 to celebrate the 25th anniversary of the T.M.C. Asser Institute were of the same opinion: see Henry G. Schermers, Cees Flinterman, Alfred E. Kellermann et al. (eds), *Free Movement of Persons in Europe* (T.M.C. Asser Institute 1993) p. 541 et seq. (Taschner, d'Oliveira, Weiler, O'Keeffe).

[28] Nicholas Blake, "Family Life in Community Law: the Limits of Freedom and Dignity", in: Elspeth Guild (ed.), *The Legal Framework and Social Consequences of Free Movement of Persons in the European Union* (Kluwer Law International 1999) p. 13.

being validly celebrated. The *lex loci celebrationis* is of primordial importance in its recognition elsewhere. The same reasoning would apply to the recognition of registered partnerships. The proposal for a number of provisions of private international law regarding registerd partnerships, developed by the Dutch Standing Committee on Private International Law,[29] provides in s. 18:

> "A registered partnership validly entered into outside the Netherlands in accordance with the law of the state of celebration or which subsequently becomes legally valid, shall be recognised as such."

Legislation along the lines developed by the Standing Committee is now under preparation. It may be interesting to note that there is in existence a letter by the Dutch Minister of Foreign Affairs to the French Embassy in the Netherlands dated 8 December 1999, in which the Minister declares that a PACS, validly concluded in France or elsewhere, shall be recognized in the Netherlands and registered at the Registry on the same footing as registered partnerships.[30] The letter even declares – erroneously in my mind – the conflict rules contained in the Act on conflicts of law on marriage applicable on recognition and registration, thus implying that, in the Netherlands, the PACS is considered as being equivalent to marriage.

Returning to the Commission's proposals, reference to the legislation of the host State implies the application of its rules of private international law on recognition of non-marital relationships. These rules would presumably look into the *lex loci celebrationis* or *registrationis* – if I may use this dog-Latin expression – in order to find out whether the person involved "corresponds to a spouse". In case of doubt, as regarding the PACS or the Belgian *cohabitation légale* characterization has to take place in a more autonomous, comparative way, under the auspices of the *lex fori*. In this manner, the PACS, for example, is to be considered as fulfilling the condition of the Commission proposal, because although it is characterized in the official documents as a contract *sui generis*, it nevertheless finds its place in the book on persons of the Code civil, and it amounts to a marriage impediment, and stands in the way of concurring PACS-es. All Scandinavian countries (similarly to the Dutch) emphasize the equality between marriage and the registered partnership.

---

[29] Cf. for the text and Explanatory Memorandum *Tijdschrift voor Familie- en Jeugdrecht* (1998) pp. 146-159; see for the English text of the draft http://www.minjust.nl: 8080/e. For a comparative review on the conflicts of law of registered partnerships and similar affiliations see: Jessurun d'Oliveira, "Registered Partnerships, PACSes and Private International Law: some reflections", *Rivista di diritto internazionale privato e processuale* (2000) (forthcoming); Id., "Registered Partnerships, PACSes and Private International Law: some reflections", in: Florence Guillaume/ Raphaël Arn (eds.), *Cohabitation non maritale – Évolution récente en droit suisse et étranger, actes du colloque de Lausanne du 23 février 2000* (Droz, Genève 2000) pp. 33-60.

[30] See D'Oliveira, "Het Pacte Civil de Solidarité, het geregistreerd partnerschap, het opengestelde huwelijk en het Nederlandse internationaal privaatrecht", *NJB* (2000) 884.

These should be recognized *qua tales* in the other Member States (and elsewhere). This implies that a registered partnership entered into in Norway, recognized in Denmark or in the UK,[31] should be recognized in such a way that a partner *eo ipso* corresponds to a spouse. Only when such recognition is manifestly incompatible with the public policy of the host State may this State refuse to recognize the registered partnership.[32] The *ordre public* of the Community may scrutinize and curtail the exercise of the discretion by the Member States in invoking their municipal public policy.

In that case the State denying recognition may thereby allow for the establishment of bigamous relationships in the broad sense of this term. By not recognizing the existence of a registered partnership, or a PACS, that State would permit the conclusion of a marriage concurrent with the partnership already established and registered in another State which, moreover, considers the concurrent marriage as a bigamous, prohibited relationship. This would offend public policy in the host state to more or less the same degree as recognition of same-sex registered partnerships or marriages, and would constitute the awkward choice between "hanging and burning".

Just as the private international law on recognition and celebration of marriages is imbued by the *favor*-principle in order to avoid limping marriages, private international law and European law should avoid limping registered partnerships, valid in one country, ignored in another. It remains to be seen whether EC countries would go so far as to invoke their public policy in refusing to recognize partnerships. I doubt this for the reasons stated earlier.

6.   SOME CRITICAL CONCLUSIONS

It is clear from the preceding paragraphs that case-law and proposed legislation in the European Union are unsatisfactory as regards the recognition of registered partnerships. The courts stick to marriage as the criterion for establishing who will count as a spouse, and refer to the legislator for further development. The evolution of the consecutive proposals by the Commission and the reactions of Parliament and the Council demonstrate a regression rather than a willingness to accept the fact

---

[31] Cf. the plea by Kenneth McK. Norrie, "Reproductive Technology, Transsexualism and Homosexuality: New Problems for Private International Law",43 *ICLQ* (1994) pp. 757-775; see also Clarkson and Hill (eds.), *Jaffey on the Conflict of Law* (Butterworths 1997) p. 339 "(...) It is hoped that in today's climate an English court would not hold a registered partnership between two Danes to be contrary to public policy. However, it is conceded that the English court is likely to be influenced by the nature of the issue before it".

[32] Cf. Ch. II of the Hague Convention on Celebration and Recognition of the Validity of Marriage, 14 March 1978, Arts. 9 and 14.

that a growing number of Member States are quickly developing a new branch of family law in order to primarily accommodate same-sex relationships. The Netherlands is even introducing legislation in order to allow same-sex partners to marry. It remains to be seen whether the European Courts will stick to their case-law in allowing these spouses to join their husbands and wives who make use of their right to freedom of movement, and to allow European Community staff members to take their spouse with them.

The attempt to reduce the impact of these new branches of family law on the law of the Communities by introducing as a kind of connecting factor the law of the various host countries is contrary to the principles of private international law. These refer mostly to the law of the place where the partnership (marriage) is registered.

Once validly entered into and registered, a registered parnership, a PACS and the like should entitle the partners to settle in the other Member States on the basis of the entitlement to freedom of movement of one of them.

If the Community legislator drags its feet, as it did during the last decade, the Courts should not shrink from taking the initiative again, and to do what the legislator is unable to.

As for legislative measures emanating from the Action Plan of the Council and Commission (Tampere, 3 December 1998),[33] these will not only be piecemeal, but, as they will contain public policy exceptions, will not in themselves be sufficient. Furthermore, these private law instruments may have implications for Community freedoms, and indeed are based on their connection with, amongst other things, the basic principle of "free movement of people within the European Union", but Community rules on the private international law of registered partnerships are still far off. They will not necessarily bring about the extension of the freedom of movement of partners, as long as the secondary legislation on the fundamental right itself remains unchanged. It is therefore essential to revise Regulation 1612/68, the Staff Regulations and the flanking directives in a way which does not deny the right to protection of family life or private life to partners in registered partnerships and similar relationships, including same-sex marriages.

*_*_*

This article is dedicated to KURT SIEHR, who takes a keen interest in this area of private international law. We have known each other for over thirty years – we started exchanging *separata* in the early 1970s – and have developed a warm friendship during the innumerable occasions on which we have met and eaten in the

---

[33] Action Plan of the Council and the Commission on how best to implement the provisions of the Treaty of Amsterdam on an Area of Freedom, Security and Justice, 3 December 1998, *OJ* [1999] C 19/1ff.

context of various organizations. His cosmopolitan and omnivorous interest in all matters pertaining to private international law has made him a subtle master of comparative conflicts law. Hundreds of publications bear witness to his virtuosity, which combines seriousness with sometimes frivolous anecdotes. Although always looking for progress, he has also taken heed of the *mèden agán* of the ancients. May he continue his precious work in good health!

De quelques règles générales de conflits de lois dans les codifications récentes

Alfred E. von Overbeck[*]

1. INTRODUCTION

Très récemment, le Professeur Siehr et quatre de ses collègues ont publié un Recueil contenant le texte original et la traduction allemande d'une soixantaine de lois extra-européennes de droit international privé.[1] Cet ouvrage exemplaire, qui facilite énormément les recherches comparatives sur le codifications, nous a donné l'idée d'esquisser l'évolution de quelques règles générales édictées postérieurement au cours général que nous avons consacré à ces questions en 1982.[2] Dans le présent cadre, nous nous limiterons à quatre de ces questions: le renvoi, le principe de proximité et la clause d'exception, les lois d'application immédiate ou lois de police étrangères et la détermination du contenu de la loi étrangère.

---

[*] Professeur émerite à l'Université de Fribourg (Suisse), ancien Directeur de l'Institut suisse de droit comparé.

[1] Jan Kropholler/ Hilmar Krüger/ Wolfgang Riering/ Jürgen Samtleben/ Kurt Siehr (Hrsg.), *Aussereuropäische IPR-Gesetze* (Hamburg/Würzburg 1999).

[2] Alfred E. von Overbeck, « Les questions générales du DIP à la lumière des codifications et projets récents, Cours général », 176 *Recueil des cours de l'Académie de droit international* (1982-III) p. 9.

J. Basedow et al., eds., Private Law in the International Arena – Liber Amicorum Kurt Siehr
© 2000, T.M.C.Asser Press, The Hague, The Netherlands

Laissant de côté des dispositions ponctuelles, nous examinerons dix-sept codifi-cations européennes et extra-européennes[3] ainsi que le projet néerlandais.[4] Tous ces codes appartiennent à des pays de *civil law.* Il faut toutefois ajouter que la loi de Louisiane, bien que régissant une juridiction en principe de *civil law,* cherche à concilier une codification avec les solutions ayant cours aux États-Unis.

Les contours des lois allemande et suisse étaient connus lorsque nous avons rédi-gé le cours de 1982, il en va de même pour la loi du Venezuela. Relevons l'intérêt que revêtent deux récentes codification africaines fortement influencées par la doc-trine française, celle du Burkina Faso et celle de la Tunisie. La première doit sans doute beaucoup au professeur français qui en a rendu compte à la Revue critique de droit international privé.

On sait que l'idée de codification, généralement rejetée dans le monde de la *com-mon law,* est aussi regardée avec scepticisme par une partie de la doctrine euro-péenne et surtout française.[5] Cette opposition a divers motifs: pour les uns les codifications nationales barrent le chemin vers l'unification internationale des rè-gles de conflit, pour d'autres elles enserrent des situations très diverses dans le car-can de règles rigides, alors qu'il vaudrait mieux s'en remettre à la sagesse des juges. Aux premiers on pourrait répondre que le droit conventionnel ne couvre pas encore tous les domaines et que rien n'empêche qu'il remplace peu à peu les règles particu-lières des divers pays. D'autre part la pratique dans les pays à droit écrit semble avoir besoin de règles précises, on ne saurait demander aux juges de se plonger dans

---

[3] Codifications examinées (Références aux textes et traductions parus à la Revue critique de droit international privé, citée Revue critique, généralement avec une note ou un commentaire. Pour les au-tres pays, voir l'ouvrage cité supra n. 1) : Allemagne : Loi du 25 juillet 1986 portant réforme du droit in-ternational privé (Revue critique 1987 p. 170). Burkina Faso : Code des personnes et de la famille du 16 novembre 1989 (Revue critique 1991 p. 220). Congo Brazzaville : Code de la famille du 17 octobre 1984. Cuba : Code civil du 16 juillet 1987. Emirat Arabes Unis : Code des transaction civiles du 15 dé-cembre 1985 (Revue critique 1986 p. 390). Italie : Loi du 31 mai 1995 N° 218 (Revue critique 1996 p. 174). Liechtenstein : Loi du 19 septembre 1996 sur le droit international privé (Revue critique 1997 p. 859). Louisiane : Code civil, Act N° 923 of 1991. Pérou : Code civil du 24 juillet 1884 (Revue cri-tique 1986 p. 192). Québec : Code civil, Loi du 18 décembre 1991 (Revue critique 1992 p. 574). Rou-manie : Loi du 22 septembre 1992 sur le règlement des rapports de droit international privé (Revue critique 1994 p. 172). Suisse : Loi fédérale sur le droit international privé du 18 décembre 1987 (Revue critique 1988 p. 409). Tunisie : Code de droit international privé du 17 novembre 1998 (Revue critique 1999 p. 382). Ouzbékistan : Code civil de 1997. Venezuela : Loi de droit international privé du 6 août 1998 (Revue critique 1999 p. 392). Vietnam : Code civil de 1995. Yougoslavie : Loi du 15 juillet 1982 (Revue critique 1983 p. 353).

[4] Schets van een algemene wet betreffende het internationaal privaatrecht, Ministère de la Justice, août 1992. Aux Pays-Bas, la plupart des matières ont été réglées par des lois spéciales ou sont en cours de règlement. La partie générale doit être codifiée en dernier lieu et toutes ces dispositions devraient être intégrées dans un livre X du nouveau Code civil. (Renseignements obligeamment communiquées par *M. H van Loon*, Secrétaire général de la Conférence de La Haye de droit international privé et *Mme C. Kessedjian*, Secrétaire général adjoint.)

[5] Voir Horatia Muir Watt, *La codification en droit international privé* (Droits 1998) p. 149.

une étude approfondie de la jurisprudence et de la doctrine à propos de chaque espèce contenant un élément international. Force est en tous cas de constater que le mouvement de codification amorcé après la guerre de 1939/45 se poursuit.

2. LE RENVOI

Certains on pensé pouvoir prononcer un « requiem pour le renvoi ».[6] Un coup d'oeil sur les codifications examinées montre que ni le renvoi, ni les controverses qu'il suscite ne sont prêts à disparaître. Tous les textes abordent la question. Les réponses, nous le verrons, divergent beaucoup. L'Institut de Droit international, qui avait condamné le renvoi en 1900, et essayé en vain de formuler une Résolution dans les années 60, a décidé d'englober le problème dans le cadre plus général de l'application des règles de droit international privé étranger. Mais la Résolution d'août 1999 a dû se borner à énumérer une certain nombre d'hypothèses dans lesquelles cette prise en considération est souhaitable, ou au contraire à écarter.[7] Et le renvoi reste son objet principal.

2.1 **Les diverses solutions**

Quatre groupes de législations peuvent être distingués quant au renvoi :
1)   Le projet des Pays-Bas (art. 1), le Pérou (art. 2048) le Québec (art. 3080) la Tunisie (art. 35) et l'Ouzbékistan (art. 1161) rejettent le renvoi, les deux derniers avec des exceptions en sa faveur (au premier et deuxième degré, semble-t-il), non spécifiés pour la Tunisie, pour un certain nombre de matières de droit de famille dans le cas de l'Ouzbékistan.
     La codification de la Louisiane (art. 3517) occupe une place à part. Elle exclut le renvoi sauf disposition contraire, mais permet de tenir compte des règles de conflits de lois étrangères (. . . *may be taken into consideration*. . .) lors de l'application de quatre articles spécifiés.
2)   Le Congo Brazzaville (art. 830), les Émirats Arabes Unis (art. 26), le Liechtenstein (art. 5), la Roumanie (art. 4) et le Vietnam (art. 827, 3) acceptent de manière générale le renvoi à la *lex fori*. Leurs lois visent en premier lieu le renvoi au premier degré, mais pourraient aussi permettre un renvoi circulaire aboutissant à la *lex fori*. Toutefois la Roumanie exclut expressément le renvoi au second degré et réserve les dispositions contraires, notamment en matière d'obligations contractuel-

---

[6] Jacques Foyer, „Requiem pour le renvoi", *Travaux du Comité français de droit international privé, années 1980/81* p. 105.
[7] La prise en considération du droit international privé étranger, Rapporteur : M. Kurt Lipstein, „Rapport et projet de Résolution", *Annuaire de l'Institut de Droit international*, vol. 68, tome I (Paris 1999) p. 13. Résolution à paraître, ibid., vol. 68 tome II, reproduite dans *RabelsZ* (2000) p. 335.

les et extra-contractuelles (art. 85).

La loi suisse (art. 14) peut être rangée dans le même groupe, elle ne prévoit en principe le renvoi (au premier et au second degré) que pour les seul cas prévus par la loi.[8] Toutefois elle accepte aussi le renvoi au premier degré à la loi suisse « en matière d'état », sans tenir compte d'un renvoi en retour éventuel du premier État désigné. Cette dernière règle, qui ne figurait pas dans l'avant-projet de la Commission d'experts, a été introduite à la demande des autorités de l'état civil. Elle permet d'appliquer le droit suisse aux Suisses domiciliés dans d'autres États européens, dont la plupart appliquent le principe de nationalité. En revanche l'harmonie des décisions n'est atteinte qu'avec les États dont les règles de conflit désignent la loi nationale matérielle ou pratiquent la *foreign court theory*. On remarquera d'ailleurs que toutes les législations, de ce groupe et des autres groupes, qui acceptent le renvoi au premier degré, prescrivent alors l'application de la *lex fori* sans égard à la position en matière de renvoi de l'Etat désigné.

3)   Les droits d'un troisième groupe admettent le renvoi au premier de gré à la *lex fori*, et le renvoi au second degré s'il est accepté par le pays tiers. Il s'agit du Burkina Faso (art. 1005) et de l'Italie (art. 13). La solution italienne est particulièrement surprenante étant donné l'hostilité traditionnelle au renvoi dans ce pays.[9] La règle actuelle ne fut introduite qu'au stade de la discussion parlementaire. Il semble que les partisans du rattachement au domicile, qui n'ont pas prévalu lors de l'élaboration de la loi, aient préconisé ce moyen de soumettre plus souvent des étrangers domiciliés en Italie à la loi italienne. Selon le texte clair, le renvoi au second degré n'est admis que si le droit de l'Etat tiers se déclare compétent, certains ont cependant soutenu qu'on pouvait aller plus loin dans l'acceptation du renvoi au second degré. L'art. 13 contient quelques restrictions. Le renvoi n'est accepté ni en cas de choix de la loi applicable par les parties, ce qui va de soi, ni pour les obligations contractuelles (art. 57 renvoyant à la Convention de Rome) ou extra-contractuelles (art. 58), ni pour les dispositions concernant la forme des actes. Il n'est appliquée en matière de filiation que s'il conduit à une loi permettant l'établissement de la filiation.

4)   Enfin, selon les lois allemande (art. 4, 1) et cubaine (art. 19), le renvoi au premier degré (suivi dans tous les cas de l'application de la *lex fori*) et au second degré

---

[8] Les seuls cas de renvoi proprement dit concernent le droit du nom et la loi applicable aux successions. Nous ne saurions partager l'opinion de M. I. Schwander, « qui entend étend englober d'autres cas par voie d'interprétation », dans: *Methodische Defizite des IPR-Kollisionsrechts – wie weiter? Rechtskollisionen, Festschrift für Anton Heini* (Zurich 1995) p. 389, 397 note 17. Voir en général Peter A. Reichart, *Der Renvoi im schweizerischen IPR, Funktion und Bedeutung*, (Etudes suisses de droit international vol. 94, Zurich 1996).

[9] Voir Susanne Kapellmann, « Der 'rinvio' im italienischen Internationalen Privatrecht – Hintergründe und Auswirkungen », *Zeitschrift für Rechtsvergleichung, Int. Privatrecht und Europarecht* (1997) p. 177; Fausto Pocar, « Das neue italienische Internationale Privatrecht », *IPRax* (1997) p. 145, 150.

sont admis. La loi cubaine autorise le renvoi au second degré à condition que la loi ainsi désignée ne soit pas contraire à l'ordre public cubain. Selon la loi allemande les règles de conflit étrangères sont appliquées « pour autant qu'elles n'aillent pas à l'encontre du sens de la règles de conflit allemande » (*Sinn der Verweisung).* Les opinions sur la portée de cette restriction sont fort divisées.[10] Le choix de la loi applicable par les parties ne peut porter que sur les règles substantielles (art. 4, 2). En vertu de l'incorporation de la Convention de Rome (art. 35, 1) le renvoi est exclu en matière de contrats.

2.2 Conclusions en matière de renvoi

L'examen qui précède montre que l'on est loin d'une opinion commune en matière de renvoi. La seule solution commune à la majorité des codifications est le renvoi du premier degré, accepté quelle que soit la position en matière de renvoi de l'Etat désigné par la règle de conflits du for. C'est ce que nous avons appelé « le principe égoïste » qui impose le retour à la *lex fori.*[11] Au contraire le « principe altruiste » veut réaliser l'harmonie des décisions (ou la coordination des systèmes). Le renvoi au premier degré n'atteint cet objectif que si les règles de conflits de l'Etat désigné en premier renvoient aux règles substantielles du for, ou si cet État pratique la *foreign court theory.* Lorsque tel est le cas, le renvoi permet de concilier les principes du domicile et de la nationalité. On notera aussi que le renvoi est exclu lorsque les parties on choisi la loi applicable et souvent en matière d'obligations.[12]

L'harmonie des décisions est atteinte chaque fois qu'un renvoi au second degré aboutit à un loi qui admet sa propre compétence, ou à un retour à la *lex fori.* Vu sous cet angle, il y a plus de raisons d'admettre le renvoi au second degré qu'un renvoi inconditionnel au premier degré.

En conclusion, on constatera que le renvoi permet le *Heimwärtstreben,* le retour à la *lex fori,* qui a parfois des avantages pratiques mais qui est contestable au niveau théorique. Dans certains cas, pratiquement limités à l'opposition nationalité – domicile, il assure l'harmonie des décisions. Occasionnellement il conduit à une loi permettant d'assurer la validité d'un acte ou à une loi ayant des liens plus étroits avec la cas d'espèce. Mais le contraire peut aussi bien se produire. Les objectifs de validité et de proximité peuvent plus facilement être atteints lorsque la disposition sur le renvoi le prévoit expressément (ainsi pour la validité la loi italienne) ou

---

[10] Voir par exemple G. Mäsch, „Der Renvoi – Plädoyer für die Begrenzung einer überflüssigen Rechtsfigur", 61 *Rabels Zeitschrift für ausländisches und internationales Privatrecht* (1997) p. 285 (restriction du renvoi au minimum) et R. Michaels, „Der Abbruch der Weiterverweisung im deutschen Internationalen Privatrecht", ibid. p. 685 (favorable au renvoi).

[11] Alfred E. von Overbeck, Cours général (supra n. 2) p. 133.

[12] Les lois du Burkina Faso et du Congo Brazzaville ne concernent que le droit des personnes et des familles.

lorsque le renvoi est facultatif. Mais pour assurer la validité d'un acte (forme, établissement de la filiation, etc.) mieux vaut prévoir des rattachements alternatifs. Et le principe de proximité sera bien plus facile à assurer par des rattachements flexibles tels qu'on les rencontre en droit des contrats, ou par une clause d'exception. La solution du droit du Québec et du projet néerlandais, qui excluent le renvoi mais connaissent une clause d'exception, est à cet égard la plus satisfaisante.

3.   LE PRINCIPE DE PROXIMITÉ ET LA CLAUSE D'EXCEPTION[13]

Le principe de proximité « exprime simplement l'idée du rattachement d'un rapport de droit à l'ordre juridique du pays avec lequel il présente les liens les plus étroits. . . ».[14] C'est en ces termes que M. Paul Lagarde définit le principe dont il est question ici. A la suite de son cours général de 1985 l'expression de « principe de proximité » s'est généralisée. L'abandon de règles de conflit rigides et leur remplacement par des systèmes plus flexibles a surtout eu lieu pour le rattachement objectif des contrats et avec plus d'hésitations en droit des obligations extra-contractuelles. La clause d'exception est un autre moyen de mettre en oeuvre le principe de proximité, sans abandonner complètement des règles de conflits fixes, mais en permettant de s'en écarter dans certains cas. Nous exposerons les règles sur le rattachement objectif des contrats[15] puis passerons aux clauses d'exception générales.

3.1   Le rattachement objectif des contrats

Les règles de conflits de loi en matière de contrats des pays examinés ont suivi la tendance vers plus de flexibilité de façon inégale.

La loi vénézuélienne se réfère directement aux liens le plus étroits (art. 30). Le tribunal devra tenir compte de tous les éléments subjectifs et objectifs et des princi-

---

[13] Voir notamment D. Kokkini-Iatridou (éd.), *Les clauses d'exception en matière de conflits de lois et de conflits de juridictions – ou le principe de proximité* (Dordrecht 1994); C. Dubler, *Les clauses d'exception en droit international privé* (Etudes suisses de droit international, vol. 35, Genève 1983); K. Kreuzer, « Berichtigungsklauseln im Internationalen Privatrecht », dans: *Mélanges en l'honneur d'Imre Zajtay* (Tübingen 1982) p. 295, « Zur Funktion von kollisionsrechtlichen Berichtigungsnormen », *Zeitschrift für Rechtsvergleichung* (1992) p. 168; K.H. Nadelmann, « Choice of Law Resolved by Rules or Presumptions with an Escape Clause », *The American Journal of Comparative Law* (1985) p. 297; P. Lagarde, « Le principe de proximité dans le droit international privé contemporain », 196 *Recueil des Cours de l'Académie de droit international* (1986-I) p. 97; S. Alvarez Gonzalez, « Objecto del derecho internacional privado y especialication normativa », 46 *Anuario de derecho civil* (1994) p. 1109.

[14] P. Lagarde, ibid., p. 25.

[15] Voir P. Lagarde, ibid., p. 32.

pes généraux du droit du commerce international reconnus par les organisations internationales.

L'Allemagne, l'Italie et les Pays-Bas sont liés par la Convention de Rome sur la loi applicable aux obligations contractuelles, du 19 juin 1980. L'art. 4 se réfère aux liens les plus étroits, précisés par des présomptions, et ajoute des règles pour certains contrats. Il est couronnée par une clause d'exception. La loi suisse (art. 117) suit un système semblable, toutefois en matière de vente (art. 118) elle renvoie au système plus rigide de la Convention de La Haye sur la loi applicable aux ventes à caractère international d'objets mobiliers corporels, du 15 juin 1955. En plus elle contient une clause d'exception générale. La loi roumaine se réfère aux liens les plus étroits pour les actes juridiques (art. 69, 2) et pour les contrats (art. 77), dans ce dernier cas avec un système élaboré de règles sur la prestation caractéristique qui semblent avoir le caractère de présomptions (art. 78 et 79). Elle ajoute des règles sur la vente inspirées de la Convention de La Haye de 1955, et sur d'autres contrats.

Le Québec (art. 3112) prévoit la loi des liens les plus étroits pour les actes juridiques, mais ajoute des règles spéciales pour certain contrats. En particulier, la vente (art. 3114) est régie par un système qui développe celui de la Convention de La Haye de 1955. On verra qu'en plus, ce droit comporte une clause générale d'exception (art. 3082).

Le droit de Louisiane occupe une place à part, il se réfère à la loi de l'Etat donc les *policies* seraient le plus fortement atteintes si sa loi n'était pas appliquée.

Les Émirats Arabes Unis (art. 19, 1) prévoient le domicile commun des parties, à défaut de domicile commun le lieu de conclusion, mais cela à moins qu'il ne résulte des circonstances qu'une autre loi devra être appliquée. La loi yougoslave (art. 20) prévoit un catalogue étendu, mais qui s'applique seulement „si les circonstances n'indiquent pas un autre droit ». L'idée du domicile de la partie qui fournit la prestation caractéristique, que la Convention de Rome et le droit suisse prévoient comme présomption, se traduit par un rattachement fixe dans les lois du Liechtenstein (art. 40, pour les contrats synallagmatiques) et de la Tunisie (art. 62). L'Ouzbékistan (art. 1190) prévoit cette solution pour les contrats ne tombant pas dans une longue liste de contrats indiquant la partie dont le domicile est déterminant.

Enfin, des solutions plus anciennes,, telles que la loi du lieu de conclusion ou du lieu d'exécution, ou leur combinaison, sont en vigueur dans les autres pays ayant codifié les règles de conflit en matière de contrats (Cuba, art. 17; Pérou, art. 2095 ; Vietnam art. 834, 2).

3.2   Les clauses d'exception générales

Une clause d'exception expresse figurait dès le début dans le projet suisse. Elle se retrouve presque inchangée dans la loi (art. 15).[16] Mais cette exemple n'a été suivi que par le Québec, dans un texte presque identique (art. 3082)[17] et par le projet néerlandais dans une disposition (art. 8, 2e phrase) proposée à titre éventuel et curieusement rattachée à l'ordre public.[18] La clause suisse reste sur un terrain strictement conflictuel, on ne saurait s'en servir pour rechercher la *better law*. Elle a un caractère exceptionnel et la jurisprudence suisse de ces dix dernières années l'a appliquée avec prudence.[19] Son texte est le suivant :

> Le droit désigné par la présente loi n'est exceptionnellement pas applicable si, au regard de l'ensemble des circonstances, il est manifeste que la cause n'a qu'un lien très lâche avec ce droit et qu'elle se trouve dans une relation beaucoup plus étroite avec un autre droit.
> Cette disposition n'est pas applicable en cas d'élection de droit.

La solution la plus intéressante dans ce domaine est sans doute la clause d'exception « cachée » de la loi du Burkina Faso (art. 103):

> Les rapports juridiques visés à l'article précédent sont régis par le droit à l'égard duquel le rattachement est le plus étroit.
> Les règles de conflits de lois du présent chapitre doivent être considérées comme l'expression du principe général énoncé à l'article premier.
> En cas de lacune ou d'insuffisance des dispositions du présent chapitre, le juge s'inspirera du principe énoncé à l'article premier.

Les deux premiers alinéas correspondent exactement au paragraphe premier de la loi autrichienne sur le droit international privé du 15 juin 1978 (Revue critique 1979

---

[16] Sur l'art. 15 voir B. Dutoit, *Commentaire de la loi fédérale du 18 décembre 1987*, 2e éd. (Bâle et Francfort 1997) Art. 15 p. 36; Keller/Girsberger, dans: *IPRG Kommentar* (Zurich 1993) p. 118; M. Mächler-Erne dans: *Internationales Privatrecht* (H. Honsell/ N.P. Vogt/ A.K. Schnyder éd.) (Bâle et Francfort 1996) p. 130; A. Bucher, *Droit international privé suisse, Tome I/2: Partie générale – Droit applicable* (Bâle 1995) p. 82; F. Knoepfler, *Utilité et dangers d'une clause d'exception en droit international privé, Hommage à Raymond Jeanprêtre* (Neuchâtel 1982) p. 113; A.K. Schnyder, « Ausweichklausel und Verbraucherschutz : Herausforderung des Schweizer Internationalprivatrechts » dans: A.K. Schnyder et al (éd.), *Internationales Verbraucherschutzrecht: Referate und Diskussionsberichte des Kolloquiums zu Ehren von Fritz Reichert-Facilides* (Tübingen 1995) p. 57.
[17] Les deux textes précisent qu'il ne sont pas applicables en cas d'élection de droit.
[18] Voir A.E. von Overbeck, « L'article 8 du projet néerlandais et la clause d'exception », *Nederlands Internationaal Privaatrecht* (1994) Speciale Aflevering p. 36.
[19] Voir A.E. von Overbeck, « The Fate of Two Remarkable Provisions of the Swiss Statute on Private International Law », 1 *Yearbook of Private International Law* (1999) p. 119.

p. 177)! Cette formule avait été choisie comme le maximum de ce qui pouvait être atteint en matière de flexibilité et de fonctionnalité, elle a fini par évoluer vers une véritable clause d'exception.[20] Il sera intéressant de savoir comment cette clause sera interprétée au Burkina Faso.

En conclusion, on peut constater que le principe de proximité a largement pénétré le droit des contrats tandis que les véritables clauses d'exception demeurent rares.[21]

4.   LES LOIS D'APPLICATION IMMÉDIATE

Le problème des lois d'application immédiate étrangères (ou lois d'application nécessaire, ordre public positif, *Eingriffsnormen, mandatory rules, specially mandatory rules* – nous n'entrerons pas dans les querelles de terminologie) a fait couler beaucoup d'encre, mais les textes relatifs à leur sort ne sont pas nombreux. Il en est différemment des lois d'application immédiate du for qui font l'objet de nombre de dispositions et dont l'application va de soi même à défaut de textes. Enfin, lorsque les lois d'application immédiate figurent dans la loi désignée par les règles de conflit du for, leur application dépend de la mesure dans laquelle le for applique la loi étrangère.

Nous nous en tiendrons donc aux lois d'application immédiate étrangères qui ne font pas partie de la *lex causae*.[22] L'article 7, 1 de la Convention de Rome du 19 juin 1980 sur les contrats permet de leur donner effet, mais cette disposition a été écartée par nombre d'États au moyen de la réserve permise par l'art. 22, a. Les controverses sur l'opportunité d'une telle règle sont loin d'être terminées, ainsi le projet de l'Union européenne pour une Convention sur les obligations extra-contractuelles (Rome II) ne la contient pas ; au contraire elle figure dans le projet sur le même objet élaboré par le Groupe européen de droit international privé.

L'art. 1165, 2 du Code de l'Ouzbékistan et l'art. 10 du projet néerlandais généralisent la clause au delà du seul domaine des contrats par des textes très proches de celui de la Convention de Rome. Il en est de même de l'art. 3079 du Code du Québec, mais ce texte ajoute l'exigence d'intérêts légitimes et manifestement prépondérants. Le projet gouvernemental suisse avait presque la même teneur. Le texte

---

[20] Voir Fritz Schwind, « § 1 IPRG Rechtsicherheit und Funktionalität im Licht der Historischen Entwicklung », *Zeitschrift für Rechtsvergleichung, Internat. Privatrecht und Europarecht* (1991) p. 255, 259, 260 et les arrêts de la Cour suprême consacrant la clause d'exception cités note 20.

[21] Nous n'avons pas recherché les clauses d'exception spéciales dans d'autres matières que les contrats.

[22] Nous nous bornerons à signaler l'ouvrage récent et complet de M. Andrea Bonomi, *Le norme imperative nel diritto internazionale privato* (Publications de l'Institut suisse de droit comparé vol. 33, Zurich 1998) qui contient aussi une bibliographie complète. Voir aussi M. Wojewoda, « Mandatory Rules in Private International Law », 7 *Maastricht Journal of European and Comparative Law* (2000) p. 183.

définitif (art. 19) a été garni de restrictions supplémentaires, notamment d'une double référence à « la conception suisse du droit ». Puis surtout, il y a une divergence entre le texte français d'une part, les textes allemand et italien de l'autre. Ces derniers textes exigent « des intérêts d'une partie » alors que cette restriction ne figure pas dans le texte français. L'histoire législative indique qu'il s'agit d'une erreur et que le texte français est déterminant.[23] Cela découle aussi de la *ratio legis* : le juge doit pouvoir prendre en considération une loi étrangère qui exprime un intérêt digne de protection, même si cela est contraire aux intérêts des deux parties. On pensera à des dispositions visant à maintenir la concurrence ou à protéger des biens culturels.

Toutes les dispositions considérées jusqu'ici ne donnent qu'une faculté au juge. Au contraire, le dernier en date des textes, celui de l'art 38, 2 du Code tunisien contient une formule impérative, le juge doit appliquer la loi de police étrangère si les conditions énoncés par le texte sont remplies :

> Le juge donne effet aux dispositions d'un droit étranger non désigné par les règles de conflit, s'il s'avère que ce droit a des liens étroits avec la situation juridique envisagée et que l'application des dites dispositions est indispensable, eu égard à la fin poursuivie.

Ni l'art. 7, 1 de la Convention de Rome, ni l'art 19 de la loi suisse n'ont eu les effets désastreux que certains craignaient.[24] Peut-être cette constatation amènera-t-elle de futurs législateurs a inclure une telle clause.

5.   LA DÉTERMINATION DU CONTENU DU DROIT ÉTRANGER

Les anciennes discussions sur le caractère – de fait ou de droit – du droit étranger ne semblent plus présenter d'intérêt. Les législations anciennes ou nouvelles ne distinguent pas toujours clairement la question de l'application d'office de la règle de conflits, et par conséquent du droit étranger, de celle de la recherche du contenu de ce droit. Seules les lois du Burkina Faso (art. 1004 et 1008), du Liechtenstein (art. 3 et 4) et du Pérou (art. 2051 et art. 2052 et s.) distinguent expressément les deux questions.[25] On ne saurait d'ailleurs tirer du silence de la loi la conclusion que dans les autres pays la règle de conflit ne s'applique pas d'office ; dans certain pays cela va de soi, dans d'autres des règles de procédure, que nous n'avons pas recherchées, peuvent régir la question.

---

[23] Ce point est controversé, voir Bonomi, *ibid.*, p. 31.

[24] Sur la jurisprudence suisse voir A.E. von Overbeck (supra n. 19).

[25] Cela à la différence de législations africaines antérieures, voir le commentaire de P. Mayer, *Revue critique* (1991) p. 231. Voir aussi P. Mayer, « Réflexions relatives aux sources internes en droit international privé burkinabé », *Revue burkinabé de droit*, N° 12 décembre 1987, p. 435.

Les lois du Burkina Faso (art 1008), de l'Italie (art. 14), du Liechtenstein (art. 4), de la Roumanie (art. 7), de la Suisse (art. 16), de Tunisie (art. 32), de l'Ouzbékistan (art. 1160) du Venezuela (art. 60) et de la Yougoslavie (art. 13) prescrivent, selon diverses formules, l'application d'office du droit étranger, la collaboration des parties ou l'apport de preuves par celles-ci, et parfois d'autres moyens d'investigation. Toutefois, selon les lois roumaine, suisse et tunisienne, les parties doivent dans certains cas prouver ce contenu. La loi du Congo Brazzaville est ambiguë: « Le contenu . . . est établi . . . par tous les moyens par le plaideur qui s'en prévaut et, au besoin à la diligence du juge » (art. 828). A l'exception de celles du Venezuela et de la Yougoslavie, ces lois prévoient l'application de la *lex fori* en cas d'impossibilité d'établir le contenu du droit étranger.

Dans l'ensemble, le constat en matière d'application d'office de la règle de conflit et du droit étranger, et la recherche du contenu de ce dernier, est satisfaisant On pourrait encore mentionner nombre de dispositions prescrivant l'application du droit étranger tel qu'il est compris dans son pays d'origine. L'idée de la collaboration entre juge et parties, qui semble avoir été lancée par H. Motulsky, a fait son chemin.[26] Les dispositions examinées satisfont largement au postulat énoncé par l'Institut de Droit international dans sa Résolution de 1989 sur : *L'égalité de traitement entre la loi du for et la loi étrangère dans les codifications nationales de droit international privé.*[27]

6.   CONCLUSIONS

Les nouvelles codifications ne révèlent pas de développements spectaculaires. Les clauses d'exception et les dispositions sur les lois d'application immédiate demeurent peu nombreuses. Des différences considérables subsistent entre les systèmes, notamment en ce qui concerne le renvoi. Mais des convergences, et des influences réciproques, entre codifications peuvent aussi être décelées. De manière générale, on peut constater une évolution vers des systèmes plus souples et des solutions conformes aux besoins des relations juridiques internationales. Des principes rigides qui étaient à la base de certains textes plus anciens, tels que la souveraineté, n'ont plus cours. Si à l'avenir de nouvelles lois tiennent compte des textes existants et de leur application, on peut espérer de nouveaux progrès.

---

[26] *L'office du juge et la loi étrangère, Mélanges Maury*, tome I (Paris 1960) p. 337, 357, 366, repris dans: H. Motulsky, *Écrits*, vol III (Études et notes de droit international privé, Paris 1978) p. 87.
[27] *Annuaire de l'Institut de Droit international*, vol. 63 tome II, 1990 p. 332, Rapports de *M. Pierre* Gannagé, *Annuaire de l'Institut de Droit international,* vol. 63 tome I, p. 205.

SUMMARY
ON SOME GENERAL RULES OF CONFLICT OF LAWS IN RECENT
CODIFICATIONS

The author gives a critical appraisal of general provisions on *renvoi*, closest
connection and exception clauses, foreign specially mandatory rules, and research
of the content of foreign law, contained in seventeen legislations enacted after
1982[28] as well as the Netherlands draft. On *renvoi*, one finds a large variety of
solutions ranging from its exclusion to its general acceptance. The principle of the
closest connection is mostly realised as far as the objective connection of contracts
is concerned, with only a few general exception clauses. Provisions on foreign
specially mandatory rules, such as art. 7, 1 of the Rome Convention on the Law
Applicable to Contractual Obligations, of 19 June 1980, are also few. Many of the
texts considered provide for some measure of *ex officio* research of the content of
the foreign law by the judge, but some provisions provide for assistance by the
parties or other means of investigation. Generally, one can say that the new
codifications tend to provide flexible solutions dealing in an appropriate way with
international situations rather than to embody rigid principles such as sovereignty.

---

[28] The countries are listed in n. 3.

Choice of Law Applicable to the Dispute in Recent Legislation on International Commercial Arbitration

Gonzalo Parra-Aranguren[*]

1.   THE SUBSTANTIVE DECISION OF DISPUTE NOWADAYS

The United Nations Commission for International Trade Law (UNCITRAL) included arbitration as one of the items of its first Working Program and decided to prepare some rules for special arbitrations (*ad hoc*) related to international commerce. Seven years later the *UNCITRAL Arbitration Rules* (hereafter UNCITRAL Rules) were approved and United Nations General Assembly Resolution 31/98 of 15 December 1976 recommended their use "in the settlement of disputes arising in the context of international commercial relations, particularly by reference to the Arbitration Rules in commercial contracts".

The work of the United Nations Commission for International Trade Law (UNCITRAL) on arbitration continued. Simultaneously with the preparation of the *UNCITRAL Rules of Conciliation*, approved in 1980, it examined the feasibility of a model Law on arbitration. Preparatory research was satisfactory and the *Model Law on International Commercial Arbitration* (hereafter UNCITRAL Model Law) was adopted in 1985. Some months later, United Nations General Assembly Resolution 40/72 of 11 December 1985 recommended that all States give due consideration to its contents, "in view of the desirability of uniformity of the law of arbitral procedures and the specific needs of international commercial arbitration practice".

States followed the recommendation made by the General Assembly. Thus an important degree of uniformity has been achieved. Nowadays it is generally admit-

[*] Professor emeritus of Private Internatioanl Law, University of Caracas, Venezuela; Judge at the International Court of Justice, The Hague.

J. Basedow et al., eds., Private Law in the International Arena – Liber Amicorum Kurt Siehr
© 2000, *T.M.C.Asser Press, The Hague, The Netherlands*

ted that parties to a dispute have the right to choose between arbitration *de iure* and arbitration *ex aequo et bono* or *amiable composition*. Article 28, paragraph 3, of the UNCITRAL Model law uses both expressions, because some legal systems only utilize one of them, other countries refer to equity (Venezuela), or to honorable composition (Great Britain). Moreover, there is no agreement as to the exact meaning of *amiable composition*, which sometimes is distinguished from the arbitrator's power to decide *ex aequo et bono* or from the concept of equity.

Recent legislation does not accept the same criteria to determine the kind of arbitration agreed by the parties when they fail to do so. UNCITRAL Model Law provides that in such case arbitrators shall decide *de jure*, solution adopted by some countries, like Venezuela; but Peru and Ecuador, for example, adopt a different presumption favoring *ex aequo et bono* arbitration.

For arbitrations *de jure*, the 1981 Report of the Secretary General on the possible features of a model law on international commercial arbitration already indicated the possibility to "empower the arbitral tribunal to determine what law is applicable to the dispute unless the parties have designated a certain law to be applied". He also mentioned that "as to the facility of designating a law, the model law might recognize not only the choice of a specific national law but also allow reference to a uniform law or convention even if not yet in force"; and indicated that it would be useful "to include a provision to the effect that any choice of law of a given State means direct reference to the substantive law of that State and not to its conflict rules".

The 1984 draft adopted by the Working Group on International Contractual Practices included Article 28 on the "rules applicable to substance of dispute". In his analytical commentary on the text the Secretary General reminded that such question, "which should be distinguished from the issue of the law applicable to the arbitral procedure or the arbitration agreement, is often dealt with in conventions and national laws devoted to private international law or conflict of laws", although "it is sometimes covered by national laws on arbitration and often by arbitration conventions an arbitration rules". The Secretary General added that the draft "follows this latter practice with a view to providing guidance on this important point and to meet the needs of international commercial arbitration".

UNCITRAL Model Law decision to include a provision determining the law applicable to the dispute has been generally adopted by the latest European and Latin-American statutes on arbitration. In Europe this is the case in **France** (Decree of 12 May 1981 *No. 81-500, instituant les dispositions des livres III et IV de nouveau Code de procédure civile et modificant certains disposiciones de ce Code*), **The Netherlands** (Act of 2 July 1986),**Portugal** (Act 31/86, 29 August 1986), **Switzerland** (Federal Act on Private International Law, 18 December 1987), **Spain** (Arbitration Law, Nr. 36/1988, 5 December 1988), **Italy** (Act Nr. 25, 5 January 1994, modifying Articles 806-840 of the Code of Civil Procedure), **Great Britain** (Act approved by Parliament in June 1996) and **Germany** (Gesetz zur Neuregelung des

Schiedsverahrensrechts (*Schiedsverfahrens – Neuregelungsgesetz – SchiedsVfG*), *von 22 Dezember 1997*).

With the exception of **Argentine** (Act Mr. 17454, 19 September 1967, as amended by Act Nr. 22434, 16 March 1981) and **Venezuela** (Act of 7 April 1998), recent Latin-American Statutes on arbitration have included similar provision, as it is evidenced by Statutes Acts recently enacted in **Mexico** (22 July 1993 Decree reforming arts. 1415-1463 of the Commercial Code and the Federal Code of Civil Procedure), **Guatemala** (Decree 67-95 of 17 November 1995), **Peru** (General Law of Arbitration, Act Nr. 26572, 3 January 1996), **Colombia** (Act 315, 1996, reproduced in Decree Nr. 1818, 7 September 1998), **Brasil** (Act Nr. 9307 of 23 September 1996), **Bolivia** (Arbitration and Conciliation Act, n° 1770, 10 March 1997), **Ecuador** (Act N. 000.RO/145, 4 September 1997) and **Costa Rica** (Act on the alternative solution of conflicts and on the promotion of social peace, Nr. 7727 of 9 December 1997). A provision on the law applicable to the substance of the dispute has also been included in the 1988 Inter-American Commission of Commercial Arbitration, in the 1997 American Arbitration Association Rules, in the 1998 London Court of International Arbitration Rules and in the 1998 International Chamber of Commerce.

2.   THE AUTONOMY OF THE PARTIES TO MAKE THE SELECTION

Article 28, first paragraph, of the UNCITRAL Law prescribes that "the arbitral tribunal shall decide the dispute in accordance with such rules of law as are chosen by the parties as applicable to the substance of the dispute". This solution is to be read in connection with letter d) of Article 2, providing that "where a provision of this Law, except Article 28, leaves the parties free to determine a certain issue, such freedom include the right of the parties to authorize a third party, including an institution, to make that determination".

Article 28, paragraph 1, of the Model Law authorizes the parties to choose the "rules of law" and not merely the "law" applicable to the dispute. The term "law" is normally understood to signify one or several particular national laws, while the expression "rules of law" denotes a wider notion, since it may also mean general principles of law, the rules embodied in a convention or similar legal text elaborated on the international level, even if not yet in force", often referred to collectively, together with trade usages, as *lex mercatoria*.

The decision to include the provision was not an easy one. Some participants advanced the idea that any reference to general principles of law would open the doors for totally unpredictable vicissitudes and to arbitrariness. After extensive discussion a compromise solution was adopted, granting more freedom in the selection to the parties (paragraph 1) than to the arbitral tribunal (paragraph 2). It was acknowledged that the choice made by the parties should not be limited, taking into account that they are empowered to authorize the arbitral tribunal to incorporate as a contractual term virtually any rule they wish and to authorize the arbitral tribunal to render decisions *ex aequo et bono*, i.e. based on equity and divorced from strict legal standards.

The authorization to choose "rules of law" had already been accepted in the 1981 French Decree on international arbitration (Article 1496 of the *Nouveau Code de Procedure Civile*) and, in Europe, it is granted in the Netherlands (Art. 1054, 2), Switzerland (Art. 187), Italy (Art. 834, paragraph 1), Great Britain (Art. 46, 1) and Germany (Art. 1051). The wording of the UNCITRAL Model Law has been reproduced, in Latin-America, by Mexico (Art. 1445, paragraph 1), Guatemala (Art. 36, paragraph 1), Peru (Art. 117, paragraph 1), Brazil (Art. 2) and Bolivia (Article 73, paragraph I). Article 197 of the 1998 Colombian Decree, repeating the provision adopted in 1996, seems to accept this broad approach because it authorizes the parties to determine the "substantial rule" applicable to the dispute, not restricting their freedom of choice to national statutes. The 1998 Arbitration Rules of the International Chamber of Commerce of Paris (Article 17, paragraph 1) copies UNCITRAL's Model Law wording; the same solution is adopted in the 1997 American Association Arbitration Rules (Article 28, paragraph 1) and in the 1998 Arbitration Rules of the London Court of International Arbitration (Art. 22, par. 3), both of them expressly specifying that the parties may chose the "law", "laws" or "rules of law" applicable to the dispute.

More explicitly, Article 2, para. 2, of the Brazilian law indicates that the parties may agree to have the arbitration conducted following general principles of law, customs and international regulations of commerce; and the 1996 England Act prescribes to decide "if the parties so agree, in accordance with such other considerations as are agreed by them or determined by the tribunal" (Section 46, paragraph 1, letter b). A step further goes Article 3, paragraph 3, of the law of Equator providing that the arbitral tribunal, in cases of arbitrations governed by law, has the obligation to respect the rules of law, the universal principles of law, the jurisprudence and doctrine; the reference to universal principles of law being not clear enough, its exact meaning shall be determined by practice, in particular, whether it includes the *lex mercatoria*.

Article 33, paragraph 1, of the UNCITRAL Rules adopts a more classical position, following Article VIII of the Geneva Convention which only authorize the parties to chose the "law" applicable to the dispute. So did also Portugal (Art. 33, paragraph 1), Costa Rica (Art. 22, paragraph 1) and the 1988 Arbitration Rules of the Inter-American Commission of Commercial Arbitration (Art. 33, paragraph 1).

Therefore, the main difference between the UNCITRAL Model Law and the UNCITRAL Rules is that the former grants greater freedom to the parties, permitting them to chose also rules of the *lex mercatoria*. However the importance of the distinction is not reflected in the Spanish official translation of Article 28, second paragraph, of the UNCITRAL Model Law which refers to its first paragraph as authorizing the parties to choose the "**law**" applicable ("*Si las partes no indican la ley aplicabl*e")

Something similar occurs with official versions of the 1987 Swiss Act. The French text authorizes the parties to chose "rules of law" (*règles de droit*); but the German and the Italian text translate "*règles de droit*" into "*Recht*" and "*diritto*", respectively. Marc Blessing explains the difference recalling that during the final parliamentary debates the French text was the one principally used by the parliamentarians; and that the official translation into German and Italian was incorrectly made by drafting committee.[1]

The UNCITRAL Model Law and the UNCITRAL Rules permit the parties to select the national law of any State or the national laws of different States to govern various aspects of their relationship, accepting therefore *depeçage*. Notwithstanding this freedom acknowledged to the parties, it shall be kept in mind that "a multiplicity of applicable laws is liable to create unnecessary disputes over the scope of each, and may generate inconsistencies or imbalances as a result of their juxtaposition".

Probably the UNCITRAL Model Law and the UNCITRAL Rules, as well as the national Acts based upon them, authorize the parties to agree on the application of the law of a State but excluding its provisions on a specific topic. This conclusion finds support on the *travaux préparatoires* because it was mentioned, as an example, the possibility to chose Swiss law, except for the rules governing judicially ordered set-off, viewed by some participants as providing too much authority to the court.

The freedom granted to the parties by recent national legislation is generally understood as permitting them to choose the law they consider more appropriate, even though not connected with their dispute. Article 62 of the Spanish Act is an exception because it requires some connection between the law chosen and the main juridical transaction (*negocio jurídico principal*) or with the dispute, reproducing the solution adopted in article 10, paragraph 5, of the Civil Code for the determination of the law applicable to contractual obligations. The underlying idea of the provision seems to be the desire to avoid, via arbitration, evasion of the law applicable to certain international transactions; and it was adopted notwithstanding it contradicts Article VIII of the Geneva Convention, ratified by Spain, and therefore applicable on a priority basis.

A different question is the possibility to freeze the chosen national law at a particular point in time, rather frequently when a private party negotiates with a state and desires to obtain protection from the legislative power of its contractual partner. The answer seems to be affirmative, at least where the parties are empowered to select the "rules of law" applicable to their dispute.

---

[1] Marc Blessing. *Introduction to Arbitration – Swiss and International Perspectives* (Basle, Helbing & Lichtenhahn 1999) para. 446, p. 175.

It is generally accepted in international arbitration and in private international law that "the word "law" encompasses all rules belonging to the legal system in question, with each source (including statute, case law and custom) having the authority attributed to it by that legal system. Thus, for example, by referring to "Venezuelan Law", the parties include all of the sources recognized by the Venezuelan legal system, following the hierarchy established therein".[2]

Notwithstanding this common understanding of the word "law", the choice of a national law by the parties is generally taken to mean the designation of the internal rules of that law, unless otherwise provided by them. This approach, rejecting *renvoi* in principle, is adopted in the second sentence of paragraph 1, Article 28, of the UNCITRAL Model Law. The same wording was reproduced in Europe by Germany (Article 1501, paragraph 1) and Great Britain (Section 46, paragraph 2); and in Latin-America by Mexico (Article 1445, paragraph 1), Guatemala (Article 34, paragraph 1) and Peru (Article 117, paragraph 1). Similar presumption seems to be accepted in Costa Rica (Article 22, paragraph 1) and Colombia (Article 197), because they permit the parties to choose the substantive rules ("*ley sustantiva*", "*norma sustancial*", respectively).

Generally the parties are free to make the selection at any time, either before or after the dispute has arisen, and their choice is not submitted to the compliance with special formalities. It may be express or tacit, but in any case their intention must be certain; therefore, it is advisable to make the selection as clear as possible. The 1975 draft of the UNCITRAL Rules suggested a different solution becase its Article 28, paragraph 1, required that the "designation must be contained in an express clause or unambiguously result from the terms of the contract". However the proposal did not succeed.

Recent statutes on international arbitration allow the parties to choose the rules of law or the law applicable to their "dispute" in general terms, i.e. not restricted to disputes arising out of contractual relationships. Therefore it has been inferred that the parties have the same freedom of choice regarding non-contractual issues between them (such as tortuous liability, questions of title to property and abuse of rights issues), despite the fact that, according to traditional private international law thinking, the principle of party autonomy does not apply in such matters. In any case, the intention of the parties shall be clearly determined because the scope of the law chosen cannot go beyond it.

---

[2] Fouchard, Gaillard, Goldman in: Emmanuel Gaillard and John Savage (eds.), *International Commercial Arbitration* (The Hague, Kluwer 1999) nr. 1432, p. 791.

3.   THE SELECTION MADE BY THE ARBITRAL TRIBUNAL

Practice demonstrate that the parties do not always determine the law applicable to the dispute or that the law chosen is irrelevant, i.e. when they have chosen the law of a Federal State, but arbitration matters are regulated by the Members of the Federation, as it occurs in the United States of America.

Participants in the *travaux preparatoires* of the UNCITRAL Model Law advanced different positions on two interrelated issues when this question was examined in the Working Group on International Contractual Practices. The first one was whether the arbitral tribunal should choose directly the substantive law applicable to the dispute, or to make the previous choice of a particular set of conflict rules; the second problem was whether the arbitral tribunal should be entitled to choose the "law" of a given national State or "rules of law" in general, as the parties had been authorized by the first paragraph, of Article 28.

The "direct" method to make the selection had already been accepted by France in 1981. Article 1491, paragraph 1, of its *nouveau Code de procédure civile* prescribes that, "failing a choice by the parties, the arbitral tribunal shall decide the dispute in accordance with the 'rules of law' it considers appropriate". This wider approach, was followed in The Netherlands (Article 1054, paragraph 2), Bolivia (Article 73, paragraph II) and in the 1998 Arbitration Rules of the International Chamber of Commerce of Paris (Article 17, paragraph 1); the 1997 American Association Arbitration Rules (Article 28, paragraph 1) and the 1998 Arbitration Rules of the London Court of International Arbitration (Article 22, paragraph 3) also adopt this liberal solution, specifying that the arbitral tribunal may chose the "law(s)" or "rules of law" applicable to the dispute.

Notwithstanding the adoption of the "direct" method, Portugal (Article 33, paragraph 2) and Peru (Article 117, paragraph 2) follow a more restricted approach because they authorize to select the "law", not the "rules of law", considered most appropriate by the arbitral tribunal. Similarly, the Guatemalan Decree prescribes that arbitrators shall determine the applicable "law", taking into account the characteristics or connections of the transaction (Article 34, paragraph 1). Thus, even though not compelled to use any conflict rule, the arbitral tribunal is only entitled to make the choice among national laws, *depeçage* being generally permitted; therefore it does not have the same freedom granted to the parties, who can also select the "rules of law" applicable, including those of the *lex mercatoria*.

Article 28, paragraph 2, of the UNCITRAL Model Law adopts a "more cautious approach" because it prescribes that, failing any designation of the applicable rules of law by the parties "the arbitral tribunal shall apply the law determined by the conflict of laws rules which it considers applicable". It reproduces Article 33, paragraph 1, of the UNCITRAL Rules, which in turn followed Article VII, paragraph 1, of the 1961 European Convention. Therefore the determination of the law applicable is to be made via a conflicts rule, but the arbitral tribunal is free to decide which conflicts rule is the most appropriate. The same solution has been adopted by Section 46, paragraph 3, of the 1996 English Arbitration Act, as explained by Lord Justice Saville in May 1996.

Notwithstanding the different regulation, it is acknowledged that the practical result of the UNCITRAL Model Law prescribing that arbitrators shall start choosing a conflicts rule to determine the applicable the "law" of a given national State, would generally be the same as if it had authorized the arbitral tribunal to utilize the *voie directe*. This conclusion finds support, first of all, because *depeçage* is admitted, permitting therefore the application of different laws to various parts of the dispute; and secondly, since the reasons invoked in practice by arbitrators when selecting directly the governing law, without reference to the conflict rules, are generally the same to those advanced by them when selecting the appropriate conflicts rule, the only difference being that when using the *voie directe* method the arbitral tribunal is under no obligation to explain the legal grounds for the determination of the applicable law or rules of law, as the case may be.

One "outdated theory" places excessive emphasis on the judicial nature of arbitration and for this reason assimilates arbitrators and judges of the seat of arbitration. This doctrine inspires Article 11 of the Resolution adopted by the Institute of International Law in its Amsterdam Session (1957), indicating that "the rules of choice of law in force in the state of the seat of the arbitral tribunal must be followed to settle the law applicable to the substance of the difference".

Notwithstanding that the determination of the law applicable via the conflict rules of the *forum* does not permit to foresee the results, recent arbitration statutes include special conflict rules specifically intended to be applied by arbitrators. Switzerland (Article 187, paragraph 1), Mexico (Article 1445, paragraph 2), Italy (Article 834, paragraph 1) and Germany (Article 1501, paragraph 2) reproduce their conflict of laws rule on the law applicable to contractual obligations and prescribe that the arbitral tribunal shall apply the law most closely connected with the dispute, even though it may be an extra-contractual one.

An "hybrid system" prevails in Spain. Article 62 of the Spanish Decree stipulates that arbitrators shall apply the law governing the relationship from which the dispute arises or, if there is none, the law they consider to be the most appropriate in the circumstances. Therefore, in first place the arbitral tribunal has to follow the prescriptions of an special conflict rule, which differs from the Spanish solution for contractual obligations (Article 10, paragraph 5, of the Spanish Civil Code). It is only where this solution is not workable that the "direct" method enters into play, permitting arbitrators to choose the law they consider the most appropriate.

The matter is not regulated in Argentina and Venezuela. Therefore, it seems that arbitrators are entitled to decide the case as they consider more appropriate, possibly taking into account whether the dispute between the parties has arisen out of a contractual or a non-contractual obligation.

4.   THE TERMS OF THE CONTRACT AND TRADE USAGES

The Report on the possible features of a model law on international commercial arbitration presented by the Secretary General to the United Nations Commission on International Trade Law (A/CN.9/207) already indicated the importance for arbitrators to decide, whether or not acting as *amiable compositeurs*, "in accordance with the terms of the contract, taking into account the pertinent usages".

The suggestion was considered by the Working Group on International Contractual Practices during its third session (16 – 26 February 1982). Then it was agreed that, in arbitration *de jure*, the arbitral tribunal should have regard to the terms of the contract and relevant trade usages: however divergent opinions were expressed as to whether the decision reached should be expressed in the model law, and if so in what manner. The prevailing view was that no provision regarding the terms of the contract should be incorporated in the model law since their observance was self-evident and because the inclusion of such rule would possible be misleading or incorrect, for a contract provision could be invalid under the applicable substantive law. On the contrary, it was agreed that an attempt be made to draft an appropriate disposition prescribing to take into account trade usages, in the terms formulated in the UNCITRAL Arbitration Rules, the Geneva Convention (1961) or the UN Vienna Sales Convention (1980), although not applicable in cases of arbitrations *ex aequo et bono*.

Therefore Article 31 of the Draft prepared by the Secretariat contained two proposals on the matter, none of them being applicable to arbitrations *ex aequo et bono*. The first one was based on Article 33, paragraph 3, of the UNCITRAL Rules, which prescribes that "in all cases, the arbitral tribunal shall decide in accordance with the terms of the contract and shall take into account the usages of the trade applicable to the transaction"; the expression "in all cases" referring to the situations whenever the law had been chosen by the parties or by the arbitral tribunal failing the parties to do so. The alternative proposal, based upon Article 9 of the United Nations Vienna Convention on Contracts for the International Sale of Goods (Vienna 1980), attempted to define the term "trade usage". Thus, it stated that the arbitral tribunal shall apply any usage to which the parties have consented to; and explained further that "the parties are considered, unless otherwise agreed, to have impliedly made applicable to their contract or its formation a usage of which they knew or ought to have known and which in international trade is widely known to, and regularly observed by, parties to contracts of the type involved in the particular trade concerned".

The Working Group on International Contractual Practices adopted the first proposal in its fourth session (4-15 October 1982), even though one participant maintained the view that "trade usages are part of the applicable law, therefore the obligation to apply them was implied incorporated in paragraph (1)" of Article 28.

However, this decision was reversed by the Working Group on International

Contractual Practices in its sixth session (29 August – 9 September 1983). Then the prevailing opinion was against its inclusion, "in view of the many questions and concerns it raised". As the Secretary General recalls in his analytical comentary of the draft, the reference to the terms of the contract was deleted "because it did not belong in an article dealing with the law applicable to the substance of the dispute and was not needed in a law of arbitration, though appropriate in arbitration rules, or that such reference could be misleading where the terms of the contract were in conflict with mandatory provisions of law or did not express the true intent of the parties". The Secretary General informs further that the reference to trade usages was considered not only redundant, since it is frequently required by the national law applicable to the dispute, but also dangerous, because "their legal effect and qualification were not uniform in all legal systems. For example, they may form part of the applicable law, in which case they were already covered by paragraph (1) or (2) of article 28".

Paragraph 4 of Article 28 was reinstated at the very end of the deliberations at the request of the United States of America. It reproduces the text of the UNCITRAL Rules and prescribes that "in all cases the arbitral tribunal shall decide in accordance with the terms of the contract and shall take into account the usages of the trade applicable to the transaction".

The Secretary General, commenting the UNCITRAL Rule, explains that it would apply "in any case", i.e. regardless of whether the law governing the substance of the dispute "was determined according to paragraph 1 o 2 of this article, or whether the arbitrators were authorized by the parties to decide the dispute *ex aequo et bono* or as "*amiables compositeurs*"; and stresses the point that the terms of the contract and trade usages shall be taken into account by arbitrators throughout the arbitral proceedings and particularly in the making of their award. The Secretary General also indicates that the provision gives arbitrators considerable latitude in arriving at their decision and that in the sphere of international commercial arbitration "this result corresponds with the intentions and expectations of the parties".

The UNCITRAL Model Law therefore provides some support for the position that an *amiable compositeur* cannot directly violate the terms of the contract. However, this is a delicate issue. The contrary view seems to prevail, at least whenever arbitrators are entitled in general not to apply the governing substantive rules if they would lead to an inequitable result, because in such case they may disregard the substantive rule which prescribes that contracts are binding between the parties.

Paragraph 4 of Article 28 distinguishes between the terms of the contract and trade usages, because of "the desirability of formulating in stricter terms the arbitrator's obligation to observe the provisions of the contract that their obligation to observe the usages of the trade". This distinction had already been made in the UNCITRAL Rules.

The categorical terms of Article 28, paragraph 4, seem not to accept any exception. However its operation may be difficult in cases of extracontractual disputes, and for this reason the 1997 Arbitration Rules of the American Arbitration Association restrict its application to disputes involving a contract (Article 28, paragraph 2).

The wording of Article 28, paragraph 4, of the UNCITRAL Model Law was copied in Mexico (Article 1445, paragraph 4), Peru (Article 117, paragraph 4, dealing with commercial arbitrations), Guatemala (Article 36, paragraph 3), Germany (Article 1051, paragraph 4), and in the 1988 Arbitration's Rules of the Inter-American Commercial Arbitration Commission (Article 33, paragraph 3). Therefore, the arbitral tribunal shall decide in accordance with the terms of the contract and take into account the usages of trade applicable to the transaction not only in arbitrations *de iure* and in arbitrations *ex aequo et bono* but also whenever the choice has been made by the parties or by the arbitral tribunal, failing the parties to do so.

The Guatemalan Decree goes an step further. Its Article 36 repeats the text of the UNCITRAL Model Law adding that in cases of international arbitrations, the arbitral tribunal "may take into account practices and principles of International Commercial Law, as well as commercial usages and practices of general acceptation" (paragraph 2).

The Italian Code of Civil Procedure, as amended in 1995, (Article 834, second paragraph) did not reproduce the final version of the UNCITRAL Rules but the provision included in its 1974 Draft; and the same formulation has been adopted in the 1998 Arbitration Rules of the International Chamber of Commerce (Article 17, paragraph 2). Therefore, they do not make any difference between the terms of the contract and trade usages prescribing that "in all cases, the arbitrator shall take into account of the provisions of the contract and the relevant trade usages". In both cases the sentence "in all cases" seems to refer only to the situations regulated by paragraphs 1 and 2, Article 28, of the UNCITRAL Model Law, not contemplating arbitrations *ex aequo et bono*.

Similarly, the 1998 Venezuelan Act does not make any difference between the terms of the contract and trade usages (*usos y costumbres mercantiles*). However, its Article 8 prescribes that arbitrators shall always (*siempre*) take them into consideration, being for this reason applicable to arbitrations *de jure* and to arbitration in equity.

Article 1054, paragraph 4, of the Dutch Statute does not mention the terms of the contract. It provides that : "In all cases the arbitral tribunal shall take into account any applicable trade usages"; the expression "in all cases" alluding to the situations regulated by paragraphs 1 and 2, Article 28, of the UNCITRAL Model Law and not to arbitrations *ex aequo et bono*.

The Costa Rican Act takes a particular stand. Its Article 22, second paragraph, prescribes that "in all cases, the arbitral tribunal shall decide according to the terms of the arbitration agreement and shall additionally take into account the uses and practices applicable to the case, even written regulations, where appropriate".

The obligation to decide in accordance with the terms of the contract and to take into account trade usages is not expressly mentioned neither in the statutes enacted in Portugal (Article 33), Spain (Article 62), Brazil (Article 2), Colombia (Article 197) and Great Britain (Section 46) nor in the 1998 Arbitration Rules of the London Court of International Arbitration (Article 22, paragraph 3). Therefore arbitrators are entitled to act as they may consider appropriate.

5.   CONCLUSION

Recent statutes on arbitrations generally accept party autonomy to decide the dispute and authorize the arbitral tribunal to make the choice, failing the parties to do so. In the second case a different regulation exists but, as indicated above, it seems to be irrelevant in practice. Moreover, modern legislation strongly substantiates the freedom of arbitrators to take the decision they consider most appropriate because the merits of the dispute is not a matter that can be reviewed by national courts, and for this reason errors in judgment, whether of fact or of law, are not in themselves grounds on which an award can be set aside or refused enforcement.

Die „Anwendung" einer ausländischen „Rechtsordnung" im Forumstaat: ... *perseverare est diabolicum!*

Paolo Picone[*]

1. DIE MÖGLICHKEIT DER ANWENDUNG EINER AUSLÄNDISCHEN RECHTSORDNUNG IM FORUMSTAAT ALS ZU UNTERSUCHENDES PROBLEM

In der juristischen Terminologie werden manchmal aus Tradition oder Gewohnheit einige Fachausdrücke verwendet, ohne daß man sich fragt, ob sie richtig sind. Ein Beispiel dafür ist nach der hier vertretenen Meinung in der Tendenz zu sehen, die Ausdrücke „Anwendung eines ausländischen *Rechts*" (oder *Gesetzes*) und „Anwendung einer ausländischen *Rechtsordnung*" als gleichwertig und untereinander austauschbar zu betrachten. Diese Sprachweise soll hier einer kritischen Analyse unterzogen werden, da sie auf einem theoretischen Fehler beruht (der Möglichkeit

[*] Professor für internationales Recht an der juristischen Fakultät der Universität „La Sapienza" in Rom.

J. Basedow et al., eds., Private Law in the International Arena – Liber Amicorum Kurt Siehr
© 2000, T.M.C.Asser Press, The Hague, The Netherlands

der formellen Anwendung einer ausländischen Rechtsordnung im Forumstaat). Dadurch wird die korrekte Lösung einiger Probleme verhindert.

Die besagte Terminologie wird von der Lehre in einigen Ländern, wie z.b. in Deutschland, in Österreich und auch in Italien üblicherweise verwendet, so daß sich jegliche Hinweise auf die Literatur erübrigen. Unlängst hat sie sogar in einigen Reformgesetzen des internationalen Privatrechts ihren Einzug gehalten. Das österreichische IPR-Gesetz vom 15. Juni 1978 bezeichnet z.b. in § 1 Abs. 2 die Kollisionsnormen („Verweisungsnormen") als „Regelungen über die anzuwendende Rechtsordnung", während bei den einzelnen zu regelnden Sachverhalten der Ausdruck „nach dem Recht zu beurteilen" üblich ist. Das deutsche Gesetz zur Reform des internationalen Privatrechts vom 25. Juli 1986 verwendet die gleiche Terminologie, indem es den Kollisionsnormen ganz allgemein in § 3 Abs. 1 die Aufgabe zuschreibt zu bestimmen, „bei Sachverhalten mit einer Verbindung zum Recht eines ausländischen Staates . . . welche Rechtsordnungen anzuwenden sind."

Im allgemeinen haben diese Formulierungen im Schrifttum keine Reaktion geweckt. Der Wortlaut der letztgenannten deutschen Vorschrift ist offensichtlich nur von Wengler kritisiert worden. Dieser wies ausdrücklich darauf hin, daß das deutsche Reformgesetz den Unterschied zwischen < „Rechtsordnung" und „Recht" eines bestimmten Staates > nicht klargestellt habe.[1]

2.   DAS NOTWENDIGE OPERIEREN DER INLÄNDISCHEN RECHTSORDNUNG
     BEI DER ANWENDUNG EINES FREMDEN RECHTS ODER GESETZES

Die Auffassung, daß die Kollisionsnormen die *Anwendung* der berufenen ausländischen Rechtsordnung im Forumstaat ermöglichen, stellt eine juristische Ungenauigkeit dar, da sie den Begriff Rechtsordnung im Grunde mißversteht.[2]

---

[1] Vgl. Wilhelm Wengler, „Zur Technik der internationalprivatrechtlichen Rechtsanwendungsanweisungen des IPR-‹‹Reform›› gesetzes von 1986", 53 *RabelsZ* (1989) S. 409ff., S. 411.

[2] Der Ausdruck „Rechtsordnung" wird in der Lehre in unterschiedlichem Sinne verwendet: siehe für eine zusammenfassende Darstellung Giovanni Tarello, „Prospetto per la voce" Ordinamento giuridico ‹‹ di una enciclopedia", 6 *Politica del diritto* (1975) S. 73ff. Der Ausdruck dient ebenfalls dazu, das Bestehen eines aus verschiedenen in gegenseitiger Beziehung stehenden Elementen resultierenden „integrierten" Rechtssystems zu bezeichnen. Dieses System wird in den früheren theoretischen Konstruktionen entweder rein formell als „Normensystem" im engeren Sinne verstanden (man denke an die ersten Schriften von Kelsen), oder mit Bezug auf die einschlägige soziale Gesamtstruktur (wie in der bekannten „institutionistischen" Theorie von Santi Romano) rekonstruiert.
In den neuesten Entwicklungen ist der Begriff (infolge derselben Evolution der Systemtheorien) weiter vertieft worden. Er bezeichnet meist die Integration in ein einheitliches und ganzheitliches normative System sowohl der Rechtserzeugungsquellen im engeren Sinne als der unterschiedlichen rechtlichen Garantie- und Durchsetzungsmechanismen. Siehe z.B. Neil MacCormick, „Law as Institutional Normative Order", 28 *Rechtstheorie* (1997) S. 219ff.; und in der italienischen Doktrin Mario G. Losano, *Sistema e struttura nel diritto. I. Dalle origini alla scuola storica* (Torino, Giappichelli 1968); Vittorio

Unter einer Rechtsordnung ist ein gesamtes und einheitliches normatives System zu verstehen, welches sich nicht an der Grenze der internen Gesetzgebung erschöpft, sondern auch alle aus ausländischen Gesetzen (oder aus dem Völkerrecht) abzuleitenden Regelungen oder konkreten normativen Beurteilungen enthält, auf die sie verweist und die sie in ihrem Bereich konkret geltend macht.[3] Diese externen Regelungen werden, so wie die ursprünglich inneren Regelungen, von den gleichen Rechtsschutz- und Durchsetzungsmechanismen der in Frage kommenden Rechtsordnung umfaßt, die das Funktionieren des *gesamten* Systems über die Grenzen der inneren Rechtsquellen im engeren Sinne des Wortes hinaus ermöglichen.[4]

Geht man von einer derartigen Konzeption der Rechtsordnung aus, so ist es die Rechtsordnung des Forums, die bei jeder Anwendung eines ausländischen Rechts oder Gesetzes tätig wird und sich im weiteren Sinne durchsetzt. Es ist der Forumstaat, der zunächst inländische Rechtslagen formell und ursprünglich erzeugt und zustande kommen läßt, wenn er den rechtsgestaltenden Akt solcher Situationen aufstellt (durch Urteil, Verwaltungsakt, Maßnahmen der freiwilligen Gerichtsbarkeit usw.): Aus dieser Sicht macht es keinen Unterschied, ob auf die entsprechenden Sachverhalte das inländische oder ein ausländisches Recht angewendet worden ist.[5] Man denke als Beispiel an den Fall, daß ein inländisches Gericht die Ehescheidung zwischen zwei Ausländern durch Anwendung ihres gemeinsamen Heimatrechts ausgesprochen hat. In diesem Fall ist unstreitig, daß die inländische Rechtsordnung durch das eigene Ehescheidungsurteil eine Rechtslage geschaffen hat, die formell nur von ihr herzuleiten ist und selbstverständlich nicht von der ausländischen Rechtsordnung, deren Recht im Forumstaat angewendet worden ist. Die inländische Ehescheidung kann im übrigen nicht einmal in der ausländischen Rechtsordnung anerkennungsfähig sein! In dem genannten Beispiel ist es daher widersinnig, von der Anwendung im Forumstaat einer „ausländischen Rechtsordnung" auszugehen, da gerade und ausschließlich die *inländische* Rechtsordnung durch ihr Operieren eine formell inländische Ehescheidung ausgesprochen hat,

---

Frosini, „Ordinamento giuridico (Filosofia del diritto)", *Enciclopedia del diritto*, Bd. XXX (Milano, Giuffré 1980) S. 639ff., S. 645ff.; Massimo Corsale, „Pluralismo giuridico", ibid., Bd. XXXIII (Milano, Giuffré 1983) S. 1003ff., S. 1005ff.

[3] Vgl. ausführlicher Paolo Picone, *Norme di diritto internazionale privato e norme materiali del foro* (Napoli, Jovene 1970) vor allem S. 28ff., 40ff.

[4] Siehe in der internationalprivatrechtlichen Lehre Wilhelm Wengler, „Die Belegenheit von Rechten", in: *Festschrift der Juristischen Fakultät der Freien Universität Berlin zum 41. Deutschen Juristentag in Berlin* (Berlin und Frankfurt, Verlag F. Vahlen 1955) S. 285ff., vor allem S. 293ff., 296ff.; ders. (oben N. 1) der als „Rechtsordnung" den Komplex von Rechtsnormen bezeichnen will, der aus der „Gesamtheit der vom deutschen Richter befolgten Rechtsanwendungsanweisungen, Prozeßnormen und auch der anzuwendenden inländischen und ausländischen Sachnormen" besteht; Rolando Quadri, *Lezioni di diritto internazionale privato*, 5. Aufl. (Napoli, Liguori 1969) S. 215ff.; Picone (oben N. 3) S. 40ff.

[5] Vgl. Paolo Picone, *Norme di conflitto speciali per la valutazione di norme materiali* (Napoli, Jovene 1969) S. 72ff.

wenn auch durch Anwendung der aus einem ausländischen „Gesetz" berufenen „Sachnormen".[6]

An diesen Folgerungen ändert sich auch dann nichts, wenn die in Frage kommenden Rechtslagen, die im Forumstaat einem ausländischen Recht unterstellt werden müssen, aus der automatischen (d.h. *ex lege*) Wirksamkeit der zuständigen fremden Sachnormen herrühren: so z.B. in den Fällen, in denen das berufene ausländische Recht die eheliche Abstammung eines Kindes oder dessen Legitimation durch nachträgliche Eheschließung der Eltern bestimmen muß. In diesen Fällen ist es aber notwendig, zwei unterschiedliche Konstellationen zu unterscheiden.[7]

Zu der ersten Konstellation zählen die Fälle, in denen das berufene ausländische Recht den ihm unterstellten Sachverhalt von seinem eigenen Gesichtspunkt aus *nicht* regeln will. Die betreffende Rechtslage (Ehelichkeit eines Kindes oder Legitimation, je nach den angegebenen Beispielen) entstammt dann formell der Anwendung solcher *inländischen* neu geschaffenen Rechtsnormen, die zumindest ihrem räumlichen und/oder persönlichen Anwendungsbereich nach *nicht* den im Ausland geltenden Sachnormen entsprechen. Sie begründet daher noch einmal eine formell und ursprünglich *inländische* Rechtslage, die von vornherein nach dem *ausländischen* Recht (und *in der ausländischen* Rechtsordnung) kein Äquivalent findet. Es ist deswegen nicht nur unrichtig, von der Anwendung im Forumstaat einer ausländischen Rechtsordnung auszugehen, sondern darüber hinaus sogar unbegründet, von der Anwendung eines im formellen Sinne des Wortes echten „ausländischen" Rechts zu sprechen!

Anders ist diejenige Konstellation zu beurteilen, in denen das ausländische berufene Recht den ihm von der inländischen Kollisionsnorm unterstellten Sachverhalt auch nach *seinem* eigenen Anwendungswillen regeln will. In diesen Fällen ist die in Frage kommende Rechtslage (Ehelichkeit eines Kindes oder Legitimation) schon das Ergebnis oder Produkt der automatischen Wirksamkeit der ausländischen anwendungswilligen Sachnormen: die Berufung und die Anwendung dieser Sachnormen im Forumstaat dienen daher formell dem Zweck, eine ausländische Rechtslage anzuerkennen. Diese Rechtslage wird aber durch die Anerkennung in die inländische Rechtsordnung umgesetzt (auf die inländische Rechtsordnung „übertragen"), um – wenn auch nur potentiell – den juristischen Ermittlungs- und Durchsetzungsmechanismen des Forums unterstellt zu werden. Auch diese Anerkennung beruht deswegen nicht auf der Anwendung im Forumstaat einer ausländischen Rechtsordnung, da infolge der Anerkennung die ausländische Rechtslage von einer anderen

---

[6] Die kritisierte Terminologie wird häufig von Rainer Hausmann, *Kollisionsrechtliche Schranken von Scheidungsurteilen* (München, Beck 1980) verwendet, der vielleicht aus diesem Grunde die Fälle einer echten kollisionsrechtlichen Verweisung auf eine ausländische Rechtsordnung in ihrer Gesamtheit (siehe unten, Nr. 5 und 6) mißversteht: siehe unsere Besprechung in 18 *Rivista di diritto internazionale privato e processuale* (1982) S. 192ff.

[7] Siehe noch Picone (oben N. 5) S. 76ff.

Rechtsordnung als derjenigen, in der sie ursprünglich entstanden war, geltend gemacht wird.[8]

3. KEINE ANWENDUNG EINER AUSLÄNDISCHEN RECHTSORDNUNG INFOLGE EINES „RINVIO FORMALE" AUF DAS FREMDE RECHT

Die vertretene Auffassung, nach der die Möglichkeit der Anwendung im Forumstaat einer ausländischen Rechtsordnung abgelehnt werden muß, ist nicht von der Natur der Verweisung auf das ausländische Recht beeinflußt, die von den inländischen Kollisionsnormen ausgesprochen wird.

Wie bekannt ist, hat sich besonders die ältere Lehre ausführlich mit der Frage auseinandergesetzt, ob die Kollisionsnormen durch diese Verweisung zu einer Rezeption oder Inkorporation des ausländischen Rechts in die inländische Rechtsordnung führen würden (sog. „rinvio materiale" oder „ricettizio"), oder ob sie nur eine formale Weisung enthalten würden, das ausländische Recht als „fremdes Recht" anzuwenden (sog. „rinvio formale").[9]

Die erste Lösung ist lange von der früheren italienischen Lehre (sowie in den Vereinigten Staaten von Cook und den Anhängern der < local-law-Theorie >) vertreten worden; sie geht in ihren radikalsten Versionen von einer vollständigen „Nationalisierung" des ausländischen Rechts aus, und teilt bisweilen den betreffenden inländischen Kollisionsnormen die Aufgabe zu, die entsprechenden Sachverhalte durch „Aneignung" des materiellen Inhalts der ausländischen Sachnormen *direkt* zu regeln.[10] In vielen Ländern jedoch hat sich die überwiegende Mehrheit der Lehre für das „rinvio formale" ausgesprochen, so auch in Deutschland. Hier wird fast einhellig betont, daß das ausländische Recht als „fremdes" Recht im Forumstaat anzuwenden ist.[11]

Die dargestellte Alternative ist zum großen Teil das Ergebnis abstrakter Spekulationen, die – abgesehen von dem nur indirekt damit verbundenen und im Grunde autonomen Problem der prozeßrechtlichen Behandlung des ausländischen Rechts –

---

[8] Diese Perspektive ist ursprünglich von Wengler (oben N. 4) S. 303ff., so weit geführt worden, daß er sogar auf die übliche Kategorie der „Anerkennung" verzichten wollte.

[9] Siehe z.B. Werner Niederer, *Einführung in die allgemeinen Lehren des internationalen Privatrechts*, 3. Aufl. (Zürich, Schulthess 1961) S. 341ff.; und später Max Keller/Kurt Siehr, *Allgemeine Lehren des internationalen Privatrechts* (Zürich, Schulthess 1986) S. 117ff.

[10] Siehe für diese Version des „rinvio ricettizio" im echten Sinne Mario Marinoni, „La natura giuridica del diritto internazionale privato", 7 *Rivista di diritto internazionale* (1913) S. 346ff., S. 354; und für eine kritische Darstellung Rodolfo De Nova, „New Trends in Private International Law", 28 *Law and Contemporary Problems* (1963) S. 808ff., S. 812ff.; Quadri (oben N. 4) S. 215ff.

[11] Vgl. neulich Kurt Siehr, „A Statute of Private International Law for Israel", in: Alfred E. Kellermann/Kurt Siehr/Talia Einhorn, *Israel among the Nations* (The Hague/Boston/London, Kluwer 1998) S. 353ff., S. 360 („Foreign law is applied as foreign law . . . ").

keine praktischen Konsequenzen nach sich ziehen. Beide Sichtweisen sind, wenn auch aus unterschiedlichen Gründen, nicht völlig überzeugend. Eine vollständige „Nationalisierung" des ausländischen Rechts kann dem Sinn und der Funktion der Kollisionsnormen nicht gerecht werden, da sie das ausländische Recht zum Bestandteil der *lex fori* erheben würde. Sie steht darüber hinaus auch praktisch im Widerspruch zu dem Erfordernis, das ausländische Recht nach den Maßstäben der entsprechenden Rechtsordnung auszulegen und im Prinzip auch anzuwenden. Die Annahme eines „rinvio formale" anderseits kann die zahlreichen Fälle nicht erfassen und verständlich machen, in denen die Kollisionsnormen von vornherein ein nicht anwendungswilliges fremdes Recht für zuständig erklären, oder dieses Recht bei seiner Berufung (wegen « dépeçage », Anpassung usw.) verschiedene Veränderungen seines ursprünglichen materiellen Inhalts erfahren muß.[12] Es ist deswegen besser, der von der neuesten italienischen Lehre vorgeschlagenen Lösung zu folgen. Diese geht davon aus, daß die Kollisionsnormen eine Art rechtserzeugende Verweisung auf das ausländische Recht (sog. "rinvio di produzione giuridica") hervorbringen, um die Schaffung von neuen Sachnormen im Forumstaat zu ermöglichen, die in ihrem Inhalt – je nach der Fallgestaltung – mehr oder weniger den im Ausland geltenden Rechtsnormen entsprechen.[13]

Unabhängig davon, welcher Lösung der Vorzug gebührt, muß doch an dieser Stelle betont werden, daß die verbreitete Annahme der These des „rinvio formale" (mit der Anwendung des ausländischen Rechts in seiner formellen Natur als „fremdes" Recht) nicht zu der Behauptung führen kann, die Anwendung eines ausländischen Rechts mit einer Berufung derselben . . . ausländischen Rechtsordnung gleichzusetzen (oder als gleichwertig zu betrachten).[14] Vergegenwärtigt man sich die logischen Konsequenzen, so erweist sich eine solche Behauptung von vornherein als völlig unhaltbar. In dem bereits geschilderten Fall einer im Inland ausgesprochenen Ehescheidung in Anwendung ausländischer Sachnormen könnte diese Behauptung z.B. zu der Schlußfolgerung führen, daß der inländische Richter in der Tat als . . . Organ der ausländischen Rechtsordnung tätig geworden sei!

---

[12] Dieses mehr „praktische" Argument wird üblicherweise von den Anhängern des „rinvio formale" vollkommen vernachlässigt. Für eine ausführliche Kritik dieser These siehe vor allem Quadri (oben N. 4) S. 218ff.

[13] Vgl. Quadri (oben N. 4) S. 215ff.; Piero Bernardini, *Produzione di norme giuridiche mediante rinvio* (Milano, Giuffré 1966) S. 163ff.; Picone (oben N. 3) S. 15. Die These des „rinvio di produzione giuridica" wird häufig in der ausländischen Lehre mit der früheren und total überholten Konstruktion des „rinvio ricettizio" irrtümlicherweise identifiziert. Vgl. auch für eine ähnliche Konstruktion in der österreichischen Lehre Franz Mänhardt, *Die Kodifikation des österreichischen Internationalen Privatrechts* (Berlin, Duncker & Humblot 1978) S. 50ff.; Kurt Heller, „Das internationale Privatrecht in der österreichischen Rechtsordnung", in: Fritz Schwind (Hrsg.), *Europarecht. Internationales Privatrecht. Rechtsvergleichung* (Wien, Verlag der österreichischen Akademie der Wissenschaften 1988) S. 9ff., S. 33ff.

[14] Siehe für eine Verbindung der zwei Aspekte innerhalb der „teoria istituzionistica" des Rechts Santi Romano, *L'ordinamento giuridico*, 2. Aufl. (Firenze, Sansoni 1946) S. 171ff.

Diese hypothetische und absurde Schlußfolgerung ist keine bloße Theorie. Sie hat vielmehr die Gedankengänge eines italienischen Autors beeinflußt. Dieser Autor hat die These vertreten, nach der die Kollisionsnormen durch ihre Verweisungen die Geltung der berufenen ausländischen Rechtsordnungen an Stelle der inländischen Rechtsordnung herbeiführen würden.[15] Den inländischen Richtern wurde konsequenterweise nicht zufällig die Aufgabe zugeschrieben, gerade durch ihre Tätigkeit der in Frage kommenden ausländischen Rechtsordnung „Wirkung" und „Geltung" im Forumstaat zu verleihen.[16]

4. KEINE ANWENDUNG EINER AUSLÄNDISCHEN RECHTSORDNUNG BEI DER ANNAHME EINER „GESAMTVERWEISUNG" AUF DAS FREMDE RECHT

Wenn die Annahme eines „rinvio formale" für das postulierte Ergebnis nicht von Bedeutung ist, kann ebensowenig von der Anwendung ausländischer Rechtsordnungen dann die Rede sein, wenn die Kollisionsnormen den Renvoi (vor allem in der Form sowohl der Rück- als auch der Weiterverweisung) beachten. Die letztgenannte Perspektive hat einen mehr empirischen Charakter, findet ihre terminologische Bestätigung aber sowohl in der Literatur, als auch im Wortlaut einzelner Vorschriften. In der Doktrin wird gelegentlich die Alternative zwischen dem Ausschluß und der Annahme des Renvoi mit derjenigen zwischen einer Verweisung auf die ausländischen Sachnormen oder auf die fremden Rechtsordnungen *in toto* gleichgesetzt.[17] In diese Richtung weist auch der verbreitete Unterschied zwischen Sachnorm- und Gesamtverweisung.[18] In den aktuellsten Reformgesetzen des internationalen Privatrechts sind ferner Vorschriften zu finden, die bei der Annah-

---

[15] Siehe, auf Santi Romano zurückgehend, Francesco Capotorti, *La nazionalità delle società* (Napoli, Jovene 1953) S. 57ff.

[16] Siehe noch Capotorti (oben N. 15) S. 88ff.; und die zutreffende Kritik von Quadri (oben N. 4) S. 219.

[17] Diese Terminologie verwendet z.B. Adolf F. Schnitzer, *Handbuch des internationalen Privatrechts*, Bd. I (Basel, Verlag für Recht und Gesellschaft 1957) S. 207. Vgl. noch in der deutschen Lehre Alexander N. Makarov, *Grundriß des internationalen Privatrechts* (Frankfurt am Main, Metzner 1970) S. 81 („. . . oder muß diese fremde Rechtsordnung in ihrem vollen Umfang angewandt werden. . . . ?"); und kürzlich Jan Kropholler, *Internationales Privatrecht*, 3. Aufl. (Tübingen, Mohr 1997) S. 149 („. . . . Theorie der ‚Gesamtverweisung', wonach jede Kollisionsnorm auf eine Rechtsordnung in ihrer Gesamtheit . . . verweist").

[18] Die Ursprünge des Ausdrucks „Gesamtverweisung" sind in der Rechtsprechung des Reichsgerichts in Deutschland zu finden: siehe George Melchior, *Die Grundlagen des deutschen internationalen Privatrechts* (Berlin und Leipzig, Walter de Gruyter 1932) S. 194, 207ff. Die Gesamtverweisung war aber bei den früheren Entscheidungen auf die Anwendung eines ausländischen „Rechts" in vollem Umfang oder in seiner Gesamtheit gerichtet: siehe z.B. Reichsgericht, 15. Februar 1912, *Entscheidungen des Reichsgerichts in Zivilsachen* 78, S. 234ff., S. 236ff (1912).

me des Renvoi ausdrücklich von der Verweisung auf ausländische Rechtsordnungen ausgehen.[19]

Besonders verbreitet ist diese Sichtweise in den Fällen, in denen das Forum den Renvoi in der Form der < foreign court theory > annimmt, wobei der inländische Richter das anwendbare Recht so bestimmen soll, wie es ein Richter der berufenen ausländischen Rechtsordnung täte. Es kommt in der Tat häufig vor, daß gerade in diesen Fällen nicht nur von einer Verweisung auf ausländische Rechtsordnungen *in toto* gesprochen wird, sondern auch von einer praktischen (wenn nicht sogar funktionellen) „Gleichstellung" des inländischen mit dem ausländischen Richter.[20]

Der aufgezeigte Ansatz ist nach der hier vertretenen Ansicht ein fortbestehendes Produkt der früheren und überholten Theorien der Rechtskollisionen als Souveränitätskonflikte, und der Kollisionsnormen als funktionell „überstaatliche" Rechtsanwendbarkeitsnormen, die eine Verteilung der Gesetzgebungskompetenz zwischen den Staaten und den entsprechenden Rechtsordnungen zur Aufgabe hätten.[21] Faßt man die Gesetzgebungskompetenz als eine typische hoheitliche Funktion des Staates auf, führt das in der Tat dazu, in der Befolgung des Renvoi (und der von einem ausländischen Staat getroffenen Bestimmungen über das anwendbare Recht) eine Art „Unterwerfung" des Forums einer von diesem ausländischen Staat ausgeübten hoheitlichen Funktion, und konsequenterweise eine Verweisung oder „Delegation" an eine ausländische Rechtsordnung „in ihrer Gesamtheit" zu sehen.[22]

Vor dem Hintergrund der an dieser Stelle interessierenden Fragen ist diese Sichtweise jedoch nachdrücklich abzulehnen, welche auch immer die ihr zugrundeliegenden theoretischen Prämissen sein mögen. Die Annahme des Renvoi kann nicht als brauchbares Element für die Behauptung herangezogen werden, daß eine ausländische Rechtsordnung *in toto* im Forumstaat berufen und sogar angewendet würde.

Unstreitig ist, daß ausländische Kollisionsnormen durch ihre Verweisungen den normativen „Bestand" der einschlägigen Rechtsordnung bereichern. Das „Gesamtoperieren" derselben wird damit aber nicht erfasst. Neben den Kollisionsnormen sind darüber hinaus zumindest die Vorschriften über die Anerkennung und Vollstreckung ausländischer Entscheide und andere hoheitliche Rechtsakte in Betracht

---

[19] Siehe z.B. § 5 Abs. 1 des österreichischen IPR-Gesetzes vom 15. Juni 1978. Siehe auch als Bestätigung dieser Tendenz die falsche Übersetzung von "lei" und "legislaçao" durch „Rechtsordnung" im Art. 17, Abs. 1 des portugiesischen Zivilgesetzbuches bei Wolfgang Riering (Hrsg.), *IPR-Gesetze in Europa* (Bern/München, Stämpfli und Beck 1997) S. 108/109.

[20] Vgl. Paul Lagarde, « Le principe de proximité dans le droit international privé contemporain. Cours général de droit international privé », *Recueil des cours*, Bd. 196 (1986-I) S. 9ff., S. 157ff. (S. 159: « ...un cas où une juridiction statue en quelque sorte par délégation d'une autre et en appliquant les règles de conflit de cette dernière »).

[21] Siehe für eine kritische Darstellung dieser Theorien Quadri (oben N. 4) S. 80ff., S. 90ff.

[22] Vgl. dazu Phocion Francescakis, *La théorie du renvoi et les conflits de systèmes en droit international privé* (Paris, Sirey 1958) S. 121ff., 124ff.

zu ziehen. Diese erweitern ebenfalls den besagten normativen Bestand, indem sie konkrete drittstaatliche Rechtslagen in die gesamte ausländische Rechtsordnung berufen und gelten lassen. Die Beachtung des Renvoi verwirklicht daher keine Verweisung des Forums auf eine ausländische Rechtsordnung in ihrer Gesamtheit, sondern nur eine normalerweise beschränkte Koordinierung mit derselben auf der Ebene der Suche des anwendbaren Rechts.[23]

Es muß weiterhin als zentrales Argument hinzugefügt werden, daß der Forumstaat die ausländischen Kollisionsnormen letztlich nicht deshalb berücksichtigt um festzustellen, welche abstrakte oder konkrete Rechtsregeln dritter Staaten *in der ausländischen Rechtsordnung* zu einer einschlägigen Wirkung gelangen können, sondern um das anwendbare Recht *im Inland* zu bestimmen.[24] Man kann daher davon ausgehen, daß diese „Beachtung" der ausländischen Kollisionsnormen zu einer „Anwendung" im *weiteren* Sinne derselben (aber *nur* der Kollisionsnormen!) im Forumstaat hinausläuft.[25] Es ist jedoch nicht angebracht, eine Anwendung der ausländischen Rechtsordnung in ihrer Gesamtheit im Forumstaat zu postulieren. Wie könnte übrigens eine solche Anwendung – nur infolge der Annahme des Renvoi – gerechtfertigt werden, wenn die ausländischen Kollisionsnormen . . . zurück auf die *lex fori* verweisen würden?!

---

[23] Diese selbstverständliche Wahrheit ist im Grunde von den Autoren anerkannt, die richtigerweise den Ausdruck „Gesamtverweisung" nicht verwenden, und an seiner Stelle nur von einer „IPR-Verweisung" sprechen: siehe ausdrücklich zu dieser terminologischen Frage Abbo Junker, *Internationales Privatrecht* (München, Beck 1998) S. 171.

[24] Auch nach den früheren Auffassungen, wonach infolge einer „Gesamtverweisung" der inländische Richter, der fremdes Recht anzuwenden hatte, genau so entscheiden sollte wie ein Richter des Landes, dessen Recht die inländische Kollisionsnorm für anwendbar erklärt hätte (siehe Melchior (oben N. 18) S. 208), hat die deutsche Lehre im Grunde vergeblich vorgeschlagen, bei der Anwendung der rück- und weiterverweisenden fremden Kollisionsnorm auch den *fremden* ordre public zu beachten (siehe Melchior (oben N. 18) S. 212ff., wo die Entscheidung Reichsgericht, 16. Mai 1931, *Entscheidungen des Reichsgerichts in Zivilsachen* 132, S. 416ff. (1931), völlig mißverstanden wird). Die Aufgabe der inländischen Richter, innerhalb und für das Tätigwerden der *inländischen* Rechtsordnung das anwendbare Recht, wenn auch „durch die Brille" der ausländischen Kollisionsnormen zu bestimmen, stand somit letzten Endes außer Frage.
Es muß auf jedem Fall betont werden, daß in den modernen kollisionsrechtlichen Systemen der Renvoi immer weniger dazu dient, eine vollständige Koordinierung des Forums *nur* mit der ausländischen Rechtsordnung zu verwirklichen, dessen Recht die inländische Kollisionsnorm ursprünglich für anwendbar erklärt hat, sondern sich als ein Mechanismus erweist, um zu der Anwendung im Forumstaat (wenn man von der Rückverweisung absieht) eines „anwendungswilligen" ausländischen Rechts zu gelangen: vgl. dazu Paolo Picone, „Caratteri ed evoluzione del metodo tradizionale dei conflitti di leggi", 81 *Rivista di diritto internazionale* (1998) S. 5ff., S. 18ff (und in: *La riforma italiana del diritto internazionale privato* (Padova, Cedam 1998) S. 243ff., S. 254ff.)

[25] Siehe z.B. Rainer Hausmann, in: *Staudingers Kommentar zum Bürgerlichen Gesetzbuch mit Einführungsgesetz und Nebengesetzen*, 13. Bearbeitung (Berlin, Sellier/De Gruyter 1996) „Art. 4 EGBGB", S. 254ff. (Rdnr. 56ff.), der aber auch auf die mangelnde Revisibilität der Anwendung ausländischer Kollisionsnormen hinweisen muß (S. 274, Rdnr. 108). In der Tat werden die ausländischen Kollisionsnormen nur von den Richtern der entsprechenden ausländischen Rechtsordnung im *engeren* Sinne angewendet, für die sie als rechtserzeugende kollisionsrechtliche Techniken operieren.

5.   DIE BERÜCKSICHTIGUNG EINER AUSLÄNDISCHEN RECHTSORDNUNG
     IN IHRER GESAMTHEIT BEI DER UNSELBSTÄNDIGEN BEURTEILUNG
     EINER VORFRAGE

Die dargelegten Analysen gründen auf einer allgemeineren Behauptung, die syn-
thetisch folgendermaßen zusammengefaßt werden kann. Wird der Begriff „Rechtsordnung" richtigerweise in dem oben beschriebenen Sinne verstanden, so ist es auf
derselben logischen Ebene ausgeschlossen, daß die Kollisionsnormen durch ihre
Verweisungen die Anwendung einer ausländischen Rechtsordnung innerhalb des
Forumstaats ermöglichen (und nicht nur die Anwendung eines ausländischen
„Rechts" oder „Gesetzes" und der einschlägigen fremden „Sachnormen"). Wie
könnte wohl die inländische Rechtsordnung, als integriertes System von Rechtser-
zeugungs- und Rechtsdurchsetzungsmechanismen verstanden, ein anderes globales
und integriertes ausländisches normatives System in seinem Geltungsbereich „anwenden"?[26]

Die mangelnde Unterscheidung zwischen „Recht" und „Rechtsordnung" kann
zu vielen fehlerhaften Ergebnissen führen, auf die im Rahmen dieser Untersuchung
nicht näher eingegangen werden kann. Es muß jedoch betont werden, daß einige
Fehler bisweilen nicht aus der dargestellten Perspektive hervorgehen, nach der von
der Anwendung einer ausländischen Rechtsordnung anstelle eines ausländischen
Rechts oder Gesetzes die Rede ist. Sie sind umgekehrt auf die gegenteilige Sichtweise zurückzuführen, nach der von der Anwendung eines ausländischen Rechts
oder Gesetzes gesprochen wird, während es korrekt wäre, sich *auf die Berücksichtigung einer ausländischen Rechtsordnung „in ihrer Gesamtheit"* (um diese letzte an
sich nicht notwendige Bezeichnung weiter zu benutzen) zu beziehen.

Diese Situation kann anhand der traditionellen Art und Weise, wie die Lehre das
klassische Problem der „Vorfrage" im internationalen Privatrecht rekonstruiert,
verdeutlicht und kritisch analysiert werden. Das Problem stellt sich, wenn die Anwendung einer *ausländischen* Sachnorm im Forumstaat von der Entscheidung über
das Bestehen, das Nichtbestehen oder den Inhalt einer „vorausgesetzten" Rechtslage abhängt (zum Beispiel das Bestehen einer gültigen Ehe als Voraussetzung einer
von einem ausländischen Recht zu regelnden ehelichen Abstammung).[27]

---

[26] Siehe supra N. 2.; und schon Paolo Picone, *Ordinamento competente e diritto internazionale pri-*
vato (Padova, Cedam 1986) S. 57 N. 20.

[27] Siehe Melchior (oben N. 18) S. 245ff.; Wilhelm Wengler, „Die Vorfrage im Kollisionsrecht",
8 *RabelsZ* (1934) S. 148ff.; und danach statt vieler Volkert Hoffmeyer, *Das internationalprivatrechtli-*
che Vorfragenproblem (Bremerhaven 1957); Paul Lagarde, « La règle de conflit applicable aux questions préalables », 49 *Revue critique de droit international privé* (1960) S. 459ff.; Paolo Picone,
Saggio sulla struttura formale del problema delle questioni preliminari nel diritto internazionale pri-
vato (Napoli, Jovene 1971); Klaus Schurig, „Die Struktur des kollisionsrechtlichen Vorfragenpro-
blems", in: Hans Joachim Musielak/Klaus Schurig (Hrsg.), *Festschrift für G. Kegel zum 75. Geburtstag*
(Stuttgart, Kohlhammer 1987) S. 549ff.; Torben Svenné Schmidt, "The Incidental Question in Private

Bekanntermaßen gehen die von der Lehre vorgeschlagenen Lösungen dieses Problems (auf die Untersuchungen vor allem von Wengler zurückgehend) von einer allgemeinen potentiellen „Alternative" aus, nach der es möglich wäre, die Vorfrage nach dem vom inländischen Kollisionsrecht berufenen Recht oder Gesetz (selbständige Anknüpfung) oder nach dem vom Kollisionsrecht der *lex causae* für zuständig erklärten Recht oder Gesetz (unselbständige Anknüpfung) zu entscheiden.[28] Auch in diesem Fall wird die übliche Terminologie der Anwendung von Rechtsordnungen seitens der Kollisionsnormen häufig verwendet. Dennoch betonen praktisch alle Autoren die Bezugnahme auf potentiell konkurrierende „Rechte" und „Gesetze" im engeren Sinne, vor allem dann, wenn sie ausdrücklich darauf hinweisen, daß dieser Konflikt bei inhaltlich gleichlautenden oder materiell äquivalenten anwendbaren „Sachnormen" unterbleiben würde.[29]

Die Grenzen dieses traditionellen Lösungsansatzes werden in der Fallgestaltung deutlich, in der die vorausgesetzte Rechtslage ihre Quelle in dem rechtsgestaltenden Akt (Urteil, Verwaltungsakt usw.) eines staatlichen Organs findet. In diesem Fall hängt die internationalprivatrechtliche Beurteilung der Vorfrage nicht mehr von den Kollisionsnormen der zwei in Frage kommenden Rechtsordnungen (des Forums und der *lex causae*) ab, sondern von den verfahrensrechtlichen Bestimmungen, die in diesen Rechtsordnungen für das Wirksamwerden (Entstehung oder Anerkennung) von Entscheidungen und anderen Akten staatlicher Organe vorgesehen sind. Um ein Beispiel zu geben, sei hier der in der älteren Rechtsprechung zu findende klassische Fall angeführt, in dem die frühere Ehe eines Ausländers, die als Vorfrage zur Beurteilung einer neuen Ehe desselben im Inland in Betracht zu ziehen war, durch eine Entscheidung aufgelöst worden war, die nur in der inländischen Rechtsordnung und nicht in derjenigen der *lex causae* bestehen würde oder umgekehrt.[30]

Bezüglich dieser letztgenannten Fallkonstellationen sind die Meinungen in der Literatur gespalten. Einige Autoren sind der Ansicht, bei Fällen dieser Art handele es sich nicht mehr um das klassische Problem der Vorfrage, da solche Fälle keine

---

International Law", in: *Recueil des cours*, Bd. 233 (1992-II) S. 305ff.

[28] Vgl. Wengler (oben N. 27) S. 188ff.

[29] Siehe z.B. Melchior (oben N. 18) S. 247; Hoffmeyer (oben N. 27) S. 43ff., 46.

[30] Siehe für die frühere Rechtsprechung zu dieser Frage in einigen Ländern Paolo Picone, *La capacità matrimoniale dello straniero divorziato* (Napoli, Jovene 1970); Kristian Dorenberg, *Hinkende Rechtsverhältnisse im internationalen Familienrecht* (Berlin, Duncker & Humblot 1968) S. 137ff.; Hausmann (oben N. 6) vor allem S. 85ff.; und jetzt für eine Behandlung des Problems vom Gesichtspunkt der englischen Lehre Rhona Schutz, *A Modern Approach to the Incidental Question* (London/ The Hague/Boston, Kluwer 1997). Die Frage hat heutzutage einigermaßen an Bedeutung verloren, nachdem in vielen neuen kollisionsrechtlichen Systemen Vorschriften eingeführt worden sind, die den Vorrang einer inländischen Ehescheidung festsetzen: siehe § 17, Abs. 2 des österreichischen IPR-Gesetzes; Art. 13, Abs. 2 EGBGB; Art. 43, Abs. 3 des schweizerischen IPR-Gesetzes; und Art. 27 des italienischen Reformgesetzes vom 31. Mai 1995.

echten „Gesetzeskollisionen" darstellen würden.[31] Die überwiegende Mehrheit der
Lehre schließt jedoch auch diese Fälle in das genannte Problem ein und geht von
der üblichen kollisionsrechtlichen Alternative aus. Auch die Vorfrage der Ehescheidung wäre demzufolge für ihre Beurteilung der Alternative unterstellt, das
vom inländischen Kollisionsrecht berufene Recht oder das nach dem Kollisionsrecht der *lex causae* zuständige Recht anzuwenden.[32]

Nach der hier vertretenen Ansicht ist die Einbeziehung dieser letzten Konstellationen in den Anwendungsbereich des klassischen Problems der Vorfrage zutreffend: sie kann aber nur durch eine radikale Umstellung der gängigen theoretischen
Darstellung des Problems gerechtfertigt werden. Wie bereits ausführlich an anderer
Stelle aufgezeigt wurde,[33] ist das Problem der Vorfrage nicht auf eine Wahl zwischen zwei abstrakt konkurrierenden Kollisionsrechtssystemen (und den von ihnen
für zuständig gehaltenen „Rechten" oder „Gesetzen"), sondern auf einen Konflikt
zwischen den einschlägigen „Rechtsordnungen" in ihrer Gesamtheit zurückzuführen.[34] In der Tat besteht das Problem darin zu bestimmen, ob die von der auf die

---

[31] Siehe z.B. Walter Dehner, „Die Wiederheirat in Deutschland geschiedener Ausländer", 48 *Neue
Juristische Wochenschrift* (1963), S. 2201ff.; Gerhard Kegel/Alexander Lüderitz, „Hindernis des Ban-
des für Ausländer trotz Scheidung in Deutschland?", 11 *Zeitschrift für das gesamte Familienrecht*
(1964) S. 57ff., S. 59 ff.; Hoffmeyer (oben N. 27) S. 81, 92, 99; Pierre Mayer, *La distinction entre règles et décisions et le droit international privé* (Paris, Dalloz 1973) S. 146ff.

[32] Im Falle der Wiederheirat eines Ausländers nach einer *inländischen* „hinkenden" Scheidung ist
von dem früher überwiegenden Teil der deutschen Lehre ein Konflikt zwischen dem auf die Scheidung
anwendbaren „deutschen" Recht und dem auf die Ehefähigkeit des Ausländers anwendbaren „Heimatrecht" angenommen worden. Die unselbständige Lösung der Vorfrage wird häufig auf eine „Gesamtverweisung" auf das Heimatrecht des Ausländers zurückgeführt, wonach auch „die Frage der
Gültigkeit der früheren Ehe eines der Verlobten nach ausländischem Recht zu beurteilen" wäre (so die
berühmte Entscheidung Bundesgerichtshof, 12. Februar 1964, *IPRspr. 1964-1965*, Nr. 74, S. 238ff.,
S. 244). Manchmal wird aber auch die irreführende These vertreten, die Anwendung des „Heimatrechts" des Ausländers würde ein Hindernis der Gestaltungswirkung des inländischen Ehescheidungs-
urteils im Ausland setzen, da ein solches Urteil „nicht weiter als die Geltung der deutschen
Rechtsordnung" (!) reichen würde: vgl. z.B. Oberlandesgericht Celle, 26. Juni 1963, 10 *Zeitschrift für
das gesamte Familienrecht* (1963), S. 570ff., S. 571. Vgl. auch für den Stand der Debatte in der damaligen deutschen Lehre Karl H. Neumayer, „Ehescheidung und Wiedererlangung der Ehefähigkeit",
20 *RabelsZ* (1955) S. 66ff., S. 74ff.; Franz Gamillscheg, *Internationales Privatrecht, Band II*, in: *Staudingers Kommentar zum BGB*, 10/11 Aufl. (Berlin, Schweitzer Verlag 1973) S. 250ff.; und vor allem
Hausmann (oben N. 6) S. 85ff.
Es ist zu betonen, daß auch Wengler anfänglich von dem Bestand *in allen Fällen* einer Gesetzeskollisi-
on bei der Beurteilung einer Vorfrage ausgegangen ist, indem er den falschen Standpunkt vertreten hat,
daß eine solche Kollision sich auch auf das von einer Entscheidung angewendete Recht erstrecken würde und eventuell zu einer kollisionsrechtlichen Einschränkung der Rechtskraft dieser Entscheidung mit
Bezug auf das auf die Vorfrage anzuwendende Recht führen könnte: vgl. oben N. 27, S. 202ff.

[33] Siehe Picone (oben N. 27) vor allem S. 36ff.; Id., « La méthode de la référence à l'ordre juridique
compétent en droit international privé », in: *Recueil des cours*, Bd. 197 (1986-II) S. 229ff., S. 303ff.

[34] Siehe für diese Lösung Picone (oben N. 27) S. 41ff.; und zustimmend Hausmann (oben N. 6)
S. 63ff.; Davì, *L'adozione nel diritto internazionale privato, I, Conflitti di leggi* (Milano, Giuffré 1981)
S. 297, 315ff.; Bischoff, Anmerkung in 77 *Revue critique de droit international privé* (1988) S. 306ff.,

Hauptfrage anwendbaren ausländischen Sachnorm herrührenden Rechtsfolgen auch mit einer vorausgesetzten Rechtslage zu verknüpfen sind, die als *hinkende* Rechtslage nur in der inländischen Rechtsordnung und nicht in derjenigen der *lex causae* wirksam ist oder aber umgekehrt.[35] Das Problem der Vorfrage findet seinen Ausdruck folglich in der Alternative, entweder auf das wirksame Bestehen der vorausgesetzten Rechtslage in der (und *aus der Sicht der*) inländischen Rechtsordnung in ihrer Gesamtheit (will man von der Beurteilung im Inland der entsprechenden Rechtsfrage ausgehen) oder auf die bestehende Rechtslage in der (und *aus der Sicht der)* in Frage kommenden ausländischen Rechtsordnung abzustellen.[36]

Diese Lösung überzeugt besonders dann, wenn die vorausgesetzte Rechtslage durch eine drittstaatliche Ehescheidung erzeugt wird und beispielsweise wie in dem oben geschilderten Fall die Ehefähigkeit eines Ausländers betrifft. In diesem Fall kann die Beurteilung der Vorfrage offensichtlich nicht von einer abstrakten Konkurrenz im Forumstaat der inländischen und der ausländischen Vorschriften über die Anerkennung ausländischer Entscheide abhängen: Während erstere Vorschriften nur dazu dienen können, die Anerkennung oder Anerkennungsfähigkeit *im Forumstaat* der drittstaatlichen Entscheidung *konkret* zu beantworten, können die Anerkennungsvorschriften der Rechtsordnung der *lex causae* die gleiche Funktion nur in Bezug gerade auf *diese* Rechtsordnung erfüllen.

Der vorgeschlagenen Lösung ist aber auch dann zu folgen, wenn die Beurteilung der Vorfrage (z.B. Gültigkeit einer Ehe als Voraussetzung einer ehelichen Abstammung) von der Konkurrenz der zwei in Frage kommenden kollisionsrechtlichen Systeme (und der von ihnen berufenen unterschiedlichen Rechte oder Gesetze) zumindest *prima facie* abhängt. Will man in diesen Fällen von einer unselbständigen

---

S. 309ff.; Lagarde, « Observations sur l'articulation des questions de statut personnel et des questions alimentaires dans l'application des conventions de droit international privé », in: *Conflits et harmonisation. Mélanges en l'honneur d'Alfred E. von Overbeck* (Fribourg, Ed. Universitaires 1990), S. 511ff.; Siehr, „Renvoi und wohlerworbene Rechte", in: Isaak Meier/Kurt Siehr (Hrsg.), *Rechtskollisionen. Festschrift für Anton Heini zum 65. Geburtstag* (Zürich, Schulthess 1995) S. 407ff., S. 426. Siehe auch Verena Füllemann-Kuhn, *Die Vorfrage im internationalen Privatrecht* (Zürich, Schulthess 1977) S. 29.

[35] Siehe ausführlich vor allem Dorenberg (oben N. 30).

[36] Es ist interessant darauf hinzuweisen, daß selbst Wengler diese Perspektive in seinen letzten Schriften akzeptiert hat. Er hat in der Tat zunächst die anfänglich vertretene mißverständliche These aufgegeben, nach welcher das Problem der Vorfrage in der „Bildung des Inhalts präjudizieller Begriffe" bestehen würde (siehe Wilhelm Wengler, « Nouvelles réflexions sur les 'questions préalables' », 55 *Revue critique de droit international privé* (1966) S. 165ff.) und am Ende dieselbe ursprünglich irreführende Konstruktion der „kollisionsrechtlichen Rechtskraft" (oben N. 32) durch eine andere Konstruktion ersetzt, die auf der notwendigen Unterscheidung in unserem Sinne zwischen „Recht" und „Rechtsordnung" beruht. Siehe Wilhelm Wengler, *Internationales Privatrecht* (Berlin-New York, de Gruyter 1981) S. 387ff. („. . . Der Rechtssatz des ausländischen Staates will eben in einer in der Rechtsordnung *dieses* Staates bestehenden bzw. noch bestehenden Vorehe das Ehehindernis sehen"); und ausführlich Picone (oben N. 27) S. 93ff.; ders. (oben N. 26) S. 214ff.

Anknüpfung der Vorfrage ausgehen, so kann man nicht von einer direkten und traditionellen Anwendung im Forumstaat (zum Zweck einer abstrakten Beurteilung der Vorfrage) des vom Kollisionsrecht der *lex causae* berufenen Rechts anstelle des im Prinzip nach dem Kollisionsrecht des Forum zuständigem Recht sprechen, wie es im Falle eines Renvoi üblich ist, dem nicht zufällig und sehr häufig nach der herrschenden Lehre eine solche Lösung nahekommen würde.[37] Das ausländische Kollisionsrecht ist hingegen nur aus dem Grunde zu beachten, um das Bestehen und die Wirksamkeit der vorausgesetzten Rechtslage als konkrete Rechtslage in der *ausländischen Rechtsordnung* festzustellen.[38]

Die „Berufung" in dem Forumstaat der konkret im Ausland bestehenden „hinkenden" Rechtslage erfolgt deswegen niemals durch eine Anwendung derselben ausländischen internationalprivatrechtlichen Techniken, was im Falle von ausländischen Anerkennungsverfahren schon von vornherein auf derselben logischen Ebene unmöglich wäre. Sie ist im Gegenteil auf das Operieren von inländischen *ad hoc* geschaffenen *speziellen* Kollisionsnormen eigener Art zurückzuführen, die (wie sogleich gezeigt werden wird) auf die Rechtsordnung der *lex causae* in ihrer Gesamtheit verweisen. Diese Kollisionsnormen schaffen aufgrund ihrer Sondernatur Rechtsfolgen, die im Prinzip nur für die Beurteilung der Vorfrage der einschlägigen Hauptfrage „relevant" bleiben.[39]

---

[37] Die Perspektive einer „Anwendung" der ausländischen an Stelle der sonst im Prinzip zuständigen inländischen Kollisionsnorm wird ausdrücklich oder implizit von der überwiegenden Mehrheit der traditionellen Lehre angenommen: siehe ausführlich Lagarde (oben N. 27) S. 466ff.; und für eine umfassende Kritik Picone (op. cit. ibid.) S. 67ff.

[38] Siehe auch oben N. 36.

[39] Siehe ausführlich Picone (oben N. 27) S. 78ff.; und zustimmend Davì (oben N. 34) S. 313ff.; Bischoff (oben N. 34). Auch Schurig (oben N. 34) S. 564, spricht jetzt von der Bildung neuer Anknüpfungsnormen, die „mit der Verweisung für die Hauptfrage zu einer ,Blockverweisung' verbunden werden", ohne allerdings auf die Natur dieser Anknüpfungsnormen einzugehen.
Der bei der Beurteilung einer Vorfrage potentiell entstehende Konflikt besteht insofern nach dem Gesagten zwischen den allgemein operierenden kollisionsrechtlichen Techniken des Forums (vor allem Kollisionsnormen und Vorschriften über die Anerkennung ausländischer Entscheidungen) und den *ad hoc* geschaffenen *inländischen speziellen* Kollisionsnormen, die eine Verweisung auf die ausländische Rechtsordnung in ihrer Gesamtheit in dem oben beschriebenen Sinne durchführen. Auch nach Schutz (oben N. 30) S. 7ff., würde der Konflikt zwischen "two conflicts rules of the forum" bestehen: der von der Autorin angenommene "new approach" ist aber methodologisch irreführend, da als Prämisse die "recognition rules" ohne irgendeine Erklärung als "conflict rules" verstanden werden, und sogar von einem *Renvoi* im echten Sinne der *lex causae* auf die ausländischen "recognition rules" gesprochen wird (op. cit. ibid., S. 27!).

6. DIE BERÜCKSICHTIGUNG EINER AUSLÄNDISCHEN RECHTSORDNUNG
   IN IHRER GESAMTHEIT INNERHALB DER KOLLISIONSRECHTLICHEN
   METHODE DER VERWEISUNG AUF EINE ZUSTÄNDIGE
   RECHTSORDNUNG

Die notwendige Unterscheidung zwischen „Recht" und „Rechtsordnung" und die
Unmöglichkeit der Anwendung einer ausländischen Rechtsordnung im Forumstaat
hindern die inländische Rechtsordnung nach den obigen Ausführungen nicht, in einigen Fällen aus rein internationalprivatrechtlichen Gründen eine echte konkrete
Verweisung auf eine ausländische Rechtsordnung in ihrer Gesamtheit auszusprechen, um durch Berücksichtigung ihres kollisionsrechtlichen Standpunktes den tatsächlichen Bestand oder die potentielle Wirksamkeit gerade *in ihrem Wirkungsbe-
reich* von einigen schon existierenden oder zu schaffenden Rechtslagen zu
bestimmen. Eine solche Verweisung ist selbstverständlich nicht mit einer an sich
unmöglichen echten „Berufung" oder sogar „Anwendung" der ausländischen
Rechtsordnung im Forumstaat zu verwechseln. Im Forumstaat werden nachher aufgrund dieser Verweisung wie üblich nur ausländische Sachnormen angewendet
oder ausländische Rechtslagen berufen, wenn auch unter Befolgung (wie im Falle
der unselbständigen Anknüpfung einer Vorfrage) des gesamtkollisionsrechtlichen
Standpunktes der in Frage kommenden ausländischen Rechtsordnung.

Die letztgenannten Hypothesen gehen über den dargestellten Fall der Vorfrage
hinaus. Sie können an dieser Stelle nicht weiter vertieft und typisiert werden. Es
muß jedoch darauf hingewiesen werden, daß der zuletzt dargestellte methodologische Ansatz dem allgemeinen Operieren einer spezifischen kollisionsrechtlichen
Methode zugrundeliegt, die wir als „Methode der Verweisung auf die zuständige
(fremde) Rechtsordnung" bezeichnet haben. Diese Methode ist von der traditionellen Methode (d.h. von der klassischen Perspektive, auf Savigny zurückgehend, die
jeden Tatbestand durch Lokalisierung seines „Sitzes" dem richtigen anwendbaren
Recht zu unterstellen versucht) scharf zu unterscheiden. Auf die Schriften, die sich
an anderer Stelle ausführlich mit der Thematik befaßt haben, muß verwiesen werden.[40] Hier läßt sich zusammenfassend nur folgendes sagen:

Die aufgezeigte Methode ist auf der Ebene der Gesetzgebungstechnik vor allem
nützlich, um diejenigen Rechtslagen (oder „Unterklassen" von Rechtslagen) kollisionsrechtlich zu beurteilen, die die geringsten Beziehungen zum Recht des Forums
darstellen (z.B. Ehen oder Ehescheidungen zwischen Ausländern, Rechte über un-
bewegliche Sachen im Ausland usw.).[41] Sie dient praktisch dazu, die Entstehung
von „hinkenden" Rechtslagen und Rechtsverhältnissen im Forumstaat zu vermeiden, die nicht in der Lage wären, ihre Wirkungen in der oder den „meist betroffe-

---

[40] Siehe ausführlich Picone (oben N. 33); ders. (oben N. 26).
[41] Siehe Picone (oben N. 33) S. 321ff.

nen" ausländischen Rechtsordnungen zu entfalten. Im Prinzip ist die Methode daher nur komplementär neben oder zusammen mit der traditionellen international-privatrechtlichen Methode zu gebrauchen (ohne allerdings durch dieses Zusammenspiel ihre Autonomie als selbständige kollisionsrechtliche Methode zu verlieren).

Zur Koordinierung des Forumstaats mit einer oder mehrerer ausländischen Rechtsordnungen in ihrer Gesamtheit bedient sich diese Methode unterschiedlicher Modalitäten, je nachdem, ob sie für die Schaffung gewisser Rechtslagen im Inland oder für die Anerkennung ausländischer Rechtslagen angewendet wird.

Im ersten Fall sorgt die inländische Rechtsordnung dafür, daß die in ihrem Bereich durch Urteil oder sonstigen rechtsgestaltenden Akt eines öffentlichen Organs zu schaffenden Rechtslagen in der oder den ausländischen Rechtsordnungen anerkannt werden können, mit denen das Forum sich koordinieren will.[42] Um dieses Ziel zu erreichen, müssen Kollisionsnormen einer spezifischen Art geschaffen werden, die als „Verweisungsvorschriften auf die zuständige Rechtsordnung" ("norme di rinvio all´ordinamento competente") bezeichnet werden können. Diese spezifischen Verweisungsnormen besitzen bisweilen von vornherein einen einheitlichen Inhalt, wie es beispielsweise bei Art. 77, Abs. 2 (Adoption) des geltenden schweizerischen IPR-Gesetzes der Fall ist.[43] In den meisten Fällen sind sie aber aus der Zusammensetzung unterschiedlicher Vorschriften in einer einzigen Verweisungsregel herzuleiten, und zwar normalerweise aus der Zusammensetzung einer Vorschrift, die eine *bedingte* internationale Zuständigkeit der nationalen Richter vorsieht und der Vorschrift über das anwendbare Recht.[44]

In beiden Fällen ist aber klar, daß die Forderung nach der Anerkennungsfähigkeit im Ausland der im Forumstaat durch Urteil oder anderen rechtsgestaltenden Akt eines öffentlichen Organs zu schaffenden Rechtslage eine Berücksichtigung aller Kriterien voraussetzt, die die in Frage kommenden ausländischen Rechtsordnungen für die Anerkennung dieser Rechtslage (und also für die Anerkennung ausländischer Entscheidungen und anderer Akte staatlicher Organe) festsetzen. Die Verweisungsvorschriften des Forumstaates müssen konsequenterweise eine ganzheitliche Betrachtung des internationalprivatrechtlichen Systems des oder der einschlägigen „zuständigen" ausländischen Staaten durchführen, wobei nicht nur auf

---

[42] Siehe noch Picone, ibid., S. 274ff.

[43] Diese Vorschrift macht die Entstehung einer Adoption in der Schweiz von ihrer Anerkennung im Wohnsitz- oder im Heimatstaat der adoptierenden Person oder adoptierenden Ehegatten abhängig, wenn dem Kind anderswo „ein schwerwiegender Nachteil erwachsen würde".

[44] Das war der Fall im früher geltenden IPR-System der Bundesrepublik Deutschland bei dem notwendigen Operieren von § 606 b Nr. 1 ZPO (von dem unten die Rede sein wird) in Verbindung mit den einschlägigen deutschen Kollisionsnormen: siehe Picone (oben N. 33) S. 266ff. Vgl. jetzt im schweizerischen IPR-Gesetz Art. 43, Abs. 2 (Eheschließung ausländischer Brautleute ohne Wohnsitz in der Schweiz). Die Auslegungsprobleme dieser spezifischen Kollisionsnormen sind ausführlich in: *Ordinamento competente* (oben N. 26) S. 165ff. untersucht worden.

die Kollisionsnormen, sondern auf das Zusammenwirken aller internationalprivat-rechtlichen Techniken dieser Staaten Rücksicht genommen werden muß. Sie bezie-hen sich demnach in dem geschilderten Sinne auf einige ausländische Rechtsordnungen in ihrer Gesamtheit, als einheitliche und integrierte Rechtssyste-me, die gleichzeitig sowohl die ursprünglich eigenen als auch die vom Ausland be-rufenen und geltend zu machenden Gesetze und Entscheidungen durch ihre Feststellungs- und Durchsetzungsmechanismen garantieren.[45]

Anders drückt sich das Tätigwerden der Methode aus, wenn sie auf die Anerken-nung ausländischer Rechtslagen angewendet wird. Die Verweisung auf eine oder mehrere ausländische Rechtsordnungen in ihrer Gesamtheit dient in diesem Fall dazu, alle diejenigen Rechtslagen der in Frage kommenden Kategorie im Forum-staat anzuerkennen (im Ausland geschlossene Ehen oder ausgesprochene Ehe-scheidungen zwischen zwei Ausländern, usw.), die gerade in diesen Rechtsordnungen konkret bestehen und wirksam sind – ohne Rücksicht darauf, ob es sich um als dort „entstandene" oder nur aus dritten Staaten „anerkannte" Rechts-lagen handelt. Diese vollständige Koordinierung des Forums mit den einschlägigen ausländischen Rechtsordnungen führt in diesen Fällen dazu, daß die inländische Rechtsordnung davon absieht, die anzuerkennenden ausländischen Rechtslagen auf Grund der in der traditionellen Methode üblichen Kriterien (u.a. Anwendung des „richtigen" Rechts, Bestehen der indirekten internationalen Zuständigkeit des ausländischen Richters, usw.) aus eigener Sicht zu kontrollieren.[46]

Die Methode der Verweisung auf eine (fremde) zuständige Rechtsordnung hat heutzutage als autonome und spezifische kollisionsrechtliche Methode eine sichere Stellung in der Lehre vieler Länder erreicht.[47] Der geringe Widerhall gerade in der deutschsprachigen Literatur kann überraschend erscheinen, wenn man bedenkt, daß nicht wenige Beispiele ihres Operierens sowohl in der früheren als auch in den heute geltenden Kollisionsrechtssystemen der Bundesrepublik Deutschland und

---

[45] Siehe ausführlich Picone (oben N. 33) S. 278ff.

[46] Siehe noch Picone, ibid., S. 287ff.

[47] Siehe z.B. in der nicht-italienischen Lehre Paul Lagarde (oben N. 20) S. 163ff., S. 179ff.; Anto-nio Boggiano, *Derecho internacional privado*, Bd. III (Buenos Aires, Depalma 1988) vor allem S. VII-Iff., 117 ff.; Rui Moura Ramos, *Da lei aplicável ao contrato de trabalho internacional* (Coimbra, Almedina 1990) S. 195ff.; Georges Droz, « Regards sur le droit international privé comparé. Cours général de droit international privé », *Recueil des cours*, Bd. 229 (1991-IV) S. 9ff., S. 367ff.; und für ei-nige praktische Anwendungen Alejandro Radzyminski, „Das argentinische internationale Insolvenz-recht", 89 *Zeitschrift für vergleichende Rechtswissenschaft* (1990) S. 466ff., S. 484ff.; Angeles Lara Aguado, *El nombre en derecho internacional privado* (Granada, Comares 1998) *passim*; Etienne Pa-taut, *Principe de souveraineté et conflits de juridictions (étude de droit international privé)* (Paris, L. G. D. J. 1998) vor allem S. 122ff., 281ff.

der Schweiz zu finden sind.[48] Ein sogar klassischer Anwendungsfall dieser Methode beruhte früher auf dem Bestehen von § 606 b Nr. 1 ZPO a.f. (heute in einschränkender Perspektive durch den geltenden § 606 a Abs. I Satz 1 Ziff. 4 ZPO n.F. ersetzt), welcher die internationale Zuständigkeit der deutschen Gerichte in Bezug auf „Ehesachen" zwischen zwei Ausländern regelte und eine zentrale Bedeutung der Anerkennung der deutschen Entscheidung „nach dem Recht des Ehemannes" (aber richtigerweise in der entsprechenden „Rechtsordnung"!) beimaß.[49] Es fragt sich daher, ob die fehlende Unterscheidung zwischen den Begriffen „Recht" und „Rechtsordnung" nicht auch in diesem Fall eine Rolle gespielt haben dürfte. Diese übliche Sichtweise könnte wohl zu dem Mißverständnis der Tatsache geführt haben, daß die deutsche Rechtsordnung durch die genannte Vorschrift nicht ein zusätzliches und isoliertes Kriterium für eine legitime Anwendung des ausländischen „Rechts" aufstellen wollte, sondern die spezifische Perspektive der Verweisung auf eine „ausländische Rechtsordnung" in ihrer Gesamtheit verfolgte.[50]

Erst kürzlich hat der hier gefeierte Kollege SIEHR in einer umfassenden Studie viele vom neuen schweizerischen IPR-Gesetz vorgesehene Fälle der Anerkennung ausländischer Entscheidungen auf die Methode der Verweisung auf die zuständige Rechtsordnung zurückgeführt.[51] Zu diesen zählen, wie wir von Anfang an vertreten haben, alle Vorschriften, die zum Zweck der Anerkennung darauf Rücksicht nehmen, daß die einschlägigen Entscheidungen in einigen bestimmten ausländischen Rechtsordnungen ausgesprochen oder (als drittstaatliche Entscheidungen) anerkannt worden sind.[52]

Die Fälle, in denen der Forumstaat den kollisionsrechtlichen Standpunkt einer ausländischen Rechtsordnung in dem oben geschilderten Sinne berücksichtigt oder

---

[48] Siehe für die früher geltenden Systeme Picone (oben N. 33) S. 274ff., 287ff. Im geltenden schweizerischen IPR-Gesetz kann man sich wieder auf die schon zitierten Art. 77, Abs. 2 und Art. 43, Abs. 2 sowie auf die Vorschriften über die Anerkennung ausländischer Entscheidungen, von denen unten die Rede sein wird, beziehen.

[49] Siehe schon oben, N. 44. Diese Vorschrift ist von der anderen im Text genannten Vorschrift ersetzt worden, die in gleicher Weise die Basis für die Bildung in den entsprechenden Fällen einer auf ausländische zuständige Rechtsordnungen verweisenden Kollisionsnorm darstellt: siehe Paolo Picone, "La teoria generale del diritto internazionale privato nella legge italiana di riforma della materia", 79 *Rivista di diritto internazionale* (1996) S. 289ff., S. 299, und in: *La riforma italiana* (oben N. 24), S. 137ff., S. 146ff.

[50] Der spezifische kollisionsrechtliche Gehalt der genannten Vorschrift ist in Deutschland von Johannes Dessauer, *Internationales Privatrecht, Ethik und Politik: Betrachtungen zur Reform des internationalen Privatrechts am Beispiel der Anerkennungsprognose als Zuständigkeitsvoraussetzung im internationalen Eherecht* (Frankfurt am Main, Peter Lang 1986) untersucht worden, ohne allerdings unsere früheren Schriften ausdrücklich zu berücksichtigen (siehe unsere Besprechung in 70 *Rivista di diritto internazionale* (1987) S. 1039ff.).

[51] Vgl. Siehr (oben N. 34) S. 413ff.

[52] Siehe schon mit Bezug auf den Entwurf des schweizerischen IPR-Gesetzes Picone (oben N. 33) S. 296ff.; und jetzt ausführlicher ders., "Sentenze straniere e norme italiane di conflitto", 80 *Rivista di diritto internazionale* (1997) S. 913ff., S. 924ff., und in: *La riforma* (oben N. 24) S. 477ff., S. 487ff.

von vornherein eine Verweisung auf ausländische Rechtsordnungen in ihrer Gesamtheit durchführt, scheinen so allmählich einem besseren Verständnis zugänglich zu werden. Die Voraussetzung dafür ist allerdings, daß sowohl die fehlende Unterscheidung zwischen den Begriffen „Recht" und „Rechtsordnung", als auch die damit verbundenen Mißverständnisse endgültig überwunden werden.

7.   DARSTELLUNG DER WICHTIGSTEN ERGEBNISSE

Die wichtigsten Ergebnisse der vorherigen Ausführungen sind wie folgt zusammenzufassen:

– Der Ausdruck „Anwendung" einer ausländischen „Rechtsordnung" im Forumstaat ist unrichtig und deshalb abzulehnen, da jede Rechtsordnung ein integriertes System von Rechtserzeugungs- und Rechtssetzungsmechanismen darstellt, das selbstverständlich als solches nicht in einer anderen Rechtsordnung „angewendet" werden kann;

– Bei jeder Anwendung im Forumstaat eines ausländischen Rechts oder Gesetzes, und der einschlägigen fremden Sachnormen, ist es stets die *inländische* Rechtsordnung, die sozusagen tätig wird und sich durchsetzt;

– Die Anwendung einer ausländischen Rechtsordnung im weiteren Sinne kann nicht darauf zurückgeführt werden, daß man davon ausgeht, daß die Kollisionsnormen des Forums eine Berufung des ausländischen Rechts in seiner formellen Natur als „fremdes" Recht verwirklichen;

– Der Ausdruck „Gesamtverweisung" bei der Annahme eines Renvoi ist mißverständlich, da er ein Produkt früherer überholter Theorien ist, wonach der Renvoi sich in der Berufung einer ausländischen Rechtsordung in ihrer Gesamtheit, wenn nicht sogar in einer Art „Ersetzung" der ausländischen Richter seitens der inländischen Richter äußern würde;

– Die genannten Fälle einer irrtümlicherweise angenommenen „Anwendung" einer ausländischen Rechtsordnung sind von den Fällen klar zu unterscheiden, in denen der Forumstaat den kollisionsrechtlichen Standpunkt einer ausländischen Rechtsordnung in ihrer Gesamtheit „berücksichtigt", um für die Entstehung oder die Anerkennung gewisser Rechtslagen auf die konkrete oder nur potentielle *Wirksamkeit derselben gerade in dieser ausländischen Rechtsordnung* Rücksicht zu nehmen;

– Ein Fall der letztgenannten Art entsteht bei dem klassischen Problem der Vorfrage, das nicht in der Konkurrenz zweier unterschiedlicher Kollisionsnormen (des Forums und der *lex causae*) besteht, sondern in der alternativen Beurteilung einer vorausgesetzten „hinkenden" Rechtslage vom Gesichtspunkt der inländischen oder der ausländischen Rechtsordnung; eine unselbständige Beurteilung der Vorfrage ist konsequenterweise dem Tätigwerden von *ad hoc* im Forumstaat geschaffenen speziellen Kollisionsnormen zu verdanken, die auf die ausländische Rechtsordnung der *lex causae* in ihrer Gesamtheit verweisen, um derjenigen in dieser Rechtsordnung bestehenden hinkenden Rechtslage auch im Inland Wirkung zu verleihen;

–   Eine allgemeine Berücksichtigung des kollisionsrechtlichen Standpunktes einer ausländischen Rechtsordnung in ihrer Gesamtheit wird von jener selbständigen Koordinierungsmethode zwischen Rechtsordnungen unternommen, die als „Methode der Verweisung auf eine fremde zuständige Rechtsordnung" bekannt ist; diese Methode beruht bei den unterschiedlichen Fallkonstellationen der Entstehung und der Anerkennung im Forum der einschlägigen Rechtslagen auf einigen *spezifischen* kollisionsrechtlichen Techniken (Kollisionsnormen eigener Art und besonderen Verfahren der Anerkennung ausländischer Entscheidungen), die oben zumindest in einigen ihrer wesentlichen Aspekte dargestellt worden sind.

SUMMARY
THE "APPLICATION" OF A FOREIGN "LEGAL ORDER" IN THE FORUM
STATE: . . . PERSEVERARE EST DIABOLICUM!

The author criticizes the terminology followed by the legal literature and case law in several European countries (but also explicitly utilized in Article 1, para. 2 of the Austrian law on Private International Law of 15 June 1978 and Article 3, para. 1 of the corresponding German law of 25 July 1986) according to which the choice of law rules enable the forum to apply foreign "legal orders" rather than merely foreign "laws" or "rules". This terminology is incorrect, as every legal order constitutes an integrated normative system based upon sources of law and enforcement mechanisms, which "nationalizes" and makes enforceable the applicable foreign rules and the foreign judgments concretely recognized at the same level as its "internal" law. Accordingly, it is impossible, from a logical point of view, to speak in a formal sense of the "application" within the forum of a foreign legal order "as a whole".

     The indicated terminology cannot be upheld on an empirical basis either, for example as a consequence of the conceptual position whereby the foreign law would be applied in the forum as "foreign law" (the theory of *rinvio formale*), or more generally in those cases where the conflict rules are supposed to lead to a *Gesamtverweisung* to foreign legal orders, applying the *renvoi* mechanism, especially in the form of the "foreign court theory".

The necessary distinction between foreign "law" and foreign "legal order" helps to clarify the cases in which the forum refers to one or more foreign legal orders considered "as a whole", in order to regulate some legal situations with regard to their (possible or actual) existence and validity from the point of view of those foreign legal orders. This approach is followed when the forum decides to create a legal situation aimed at producing its effects primarily in some foreign legal order, or when the recognition of some (categories of) foreign legal situations depends only on their validity and effectiveness within the foreign legal order or orders referred to (as they have been established or recognized in those legal orders). Some applications of this particular conflictual perspective may be found whenever the forum solves the incidental question raised by the foreign legal rule applicable to the main question according to the conflict rules of the *lex causae*; and, more generally, with regard to the operation of that peculiar method for coordinating legal systems known as the "method of reference to a foreign legal order".

Quelques observations sur la continuité des contrats face à l'introduction de l'euro

Fausto Pocar[*]

1. LES DISPOSITIONS SUR LA CONTINUITÉ DES CONTRATS DANS LE RÈGLEMENT COMMUNAUTAIRE N° 1103/97

La normative communautaire sur l'introduction de l'euro, telle qu'elle résulte notamment du règlement n° 1103/97 du 17 juin 1997, adopté en vertu de l'article 235 du traité instituant la Communauté européenne,[1] s'inspire des principes de la substitution automatique de l'euro aux monnaies nationales, de la continuité des contrats (et en général des instruments juridiques) et du respect de la volonté des parties contractantes. Il s'agit de principes qui présentent un haut degré d'interaction : ce n'est pas par hasard qu'on les retrouve réunis dans la même disposition du règlement, à savoir l'article 3, aux termes duquel « l'introduction de l'euro n'a pas pour effet de modifier les termes d'un instrument juridique ou de libérer ou de dispenser de son exécution, et elle ne donne pas à une partie le droit de modifier un tel instrument ou

---

[*] Professeur de droit international à la Faculté de droit de l'Université de Milan.
[1] Règlement (CE) 1103/97 du Conseil fixant certaines dispositions relatives à l'introduction de l'euro, *JO(CE)* [1997] L 162/1 (19 juin 1997).

J. Basedow et al., eds., Private Law in the International Arena – Liber Amicorum Kurt Siehr
© *2000, T.M.C.Asser Press, The Hague, The Netherlands*

d'y mettre fin unilatéralement. La présente disposition s'applique sans préjudice de ce dont les parties sont convenues ».

L'énonciation du principe de continuité dans un règlement à une date largement antérieure à celle de l'adoption de la monnaie unique répond à la préoccupation évidente de rassurer les marchés et les opérateurs moyennant une loi qui indique avec précision l'influence de l'introduction de la nouvelle monnaie sur les instruments juridiques intervenus avant le 1er janvier 1999 mais destinés à produire des effets aussi après une telle date.[2]

Il y a lieu toutefois de remarquer que, si la disposition mentionnée peut sembler claire à première vue, on lui a donné des interprétations différentes. Celles-ci se situent, avec des nuances, entre l'extrême de lui attribuer une valeur pleinement dispositive ou même impérative d'application nécessaire, et celui de ne lui reconnaître qu'une nature déclarative d'un principe existant, qui rendrait sa présence dans le règlement presque superflue.

Dans cette deuxième perspective, on a rappelé notamment le septième considérant du préambule du règlement, d'après lequel c'est un « principe général de droit » que la continuité des contrats n'est pas affectée par l'introduction d'une nouvelle monnaie et qu'il convient d'en confirmer explicitement l'applicabilité à l'introduction de l'euro « en vue de renforcer la sécurité et la clarté du droit ». On en a déduit que l'article 3 du règlement aurait une nature déclarative et n'affecterait pas les dispositions sur les contrats du droit interne des États membres, qui demeureraient pleinement applicables quant aux remèdes éventuellement à la disposition des parties, alors même que ces remèdes dépendent de la conversion de la monnaie contractuelle dans la nouvelle monnaie, pourvu que celle-ci implique un changement des conditions du contrat qui corresponde aux circonstances prévues par le droit interne pour justifier de telles remèdes. En d'autres termes, la disposition sur la continuité ne prendrait en compte la substitution monétaire qu'en tant que telle, mais elle ne viserait pas les conséquences qui pourraient découler directement ou indirectement d'un tel remplacement : l'appréciation de ces conséquences continuerait à dépendre du droit applicable à l'instrument juridique concerné, auquel le règlement n'apporterait aucune modification.

On a encore souligné qu'il serait inconcevable que le règlement puisse modifier le droit interne des États membres sur l'adaptation des contrats, car un effet modifi-

---

[2] Cette préoccupation est expressément mentionnée dans le préambule du règlement, où l'on observe que « les dispositions relatives à la continuité ne peuvent atteindre leur objectif, qui est de fournir la sécurité juridique et la transparence pour les agents économiques, en particulier les consommateurs, qu'à condition d'entrer en vigueur le plus rapidement possible » (septième considérant). Voir à ce propos Wölker, « The Continuity of Contracts in the Transition to the third Stage of Economic and Monetary Union », 33 *Common Market Law Review* (1996) p. 1117 et suiv. La nécessité de règles précises en la matière avait été aussi soulignée par le Comité économique et social : Voir doc. ECO/204 du 8 mai 1995.

catif de cette portée serait contraire aux principes généraux communs aux États membres, que l'ordre juridique communautaire serait nécessairement tenu de respecter.[3]

Bien qu'intéressante, l'interprétation qu'on vient de mentionner ne peut pas être suivie. D'abord, elle s'appuie essentiellement sur un considérant du préambule du règlement, qui par sa nature n'a pas de valeur dispositive. En outre elle ne met en valeur que la partie du considérant qui souligne le principe que la continuité des contrats n'est pas affectée par l'introduction d'une nouvelle monnaie et exprime l'intention de confirmer ce principe à l'égard des relations entre monnaies nationales et euro. Mais elle oublie que le même considérant contient d'autres déclarations susceptibles d'être interprétées en tant qu'indiquant l'intention de modifier le droit interne, telle la déclaration que, pour les instruments à taux d'intérêts fixes, l'introduction de l'euro ne modifie pas le taux d'intérêt nominal à payer par le débiteur. De toute façon, l'intention exprimée par le législateur communautaire de confirmer un principe existant n'exclut pas automatiquement que la règle qui le reflète ait également un contenu dispositif autonome visant à en préciser la portée et les modalités d'application aux situations visées par la règle même.

Il faut encore souligner que l'opinion qui attribue à l'article 3 du règlement une fonction purement déclarative ne tient pas compte de sa teneur littérale. L'article 3 n'est pas rédigé dans les termes génériques de la confirmation d'un principe ; il est au contraire précis et détaillé lorsqu'il déclare que l'introduction de l'euro ne comporte aucune modification des termes d'un instrument juridique et ne dispense pas de son exécution, ni donne à une partie le droit de le modifier ou d'y mettre fin unilatéralement. À l'encontre de l'opinion qui réduit la portée de la règle a la substitution des monnaies nationales par la nouvelle monnaie unique on peut d'ailleurs remarquer que l'article 3 ne fait pas dépendre les effets susmentionnés de cette substitution en tant que telle, mais plutôt de « l'introduction de l'euro » : cette expression a une portée bien plus large, susceptible d'étendre la portée du principe en le rendant applicable aussi à des circonstances différentes de la simple substitution monétaire, tout en s'y rattachant directement.

En d'autres termes, la disposition communautaire a la fonction d'exclure que toutes les circonstances se rattachant directement à l'introduction de l'euro, y compris celles produites par des règles internes de mise en œuvre des règles communautaires, puissent être utilisées pour invoquer le droit national sur l'adaptation des contrats et des instruments juridiques en général. Une conclusion différente doit être tirée des circonstances ne se rattachant qu'indirectement à la création de la nou-

---

[3] Cf. en ce sens spécialement Draetta, « L'euro e la continuità dei contratti in corso », *Diritto del commercio internazionale* (1997) p. 7 et suiv. ; Sacerdoti, « Aspetti giuridici dell'introduzione dell'euro », *Diritto comunitario e degli scambi internazionali* (1997) p. 349 ; Visco et Simonetti, « L'euro e il problema della continuità dei contratti », *Diritto del commercio internazionale* (1998) p. 113 et suiv.

velle monnaie ; il est certes possible d'interpréter l'expression « introduction de
l'euro » au sens large, mais il ne semble pas logique d'y inclure aussi les circonstances qui, tout en s'étant produites à l'occasion ou en vue de l'introduction de l'euro,
auraient pu se produire indépendamment de cette dernière.

Par exemple, le fait que le taux d'intérêt sur l'euro puisse être moins élevé que le
taux sur la monnaie contractuelle nationale doit être considéré comme une conséquence directe de l'introduction de l'euro et tombe ainsi dans les prévisions de l'article 3. Au contraire la circonstance qu'en vue de l'adoption de la monnaie unique le
taux d'intérêt sur la monnaie nationale ait subi une réduction sensible dans l'État
membre concerné constitue un événement qui ne se rattache qu'indirectement à
l'introduction de la nouvelle monnaie. Il aurait bien pu se produire, en effet, dans le
cadre d'un accord de stabilité entre les États membres, aux fins d'une meilleure coordination de leurs politiques économique et monétaire, même dans le cas ou ledit
accord ne prévoyait pas l'unification monétaire.

Enfin, il est contestable qu'une obligation des institutions communautaires de
respecter intégralement les principes généraux de droit communs aux États membres puisse être invoquée en faveur d'une fonction purement déclarative de l'article
3. Dans le traité instituant la Communauté, on ne retrouve aucune trace d'une obligation de ce genre, qui impliquerait une faute de compétence des institutions communautaires pour adopter des règles susceptibles de modifier le droit interne si ces
principes sont affectés. A ce propos, il ne faut pas confondre l'affirmation incon-
testée que les principes communs du droit interne peuvent être utilisés pour définir
le contenu de règles communautaire, ou même qu'on doit présumer la conformité
de ces dernières à de tels principes, avec une prétendue incompétence des institutions à émaner des règles affectant les mêmes principes. Une pareille déduction
semble d'autant plus injustifiée lorsqu'il s'agit de règles qui précisent la portée des
principes, ou y dérogent dans des situations spéciales, ainsi qu'il arrive fréquem-
ment aussi au niveau de la législation interne des États membres qui seraient les ga-
rants des principes considérés.

Il ne faut pas oublier non plus, dans ce même contexte, les pouvoirs normatifs at-
tribués aux institutions par l'article 308 CE [ex article 235 TCE] du traité instituant
la Communauté européenne, selon lequel elles peuvent prendre toute disposition
utile à la mise en œuvre d'une action nécessaire pour atteindre, dans le fonctionnement du marché commun, un de buts de la Communauté. Cet article du traité – qui
prévoit des pouvoirs ordinaires et non pas exceptionnels, ainsi qu'on l'a parfois affirmé – représente d'ailleurs la base juridique d'une grande partie de la législation
communautaire, y compris en particulier le règlement n° 1103/97.

La conclusion que la législation communautaire sur la continuité des instruments juridiques peut modifier le droit national sur l'adaptation des contrats, et que
l'article 3 du règlement concerné a précisément ce but, implique toutefois des
conséquences dont la portée à été souvent exagérée, probablement parce qu'on a
souligné leur influence sur les principes plutôt que leur effet concret. Ainsi qu'on

vient de le mentionner, en effet, la portée modificatrice du droit interne se limite aux circonstances qui se rattachent directement à l'introduction de l'euro, tandis qu'elle ne touche pas celles qui ne s'y rattachent qu'indirectement, et en particulier ne touche pas les mesures internes qui ont déterminé la vie de la monnaie nationale avant son remplacement par l'euro. Il est naturellement plus difficile de définir le rôle des circonstances postérieures à l'introduction de la nouvelle monnaie, vu la difficulté d'apprécier quand elles sont la conséquence directe de l'adoption de l'euro ou au contraire la conséquence de conditions du marché indépendant du changement des monnaies des États membres de l'Union européenne. C'est une appréciation qu'on ne pourra faire que cas par cas, à la lumière de la situation qui s'est produite concrètement à un moment déterminé.

2.   LE PRINCIPE D'AUTONOMIE DES PARTIES ET SA PORTÉE EN MATIÈRE DE CONTINUITÉ DES CONTRATS

L'application de la disposition communautaire sur la continuité des contrats rencontre une limitation dans l'autonomie des parties contractantes et doit être harmonisée avec celle-ci. En vertu de l'article 3 du règlement, cette disposition « s'applique sans préjudice de ce dont les parties sont convenues ».

L'importance ainsi accordée au principe d'autonomie comme fondement du contenu du contrat suffit à exclure que la disposition sur la continuité des contrats soit une règle impérative, à laquelle les parties ne peuvent pas déroger, et à plus fort raison qu'elle puisse être considérée une règle d'application immédiate, applicable indépendamment de la loi qui régit le contrat.[4] En vertu de son applicabilité directe dans l'ordre juridique interne, cette disposition ne déroge au droit national sur l'adaptation des contrats que dans la mesure où les parties ne l'ont pas regardée comme applicable ou n'ont pas prévu des procédures spécifiques d'adaptation du contrat.

Le problème qui se pose à cet égard consiste plutôt à définir les conditions de forme et de substance auxquelles doit répondre l'accord des parties pour exclure l'application du principe de continuité affirmé par le règlement. Pour ce qui est de la forme, l'absence de toute indication dans la rédaction générique de l'article 3 semble impliquer que l'accord des parties puisse être exprès ou même tacite, s'il résulte avec certitude raisonnable des clauses du contrat ou des circonstances de celui-ci.

La question de savoir si les parties doivent se référer spécifiquement à l'euro ou s'il suffit qu'elles rappellent en général les événements susceptibles de changer

---

[4] Ainsi qu'il est bien connu, la notion de « règles d'application immédiate » est codifiée au niveau communautaire dans l'article 7 de la Convention de Rome du 19 juin 1980 sur la loi applicable aux obligations contractuelles.

l'équilibre du contrat est au contraire plus douteuse. La lettre de l'article 3 permet sans doute de donner un rôle également aux clauses contractuelles ayant un contenu générique et rappelant l'onérosité survenue ou le changement de circonstances du contrat. En revanche, un sens plus restrictif semble découler du préambule qui affirme que « le principe de continuité doit être compatible avec toute convention entre les parties *en ce qui concerne l'introduction de l'euro* ».[5] La valeur de cette dernière précision est toutefois problématique, non seulement parce qu'elle se trouve dans le préambule qui n'a pas de contenu dispositif mais surtout parce que sa présence dans le préambule est le résultat d'un compromis à la suite de l'opposition à son inclusion dans la partie dispositive du règlement.

Par ailleurs, l'interprétation restrictive suggérée par une lecture de l'article 3 à la lumière du préambule ne résout pas tous les doutes, si l'on considère la variété des clauses contractuelles employées dans la pratique. Une solution consisterait à les considérer comme une manifestation de volonté contraire à l'immutabilité du contrat non seulement lorsqu'elles mentionnent expressément l'introduction de l'euro, mais également lorsqu'elles prennent en compte les changements de la monnaie contractuelle en général. Une conclusion opposée s'imposerait en présence d'un simple rappel de l'onérosité survenue ou de la stabilité des conditions contractuelles, ou encore, et à plus forte raison, lorsque ce rappel est fait par une expression générique ou une clause de style. Mais il serait imprudent de formuler des critères d'appréciation de portée générale dans une matière dans laquelle l'autonomie des parties s'exprime de la manière la plus variée et leur intention ne peut être établie qu'à l'égard de chaque cas d'espèce.

L'interprétation des clauses contractuelles en la matière se présente comme spécialement complexe lorsque ces clauses ont été insérées dans des contrats conclus à une date précédant largement l'introduction de l'euro. Il faut noter par ailleurs que le libellé de l'article 3 ne permet pas de limiter son domaine aux contrats postérieurs à l'adoption de la nouvelle monnaie ou intervenus après l'entrée en vigueur du règlement.[6] Tout au contraire, c'est précisément pour les contrats conclus avant que l'introduction de l'euro puisse être considérée imminente ou probable que l'on pourra plus facilement attribuer un rôle à des clauses moins spécifiques : il semble logique en effet que dans les contrats plus récents, les parties, si elles veulent déroger au principe de continuité prévu par le règlement, le fassent d'une manière explicite et ponctuelle.

---

[5] Italique ajouté par l'auteur.

[6] Voir De Nova, « Il principio di continuità dei contratti dopo l'introduzione dell'euro », *I contratti* (1998) p. 7, et Alpa, « Introduzione dell'Euro e disciplina del contratto. Note minime », *Contratto e impresa. Europa* (1998) p. 657, lequel affirme que la disposition de l'article 3 sur la continuité implique aussi l'inefficacité des clauses contractuelles sur l'adaptation du contrat stipulées avant l'entrée en vigueur du règlement.

La possibilité susmentionnée d'un accord tacite découlant avec certitude du contrat permet d'autre part de résoudre aussi le problème soulevé par les contrats portant sur les risques de change et les variations de taux, qui perdraient leur objet ou leur cause avec l'unification de la monnaie.[7] On pourrait dans ce cas déduire de la teneur du contrat l'intention des parties de le conserver seulement en présence de conditions permettant une marge de fluctuation de la monnaie, devenue impossible à cause de sa substitution par une autre à un taux fixe de conversion.

Il y a lieu enfin de remarquer que le rôle attribuée à l'autonomie des parties dans la détermination de l'influence de l'introduction de l'euro sur la vie du contrat répond aussi à l'exigence d'atténuer les effets d'une règle trop rigoureuse sur l'immutabilité des conditions contractuelles. De ce point de vue l'article 3 du règlement peut s'entendre comme une invitation aux parties à réglementer directement et au préalable les conséquences du passage à la nouvelle monnaie par le moyen de clauses spécifiques. Il faut rappeler à cet égard que des clauses relatives à l'euro ont été suggérées par plusieurs associations professionnelles surtout pour ce qui a trait aux contrats qu'on qualifie normalement de « dérivés » car leur valeur découle d'éléments de référence représentés par le prix d'une activité financière.[8]

Lorsque des clauses relatives à l'euro n'ont pas été inclues dans un contrat, la disposition de l'article 3 sur l'autonomie contractuelle peut aussi jouer le rôle d'une recommandation aux parties de se servir de l'instrument conventionnel, même après l'introduction de la nouvelle monnaie, pour résoudre les difficultés découlant des variations intervenues dans les conditions contractuelles, et de renégocier les termes du contrat de manière plus conforme à leurs intérêts.

3.   PRINCIPE DE CONTINUITÉ ET LOI APPLICABLE AUX CONTRATS INTERNATIONAUX

Il reste à examiner le rôle du principe de continuité des contrats, tel qu'il est retenu par l'article 3 du règlement n° 1103/97, lorsqu'il s'agit de contrats internationaux, dont la monnaie contractuelle est remplacée par l'euro.

Il ne faut pas oublier à cet égard que l'article 3 est une règle de droit matériel uniforme, qui déroge au droit interne en matière de contrats dans la mesure nécessaire pour en assurer l'application ; et qu'elle a cet effet dérogatoire par rapport au droit interne de tous les États membres de la Communauté européenne, y compris les

---

[7] Cf. Alpa, ibid., p. 659 ; Carriero, « I contratti in moneta unica: riflessi civilistici », *Foro italiano* (1997 – V) 240 et suiv.

[8] Cf. Draetta (supra n. 3) p. 20.

États « avec dérogation »,[9] qui n'ont pas encore adopté la monnaie unique. Il en découle que le principe de continuité joue son rôle à l'égard de tous les contrats, internes ou internationaux, régis par la loi d'un État membre.

Tandis que la substitution de la monnaie contractuelle nationale par l'euro dépend de la *lex monetae* et doit être respectée en toute occasion, la règle sur la continuité se rapporte à la *lex contractus* (ou *lex obligationis*) et n'exerce son influence que sur la loi applicable au contrat, en la modifiant où elle contient une réglementation différente en matière d'adaptation des contrats, sauf si les parties en ont décidé autrement.

Par conséquent, lorsque la loi d'un État membre de la Communauté européenne régit le contrat, celui-ci est affecté par le principe de continuité prévu par le règlement communautaire, qui déroge aux dispositions contraires éventuelles du droit interne, tant en ce qui concerne les effets du changement des conditions contractuelles et des circonstances dans lesquelles le contrat a été conclu, qu'en ce qui a trait au rôle de l'autonomie des parties. Cette conclusion s'applique également à la désignation par les parties de la loi d'un État tiers pour régir le contrat, lorsque tous les autres éléments de fait, sauf le choix de la loi applicable, sont localisés dans un même État membre de la Communauté. Le choix d'une loi étrangère ne constituant dans un pareil cas qu'une simple réception matérielle (*materielle Rechtsverweisung*) du droit étranger – ainsi que le confirme l'article 3 paragraphe 3 de la convention de Rome du 19 juin 1980 sur la loi applicable aux obligations contractuelles[10] –, c'est l'article 3 du règlement qui fixe le domaine dans lequel l'autonomie des parties peut être exercée aux fins d'une telle réception matérielle.

Une conclusion différente s'impose lorsque le choix des parties s'exprime en faveur de la loi d'un État tiers dans un contrat international, qui présente donc des éléments qui se rapportent à des pays différents. Dans ce cas l'autonomie des parties peut jouer en tant que rattachement de droit international privé (*internationalrechtliche Rechtsverweisung*), en soumettant le contrat à la loi de l'État tiers désigné, sur laquelle l'article 3 du règlement ne peut exercer aucune influence. Il en est de même lorsque les parties à un contrat international n'ont pas choisi la loi applicable et qu'un rattachement objectif désigne la loi d'un État non membre de la Communauté européenne. Puisque le règlement a une portée spatiale limitée au territoire des États membres, il ne saurait influencer la loi applicable. Les conséquences de l'introduction de l'euro, lorsqu'il remplace la monnaie contractuelle, ne devraient alors être appréciées qu'à la lumière de la teneur de la loi applicable de manière à ce que les dispositions de celle-ci sur l'adaptation des contrats devraient en principe être

---

[9] Le traité instituant la Communauté européenne indique avec cette expression les États membres qui ne font pas partie du premier groupe d'États qui adoptent la monnaie unique (cf. article 122, tel que résultant des traités de Maastricht et d'Amsterdam).

[10] Voir Pocar, « Brevi appunti sull'incidenza della convenzione di Roma relativa alla legge applicabile ai contratti sul diritto italiano », *Studi in ricordo di A. F. Panzera,* II (Bari 1995) p. 692.

prises en compte sans les restrictions auxquelles elles seraient soumises si le règlement était en vigueur dans l'État tiers concerné.

4.   LE PROBLÈME DE LA VARIATION DES TAUX D'INTÉRÊT À LA LUMIÈRE DE LA LOI RÉGISSANT LE CONTRAT

Le sujet des intérêts que le débiteur doit payer en vertu du contrat mérite une attention spéciale à la lumière de son incidence éventuelle sur le changement des conditions du contrat, surtout lorsque le taux d'intérêt sur l'euro est sensiblement plus bas du taux pratiqué sur la monnaie nationale. Il faut distinguer en la matière entre intérêts légaux et contractuels et, pour ces derniers, entre intérêts à taux fixe ou variable.

Lorsqu'il s'agit d'intérêts légaux, leur montant dépend de la loi applicable au contrat, sauf si les parties les ont expressément soumis à la *lex monetae* en choisissant la monnaie contractuelle. Par conséquent, c'est en principe à la *lex contractus* qu'il faut se référer pour établir le taux des intérêts légaux et pour vérifier s'il a été modifié à la suite de l'introduction de la nouvelle monnaie. La même loi doit être utilisée pour trancher la question de savoir si l'application du taux des intérêts légaux à l'euro constitue un changement des conditions contractuelles qui demande leur adaptation.[11]

Si l'on en vient maintenant aux intérêts contractuels, aucun problème ne semble se poser lorsqu'il s'agit d'intérêts variables dont le taux de référence de la monnaie contractuelle correspond à des taux de référence existants. Il semble approprié que la substitution de la monnaie contractuelle par l'euro implique que le débiteur doive payer le taux d'intérêt défini pour l'euro dans le même cadre. Si par exemple une société à emprunté une somme en florins néerlandais en payant des intérêts au taux interbancaire offert à Londres (*London Inter-Bank Offered Rate, LIBOR*), elle continuera à payer les intérêts sur la somme renommée en euro au taux interbancaire offert à Londres pour la nouvelle monnaie. Ce n'est qu'en cas de disparition d'un taux de référence, ce qui peut arriver notamment lorsque celui-ci est défini par une entité privé, que son remplacement pourrait être problématique. Il reviendrait alors aux parties de désigner un nouveau taux de référence ou, si elles ne parviendraient pas à s'entendre sur le remplacement, au juge d'assurer l'exécution du con-

---

[11] La réponse à cette question ne pourra naturellement être que négative lorsque la loi applicable au contrat est la loi d'un État membre de la Communauté européenne, où la disposition de l'article 3 du règlement n° 1103/97 s'applique ; et cela même s'il est possible que la même monnaie, à savoir l'euro, puisse comporter un taux d'intérêt légal différent, selon l'État membre prise en compte. Bien qu'une telle situation ne soit pas souhaitable, c'est une situation à laquelle seulement les législations nationales peuvent remédier, spontanément ou en exécution d'une règle communautaire qui adopte un taux d'intérêt uniforme pour tout le territoire de l'Union.

trat en adoptant un nouveau taux de référence, aussi proche que possible de l'ancien. Mais il s'agit là d'une question qui pourrait également se présenter indépendamment d'un changement de la monnaie contractuelle.

Lorsque les parties ont convenu un taux d'intérêt fixe, ce taux doit en principe s'appliquer également à la nouvelle monnaie. La circonstance que, pour l'euro, soient offerts sur les marchés financiers des intérêts plus élevés, ou plus bas, que ceux offerts pour la monnaie contractuelle, ne constitue pas en soi un motif pour demander une adaptation du contrat, sauf si la différence des taux est d'une telle ampleur qu'elle modifie sensiblement la prestation d'une partie en donnant à l'autre un avantage injustifié. Toutefois, même dans ce cas, la possibilité d'invoquer les règles sur l'adaptation des contrats dépend de la loi applicable au contrat et ne peut donc exister que si cette loi est celle d'un État tiers. Lorsque le contrat est régi par la loi d'un État membre de la Communauté européenne, cette possibilité est exclue part l'article 3 du règlement n° 1103/97, ainsi qu'on l'a déjà indiqué. Il y a lieu d'ajouter que le septième considérant du préambule du règlement réaffirme cette conclusion, en précisant que le principe de la continuité des contrats « signifie en particulier que, pour les instruments à taux d'intérêt fixe, l'introduction de l'euro ne modifie pas le taux d'intérêts nominal payable par le débiteur ».

Il y a lieu également de remarquer que cette conclusion n'est pas affectée par la condition de consommateur de la partie qui doit payer les intérêts, bien que cette condition puisse constituer un élément qui doit être apprécié pour la détermination du droit applicable au contrat.[12]

5.   L'INFLUENCE DE LA COMPÉTENCE JURIDICTIONNELLE SUR
      L'APPLICATION DU PRINCIPE DE CONTINUITÉ DES CONTRATS
      INTERNATIONAUX

Les relations entre le principe de continuité et la loi applicable au contrat, telles qu'on vient de les esquisser, demandent toutefois des précisions ultérieures, qui tiennent compte de la juridiction saisie par les parties pour statuer sur la portée des clauses contractuelles.

Lorsque le contrat est soumis aux tribunaux d'un État membre de l'Union européenne, on pourrait également envisager une incidence du principe de continuité, tel que prévu par le règlement, sur la loi étrangère applicable au contrat, dans la mesure où le tribunal saisi estime que la continuité constitue un principe fondamental de son système juridique, faisant partie de l'ordre public. Le principe limiterait dans ce cas l'application du droit étranger s'exprimant en sens contraire – excluant, par

---

[12] Voir toutefois Malatesta, « Il principio di continuità dei contratti dopo l'euro al vaglio della disciplina sulle clausole abusive », *Diritto del commercio internazionale* (1999) p. 205 et suiv.

exemple, toute influence du principe de continuité – dans la mesure où l'on pourrait parler d'une incompatibilité manifeste de ce droit avec le principe même. On ne peut exclure non plus *a priori* que le juge d'un État membre de la Communauté puisse utiliser la possibilité offerte par l'article 4 de la Convention de Rome du 19 juin 1980, de dépecer le contrat et d'identifier un lien plus étroit pour une partie de celui-ci. Bien que seulement dans des cas exceptionnels, le juge pourrait alors déterminer ce lien plus étroit pour la partie du contrat concernant les effets du changement de la monnaie contractuelle, en fonction de cette dernière, et par conséquent avec un État membre de l'Union. Le contrat resterait dans son ensemble régit par la loi d'un État tiers, mais le principe de continuité affirmé par le règlement pourrait être « récupéré » et appliqué dans un cas donné.

Toute influence du règlement communautaire devrait au contraire être exclue si le contrat régi par la loi d'un État tiers était soumis à la juridiction de cet État ou d'un autre État tiers. Dans ce cas il n'y aurait aucune raison de prendre en compte la loi d'un État autre que celui dont la loi régit le contrat. La juridiction saisie serait, elle aussi, tenue de respecter la *lex monetae* pour ce qui est de la substitution de la monnaie contractuelle par l'euro, mais elle ne serait pas obligée de prendre en considération les règles et les principes concernant le changement des circonstances contractuelles édictée par l'État qui a modifié sa monnaie. En outre, on a déjà précisé plus haut que l'article 3 du règlement n'a pas la nature de règle d'application immédiate, qui pourrait jouer un rôle même lorsqu'elle n'appartient pas à la loi applicable au contrat tout en ayant un lien étroit avec celui-ci, ainsi que cela serait sans doute le cas de la loi de la monnaie contractuelle. La seule possibilité d'une prise en compte du règlement, en tant qu'en vigueur dans le cadre du droit matériel de l'État de la monnaie contractuelle, serait liée à un dépeçage du contrat dans les termes indiqués plus haut, dans la mesure où ce dépeçage est permis par le système de droit international privé du for.

Si l'on fait abstraction de cette possibilité, on devrait exclure que le règlement puisse en tant que tel affecter la vie d'un contrat soumis à la loi et à la juridiction d'un État tiers, car ce dernier n'a aucune obligation d'en faire application. Le législateur communautaire en était bien conscient, lorsqu'il a écrit dans le huitième considérant du préambule du règlement n° 1103/97 que « la confirmation explicite du principe de continuité doit entraîner la reconnaissance de la continuité des contrats et autres instruments juridiques dans l'ordre juridique des pays tiers », exprimant par cela un souhait plutôt qu'une conviction quant à l'existence d'une obligation de reconnaissance du principe.[13]

On pourrait faire des remarques analogues lorsque la juridiction en la matière est

---

[13] Le principe à été en effet reconnu expressément par la législation de quelques États tiers. Voir en particulier, quant aux États Unies Lenihan, « The Legal Implications of the European Monetary Union under U.S. and New York Law », *European Commission, D. G. for Economic and Financial Affairs, Economic Papers,* n° 126 (1998) p. 215 et suiv.

exercée par un tribunal arbitral. Ce dernier n'a pas non plus un devoir de prendre en compte le règlement communautaire lorsque la loi régissant le contrat est la loi d'un État non membre de la Communauté européenne. Par conséquent, si les parties ont soumis le contrat à la loi d'un État tiers ou si cette dernière loi s'applique en vertu de critères de rattachement objectifs, le tribunal arbitral ne devra pas tenir compte, en principe, du règlement communautaire. Il y a lieu toutefois de remarquer que la liberté dont souvent disposent les arbitres dans la détermination du droit applicable au litige pourrait également permettre dans des cas d'espèce d'aboutir à une solution moins rigide, compte tenu notamment de la possibilité de se référer aux usages du commerce international. Par contre, il ne faut pas oublier que lorsque la loi applicable est celle d'un État membre de l'Union européenne, l'appréciation de la volonté des parties contractantes pourra porter à des solutions plus flexibles que celles qui pourraient résulter de l'application rigoureuse du principe de continuité tel que visé par le règlement communautaire.

ENGLISH SUMMARY
NOTES ON THE CONTINUITY OF CONTRACTS FOLLOWING THE
INTRODUCTION OF THE EURO

Article 3 of EC Regulation 1103/97 provides that the introduction of the single currency will not affect any contractual obligation entered by the parties, unless the parties agree otherwise. Notwithstanding its apparent clarity, this provision has received a variety of interpretations. These include its definition as a mandatory rule, as well as its description as merely declaratory of a general principle which would not affect the application of the substantive law governing the contract, which would continue to dictate the consequences of the replacement of the contractual currency by the Euro. The former approach appears to be too radical, especially in the light of the fact that the provision does not exclude party autonomy. The latter is clearly contradicted by the text of the Regulation, which suggests that no circumstance directly related to the introduction of the Euro can be invoked as a ground for modification of the terms of the contract. It runs also against the finality of the provision, which is precisely to prevent commercial transactions from being disturbed by a different appreciation of the consequences of the introduction of the Euro under domestic laws.

As mentioned above, the principle of continuity may be derogated from by the parties. The extent to which such a derogation applies is largely a matter for interpretation of the contractual clauses, in particular when the latter do not contain an express reference to the introduction of the Euro. Furthermore, the role that party autonomy is given in the Regulation could also be seen as a recommendation to contracting parties to agree on specific clauses dealing with the introduction of the new currency, especially as far as long term or financial contracts are concerned.

The payment of interests related to monetary obligations is also a matter for concern. Legal interests clearly depend on the *lex contractus*, it being understood that no problem will arise whenever the latter is the law of a EU state within the Euro area. While the same applies to contractual interests at a fixed rate, a reference made by the parties to interests rates offered for the contractual currency within a particular financial framework should lead to the application of the interest offered for the Euro within the same framework.

Finally, the impact of questions of jurisdiction cannot be underestimated. Indeed, should a dispute arising out of the contract be submitted to a court in a EU State participating in the Euro, the Regulation might still play a role, even if the contract is governed by the law of a State which is not bound by the Regulation. This would not be the case if the contract is put before a court in a State which is not a member of the EU, unless that State has adopted specific rules to this effect. Other issues may also arise when the dispute is submitted to an arbitral tribunal.

Juristische Personen im polnischen IPR – Geschichte, heutiger Stand und Novellierungsentwurf

Jerzy Poczobut[*]

1. REGELUNG IM IPR-GESETZ VON 1926

Das erste polnische IPR-Gesetz ging für die Bestimmung des Personalstatuts der juristischen Personen von der Sitztheorie als Grundsatz aus: Gemäß Art. 1 Abs. 3 des polnischen Gesetzes vom 2. August 1926 betreffend das für internationale Privatverhältnisse geltende Recht[1] (im folgenden „IPRG von 1926") ist die Fähigkeit juristischer Personen sowie aller Gesellschaften und Vereinigungen nach dem an ihrem Sitz geltenden Recht zu beurteilen. Unter „Fähigkeit" wurde dabei die

---

[*] Prof. Dr. iur., Direktor des Instituts für Internationales Recht, Fakultät für Recht und Verwaltung, Universität Warschau.

[1] Dziennik Ustaw (poln. Gesetzblatt) Nr. 101, Pos. 581; geänd. Dziennik Ustaw 1936 Nr. 3, Pos. 22.

J. Basedow et al., eds., Private Law in the International Arena – Liber Amicorum Kurt Siehr
© *2000, T.M.C.Asser Press, The Hague, The Netherlands*

Rechts- und Handlungsfähigkeit verstanden.[2] In der polnischen IPR-Lehre wies man darauf hin, daß der Sitz einer juristischen Person in der Regel der Sitz ihrer Hauptverwaltung sein wird.[3] Es wurde auch betont, für die Feststellung des Sitzes einer juristischen Person komme es maßgeblich auf eine Gesamtbewertung der tatsächlichen Sachlage an, während andererseits die Bedeutung von Satzungsbestimmungen über den Sitz in Frage gestellt wurde.[4]

2.   REGELUNG IM IPR-GESETZ VON 1965

2.1   Grundsatz

Das Gesetz vom 12. November 1965 – Internationales Privatrecht[5] (im folgenden „IPRG") hat die soeben dargestellte Lösung übernommen, sie jedoch expressis verbis auf die juristischen Personen begrenzt. Artikel 9 § 2 IPRG erhielt in der Schlußfassung folgenden Wortlaut: „Die Fähigkeit einer juristischen Person wird nach dem Recht des Staates beurteilt, in dem sie ihren Sitz hat." Dieses Abstellen auf den Sitz einer juristischen Person findet eine Entsprechung in folgendem in Art. 1103 Pkt. 1 des polnischen Zivilverfahrensgesetzbuches von 1964 für die inländische Gerichtsbarkeit im Prozeß verankerten Grundsatz: Die im Prozeßwege verhandelten Rechtsstreitigkeiten, mit Vorbehalt einer besonderen Regelung der Ehesachen, der Sachen aus den Beziehungen zwischen Eltern und Kindern sowie eine Adoption betreffender Sachen, der Sachen wegen dinglicher Rechte und wegen des Besitzes eines Grundstücks sowie auch der Sachen aus einem Miet- oder Pachtverhältnis an einem Grundstück mit Ausnahme von Sachen wegen des Zinses, gehören zur in-

---

[2] Vgl. K. Przybyłowski, *Polskie prawo międzynarodowe prywatne. Część szczegółowa* (Polnisches internationales Privatrecht. Besonderer Teil) Manuskript (vervielfältigte Maschinenschrift) (Lwów 1935) S. 99-100; F. Zoll, *Międzynarodowe prawo prywatne w zarysie* (Abriß des internationalen Privatrechts) 4. Aufl. (Kraków 1947) S. 46 sowie J. Kosik, *Zdolność państwowych osób prawnych w zakresie prawa cywilnego* (Fähigkeit staatlicher juristischer Personen im Bereich des Zivilrechts) (Warszawa 1963) S. 34. Anders A. N. Makarov, *Quellen des internationalen Privatrechts*, Loseblattsammlung, 2. Aufl., Bd. I, Gesetzestexte (Berlin, Tübingen 1953) – Polen, S. 4, nach dessen Ansicht es in dieser Vorschrift um die Rechts- und Geschäftsfähigkeit juristischer Personen geht.

[3] Vgl. Z. Cybichowski, *Prawo międzynarodowe publiczne i prywatne* (Internationales Völker- und Privatrecht) 4. Aufl. (Warszawa 1932) S. 454; Z. Fenichel, „Polskie prywatne prawo handlowe międzynarodowe i międzydzielnicowe" (Das polnische internationale Privathandelsrecht und interterritoriale Recht) *Przegląd Prawa Handlowego* (Revue des Handelsrechts) (1932) S. 353-366, 409-426 – Abdruck, S. 8; Zoll, vorige Note, S. 46, sowie L. Babiński, *Zagadnienia współczesnego polskiego prawa międzynarodowego prywatnego* (Fragen des heutigen polnischen internationalen Privatrechts) (Warszawa 1958) S. 125; Kosik, vorige Note, S. 34.

[4] Vgl. K. Przybyłowski, *Prawo prywatne międzynarodowe. Część ogólna* (Internationales Privatrecht. Allgemeiner Teil) (Lwów 1935) S. 129.

[5] Dziennik Ustaw (poln. Gesetzblatt) Nr. 46, Pos. 290; geänd. Dziennik Ustaw 1995 Nr. 83, Pos. 417 und 1999 Nr. 52, Pos. 532.

ländischen Gerichtsbarkeit, wenn die beklagte Partei im Zeitpunkt der Zustellung der Klage sich in Polen aufhält, wohnt oder ihren Sitz in Polen hat.

2.2 Bedeutung des Begriffes „Fähigkeit"

Ungeachtet dessen, daß Art. 9 § 2 IPRG nur die „Fähigkeit" regelt, ist es die übereinstimmende Auffassung der polnischen Lehre und Rechtsprechung, daß auch die meisten übrigen Elemente des Personalstatuts einer juristischen Person nach dem an deren Sitz geltenden Recht zu beurteilen sind.[6] Ein ausführlicher und abschließender Katalog dieser Elemente wurde jedoch ausdrücklich nicht festgelegt.[7] Zum Beispiel ist es streitig, ob die Gründungsform und mit der Entstehung, Auflösung, Umwandlung und Fusion der Gesellschaften verbundene Rechtsgeschäfte, sowie die Aktien- oder Anteilsübertragung vom Gesellschaftsstatut erfaßt wird.[8]

Um Meinungsverschiedenheiten bei der Bestimmung des auf die wichtigsten Elemente des Personalstatuts anwendbaren Rechts und über den Umfang des Personalstatuts vorzubeugen, sollte das Gesetz die wichtigsten dieser Elemente in einem Katalog aufzählen, wie dies die geltenden Kollisionsgesetze Italiens, Rumäniens und der Schweiz tun. Die Festlegung scharfer Grenzen des Personalstatuts in einem novellierten Kollisionsgesetz erscheint hingegen weder möglich noch notwendig; streitige Fragen hinsichtlich dieses sehr komplizierten und facettenreichen Problems sollten wie bisher der Entscheidung durch die für die Rechtsanwendung berufenen Organe und die Lehre überlassen bleiben.

2.3 Die Frage der „hinkenden" juristischen Personen

Ob auch Organisationseinheiten mit Vereinigungscharakter und in bestimmter Weise gestalteten Vermögensmassen, die zwar keine juristische Persönlichkeit ha-

---

[6] Vgl. J. Jakubowski, *Prawo międzynarodowe prywatne. Zarys wykładu* (Internationales Privatrecht. Abriß der Vorlesung) (Warszawa 1984) S. 76; W. Ludwiczak, *Międzynarodowe prawo prywatne* (Internationales Privatrecht) 5. Aufl. (Poznań 1996) S. 171; M. Pazdan, *Prawo prywatne międzynarodowe* (Internationales Privatrecht) 5. Aufl. (Warszawa 1999) S. 96; ders., *Założenia zmian w ustawie o prawie prywatnym międzynarodowym* (Prämissen der Änderungen im IPR-Gesetz) vervielfältigte Maschinenschrift (Warszawa 1988) S. 4; K. Przybyłowski, *Kodyfikacyjne zagadnienia polskiego prawa międzynarodowego prywatnego* (Kodifikationsfragen des polnischen IPR) Studia Cywilistyczne (Zivilistische Studien) (1964) Bd.V, S. 21; S. Sołtysiński, *Wprowadzenie* (Einführung) in: S. Sołtysiński / A. Szajkowski / J. Szwaja, *Kodeks handlowy. Komentarz* (Handelsgesetzbuch. Kommentar) Bd. I (Warszawa 1994) S. 198-199; M. Sośniak, *Prawo prywatne międzynarodowe* (Internationales Privatrecht) 3. Aufl. (Katowice 1991) S. 104.

[7] Zum Anwendungsbereich des Personalstatuts einer juristischen Person siehe vor allem J. Jakubowski, „Osoby prawne w polskim prawie prywatnym międzynarodowym" (Juristische Personen im polnischen internationalen Privatrecht) *Państwo i Prawo* (Staat und Recht) (1969) H. 8-9, S. 278-279; Pazdan, vorige Note, S. 98; Sołtysiński, vorige Note, S. 198-203.

[8] Vgl. Sołtysiński (oben N. 6) S. 199.

ben, häufig aber mit Gerichts- und Prozeßfähigkeit ausgestattet sind (sog. „hinkende" juristische Personen), nach Art. 9 § 2 IPRG beurteilt werden sollen, ist der jetzi-
gen Formulierung dieser Vorschrift nicht zu entnehmen. Zwar sah der Entwurf des
polnischen IPR-Gesetzes von 1954 vor, die Vorschrift um die Feststellung zu ergänzen, daß „für Vereinigungen und Institutionen ohne juristische Persönlichkeit"
dieselbe Regelung gelten soll, schließlich wurde hiervon jedoch abgesehen, da man
„mit der starren Vorschrift der streitigen und komplizierten Problematik nicht vor-
greifen" wollte.[9] Einige Vertreter der polnischen Rechtskollisionslehre postulieren
die entsprechende Anwendung des Art. 9 § 2 IPRG[10] auf die „hinkenden,, juristischen Personen. Nach der Gegenansicht fallen dagegen unter den breit verstandenen Begriff der „juristischen Person" auch die „Organisationen mit partieller juristischer Persönlichkeit",[11] im Ergebnis fordern die Vertreter dieser Ansicht die
direkte Anwendung des Art. 9 § 2 IPRG auf diese Organisationen.

In Anbetracht der Existenz verschiedener Kategorien der „hinkenden" juristischen Personen und der Schwierigkeit einer allgemeinen Definition, sollte die Frage der Anwendung des Art. 9 § 2 IPRG auf diese Organisationen auch weiterhin
den rechtsanwendenden Organen zur Entscheidung nach den allgemeinen Regeln
überlassen bleiben.

2.4 Charakter des Sitzes einer juristischen Person

In Art. 9 § 2 IPRG von 1965 wurde weder der Charakter des Sitzes einer juristischen Person bestimmt noch eine Grundlage für seine Bestimmung gegeben. In der
polnischen IPR-Lehre fehlt es an Gewißheit über die Auslegung dieses Begriffes.
Unter diesem Vorbehalt und ohne überzeugende Begründung nimmt man jedoch
relativ allgemein an, daß unter dem Sitz im Sinne dieser Vorschrift der tatsächliche
Sitz der Hauptverwaltung (Direktion) einer juristischen Person zu verstehen ist.[12]
Vereinzelt wird die Meinung vertreten, bei der Feststellung des Verwaltungssitzes
einer juristischen Person sollten sowohl die tatsächlichen Umstände als auch die
Bestimmungen der Satzung in Betracht gezogen werden.[13]

---

[9] Vgl. B. Walaszek, M. Sośniak, *Zarys międzynarodowego prawa prywatnego* (Abriß des internationalen Privatrechts) (Warszawa 1968) S. 73. In erwähnter Ergänzung knüpfte man an Art. 1 Abs. 3
IPRG von 1926 an.

[10] Vgl. Pazdan (oben N. 6) S. 99; Sołtysiński (oben N. 6) S. 195-196; Sośniak (oben N. 6) S. 103-
104.

[11] Anders Jakubowski (oben N. 7) S. 270; ders., Prawo międzynarodowe (oben N. 6) S. 76; Ludwiczak (oben N. 6) S. 171; Walaszek / Sośniak (oben N. 9) S. 73; E. Wierzbowski, *Międzynarodowy
obrót prawny w sprawach cywilnych* (Internationaler Verkehr in Zivilsachen) (Warszawa 1971) S. 236.

[12] Vgl. Ludwiczak (oben N. 6) S. 170; Jakubowski (oben N. 7) S. 270, 276; Pazdan (oben N. 6) S.
97; Sołtysiński (oben N. 6) S. 193-194.

[13] So wahrscheinlich (die Aussage ist nicht klar) Sośniak (oben N. 6) S. 104 sowie Walaszek /
Sośniak (oben N. 9) S. 74.

Angesichts der allgemein bekannten Mängel der Konzeption eines tatsächlichen Verwaltungssitzes erscheint jedoch der Standpunkt, nach dem unter dem Sitz einer juristischen Person i. S. v. Art. 9 § 2 IPRG der tatsächliche Verwaltungssitz zu verstehen sein soll, schwierig aufrechtzuerhalten.

2.5 Elastizität des Grundsatzes

In der polnischen IPR-Lehre wird auf die mangelnde Flexibilität der sich aus Art. 9 § 2 IPRG im Zusammenhang mit Art. 4 IPRG ergebenden Regelung hingewiesen; in Art. 4 IPRG wurde lediglich die Rückverweisung ohne Einschränkung zugelassen (§ 1), die Anwendungsmöglichkeit der Weiterverweisung hingegen durch die Anforderung begrenzt, daß das durch das polnische IPR-Gesetz als maßgeblich erklärte ausländische Recht für ein bestimmtes Rechtsverhältnis ein Heimatrecht sein soll (§ 2).[14] Diese Lösung schließt die Anwendung der einstufigen Weiterverweisung aus. Eine solche scheint jedoch geboten zu sein, weil sie der gesamten Regelung des Personalstatuts die Elastizität verleihen würde, die für die internationale Entscheidungsharmonisierung und wenigstens partielle Minderung der Auffassungskollisionen im besprochenen Bereich unerläßlich ist.

Nach Maksymilian Pazdan erscheint es wünschenswert, die Kollisionsnormen des Staates zu beachten, in dem eine juristische Person ihren Sitz hat, insbesondere dann, wenn diese Normen an andere Kriterien anknüpfen als das polnische IPR-Gesetz (z.B. das Kriterium der Gründung einer juristischen Person) oder zwar dieselbe Anknüpfung enthalten, diese aber anders verstehen (In diesem Falle tritt ein Qualifikationskonflikt im Anknüpfungsbereich ein). Das spricht für die Zulassung nicht nur der Rückverweisung, sondern auch der einstufigen Weiterverweisung.[15] Dies entspricht dem Vorschlag der Expertenkommission im Entwurf des polnischen internationales Privatrechts von 1965, Art. 9 § 2 IPRG um einen Satz 2 mit folgendem Wortlaut zu ergänzen: „Wenn jedoch dieses Recht ein anderes Recht als maßgeblich im obigen Umfang, so ist dieses andere Recht anzuwenden".[16] In dieser Fassung würde die Verweisung nicht nur dann eingreifen, wenn das Kollisionsrecht

---

[14] Vgl. Jakubowski(oben N. 7) S. 276-277; Pazdan (oben N. 6) S. 3. Art. 4 IPRG: § 1. „Verweist das durch dieses Gesetz als maßgeblich erklärte ausländische Recht für ein bestimmtes Rechtsverhältnis auf polnisches Recht, so ist polnisches Recht anzuwenden. § 2. Verweist das durch dieses Gesetz als maßgeblich erklärte ausländische Heimatrecht für ein bestimmtes Rechtsverhältnis auf ein anderes ausländisches Recht, so ist dieses andere Recht anzuwenden" (siehe A. N. Makarov, *Quellen des internationalen Privatrecht. Nationale Kodifikationen* (Tübingen 1978) S. 185).

[15] So Pazdan (oben N. 6) S. 3.

[16] Ebd., S. 3-4. Dies wurde von Pazdan im Laufe der durch die Arbeitsgruppe für die Fragen der Rechtsverhältnisse im internationalen Verkehr (die im Rahmen der Kommission für die Reform des Zivilrechts tätig war) geführten Arbeit an den Prämissen der Änderungen im polnischen Kollisionsrecht erneut vorgeschlagen. Näher zu der erwähnten Kommission im deutschen Schrifttum siehe J. Poczobut, „Zur Reform des polnischen Zivilrechts", *ZEuP* (1999) S. 80 und die dort zitierte Literatur.

des Staates, in dem eine juristische Person ihren Sitz hat, das Kriterium der Gründung dieser Person vorsieht, sondern auch dann, wenn an ein anderes Kriterium angeknüpft wird (selten) und außerdem, wenn dieses Recht zwar an den Sitz der juristischen Person anknüpft, diese Anknüpfung jedoch anders verstanden wird als im polnischen internationalen Privatrecht (zu erwähnen wäre hier die Konkurrenz zwischen den Konzeptionen des tatsächlichen und des in der Satzung einer juristischen Person vorgesehenen Sitzes).[17]. Die Abfassung der vorgeschlagenen Vorschrift könnte jedoch sprachlich verbessert werden.

2.6   Ausnahme vom Grundsatz

Eine Ausnahme vom Grundsatz des Art. 9 § 2 IPRG wurde in § 3 desselben Artikels vorgesehen: Nimmt eine juristischen Person ein Rechtsgeschäft im Bereich ihres Unternehmens vor, so wird ihre Fähigkeit nach dem Recht des Staates beurteilt, in dem sich der Sitz dieses Unternehmens befindet. Bei der Ausgestaltung dieser Vorschrift wurde Art. 2 IPRG von 1926 zum Vorbild genommen, wonach sich die persönliche Fähigkeit eines Kaufmannes nach dem am Sitze seines Unternehmens geltenden Recht bestimmt. In der polnischen IPR-Lehre ist die Auffassung herrschend, trotz der Verwendung des Begriffes „Fähigkeit einer juristischen Person" in Art. 9 § 3 IPRG betreffe die erwähnte Ausnahme lediglich die Geschäftsfähigkeit dieser Person, nicht hingegen die übrigen Elemente ihres Personalstatus, z.B. die Rechtsfähigkeit, die dem in Art. 9 § 2 IPRG vorgesehenen Recht unterliegt.[18]

Es liegt auf der Hand, daß eine solche Bestimmung des Anwendungsbereiches des Art. 9 § 3 IPRG[19] nicht alle Zweifel beseitigen kann, die hinsichtlich des Verhältnisses dieses Bereiches zum Anwendungsbereich des Art. 9 § 2 IPRG auftreten können.[20] Insbesondere wäre im Falle einer juristischen Person die Unterscheidung zwischen der Rechts- und der Gechäftsfähigkeit unnötig, da beide denselben Umfang haben.[21] Der in Art. 9 § 3 IPRG benutzte allgemeine Begriff der „Fähigkeit" einer juristischen Person sollte daher beibehalten werden.

In der Lehre wird in Hinblick auf Gesellschaften auch postuliert, der Anwendungsbereich des am Sitz eines Unternehmens geltenden Rechts solle nicht nur die Fragen der Fähigkeit sondern auch der Vertretung einer Filiale (Zweigstelle) der

---

[17] Vgl. Pazdan (oben N. 6) S. 4.

[18] Vgl. Pazdan (oben N. 6) S. 93, 98.

[19] Z.B. in einer Weise, die dem Entwurf eines neuen Art. 9 § 3 IPRG ähnlich ist, der von der Experten-Kommission für Fragen des Gesetzes über die zivilrechtlichen Verhältnisse im internationalen Handel in 1979 vorgeschlagen wurde. Dieser Entwurf knüpfte an den von H. Trammer im Laufe der Arbeit am polnischen IPRG von 1965 vorgebrachten Vorschlag an (vgl. Przybyłowski (oben N. 6) S. 22).

[20] Ähnlich Pazdan (oben N. 6) S. 5.

[21] Von der so vestandenen Fähigkeit einer juristischen Person soll man ihre besondere Fähigkeit zu einigen Handlungsarten unterscheiden.

Firma usw. Erfassen.[22] Dies würde jedoch eine genaue Abgrenzung der Elemente des Personalstatus am Sitz einer juristischen Person einerseits und am Sitz ihres Unternehmens andererseits erfordern. Bisher gibt es aber noch keine ausführlichen Bemühungen in dieser Richtung.

Der Begriff des „Unternehmens" soll im funktionalen Sinne verstanden werden: Unternehmen ist das berufliche, auf Gewinn gerichtete Betreiben einer organisierten Wirtschaftstätigkeit (vor allem im Bereich der Produktion, der Dienstleistungen und des Handels).[23] Unter dem Sitz des Unternehmens versteht man den Ort, an dem sich das Zentrum dieser Tätigkeit (der tatsächliche Sitz) befindet.[24] Die Vorschrift des Art. 9 § 3 IPRG findet Anwendung, wenn eine juristische Person organisierte und ständig funktionierende Zentren ihrer Wirtschaftstätigkeit außerhalb des Hoheitsgebietes des Staates hat, in dem der Sitz dieser Person sich befindet. Solche Unternehmen können Filialen (Zweigstellen) ohne eigene juristische Persönlichkeit sein, deren Mutterunternehmen sich am Sitz der juristischen Person befindet.[25]

Die Ausnahmeregelung des Art. 9 § 3 IPRG hinsichtlich einer im Bereich ihres Unternehmens tätigen juristischen Person wurde mit dem Bedürfnis der Sicherheit des Rechtsverkehrs begründet, das sich vor allem unter dem Gesichtspunkt der Sicherung der Interessen eines Vertragspartners einer solchen juristischen Person ergibt, der im guten Glauben und im Vertrauen auf die Rechtsordnung des Staates handelt, in dem ein solches Unternehmen sich befindet und die Tätigkeit betreibt.[26] Nach Kazimierz Przyby»owski ist statt des Heimatrechts einer natürlichen Person (bzw. des Rechts des Staates, in dem eine juristische Person ihren Sitz hat) das am Sitz des Unternehmens geltende Recht maßgebend, und zwar ohne Rücksicht darauf, ob dieses Recht zu Gunsten der Fähigkeit wirkt oder nicht. Es geht darum, im Umgang mit einem Unternehmen leicht feststellen zu können, welche Rechtsordnung maßgeblich ist, ohne prüfen zu müssen, wer der Eigentümer des Unternehmens ist und welche Staatsangehörigkeit dieser Eigentümer hat.[27] Man hat auch darauf hingewiesen, daß die Anknüpfung an den Unternehmenssitz in Art. 27 § 2 IPRG für die Bestimmung des Statutes der Schuldverbindlichkeiten angewandt wird, die aus im Bereich des Unternehmens geschlossenen Verträgen entstehen.[28]

---

[22] Vgl. Sołtysiński (oben N. 6) S. 198. Nach dem Personalstatut der „Zentrale" einer Gesellschaft würde dagegen die Frage beurteilt, wer Eigentümer des Vermögens einer Filiale ist sowie die Verhältnisse zwischen der „Zentrale" und der Filiale (ebd.).

[23] Siehe Pazdan (oben N. 6) S. 93. Jakubowski (oben N. 6) S. 77 betont dagegen den sachlichen Aspekt des Begriffes „Unternehmen"; seiner Meinung nach ist Unternehmen eine organisierte Gesamtheit von Mitteln, die die Verfolgung einer Wirtschaftstätigkeit ermöglicht.

[24] Vgl. Jakubowski (oben N. 7) S. 276; Pazdan (oben N. 6) S. 93, 99.

[25] Vgl. Pazdan (oben N. 6) S. 99.

[26] Vgl. Jakubowski (oben N. 7) S. 270, 277; Ludwiczak (oben N. 6) S. 171; Sośniak (oben N. 6) S. 104; Walaszek / Sośniak (oben N. 9) S. 75.

[27] So Przybyłowski (oben N. 6) S. 22.

[28] Vgl. Jakubowski (oben N. 7) S. 270.

In bilateralen Staatsverträgen über den Rechtsverkehr und die Rechtshilfe zwischen Polen und anderen Staaten wurde bei der Regelung des Personalstatuts juristischer Personen häufiger an die Sitz- als an die Gründungstheorie angeknüpft.[29]

3. VORSCHLAG ZUR ÄNDERUNG DER JETZIGEN REGELUNG

3.1 Rahmen der möglichen Lösungen

Die Mehrheit der innerstaatlichen Regelungen des Personalstatuts einer juristischen Person folgt entweder der anglo-amerikanischen Gründungstheorie (Inkorporations-, Registrierungs-, Entstehungs- oder Errichtungstheorie) oder der kontinentaleuropäischen Sitztheorie. Gemäß der ersten Theorie unterliegt das Personalstatut einer juristischen Person dem Recht desjenigen Staates, in dem und nach dessen Regeln sie sich gebildet hat. Nach der zweiten Theorie dagegen unterliegt es dem Recht desjenigen Staates, in dem sich der Sitz der juristischen Person befindet. Der Sitz einer juristischen Person kann sein: a) der im Gründungsakt bestimmte Sitz (Satzungssitz), b) der tatsächliche (faktische) Sitz des diese Person verwaltenden Hauptorganes (der Verwaltung), d. h. der Ort, an dem tatsächlich die Verwaltung ausgeübt wird, die in der Regel entweder als Willensgestaltung des Verwaltungsorganes einer juristischen Person oder als Umsetzung der Hauptentscheidungen der Unternehmensleitung in laufende Verwaltungsakte verstanden wird, c) das Exploatationszentrum einer juristischen Person, d.h. der Ort, an dem ihre Tätigkeit sich konzentriert hat.[30]

---

[29] Siehe Ludwiczak (oben N. 6) S. 169.

[30] Siehe vor allem im polnischen Schrifttum – Jakubowski (oben N. 7) S. 272-277; ders. (oben N. 6) S. 75-76; W. Klyta, „Łącznik siedziby w niemieckim międzynarodowym prawie spółek" (Sitzanknüpfung im deutschen internationalen Gesellschaftsrecht) *Kwartalnik Prawa Prywatnego* (Vierteljahresschrift für Privatrecht) (1998) H. 2, S. 243-253; Ludwiczak (oben N. 6) S. 168-170; Pazdan (oben N. 6) S. 96; Sołtysiński (oben N. 6) S. 193; Walaszek / Sośniak (oben N. 9) S. 72-73; A. W. Wiśniewski, *Prawo spółek. Podręcznik praktyczny* (Gesellschaftsrecht. Praktisches Handbuch) Bd. II (Warszawa 1991) S. 81-82, im deutschen Schrifttum – Ch. von Bar, *Internationales Privatrecht, Bd. II, Besonderer Teil* (München 1991) S. 449-459; B. Grossfeld, *Praxis des internationalen Privat- und Wirtschaftsrechts: Rechtsprobleme multinationaler Unternehmen* (Reinbek b. Hamburg 1975) S. 41ff.; ders., „Internationales Gesellschaftsrecht", in: J. von Staudinger, *Kommentar zum Bürgerlichen Gesetzbuch. Einführungsgesetz zum Bürgerlichen Gesetzbuche / IPR*, 13. Aufl. (Berlin 1993) S. 4-19; G. Kegel, *Internationales Privatrecht*, 7. Aufl. (München 1995) S. 408-416; H. Koch/ U. Magnus/ P. W. von Mohrenfels, *IPR und Rechtsvergleichung*, 2. Aufl. (München 1996) S. 157-159; D. Zimmer, *Internationales Gesellschaftsrecht* (Heidelberg 1995) S. 27-29, im schweizerischen Schrifttum – F. Vischer, Zu Art. 154, in: *IPRG Kommentar* (A. Heini, M. Keller, K. Siehr, F. Vischer, P. Volken (Hrsg.)) (Zürich 1993) S. 1341-1343, im französischen Schrifttum – H. Batiffol/ P. Lagarde, *Droit international privé*, Bd. I (Paris 1981) S. 224-253, Bd. II (Paris 1983) S. 21ff.; P. Bourel, Y. Loussouam, *Droit international privé*, 4. Aufl. (Paris 1993) S. 653-669; P. Mayer, *Droit international privé*, 4. Aufl. (Paris 1991) S. 605-638 und die dort zitierte Literatur. Zu den kollisionsrechtlichen Systemen außerhalb Europa siehe *Au-*

3.2 Ausbreitung und Implementierung der Gründungstheorie in Europa

Die Gründungstheorie wurde im Kollisionsrecht von sieben EU-Mitgliedstaaten (Dänemark, Finnland, Großbritannien, Holland, Irland, Italien und Schweden) sowie von anderen Staaten Europas, u.a. Jugoslawien, Liechtenstein, Schweiz und Ungarn angenommen.[31] Diese Theorie scheint immer mehr Anhänger zu finden und immer häufiger in Rechtssystemen Kontinentaleuropas übernommen zu werden.

Von den neueren Kollisionskodifikationen ist die Umsetzung einer vervollkommneten Fassung dieser Theorie im schweizerischen Bundesgesetz vom 18. Dezember 1987 über das internationale Privatrecht (im folgenden „schw. IPRG") charakteristisch. Nach dem Grundsatz von Art. 154 Abs. 1 schw. IPRG, der die breit verstandenen Gesellschaften betrifft,[32] unterstehen diese dem Recht des Staates, nach dessen Vorschriften sie organisiert sind, wenn sie die vorgeschriebenen Publizitäts- oder Registrierungsanforderungen dieser Rechtsordnung erfüllen oder, falls solche Vorschriften nicht bestehen, wenn sie sich nach dem Recht dieses Staates organisiert haben. Erfüllt eine Gesellschaft diese Voraussetzungen nicht, so untersteht sie dem Recht des Staates, in dem sie tatsächlich verwaltet wird (Art. 154 Abs. 2 schw. IPRG).

Für die grundsätzlichen Prämissen der schweizerischen Konzeption des Personalstatuts von Gesellschaften ist bezeichnend, daß der schweizerische Gesetzgeber in der Kollisionskodifikation nicht die Gründungstheorie in „reiner„ Form im Sinne der alleinigen Anknüpfung an die Gründung (Organisierung) einer Gesellschaft umgesetzt hat, sondern es notwendig fand, diesen Ansatz mit der Sitztheorie in Gestalt der Anknüpfung an den Ort der tatsächlichen Verwaltung zu ergänzen. Um die jeweiligen Vorzüge der Gründungs- und Sitztheorie zu nutzen und die Auswirkung ihrer Mängel zu beschränken, folgte man daher in der Schweiz einer Kombinationstheorie, die eine Vereinigung von Elementen beider Theorien darstellt, jedoch mit dem Vorrang der Gründungstheorie.

Grundsätzlich ähnliche Hybridlösungen, mit Vorrang der Gründungstheorie, wurden in Art. 25 Abs. 1 des italienischen Gesetzes Nr. 218 vom 31. Mai 1995 –

ßereuropäische IPR-Gesetze, (J. Kropholler, H. Krueger, W. Riering, J. Samtleben, K. Siehr (Hrsg.)) (Hamburg, Würzburg 1999) *passim.*

[31] Die Gründungstheorie wurde in dieser Dekade auch im Zivilgesetzbuch von Quebec vom 18. Dezember 1991 umgesetzt. Gemäß Art. 3083 Abs. 2 dieses Gesetzbuches findet auf den Status und die Geschäftsfähigkeit einer juristischen Person das Recht des Staates Anwendung, in dem sie gegründet worden ist, unter dem Vorbehalt, daß auf ihre Handlungen das Recht des Staates anzuwenden ist, in dem diese Handlungen vorgenommen werden (siehe Außereuropäische IPR-Gesetze (vorige Note) S. 335).

[32] Gemäß Art. 150 Abs. 1 schw. IPRG gelten als Gesellschaften im Sinne dieses Gesetzes organisierte Personenzusammenschlüsse und organisierte Vermögenseinheiten. Für einfache Gesellschaften, die sich keine Organisation gegeben haben, gilt dennoch das auf Verträge anwendbare Recht (Art. 150 Abs. 2 schw. IPRG).

Reform des italienischen Systems des internationalen Privatrechts, in Art. 17 des jugoslawischen Gesetzes vom 15. Juli 1982 über die Entscheidung der Gesetzkollisionen mit den Vorschriften der Fremdstaaten in bestimmten Verhältnissen] sowie in § 18 Abs. 1-2 des ungarischen Erlasses Nr. 13 vom 13. Mai 1979 über das internationale Privatrecht (im folgenden „ung. IPRD") übernommen.

Schon anhand einer flüchtiger Analyse der verschiedenen Lösungen, die in den europäischen Systemen des internationalen Privatrechts während der letzten zwanzig Jahre hinsichtlich des Personalstatuts juristischer Personen gewählt wurden, kann man feststellen, daß in allen Systemen, in denen die Gründungstheorie den Ausgangspunkt darstellt, eine Ergänzung mittels der Sitztheorie vorgenommen wurde und sich die beiden Theorien so einander angenähert haben. Die erwähnten Ergänzungen bestehen in verschiedenen Begrenzungen und Korrekturen der Gründungstheorie im Interesse der Gesellschafter, der Arbeitnehmer, der Gläubiger, der Dritten und anderer Rechtssubjekte. In diesem Sinne enthalten die erwähnten Rechtssysteme Regelungen, die an die Kompromiss-Kombinationstheorie des Personalstatuts juristischer Personen anknüpfen. Diese Tendenz, die in Kontinentaleuropa schon deutlich sichtbar ist, fördert die internationale Harmonisierung der Entscheidungen.

Eine nahezu gleichgewichtige Verbindung der Prämissen von Gründungs- und Sitztheorie wurde im Brüsseler EWG-Übereinkommen vom 29. Februar 1968 über die gegenseitige Anerkennung von Gesellschaften und juristischen Personen vorgesehen, das jedoch nicht in Kraft getreten ist.[33] Gemäß Art. 1 dieses Übereinkommens werden die Gesellschaften des bürgerlichen und des Handelsrechts einschließlich der Genossenschaften ohne weiteres anerkannt, wenn sie nach dem Recht eines Vertragsstaates gegründet worden sind, das ihnen die Fähigkeit zuerkennt, Träger von Rechten und Pflichten zu sein, und wenn sie ihren satzungsmäßigen Sitz innerhalb eines der Hoheitsgebiete haben, für die dieses Übereinkommen gilt.[34]

Auch im Haager Übereinkommen vom 1. Juni 1956 über die Anerkennung der Rechtspersönlichkeit ausländischer Gesellschaften, Personenverbindungen und Stiftungen (ausgearbeitet im Rahmen der Haager Konferenz für das Internationale Privatrecht, noch nicht in Kraft getreten[35]), sowie in der Resolution des Instituts für Internationales Recht, die während der Warschauer Session im Jahre 1965 verfaßt wurde,[36] finden sich Kombinationen der Gründungs- und Sitztheorie.

---

[33] Das Übereinkommen ist von Belgien, Deutschland, Frankreich, Italien und Luxemburg ratifiziert worden.

[34] Anders wurde diese Vorschrift von Jakubowski (oben N. 7) S. 274-275 beurteilt.

[35] Das Übereinkommen ist von Belgien, Frankreich, Luxemburg, den Niederlanden und Spanien ratifiziert worden.

[36] Siehe Jakubowski (oben N. 7) S. 275.

Trotz der gegenseitigen Durchdringung und Ergänzung der Prämissen von Gründungs- und Sitztheorie in der Praxis scheinen aber die Kontroversen zwischen diesen Theorien auch weiterhin über das Problem der „Zulässigkeit der Gründung juristischer Personen nach dem Recht des Staates, in dem der Sitz einer bestimmten juristischen Person sich nicht befindet und befinden wird", hinauszugehen.[37] Die Kontroversen betreffen denn auch u.a. solche wichtigen Fragen wie die Anforderungen, die nach jeder dieser Theorien für den Statutwechsel einer juristischen Person zu erfüllen sind, die Zulässigkeit und die kollisionsrechtlichen Folgen der Sitzverlegung einer juristischen Person ins Ausland und – was für die EU-Mitgliedstaaten und EU-Beitrittskandidaten von wesentlicher Bedeutung ist – die Übereinstimmung der Prämissen beider Theorien, insbesondere aber der Sitztheorie, mit den Bestimmungen über die Niederlassungsfreiheit im Römischen Vertrag vom 25. März 1957 zur Gründung der Europäischen Wirtschaftsgemeinschaft.

3.3 Ausbreitung und Implementierung der Sitztheorie in Europa

Die Sitztheorie wurde für die Bestimmung des Personalstatuts juristischer Personen im Kollisionsrecht der meisten EU-Mitgliedstaaten (Belgien, Deutschland, Frankreich, Griechenland, Luxemburg, Österreich, Portugal und Spanien) sowie in anderen Staaten Europas (u.a. Rumänien und Estland), darunter auch in Polen übernommen.

Von den neueren Regelungen, in denen die Prämissen dieser Theorie angewandt wurden, ist die im rumänischen Gesetz vom 7. September 1992 zur Regelung der Rechtsverhältnisse des internationalen Privatrechts (im folgenden „rum. IPRG") vorgesehene Lösung beachtenswert, die in der konsequenten Anwendung der Prämissen der Sitztheorie und in einer originellen Verbindung der Konzeption des Satzungssitzes mit der Konzeption des tatsächlichen Sitzes besteht. Gemäß Art. 40 rum. IPRG ist eine juristische Person der Rechtsordnung des Staates unterstellt, in dessen Hoheitsgebiet gemäß ihrer Gründungsurkunde ihr Sitz liegt; hat die juristische Person danach Sitze in mehreren Staaten, so ist der tatsächliche Sitz maßgebend für die Bestimmung der Rechtsordnung, der die juristische Person unterstellt ist; unter dem tatsächlichen Sitz wird der Ort verstanden, an dem sich der Hauptsitz der Leitung und Verwaltung der satzungsmäßigen Tätigkeit befindet, selbst wenn die Beschlüsse dieser Stelle auf Weisung von Aktionären und Gesellschaftern aus anderen Staaten gefaßt werden.[38]

Dagegen hat der estnische Gesetzgeber in der neuen Kodifikation des Kollisionsrechts eine Kombination der Sitztheorie (die Konzeption des tatsächlichen Verwaltungssitzes wurde durch die Konzeption des Exploatationszentrums er-

---

[37] So Jakubowski (oben N. 6) S. 76.
[38] Siehe Ch. Mindach, *Das neue rumänische IPR-Gesetz von 1992*, BfAI (Köln 1993) S. 30.

gänzt) mit der Gründungstheorie umgesetzt. Gemäß § 133 des estnischen Zivilgesetzbuches vom 13. Juni 1994 (im folgenden „estn. ZGB") unterliegt nur die
Gründung einer juristischen Person in Estland dem estnischen Recht. Für die
Rechts- und Geschäftsfähigkeit einer ausländischen juristischen Person ist dagegen
das Recht des Staates maßgebend, in dem ihre Hauptverwaltung sich befindet; wird
die Haupttätigkeit einer ausländischen juristischen Person nicht in demselben Staat
betrieben, in dem ihre Hauptverwaltung sich befindet, so ist das Recht des Staates
maßgebend, in dem sie ihre Haupttätigkeit betreibt; diese Regel findet auch auf Filialen ausländischer juristischer Personen Anwendung (Art. 134 estn. ZGB).[39]

3.4   Hauptsächliche Kollisionsentscheidung

Die bisher gemachten Bemerkungen und Empfehlungen, die den Anwendungsbereich und die Anknüpfungskriterien der das Personalstatut juristischer Personen be-
stimmenden Kollisionsnormen im polnischen IPR-Gesetz von 1965 betreffen, ergänzt um die ausgewählten Grundinformationen über die Natur, die Ausbreitung
sowie die Implementierung der Gründungs- und Sitztheorie (eine tiefgreifendere
Beschreibung und Vergleichung dieser Theorien würde den Rahmen dieses Beitrages sprengen[40]), helfen noch nicht bei der Entscheidung über das grundsätzliche
Problem, das auf folgende Frage zurückgeführt werden kann: Besteht Bedarf für
eine Abkehr von der in diesem Bereich angenommenen Sitztheorie zu Gunsten der
Gründungstheorie oder der Kombinationstheorie und wenn ja, welche Variante dieser Theorien verdient den Vorzug? Auf Grund einer allgemeinen Beurteilung der
Tauglichkeit der Gründungs- und Sitztheorie für die Kollisionslegislatur muß man
feststellen, daß die Entscheidung für eine dieser Theorien vor allem von der Beant-
wortung folgender, hauptsächlich aus dem Bereich der Rechtspolitik stammenden,
Fragen abhängt: Wie beurteilt man wirtschaftliche und politische Einflüsse sowie
das Bedürfnis der Kontrolle der Großbetriebe und welcher Umfang soll der Wil-
lensautonomie im internationalen Privatrecht zuerkannt werden?[41] Es ist schwierig,
die Antwort ohne Berücksichtigung der im innerstaatlichen materiellen Recht be-
vorzugten Interessen und Werte zu geben. Wendet man die aufgezählten Kriterien
auf das polnische Recht an, so scheint die Auffassung begründet, daß in dieser Sache entscheidende Bedeutung einem vernünftigen Kompromiß zwischen den Interessen verschiedener Sozialgruppen und Teilnehmer des zivilrechtlichen Verkehrs
zukommen soll.

Die unter verschiedenen Gesichtspunkten und mit unterschiedlichen Argumenten vorgebrachte Kritik an der Tauglichkeit der Gründungs- und der Sitztheorie für

---

[39] Siehe Estland: Neues IPR, *IPRax* (1996) S. 440.
[40] Dazu siehe oben N. 30 und das dort zitierte Schrifttum.
[41] Vgl. B. Grossfeld (oben N. 30) S. 6.

die Bestimmung des Personalstatuts einer juristischen Person führt zu der Folgerung, daß jede dieser Theorien bedeutende Vorzüge und Mängel hat, die sich, von ihrem verschiedenen Charakter unabhängig, im Prinzip ausgleichen (insbesondere kann die Anwendung beider Theorien zu ähnlichen Resultaten führen). Allerdings scheint die Konzeption des Satzungssitzes den übrigen Personalstatutskonzeptionen möglicherweise geringfügig überlegen zu sein. Diese Konzeption gewährt nämlich in größerem Ausmaß die Rechtssicherheit, die als Universalwert nicht nur den Schutz der Mitglieder, der Arbeitnehmer, der Gläubiger und der anderen mit der juristischen Person in Form verschiedener Rechtsverhältnisse verbundenen Personen, sondern im bestimmten Umfang und trotz zu geringer Elastizität auch den Schutz und die Entwicklung des internationalen Kapitalmarktes gewährleistet.

Für die Entscheidung über den Grundsatz der Bestimmung des Personalstatuts juristischer Personen im novellierten polnischen IPR-Gesetz sollte man jedoch auch andere Argumente zusätzlich in Betracht ziehen, insbesondere den aktuellen Stand und die Tendenzen im Bereich der Regelung des Personalstatuts juristischer Personen sowie heimische Traditionen in diesem Bereich. Sowohl in der Europäischen Union als auch im gesamten Europa überwiegen die Kollisionsrechtssysteme, die der Sitztheorie folgen. Auch die Umsetzung der Gründungstheorie im neuen internationalen Privatrecht der Schweiz und Italiens kann man nur schwerlich als Anzeichen einer in Europa sich abzeichnenden gegenläufigen Tendenz werten, wenn man berücksichtigt, daß a) in Italien die Entscheidung in dieser Sache ziemlich unerwartet in der Schlußetappe des Legislationsprozesses getroffen wurde, b) in den beiden erwähnten Rechtssystemen die ergänzende Anwendung der Sitztheorie vorgesehen wurde, und c) z.B. der rumänische und der estnische Gesetzgeber sich in ihren neuen Kollisionskodifikationen für die Sitztheorie entschieden haben.

Die polnische Rechtstradition im Bereich der Regelung des Personalstatuts der juristischen Personen ist, soweit es um das Hauptprinzip geht, eindeutig: In beiden polnischen Kollisionsgesetzen wurden die Prämissen der Sitztheorie umgesetzt. In den Vorschriften dieser Gesetze fehlten jedoch Hinweise für die Bestimmung, wie das Kriterium des Sitzes einer juristischen Person zu verstehen ist. Vor diesem Hintergrund entspricht die ausdrückliche Feststellung, daß diese Anknüpfung den Ort des satzungsmäßigen Sitzes einer juristischen Person betrifft, der polnischen Rechtstradition. Die Konzeption des satzungsmäßigen Sitzes einer juristischen Person entspricht auch dem Sprachgebrauch des diese Personen betreffenden polnischen materiellen Privat- und öffentlichen Rechts hinsichtlich des Begriffes „Sitz".

Die Konzeption des satzungsmäßigen Sitzes einer juristischen Person würde der Ergänzung bedürfen, weil die Bestimmung des Sitzes im Gründungsakt einer juristischen Person nach dem Recht einiger Staaten nicht erforderlich ist. Für diese Fälle sollte man die Anwendung der Gründungstheorie erwägen, etwa an den im § 18 ung. IPRD enthaltenen Begriff der „Registrierung" anknüpfend. Erst in Ermangelung einer Registrierung könnte die Konzeption des tatsächlichen Verwaltungssitzes einer juristischen Person in Frage kommen, in ähnlicher Weise wie dies im Falle mehrfacher Sitze in Art. 40 rum. IPRD vorgesehen ist. Im Ergebnis würde die grundsätzliche Anknüpfung an die Kombinationstheorie mit Vorrang der Sitztheorie erreicht, wobei unter „Sitz„ der im Gründungsakt einer juristischen Person bestimmte Sitz zu verstehen ist.

4.   NOVELLIERUNGSENTWURF

Als Ergebnis der obigen Erwägungen ergibt sich folgender Vorschlag: a) Die Erweiterung des Art. 9 § 2 IPRG über die Regelung der Fähigkeit einer juristischen Person hinaus im Sinne einer grundsätzlichen Maßgeblichkeit des am satzungsmäßigen Sitz einer juristischen Person geltenden Rechtes b) die Ergänzung des in dieser Weise geänderten Art. 9 § 2 IPRG um einen zweiten Satz, der für den Fall des Fehlens eines Satzungssitzes das Recht desjenigen Staates für anwendbar erklärt, in dem die Registrierung der juristischen Person erfolgt ist, und in Ermangelung der Registrierung das Recht desjenigen Staates, in dem sich der tatsächliche Sitz des Verwaltungsorganes der juristischen Person befindet, c) die Zulassung der einstufigen Weiterverweisung in einem an Art. 9 § 2 IPRG anzufügenden weiteren Paragraphen, d) die Beibehaltung der Ausnahme des Art. 9 § 3 IPRG in Hinblick auf juristische Personen (dieser Paragraph betrifft jetzt sowohl juristische als auch natürliche Personen), e) die Aufnahme eines Kataloges der wichtigsten von der Reichweite des Personalstatuts juristischer Personen erfaßten Punkte f) die Aufnahme der das Personalstatut juristischer Personen betreffenden Vorschriften in einem abgesonderten, in vier Paragraphen geteilten Artikel, es sei denn, daß dies infolge der neuen Abfassung dieser Vorschriften unmöglich wäre.

Die neue Fassung des Personalstatuts juristischer Personen im polnischen internationalen Privatrecht könnte folgenden Wortlaut haben:

§ 1. Eine juristische Person wird nach dem Recht des Staates beurteilt, in dem sich ihr im Gründungsakt bestimmter Sitz befindet. In Ermangelung eines solchen Sitzes ist das Rechts des Staates maßgebend, in dem die juristische Person registriert wurde und in Ermangelung der Registrierung das Rechts des Staates, im dem das Verwaltungsorgan der juristischen Person tätig ist.

§ 2. Verweist das für eine juristische Person maßgebende Recht auf ein anderes Recht, so ist dieses andere Recht anzuwenden.

§ 3. Wenn eine juristische Person jedoch ein Rechtsgeschäft im Bereich ihres Unternehmens vornimmt, so wird ihre Fähigkeit nach dem Recht des Staates beurteilt, in dem sich der Sitz dieses Unternehmens befindet.

§ 4. Insbesondere unterliegen dem [nach den vorstehenden Vorschriften] für eine juristische Person maßgebenden Recht:
1)   die Gründung, Umwandlung und Auflösung;
2)   die Rechtsnatur;

3) der Name oder die Firmenbezeichnung;
4) die Rechts- und Handlungsfähigkeit;
5) die innere Struktur und die Tätigkeitsgrundsätze der Organe;
6) die Vertretung der juristischen Person;
7) der Erwerb und Verlust der Mitgliedschaft sowie die damit verbundenen Rechte und Pflichten;
8) die Haftung der Mitglieder für die Verpflichtungen der juristischen Person;
9) die Änderung des Gründungsaktes.

SUMMARY
LEGAL PERSONS IN POLISH PIL – PAST, PRESENT AND THE NEW DRAFT LEGISLATION

1. According to Art. 1 § 1 of the old Polish private international law of 1926 the capacity of legal persons, companies and associations was governed by the law of the state where their seat was located. The term "capacity" was understood as relating to both the legal capacity and the capacity to act. It was as a rule the seat of the main administration of such entities.

2. Similarly, under Art. 9 § 2 of the new Polish private international law of 1965 (referred to as „P.I.L.") the capacity of a legal person is governed by the law of the state in which this person has its seat. This provision gives no further guidance as to the meaning of the term „seat". This term is commonly understood as the real seat of the central management (directorate) of a legal person.
However, if a legal person performs legal transactions through its enterprise, the capacity of that person shall be governed by the law of the state where the seat of this enterprise is located (Art. 9 § 3 P.I.L.).

3. The proposed new version of the statutory regulation of the law applicable to the legal person contains the following provisions:
Art. ...
§ 1. A legal person is governed by the law of the state where its seat is located, as determined in the foundation charter. In the absence of such a seat, the law of the state where a legal person is registered shall apply, and in the absence of a registration, the law of the state where the governing body of the legal person is acting shall apply.
§ 2. If the law applicable to a legal person refers to another law, this law is to apply.
§ 3. However, if a legal person performs legal transactions through its enterprise, the capacity of that person shall be governed by the law of the state where the seat of this enterprise is located.

§ 4. The applicable law governs particularly the following questions:
1) foundation, transformation and liquidation;
2) legal nature;
3) name or firm name;
4) capacity;
5) internal structure and activity principles of the organs;
6) representation;
7) acquisition and loss of membership as well as rights and duties connected with it;
8) responsibility of members for obligations of legal persons;
9) changes of the foundation charter.

Interim Relief under the Brussels and Lugano Conventions

Lennart Pålsson[*]

1.   INTRODUCTION

The title of this essay in honour of my learned friend and colleague KURT SIEHR may call for a few comments: The term "interim relief" will be used synonymously and interchangeably with the term "provisional, including protective, measures" figuring in Article 24 of the Brussels and Lugano Conventions. Those two conventions are identical for all purposes relevant to this contribution and will, for convenience, be referred to as "the Convention", except where it appears necessary to distinguish between them. Finally, the title ought perhaps to have been preceded by words indicating that my contribution is limited to *selected* problems relating to the present theme. Indeed, this theme is a fairly vast one, which has already been treated in several monographs and numerous articles, as well as in all handbooks on the Convention. There can be no question of dealing with it comprehensively or exhaustively within the necessarily limited space conceded to the contributors to this *Festschrift*.

---

[*]   Professor emeritus of International Law, Lund University, Sweden.

J. Basedow et al., eds., Private Law in the International Arena – Liber Amicorum Kurt Siehr
© 2000, T.M.C.Asser Press, The Hague, The Netherlands

In the first place, I shall confine myself to provisional measures directly relating to the defendant's property. Other kinds of interim relief – such as, for instance, orders for the disclosure of information, for the discovery of documents or for the designation of a court expert or other orders for obtaining evidence – may require some special considerations and will in any event not be treated here.

Secondly, my contribution is limited to problems of jurisdiction to grant interim relief and to the recognition and enforcement of orders for such relief. Even within the area so defined several issues will be dealt with only in outline. Other questions which may arise in relation to the grant of interim relief in international cases, such as choice of law and *lis pendens*, will not be considered at all.

Although the present subject is within the ambit of the Convention, it involves numerous aspects pertaining to the national laws of the Contracting States and could well be treated from the specific point of view of one or other of those States (such as the writer's own State). It is nevertheless not my intention to do so. Focus will largely be placed on the relevant cases decided by the European Court. Decisions of national courts and other national source material will only be used for the purpose of illustrating various problems.

Before embarking on the subject, it should be noted that the Convention, pursuant to Article 57(1), does not affect any conventions to which the Contracting States are or will be parties and which in relation to particular matters, govern jurisdiction or the recognition or enforcement of judgments. There are a number of such conventions containing provisions on provisional measures. They include the 1926 Brussels Convention Relating to the Immunity of State-owned Ships, the 1933 Rome Convention Relating to the Precautionary Attachment of Aircraft and the 1952 Brussels Convention Relating to the Arrest of Sea-going Ships. Interim orders for maintenance are covered by the two Hague Conventions of 1958 and 1973 on the Recognition and Enforcement of Decisions Relating to Maintenance Obligations and by the Nordic Convention of 1962 on the Recovery of Maintenance Contributions. None of these instruments will be adverted to in what follows.

At the time of writing it seems unlikely that the substance of the questions to be treated in this paper will be affected by the current work aimed at revising the Convention. However this may be, it has not been possible to take account of any material which was not available by the end of May, 1999.

2.   JURISDICTION

2.1 **Based on the General Rules of the Convention**

It is well settled that a court having jurisdiction as to the substance of a case under one of the heads of jurisdiction laid down in Articles 2 and 5 to 18 also has jurisdiction to order provisional or protective measures.[1] This is not subject to any further conditions being fulfilled.[2] It is immaterial, for instance, that the defendant may not have any assets in the country where the application for provisional measures is made and that, therefore, the order requested may not be susceptible of enforcement in that country. The rule applies before as well as after commencement of the main proceedings.

If, however, the parties have validly excluded the jurisdiction of the courts in a dispute arising under a contract and have referred that dispute to arbitration, there are no courts of any Contracting State that have jurisdiction over the principal proceedings. Consequently, a party to such a contract is not in a position to make an application for provisional or protective measures to a court that would have jurisdiction under the Convention as to the substance of the case.[3] In these circumstances it is only under Article 24, if at all, that a court may be empowered under the Convention to order such measures.

2.2   Based on Article 24

2.2.1   *General*

Without in any way detracting from the principle set out above, Article 24 provides an additional rule of jurisdiction. That provision reads:

"Application may be made to the courts of a Contracting State for such provisional, including protective, measures as may be available under the law of that State, even if, under this Convention, the courts of another Contracting State have jurisdiction as to the substance of the matter."

Article 24 constitutes an exception to the general system for allocating jurisdiction under the Convention. Its purpose is to strengthen the creditor's position by enabling him to seek interim relief in his "nearest" court, even if that court lacks jurisdiction to adjudicate on the merits of the claim. This situation occurs mainly where the case does not present any connection with the country of the forum sufficient to found jurisdiction under Articles 2 or 5 to 18 (as, for example, where the only connection is the presence of the defendant's assets in that country). In addition, Article 24 covers the situation in which such a connection does exist, but where the court nevertheless lacks jurisdiction over the merits because the courts of another Contracting State were first seised of proceedings involving the same cause of action and between the same parties (*lis pendens* under Article 21).

The jurisdiction afforded by Article 24 may be of substantial practical impor-

---

[1] A different view has been put forward by Schlosser, *EuGVÜ* (Munich 1996), Art. 24 no. 1.

[2] See Case C-391/95 *Van Uden* v. *Deco-Line* [1998] ECR I-7091, paras. 19 and 22. Followed in Case C-99/96 *Mietz* v. *Intership Yachting* [1999] ECR I-2277, paras. 40-41.

[3] *Van Uden* (preceding note) para. 24.

tance for the creditor, especially in cases where assets belonging to the defendant are located in the country in which interim relief is sought (whereas, perhaps, no such assets exist in the country whose courts have jurisdiction to try the substantive dispute). The courts of the country where such assets are present and where the interim order, if made, is capable of enforcement are often in a better position than other courts to act swiftly and efficiently and to deal with the various issues raised by an application for interim relief. This idea has been expressed by the European Court in the *Denilauler* case, where the Court emphasised that the granting of the type of measures envisaged in Article 24 requires particular care on the part of the court and detailed knowledge of the actual circumstances in which the measure is to take effect, and went on to state that:[4]

> "The courts of the place or, in any event, of the Contracting State, where the assets subject to the measures sought are located, are those best able to assess the circumstances which may lead to the grant or refusal of the measures sought or to the laying down of procedures and conditions which the plaintiff must observe in order to guarantee the provisional and protective character of the measures ordered. The Convention has taken account of these requirements by providing in Article 24 that application may be made to the courts of a Contracting State for such provisional, including protective, measures as may be available under the law of that State, even if, under the Convention, the courts of another Contracting State have jurisdiction as to the substance of the matter."

The provision does, however, give rise to several problems. It is couched in rather vague terms, which leave a wide scope for different interpretations, and its relationship and interplay with other provisions of the Convention and with the national laws of the Contracting States are not very clear, to say the least. In addition, there is the risk that Article 24, when combined with certain national rules of jurisdiction, may prove to be unduly "generous" towards the creditor. The weight of this argument depends on the answers given to the questions to be treated in the following sections.

2.2.2 *Measures covered by Article 24*

Article 24 applies to "such provisional, including protective, measures" as may be available under the law of the forum. It does not specify what measures are included within this concept. Nor do the official reports on the Convention or on the various Accession Conventions shed any light on the question. In the national laws of the Contracting States the concept embraces a wide and variegated range of orders.[5]

---

[4] Case 125/79 *Denilauler* v. *Couchet Frères* [1980] ECR 1553, paras. 15-16.
[5] For comparative surveys see, e.g., Heiss, *Einstweiliger Rechtsschutz im europäischen Zivilrechtsverkehr (Art. 24 EuGVÜ)* (Berlin 1987) p. 51-102; Merkt, *Les mesures provisoires en droit*

Obviously, however, the concept as used in the Convention must be given an autonomous interpretation, to be based primarily on the objectives and scheme of the Convention. It cannot be taken for granted, therefore, that a measure characterised as provisional or protective in a national legal system is to be so treated for the purposes of the Convention.

A definition of the concept was given by the European Court in *Reichert (No. 2)*.[6] It was stated there that the expression "provisional, including protective, measures" must be understood as referring to "measures which, in matters within the scope of the Convention, are intended to preserve a factual or legal situation so as to safeguard rights the recognition of which is sought elsewhere from the court having jurisdiction as to the substance of the matter". The case itself involved an *action paulienne* under French law (Article 1167 of the Civil Code) brought by a creditor challenging a donation of immovable property which had been made by his debtor. Whilst such an action enables the creditor's security to be protected by preventing the dissipation of his debtor's assets, it does not seek to preserve a factual or legal situation. On the contrary, its purpose is to obtain a judgment varying the legal situation of the assets of the debtor and that of the beneficiary of the transaction by ordering the revocation as against the creditor of the disposition effected by the debtor in fraud of the creditor's rights. Such an action, therefore, was held not to come within the scope of Article 24.

Judging from the definition provided by the European Court, it seems that the "core" of the scope of Article 24 consists of safeguarding measures designed to preserve the *status quo* pending the final adjudication of the case, thereby preventing the debtor from dealing with his assets in such a way as to risk frustrating the enforcement of any judgment against him obtained by the creditor in due course. Typical examples are *Mareva* injunctions under English law, orders for *saisie conservatoire* or *saisie-arrêt* under French law and *Arrest* orders under German or Swiss law.

The national laws of the Contracting States, however, also provide for a variety of interim orders whose purpose is not to preserve the *status quo*, but which rather enable the creditor to obtain provisional satisfaction, wholly or in part, of his claim (*Befriedigungsverfügungen*). Such orders may be for the performance of some act such as the delivery-up of goods or the payment of a sum of money. They tend in practice often to render the conduct of the principal proceedings unnecessary and thus to become definitive. It may be very difficult, if not impossible, especially in international cases, to secure the return of assets handed over or repayment of the sum awarded, as the case may be, if the creditor's claim ultimately fails.

---

international privé (Neuchâtel 1993) p. 22-52; Rose (ed.), *Pre-emptive Remedies in Europe* (London 1992).

[6] Case C-261/90 *Reichert* v. *Dresdner Bank* [1992] ECR I-2149, para. 34.

In French law, for instance, an important remedy is that known as *référé-provision*. By such an order the creditor may provisionally be granted full or partial satisfaction of his claim, provided that there is no serious dispute as to the debtor's liability.[7] In Dutch law a similar function is fulfilled by measures ordered in the proceedings known as *kort geding*.[8] A third example is the *Leistungsverfügung* developed in German law. This is an interim order, usually for the payment of a sum of money, requiring the debtor to perform his obligation immediately, which can be made if there is a pressing need for provisional satisfaction of the applicant's claim.[9] The legal systems of other Contracting States make provision for injunctions more or less similar to those mentioned here.[10]

Do orders of this type qualify as provisional measures within the meaning of Article 24? Some writers are inclined to answer this question in the negative.[11] The reason is essentially that such orders are likely to preempt the decision on the substance of the case, or even to dispose effectively of the whole action in favour of the plaintiff, and that they may be recognised and enforced in other Contracting States. If these orders could be made by a court which lacks jurisdiction over the merits, the door would largely be open to circumvention or even subversion of the ordinary rules of jurisdiction laid down by the Convention. It would also seem to be difficult to bring orders of the present type within the definition of provisional measures given by the European Court in *Reichert* (*No. 2*), since apparently that definition is limited to measures which involve a freezing of an existing factual or legal situation.

Nevertheless, other writers have argued – with some support in national case law – that these orders do amount to provisional (albeit not protective) measures for the purposes of Article 24, at least in certain circumstances.[12] This view has in part been endorsed by the European Court in the *Van Uden* case.[13] That case involved a contract between the Dutch company Van Uden and a German company. The contract contained an arbitration clause. Pursuant to that clause, Van Uden instituted arbitration proceedings in the Netherlands claiming payment of certain sums due from the

---

[7] "Dans les cas où l'existence de l'obligation n'est pas sérieusement contestable", see *inter alia* Article 809 of the New Code of Civil Procedure (*Nouveau Code de procédure civile*).

[8] Such orders were involved in the *Van Uden* and the *Mietz* cases cited supra n. 2.

[9] See Heiss (supra n. 5) p. 57-61.

[10] For Swedish law see Pålsson, 1996 *Svensk Juristtidning* 385, at 398.

[11] E.g., Collins, *Essays in International Litigation and the Conflict of Laws* (Oxford 1994) p. 37-39; Heiss (supra n. 5) p. 44-49 and *passim*; Huet, *Clunet* (1989) 96-99. Cf. point 22 of the "Principles on Provisional and Protective Measures in International Litigation" adopted by the International Law Association, *ILARep. of the 67th Conf.* (Helsinki 1996) p. 202.

[12] See, e.g., Gaudemet-Tallon, *Les Conventions de Bruxelles et de Lugano* (2nd ed., Paris 1996) p. 194-195; Geimer/Schütze, *Europäisches Zivilverfahrensrecht* (Munich 1997) Art. 24 nos. 20-22; Kropholler, *Europäisches Zivilprozeßrecht* (6th ed., Heidelberg 1998) Art. 24 no. 5.

[13] *Van Uden* v. *Deco-Line* (supra n. 2). See also *Mietz* v. *Intership Yachting*, ibid.

German company under the contract. Van Uden also applied to a Dutch court (that of its own domicile) for interim relief in *kort geding* proceedings. In its application, it sought an order for payment of an amount apparently corresponding to that claimed in the arbitration proceedings.

The European Court, to which several questions were referred, held first that Article 24 may confer jurisdiction on the court hearing an application for provisional measures even where the proceedings on the substance of the case have been commenced, or are to be conducted, before arbitrators. Concerning the nature of Van Uden's application, the Court took the view that it is not possible to rule out in advance, in a general and abstract manner, that interim payment of a contractual consideration, even in an amount corresponding to that sought as principal relief, may be necessary in order to ensure the practical effect of the decision on the substance of the case and may, in certain cases, appear justified with regard to the interests involved.[14] However, the Court then gave consideration to the objections raised against including such orders within the scope of Article 24 and ultimately held that interim payment of a contractual consideration does *not* constitute a provisional measure within the meaning of that provision unless two conditions are met. First, repayment to the defendant of the sum awarded must be guaranteed if the plaintiff is unsuccessful as regards the substance of the case. Second, the measure sought must relate only to specific assets of the defendant located or to be located within the confines of the territorial jurisdiction of the court to which application is made.

These restrictions, it is submitted, are quite apposite and badly needed if evasion of the jurisdictional rules of the Convention is to be forestalled. Although the judgment is only concerned with contractual considerations, it must probably be assumed that similar restrictions apply, for instance, in respect of interim orders for the payment of damages or for the delivery-up of property.

Interim relief plays a significant part in several branches of *family law*. Most matters of family law, however, are excluded from the scope of the Convention by virtue of Article 1, paragraph 2(1). One important exception is maintenance obligations, which are fully governed by the rules of the Convention. The same is also true of interim orders for maintenance, which fall within the scope of Article 24.[15] Although such orders go far beyond the limit of merely safeguarding the creditor – indeed, they secure him full satisfaction for the period specified in the order – they seem unlikely to be affected by the decision of the European Court in *Van Uden*.

---

[14] For an earlier decision to the same effect rendered in the context of Community law, see Case C-393/96 P(R) *Antonissen* v. *Council and Commission* [1997] ECR I-441, para. 37.

[15] See Case 120/79 *De Cavel* v. *De Cavel* [1980] ECR 731.

2.2.3 *Effect of Article 24 on jurisdiction*

There are two basically different conceptions of Article 24. According to one view, that provision is of the same nature as the rules of jurisdiction contained in Articles 2 to 18, providing an independent and mandatory ground of jurisdiction to grant interim relief. It operates to confer such jurisdiction on the courts of any Contracting State in circumstances in which the courts of another Contracting State possess jurisdiction as to substance and without regard to national rules requiring some kind of connection to be shown to exist between the parties to or subject-matter of the litigation and the country of the court applied to.[16] This view seems to have been squarely endorsed in an English case, in which it was stated that "the Convention *requires* each contracting state to make available, in aid of the court of another contracting state, such provisional and protective measures as its own domestic law would afford if its courts were trying the substantive action".[17]

According to the rival conception, Article 24 is merely permissive in nature: it authorises, but does not require, the national laws of Contracting States to provide for jurisdiction to grant interim relief in support of substantive proceedings pending or contemplated in the courts of another Contracting State. On this view Article 24 does not, of itself, confer jurisdiction on any court, but does so only in conjunction with national rules of jurisdiction to grant such relief. Its function is to clarify that this type of jurisdiction is not limited to the courts having jurisdiction over the merits but that it can, alternatively, be based on relevant national rules. The Contracting States are left free to preserve those rules, to amend them, or to enact entirely new provisions on the subject.[18] By and large, this appears to be the prevailing view in most Contracting States.[19]

In principle, the reference to national law thus considered to form the gist of Article 24 includes the rules of exorbitant jurisdiction listed in Article 3, paragraph 2.[20] Indeed, although those rules cannot be invoked against defendants domiciled in a Contracting State, this prohibition applies only as far as Articles 5 to 18 are concerned. It does not extend to the special regime provided for by Article 24.[21]

---

[16] See, e.g., Grundmann, *Anerkennung und Vollstreckung ausländischer einstweiliger Massnahmen nach IPRG und Lugano-Übereinkommen* (Basle & Frankfurt a.M. 1996) p. 130-146; Kaye, *Civil Jurisdiction and Enforcement of Foreign Judgments* (Abingdon 1987) p. 1146-1148.

[17] *Republic of Haiti* v. *Duvalier* [1990] 1 QB 202, at 212 (CA). For criticism see Collins (supra n. 11), p. 37, characterising this suggestion as "almost certainly wrong as a matter of law".

[18] In the United Kingdom no jurisdiction of the present type existed prior to the coming into force (in 1987) of the Civil Jurisdiction and Judgments Act 1982. S. 25 of that Act gives effect to Article 24 of the Convention.

[19] See, e.g., Gaudemet-Tallon (supra n. 12) p. 197; Kropholler (supra n. 12) Art. 24 nos. 6-9; O'Malley/Layton, *European Civil Practice* (London 1989) p. 649-650.

[20] Provided that they are not discriminatory within the meaning of (what is now) Article 12 of the EC Treaty. See Case C-398/92 *Mund & Fester* v. *Hatrex* [1994] ECR I-467.

[21] See the *Van Uden* case (supra n. 2) at para. 42.

Much could be added to the discussion of these questions. Suffice it to say, however, that jurisdiction to grant interim relief in the circumstances envisaged by Article 24 seems in fact to be available in all Contracting States, albeit subject to conditions differing from one State to the other.

Whichever basic conception is adopted, the further and perhaps more interesting question arises as to whether, as has often been suggested by writers, Article 24 can (and must) be interpreted so as to impose some limitations on the jurisdiction to grant interim relief. An affirmative answer to this question has been given by the European Court.

The first time the question came up for consideration, although it did not have to be decided, was in the *Denilauler* case.[22] In that case, it will be recalled, the European Court clearly indicated that it is primarily for the courts of the State where the defendant' s assets are located to determine whether and, if so, what protective measures should be ordered.

This idea was followed up in the *Van Uden* case.[23] In that case the only connection with the Netherlands, before whose courts the question of granting interim relief arose, was apparently that the plaintiff was domiciled there. The defendant German company did not have any assets in the Netherlands, but it was engaged in international trade and could be expected to become a creditor there (so that any judgment against it could be enforced there). The referring Dutch court asked, *inter alia*, whether it is required, in order for the court hearing an application for interim relief to have jurisdiction, that the relief sought from it must take effect (or be capable of taking effect) in the Contracting State concerned and, if so, whether that means that the order applied for must be capable of enforcement in that State and whether it is then necessary for this condition to be fulfilled when the interim application is made, or whether it is sufficient that it can be reasonably expected to be fulfilled in the future. In other words, is it necessary for the defendant to have, or at least reasonably to be expected to have at a later point of time, assets in the country concerned?

The European Court ruled that "the granting of provisional or protective measures on the basis of Article 24 is conditional on, *inter alia*, the existence of a real connecting link between the subject-matter of the measures sought and the territorial jurisdiction of the Contracting State of the court before which those measures are sought". It was added that a court ordering measures on the basis of Article 24 must take into consideration the need to impose conditions or stipulations such as to guarantee their provisional or protective character.

This ruling does not seem to give a fully satisfactory answer to the question posed by the Dutch court. For whilst it is clear that the European Court wanted to

---

[22] *Denilauler* v. *Couchet Frères* (supra n. 4).
[23] *Van Uden* v. *Deco-Line* (supra n. 2).

impose a restriction on the use of national fora for the purpose of granting interim relief, it did not specify what is to be understood, more exactly, by "a real connecting link" required to exist between the subject-matter of the measures sought and the country whose courts are hearing the application. It seems safe to assume that it is sufficient for that requirement to be met if, at the time of application, the defendant possesses property in the country in question, so that the order requested will be susceptible of enforcement there. But does the same hold true in the other hypothesis submitted by the Dutch court, i.e. where this condition can reasonably be expected to be fulfilled in the future (a situation that may be quite practical in the case of a defendant engaged in international trade)? And is it conceivable, in the case of a request for an interim order *in personam*, that the requisite "real connecting link" would be held to exist if the defendant, although not having any assets in the country of the forum, was domiciled and resident there?[24] On these points there would seem to be a need for further clarification in the future.

Miscellaneous issues. Although a court may have jurisdiction to grant interim relief even if it lacks jurisdiction as to the main dispute, it has been suggested that the principle may not extend to cases where exclusive jurisdiction over the subject-matter of the proceedings is accorded to the courts of one Contracting State under Article 16.[25] In view of the paramount status of Article 16 this may well be true. No reported cases on this issue have been found.

No such doubts ought to exist in the case of exclusive jurisdiction being vested in the courts of a Contracting State by virtue of a prorogation agreement validly entered into under Article 17. That provision can hardly be interpreted so as to affect the jurisdiction of other courts to grant interim relief.[26] It may be the case, however, that the prorogation clause itself reserves, or must be interpreted as reserving, that power to the chosen court. Whether such a clause is effective to rule out the jurisdiction of other courts to grant interim relief is probably a matter to be determined according to the national law of the court to which application for provisional measures is made.[27]

The position is similar in the case of an arbitration agreement. Such an agreement will not, normally, have the effect of excluding the jurisdiction of courts to grant interim protection.[28] It is in accordance with this view that the European Court

---

[24] For an English case involving such a situation see *Crédit Suisse Fides Trust SA* v. *Cuoghi* [1997] 3 All ER 724 (CA).

[25] O'Malley/Layton (supra n. 19) p. 652. *Contra*, Geimer/ Schütze (supra n. 12) Art. 16 no. 29. For distinctions see Merkt (supra n. 5) p. 119-122.

[26] Cf. Collins (supra n. 11) p. 41-44; O'Malley/Layton (supra n. 19) p. 171, 652. But see Geimer/ Schütze (supra n. 12) Art. 17 no. 192; Merkt (supra n. 5) p. 122-125.

[27] For French cases involving this problem see Paris 17 November 1987, *Clunet* (1989) 96, note Huet, and Cass.civ. 17 December 1985, *Rev.crit.* (1986) 537, note Gaudemet-Tallon (the latter case is one falling outside the scope of the Convention).

[28] See on this subject, Collins (supra n. 11) p. 48-67.

held in *Van Uden* that a court may have jurisdiction to grant such relief under Article 24, even though the substance of the case is to be resolved by arbitration.[29] If, however, the arbitration agreement excludes, or must be interpreted as excluding, any judicial interference even as regards interim relief, it seems to be a matter for the national law of the court asked to grant such relief to decide whether effect is to be given to such a clause. This conclusion, it is submitted, is not incompatible with the ruling of the European Court in *Van Uden*.[30]

As has been seen, the principal effect of Article 24 is to enable a person to seek interim relief in a court which lacks jurisdiction over the merits. In many cases, however, it may be more or less uncertain, at the time when the application for such relief is made, whether the court applied to does or does not possess jurisdiction as to the merits of the dispute. In this situation, it is submitted, there is nothing to prevent the court from hearing the application for interim measures on the strength of Article 24 (in conjunction with relevant national rules). If such measures have been granted, there is no reason why their validity should lapse even if the court, at a later stage, should find that it has no jurisdiction over the main dispute.

The jurisdiction to grant interim relief conferred on a court under Article 24 includes the power to vary or to discharge any order made by that court.[31] There may be some room for doubt on this point in the case of an order issued at a time before the main proceedings were commenced in another Contracting State. Suppose, for instance, that an interim order is made by a court in Sweden, where assets belonging to the defendant are located, and that the main proceedings are subsequently instituted in Norway, where the defendant is domiciled. In Swedish law there is a provision to the effect that, once the main proceedings have become pending, it is for the court entertaining those proceedings alone to decide on the termination of the order even if it was made by another court.[32] Does this mean that the institution of the Norwegian proceedings has the effect of depriving the Swedish court of its power to discharge the order made by it? It is suggested that this question should be answered in the negative. The reason is that provisions of the type existing in Swedish law must probably be regarded as going to the question of local venue only and as having no application when the substantive claim is pursued in a foreign court.

---

[29] *Van Uden* v. *Deco-Line* (supra n. 2), paras. 23-34.

[30] In that case there was an express provision in Dutch law that an arbitration clause cannot preclude a party's right to seek interim relief (from the courts). Cf. the submissions of Advocate-General Léger, paras. 68-70.

[31] See, e.g., Geimer/ Schütze (supra n. 12) Art. 24 no. 17; Merkt (supra n. 5) p. 132-133.

[32] Ch. 15 s. 8 of the Code of Judicial Procedure (*rättegångsbalken*). For a similar provision in German law see s. 927, para. 2, of the Code of Civil Procedure (*Zivilprozeßordnung*).

2.2.4 *Material scope of Article 24*

Article 24 has the same material scope as the Convention as a whole. It applies in civil and commercial matters, subject to certain exceptions, see Article 1. This follows from the wording of the provision, which presupposes that, *under this Convention*, the courts of another Contracting State have jurisdiction as to the substance of the matter. That condition can only be met if the subject-matter of the proceedings, pursuant to Article 1, is within the scope of the Convention.

This proposition is fully borne out by the cases decided by the European Court. The Court has consistently held that the inclusion of provisional measures in the scope of the Convention must be determined, not by their own nature but by the nature of the rights which they serve to protect.[33]

On the one hand, Article 24 cannot be relied on to bring within the scope of the Convention provisional or protective measures relating to matters which are excluded from it. Accordingly, since the status of natural persons and rights in property arising out of a matrimonial relationship are so excluded by the second paragraph of Article 1, it has been held that provisional protective measures – such as the placing under seal or the freezing of the assets of the spouses – in the course of proceedings for divorce equally do not fall within the scope of the Convention if they concern or are closely connected with such questions.[34]

On the other hand, the Convention, including its Article 24, is applicable where the provisional measures sought relate to matters falling within the scope *ratione materiae* of the Convention.[35] This is so, for instance, in the case of a claim for interim payment of maintenance even if that question is ancillary to a principal claim, such as a petition for divorce, which is outside the scope of the Convention.[36]

2.2.5 *Relevance of the defendant's domicile?*

It is often assumed that, for Article 24 to apply, the defendant must be domiciled in a Contracting State.[37] On this view, where the defendant is not so domiciled the jurisdiction of the courts of each Contracting State must be determined solely by reference to the (autonomous) law of that State. This is, of course, in accordance with the general system for allocating jurisdiction laid down in Articles 2 to 4 of the Convention.

---

[33] Case 143/78 *de Cavel* v. *de Cavel* [1979] ECR 1055, para. 8; *Reichert* (*No. 2*) (supra n. 6), para. 32.
[34] *De Cavel* (*No. 1*) (preceding note). See also Case 25/81 *C.H.W.* v. *G.J.H.* [1982] ECR 1189.
[35] *De Cavel* (*No. 2*) (supra note 15); *Van Uden* (supra note 2) para. 34.
[36] *De Cavel* (*No. 2*), ibid.
[37] See, e.g., Geimer/ Schütze (supra n. 12) Art. 24 no. 5; Kropholler (supra n. 12) Art. 24 no. 2.

Nevertheless, the better view would seem to be that this system does not extend to Article 24. As has been argued especially in England, that provision should be held to apply independently of the defendant's domicile.[38] The reason is that the judgment to be rendered by the court entertaining the substantive claim will be entitled to recognition and enforcement in the country in which provisional measures are sought even where the defendant is not domiciled in a Contracting State and where jurisdiction to hear the substantive proceedings is therefore based on national law. This being so, the creditor has a legitimate interest in being able to obtain provisional measures under Article 24 in order to safeguard the enforcement of the future judgment in that country. It is reasonable that this interest should be protected by the Convention. Nor should it make any difference that, in the case of a defendant not domiciled within the Convention area, jurisdiction for the main proceedings is only indirectly, via Article 4, based on the Convention. It may also be noted in this connection that, for similar reasons, the provision in Article 21 on *lis pendens* has been held to apply irrespective of the domicile of the parties to the proceedings involved.[39]

If the view supported here is adopted, it follows that jurisdiction to grant interim relief under Article 24 will be subject to the limitations enunciated in the *Van Uden* case (see above, section 2.2.3) even if the defendant is not domiciled in a Contracting State.

3. RECOGNITION AND ENFORCEMENT

3.1 General

Questions of international recognition and enforcement of orders for interim relief used to be of rare occurrence in the past. In the first place, many, perhaps most, such orders were themselves, expressly or implicitly, "territorially limited", i.e. confined to assets situated within the territory of the forum State. Where an order is so re-stricted there can obviously be no question of enforcing it in other countries.

In this respect, however, a gradual change has been taking place in recent years.[40] A rather spectacular example is the development of the Mareva injunction in English law. Such an injunction, which originally could only be granted in respect

---

[38] There is at least one English case so holding, *X* v. *Y* [1990] 1 QB 220, at 229. And see Kaye (supra n. 16) p. 1144-1145; O'Malley/ Layton (supra n. 19) p. 168.

[39] Case C-351/89 *Overseas Union* v. *New Hampshire Ins.* [1991] ECR I-3317. In all probability the same holds true of Articles 22 and 23.

[40] Cf. Muir Watt, *Rev.crit.* (1998) 27-50.

of property in England, can now be granted worldwide.[41] Many other examples of provisional measures extending to assets abroad can be found in cases decided by the European Court and by national courts.

Sometimes it may be doubtful whether an order for interim relief does or does not claim to have extraterritorial reach. This is a research subject of its own which must here be left unexplored. Suffice it to say that, in order for the present problem to arise, it is necessary that the decision presented for recognition or enforcement should be intended to have extraterritorial effect.

Secondly, national legislation usually gave little scope for the recognition or enforcement of orders purporting to have such effect. Subject to some exceptions, in particular as regards interim orders for maintenance, international conventions did not alter this position. In this respect, however, the Brussels Convention, and in its wake the Lugano Convention, broke new ground.

Indeed, interim orders are within the definition of judgments provided by Article 25 of the Convention. There is no requirement, similar to those usually found in earlier enforcement treaties, that the decision must be final and conclusive, or that it must have become *res judicata*.[42] In principle, therefore, interim orders benefit from the system of free movement of judgments laid down in the provisions of Title III of the Convention.

Accordingly, an interim measure issued by a court in a Contracting State, which is within the material scope of the Convention and which is enforceable in the State of origin, may be declared enforceable in other Contracting States, subject to the same conditions as those applicable to ordinary judgments. In particular, no review of the jurisdiction of the adjudicating court is normally permitted, not even where the court has based its jurisdiction on, possibly exorbitant, rules of national law.

The principle is, however, subject to significant exceptions. The first of these results from the decision of the European Court in the *Denilauler* case.[43] In that case, which involved an *ex parte* order made by a French court for the freezing of the defendant's bank account in Germany, it was held that judicial decisions authorising provisional or protective measures, which are delivered without the party against which they are directed having been summoned to appear and which are intended to be enforced without prior service, do not come within the system of recognition and enforcement provided for by Title III of the Convention. In other words, that system of rules only applies to such provisional measures as are ordered pursuant to adversary proceedings. This is so regardless of whether the order emanates from a court having or from a court not having jurisdiction to entertain the main action.

---

[41] This change was brought about by the decision in *Babanaft International Co.* v. *Bassatne* [1990] Ch 13 (CA). A worldwide order can also be made in aid of main proceedings taking place abroad. Illustrative examples are the *Republic of Haiti* and the *Crédit Suisse* cases (supra n. 17 and 24, respectively).

[42] Cf. the Jenard Report, OJ [1979] C 59/1 at 44.

[43] *Denilauler* v. *Couchet Frères* (supra n. 4).

The reasons given by the European Court for this restriction were essentially that:

All the provisions of the Convention, both those contained in Title II on jurisdiction and those contained in Title III on recognition and enforcement, express the intention to ensure that, within the scope of the objectives of the Convention, proceedings leading to the delivery of judicial decisions take place in such a way that the rights of the defence are observed. It is because of the guarantee given to the defendant in the original proceedings that the Convention, in Title III, is very liberal in regard to recognition and enforcement. In the light of these considerations it is clear that the Convention is fundamentally concerned with judicial decisions which, before the recognition and enforcement of them are sought in a State other than the State of origin, have been, or have been capable of being, the subject in that State of origin and under various procedures, of an inquiry in adversary proceedings. It cannot therefore be deduced from the general scheme of the Convention that a formal expression of intention was needed in order to exclude judgments of the type in question from recognition and enforcement.

Since it is in practice quite common for interim orders to be sought and obtained in *ex parte* proceedings, the rule in *Denilauler* is likely to assume considerable importance. It should be noted, however, that an order originally made *ex parte* can be brought within the provisions of Title III of the Convention if the defendant has had an opportunity to apply for the order to be set aside, at least if he has (unsuccessfully) availed himself of the opportunity to do so. In any event the creditor seems to be well advised, in light of the *Denilauler* case, to consider his strategic choices before applying for interim relief.[44]

Secondly, it follows from the rule in *Van Uden* (see above, section 2.2.2) that an order for interim payment of a contractual consideration (and, presumably, other interim payment orders) which does not guarantee the repayment to the defendant of the sum awarded if the plaintiff is unsuccessful as regards the substance of his claim, or which does not relate to specific assets located or to be located within the confines of the territorial jurisdiction of the court to which application is made, is not to be regarded as a provisional measure within the meaning of Article 24. In the recently decided *Mietz* case[45] the European Court has inferred that such a measure cannot be the subject of an enforcement order under Title III of the Convention. This ruling, in contrast to that of the *Denilauler* case, applies even if the defendant appeared before the court ordering the measure in question, though only where that court did not have jurisdiction under the Convention as to the substance of the matter.

Finally, as has been seen (above, section 2.2.3), it was held in *Van Uden* that ju-

---

[44] On this aspect see Hausmann, *IPRax* (1981) 79, at 82.
[45] *Mietz* v. *Intership Yachting* (supra n. 2).

risdiction to grant interim relief on the basis of Article 24 is only available if there exists a real connecting link between the subject-matter of the measures sought and the country to whose courts application for those measures is made. This ruling, although directly concerned only with jurisdiction, is very likely to have an impact on the practical significance of the rules for recognition and enforcement of interim orders. Indeed, it can be expected to reduce considerably, if not to eliminate, the need for international recognition and enforcement of orders made under Article 24.

In any event, the rules of the Convention concerning recognition and enforcement will retain their interest for interim orders in so far as such orders are made in proceedings *inter partes* and by a court having jurisdiction over the substance of the matter. It may indeed well be that the defendant does not have any assets at all in the country of that court or, if he does, that those assets are not sufficient to cover the amount due under the interim order. In both cases the order may come up for recognition and enforcement in another Contracting State.

3.2   Actual Enforcement (Execution)

Apart from Article 39, the Convention does not contain any provisions as to the measures of enforcement – as distinct from the procedure for obtaining an order authorising the enforcement (*exequatur*) – of foreign judgments. These questions are left to be determined by the law of the State in which execution is sought, the *lex fori*.[46]

Nevertheless, some problems are bound to arise in this connection. One of them is that the type of order made by the foreign court may differ more or less substantially from the provisional measures available under the *lex fori*. In such cases it seems desirable – so far as is possible within the framework of the *lex fori* – that the means of enforcement chosen should reflect the sort of enforcement which would be ordered in the State of origin.

A special situation occurs if the foreign interim order contains provisions relating to the manner in which it is to be enforced. To that extent it follows from Articles 28 and 34 that the order cannot be recognised or enforced, since pursuant to Article 16(5) such questions fall within the exclusive jurisdiction of the courts of the State of enforcement.

Sometimes, however, it is difficult to draw the line between what in German terminology is called *Erkenntnisverfahren* and *Vollstreckungsverfahren*, that is to say, between such parts of the foreign judgment as affect the substance of the case and those relating to the manner of its enforcement. This is especially so in the case of

---

[46] See, e.g., Case 148/84 *Deutsche Genossenschaftsbank* v. *Brasserie du Pêcheur* [1985] ECR 1981, para. 18.

orders for interim relief. A good illustration of this point is afforded by the *Preziosi* case decided by the Supreme Court of Sweden:[47]

An Italian company (P) brought an action against a Swedish company in an Italian court concerning the ownership of some machinery which was in the latter company's possession in Sweden. On the application of P, the Italian court made an order for sequestration (*sequestro giudiziario*) of the property in question and, in accordance with Italian law,[48] appointed P itself as custodian of the property. The Italian order was declared enforceable in Sweden on the strength of the Lugano Convention. So far there was apparently no problem. P then sought execution of the order and demanded the property to be handed over and placed in P's custody, as provided by the Italian court. The Swedish enforcement authority officer did not accede to the latter request, but executed the order in accordance with Swedish law by taking the property into his own custody. P appealed, and the case went all the way up to the Supreme Court.

The Supreme Court, by a majority of three votes to two, affirmed the decisions of the courts below to the effect that the enforcement officer's action should be upheld. In so far as P was appointed as custodian of the property, the Italian order was held to concern the method of its enforcement. There was no support in the Convention for the proposition that the courts of the State of origin could decide on such questions with binding effect in the State of enforcement of the order.[49] Instead, the Italian order had to be treated in the same way as a corresponding Swedish order, as provided by the Swedish Act 1992:794 incorporating the Convention. The nearest counterpart (there being no exact equivalent) in Swedish law to the Italian type of measure was an order for *kvarstad* (provisional attachment), which is executed by the property in question being placed in the enforcement officer's custody. Hence, that was the proper way in which to deal with the Italian order.

The minority would have allowed P's claim to succeed. In their view, the appointment of P as custodian formed an integral part of the substance of the Italian order and therefore, under the Lugano Convention, had to be respected in Sweden. It was argued, *inter alia*, on the strength of the decision of the European Court in the *Hoffmann* case,[50] that a judgment recognised under the Convention must in principle have the same effects in the State of enforcement as it did in the State of origin. In the present case this would not be so if the property in question were taken into the enforcement officer's custody rather than being handed over to P, in particular because the costs of administering the property would be higher, and the value of the protective measure lower for P, in the former alternative than in the

---

[47] *Nytt juridiskt arkiv* (1995) 495.

[48] Article 676 of the Code of Civil Procedure (*Codice di procedura civile*).

[49] Indeed, the State of enforcement has exclusive jurisdiction under Article 16(5) of the Convention.

[50] Case 145/86 *Hoffmann* v. *Krieg* [1988] ECR 645.

latter. The minority also pointed out that the Swedish Enforcement Code (*utsökningsbalken*) gave scope for arrangements of the type prescribed by the Italian order.

As highlighted by the split of opinion in the Supreme Court, respectable arguments – which were rather extensively developed both by the majority and by the minority – can be adduced in favour of either solution. Obviously, this is a case which should have been referred to the European Court for a preliminary ruling if this course had been available, i.e. if the case had come up for decision under the Brussels rather than under the Lugano Convention.

Berührungspunkte zwischen IPRG und beruflicher Vorsorge

Hans Michael Riemer[*]

1. EINLEITUNG

Die schweizerische berufliche Vorsorge (2. Säule der Alters-, Hinterlassenen- und Invalidenvorsorge; im Ausland oft mit „Betriebspensionen", „betriebliche Altersvorsorge" und dgl. umschrieben) ist heute, d.h. seit Inkrafttreten des Bundesgesetzes über die berufliche Alters-, Hinterlassenen- und Invalidenvorsorge (BVG, SR 831.40) am 1. Januar 1985 und des Bundesgesetzes über die Freizügigkeit in der beruflichen Alters-, Hinterlassenen- und Invalidenvorsorge (Freizügigkeitsgesetz,

---

* Dr.iur., o. Professor an der Universität Zürich.

J. Basedow et al., eds., Private Law in the International Arena – Liber Amicorum Kurt Siehr
© 2000, T.M.C.Asser Press, The Hague, The Netherlands

FZG, SR 831.42) am 1. Januar 1995, nicht nur in ihrem obligatorischen sondern auch in ihrem überobligatorischen (freiwilligen) Bereich stark *öffentlich* – rechtlich (sozialversicherungsrechtlich) geprägt und zudem nach wie vor *territorial* orientiert. Dennoch bestehen einige internationalprivatrechtliche Bezüge: Behandlung von Arbeitnehmern, welche für einen schweizerischen Arbeitgeber im Ausland tätig sind, und von Arbeitnehmern, welche für einen ausländischen Arbeitgeber in der Schweiz arbeiten (Unterstellung unter eine Versicherung und anwendbares Recht; nachfolgend Ziff. 2), internationale Verhältnisse und Familienrecht (Ziff. 3), internationale Verhältnisse und Erbrecht (Ziff. 4), Kapitalanlagen von Vorsorgeeinrichtungen im Ausland (Ziff. 5), internationale Schiedsgerichtsbarkeit (Ziff. 6).

Dabei sind die diesbezüglichen Fragen im Bereiche der beruflichen Vorsorge teilweise nur insoweit international*privat*rechtlicher Natur, als es um den *überobligatorischen (freiwilligen)* Bereich der beruflichen Vorsorge geht (vgl. nachfolgend Ziff. 2 und auch Ziff. 3.1).

2.   BEHANDLUNG VON IM AUSLAND TÄTIGEN ARBEITNEHMERN EINES SCHWEIZERISCHEN ARBEITGEBERS UND VON IN DER SCHWEIZ TÄTIGEN ARBEITNEHMERN EINES AUSLÄNDISCHEN ARBEITGEBERS

2.1   Unterstellung unter eine Versicherung

Ob Arbeitnehmer der hier in Frage stehenden Kategorien dem BVG-*Obligatorium* unterstellt sind, richtet sich nach Artikel 2 Absatz 2 und Artikel 5 BVG sowie nach Artikel 1 Absatz 1 lit. a und Absatz 2 BVV2 (Verordnung über die berufliche Alters-, Hinterlassenen- und Invalidenvorsorge, SR 831.401) und wird im Wesentlichen durch die AHV/IV-Gesetzgebung (erste – d.h. staatliche – Säule der Alters-, Hinterlassenen- und Invalidenvorsorge) präjudiziert;[1] es ist *öffentlich*-rechtlicher Natur und daher hier nicht weiter zu verfolgen.

Im *freiwilligen* Bereich der beruflichen Vorsorge (vgl. Art. 48/49 Abs. 2 BVG, Art. 89bis ZGB Schweizerisches Zivilgesetzbuch vom 10. Dezember 1907. SR 210, Art. 331 ff. OR Bundesgesetz betreffend die Ergänzung des Schweizerischen Zivilgesetzbuches (fünfter Teil: Obligationenrecht) vom 30. März 1911. SR 220), handle es sich um die blosse Aufstockung der Versicherung von – trotz ihres Auslandsbezugs – obligatorisch Versicherten (sodass u.U. obligatorisch und freiwilliger Bereich nicht demselben Recht unterstehen, vgl. nachfolgend lit. B) oder handle es sich um Personen, die zufolge ihres Auslandsbezugs nicht obligatorisch versichert sind, richtet sich die Frage der Unterstellung primär nach den einzelnen Ar-

---

[1] Vgl. Brühwiler, *Die betriebliche Personalvorsorge in der Schweiz* (Bern, Stämpfli 1989) (ASR Bd 521) S. 268ff.

beitsverträgen und sodann nach den darauf beruhenden individuellen Vorsorgeverträgen bzw. nach den ihre Basis bildenden Vorsorgereglementen der einzelnen privatrechtlichen Vorsorgeeinrichtungen (in aller Regel Personalvorsorgestiftungen[2]) als Trägerinnen dieser Vorsorgeverhältnisse.

2.2 Anwendbares Recht

2.2.1 *Arbeitsvertrag*

Bei dem die Grundlage der freiwilligen beruflichen Vorsorge bildenden Arbeitsvertrag richtet sich die Frage der Rechtsanwendung grundsätzlich nach *Artikel 121 Absatz 1 und 2 des Bundesgesetzes über das Internationale Privatrecht vom 18. Dezember 1987, SR 291*. Soweit schweizerisches Arbeitsvertragsrecht anwendbar ist, umfasst dieses auch – obwohl im Rahmen des Arbeitsvertragsrechts materiell eher einen „Fremdkörper" darstellend,[3] zumal sie sich teilweise direkt auf das Vorsorgeverhältnis (zwischen Begünstigten und Vorsorgeeinrichtungen) beziehen – die formell zum Arbeitsvertragsrecht gehörenden Artikel 331 – 331c OR („Personalvorsorge"), Artikel 331d/331e OR (Wohneigentumsförderung mit Mitteln der Personalvorsorge) je i.V.m. Artikel 341 OR (Unverzichtbarkeit und Verjährung) und Artikel 361/362 OR (Unabänderlichkeit).[4] Nach Massgabe von *Artikel 121 Absatz 3 IPRG* ist allerdings auch eine – diese Bestimmungen ebenfalls betreffende – *Rechtswahl* zulässig. Wie allgemein im Vertragsrecht bezüglich „innerlich zusammenhängender Komplexe"[5] ist aber auch im Arbeitsvertragsrecht – im Rahmen von Artikel 121 Absatz 3 IPRG – eine *Teilrechtswahl* zulässig, wobei gerade eine – im Verhältnis zum „eigentlichen Arbeitsvertrag" – *besondere* Rechtswahl bezüglich „Zusage und Durchführung einer betrieblichen Altersversorgung" als zulässig angesehen wird;[6] das muss selbstverständlich auch bezüglich der anderen Zwecke der beruflichen Vorsorge gelten und im übrigen auch in Gestalt einer „Teilrechtsbelassung" zulässig sein (die Rechtswahl wird nur bezüglich des „eigentlichen" Arbeits-

---

[2] Der seltene Ausnahmefall der Personalvorsorgegenossenschaft (vgl. Art. 331 Abs. 1 OR, Art. 48 Abs. 2 BVG) wird hier nicht weiterverfolgt, ebensowenig naturgemäss der Fall der „Einrichtung des öffentlichen Rechts" für die Arbeitnehmer der öffentlichen Hand.

[3] Vgl. meine Ausführungen in *SZS* (Schweizerische Zeitschrift für Sozialversicherung und berufliche Vorsorge) (1988) S. 335.

[4] So offenbar auch Keller/Kren Kostkiewicz, N 41 zu Art. 121 IPRG, in: Heini/ Keller/ Siehr/ Vischer/ Volken, *Kommentar zum Bundesgesetz über das Internationale Privatrecht (IPRG) vom 1. Januar 1989* (Zürich, Schulthess 1993): „*Arbeitgeberpflichten* (insbesondere . . . Altersversorgung)".

[5] Vgl. Keller/Kren Kostkiewicz, ibid., N 92ff., bes. N 97, zu Art. 116 IPRG.

[6] Vgl. Hischier, *Das Statut des Arbeitsverhältnisses entsandter Arbeitnehmer schweizerischer Unternehmen*, (Diss. Zürich, Schulthess 1995), Schweizer Studien zum internationalen Recht, Bd. 91, S. 39.

vertragsrechts vorgenommen, und die berufliche Vorsorge bleibt dem nach Art. 121 Abs. 1 und 2 IPRG massgebenden Recht unterstellt).

2.2.2 Vorsorgeverhältnis

2.2.2.1 Institutionelle Komponente (Trägerschaft)

Sofern aufgrund des vorstehend unter Ziffer 2.2.1 Gesagten (u.a.) eine Anwendbarkeit von Artikel 331 OR zu bejahen und gemäss dessen Absatz 1 (vgl. demgegenüber dessen Abs. 2) eine Stiftung zu errichten ist (und zwar – auch für den Obligatoriumsbereich – eine privatrechtliche), muss es sich um eine nach schweizerischem Recht inkorporierte (und diesem unterstehende) Personalvorsorgestiftung (Art. 89 bis ZGB) handeln (vgl. 150 Abs. 1, 154 Abs. 1, 155 IPRG[7]).

2.2.2.2 Vertragliche Komponente

Diesbezüglich involviert eine Bejahung der Anwendbarkeit der vorstehend unter Ziffer 2.2.1 aufgeführten OR-Bestimmungen m. E. zwingend die Anwendbarkeit des schweizerischen Rechts auf das *gesamte* Vorsorgeverhältnis zwischen der Personalvorsorgestiftung und den Destinatären, d.h. auch auf den Vorsorgevertrag (keine Teilrechtswahl *innerhalb* des Vorsorgeverhältnisses, da sonst „innerlich zusammenhängende Komplexe" auseinandergerissen würden;[8] Entsprechendes muss für ausländische Vorsorgeträger gelten). Das gilt im übrigen auch im Verhältnis zwischen Arbeitgeber und Personalvorsorgestiftung.

3. INTERNATIONALE VERHÄLTNISSE UND FAMILIENRECHT

3.1 Auslegung von Vorsorgereglementen bzw.–verträgen bezüglich familiärer Beziehungen von Ausländern

Soweit in Vorsorgereglementen bzw.–verträgen auf familiäre Beziehungen von Destinatären Bezug genommen wird (z.B. „Kinder", „Adoption", „Ehe", „Ehefrau", „Ehescheidung"), müssen aufgrund des Gleichbehandlungsgebotes, das auch

---

[7] Zur Inkorporationstheorie bereits Keller/Siehr, *Allgemeine Lehren des internationalen Privatrechts* (Zürich, Schulthess 1986) S. 331.

[8] Demgegenüber würde der Grundsatz der einheitlichen Rechtsanwendung im „Gesellschaftsrecht" (vgl. Vischer, in: *Kommentar zum IPRG* (oben N. 4) N 31 zu Art. 150, N 1 und 2 zu Art. 155 IPRG) – worunter aufgrund der Begriffsbildung gemäss Art. 150 Abs. 1 IPRG auch Stiftungen fallen – nicht verletzt, da es sich bei den Beziehungen zwischen Stiftungen und ihren Destinatären um externe, vertragliche, nicht um mitgliedschaftliche Beziehungen i.S.v. Art. 155 lit. f IPRG handelt.

in diesem Bereich zu beachten ist,[9] die Vorsorgereglemente bzw.–verträge für alle Destinatäre einheitlich nach Massgabe der entsprechenden *schweizerischen* Rechtsbegriffe ausgelegt werden, ohne dass Ausländer aufgrund des Vertrauensprinzips annehmen dürften, für sie gelte eine Auslegung gemäss ihrem allfällig abweichenden heimatlichen Recht.

3.2   Ehescheidung, einschliesslich eheliches Güterrecht

Auch wenn im Gesetzgebungsverfahren zum IPRG die rechtliche Behandlung von Pensionskassenansprüchen nicht erörtert wurde,[10] findet sich im IPRG eine einschlägige Norm: Anwendbar ist in der Regel (Ausnahme: Art. 61 Abs. 2 IPRG) *schweizerisches* Recht (*Art. 63 Abs. 2 Satz 1 i.V.m. Art. 61 Abs. 1 IPRG*), denn diese Frage gehört durchaus zu den „Nebenfolgen der Scheidung" i.S.v. Artikel 63 Absatz 2 Satz 1 IPRG (vgl. auch die Überschrift „Die Scheidungsfolgen" vor Art. 119 ff. ZGB, bes. Art. 122 – 124 ZGB, wobei sich diese Bestimmungen auch auf den überobligatorischen Bereich der beruflichen Vorsorge beziehen). Eine *Rechtswahl* ist in diesem Bereich der Pensionskassenansprüche *nicht* vorgesehen (die berufliche Vorsorge gehört nicht zu den „güterrechtlichen Verhältnissen" i.S.v. Art. 52 Abs. 1 IPRG, vgl. auch den Randtitel zu Art. 120 ZGB mit demjenigen zu Art. 122 – 124 ZGB,[11] ausgenommen – und zwar auch im überobligatorischen Bereich – bei aufgrund eines eingetretenen Vorsorgefalles bereits *erfolgten* Leistungen,[12] welche denn auch von einer Rechtswahl i.S.v. Art. 52 IPRG miterfasst werden).

4.   INTERNATIONALE VERHÄLTNISSE UND ERBRECHT

Auch im überobligatorischen Bereich haben die Hinterlassenen des Arbeitnehmers – aufgrund eines im Vorsorgevertrag enthaltenen Vertrages zugunsten eines Dritten (Art. 112 OR) – in der Regel einen *eigenen vertraglichen (schuldrechtlichen)* Anspruch auf die Hinterlassenenleistung, welchen sie direkt gegenüber der Personalvorsorgestiftung geltend machen können und müssen.[13] Die betreffenden Leistungen fallen also nicht in die Erbmasse des Verstorbenen. Ob *versicherungsmässig* konzipierte Vorsorgeansprüche (d.h. nicht Ansprüche auf blosses *Spar*kapital) im

---

[9] Vgl. BGE 110 II 443/444, 121 II 201, 124 II 577.

[10] Vgl. Volken, in: *Kommentar zum IPRG* (oben N. 4) N 9 zu Art. 63 IPRG.

[11] Aus dem Vergleich der einschlägigen Randtitel ergibt sich im übrigen, dass die berufliche Vorsorge auch nicht zum *nachehelichen Unterhalt* i.S.v. Art. 125ff. ZGB gehört.

[12] Vgl. im einzelnen meine Ausführungen unter dem Titel „Berufliche Vorsorge und eheliches Vermögensrecht (eheliches Güterrecht; Austrittsleistung bei Ehescheidung i.S.v. Art. 22 FZG; Entwurf zur Revision des Ehescheidungsrechts)", *SZS* (1997) S. 106ff., bes. S. 108 Ziff. 5, 118/119.

[13] Vgl. BGE v. 31.1.1995 in *SZS* (1997) S. 405ff. (mit zahlreichen Verweisungen).

Zusammenhang mit dem Pflichtteilsschutz (Art. 476, 529 ZGB) bei der Berechnung des verfügbaren Teils des Nachlassvermögens zu berücksichtigen sind, ist für das schweizerische Recht zu bejahen (was allerdings umstritten ist). Soweit dagegen nach Massgabe der einschlägigen Vorschriften (Art. 90 ff. IPRG) auf den Nachlass des Arbeitnehmers ausländisches Recht anwendbar ist, ist es denkbar, dass dieses – welches auch in vorliegendem Zusammenhang massgebend ist (vgl. *Art. 92 Abs. 1 IPRG*: „was zum Nachlass gehört") – für solche Leistungen (wie auch für Leistungen im Obligatoriumsbereich sowie für Sparkapital) eine eindeutige Regelung enthält (Zurechnung oder Nichtzurechnung).

5.   KAPITALANLAGEN VON VORSORGEEINRICHTUNGEN IM AUSLAND

Kapitalanlagen von Vorsorgeeinrichtungen im Ausland sind zulässig (Art. 53 lit. e/ 54 BVV2), wenn auch nur in begrenztem Umfang (Art. 55 BVV2). Die daraus entstehenden internationalen Rechtsbeziehungen der Personalvorsorgeeinrichtungen unterliegen naturgemäss hinsichtlich der Frage der Rechtsanwendung denselben Vorschriften wie die entsprechenden Rechtsbeziehungen anderer Anleger (vgl. z.B. Art. 154/155 IPRG betr. Aktionäre einer ausländischen AG, Art. 156 IPRG betr. Gläubiger bei ausländischen Anleihensobligationen).

6.   INTERNATIONALE SCHIEDSGERICHTSBARKEIT

Streitigkeiten aus dem eigentlichen Vorsorgeverhältnis (vorn Ziff. 2.2.2 und auch Ziff. 3.1), welche auch im überobligatorischen Bereich unter Artikel 73 BVG (Zuständigkeit entsprechender kantonaler Gerichte sowie des Eidgenössischen Versicherungsgerichtes) fallen (Art. 89 bis Abs. 6 ZGB), sind *nicht schiedsfähig*, was aufgrund von *Artikel 18 IPRG* (ordre public) auch in internationalen Verhältnissen zu beachten ist.[14] Entsprechendes gilt für Ehescheidungsklagen samt Nebenfolgen der Ehescheidung (vorn Ziff. 3.2) ohnehin und generell.[15] Hingegen sind die sich auf die berufliche Vorsorge beziehenden eigentlichen erbrechtlichen Auseinandersetzungen (vorn Ziff. 4) schiedsfähig, ebenso Streitigkeiten im Zusammenhang mit Kapitalanlagen von Vorsorgeeinrichtungen im Ausland (vorn Ziff. 5).

---

[14] Vgl. auch meine Ausführungen unter dem Titel „Schiedsfähigkeit von Klagen des ZGB bei internationalen Schiedsgerichten (Art. 177 Abs. 1 IPRG)", in *Rechtsschutz, Festschrift zum 70. Geburtstag von Guido von Castelberg* (Zürich, Schulthess 1997) S. 216/217.

[15] Vgl. Riemer (oben N. 14) S. 218 (und im übrigen auch Art. 25a FZG betr. die Zuständigkeit gemäss Art. 73 BVG).

SUMMARY
THE INTERFACE BETWEEN SWISS PIL AND EMPLOYMENT SOCIAL
BENEFITS

The Swiss employment, retirement and pension plan schemes are primarily governed by administrative law; nevertheless, there are a number of aspects relating to private international law, such as issues arising in connection with the optional insurance of employees working for Swiss employers abroad, and for employees of foreign employers working in Switzerland, as well as questions arising in international divorces.

The Law Applicable to Non Traditional Families

François Rigaux[*]

Family law has never been an exhilarating part of private international law. Judicial decisions flow in abundance but their interest from a scholarly point of view is meager. Up to a recent date the basic notions seemed almost universal and easy to tackle, but for polygamy, repudiation and trust – the last institution belonging only partially to family law. Adoption and divorce which some countries were ignorant of are more universally accepted nowadays. Of course the rules of municipal family law differ from one another as much as the rules of contracts or torts but until recently the fundamental institutions were basically alike and the main problem was to make the appropriate choice of law and to apply correctly the foreign law or to grant recognition to a foreign judgment. What has changed during the recent years?

1. THE FAMILY LAW MALAISE

A first paradox is that polygamy and repudiation which were until recently exhibited in all private international law treatises as exotic plants difficult to acclimate in Western countries have become more familiar, and our courts have learned how far they can go in recognizing their effects. The pluralist secularization of our *Weltanschauungen* renders it easier to take into account foreign institutions, even when they are religiously inspired.

But that very secularization and the diminishing impact of traditional values, of

---

[*] Professor emeritus, Université catholique de Louvain; Member of the International Law Institute.

J. Basedow et al., eds., Private Law in the International Arena – Liber Amicorum Kurt Siehr
© 2000, *T.M.C.Asser Press, The Hague, The Netherlands*

the Christian impregnation of Western family law have brought forth two results which are significant for the lawyers in the field of private international law. One is that the group of countries which according to Savigny belonged to the community of Christian nations do not share any more the same basic concepts of family law. The main differences concern the scientific evaluation of gender, of sex and of the capacity to marry, but also new hesitations as to the parental roles due in part to new procreation techniques and in part to the success story of adoption. The second result is even more perverse: not only is it the case that these developments do not follow the same pace in countries which in the recent past still shared traditional or conventional values. Still worse, no legal order is any more at peace with that field. Conflicting views and policies are voiced within the same country. Courts and legal scholars are deeply divided among themselves and the legislatures are dubious on the course to follow. These are the main new factors in the field of the family department of private international law.

After this short introduction, the present contribution to Kurt Siehr's Festschrift will be divided into two parts: 1) legal parentage in private international law; 2) The legal condition of same-sex partners in private international law.

2.   LEGAL PARENTAGE IN PRIVATE INTERNATIONAL LAW

Two sets of fresh difficulties are developing in private international law from the new trends which can be observed in municipal laws. As far as nationality remains a relevant connecting factor the difference of nationalities among persons involved in a determinate situation has given rise to new problems. Moreover, the same person can have more than one nationality. But even the reliance on domicile or residence does not spare municipal law from awkward problems: traveling has become so easy that emotional links can be maintained across national borders. That first difficulty is compounded by the second one, probably the most decisive. New non-traditional families are made up of disjointed parts which combine together differently at successive moments of the narrative. After having given birth to a child the woman gets married to a man who is not that child's father. They divorce, the mother remarries, and the child now lives with his mother and stepfather. The facts of life for such a child are that he has three fathers, a biological or genetic one (his mother's first lover), a legal one (the first husband who did not disclaim his paternity) and two nurturing fathers, that same ex-husband and the second one who is functioning as stepfather. To complicate matters one can suppose that the third man adopts the child. Such a case is all the more relevant for private international law if these persons neither share a common nationality nor do they reside in the same state. Moreover, one element of the restless life of the young woman can be her desire to move from state to state at the same pace that she updates her feelings. Not only does such a situation entertain links with different countries but the traditional choice of law methods map out the field under different headings. There is a connecting factor for adoption, another one for determining the denial of the paternity of the husband of a pregnant woman, still another one for the right of a biological father to establish his right to take charge of his child or to obtain a visitation right. Even if all legal questions are raised in the same jurisdiction it is not at all certain that the local court will apply the same law to each of the intermingling aspects of a unique situation. Finally, if one of the parties had recourse to assisted procreation, either through artificial insemination or through surrogate motherhood, another batch of problems will have to be dealt with.

The care of such conflicts of laws resides in the indeterminacy of the basic concepts of family law. The traditional unifying semantics is gone: who is the mother of a child? The woman whose gametes afforded the child its genetic heritage? The woman in whose womb the embryo became a foetus and who gave birth to the child? The woman who engineered the whole scheme and intended to take charge of the new-born for the whole of his or her life? In a case of artificial insemination is the man whose semen was put to good use the father? Of course he is genetically. But what is the counterbalancing value of socio-effective paternity?

Needless to say, all this will have a devastating influence on the methods of private international law. Until now we worked with well known tools. We had to determine the law applicable to motherhood or to fatherhood, but we knew what a mother or a father was. Now we have to navigate on almost uncharted seas: what law is applicable to the definition of the basic concepts?

One could suggest that such problems are not entirely new, perhaps not new at all. Does it not suffice to revisit the conflict of characterization according to the pattern set up by Kahn and Bartin almost a century ago? Eventually we get a reversal of the Bartinian scheme. For him as for Kahn characterization was with *renvoi* and public policy a three-pronged challenge to a universalistic theory of private international law. Their point was of course that municipal law concepts did not coincide in the countries which shared the same conflict of laws rules and they entertained a reified vision of those concepts which clashed with one another. Already then the basic core of civil law concepts was surrounded by veils of indeterminacy the result of which was that the so-called problem of characterization was intractable. That was a far cry from the actual seismic events which later destroyed family law. The basic solution of characterization, the reliance on the secure concepts of the *lex fori,* is not valuable any more. Of course it was illusory but it did not seem so to clever scholars. Now the illusion is lost since the disease strikes municipal law which far from offering the appearance of a solution has become the problem.

Not only is characterization *lege fori* obsolete but even clear-cut rules of conflicts have to give way to a more flexible, judiciary approach. Let us propose some scenarios in order to show that conflict of laws rules are also part of the problem.

A Belgian married woman who cannot bring her pregnancies to their successful conclusion and yet wants to bear her husband a child provides for the insemination to be performed *in vitro*, in the State of New York, the embryo being implanted in the womb of a Californian woman in California. After childbirth in Arizona, the Californian woman refuses to hand the child over. According to what criterion shall we apply Belgian, Arizona, Californian or New York law to that case? If the Belgian husband and wife intend to adopt the child, who has to consent to the adoption. More precisely, which law applies to that question? In case of the husband's sterility it is possible that the semen for the insemination was, with his consent, provided by his twin brother or by an unrelated man. If after the insemination the donor, whoever he is, has lost the possibility to beget a child, has he a standing to claim the child as his? The dissemination of the connecting factors which should entail the application of different laws to the right of the surrogate mother, to the claims of the genetic father, to the consent required for an eventual adoption makes it peremptory to abandon the preconceived conflict rules whose performance is unsatisfactory as soon as they are not applied separately to the sole legal questions for which each is competent. Under less favourable circumstances, the unique outcome is to give the judge free reins to choose the adequate solution. Needless to say that solution will not be the same in Belgium, in New York or in California but the risks of discrepancy are not higher than through the mechanical application of rigid conflict rules.

According to a news item published in the *Corriere della Sera* of Friday 7 March 1997, an Italian woman had agreed to be the surrogate mother of two embryos coming from two different couples. The Italian physician of both women conceived that scheme because neither could go through pregnancy. After the birth of those false twins, each was to be attributed to its own biological parents by genetic testing. All parties were Italian but the medical interventions occurred in Switzerland where the birth was also planned, since that country does not have the restrictive legislation which renders such manipulations illegal in Italy. The conflict of laws is apparently not very acute but what would seem in this case as in all other similar and more complicated issues a useful solution – the application of the personal status of the children – is of no avail: at the time of their birth the children have neither domicile nor nationality but need to acquire the domicile or the nationality of at least one of their biological parents. So the status is dependent on filiation. Has one to accept that the children acquire on a provisional level the nationality of the surrogate mother until the moment of their attribution to their "legal" biological parents? But if the surrogate mother is German or Brazilian the case becomes more awkward. Moreover the private international law element is inherent in such a case, since the medical manipulations would have been impossible in the country which has the strongest links with the case.

The second scenario is the transposition of a case decided by the United States Supreme Court, *Michael H.* v. *Gerard D.*[1] It included eventually connections with a

---

[1] 109 S. Ct. 2333 (1989).

state other than California but no conflict of laws question was raised. A married woman leaves her husband and lives several years with a lover who is the father of their child. Later on the woman resumes her conjugal life and the child who is legally her husband's one is treated by him as his daughter. With the consent of the mother the child spends holidays with her biological father who contributes to her support. When the mother imposes the severing of any links of the child with her former lover, the latter claims the establishment of his paternity and demands visitation rights. In the real case the biological father was French and part of their life in common occurred in New York, but the California Supreme Court treated the case as purely Californian without any hint at a conflict of laws problem. Let us suppose that the woman is an Italian married to a Belgian. The lover is German and the child is born in France. The biological father's action is linked to the legal paternity of the husband. One cannot contemplate the application of two different conflict of laws rules to the factual situation for defeating the husband's paternity and to the establishment of a new link with the biological father. But the main question is whether both links can coexist. Do we accept dual fatherhood? Whatever the solution, the conflictual method is entirely inadequate.

The same Italian newspaper relates the revendication of American gay men to reproduce themselves through cloning. What will be the legal status of a cloned child? Are its father and mother the legal parents of the person of whom the child is the reproduction?

A third scenario concerns the conflict between biological and adoptive families. Has the law applicable to adoption jurisdiction on the termination of any links with the family of origin? Do cooperative adoption or open adoptions, according to which personal relationships with both families can be concurrent depend on the law applicable to the biological family or on the adoption status?

When contemplating those three scenarios which are not the most cumbersome ones, it is necessary to be conscious of the underlying constitutional questions. The right to respect of the family life (European Convention of Human Rights, ECHR, Art. 8), the protection of family (German GG, Art. 6), the *due process clause* of the XIVth Amendment to the United States Constitution are *individual* rights which can be asserted by each of the persons involved in a family relationship. Normally constitutional protection is afforded in the country where litigation is being conducted, which does not necessarily coincide with the country of which claimant is a national since aliens are not denied constitutional rights. Regarding the application of the ECHR the European Court of Human Rights will some day have to rule on choice of law problems. Constitutionalization of private international law problems is still a step further away from traditional conflict of laws rules.

Legal parenthood is not any more a concept at peace with itself. The characterization problem, if one wants to call it so, goes to the roots of family law. There is no agreement any more neither on the facts of life which can bring forth a child, nor on the splitting of biological or genetic parentage and the will to take care of a child and for bringing it up. Just as someone needs to be perfectly acquainted with his or her native language before learning a foreign one, so the technique of private international law needs the support of a sufficiently secure system of municipal law. The idea of Kahn and Bartin that the specificity of a municipal legal order poses an obstacle to the building up of universal systems of private international law has been turned upside down. Now we have to put up with the very disturbing fact that the dislocation of the social and cultural fabric inside the countries is much more damaging to a smooth functioning of conflict of law rules. Private international law needs the support of strong institutions of municipal law which are progressively disappearing.

3.   THE NEW FORMS OF LIVING TOGETHER

Besides the unconventional modes of insertion in traditional molds such as divorce and successive marriages, adultery and conception of children of plural maternity and dubious paternity, there exist strongly offensive brands of non-traditional families. Four of them will be considered: (1) adoption by two unrelated parents; (2) cohabitation out of wedlock; (3) cohabitation contracts in conformity with some statute; (4) same-sex marriage.

There are two main approaches to the problems such situations give rise to in the field of private international law. One is to look into the conflict of laws rules applicable to each typical situation. The other deals with a differentiation between structural aspects of the application of any rule of private international law. The distinctions bears on different phases or moments of the application of private international law. An old but still useful criterion goes back to the vested rights theory. For a system of municipal law it is one thing to recognize a right duly acquired in another country and another one to allow the acquisition of an analogous right according to the local law. That difference was and remained paramount with regard to divorce and polygamy. In some jurisdictions divorce cannot be obtained and in most a second marriage may not be entered into before the dissolution of the former one. But in the same jurisdictions a right regularly acquired in another country under the application of the foreign law can produce some effects. It is worthwhile mentioning that old cases about polygamy, bigamy, incest and miscegenation are presented as useful precedents for the extent to which same-sex marriages may be recognized.[2]

---

[2] David L. Chambers, "Polygamy and Same-Sex Marriage", 26 *Hofstra LR* (1997) 53-83; Andrew Koppelman, "The Miscegenation Analogy: Sodomy Law as Sex Discrimination", 98 *The Yale LJ* (1988) 145-164; James Trosino, "American Wedding: Same-Sex Marriage and the Miscegenation Analogy", 73 *Boston Univ. LR* (1993) 93-120.

The distinction just hinted at is easily explicable on the ground of more or less extensive involvement of state authorities with the state-sponsored acquisition or recognition of a right: those authorities are much more involved when directly associated with the creation of a right. They are not so profoundly entangled when they only recognize some effects of a right regularly acquired abroad. That distinction brings to another one. If a legal situation has been adjudicated by a foreign court, it is easier to give effect to that decision than to start proceedings afresh on the same issue. Regarding the legal consequences of a legal situation they may differ. Concerning polygamy, one has to distinguish between the case of a husband intending to coerce any of his women to cohabit with the others in a country where monogamy is the expression of a strong public policy of the state and the case of a claim brought by the surviving wives to get reparation for the wrongful death of their husband.

As in the first part, the best method is to produce different scenarios.

3.1 Adoption

In countries where adoption by two persons is only allowed to husband and wife, it will be difficult to obtain an adoption decree applied for by two unmarried partners, let alone by two women[3] or two men. The recognition of an adoption regularly entered into under a foreign jurisdiction is a different matter. If two women have jointly adopted a child in California and later emigrate to be employed at the American Embassy in Paris or at the European headquarters of an American transnational company in Brussels or in Geneva there are strong arguments to recognize the parental authority of both of them.

3.2 Cohabitation out of Wedlock

Factual cohabitation has become common in many countries where marriage remains however a living institution. Such cohabitations are more or less permanent, whether between opposite sex or same-sex partners. Such cohabitations have effect between the partners or against third parties. On the first level they can concern the administration of common property or, in case of separation, the partition thereof, perhaps also the liberty to put to an end such union, the rights to a shared lodging and so on. In many jurisdictions and in purely municipal cases such cohabitation are not devoid of some legal consequences. In the field of private international law the question is whether the formation of a factual companionship or partnership in

---

[3] Adoptions by a lesbian couple or by the female companion of the biological mother are admitted in some jurisdictions of the United States: Nancy D. Polikoff, "This Child Does Have Two Mothers: Redefining Parenthood to Meet the Needs of Children in Lesbian-Mother and other Nontraditional Families", 78 *Georgetown LJ* (1990) 459-575.

country A can create in country B to which the parties have moved some effects which are not usual under the law of B. The relationships with third parties are easier to deal with. If for instance one of the partners in an opposite or same-sex cohabitation dies through the wrongful action of a third party, the local law applicable to that act is principally competent to determine how far the liability extends to damages suffered by a mere cohabitant.

3.3   LEGAL RECOGNITION OF REGISTERED CONTRACTS OF COHABITATION

In Scandinavian countries special statutes have provided for the legalization of contracts of cohabitation out of wedlock.[4] More recently France and Belgium have followed suit.[5] In most cases the statute is also applicable to same-sex partners and sometimes only to them.

According to the traditional schemes of conflict of laws, such agreements have to be contemplated either according to the law applicable to the contracts or under the heading of personal status. The problem of characterization as such is irrelevant. It concerns a contractual agreement set up by a special statute in the field of personal relationships and therefore it is not without analogy to family law affiliations or conjugal status. Contracts in those fields are generally submitted to a close legal scrutiny. For instance, it can be assumed that contracts regarding out-of-wedlock sexual activity are against the law. The relevant question is twofold. The registration of such unions is only possible in the country whose statute has made them possible, under the conditions laid down in that statute. For instance such registration according to the Danish act requires that one partner has Danish nationality and is residing in that country.[6] The same partners would not find everywhere a foreign public official having jurisdiction for the solemnization of such a contract. Conversely the recognition of the effects of such agreements in a foreign jurisdiction should not be discarded without further inquiry. The question will come up again when we deal with the issue of same-sex marriage. Suffice it to note that the recognition of the effects of an act of cohabitation even between same-sex partners will not meet with such strong objections as a same-sex marriage proper.

[4] Martin D. Dupuis, "The Impact of Culture, Society, and History on the Legal Process: an Analysis of the Legal Status of Same-Sex Relationships in the United States and Denmark", 9 *Int. J. of Law and the Family* (1995) 86-118.

[5] Loi n° 99-944 du 15 novembre 1999 relative au pacte civil de solidarité, published in the *JO(RF)* n° 265, 16 November 1999, p. 16959; loi du 23 novembre 1998 (*Moniteur belge*, 12 January 1999, p. 786), entered into force on 1 January 2000.

3.4   Same-sex Marriages

Four different scenarios have to be considered regarding the question of same-sex marriages.

A.   If two men or two women residing in Hawaii have entered into a "marriage" in their home state[7] and later move to a country where such unions are not accepted by the law, the recognition of some effects of such unions can depend upon an analogous application of the conflict rules on personal status. Of course, even without any interference of public policy, some jurisdictions may assume that the *lex fori* concept of marriage cannot be extended to same-sex unions. Countries such as Denmark which provide for the registration of same-sex partnerships could accept more liberally the recognition of same-sex marriages. In the United States the Full Faith and Credit Clause and the Due Process Clause obliges every state in the Union to give full faith and credit to the operation of law and judgments in the sister states, and to guarantee the due process of law, the second clause being also applicable to international conflicts.[8] Even if the conceptual schemes of the *lex fori* do not resent the characterization as marriages, for the purpose of conflicts of law, of a union which satisfies a foreign country's requirements, nonetheless public policy could be strongly challenged by any hint at recognizing foreign same-sex marriages.

The impact of public policy depends on the nature of the effect based on the same-sex marriage. The effect may be purely incidental and similar to the consequence of a factual relationship. It also depends on the links between the factual situation and the former state. The German concept of *Inlandsbeziehung* or *Binnenbeziehung* can be useful here. When the same-sex marriage has been formalized in the foreign country where the parties are resident, their occasional, perhaps fortuitous, presence in the territory of another country renders the public policy argument almost negligible.

---

[6] Act N° 372 of 7 June 1989, known as the Registered Partnership Act, section 2 (2). For a comparative study, see: *Civil Law Aspects of Emerging Forms of Registered Partnerships*, by Dr Caroline Forder, assisted by Silvina H. Lombardo (Ministry of Justice of the Netherlands 1999).

[7] The possibility of such a marriage has to be taken account of since the Supreme Court of Hawaii did not discard it: *Baehr* v. *Levin,* 74 Haw. 530, 852 P 2d 44 (1993); 74 Haw. 645, 852 P 2d 74 (1993); see also *Baehr* v. *Miike*, 950 P 2d 1231 (Haw. 1997). Meanwhile a constitutional amendment has been introduced to define marriage as the union of two persons of opposite sex: W. Brian Burnette, "Hawaii's Reciprocal Beneficiaries Act : An Effective Way in Resolving the Controversy Surrounding Same-Sex Marriage", 37 *Brandeis LJ* (1998-1999) 81-88.

[8] David L. Chambers, "What if? The Legal Consequences of Marriage and the Legal Needs of Lesbian and Gay Male Couples", 95 *Michigan LR* (1996) 447-491; Robert Cordell II, "Same-Sex Marriage: the Fundamental Right of Marriage and an Examination of Conflict of Laws and the Full Faith and Credit Clause", 26 *Columbia Human Rights LR* (1994) 247-272; Anthony Dominic D'Amato,

B.   If the same-sex couple has taken up a regular residence in a country where they risk to meet resistance to the recognition of their union on the ground of public policy the question is more awkward. If for instance a Danish same-sex couple resides in Berlin as public officials of the European Community or if one of them has that capacity, are the European authorities under a duty to accept the effects of the laws in force in a Member State? What are the duties of the State where an institution of the Union has its seat? The duties of Member States of the Community towards one another are not entirely dissimilar from those imposed on federated states in the United States on the basis of the Full Faith and Credit Clause and the Due Process Clause.

C.   If two persons resident in Hawaii enter into a same-sex marriage and immediately afterwards emigrate to a country where such unions are not admitted by the municipal law, it can be doubted whether the latter country is under any duty to implement the effects of the foreign marriage.

D.   The easiest scenario is the last one. A same-sex couple who resides in a country where their union cannot be formalized travels to a country where, let us assume, they can get married or be registered as living together. After their return to their country of origin there is very small chance that their union will be recognized notwithstanding that it was performed in accordance with *the lex loci celebrationis*.

Equal Treatment of the Parties in International Maintenance Cases

Guus E. Schmidt[*]

1. INTRODUCTION

One of the basic principles of civil procedure is that there must be equality of arms between the parties. The plaintiff and the defendant should have an equal right to defend their position. They should have equal access to facilities such as state-financed legal aid and they should – as long as there is no reason to distinguish between them – be treated equally.

This does not mean, however, that the parties must be treated in exactly the same way in all circumstances. Especially individuals who are in conflict with commercial enterprises – e.g. consumers against suppliers, employees against employers – often receive extra legal protection, both in domestic law and in private international law. For instance, employees and consumers may, under the Brussels Convention, start proceedings in their home country more often than other contracting parties and they are, at the same time, better protected against being sued abroad.

Weaker party protection exists not only in the relation between individuals and commercial enterprises. For instance, maintenance creditors are often considered as being in a weaker position than their debtors and therefore as deserving extra protection. Having regard to their dependency on the payments of the debtor, this seems a very justifiable standpoint. But at the same time one should bear in mind that the difference between the maintenance debtor and the creditor is not as obvious as the difference between, for instance, a supplier and a consumer. The (al-

---

[*] Dr.iur., Senior Researcher, T.M.C. Asser Instituut, The Hague.

J. Basedow et al., eds., Private Law in the International Arena – Liber Amicorum Kurt Siehr
© 2000, *T.M.C.Asser Press, The Hague, The Netherlands*

leged) debtor may be out of work and without any financial resources and the creditor may have a well paid job. Of course, this is not the typical situation but still the differences between the creditor and the debtor will, generally speaking, not be extreme. Quite often the debtor will be the type of person who in a consumer case or in an employment dispute would be regarded as a party deserving special protection – someone not at home in (international) litigation, not equipped to communicate with foreign lawyers and lacking the financial resources needed for participating in complicated proceedings.

This does not, of course, mean that maintenance debtors and their creditors may never be treated in different ways. But in drafting legislation or conventions one should be careful when it comes to the protection of the position of maintenance creditors. Such protection should not be detrimental to the position of the maintenance debtor, and neither should the debtor be deprived of governmental assistance such as state-financed legal aid when such assistance is given to the creditor in comparable circumstances. The importance of this is underlined by the fact that the principle of the equality of arms is incorporated in Article 6 of the European Human Rights Convention[1] and in Article 14 of the International Covenant on Civil and Political Rights.[2]

In this contribution to Festschrift KURT SIEHR I will in the first place discuss to what extent the principle of the equality of arms is respected in the relevant multilateral conventions that are in force in European countries. This question will be raised with respect to jurisdiction (Article 5(2) of the Brussels and Lugano Conventions[3]), to applicable law (especially with regard to the "cascades" of Articles 1 and 3 of the 1956 Hague Convention[4] and Articles 4, 5 and 6 of the 1973 Hague Convention[5]) and to international legal aid (as provided for in the 1956 New York Maintenance Recovery Convention[6]).[7] Thereafter, I will pay attention to some questions that

---

[1] Convention for the Protection of Human Rights and Fundamental Freedoms, Rome, 4 November 1950.

[2] International Covenant on Civil and Political Rights, New York, 16 December 1966.

[3] Convention on Jurisdiction and the Enforcement of Judgements in Civil and Commercial Matters, Brussels, 27 September 1968 (amended by Accession Conventions in 1978, 1982 and 1989); Convention on Jurisdiction and the Enforcement of Judgements in Civil and Commercial Matters, Lugano, 16 September 1988.

[4] Convention on the Law Applicable to Maintenance Obligations towards Children, The Hague, 24 October 1956.

[5] Convention on the Recognition and Enforcement of Decisions Relating to Maintenance Obligations, The Hague, 2 October 1973.

[6] Convention on the Recovery Abroad of Maintenance, New York, 20 June 1956.

[7] The Hague Convention of 15 April 1958 Concerning the Recognition and Enforcement of Decisions Relating to Maintenance Obligations Towards Children and the Hague Convention of 2 October 1973 on the Recognition and Enforcement of Decisions Relating to Maintenance Obligations will not be discussed as they do, to my opinion, not raise questions with regard to the equality of arms.

should be discussed if a new Hague Convention on Maintenance Obligations will be drafted.

2.   THE EXISTING INSTRUMENTS

2.1   Direct Jurisdiction: Article 5(2) of the Brussels and Lugano Conventions[8]

According to Article 2 of the Brussels and Lugano Conventions, persons domiciled in a Contracting State shall, whatever their nationality, be sued in the courts of that State. There is, however, an important exception: Article 5(2) provides that a person who is domiciled in a Contracting State may, in matters relating to maintenance, be sued "in the courts for the place where the maintenance creditor is domiciled or habitually resident (...)".[9] These are rules of direct jurisdiction: if a court of a Contracting State is seized without regard to these rules, it shall declare itself to have no jurisdiction unless the defendant enters an appearance without contesting the jurisdiction of the court before raising any substantive defence.

So, if the maintenance creditor lives in Contracting State C and the maintenance debtor lives in Contracting State D, the creditor may start proceedings either in D (under Article 2) or in C (under Article 5(2)). If, on the other hand, the debtor wants to sue the creditor, for instance when he wants a modification of an earlier decision, he may, by virtue of Article 2, only do so in State C.

In the Jenard Report, two reasons are mentioned for giving jurisdiction to the forum of the creditor. The first of these is that a convention which did not recognise the forum of the maintenance creditor would be of only limited value, "since the creditor would be obliged to bring the claim before the court having jurisdiction over the defendant. If the Convention did not confer jurisdiction on the forum of the maintenance creditor, it would apply only in those situations where the defendant against whom an order had been made subsequently changed residence, or where the defendant possessed property in a country other than that in which the order was made". This argument is not correct. A convention only permitting the creditor to sue the debtor in the *forum rei* would certainly not be of limited value. It would, on the contrary, oblige all other courts in the Contracting States to refuse jurisdiction.

---

[8] The relevant Article of the Lugano Convention is similar to that of the Brussels Convention. Therefore, when reference is made to the Brussels Convention this may be understood as refering to both Conventions, where appropriate.

[9] In addition, but not relevant to the discussion held here, Article 5(2) provides that the defendant may also be sued "if the matter is ancillary to proceedings concerning the status of a person, in the court which, according to its own law, has jurisdiction to entertain those proceedings, unless that jurisdiction is based solely on the nationality of the parties".

But even if a convention confining itself to the *forum rei* would be of a restricted importance, this would not be a reason to introduce other grounds for jurisdiction. It almost seems as if, according to the Jenard Report, a convention on jurisdiction, recognition and enforcement is only useful if it leads to increasing international litigation instead of reducing it.

The second argument given in the Jenard Report is more convincing. "[T]he court for the place of domicile of the maintenance creditor is in the best position to know whether the creditor is in need and to determine the extent of such need". In addition to this, it may be pointed out that in a considerable number of Contracting States the courts will apply the law of the habitual residence of the maintenance creditor. Thus, the jurisdiction of Article 5(2) is not based on the protection of the maintenance creditor as a weaker party but, as in the case of the other rules of special jurisdiction included in Article 5, on the close connection that generally exists between the dispute and the court to which jurisdiction is given. This, however, does not take away the fact that the maintenance creditor is given an advantage by Article 5 (2). Is there enough justification for this? To my opinion: yes. Whether the proceedings take place in the *forum rei* or in the *forum actoris*, one of the parties is necessarily disadvantaged, unless one would decide to have proceedings in a neutral third State on the "equally bad is equal as well" basis. Therefore, the jurisdiction of Article 5 (2) should not be regarded as infringing the principle of the equality of arms.

2.2   The Cascades of the Applicable Law Conventions

The equality of arms is basically a concept of procedural law. But neither may it be accepted that the substantive conflict rules would give a preferential treatment to one of the parties without sufficient reason. In this paragraph I want to examine whether the conflict rules included in the 1956 Hague Convention on the Law Applicable to Maintenance Obligations in Respect of Children and in the 1973 Hague Convention on the Law Applicable to Maintenance Obligations can stand up to a test in this respect.

Both conventions prescribe the application of the law of the habitual residence of the creditor as the main rule. For the 1973 Convention, this rule is primarily justi-fied in the Verwilghen Report by pointing out that it is the creditor who is to be pro-tected by the maintenance obligation and that the creditor will use the maintenance to enable him to live. Further, the Verwilghen Report points out that this system fa-cilitates a degree of harmonisation within each State: all maintenance creditors will be put on the same footing.

The rule in itself does not put either of the parties at a disadvantage. The law of the habitual residence of the creditor may award more maintenance to the creditor than the law of the debtor's habitual residence does, but it may also award less. Per-haps the application of the law of the creditor's habitual residence is even safer for the debtor than the application of his own law. If the creditor receives hardly any money or even no money at all, this will be easier to accept if it is determined by his own law than if it is the outcome of the application of the law of the debtor. In the first case, the creditor will find himself in the same position as any maintenance creditor living in the same country and no difference will be felt between domestic and international cases. In the second case however, such a difference exists and the court could be tempted to find a way out, either by interpreting the applicable law in a way that is favourable to the creditor or by applying an exception such as Article 11 of the 1973 Convention.

In both conventions, exceptions are made to the main rule. Article 2 of the 1956 Convention allows the Contracting States to refer to the *lex fori* if both of the parties have the nationality of the forum and the debtor has his habitual residence in that state. Article 8 of the 1973 Convention makes an important exception for divorce cases: maintenance obligations between ex-spouses are governed by the law that has been applied to the divorce. Both of these exceptions replace one law by another without having any concern with the substantive outcome of the applicable law. Therefore, neither of these exceptions gives reason for suspicion that the rules of the conventions would not be impartial.

This cannot be said, however, with regard to some other exceptional rules contained in both of the conventions. Both the 1956 and the 1973 Conventions give a cascade of conflict rules. If the law determined by the main rule does not allow the creditor any maintenance at all, he will have a second or even a third chance. Under the 1956 Convention, if the law declared applicable by the Convention refuses the creditor any right to maintenance, the law referred to by the municipal private international law of the court will be applied by virtue of Article 3.[10] Article 5 of the 1973 Convention provides that if the creditor is unable, by virtue of the law referred to in Article 4, to obtain maintenance from the debtor, the law of their common nationality will apply. And, if the parties have no common nationality or if the creditor is unable to obtain maintenance under that law as well, he receives a third chance by Article 6: in that case the *lex fori* will be applicable.

According to the Verwilghen Report to the 1973 Convention, the subsidiary conflict rule of the 1956 Convention had been introduced "to put children in the most favourable position possible". In 1973, according to the Report, the Special Commission was confronted with the same problem and "actuated by the same laudable intention in relation to the creditor". But it appeared impossible to repeat the solution of the 1956 Convention in 1973. As the 1956 Convention only applies if the law referred to in Article 1 is the law of a Contracting State, it leaves room for

---

[10] The 1956 Convention is only applicable if Article 1 of that Convention refers to the law of a Contracting State. If not, the municipal conflict rules of the forum remain in force.

the continued existence of a municipal private international law. The 1973 Convention, however, has a universal scope. All cases are governed by the law designated by the Convention, whether or not it is the law of a Contracting State. This leaves no room for municipal conflict rules and therefore it is not possible to refer to these rules as an alternative for the rules of the Convention. Therefore, another subsidiary connecting factor was sought. The authors of the Convention found even two of them: the common nationality of the creditor and the debtor and the *lex fori*. After it appeared that both of these connecting factors had their supporters it was agreed that both of them would be included in the Convention as subsidiary connecting factors in the way described above.

This cascade is defended with the argument that it protects the maintenance creditor since it removes any excessive feature which may result from the systematic application of the law of the habitual residence of the creditor and, further, that it favours the maintenance creditor, who is regarded as being in a weaker situation than the debtor.[11] It remains unclear what is to be understood by "excessive features" but whatever they may be, it is preferable not to take them away by taking refuge in subsidiary conflict rules. Denying a right to maintenance is not always excessive and excessive rules will not always lead to a total denial of maintenance. Therefore, if the application of the law of the habitual residence would lead to an outcome which is incompatible with the basic essentials of the legal system of the forum – either because the amount due is excessively high or excessively low – recourse should be had to the provision that has been written for this purpose: the public policy exception of Article 11 of the Convention. Section 2 of this Article expressly provides that, even if the applicable law provides otherwise, the needs of the creditor and the resources of the debtor shall be taken into account in determining the amount of maintenance. So, any excessive outcomes of the application of the law of the habitual residence of the creditor will be corrected by the application of Article 11, Section 2. The only effect of the subsidiary conflict rules is that they put a premium on international cases as in those cases the creditor has one or more extra chances that he will receive money from the debtor. Although one would not begrudge the creditor this extra chance, it does mean that the debtor faces in international cases a higher risk that he must pay than in a domestic case.

This inequality is not as strong as the straightforward favour approach of Article 6 of the Inter-American Convention on Support Obligations[12], determining that the law should be applied which is most favourable to the creditor. The cascades of the Hague Conventions will only have effect if the law which is primarily designated does not oblige the debtor to pay any maintenance at all *and* one of the subsidiary

[11] Actes et documents de la douzième session 2 au 21 octobre 1972 (The Hague 1975) p. 444, no. 144 (Verwilghen Report).
[12] Inter-American Convention on Support Obligations, Montevideo, 15 July 1989.

laws does. However, principally speaking, it is an unjustified disturbance of the balance between the parties.[13]

2.3   Legal Aid: the New York Maintenance Convention

Whatever the rules are with regard to jurisdiction, applicable law and recognition and enforcement, the maintenance creditor who wants to obtain money from a debtor abroad faces a difficult task. Communication with foreign lawyers and courts may be troublesome and international proceedings are often time consuming and very expensive. All the problems that may occur in domestic proceedings are exacerbated in international cases and new problems – e.g. with regard to language – may be added. Therefore, the New York Convention on the Recovery of Maintenance Abroad facilitates the recovery of maintenance in international cases. If the maintenance creditor and the debtor live in different Contracting States, the creditor hands over the relevant documents and data to an authority in his own country – the Transmitting Agency – who will send the case to the Receiving Agency of the other state. The Receiving Agency will then take, on behalf of the claimant, all appropriate steps for the recovery of maintenance. By virtue of Article 6, this may include the settlement of the claim and, where necessary, the institution and prosecution of an action for maintenance and the enforcement of a judgement given in the creditor's country. So, the Receiving Agency provides for a kind of legal aid that would normally speaking be given by practising lawyers or other professionals. As Article 9, Section 3, forbids the Transmitting and Receiving Agencies to charge any fees in respect of their services rendered under the Convention, this means that the claimant receives free legal aid without being subject to a means test, at least as long as the Receiving Agency can handle the case itself. If, for instance, court proceedings must be started, it will often (but not always[14]) be necessary to call in a solicitor. With regard to his assistance the claimant will receive state-financed legal aid on the same basis as any resident or national of the country where the proceedings are instituted.[15]

The Transmitting and Receiving Agencies act on behalf of the claimant only. The defendant is dependant on legal aid under the same conditions and restrictions as in domestic cases. There may be a good argument for this inequal treatment of

---

[13] It is somewhat peculiar that the Verwilghen Report (p. 444, no. 144) regards it as "not satisfactory, from a purely logical point of view" that the creditor who has the same nationality as the debtor receives a triple chance of obtaining maintenance whereas the creditor who has another nationality than the debtor has only a double chance, without explaining why creditors in international cases should receive extra chances at all in comparison to creditors in domestic cases.

[14] E.g. Article 8 of the Dutch Act implementing the Convention (Wet van 27 september 1961, Stb. 303) provides that the Receiving Agency acting in court does not need the assistance of a solicitor which otherwise would be necessary.

[15] Article 9, Section 1.

the parties when proceedings – either substantive or for the enforcement of a foreign decision – are brought in the country of the habitual residence of the debtor. In that case, the creditor must solve the problems of proceeding abroad and the debtor plays the home game. But if proceedings are started in the court of the creditor's habitual residence, it is the debtor who has to conquer the difficulties of litigating abroad. In that case, one would expect that provisions would be made to assist the debtor.

Litigation in the court for the habitual residence of the creditor may take place on the initiative of the creditor, e.g. on the basis of a jurisdictional ground such as contained in Article 5 (2) of the Brussels and Lugano Conventions, but proceedings may also be initiated by the debtor, especially when he applies for a modification of a decision that has been rendered earlier. The latter cases have been discussed in the meeting of the Special Commission of the Hague Conference on Private International Law in April 1999. The question was whether a maintenance debtor who applies for modification can invoke the services of the Transmitting and Receiving Agencies on the basis of Article 8 New York Convention.[16] Some delegates interpreted Article 8 as applying also to modification requests made by the debtor. In contrast, others did not accept that view.[17] They denied that the Transmitting and Receiving Agencies are obliged to provide their services to debtors who apply for modification and based this opinion on the overall purpose of the New York Convention, as reflected in its other provisions, in particular Article 1(1). Article 1 provides that "the purpose of this Convention is to facilitate the recovery of maintenance to which a person, hereinafter referred to as claimant, (...) claims to be entitled from another person, hereinafter referred to as respondent, (...). This purpose shall be effected through the office of agencies which will hereinafter be referred to as Transmitting and Receiving Agencies". Taking into account this provision, it seems hardly possible for a debtor who wants modification of a decision to invoke Article 8 of the Convention. Any help by the Transmitting and Receiving Agencies will be rendered on a voluntary basis.

The only argument one can imagine for this unequal treatment is that the creditor is generally speaking a weaker party than the debtor. But, as we have seen, this is not always the case. First, cases are more and more brought by public authorities such as social security agencies seeking recovery for allowances paid to the creditor. In itself, it is positive that public authorities make use of the services of the specialised agencies that are better equipped to recover maintenance than they are themselves, but public authorities cannot be considered as a weaker party than the maintenance debtor – on the contrary. Second, even if the dispute is between the

---

[16] Article 8 reads: "The provisions of this Convention apply also to applications for the variation of maintenance orders".

[17] Report on and Conclusions of the Special Commission on Maintenance Obligations of April 1999, Document Drawn up by the Permanent Bureau, December 1999, p. 17, no. 29.

creditor and the debtor themselves, the creditor is not always the weaker party. As we have seen, the creditor may have a good income and the debtor may be out of work. Especially when the debtor applies for modification – obviously stating that circumstances have changed and that he is no longer able to pay the amount to which he was obliged by the decision – it is unconvincing to regard him by definition as the stronger party.

So, by assisting the creditor and not the debtor, the New York Convention does not meet the standards of equal treatment that should be observed by a convention like this. The question arises how to meet this shortcoming. It seems difficult to make any improvements within the framework of the present Convention and therefore I will pay some attention in the next paragraph to the questions that should be discussed within the framework of the Hague Conference when drafting a new instrument.

3. CONSEQUENCES FOR A NEW HAGUE CONVENTION ON MAINTENANCE OBLIGATIONS

In April 1999, a Special Commission on Maintenance Obligations was convened by the Hague Conference on Private International Law, with instructions "to examine the operation of the Hague Conventions on maintenance obligations and the New York Convention of 20 June 1956 on the Recovery Abroad of Maintenance and to examine (…) the desirability of revising those Hague Conventions, and the inclusion in a new instrument of judicial and administrative co-operation."

In its conclusions, the Special Commission recommends that the Hague Conference should commence work on the elaboration of a new worldwide international instrument. This new instrument should, among other things, "contain as an essential element provisions relating to administrative co-operation", and "be comprehensive in nature, building upon the best features of the existing Conventions, including in particular those concerning the recognition and enforcement of maintenance obligations".[18]

Developing a new convention opens up the opportunity to reconsider the position of the maintenance creditor and the debtor. The drafters should take this opportunity seriously. It would be highly unwelcome if there were serious doubts as to whether a new instrument would be compatible with Article 6 of the European Human Rights Convention or Article 14 of the International Covenant on Civil and Political Rights. Therefore, the creditor and the debtor should be treated equally or, if they are unequally treated, there should be a good argument for it. That the

---

[18] Report on and Conclusions of the Special Commission on Maintenance Obligations of April 1999, Document Drawn up by the Permanent Bureau, December 1999, p. 22, no. 46.

creditor is, generally speaking, the weaker party does not suffice as a justification for a different treatment.

How can the drafters ensure that in a new convention the parties will be treated equally? We have seen that the present conventions that have been studied give rise to difficulties in the fields of applicable law and international judicial co-operation. The recommendation by the Special Commission of April 1999 does not explicitly mention that the new convention should deal with determining the applicable law. If it will nevertheless cover this topic, a critical attitude will be necessary if proposals are made to include a cascade of conflict rules or to favour the creditor in another way.

The most important aspect of the possible new convention will, however, probably be the international co-operation, resulting in legal assistance to the parties. It is in this respect that the balance between the positions of the creditor and the debtor should seriously be considered. The facilities offered by a system such as that of the Transmitting and Receiving Agencies under the New York Convention should not be reserved to the creditor, but the debtor should benefit from them as well. As a consequence, it should be possible for the debtor to invoke the services of the Transmitting and Receiving Agencies if he wants to apply for modification of a maintenance decision abroad. Further, facilities offered to the creditor with regard to legal aid, costs and – for example – translations should also be available to the debtor. This should not be restricted to proceedings initiated by the Receiving Agencies. The debtor will need assistance especially when he must appear in the courts of the habitual residence of the creditor. As these proceedings will often be initiated by the creditor, the debtor should profit from the same type of facilities as are offered to the creditor when litigation takes place in the court of the habitual residence of the debtor. By offering such facilities one will not only prevent the new convention from being under the suspicion of being incompatible with human rights conventions. One will also reduce the chance that the debtor will not appear in the foreign court and later try to evade the negative consequences by frustrating the enforcement of the decision.

Parteiautonomie im Internationalen Namensrecht

Anton K. Schnyder[*]

1.   VERWIRKLICHUNG DER PARTEIAUTONOMIE IM SCHWEIZER IPR-GESETZ

Wem die Ehre zufällt, in der Festschrift für KURT SIEHR einen Beitrag verfassen zu dürfen, der steht zunächst vor einem schier unauflösbaren Dilemma. Worüber hat der Jubilar nicht geschrieben, und wieviel Exklusives sowie Weiterführendes hat er nicht zum Kollisionsrecht und zur Rechtsvergleichung verfasst? Trotzdem: Gerade als Lehrer, Kollege und Freund hat KURT SIEHR einen angehalten, sich durch den Wust des Vorhandenen durchzukämpfen und die eigene Neugierde nicht absterben zu lassen. Dabei gehört es zu den besonderen Markenzeichen des Jubilars, dass er seinen unzähligen Schülerinnen und Schülern – trotz seiner nie erreichten Souveränität und seinen strengen Anforderungen an Leistung – mit einer ganz spezifischen, ja herzlichen Liberalität begegnet ist. Liberales Denken und Handeln impliziert zugleich Freiheit und Verantwortung, so dass es angebracht erscheint, mit den nachstehenden Ausführungen einen kleinen Beitrag zu leisten zu dem dadurch vorgegebenen Spannungsverhältnis auf dem Gebiet des Privatkollisionsrechts. Es lässt sich damit für einen Mikrobereich auch nachzeichnen, mit was für Herausforderungen der Makrokosmos von Freiheit und insonderheit der kollisionsrechtlichen Parteiautonomie konfrontiert ist.

---

[*] Dr.iur. LL.M., Professor an der Universität Basel.

J. Basedow et al., eds., Private Law in the International Arena – Liber Amicorum Kurt Siehr
© 2000, T.M.C.Asser Press, The Hague, The Netherlands

Das Schweizer IPR-Gesetz (Bundesgesetz vom 18. Dezember 1987 über das Internationale Privatrecht) eröffnet dem Parteiwillen einen weiten *Gestaltungsspielraum*. Die kollisionsrechtliche Parteiautonomie ist – zumindest partiell – in praktisch allen Regelungsbereichen des IPRG verwirklicht. Zu nennen sind das Namensrecht (Art. 37 Abs. 2); das Ehegüterrecht (Art. 52 f.); die scheidungsrechtliche Anerkennung einer ausländischen Entscheidung (Art. 65 Abs. 2 lit. c); das Erbrecht (Art. 87 ff.); das Sachenrecht (Art. 104); das Vertragsrecht (Art. 116); eine begrenzte allgemeine Rechtswahlmöglichkeit im Deliktsrecht (Art. 132); Wahlrechte der geschädigten Person bei besonderen Deliktskollisionsnormen (Art. 135 Abs. 1, 138 sowie 139 Abs. 1); die Inkorporationsautonomie im Gesellschaftsrecht (Art. 21 Abs. 2, 154 Abs. 1); und schliesslich die internationale Schiedsgerichtsbarkeit (Art. 187).

Die Gestaltungsfreiheit der Partei(en) findet dort ihre *Grenze*, wo qualifizierte Schutzanliegen zumindest einer Partei es gebieten. Dabei ist zu unterscheiden zwischen dem gänzlichen Ausschluss der Parteiautonomie – wie in Art. 120 Abs. 2 (Verträge mit Konsumenten) oder Art. 151 Abs. 3 (zwingende Zuständigkeit für Verantwortlichkeitsklagen infolge öffentlicher Ausgabe von Beteiligungspapieren und Anleihen) – und einer gesetzlichen Beschränkung der wählbaren Rechtsordnungen – wie bei Art. 121 Abs. 3 (Arbeitsverträge) oder Art. 52 Abs. 2 (Vereinbarungen des ehelichen Güterrechts). Hinzuweisen ist sodann auf Art. 5 Abs. 2 IPRG, welche Bestimmung eine (an sich zulässige) Gerichtsstandsvereinbarung als unwirksam erklärt, „wenn einer Partei ein Gerichtsstand des schweizerischen Rechts missbräuchlich entzogen wird."

Zwei Aspekte der umfassend gewährten Parteiautonomie haben sich eröffnet, die noch nicht überall ins Bewusstsein der Praxis gedrungen sind. Zum einen scheint noch bei manchen Personen die nötige Kenntnis in Bezug auf die vielen „Spiel"möglichkeiten der kollisionsrechtlichen Parteiautonomie zu fehlen. Das gilt etwa für die Abstimmung von vertrags- und sachenrechtlichen Rechtsfragen (insbesondere mit Bezug auf Art. 104 IPRG). Aber auch in vielleicht vertrauteren Bereichen – wie hinsichtlich des Ehegüter- und des Erbrechts – vermisst man für internationale Sachverhalte mitunter einen im Hinblick auf die Rechtsplanung und -koordinierung gebotenen Kenntnisstand.

Ein weiterer offener Punkt ist der mögliche Zwang zur „Rücknahme" gewisser Wahlfreiheiten in Einzelfällen. Namentlich Konflikte mit ausländischen Ordnungs- und sonstigen Eingriffsnormen (des Wettbewerbsrechts, des Devisenrechts, von Handelsrestriktionen u.a.) mögen nach differenzierten Lösungsansätzen rufen. Das Gesetz bietet dazu seinerseits Hand (vgl. vor allem Art. 13 und 19), und selbst im „liberalen" Schiedsgerichtsdenken stellen bezügliche Überlegungen für falladäquate Konfliktlösung keinen Fremdkörper mehr dar.

2. Objektive Anknüpfung des Namens

2.1 Allgemeines

Der Name einer Person ist Ausdruck ihrer Persönlichkeit und ihrer Identität; darüber hinaus kennzeichnet er Familienzugehörigkeit. Trotz des letzteren Zusammenhangs wurde im IPR-Gesetz keine akzessorische, sondern eine *selbständige* Anknüpfung des Namens vorgesehen: Art. 37 ff. IPRG. Entsprechend werden im Scheidungsrecht (Art. 63 Abs. 2, 64 Abs. 2 IPRG) und im Kindesrecht (Art. 82 Abs. 3 IPRG) die Sonderkollisionsnormen für den Namen vorbehalten.

Grundsätzlicher Anknüpfungspunkt für namensrechtliche Fragen ist der *Wohnsitz* einer betroffenen Person. Befindet sich dieser in der Schweiz, so untersteht der Name dem schweizerischen Recht. Der Name einer Person mit Wohnsitz im Ausland untersteht jenem Recht, auf welches das *Kollisionsrecht* des Domizilstaates verweist (Art. 37 Abs. 1 IPRG). Hierbei handelt es sich um einen der wenigen Fälle, in denen das IPR-Gesetz einen ausländischen Renvoi vollumfänglich – d.h. sowohl als Rückverweisung auf schweizerisches Recht als auch als Weiterverweisung auf ein drittes Recht – anerkennt (vgl. Art. 14 Abs. 1 IPRG).

2.2 Flexibilisierung der Anknüpfung durch das Schweizer Bundesgericht

In einem bemerkenswerten Entscheid hatte sich das Bundesgericht mit der Frage zu befassen, wo der Wohnsitz einer Person zu lokalisieren ist, wenn es um die Namensbestimmung im Zusammenhang mit einer *Eheschliessung* geht.[1] In casu ging es um Folgendes: Gerhard Koch – so das Bundesgericht – war deutscher Staatsangehöriger mit langjährigem Wohnsitz in der Schweiz, seit 1970 in Reinach (BL). Léone Grayo, die sich am 24. Februar 1989 mit Gerhard Koch verheiratet hat, war französische Staatsangehörige und wohnte bis zu ihrer Trauung in Guebwiller (Frankreich). Bei der Eheschliessung verurkundete die Zivilstandsbeamtin von Reinach unter der Rubrik „Familienname des Mannes/der Frau nach der Eheschliessung„ je den ledigen Namen der Brautleute. Das Ehepaar war damit nicht einverstanden und argumentierte, die Pflicht zur unterschiedlichen Namensführung innerhalb derselben Ehegemeinschaft sei ihnen unverständlich, und sie empfänden das als diskriminierend. Die Behörden waren also mit dem sonderbaren Namensproblem konfrontiert, der Gleichberechtigung gleichsam in umgekehrter Richtung zum Durchbruch zu verhelfen!

Das war vorliegend gar nicht so einfach. Zwar hält Art. 160 Abs. 1 des Schweizerischen Zivilgesetzbuches als Regel nach wie vor fest: „Der Name des Ehemannes ist der Familienname der Ehegatten." Um in den Genuss dieser helvetischen Schutzvorschrift zu gelangen, mussten die Eheleute jedoch namensrechtlich dem

---

[1] BGr. 26.04.1990, BGE 116 II 202.

Schweizer Recht unterstehen. Diese Frage – eine typisch kollisionsrechtliche – war indessen zunächst zu klären, wies der Sachverhalt doch Beziehungen zu drei verschiedenen Staaten auf: Frankreich, Deutschland, Schweiz. Mithin waren die für inländische Behörden massgebenden Kollisionsnormen zu beachten – hier in erster Linie Art. 37 Abs. 1 IPRG. Die Vorschrift unterscheidet für das auf den Namen einer Person anwendbare Recht danach, ob die Person Wohnsitz in der Schweiz hat oder nicht. Herr Koch wohnte seit langem in der Schweiz, Frau Grayo jedoch erst nach der Eheschliessung. Bis zur Trauung hatte sie Wohnsitz in Frankreich. Nach Auffassung der zuständigen Zivilstandsbehörden verwies das französische Recht nicht auf die Schweiz zurück, so dass auf den Namen der Frau und auf eine etwaige Namensänderung infolge Heirat französisches Recht zur Anwendung gelangen musste. Gemäss französischem Recht hatte die Eheschliessung auf den Namen von Frau Grayo aber keinen Einfluss, soweit es um den Familiennamen im Rechtssinne ging. Eine Hinzufügung oder gar Übernahme des Namens Koch in Zivilstandsregister und Familienbücher kam für Frau Grayo nicht in Betracht.

Mit diesem Ergebnis, das durch korrekte, wenn auch strenge Auslegung des IPR-Gesetzes zustande gekommen war, wollte das Bundesgericht die Eheleute Koch-Grayo nicht sich selbst überlassen. Vielleicht auch bewegt durch die materiale Überlegung, den Schutz der ehelichen Gemeinschaft nicht mittels kollisionsrechtlicher Kapriolen zu sehr zu gefährden, fand es eine Lösung, die von den basellandschaftlichen Entscheiden abwich, indessen die Betroffenen befriedigte und auch mit dem Gesetz in Einklang steht. Nach Bundesgericht soll nämlich für die Frage des Wohnsitzes in diesem Zusammenhang nicht auf die tatsächlichen Verhältnisse am Tag der Trauung, sondern auf den von den Brautleuten bezeichneten *ersten ehelichen Wohnsitz* abgestellt werden. Dieser aber befand sich in casu zweifelsfrei in Reinach, so dass ebenfalls für Frau Grayo – wegen der Anknüpfung an ihren künftigen Wohnsitz in der Schweiz – die Anwendung schweizerischen Rechts, und somit von Art. 160 Abs. 1 ZGB, resultieren konnte. Der Entscheid des Bundesgerichts offenbarte teleologische Flexibilität und nahm auch Rücksicht auf den konkreten Parteiwillen.

3.   UNTERSTELLUNG DES NAMENS UNTER DAS HEIMATRECHT

3.1   Tragweite

Art. 37 Abs. 2 IPRG eröffnet den Namensträgern die Möglichkeit, anstelle der objektiven Anknüpfung nach dem Wohnsitzprinzip den Namen parteiautonom dem Heimatrecht zu unterstellen. Die Bestimmung ist ein (weiterer) Beleg für die Beachtung des Parteiwillens und der Parteierwartungen im Namensrecht – so wie auch das Bundesgericht diesem Aspekt bei der Lokalisierung des Wohnsitzes im Zusammenhang mit einer Eheschliessung Rechnung getragen hat (vgl. hiervor).

Die subjektive Anknüpfung steht sowohl Auslandschweizern als auch ausländischen Staatsangehörigen mit Wohnsitz in der Schweiz zur Verfügung.

In der Lehre umstritten ist die Frage, ob Art. 37 Abs. 2 IPRG eine *Sachnormverweisung* darstellt oder ob dabei – wie in Art. 37 Abs. 1 – im Sinne einer Gesamtverweisung auf die Kollisionsnormen des Heimatrechts verwiesen wird.[2] Für die letztere Lösung und damit für die Anerkennung eines etwaigen Renvoi durch das Heimatrecht spricht der Gedanke, hinsichtlich des Namens einen Entscheidungseinklang zwischen Heimat- und Wohnsitzstaat herbeizuführen. Insbesondere in Fällen, in denen die Namensträgerin oder der Namensträger dereinst wieder in den Heimatstaat zurückkehrt, könnten dadurch Namenskonflikte vermieden werden. Andererseits führte eine Gesamtverweisung mitunter dazu, dass eine Unterstellungserklärung wirkungslos bliebe, wenn das ausländische IPR des Namens seinerseits dem Wohnsitzprinzip folgt. Zeigt sich in einem Fall, dass eine Person mit einer Rechtswahl ihre „persönliche Präferenz in der Namensgestaltung" verwirklichen möchte,[3] spricht einiges dafür, diese Rechtswahl (wie allgemein bei der Rechtswahl) als *Sachnormverweisung* zu akzeptieren. Streben nach etwaigem Entscheidungseinklang hat hier demgegenüber in den Hintergrund zu treten. Auch stellte es für das IPRG einen Fremdkörper dar, die subjektive Anknüpfung zunächst zuzulassen, sie aber danach – mittels eines Renvoi – möglicherweise wieder zu unterminieren.

3.2 Zeitpunkt der Unterstellung

Art. 37 Abs. 2 IPRG enthält keine Regelung hinsichtlich der Frage, wann eine etwaige Rechtswahl zu erfolgen habe. Es wird (mit durchaus guten Gründen) argumentiert, trotz des Schweigens des Gesetzgebers müsse „davon ausgegangen werden, dass die Rechtswahl dann anzumelden ist, wenn sich die Namensfrage konkret stellt".[4] Dieser Auffassung kann zugestimmt werden, insbesondere im Zusammenhang mit relevanten Statusakten. Allerdings können auch diesbezüglich Fälle nicht völlig ausgeschlossen werden, in denen ausnahmsweise eine Unterstellung noch zu späteren Zeitpunkten zugelassen werden sollte, sofern dafür stichhaltige Gründe vorliegen.

---

[2] Vgl. Jametti Greiner/ Geiser in: Honsell/ Vogt/ Schnyder, *Kommentar zum schweizerischen Privatrecht, Internationales Privatrecht* (Basel 1995), Art. 37 N 28; Vischer in: Heini/ Keller/ Siehr/ Vischer/ Volken, *IPRG-Kommentar* (Zürich 1993) Art. 37 N 26.

[3] So Vischer, ibid.

[4] Jametti Greiner/Geiser (oben N. 2) Art. 37 N 29.

SUMMARY
PRIVATE AUTONOMY IN THE INTERNATIONAL LAW OF NAMES

The Swiss Federal Act on Private International Law (IPRG) opens up a wide range of possibilities concerning party autonomy. The law only fixes limits with respect to the protection of the parties. As an example for this liberal approach the author discusses the right of a person to the use of his or her name which follows autonomous connecting factors. Beside the parties' right to submit the name to the law of their country of origin (Article 37 Paragraph 2 IPRG) the law states the principle of the right of domicile (Article 37 Paragraph 1 IPRG). Applying this to the marriage between a German husband and his French wife in Switzerland, the Supreme Court of Switzerland remarkably decided, contrary to the civil registry office, that the first domicile indicated by the engaged couple is relevant for the stipulation of the applicable law rather than the actual circumstances (residence in France) at the moment of marriage. Due to this flexible interpretation the bride's will to assume the name of her husband could be given effect, since, according to French law, marriage did not have any effect on the names of the engaged couple.

Wie kann nationales IPR zu vermehrt internationaler Optik gelangen?

Ivo Schwander[*]

1. EINLEITUNG

Selten ist der national-rechtliche Ausgangspunkt des IPR so selbstverständlich akzeptiert worden wie heute, was in einem krassen Gegensatz zu den Bedürfnissen der sich globalisierenden Wirtschaft und der sich weiter gegenseitig angleichenden Informationsgesellschaft steht. In den USA war es die Materialisierung des IPR, im kontinentalen Europa die systematischere Unterstellung des IPR unter das Diktat der Zuständigkeitsordnungen des Internationalen Zivilprozessrechts (IZPR), welche im Verlaufe des 20. Jahrhunderts das IPR immer mehr in positivistische und nationalrechtliche Fesseln legte.

Mit diesem Aufsatz soll kurz zusammengefasst werden, wie der dem Gegenstand des IPR einzig adäquate universalistische Gesichtspunkt, den FRIEDRICH CARL VON SAVIGNY, der geniale Erneuerer und Denker des IPR, als stete Herausforderung definiert hat[1], in den heutigen positivrechtlichen IPR-Systemen der Staaten an Boden gewinnen könnte.

---

[*] Dr. iur., Professor an der Universität St. Gallen.

[1] Friedrich Carl von Savigny, *System des heutigen Römischen Rechts*, Bd. 8 (Berlin 1849) S. 24ff. Zum universalistischen Ausgangspunkt Savignys: Max Gutzwiller, *Der Einfluss Savignys auf die Entwicklung des Internationalprivatrechts* (Fribourg 1923) und Paul Heinrich Neuhaus, „Abschied von Savigny?" 46 *RabelsZ* (1982) S. 4ff.

J. Basedow et al., eds., Private Law in the International Arena – Liber Amicorum Kurt Siehr
© 2000, T.M.C.Asser Press, The Hague, The Netherlands

Dabei soll zuerst an die ihrer Natur nach beschränkte Bedeutung nationalrechtlicher IPR-Kollisionsregeln erinnert werden (2). Es folgen Ausführungen dazu, wie im Verhältnis zum internationalen Zivilprozessrecht den IPR-Gesichtspunkten autonomere Bedeutung zukommen könnte (3) und wie im IPR selbst ein vom Forum losgelöster methodischer Ausgangspunkt angestrebt werden könnte (4). Schliesslich sei an die Aufgabe des IPR erinnert, vermehrt eigenständige, vom nationalen Privatrecht unabhängige Werturteile und Gerechtigkeitsmassstäbe zu entwickeln (5).

2.   BEGRENZTHEIT DER AUSSAGEN DER NATIONALRECHTLICHEN IPR-KOLLISIONSREGELN

Die Begrenztheit der Aussagen und der Relevanz einzelstaatlicher IPR-Systeme und von deren Kollisionsregeln ist allgemein bekannt, und dennoch zieht kaum jemand die sich daraus ergebenden Schlüsse. Diese Einengungen können wie folgt gegliedert werden:

1.   Zunächst ist zwischen dem *IPR als allgemeiner, zeitloser und überstaatlicher Fragestellung* danach, wie Rechtsbeziehungen zwischen Privaten mit Berührungen zu mehreren staatlichen Rechtsordnungen aus einer quasi-überstaatlichen Sichtweise gerechten und der Plurinationalität der Sachverhalte angemessenen Rechtsfolgen zugeführt werden sollen, einerseits, und den *unvollkommenen und partiellen, einer einseitigen nationalen Optik entspringenden Antworten der zahlreichen positivrechtlichen staatlichen IPR-Systeme*, andererseits, zu unterscheiden.

Was die IPR-Lehre an hehren Grundsätzen im Allgemeinen Teil – durchaus im Sinne des IPR als allgemeiner Fragestellung – pflegt, macht sie nur zu oft mit kleinlicher Auslegung der positivierten nationalen Kollisionsregeln des Besonderen Teils illusorisch. Wenn z.B. im Allgemeinen Teil gesagt wird, Korrekturen am anwendbaren fremden Recht mittels Ordre public seien nur mit grösster Zurückhaltung in Erwägung zu ziehen, so entbinden die Kollisionsregeln im Besonderen Teil, die auf direktem Weg zum inländischen Recht führen, von vorneherein von der Anwendung fremden Rechts.

2.   Aus einer überstaatlichen Betrachtung heraus erweisen sich die IPR-Kollisionsregeln der nationalen IPR-Systeme in mehrfacher Hinsicht als höchst *unvollkommene Lösungsversuche*:

(1) *Auf die Fragestellung, wie sich Private rechtens zu verhalten haben*, wenn sie in verschiedenen Staaten leben oder ihre vertraglichen Leistungen erbringen – und wenn dementsprechend a fortiori weder die Anwendung des einen noch des anderen Rechts naheliegt, sondern die Rechte und Pflichten die Besonderheit aufweisen, dass sie eben nicht von vorneherein einer nationalen Rechtsordnung zuzuordnen sind – *geben einzig materiell-privatrechtliche Rechtssätze eine vollkommene Antwort*.

Kollisionsregeln verweisen auf eine einzige Rechtsordnung, ohne sich zum gebotenen Verhalten im Verhältnis zwischen den je in einer anderen Rechtssphäre lebenden Personen zu äussern und dieses zu bewerten. Die Verweisung auf ein nationales Privatrecht verweigert ein allenfalls gebotenes spezifisches Werturteil über das richtige Verhalten zwischen Personen, die in verschiedenen Staaten mit je verschiedenen Rechtsordnungen leben. Der Lebenssachverhalt, der sich im Geltungsbereich zweier verschiedener Rechtsordnungen abspielt, wird behandelt, wie wenn er sich im Geltungsbereich einer einzigen Rechtsordnung zutragen würde. Die plurinationale Komponente wird, sozusagen wider besseres Wissen, negiert.

Diese kollisionsrechtliche Methode hat sich ihrer praktischen Vorteile wegen (grundsätzlich mögliche Vorhersehbarkeit des Ergebnisses, Verweisung auf das den Parteien bekannte nationale Privatrecht) durchgesetzt. In der Mehrzahl der Konstellationen führt sie zu befriedigenden Ergebnissen. Rechtslogisch überzeugt sie aber nicht, und in den minderheitlichen Konstellationen, in denen ein spezifisches Werturteil über das ausgeprägt zwischenstaatliche Element des Sachverhalts (Spezifika des internationalen Rechtsverkehrs) notwendig ist, versagt sie.

(2) Soweit materiell-rechtliche Rechtssätze eine spezifische Antwort geben, ist diese daher dem durch die kollisionsrechtliche Methode gefundenen Ergebnis vorzuziehen. Die materiell-rechtliche IPR-Methode befasst sich mit dem Spezifischen des IPR-Sachverhaltes, nämlich dem Plurinationalen, und schafft für dieses ein eigenes Werturteil. Sie ist in diesem Sinn *lex specialis* und gibt eine umfassendere, direkte Antwort auf die eigentliche IPR-Fragestellung[2].

Jedoch gibt es im heutigen Rechtszustand wenige materiell-rechtliche Rechtssätze, welche unmittelbar Rechte und Pflichten der Privaten im grenzüberschreitenden Rechtsverkehr begründen. Es handelt sich um vereinheitlichtes Sachrecht (wie das Wiener Kaufrecht) oder um gesetzlich oder richterrechtlich entwickelte spezielle IPR-Sachnormen oder um internationale Handelsbräuche (lex mercatoria). Das ist der faktische Nachteil dieser Methode; *es gibt zu wenige allgemein anerkannte oder international vereinheitlichte spezielle Sachnormen für grenzüberschreitende Sachverhalte*, sodass international-privatrechtliche Streitigkeiten nur selten auf ihrer Basis allein gelöst werden können.

Eine weitere Schwäche der materiell-rechtlichen Methode besteht darin, dass allzu oft Wertungen des nationalen Privatrechts (*materielle lex fori*) zum Massstab gewählt werden. Wenn hier von einer der kollisionsrechtlichen IPR-Methode überlegenen materiellrechtlichen IPR-Methode die Rede ist, so nur insoweit, als es um *spezifische materiellrechtliche Werturteile und Rechtssätze für den internationalen Rechtsverkehr* geht.

---

[2] Die eigentliche IPR-Frage lautet: *Welches sind die Rechte und Pflichten der Privaten im grenzüberschreitenden Rechtsverkehr?* Die in Lehrbüchern tradierte Fragestellung: *Welches Recht ist auf einen plurinationalen Sachverhalt anwendbar?* ist unzulässig verkürzt, da sie die allgemeine IPR-Fragestellung auf die von der kollisionsrechtlichen IPR-Methode bewältigbare Fragestellung reduziert.

(3) Beide IPR-Methoden verknüpfen die modernen Varianten des alten statutarischen Methodenansatzes, nämlich die *lois d'application immédiate* und die *Sonderanknüpfung fremden zwingenden Rechts.* Die materiellrechtlichen Wertungen werden zwar dem nationalen Recht entnommen, es findet aber eine spezifische, auf den Inhalt dieser Rechtssätze ausgerichtete kollisionsrechtliche Abwägung statt, welcher der beteiligten nationalen Rechtsordnungen sie entnommen werden sollen. Beispielsweise wird eine zwingende wirtschaftsrechtliche Verbotsnorm (Nichtigkeit einer Kartellabrede) derjenigen nationalen Rechtsordnung entnommen, auf deren Markt sich die Absprache auswirkt und deren Markt diese Verbotsnorm schützt.

Die modernen Statutenmethoden verbinden die vorhin erwähnten Vor- und Nachteile der kollisionsrechtlichen und der materiellrechtlichen Methoden. Ihre weiteren Schwächen liegen in den in der Praxis zu beobachtenden unterschiedlichen Bewertungen, je nachdem ob es um *eigene oder fremde zwingende Normen* geht, und auch in den *Unsicherheiten der Teleologie* der zwingenden Rechtssätze.

(4) Der grundsätzliche *Methodenpluralismus*, von welchem moderne IPR-Systeme ausgehen, würde es den rechtsanwendenden Gerichten und Behörden an sich gestatten, IPR-Sachverhalte vermehrt aus einer überstaatlichen Optik anzugehen. Die Praxis scheint hingegen vielfach in die gegenteilige Richtung zu verlaufen.

(5) Weiter helfen könnte hier die konsequente Analyse des Verhältnisses zwischen der allgemeinen IPR-Fragestellung einerseits und der verkürzten, vorwiegend auf die Auswahl zwischen zwei nationalen Rechtsordnungen ausgerichteten kollisionsrechtlichen Fragestellung der positivierten nationalen IPR-Systeme.

Weil es keine dem nationalen Recht übergeordneten, allgemeinen völkerrechtlichen Grundsätze zur Lösung von IPR-Sachverhalten gibt und auf Staatsvertragsweg nur eine verhältnismässig geringfügige Menge an Rechtssätzen vereinheitlicht worden ist, bieten die positivierten IPR-Systeme der verschiedenen Staaten nur unvollkommene Lösungsvorschläge.

Unvollkommen sind diese Lösungsvorschläge:

a. *weil sie nicht alle Staaten binden.* Die fehlende Durchsetzbarkeit der IPR-Regeln der einzelnen Staaten im Verhältnis zur Jurisdiktion der anderen Staaten führt zwar nicht zur Negierung ihres Charakters als Rechtssätze, aber die grundsätzliche Beschränkung ihrer Durchsetzbarkeit ausserhalb der eigenen Jurisdiktion trifft sie im eigentlichen Kern des Regelungsgegenstandes. Im Gegensatz zu Rechtssätzen des materiellen Privatrechts eines Staates, die primär Inlandsachverhalte regulieren wollen und in der Regel auch in Inlandsachverhalten durchgesetzt werden können, wollen IPR-Rechtssätze ja gerade Sachverhalte mit Berührung zu mehreren Rechtsordnungen ordnen, was ihnen – in der Annahme, dass es nicht nur IPR-Sachverhalte zu bloss zwei Rechtsordnungen gibt, und in der Annahme, dass die beteiligten Staaten ihre Gerichtszuständigkeit ungefähr gleich weit ausdehnen – in logischerweise weniger als 50 % der Fälle gelingt.

b. *weil sie in ihrem Ausgangspunkt vom einzelnen Staat her konzipiert sind.* Es fehlt die echt überstaatliche Optik. Die Staaten, deren IPR-Systeme hinsichtlich der anwendbaren Rechtsordnung konsultiert werden, sind selbst in den Fällen, in denen Privatrechtssachverhalte eine wesentliche Berührung zu einer anderen Rechtsordnung aufweisen, im allgemeinen an der Anwendung der eigenen Rechtssätze interessiert, sei es zum Zwecke einer kohärenten Rechtspolitik der eigenen Gerichte und Behörden, sei es weil sie in guten Treuen die Werturteile der eigenen Rechtsordnung für überzeugend ansehen. Wenn es darum geht, zu entscheiden, unter welchen Voraussetzungen das eigene oder ein fremdes Recht angewendet werden soll, ist jeder Staat „befangen", nicht unparteiisch. Ein staatliches IPR-System überfordert schon im Ansatz die gesetzgebenden Organe. Ein nationales IPR kann letztlich nicht sagen, welche Rechtsordnung objektiv anwendbar ist, sondern höchstens, welche Rechtsordnung die Gerichte und Behörden dieses Staates anzuwenden haben. Die Anknüpfungsbegriffe der IPR-Kollisionsregeln (wie „Sitz" der Erbringerin der für den Schuldvertrag charakteristischen Leistung oder „gewöhnlicher Aufenthalt" des Kindes) sind Argumente, die sich im internationalen Diskurs mit anderen Argumenten auseinander setzen müssen. Weil der Regelungsgegenstand des IPR sich naturgemäss der Jurisdiktion eines einzigen Staates entzieht, findet er eine gerechte Lösung nur in der übereinstimmenden argumentativen Bewertung im Lichte aller beteiligten Rechtsordnungen. Die IPR-Systeme der einzelnen Staaten drücken aus, was aus ihrer Sicht entscheidend sein soll; sie können sich durchsetzen, soweit ihre Gerichte zuständig sind und ein Privater in diesem Staat klagt und das Urteil entweder im eigenen Staatsgebiet Vollstreckungssubstrat findet oder in den anderen Staaten vollstreckbar ist. Die Selbstbeschränkung des nationalen IPR auf das von diesem Staat Durchsetzbare lässt tendenziell Rechtsüberzeugungen hinter Machbarkeit zurücktreten.

c. *weil sie mehrheitlich der kollisionsrechtlichen IPR-Methode folgen.* Zur Schwäche dieser Methode wurden vorne, sub 2 (1), Ausführungen gemacht. Zusammengefasst sei hier wiederholt: Die kollisionsrechtliche Methode reduziert künstlich die Fragestellung nach der adäquaten rechtsfolgemässigen Behandlung von plurinationalen Sachverhalten auf die Auswahl zweier Rechtsordnungen und führt zur Anwendung einer einzigen nationalen Rechtsordnung, wie wenn ein Inlandsachverhalt vorläge. Es fehlt damit eine Bewertung der Plurinationalität, also des Charakteristischen dieses Sachverhaltes. Das ist nur eine Verlegenheitslösung. Auch äussert sich die IPR-Kollisionsregel einzig zum anwendbaren Recht und sagt nicht, wie sich die Parteien gerade mit Rücksicht darauf, dass die Sphären zweier Rechtsordnungen betroffen sind, zu verhalten haben. Hinzu kommt, dass IPR-Kollisionsregeln sehr allgemein gehaltene leges generales sind, was sich schon aus ihren sehr weiten Verweisungsbegriffen ergibt. Die IPR-Kollisionsregeln verweisen aufgrund ihrer Anknüpfungsbegriffe auf nationales Recht, vorerst unbesehen, welchen Inhalt die kollidierenden Rechtsordnungen konkret aufweisen. Mit Rücksicht auf den Umfang und die Differenziertheit der nationalen Privatrechtsordnungen (z.B. über zweitausend Gesetzesartikel im schweizerischen ZGB und OR, sowie zusätzliche Spezialgesetze wie UWG usw.) und auf die grundsätzlich unterschiedliche Ausgestaltung der vielen hundert staatlichen Rechtsordnungen kann auch ein so ausführliches IPR-Gesetz wie dasjenige der Schweiz aus dem Jahr 1987 (mit über hundert Gesetzesbestimmungen kollisionsrechtlichen Inhaltes) bei weitem nicht die Vielfalt möglicher Kollisionen von Rechtssätzen und Rechtspflichten erfassen. Die IPR-Kollisionsregeln sind nur erste Wegweiser in der Rechtsfindung, gestatten allein aber keine befriedigende Lösung der IPR-Fragestellung.

Aus dem Gesagten ergibt sich die selbstverständliche Folgerung, dass wir uns im heutigen Rechtszustand bei der Lösung von IPR-Fragen noch ganz mehrheitlich der *topischen Methode* bedienen müssen. Das IPR ist heute mehr Problem und Frage als System und Antwort. Die positivrechtlichen IPR-Systeme der verschiedenen Staaten sind in ihrer relativ engen Aussagemöglichkeit zu erkennen. Die Kollisionsregeln der nationalen IPR-Systeme sind darauf hin zu prüfen, ob sie sich überhaupt dafür eignen, die gestellte wirkliche, vollständige Frage zu beantworten. Häufig operieren Gerichte innerhalb der nationalen IPR-Systeme mit vermeintlichen Axiomen, denen jede innere Rechtfertigung abgeht.

Richtig ist es daher m.E., in jedem IPR-Fall von der allgemeinen Fragestellung (welches sind die Rechte und Pflichten der Privaten in dieser Sachverhaltskonstellation mit Berührung mehrerer staatlicher Territorien bzw. Rechtsordnungen?) auszugehen, und dann zu prüfen, ob die sich anbietenden nationalen IPR-Systeme (die im wesentlichen nur sagen, welches Recht die Gerichte und Behörden ihres Staates anwenden) überhaupt eine taugliche Antwort geben (können). Eine unvollständige oder parteiische Antwort, eine Antwort, die auf die Besonderheit des plurinationalen Sachverhalts nicht eingeht und nicht auf einem für den grenzüberschreitenden Rechtsverkehr spezifischen Werturteil beruht, kann nicht unfraglich richtig sein. Sie kann daher auch nicht die einzige verbindliche sein. Weil die Kollisionsregeln der einzelnen staatlichen IPR-Systeme nicht auf die echte, vollständige Fragestellung eingehen, weil sie den Regelungsgegenstand nicht voll erfassen und als Antwort in der Regel das Wesen des plurinationalen Sachverhalts ignorieren und diesen wie einen Inlandsachverhalt und zudem oft nach den der eigenen Rechtsordnung entnommenen Werturteilen behandeln, können sie nicht in Anspruch nehmen, einzige Entscheidungsgrundlage zu sein. Die rechtsanwendenden Gerichte und Behörden müssen sich, wollen sie den Gegenstand des IPR adäquat beurteilen, vom einzelstaatlichen Gesichtspunkt lösen und eine überstaatliche Optik wagen.[3]

---

[3] Einige der hier dargestellten Überlegungen hat der Verfasser in früheren Publikationen näher begründet. Vgl. zur Unterscheidung zwischen allgemeiner IPR-Fragestellung und deren topischem Charakter einerseits und der verengten Fragestellung der kollisionsrechtlichen Methode andererseits: Ivo Schwander, *Lois d'application immédiate, Sonderanknüpfung, IPR-Sachnormen und andere Ausnahmen von der gewöhnlichen Anknüpfung im IPR* (Zürich 1975) S. 235ff.; Ivo Schwander, *Einführung in das internationale Privatrecht, Bd. 1: Allg. Teil*, 2. Aufl. (St. Gallen 1990) S. 52, Nr. 56; zum Gegen-

Solchen Mut zeigte z.B. das schweizerische Bundesgericht in seinen Entscheiden vom 3. Juni 1971[4] und vom 27. September 1973,[5] in denen es zunächst in herkömmlicher Auslegung von gesetzlichen IPR-Rechtssätzen zu einem Resultat kam, das es als unbefriedigend bewertete, und in denen es danach gestützt auf „menschliche und soziale" Gesichtspunkte bzw. aus Gründen „d'humanité ou d'équité" andere Entscheidregeln bildete. Als weiteres Beispiel für eine klare und konsequente besondere Behandlung plurinationaler Sachverhalte kann ein über siebzigjähriger Entscheid des schweizerischen Bundesrates erwähnt werden, in welchem sich der Bundesrat – bei an sich anwendbarem schweizerischen Aktienrecht – über eine zwingende Gesetzesnorm des schweizerischen Rechts hinweggesetzt hat, mit der doppelsinnigen Formulierung: „Allein für eine internationale Gesellschaft wie hier kann das nationale Recht nicht uneingeschränkt angewendet werden."[6]

3. Vermehrte Beachtung von IPR-Gesichtspunkten im Rahmen des Internationalen Zivilprozessrechts

Es gehört zu den Fortschritten der IPR-Dogmatik des 20. Jahrhunderts, dass vermehrt gegenseitige Einflüsse und Abhängigkeiten zwischen den Zuständigkeits- und Anerkennungsregeln des Internationalen Zivilprozessrechts einerseits und des IPR andererseits bewusst gemacht worden sind. Auch haben die Konventionen des Internationalen Zivilprozessrechts, allen voran das Brüsseler- bzw. das Lugano-Übereinkommen, sowie die erleichterten Anerkennungsvoraussetzungen massgeblich zu vermehrter Rechtssicherheit im internationalen Rechtsverkehr beigetragen.

Das IPR begab sich damit jedoch in vermehrte Abhängigkeiten von Zuständigkeitsordnungen und von den Voraussetzungen der Anerkennung ausländischer Entscheidungen. Für die Rechtsgeschäftsplanung und das Ausarbeiten von Prozessstrategien wird folgerichtig primär auf die Frage, wo ein allfälliger Prozess ausgetragen würde, geachtet, weniger auf die Frage des anwendbaren Rechts. Dabei wird m.E. zu wenig thematisiert, dass die Kriterien zur Begründung einer internationalen Gerichtszuständigkeit (wie Bedürfnis nach Rechtsschutz und Rechtsfriede in einem bestimmten Territorium, Nähe des Gerichts zur effizienten Durchführung

---

stand des IPR: Ivo Schwander, „Zum Gegenstand des internationalen Privatrechts", in: E. Brem/ J. N. Druey/ E. A. Kramer/ I. Schwander (Hrsg.), *Festschrift Mario M. Pedrazzini* (Bern 1990) S. 355ff.; zur Kritik an den IPR-Methoden: Ivo Schwander, „Methodische Defizite des IPR-Kollisionsrechts – wie weiter?" in: I. Meier/ K. Siehr (Hrsg.), *Festschrift für Anton Heini* (Zürich 1995) S. 389ff.

[4] Urteil vom 3.6.1971 i.S. *Dal Bosco und Walther* c. *Regierungsrat des Kantons Bern*, BGE 97 I 389ff.

[5] Urteil vom 27.9.1973 i.S. *Brulhart* c. *Conseil d'Etat du canton de Fribourg*, BGE 99 Ib 240ff.

[6] Walther Burckhardt, *Schweizerisches Bundesrecht, Staats- und verwaltungsrechtliche Praxis des Bundesrates und der Bundesversammlung 1903-1926*, Bd. III (Frauenfeld 1931) S. 471.

des Prozesses usw.) andere sind als diejenigen zur Bestimmung des anwendbaren Rechts (des IPR oder des materiellen Rechts).

Eine sachlich gerechtfertigte, intensivere Berücksichtigung von Rechtsanwendungsfragen im IZPR könnte z.B. dadurch erreicht werden, dass die *Beachtung ausländischer Litispendenzen* und von im Zusammenhang stehenden Verfahren (z.B. Art. 21 und 22 Brüsseler- bzw. Lugano-Übereinkommen) nicht (nur) im Falle der zeitlichen Priorität der ausländischen Rechtshängigkeit in Frage käme, sondern (ebenfalls) entsprechend einer Beurteilung der inneren Begründetheit bzw. einer Abschätzung der fehlenden oder gleichwohl noch bestehenden Rechtsschutzbedürfnisse. Zu den kreativen Vorschlägen zu einer intensiveren internationalen Zusammenarbeit der Zivilgerichte gehört die Idee der grenzüberschreitenden *Koordination von Gerichtsverfahren* (gemeinsames „management" von Parallelprozessen in verschiedenen Staaten). Denkbar wären sowohl Überweisungen von Prozessen oder Teilen davon ohne Unterbruch der Rechtshängigkeit über die Grenzen, als auch Absprachen darüber, dass z.B. im Staat A die Frage der Handlungsfähigkeit als Hauptfrage entschieden wird, im Staat B die Frage des Zustandekommens des Vertrages und im Staat A wiederum alle im Zusammenhang mit der Erfüllung der strittigen vertraglichen Leistung stehenden Aspekte beurteilt werden.

Im Bereich der Zuständigkeitsregeln ist m.E. beim Mechanismus der nur einmaligen Prüfung sogenannt *doppelt relevanter Tatsachen oder Rechtsfragen* vermehrt der Akzent auf die Würdigung unter dem Gesichtspunkt des anwendbaren Rechts zu setzen. Doppelt relevante Tatsachen wie z.B. der gewöhnliche Aufenthalt einer Person oder der Erfüllungsort, haben meistens im IPR eine konstantere und aufgrund der Rechtsvergleichung vertieftere Auslegung erfahren als im Zuständigkeitsrecht des IZPR.

Im Anerkennungsrecht könnte die Einführung der sog. *kollisionsrechtlichen Anerkennung* den IPR-Gesichtspunkten mehr Kohärenz auch bei der Anerkennung und Vollstreckbarerklärung ausländischer Entscheidungen verleihen. So ist z.B. dem italienischen Recht die Anerkennung ausländischer Entscheidungen über das IPR-Kollisionsrecht bekannt; vgl. z.B. Art. 65 und 66 des Revisionsgesetzes 218/1995. Hat eine Behörde des Staates entschieden, dessen Rechtsordnung nach italienischem IPR anwendbar ist, so wird deren Entscheid in Italien anerkannt, ebenso der Entscheid eines dritten Staates, welcher in dem Staat anerkannt wird, dessen Rechtsordnung nach italienischem IPR anwendbar wäre.

4.   Ein vom Forum unabhängigerer Ausgangspunkt des IPR

Will man das IPR wegen seiner überstaatlichen Aufgabe von den Fesseln der nationalrechtlichen Herkunft der positivrechtlichen IPR-Kollisionsregeln lösen, geht es vor allem darum, dem IPR eine gewisse Autonomie von Begriffen und Wertungen des Rechts am Forum zu verschaffen.

Dies kann beispielsweise dadurch angestrebt werden, dass im nationalen IPR *Begriffe und Regeln aus internationalen Konventionen* auch in Bereichen übernommen werden, in denen diese Konventionen an sich nicht anwendbar wären. Im schweizerischen IPR-Gesetz von 1987 wurden einige internationale Konventionen in ihrem persönlich-räumlichen oder sachlichen Anwendungsbereich nationalrechtlich ausgedehnt, sodass auf eine davon abweichende nationalrechtliche IPR-Kollisionsregel für den konventionsrechtlich nicht geregelten Bereich verzichtet wurde; so in Art. 83 Abs. 2 oder Art. 85 Abs. 2 IPR-Gesetz. Denkbar wäre es auch, auf einen nationalrechtlichen Anknüpfungsbegriff des gewöhnlichen Aufenthalts zu verzichten und statt dessen denjenigen der Haager IPR-Konferenz zu übernehmen.

Wenn im Rahmen des Haager Unterhaltsstatutsabkommens von 1973 die *Vorfrage* nach dem Bestand eines familienrechtlichen Statusverhältnisses unselbständig (also nach dem IPR der für den Unterhalt massgeblichen Rechtsordnung) angeknüpft wird, so wird das IPR des Forums ausgeschaltet.

Traditionell und einfach zu bewerkstelligen ist eine gewisse Loslösung des IPR vom nationalrechtlichen Kontext dadurch, dass feste *Anknüpfungskriterien* verwendet werden, *welche auf äusserlich wahrnehmbaren und von einer Vielzahl von Staaten anerkannten territorialen Verknüpfungen beruhen*. Der Trend zur vermehrten Anknüpfung an den gewöhnlichen Aufenthalt einer Person erklärt sich u.a. gerade damit, dass dieses Kriterium in der Regel gleichförmig ausgelegt wird und sich im Einzelfall aufgrund äusserlich wahrnehmbarer Umstände leicht feststellen lässt. Im IPR des Schuldvertragsrechts kommt es zuweilen nicht auf den Sitz oder den Wohnsitz der Erbringerin der charakteristischen Leistung an, sondern statt dessen auf den Ort von deren Erfüllung.

Ausländisches IPR und nicht das IPR des Forums kommt bis zu einem gewissen Grade in einigen bekannten Problematiken des allgemeinen Teils des IPR zum Zuge, so beim *Renvoi*, bei der *Anpassung*, beim *Statutenwechsel*, bei der Erörterung des *Handelns unter falschem Recht*. Das auf *vorsorgliche Massnahmen* anzuwendende Recht soll nach neuerer Auffassung nach dem IPR des Staates bestimmt werden, in welchem der Hauptprozess stattfindet, und nicht des Staates, der für die vorsorglichen Massnahmen zuständig ist. Entsprechendes sollte gelten, wenn der Gerichtsstand des *Arrestorts* (soweit überhaupt noch zulässig) beziehungsarm bleibt; dann wird m.E. zweckmässigerweise das IPR desjenigen Staates konsultiert, in welchem sich der ordentliche Gerichtsstand befindet.

Moderne Kodifikationen des IPR formulieren ihre Kollisionsregeln oft mit sehr *differenzierten Rücksichtnahmen auf den Inhalt fremder IPR-Kollisionsregeln oder Sachnormen*. Beispiele dafür bieten im schweizerischen IPR-Gesetz Art. 119 Abs. 3 Satz 1 (wonach die Form von Verträgen über Grundstücke oder deren Gebrauch dem Recht des Lageorts des Grundstückes untersteht, es sei denn, dieses Recht lasse die Anwendung eines anderen Rechts zu) und Art. 124 Abs. 3 Satz 1 (wonach sich die Formgültigkeit eines Vertrages ausschliesslich nach dem auf den Schuldvertrag anwendbaren Recht richtet, wenn dieses Recht die Beachtung einer Form zum Schutz einer Partei vorsieht, es sei denn, es lasse die Anwendung eines anderen Rechts zu). Art. 77 Abs. 2 nimmt ausdrücklich darauf Rücksicht, ob die in der Schweiz vorgesehene Adoption – deren Voraussetzungen gemäss Abs. 1 derselben Bestimmung schweizerischem Recht unterstehen – im Wohnsitz- oder im Heimatstaat der Adoptierenden nicht anerkannt und dem Kind daraus ein schwerwiegender Nachteil erwachsen würde.

Noch weiter gehen moderne IPR-Gesetze, welche *offene Lücken* aufweisen bzw. *bewusst vor ausländischem Kollisionsrecht zurücktreten.* Art. 37 Abs. 1 Satzteil 2 des schweizerischen IPR-Gesetzes bestimmt, dass der Name einer Person mit Wohnsitz im Ausland der Rechtsordnung untersteht, auf welche das Kollisionsrecht des Wohnsitzstaats verweist. Art. 91 Abs. 1 desselben Gesetzes unterstellt den Nachlass einer Person mit letztem Wohnsitz im Ausland derjenigen Rechtsordnung, auf welche das Kollisionsrecht des Wohnsitzstaates verweist. Der Technik der ausdrücklichen Nichtregelung oder der Technik des Verweises auf das IPR eines anderen Staates sollte m.E. vermehrt gefolgt werden, denn nationales IPR ist glaubwürdiger, wenn es seine eigenen Kollisionsregeln auf diejenigen Konstellationen beschränkt, in denen sie auch durchsetzbar sind.

Noch konsequenter in diese Richtung weisen die de lege ferenda diskutierten Auffassungen, wonach versucht werden soll, mit einfachen Regeln den „Sitz" des Lebensverhältnisses durch die *Wahl des dem Lebensverhältnis am nächsten stehenden nationalen IPR* als Ausgangspunkt zu bestimmen. Massgeblich wäre dann primär das IPR nicht des Forums, sondern z.B. im Personen- und Gesellschaftsrecht das IPR des Staates am Wohnsitz oder Sitz der natürlichen Person bzw. der Gesellschaft, im Familienrecht das IPR des Staates, wo sich der gemeinsame Lebensmittelpunkt der Familie oder der Wohnsitz der hauptsächlich betroffenen Person befindet, im Erbrecht das IPR am letzten Wohnsitz des Erblassers, im Sachenrecht das IPR am Lageort. Solche Gesichtspunkte würden den prioritären Ausgangspunkt der kollisionsrechtlichen Rechtsfindung aus einer überstaatlichen Optik bestimmen. Ferner könnte jeder Staat mit primären oder mit sekundären Kollisionsregeln signalisieren, welche Kollisionsregeln oder Eingriffsnormen er in jedem IPR-Sachverhalt mit Berührung zur eigenen Rechtsordnung durchsetzen will und welche Kollisionsregeln er in Konkurrenz zu anders wertenden Kollisionsregeln ausländischer IPR-Systeme zurücktreten lassen will.

In Zukunft sollten m.E. auch vermehrt in Europa die in den USA geführten Diskussionen um „true" und „false" *conflicts* wieder aufgenommen werden. Wenn aus dem unter Ziffer 2 vorstehend Ausgeführten gefolgt wird, dass einheitliche materiellrechtliche Beurteilungen an sich die umfassendste Antwort auf die natürliche und allgemeine Fragestellung des IPR nach den Rechten und Pflichten der Privaten im internationalen Rechtsverkehr geben, dann sollte in problemorientierter (topischer) Methode klar sein, dass *einer übereinstimmenden materiellrechtlichen Beurteilung* (sei es in Form von gemeinsamen IPR-Sachnormen oder Handelsgebräuchen, sei es in Form von im wesentlichen übereinstimmendem Privatrecht der beiden hauptsächlich betroffenen Rechtsordnungen) Vorrang zukommen soll. In zweiter Linie soll es auf *übereinstimmende Lösungen der IPR-Systeme der hauptsächlich betroffenen Staaten* ankommen. Eine IPR-Kollisionsregel überzeugt nicht allein deswegen, weil sie vom Forumstaat aufgestellt worden ist, sondern weil sie im Ergebnis mit der IPR-Kollisionsregel des Staates übereinstimmt, zu welchem der Sachverhalt ebenfalls einen wesentlichen Bezug aufweist. Divergieren die IPR-Kollisionsregeln der beteiligten Rechtsordnungen, so kann auf das Ergebnis der IPR-Kollisionsregel des Forums nur dann abgestellt werden, wenn hier auch der *Schwerpunkt* (Sitz des Lebensverhältnisses) im soeben umschriebenen Sinn (prioritäre Regel) liegt. Die Unterscheidung von *primären und sekundären Kollisionsregeln* entsprechend der ihnen vom nationalen IPR-System zuerkannten Relevanz im Konfliktfall spielt wiederum eine Rolle, wenn man echte von falschen Konflikten unterscheiden will; in Konkurrenz zu solchen IPR-Kollisionsregeln stehen aber auch weitere kollisions- und materiellrechtliche Erwägungen.[7]

5. ZUR AUFGABE DES IPR, VOM NATIONALEN RECHT UNABHÄNGIGE WERTURTEILE ZU ENTWICKELN

Werturteile, mit denen das IPR arbeitet, weisen teils eher kollisionsrechtlichen, teils eher materiell-privatrechtlichen Charakter auf. Insbesondere bei letzteren besteht das Risiko einer zu starken Gewichtung von dem nationalen Recht (Verfassungsrecht, übriges öffentliches Recht, Privat- und Wirtschaftsrecht) entnommenen Werturteilen. Eine stärker materiellrechtlich orientierte IPR-Disziplin rechtfertigt sich jedoch nur mit spezifisch für den internationalen Rechtsverkehr entwickelten Werturteilen. Dass z.B. das neuere schweizerische Verfassungsrecht eine engagiertere Rechtspolitik im Bereich der Herstellung einer echten Gleichstellung von Frau und Mann fordert, rechtfertigt es noch nicht, zu diesem Zweck den Ordre public gegen rechtsungleiches fremdes Recht einzusetzen; wohl aber der Umstand, dass die Schweiz die UNO-Menschenrechtspakte, die UNO-Frauendiskriminierungsverbotskonvention und weitere einschlägige Konventionen ratifiziert hat und diese Konventionen Ausdruck einer weltweit übereinstimmenden Bewertung dieser zentralen Menschenrechtsfrage sind. Auch andere Wertungen der neueren Gesetzgebung entsprechen allgemeinen Entwicklungen von Gesellschaft, Wirt-

---

[7] Einige dieser Gedanken sind näher oder unter anderen Gesichtspunkten erörtert worden in: Ivo Schwander, „Tentativo di determinare nel diritto internazionale privato e nella procedura civile internazionale un punto di vista fisso al di là della disciplina del foro", in: Alfred E. von Overbeck/ Fausto Pocar/ Kurt Siehr (Hrsg.), *Collisio Legum, Studi di diritto internazionale privato per Gerardo Broggini* (Milano 1997) p. 497ff.

schaft und Technik über nationale Grenzen hinaus, sodass sie legitimerweise in Werturteilen des IPR Eingang finden.

Es geht um von der internationalen Rechtsgemeinschaft – sie ist im IPR der Kreis der mobilen und grenzüberschreitend handelnden Privaten – akzeptierbare Wertungen, welche dem internationalen Rechtsverkehr dienen. Zu denken ist etwa an: striktere Handhabung des Grundsatzes „pacta sunt servanda" und grösserer Spielraum in der Gestaltung von Rechtsgeschäften im kommerziellen Rechtsverkehr; Rechtsgeschäfte zur Sicherung von Kredit und Geschäftsabwicklungen über die Grenze sollen nicht durch staatliche Vorschriften in der Wirksamkeit eingeschränkt werden; Recht auf Zusammenführung von Familien und Schutz des Kindes; Erleichterung von Ehescheidungen; Verbot des Eindringens des Staates und anderer Privater in die Privatsphäre.

Die Bemühungen um weitere Rechtsvereinheitlichung und Rechtsangleichung, die rege Schiedsgerichtstätigkeit, die lex mercatoria sowie Annäherungen an einen „transnationalen" Ordre public können ebenfalls als Anzeichen dafür bezeichnet werden, dass eine vermehrt „materiellrechtliche" Ausrichtung des IPR nicht notwendigerweise dessen Fixierung auf nationales Recht bedeutet.

SUMMARY
HOW CAN PRIVATE INTERNATIONAL LAW ACQUIRE A MORE
INTERNATIONAL VIEWPOINT?

This essay summarizes briefly how the only adequate *universal viewpoint* of PIL can gain ground in today's national PIL codifications. The object of PIL has been referred to as a continuous challenge by the genius PIL restorer and thinker, Friedrich Carl von Savigny.

One needs to remain mindful of the explicit *meaning of the national rules on conflict of laws* due to their nature (section 2). Only substantive rules are capable of providing an answer to the problem in question, as the rules on conflict of laws refrain from deciding which of the two or more material statutes in question is to be applied. As soon as there are substantive acts which themselves answer specific legal problems, the solutions offered by those should be favoured over solutions resulting from the use of conflict rules. However, today we have only very few rules of PIL which directly answer problems by imposing rights and duties upon private persons.

We shall see how, based upon a comparison with international civil procedure law, the *PIL-viewpoints* could be revised to acquire *a more autonomous meaning* (section 3). We shall then see how to achieve a *methodical starting point separate from the forum* (section 4). Finally, we should be reminded that the task of the PIL is to develop more *autonomous value judgements and judicial measures*.

Tort Choice of Law in Israel: Putting Order in a Methodological Chaos

Amos Shapira[*]

1.	The Case.	685
2.	The Present Methodological Chaos	687
3.	A Restatement of the Principal Choice of Law Policy-Goals.	691
4.	A Proposed Scheme for Tort Choice of Law	697
5.	Resolving the Case under the Proposed Scheme	700

1. THE CASE

Consider the following case:

An Israeli young man afflicted with a brain tumor that necessitated brain surgery sought the services of an internationally renowned Romanian surgeon. The patient established contact with the surgeon through a liaison office maintained by the latter in Virginia, the United States. That office referred the patient to a hospital in Lubliana, Slovenia where the surgeon is habitually employed. It should be noted that, in addition to practicing in Slovenia, the surgeon quite regularly performs brain surgery worldwide, including in Israel. The operation proved unsuccessful and the patient brought a tort compensation action against the surgeon before the Tel Aviv District Court in Israel. Israeli judicial jurisdiction was based on the service of process on the defendant-surgeon upon one of his occasional visits to Israel. A Forum Non Convenience allegation was dismissed by the Israeli forum.

The plaintiff-patient founded his lawsuit against the defendant-surgeon on two grounds: assault (performing the operation without the informed consent of the patient who, allegedly, was not informed properly as to the risks involved) and malpractice (executing the surgical procedure in a professionally negligent manner). Under Israeli tort law, the plaintiff would be entitled to recovery on both grounds, if supported by the evidence. The claim, which was brought three years subsequent to

---

[*] M.Jur. (Hebrew University of Jerusalem), M.C.L. (Columbia University), J.S.D. (Yale University); Professor of Law, Tel-Aviv University; K. Lubowski Chair of Law and Biomedical Ethics; Co-Director, The Minerva Center for Human Rights, Tel-Aviv University, Israel.

J. Basedow et al., eds., Private Law in the International Arena – Liber Amicorum Kurt Siehr
© 2000, T.M.C.Asser Press, The Hague, The Netherlands

the event, would not be time-barred by Israeli law that provides for a seven years limitation period. The defendant-surgeon argues, however, that the action against him should be dismissed under the allegedly applicable Slovenian law. An expert opinion submitted by the defendant-surgeon stipulates that under Slovenian law such an action would be time-barred two years after the event. Slovenian law, more-over, does not recognize a tort cause-of-action for a medical intervention allegedly performed without the informed consent of the patient and a medical malpractice action may only be brought against the hospital concerned but not against the hospi-tal's employees, agents or physicians (except where it is claimed that they acted ma-liciously). It follows that if the Israeli *lex fori* applies the plaintiff-patient may win whereas if the Slovenian *lex loci delicti* governs he must lose.

In support of his claim that the Israeli *lex fori* should be the applicable law, the plaintiff-patient argues, *inter alia*, that he sought the personal-professional services of the world famous defendant-surgeon through the latter's Virginia, U.S.A. liaison office. There the plaintiff-patient was indeed referred to the Lubliana, Slovenia hos-pital but, as far as he was concerned, he could have been referred to any other venue where the defendant-surgeon occasionally performs brain-surgery, including Is-rael. The Lubliana, Slovenia *locus delicti* is, therefore, utterly fortuitous as regards the plaintiff-patient. Furthermore, the defendant-surgeon in any event exposes him-self regularly to the legal regimes of the various countries where he periodically renders his professional services. From his perspective, so the argument runs, it does not really matter whether, say, Japanese law becomes applicable to his con-duct by dint of operating in Japan or in consequence of performing surgery on a Japanese patient in Slovenia. The defendant-surgeon counters that, due to his inter-national professional reputation, patients from all over the world seek his services at the Lubliana, Slovenia hospital where he is habitually employed. It would be grossly unsensible and unfair, so he argues, to subject him to Japanese law on Mon-day morning, when he operates on a Japanese patient, and to Israeli law on Monday afternoon, when he performs surgery on an Israeli. The Slovenian *lex loci delicti* should govern in both instances.

In a decision rendered in February 1999, the Tel Aviv District Court found for the plaintiff-patient.[1] Although seemingly acknowledging the prima facie primacy of the hard-and-fast *lex loci delicti* choice of law rule, the Court cited approvingly American and English judicial opinions that favored more flexible, case-specific, result-sensitive and discretion-laden choice-of-law standards such as "the center of gravity", "the most significant relationship" and "the predominant state interest". The case at bar, the Court intimated, is neither about a tort committed at a Slovenian hospital and involving two Slovenians nor about a patient who sorted out the

---

[1] Civil Action 823/95 *Mesika v. Prof. Dr. Dolens et al* (Tel Aviv-Jaffa District Court, decision ren-dered on February 14, 1999).

Slovenian hospital to be operated there by one of its physicians. Rather, it is a case about an Israeli patient who sought the personal-professional services of an internationally renowned surgeon and was referred to be operated in one of the theatres of operation frequented by that surgeon. As far as the patient is concerned, he would have pursued this surgeon of his choice anywhere. The *locus delicti*, under these circumstances, is indeed merely accidental and clearly outweighed by other and more dominant contacts such as the plaintiff-patient's habitual residence and the location of his pre and post surgery treatment. These significant contacts, the Court reasoned, point to Israel and to Israeli law as the proper *lex causae*. It is noteworthy that the Court then went beyond this rather conventional process of grouping, counting and weighing territorial and personal contacts and ventured a kind of policy analysis focusing on the merits and concrete consequences of the implicated substantive laws. The Slovenian two-years time bar and exemption of physicians employed by hospitals from personal malpractice liability were branded by the Israeli forum as unfair and anachronistic. The forum deemed it as its duty to protect the Israeli plaintiff against such unjust and archaic foreign laws. All the more so considering that denial of recovery under the Slovenian *lex loci delicti* would leave the Israeli plaintiff destitute, a public charge, a burden on the Israeli society.

2.   THE PRESENT METHODOLOGICAL CHAOS

Until the early seventies, Israeli courts followed faithfully the English common law traditional dual-limb rule on choice of law in tort.[2] Torts committed in Israel were regarded as purely domestic situations, regulated as a matter of course by Israeli tort law, even if one or both parties were foreigners. In claims based on the defendant's conduct abroad, liability would accrue if such conduct is actionable as a tort (namely, gives rise to tort liability) according to Israeli tort law and not justifiable (namely, non-innocent, unauthorized or inexcusable) according to the law of the foreign place of conduct. In theory, only a convergence of actionability under the Israeli *lex fori* and non-justifiability under the foreign *lex loci delicti commissi* could lead an Israeli forum to find for a plaintiff suing on a foreign tort. Practically speaking, if the defendant failed to assert and prove the justifiability of his behavior under the law of the foreign location, the plaintiff would be likely to win merely by establishing that tort liability would have attached under Israeli tort law had the conduct taken place in Israel. Such a conclusion was bound to be reached in consequence of the forum's propensity to invoke the presumption of similarity of laws or

---

[2] On the English common law traditional dual-limb rule see J.H.C. Morris, *The Conflict of Laws*, 4th ed. (by D. McClean) (London, Sweet & Maxwell LTD 1993) pp. 280-286; J.G. Collier, *Conflict of Laws* (Cambridge University Press 1987) pp. 184-186.

simply to ignore the foreign location of the alleged tort. Viewed from the perspective of this common law traditional dual-limb rule it appears that the plaintiff-patient in the case at hand would prevail. The defendant-surgeon's conduct (alleged assault and malpractice) is actionable as a tort under the Israeli *lex fori* and, presumably, would not be considered justifiable (even though it does not import tort liability) by the Slovenian *lex loci delicti*.

In 1969 the House of Lords modified substantially the traditional common law position on tort choice of law.[3] The "double actionability" rule fashioned by the House of Lords in *Chaplin* v. *Boys* was invoked, although not consistently, by Israeli courts in the seventies and early eighties. Under this rule, a plaintiff suing in Israel for a tort allegedly committed in a foreign country will only win if the claim's actionability can be established both under the Israeli *lex fori* and the foreign *lex loci delicti*. There is, however, a flexible exception that is designed to mitigate the strictness of the "double actionability" requirement. Under this exception, an Israeli forum may on occasion consider it unreasonable or unfair to subject the plaintiff's claim to the legal standards (denying or limiting tort liability) of either the *lex loci delicti* or the *lex fori*. This might be the case where the contact between the country invoking such restrictive legal standards and the occurrence and the parties is deemed by the forum as too tenuous or fortuitous. In such a case, the plaintiff may recover under the law favorable to his or her claim of the one country (be it the forum or the *locus delicti*) having the significant connection with the occurrence and the parties. Applying the "double actionability" rule to the case at bar produces a clear result: The Israeli plaintiff-patient loses, since his tort claim against the defendant-surgeon is not vindicated by the Slovenian *lex loci delicti*. One could, nonetheless, argue that the particular circumstances of the case at hand may justify having resort to the flexible exception on the ground that the connection between the Slovenian *locus delicti* and the occurrence and the parties is merely accidental or tenuous. If the Slovenian *lex loci delicti* denying tort liability can thus be brushed aside, the Israeli plaintiff-patient would prevail on the basis of the supportive Israeli *lex fori* alone.

In 1983 the Israeli Supreme Court endorsed (though merely by dictum and without systematic elaboration)[4] the flexible, some would say open-ended, "most significant relationship" formula championed by the American Restatement (Second), Conflict of Laws, 1971.[5] Under this choice of law criterion, the rights and liabilities of the parties with respect to an issue in tort are determined by the domestic law of the state which, as to that issue, has the most significant relationship to the occur-

---

[3] *Chaplin* v. *Boys*, [1969] 2 All E.R. 1085.

[4] See Civil Appeal 750/79, *Klausner* v. *Berkovitz* et al, 37 (4) P.D. (Israel Supreme Court Judgments) 449.

[5] Restatement of the Law Second, Conflict of Laws 2d §145 (St. Paul, Minn., American Law Institute Publishers, 1971).

rence and the parties. The American Restatement (Second) choice of law prescription found favor with Israeli district court judges in the mid and late eighties and the early nineties. They clearly cherished the flexibility offered them by the Restatement's formula, that was understood as undercutting the undue monopoly of the *lex loci delicti* and enhancing the role played by personal links (such as the plaintiff's habitual residence) in the choice of law process. Typically, the "most significant relationship" nebulous standard can hardly provide us with a ready-made, clear-cut solution to the choice of law dilemma presented by the case at hand: Does Israel (the location of the forum of litigation and the place of habitual residence of the plaintiff-patient) or Slovenia (the *locus delicti* and where the defendant-surgeon is habitually employed) have the most significant relationship with the occurrence and the parties? It is noteworthy that the American Restatement (Second) offers a presumptive rule to the effect that whenever the injury and the conduct causing it occur in the same state it would usually be designated as having the most significant relationship and consequently its law should govern. Following this presumptive rule, if applicable, the plaintiff-patient's tort action ought to be dismissed.

The last development to date in the Israeli case law regarding choice of law in torts occurred in 1994 when the Israeli Supreme Court expressed gross dissatisfaction with what it considered as chaos in the English and American tort choice of law jurisprudence.[6] As the case before it involved a tort allegedly committed in Israel, the Supreme Court opted to view it – much in the English common law tradition – as a purely domestic controversy devoid of any choice of law connotations (even though the plaintiff was a foreigner injured during a touristic visit to Israel). Thus Israeli domestic law was applied as a matter-of-course. The Supreme Court seemed quite eager to relieve itself of the task of consolidating a definitive position on the appropriate methodological approach to the choice of the applicable law in cases of a tort allegedly committed abroad. This question was emphatically left open for future deliberation.

A year later, in 1995, the British Parliament enacted the Private International Law (Miscellaneous Provisions) Act, 1995.[7] The Act explicitly abolishes the "double actionability" rule and the exception thereto. Instead it adopts a general rule under which the applicable law in tort claims entailing foreign elements is the law of the country in which the events constituting the tort in question occur. Where those events occur in different countries, the applicable law for personal injury cases is the law of the place of injury, for damage to property cases is the *lex situs*, and for other cases is the law of the country where the most significant elements of those events occurred. The Act provides further for an exception to the general rule.

---

[6] Civil Appeal 702/87, *State of Israel* v. *John Cohn* et al, 48 (2) P.D. 705.
[7] Private International Law (Miscellaneous Provisions) Act, 1995 (1995 Chapter 42, Part III, sections 9-15).

According to the exception, the applicable law indicated by the general rule may be displaced by the law of another country if it appears that, considering the significance of the factors connecting it with the tort in question, it would be substantially more appropriate for its law to govern. Under the British 1995 Act the plaintiff-patient would lose if the general rule (mandating the applicability of the law of the country where the events constituting the tort occur) should control the case at bar. Yet the Slovenian law indicated as applicable by this general rule may be displaced by the plaintiff-favoring Israeli law if the latter is deemed substantially more appropriate to govern the situation at hand.

In a comparative law setting one should note the Proposal for a European Convention on the Law Applicable to Non-Contractual Obligations (Text adopted in Luxembourg on 25-27 September 1998). The proposed convention mandates (much in the vein of the American Restatement (Second), Conflict of Laws) that a non-contractual obligation arising out of a harmful event shall be governed by the law of the country with which it is most closely connected. It provides further that when the parties to the litigation are habitually resident in different countries, and the event and the resulting injury occurred in the same country, it shall be presumed that the obligation is most closely connected with that latter country (unless it appears from the circumstances as a whole that the obligation is more closely connected with some other country). It seems that, under this approach, the law of Slovenia (where the event as well as the injury occurred) is likely to be considered as the presumptive applicable law and, if so, the plaintiff-patient is doomed to lose.

To add yet another comparative law perspective let me mention also the new German Statute on Private International Law of Non-Contractual Obligations and Property of 21 May, 1999.[8] The German Statute decrees that claims arising out of a tortious event are governed by the law of the country where the defendant has acted or by the law of the country where the injury has occurred – depending on the plaintiff's choice. It provides further that in case the parties were, at the time of the occurrence, habitually resident in the same country its law shall apply. These hard-and-fast choice of law directives are then qualified by a provision mandating the applicability of the law of another country (rather than the country otherwise indicated) if it has an essentially closer connection to the matter. Such an essentially closer connection may result, in particular, from a special legal or factual relationship between the parties. It is quite obvious that, under the German position, the law of Slovenia (where the defendant acted and the injury occurred) will apply and, in consequence, the defendant-surgeon will prevail.

---

[8] Published in the Official Gazette 1(26), 31 May 1999.

3. A RESTATEMENT OF THE PRINCIPAL CHOICE OF LAW POLICY-GOALS

Choice of law theorists are characteristically prone to assign a host of frequently incompatible policy goals to be furthered through the workings of choice of law prescriptions. Yet inflated expectations regarding the potential accomplishments of the choice of law machinery are doomed to frustration: The choice of law process, even in its most sophisticated version, just cannot faithfully and effectively serve too many, often irreconcilable, masters simultaneously. One should therefore refrain from overstating choice of law methodological desiderata. An overloaded choice of law apparatus just cannot carry the burden and deliver the goods.

Still, a fair, rational and functional choice of law method ought to be responsive – to a carefully measured, proportionately shaped extent – to the following four policy objectives:

A.   Ease of judicial administration.
B.   Uniformity and predictability of the result of litigation.
C.   Vindication of parties' expectations and fair notice as to the applicable law.
D.   Advancement of the substantive law concerns of the implicated legal orders through the elucidation and evaluation of the underlying concrete policies of the various legal standards involved.

Let me briefly elaborate.

A.   Ease of judicial administration

An appropriate choice of law methodology should avoid confronting the forum of litigation with insurmountable practical difficulties in its routine implementation. The need to economize on judicial time and effort is all the more pressing where courts' dockets are crowded in general and choice of law litigation is not a rarity. Surely, the virtues of a simple, convenient and efficient adjudicatory apparatus for the handling of choice of law controversies are self evident. No one can deny that litigants, lawyers and judges are bound to benefit from an easily workable, smoothly operational choice of law machinery.

Specific and simple choice of law rules forged ex ante by the legislature are conducive to judicial economy. By the same token, open-ended and complex choice of law standards, that can only be invoked through an ad hoc exercise of broad and essentially unguided judicial discretion, will hardly serve the need for ease of judicial administration. Yet the borderline between guiding clarity and mechanical rigidity is often frustratingly blurred. To be sure, judges are likely to welcome brightline, hard-and-fast legislative directives that are designed to facilitate the task of judicial decision making. But at the same time they are prone also to shun overly mechanical and rigid statutory formulas and to seek ingenious escape devices in order to avoid an unfair or unsound, and therefore unacceptable, result otherwise dictated by the ostensibly governing black-letter rule. The truth of the matter is that sometimes simplicity in judicial administration is incompatible with the complexity inherent in a certain branch of the law. A modality proposed for the regulation of a given problem-area is bound – if it purports to be rational, principled and directive – to reflect the intrinsic complications of that same problem-area. An attempt to create ease of administration in a legal field which is not endowed with the virtue of simplicity is doomed to breed confusion and frustration. It is always better, in the final analysis, to face up to the problem in its true dimensions and with its unconcealed complexities while striving to maximize realistically the ease of judicial administration.

B.   Uniformity and predictability of the result of litigation

The traditionally asserted overriding policy objective of the choice of law process has been uniformity and predictability of the result of litigation irrespective of the location of the forum. Uniformity of result is expected to promote international harmony and cooperation in socioeconomic matters and to foster predictability as to the governing law, thus facilitating private legal ordering, ensuring stability and eliminating forum shopping. It is also designed to guarantee equal treatment and impartiality in choice of law adjudication. It goes without saying that all these are values worthy of promotion in any legal discipline. Yet a substantial measure of uniform judicial decision making in choice of law matters across national boundaries requires a uniform choice of law instrumentality common to all legal systems – an ideal that is still largely unrealized. Also, judges' propensity to resort to side-stepping techniques in order to escape unacceptable results otherwise dictated by mechanical – even if uniform – choice of law rules is bound to undermine decisional uniformity and predictability.

Looking around we must realize that practitioners learn how to function in the legal sphere without absolute certainty, resorting to educated guesses and conducting their affairs with some doubt at the edges. This is so in a host of wholly domestic legal settings and a fortiori in the real world of transnational choice of law. Realistically viewed, the need for uniformity of result is not equally pressing in each and every choice of law problem area. As a corollary, the prospects of the actual realization of this policy goal range over a wide spectrum from reasonably promising to virtually non existent. Universal uniformity of result is truly not required in many instances or is overshadowed by other policy goals of the choice of law process. Conversely, there are situations where – due to political, socioeconomic, humanistic or technological constraints – a uniform pattern of decision making across national frontiers is clearly indicated. Where the need to secure accommodation of concrete transnational concerns – such as the facilitation of multinational commercial activity – is acutely felt and widely shared, similar choice of law standards are prone to emerge, either through independent legal evolution in the various national communities or by concerted international or regional effort in the form of multilateral conventions. Such choice of law standards usually point to the application of the rule of decision of that one of the involved legal systems which displays a paramount interest in controlling the matter at hand. Thus, for instance, the home community of a person is preeminently concerned with his or her marital status. Similarly, the *situs* country has a predominant interest in safeguarding its system of registration and ascertainment of title to local land.

A fair degree of uniformity of result, where it really presents a compelling necessity of international life, can best be secured through multinational collaboration with a view to the mutual adoption of uniform choice of law standards. To be uniformly adoptable and operative, such standards must be simple, "shortcut" choice of law directives, much in the traditional system-pointing mold. Adherents of some of the modern approaches who recoil from the very notion of system-selecting rules must realize that uniformity of result in distinctive problem areas is not a cost-free objective. Its promotion as a peculiar transnational concern inhering in the multi-jurisdictional context must be paid for at the expense of other choice of law policy goals.

C.   Vindication of parties' expectations and fair notice as to the applicable law

Situations involving foreign ingredients present a fundamental jurisprudential dilemma: the reasonableness and fairness of judging human conduct by foreign legal standards. The concept of legal fairness postulates the existence of an appropriate connection between the parties to the controversy at hand and the legal norms in the light of which their rights and obligations are to be assessed. This notion of an appropriate connection between parties and the law governing them is frequently depicted in terms of vindication of justified expectations as to the applicable law.

The protection of the justified expectations of parties to legal relationships is a much-acclaimed goal in all branches of law, including private international law. It would clearly be unfair to charge a person with liability under the laws of country A, for conduct undertaken by him or her with reasonable reliance on the different laws of country B. It would likewise be unjust suddenly to saddle one's transactions with a prohibitory or regulatory law, the applicability of which could not have been foreseen at the relevant time. Thus the "vindication of justified expectations" desideratum weighs very heavily in choice of law literature. It imparts life to some cardinal choice of law principles, such as the "party autonomy" rule enabling the parties to a transnational contract to choose for themselves the governing law. It also lends support to the idea of allowing the litigants in a transnational tort case to agree, after the dispute has arisen, on the applicable law (without prejudice to the rights of third parties).

Nonetheless, one should be cautious not to overstate the significance of subjective foreseeability and reliance in cases entailing foreign elements. After all, to be

deserving of legal protection, alleged party expectations must first be actually existing and susceptible of realistic ascertainment. To attribute concrete expectations to
litigants where such expectations have never really existed or are incapable of verification is to obfuscate legal reasoning. Indeed, the hypothesis that parties to legal
relationships invariably form specific expectations as to the legal norms that will
govern their interactions is highly questionable in many instances, especially in
contexts fraught with foreign factors.

It may well make sense to reason in terms of concrete expectations regarding the
applicable law in the domain of privately ordered, preplanned activity, such as in
the field of transnational commercial transactions. In many cases falling within this
category, the parties indeed are prone to be mindful of the juridical implications of
their planned activity and to fashion their business policy upon an informed
consideration of relevant legal standards, local and foreign. Thus, for instance, a
manufacturer whose commercial engagements cut across national boundaries is
likely to foresee contingencies of involvement with foreign laws (pertaining, say, to
products liability) and to account for them when determining prices or acquiring
insurance coverage. It would, therefore, only be fair to vindicate as fully as possible
(barring countervailing policy and fairness considerations such as consumer
protection) the conduct-influencing expectations formed by parties with regard to
the legal regulation of their transnational activities. The situation is utterly
different, however, concerning a wide range of human interactions that ordinarily
are devoid of any meaningful prior legal ordering. These are not readily amenable
to judicial elaboration in terms of subjective expectations as to the applicable rule of
decision. Where people usually interact with little or no awareness of the possible
legal ramifications of their actions, the "upholding of the parties' expectations"
desideratum may be nothing but an empty slogan. Thus a host of ordinary personal
injury tort cases are simply not amenable to judicial reasoning based upon the
concept of subjective party expectations. The very notion of crystallized choice of
law expectations is incongruous in a context of social interaction where the
participants are not disposed to fashion their conduct upon a prior consideration of
potentially applicable laws.

The notion of a required appropriate connection between parties and applicable
laws in cases entailing foreign elements has thus far been addressed in terms of
vindication of subjective choice of law expectations whenever they actually exist.
Yet the fundamental principle of fairness embodied in this notion transcends the
goal of upholding parties' concrete choice of law expectations. This principle
conveys the basic idea that it is a threshold requirement of fairness in the choice of
law process that a sufficiently significant relationship exist between a party and the
legal regime by which his or her situation is to be judged. This is an objective
criterion that is not necessarily related to any actual or presumed subjective
expectations as to the governing law. Under this criterion, the fairness of judging
conduct by foreign legal prescriptions is ultimately dependent on whether it would

be reasonable to charge the party concerned with prior notice regarding the potential foreign law connotations of the occurrence at bar. If the party can reasonably be charged with fair notice as to the possible transnational ramifications of the affair at hand then one may conclude that an appropriate connection does exist between that party and the foreign law which is to be applied. Fair notice means that the party in question could have reasonably perceived at the relevant time a possible contact with, or potential impact upon, persons, property, institutions or events that might fall within the prescriptive domain of a given legal system. Hence a litigant who actually was, or reasonably could have been, mindful of possible involvement with matters potentially subject to the legal management of a foreign country may not complain of lack of sufficient connection between himself or herself and the normative order upheld by that country. By the same token, a choice of law methodology that aspires to promote the idea of objective fair notice ought to refrain from designating as applicable a system of law that clearly has no appropriate relationship with a party to the litigation.

D. Advancement of the substantive law concerns of the implicated legal orders through the elucidation and evaluation of the underlying concrete policies of the various legal standards involved

The traditional approach builds on system-pointing choice of law rules, that purport to designate the governing *lex causae* (whether domestic or foreign) in cases involving foreign elements. A conventional system-pointing choice of law rule comprises two structural components: a category of type-situations (e.g., tort claims) linked to a connecting factor (namely, a spatial contact between a person, a relationship or an event and a given country, e.g., the place of the tort). Once the matter at bar is characterized as falling within a given category of type-situations, the connecting factor attached to that category will lead the forum to the designated governing legal system, be it the *lex fori* or the law of a foreign country. Thus, conventional choice of law rules are in essence system-selecting. They are intended to furnish a reference to a country the law of which would ultimately provide the controlling rule of decision. And such reference is supposed to be effected in deliberate disregard of the content of the specific rule of decision (local or foreign) finally to be applied and in an acknowledged indifference as to the merits of the concrete resulting outcome of the dispute. Such multilateral directives are designed to furnish impartiality, reciprocity, certainty, uniformity and ease of application to the choice of law process. Critics of the traditional system, however, have persistently challenged its actual ability to deliver these promised goods. In particular, they have pointed to the public policy barrier and to the notion of substantive rules of direct ("immediate") or mandatory application as escape devices, or longstop techniques, that in fact infuse a seemingly multilateralistic system-pointing apparatus with unabashed unilateralistic, often parochial, choice-influencing considerations.

In sharp contrast to the traditional system-pointing paradigm, current rule-selecting methods seek the maximization of the substantive law concerns of the socio-legal systems entangled in a choice of law situation. Rather than relying on stereotyped connecting factors, rule-selecting approaches call for a functional analysis of the specific substantive legal rules potentially involved as the very core of the choice of law process. The distinguishing mark of this school of thought lies in its fundamental assumption that all standards of law are designed to further some distinct social concerns, randomly defined as "public policies", "governmental interests", "socioeconomic goals" and the like. The application of these standards in concrete situations, both purely local and those involving foreign ingredients, must therefore entail a systematic probe into their supporting purposes to determine their contemplated scope of personal and territorial coverage. In this view, the appropriate reach of all legal standards, domestic and foreign, can only be delineated through an examination and evaluation of their particular underlying rationale. Choosing the governing law solely on the basis of stereotyped spatial connecting-factors, and in deliberate ignorance of the tenor and purpose of the potentially applicable laws, is therefore an irrational exercise in futility. The choice of law process must be based on a functional analysis of the social objectives underlying the substantive rules, local and foreign, implicated in the dispute at bar.

It goes without saying that rule-selecting methods, like the American "govern-mental interests" approach, are not conducive to judicial ease of application. And the ad hoc exercise of broad, potentially freewheeling, judicial discretion that is mandated by such methods is hardly compatible with the goals of uniformity and predictability of result. Moreover, "governmental interests" enthusiasts are predis-posed to impute to virtually every legal norm some underlying concrete socioeco-nomic or political purpose. The intellectual premise of such a process may become rather shaky as one encounters legal rules whose supporting policy goals are unascertainable, obscure, tenuous, cumulative, or even contradictory. In the ab-sence of reliable information as to the intended policy function of the legal norm in question, the process may readily degenerate into a speculative postulation, or even an outright fabrication, of putative underlying policies, merely on the ground of their assumed plausibility. To ascribe hypothetical purposes to concrete legal rules, particularly foreign ones, on the basis of mere conjecture is a judicial enterprise of dubious validity and utility.

Still, the advancement of the substantive law concerns of the legal orders implicated in a choice of law situation is a worthy policy objective in appropriate instances. Thus certain normative arrangements – pertaining, for example, to matters of social welfare, economic regulation, fiscal stability and market institutions – are sometimes likely to be adversely affected unless the particular substantive law supporting them is applied. Substantial and readily discernible socioeconomic benefits or detriments may well count in the choice of the applicable law. Indeed, it hardly makes sense to designate as applicable a legal system whose relevant rule of decision is manifestly "uninterested" functionally in controlling the matter at hand or, conversely, to exclude the applicability of a legal system whose relevant rule of decision is evidently "interested", given its underlying objective, to govern the situation at bar. A choice of law methodology that repeatedly and haphazardly produces such unsound results cannot be accepted as rational. To be sound and functional, it should be responsive, in proper cases, to a measured consideration of the intrinsic particular policies animating the substantive laws that are candidates for application.

4.   A Proposed Scheme for Tort Choice of Law

As noted above, in 1994 the Israeli Supreme Court, unabashedly criticizing the Tort choice of law methodological chaos in English and American jurisprudence, opted to refrain from taking a general position on this matter while decreeing Israeli tort law as the law invariably applicable to torts allegedly committed in Israel. This is patently an unsatisfactory situation. The time has come to forge appropriate, preferably statutory, standards for choice of law in torts. How should one go about it?

It has already been indicated that a functional choice of law scheme ought to be sensitive to a soundly balanced matrix of four policy concerns: Ease of judicial administration, uniformity and predictability of result, parties' fair notice as to the applicable law, and advancement of the domestic law concerns of the countries involved. I believe that the ground rule of such a scheme should decree that the law applicable to the rights and liabilities of the parties with respect to an issue in tort is the law of the country which has the most significant relationship with the event and the parties. This is the position taken by the American Restatement (Second), Conflict of Laws, 1971 as well as by the proposed European Convention on the Law Applicable to Non-Contractual Obligations (Luxembourg, 25-27 September 1998). It plays a material role – although not as a starting point – also in the British Private International Law (Miscellaneous Provisions) Act 1995. To be sure, the "most significant relationship" (or "the closest connection") quite nebulous formula as such is hardly supportive of the policy aims of ease of judicial administration and uniformity and predictability of result. But it signals to judges that the choice of the applicable law must never be considered as a mechanical, automatic and arbitrary enterprise. This, I submit, is an all-important message, designed to enhance the values of legitimacy, rationality and fairness in the choice of law process.

The flexible "most significant relationship" standard must then be coupled with a series of presumptive localizing rules that are designed to indicate the country ordinarily regarded as most closely connected to certain type-situations – again, much like the modality adopted by the American Restatement (Second) and the proposed European convention. Principal among such rules would be the presumptions that designate as most closely connected – and hence applicable – the law of the parties' common habitual residence (if this is the case) and the law of the place where both the harmful event – e.g., the negligent conduct – and the ensuing damage – e.g., the personal injury – have occurred (if this is the case and the parties do not have a common habitual residence). Additional presumptions could point to the plaintiff's habitual residence as most significantly related to defamation and invasion of privacy tort actions, and to the location of the affected market for unfair competition law suits. These and similar presumptive choice of law directives are calculated to contribute substantially to ease of judicial administration and uniformity and predictability of result in the tort choice of law process.

Yet these specific choice of law indicators are no more than presumptions that point to the prima facie applicable law in certain well-defined type-situations. To be sure, courts should take these presumptive rules seriously enough or else their facilitating utility will be eroded. But means should not be confused with ends. The choice of law process must ultimately strive to maximize the rationality and fairness of the concrete results of litigation in particular cases. And this goal can only be furthered if judges are prepared on occasion to displace the otherwise applicable law indicated by the relevant presumptive directive if convinced by an interested party that, in all the circumstances, some other country has the most significant relationship and therefore it is clearly more appropriate that its law should govern the matter at bar.

In determining whether the presumptively applicable law ought to be displaced by a more closely connected normative regime, the forum of litigation may take into account a comprehensive array of factors including "factors relating to the parties, to any of the events which constitute the tort...in question or to any of the circumstances or consequences of those events" (this is the terminology adopted by the British Act of 1995). In appropriate instances I would include among these factors the substantive law concerns of the legal systems involved in the case at bar. Thus a displacement of an otherwise applicable law indicated by a presumptive choice of law directive might be justified if an interested party could demonstrate that the rule of decision of the presumptively governing law is manifestly inapplicable to the situation at hand given its own particular underlying objective. By the same token, a country whose relevant rule of decision evidently extends to the matter in question in terms of its intrinsic supporting rationale may well be regarded as having the closest connection for choice of law purposes. Indeed, to mechanically apply a functionally "uninterested" rule of decision of the presumptively governing law while blindly brushing aside the clearly policy-relevant legal standard of a country not presumptively indicated as most closely connected is not to indulge in rational choice of the applicable law. It is noteworthy, in this connection, that the proposed European Convention on the Law Applicable to Non-Contractual Obligations accords qualified consideration in the choice of the applicable law to the substantive law concerns of the implicated countries. Thus it decrees that effect may be given to the "mandatory" rules of law of a closely connected country (including the forum) irrespective of the law otherwise applicable under the proposed convention's choice of law directives. And it provides further that in considering whether to give effect to such mandatory rules "regard shall be had to their nature and purpose and to the consequences of their application or non-application". Let me stress that according due weight, in appropriate cases, to the substantive law concerns of the legal systems involved should not be confused with engaging in a freewheeling, unilateral reasoning that would invariably lead to the application of the substantive law position favored by the forum (such as a sweeping pro-plaintiff orientation in civil injury actions). A carefully calculated resort to the "public policy" backstopping device can be counted on to introduce a necessary measure of substantive justice as a choice-influencing consideration in situations that manifestly require such a corrective.

The factors taken into account in deciding whether the presumptively applicable law should be displaced by a more significantly related legal order ought to encompass also, where appropriate, the consideration of parties' expectations and fair notice as to the applicable law. Thus a presumptive choice of law directive might lead, on occasion, to the application of a legal regime contrary to the actual conduct-influencing expectations of the parties regarding the applicable law. Likewise, the law indicated as prima facie applicable could sometimes fail to satisfy the threshold requirement of objective fair notice. This may happen where it would demonstrably be unreasonable to charge the party concerned with prior notice regarding a potential involvement with the prescriptive domain of the presumptively indicated governing legal system. A displacement of an otherwise applicable law designated by a presumptive choice of law directive may well be justified in order to avoid gross frustration of party actual expectations or violation of the objective fair notice requirement.

It is beyond the scope of this essay to elaborate in detail on additional components of the proposed tort choice of law scheme. Let me just briefly offer the following supplementary propositions. First, the scope of the applicable law once selected ought to be broad, including matters such as the measure of damages, injunctions (subject to limits set by the procedural *lex fori*), prescription or limitation of actions, legal presumptions and burden of proof. Second, the choice of the applicable law should be issue-specific while being mindful of the potential pitfalls of *depeçage*. Third, *renvoi* ought to be excluded. Fourth, a carefully delineated, narrowly drawn "public policy" exception to the application of foreign law could be introduced. Fifth, the litigants may be allowed to agree, after the dispute has arisen, on the applicable law. Sixth, the forum of litigation may have recourse to the *lex fori* in its residuary capacity, as a last resort.

5.   RESOLVING THE CASE UNDER THE PROPOSED SCHEME

Returning finally to our case, how should the malpractice dispute be resolved in terms of the proposed tort choice of law methodology? Admittedly, this is not an easy case to decide. As recounted above, the plaintiff-patient is an Israeli habitual resident. The defendant-surgeon is an internationally renowned Romanian expert. The plaintiff-patient sought the professional services of the defendant-surgeon through a liaison office located in the United States. That office referred the plaintiff-patient to a hospital in Slovenia where the defendant-surgeon performed the brain operation. While being habitually employed in Slovenia, the world famous defendant-surgeon quite regularly performs brain surgery worldwide, including in Israel. The operation proved unsuccessful and the plaintiff-patient brought in Israel a tort action on the grounds of assault (performing the operation without informed consent) and malpractice (professional negligence). Under Israeli law, the action is not time barred and the plaintiff may win on both grounds. Under Slovenian law, the action is time barred and would in any event be dismissed since a tort cause-of-action for a medical intervention conducted without informed consent is not at all recognized and a medical malpractice suit may only be brought against the hospital concerned but not against any of its physicians personally.

The plaintiff-patient claims that Israeli law should apply to all outstanding issues while the defendant-surgeon maintains that Slovenian law ought to govern. Does Israel or Slovenia have the most significant relationship with the event and the parties as to the issues in dispute? The parties do not have a common habitual residence and both the alleged harmful conduct and the resulting injury occurred in Slovenia. In consequence, the presumptive choice of law rule referred to above points to Slovenia as the country most closely connected and its law must therefore prevail. Should, however, the prima facie applicable Slovenian law be displaced by Israeli law on the ground that, in all the circumstances, Israel has the demonstrably more significant relationship and hence it is patently more appropriate that its law will govern the issues at bar? Evidently, the Israeli plaintiff-patient sought the personal-professional services of the internationally renowned defendant-surgeon and was prepared to undergo surgery wherever the liaison office would refer him to. As concerns the plaintiff-patient, the Slovenian *locus delicti* is indeed utterly fortuitous. But not so as regards the defendant-surgeon. True, he periodically renders professional services worldwide yet the hospital in Slovenia is where he is habitually employed. From his vantage point, the contact with Slovenia can hardly be viewed as fortuitous or tenuous. The prima facie applicable Slovenian law may, therefore, not be displaced on the ground that the event and the parties lack a substantial enough contact with Slovenia.

Is an assessment of the substantive law concerns of the involved legal systems bound to tip the scales of decision in favor of applying Israeli law? The implicated Israeli law standards – a rather lengthy limitation period and physician's personal liability for medical procedures performed without the patient's informed consent and for malpractice – are manifestly supportive of tort compensation recovery and hence are pro-plaintiff. They are clearly policy-relevant and functionally engaged where, as here, the plaintiff-patient is an Israeli habitual resident. The involved Slovenian law standards – a rather short limitation period, non-recognition of liability for medical interventions conducted without informed consent, and exemption of physicians from personal liability for malpractice – are patently designed to restrict tort compensation recovery and hence are pro-defendant. As such, one can hardly argue that they are substantively irrelevant and functionally "uninterested" in controlling a tort compensation claim implicating as the defendant a Slovenian habitually-employed physician. An assessment of the substantive law concerns of the Israeli and Slovenian normative systems thus produces a tie, or a true conflict, and hence the presumption designating Slovenian law as applicable is not rebutted.

Is a calculus of the parties' choice of law expectations and reliances likely to support resort to Israeli law in displacement of the otherwise governing Slovenian law? More precisely, can the Israeli plaintiff-patient claim convincingly that having recourse to the presumptively applicable Slovenian law would be grossly unfair to him for it would unduly frustrate his actual expectations or violate the objective fair notice requirement concerning the applicable law? It is highly doubtful that the plaintiff-patient in fact has formed any concrete expectations as to the law applicable to the relationship between him and the defendant-surgeon. And it is hardly unreasonable to charge the Israeli plaintiff-patient, who sought the services of a world famous brain surgeon habitually employed in Slovenia and traveled abroad to be operated there, with fair notice regarding a possible entanglement with the Slovenian legal order. Thus a calculus of the parties' choice of law expectations and reliances fails to provide a good reason for displacing the presumptively applicable Slovenian law.

Finally, one cannot rule out the possibility that the Israeli forum might wish to invoke the "public policy" longstop device and thus decline to give effect to the otherwise applicable Slovenian law. Indeed, an Israeli court is likely to regard the Slovenian highly restrictive recovery standards as parochial, archaic, unsound and regressive. It is prone to find it hard to deny compensation to a deserving (from the forum's normative perspective) Israeli plaintiff on the basis of such unpalatable standards. The shielding of presumably negligent physicians from personal liability in particular is bound to be deemed objectionable. Still, as observed above, the narrowly drawn "public policy" exception to the application of the otherwise indicated foreign *lex causae* must be invoked with much perception and caution. One should realize that an overdose of the "public policy" preventive medicine might upset the orderly functioning of the choice of law apparatus. Admittedly, the Slovenian legal stance on physician's tort liability comes very close to the forbidden zone of repugnant, repulsive and offensive foreign law that may not penetrate the public policy protective shield. Yet, all things considered,[9] the Israeli forum is well advised to exercise self restraint, to refrain from seeking refuge behind the "public policy" barrier, and to dismiss the action as decreed by the applicable Slovenian law. Hard cases must not make bad choice of law.

---

[9] Including a wish to guarantee the continuous availability of the internationally renowned defendant-surgeon to Israeli patients who may seek his expert services in the future.

The 1996 Convention on Jurisdiction, Applicable Law, Recognition, Enforcement and Co-operation in Respect of Parental Responsibility and Measures for the Protection of Children: A Perspective from the United States

Linda Silberman[*]

1. INTRODUCTION

It is a pleasure to be asked to join this special *Festschrift* in honor of Professor KURT SIEHR. The topic of my paper, the 1996 Convention on Jurisdiction, Applicable

---

[*] Professor of Law, New York University. Special thanks to my research assistant, Ms. Karin Wolfe, a third-year student at New York University School of Law, who provided valuable research help, particularly in translating and summarizing the German sources.

J. Basedow et al., eds., Private Law in the International Arena – Liber Amicorum Kurt Siehr
© 2000, T.M.C.Asser Press, The Hague, The Netherlands

Law, Recognition, Enforcement, and Co-operation in Respect of Parental Responsibility and Measures for the Protection of Children[1] [hereinafter the 1996 Convention], is one of several collaborative efforts I have had with Professor SIEHR.[2] Professor SIEHR's participation in the Special Commission on the 1996 Convention was extraordinarily influential. His understanding of common and civil law systems and the importance of finding compromises compatible with both systems proved critical in molding consensus on a variety of issues. I believe KURT's efforts helped make possible a successful conclusion to the negotiations on the 1996 Convention. Whether or not the rules of private international law for jurisdiction, choice of law, and enforcement adopted in the 1996 Convention will be effective remains to be seen. But I am convinced that Professor SIEHR deserves much of the credit for trying to achieve the correct objectives in the 1996 Convention, and I hope that he will find my perspective on the 1996 Convention a focus for a continuing dialogue.

2. SOME PRELIMINARY OBSERVATIONS ON THE 1996 CONVENTION

Commentary on the 1996 Protection of Children Convention at this point in time can only be speculative. What exists is a formal structure and design for the 1996 Convention; but there is not much sense of how it will really operate in practice. The 1996 Convention has been signed by five countries – Monaco, Morocco, the Netherlands, the Czech Republic, and Slovakia – but only Monaco has ratified; thus, the 1996 Convention is not yet in force.

The 1996 Convention has many dimensions as its formal title indicates. In light of its connection to the earlier Convention Concerning the Powers of Authorities and the Law Applicable in Respect of the Protection of Infants [hereinafter 1961 Protection of Minors Convention],[3] much attention has been directed to its impact as a jurisdiction and recognition of judgments convention and its effect on custody orders. Indeed, it is that aspect on which I will concentrate most extensively in this essay, and where I believe most of the complexities lie. But the 1996 Convention has a broader impact, and at the outset I want to underscore several other aspects of this Convention.

---

[1] Convention of 19 October 1996 on Jurisdiction, Applicable Law, Recognition, Enforcement and Co-operation in Respect of Parental Responsibility and Measure for the Protection of Children [hereinafter 1996 Convention], mulitlateral, Oct. 19, 1996, 35 *ILM* 1391, 1396 (1996).

[2] Professor Siehr and I were also involved in the Second and Third Special Commissions reviewing the operation of the 1980 Hague Convention on the Civil Aspects of International Child Abduction.

[3] Convention Concerning the Powers of Authorities and the Law Applicable in Respect of the Protection of Infants [hereinafter 1961 Protection of Minors Convention], Oct. 5, 1961, multilateral, (1969) *UNTS* 145.

First, measures taken with respect to a child will have effect in other Convention States. Under Article 23 of the 1996 Convention, measures taken relating to the protection of a child or an order attributing parental responsibility to a particular adult are entitled to recognition in other Convention countries. If an order entitles someone to act for a child with respect to a social, education, or medical situation, the order is entitled to recognition. Article 40 permits a party given such authority to request a certificate from the authorities that granted the measure of protection indicating the capacity in which that person is entitled to act and the powers conferred. Thus, in many situations, the 1996 Convention makes possible the recognition of simple and straightforward measures taken in other countries without necessitating additional action in another country.

The provisions on co-operation in Chapter V will also be extremely useful. The ability to bring together all the relevant information concerning the child and family is often critical. Mechanisms for co-operation are established for public bodies as well as judicial authorities, and both formal and informal co-operation is contemplated. Like both the 1980 Abduction Convention[4] and the Convention on Protection of Children and Co-operation in Respect of Intercountry Adoption [hereinafter 1993 Adoption Convention],[5] the 1996 Convention provides for the establishment of a Central Authority to facilitate communication and exchanges of information between Contracting States, but the role for Central Authorities in the 1996 Convention is much more amorphous than in the other Conventions. In part, that is because responsibilities under the 1996 Convention fall to a variety of different local authorities and institutions, and they are difficult to centralize. Because a number of states may have authority to act under the 1996 Convention, provisions providing for exchanges of information between those authorities may be critical in ensuring that appropriate action is taken.

These merits of the 1996 Convention should lead States, including the United States, to give serious consideration to signing and ratifying the Convention. At the same time, other aspects of the 1996 Convention are more complex and not always clear in their meaning. The particular attraction of the 1996 Convention for the United States is its operation as a jurisdiction and judgments convention for custody orders and as an additional weapon in the fight against international child abduc-

---

[4] Convention on the Civil Aspects of International Child Abduction [hereinafter 1980 Abduction Convention], Oct. 25, 1980, multilateral, 19 *ILM* 1501 (1980).

[5] Convention on Protection of Children and Co-Operation in Respect of Intercountry Adoption [hereinafter 1993 Adoption Convention], 17th Session, multilateral, May 29, 1993, 32 *ILM* 1134 (1993).

tion.[6] The remainder of this essay explores this and other details of the 1996 Convention.[7]

3.   THE BACKDROP FOR THE 1996 CONVENTION: THE 1902 AND 1961
      HAGUE CONVENTIONS

The 1996 Convention has a long lineage, dating back to the 1902 Hague Convention Governing the Guardianship of Minors.[8] That early 1902 Convention allocated to the State of nationality jurisdictional authority to control the guardianship of minors. But nationality as the exclusive basis for jurisdiction became increasingly untenable as states where children lived promulgated laws and regulations for protection of children within their domestic public and administrative laws.

The deficiencies of the 1902 Convention were highlighted by the 1958 *Boll* case before the International Court of Justice,[9] which gave a narrow construction to the term "guardianship" (*tutelle* in French) and allowed states to use their own domestic rules with respect to the care and protection of minors, thus eviscerating a guardianship established by another State of much of its content.[10]

In March 1960, the Ninth Diplomatic Session of the Hague Conference convened to revise the 1902 Guardianship Convention, which culminated in a new convention. The new 1961 Protection of Minors Convention sought to resolve such conflicts of jurisdiction and to expand the scope of an international convention to encompass a broader array of protective measures over children. With respect to a minor, the 1961 Protection of Minors Convention covered "measures directed to the protection of his person or property"[11]; the measures included those arising both in the context of private family law as well as those taken by public authorities to protect the welfare of the child.[12] The Convention adopted as its primary rule of jurisdiction the State of habitual residence of the minor and entrusted to the authori-

---

[6] For a more detailed account of the issues posed by the Convention for the United States, see Linda Silberman, "The 1996 Hague Convention on the Protection of Children: Should the United States Join?" 34 *Fam.L.Q.* (2000) (forthcoming).

[7] The Convention's provisions dealing with property of the child are omitted from the discussion.

[8] For excellent coverage of that lineage, see A. Dyer, "Report on the Revision of the 1961 Hague Convention on Protection of Minors—Part One", Preliminary Document No. 1, *Hague Conference on Private International Law, Proceedings of the Eighteenth Session* (1996) Vol. 2, 11-57 [hereinafter *Dyer Report*].

[9] *The Netherlands* v. *Sweden* (1958) ICJ 55 (Nov.28, 1958).

[10] *See* A. Dyer, "The Internationalization of Family Law", 30 *University of California Davis Law Review* (1997) pp. 625, 627-32 (citing the *Boll* Case (*The Netherlands*. v. *Sweden*, ibid.)).

[11] Art. 1, 1961 Convention on the Protection of Minors (supra note 3).

[12] See A. Bucher, "Personnes, Familles, Successions", *Droit international privé suisse*, Tome II (1992), Nos. 838-843, pp. 275-76, cited in: *Dyer Report* (supra n. 8) at p. 15.

ties of that State the competence to take the necessary "protective measures."[13] The 1961 Convention entered into force on February 4, 1969, and was ratified or acceded to by a number of European countries.[14] No common law countries became parties to the 1961 Protection of Minors Convention.

Much of the difficulty with the 1961 Protection of Minors Convention was the result of competing rules of jurisdiction permitted under Articles 3 and 4 of the Convention,[15] and the failure to identify them as subsidiary rules of jurisdiction to the authority of the State of habitual residence.[16] Thus, if measures arrived at by the authorities of the State of habitual residence were seen to be detrimental, authorities of the State of nationality could override them and institute their own measures.

The provisions on recognition and enforcement under the 1961 Protection of Minors Convention had an equally schizophrenic quality. Article 7 provided that the measures taken under prior articles of the Convention "shall be recognized in all contracting States." But to the extent the measures involved "acts of enforcement" in another State, "recognition and enforcement" of those measures was to be governed by the domestic law in which enforcement was sought or by another applicable international convention.[17] Moreover, under Article 8, the State of habitual

---

[13] Art. 1, 1961 Convention on the Protection of Minors (supra n. 3).

[14] The following states ratified or acceded to the 1961 Convention: Austria, France, Germany, Italy, Luxembourg, Netherlands, Poland, Portugal, Spain, Switzerland, and Turkey. See 35 *Netherlands International Law Review* (1998) pp. 277-278.

[15] Art. 3 of the 1961 Convention provides: "A relationship subjecting the infant to authority, which arises directly from the domestic law of the State of the infant's nationality, shall be recognized in all the Contracting States" (supra n. 3) at p. 146.

Art. 4 of the 1961 Convention provides:

If the authorities of the State of the infant's nationality consider that the interests of the infant so require, they may, after having informed the authorities of the State of his habitual residence, take measures according to their own law for the protection of his person or property. That law shall determine the conditions for the initiation, modification and termination of the said measures. It shall also govern their effects both in respect of relations between the infant and the persons or institutions responsible for his care, and in respect of third persons. The application of the measures taken shall be assured by the authorities of the State of the infant's nationality. The measures taken by virtue of the preceding paragraphs of the present article shall replace any measures which may have been taken by the authorities of the State where the infant has his habitual residence.

[16] The drafters of the 1961 Protection of Minors Convention began with the intention of prioritizing jurisdiction in the State of habitual residence but many delegates to the negotiations had insisted on the more traditional rule allocating authority to the State of nationality. A compromise solution provided authorities of the State of habitual residence with primary jurisdiction, but (1) required recognition of *ex lege* relationships created by the law of the State of nationality and (2) allowed the authorities of the State of nationality to issue protective measures when in the best interests of the minor. See generally W. von Steiger, "Die IX. Haager Konferenz für Internationales Privatrecht", 57 *Schweizerische Juristen-Zeitung* (1961) pp. 150-51; see also W. von Steiger, "Die Revision des Haager Abkommens von 1902 zur Regelung der Vormundschaft über Minderjährige", 56 *Schweizerische Juristen-Zeitung* (1960) pp. 257-58.

[17] See Art. 7, 1961 Protection of Minors Convention (supra n. 3) at p. 149.

residence was given authority to take measures of protection to protect the minor from "serious danger" to person or property, but other Contracting States were not bound to recognize those measures.

Another difficulty came from the provision in Article 15, which permitted a reservation of jurisdiction over minors in cases involving the validity of the marital relationship, thus increasing the likelihood of conflicting decisions and resulting impasse in those states that made the reservation.[18] The provision in Article 16 of the 1961 Protection of Minors Convention allowing for "refusal" of Convention provisions if their application is "manifestly contrary to public policy" did not create unusual problems, but nonetheless offered another basis for refusing to honor foreign orders.[19]

4.   THE 1996 CONVENTION ON JURISDICTION, APPLICABLE LAW, RECOGNITION, ENFORCEMENT AND CO-OPERATION IN RESPECT OF PARENTAL RESPONSIBILITY AND MEASURES FOR THE PROTECTION OF CHILDREN

The frequency of conflicting protective measures and the lack of predictability and certainty under the 1961 Protection of Minors Convention produced a call for its reform and revision.[20] In addition, the success of the 1980 Abduction Convention, adopted then by over 50 states, including most of the countries party to the 1961 Protection of Minors Convention, suggested that a revised jurisdiction and judgments convention might gain more universal acceptance, including interest by common law countries, none of which had become parties to the 1961 Convention. Preparation of the 1996 Convention was initiated at three Special Commissions.[21] The Convention was finalized at the Hague Conference's Eighteenth Session in 1996.[22]

---

[18] Luxembourg, Poland, Spain and Turkey. See *Dyer Report* (supra n. 8) p. 29.

[19] Some courts continued to equate the Article 16 defense with a "best interests" test and refused to enforce a foreign custody order when it was thought not to be in the child's best interests. See generally J. Kropholler, "Vorbemerkungen zu Artikel 19 EGBGB: Das Internationale Kindschaftsrecht der Übereinkommen", in: *v. Staudingers Kommentar, EGBGB/IPR Kindschaftsrechtliche Übereinkommen*; Art. 19 EGBGB, 13th ed. (Berlin, de Gruyter 1994) pp. 199-202.

[20] See generally J. Kropholler, "Gedanken zur Reform des Haager Minderjährigenschutzabkommens", 58 *RabelsZ* (1994) pp. 1 et seq.; Helga Oberloskamp, "Reformüberlegungen zum Haager Minderjährigenschutzabkommen von 1961", 43 *Zeitschrift für das Gesamte Familienrecht* (1996) pp. 918 et seq.; K. Siehr, "Die Rechtslage der Minderjährigen im Internationalen Recht und die Entwicklung in diesem Bereich: Zur Revision des Haager Minderjährigenschutzabkommens", 43 *Zeitschrift für das Gesamte Familienrecht* (1996), pp. 1047 et seq.

[21] Only 29 of the 40 member states of the Hague Conference on Private International Law participated in the preparatory meetings for the 1996 revisions. See K. Siehr, "Die Rechtslage der Minderjährigen im Internationalen Recht und die Entwicklung in diesem Bereich" (supra n. 20) p. 1048.

[22] Art. 61 provides the 1996 Convention "shall enter into force on the first day of the month follow-

4.1   Defining Protective Measures

A first task of the 1996 Convention was to clarify its scope since "measures of protection" had not always been well understood under the 1961 Convention;[23] thus, Article 3 of the 1996 Convention specifies various categories of such measures. The list is not exhaustive, but it would be very difficult to find a measure that could not be classified under one of these headings.[24] The measures include attribution, exercise, termination or restriction of parental responsibility (Article 3(a)), rights of custody and rights of access (Article 3(b)), and measures relating to guardianship, curatorship, and analogous institutions (Article 3(c)). The designation and determination of the functions of any person or body taking responsibility for the child or representing the child constitute measures (Article 3(d)), just as placement of the child in a foster family or supervision by a public authority of any person having charge of the care of a child (Article 3(e) and (f)) also constitute measures. The 1996 Convention also makes express mention of the Islamic care provision of *kafala*. The 1996 Convention also covers the administration, conservation or disposal of the child's property (Article 3(g)).

Specific exclusions from the 1996 Convention are set forth in Article 4. Some of those subjects – such as adoption and maintenance (support) are covered by other conventions – and certain others were thought to raise sovereignty interests (criminal law, social security and immigration) outside of the immediate Convention needs. Two of the more significant exclusions are paragraph a – the decision on establishing or contesting a parent-child relationship – and paragraph d – emancipation. These exclusions mean that the creation of the parent-child relationship via paternity is excluded as is the more general concept of emancipation from parental authority.[25]

---

ing the expiration of three months after the deposit of the third instrument of ratification, acceptance or approval." (supra n. 1) 35 *I.L.M.* 1391, 1404. Morocco, Monaco, Netherlands, and the Czech Republic have signed the Convention, but only Monaco has deposited its instrument of ratification, acceding to the Convention on May 14, 1997. See 35 *Netherlands International Law Review* (1998) p. 312.

[23] For example, under the 1961 Protection of Minors Convention, most Contracting States viewed a custody order following a divorce as within the scope of protective measures, but not all states included visitation or access rights. See *Dyer Report* (supra n. 8) p. 15 (noting that German and French courts considered visitation rights granted post divorce as within the 1961 Protection of Minors Convention while the court at the Hague did not). See also P. Pfund, "Protecting Children's Rights through the Hague Conventions", 4 *Loyola Poverty Law Journal* (1998) p. 217.

[24] A. Bucher, "La Dix-huitième session de la Conférence de la Haye de droit international privé", 7 *Swiss Review of International and European Law* (1997) p. 67.

[25] For a somewhat unsatisfactory explanation of the reason for the exclusion, see P. Lagarde, "Explanatory Report: on the Convention of 19 October 1996 on Jurisdiction, Applicable Law, Recognition, Enforcement and Co-Operation in Respect of Parental Responsibility and Measures for the Protection of Children" [hereinafter *Lagarde Report*], *Hague Conference on Private International Law, Proceedings of the Eighteenth Session* (1996) Vol. 2, 533, at p. 549.

4.2   Habitual Residence as the Primary Basis of Jurisdiction

The primary objective of the 1996 Convention was to resolve the conflicts of jurisdiction in the 1961 Protection of Minors Convention between the State of nationality and the State of habitual residence. Under the 1996 Convention, the authorities
of the State of habitual residence are granted jurisdiction over the child to the exclusion of the authorities of the State of nationality.[26] As explained in the Preparatory
Report on the Revision of the 1961 Protection of Minors Convention by then Deputy Secretary Adair Dyer, the authorities of the State of habitual residence are in the
best position to ascertain the needs of protection for minor children.[27] Moreover,
those authorities will be most effective if they apply their own law.[28] To that end,
Article 5 of the 1996 Convention provides for the judicial or administrative authorities of the Contracting State of the habitual residence of the child to have jurisdiction to take measures "directed to the protection of the child's person or property."[29]
Article 15 provides that in exercising jurisdiction, the authorities "shall apply their
own law," although a proviso paragraph allows the State exercising jurisdiction to
"apply or take into consideration the law of another State with which the situation
has substantial connection."

The "supremacy" of habitual residence jurisdiction is not absolute, and I will return shortly to other provisions of the 1996 Convention which provide for temporary and urgent measures, a special divorce jurisdiction, as well as a unique
provision which permits a transfer and/or relinquishment of jurisdiction in favor of
another State when certain criteria are met. But there are a number of potentially
complicating factors with respect to the "habitual residence" jurisdiction itself.

First, the difficulty of defining "habitual residence" remains a serious problem.[30]
Second, a change in the child's habitual residence raises the question of whether jurisdiction should automatically shift or whether the general rule should be qualified
in this circumstance. And finally, abductions will be encouraged and not deterred if
wrongful removals and/or wrongful retentions can create habitual residence jurisdiction.

---

[26] See Art. 5, 1996 Convention (supra n. 4) at p. 1397. See also K. Siehr, "Die Rechtslage der
Minderjährigen im Internationalen Recht" (supra n. 20) p. 1049.

[27] See *Dyer Report* (supra n. 8) p. 43.

[28] See ibid.

[29] It should be noted that in a situation where the habitual residence of a child is not in a Contracting
State, Article 5 is not applicable. The authorities of Contracting States have jurisdiction under the Convention only on the basis of other provisions (Articles 11 and 12, discussed infra at p. 719). Of course,
Contracting States can exercise jurisdiction outside of the Convention on the basis of their own rules of
private international law. See *Lagarde Report* (supra n. 25) p. 553.

[30] For the most comprehensive article on the concept of habitual residence as used in multilateral
conventions, see E.M. Clive, "The Concept of Habitual Residence", *Juridical Review* (1997) Part 3.

As early as the first preparatory session, then Deputy Secretary Adair Dyer raised in his "Checklist of provisions which might be included in the Revised Convention" the possibility of including "a presumption that six months of ordinary residence in a locality constitutes 'habitual residence' there."[31] A similar definition exists in United States law under the Uniform Child Custody Jurisdiction Act[32] [hereinafter UCCJA] and the Uniform Child Custody Jurisdiction and Enforcement Act[33] [hereinafter UCCJEA]. However, the tradition of the Hague Conference has consistently resisted formally defining "habitual residence", and there was concern among the delegates that including such a definition in the 1996 Convention would have risked disturbing interpretations of that concept in other Hague Conventions.[34] Although no definition was included, discussions during the negotiations make clear the understanding that temporary absence of a child from its habitual residence for reasons of vacation, school attendance or of the exercise of access rights would not change the child's habitual residence.[35]

The question of the impact of a change of habitual residence to another Contracting State was a more controversial issue. The rationale that the State of "habitual residence" is the one best situated to examine the child's circumstances is not completely convincing because the authorities in the child's previous residence may be better placed to assess the family and social circumstances. Morever, there is the additional danger that measures taken in the previous residence could be immediately replaced by authorities in the new habitual residence – a situation particularly likely in the context of custody and access disputes.[36]

Let me offer a hypothetical case as a concrete example. Two law students – Pierre from France, and Ellen, an American – each decide to spend a semester abroad at the University of Zürich in order to further their interest and study of private in-

---

[31] See A. Dyer, "Checklist of Provisions which might be included in the Revised Convention", Preliminary Document No. 2, *Hague Conference on Private International Law, Proceedings of the Eighteenth Session* (1996) Vol. 2, 59. Mr. Dyer referred to such a "rule of thumb" having developed in the German and Austrian courts and a six-month time period having been adopted formally in United States analogous legislation, the Uniform Child Custody Jurisdiction Act and the Parental Kidnaping Protection Act of 1980.

[32] See Uniform Child Custody Jurisdiction Act (UCCJA), 9 (Part 1A) Uniform Laws Annotated 271 et seq. (1999).

[33] See Uniform Child Custody Jurisdiction and Enforcement Act (UCCJEA), 9 (Part 1A) Uniform Laws Annotated 657 et seq. (1999).

[34] See *Lagarde Report* (supra n. 25) p. 553. "Habitual residence" is also the central focus of the 1980 Abduction Convention.

[35] See ibid. Notwithstanding this general approach to the determination of habitual residence, there are several categories of cases where the 1996 Convention provides more direction. For "refugee children and those children who due to disturbances in their country, are internationally displaced", the 1996 Convention equates presence in the territory with habitual residence. Also when habitual residence cannot be established, presence in the territory is the basic jurisdictional rule.

[36] See ibid.

ternational law by taking classes from the renowned professor, KURT SIEHR. They meet while there, fall in love, and continue their relationship for several years. Eventually they marry and decide that they will live in France. They have a child, Paul, but when their son is five, the marriage deteriorates, and Pierre and Ellen divorce in France, their habitual residence. Primary custody is awarded to Ellen and liberal access rights are given to Pierre. Ellen eventually changes her habitual residence to the United States and then seeks to restrict or eliminate Pierre's access rights by bringing a suit in the United States to modify the custody order.

When similar issues arise in the domestic interstate situation in the United States, United States law adopts a rule of "exclusive continuing jurisdiction." The recent amendment to the U.S. Uniform Law, the UCCJEA, grants jurisdiction to the state that rendered the initial decree to retain jurisdiction, unless that state prefers to decline jurisdiction and defer to the new state of habitual residence.[37] Such a rule minimizes the ability to seek a new and different forum to gain a merits advantage in the custody proceeding; and it attempts to create stability with respect to decision-making about custody and access arrangements. In the international context, however, where the change of habitual residence involves relocation to another country, often at a substantial distance from the former habitual residence, an unlimited rule of "continuing jurisdiction" may be impractical. As a compromise, the United States delegation on the 1996 Convention proposed that the authorities of the child's habitual residence, which had taken measures concerning custody or access, should retain exclusive jurisdiction of these issues after the child's departure *for a period of two years*, if at least one of the parents continued to reside in that State and maintained a continuing relationship with the child.[38] But the Convention delegates found any rule of continuing jurisdiction too burdensome once there had been a permanent relocation, and preferred that jurisdiction be ceded to the new State of habitual residence. Thus, Article 5(2) of the 1996 Convention provides that in the case of a change of the "child's habitual residence to another Contracting State, the authorities of the State of the new habitual residence have jurisdiction." The task of the relevant authorities will be to consider when a child's move from one country to another, considering all the circumstances, brings about a sufficient integration of the child into its new environment. Of course, if measures were under consideration – or were taken – in the prior habitual residence, other provisions of the Convention may work to assure continuity. Article 13 establishes a rule of *lis pendens* and Article 23 requires recognition and enforcement of measures taken by the original state of habitual residence. Indeed, the concept of continuing jurisdic-

---

[37] See UCCJEA (supra n. 33) Sec. 202.
[38] See Comments of the United States in Comments of the Governments and International Organizations, Preliminary Document No. 8 of September 1996, *Hague Conference on Private International Law, Proceedings of the Eighteenth Session* (1996) Vol. 2, 195-196.

tion was rejected in part because it was widely accepted that any new habitual residence would not act to modify an order absent a change in circumstances.

4.3   The Special Problem of "Child Abduction"

The most difficult problem for the Special Commission remained the impact of a
wrongful removal or retention on the concept of habitual residence. Several delegations argued that a wrongful removal or retention should never result in establishment of a new habitual residence. Other delegations took a more pragmatic view
that when wrongful removals and retentions are perpetuated and a new habitual residence created, it is authorities in the new habitual residence that are best situated to
assess the child's needs.

For countries that have adopted the 1980 Abduction Convention, there is a partial solution. Article 16 of that Convention prevents the judicial or administrative
authorities of the Contracting State to which a child has been removed or in which it
has been retained – once it is informed of a wrongful removal or retention – from
deciding on the merits of rights of custody until it has been determined that the child
is not to be returned or unless an application for return under the Convention has not
been lodged. But countries which join the 1996 Convention will not necessarily be
parties to the 1980 Abduction Convention, so an independent provision was necessary. Moreover, the question of whether a wrongful removal or retention should
create a permanent bar to a shift of habitual residence had to be confronted.

Paragraph 1 of Article 7 of the 1996 Convention provides that in case of a
wrongful removal or retention, the State with jurisdiction at the time of removal or
retention retains jurisdiction until the child acquires a new habitual residence *and*
either of two situations occurs: (1) each person, institution or other body with a right
of custody has acquiesced in the removal or retention, *or* (2) the child has resided in
the other State for at least a year after the person, institution or other body having a
right of custody has or should have had knowledge of the whereabouts of the child,
no request for return lodged within that period is still pending, and the child is settled in its new environment.

The purpose of Article 7 is to prevent a person who abducts a child from gaining
any advantage by creating a basis of jurisdiction in the State to which the child has
been taken. In addition, Article 7 attempts to mesh the 1996 Convention and provisions in the 1980 Abduction Convention, which does not deal with jurisdiction at all
but is effectively a provisional remedy limited to the restoration of the *status quo
ante*. The 1996 Convention underscores the fact that non-return of a child (under the
1980 Abduction Convention or otherwise) does not create jurisdiction in the State
that refuses to return a child. The United States delegation, particularly, wanted to
assure that jurisdiction to take measures of protection would not automatically result from a decision that a child not be returned. It feared that a contrary rule would
create incentives for non-return and possibly influence courts in deciding petitions

for return under the 1980 Abduction Convention. Thus the 1996 Convention is clear that only when a new habitual residence is established *and other conditions are met* will the new State of habitual residence be authorized to assert jurisdiction. The first situation – acquiescence in the removal of the child – is also a ground for non-return of a child under the Abduction Convention. Here, the view is that both parties have accepted the establishment of a new habitual residence, even though it may have begun with a wrongful removal or retention.

The second category presents a more complex regime. There must first be a factual finding that the child has obtained a new habitual residence. In addition, the child must maintain that residence for a one-year period from the time that the person with custody rights has knowledge of the child's whereabouts, no request for return presented during this period can still be pending, and the child must be settled in this new environment. The provision represents a compromise between delegations that favored an absolute prohibition on a wrongful removal ever maturing into a recognized habitual residence, and those that believed that after some period of time, the State of habitual residence – regardless of how that status was obtained – must be permitted to take measures with respect to the child. The compromise highlights that a State that makes a decision not to return a child does not create for itself jurisdiction to make appropriate custody and access orders. Jurisdiction under the 1996 Convention still belongs to the authorities of the State in which the child had its habitual residence immediately before the wrongful removal or retention. And if the original State of habitual residence exercises its jurisdiction even after the child has been removed, authorities of the State to which the child has been wrongfully taken or where it has been retained will be required to recognize and enforce such a decision in accordance with Article 23 of the new Convention.[39] But because the more general concept of continuing jurisdiction has been rejected by the 1996 Convention, once there is no longer a petition for return pending, a year has passed, and once the child is settled in the new habitual residence, the new habitual residence to which the child has been taken may be able to change whatever measures were taken in the first State.

However, there is a possible reading of Article 7 that would continue to limit jurisdiction in the abducted-to State. If a request for return of the child is made *in the original State of habitual residence* and those proceedings are not dismissed, the formal conditions of Article 7(1)(b) would not seem to be met. In those circumstances, jurisdiction could not be assumed by the new State of habitual residence to which the child had been removed. Such an interpretation is consistent with one objective of Article 7 – that jurisdiction in wrongful removal situations should shift only when there is either acquiescence or "laches".[40] So long as jurisdiction remains

---

[39] See *Lagarde Report* (supra n. 25) p. 559
[40] See G. de Hart, "Introductory Note", 35 *ILM* 1391, 1392 (1996).

in the original State of habitual residence, under paragraph 3 of Article 7, the new State can exercise jurisdiction only for the purpose of emergency measures. On the other hand, it is possible to read Article 7 as referring only to return proceedings brought in the abducted-to State. Thus, if that court has decided not to return the child and the child is settled there after one-year, that State can achieve status as the habitual residence – even though obtained as the result of a wrongful removal.

4.4   Introduction of the Concept of Transferring Jurisdiction

A unique concept emerged in the 1996 Convention – permitting a transfer of juris- diction by the State of habitual residence to specified Contracting States that may be better placed in a particular case to assess the best interests of the child.[41] Concomi- tantly, authorities in the identified Contracting States – State of nationality, State in which property of the child is located, State where a divorce, separation, or annul- ment action is being heard, or State with which the child has a substantial con- nection[42] – are also permitted to make a request to authorities in the State of habitual residence[43] that they be permitted to exercise jurisdiction to take measures or to in- vite the parties to make such a request of the authorities in the State of habitual resi-

---

[41] Art. 8 provides:

1   By way of exception, the authority of a Contracting State having jurisdiction under Arti- cle 5 or 6, if it considers that the authority of another Contracting State would be better placed in the particular case to assess the best interests of the child, may either request that other authority, directly or with the assistance of the Central Authority of its State, to assume jurisdiction to take such measures of protection as it considers to be necessary, or suspend consideration of the case and invite the parties to introduce such a request before the authority of that other State.

2   The Contracting States whose authorities may be addressed as provided in the preceding paragraph are

a   a State in which the child is a national,

b   a State in which property of the child is located,

c   a State whose authorities are seised of an application for divorce or legal separation of the child's parents, or for the annulment of their marriage,

d   a State with which the child has a substantial connection.

3   The authorities concerned may proceed to an exchange of views.

4   The authority addressed as provided in paragraph 1 may assume jurisdiction, in place of the authority having jurisdiction under Article 5 or 6, if it considers that this is in the child's best inter- ests – 1996 Convetion (supra n. 1) at pp. 1397-1398.

[42] See Art. 8(2), ibid.

[43] Such a transfer can also be requested from the authorities that have jurisdiction under Article 6 — the State where the child is present — in those limited circumstances where there is no State of habitual residence. This is clear from the reference to Article 8 that is made in Article 9. Article 8 makes clear that the authorities who may transfer include both Article 5 and Article 6. Thus the reference to making a request of the State of habitual residence in Article 9 must be understood in that context. For a similar view, see A. Bucher (supra n. 24). See also *Lagarde Report* (supra n. 25) p. 563. (Any "dissymmetry with Article 8 appears to be due to an oversight" . . . "The Reporter is of the opinion that on this point Article 9 should be aligned on Article 8.")

dence.[44] These two articles, Articles 8 and 9, are the result of a confluence of factors. From the perspective of civil law countries, several states, particularly those with experience under the 1961 Protection of Minors Convention, were reluctant to completely surrender jurisdiction by the State of nationality. Their goal had been to find a way of allocating jurisdiction between the State of habitual residence and the State of nationality so as to avoid the conflicts that had developed under the 1961 Protection of Minors Convention.[45] Similarly, the 1961 Protection of Minors Convention included a reservation of "child protection jurisdiction" in a State with jurisdiction over the status of the marital relationship.[46] Although only a small number of states had made the reservation, the European Union was preparing a Convention concerning the scope, the judicial jurisdiction and the enforcement of decisions in matrimonial matters [hereinafter Brussels II], which authorized states with "divorce" jurisdiction to also regulate the exercise of parental authority in particular situations.[47] It was deemed advisable to find ways to prevent inconsistencies with the proposals being drafted in the European Union and to avoid disparities between the two Conventions.[48] From the perspective of the common law countries, particularly the United States, different considerations were at work. It was thought that some discretion in the exercise of jurisdiction by the State of habitual residence, akin to the doctrine of *forum non conveniens*, was desirable.[49] In child custody matters in the interstate context, the states of the United States had initially structured through the UCCJA a "cascade" of jurisdictional grounds, which included "home state" jurisdiction, a "significant connection" basis of jurisdiction, an "emergency jurisdic-

---

[44] See Art. 9(1), 1996 Convention (supra n. 1) at p. 1398.

[45] See A. Bucher (supra n. 24).

[46] Art. 15, 1961 Convention on the Protection of Minors (supra n. 3) at p. 151.

[47] See Convention on Jurisdiction and the Recognition and Enforcement of Judgments in Matrimonial Matters (Brussels II), Article 3. On an application for divorce, separation, or annulment, jurisdiction over matters relating to parental responsibility of a child can be exercised in the member State where the child is habitually resident; the courts of a State where the child is not habitually resident can also exercise jurisdiction on parental responsibility issues as part of a matrimonial application if the child is habitually resident in another Member State and (a) one of the spouses has parental responsibility, and (b) the spouses have accepted the court's jurisdiction and it is in the best interests of the child.

[48] The 1996 Convention made two such accommodations. The divorce court, whose jurisdiction could be reserved under Article 15 of the 1961 Protection of Minors Convention, has concurrent jurisdiction under Article 10 of the 1996 Convention. See discussion infra at pp. 719-720. Articles 8 and 9 – through the vehicle of transfer to the divorce jurisdiction – provides additional flexibility, in those situations where the conditions of Article 10 are not met and where it appears that the divorce court is the more appropriate forum. See *Lagarde Report* (supra n. 25) p. 561.

[49] The doctrine of *forum non conveniens* – permitting a forum to refuse to exercise its jurisdiction when an alternative forum is more appropriate – is a feature in many common law countries. *See* P. Blair, "The Doctrine of Forum Non Conveniens in Anglo-American Law", 29 *Columbia Law Review* (1929), p. 1 et seq. For a synthesis of the reception of the doctrine in various countries, see J.J. Fawcett (ed.), *Declining Jurisdiction in Private International Law: Reports to the XIVth Congress of the International Academy of Comparative Law* (Oxford, Clarendon 1995).

tion based on presence", and a jurisdiction by necessity.[50] To allocate jurisdiction, the UCCJA included a provision allowing a court with jurisdiction to "decline to exercise its jurisdiction any time before making a decree if it finds that it is an inconvenient forum to make a custody determination under the circumstances of the case and that a court of another state is a more appropriate forum."[51] The recent amendments to the UCCJA – in what is known as the UCCJEA[52]– as well as the federal Parental Kidnaping Prevention Act [hereinafter PKPA][53] prioritize "home state" jurisdiction and permit jurisdiction on the other specified grounds only when there is no "home state" jurisdiction or when there has been a declination of such jurisdiction.[54] This domestic interstate scheme within the United States for child custody matters provided something of a model for the concept of a transfer of jurisdiction in situations where another court is better placed to assess the child's best interest. Although the concept of transferring jurisdiction is not generally accepted in Europe, the provision created flexibility for the particular circumstances of an international case and introduced subsidiary jurisdiction for the State of nationality as well as other "interested" states, subject to control by the State of habitual residence.

It should be underscored that the 1996 Convention provides for a transfer of jurisdiction to authorities only in other Contracting States. The Commission rejected various proposals to transfer authority to non-Contracting States based on the best interests of the child.[55] As the *Lagarde Report* explains, it was necessary to limit jurisdiction to Contracting States in order to assure that there would be appropriate authority in the transferee jurisdiction.[56]

There are two methods for the habitual residence jurisdiction to transfer its authority. It may contact the authority that it considers to be more appropriate jurisdiction and request it to "assume jurisdiction to take such measures of protection as it considers to be necessary."[57] Alternatively, it may "suspend consideration of the case and invite the parties to introduce such a request before the authority of that other State."[58] The 1996 Convention, though recognizing that these options may turn on whether an action is before a judicial or administrative body, does not link the procedure to the nature of the authority in question. Because the allocation of powers between administrative and judicial authorities differs from State to State, it was left to Contracting States themselves when ratifying the 1996 Convention to provide in legislation for methods of addressing authorities in other

[50] See UCCJA (supra n. 32) Sec. 3.
[51] See ibid., Sec. 7.
[52] See UCCJEA (supra n. 33).
[53] See Parental Kidnaping Prevention Act [PKPA], Title 28 U.S.C. Sec. 1738A (1980).
[54] See UCCJEA (supra n. 33) Sec. 201. See also PKPA, 28 U.S.C. Sec. 1738A (c).
[55] See *Lagarde Report* (supra n. 25) p. 559
[56] See ibid.
[57] Art. 8(1), 1996 Convention (supra n. 1) at pp. 1397-1398.
[58] Ibid.

States.[59] Articles 8 and 9 specify only that the authorities may proceed to an exchange of views,[60] and both articles authorize communication between authorities directly or with the assistance of the Central Authority. In the section of the Convention on co-operation, Chapter V, provision is made for the establishment of a Central Authority.[61] Central Authorities are directed, either directly or through other bodies, to take appropriate steps to facilitate communication and offer assistance as provided for in Articles 8 and 9.[62] The provisions on co-operation are another important feature of this Convention, borrowed to some degree from the co-operation provisions in the American UCCJA and UCCJEA.

The authority addressed may assume or refuse jurisdiction in light of its own assessment of the necessity and propriety of its intervention based on the best interests of the child.[63] If it assumes jurisdiction, it acts in place of the authority addressed under Articles 5 and 6. The jurisdiction extends to all measures which the accepting authority deems necessary "in the particular case" and is not bound to a pre-determined measure suggested by the requesting authority.[64]

Article 9 is the mirror image of Article 8 and the procedure provided is in symmetry with that provided in Article 8. A requesting authority – one of those identified in Article 8 – that has had its jurisdiction invoked by a party should normally decline jurisdiction in favor of the primary jurisdiction as defined in Articles 5 and 6. However, if the authority believes that in the circumstances of the particular case it is better placed to exercise jurisdiction, it can proceed in one of two ways: (1) it can request from the authority in the State of primary jurisdiction[65] permission to take the measures it deems appropriate or (2) it can stay the proceedings and invite the parties to bring such a request before that authority. But jurisdiction can be exercised by the requesting State only if the authority of the Contracting State of habitual residence accepts the request to act. A failure to respond by the State of habitual residence is taken as a rejection of the request. The requirement of a formal acceptance for action by a subsidiary jurisdiction was necessary to prevent conflicts of jurisdiction and competing requests by various states that are entitled to make such requests.

---

[59] See *Lagarde Report* (supra n. 25) p. 561.
[60] See Arts. 8(3), 9(2), 1996 Convention (supra n. 1) at pp. 1397-1398.
[61] Art. 29(1) of the 1996 Convention provides: "A Contracting State shall designate a Central Authority to discharge the duties which are imposed by the Convention on such authorities." Ibid., at p. 1400.
[62] See Art. 31(a), ibid., at p. 1400.
[63] See Art. 8(4), ibid., at pp. 1397-1398.
[64] See A. Bucher (supra n. 24).
[65] This will usually be the State of habitual residence.

4.5   The Provisions for Concurrent Jurisdiction

An authority originating a request may take urgent or provisional measures without approval of the State of habitual residence *if* it meets the jurisdictional requirements set forth in Articles 11 and 12. Articles 11 and 12 provide for jurisdiction based on the presence of the child within the territory in limited circumstances. Article 11 is an "urgency" or "emergency" jurisdiction; Article 12 calls for measures of a "provisional" or "temporary" nature limited to the territory. Both particular provisions have a broader scope than other 1996 Convention provisions and apply to all children present (or having property) in a Contracting State regardless of their habitual residence. Limitations in both provisions are designed to prevent any serious conflict of jurisdiction with the State of habitual residence. The measures taken lapse as soon as the appropriate authority of the Contracting State with jurisdiction has taken measures or recognizes measures taken by the authorities of another State.

As noted earlier, the concurrent negotiations of a Brussels II Convention extending the 1968 Brussels Convention to "matrimonial causes" were the catalyst for adding a special divorce jurisdiction in Article 10 of the 1996 Convention. This provision is independent of the discretionary "transfer" jurisdiction that is permitted under Articles 8 and 9. Moreover, the jurisdiction under Article 10 is concurrent and not exclusive. Under Article 10, a court exercising jurisdiction over a divorce, separation or annulment may, when consistent with its internal law, decide on measures of protection for a child not habitually resident there if certain cumulative conditions are satisfied. One of the parents must reside in the State with jurisdiction over the divorce and one of the parents must have parental responsibility; both parents must agree to the jurisdiction of the divorce court, and the exercise of jurisdiction must be in the best interests of the child.

Acceptance in the 1996 Convention of a number of limited – yet concurrent bases of jurisdiction (as in Article 10's divorce jurisdiction and Article 11 and 12 authority for "urgent" and "temporary" measures to be taken by a State where the child is present) – creates the possibility of potential conflicts of jurisdiction. It was just such overlaps of jurisdiction without clear priorities that made the 1961 Protection of Minors Convention unworkable. Article 13 of the 1996 Convention offers a rule in the manner of *lis pendens* and requires a State to abstain from exercising jurisdiction if corresponding measures have been requested from authorities in another Contracting State, which has jurisdiction and that request is still under consideration.[66] However, the abstention principle does not apply to the exercise of

---

[66] Art. 13 provides:

1   The authorities of a Contracting State which have jurisdiction under Articles 5 to 10 to take measures for the protection of the person or property of the child must abstain from exercising this jurisdiction if, at the time of the commencement of the proceedings, corresponding measures have been requested from the authorities of another Contracting State having jurisdiction under Articles 5 to 10 at

jurisdiction for urgent or temporary measures; there is less need for a *lis pendens* rule in connection with such jurisdiction because the measures taken lapse automatically once other measures are taken by Contracting States exercising the basic jurisdiction. Because of the inherent nature of "urgent" and "provisional" relief, it is important that there be opportunity to issue protective measures even when a request is pending elsewhere. The more general problem of assuring that measures do not lapse once in place is handled by the "continuing in force" jurisdiction provision of Article 14. It provides that the measures taken under Articles 5 through 10 "remain in force according to their terms" even if a change of circumstances has eliminated the basis upon which jurisdiction is founded. Of course, once jurisdiction is created in another State – such as a new habitual residence – that State may modify, replace, or terminate such measures, but the earlier measures continue in force until the Contracting State with the "new" jurisdiction has acted.

4.6   Applicable Law

Formal choice of law rules are probably less important in the context of the "children conventions" than they are in other Hague Conventions. Nonetheless, the issue of applicable law does often arise, and the 1996 Convention brings together in Articles 15 through 22 the entirety of the rules of conflict of laws operating in the Convention.[67] The basic principle is found in Article 15, which provides that the authorities of the Contracting States shall apply their own law (i.e. forum law). In the usual situation, the State exercising jurisdiction will be that of the "habitual residence", and thus the law of habitual residence will usually be applicable. However, under the jurisdictional provisions of the 1996 Convention, measures may, in some situations, be taken by the divorce court (via Article 10 or through transfer pursuant to Articles 8 and 9), by the State of nationality (in case of a transfer of jurisdiction under Article 8 and 9), or by an authority exercising "emergency" or "provisional" jurisdiction under Articles 11 and 12. There were various proposals to impose a single applicable law – that of habitual residence – in all situations.[68] Despite the attraction of such a rule – in particular relating to situations where the divorce court takes measures with respect to the child – the Commission reached a judgment that the forum was best equipped to apply its own domestic law on the subject of appropriate measures. Recognizing that certain situations might warrant a different rule, para-

---

the time of the request and are still under consideration.

2   The provisions of the preceding paragraph shall not apply if the authorities before whom the request for measures was initially introduced have declined jurisdiction (supra n. 1) at p. 1398.

[67] This structure is in contrast to the conflict of laws rules in the 1961 Protection of Minors Convention which were spread out in the separate sections governing conflicts of jurisdiction. *See Lagarde Report* (supra n. 25) p. 573.

[68] See *Lagarde Report* (supra n. 25) p. 573.

graph 2 allows by way of exception the application or taking into consideration of "the law of another State with which the situation has a substantial connection."[69]

Paragraph 3 of Article 15 draws another distinction, sometimes difficult to comprehend and apply. It addresses the situation when there has been a change of habitual residence of the child. As we saw in Article 14, measures previously taken by other authorities remain in effect, but under paragraph 3 of Article 15, the law of the new habitual residence will control the "conditions of application of the measures taken in the State of the former habitual residence."[70] Obviously, care must also be taken to assure that the substance of the measure is not denuded by imposing "conditions of application."

The remaining choice of law provisions deal with the particular issue of parental responsibility – its attribution/extinction by operation of law[71] and its exercise.[72] These Articles do not deal with "measures" at all, but rather the recognition and continuity of existing *ex lege* relationships. Article 16 was originally intended to ensure the protection in a new habitual residence of the rights and responsibilities accorded to a parent (focusing primarily on the attribution of parental rights of unmarried fathers) in the original State of habitual residence. During the Convention deliberations, the concept was expanded to accord additional rights of parental responsibility if the law of the new habitual residence was more "generous" than was the original habitual residence. Such increased rights are not extinguished by a later change of residence of the child, even if the child moves back to the original State which did not accord such rights.[73] In this instance, stability (at least in one direction) gave way to a substantive judgment in favor of equal parental rights.

Nonetheless, there are limitations that operate with respect to the rules on parental responsibility. First, under Article 17, the *exercise* – in contrast to the

---

[69] Ibid., p. 575. The *Lagarde Report* offers the example of authorities of the habitual residence of a minor "taking measures" to sell property located abroad. If there is authorization under the law of the *situs* (but not of the habitual residence), it is suggested that the *situs* rule should prevail and the authorization be given.

[70] Here again the *Lagarde Report*, ibid., offers an example. Assume a guardianship imposed by authorities in the State of habitual residence requires that the guardian obtain permission from the judge before taking certain actions. If the law in the new State of habitual residence would not require permission from the judge, the suggestion is that the guardian could act alone. Professor Lagarde may be correct about this interpretation of Art. 15, para. 3, and the term "conditions of application". Nonetheless, the example exhibits some of the dangers in divorcing conditions that may have attached to the original measure. If a particular guardian or guardianship was permitted only because there was a measure of oversight by the judge, it might be short-sighted to continue that guardianship without such a condition and without a review of the circumstances by the authorities in the new State of habitual residence.

[71] The attribution or extinction of parental responsibility by operation of law is governed by the law of the State of habitual residence. See Art. 16, 1996 Convention (supra n. 1) at p. 1398.

[72] The exercise of parental responsibility is governed by the law of the State of the child's habitual residence. However, if the child's habitual residence changes, the exercise is now governed by the law of the State of the new habitual residence.

[73] See G. de Hart (supra n. 40) at pp. 1392-1393.

attribution – of parental rights is governed by the law of the new habitual residence when a change in habitual residence occurs. Second, under Article 18, the attribution of parental responsibility can be terminated or modified by measures taken by the State with jurisdiction under the 1996 Convention. This power in the new State of habitual residence – along with the ability of that State to apply the law of the former State of habitual residence under Article 15, paragraph b – mitigates the potentially harsh effect of attributing rights of parental responsibility where they did not exist in the original State of habitual residence. Finally, the choice of law provisions are all subject to Article 22,[74] which allows deviation from the designated provisions if "manifestly contrary to public policy, taking into account the best interests of the child."

4.7 Recognition and Enforcement

One of the most serious limitations of the earlier 1961 Protection of Minors Convention was its weak provisions on recognition and enforcement.[75] So long as steps for enforcement of measures were required, the recognizing State – with either nationality or habitual residence jurisdiction – was able to modify those measures. Thus, a custody/visitation order obtained in the State of habitual residence might be recognized – but could also be modified – by the State of nationality.[76]

The 1996 Convention attempts to strengthen provisions on recognition and enforcement. Article 23 imposes a mandatory obligation of recognition ("measures . . . shall be recognized"), and Article 26 provides that if enforcement elsewhere is required, the measures shall be "declared enforceable or registered for the purpose of enforcement" according to the procedures in the enforcing State. Authorities of the requested State are bound by the findings of fact on which jurisdiction was based,[77] and no review of the merits is permitted in the requested State.[78]

One potential loophole to evade enforcement is found in Article 28, which provides for enforcement of measures declared or registered for enforcement "as if they had been taken by the authorities of the requested state." However, a second

---

[74] See Art. 22, 1996 Convention (supra n. 1) at p. 1399 ("The application of the law designated by the provisions of this Chapter can be refused only if this application would be manifestly contrary to public policy, taking into account the best interests of the child.").

[75] Art. 7 of the 1961 Protection of Minors Convention provides:

The measures taken by the competent authorities by virtue of the preceding articles of the present Convention shall be recognized in all contracting States. However, if these measures involve acts of enforcement in a State other than that in which they have been taken, their recognition and enforcement shall be governed either by the domestic law of the country in which enforcement is sought, or by the relevant international conventions. (supra n. 3) at p. 149.

[76] See *Dyer Report* (supra n. 8) p. 21.

[77] See Art. 25, 1996 Convention (supra n. 1) at p. 1400.

[78] See ibid.

sentence in Article 28 adds that enforcement shall take place "in accordance with the law of the requested State to the extent provided by such law, *taking into consideration the best interests of the child*." (Emphasis added.) Though intended only to accommodate the law of the requested State,[79] one fears that the requested State might use this provision to superimpose a "best interests" test at the enforcement stage, thereby undermining the objectives of a jurisdiction and judgments convention of this kind. Not surprisingly, there was a strong sense that the quasi-automatic system of enforcement established by the Brussels and Lugano Conventions was not appropriate for a convention dealing with child protective measures, where additional flexibility was desired.[80] Nonetheless, too great a dosage of "ad hoc" best interests could distort the overall design of jurisdiction and recognition/enforcement in the 1996 Convention, which itself has the "best interests" of children at its core.

Similar tensions are found in the basic provision on enforcement in Article 23(2), which lists those grounds on which recognition may – but is not required to – be refused. Several of the defenses are to be expected: an exercise of jurisdiction outside the grounds approved in the 1996 Convention,[81] infringement of parental responsibility without an opportunity of the parent to be heard, except in a case of urgency,[82] and "manifestly contrary to the public policy of the requested State." Note that the public policy defense is limited: it must be "manifestly contrary" to the policy and the policy is limited to one which takes "into account the best interests of the child."[83]

A more controversial provision is found in Article 23(2)(b), which permits refusal of recognition "if the measure was taken, except in a case of urgency, in a judicial or administrative proceeding, without the child having been provided the opportunity to be heard, in violation of fundamental principles of procedure of the requested State."[84] The procedures of many countries do not provide for an across-the-board right of a child to be heard in proceedings; often the right to be heard is contingent on context as well as the age of the child. Thus, there was a danger that the 1996 Convention was imposing uniformity of procedural practice on States party to the Convention. However, the phrasing "in violation of fundamental principles of procedure" indicates that the exception is only intended to apply where the

---

[79] See *Lagarde Report* (supra n. 25) p. 589.
[80] See A. Bucher (supra n. 24).
[81] See Art. 23(2)(a), 1996 Convention (supra n. 1) at pp. 1399-1400.
[82] See Art. 23(2)(c) ibid.
[83] See Art. 23(2)(d), ibid. Two additional defenses are quite specific to the coverage of the 1996 Convention. Under paragraph 2(e), recognition may be refused if the measure is incompatible with a later measure taken in a non-Contracting State of the child's habitual residence if it fulfills the requirement for recognition in the requested State, and under paragraph 2(f) there is a defense if the procedure of Article 33(1) (consent to placement for care in another State) has not been complied with.
[84] See Art. 23(2)(b), ibid.

failure to hear the child is contrary to the fundamental procedural principles of the requested State.[85]

4.8   Co-Operation and Mutual Assistance

The innovations in the 1996 Convention with respect to co-operation and mutual assistance have already been noted. The obligations imposed on the Central Authority are quite genuine but designed to fit with various mechanisms in the 1996 Convention.[86]

Pursuant to Article 30, Central authorities (1) "shall co-operate with each other and promote co-operation amongst the competent Authorities in their States" and (2) "shall take appropriate steps to provide information as to the law of, and services available" in their State. In addition, under Article 31 Central Authorities shall take steps either directly – or through public authorities or other bodies – to facilitate communications with respect to the transfer of jurisdiction under Articles 8 and 9, to facilitate by mediation or other means possible solutions to situations arising under the 1996 Convention, and to provide, on request of a competent authority of another Contracting State, assistance in discovering the whereabouts of the child, if it appears the child is in that State and in need of protection. Note that there is no obligation to take a particular initiative or to co-ordinate in advance the taking of any measure, except in the case of trans-border placements under Article 33. Under Article 33, when a child is to be moved to another State for foster or other institutional care, there shall be consultation with authorities in the second State and a report on the child as well as the reasons for the proposed placement shall be transmitted.

In conjunction with the 1996 Convention's design that a number of States may have jurisdiction to take measures, there are several other provisions detailing situations calling for co-operation and communication. Pursuant to Article 32, a Contracting State with which a child has a substantial connection may (through its authorities) request (if it provides supporting reasons) the Central Authority of the State of habitual residence to provide a report on the situation of the child or to consider that measures be taken. The provision is in effect a substitute for the more dramatic request by a State to transfer jurisdiction to it under Article 9. Article 34 is the mirror provision for authorities contemplating "measures" under the 1996 Convention; they may request any authority of another Contracting State to provide and communicate information relevant to the protection of the child. To avoid confusion as to when a proper request has been made, a Contracting State may declare that such requests be routed only through its Central Authority.[87] There does not ap-

---

[85]   See *Lagarde Report* (supra n. 25) p. 583.

[86]   There was also a concern in many countries that any provision that operated to impose heavy burdens or costs on the Central Authority would be unacceptable internally.

[87]   See Art. 34(2), 1996 Convention (supra n. 1) at p. 1401.

pear to be any obligation on the part of the requested State to furnish information in response to requests made under Articles 32 and 34. However, under Article 36, if a Contracting State, which has taken or is contemplating measures of protection in the case of a child exposed to serious danger, is informed that the child is elsewhere, it must inform authorities in the other State about the danger. However, no request or transmission of information can take place if it is likely to place the child or family member in danger,[88] and other rules of confidentiality are imposed by the 1996 Convention.[89]

One specific Article of co-operation (Article 35) addresses the particular problem of access (visitation) rights in a custody dispute.[90] The 1980 Abduction Convention, which contains a provision requiring a State to assist in organizing access to the child but establishes no specific procedures,[91] has been disappointing as a means of ensuring and enforcing access rights. The 1996 Convention has tried to fill that gap by authorizing a parent residing in a State other than that of the child's habitual residence to request that State to gather information and evidence and make a finding on the suitability of that parent to exercise access and under what conditions. The authority that has jurisdiction to determine an application for access is required to admit and consider such information before reaching its decision; if a proceeding before it is already pending, it may adjourn to take advantage of this procedure, in particular, when it is considering an application to restrict or terminate access rights granted in a State of former habitual residence.

5.   RELATIONSHIP TO OTHER CONVENTIONS

The emerging Brussels II Convention was a constant backdrop in the negotiations of the 1996 Convention. Given the solutions crafted by the 1996 Convention, e.g. the acceptance of the divorce jurisdiction in Article 10, the potential conflicts do not seem serious. In any event, a "disconnect" clause in Article 52, paragraph 2 allows for Contracting States to conclude agreements among themselves pertaining to children habitually resident in any of the States Parties to such agreements. The rule allows a group of Contracting States and particularly those States that are members of the European Union to create their own system of protection between States for children that will have priority over the 1996 Convention in those States to the

---

[88] See Art. 37, ibid.

[89] See Art. 41, (limiting the use of personal data), Art. 42 (guaranteeing confidentiality according to local law), ibid.

[90] Paragraph 1 of Art. 35 is more general and authorizes a request to another State for assistance in the "implementation of measures of protection taken under the Convention." Paragraphs 2-4 address the specific issues of access rights.

[91] See Art. 21, 1980 Abduction Convention (supra n. 4) at p. 1503.

extent that it applies to children habitually resident in a State that is party to the agreement.[92]

The less clear interrelationship is with the 1980 Abduction Convention. It has always been thought that the two Conventions had different objectives and did not overlap, but there was great concern that the 1996 Convention not undermine in any way the 1980 Abduction Convention. Article 50 of the 1996 Convention contains an express provisions that the Convention "shall not affect the application of the [1980 Abduction Convention], as between Parties to both Conventions"; but emphasizes that nothing precludes the 1996 Convention from being invoked to obtain the return of a child wrongfully removed or retained or of organizing access rights. Possibly, the primacy of the 1980 Abduction Convention should have been stated more forcefully as it was in relation to the 1961 Protection of Minors Convention.[93]

Nonetheless, there are various interplays between the two Conventions, all of which may not have been foreseen. The 1980 Abduction Convention owes its structure in part to the absence of other effective mechanisms for enforcement of child custody decisions. It is quite possible that when a custody decision has been made by an appropriate court, the recognition and enforcement provisions of Chapter IV of the 1996 Convention will be more effective than a request for return under the 1980 Abduction Convention, where additional defenses, such as the objection of the child to return, may be invoked. On the other hand, the 1980 Abduction Convention has the advantage of providing a remedy in the absence of any decree or order, and contains a more dynamic and activist role for Central Authorities in locating the child and initiating proceedings. In addition, there are legal assistance provisions (when no reservation has been made) in the 1980 Abduction Convention,[94] which do not exist under the 1996 Convention.

A more troubling connection stems from the intersection of a no-return order under the 1980 Abduction Convention and assertions of jurisdiction under the 1996 Convention. The United States delegation consistently pressed for a provision that would make clear that a wrongful removal or retention could *never* give rise to habitual residence jurisdiction. Otherwise, courts entertaining applications for return might have an incentive to accept a defense to return a child, and as a result, obtain jurisdiction to make a subsequent custody order. As discussed earlier, Article 7 of the 1996 Convention attempts to limit (though it does not eliminate) situations in which a new habitual residence can be established once there has been a refusal to return. And notwithstanding the *lis pendens* provisions of Article 13 and the enforcement provisions of Article 23, a new habitual residence can always modify prior measures.

---

[92] See A. Bucher (supra n. 24).
[93] See Art. 34, 1980 Abduction Convention (supra n. 4) at p. 1504.
[94] See Art. 25, ibid., at p. 1503.

6.   CONCLUSION

The 1996 Convention on the Protection of Minors reflects a Herculean effort to articulate appropriate standards for the assertion of jurisdiction and recognition of judgments on matters relating to children across transnational borders. Professor SIEHR's contributions to that effort were invaluable. One can only hope that the future operation and interpretation of the 1996 Convention will develop in a way consistent with his insight, wisdom, and vision.

Parental Responsibility under Brussels II

Mathilde Sumampouw[*]

1. INTRODUCTION

The Brussels Convention of 27 September 1968 on Jurisdiction and Enforcement of Judgments in Civil and Commercial Matters (hereinafter Brussels I) was designed to meet the economic needs of the European integration of the sixties. In the past 30 years Brussels I and the various amendments required by the enlargement of the European Community fulfilled its promises of legal protection and, hence, legal certainty in the Community. At present European integration is not mainly an economic affair any more. According to the drafters of the Convention of 28 may 1998 on Jurisdiction and the Recognition and Enforcement of Judgments in Matrimonial Matters, drawn up on the basis of Article K3 of the Treaty on European Union, the achievement of free movement of persons and more frequent establishment of family links between individuals who are nationals or residents of different countries

---

[*] Former Head of the Private International Law Department at the T.M.C. Asser Institute, The Hague.

J. Basedow et al., eds., Private Law in the International Arena – Liber Amicorum Kurt Siehr
© *2000, T.M.C.Asser Press, The Hague, The Netherlands*

demanded a judicial response, which is provided by this Convention.[1] The question is, will this so-called Brussels II Convention have the same beneficial effects as Brussels I? The merits of Brussels I are not only because it meets the economic needs of the Community, but also because it is the only multilateral convention of this sort which operates in the European region. Unlike Brussels I, Brussels II has no monopoly in providing legal protection and, hence, legal certainty for European citizens. Several other multilateral conventions meet those needs as well.[2] Taking account of these concurrent international instruments that also operate in the European region, this study analyses the benefits of Brussels II, limited to questions of parental responsibility governed by this Convention.

2. SCOPE OF THE CONVENTION

The Convention provides a set of rules governing the jurisdiction of Member States' courts and the recognition and enforcement of judgments of these courts in civil proceedings related to the matters specified below.

2.1 **Material Scope**

Brussels II is primarily designed to cover proceedings concerning matters of divorce, legal separation, and annulment of marriages: the Preamble and Article l (1a). In addition to these matrimonial issues the Convention covers proceedings in matters of parental responsibility on the occasion of matrimonial proceedings: the Preamble and Article 1 (1b). As noted above this contribution will focus on these additional issues of Brussels II.

The crucial question regarding the scope of Brussels II in respect of these matters is to ascertain the issues incorporated in the wording "parental responsibility on the occasion of proceedings as to divorce, legal separation, and annulment of marriages".[3] The Borrás Report states that the wording only covers "matters relating to parental responsibility that appear to be linked to the matrimonial proceedings when those take place". As regards the concept of "parental responsibility" the Report holds that this concept "has to be defined by the legal system of the Member State in which responsibility is under consideration". It was acknowledged that the national interpretation is likely to engender some problems. Nonetheless, the expectation was that a uniform interpretation will gradually develop because the term

---

[1] Alegría Borrás, *Explanatory Report on the Convention of 28 May 1998 on Jurisdiction and the Recognition and Enforcement of Judgments in Matrimonial Matters* (hereinafter – Borrás Report), *OJ(EC)* [1998] C 221/29 (16 July 1998).

[2] See also K. Boele-Woelki, "Waarom Brussel II?" (Why Brussels II?) *FJR* (1998) p. 125.

[3] Hereinafter, for sake of brevity, the reference will be made only to the divorce proceedings.

"parental responsibility" is employed in various international conventions, and in particular in the Hague Convention of 19 October 1996, on Jurisdiction, Applicable Law, Recognition, Enforcement and Co-operation in Respect of Parental Responsibility and Measures for the Protection of Children.[4] This Convention (hereinafter Hague Convention 1996) is one of the multilateral conventions which a.o. covers similar matters of parental responsibility as Brussels II.[5] It should be noted that at the time when the Hague Conference on Private International Law (hereinafter Hague Conference) was drafting the Hague Convention 1996, the Member States of the European Union (hereinafter EU) were negotiating the draft of Brussels II. During the preparatory work of the two Conventions, frequent consultations have taken place between the EU and the Hague Conference.[6] The Hague Convention 1996 has also frequently been referred to in the Borrás Report. In view of these references and the said background of Brussels II it seemed opportune to explore the provisions of The Hague Convention 1996 related to the critical question stated above.

The concurring aspect of the Hague Convention 1996 is that it also provides a set of rules governing jurisdiction, recognition and enforcement of judgments regarding parental responsibility. Unlike Brussels II, the concept of parental responsibility is defined in the Hague Convention 1996 itself. Article 1(2) of this Convention reads as follows:

> For the purpose of this Convention, the term "parental responsibility" includes parental authority, or any analogous relationship of authority determining the rights, powers and responsibilities of parents, guardians or other legal representatives in relation to the person or the property of the child.

Furthermore, Article 3 of the Hague Convention 1996 provides a non exhaustive list of measures which fall within the scope of that Convention. Relevant for the question at hand is the enumeration in Article 3(b). It gives a list of custodial issues which frequently are at stake when a marriage relation breaks up, such as rights relating to the care of the person of the child, the right to determine the child's place of residence, rights of access including the right to take a child for a limited period of time to a place other than the child's habitual residence.[7] These custodial issues may rightly fall within the scope of the present Convention as well. Brussels II, however,

---

[4] Borrás Report (supra n. 1) p. 36 nrs. 23 and 24.

[5] See Final Act of the 18th Session of the Hague Conference on Private International Law; The Hague, 19 October 1996.

[6] See Borrás Report (supra n. 1) p. 31 nr. 9.

[7] P. Lagarde, *Explanatory Report on the Convention of 19 October 1996 on Jurisdiction, Applicable Law, Recognition, Enforcement and Cooperation in Respect of Parental Responsibility and Measures for the Protection of Children* (hereinafter Lagarde Report); Provisional edition 15 January 1997; Permanent Bureau of the Hague Conference on Private International Law; pp. 1-141, p. 43 nr. 18 and p. 45 nr.20.

requires an additional time-limit: the proceedings have to be initiated either together with or pending the divorce proceedings. This restriction is embodied in the
term "on the occasion",[8] and indirectly in the exclusive jurisdiction rule of Article 3.
(see *infra* section 3.2). Consequently, custody proceedings initiated after the divorce decree has become final and the recognition and enforcement of the judgments in these custody proceedings are not covered by Brussels II.

With respect to variation orders, the following distinction should be made. A petition to modify an initial custody decree rendered on the occasion of divorce proceedings is generally instituted after the divorce has become final. As such, the
jurisdiction over the said petition and the recognition and enforcement of the variation order in question are not covered by Brussels II. However, custody decrees rendered on the occasion of a legal separation could be modified in the event that the
legal separation is converted into a divorce. Unlike the former situation, these variation orders do fall within the scope of Brussels II.

2.2   Personal Scope

The personal scope of Brussels II in relation to the present study is limited to children of both spouses: Article 1(1b). According to the Borrás Report this provision
covers both biological and adopted children.[9]

2.3   Transitional Scope

Under Article 37(l), Brussels II covers jurisdiction only in legal proceedings instituted after its entry into force in the State of origin, and as regards recognition and
enforcement, after its entry into force in the State addressed. Pursuant to Article
37(2), however, the recognition and enforcement of judgments rendered after
Brussels II has entered into force between the State of origin and the State addressed
and instituted before that date are governed by Brussels II, provided that jurisdiction was based either on rules which correspond to those of Brussels II or on rules
provided in another Convention which was in force between the State of origin and
the State addressed when the proceedings were initiated.

2.4   Concurring Conventions

Brussels II claims exclusive application in the relation between Member States as
from the date of its entry into force. It supersedes any convention existing at that
date which covers matters falling within the scope of Brussels II: Article 38(1).

---

[8]   See also the citation from the Borrás Report (supra n. 4).
[9]   Borrás Report (supra n. 1) p. 36 nr. 25.

With respect to the present study, three conventions over which Brussels II claims to take precedence are specifically mentioned: Article 39. These are: the Hague Convention of 5 October 1961 concerning the Powers of Authorities and the Law Applicable in Respect of the Protection of Minors (hereinafter Hague Convention 1961), the European Convention of 20 May 1980 on Recognition and Enforcement of Decisions concerning Custody of Children and on Restoration of Custody of Children, and the Hague Convention 1996 mentioned before. The primacy of Brussels II over these Conventions is limited to those matters which fall within the scope of Brussels II: Articles 39 and 40.

After Brussels II enters into force Member States may only conclude conventions or apply agreements which are to supplement the provisions of Brussels II, or to facilitate the application of the principles of Brussels II: Article 38(3). The Borrás Report mentions as an example of such supplementary agreement a convention dispensing with all or some of the grounds of non-recognition stated in Article 15.[10] Article 38(3) does not mean that after the entry into force of Brussels II Member States are prohibited to ratify the Hague Convention 1996 or other concurring conventions, because – as stated earlier – the precedence of Brussels II over concurring conventions is limited to those matters which also fall within the scope of Brussels II.

With respect to the exclusive application of Brussels II in relation to other conventions, two exceptions are made. The first one is the Convention of 6 February 1931 between Denmark, Finland, Iceland, Norway and Sweden, containing international private law provisions concerning marriage, adoption and guardianship. The EU Contracting States: Denmark, Finland and Sweden, have the option of declaring that said Convention together with the Final Protocol thereto will apply whole or in part, in their mutual relations, in place of Brussels II: Article 38(2a). The second exception is the Hague Convention of 25 October 1980 on the Civil Aspects of International Child Abduction. (See *infra* section 3.5).

3. JURISDICTION

3.1 Conditions

The jurisdiction over the custody issues at hand is connected to the divorce jurisdiction under Article 2. According to Article 3 the divorce court exercising jurisdiction under Article 2 has jurisdiction as a custody court provided the child is habitually resident in the State of the divorce court in question: Article 3(1), or in another Contracting State: Article 3(2). In the latter event two additional conditions have to be

---

[10] Borrás Report (supra n. 1) p. 60 nr. 114.

met. First, at least one of the spouses must have parental responsibility in relation to the child: Article 3(2a). Second, the jurisdiction has been accepted by the spouses and is in the best interests of the child: Article 3(2b). There are no difficulties if the child is habitually resident in the State of the divorce court. Some questions arise, however, as to the conditions of Article 3(2). First, regarding the title to parental responsibility. The Borrás Report is silent on this question. It is reasonable to assume that the title to parental responsibility could either be by operation of law, or by a court decision or court settlement.[11] The latter two imply that parental responsibility could be shared between one parent and a third person. This situation could affect the requirement as regards the acceptance of the divorce court's jurisdiction.

A second question is about the interpretation of the words "has been accepted". The Borrás Report is silent on this issue as well. Since the principles of Brussels I were taken into account when the present Convention was drafted – as mentioned in the Preamble – it seems logical to interpret the words in question in analogy to the interpretation of Article 18 of Brussels I. This implies that a respondent who enters an appearance without contesting the court's jurisdiction is considered to accept this jurisdiction. A respondent is entitled to contest the court's jurisdiction and make submissions to the substance of the action as well, "provided that, if the challenge to jurisdiction is not preliminary to any defence as to the substance, it does not occur after the making of the submissions which under national procedural law are considered to be the first defence addressed to the court seized."[12] It goes without saying that a respondent, who does not enter an appearance after having duly been served, cannot be considered to have accepted the court's jurisdiction.

A third question arises since Article 3(2b) is silent on the possibility that parental responsibility is shared with a third person.[13] Example: On the occasion of a legal separation the parental responsibility in relation to the child was attributed to the child's mother and the child's grandfather. After a time the child's father filed for the conversion of the legal separation into divorce and for a new custody order. Article 3(2b) is silent as to whether a grandfather, who shares the custody with the child's mother, has also a say in the matter of the jurisdiction of the divorce court. The Borrás Report does not cover this problem either. In my view, the custody claim in question falls within the material and personal scope of Brussels II. Thus, when the child's parents, of whom one is a co-custodian, are granted a say in the attribution of jurisdiction to hear the custody claim, I see no reason why another co-

---

[11] See also Th. M. de Boer, "Favor divortii en rechtsmacht. Comentaar op artikel 2 van het voorstel voor een bevoegdheids- en executieveverdrag in zaken van familie- en erfrecht" (Favor divortii and Jurisdiction. Comment on Article 2 of the proposal for a jurisdiction and enforcement convention on matters of family law and law of succession) in: *Op Recht, Liber Amicorum A.V.M. Struycken* (S.C.J.J. Kortmann et al (eds.)) (1996) p. 19-31, p. 27.

[12] *Elefanten Schuh GmbH* v. *Jackmain*, case 150/80, [1981] ECR 1971.

[13] Lagarde Report (supra n. 7) p. 75 nr. 65.

custodian, in this case a third person, should not be granted the same right. To exclude this custody matter from the scope of Brussels II could result in different jurisdiction rules being applied if the spouses have more than one child.

Unlike Brussels II, the Hague Convention 1996 has not mentioned the question as regards the acceptance of the divorce court's jurisdiction by a third person. Article 10 of this Convention, which is basically similar to Article 3(2) of Brussels II, requires that the jurisdiction of the divorce court has been accepted, not only by the child's parents, but also "by any other person who has parental responsibility in relation to the child."

3.2   Territorial Scope; Time-Limit; *Perpetuatio Fori*

The text of Article 3 suggests that the scope of this jurisdiction rule is limited to children habitually resident in a Contracting State. Referring to the compatibility of Article 3 with the provisions of the Hague Convention 1996, the Borrás Report remarks: "The fact that the *Community Convention limits itself* to children habitually resident in the Member States facilitates its compatibility with the Hague Convention 1996".[14] (Italics added – M.S.). The wording in italic is misleading, for the limitation does not concern the scope of the Convention but the scope of a conventional rule. A limitation as stated in the Report would mean that custody matters in relation to children habitually resident in a non-Contracting State fall outside the scope of Brussels II, and thus not governed by its provisions. Its drafters apparently did not intend such a limited scope of Brussels II. (See *infra* section 4.). The territorial scope of Article 3 affects the applicability of Article 7 in which the exclusive nature of Article 3 is laid down. (See *infra* section 3.3).

Another limitation of the scope of Article 3 is a time-limit to the jurisdiction of the custody court. As observed earlier regarding the scope of Brussels II, Article 3(3) implies that only custody proceedings instituted together with or pending the divorce proceedings are covered by Brussels II. For under Article 3(3a) the jurisdiction conferred by Articles 3(1) and 3(2) only ceases when the judgment in the divorce proceeding has become final. If the custody proceeding is still pending on the latter date, the jurisdiction of the custody court ceases when the judgment on the custody proceeding has become final: Article 3(3b). A third possibility provided by Article 3(3c) is when the divorce or custody proceeding has come to an end for another reason, such as the withdrawal of the application or the death of the relevant party.[15]

Another implication of Article 3(3) is that Brussels II upholds the principle of *perpetuatio fori* which follows from the consequence of Articles 3(3a) and 3(3b),

---

[14] Borrás Report (supra n. 1) p. 40 nr. 36.
[15] Borrás Report (supra n. 1) p. 41 nr. 39c.

that a court retains its jurisdiction conferred by Articles 3(1) and 3(2) if a child changed its habitual residence pending the proceeding.

3.3 Exclusive and Residual Jurisdiction

Pursuant to Article 7 the jurisdiction under Article 3 is exclusive. Since Article 3 is territorially limited to children habitually resident in a Contracting State, Article 7 is not applicable if the child's habitual residence is in a non-Contracting State. Hence, in this event no court of a Contracting State has jurisdiction pursuant to Article 3. Therefore, under Article 8(1) the jurisdiction over custody matters in relation to children habitually resident in a non-Contracting State is governed by "the laws" of the Contracting State where the proceeding takes place.

The question arises regarding the interpretation of the term "the laws" laid down in Article 8(1). According to the Borrás Report the jurisdiction under Article 8, named residual jurisdiction, corresponds to the exorbitant jurisdiction under Articles 3 and 4 of Brussels I. In addition, the Report mentions some examples of national (i.e. non-conventional) jurisdiction rules on divorce of several Contracting States which according to the Report "can be defined as residual for the purpose of Article 2 of the Convention".[16] This explanation suggests that the term "the laws" refers to the non-conventional exorbitant jurisdiction rules of a Contracting State.

It seems more reasonable, however, to suggest that the term "the laws" means not only the non-conventional rules but also the conventional rules of the Contracting State in question. Accordingly, with respect to jurisdiction over custody issues regarding children habitually resident in a non-Contracting State, the Hague Convention 1996 or the Hague Convention 1961 could be applicable if the Contracting State is a Party to these Conventions. In light of Article 40(1) of Brussels II, the primacy of Brussels II over these two Hague Conventions under Article 39 of Brussels II is not applicable here, because the custody issue at hand is not governed by the proper jurisdiction rule of Brussels II. The following examples will illustrate that this interpretation of the term "the laws" could avoid a discrepancy between custody jurisdiction as regards children habitually resident in a Contracting State and those in a non-Contracting State.

Example A. A child of Dutch and German nationality is habitually resident in Germany together with his German mother. His father, a Dutch national, filed for divorce and custody in the Netherlands where he is habitually resident, and which is the last habitual residence of the spouses before the marriage breakdown. The mother enters an appearance to contest the Dutch court's jurisdiction over the custody claim.

---

[16] Borrás Report (supra n. 1) p. 43 nr. 46 and p. 44 nr. 47

The Dutch court having divorce jurisdiction under Article 2(1) second indent has no jurisdiction over the custody claim pursuant to Article 3(2). Due to the exclusive nature of Article 3 as provided for in Article 7, the Dutch court has to decline jurisdiction by its own motion based on Article 9. Another consequence is the absence of an alternative court for the parents to obtain a custody order pending the divorce proceeding. This situation could harm the child's interests. In an urgent case, however, either parent can apply for provisional or protective measures related to the person or property of the child under the urgent jurisdiction of Article 12. When the mother intends to have a custody order from the German court as the court of the child's habitual residence, she has to wait till the divorce proceedings have become final after which Brussels II is not applicable any more.

Example B. The facts are the same as in *example A*, except that mother and child are habitually resident in Switzerland. Assuming that under Article 2(2) both the Netherlands and Germany have made the option to apply the criterion of nationality, the Dutch court has jurisdiction over the divorce action pursuant to Article 2(1) second indent. With respect to the custody claim Articles 3 and 7 are not applicable because the child is habitually resident in a non-Contracting State. Hence, the custody claim is governed by the residual jurisdiction of Article 8(1): the national law, including the conventional law of the Netherlands. As remarked earlier the relevant conventions are the Hague Convention 1961 to which both the Netherlands and Switzerland are Parties, and the Hague Convention 1996, which is not yet in force.

Let us assume for the sake of argument that the Hague Convention 1996 has meanwhile entered into force, and both the Netherlands and Switzerland have become Contracting States. Under Article 51 of the Hague Convention 1996 this Convention replaces the Hague Convention 1961 between the Netherlands and Switzerland. Under Articles 1 and 3 of the Hague Convention 1996 the custody claim falls within the scope of this Convention. Hence, the jurisdiction is governed by Article 10 of this Convention.

Article 10 was added to the primary jurisdiction rules of Articles 5 to 9 of the Hague Convention 1996 at the request of the EU Member States to avoid a too great discrepancy between the Hague convention 1996 and Brussels II.[17] The conditions of Article 10 are essentially similar to those of Article 3 of Brussels II, but for two additional requirements in Article 10.[18] One is the additional consent of a third per-

---

[17]   Lagarde Report (supra n. 7) p. 73 nr. 61.
[18]   Article 10 reads:
1.   Without prejudice to Articles 5 to 9, the authority of a Contracting State exercising jurisdiction to decide on an application for divorce or legal separation of the parents of a child habitually resident in another Contracting State, or for annulment of their marriage, may, if the law of their State so provides, take measures directed to the protection of the person or property of the child if
a.   at the time of the commencement of the proceedings, one of his or her parents habitually resides in that State and one of them has parental responsibility in relation to the child, and
b.   the jurisdiction of these authorities to take measures has been accepted by the parents, as

son as (co-) custodian to the jurisdiction of the divorce court: Article 10(1b). This condition has been observed earlier. The second is that at the time of the commencement of the divorce proceeding one of the parents is habitually resident in the divorce State: Article 10(1a). There is, however, no essential difference between the latter condition and Article 3(2) of Brussels II, because the custody jurisdiction under Brussels II is connected to the divorce jurisdiction. Thus, when the divorce jurisdiction is based on Article 2(1) of Brussels II, at least one of the spouses is habitually resident in the divorce State at the commencement of the divorce proceeding. Only when the divorce jurisdiction is based on the common nationality or "domicile" of the spouses pursuant to Article 2(2) of Brussels II, there might be a difference between Article 10 of the Hague Convention 1996 and Article 3(2) of Brussels II. In these cases, it is not necessary that one of the spouses is habitually resident in the divorce State at the time of the commencement of the divorce proceeding.

The foregoing illustrates that also under Article 10 of the Hague Convention 1996 the Dutch court has no jurisdiction. Unlike Article 3 of Brussels II, however, Article 10 of the Hague Convention 1996 is not exclusive. The latter Convention provides concurring *fora* of which the forum of the child's habitual residence is the main one: Article 5. If the child's best interests so required, the authorities of the State of the child's habitual residence may transfer or authorise a request for transfer of its jurisdiction to the authorities of another Contracting State, a.o. the State of which the child is a national: Articles 8 and 9. Given the challenge to jurisdiction of the Dutch divorce court by the mother, a possible request by the Dutch father under Article 9 of the Hague Convention 1996 to the Swiss court to transfer its jurisdiction to the Dutch court would most probably be denied. As far as the mother is concerned, she can file a custody claim with the Swiss court. Under Article 5 of the Hague Convention 1996 (as well as under Article 1, the Hague Convention 1961) the Swiss court has jurisdiction as the court of the child's habitual residence. This action, however, falls outside the scope of Brussels II.

The two examples above demonstrate that under the same circumstances the application of Brussels II as regards a child habitually resident in a Contracting State, as well as of the Hague Convention 1996 as regards a child habitually resident in a non-Contracting State, leads to a similar result.

---

well as by any other person who has parental responsibility in relation to the child, and is in the best interest of the child.

2.   The jurisdiction provided for by paragraph 1 to take measures for the protection of the child ceases as soon as the decision allowing or refusing the application for divorce, legal separation or annulment of marriage has become final or the proceedings have come to an end for another reason.

3.4   Urgent Jurisdiction

In urgent cases the jurisdiction rule of Article 3 may be set aside: Article 12. The text implies that Article 12 is limited to children and their property present in the territory of the Contracting State where the urgent measures are taken. Furthermore, that the type of measures and the jurisdiction to take these measures are governed by the domestic law of the Contracting State.

Article 9(1) of the Hague Convention 1961 and Article 11(1) of the Hague Convention 1996 provide a similar rule, but with an explicit addition. Articles 9(2) and 11(2) provide that the urgent measures lapse as soon as the authorities which have normally jurisdiction under the Convention have taken the measures required by the situation. According to the Lagarde Report, the provision of Article 11(2) presupposes that the measures taken on the basis of urgency are recognised in all other Contracting States.[19]

Article 12 of Brussels II does not provide the explicit addition as mentioned above, but it lapses in a similar way. According to the Borrás Report, the measures cease to apply once the court having jurisdiction under the Convention gives a judgment which is recognised (or enforced) under the Convention.[20] Due to the exclusive nature of Article 3, however, a replacement of an urgent measure as suggested by the Borrás Report is not feasible if the child is not habitually resident in the divorce State, but in another Contracting State, and the jurisdiction of the divorce court is not accepted by both spouses as provided for in Article 3(2).

As regards the scope of Article 12 the Borrás Report gives the following explanation. The measures taken under Article 12 can affect both persons and assets; the Convention is silent about the type of the measures and about their connection with the matrimonial proceedings. Based on these observations the Report then concludes that "these measures, accordingly, affect even matters that do not come within the scope of the Convention". Furthermore, the Report states that the rule laid down in Article 12 "is confined to establishing territorial effects in the State in which the measures are adopted".[21] These conclusions are questionable.

As regards the type of measures, the words "measures (—) as may be available under the law of that Member State" leave no doubt that this question is governed by the law of the Contracting State where the measures are taken, as has already been suggested earlier. With respect to the scope of Article 12, the Report apparently focused attention only on the question of matrimonial property, which indeed is excluded from the scope of Brussels II.[22] Parental responsibility, however, in-

---

[19]   Lagarde Report (supra n. 7) p. 79 nr. 72. Lagarde adds in a footnote that the extra-territorial effects are regulated in Article 23.
[20]   Borrás Report (supra n. 1) p. 48 nr. 59.
[21]   Borrás Report (supra n. 1) p. 47/48 nr. 59.
[22]   Borrás Report (supra n. 1) p. 35 nr. 22.

cludes the rights, powers and responsibilities of parents in relation, not only to the person of the child, but also to the child's property.[23] There is no indication in the text of Brussels II that the latter issue of parental responsibility is excluded from the scope of the Convention. Accordingly the word "assets" does not imply that Article 12 also covers matters outside the scope of Brussels II. In fact, Article 12 might be intended to cover only issues of parental responsibility. This suggestion is corroborated by the provision on the grounds of non-recognition. Under article 15(2b) recognition shall be refused, *except in case of urgency*, if the judgment was rendered without the child having been given the opportunity to be heard in violation of fundamental principles of procedure of the requested State. This provision implies that measures taken under Article 12 do have extra-territorial effects. Contrary to Article 15(2b), the question of urgent measures is not mentioned at all in Article 15(1), which regulates the non-recognition of judgements relating to divorce. Hence, the conclusion must be that Article 12 only covers matters within the scope of the Convention, and that the measures taken under Article 12 have extra-territorial effects.

3.5   Hague Child Abduction Convention

Article 4 of Brussels II instructs the court having jurisdiction under Article 3 to exercise its jurisdiction in conformity with the Hague Child Abduction Convention of 1980, and in particular Articles 3 and 16 thereof. The objective of this Convention is to provide a set of rules for obtaining the prompt return of children who have been taken to another country in violation of custody and access rights. It does not provide rules governing jurisdiction, recognition and enforcement of judgments regarding custody issues like Brussels II and other concurring conventions mentioned in section 2.4 above. Article 3 of the Hague Child Abduction Convention defines a wrongful removal or retention of a child within the meaning of this Convention. Article 16 provides that after receiving notice of a wrongful removal or retention in the sense of Article 3, the judicial and administrative authorities of a Contracting State of the Hague Child Abduction Convention to which the child has been removed or in which it has been retained shall not decide on the merits of rights of custody until it has been determined that the child is not to be returned under the Hague Child Abduction Convention or unless an application under the latter Convention is not lodged within a reasonable time following receipt of the notice of the wrongful conduct.

   According to the Borrás Report, Article 4 "assumes" that the Contracting States of Brussels II are parties to the Hague Child Abduction Convention.[24] The wording

---

[23]   Compare the above mentioned definition of "parental responsibility" laid down in article 1(2) of the Hague Convention 1996.
[24]   Borrás Report (supra n. 1) p. 42 nr. 41.

of Article 4 does not seem to suggest that assumption. It rather seems to imply the incorporation of Articles 3 and 16 of the Hague Child Abduction Convention into Brussels II. True, it would be more advantageous if Member States would ratify the said Hague Convention. Yet, even if they have not yet ratified it, the relevant provisions of the Hague Child Abduction Convention could well be applied by analogy. At present this question only concerns Belgium. All other EU Member States have ratified the Hague Child Abduction Convention.

As regards the impact of Article 16 on Brussels II, it should be noted that this provision is not a jurisdiction rule, but it does affect the adjudication of a court in the State of refuge. Such a situation occurs if a child has wrongfully been removed to or retained in a Contracting State of Brussels II in the sense of Article 3 of the Hague Child Abduction Convention, and the parent who committed the wrongful removal or retention filed for divorce and custody in that State. The court in that State, the State of refuge, has first to decide whether it has jurisdiction pursuant to Articles 2 and 3 of Brussels II. Only after the court has determined that it has jurisdiction under Brussels II, Article 16 of the Hague Child Abduction Convention becomes relevant and determines whether the court is allowed to decide on the merits of rights of custody.

Article 16 of the Hague Child Abduction Convention addresses the respective authorities of the State of refuge. It does not affect the adjudication of a court in the State from where the child has wrongfully been removed. If pending a proceeding where the court has jurisdiction under Article 3(1) of Brussels II, the child is wrongfully removed to another Contracting State or a non-Contracting State, the said court retains its jurisdiction based on the principle of *perputuatio fori* to decide on rights of custody. (See *supra* section 3.2). Article 16 of the Hague Child Abduction Convention does not interfere in the adjudication of this court. The problem is that the decision of this court – which must be recognised in the Contracting State where the child has been removed to or retained in – might be contrary to a decision of a court in the State of refuge not to return the child pursuant to the provisions of the Hague Child Abduction Convention.

4.   RECOGNITION

Article 14(1) states that judgments given in a Contracting State are recognised automatically in other Contracting States. It is obvious that only judgments within the scope of the present Convention are entitled to recognition under Article 14(1). The Convention does not require that the judgment be final. Hence, provisional measures within the scope of Brussels II are also governed by Article 14(1). So are measures taken in urgent cases pursuant to Article 12, as implicitly provided for in Article 15(2b). If an ordinary appeal has been lodged against the judgement, a court in the State addressed may stay the proceedings: Article 19(1).

Recognition may only be refused on the grounds specified in Article 15(2). If one of these grounds exists, non-recognition is apparently obligatory.[25] Article 15(2) corresponds for the main part to Article 23 of the Hague Convention 1996. This similarity is another result of the consultation between the EU and the Hague Conference.[26] The present grounds of non-recognition can be divided in three groups: general, persons directly involved with the custody issue, and conflicting judgments. The general grounds of non-recognition, usually provided for in any convention on recognition and enforcement of foreign judgements, are the following. Article 15(2a): recognition is manifest contrary to the public policy of the State addressed, taking into account the best interests of the child. In practice these two elements, public policy and the child's best interests, usually overlap each other. This ground of non-recognition is exactly the same as the one provided for in Article 23(2d) of the Hague Convention 1996. The second general ground is failure of the court of origin to respect the rights of defence: Article 15(2c).

The second group is provided for in Article 15(2b): except in case of urgency, failure to hear the child, in violation of fundamental principles of procedure of the State addressed, and in Article 15(2d): failure to hear a person who claims that the judgement infringes his/ her parental responsibility. These two grounds are also grounds of non-recognition under the Hague Convention 1996: Article 23(2b) and 23(2c). However, unlike Article 15(2d) of Brussels II, under the Hague Convention 1996 the exception of a case of urgency also applies as regards the second ground: Article 23(2c). The Borrás Report gives no explanation regarding the omission of this exception in Article 15(2d). According to the Lagarde Report, Article 23(2c) of the Hague Convention 1996 manifests the sanction against the violation of the defendant's rights of due process of law.[27] Under Brussels II this sanction is laid down in Article 15(2c) mentioned above.

As regards the ground of non-recognition related to the child in question, the interpretation of the Borrás Report is that the child must be heard in accordance with the rules applicable in the Contracting State concerned, which must include the rules of the UN Convention of 20 November 1989 on the Rights of the Child and in particular Article 12 thereof.[28] As regards the same ground of non- recognition in the Hague Convention 1996, the Lagarde Report mentions that this ground is directly inspired by Article 12 of the said UN Convention. It does not imply that the child ought to be heard in every case. It is only where the failure to hear the child is contrary to the fundamental principles of procedure of the requested State that this may justify a refusal of recognition.[29]

---

[25] See, however, supra n. 10 and infra n. 31.
[26] Compare Borrás Report (supra n. 1) p. 50 nr. 67.
[27] Lagarde Report (supra n. 7) p. 107 nr. 124.
[28] Borrás Report (supra n. 1) p. 52 nr. 73.
[29] Lagarde Report (supra n. 7) p. 107 nr. 123.

The third group of grounds of non-recognition is as follows. The judgment is irreconcilable with a later judgment relating to parental responsibility given in the State addressed: Article 15(2e), or in another Contracting State or non-Contracting State: Article 15(2f). In the latter event, the later judgment must meet the conditions required for its recognition in the State addressed. The text of Articles 15(2e) and 15(2f) implies that the later judgment relating to parental responsibility could also fall outside the scope of Brussels II. An example of this is a custody decree of which the proceedings are initiated after the divorce has become final, and which modifies the earlier custody order given on the occasion of the divorce. (See *supra* section 2.1).

In respect of the rules of recognition, two differences between Brussels II and the Hague Convention 1996 should be mentioned. Under Article 23(2a) of the Hague Convention 1996 failure to comply with the jurisdiction rules of that Convention is a ground of non-recognition. Hence, this provision authorises a review of the jurisdiction of the court of origin. Under Article 16(3) of Brussels II such a review is prohibited, except as regards judgments provided for in Articles 37(2), 38(2d), 41 and 43 mentioned below. The second difference: if one of the grounds for non-recognition exists, under the Hague Convention 1996 refusal of recognition is not compulsory, as under Brussels II, but it authorises a Contracting State to decide so.[30] However, according to the example given by the Borrás Report, the obligation to refuse recognition under Brussels II can be withdrawn by a supplementary agreement under Article 38(3) between the Contracting States.[31]

In reviewing the court of origin's jurisdiction, both Conventions provide that the court addressed is bound by the findings of fact on which the court of origin based its jurisdiction: Article 16(2) of Brussels II and Article 25 of the Hague Convention 1996. Also, under both Conventions a review of the merits of a judgment is prohibited: Article 18 of Brussels II and Article 27 of the Hague Convention 1996.

The rules on recognition and enforcement of judgments laid down in Title III of Brussels II also apply to the following three types of judgments. Judgments related to a transitional situation of Brussels II: Article 37(2), judgments based on the Nordic Convention of 1931: Article 38(2d), and judgments based on a supplementary agreement: Article 41. However, apart from the grounds of non-recognition of Article 15 mentioned earlier, the recognition of these judgments are also subject to the condition that the jurisdiction of the court of origin was based on rules which correspond with Articles 2 to 7. As already indicated before this means that unlike the general prohibition to review the court of origin's jurisdiction, such a review is authorised regarding these judgments. Also indicated above, a review of the court of origin's jurisdiction is explicitly authorised in a case provided for in Article 43:

---

[30] Lagarde Report (op. cit. n.7) p. 107 nr. 121.
[31] See Supra n.10.

Article 16(2). Under Article 16(1) a judgment which meets the conditions of Article 43 shall not be recognised. Article 43 is a copy of the rule laid down in Article 59 of Brussels 1.[32] The text of Article 43 , however, is less precise. In the light of the foregoing explanation of the Borrás Report as regards Article 8 and my suggestion regarding this provision (see *supra* section 3.3), Article 43 should not be interpreted as referring to any judgment rendered under Article 8, but only to judgments founded on a national exorbitant jurisdiction rule.

Authentic instruments which are enforceable in a Contracting State and court settlements which are enforceable in the Contracting State in which they were concluded are recognised and enforceable in other Contracting States under the same conditions as judgments given in a Contracting State: Article 13(3).

The rules on enforcement of judgments will not be examined in this contribution. These rules follow the rules on enforcement of Brussels I.

5.   CONCLUSION

The initial intention of Brussels II was to extend Brussels I to cover matrimonial matters. A draft convention of 1994 only covered divorce, legal separation and annulment of marriage. It was on the request of the French and Spanish delegations that custody issues were later on included within the scope of the Convention. A year later, on 25 September 1995, the Council of Ministers of Justice and Home Affairs decided that custody matters are to be provided for in the context of matrimonial proceedings, "in the form of measures supplementary to those laid down in the Hague Convention".[33] The latter Convention refers to the Convention which at that time was being prepared by the Hague Conference to revise the Hague Convention 1961, and which in October 1996 became the Hague Convention 1996.

At present, one could say that the Hague Convention 1996 is the most relevant multilateral instrument in the field of private international law on questions of parental responsibility. The scope of this Convention is much broader than that of Brussels II. Apart from that it is an "integral" private international law convention, in the sense that it not only governs questions of jurisdiction, recognition and enforcement of foreign judgments, but also the question of the applicable law. It must be commended that during the preparatory work and drafting of Brussels II frequent consultations between the EU and the Hague Conference have taken place.[34] The result of this is that the rules of Brussels II harmonise with those of the Hague Convention 1996, particularly regarding jurisdiction. In fact, the jurisdiction rules are

---

[32] Seel also Borrás Report (supra n. 1) p. 61 nr. 125.
[33] Borrás Report (supra n. 1) p. 31 nrs. 8 and 9.
[34]   Borrás Report, (supra n. 1) p. 61 nr. 125.

practically similar. Article 3(1) of Brussels II comes down to the rule that the court in the State of the habitual residence of the child has jurisdiction. This rule is exactly similar to the primary jurisdiction rule of the Hague Convention 1996: Article 5. The similarity between Article 3(2) of Brussels II and Article 10 of the Hague Convention 1996 has been illustrated before. The rules on recognition of both Conventions correspond with each other too, except as regards the review of the court of origin's jurisdiction and the question whether the refusal of recognition is compulsory if one of the grounds of non-recognition exists. The requirements of enforcement are similar as well. It is with respect to the procedure of enforcement that the rules of both Conventions do not completely correspond with each other. The rules of Brussels II follow those of Brussels I, in which the Convention provides some main rules, while other procedural rules are left to the law of the State addressed. The Hague Convention 1996 limits itself to the instruction that the law of the State addressed governs the procedure: Article 26(1), and that the Contracting States are to provide a "simple and rapid procedure": Article 26(2).

As indicated above, the objective of the decision of the Council of Ministers of Justice and Home Affairs on 25 September 1995 was to provide provisions on custody matters supplementary to those of the Hague Convention 1996. Instead, the only beneficial effect of Brussels II is the harmonisation with the Hague Convention 1996. However, at the same time this benefit, the similarity between the respective provisions of Brussels II and the Hague Convention 1996, demonstrates that the provisions of Brussels II on matters of parental responsibility are superfluous. One cannot but wonder that the frequent consultations with the Hague Conference during the preparatory work and the drafting of Brussels II – commendable as they are – did not result in the understanding on the part of the EU Member States – which are Member States of the Hague Conference too – of the redundancy of providing the so-called "supplementary rules to the Hague Convention 1996".[35] Due to the fact that the Hague Convention 1996 has a broader scope than Brussels II, the Hague Convention 1996 has more to offer as regards legal protection and, hence, legal certainty than the same provisions of Brussels II. The very limited scope of Brussels II and its self-proclaimed supremacy combined with the exclusive nature of its jurisdiction rules, might not always be advantageous to European citizens. Therefore, ratifying the Hague Convention 1996 by all the EU Member States is advisable.

---

[35] As regards this type of efforts of the EU, compare H. Duintjer Tebbens, "De Haagse Conferentie, de Europese Gemeenschap en de subsidiariteit" (The Hague Conference, the European Community and the Subsidiarity) *NJB* (1993) p. 671-672.

On the Side of the Angels: Choice of Law and Stolen Cultural Property

Symeon C. Symeonides

1. INTRODUCTION

KURT SIEHR's Hague lectures on International Art Trade and the Law[1] remain one of the most comprehensive and incisive discussions of conflicts resulting from trans-border trade in stolen art and antiquities. One of the cases Siehr discusses at length[2] is *Autocephalous Greek-Orthodox Church of Cyprus v. Goldberg & Feldman Fine Arts, Inc.*,[3] which may be called *the case of the stolen angels*.[4] This case

---

  * LL.B, LL.B, LL.M, S.J.D., Dean & Professor of Law, Willamette University College of Law, Salem, Oregon, USA.

  [1] Siehr, "International Art Trade and the Law", 243 *Recueil des Cours* 9 (1993-VI).

  [2] See ibid., 53, 62-63, 75-76, 79, 107, *et passim*.

  [3] 717 F.Supp. 1374 (S.D. Ind. 1989). The district court decision was affirmed on appeal. See 917 F.2d 278 (7th Cir. 1990). The discussion hereinafter is confined to the district court decision.

  [4] As explained below, this case involved four stolen mosaics, one of which depicted Archangel Ga-

J. Basedow et al., eds., Private Law in the International Arena – Liber Amicorum Kurt Siehr
© 2000, T.M.C.Asser Press, The Hague, The Netherlands

involved Switzerland, Siehr's professional home for the last two decades, and also Cyprus, my own home country for the first two decades of my life. Thus, this case would seem to be a fitting subject for this brief commentary dedicated to him.

On the other hand, *Autocephalous* is also a case with which I have had a professional involvement, having served *pro bono* as consultant for the successful plaintiffs.[5] Because of this involvement, I claim no impartiality, either with regard to the intrinsic merits of the plaintiffs' case or with regard to the fundamental right of countries like Cyprus to protect their cultural heritage. Nevertheless, because of my own partiality, I have chosen to steer away from the political dimensions of the case and to confine my discussion to the less political choice-of-law questions posed by cases involving trans-border trade in stolen art or antiquities.[6]

Unfortunately, the space limitations of this volume do not permit an in-depth discussion nor extensive documentation of this large topic. Fortunately, these deficiencies are remedied by the availability of Siehr's own comprehensive and competent work cited above, to which the reader can resort for both depth and documentation.

2.   THE CASE OF THE STOLEN ANGELS

2.1   **The Facts**

Although the *Autocephalous* case is well known,[7] a brief summary of the facts would facilitate the ensuing discussion. *Autocephalous* involved four six-century

---

briel. Also stolen, and still missing, is the depiction of Archangel Michael.

[5] More precisely, I served as consultant to the lawyers Thomas Kline and Tom Starnes, then of the law firm of Andrews & Kurth, who ably represented the plaintiffs, the Republic of Cyprus and the Greek-Orthodox Church of Cyprus. The views expressed herein do not necessarily reflect the views of the plaintiffs or their attorneys.

[6] This discussion is further limited to the sphere of private law and does not encompass the many pertinent international treaties and other public law means. For an excellent discussion of these, see J. Nafziger, "Toward a More Collaborative Regime of Transnational Cultural Property Law", in: *Liber Amicorum Kurt Siehr* (The Hague 2000)   ??.

[7] For writings devoted exclusively to this case, see 86 *Am. J. Int'l L.* 128 (1992); 15 *Suffolk Transnat'l L.J.* 790 (1992); 43 *Vand. L. Rev.* 1839 (1990). For other discussions of this case, see, *inter alia*, 9 *Am. U. J. Int'l L. & Pol'y* 225, 242 (1993); 14 *Ariz. J. Int'l & Comp. L.* 527, 549 (1997); 4 *Cardozo J. Int'l & Comp. L.* 23, 41 (1996); 22 *Case W. Res. J. Int'l L.* 1, 29 (1990); 32 *Colum. J.L. & Soc. Probs.* 1, 33 (1998); 30 *Colum. J. Transnat'l L.* 179, 229 (1992); 95 *Colum. L. Rev.* 377, 417 (1995); 18 *Colum – VLA J.L. & Arts* 75, 101 (1993); 6 *DePaul – LCA J. Art & Ent. L.* 39, 60 (1995); 14 *Dick. J. Int'l L.* 31, 55 (1995); 43 *Duke L.J.* 337, 383 (1993); 7 *Emory Int'l L. Rev.* 457, 536 (1993); 64 *Fordham L. Rev.* 49, 96 (1995); 49 *Hastings L. J.* 225 (1997); 36 *How. L.J.* 17, 42 (1993); 29 *Ind. L. Rev.* 1201, 1210 (1996); 28 *Law & Pol'y Int'l Bus.* 123, 138 (1996); 13 *Loy. L.A. Int'l & Comp. L.J.* 427, 458 (1990); 13 *N.Y.L. Sch. J. Int'l & Comp. L.* 125, 151 (1992); 31 *N.Y.U. J. Int'l L. & Pol.* 79, 94 (1998); 22 *Pepp. L. Rev.* 1772, 1776 (1995); 30 *Rutgers L.J.* 441, 459 (1999); 15 *Suffolk Transnat'l L.J.*

mosaic depictions of Jesus and the Virgin Mary, an archangel, and two apostles. These mosaics were imbedded in the hallowed sanctuary of the early Christian church of *Panayia Kanakaria* (Virgin Mary the Affectionate). The church is situated in that part of the Republic of Cyprus that has been occupied by Turkey since 1974. Sometime in the latter 1970s, these mosaics were illegally removed from the church and transported to Turkey by a Mr. Aydin Dikman, a Turkish national. From there Mr. Dikman smuggled them into Germany and kept them hidden behind fake walls in his apartment for about ten years. In July 1988, following a sale agreement negotiated through intermediaries in a Dutch restaurant, Dikman transported the mosaics to the free-port area of the Geneva airport where he delivered them to defendant Ms. Goldberg, an Indiana art dealer, upon receipt of $350,000 in dollar bills contained in paper bags. Ms. Goldberg shipped the mosaics to Indiana on the same day, and a few weeks later offered to sell them to the Getty Museum in California for about $20 million. The museum's curator, who was familiar with these internationally-known mosaics, refused the offer and promptly notified the Republic of Cyprus. The Republic and the Church of Cyprus offered to reimburse Ms. Goldberg for the purchase price in exchange for surrendering the mosaics. Following her refusal, the Republic and the Church filed against her an action in the federal district court for the district of Indiana, in March 1989.

2.2 The Laws

As is typical in cases of trans-border trade in stolen property, *Autocephalous* implicated the laws of at least three[8] countries or states, Cyprus, Switzerland, and Indiana. These laws differed in significant respects.

Under the law of Cyprus, antiquities and things dedicated to worship are "out of commerce" and cannot be acquired by a private person, whether through sale, prescription, or otherwise. Thus, if the Church of Cyprus could establish ownership under Cypriot law, the Church could not under that law lose that ownership by any of the facts or transactions invoked by the defendant. The Church did in fact prove such ownership.[9]

Under Swiss law, if read in the light most favorable to the defendant,[10] the defendant could prevail if she purchased the mosaics in good faith and the plaintiff's action was filed more than five years after the time of the theft.

609, 637 (1992); 74 *Tex. L. Rev.* 615, 653 (1996); 70 *Tex. L. Rev.* 1431, 1467 (1992); 9 *Transnat'l Law.* 235, 257 (1996); 31 *Va. J. Int'l L.* 1, 51 (1990); 103 *Yale L.J.* 2437, 2469 (1994).

[8] Germany was also involved in that Dikman kept the mosaics there for about ten years before selling them to defendant. However, German law did not vest Dikman with ownership of the mosaics and thus defendant did not invoke that law.

[9] See *Autocephalous*, 717 F.Supp. at 1397.

[10] See pertinent discussion infra at 4.2.

Under Indiana law, a thief does not acquire and thus cannot convey ownership of the stolen property. However, the owner's action to recover the property must be filed within "six (6) years after the action has accrued and not afterwards."[11]

2.3   The Court's Choice of Law

The court held that Indiana had the "most significant contacts"[12] or the "more significant relationship"[13] to this suit and thus its law applied. Under that law, the defendant did not acquire ownership of the mosaics. However, the defendant argued that the plaintiffs' action to recover the mosaics was untimely because it was filed more than six years form the time of the theft (which occurred in the late 1970s). The court dismissed the argument and held that the plaintiffs' action did not "accrue," and thus the statute of limitation did not commence until the plaintiff, using due diligence, knew or should have known of the identity of the possessor of the mosaics.[14] This part of the opinion is known as the Discovery Rule and is discussed at length later.[15] The court then described the plaintiffs' unsuccessful but diligent efforts to determine the whereabouts of the mosaics as soon as plaintiffs knew of the occurrence of the theft and explained why the plaintiffs could not have discovered the identity of the mosaics' possessor until she attempted to sell them to the Getty museum in late 1988.[16] The court held further that, even if the statute of limitation had begun running at an earlier time, the doctrine of fraudulent concealment tolled or suspended the running of the statute for the ten-year period during which the mosaics were hidden in Germany.[17]

The court also held in the alternative that, even if Swiss law applied, the defendant could not have prevailed because she was clearly not in good faith when she bought the mosaics. The court discussed pointedly and at length the suspicious circumstances under which she bought the mosaics[18] and her failure to undertake even a minimally prudent inquiry into the seller's title.[19]

Thus, under either Indiana or Swiss law, the plaintiffs were entitled to recover the mosaics and the court so ordered.[20]

---

[11] *Autocephalous*, 717 F.Supp. at 1385.

[12] Ibid., at 1394.

[13] Ibid., at 1376, 1394.

[14] See ibid., at 1386-87, 1388-91.

[15] See infra at 3.2, 4.

[16] See *Autocephalous*, 717 F.Supp. at 1388-91.

[17] See ibid., at 1387-88, 1391-93.

[18] See ibid., at 1400-03. The court concluded by quoting from the testimony of an expert witness: "The Court cannot improve on Dr. Vikan's summation of the suspicious circumstances surrounding this sale: 'All the red flags are up, all the red lights are on, all the sirens are blaring.'" Id. at 1402.

[19] See ibid., at 1403-04.

[20] After the Court of Appeals affirmed the trial court decision, see 917 F.2d.278 (7th Cir. 1990), the

3.   The Proper Choice of Law

Because the plaintiffs could prevail under the laws of both Switzerland and Indiana, the plaintiffs did not argue vigorously against the application of these laws nor for the application of the law of Cyprus. Litigants who can win on the facts rarely quarrel with the law. In this sense the *Autocephalous* case could be characterized as a sub-species of false conflict – the type in which the laws of the involved states are different in content but in ways that, under the facts of the particular case, do not affect the outcome. For this reason, the court's choice-of-law analysis need not be particularly categorical or precise, and its willingness to apply Indiana law and especially Swiss law should be understood in that light.

More precision is necessary, however, in cases in which the laws of the involved states differ in ways that would produce a different result. For example, when under the facts of the particular case, the owner of the stolen property is protected by the law of the country of origin but not by the law of the country or countries to which the property is removed, the resulting conflict is as true as they come. The following discussion focuses on this hypothetical pattern of cases.

3.1   *Lex Rei Originis*

Strong arguments can be made that in cases of this pattern, the law of the situs of origin should remain applicable, to the exclusion of the law of any subsequent situs. No lesser a body than the *Institut de droit international* has advocated the adoption of precisely such a rule. In its 1991 session in Basle, held less than a year after the *Autocephalous* case, the Institut adopted a resolution providing that "[t]he transfer of ownership of works of art belonging to the cultural heritage of the country of origin shall be governed by the law of that country."[21] Indeed, there should be little argument that the country of origin has the closest connection and the most legitimate claim to determine ownership of objects of cultural heritage. I would therefore wholeheartedly endorse this resolution.

At the same time, I am painfully aware that certain western countries whose markets tend to attract stolen antiquities are unlikely to subscribe to this resolution. The typical argument of these countries is that the application of the *lex rei originis* deprives them of the ability to protect third parties who in good faith have acquired rights in the stolen property after its removal to these states. This argument has merit provided it is confined to third parties who in fact act in good faith. Even so, this simply means that these other states also acquire an interest in applying their

---

mosaics were returned to Cyprus and are now exhibited in a special museum in Nicosia, until such time as will become possible to be returned to their proper place in the now occupied part of Cyprus.

[21] Institut de droit international, Resolution of September 1999, 81 *Revue critique de droit international privé* 203 (1992).

law. It does not mean that this interest is necessarily greater than that of the situs of origin. Which of the two interests should prevail in a given case is a difficult question that admits different answers. For what is worth, my answer is given below. It consists of a compromise choice-of-law approach that retains the *lex rei originis* but reduces its role to that of a strong but rebuttable presumption.

3.2 **A Compromise**

My proposed choice-of-law compromise is as follows:

> A person who is considered the owner of a thing under the law of the state in which the thing is situated at the time of the theft shall be entitled to the protection of that law even if the thing is later removed to another state whose law denies such protection, unless:
> (a)   the other state has a materially greater connection to the case;
> *and*
> (b)   the person knew or should have known of facts that would enable a diligent owner to take effective legal action against the possessor of the thing.

This proposal consists of three elements: a presumption in favor of the law of the situs of origin and two conditions, both of which must be met for that presumption to be rebutted. The latter of the two conditions is a restatement of the discovery rule enunciated in *Autocephalous*. The other two elements are partly a variation and partly a refinement of the approach followed in that case. The space limitations of this volume do not permit a full development of this proposal here. The following is simply a brief sketch of these three elements.

3.2.1 *Presumption in favor of the lex rei originis*

In cases such as *Autocephalous* which involve stolen property, the presumption in favor of the law of the situs of origin makes perfect sense because, *ex hypothesi*, theft is a unilateral act of another to which the owner neither participates nor acquiesces. As in the *Autocephalous* case, the owner may be justifiably unaware of both the identity of the thief and the very fact of the theft. The unilateral removal of the thing to another state should not deprive the owner of the protection provided by the law of the first situs.[22] The owner should be entitled to the protection of that law unless such protection is contrary to the law of another state that acquires a materially closer connection to the case and thus a more justified claim to apply its law, as explained below.

---

[22] See American Law Institute, *Restatement (Second) Conflict of Laws*, § 247 (1971): "interests in a chattel are not affected by the mere removal of the chattel to another state."

3.2.2 *The state of the materially closer connection*

The proposal allows displacement of the *lex rei originis*, but that displacement can be only in favor of a country that has a materially closer connection with the case than the country of origin. Other iterations of this concept are a "manifestly more significant relationship," a "manifestly greater interest," etc. The precise choice of words is less significant than the basic notion that the threshold for rebutting the presumption in favor of the *lex rei originis* should be very high indeed. As the *Autocephalous* case demonstrates,[23] a relationship such as the one claimed by the defendant with regard to Switzerland does not even come close to this threshold and should not be sufficient to displace the right of the situs of origin to apply its law. A transitory, artificial relationship unilaterally fabricated by the defendant (or by persons through whom she claims) should never be considered more significant than the relationship of the situs of origin.

As importantly, however, under the above proposal, even Indiana's relationship should not be considered more significant than that of Cyprus, although it was clearly more significant than that of Switzerland. The *Autocephalous* court correctly concluded that, as between Indiana and Switzerland, Indiana had "the *most* significant"[24] relationship. However, to the extent that the use of the superlative "most" may encompass a juxtaposition of more than two comparables, the quoted statement is less accurate.

Indeed, if Cyprus were to be included in this comparison, it should be readily obvious that Indiana's relationship with the case was clearly less significant than that of Cyprus. The defendant's domicile in Indiana could not be deemed as more weighty than the plaintiffs' domicile in Cyprus. Unlike the plaintiffs who had every reason to rely on the protective law of their domicile, the defendant could not claim any reliance on the non-protective law of her domicile, especially since none of the acts pertaining to the purchase took place in that state. Similarly, the situs of the mosaics at the time of the trial should not be deemed any more significant than the situs at the time of the theft, especially because the mosaics were not even movable before the theft. After all, the mosaics had been lawfully and publicly kept in Cyprus for over fourteen centuries and were brought to Indiana unilaterally, secretively, and recently. Finally, the fact that Indiana was the forum state should not in and of itself make its relationship any more significant. The mere fact that litigation takes place there may justify the application of the forum's procedural laws, but rules pertaining to the loss and acquisition of ownership of stolen property should not be

---

[23] See *Autocephalous*, 717 F.Supp. at 1393-94, describing Switzerland's "lack of significant contacts."

[24] Ibid. at 1394 (emphasis added).

classified as procedural.[25] If the forum *qua forum* were to automatically apply its statute of limitation, then states that have short statutes of limitations would become safe heavens for thieves of cultural property or their transferees. The *Autocephalous* court avoided that possibility, but only because it applied the discovery rule.

Indiana's relationship might have been considered "significant" if, for example, the property had been situated in Indiana for a relatively long time and third parties had dealt with the property in good faith and in justifiable reliance on Indiana law. For example, if the stolen mosaics had been publicly exhibited for some time in the Indianapolis Museum of Fine Arts, and then they were sold at a public auction to a person who was in good faith, that person's reliance on Indiana law should be given due weight. Thus, if under Indiana law that person would be entitled to reimbursement of the purchase price from the owner, such reimbursement should be due even if it would not be available under the law of the situs of origin. Under these circumstances, Indiana would qualify as the state that, with regard to the narrow issue of reimbursement, had a materially closer connection.

3.2.3 *The discovery rule*

The third element of the above proposal is a discovery rule or proviso, such as the one enunciated in *Autocephalous*. The effect of this rule is to suspend the running of time against the owner for as long as he, for reasons beyond his control, is unable to protect his ownership. While there is room for disagreement on the exact phrasing of this rule, there should be little disagreement about the need for it. In today's extremely mobile market, the discovery rule is a sensible, equitable, and indispensable vehicle for furnishing diligent owners with a fighting chance to recover their stolen property. Without such a rule, any pretense of protecting owners of stolen property is truly a sham. For example, in *Autocephalous*, the owner could not even know of the exact time of the theft. Even when the theft became known some years later, the thief's identity could not be ascertained. Thus he could not be sued in any court, in any country. The application of the discovery rule was the only way to prevent the thief from benefiting from his own wrongdoing.

The *Autocephalous* court applied the discovery rule as a part of Indiana law, and, in so doing, avoided the risk of turning Indiana into a heaven for possessors of stolen property. As said above, that risk is particularly high when one proceeds on the assumption that the forum can always apply its statute of limitations on the theory that such statutes are procedural. Thus, one can easily conclude that the discovery rule is particularly necessary in cases in which the court proceeds on the above assumption.

---

[25] See S. Symeonides, W. Perdue & A. von Mehren, *Conflict of Laws, American, Comparative, International* 377-378, 386 (1998).

As importantly, however, the discovery rule is also necessary in cases in which the court is prepared to apply non-forum law, such as Swiss law in the *Autocephalous* case. In that case, the court did not need to subject Swiss law to a discovery because the defendant's lack of good faith when she took delivery of the property at the Geneva airport was fatal to her claim under Swiss law. Had the defendant been in good faith, however, one might argue that the defendant would prevail, even though the owner could not have been aware that the property was ever near Switzerland. A basic premise of such an argument is that Swiss law does not recognize a discovery-type rule which would suspend the running of time. In the next section, I explain why I believe that Swiss substantive law does or should recognize such a rule. My main thesis, however, is that, even if this rule is not part of Swiss substantive law, it should be a integral part of the choice-of-law decision in any forum that does not want to aid and abet the laundering of stolen cultural property.

4. EXCURSUS IN SWISS LAW

It would be presumptuous of me to claim any expertise in Swiss law, and thus this section is no more than an amateur's excursus in unknown terrain. Even so, however, I would be very surprised if a civil law system would be oblivious to the equitable principles embodied in the ancient civilian maxim of *contra non valentem agere non currit prescriptio*,[26] which is at the heart of the discovery rule.

It may, of course, be countered that this maxim is confined to cases of *liberative* prescription (statute of limitations) and is inapplicable to cases of *acquisitive* prescription (*Ersitzung*).[27] My arguments are: (a) that the above maxim is or should be applicable to cases of acquisitive prescription or other acquisition of stolen and *concealed movables*; and (b) that the above maxim is or should be applicable *a fortiori* to the extent that the *Autocephalous* defendant's claim was based on liberative prescription.

---

[26] Prescription does not run against those who are unable to act.

[27] In the interest of consistent terminology, the term liberative prescription (statute of limitations) is used hereafter in the sense of a mode of barring of personal actions as a result of inaction for a period of time. The term acquisitive prescription (adverse possession) is used in the sense of a mode of acquiring ownership (or other real rights) as a result of adverse possession for a period of time. Unlike liberative prescription which focuses on the inaction of the obligee, acquisitive prescription focuses not on the inaction of the owner but on the actions of the adverse possessor.

4.1   Civil Code Article 728 (Acquisitive Prescription)

The *Autocephalous* defendant did not base her claim on acquisitive prescription as provided by Swiss Civil Code Article 728[28] for the simple reason that she had absolutely no chance to prevail under that article.[29] Nevertheless, the discussion begins with this article because of its potential importance in other cases in which the defendant does satisfy the requirements of the article. One such case was *Koerfer* v. *Goldsmith*[30] which involved paintings allegedly stolen from the German owner during the Nazi period. Apparently employing a *contra non valentem* rationale, the Swiss Federal Court held that because the owner lacked a fair judicial forum in which to bring an action during the war, the five-year acquisitive prescriptive period of Article 728 did not commence until after the end of the war.

This case is particularly revealing precisely because it runs contrary to certain entrenched assumptions about the operation of the rules of acquisitive prescription and liberative prescription, respectively. For example, it is often said that, although under the law of liberative prescription the plaintiff's (obligee's) objective inability to bring the action may exceptionally suspend the running of prescription, no such exception is recognized in the law of acquisitive prescription. The plaintiff's (owner's) inaction is in principle immaterial and, one would argue, so are the reasons for such inaction. Yet, as the *Koerfer* case suggests, the law is neither as mechanical nor as indifferent to equitable considerations. The owner's non-negligent objective inability to protect his rights, either because of the lack of a fair forum as in *Koerfer* or because of justifiable lack of knowledge of the whereabouts of his stolen property as in *Autocephalous*, is a factor that any fair legal system would want to take into account. A discovery rule is a flexible tool for doing so.

The fact that Article 728 does not *expressly* authorize exceptions for cases in which the owner is justifiably unable to protect his rights does not necessarily preclude such exceptions. For example, Article 728 contains an implicit exception for cases in which the owner's inability is attributable to the adverse possessor's violence.[31] Another implicit exception is available for cases in which the adverse pos-

---

[28] This article provides that "[w]hen a person has been continuously in *bona fide* and peaceful possession of another's movable for five years as owner, he is held to have acquired the ownership of it by prescription."

[29] In addition to her lack of good faith, the defendant could not satisfy the possession requirements of Article 728 because: (a) she did not herself possessed the property for five years, and (b) she could not benefit from the tacking rule of Article 941 because the possession of her transferor, Mr. Dikman, was clandestine and thus legally ineffective. Article 941 permits tacking or joining of the two possessions but properly requires that the transferor's possession be "such that a prescriptive title could be based on it."

[30] Bundesgericht 13 December 1968, Entscheidungen des Schweitzerischen Bundesgerichts (BGE) 94 II 297.

[31] This exception derives from the requirement that the possession be "peaceable." Civ. Code Art. 728(1). See also Art. 926.

session is clandestine, as Dikman's possession was in *Autocephalous* for as long as he was hiding the mosaics behind fake walls in his Munich apartment. A third exception is revealed by reading Article 728 in *pari materia* with Article 134(1)6 of the Swiss Code of Obligations. The latter article provides that "[t]he period of limitation does not begin to runs and in case it has begun to run, it is suspended . . . as long as the claim cannot be enforced before a Swiss court."[32] Surely, even leaving aside questions of jurisdiction, the plaintiffs' claim in *Autocephalous* could not have been enforced before a Swiss court – or for that matter any court – throughout the time Dikman kept the mosaics hidden in his Munich apartment. Similarly, as the *Koerfer* case demonstrates, other exceptions are possible if the law is to remain as fair as originally conceived and to continue meeting contemporary needs. One such exception could be adopted for cases in which the owner's inability to act was the result of his justifiable lack of knowledge of the whereabouts of his property, even if the property is not actively concealed.

Despite contrary appearances, such an exception would not contradict but would in fact be in harmony with the ancient institution of *usucaptio* from which Article 782 originates. In the context of the small rural societies in which that institution developed, there was no need to expressly make the running of acquisitive prescription dependent on the owner's knowledge of adverse possession. Such knowledge was almost taken for granted because of the requirement that, in order to lead to acquisitive prescription, possession must be open and public. Thus, a reasonably diligent owner would likely find out about it and would be in a position to react to it. This is not so in contemporary cases of cross-border trade in stolen goods. With the speed of today's transportation, a stolen thing may be removed thousands of miles away in the course of a single day. Even if the thing is possessed "openly and publicly" in the second situs, it may be extremely difficult for the owner to find out about such possession. As one author noted, "[u]nlike domestic animals, to which much of the early adverse possession cases apply, art is seldom open to view by the general public in the way that horses and cows are."[33] In such a case, to allow loss of ownership without regard to knowledge would be extremely inequitable and would facilitate the launders of stolen goods. In contrast, the introduction of a discovery rule would restore the equitable balance between owners and possessors that was implicit in the ancient *usucaptio* scheme.

---

[32] This article becomes applicable to acquisitive prescription cases by virtue of Civil Code Article 728(3) which provides that "[t]he rules laid down in regard to the limitation of actions apply here by analogy for the purpose of . . . determining in what cases the running of years is stopped or suspended."

[33] Preziosi, "Applying a Strict Discovery Rule to Art Stolen in the Past", 49 *Hastings L.J.* 225 at 234 (1997). See also Bibas, "The Case Against Statutes of Limitations for Stolen Art", 103 *Yale L.J.* 2437 at 2442 (1994) (noting that law developed for "horses, cattle, sheep, and mules" does not work well when used to cover more easily concealed objects).

4.2   Civil Code Article 934(1)

As said above, the defendant in *Autocephalous* did not rely on Civil Code Article 728 because she could not meet its requirements. Rather, the defendant relied on the seemingly more favorable Article 934(1). This article provides that "[w]hen a person in possession of a movable thing loses it or has it stolen from him . . ., he can demand it back within a period of five years from any person who is detaining it."[34] To begin with, there are serious doubts as to whether this article is even applicable to cases such as *Autocephalous*.[35] But even in the absence of such doubts, the defendant's victory would be far from assured. For, if this article is based on an acquisitive prescription rationale,[36] then it could be subject to the same exceptions discussed above. If the article establishes a rule of liberative prescription, then *a fortiori* it should be subject to these and other exceptions, including, as a last resort, the generic *contra non valentem* exception.

Indeed, even leaving aside for now the question of the detainer's good faith, the question of whether the five-year period of Article 934(1) begins to run from the date of the theft rather from the date the thing came to the hands of the present detainer is not free from ambiguity. The wording of the article as well as pertinent jurisprudence[37] suggest that the period begins running from the date of the theft. This, however, is tantamount to subjecting the owner's action to a liberative pre-

---

[34] The second paragraph of the same article provides that if the thing has been bought "at a public auction or in market overt or from a dealer in property of the same kind" then "it cannot be recovered from the first purchaser or any subsequent *bona fide* purchaser, unless he is compensated for the purchase-money paid." This provision could not benefit the defendant in *Autocephalous* because her purchase was not at a public auction or in market overt and the seller was not a "dealer" within the meaning of this provision.

[35] The wording of Article 934(1) (e.g., "person in possession" versus one who "is detaining" the thing) as well as its location in the Civil Code's Title dealing with Possession rather than in the Title dealing with Ownership suggest that the article was intended only for cases in which the plaintiff proves mere possession, rather than ownership, prior to the theft. Thus interpreted, the article would make perfect sense and would be consistent with the principle that, while ownership is never lost by mere non-use alone (see Swiss Civil Code Article 729), possession may be lost by failure to exercise it for a specified period of time (see, e.g., Swiss Civil Code Article 929(3)). Put another way, Article 934(1) may have been intended as a bar to an untimely *possessory* action (i.e., an action in which the plaintiff only asserts his right to possess the property) rather than as a defense to a *revendicatory* action (i.e., an action in which the plaintiff asserts and proves *ownership*, as opposed to mere possession, prior to the theft).

[36] For example, one could argue that Article 934(1) simply parallels Article 728 in that both articles contemplate the possibility of loss of the ownership of a movable thing after five years from the time the owner loses possession of it. If this argument is accepted, then the person who presently detains the thing under Article 934(1) must meet the qualifications of a possessor as provided by Article 728, that is, he must be in good faith and must have possessed the thing openly and publicly for five years. The *Autocephalous* defendant would of course fail on both counts. See supra n. 29.

[37] See Judgment of July 25, 1953 [Civil Court of Baselstadt Canton], *Schweizerische Juristen-Zeitung* (1955) 55.

scription (statute of limitation). In turn, this creates at least two problems for defendant.

The first problem is that it renders more directly applicable Article 134(1)6 of the Swiss Code of Obligations which, as explained above, suspends the running of liberative prescription for "as long as the claim cannot be enforced before a Swiss court."[38] At a minimum, this would include the time during which Dikman kept the mosaics hidden in Germany and his identity was unknowable.[39]

The second problem is that subjecting the owner's revendicatory action to a liberative prescription is contrary to a fundamental principle of the civil law – that ownership is not lost by mere non-use alone, that is, by the mere failure of the owner, however prolonged, to exercise the prerogatives of ownership, *unless* someone else has acquired ownership in the meantime, for example, through acquisitive prescription. The Swiss Civil Code recognizes this principle in Article 729 which provides that "[t]he ownership of a movable is not destroyed by loss of possession, provided the owner has not abandoned the right to it or the movable has not been acquired by a third person."

It could, of course, be countered that Article 934(1) does vest the detainer with ownership and thus does not contradict Article 729, but rather is simply an exception thereto. If so, however, one is hard pressed to explain the anomaly of ownership being acquired because of someone else's omission and without regard to the acquirer's circumstances. In any event, if Article 934(1) is interpreted as vesting ownership, then one must wonder about its inherent fairness. For, literally speaking, it could be invoked even by the thief himself or by someone holding for the thief. After all, this provision does not require open possession (it simply speaks of "detaining" the thing) and does not require good faith. Is it possible that the Swiss Civil Code intended to vest ownership in a thief who simply kept the thing in hiding for five years? If so, this would render superfluous Article 728 of the Code, which requires five years of public possession in good faith before vesting a possessor with ownership.

One could still counter that the possibility of a thief acquiring ownership is only theoretical because, as *Autocephalous* held, to avail himself of the protection provided in 934(1) the detainer of the thing must be in good faith. This is reassuring, to be sure, except that this provision makes no reference to good faith. Good faith is

---

[38] Cod. Oblig. Art. 134(1)6.

[39] It should also be noted that, although Article 934(1) makes no reference to the plaintiff's lack of knowledge of the whereabouts of the property or of the identity of the detainer, the article does not provide that such lack of knowledge is immaterial. In contrast, Article 929, which applies to possessory actions, does provide that the plaintiff's lack of knowledge is immaterial ("even though the plaintiff did not know of the wrong or the identity of the wrongdoer"). The juxtaposition of the two articles supports an *a contrario* argument that the plaintiff's justifiable lack of knowledge is material under Article 934(1).

mentioned in the article' second paragraph which deals with things sold at a public auction or in market overt or by dealers selling similar things.[40] The secretive sale at the airport warehouse did not meet any of these requirements. Thus the defendant's subjective good faith, even if present, would have been immaterial in the eyes of the law. As Professor Siehr correctly observes, "[a]s . . . the [mosaics] were not sold by a merchant at his business but rather clandestinely in the airport, there could not have been a bona fide purchase of stolen things under the Swiss Civil Code Article 934. There was a false conflict between Swiss and American law as both refuse to acknowledge a bona fide purchase."[41]

Be that as it may, because the plaintiffs were confident of their ability to prevail on the facts, they did not strongly protest this erroneous transposition of the two paragraphs of Article 934. Perhaps for the same reason, the court felt free to give defendant the benefit of the doubt and provide her a chance to prove her case. She failed because of her lack of good faith.

Such liberality is understandable in some cases but should not be allowed to become a permanent interpolation in future applications of Article 934(1). To do otherwise would be to create a huge equity deficit at the expense of the owner and to facilitate the laundering of stolen goods. The owner whose thing is stolen and kept in hiding for more than five years would lose ownership of it without ever being in a position to protect his ownership. This is not only inequitable, it is also anomalous. It is anomalous in that the plaintiff's action to protect his ownership is barred even though his ownership is not lost. One way to avoid both the inequity and the anomaly is to enunciate a discovery rule, such as the one adopted in *Autocephalous*, which would suspend the running of time for as long as the owner is justifiably and objectively unable to protect his ownership. Such suspension is already dictated by the law of acquisitive prescriptions for the time during which the possession is clandestine. A similar suspension should also be adopted if Article 934(1) is to be interpreted as imposing a rule of liberative prescription so that this prescription should not run during the time at which the owner, using due diligence, could not have ascertained the whereabouts of the property and the possessor's identity. This suspension could be based on several provisions of the Civil Code and the Code of Obligations discussed earlier or, as a last resort, it could be derived from the doctrine of *contra non valentem* which, after all, is fully operational in cases of liberative prescription.

---

[40] See supra n. 34.
[41] Siehr (supra n. 1) at 79.
[42] See Siehr (supra n. 1) at 264-269.

5. CONCLUSIONS

In this brief commentary I have proposed a choice-of-law compromise between the conflicting interests of the law of the situs of origin of stolen cultural property and the potential interest of other countries in which that property is subsequently removed. This compromise takes into account not only the expectations of the buyer and the interest of the second situs in protecting her, but also the expectations of the owner and the interest of first situs in protecting him. When the owner has no way of knowing that the stolen property has been moved to the second situs or cannot ascertain the identity of the possessor, the owner has no way of availing himself of any protection accorded owners by the law of the second situs. The discovery rule will simply buy some time for obtaining this protection and will thus level the playing field. In this sense, the discovery rule is the key to any private international law effort to accommodate the above conflicting interests.

I have also tried to demonstrate that a discovery-type rule either is available or should be available under Swiss substantive law, and that this is so whether the defendant invokes the acquisitive or the liberative prescription. It is entirely possible that I may be wrong on any or all counts. This, however, is not my main point. My point is that a discovery-type rule is a necessary rule *for private international law*. Indeed, the thrust of my proposal is that a discovery-type rule should be part of the choice-of-law decision even when it is not part of the applicable substantive law. In this sense, I view the discovery rule as an international *règle materiel*.

I am gratified to see that Professor Siehr does not disagree with this notion and in fact proposes a discovery rule in his Hague lectures. This rule figures prominently in his own Draft Convention on the Return of Stolen Works of Arts and on Illegally Removed Objects on National Cultural Heritage.[42] Article 4 of the Convention provides that the limitation period for recovering the stolen object does not begin to run until the owner "could have known the location and the holder of the object and could have brought the suit for return."[43] This alone allows the conclusion that KURT SIEHR is indeed *on the side of the angels!*

---

[43] See ibid., at 265. See also Article 12 at 268.

The Most Recent Case-Law on the Subject of Jurisdiction Agreements by the Assembly of the Civil Chamber of the Turkish Supreme Court of Appeals

Gülören Tekinalp[*]/ Ünal Tekinalp[**]

1. RELATED LEGISLATION AND EARLIER STANDING OF THE SUPREME COURT OF APPEALS

The Law Concerning Private International Law and the Law of Civil Procedure (hereinafter "PIL") contains a general provision relating to agreements on the submission of disputes to foreign courts. According to Article 31(1) PIL parties to a dispute having a foreign element which arises in relation to their obligations, may submit their dispute to a foreign court, unless this would be contrary to public order or to the rules determining the exclusive jurisdiction of the Turkish courts. Pursuant to the second clause of the same article, if the foreign court considers itself to lack jurisdiction, then the case is to be heard by a Turkish court. As may be clearly understood from these provisions, in situations where Turkish courts have jurisdiction, the parties may invoke the jurisdiction agreement (clause) and submit the dispute to the jurisdiction of a foreign court. On the other hand, in situations where Turkish courts lack international jurisdiction – that is to say, in situations where there is no court in Turkey which has jurisdiction – then the fact that the parties have designated a court in a foreign country as having jurisdiction, is not a matter of concern for Turkish law.[1]

---

[*] Prof. Dr. Gülören Tekinalp, Professor of Private International Law at the Law Faculty, University of Istanbul.
[**] Prof. Dr. Ünal Tekinalp, Professor of Commercial Law and Banking Law at the Law Faculty, University of Istanbul.
[1] Ergin Nomer, *Devletler Hususî Hukuku*, 9 Bası [Private International Law, 9th ed.] (Istanbul 1998) p. 372.

J. Basedow et al., eds., Private Law in the International Arena – Liber Amicorum Kurt Siehr
© 2000, T.M.C.Asser Press, The Hague, The Netherlands

The Turkish Supreme Court's interpretation of Article 31 PIL is somewhat different. In a decision delivered by the Assembly of the Civil Chamber of the Supreme Court of Appeals (hereinafter "ACC. Sup. Court") on 15 June 1988,[2] the court indicated that a contractual provision granting jurisdiction to a foreign court could not abrogate the jurisdiction of a Turkish court and the court therefore concluded that the case could be brought before a "competent Turkish court" in spite of any such jurisdiction agreement. Pursuant to the ACC. Sup. Court's decision, any agreement to the contrary is tantamount to creating *a lack of confidence* in a Turkish court that is competent according to domestic law and such a contractual provision must be considered null and void because it is contrary to the rule of public order. This decision notwithstanding, there were a number of decisions delivered by the 11th Civil Chamber of the Supreme Court[3] (hereinafter "11th C. Chamb. Sup. Court") in which it was clearly stated that contractual provisions granting jurisdiction to a foreign court give that foreign court exclusive jurisdiction, and that, therefore, in such situations, the jurisdiction of the Turkish court competent under domestic law has been abrogated; in other decisions,[4] the Chamber adopted the view held by the ACC. Sup. Court: that is, a jurisdiction agreement does not assign jurisdiction exclusively to a foreign court and the case may also be heard by a competent Turkish court. This divergence of opinion between the 11th C. Chamb Sup. Court and the ACC. Sup. Court, compounded by the inconsistencies in the 11th C. Chamb Sup. Court's own decisions on such matters, led to confusion and doubts concerning Turkish practice in these matters. These in turn formed the basis for disputes as to how the Supreme Court had interpreted or would interpret contractual provisions granting jurisdiction to foreign courts. Lower courts, for the most part, nevertheless follow the ACC. Sup. Court's view.

The ACC. Sup. Court's view and some of the decisions delivered by the 11th C. Chamb Sup. Court have been the subject of fierce criticism and are generally rejected by nearly all academics. According to some authors,[5] the 1988 decision by the ACC. Sup. Court (which is entirely at odds with Article 31(2) PIL) disregards

---

[2] Jud. [ACC. Sup. Court], No. 11-246/476 [15 June 1988], Reports, Vol. XIV (1988) pp. 1486-1490.

[3] Jud. [11th C. Cham. Sup. Court], No. 7190/560, [6 February 1987], Reports, Vol. XIV (1988) p. 1486; Jud. [11th C. Cham. Sup. Court] No. 7016/7400 [19 November 1990], in: Batider, 15 *Banking and Commercial Law Review* (1989-1990) pp. 145, 146.

[4] Jud. [11th C. Cham. Sup. Court], No. 5757/2881 [15 May 1989], in: Fügen Sargın, *Milletlerarası Usul Hukukunda Yetki Anlaşmaları* [Jurisdiction Agreements in International Civil Procedure Law] (Ankara 1996) p. 198; Jud. [11th C. Cham. Sup. Court], No. 8607/8 [22 January 1996], in: Sargın, ibid., p. 198; Jud. [19th C. Cham. Sup. Court], No. 1632/9151 [2 November 1995], in: Sargın, ibid., p. 199.

[5] Nomer, op.cit.n.1, p. 376; Hilmar Krüger and Ergin Nomer, "Gerichtsstandsvereinbarung nach türkischem Recht", *RIW* (1989) p. 376; Aysel Çelikel, *Milletlerarası Özel Hukuk*, 4 Bası [Private International Law, 4th ed.] (Istanbul 1995); Nuray Ekşi, *Türk Mahkemelerinin Milletlerarası Yetkisi* [International Jurisdiction of the Turkish Court] (Istanbul 1996) p. 163.

Article 31 PIL by adopting the mistaken view that exclusive jurisdiction *encourages a lack of confidence in the Turkish courts* and thus deprives this clause of any practical importance.

Criticism of the ACC. Sup. Court's ruling was based on Article 31 PIL, and especially on the second clause of that article. Kuru[6] and three Supreme Court judges who dissented in the 15 June 1988 judgement chose to support their views by pointing to the recommendations and arguments that had been set forth, especially with respect to the second clause, when the PIL was being drafted. In 1978 a symposium (hereinafter the "Symposium") was held in Istanbul concerning the PIL, which was then in its draft form. In discussing the meaning of Article 28(2) of Prof. Ergin Nomer's draft (which subsequently became Article 31(2) PIL) Prof. Kuru and the dissenting Supreme Court judges stated that, under this provision, a jurisdiction agreement gave an exclusive right of jurisdiction to hear a case; that if such a jurisdiction agreement existed, then the case could not be brought before the Turkish courts; and that any attempt to do so would only be possible if the foreign court designated as having exclusive jurisdiction, was to determine that in fact it did not have such jurisdiction. Prof. Dr. Gülören Tekinalp stated that she shared the same view and that for this reason she had recommended that the draft article 28(2) (that is Article 31(2) PIL) be amended to make it possible for the Turkish courts also to have jurisdiction in such cases. She added that the draft provision had been enacted without any changes having been made. According to Kuru, if jurisdiction has been given to a foreign court under a jurisdiction agreement, it is no longer possible to directly initiate a case in a Turkish court on the grounds of Article 31(2) PIL. Such a case could be heard by a competent Turkish court only if the foreign court to which jurisdiction has been submitted under the jurisdiction agreement declares itself to be lacking jurisdiction and, for that reason, refuses to hear the case.

In addition to these grounds, it has also been pointed out in academic texts that the existence of practices that reject the exclusive jurisdiction of a foreign court (despite the explicit rule of law accepting such jurisdiction) vitiate legal certainty and foreseeability[7] that are the basis of international law and international relations. Authors have also expressed the view that granting exclusive jurisdiction to a foreign court does not generally imply a lack of confidence in the Turkish courts. These academics draw attention to the fact that stipulating in advance which court will have jurisdiction – even if that court is a foreign one – is in the interests of the parties insofar as they will have gained additional security for themselves by eliminating an element of uncertainty. They also point out that parties which are considered equally strong in international trade are not in need of being "nannied" by the courts

---

[6] Baki Kuru, *Hukuk Muhakemeleri Usulü*, C. I, 5 Bası, [The Law of Civil Procedure Law, Vol. 1, 5th edn.], Istanbul (1990) p. 1072/32-33.

[7] Krüger and Nomer (supra n. 5) p. 161.

and that everyone is at liberty to reject the protection of the law of his own country.[8] Not a single author has sided with the *lack of confidence in the Turkish courts* argument put forth by the ACC. Sup. Court.[9] In the dissenting opinions written by the three Supreme Court judges who objected to the 15 June 1988 ruling, it is stated that if a jurisdiction agreement exists granting jurisdiction to a foreign court, then that foreign court has exclusive jurisdiction in the matter at hand, and that that case can no longer be initiated in any competent Turkish court. They based this view, as stated above, on Article 31(2) PIL, an interpretation which was in turn based on the preliminary work on the PIL and on the debates which took place during the Symposium.

In the flawed ruling delivered by the ACC. Sup. Court on 15 June 1988, Article 22 of the Code of Civil Procedure ("CCP") which governs jurisdiction agreements in domestic law, was at least as instrumental as the extra-legal (we might even call it "emotional") justification of *encouraging a lack of confidence in the Turkish courts*. Also instrumental was the failure to delineate a distinction between Article 22 CCP and Article 31 PIL. Under Article 22 CCP, which is concerned with domestic law, in situations where a court's jurisdiction is not based upon the principle of public order, the parties involved may conclude a written agreement stipulating that legal disputes concerning with one or more matters may be brought before a court not specifically designated as having jurisdiction. In such situations, a court that has been identified in the jurisdiction agreement as being the court of jurisdiction cannot refuse to hear the case. As we see, under Article 22 CCP, the fact that parties have made a jurisdiction agreement does not overrule the general provisions concerning jurisdiction laid down in the CCP. That is, if one of the parties brings an action in a court having jurisdiction under general CCP rules governing jurisdiction, that court may hear the case. Article 27 PIL further provides: "The jurisdictional rules of domestic law governing the venue of adjudication shall determine the international jurisdiction of Turkish courts." However, this provision becomes inoperable if a jurisdiction agreement exists as specified in Article 31 PIL. If there exists a jurisdiction agreement that has been concluded in accordance with Article 31 PIL, that agreement determines jurisdiction. In their dissenting opinions, the three Supreme Court judges drew attention to this feature of the CCP and noted the difference between it and Article 31 PIL.

---

[8] Çelikel (supra n. 5) p. 317; Ekşi (supra n. 5) p. 163; Krüger and Nomer (supra n. 5) p. 159; Sargın (supra n. 4) p. 201.
[9] Çelikel (supra n. 5) p. 317; Ekşi (supra n. 5) p. 163; Krüger and Nomer (supra n. 5) p. 159, Sargın, (supra n. 4) p. 201.

2.   RECENT DECISIONS OF THE SUPREME COURT OF APPEALS

In a recent decision delivered by the ACC. Sup. Court, the court addressed the issue
of the effects that a jurisdiction agreement granting jurisdiction to a foreign court
has on the jurisdiction of the Turkish courts and it has reversed its previous opinion
on this matter. The text of the decision (E.1998-12-287, K.1998-325, 6 May 1998)[10]
reads as follows:

> *For the purpose of clarifying the subject, the ACC. Sup. Court judgements E.60-K.394
> (26 March 1975) and E.11-K.246-476 (15 June 1988) were referred to and debated. It
> was agreed that the view advocating that [such agreements on jurisdiction][11] must be
> considered null and void on the grounds of these ACC. Sup. Court judgements, due to the
> fact that they are contrary to the rule of public order, and that, for this reason, a plaintiff
> has the right to bring suit before a legally competent court in Turkey and that the juris-
> diction of a competent court cannot be eliminated by means of jurisdiction agreements
> because the general rules of jurisdiction set forth in law under the rule of CCP Article 22
> cannot be abrogated by agreements among parties and because holding a contrary view
> was tantamount to creating a lack of confidence in a Turkish court that had been duly
> granted jurisdiction in accordance with the requirements of domestic law, should be re-
> versed.*

This ruling, which was unanimous, has the nature of a determined legal principle
and therefore the differences of opinion and inconsistencies among previous judgments in the Turkish legal system have now been eliminated and the implementation of this principle has been clarified.

The facts of the case leading up to the ACC. Sup. Court's ruling of 6 May 1998
concerned a plaintiff bank that had sought and obtained in a Turkish court an order
of attachment against a defendant company. The defendants objected to this ruling,
arguing that the Court issuing the order had no jurisdiction in the matter. The defendants produced a contract between themselves and the plaintiffs, Article 20 of
which stated that German law would govern the contract and that the German courts
would have jurisdiction to resolve any disputes arising under it. The Bailiff's Court
rejected the defendants' objection on the grounds that "*the general rules of jurisdiction set forth in law cannot be abrogated by jurisdiction agreements and that an objection that would create a lack of confidence in a Turkish court that has been
granted jurisdiction by law cannot be allowed.*" It should be noted that the local
court essentially repeated the justification of the ACC. Sup. Court's ruling of 15

---

[10] Jud. [ACC. Sup. Court], No. 1998-12-287/1998-325, Reports, Vol. 24 (1998) pp. 1269-1272.
[11] Added by the authors.

June 1988. This is illustrative of how that ruling influenced local courts and, consequently, their interpretation of the law as well. The defendants appealed against the
local court's decision. The case was heard by the 12th Chamber of the ACC. Sup.
Court. In judgement 6906-8220 (9 July 1997), the court held:

> *In Article 20/1 of the lending agreement dated 14 October 1992 on which the creditor has*
> *based its action is a provision that states "This agreement and the rights and obligations*
> *of the parties thereto shall be executed and interpreted in accordance with German law".*
> *Similarly the second paragraph of the same article contains an agreement that German*
> *courts will also have jurisdiction in the resolution of any disputes. Article 24 of Statute*
> *2675 (PIL) stipulates that relationships arising from a contract are to be subject to the*
> *laws of whatever country the contractual parties have specifically chosen. In violation of*
> *the aforementioned provisions of law and contract, the creditor applied to the Serik Bai-*
> *liff's Office, which is authorized to take action in such cases under Turkish law, for an or-*
> *der of precautionary distress. The objection on the grounds of jurisdiction should have*
> *been resolved within the framework of the aforementioned contractual provisions; as-*
> *sessing it as described in accordance with Turkish law is a misjudgment.*

On these grounds the court quashed the order. The local court, however, remained
adamant as regards its earlier decision and so the matter came before the ACC. Sup.
Court. This case demonstrates that not only the 11th C. Chamb. Sup. Court but also
the 12th C. Chamb. Sup. Court (which has responsibility for hearing appeals in
cases involving seizures and bankruptcies) had a different opinion to that of the
ACC. Sup. Court and also that this difference of opinion was quite diverse and far-
reaching within the Supreme Court community.

The matter at issue in the ACC. Sup. Court's latest decision of 6 May 1998 appears to be basically concerned with a court that is authorized to issue orders of attachment and with the question of whether or not a contractual clause granting
jurisdiction to a foreign court is also applicable to orders of attachment – in other
words, is the foreign court also authorized to issue orders of attachment or not? In
fact, at the heart of this dispute is the question of whether or not the jurisdiction
clause gives the foreign court exclusive jurisdiction in all disputes arising under the
contract and whether or not this clause abrogates the jurisdiction of the Turkish
courts. Indeed, in order to resolve this question concerning the core issue, the ACC.
Sup. Court felt it necessary to interpret the rule contained in Article 31 PIL and, after stating its opinion concerning that provision, it gave its decision on the fundamental issue of the case. This attitude on the part of the ACC. Sup. Court suggests
that the court was ill at ease with the decision of 15 June 1988, that it acknowledged
the criticism of academics as being justified, that it was looking for an opportunity
to reverse this ruling, and that it treated the Serik court's decision as the appropriate
opportunity to do so. This, in turn, proves that the 6 May 1998 ruling by the ACC.
Sup. Court was not an ordinary decision limited to the material facts of the case at

hand, but that it was a ruling that was intended as a precedent. That of course increases the importance of this ruling. Furthermore, in reversing the previous decision, the ACC. Sup. Court noted that the judgement was based on Article 22 CCP, which is concerned with domestic law and in doing so, it pointed to the source from which the earlier decision's invalidity arose and also indicated that only Article 31 PIL was applicable to such matters.

In its reversal, the ACC. Sup. Court referred not only to the ruling of 15 June 1988, but also to another ruling (E.60/K.394, 26 March 1975), which was along the same lines and which had been delivered before the PIL had entered into effect. This reference amounts to a re-emphasis of the attitude that the previous rulings had been made under the influence of Article 22 CCP because both cite that article as their basis.

In the ACC. Sup. Court's view, if there exists a jurisdiction clause that grants jurisdiction to a court of a foreign State and if that clause conforms with the provisions of Article 31(1) PIL, then the foreign court acquires the status of a court having *exclusive* jurisdiction. As nearly all of the authors cited above point out, the basis for this interpretation is Article 31(2) PIL, and this is the ACC. Sup. Court's position as well. The reason for this is that this provision explicitly states that a case can be heard in a Turkish court only if the foreign court has declared that it lacks in jurisdiction. The ACC. Sup. Court's statement that a jurisdiction agreement drawn up in accordance with the substance and wording of Article 31(1) PIL precludes the jurisdiction of the Turkish courts is simply another formulation of this new opinion. That the ACC. Sup. Court was influenced by criticism levelled by academics, can be understood from the following passage taken from its ruling:

> In the face of the essential social and industrial needs that states have of one another in the Information Age today, it cannot be denied that economic relations have become more intense thanks to easy communication and rapid transportation or that, because of this, it is necessary to enter into contracts that reach beyond countries' borders. As an integral member of the world's nations and a participant in the world economy, it is inconceivable that Turkey should divorce itself from this reality. In point of fact, in the face of the demands imposed by the social and economic conditions of our times, every State must keep in mind the fact that it is a part of the system of international law and must make an effort to eschew all forms of legal egotism. For this reason, jurisdiction clauses that have been decided upon in contracts based on commercial relationships of this sort have become an indispensable element of such agreements. Indeed there are many benefits to be had if parties know at the very outset of a contract which country's competent courts they may have recourse to and if they identify and set down the rules of law that are to apply to themselves in advance.

If a case should be brought before a competent Turkish court despite a jurisdiction agreement granting jurisdiction to a foreign court, then upon the defendant's objection the Turkish court should rule (assuming, of course, that the jurisdiction agreement is valid under Turkish law) that it lacks jurisdiction in the case. Under Turkish law, this objection on the part of the defendant is called *ilk itiraz* ("initial objection") and it is the counterpart of *prozeßhindernde Einreden* in German law and of *moyens préjudiciels* in French law. In such cases, the plaintiff must bring the action in a court having jurisdiction as designated in the jurisdiction agreement. Only if the foreign court itself decides that it lacks jurisdiction may the plaintiff then bring the case before a Turkish court as specified in Article 31(2) PIL. Some scholars[12] consider this to be contrary to the principle of *procedural economy*. In their view, if a case is brought first before a Turkish court despite the existence of a jurisdiction agreement then the Turkish court should agree to hear the case (a) if it is apparent in advance that the foreign court is going to rule that it lacks jurisdiction, or (b) if the decision rendered by the foreign court is incapable of being executed in Turkey, or (c) if there is no possibility of the decision being executed in foreign countries. It is impossible to concur with this view, however. First of all, even if it is known in advance that the foreign court will declare itself to lack jurisdiction, it is the duty of the foreign court to make that declaration. Secondly, in order for a Turkish court to conclude that a foreign court's judgement is incapable of being executed in Turkey, it must weigh the pertinent issues and come to a decision accordingly; but this is something that is governed by special rules in the PIL. The case before the judge is not one involving the execution of a foreign court's decision: indeed, in order for such a hearing to take place, there must first of all be a foreign court's decision to be considered by the Turkish judge. A judge cannot deliver a ruling on the basis of what someone might imagine another court's decision will be. Finally, we do not believe it possible for Turkish courts to investigate whether or not a foreign court's decision is capable of being executed in foreign countries, nor do we think that they even have the authority to make such an assessment. Such competence is not granted to Turkish judges either by the CCP or by the PIL.

The same authors[13] also contend that, even when there exists a jurisdiction agreement granting jurisdiction to a foreign court, which is valid in the eyes of Turkish law, a litigant's objection on jurisdictional grounds should be rejected if it appears that the objection is contrary to the principles of good faith that are laid down in Article 2 of the Turkish Civil Code. On this issue, they propose the following example. Let us suppose that there is a sales agreement in which the seller is a German and the buyer a Turk and in which jurisdiction is assigned to a court in Munich. If the German seller were to bring an action in Turkey under the contract and the Turkish buyer were to object to this on jurisdictional grounds, that objection would be contrary to the principles of good faith because the defending party in this case would

---

[12] Kuru (supra n. 6) p. 1072/33; Sargın (supra n. 4) p. 198.
[13] Kuru (supra n. 6) p. 1072/33.

be in a better position to mount a defence in Turkey: from the defendant's point of view, there is no meritorious benefit to be had in the case being heard in Munich. These authors point to a Supreme Court decision in which the court held that a defendant's objection to enforcement proceedings that had been initiated with a court at the defendant's place of residence despite the existence of a jurisdiction agreement stipulating another court as having contractual jurisdiction was in violation of Article 2 of the Turkish Civil Code – in other words it was contrary to the principle of good faith. It is also impossible to concur with this view. The first reason is the important difference between Article 22 CCP and Article 31 PIL: a judgement rendered on the basis of Article 22 CCP cannot be adduced as a precedent for an issue being contested under the PIL. Secondly, a court in a litigant's country of residence may not always be more advantageous for the litigant than one with jurisdiction in a foreign country. It might be so, for example, that a litigant's opportunities to prove his case are more readily available in the country in which the foreign court is located or that the procedural law that the foreign court will adhere to is in the litigant's better interests. Finally, providing one of the parties to a contract with the means to escape his contractual obligations on the basis of Article 2 of the Turkish Civil Code is inconsistent with the rule of contractual law.

If a case is brought before a competent Turkish court rather than in a foreign court that has been granted jurisdiction under a jurisdiction agreement and if this action is not objected to, then the court may hear the case.

Some authors[14] assert the view that under a jurisdiction agreement, a foreign court is selected that is in the best interests of both contractual parties and that the conduct of a case in a court so identified is also in the interests of both parties; but that in situations where a jurisdiction agreement has been entered into in which *only one litigant's interests have been considered*, then the exclusive jurisdiction of the foreign court can be objected to and a case can be brought in a Turkish court. This is another opinion in which it is impossible to concur: first, because it is presumptuous to suppose that a court chosen under a jurisdiction agreement is always going to be in the best interests of both parties and, second, because Article 31 PIL provides no grounds whatsoever to authorize a Turkish court to advance such a hypothesis. The latter article is explicit and clear-cut on the subject of when Turkish courts may have jurisdiction. It is possible to say that this view has also been influenced by Article 22 CCP. One such author also offers an equally nebulous view:

> Nevertheless it is also possible that a jurisdiction agreement may be made taking into account the interests of only one of the parties. Such an agreement on the part of those involved rules out exclusivity of jurisdiction and grants one of the parties the possibility of

---

[14] Sargın (supra n. 4) p. 199.

an alternative. For in such a situation, the party in whose benefit the jurisdiction agreement was concluded could, if he so wished, forgo his right to apply to the chosen court and instead initiate proceedings in a Turkish court. In the event of such proceedings, the Turkish court would no longer take into account any objections on the grounds that the chosen court had exclusive jurisdiction.

In our opinion, the concept of the "party in whose benefit the jurisdiction agreement was concluded" is somewhat cloudy and apt to lead to misjudgments and to erroneous conclusions.

The question that needs to be examined here is whether or not Article 31 PIL allows non-exclusive jurisdiction. That Article 31 PIL does not exclude this possibility is certain, the reason being that, if a legal system recognizes and allows for jurisdictional exclusivity, it is unreasonable for it to reject non-exclusivity.

That having been said, it is also essential that the courts having jurisdiction are not left undefined. Contracts that incorporate a jurisdiction clause that charges one of the parties with an absolute obligation to initiate proceedings in a court having jurisdiction while allowing the other the right to initiate a case in other – specified – courts are in accordance with Article 31 PIL.

In its 1988 ruling, the ACC. Sup. Court did not touch upon these issues.

In its ruling of 6 May 1998, the ACC. Sup. Court laid down its views on matters such as the forms, conditions of validity, and limits of jurisdiction agreements. According to the ACC. Sup. Court, Turkish law imposes no requirements with respect to matters of form where the granting of jurisdiction to a foreign court is concerned. In so doing, the ACC. Sup. Court indicated its complete agreement with the view that is shared unanimously by academic authors. Quite correctly, academics indicate that jurisdiction agreements are not bound to any specific form: that is, they may be concluded in writing or verbally, explicitly or by implication. The reason for this is that Turkish law is silent on this point. From the standpoint of clarity or probative value of course, the written form is to be recommended.

In order for jurisdiction clauses to be valid, they must not be contrary to Turkish public order and they must not incorporate any issue in which Turkish courts have exclusive jurisdiction. According to the ACC. Sup. Court, jurisdiction clauses are applicable in disputes arising from what is called a *borç iliskisi* ("obligational relationship") in Turkish law, but are invalid in disputes concerning issues pertaining to personal or family law. This Turkish legal concept may be understood as a form of *lex fori*. Authors regard this concept as also including relationships that involve torts and unjustified enrichment. In addition, the relationship in question must incorporate an element of extra-nationality, which is said to exist if one or all of the parties to the dispute are foreign nationals, or if the place where the contract has been entered into or carried out is in a foreign country, or if the relationship arises in a foreign country, or if the law applicable to the relationship is that of a foreign country. In the eyes of Turkish law, a jurisdiction agreement that grants jurisdiction to a foreign court in a debt relationship that lacks a foreign element is invalid.

3.   CONCLUSION

Having thus set out the justifications for reversing its earlier ruling and explaining in detail its opinions on the matter of jurisdiction agreements, the ACC. Sup. Court returned to the case at hand and declared that the case in question entailed a legal procedure of an entirely different nature insofar as it was concerned with a matter of precautionary distress: it was an issue, in other words, involving compulsory execution and the laws applicable thereto. As the ACC. Sup. Court was quite right to point out, jurisdictional objections will come into play at the stage when the interlocutory order for attachment issued by the court of first instance is to be enforced by the Serik Bailiff's Office. For this reason, the dispute needs to be assessed within the limits of this legal consideration. There cannot be the slightest doubt that the legal consequences and provisions of executing an order for attachment are concerned with compulsory execution law. Compulsory execution in turn is an absolute power and authority that every State possesses within the borders of its own territory. Compulsory execution is furthermore a consequence arising directly from a State's exercise of its sovereign rights. For this reason, the authority to enforce an order for attachment issued by a Turkish court is a manifestation of the ability of a State to exercise its power over its own territory and is, for that reason, a matter of its exclusive authority. This being so, when the case is considered solely in the light of this specific legal aspect and scope, the acknowledgement of the Turkish court's domestic jurisdiction and the international jurisdiction associated with it becomes unavoidable.

Antizipierte Umsetzung von Verbraucherrichtlinien und das Internationale Privatrecht

Lajos Vékás[*]

1. EINLEITUNG: POINTILLISMUS UND TROTZDEM?

1.1 EG-Richtlinien als Mittel fragmentarischer Rechtsangleichung

Gemeinschaftsprivatrecht[1] breitet sich langsam auch ausserhalb der Europäischen Union aus. Die autonome Übernahme von zivilrechtlichen Regelungen aus der Gemeinschaft, das freiwillige Kopieren des EVÜ, der Beitritt zum Lugano-Übereinkommen – sie sind nicht mehr reine Phantasieträume von besessenen Rechtsver-

---

[*] Dr.iur., Professor, University of Budapest.
[1] Zum Begriff „Gemeinschaftsprivatrecht": P.-Ch. Müller-Graff, *Privatrecht und europäisches Gemeinschaftsrecht, Gemeinschaftsprivatrecht*, 2. Auflage (Baden-Baden, Nomos 1991)

J. Basedow et al., eds., Private Law in the International Arena – Liber Amicorum Kurt Siehr
© *2000, T.M.C.Asser Press, The Hague, The Netherlands*

gleichern und Rechtsvereinheitlichern. Auch die antizipierten Umsetzungen von Richtlinien stehen auf der Tagesordnung.

„Fragmentarische Rechtsvereinheitlichung, die in einem Meer nationalen Rechts winzige Inseln vereinheitlichten Rechts schafft"?[2] Sie zeigen doch in eine zukunftsversprechende Richtung, auch wenn dieser Prozess lange dauern und von unerwünschten Nebenwirkungen, von Systembrüchen in den nationalen Privatrechtsordnungen, methodologischen Irrwegen, überflüssigen Parallelaktionen und anderen Rückschlägen, begleitet sein wird. Historisch gesehen gehören die Richtlinien mit ihrem Pointillismus[3] und ihrer konzeptionellen Beschränktheit wohl zu den Übergangserscheinungen des Rechtsangleichungs- und Rechtsvereinheitlichungsprozesses in Europa, genauso wie ihre rechtstechnisch unvollkommenen und divergierenden Umsetzungen (seien sie obligatorisch oder autonom) in die nationalen Rechtsordnungen. Trotzdem meine ich: sie dienen einem guten Ziel. Wie ihre Kosten- Nutzen-Analyse[4] ausgehen wird – diese Frage steht heute noch offen.

1.2 Autonome Rechtsangleichung in Nichtmitgliedsstaaten

Mit einer autonomen Rechtsangleichung und – in ihrem Rahmen – mit freiwilliger Umsetzung von Richtlinien hat es Ende der 80er Jahre begonnen. Vor allem die EFTA-Staaten (im Rahmen des EWR) haben dafür gute Beispiele gegeben: die antizipierte Übernahme des EVÜ und der Produkthaftungsrichtlinie in Finnland[5] und in einigen anderen (ehemaligen) EFTA-Staaten,[6] die Umsetzung anderer verbraucherrechtlicher Richtlinien[7] usw.

---

[2] H. Kötz, „Rechtsvergleichung – Nutzen, Kosten, Methoden, Ziele", 50 *RabelsZ* (1986) S. 1ff., 12.

[3] So auch über den „punktuellen und fragmentarischen Charakter" der Rechtsvereinheitlichung Kötz (oben N. 2) S. 3, 5.; hinsichtlich unseres Themas kritisch E. Jayme/ Ch. Kohler, „Europäisches Kollisionsrecht 1996 – Anpassung und Transformation der nationalen Rechte", *IPRax* (1996) S. 377ff., 389; D. Martiny, „Europäisches internationales Vertragsrecht – Erosion der Römischen Konvention?" *ZEuP* (1997) S. 107ff., 108.; Über „pointillistische Rechtsangleichung ohne System und Konzept": A. Junker, „Der EuGH im Arbeitsrecht – die schwarze Serie geht weiter", *NJW* (1994) S. 2527f., 2528.

[4] Kötz (oben N. 2) S. 3ff.

[5] K. Buure-Hägglund, „New Finnish Legislation on Law Applicable to Contracts", *IPRax* (1989) S. 407ff.; R. Paanila, „Das finnische Produkthaftungsgesetz", *RIW* (1991) S. 560ff.

[6] W. Posch, „Probleme ‚autonomer Rechtsangleichung' – dargestellt am Produkthaftungsgesetz", in: *FS Ostheim* (Wien, Manz 1990) S. 665ff.; M. Will, „Autonome Rechtsangleichung in Europa", in:f. Schwind. (Hrsg.), *Österreichs Weg in die EG* (Wien, Verlag der Akademie 1991) S. 53ff.; vgl. auch hinsichtlich der Schweiz, die weder der EU noch dem EWR angehört: C. Baudenbacher, „Zum Nachvollzug europäischen Rechts in der Schweiz", *EuR* (1992) S. 309ff.; E.A. Kramer, „Das schweizerische Schuldrecht vor der Herausforderung des Europarechts", *ZEuP* (1995) S. 500ff., 504ff.

[7] S. hierzu W. Posch, „Zur EWR-bedingten Umsetzung von Richtlinien verbraucherprivatrechtlichen Inhalts in das österreichische Recht; oder ‚aller Anfang ist schwer'", in: *FS Everling*, Band II (Baden-Baden, Nomos 1995) S. 1141ff.; vgl. auch die jährlichen Berichte von Jayme/ Kohler zum Europäischen Kollisionsrecht in der *IPRax*.

Ein ähnlicher Prozess hat seinen Anfang in den 90er Jahren in den mit der EG assoziierten Staaten Mittel- und Osteuropas genommen. Ungarn wird zum Beispiel bald dem Lugano-Übereinkommen beitreten, und auch die autonome Übernahme des EVÜ ist ernsthaft im Gespräch.[8]

Einen quantitativen neuen Schritt in diese Richtung stellen die Assoziationsabkommen der letztgenannten Staaten mit der EG dar. Mit dem Europa-Abkommen zur Gründung einer Assoziation zwischen der EG und ihren Mitgliedsstaaten einerseits und der Republik Ungarn andererseits vom 16.12.1991[9] hat sich Ungarn verpflichtet, seine Rechtsvorschriften u. a. im Bereich des Verbraucherschutzes an das Gemeinschaftsrecht anzugleichen.[10] Im Rahmen dieses Angleichungsprozesses hat Ungarn inzwischen die Produkthaftungsrichtlinie (85/374/EWG[11]), die Haustürwiderrufs-Richtlinie (85/577/EWG[12]), die Verbraucherkredit-Richtlinie (87/102/EWG, geändert durch 90/88/EWG[13]), die Pauschalreise-Richtlinie (90/314/EWG[14]),

---

[8] M. Kengyel, „Die ungarischen Perspektiven für einen Beitritt zum EuGVÜ oder zum Lugano-Übereinkommen", in: Tomuschat/ Kötz/ von Maydell (Hrsg.), *Europäische Integration und nationale Rechtskulturen* (Köln, Heymann 1995) S. 63ff.; ders., „Magyarország a Luganói Egyezmény kapujában" (Ungarn vor dem Tore des Lugano-Übereinkommens, ungar.), *Magyar Jog* (1999) S. 329ff.; ders., „Ungarn vor dem Tor des Lugano-übereinkommens", in: R. Geimer (Hrsg.), *Festschrift Schütze* (München, Beck 1999) S. 347ff.; L. Burián, „Die Anpassung des IPR-Gesetzes an das vereinheitlichte IPR der Europäischen Union", in: *FS Posch* (Wien 1996) S. 29ff.; zur autonomen Rechstangleichung in Polen s. Jayme/ Kohler (oben N. 7) (1996) S. 377ff., 378f. mit N. 24 und Jayme/ Geckler, *IPRax* (1997) S. 66f.; in Rumänien s. Jayme/ Kohler (oben N. 7) (1995) S. 343ff., 344 mit N. 11.

[9] ABl. EG Nr. L 32 v. 5. 2. 1994, S. 3ff.

[10] S. Art. 68 des Europa-Abkomens mit der Republik Ungarn. Ganz ähnlich Art. 69 des Europa-Abkommens mit der Republik Polen (*ABl.(EG)* [1993] L 348/II. v. 31.12.1993), Art. 69 des Europa-Abkommens mit der Tschechischen Republik (*ABl.(EG)* [1994] L 360/2 v. 31.12.1994), Art. 69 des Europa-Abkommens mit Rumänien (*ABl.(EG)* [1994] L 357 v. 31.12.1994), Art. 69 des Europa-Abkommens mit der Republik Bulgarien (*ABl.(EG)* L [1994] 358 v. 31.12.1994), Art. 69 des Europa-Abkommens mit der Slowakischen Republik (*ABl.(EG)* [1994] L 359 v. 31.12.1994), Art. 70 des Europa-Abkommens mit der Republik Litauen (*ABl.(EG)* [1995] L 51 v. 12.6.1995), Art. 70 des Europa-Abkommens mit der Republik Lettland (*ABl.(EG)* [1998] L 26 v. 2.2.1998), Art. 69 des Europa-Abkommens mit der Republik Estland (*ABl.(EG)* [1998] L 68 v. 9.3.1998), Art. 71 des Europa-Abkommens mit der Republik Slowenien (*ABl.(EG)* [1999] L 51 v. 26.2.1999).

[11] Gesetz Nr. X/1993 über die Produkthaftung (Deutsche Übersetzung in: Brunner/ Schmid/ Westen, *Wirtschaftsrecht der Osteuropäischen Staaten* [Loseblatt] (Baden-Baden, Nomos) Band I 3 Ungarn, Dok. IV 4 a.

[12] § 377 n.F. ZGB sowie Regierungsverordnung [RVO] 44/1998 über die Haustürgeschäfte (M. K. Nr. 18/1998, S. 1514).

[13] § 7 des Gesetzes Nr. CLV/1997 über den Verbraucherschutz (Magyar Közlöny [M. K.] Nr. 119/1997, S. 9558ff.) sowie die §§ 212-214 des Gesetzes CXII/1996 über die Kreditinstitute und Finanzunternehmungen (M. K. Nr. 109/1996, S. 6164ff.).

[14] RVO Nr. 213/1996 über die Reiseveranstaltungs- und Reisevermittlungstätigkeit (M. K. Nr. 117/1996, S. 6943ff.) und RVO 214/1996 über die Reise- und Reisevermittlungsverträge (M. K. Nr. 117/1997 S. 6948ff.).

die Klauselrichtlinie (93/13/EWG[15]), die Timesharing-Richtlinie (94/47/EG[16]) sowie die Fernabsatz-Richtlinie (97/7/EG[17]) in das eigene Rechtssystem umgesetzt. Es ist vorauszusehen, dass der ungarische Gesetzgeber und noch früher die Rechtsliteratur sich auch mit den Angleichungsmodalitäten der Verbrauchsgüterkauf-Richtlinie[18] und bald auch mit der FinanzFernabsatz-Richtlinie[19] auseinandersetzen sollen.

2. DIE KOLLISIONSRECHTLICHE PROBLEMATIK

2.1 Richtlinienwirkung bei länderübergreifenden Sachverhalten

Die verbraucherrechtlichen Richtlinien wollen das herkömmliche materielle Privatrecht verbraucherfreundlicher gestalten. Dementsprechend steht die Angleichung der jeweiligen materiellrechtlichen Regelung[20] in ihrem Mittelpunkt. Bekanntlich enthalten viele von ihnen auch Kollisionsnormen, die nach Art. 20 EVÜ Vorrang genießen, also die eigentlich einschlägigen Normen des EVÜ verdrängen. Diese Kollisionsnormen (ohne ein allgemein-verbraucherrechtliches Konzept) ha-

---

[15] Gesetz Nr. CXLIX/1997 über die Änderung des ZGB, insb. § 205 Abs. 3 n.F., und die neu eingefügten Abs. 5 und 6, § 207 Abs. 2 n.f., § 209 n.f., die neu eingefügten §§ 209/A – 209/D und § 685 lit. d ZGB sowie die neu eingefügten §§ 5/A – 5/C der Gesetzesverordnung Nr. 2/1978 (Deutsche Übersetzung in: Brunner/ Schmid/ Westen (oben N. 11) Band I 3 Ungarn, Dok. IV 1.

[16] RVO Nr. 20/1999 über die Teilzeit-Immobilinennutzungsverträge (M. K. Nr. 8/1999, S. 569ff.)

[17] RVO Nr. 17/1999 über die Fernabsatzverträge (M. K. Nr. 8/1999, S. 535ff.).

[18] 1999/44/EG vom 25.05.1999, ABl.(EG) [1999] L 171/12, 7.7.1999; vgl. dazu Beale/ Howells, „EC Harmonisation of Consumer Sales Law – A Missed Opportunity?", Journal of Contract Law (9/ 1997) S. 21ff.; Ehmann/ Rust, "Die Verbrauchsgüterkaufrichtlinie", JZ (1999) S. 853ff.; Hondius, "Kaufen ohne Risiko: Der europäische Richtlinienentwurf zum Verbraucherkauf und zur Verbrauchergarantie", ZEuP (1997) S. 130ff.; Lehr/ Wendel, „Die EU-Richtlinie über Verbrauchsgüterkauf und - garantien", EWS (1999) S. 321ff.; Medicus, „Ein neues Kaufrecht für Verbraucher?", ZIP (1996) S. 1925ff.; Micklitz, „Die Verbrauchsgüterkauf-Richtlinie", EuZW (1999) S. 485ff.; Reich, „Die Umsetzung der Richtlinie 1999/44/EG in das deutsche Recht", NJW (1999) S. 2397ff.; Schlechtriem, „Verbraucherkaufverträge – ein neuer Richtlinienentwurf", JZ (1997) S. 441ff.; Schmidt-Räntsch, „Gedanken zur Umsetzung der kommenden Kaufrechtsrichtlinie", ZEuP (1999) S. 294ff.; Schurr, „Die neue Richtlinie 99/44/EG über den Verbrauchsgüterkauf und ihre Umsetzung – Chancen und Gefahren für das deutsche Kaufrecht", ZfRV (1999) S. 222ff.; Staudenmayer, „Die EG-Richtlinie über den Verbrauchsgüterkauf", NJW (1999) S. 2393ff.; Tonner, „Verbrauchsgüterkauf-Richtlinie und Europäisierung des Zivilrechts", BB (1999) S. 1769ff.

[19] FinanzFernabsatz-Richtlinienvorschlag: KOM (98) 468 endg., ABl.(EG) [1998] C 385/10 (abgdr. mit Begr. auch in WM (1999) S. 1477ff.); vgl. dazu K. Riesenhuber, „Fernabsatz von Finanzdienstleistungen im europäischen Schuldvertragsrecht", WM (1999) S. 1441ff.; Kurzberichte von W. Mayer, WM (1998) S. 2445f. und R. Wägenbaur, EuZW (1999) S. 34f.

[20] Zum Problem des Fehlens der entsprechenden Gerichtszuständigkeiten s. Jayme/ Kohler (oben N. 7) (1997) S. 385ff., 391f. und (1998) S. 417ff., 427. Ein Fortschritt stellt die Richtlinie 98/27/EG über Unterlassungsklagen zum Schutz von Verbraucherinteressen dar.

ben inzwischen eine neue internationalprivatrechtliche Problematik und ein Spannungsfeld zwischen Europarecht und Kollisionsrecht bewirkt.[21]

Mit der Behandlung einiger Aspekte dieses Gebiets soll dieser Aufsatz unserem Jubilar eine Freude bereiten. Es hat mich, den Verehrer seiner breit angelegten, internationalprivatrechtlichen schöpferischen Tätigkeit, gar nicht überrascht, als er nach Fertigstellung dieses Beitrags einen Aufsatz zum Thema veröffentlicht und mir als Sonderdruck überreicht hat.[22]

Die wichtigste Ursache der turbulenten internationalprivatrechtlichen Problematik liegt darin, dass die verbraucherrechtlichen Richtlinien bei internationalen Sachverhalten sich nicht auf die bewährten Lösungen des Art. 5 EVÜ verlassen. Sie bestimmen gar ganz unterschiedlich und rechtsdogmatisch unscharf ihren eigenen räumlich-persönlichen Anwendungsbereich.[23]

In den hier zu besprechenden verbraucherrechtlichen Richtlinien wurden hinsichtlich der Bestimmung ihres Anwendungsbereichs nicht weniger als drei Lösungsvarianten (die eine von ihnen gar mit zwei Untertypen) „erprobt". Dies zeigt den „erfinderischen Schöpfungsgeist" in Brüssel. So ist es kein Wunder, dass „die in den Richtlinien enthaltenen Kollisionsnormen in manchen Staaten als ein Appell an die Phantasie des Gesetzgebers verstanden werden".[24]

---

[21] S. hierzu Brödermann/ Iversen, *Europäisches Gemeinschaftsrecht und Internationales Privatrecht* (Tübingen, Mohr 1994); E. Jayme, *Ein Internationales Privatrecht für Europa* (Heidelberg, Decker und Müller 1991); W.-H. Roth, „Der Einfluss des europäischen Gemeinschaftsrechts auf das Internationale Privatrecht", *RabelsZ* (1991) S. 623ff.; ders., „Angleichung des IPR durch sekundäres Gemeinschaftsrecht", *IPRax* (1994) S. 165ff.; K.-F. Kreuzer, „Die Europäisierung des Internationalen Privatrechts – Vorgaben des Gemeinschaftsrechts", in: P-Ch. Müller-Graff (Hrsg.), *Gemeinsames Privatrecht in der Europäischen Gemeinschaft* (Baden-Baden, Nomos 1993) S. 373ff.; B. von Hoffmann, „Richtlinien der Europäischen Gemeinschaft und Internationales Privatrecht", *ZfRV* (1995) S. 45ff.; J. Basedow, „Matreielle Rechtsangleichung und Kollisionsrecht", in: Schnyder/ Heiss/ Rudisch (Hrsg.), *Internationales Verbraucherschutzrecht* (Tübingen, Mohr 1995) S. 11ff.; Jayme/ Kohler, „L'interaction des règles de conflit contenues dans le droit dérivé de la Communauté européenne et des conventions de Bruxelles et de Rome", *Rev.crit.d.i.p.* (1995) S. 1ff.; dies. (oben N. 7); H. J. Sonnenberger, „Die Umsetzung kollisionsrechlicher Regelungsgebote in EG-Richtlinien", *ZEuP* (1996) S. 382ff.; D. Martiny (oben N. 3); ders., „Europäisches Internationales Vertragsrecht – Ausbau und Konsolidierung", *ZEuP* (1999) S. 246ff.; A. Junker, „Vom Citoyen zum Consommateur – Entwicklungen des internationalen Verbraucherschutzrechts", *IPRax* (1998) S. 65ff.; S. Krebber, „Die volle Wirksamkeit von Richtlinien in länderübergreifenden Sachverhalten", *ZVglRWiss* (1998) S. 124ff.; Ch. Kretschmar, *Die Richtlinie 93/13/EWG . . . und das deutsche AGB-Gesetz* (Frankfurt a.M. 1998).

[22] K. Siehr, „Drittstaatklauseln in Europäischen Richtlinien zum Verbraucherschutz und die Schweiz", in: *Der Einfluss des europäischen Rechts auf die Schweiz. FS Roger Zäch* (Zürich, Schulthess 1999) S. 593ff.

[23] Dieser Umstand hat auch die *Groupe européen de droit international privé* zu einer Deklaration veranlasst: „Conclusions concernant l'interaction du droit communautaire dérivé et des conventions de Bruxelles du 27 septembre 1968 et de Rome du 19 juin 1980", *Rev.crit.d.i.p.* (1995) S. 39f.; vgl. hierzu auch J. Basedow, „Europäisches Internationales Privatrecht", *NJW* (1996) S. 1921ff., 1923, 1926.

[24] Jayme/ Kohler (oben N. 7) (1997) S. 385ff., 389.

2.2   Schwierigkeiten bei fehlender Bestimmung des internationalen Geltungsanspruchs

Drei von den in Betracht gezogenen Richtlinien (nämlich die Produkthaftungs-, die Haustürwiderrufs- und die Verbraucherkredit-Richtlinie[25]) enthalten weder eine unmittelbare noch eine mittelbare Regelung zur Feststellung ihres Geltungsanspruchs. Bei ihnen ist also der Anwendungswille alleine durch Auslegung zu ermitteln.[26] Die lückenhafte Lösung hat zur Folge, dass sich bei internationalen Sachverhalten Schwierigkeiten bei der Anknüpfung an das Recht sowohl eines Mitgliedsstaates als auch eines Drittstaates einstellen können.

a)   Bei länderübergreifenden Sachverhalten entstanden innerhalb der EU Schwierigkeiten hinsichtlich dieser Richtlinien, falls das Kollisionsrecht der lex fori zur Anwendung einer mitgliedsstaatlichen Rechtsordnung geführt hat, in der eine Richtlinie noch nicht umgesetzt worden war.

In den sogenannten „Grand-Canaria"-Fällen hat z.B. die deutsche Rechtsprechung und das Schrifttum auf mehreren kollisionsrechtlichen Wegen versucht, das Problem zu lösen, welches sich aus der (damals noch) nicht erfolgten Umsetzung der Haustürwiderrufs-Richtlinie in allen Teilrechten des territorial gespaltenen spanischen Verbraucherrechts ergeben hat. Sämtliche kollisionsrechtlichen Mittel wurden durch die Gerichte in Anspruch genommen bzw. in der Literatur diskutiert,[27] um deutsches anstelle des gewählten spanischen Rechts anwenden und so ein Rücktrittsrecht für die Käufer gewähren zu können. Eine Sonderanknüpfung gemäss Art. 27 Abs. 3 EGBGB für das deutsche AGB-Gesetz bzw. HausTWG wurde befürwortet;[28] ähnlich wurde die analoge Anwendung von Art. 29 Abs. 1 EGBGB und mit Hilfe dessen wieder die Anwendbarkeit des deutschen HausTWG stark vertreten.[29] Als eine dritte Möglichkeit wurde vorgeschlagen, das HausTWG als eine verbraucherschützende Eingriffsnorm[30] oder aber als richtlinienkonformes nationales Recht anstelle des richtlinienwidrigen gewählten mitgliedsstaatlichen

---

[25]   Auch der zurückgenommene Vorschlag für eine Richtlinie des Rates über die Haftung bei Dienstleistungen (KOM/90 482 endg.-SYN 308, von der Kommission vorgelegt am 9. Nov. 1990) bestimmt nicht näher ihren räumlich-persönlichen Anwendungsbereich, sie betrachtet sich lediglich als „Massnahme auf Gemeinschaftsebene", definiert der Dienstleistungsmarkt als „die gesamte Gemeinschaft" und will die „Dienstleistungsfreiheit gemeinschaftsweit fördern" (Präambel).

[26]   So auch Krebber (oben N. 21) S. 139; zu den verschiedenen Lösungsmöglichkeiten s. von Hoffmann (oben N. 21) S. 49ff.

[27]   Eine ausführliche und kritische Besprechung der Gerichtsentscheidungen und eine Darstellung der Literaturmeinungen s. Brödermann/ Iversen (oben N. 21) S. 387ff.

[28]   Fundstellen bei Brödermann/Iversen, ibid., Teil II, N. 265, 266, die Gegenmeinungen in N. 268-272.

[29]   Fundstellen bei Brödermann/Iversen, ibid., Teil II, N. 277-280, die verschiedenen Analogievarianten in N. 281-285, die Gegenmeinungen in N. 291-292.

[30]   B. von Hoffmann, „Inländische Sachnormen mit zwingendem internationalem Anwendungsbereich", *IPRax* (1989) S. 261ff., 268; Brödermann/ Iversen (oben N. 21) S. 411ff.

Sachstatuts[31] über Art. 34 EGBGB anzuwenden. Schliesslich wurde auch die allgemeine Vorbehaltsklausel des Art. 6 EGBGB[32] und sogar die Gesetzesumgehung[33] ins Feld geführt.

Die meisten Lösungsansätze wollten deutsches IPR in seiner traditionellen Form anwenden und haben dabei die gemeinschaftsrechtliche Einbettung der Sachverhalte ausser acht gelassen.[34] Hingegen hat *Jayme* seine Auffassung auf die Richtlinienkonformität bzw. auf deren Fehlen in den konkurrierenden mitgliedsstaatlichen Rechten gestützt und mit Hilfe des Art. 34 EGBGB die „mittelbare horizontale Wirkung von EG-Richtlinien" angenommen.[35] Dieser „Umweg" musste gewählt werden, weil der EuGH in ständiger Rechtsprechung eine unmittelbare Wirkung der Richtlinien nur gegenüber einem Mitgliedsstaat (d.h.: im vertikalen Verhältnis zwischen Marktbürger und Staat), nicht jedoch gegenüber einzelnen natürlichen und juristischen Personen (d.h.: im horizontalen Verhältnis zwischen Privatrechtssubjekten) anerkennt.[36] Statt dessen verlangt der EuGH die richtlinienkonforme Auslegung des nationalen Rechts.

Iversen akzeptiert – allerdings nicht vorbehaltlos – die Rechtsprechung des EuGH.[37] Dementsprechend kritisiert er den Vorschlag von *Jayme* nicht unter diesem Gesichtspunkt. Vielmehr meint er, dass die Anknüpfung gemäss Art. 34 EGBGB zu einer „Internationalisierung der nationalen Rechtsauffassungen" führe

---

[31] E. Jayme, „Haustürgeschäfte deutscher Urlauber in Spanien: Horizontale Wirkungen der EG-Richtlinien und internationales Vertragsrecht", *IPRax* (1990) S. 220ff.; Ch. Langenfeld, „Noch einmal: Die EG-Richtlinie zum Haustürwiderrufsgesetz und deutsches IPR", *IPRax* (1993) S. 155.ff.; so auch Jayme/ Kohler (oben N. 7) (1994) S. 407; kritisch zu dieser Auffassung Brödermann/ Iversen (oben N. 21) S. 429ff. und D. Martiny, „Internationales Vertragsrecht zwischen Rechtsgefälle und Vereinheitlichung", *ZEuP* (1995) S. 67ff. 80f.; „internationalprivatrechtlich für völlig einwandfrei" hält dagegen Kronke die Anwendung des Art. 34 EGBGB (bzw. Art. 7 Abs. 2 EVÜ) für die Durchsetzung des europäischen Verbraucherschutzstandards: H. Kronke, „Electronic Commerce und Europäisches Verbrauchervertrags-IPR – Zur Umsetzung der Fernabsatzrichtlinie", *RIW* (1996) S. 985ff., 992.

[32] Brödermann/ Iversen (oben N. 21) S. 415f.

[33] Brödermann/Iversen, ibid., S. 416f.

[34] Zu Recht kritisch dazu Brödermann/Iversen, ibid., S. 388, 431ff.; Krebber (oben N. 21) S. 148f.

[35] Jayme (oben N. 31) S. 222; vgl. auch Jayme/ Kohler (oben N. 7) (1990) S. 361; Langenfeld (oben N. 31) S. 157.

[36] EuGH 26.2.1986, Rs. 152/84 (Marshall), Slg. 1986, 723ff.; EuGH 12.5.1987, Rs. 372-374/85 (*Oscar Traen ua.*), Slg. 1987, 2153ff.; zur Haustürwiderrufs-Richtlinie: EuGH 14.7.1994 Rs.C-91/92 (*Paola Faccini Dori*), Slg. 1994 I 3325ff.; zur Verbraucherkredit-Richtlinie: EuGH 7.3.1996, Rs. C-192/94 (*El Corte Inglés SA*), Slg. 1996, I 1281ff. In seiner jüngsten Entscheidung beschränkt sich sogar der EuGH auf eine Wiederholung seiner ständigen Rechtsprechung: 4.12.1997, Rs. C-97/96 (*Verband deutscher Daihatshu-Händler e.V.*), Slg. 1997, I. 6843ff. Die Rechtsprechung des EUGH wird zum Teil auch kritisiert: G. Nicolaysen, „Richtlinienwirkung und Gleichbehandlung von Männern und Frauen beim Zugang zum Beruf", *EuR* (1984) S. 380ff. 387ff; ders., „Keine horizontale Wirkung von Richtlinienbestimmungen", *EuR* (1986) S. 370f.; S. Richter, „Die unmittelbare Wirkung von EG-Richtlinien zu Lasten Einzelner", *EuR* (1988) S. 394ff.; zum Problem generell s. I. Klauer, *Die Europäisierung des Privatrechts* (Baden-Baden, Nomos 1998) S. 44ff.

[37] Brödermann/ Iversen (oben N. 21) S. 374ff., 382f.

und für eine Sonderanknüpfung „ein konkreter, auf Privatrechtsverhältnisse bezogener gemeinschaftsrechtlicher Rechtsgrundsatz" fehle. *Iversen* vertritt zu Recht den Standpunkt, dass der Rechtsanwendungsbefehl bei einer mittelbaren horizontalen Richtlinienwirkung nicht aus dem Gemeinschaftsrecht, sondern aus dem nationalen Kollisionsrecht folge und im Unterschied zur unmittelbaren Richtlinienwirkung nicht die Richtlinie selbst, sondern das nationale Umsetzungsrecht angewendet werde.[38] Im übrigen schlägt er einen ähnlichen Weg wie *Jayme,* nämlich den der allgemeinen Vorbehaltsklausel des Art. 6 EGBGB ein. Er kommt zur Folgerung, dass die Anwendung richtlinienwidrigen mitgliedstaatlichen Rechts einen Verstoss gegen Art. 5 (Art. 10 kons. F.) EG-Vertrag, und somit auch gegen den ordre public des Forumstaates darstelle, falls dieser die Richtlinie ordnungsgemäss umgesetzt habe und die Richtlinienbestimmungen hinreichend genau seien.[39] Dieser Auffassung ist grundsätzlich beizupflichten. Sie ist juristisch fundiert und logisch konsequent durchdacht. Sie schafft ausserdem den nötigen Ausgleich zwischen den europarechtlichen und kollisionsrechtlichen Gesichtspunkten.

Bei nicht rechtzeitig erfolgter[40] oder inhaltlich unzureichender Umsetzung lassen sich die Probleme allein mit Hilfe des „Grundsatzes der vollen Richtlinienwirksamkeit" m. E. nicht lösen.[41] Man muss einsehen, dass eine Richtlinie bei hinkender Umsetzung in den betroffenen Mitgliedstaaten und bei länderübergreifenden Sachverhalten nur dann durchsetzbar ist, wenn (mangels einer unmittelbaren) eine „mittelbare horizontale Richtlinienwirkung" anerkannt wird. Dazu ist jedoch die Vorschaltung des (nationalen bzw. vereinheitlichten: EVÜ-) Kollisionsrechts unerlässlich. Eine andere Frage ist, ob bei einer richtlinienkonformen Umsetzung ein „Offenlassen der Rechtswahl" zulässig ist, wenn ein Sachverhalt nur zu Mitgliedsstaaten Verbindung hat und in den Regelungsbereich einer insoweit abschliessende und verbindliche Rechtsvorschriften enthaltenden Richtlinie fällt.[42]

Hier nur kurz zu erwähnen, dass eine ähnliche Konfliktsituation hinsichtlich der Timesharing-Richtlinie entstanden ist, die die Gerichte[43] und auch die Literatur[44] für

---

[38] Brödermann/ Iversen, ibid., S. 430f; vgl. hierzu Kropholler, 56 *RabelZ* (1992) S. 331.

[39] Brödermann/Iversen, ibid., S. 431ff., zusammenfassend S. 447f. Als Ersatzrecht anstelle des Richtlinienwidrigen Sachstatuts schlägt Iversen nicht die Anwendung der Regeln der lex fori, sondern die der Richtlinienbestimmungen vor (S. 448).

[40] Die Produkthaftung-Richtlinie wurde zum Beispiel in das französische Recht mit knapp zehnjähriger Verspätung umgesetzt. S. hierzu M. Leonhard, „Das neue französische Produkthaftungsrecht", *ZVglWiss* (1999) S. 101ff.; zur schlechten Umsetzungsmoral s. generell Klauer (oben N. 36) S. 35.

[41] So aber Krebber (oben N. 21) insb. S. 148f., zusammenfassend S. 160.

[42] Vgl. hierzu Brödermann/ Iversen (oben N. 21) S. 319ff. 330f. mit N. 303; Krebber (oben N. 21) S. 127f.; Roth (oben N. 21) *RabelsZ* S. 639.

[43] BGH 19.3.1997, *JZ* (1997) S. 612ff., zu Recht kritisiert von Jayme/Kohler (oben N. 7) (1997) S. 400. Weitere Nachweise bei Martiny (oben N. 3) S. 112 in N. 28-30. Das Problem wurde inzwischen grösstenteils gelöst, indem die meisten Mitgliedstaaten die Timesharing-Richtlinie in ihr nationales Recht umgesetzt haben. Der Anwendungsbereich der entsprechenden britischen Rechtssvorschriften (Timeshare Regulations 1997, i.K. seit 1.12.1997) sollen durch eine entsprechende *Regulation* auch für

einige Zeit beschäftigt hat. Diese Konfliktsituation ist schon deshalb bemerkenswert, weil diese Richtlinie ihren Geltungsbereich mit einer speziellen Kollisionsnorm abzugrenzen versucht. (Die Timesharing-Richtlinie gehört somit zur zweiten Gruppe in unserer Typisierung.)

b)   Noch schwieriger sind die Probleme, die sich dann einstellen, wenn der länderübergreifende Sachverhalt nicht einen anderen Mitgliedstaat, sondern einen Drittsaat berührt und nach der kollisionsrechtlichen lex fori das Recht dieses Drittstaates zur Anwendung kommen soll. Zur Lösung dieses Problems sind mehrere Methoden vorgeschlagen worden.[45]

Einige Autoren wollen den Anwendungsbereich der Richtlinie aus dem Richtlinienzweck ableiten.[46] Zu diesem Lösungsversuch bieten die am Beginn der jeweiligen Richtlinie aufgeführten Begründungserwägungen einen Anhaltspunkt. Nach ständiger Rechtsprechung des EuGH „können sich jedoch diese Erwägungen darauf beschränken, die Gesamtlage anzugeben, die zum Erlass der Massnahme geführt hat, und die allgemeinen Ziele zu bezeichnen, die mit ihr erreicht werden sollen".[47] Typischerweise verfolgen die hier in Betracht gezogenen Richtlinien das Ziel, die Hindernisse der Grundfreiheiten und die Wettbewerbsverzerrungen abzubauen bzw. den Verbraucherschutz zu verbessern. Wegen ihrer Unbestimmtheit werden die Begründungserwägungen der Richtlinien für das internationale Privatrecht als „narrative Normen" qualifiziert.[48] Das Problem wird noch dadurch erschwert, dass einige Richtlinien mehrere unterschiedliche Ziele verfolgen. Die Timesharing-Richtlinie will zum Beispiel den Verbraucher schützen und ferner

---

die Verträge erstreckt werden, die dem Recht der Insel Man unterliegen: Jayme/ Kohler (oben N. 7) (1998) S. 417ff., 427.

[44] H. Beise, „Time-Sharing-Verträge und die Isle of Man", *RIW* (1995) S. 632f.; E. Jayme, „'Timesharing-Verträge' im Internationalen Privat- und Verfahrensrecht", *IPRax* (1995) S. 234ff.; P. Mankowski, „Timesharingverträge und Internationales Vertragsrecht", *RIW* (1995) S. 364ff.; G. Mäsch, „Die Time-Sharing-Richtlinie", *EuZW* (1995) S. 8ff.; A. Schomerus, „Time-Sharing-Verträge in Spanien im Lichte der EG-Richtlinie über den Erwerb von Teilnutzungsrechten an Immobilien", *NJW* (1995) S. 359ff. Zur deutschen Umsetzung s. G. Mäsch, „Das deutsche Time-Sharing-Recht nach dem neuen Teilzeit-Wohnrechte-Gesetz", *DNotZ* (1997) 180ff.; E. Jayme, „Neues Internationales Privatrecht für Timesharing-Verträge – zum Teilzeit-Wohnrechtegesetz vom 20.12.1996", *IPRax* (1997) S. 233ff., K. Otte, „Anwendbares Recht bei grenzüberschreitendem Timesharing", 62 *RabelsZ* (1998) S. 405ff.

[45] S. dazu ausführlich von Hoffmann (oben N. 21) S. 49ff.

[46] So Basedow (oben N. 21) S. 32ff.; mit der Betonung eines „Inlandsbezuges" P. Limmer, in: Reithmann/ Martiny, *Internationales Vertragsrecht*, 5. Auflage (Köln, O. Schmidt 1996) RdNr. 398; wegen der „Durchsetzung des Gemeinschaftsrechts" Krebber (oben N. 21) S. 144ff., 149f., auch er kritisiert jedoch die zufällige Lösungen in den Richtlinien: S. 150ff.; zu Recht vorsichtig und kritisch zu einem alleine aus dem Richtlinienzweck ausgehenden Lösungsansatz Roth (oben N. 21) *RabelsZ* S. 668.

[47] Grabitz/ Hilf, *Kommentar zur EU* [Loseblatt] (München, Beck 1998) Art 190, Rn. 5 mit m.N.

[48] Jayme/Kohler (oben N. 7) (1995) S. 343ff., 344 mit N. 22. Vgl. auch generell E. Jayme, *Narrative Normen im Internationalen Privat-, und Verfahrensrecht* (Tübingen, Mohr 1993) 44 S.

gleiche Wettbewerbsbedingungen im Binnenmarkt sichern.

Man kann den internationalen Anwendungsbereich aber auch mit Hilfe der An-knüpfungskriterien des Art. 5 EVÜ bestimmen.[49] Auch diese Lösungsrichtung zeigt jedoch einen Mangel insoweit auf, als der Art. 5 EVÜ selbst einige wenige Schutz-lücken enthält.[50]

Noch weniger überzeugt der dritte Vorschlag, bei fehlender Bestimmung des räumlich-persönlichen Anwendungsbereichs diese Lücke durch analoge Anwen-dung von in anderen verbraucherrechtlichen Richtlinien enthaltenen Kollisionsnor-men zu füllen.[51]

2.3 Drittstaatenklauseln, ihre Umsetzung und ihr Verhältnis zum EVÜ

In die zweite Gruppe werden diejenigen Richtlinien eingeordnet, die zwar ihren räumlich-persönlichen Anwendungsbereich nicht unmittelbar bestimmen, in denen aber eine spezielle Kollisionsnorm die unerwünschten Folgen des sonst anzuwen-denden Rechts verhindert. Unter diese Kategorie fallen die Klausel-, die Timesha-ring-, die Fernabsatz- und die Verbrauchsgüterkauf-Richtlinie sowie die kommen-de FinanzFernabsatz-Richtlinie.

a)   Auf den ersten Blick scheint es so, als hätte man bei der Ausarbeitung der spä-teren verbraucherrechtlichen Richtlinien aus den oben besprochenen Problemen die notwendigen Konsequenzen gezogen. Die in die Richtlinien aufgenommenen Kollisionsnormen haben jedoch in gewisser Hinsicht noch grössere Probleme und deshalb in der Literatur zu Recht heftige Kritik ausgelöst.[52] Die in den verbraucher-schützenden Richtlinien enthaltenen Kollisionsnormen verursachten „Wertungs-widersprüche" mit dem EVÜ, sie führten „zu einer Zersplitterung, die dem Ver-braucher mehr Nachteile als Vorteile bringen werde", durch sie werde die „Einheit des Europäischen Kollisionsrechts unnötigerweise gefährdet",[53] „auf diese Weise werden dem EVÜ kollisionsrechtliche Fragen entzogen, welche an sich in seinen Anwendungsbereich fallen".[54]

---

[49] von Hoffmann (oben N. 21) S. 49ff.; vgl. auch Jayme/ Kohler (oben N. 21) S. 19f., 25f.
[50] S. hierzu Krebber (oben N. 21) S. 151 mit N. 139; sowie E. Jayme, „Klauselrichtlinie und Inter-nationales Privatrecht", in: *FS Trinkner* (Heidelberg, Verlag Recht und Wirtschaft 1995) S. 575ff., 579.

[51] Krebber (oben N. 21) S. 149ff.
[52] S. insbesondere zum Art. 6 Abs. 2 der Klauselrichtlinie und deren Umsetzung: Jayme (oben N. 50) S. 575ff.; Sonnenberger (oben N. 21) S. 389ff.; eine Kritik genereller Art bei Jayme/ Kohler (oben N. 7) (1993) S. 357ff., 359f. und (1994) S. 405ff., 407f.; Martiny (oben N. 3) S. 106ff., ders. (oben N. 21) S. 249ff. Eine eher ambivalente Meinung vertritt Martiny (oben N. 3) S. 128; grundsätzlich beja-hend Basedow (oben N. 23) S. 1926: „Diese Entwicklung ist . . . doch durchaus folgerichtig."
[53] Jayme (oben N. 50) S. 583; Jayme/ Kohler (oben N. 7) (1996) S. 377ff. 378.
[54] Martiny (oben N. 21) S. 249.

Besonders fragwürdig ist in der Tat das Verhältnis zwischen den Richtlinienkollisionsnormen und dem Art. 5 EVÜ. Durch letzteren wird nämlich in der überwiegenden Mehrzahl der Fälle dem Verbraucher, der in einem EG-Land seinen gewöhnlichen Aufenthalt hat, der nötige Schutzstandard gewährleistet.[55] Deshalb wird zum Beispiel über die Kollisionsnorm des Art. 12 Abs. 2 der Fernabsatzrichtlinie zu Recht das schlichte Urteil gesprochen: insgesamt erscheine sie überflüssig und stifte Verwirrung.[56]

b)   Die Zielsetzung solcher Kollisionsnormen sollte sein, den für die Mitgliedsstaaten erreichten Verbraucher-Mindestschutzstandard gegen das von den Parteien gewählte Recht (bzw. in der Timesharing-Richtlinie und im FinanzFernabsatz-Richtlinienvorschlag auch gegen das objektiv anzuwendende Recht) abzusichern.[57]

Zur Verwirklichung dieser Aufgabe zielen die verbraucherrechtlichen Richtlinien auf eine einseitige Kollisionsnorm, die das umgesetzte materielle Recht gegenüber dem gewählten (bzw. sogar auch gegenüber dem objektiv anzuwendenden[58]) Recht eines Drittstaates durchsetzt. So wird den Richtlinienregelungen der Charakter des international zwingenden Rechts im Sinne des Art. 7 Abs. 2 EVÜ verliehen,[59] sofern das Recht des Drittstaates für den Verbraucher nicht vorteilhafter ist als der Umsetzungsakt der lex fori (sog. Günstigkeitsprinzip). Der unilaterale Charakter des Richtlinienkollisionsrechts wird im Schrifttum kritisch betrachtet. In der treffenden Karikatur Basedows werden die „einseitigen und sonst ungewöhnlichen Kollisionsnormen" der Richtlinien als Parvenus „vom Butler (regelmässig einem Lehrbuchautor des IPR) missbilligend in kleinere Nebenräume der herrschaftlichen Villa à la fin de siècle des klassischen IPR" geführt.[60]

c)   Man kann die Funktion der Kollisionsnormen in den verbraucherrechtlichen Richtlinien auch so verstehen, dass durch sie der räumlich-persönliche Anwendungsbereich bestimmt wird. Dann soll aber die Frage gestellt werden: Wie weit erstrecken die Kollisionsnormen den Anwendungsbereich? Typischerweise wird eine EG-Inlandsbeziehung als wichtigste Voraussetzung für das Eingreifen der

---

[55] Anders Krebber (oben N. 21) S. 151 mit N. 139.

[56] Jayme/ Kohler (oben N. 7) (1996) S. 377ff. 378 mit N. 13; i.d.S. auch hinsichtlich des Art. 6 Abs. 2 der Kollisionsrichtlinie: Jayme (oben N. 50) S. 576f. 583; zur Fernabsatz-Richtlinie vgl. noch Kronke (oben N. 31); N. Reich, „Die neue Richtlinie 97/7/EG über den Verbraucherschutz bei Vertragsabschlüssen im Fernabsatz", *EuZW* (1997) S. 581ff.; K. Thorn, „Verbraucherschutz bei Verträgen im Fernabsatz", *IPRax* (1999) S. 1ff.

[57] Vgl. hierzu: Ch. Joerges, „Die Europäisierung des Privatrechts als Rationalisierungsprozess und als Streit der Disziplinen", *ZEuP* (1995) S. 185ff., 195f.; Sonnenberger (oben N. 21) S. 383; Jayme (oben N. 50) S. 577; Krebber (oben N. 21) S. 143; Martiny (oben N. 21) S. 249.

[58] Dazu unten bei Punkt d).

[59] Roth (oben N. 21) *IPRax* S. 169.

[60] *Basedow* (oben N. 21) S. 12.

Richtlinienregeln verlangt[61]. Wie die EG-Inlandsbeziehung zu konkretisieren ist, wird in der Literatur unterschiedlich aufgefasst.[62]

Jayme und *Kohler* vertreten den Standpunkt, bei der Konkretisierung der EG-Beziehung die im EVÜ (Art. 5 Abs. 2) bestimmten objektiven Anküpfungsmerkmale anzuwenden.[63] Dieser Auffassung wird inzwischen in einigen mitgliedsstaatlichen Umsetzungsakten gefolgt (so zum Beispiel die belgische, dänische und schwedische Umsetzung des Art. 6 Abs. 2 der Klauselrichtlinie[64]). *Krebber* dagegen spricht sich für eine autonome Auslegung des „engen Zusammenhangs" aus.[65]

d)   Wie schon erwähnt, unterscheiden sich die in diese Gruppe eingeordneten Richtlinien hinsichtlich ihres Anwendungswillens voneinander. Die Klausel-, die Fernabsatz- sowie die Verbrauchsgüterkauf-Richtlinie[66] dehnen ihren Mindestsschutzstandard nur gegen ein – für den Verbraucher nachteilig wirkendes – gewähltes Recht aus. Dagegen gilt die Schutzregel in der Timesharing-Richtlinie und in dem FinanzFernabsatz-Richtlinienvorschlag auch gegen ein objektiv anzuknüpfendes Recht eines Drittstaates. Die Autoren, die die Timesharing-Verträge als gemischte Verträge, im Regelfall als Dienstleistungsverträge i.S. des Art. 5 EVÜ betrachten, stehen diesem erweiterten Geltungswillen (praktisch „auf Kosten" des Art. 5 Abs. 2 EVÜ) kritisch gegenüber.[67] Art. 5 EVÜ gilt nämlich nur in einer seltenen Fallgruppe nicht, dem Falle des Erwerbs von dinglichen oder schuldrechtlichen Nutzungsrechten an Grundstücken ohne vertraglich vereinbarte Dienstleistungen.

e)   Vielleicht das grösste Problem stellt hinsichtlich dieser Kollisionsnormen ihre uneinheitliche, gar divergierende Umsetzung in den einzelnen Mitgliedsstaaten[68]

---

[61] So Art. 6 Abs. 2 der Klauselrichtlinie, Art. 9 der Timesharing-Richtlinie, Art. 12 Abs. 2 der Fernabsatz-Richtlinie und Art. 7 Abs. 2 der Verbrauchsgüterkauf-Richtlinie (oben N. 18) sowie Art. 11 Abs. 3 des FinanzFernabsatz-Richtlinienvorschlags (oben N. 19).

[62] Zum Problem umfassend W. Brechmann, *Die richtlinienkonforme Auslegung – zugleich ein Beitrag zur Dogmatik der EG-Richtlinie*, (München, Beck 1994); R. Schulze, *Auslegung europäischen Privatrechts und ausgeglichenen Rechts* (Baden-Baden, Nomos 1999).

[63] Jayme/ Kohler (oben N. 21) S. 19f., 25f.; so auch Jayme (oben N. 50) S. 578, 582.

[64] Jayme/Kohler (oben N. 7) (1997) S. 385ff., S. 398 mit N. 128; 1995, S. 343ff., 345.

[65] Krebber (oben N. 21) S. 144ff.; vgl. auch P. Ulmer, „Zur Anpassung des AGB-Gesetzes an die EG-Richtlinie über missbräuchliche Klauseln in Verbraucherverträgen", *EuZW* (1993) S. 337ff., 346. Zur autonomen Auslegung vgl. oben Punkt 2.2).

[66] Nach dem ursprünglichen Vorschlag der letztgenannten Richtlinie sollte der Schutzstandard auch gegen das objektiv anzuknüpfende Vertragsstatut durchgesetzt werden, s. dazu P. Schlechtriem, „Verbraucherkaufverträge – ein neuer Richtlinienentwurf", *JZ* (1997) S. 441ff.; Jayme/ Kohler (oben N. 7) (1997) S. 385ff. 388, 1998 S. 417ff., 428 mit N. 125.

[67] Jayme/ Kohler (oben N. 21) S 29ff.; dies. (oben N. 7) (1994) S. 405ff., 407f.; Krebber (oben N. 21) wertet dagegen positiv – m.E. jedoch zu Unrecht – den ausgedehnten Schutzbereich in der Timesharing-Richtlinie im Vergleich zur Klauselrichtlinie, S. 143f., 151f.; über die Qualifikationsschwierigkeiten Otte (oben N. 44) S. 413ff. Der neue deutsche Referentenentwurf zum Internationalen Verbrauchervertragsrecht (oben N. 73) will die Schutzregeln des Teilzeit-Wohnrechtegesetzes zweifelsfrei durchsetzen.

[68] Die antizipierten Umsetzungen zeigen genauso eine bunte Vielfalt von Variationen auf: Time-

dar. Nicht zuletzt deshalb wird das ganze Richtlinienkollisionsrecht und die Umsetzungsmethode im Schrifttum kritisiert.[69] Es „entstehen mit der unterschiedlichen mitgliedsstaatlichen Umsetzung neue Ungleichheiten, so dass der Vereinheitlichungseffekt des EVÜ wieder teilweise zunichte gemacht wird".[70]

Es ist schwer, sich ein klares Bild darüber zu verschaffen, wo und wie die kollisionsrechtlichen Lösungen in den mitgliedsstaatlichen Umsetzungsakten divergieren. Auch die insgesamt gelungenen Umsetzungen unterscheiden sich voneinander in kleineren, aber nicht unbedeutenden Punkten (so zum Beispiel die Umsetzung der Timesharing-Richtlinie in den Niederlanden bzw. in den drei der EG angehörenden nordischen Staaten[71]).

Auf der anderen Seite muss man jedoch das legitime Bestreben nach möglicher Bewahrung des inneren Systems des nationalen Rechts und nach Ausgleich der Divergenzen innerhalb des Richtlinienkollisionsrechts in den (mitgliedsstaatlichen oder autonomen) Umsetzungsakten anerkennen. So ist es vielleicht nicht unbedingt vorzuwerfen, wenn in einem Umsetzungsakt die Übernahme der Richtlinienkollisionsnorm abgewartet wird,[72] um später eine besser durchdachte, abstraktere Lösung zu finden. Ein treffendes Beispiel für eine „zweistufige" Umsetzung (eine „Korrektur im zweiten Schritt") liefert der jüngste deutsche Referentenentwurf zum internationalen Verbrauchervertrag.[73] Das neue Gesetz sieht (neben der Umsetzung der Fernabsatzrichtlinie und anderer Fragen des Verbraucherrechts) in einem Art. 29a EGBGB eine umfassende Norm über „Verbraucherschutz für Sondergebiete" vor. Die neue Norm soll das besondere internationale Verbrauchervertragsrecht regeln und den räumlichen Anwendungsbereich des AGBG, FernabsatzG, FernunterrichtsG sowie des Teilzeit-WohnrechteG bestimmen. Gleichzeitig sollen die speziellen Kollisionsnormen der § 12 AGBG und § 8 Teilzeit-WohnrechteG aufgehoben werden.

Manche Umsetzungen stören die gewünschte Rechtsangleichung gerade dadurch, dass sie – zum Beispiel bei der Bestimmung des räumlich-persönlichen Anwendungsbereichs des Umsetzungsaktes – über die Richtlinie hinausgehen (so z.B.

---

sharing-Gesetz in Norwegen (s. dazu Jayme/ Kohler (oben N. 7) (1998) S. 417ff., 426 mit N. 109), polnischer Umsetzungsgesetzentwurf der Klauselrichtlinie (s. dazu Jayme/ Geckler (oben N. 8) S. 66).

[69] Roth (oben N. 21) *IPRax*, S. 168ff.; Basedow (oben N. 21) S. 12; ders. (oben N. 23) S. 1926; Jayme/ Kohler (oben N. 7) (1995) S. 343ff. 343, (1997) S. 385ff., 388f.; Sonnenberger (oben N. 21) S. 386.

[70] Martiny (oben N. 3) S. 109, im Endergebnis zeigt er jedoch mehr Verständnis für das Richtlinienkollisionsrecht: a.a.O., S. 128f.

[71] Jayme/ Kohler (oben N. 7) (1997) S. 385ff., 399: N. 135, (1998) S. 417ff., 427. Die nationalen Umsetzungsmassnahmen werden in *ABl.(EG)* [1998] C 354/94 aufgezählt.

[72] So hat zum Beispiel die 1997 erfolgte luxemburgische Umsetzung den Art. 6 Abs. 2 der Klauselrichtlinie nicht umgesetzt (Jayme/ Kohler [oben N. 7] (1997) S. 385ff., 398 mit N. 127) oder die irische Umsetzung der Timesharing-Richtlinie spart die Kollisionsnorm aus (Jayme/ Kohler [oben N. 7] (1997) S. 385ff. 389 mit N. 42).

[73] Referentenentwurf zum internationalen Verbrauchervertragsrecht (Stand: 31.5.1999), *IPRax* (1999) Heft 4, S. VII.

das deutsche TzWrG [§ 8] und das AGBG [§ 12] sowie das österreichische TNG und die britischen Timeshare Regulations 1997[74] und das französische Gesetz No. 98-566 vom 8.7.1998 [Art. L. 121-74, 121-75] zur Umsetzung der Timesharing-Richtlinie). Bemerkenswert ist auch der griechische Umsetzungsakt der Klausel-richtlinie, welcher auch dann anwendbar ist, wenn das objektive Vertragsstatut nach dem Art. 5 Abs. 3 des EVÜ nicht griechisches Recht ist. Das griechische Ge-setz ist dann anwendbar, wenn der Abschluss- oder der Erfüllungsort des Vertrages in Griechenland liegt.[75]

Die unterschiedlichen Auslegungsmerkmale des „engen Zusammenhangs" wir-ken auch gegen die Rechtsangleichung. Die Unterschiede bestehen schon darin, ob der Umsetzungsakt selbst die Auslgegungsmerkmale bestimmt oder aber diese den Gerichten überlässt. Einige Mitgliedsstaaten haben etwa bei der Klauselrichtlinie die Beziehung zur EG in dem Umsetzungsakt konkretisiert,[76] andere wie Grossbri-tannien haben dagegen diese Aufgabe dem Richter überlassen.[77] Die irische Umset-zung hat den Bezug zur EG ganz ausser acht gelassen.[78] Der Einfallsreichtum der Umsetzungen ist damit noch gar nicht in seiner ganzen Vielfalt dargestellt worden. Im französischen Umsetzungsgesetz[79] der Klauselrichtlinie soll die territoriale Ver-knüpfung nicht durch den gewöhnlichen Aufenthalt, sondern durch den Wohnsitz[80] des Verbrauchers oder des Nichtgewerbetreibenden hergestellt werden. Im deut-schen AGBG (§ 12 n. F.) wird das Günstigkeitsprinzip geopfert usw. Es wird auch sonst oft vergessen, dass die Richtlinien die bessere Stellung des Verbrauchers nach dem gewählten Recht nicht antasten wollen.

2.4 Misslungene Bestimmung des räumlich-persönlichen Anwendungsbereichs

Die bis jetzt einzige Verbraucherrichtlinie, die ihren räumlich-persönlichen An-wendungsbereich abgrenzen will, ist die Pauschalreise-Richtlinie. In ihrem zweck-bestimmenden Art. 1 wird gesagt, dass die Angleichung der Rechtsvorschriften hinsichtlich derjenigen Pauschalreisen bezweckt wird, „die in der Gemeinschaft

---

[74] Jayme/ Kohler (oben N. 7) (1997) S. 385ff. 389f. mit N. 46 und S. 399 mit N. 136, 137.

[75] Jayme/ Kohler, ibid. (1995) S. 343ff., 345 mit N. 28.; Martiny (oben N. 3) S. 110.

[76] S. Beispiele oben bei N. 64. Zur Umsetzung der Klauselrichtlinie in Italien: Jayme/ Kohler (oben N. 7) (1997) S. 385ff. 398 mit N. 131; zum niederländischen Umsetzungsgesetz der Timesharing-Richtlinie: ibid., S. 399: N. 135.

[77] Jayme/ Kohler (obn N. 7) (1995) S. 343ff., 345 mit N. 27.

[78] Ibid., mit N. 34.

[79] P. Brock, *Der Schutz der Verbraucher vor missbräuchlichen Klauseln im französischen Recht*, (Berlin, Verlag Spitz 1998) insb. S. 48ff. 103ff., 116ff., 175ff., 211ff.; Sonnenberger (oben N. 21) S. 386, 388, 398.

[80] Jayme/ Kohler (oben N. 7) (1995) S. 343ff., 345 mit N. 29; so im übrigen auch eine Richtlinie selbst: Art. 11 Abs. 3 FinanzFernabsatz-Richtlinienvorschlag (oben N. 19).

verkauft oder zum Kauf angeboten werden". Vergleicht man diese Regelung mit der des Art. 5 Abs. 2 EVÜ, werden die Unterschiede zwischen den beiden Regelungen deutlich. Der Art. 5 Abs.2 EVÜ, welcher im übrigen die Pauschalreiseverträge ausdrücklich erfasst,[81] differenziert nach den einzelnen Handlungen der Vertragsparteien.[82] Die Richtlinie dagegen stellt auf den Verkauf bzw. das „Kaufangebot" ab und lässt auch die Frage offen, nach welchem Recht das Vorliegen eines Verkaufs bzw. eines „Kaufangebots" geprüft und festgestellt werden soll.[83]

Der Vergleich zeigt also auf den ersten Blick, dass die Bestimmung des internationalen Anwendungsbereichs auch in der Pauschalreise-Richtlinie misslungen ist. Dem Art. 5 Abs. 2 EVÜ werden mit der internationalprivatrechtlichen Regelung des Art. 1 der Pauschalreise-Richtlinie Probleme entzogen, ohne eine einwandfreie Lösung anzubieten. Hinzu kommen die nicht immer glücklichen nationalen Umsetzungen, wie z.B. die im § 651 k Abs. 5 BGB. Letztere stellt auf die Belegenheit der Hauptniederlassung des Reiseveranstalters ab.

2.5   Zusammenfassung

Wollen wir die bisherige Bewertung zusammenfassen und die Funktion des Kollisionsrechts in den Verbraucherrichtlinien und in deren Umsetzungen in die nationalen Rechte auf eine einfache Formel bringen, so kann folgendes festgestellt werden:

–   Die Bestimmung des räumlich-persönlichen Anwendungsbereichs ist uneinheitlich, lückenhaft, dogmatisch undurchdacht und vor allem nicht auf die Regelung des Art. 5 EVÜ abgestimmt.
–   Die Richtlinienkollisionsnormen sind ausserdem überflüssig, denn in Art. 5 EVÜ werden die Verbraucherverträge einbezogen und im einzelnen wesentlich differenzierter geregelt. Auch für die Beseitigung der wenigen Schutzlücken in Art. 5 EVÜ bietet die Änderung des Schuldvertragsübereinkommens eine bessere Möglichkeit[84] als die fragmentarischen Kollisionsnormen in den einzelnen Richtlinien.[85]
–   Bei den divergierenden Umsetzungen ist der Drang zum „geringstmöglichen Eingriff"[86] in das eigene System verständlich. Dennoch lassen sich leider oft auch

---

[81]   So auch Krebber (oben N. 21) S. 142.
[82]   Soergel/ von Hoffmann, *BGB mit Einführungsgesetz und Nebengesetzen, Band 10, Einführungsgesetz*, 12. Aufl. (Stuttgart/Berlin/Köln, Kohlhammer 1996) Art. 29, RdNr. 16ff.
[83]   So auch Krebber (oben N. 21) S. 142f.
[84]   So auch Jayme (oben N. 50) S. 580.
[85]   Statt den Sondervorschriften empfiehlt auch Basedow (oben N. 23, S. 1926) „die Absicherung des Gemeinschaftsrecht gegenüber dem Recht von Drittsaaten im Bereich des Vertragsrechts in das EVÜ aufzunehmen". In diesem Sinne hinsichtlich der Umsetzung des Art. 6 Abs. 2 Klauselrichtlinie auch Sonnenberger (oben N. 21) S. 391.
[86]   So Ulmer/ Brandner/ Hensen, *AGB-Gesetz*, 8. Auflage (Köln 1997) im Vorwort, S. V.

die nötigen IPR-Kenntnisse vermissen.[87]
– Alles in allem: Die mitgliedsstaalichen Erfahrungen fördern nicht die freiwillige Umsetzung der Richtlinienkollisionsnormen.[88]

3. DIE ANTIZIPIERTE UMSETZUNG

3.1 Allgemeine Charakteristika der antizipierten Umsetzung

Während die Richtlinie hinsichtlich des zu erreichenden Ziels für jeden Mitgliedsstaat verbindlich ist und den innerstaatlichen Stellen nur die Wahl der Form und der Mittel der Umsetzung überlässt,[89] besteht eine ähnliche rechtliche Bindung, eine vollständige Richtlinienwirksamkeit, bei einer freiwilligen Umsetzung nicht.

Auch die EU-Abkommen der assoziierten Mittel- und osteuropäischen Staaten mit den Europäischen Gemeinschaften und ihren Mitgliedsstaaten[90] schreiben nur „die Angleichung der bestehenden und künftigen Rechtsvorschriften" der assoziierten Staaten an das Gemeinschaftsrecht vor. Der assoziierte Staat hat demnach dafür zu sorgen, dass „die künftigen Rechtsvorschriften möglichst weitgehend mit dem Gemeinschaftsrecht vereinbar sind". Das Europa-Abkommen präzisiert nicht, ob es um die Angleichung nur an das sekundäre oder aber auch an das primäre Gemeinschaftsrecht geht. Die Aufzählung der anzugleichenden Rechtsgebiete (u.a. geistiges Eigentum, Wettbewerbsregeln) scheint jedoch darauf hinzudeuten, dass auch das Primärrecht gemeint ist.

Es fehlt also eine echte Umsetzungspflicht. Auch eine Sperrwirkung[91] nach dem Erlass der Richtlinien i.S. des EG-Vertrages kann wohl nicht angenommen werden. Für den zur Rechtsangleichung verpflichteten Staat ist jedoch, wie schon erwähnt, durch das EU-Abkommen vorgeschrieben, nur mit den Richtlinien vereinbare Rechtsvorschriften zu erlassen. Das Mass und die Tiefe der Angleichung sind im EU-Abkommen nicht näher präzisiert worden. Noch weniger entstehen durch die autonome Übernahme besondere Anforderungen an eine einheitliche Anwendung[92]

---

[87] Dabei muss man mit Sonnenberger (oben N. 21, S. 384) anerkennen, dass „entscheidende Würfel" schon mit der Verabschiedung der Richtlinie gefallen sind.
[88] Vgl. dazu den Referentenentwurf eines Art. 29a EGBGB zum internationalen Verbrauchervertragsrecht, *IPRax* (1999) Heft 4, S. VII; A. Staudinger, „Art. 29a EGBGB des Referentenentwurfs zum Fernabsatzgesetz", *IPRax* (1999) S. 414.ff.; Freitag/ Leible, „Von den Schwierigkeiten der Umsetzung kollisionsrechtlicher Richtlinienbestimmungen", *ZIP* (1999) S. 1296ff.; Der Aufsatz wurde Ende 1999 abgeschlossen. Das deutsche Fernabsatzgesetz (Bundesgesetzblatt Teil I. Nr. 28/2000) mit dem neuen Paragraph 29a EGBGB konnte nicht mehr berücksichtigt werden. S. dazu: Wagner, *IPRax* (2000) S. 249ff.
[89] Art. 249 Abs. 3 EGV kons.f., ex-Art. 189 Abs. 3.
[90] Oben N. 10.
[91] M. Hilf, „Die Richtlinie der EG – ohne Richtung, ohne Linie?" *EuR* (1993) S. 1ff., 7.
[92] G. Nicolaysen, *Europarecht*, Bd. I (Baden-Baden, Nomos 1991) S. 39ff.

des angeglichenen Rechts. Die Richtlinie stellt doch Massstab für die Auslegung[93] auch des freiwillig umgesetzten Rechts dar. Auslegungsdifferenzen sind nicht auszuschliessen, weil die Auslegungszuständigkeit des EuGH fehlt.

Man kann auch hier die Frage stellen, ob ein „Offenlassen der Rechtswahl" möglich bzw. zulässig ist, wenn das zu entscheidende Problem durch eine Richtlinie verbindlich beantwortet wird und der Sachverhalt (neben Mitgliedsstaaten) auch einen Drittstaat berührt, welcher die Richtlinie in sein nationales Recht autonom übernommen hat.[94] Diese Frage wird im Schrifttum vor allem deswegen verneint, weil eine einheitliche Auslegung nicht gesichert sei. Drittsaaten seien an die Rechtsprechung des EuGH nicht gebunden und selbst wenn ein Drittsaat eine Richtlinie wörtlich übernehme und seine Gerichte der Auslegung des EuGH folgten, fehle dem Drittsaat die Möglichkeit, Auslegungsfragen dem Gerichtshof für eine Vorabentscheidung vorzulegen. Deshalb solle aus Gründen der Rechtssicherheit die Frage nach dem anzuwendenden Recht nicht offengelassen werden.[95] Dieser Meinung ist zuzustimmen.

3.2 Die Umsetzung der materiellrechtlichen Regeln der Verbraucherrichtlinien in das ungarische Recht

Betrachtet man die ungarische Gesetzgebung der letzten Jahre, so kann man feststellen, dass eine Angleichung an die Verbraucherrichtlinien sowohl bei den neuen Vorschriften als auch bei den Änderungen alter Gesetze (wie z.B. bei der Novellierung des ZGB) herbeigeführt worden ist. Was die Form und die Mittel der Umsetzung der verbraucherrechtlichen Richtlinien betrifft, findet man im ungarischen Privatrecht unterschiedliche Lösungsvarianten.[96] Bei neuen Rechtsinstitutionen wie Produkthaftung, Timesharing, Fernabsatz von Produkten und Dienstleistungen hat der Gesetzgeber die Methode der (beinahe) wörtlichen Übernahme des Richtlinientextes gewählt. Dies hat (in manchen Fällen unnötigerweise) dazu geführt, dass die Umsetzung in der Form eines Sondergesetzes erfolgt und nicht einmal versucht worden ist, die Richtlinienregelung in das bestehende System des Privatrechts harmonisch einzugliedern. Diese Methode ist verständlich beim Timesharingvertrag, wo die Komplexität bzw. die Typenverschiedenheit der Teilzeit-Wohnrechte einen organischen Einbau in das ZGB für sehr schwierig macht. Das Timesharing-Recht kann dinglich, treuhandschaftlich, gesellschaftsrechtlich oder aber schuldrechtlich aufgefasst und dementsprechend unterschiedlich geregelt werden. Seine privat-

---

[93] Vgl. Brechmann (oben N. 62) S. 256ff.; U. Ehricke, „Die Richtlinienkonforme und gemeinschaftskonforme Auslegung nationalen Rechts", *RabelsZ* (1995) 598ff.

[94] Zu diesem Problem zwischen Mitgliedsstaaten s. oben bei N. 42.

[95] Brödermann/ Iversen (oben N. 21) S. 333f.

[96] S. oben N. 11-17.

rechtliche Problematik ist so vielfältig,[97] dass die separate Regelung[98] vielleicht als die beste Lösung betrachtet werden kann. Anders ist die Lage bei der Produkthaftung. Obwohl die Produkthaftung-Richtlinie auch in den meisten EG-Staaten durch spezielle Gesetze umgesetzt worden ist,[99] hätte man wohl diese Richtlinie in das Deliktsrecht des ungarischen ZGB thematisch einbauen können. Ähnlich wäre auch die Umsetzung der Fernabsatz-Richtlinie[100] in das allgemeine Vertragsrecht des ZGB wohl denkbar. Die Übernahme der Pauschalreise-Richtlinie hätte bestimmt nicht vom ZGB losgelöst, wie es geschah,[101] sondern unter der Regelung über den Reisevertrag (§ 415f ZGB), erfolgen müssen.[102] Die Klausel-Richtlinie ist insofern richtig umgesetzt worden. Ihre Regelungen sind in die Vorschriften des ZGB über die Allgemeinen Geschäftsbedingungen (§§ 205, 207 und 209 ff.) integriert worden.[103] Die Verbraucherkredit-Richtlinie ist durch zwei verschiedene Gesetze[104] (Verbraucherschutzgesetz bzw. Kreditinstitutsgesetz) in das ungarische Recht übernommen worden, genauso wie die Haustürwiderrufs-Richtlinie.[105]

Diese Vielfalt, alleine in struktureller Hinsicht, hat mehrere Gründe. Sie ist nur zum Teil damit zu erklären, dass der Gesetzgeber zum „geringstmöglichen Eingriff"[106] in das eigene Recht geneigt oder bestrebt ist, die innere Harmonie seine Rechtsordnung zu wahren. Leider spielt auch die Fristwahrung bei den Umsetzungen eine gegen die Qualität wirkende Rolle.

Ungeachtet dieser kritischen Bemerkungen kann man insgesamt doch sagen, dass durch die autonome Übernahme der materiellen Regeln der Verbraucherrichtlinien ein „mit der Richtlinie vereinbares"[107] Recht entstanden ist.

3.3 Autonome Übernahme des Art. 5 EVÜ in das ungarische Recht

Im Hinblick auf die mitgliedsstaatlichen Erfahrungen ist es nicht verwunderlich, dass der Gesetzgeber sich nicht beeilt, bei antizipierter Umsetzung einer Richtlinie deren Kollisionsnorm zu übernehmen.[108] So ist es auch bei der Angleichung an die

---

[97] Vgl. Mäsch (oben N. 44) *DNotZ*; Otte (oben N. 44) S. 408ff.

[98] S. oben N. 16.

[99] Zu Ungarn s. N. 11. Die Produkthaftung ist – als ein spezieller Fall der Haftung für gefährliche Stoffe – in das niederländische BGB (Artt. 6: 185ff.) aufgenommen worden.

[100] S. oben N. 17.

[101] S. oben N. 14.

[102] So in Art. 651a BGB und Artt. 7: 500ff. niederländisches BGB.

[103] S. oben N. 15.

[104] S. oben N. 13.

[105] S. oben N. 12.

[106] Vgl. oben N. 86.

[107] So Art. 67 EU-Abkommen Ungarns (oben N. 9).

[108] Beispiele bei Jayme/ Kohler (oben N. 7) (1996) S. 377ff., S. 378 mit N. 14; Jayme/Geckler (oben N. 8); ein Gegenbespiel: norwegische Timesharing-Gesetz (Jayme/ Kohler [oben N. 7] (1998) S. 417ff., 426 mit N. 109).

Verbraucher-Richtlinie in Ungarn geschehen. Keine von den Richtlinienkollisionsnormen wurde übernommen. Stattdessen wurde bei der Umsetzung der Klausel-
Richtlinie[109] das IPR-Gesetz (fortan: IPRG) [110] modifiziert.[111] Eine Änderung war
ohnehin notwendig, weil das ungarische IPRG in seiner früheren Fassung keine besonderen Bestimmungen für Verbraucherverträge enthielt. Mit den neuen Regelungen wurde, wie im Art. 5 EVÜ, eine über die Klausel-Richtlinie hinausgehende
Möglichkeit einer Sonderanknüpfung für Verbraucherverträge eröffnet.

a) Der neu aufgenommene § 28/A Abs. 1 IPRG führt für Verbraucherverträge ein
neues objektives Vertragsstatut ein. Dieser hat – anders als Art. 6 Abs. 2 der Klausel-Richtlinie – nicht den Vertrag, sondern – wie Art. 5 EVÜ – die rechtlich relevanten Vorgänge der Vertragsbegründung im Auge:

„*Für Verbraucherverträge ist das Recht des Staates massgebend, in dem der Verbraucher seinen Wohnsitz oder gewöhnlichen Aufenthalt hat, vorausgesetzt, dass*

— *dem Vertragsabschluss ein ausdrückliches Angebot oder eine Werbung in diesem
Staat vorausgegangen ist, und wenn der Verbraucher in diesem Staat die zum Abschluss
des Vertrages erforderlichen Rechtshandlungen vorgenommen hat oder*
— *der Vertragspartner des Verbrauchers oder sein Vertreter die Bestellung des
Verbrauchers in diesem Staat entgegengenommen hat oder*
— *der Verkäufer, mit dem Ziel den Verbraucher zum Kaufvertragsabschluss zu
veranlassen, eine Reise veranstaltet hat, und der Verbraucher von diesem Staat in einen
anderen gereist ist und dort den Vertrag geschlossen oder eine darauf gerichtete
Willenserklärung abgegeben hat.*“[112]

Abgesehen von einigen kleineren Abweichungen, eher sprachlicher als inhaltlicher
Art in Punkt c), ist diese Norm bis auf einen Punkt mit Art. 5 Abs. 3 EVÜ identisch.
Der einzige inhaltliche Unterschied zum EVÜ besteht in der Bestimmung des Attri-
buts im Anküpfungsmoment. Aus unerklärlichen Gründen wird „alternativ" auf
den Wohnsitz bzw. den gewöhnlichen Aufenthalt des Verbrauchers angeknüpft.

Um Qualifikationsprobleme möglichst gering zu halten, wird im § 28/A Abs. 2
IPRG die Definition des Verbrauchervertrages weitgehend an Art. 5 Abs. 1 EVÜ
abgestimmt. Im Sinne des Gesetzes „*werden Verträge über die Lieferung beweglicher Sachen oder Erbringung von Dienstleistungen sowie Verträge zur Finanzierung eines solchen Geschäfts dann als Verbrauchervertrag betrachtet, wenn die*

[109] S. oben N. 15.
[110] Gesetzesverordnung Nr. 13/1979 über das Internationale Privatrecht, deutsche Übersetzung des
gültigen Textes v. E. Schweisguth, in: Brunner/ Schmid/ Westen (oben N. 11) Bd. I. 3 Ungarn, Dok. X.
[111] Gesetz Nr. CXLIX/1997 (oben N. 15).
[112] Übersetzung des Verfassers.

eine Vertragspartei ausserhalb ihrer gewerblichen oder beruflichen Tätigkeit handelt".[113]

Die Ausnahmevorschriften des Art. 5 Abs. 4 und 5 wurden in Abs. 3 des § 28/A IPRG aufgenommen. Die Regelungen über die Verbraucherverträge gelten demnach „*nicht für Personenbeförderungsverträge*[114] sowie für Verträge über die Erbringung von Dienstleistungen, wenn die dem Verbraucher geschuldeten Dienstleistungen ausschliesslich *in einem anderen als in dem Staat erbracht werden müssen, in dem der Verbraucher seinen Wohnsitz oder gewöhnlichen Aufenthalt hat.*[115] *Die Verbraucherschutzregeln gelten jedoch für Reiseverträge, die für einen Pauschalpreis kombinierte Beförderungs- und Unterbringungsleistungen vorsehen*".

Abgesehen von den erwähnten Fehlern, die offensichtlich auf mangelnde Kenntnisse des Kollisionsrechts zurückzuführen sind, kann man das neu geschaffene objektive Vertragsstatut für Verbraucherverträge als gelungen betrachten. Es schaffte für solche Verträge mit der Übernahme des Art. 5 EVÜ eine breit akzeptierte Sonderanküpfungsmöglichkeit, welche im ungarischen Internationalen Privatrecht ohnehin gefehlt hat. Zugleich blieben die Probleme aus, die die Umsetzung fragmentarischer Lösungsversuche der Richtlinienkollisionsnormen mit sich gebracht hätte.

b)   Die Angleichung an das EVÜ ist hinsichtlich der Rechtswahl bei Verbraucherverträgen leider misslungen.[116] Es wird bestimmt, dass „*in dem Fall, in dem die Parteien für ihren Vertrag ausländisches Recht gewählt haben, anstelle dieses Rechts die Regeln des ungarischen Verbrauchervertragsrechts anzuwenden sind, falls das IPRG – in Ermangelung einer Rechtswahl – zur Anwendung des ungarischen Rechts führte*". Richtig ist, dass hierbei zur Feststellung des engen Zusammenhangs dieselben Kriterien gewählt worden sind, wie im objektiven Vertragsstatut selbst, wie also auch durch Art. 5 EVÜ. Die in der einseitigen Kollisionsnorm[117] vorgegebene Lösung ist jedoch aus zweierlei Gründen zu kritisieren. Erstens wird das Günstigkeitsprinzip nicht befolgt. Stattdessen wird das ungarische Recht und der darin enthaltene Schutzstandard auf jeden Fall durchgesetzt, wenn der Verbraucher

---

[113]   Eine andere Lösung hat das finnische Gesetz aus 1988 (vor dem Inkrafttreten des EVÜ in Finnland) bei antizipierter Angleichung an das Gemeinschaftskollisionsrecht favorisiert. Es hat das Problem durch eine Qualifikationsverweisung auf das Recht des gewöhnlichen Aufenthaltes des Verbrauchers gelöst (Section 10 Abs. 1 des Gesetzes v. 27. 5. 1988/Nr. 466 über das auf internationale Verträge anwendbare Recht).

[114]   Das IPRG spricht – irrtümlich – auch über „Frachtverträge".

[115]   Die „alternative" Anknüpfung an den Wohnsitz des Verbrauchers wiederholt sich als Irrtum.

[116]   S. den durch das Gesetz CXLIX/1997 neu eingefügte § 5/C in der GVO Nr. 2/1978 (oben N. 15).

[117]   Kritisch auch L. Burián, „A fogyasztóvédelem az új nemzetközi magánjogi szerzÅdési szabályok tükrében" (Verbraucherschutz im Spiegel der neuen Regelungen des Vertragskollisionsrechts, ungar.) *Magyar Jog* (1999) S. 16ff., 22.

seinen Wohnsitz oder gewöhnlichen Aufenthalt in Ungarn hat. Zweitens wird dieses Schutzniveau dem Verbraucher nur dann gewährt, wenn das objektive Vertragsstatut im IPRG zur Anwendung des ungarischen Rechts führte. Dieser Schutz ist jedoch dann nicht gesichert, wenn zwar von den Parteien ein ausländisches Recht mit niedrigerem Schutzstandard gewählt wird, es aber durch das objektive Vertragsstatut zur Anwendung eines ausländischen Rechts käme.

SUMMARY

AUTONOMOUS IMPLEMENTATION OF EC CONSUMER LAW DIRECTIVES AND PRIVATE INTERNATIONAL LAW

The EC has built up a considerable body of consumer protection law. The primary legislative tool chosen to integrate the consumer laws of the Member States has been the Directive. Directives are intended to give Member States a broad degree of freedom to decide how they achieve the objectives of the harmonised rules. The Consumer Law Directives harmonise mainly the substantive rules but they include also rules concerning the applicable law (*Drittstaatenklauseln*).

This article focuses on the conflict of law issues in the EC Consumer Law Directives and examines various questions which arise concerning their autonomous implementation by non-Member States (e.g. by Hungary).

10 Jahre IPRG unter besonderer Berücksichtigung des internationalen Schuldrechts

Frank Vischer*

1. EINLEITUNG

A. Das Bundesgesetz über das internationale Privatrecht, welches dieses Jahr sein 10jähriges Bestehen feiert, ist das Resultat einer gemeinsamen Anstrengung der damals aktiven IPR-Lehrer. Die Kommission, noch unter Bundesrat Furgler eingesetzt, hat in zahlreichen Sitzungen der Unterkommissionen und des Plenums das Gesetz zusammengeschmiedet. Die lebhaften, intensiven, zuweilen spannungsgeladenen Diskussionen sind uns in bester Erinnerung. Das IPRG ist das Werk der älteren, ja der alten Generation der IPR Lehrer. Fast alle Kommissionsmitglieder sind heute emeritiert, allerdings die meisten noch recht munter und aktiv. Die intensive Beschäftigung mit dem IPR hält offensichtlich jung. Inzwischen sitzt eine neue Generation von IPR-Lehrerinnen und Lehrern auf den Lehrstühlen. Manche sind unsere Schülerinnen und Schüler, haben sich aber von ihren Lehrern glücklicherweise weitgehend emanzipiert. Ihre Bewertung des IPRG interessierte eigentlich viel mehr, als unsere nicht ganz nostalgiefreie Schau.
B. Ausgangspunkt der Revision war die Engelberger Tagung des schweizerischen Juristenvereins im Jahre 1971 mit dem Thema „Das Problem der Kodifikati-

---

* Dr. iur., Professor an der Universität Basel. Vortrag gehalten am 11e Journée des Professeurs de Droit International Privé, Schweizerisches Institut für Rechtsvergleichung, Der Vortragscharakter wurde beibehalten.

J. Basedow et al., eds., Private Law in the International Arena – Liber Amicorum Kurt Siehr
© 2000, T.M.C.Asser Press, The Hague, The Netherlands

on des schweizerischen IPR" und den Referaten von Gerardo Broggini und mir.[1]
Die Engelberger Diskussion war lebhaft und hat vielen nicht spezialisierten Juristen
die Probleme des IPR nähergebracht. Ich war eher Skeptiker gegenüber einer alle
Materien umfassenden IPR Kodifikation, die auch das Schuldrecht einbezieht. Ich
gebe gerne zu, dass ich damals von der „Revolution" des IPR in den USA beeindruckt war, vor allem von den Arbeiten David Cavers, einem Anhänger der von
Roscoe Pound und anderen in den 30-er Jahren gegründeten „school of realists".
Mit Cavers hatte ich später an der Harvard Law School, wo ich als visiting professor weilte, eine enge freundschaftliche Beziehung. In seiner Wohnung habe ich zusammen mit Paul Volken und Arthur von Mehren den ersten Vorentwurf durchdis-
kutiert. Cavers hatte schon 1933 in der Harvard Law Review[2] seinen epochalen
Aufsatz „A Critique of the Choice-of-Law Problem" veröffentlicht und darin ein-
drücklich auf den entscheidenden Punkt hingewiesen: „The court is not idly choosing a law; it is determining a controversy" (S. 189). Der Aufsatz war das Fanal für
die nach dem zweiten Weltkrieg in den 60-er Jahren sich ausweitende umfassende
Auflehnung gegen das dem herkömmlichen System verhaftete Restatement first
von Joseph Beale gegen gesetzlich fixierte ganzseitige Kollisionsnormen und die
klassische Dogmatik des IPR im allgemeinen. Die Namen von Brainerd Currie, Arthur von Mehren, R.A. Leflar u.a. stehen für die Bewegung. Mein lebhaftes Interesse am Geschehen in den USA hat in Engelberg zur Bemerkung meines Freundes
Pierre Lalive geführt, ich sei von den „syrènes d'outre mer" verführt worden.

Im IPRG hat die inzwischen weitgehend erloschene US „Revolution" einige, allerdings doch recht signifikante Spuren hinterlassen, etwa in den Art. 18 und 19 bei
der Behandlung der Eingriffsnormen legis fori und von Drittstaaten oder in der generellen Ausnahmeklausel von Art. 15 IPRG. Auch die Resultat bezogenen Lösungen, die Alternativanknüpfungen, wenn immer ein materiellrechtliches Ergebnis
gefördert werden soll, stehen zumindest in einer gewissen Nähe zum „better law approach". Die „governmental interest weighing"-Methode findet in Art. 19 ihren unmittelbaren Ausdruck. Einmalig dürfte die in Art. 19 Abs. 2 IPRG festgeschriebene
Verpflichtung des Richters auf „eine nach schweizerischen Rechtsauffassung sach-
gerechter Entscheidung" sein. In gewisser Beziehung kann auch die gleichwertige
Behandlung der Zuständigkeitsfrage auf den Einfluss der US-Doktrin und Praxis
zurückgeführt werden, steht doch in den USA bei internationalen Fällen die Zuständigkeitsfrage im Rang eindeutig vor der Frage nach dem anwendbaren Recht. Darauf werde ich zurückkommen.

Im der parlamentarischen Beratung standen vor allem folgende Bedenken im
Vordergrund:

---

[1] *ZSR* (1971 II) S.1ff., 245ff.
[2] 47 *Harv. L. Rev.* (1933) 173.

– Der föderalistische Einwand gegen eine in die Kantonshoheit eingreifende prozessuale Regelung;

– das Bedenken, es werde den Auslandschweizern der Zugang zum Heimatgerichtsstand zu sehr erschwert und bei der Rechtsanwendung das Heimatrechtsprinzip zu stark zu Gunsten des Wohnsitzrechtsprinzips verdrängt;

– die Befürchtung über die Einfalltore von Art. 13 (Anwendung ausländischen öffentlichen Rechts) und Art. 19 würden ungerechtfertigte ausländischen Machtansprüche vor schweizerischen Gerichten durchsetzbar sein.

Die Befürchtungen haben sich nicht bewahrheitet. Das Bedenken, ausländische Staaten würden ihre Machtansprüche über Art. 13 und 19 IPRG durchsetzen, findet in der Bundesgerichtspraxis keine Bestätigung. Im Fall der Banco Nacional de Cuba v. Banco Central de Chile (BGE 118 II 348) hat das Bundesgericht in aller Deutlichkeit festgehalten, dass ausländisches öffentliches Recht, das der Durchsetzung der Machtansprüche des ausländischen Staates und seinen Organisationen dienen soll, keinen Anspruch auf Anwendung in der Schweiz begründe.

Mit der zurückhaltenden Öffnung des schweizerischen Heimatgerichtsstandes, jeweils verbunden mit der Anwendung des schweizerischen Rechts, haben sich die Auslandschweizer offensichtlich abgefunden. Die Ansicht der jüngeren Generation hat Daniel Girsberger zum Ausdruck gebracht: In seiner Rückschau auf 10 Jahre IPRG tadelt er, der Gesetzgeber habe einer übertriebenen Tendenz nachgegeben, den Auslandschweizern den Zugang zu den schweizerischen Gerichten und zum schweizerischen Recht zu eröffnen.[3] Dass im Zivilprozess ein Föderalismus je länger je weniger gerechtfertigt ist, zeigt die Bestrebung nach Einführung einer eidgenössischen Zuständigkeitsordnung. Im internationalen Zuständigkeits- und Anerkennungsrecht steht mit der Ratifikation des Lugano Ue die eidgenössische Rechtshoheit heute ausserhalb jeder Diskussion. Dort, wo das IPRG den kantonalen Gerichten einen eigenständigen Entscheidungsspielraum einräumt, insbesondere in Art. 5 Abs. 3 und Art. 6, zweiter Halbsatz IPRG (Ablehnung der Zuständigkeit bei Gerichtsstandwahl oder vorbehaltloser Einlassung), enthält das IPRG seinem Geist fremde parochiale Elemente. Die Schwierigkeiten der Voraussage, ob das gewählte schweizerische Gericht dann, wenn die Voraussetzungen von Art. 5 Abs. 3 nicht erfüllt sind, seine Zuständigkeit annehmen oder ablehnen wird, sind jedem Rechtsberater bekannt. Da im Bereich des Lugano Ue der Vorbehalt der Ablehnung der Zuständigkeit ohnehin nicht gilt, wäre es Zeit, auf die Möglichkeit der Ablehnung zu verzichten.

---

[3] 10 Jahre IPRG, *SJZ* (1999) S. 95.

2.   DAS GEWANDELTE UMFELD

a.   Seit die Kommission in den siebziger Jahren mit ihrer Arbeit begann, hat sich das rechtliche Umfeld wesentlich verändert. In Europa, aber auch ausserhalb, etwa in Südamerika, hat als Folge des sozialen Wandels eine Rechtangleichung stattgefunden. In fast allen Staaten der Welt sind Eheschliessungshindernisse, etwa das berüchtigte „impedimentum ligaminis", weggefallen. Die grossen Fälle des Bundesgerichts wie etwa Caliaro,[4] Cardo[5] und Paiano[6] oder der Spanienfall des deutschen Bundesverfassungsgerichts[7] gehören endgültig der Vergangenheit an. Eine ähnliche Entwicklung ist etwa im Kindschaftsrecht mit der Gleichstellung des ausserehelich geborenen Kindes festzustellen.

Eine Sonderstellung nimmt nach wie vor der islamische Rechtskreis ein. Mit der weisen Vorherrschaft des Domizilprinzips im IPRG, welches die Tradition des NAG fortgesetzt hat, wird allerdings die Konfrontation mit islamischen Rechtsprinzipien zu einem grossen Teil vermieden. Jedenfalls sind m.W. wenig Fälle bekannt, bei welchen sich die Gerichte im familien- und erbrechtlichen Verhältnissen (hier aufgrund einer professio iuris gemäss Art. 90 Abs. 2 IPRG) mit islamischen Rechtsgrundsätzen auseinandersetzen musste. Auseinandersetzungen mit dem islamischen Rechtskreis oder mit religiös geprägten Rechten im allgemeinen ergeben sich vor allem im Zusammenhang mit der polygamischen Ehe, der Scheidung und der Kindesentführung. Selbst in Staaten, welche die Haager Konvention vom 25. Oktober 1980 über die zivilrechtlichen Aspekte internationaler Kindesentführung ratifiziert haben, können sich Schwierigkeiten ergeben, wenn religiöse Gerichte zu entscheiden haben. Diesfalls setzen sich oft religiös geprägte Anschauungen über die elterliche Gewalt gegenüber dem strikten Rückschaffungsgebot der Konvention durch.[8]

Mit dem Wandel in den sozialen Anschauungen und mit der Rechtsangleichung in den Zivilrechtsstaaten, aber auch im Verhältnis dieser zu dem angelsächsischen und amerikanischen Rechtskreis, verliert die Rechtsanwendungsfrage erheblich an Brisanz und Dramatik. Die Frage der Rechtsanwendung ist meist nicht mehr schicksalentscheidend.

b.   Im Bereich des internationalen Handelsrechts hat sich die Tendenz zur internationalen Schiedsgerichtsbarkeit und damit zur Verdrängung der staatlichen Gerichtsbarkeit verstärkt. Immer deutlicher wird auch das Bestreben der Schiedsgerichte, statt des Umwegs über das Kollisionsrecht, „par voie directe" zu

---

[4]   BGE 80 I 427.
[5]   BGE 94 II 65.
[6]   BGE 102 Ib 1.
[7]   BVerfG 31, 58.
[8]   vgl. Carol S. Bruch, „The Hague Child Abduction Convention: Past Accomplishments, Futures Challenges", *European Journal of Law Reform* 1 (1998/1999) 97ff.

materiellrechtlichen Lösungen zu gelangen. Dabei steht der Rückgriff auf ausserstaatliches Recht im Vordergrund. Als Stichworte seien nur die zunehmende Bedeutung der lex mercatoria und der Unidroit Principles of International Commercial Law genannt. Die Tendenz zum Rückgriff auf allgemeine Rechtsprinzipien hat letztlich ihren Grund darin, dass der echte internationale Handelsvertrag, insbesondere der internationale Kauf, sich nur unter Zuhilfenahme von Fiktionen „nationalisieren" lässt. Für die Bevorzugung materiellrechtlicher Lösung unter Ausschaltung des IPR und der nationalen Rechte zeugt auch der Ratifikationserfolg des Wiener Kaufrechts (CISG), wenn auch festzustellen ist, dass in den internationalen Handelskreisen das einheitliche Kaufrecht noch nicht eigentlich populär geworden ist. Die Globalisierung der Wirtschaft wirkt sich auf die internationalen Handelsverträge, dem Hauptinstrument der internationalen Handelsbeziehungen, aus. Der Rückgriff auf nationales Recht via IPR steht mit der Globalisierungstendenz der Wirtschaft in einem immer stärker werdenden Spannungsfeld. Geblieben allerdings ist das Problem nationaler Eingriffsnormen.

Während im Personen-, Familien- und Erbrecht das IPR seine grundlegende Zuordnungsfunktion behalten dürfte, wird vor allem im internationalen Handelsrecht sichtbar, dass dem IPR nur eine Übergangsfunktion zukommt, und die Zukunft in einheitlich materiellrechtlichen Lösungen liegt. Es ist einzuräumen, dass das IPR besonders im Schuldrecht den von der Wirtschaftswissenschaft geforderten „Systemwettbewerb" begünstigt. Im internationalen Vertragsrecht wird mittels der kollisionsrechtlichen Parteiautonomie das „qualitativ" beste Recht bevorzugt und damit die Staaten zur Optimierung ihrer Rechtsordnungen veranlasst, während in der Meinung der Kritiker das materielle Einheitsrecht tendenziell zur Versteinerung und Nivellierung der Lösungen führt. Der „Wettbewerb der Systeme" mag tatsächlich die „law reform" weltweit begünstigen. Der internationale Handel jedoch bedarf der einfachen und leicht zugänglichen Rechtsgrundlagen sowie der Rechtssicherheit, die der Weg über das IPR nicht gleichermassen wie das Einheitsrecht bieten kann.

3. BEHERRSCHENDE BEDEUTUNG DER ZUSTÄNDIGKEIT UND DER SICHERUNG DER ANERKENNUNG UND VOLLSTRECKUNG AUSLÄNDISCHER URTEILE

a. In den USA steht schon lange die Frage der internationalen Zuständigkeit im Vordergrund. Dem Kollisionsrecht im engeren Sinn kommt eine eher zweitrangige Bedeutung zu. Diese Tendenz zeigt sich auch in Europa zumindest auf dem Gebiet der Zivil- und Handelssachen unter Ausschluss der ZGB-Materien. Die Brüsseler/ Lugano Übereinkommen haben die Zuständigkeitsfrage ganz in den Vordergrund gestellt. Die Nachprüfung der Frage der Rechtsanwendung durch das Erstgericht (unter Vorbehalt der vorfrageweisen Entscheidungen im Gebiet der Handels-fähigkeit, des ehelichen Güterrechts und des Erbrechts[9]) ist im Anerkennungs-verfahren ausdrücklich ausgeschlossen und zeigt, dass der Rechtsanwendung kein primäres Gewicht zukommt. Diese Lösung ist bereits im IPRG enthalten, immer unter dem Vorbehalt der Kontrolle unter dem „ordre public atténué". Das Primat der Zuständigkeitsfrage wird sich verstärken, wenn das epochale Werk der Haager Konferenz über die Zuständigkeit und Anerkennung, das eine mondiale Aus-richtung hat, an der vorgesehenen Konferenz im Oktober 2000 zu einem Erfolg wird, der weltweit Ratifikationen, vor allem durch die USA, einschliesst.

b.　　Für den schweizerischen Gesetzgeber drängt sich mit dem Inkrafttreten der neuen Bundesverfassung eine Revision des IPRG bei aller Zuständigkeits- und An-erkennungsbestimmungen auf, die dem bisher heiligen Grundsatz von Art. 59 alt BV Rechnung tragen. Er war schon bei der Geburt des IPRG allen IPR-Spezialisten klar, dass die einseitige Sicherung des Gerichtsstands am Wohnsitz des Beklagten für die in der Schweiz domizilierten Personen und Gesellschaften bei gleichzeitiger Anerkennung anderer Gerichtsstände, wie etwa des Gerichtsstandes am Erfül-lungs- oder Deliktsort für die im Zeitpunkt der Klageerhebung nicht in der Schweiz domizilierten Beklagten, einen letztlich nicht zu rechtfertigenden Widerspruch be-inhaltet. Sicherlich hätte im damaligen Zeitpunkt eine andere Lösung im Parlament nicht die geringste Chance gehabt. Zuzugeben ist auch, dass gerade im Zeitalter der U.S. Class Action gegen Schweizer Firmen der Einwand der Nichtanerkennung ei-nes Urteils in der Schweiz ein wichtiges Verteidigungsmittel unter dem Gesichts-punkt des forum non conveniens war und ist, ein Einwand, der allerdings in der Re-gel die Kläger und den amerikanischen Richter nicht besonders beeindruckt, wenn immer die beklagten Schweizer Firmen über Guthaben in den USA oder anderswo ausserhalb der Schweiz verfügen.

Die neue Bundesverfassung verankert zwar in Art. 30 die Garantie des Wohn-sitzgerichtsstandes nach wie vor, behält aber im Unterschied zu Art. 59 der alten BV Ausnahmen im Wege der Gesetzgebung und internationaler Übereinkommen ausdrücklich vor. Das IPR ist sicherlich eine Materie, bei der sich eine Ausnahme aufdrängt. Es ist deshalb bei den Gerichtsständen und Anerkennungsregeln der BV 59-Vorbehalt zu beseitigen. Dies drängt sich um so mehr auf, als im Anwendungs-bereich des Lugano-Ue der schweizerische Vorbehalt bezüglich der Nichtanerken-nung der am ausländischen Erfüllungsort ergangenen Urteile wegfällt.

4.　　FEHLLEISTUNGEN IM IPRG?

a.　　Eine umfassende Bewertung des IPRG auch im Blick auf die bisherige Recht-sprechung ergibt ein insgesamt befriedigendes Ergebnis. Die Zahl der Bundesge-

---

[9] Art. 27 N. 4 Lugano Übereinkommen.

richtsentscheide hat seit Inkrafttreten des IPRG markant abgenommen. Dies darf als Zeichen dafür gewertet werden, dass die Rechtssubjekte, die mit IPR-Fragen befasst sind, im Gesetz die notwendigen Antworten und Wegweisungen finden. Der Hauptzweck jedes Gesetzes, Rechtssicherheit in einer Materie zu gewährleisten, scheint erfüllt. Dies ist um so bemerkenswerter im Blick auf die doch recht zahlreichen auslegungsbedürftigen Generalklauseln des Gesetzes. So hat sich z.B. die oft geäusserte Befürchtung, die allgemeine Ausnahmeklausel von Art. 15 IPRG werde zu grosser Unsicherheit führen, nicht erfüllt. Das Bundesgericht[10] ist der Ausnahmeklausel mit grosser, vielleicht zu grosser Zurückhaltung begegnet. Gleiches gilt für den Begriff der Unzumutbarkeit der Klageerhebung am ausländischen Wohnsitz des Beklagten. Ein Beispiel: Im Entscheid BGE 119 II 167, S.171 ging es um Massnahmen im Eheschutzverfahren (Art. 47 I IPRG). Die Begründung für einen Heimatgerichtsstand, eine Klageerhebung in Frankreich sei deshalb unzumutbar sei, weil sie zur Offenlegung von Einkommensteilen führe, die dem französische Fiskus verschwiegen wurden, wurde mit dem Hinweis abgelehnt, dass diesfalls „die Ehegatten damit nur die Konsequenzen ihres eigenen rechtswidrigen Verhaltens zu tragen" hätten.

Das Fehlen einer Bestimmung im allgemeinen Teil des IPRG über die fraus legis war wohl gerechtfertigt. Im Gesellschaftsrecht hat das Bundesgericht aufgrund des klaren Wortlautes von Art. 154 IPRG den Vorbehalt der fiktiven, zum Zwecke der Gesetzesumgehung gewählten Sitzes m.E. zu Recht abgelehnt (BGE 117 II 496). Ob in anderem Zusammenhang der fraus legis-Einwand noch möglich ist, bleibt zumindest zweifelhaft.[11] Im Unterschied zu meinen welschen Kollegen, welche offensichtlich vom Recht des Ursprungslandes der „fraude à la loi" im IPR, vom französischen Recht, beeinflusst sind, habe ich schon immer grösste Bedenken gegen die Einführung des fraus legis Vorbehalts im IPR geäussert.

Zu vielen in der Doktrin strittigen Fragen fehlen bislang Entscheidungen. Dies gilt etwa für den im Laufe der parlamentarischen Beratung verschlimmbesserten Artikel 159 IPRG, der die Haftung bei einer ausländischen Gesellschaft, die in der Schweiz oder von der Schweiz aus geführt wird, regelt.

Nach wie vor nicht völlig geklärt ist der Wortlaut und die Tragweite von Art. 19 IPRG, dessen Genesis besonders umstritten war. Art. 19 regelt bekanntlich die kollisionsrechtliche Beachtung zwingender Normen von Drittstaaten. Ob „offensichtlich überwiegende Interessen einer Partei" rechtliche Anwendungsvoraussetzung sind, wie der deutsche und italienische Text im Unterschied zum Wortlaut des französischen Textes es vorschreiben, ist weiterhin ungeklärt. Einig scheint man sich zu sein, dass das Parteiinteresse dann nicht entscheidend sein darf, wenn die Anwendung erheischende Norm der Rechtsordnung, die weder lex causae noch lex fori ist,

---

[10] vgl. BGE 118 II 80; 121 III 247.

[11] vgl. bejahend B. Dutoit, *Commentaire de la loi fédérale du 18. Dec. 1987*, 2. Aufl. (Basel/Frankfurt a.M. 1997) Art. 154, N 6.

einen ordre public international-Gehalt aufweist. Die Frage allerdings, unter welchen Voraussetzungen die ordre public-Qualität der in Frage stehenden Norm zu bejahen ist, bleibt in manchen Belangen offen. Zu denken ist insbesondere an die kartellrechtlichen Bestimmungen eines Staates und deren internationale Durchsetzung. Das Urteil des Europäischen Gerichtshofes vom 1.06.1999 i.S. *EcoSwiss China Time Ltd. / Benetton International NV*,[12] in welchem den Kartellrechtsbestimmungen der EWG für die Gerichte und Schiedsgerichte der Mitgliedstaaten verbindlich ordre public-Qualität zugesprochen wurde und deren Anwendung durch alle staatlichen Instanzen verlangt wird, und zwar unabhängig davon, ob eine Partei im Prozess sich darauf beruft oder nicht, klärt die Situation für schweizerische Gerichte und Schiedsgerichte m.E. nicht vollständig. Insbesondere stellt sich die Frage, ob die ordre public international-Qualität allen kartellrechtlichen Normen eines Staates zukommt, oder ob, im Sinne der Empfehlung der OECD,[13] nur das Verbot von horizontalen „hard core"-Kartellen (wie etwa Gebietsaufteilungen oder Preisabsprachen)[14] immer, insbesondere auch gegen den Willen der Prozessparteien, zu beachten ist.

Auslegungsschwierigkeit bereitet auch der Ausdruck „Bestimmung eines anderen Rechts, die zwingend angewendet sein will". Können damit alle zwingenden Normen des Drittstaates anstelle oder kumulativ zu den zwingenden Normen der lex causae Berücksichtigung verlangen, oder nur, wie ich meine, sog. Eingriffsnormen?

Folgt man der allgemeinen Tendenz in der Doktrin, so sind alle zwingenden Normen, insbesondere auch solche, die dem Parteischutz dienen, erfasst, selbst wenn die schwächere Partei einen besonderen kollisionsrechtlichen Schutz, wie beim Konsumenten- oder Arbeitsvertrag, geniesst. Damit würde über Art. 19 IPRG und Art. 7 Abs. 1 Römer Ue im internationalen Vertragsrecht eine Sonderanknüpfung aller zwingenden Normen auf Kosten des Vertragsstatuts bewirkt, die sich insbesondere auch gegenüber dem von den Parteien gewählten Recht durchsetzen müsste. Dass damit eine Rechtsunsicherheit grössten Ausmassen verbunden wäre, liegt auf der Hand.

b.   Rückblickend wären einige Entscheide des Gesetzes wohl zu korrigieren. Ich möchte nur zwei Beispiele nennen: Der Hauptfall betrifft den Renvoi. Die Renvoi-Bestimmung von Art. 14 IPRG ist wohl zu eng und schliesst den Einsatz der Rück- und Weiterverweisung zur Erzielung eines angemessenen Resultates aus. Zu denken ist etwa an die Anwendung des Renvois zur Aufrechterhaltung eines Rechtsaktes oder zur Anwendung des Rechts, mit dem die Parteien gerechtfertigter Weise

---

[12] C-126/97 Slg. 1999, I-1103.
[13] Recommendation of the Council concerning effective measures against hard core cartels vom 25.03.1998, C(98)35/FINAL.
[14] Vgl. auch die Vermutungstatbestände in Art. 3 KG.

rechnen durften. Auch ist zu Recht gerügt worden, dass z.B. im Ehegüterrecht, bei Fehlen einer Rechtswahl, eine Weiter- oder Rückverweisung des ausländischen Wohnsitzrechts im Unterschied zur analogen Situation im Erbrecht (Art. 91 Abs. 1 IPRG) nicht berücksichtigt werden darf. An der diesjährigen Session des Institut de droit international in Berlin wurde auf der Grundlage eines Rapports von Prof. Kurt Lipstein (Cambridge, England) eine Resolution verabschiedet, die den undogmatischen Einsatz des Renvoi als „expédient", insbesondere auch zur Herbeiführung eines als wünschbar erachteten Resultates fordert. Ob ein solcher Einsatz des Renvoi als „expédient" über die allgemeine Ausnahmeklausel von Art. 15 IPRG erfolgen kann, ist umstritten. M.E. sollte trotz des strikten Wortlautes von Art. 15 ein solcher Einbezug nicht ausgeschlossen werden.

Das weitere Beispiel betrifft den Konkurs. Im Kapitel über den Konkurs und den Nachlassvertrag (Kap. 11) wäre das Gegenseitigkeitserfordernis in Art. 166 Abs. 1 lit.c und wohl ganz allgemein die Privilegierung der schweizerischen Gläubiger (Art. 72 und 73 IPRG) neu zu überdenken. Die Bestimmungen sind m.E. zu stark vom „Heimatschutz" geprägt. Das internationale Konkursrecht ist letztlich nur durch eine umfassende Konvention befriedigend zu regeln.

Fragezeichen zu Lösungen des IPRG stellen sich wohl am ausgeprägtesten im Schuldrecht, dem ich mich nun speziell zuwenden möchte.

5. BEMERKUNGEN ZU DEN SCHULDRECHTLICHEN BESTIMMUNGEN DES IPRG

a. Ich war, wie schon angedeutet, skeptische gegenüber einer Kodifikation des Schuldrechts. Das IPR/Schuldrecht war nach meiner Meinung, wie ich sie im Referat des Juristentags vertrat, eine Materie, die sich für strikte Kollisionsnormen schwer eignet. Die „US-Revolution" hatte bekanntlich im internationalen Deliktsrecht ihren Ausgangspunkt. Die Theorien über das policies' weighing, den better law approach oder die comparative impairment method wurden am Beispiel von Deliktsfällen entwickelt.[15] Im Deliktsrecht fanden die neuen Theorien auch in der Rechtsprechung von New York bis nach Kalifornien ihren Niederschlag, wenn auch heute eine gewisse Konsolidierung der Rechtssprechung und Doktrin, ja selbst eine Tendenz zur Regelbildung feststellbar ist.

Ich habe mich allerdings davon überzeugen lassen, dass auch oder gerade im Schuldrecht ein grosses Bedürfnis nach Vorhersehbarkeit der Entscheidung, nach Rechtssicherheit allgemein besteht. Dieses Bedürfnis kann nur durch eine gesetzliche Regelung befriedigt werden, die allerdings die notwendige Flexibilität aufweisen muss.

---

[15] Vgl. dazu F. Vischer, General Course on Private International Law, 232 *Rec. des Cours* (1992-I) S. 44fff.

Rückblickend ist denn auch festzustellen, dass der Entscheid zum Einbezug des Schuldrechts in die Kodifikation richtig war. In meiner Tätigkeit als Rechtslehrer und Rechtskonsulent habe ich erfahren, dass die Studenten und die Rechtssuchenden über die Orientierung, die das Gesetz bietet, dankbar sind. Von grosser Bedeutung ist die gesetzliche Regelung etwa auch dann, wenn vor ausländischen Gerichten ein Foreign Law Expert Witness die kollisionsrechtliche Rechtslage im Schuldrecht der Schweiz nachzuweisen hat.

b.   Fast gleichzeitig mit dem IPRG ist das römische EWG Übereinkommen über das auf vertragliche Schuldverhältnisse anwendbare Recht vom 19. Juni 1980 (nachfolgend Römer Übereinkommen genannt) entstanden. Beide Regelungen haben sich gegenseitig beeinflusst. Beide beruhen auf den gleichen Grundprinzipien, enthalten aber in wichtigen Einzelfragen abweichende Lösungen. Das Römer Schuldrechtsübereinkommen, das von allen EU Staaten ratifiziert worden ist, soll durch ein das Deliktsrecht regelndes Übereinkommen ergänzt werden. Die Schweiz kann ohne Mitgliedschaft in der EU dem Römer Übereinkommen anscheinend nicht beitreten.

Beide Übereinkommen, das Römer Übereinkommen und das IPRG, anerkennen die Rechtswahl bei internationalen Verträgen ohne Begrenzung. Im Unterschied zum IPRG anerkennt Art. 3 Abs.1 des Römer Übereinkommens ausdrücklich eine Teilrechtswahl. Die schweizerische Doktrin ist sich allerdings einig, dass das IPRG zu dieser Frage kein qualifiziertes Schweigen beinhaltet, und dass auch nach unserem Recht, zumindest für zusammenhängende Rechtsfragen, eine Teilrechtswahl zu anerkennen ist.

Es ist unbestritten, dass bei schiedsgerichtlicher Entscheidung die Parteien auch ein nichtstaatliches Recht, etwa die Unidroit Principles, mit kollisionsrechtlicher Wirkung wählen können. Ich habe die vielleicht von vielen als verwegen angesehene Meinung vertreten, dass selbst ein staatliches Gericht die Wahl einer in sich zusammenhängenden ausserstaatlichen Ordnung, wie die Unidroit Principles, als verbindlich akzeptieren sollte.[16]

Beide Kodifikationen, das IPRG und das Römer Ue, gehen im Vertragsrecht bei Fehlen einer Rechtswahl vom der charakteristischen Leistung aus. Allerdings kommt in beiden Rechten dem Prinzip nur die Bedeutung einer widerlegbaren Vermutung zu. Die Lehre von der charakteristischen Leistung wird allgemein als schweizerische „Erfindung" betrachtet. Insofern könnten wir über den europäischen Erfolg dieser Anknüpfungslehre Stolz empfinden. Allerdings ist das Prinzip der charakteristischen Leistung scharfer Kritik aus verschiedenen „quarters" ausgesetzt. Insbesondere die jüngere Generation der schweizerischen IPR Spezialisten

---

[16] F. Vischer, „The Relevance of the Unidroit Principles for Judges and Arbitrators in Disputes Arising out of International Contracts", 1 *Eur. J.L. Ref.* (1998/1999) S. 210ff.

steht, wenn ich recht sehe, der Lehre zumindest skeptisch gegenüber. Die englische Doktrin bezweifelte schon immer, dass die Lokalisierung internationaler Verträge auf Grund eines im voraus festgelegten Prinzips erfolgen könne. Aber auch ausserhalb des angelsächsischen Rechtskreises wird Kritik laut. Die Lehre wird als ein „postpandektisches", pseudowissenschaftliches Konstrukt empfunden. Die Bevorzugung der Nicht-Geldleistung beruhe, so wird weiter eingewendet, im heutigen „monetären" Wirtschaftssystem, in der „monetary economy", bei welcher die Geldleistung dominiere, auf einer Fehlleistung. Jessurun d'Oliveira, ein sich geradezu ereifernder Kritiker, tadelt, dass mit dem Prinzip der Nicht-Geldleistung die stärkere Partei, die Professionellen und Gewerbetreibenden, mithin die Banken und Versicherungen, vor den Kunden und Amateuren ungerechtfertigterweise bevorzugt würden. Er erblickt darin typisch schweizerische Züge, „a reflection of the prejudices of Helvetian hotel-keepers and cockoo clock makers (!). . . ".[17] Gabrielle Kaufmann-Kohler[18] meint, das Konzept der charakteristischen Leistung sei „aujourd'hui de plus en plus souvant inadaptée à l'évolution des conditions économiques sociales et politiques" und verweist insbesondere auch auf die wachsende Zahl von komplexen Verträgen, wie Joint Ventures-, Franchise- oder Leasingverträge sowie auf die Devisenverträge, welche alle in aller Regel gar keine eindeutige charakteristische Leistung aufweisen.

Die hier angedeutete Kritik hat sicherlich Gewicht. Das Prinzip der charakteristischen Leistung ist beim internationalem Kaufvertrag entwickelt worden und hat seine extremste Formulierung im Haager IPR-Kaufabkommen vom Jahre 1954 (Art. 118 IPRG) gefunden. Es ist einzuräumen, dass der echte internationale Kaufvertrag sich der eindeutigen Lokalisierung entzieht, dass Käufer- und Verkäuferleistung gleichwertig sind und Käufer und Verkäufer im Handelsbereich oft die Rollen wechseln. Der internationale Kaufvertrag ruft geradezu zwingend nach einer einheitlichen sachrechtlichen Regelung. Doch ist m.E., wenn vom internationalen Kaufvertrag abgesehen wird, das Prinzip noch immer valabel. Eine Lösung unter umgekehrten Vorzeichen, somit Massgeblichkeit der Geldleistung, würde gerade im wichtigen Dienstleistungssektor bedeuten, dass für jede Transaktion das anwendbare Recht gesondert ermittelt werden müsste, womit jede vernünftige Rechtsplanung ausgeschlossen würde.

Der Hauptvorwurf von d'Oliveira, das Prinzip schütze die mächtigere Vertragspartei, verkennt, dass mit der Sonderregelung über die Konsumenten und Arbeitsverträge dem Schutzinteresse der schwächeren Partei Rechnung getragen wird.

Jedenfalls ist es bei einer Konzentration auf Handelsverträge im Sinne einer Vermutungsregel grundsätzlich gerechtfertigt, die berufliche bzw. gewerbliche Leistung und nicht die pekuniäre in den Vordergrund zu stellen. Bemerkenswert ist,

---

[17] Jessurun d'Oliveira, „The Characteristic Obligation in the EC-Draft Convention", *Am. J. Comp. L.* 25 (1977) S.327

[18] La prestation caractéristique en droit international privé, 14 *SJIR* (1989) S. 195ff.

dass die Kritiker, ausser der Ermittlung des anwendbaren Rechts durch eine Beurteilung aller Umstände des Einzelfalles, keine Lösung vorschlagen, jedenfalls keine, die eine vernünftige Planung, damit die Voraussehbarkeit der Entscheidung
ermöglicht. Das Prinzip der charakteristischen Leistung ist ein heuristisches Mittel,
welches auf der bewährten Dialektik von Regel und Ausnahme aufbaut und den
Richter zwingt, schrittweise zur richtigen Lösung zu gelangen. Auf der generell abstrakten Ebene wird in einem ersten Schritt von der Besonderheit des Einzelfalles
abstrahiert. Funktionell gleichgelagerte, häufig wiederkehrende Tatbestände
werden typisiert. In einem zweiten Schritt ist zu fragen, ob der zur Beurteilung vorliegende Tatbestand atypisch und einer Sonderregelung zuzuführen ist. Wiederkehrende gleichartige atypische Fälle können in Subregeln zusammengefasst werden.
Das Prinzip ist offen für adäquate Lösungen für typische atypische Verträge wie
etwa Franchise- oder Leasingsverträge. Der von Gabrielle Kaufmann-Kohler genannte Devisenaustauschvertrag ist letztlich wie der Tausch nur mit Hilfskonstruk-
tionen zu bewältigen. Bei diesen Verträgen fehlen von vornherein nicht nur eine
typische Leistung, sondern auch andere Anhaltspunkte für eine Schwerpunktsbil-
dung. Bei der Rechtsanwendung ist allerdings im Sinn von Michael Bonell[19] bei der
Anwendung zwingender Normen Zurückhaltung zu üben. Nur solche zwingende
Normen verdienen Durchsetzung, die den involvierten Rechten gemeinsam sind.[20]

c.   Das IPRG und das Römer Schuldrechts Übereinkommen enthalten Sondernor-
men für Konsumenten- und Arbeitsverträge (Art. 120 und 121 IPRG, Art.5 und 6
Römer Ue).

Die Sonderregelungen vor allem für die Konsumentenverträge haben beinahe zu
einer Zweiteilung des Kollisionsrechts der Verträge geführt. Dass die Doktrin den
Begriff des Konsumentenvertrags so weit auslegen wird, dass er – entgegen dem
Wortlaut von Art. 120 IPRG – z.B. auch Bank- und Versicherungsverträge einzu-
schliessen vermag, hat nach meiner Erinnerung niemand vorausgeahnt. Wir dach-
ten in erster Linie an Abzahlungs- und Vorauszahlungsverträge, allenfalls
Kleinkredite und ähnliche typische Konsumentenverträge. Die Frage, ob die Tendenz zur Ausdehnung des Schutzes der Konsumentenverträge nicht zu weit geht
und die Mündigkeit der Konsumenten in Frage stellt, muss zumindest gestellt werden.

Der Hauptunterschied zwischen den Regelungen des IPRG und der Römer Ue
besteht bei der Rechtswahl. Art.120 Abs.3 IPRG schliesst sie für den Konsumentenvertrag kurzer Hand aus, während Art.5 Abs.2 Römer Ue eine Rechtswahl
grundsätzlich zulässt, jedoch dem Konsumenten die Berufung auf die zwingenden

---

[19] Das autonome Recht des Welthandels, rechtsdogmatische und rechtspolitische Aspekte, 42
RabelsZ (1978) S. 485ff.
[20] vgl. zur Kritik der charakteristischen Leistung eingehend F. Vischer, „The Concept of the Characteristic Performance reviewed" in: *FS Georg A.L. Droz* (Den Haag 1996) S. 499ff.

Bestimmungen des Rechts des Staates, in dem er seinen gewöhnlichen Aufenthalt hat, erlaubt. Die EG-Lösung ist flexibler und entspricht den Bedürfnissen des internationalen Verkehrs besser. Auch behandelt das Römer Ue den Konsumenten weniger als „unmündige" Person als es das schweizerische Recht tendenziell tut.

Das Römer Schuldrechtsübereinkommen sieht die gleiche Lösung auch für den Arbeitsvertrag vor, nur lautet der Vorbehalt zu Gunsten der Schutzvorschriften am Arbeitsort. Das IPRG dagegen enthält eine abschliessende Aufzählung der wählbaren Rechte (Art. 121 Abs.3). Die schweizerische Lösung muss als Fehlleistung bezeichnet werden: Die Aufzählung ist zu eng. Insbesondere fehlt die praktische wichtige Möglichkeit, das Recht der Konzernmuttergesellschaft zu wählen. Zu denken ist etwa an die Entsendung eines leitenden Mitarbeiter eines schweizerischen Unternehmens an eine ausländische Tochtergesellschaft. Der Arbeitsvertrag wird mit der Tochtergesellschaft abgeschlossen. Warum sollte die Wahl des Rechts am schweizerischen Sitz der Konzernmuttergesellschaft ausgeschlossen sein? Ob im Wege der Auslegung, etwa mir dem Hilfsmittel der teleologischen Ausdehnung, in Umkehrung der modisch gewordenen teleologischen Reduktion, eine angemessene Lösung erzielt werden kann, ist fraglich, wenn ich auch eine solche doch recht kühne Lösung durchaus befürworte. Fehlleistungen des Gesetzgebers müssen m.E. korrigierbar sein.

d.   Bei den im IPRG abschliessend geregelten Verträgen (Art. 119-122 IPRG) stellt sich die Frage, ob eine aufgrund der konkreten Umstände sich aufdrängende, vom Gesetz abweichende Anknüpfung nur unter der allgemeinen Ausnahmeklausel (Art. 15 IPRG) möglich ist, oder ob auch bei diesen Verträgen der Vorbehalt des noch engeren Zusammenhangs gemäss Art. 117 Abs. 1 IPRG gilt. Dass besonders bei Verträgen über Immaterialgüterrechte (Art. 122 IPRG), somit vornehmlich beim Lizenzvertrag, das Bedürfnis, ja die Notwendigkeit nach flexiblen Lösungen besteht, und dass eine Modifikation der gesetzlichen Anknüpfung möglich sein muss, ist unbestritten. Wenn ich recht sehe, befürwortet die Mehrheit der Autoren heute die These, dass auch diese Verträge, im Gegensatz zum gesetzlichen Wortlaut, Vermutungsregeln sind, die unter dem Vorbehalt eines noch engeren Zusammenhangs zu einem anderen Recht stehen. Vielleicht ist im Unterschied zu den in Art. 117 Abs. 2 aufgelisteten Verträgen die Vermutung als stärker zu betrachten, weshalb erhöhte Anforderungen an die Abweichung von der Regel zu stellen wären. Es darf nicht ausser Acht gelassen werden, dass der Katalog der Sonderverträge in das Gesetz nur aufgenommen wurde, weil bei diesen das Prinzip der charakteristischen Leistung nicht oder jedenfalls nicht eindeutig zum Zuge kommt.

e.   Im Bereich des Deliktsrechts haben sich in der Bundesgerichtspraxis im allgemeinen keine besonderen Schwierigkeiten gezeigt. Letztlich ungeklärt ist noch immer die Frage, wie im Rahmen von Art. 129 Abs. 2 (Zuständigkeit) und Art. 133 Abs. 2 (anwendbares Recht) der Erfolgsort definiert werden soll. Das Problem stellt sich insbesondere beim sog. reinen Vermögensschaden, beim Schaden somit, der nicht Folge der Verletzung eines absoluten Rechts, wie des Eigentums, der persönlichen Integrität oder eines Immaterialgüterrechts, ist. Das Bundesgericht hat im Entscheid BGE 125 III 103 (1999) bei reinen Vermögensschädigungen die an sich naheliegende Lokalisierung des Erfolgsorts am Wohnsitz der geschädigten Person als nicht zwingend bezeichnet. Das absolute dictum des Bundesgerichts: „Der Erfolgsort ist derjenige Ort, wo das geschützte Rechtsgut verletzt wurde" (S. 105), und: „Massgeblich zur Bestimmung des Erfolgsortes ist mithin, wo die erste unmittelbare Einwirkung auf das durch den Tatbestand einer Deliktsnorm geschützte Rechtsgut stattgefunden hat" (S. 106), würde beim reinen Vermögensschaden die Unterscheidung zwischen Handlungs- und Erfolgsort weitgehend aufheben. Die Aussage des Bundesgerichts mag beim berühmten tödlichen Schuss über die Grenze zutreffen, wohl aber kaum beim reinen Vermögensschaden. Bei diesem stellt sich gerade die Frage, wo das geschützte Vermögen liegt. Persönlich neige ich zur Meinung, dass beim reinen Vermögensschaden, jedenfalls in der Regel, das Rechtsgut „Vermögen" am Wohnsitz des Vermögensträgers zu lokalisieren ist. Im Regest des Urteils steht der Satz, dass das Domizil des Geschädigten nicht als Erfolgsort anzusehen se, wenn sich die „konkret verletzten Vermögenswerte vom übrigen Vermögen abrenzen" lassen. Wenn der Schaden in einem lokalisierbaren Sondervermögen eingetreten ist, könnte dieser Aussage im Sinne einer Ausnahme zugestimmt werden. Nur findet sich das dictum im Regest in der Erwägung des Bundesgerichts nicht wieder.

f.   Die im 4. Abschnitt des 9. Kapitels (Obligationenrecht) unter dem Titel „Gemeinsame Bestimmungen" zusammengefassten Normen sind teilweise nicht sehr benutzerfreundlich formuliert. Dies gilt insbesondere für die Bestimmungen über den Rückgriff zwischen Schuldnern (Art. 144) und die cessio legis (Art. 146). Art. 144 Abs. 1 verlangt als Voraussetzung des Rückgriffs kumulativ die Zustimmung des Rechts, dem die Verpflichtung zur Zahlung, für welche Regress beansprucht wird, untersteht (sog. Kausalstatut, z.B. das Recht, dem der Versicherungsvertrag untersteht) und des Rechts, das die Verpflichtung des im Rückgriff belangten Schuldners gegenüber dem Gläubiger beherrscht (z.B. Delikts- oder Vertragsstatut).

Ob aber diese an sich bewährte Regel dem Wortlaut von Art. 144 Abs. 1 IPRG ohne weiteres entnommen werden kann, ist angesichts des hohen Abstraktionsgrades der Bestimmung fraglich (Art. 144 Abs. 1 lautet: „Der Rückgriff unter Schuldnern ist insoweit möglich, als es die Rechte zulassen, denen die entsprechenden Schulden unterstehen." Ein mit dem IPR und der Bundesgerichtspraxis nicht vertrauter Jurist bleibt nach meiner Erfahrung eher ratlos. Art. 13 der Römer Ue, der im Unterschied zum schweizerischen Recht allein auf das sog. Kausalstatut abstellt, ist zwar viel umständlicher formuliert, aber in der Aussage eindeutiger.

g. Eine recht bedeutsame Rolle spielt die international viel beachtete Währungsnorm (Art. 147 IPRG). Sie ist einzigartig geblieben. M.W. kennt keine neue Kodifikation eine Regelung über die Währung. Die besondere Bewährungsprobe hat Art. 147 IPRG bei der Umstellung der Währungen der Mitgliedstaaten der europäischen Währungsunion auf den Euro bestanden. Dabei hat sich in einer Grundsatzfrage eine erhebliche Meinungsverschiedenheit zwischen Prof. Wolfgang Wiegand und mir ergeben. In seinem Werk „Die Einführung des Euro/Auswirkungen auf privatrechtliche Rechtsverhältnisse in der Schweiz"[21] hat Kollege Wiegand die These vertreten, dass bei innerschweizerischen Verträgen, die jedoch auf eine ausländische, in casu auf die Währung eines Mitgliedstaates der Europäischen Währungsunion lauten, Art. 147 IPRG mangels eines internationalen Verhältnisses im Sinn von Art. 1 Abs. 1 IPRG nicht anwendbar sei. Deshalb könne nicht, wie Art. 147 Abs. 1 es vorschreibt, die lex monetae zur Bestimmung der Umstellung und des „recurrent link" zur Anwendung gelangen. Die bestehenden Verträge entbehrten deshalb eines negotium essentiale, nämlich einer Bestimmung über die Währung, nachdem die Vertragswährung untergegangen ist. Das Prinzip der Vertragskontinuität könne nicht gewährleistet werden und die Verträge müssten bis zum Zeitpunkt der Umstellung neu verhandelt werden. Zumindest sei eine der ärztlichen Aufklärungspflicht entsprechende Information der Kunden einer Bank erforderlich.

Dieser Auffassung habe ich in einem für die Schweizerische Bankiervereinigung verfassten Gutachten widersprochen. Das Gutachten wurde von der Bankiervereinigung veröffentlicht.[22] Nach meiner Überzeugung liegt ein internationales Verhältnis immer dann vor, wenn auch nur für eine Teilfrage sich die Frage nach dem anwendbaren Recht stellt. Für die Internationalität muss genügen, dass mindestens ein relevantes Element des Sachverhaltes einen Auslandbezug aufweise. Auch bei sonst rein schweizerischen Verträgen muss deshalb für Währungsfragen Art. 147 IPRG zur Anwendung gelangen.

In Übereinstimmung mit der internationalen Doktrin bestimmt gemäss Art. 147 Abs. 1 IPRG das Statut der Währung über die Währungsumstellung und ihre Modalitäten. Dabei gehe ich von einer kollisionsrechtlichen Teilverweisung auf die lex monetae aus. Die Auswirkungen der Umstellung auf den Vertrag bestimmt dagegen das Vertragsstatut (Art. 147 Abs. 2). Unter schweizerischem Recht als Vertragsstatut muss die Vertragskontinuität als gewahrt gelten. Dies ergibt sich aus der Verbindung der Sonderanknüpfung an die lex monetae für alle Fragen, welche die Währung unter Einschluss der Währungsumstellung betreffen, in Verbindung mit dem Nominalismusprinzip, das sowohl im schweizerischen wie im ausländischen Recht anerkannt ist. Jede Geldschuld ist im Prinzip eine Geldsummenschuld. Tritt

---

[21] Berner bankenrechtliche Abhandlungen, Bd. 4 (Bern 1998).
[22] *Die Währungsumstellung auf den Euro und die Auswirkung auf Verträge, die dem schweizerischen Recht unterstehen* (Basel 1998).

anstelle der vereinbarten Währung durch Anordnung der lex monetae eine neue Währung, so tritt diese automatisch anstelle der ursprünglichen Vertragswährung. Dies muss jedenfalls solange gelten, als die Umrechnungsprinzipien adäquat sind und die Wertrelation aufrechterhalten bleibt. Ist aber der „recurrent link" angemessen, so ist die Umstellung zu akzeptieren. Verschiedene Staaten, so New York und andere Gliedstaaten der USA wie auch Mitgliedstaaten der EU haben zur Sicherung der Vertragskontinuität spezielle Gesetze erlassen. Die Schweiz hat im Blick auf die Anwendbarkeit von Art. 147 zu Recht darauf verzichten können.

h.   Der Kernpunkt meiner Auseinandersetzung mit Kollege Wiegand liegt nicht bei der Auslegung der Währungsbestimmung von Art. 147 IPRG. Hier sind wir weitgehend der gleichen Meinung. Die Differenz liegt vielmehr bei der Frage: Was ist ein internationales Verhältnis im Sinne von Art. 1 Abs. 1 IPRG? Die bisherigen Erfahrungen haben gezeigt, dass keine abstrakte endgültige Definition möglich ist. Im Schuldrecht bin ich für eine eher grosszügige Auslegung.

Ich wiederhole meine Meinung: Ein internationales Verhältnis liegt immer dann vor, wenn sich zumindest für eine rechtserhebliche Teilfrage die Frage nach dem anwendbaren Recht stellt. Dann ist für diese Teilfrage das anwendbare Recht nach dem IPRG zu ermitteln. Dies gilt unzweifelhaft für diejenigen Teilfragen, für welche das Gesetz, wie im Fall der Währung, eine Sonderanknüpfung vorsieht. Besondere Probleme ergeben sich bei der kollisionsrechtlichen Parteiautonomie. Die Frage ist, welche grenzüberschreitenden Elemente der Vertrag aufweisen muss, damit den Parteien das Recht zusteht, den Vertrag kollisionsrechtlich, d.h. mit Einschluss der zwingenden Bestimmungen, einer ausländischen Rechtsordnung zu unterstellen. Dass eine materiellrechtliche Verweisung auf ausländisches Recht auch bei Inlandsverträgen zulässig ist, ist unbestritten. Art. 3 Abs. 3 des Römer Ue schliesst die kollisionsrechtliche Parteiautonomie immer dann aus, „wenn der sonstige Sachverhalt im Zeitpunkt der Rechtswahl nur mit einem Staat verbunden ist." Diesfalls können die zwingenden Bestimmungen dieses Staates nicht durch Rechtswahl wegbedungen werden. Das dürfte im Prinzip auch für das schweizerische Recht gelten. Immerhin ist denkbar, dass ein Inlandsvertrag Glied in einer Kette von Auslandverträgen ist. Diesfalls würde ich kraft Attraktionsprinzip die kollisionsrechtliche Parteiautonomie auch für diesen Gliedvertrag bejahen.

i.   Der kleine Rundgang durch die Probleme des IPRG und des Schuldrechts im Speziellen hat die überwiegenden Stärken, aber auch gewisse Schwachstellen des IPRG aufgezeigt.

Seit Erlass des IPRG hatte sich die IPR-Kodifikationwelle in Europa verstärkt. Doch bleibt das IPRG m.E. insgesamt ein gutes Gesetz. Es enthält Bestimmungen, die neue Wege im IPR aufzeigen und hat deshalb in gewisser Hinsicht noch immer Pioniercharakter. Den eidgenössischen Gesetzgeber möchte ich ermahnen, insbesondere beim oft unbekümmerten Nachvollzug des EU-Rechts die klare Linie des

IPRG zu wahren. Ich denke insbesondere an die Regelung des internationalen Versicherungsrechts im revidierten VVG, die fast unverständlich ist.

Verschiedene Ergänzungen des IPRG stehen an: Im Zusammenhang mit dem Fusionsgesetz ist die Ergänzung des IPRG durch die kollisionsrechtliche Regelung der Fusion und Spaltung von Gesellschaften vorgesehen. Die neuen Bestimmungen bemühen sich, dem System und der sprachlichen Eigenart des Gesetzes treu zu bleiben. Mit dem Bundesgesetz über die in die Schweiz entsandten Arbeitnehmerinnen und Arbeitnehmer, welches die EG-Entsenderichtlinie in das schweizerische Recht umsetzt, wird ein neuer arbeitsrechtlicher Gerichtsstand am Ort, „an dem der Arbeitnehmer für einen begrenzten Zeitraum und zur Verrichtung auch nur eines Teils seiner Arbeit aus dem Ausland entsandt worden ist", eingeführt. Für den vom Ausland entsandten Arbeitnehmer, der seinen gewöhnlichen Aufenthalt im Ausland hat, bestand bisher kein schweizerischer Gerichtsstand. Der neu eingeführte Absatz 3 von Art. 115 IPRG soll dem Arbeitnehmer ermöglichen, die im schweizerischen Entsendegesetz im Sinn von Art. 18 IPRG als unmittelbar anwendbar bezeichnete arbeitsrechtlichen Normen, mit Einschluss der in dem neu mit zwingenden Normen ausgestatteten Normalarbeitsvertrag (Art. 360a-360e OR [neu]) oder in einem allgemein verbindlich erklärten Gesamtarbeitsvertrag enthaltenen Mindestlohnvorschriften, vor einem schweizerischen Gericht durchzusetzen.

SUMMARY
10 YEARS OF PILA – APPRAISAL OF THE SWISS LAW ON INTERNATIONAL OBLIGATIONS

The Swiss Act on Private International Law (PILA) of December 18, 1987, in the preparation of which I was involved as the president of the Federal Commission, came into force on January 1, 1988. My contribution attempts an appraisal of the Act under special consideration of the law of obligations (contracts and torts) after 10 years of practice. I note the changed circumstances since the coming into force of the Act and discuss the merits and shortcomings of the Act. Special attention is given to the effects of the *lois d'application immédiate* (Art. 18 and 19 PILA) in the conflict of laws in general and in contracts in particular. I try to find an answer to the critique of the doctrine of the characteristic obligation which is retained as a presumption in Art. 117 PILA. The regulation on contracts in the PILA is confronted with the solutions of the EC Rome Convention on the Law Applicable to Contractual Obligations. The general trend to shift priority to the issue of jurisdiction and recognition of foreign decisions rather than to the applicable law is noted and discussed. As a result, it can be said that the PILA was well accepted by the community of lawyers and the courts. That the Act contains clear and valuable solutions for the practitioner is confirmed by the fact that since its coming into force the number of decisions of the Federal Tribunal dealing with conflict of law issues markedly diminished. My contribution ends with an outlook to some complementary regulations in the PILA which are in preparation, especially conflict-rules for international mergers and divisions of companies.

Wenn Wächter mit Story

Paul Volken[*]

EINLEITUNG

§ 1. Der Name unseres Jubilaren ist in der Schweiz ein erstes Mal mit der Neuausgabe des von Werner Niederer begründeten Zürcher Lehrbuches über die *Allgemeinen Lehren des internationalen Privatrechts* verbunden.[1] Schon als Student war ich fasziniert von der Leichtigkeit, mit welcher Niederer in seinem Einleitungsteil auf knappem Raum tausend Jahre Dogmengeschichte des IPR hingezaubert hat. Da stand jeder IPR-Lehrer mit seinen Gefolgsleuten am richtigen Platz und deren oft wundersame Lehren waren überzeugend zu einen systematischen Ganzen verwoben. Einfach genial. Die Neuausgabe von Keller/Siehr hat 1986 Niederer's Konzept der IPR-Ideengeschichte mit „Max-Planckscher,, Tiefenschärfe angereichert, und entsprechend übertrug sich die Bewunderung auf den neuen Band und dessen Autoren.

§ 2. Vor kurzem hat es der Zufall gewollt, dass ich nacheinander Texte von Story und Wächter zu verifizieren hatte. Dabei war mir dank der *Allgemeinen IPR-Lehren*

---

[*] Dr. iur., LL.M. (Harvard), Professor für IPR und Wirtschaftsrecht an der Rechtswissenschaftlichen Fakultät der Universität Fribourg.
[1] Werner Niederer, *Einführung in die allgemeinen Lehren des internationalen Privatre*chts, 1. Aufl. (Zürich 1954) 3. Aufl. (Zürich 1961) 405 S. Max Keller/ Kurt Siehr, *Allgemeine Lehren des internationalen Privatrechts* (Zurich 1986) LXXII, 714 S.

J. Basedow et al., eds., Private Law in the International Arena – Liber Amicorum Kurt Siehr
© 2000, T.M.C.Asser Press, The Hague, The Netherlands

vom Ansatz her klar, dass ich es mit zwei völlig verschiedenen Grössen der IPR-Dogmatik zu tun hatte: Da stand die in weissen Marmor gehauene Lichtgestalt aus der neuen Welt,[2] die das IPR-Denken in der Version der sog. *comitas*-Lehre in die englischsprachige Wissenschaft eingeführt hatte; und da war daneben dieser deutsche „Zerstörer der Statutenlehre",[3] dieser Kritikast aus dem Württembergischen, der eigentlich Strafrechtsspezialist war und der zum IPR wohl nur gekommen ist, weil er für Sachsen ein neues Zivilgesetzbuch schreiben sollte.

§ 3. Aber eben, Genosse Zufall ist ein ungemütlicher Kumpan; er kommt, wann er will, und stiftet Unruhe, wo es ihm beliebt. So ist aus der raschen Textverifikation eine Neugier entstanden, die Seelenverwandtschaften auszumachen glaubte, und zurückgeblieben ist die Frage: Wo stünden wir heute mit unserem IPR, wenn es den Zeitgenossen Story und Wächter vergönnt gewesen wäre, wissenschaftlich zusammenzuspannen? Solche Fragen stellen, heisst auch, darauf eine Antwort zu geben. Ich weiss nicht, ob ich die richtige Antwort schon habe. Aber die Festgabe zu Ehren von KURT SIEHR scheint mir eine gute Gelegenheit, für eine solche Antwort erste Ansätze zu entwickeln.

1.   JOSEPH STORY

§ 4. Unter den US-amerikanischen IPR-Wissenschaftern der erste Stunde gilt Joseph Story (1779-1845) aus Massachusetts zwar nicht als der zeitlich erste,[4] wohl aber als der fachlich wichtigste Vertreter. Mit seinen *Commentaries on the Conflict of Laws*[5] hat er ab 1834 dem internationalen Privatrecht in der englischsprachigen Welt erstmals zu einer bewussten Stimme verholfen. Es sollte eine nachhaltige Stimme werden. Nicht nur hat das Buch bis zum Ende des Jahrhunderts acht Auflagen erlebt; es sollte auch den nachfolgenden englischsprachigen IPR-Lehrbüchern – und nicht nur diesen[6] – als Vorlage dienen bis hin zu Dicey's erstem *Conflict of*

---

[2] Die Marmorbüste von Joseph Story ist im Untergeschoss des US Supreme Court in Washington zu bewundern.

[3] Vgl. Christian von Bar, *Internationales Privatrecht*, Bd. I (München 1987) S. 398; G. Kegel, *Internationales Privatrecht*, 7. Aufl. (München 1995) S. 144.

[4] Als erste auf Englisch geschriebene IPR-Bücher gelten:
James Kent, *Commentaries on American Law*, vol. 2 (1827);
Samuel Livermore, *Dissertations on the question which arise from the contrariety of positive laws of different States* (New Orleans 1828).

[5] Joseph Story, *Commentaries on the Conflict of Laws, Foreign and Domestic, in Regard to Contracts, Rights and Remedies, and especially in Regard to Marriages, Divorces, Wills, Successions and Judgments* (Boston 1834).

[6] In Frankreich hat keine zehn Jahre später Jean Foelix erklärt: „La doctrine que nous exposons dans ce chapitre est celle de M. Story; nous l'adoptons complètement, in: *Traité de droit international privé*, 1. Aufl. (Paris 1843) p. 12.

Laws aus dem Jahre 1896.[7] Und auch die später so prominent gewordenen IPR-Theorien des englischen Sprachraums, und zwar sowohl diejenige der *vested rights* wie auch diejenigen der späteren *legal realists*, haben alle letztlich bei *Story* angedockt.[8]

§ 5. Joseph Story hatte sich sein IPR-Denken noch in der Form und mit den Parametern der alten Statutenlehre erarbeitet und er hat es weitgehend auch in diesem Denkschema an die englischsprachige Welt weitergegeben.[9] Freilich ist er dabei mit einer besonderen Spätform der Statutenlehre in Berührung gekommen; konkret hat er sich an der Statutenlehre in ihrer französisch-holländischen Ausgestaltung des ausgehenden 18. Jahrhunderts orientiert. Diese Lehre hatte es nicht mehr mit der frühitalienischen Problematik betreffend die Reichweite der einzelnen Stadtrechte zu tun,[10] gefragt war vielmehr nach der räumlichen Geltung der eigenständigen französischen bzw. holländischen Provinzgesetzgebungen. Dabei sah sich Story insbesondere mit jener streng territorialistisch ausgerichteten Variante der Statutentheorie konfrontiert, die d'Argentré[11] im 16. Jahrhundert für die Bretagne zurechtgeschmiedet hatte und die in der Folge von Boullenois[12] für das Burgund übernommen wurde und in der Folge durch Rodenburg[13] und die beiden Voet[14] auf die holländischen Gegebenheiten übertragen worden war.

Story ist vor allem mit der holländischen Version der Statutenlehre in Berührung gekommen, und zwar vorzugsweise mit jener Variante, die von Ulrich Huber[15] rechtspolitisch aufmunitioniert, d.h. mit dem stark prägenden Souveränitätsdenken der *comitas*-Lehre versehen worden war.

---

[7] Albert Venn Dicey, *The Conflict of Laws*, 1st ed. (London 1896).

[8] Vgl. dazu statt vieler: John O'Brian, in: *Smith's Conflict of Laws*, 2nd ed. (London 1999) S. 15, 16; Max Gutzwiller, "Le développement historique du droit international privé", 29 *Rec. des cours* (1929 IV) S. 289ff, insbes. 343; Herma Hill Kay, „A Defence of Currie's Governmental Interest Analysis", 215 *Rec. des cours* (1989 III) S. 26.

[9] Vgl. dazu insbes. Max Gutzwiller (oben N. 7) S. 344, unten.

[10] Den Accursius (1180-1260) bewegte als ursprünglich einen der ersten die Frage: Darf man auf einen Bürger von Bologna, der den Markt von Modena besucht, das dortige Recht anwenden, dem er ja nicht untersteht?

[11] Bertrand d'Argentré (1519-1590) hat seine Ausführungen als Glosse zu Art. 218 der Coutume de Bretagne (*Commentaris in patrias britonum leges*) präsentiert und dort als zentralen Grundsatz festgehalten: „statuta extra territoria sua sine usu sunt".

[12] Louis Boullenois (1680-1762), *Traité de la personnalité et de la réalité des lois, Coutumes ou statuts* (Paris 1766).

[13] Christian Rodenburg (1618-1668), *Tractatus de jure conjugum* (Leyden 1653).

[14] Paul Voet (1619-1667), *De statutis eorunque concursu* (Brüssel 1160); Johannes Voet (1647-1716), *Commentarius ad Pandectas, Pass II, De Statutis* (Leyden 1698).

[15] Ulrich Huber (1636-1694), „De conflictu legum in diversis imperiis", in: *Praelectiones iuris romani et hodierni*, Pass II (Leyden 1689).

2. STORY UND DIE STATUTENLEHRE

§ 6. Bevor er aber seiner klar holländisch orientierten Statuten-Neigung nachgegeben hat, ist Story, der für seine *Commentaries* auf strenge Wissenschaftlichkeit bedacht war, zunächst auch den Lehren und Meinungen der älteren französischen und italienischen Schule nachgegangen.[16] Aber er scheint dies im Grunde nur getan zu haben, um sich seine holländisch und insbesondere Huber- orientierte Überzeugung mit Hilfe einiger Negativbilder zu Lasten anderer Statutentheorien bestätigen zu lassen.

In diesem Sinn liest man z.B. in Story's Einführung.[17] Die europäischen Vertreter des *civil law* haben das Problem der Statutenkollisionen für die meisten ihrer Erscheinungsweisen mit viel Akribie untersucht. Aber ihre Schriften zu diesem Thema sind derart mit subtilen theoretischen Unterscheidungen und Unterteilungen überladen, dass man vor lauter Bäumen den Wald nicht mehr erkennen kann; in Wirklichkeit scheinen diese theoretischen Ergüsse zu wenig mehr als um der reinen Diskussion willen entwickelt worden zu sein.[18] Und Story lässt die Belege für seine Wertung auf dem Fusse folgen, wenn er z.B. ausführt: Die europäischen Juristen haben die kollidierenden *statuta* in die drei Klassen der *personalia*, der *realia* und der *mixta* eingeteilt; wenn es dann aber darum geht, dieser Trias auch Inhalte zu verleihen, hört der wissenschaftliche Friede unter den Europäern schlagartig auf.[19]

§ 7. So verstehen – erklärt Story seinen Landsleuten – die Europäer unter dem Begriff des *statutum* nicht etwa einen bestimmten Gesetzeserlass, der von einem nationalen oder lokalen Gesetzgeber erlassen worden ist (wie dies etwa in England oder Amerika der Fall wäre). Vielmehr bezeichnen sie mit dem Statut die Gesamtheit des auf einem bestimmten Staatsgebiet geltenden Rechts, gleich welchen Ursprungs die einzelnen Rechtssätze sind.[20]

Entsprechend bezeichnen sie [sc. die Europäer] als *personenbezogene statuta* alle jene Rechtssätze, die für den Bürger allgemein gültige und überall geltende Verpflichtungen enthalten. In der Regel handelt es sich dabei um die Rechtssätze, die zur Hauptsache die Person als solche betreffen und höchstens indirekt mit Eigentumsfragen zu tun haben.[21]

Umgekehrt gelten den Europäern jene Rechtssätze einer Rechtsordnung als *real-statuta*, die keine extraterritoriale Wirkungen beanspruchen und nicht persönliche Verpflichtungen aufstellen. Es sind die Rechtsnormen, die zur Hauptsache Ei-

---

[16] Vgl. J. Story (oben N. 5) S. 15.
[17] Story (oben N. 5) S. 10.
[18] Story (oben N. 5) S. 27.
[19] Story (oben N. 5) S. 12, 13.
[20] Story (oben N. 5) S. 12.
[21] Story (oben N. 5) S. 13.

gentumsfragen betreffen und sich nicht auf Personen beziehen, ausser im Zusammenhang mit deren Eigentumsrechten.[22]

Und schliesslich werden jene Normen der Rechtsordnung als *gemischte statuta* bezeichnet, die sowohl Personen als auch Eigentumsrechte zum Gegenstand haben. In diesem Sinne, fügt Story ironisch an, können praktisch alle *statuta* als gemischte angesehen werden, denn es ist ja kaum ein personenbezogener Rechtssatz vorstellbar, der sich nicht zugleich irgendwie auf bestimmte Gegenstände bezöge.[23]

§ 8. Für seine Aussagen über die Grundeinteilung der Statutenlehre beruft *Story* sich zur Hauptsache auf Merlin, Rodenburg und Boullenois, und er fügt seinen Erläuterungen ergänzend noch die Feststellung hinzu: In der Frage, wie die Dreiteilung der *Statuta* in *personalia*, *realia* bzw. *mixta* im Einzelfall vorzunehmen sei, bestehen unter den europäischen Juristen grundlegende Meinungsverschiedenheiten. Auch wenn hinsichtlich des Grundsatzes, wonach die *personalia* auf personenbezogene Rechtsfragen, die *realia* hingegen auf Sachen einzuwenden sind, Einigkeit besteht, so sind doch über deren konkrete Abgrenzungen erhebliche wissenschaftliche Divergenzen auszumachen.[24]

Dies alles führt Story nach knapp fünfzehnseitiger Beschäftigung mit der Statutenlehre zu folgendem Ergebnis: Es ist, so sagt er, nicht meine Absicht, mich in die europäischen Kontroversen über die *statuta personalia*, *realia* oder *mixta* und deren allfällige Vorzüge oder Nachteile einzumischen. Mein (Story's) Ziel ist es, die wichtigsten Grundsätze, die zur Lösung der zentralen Fragestellungen im IPR in Europa entwickelt worden sind, aufzuzeigen und aus den wissenschaftlichen Arbeiten der Europäer den grösstmöglichen Nutzen zu ziehen, um die IPR-Lehre im *common law* zu erläutern, zu untermauern und weiterzuentwickeln.[25]

3.   STORY'S FOLGERUNGEN

§ 9. In Verfolgung der so umschriebenen Zielsetzung, nämlich die *leading principles* der *private international jurisprudence* der Statutisten für das *common law*-IPR fruchtbar zu machen, hält Story zunächst drei allgemeine Maximen fest, die

---

[22] Story (oben N. 5) S. 13.

[23] Story (oben N. 5) S. 14, Rdz. 14: „ In the application of this classification to particular cases, there has been no inconsiderable adversity of opinion among the civilians", und als Ergebnis hält er auf S. 19, Rdz. 16, fest: „It is not my design to engage in the controversy as to what constitutes the true distinction between personal statutes and real statutes, or to examine the merits of various systems propounded by foreign jurists on this subject (...). My object is rather to present the leading principles upon some of the more important topics of private international jurisprudence, and to use the works of the civilians to illustrate, confirm, and expand the doctrines of the common law".

[24] Story (oben N. 5) S. 21ff., insbes. Rdz. 18, 20, 23.

[25] Story (oben N. 5) S. 19.

überall und in jedem Fall zu beachten seien und die da lauten: Souveränität, territoriale Grenzen der Souveränität, Wirkungserstreckung durch Anerkennung.[26]

§ 10. Zur Souveränität hält Story fest: Jede Nation verfügt über eine exklusive Jurisdiktion auf ihrem Staatsgebiet. Entsprechend beherrschen die Gesetze eines Staates unmittelbar alle Eigentumsrecht an Gegenständen, die auf dem betreffenden Staatsgebiet belegen sind, und auch alle Personen, die Einheimischen wie die Fremden, die auf jenem Staatsgebiet wohnen, sowie alle Verträge, die auf seinem Gebiet abgeschlossen, und auch alle anderen Rechtshandlungen, die dort ausgeführt werden.[27] Als Begründung und Rechtfertigung dieser ersten Maxime beruft sich Story auf Boullenois[28] und Vattel,[29] die beide das souveräne Recht jedes nationalen Gesetzgebers zum Erlass von Gesetzen über Personen, Sachen und Rechtsverhältnisse auf seinem Staatsgebiet erörtert und begründet haben.

§ 11. Für die territoriale Begrenzung der staatlichen Souveränität argumentiert Story in Anlehnung an Rodenburg[30] und hält fest: Kein Staat kann mit seinen Gesetzen Eigentumsrechte an Sachen beeinflussen, die ausserhalb seines Staatsgebietes liegen, oder Personen verpflichten, die nicht in seinem Hoheitsgebiet wohnen. Dieses ist die natürliche Folge, die sich aus dem ersten Grundsatz ergibt, denn es wäre mit dem Grundsatz von der Gleichwertigkeit und der Ausschliesslichkeit der Souveränität völlig unvereinbar, wenn ein Staat für Personen und über Sachen sollte legiferieren dürfen, die sich nicht in seinem Herrschaftsbereich befinden.[31]

§ 12. Und zur Wirkungserstreckung fremder Entscheide hält Story fest: Die Frage, welche Bindungswirkung und Verpflichtung den Gesetzen eines Staates auf dem Hoheitsgebiet anderer Staaten zukommt, hängt allein von den Gesetzen und Regulierungen des letzteren Staates ab.[32] Diesbezüglich sind nach Story drei Grundsätze zu beachten, nämlich:
(1) Ein Staat kann ausländischen Gesetzen und davon abgeleiteten Ansprüchen auf seinem Gebiet jede Wirkung absprechen; er kann sie teilweise oder mit modifizierter Auswirkung akzeptieren oder kann sie auch ganz anerkennen.[33]

---

[26] Story (oben N. 5) S. 21: „[E]very nation possesses an exclusive sovereignty and jurisdiction within its own territory. The direct consequence of this rule is, that the laws of every state affect and bind directly all property, whether real or personal, within its territory, and all persons who are resident within it, whether natural-born subjects or aliens, and also all contracts made and acts done within it".
[27] Story (oben N. 5) S. 21, Rdz. 18, S. 22, Rdz. 20, S. 25 Rdz. 23.
[28] Vgl. Louis Boullenois (oben N. 12) S. 2.
[29] Vgl. Emer Vattel, *Le droit des gens* (Paris 1763) sect. 84, 85.
[30] Ibid. (oben N. 13) S. 7.
[31] Story (oben N. 5) S. 23, Rdz. 21.
[32] Story (oben N. 5) S. 2, Rdz. 23.
[33] Story (oben N. 5) S. 25, Rdz. 23.

(2) Wo das geschriebene oder ungeschriebene Recht eines Staates sich zu der Frage der Wirkungserstreckung ausdrücklich äussert, muss der entsprechende Rechtsbefehl von allen Personen beachtet werden, die sich im Hoheitsgebiet des betreffenden Staates befinden.[34]

(3) Wo sich weder das geschriebene noch das ungeschriebene Recht eines Staates zur Wirkungserstreckung fremder Rechtssätze und darauf beruhender Ansprüche äussern, dort und nur dort kann sich legitim fragen: Welche Rechtsordnung soll die Frage der Wirkungserstreckung beantworten, wenn sich der nationale Souverän dazu nicht klar geäussert hat?[35]

§ 13. Auf der Grundlage dieser drei Prinzipien greift Story zurück auf die Theorien der italienischen und der französischen Statutenlehre und prüft, inwieweit ihm deren Lehren Hilfestellungen geben, um diese drei Prinzipien mitzutragen. Story findet sich für seinen Geschmack von den Statutisten zuwenig unterstützt. Von den europäischen Juristen jener Zeit sagt er, sie hätten zwar mit viel intellektuellem Einsatz versucht, für die kollisionsrechtlichen Fragen allgemeingültige Regeln aufzustellen. Doch müsse bezweifelt werden, ob dabei Aufwand und Ertrag immer in einem angemessenen Verhältnis geblieben seien und ob die gefundenen Lösungen immer auch als sachlich angemessen, inhaltlich wünschbar und im Ergebnis gerecht angesehen werden können.[36] Und das Anschauungsmaterial für diese Zweifel wird sogleich nachgeliefert.[37]

Um darzutun, dass der Wirkungserstreckung ausländischer Rechtspositionen notwendig Grenzen gesetzt werden müssen, greift Story auf das altrömische Zwölftafelgesetz zurück, das es den unbefriedigten Gläubigern erlaubt habe, den Körper des insolventen Schuldners unter sich aufzuteilen.[38] Natürlich wird mit Story auch heute niemand von einem „Staat der Christenheit" verlangen, dass er solchen ausländischen Gesetzen Nachachtung verschafft.

Ähnlich unbeholfen ist in Story's Amerika von 1834 die völlig unzureichende Unterscheidung zwischen *statuta personalia* und *realia* dahergekommen, denn sie verlangte, dass ein- und dieselbe Rechtsfrage in einem Gliedstaat (mit Sklaverei) dem Real-, im anderen aber (ohne Sklaverei) dem Personalstatut unterstellt würde.[39]

§ 14. Wenn die abstrakt-theoretischen Regeln der europäischen Statutisten zu derart abscheulichen Konsequenzen führen können, so musste dies zwangsläufig die

---

[34] Story (oben N. 5) S. 25, Rdz. 23.

[35] Story (oben N. 5) S. 25, Rdz. 23.

[36] Story (oben N. 5) S. 26, 27.

[37] Story (oben N. 5) S. 27.

[38] Story (oben N. 5) S. 27, Mitte.

[39] Story (oben N. 5) S. 28, Rdz. 25, in fine. Merke: Etienne Bartin und Franz Kahn hätten das Beispiel betr. Sklaverei sicher dankbar genutzt, um ihre Qualifikationsprobleme zu veranschaulichen.

Ablehnung ihrer Lehren Folge haben. In dieser Haltung und Überzeugung fand sich Story auch bestärkt durch die Erkenntnisse von Richter Porter[40] aus Louisiana, der bereits 1827 in einem Entscheid *Saul v. His Creditors*[41] zur europäischen Statutenlehre festgehalten hatte: Wo so viele hochkarätige Wissenschaftler bei dem Versuch, konkrete Lösungsgrundsätze aufzustellen, gescheitert sind, müssen wir notwendig zu dem Ergebnis kommen, dass deren Scheitern nicht etwa mit persönlicher Unfähigkeit zu tun hatte, sondern sachbedingt war: Der Untersuchungsgegenstand, mit dem sich die Statutisten befasst haben, ist einer Regelung durch allgemeine Grundsätze schlicht nicht zugänglich. Die Statutisten wollten zu weit gehen; sie wollten allgemeingültige Regeln aufstellen für Probleme, die von der Natur der Sache her einer Regelung mittels allgemeiner Grundsätze nicht zugänglich sind. Die Statutisten haben scheinbar die Tatsache aus den Augen verloren, dass sie an einer Frage arbeiteten, welche die *comitas* unter den Nationen zum Gegenstand hatte, und dass bei der Erfassung dieser *comitas* ein unlösbarer Rest übrigbleibt und stets übrig bleiben muss.[42]

4.   DAS ERGEBNIS

§ 15.   Auf diese Weise durch ein US-amerikanisches Präzedenz in seiner eigenen Einschätzung gestärkt, kehrte Story zur *comitas*-Lehre von Ulrich Huber zurück.[43] Sie allein überzeugte ihn, ihr war er zu folgen bereit und dazu hielt er als Ergebnis fest:

Huber hat drei Axiome aufgestellt, welche seines Erachtens genügen, um alle Schwierigkeiten im IPR zu lösen, nämlich:

(1)   Die Gesetze jedes Staatswesens entfalten ihre Bindungswirkung nur in den Grenzen der staatlichen Hoheitsgewalt; sie verpflichten dort alle Rechtsunterworfenen, aber nicht darüber hinaus.

(2)   Alle Personen, die sich auf dem Hoheitsgebiet eines Staates befinden, gleichgültig, ob ihr Aufenthalt dort andauert oder nur vorübergehender Natur ist, gelten als Rechtsunterworfene dieses Staates.

(3)   Die Rechtsgrundsätze jedes Staatswesens gehen aufgrund der *comitas* davon aus, dass den Gesetzen jedes Volkes, die in seinem Herrschaftsbereich in Kraft stehen, überall die gleiche Wirkung zukommen sollte, soweit dadurch nicht die Herrschaftsgewalt oder die Rechtsansprüche anderer Regierungen oder deren Bürger beeinträchtigt werden.[44]

---

[40] Story (oben N. 5) S. 28, Rdz. 28.
[41] Vgl. 5 Mart, N.S. (La), 595/6.
[42] Story (oben N. 5) S. 28, 29.
[43] Story (oben N. 5) S. 29, Rdz. 29.
[44] Story (oben N. 5) S. 29.

§ 16.   Diesen von Ulrich Huber übernommenen Grundsätzen fügt Story bestäti-
gend hinzu: Selbstverständlich werden die ersten zwei Maximen Hubers heutzutage von kaum jemandem in Frage gestellt. Und die dritte Maxime scheint sich zwingend aus dem Recht und der Pflicht jeder Nation zu ergeben, der aufgetragen ist,
ihre eigenen Rechtsunterworfenen gegen Rechtsgutverletzungen zu schützen, die
sich aus einem ungerechten und nachteiligen Einfluss ausländischer Rechte ergeben können.[45] Und er schliesst seine theoretische Auseinandersetzung über die Statutenlehre mit der Feststellung: In der Verwendung des Huberschen Begriffes der
comity of nations ist demnach nichts Ungebührliches zu erblicken; vielmehr handelt es sich hierbei um den Grundsatz, der [zur Zeit] am besten in der Lage ist, den
theoretischen Grund dafür zu umschreiben, dass es eine Pflicht gibt zur Anwendung der Gesetze eines Staates auf dem Hoheitsgebiet eines anderen, und auch die
sachliche Reichweite dieser Pflicht zum Ausdruck zu bringen.[46]

§ 17.   Eine kritisch-nüchterne Auseinandersetzung mit Story's *General Maxims of
International Jurisprudence*[47] lässt klar erkennen, dass er auf der Grundlage einer
späten, starke territorialistisch ausgerichteten und mit viel Souveränitätsdenken an-
gereicherter Statutenlehre gearbeitet hat. Aber auch so hat die Statutenlehre in Story's Thesen zur Lösung des *Conflict of Laws* nur einen sehr kleinen Platz eingenommen. Wenn es nämlich um die Lösung von Gesetzeskollisionen ging, hat Story
– vergleichbar einem strengen Positivisten – gefordert, der Richter solle bezüglich
der Anwendung von fremdem Recht zunächst das tun, was ihm sein Gesetzgeber
oder allenfalls das einschlägige Gewohnheitsrecht vorschreibe.[48] Erst wenn Gesetz
und Gewohnheitsrecht keine Lösung enthalten, dann und nur könne eine Kontroverse um die Frage nach dem anwendbaren Recht auftreten.[49] Und erst unter dieser
Hypothese – gleichsam im Falle eines *real* oder *true conflict* – sieht Story Raum für
den Einsatz von Huber's *comitas*-Theorie.

5.   CARL GEORG WÄCHTER

§ 18.   Für seine oben erwähnte wissenschaftliche Position hätte Story – offenbar
ohne es zu wissen – in Carl Georg Wächter einen ferventen europäischen Verbündeten gehabt.
    Carl Georg von Wächter (1797-1880), aus dem württembergischen Marbach am
Neckar, wurde mit 21 Jahren Professor in Tübingen und hat sich regelmässig zwi-

---

[45] Story (oben N. 5) S. 31.
[46] Story (oben N. 5) S. 35, Rdz. 38.
[47] So der Titel seines zweiten allgemeinen Kapitels, Story (oben N. 5) S. 21.
[48] Story (oben N. 5) S. 25.
[49] Story (oben N. 5) S. 25, Mitte und S. 29, Rdz. 29.

schen Tübingen und Leipzig hin- und herbewegt. Von Haus aus war er an sich ein
Spezialist des Strafrechts; zum IPR kam er vermutlich aufgrund eines Gesetzge-
bungsauftrages. Jedenfalls hat er 1841/42 in einem vierteiligen Aufsatz „Über die
Kollision der Privatrechtsgesetze verschiedener Staaten"[50] sich seine eigene Meinung zu den umstrittenen IPR-Fragen seiner Zeit gebildet. In der Literatur wird von
Wächter immer wieder gesagt, er sei in Deutschland der grosse Kritiker der Statutenlehre gewesen; ein eigener theoretischer Wurf sei ihm aber versagt geblieben.[51]

Wächter war gewiss ein grosser Kritiker; seine radikale Kritik an der damaligen
IPR-Wissenschaft war für ihn nicht zuletzt deshalb möglich, weil er ganz einfach
die Publikationen seiner Zeitgenossen sehr genau gelesen und analysiert hatte. Diese Arbeit hat ihn auch in die Lage versetzt, den verschiedenen zeitgenössischen
(und früheren) Autoren ihre eigenen Syllogismen und Scheinbegründungen mit
entwaffnender Klarheit vor Augen zu führen.[52]

Daneben aber hat Wächter durchaus auch seine eigene IPR-Theorie entwickelt,
und zwar vertrat auch er eine streng positivistische und in diesem Sinn mit Story's
Lehren geistig stark verwandte Theorie.[53]

6.   DIE IPR-VERSTÄNDNISSE IM VERGLEICH

§ 19.   Wächter hat seine Untersuchungen zum IPR mit einer konkreten Frage begonnen: Nach welchen Rechtsnormen hat der Richter unseres Landes über ein ihm
vorgelegtes Rechtsverhältnis zu entscheiden? Diese Frage war für Wächter zunächst eine Frage nach der massgebenden Rechtsquelle, und die Antwort darauf –
hierin wird Wächter's Parallele zu Story's erster Maxime augenfällig – ist für den
Tübinger Professor ganz klar: Quelle müssen logischerweise die Gesetze sein, auf
die der urteilende Richter verpflichtet ist; massgebend sind also die am Gerichtsort,
im Gerichtsstaat, am Forum geltenden Gesetze. Mit jenen Gesetzen hat Wächter –
und hat auch Story – nicht etwa bloss die materielle, sondern ebenfalls die kollisionsrechtliche *lex fori* gemeint. Wächter hat hierzu gleichsam als *erste* Maxime
festgehalten:

„Es hat somit – dies ist der erste leitende Grundsatz – der Richter zunächst darauf
zu achten, ob nicht das positive Recht seines Landes eine ausdrückliche Entschei-

---

[50] Vgl. *Archiv für civilistische Praxis (AcP)* (1841) S. 290-311, 1842, S. 1-60, S. 161-200 und S.
361-619. Die theoretisch interessanten Aussagen finden sich in *AcP* (1841) S. 236-270.

[51] Vgl. statt vieler, z.B. Gerhard Kegel (oben N. 3) S. 117, 118.

[52] Vgl. AcP (oben N. 50) S. 235, 236: „Ich fand über das, was bis jetzt bei uns in Deutschland geleistet worden ist, nirgends eine gründliche und genügende Übersicht, und da, wo die Ansichten Anderer berührt sind, geschieht dies meist so ungenau, dass man nicht einmal einen Umriss vom Stande der
Meinungen erhält". Ferner ibid., S. 270ff.

[53] Vgl. *AcP* (oben N. 50) S. 239.

dung der Frage enthalte. Entscheidet dieses die Frage, so ist für ihn jeder Zweifel behoben; er hat dann in der Sache auf die Weise zu verfahren, welche ihm das Recht seines Landes vorschreibt, somit auf die konkreten Fälle die Gesetze, sei es des Auslandes oder des Inlandes anzuwenden, deren Anwendung sein Landesrecht gebietet.“[54]

Bei Story lautete die entsprechende Aussage:

„Wenn das Gesetzbuch des Forumstaates sich zu der Frage [des anwendbaren Rechtes] selber positiv äussert, muss dieser Gesetzesbefehl von allen Personen befolgt werden, die unter der Souveränität des betreffenden Staates stehen.“[55]

§ 20.   Wächter hat seine Untersuchung mit der Frage fortgesetzt: Was soll gelten, „[w]enn solche partikulären Normen [sc. des staatlichen Rechts dem Richter] keine bestimmte Entscheidung an die Hand geben“? Und er fragt sich: Enthält das gemeine (römische) Recht, allenfalls das deutsch-germanische Recht ausdrückliche und ausreichende Bestimmungen über die Rechtsanwendungsfrage, und hat sich darauf aufbauend ein festes und bestimmtes Gewohnheitsrecht in Deutschland herausgebildet? Aufgrund seiner Lektüre in den Publikationen, die bisher in Europa zur Statutenlehre erschienen sind, kommt Wächter zu dem Ergebnis: die Vertreter der Statutenlehre sind untereinander derart stark zerstritten und ihre Lehren sind mit so vielen Widersprüchlichkeiten behaftet, dass man wissenschaftlich nicht ernsthaft davon ausgehen kann, es habe sich auf der Grundlage der Statuten-Lehren in Deutschland ein festes Gewohnheitsrecht herausgebildet.[56] Entsprechend hält Wächter als zweite Maxime fest:

„[W]enn sonst keine allgemeine ausdrückliche Entscheidung [sc. des Gesetzgebers] vorliegt, [muss der Richter] die Entscheidung zunächst im Sinne und Geiste derjenigen besonderen, in seinem Lande geltenden Gesetze [suchen], welche das vor ihn gebrachte Verhältnis an sich zum Gegenstand haben (...). Ergibt sich aus dem Sinne und Geiste dieser Gesetze, dass eine Anwendung auf Fremde, auf Verhältnisse, die im Ausland begründet wurden, und dergl. dem Sinne und Geiste derselben gemäss oder entgegen ist, so hat der Richter lediglich hiernach zu verfahren. Denn er muss die Gesetze, unter denen er steht, ihrem Sinne gemäss zur Anwendung bringen.“[57]

In diesem zweiten Punkt hatte es Story einfacher als Wächter, denn im angelsächsischen Recht ist das durch Rechtsprechung entwickelte Gewohnheitsrecht eine unumstritten anerkannte Rechtsquelle. In diesem Sinn konnte er (Story) kurz und bündig festhalten:

---

[54] Vgl. *AcP* (oben N. 50) S. 239, 240.
[55] Story (oben N. 5) S. 25, Rdz. 23.
[56] Vgl. *AcP* (oben N. 50), S. 242-261.
[57] Vgl. *AcP* (oben N. 50) S. 261, 262.

„When its [sc. the forum States] customary, unwritten, or common law speaks directly on the subject, it is equally to be obeyed for it has an equal obligation with its positive code."[58]

§ 21. Wächter war nicht gegen das Gewohnheitsrecht; er hielt nur (aber immerhin – auch hierin trifft er sich mit Story) fest, aufgrund der in sich total zerstrittenen Statutenlehre, wie sie sich noch um 1840 in Europa präsentiert habe, könne man nicht behaupten, es habe sich auf deren Grundlage für das deutsche Kollisionsrecht ein Gewohnheitsrecht herausgebildet.[59] Angesicht dieser Sach- und Rechtslage sah sich Wächter veranlasst, für die weitere Entwicklung des deutschen IPR auf jene Grundlagen zurückzugreifen, aus denen sich ein entsprechendes kollisionsrechtliches Gewohnheitsrecht hätte entwickeln können. Das konnte nach Überzeugung der Positivisten Wächter nur der Sinn und Geist (später bei Ihering wurde es der Zweck) der einschlägigen Gesetzgebung sein.

Auch wenn es auf den ersten Blick anders aussehen mag, so ist in Bezug auf dieses zweite Prinzip der inhaltliche Unterschied zwischen Story und Wächter nicht sehr gross gewesen. Gemeinsam war beiden der inhaltliche Kern des zweiten Prinzips, nämlich die Massgeblichkeit des Gewohnheitsrechts. Ein wichtiger Unterschied ergab sich freilich aus der wissenschaftlich unterschiedlichen Beurteilung des Gewohnheitsrechts im angloamerikanischen bzw. im deutsch-europäischen Recht. Während für Story Bestand und Entwicklung eines kollisionsrechtlichen Gewohnheitsrechts für das *common law* selbstverständlich war, hatte Wächter für das deutsche IPR ohne weiteres bestreiten können, dass sich ein solches Gewohnheitsrecht auf der Grundlage der in sich zerstrittenen Statutenlehre damals habe herausbilden können.

§ 22. Ein fundamentaler Unterschied zwischen Story und Wächter bestand freilich in Bezug auf das dritte Lösungsprinzip: Für Wächter galt: Wenn weder aus dem klaren Gesetzeswortlaut des Forums (erstes Prinzip) noch aus dem Geist eines Gesetzes (zweites Prinzip) die Entscheidung über eine IPR-Frage sich mit Bestimmtheit entnehmen lässt,

„so hat der Richter im Zweifel das Recht seines Landes [die lex fori] in Anwendung zu bringen."[60]

Story hingegen hatte zur gleichen Fragestellung festgehalten:

„When both [the code as well as the customary law] are silent then, *and then only*, can the question properly arise, what law is to govern in the absence of any clear declaration of the sovereign will."[61]

---

[58] Story (oben N. 5) S. 25, Rdz. 23.
[59] Vgl. *AcP* (oben N. 50) S. 261, oben.
[60] Vgl. *AcP* (oben N. 50) S. 265.
[61] Story (oben N. 5) S. 25, Rdz. 23.

Mit anderen Worten: Wo für Wächter die IPR-Diskussion endet und er mangels anderweitiger Lösung auf die *lex fori* zurückgreifen will, dort fängt für Story die eigentliche IPR-Aufgabe erst an. Erst hier setzt nämlich Story sein drittes Prinzip, d.h. die von Huber übernommene *comitas*-Lehre ein, d.h. erst hier gilt für Story:

„that the rulers of every empire from comity admit that the laws of every people in force within ist own limits ought to have the same forces everywhere (...).“[62]

Aber die Akzeptanz der unter einer anderen Rechtsordnung entstandenen Rechtsansprüche geschieht für Story nicht vorbehaltlos, sondern, wie er es schon betont hatte, nur:

„in so far as those laws do not prejudice the powers or rights of other governments or of their citizen, for no nation can be justly required to yield up ist own fundamental policy and institution in favor of another nation.“[63]

7. Das Fazit

§ 23. Wie der vorstehende Vergleich gezeigt hat, sind sich Story und Wächter in ihren Positionen vom Vorrang der *lex fori* einerseits und der bloss kontrollierten Berücksichtigung des ausländischen Rechts andererseits ziemlich nahegestanden. Aber ihr Einfluss auf die weitere Entwicklung war sehr verschieden.

In Europa ist die theoretische Leistung Wächter's von der Wissenschaft nur halb, nämlich nur in Bezug auf seine scharfe Kritik an den Statutisten zur Kenntnis genommen worden. Hingegen waren Wächter's eigene IPR-Ideen – obwohl sie den Vergleich mit vielen Statutisten nicht hätten zu scheuen brauchen – von Anfang an chancenlos. Die europäische Wissenschaft hatte ganz einfach keine Zeit, sie zur Kenntnis zu nehmen, denn schon ganz kurz nach Erscheinen von Wächter's Analysen sollte der europäische Kontinent vollständig in den Bann der neuen Theorien Savigny's fallen.

Im angelsächsischen Raum hingegen hat Story's comity-Lehre mit ihrer Mischung aus stark territorialer Verankerung in der *lex fori* und behutsamer, vom Rechtsschutzgedanken geprägter Öffnung in Richtung ausländischen Rechts die zweite Hälfte des 19. Jahrhunderts vollständig beherrscht.

Man braucht kein Hellseher zu sein, um zu erahnen, dass der positivistische *lex fori*-Ansatz mit Hilfe der Dominanz, die ihr nach 1834 im angelsächsischen Raum zugute gekommen ist, auch auf dem europäischen Kontinent sich stärkeres Gehör verschafft hätte. Ob das ausgereicht hätte, um Savigny's Einfluss zu retardieren, und vor allem, was dann mit Mancini geschehen wäre, lässt sich höchstens erahnen. Sicher ist, dass diese beiden gegen ein *joint venture* von Wächter und Story einen erheblich schwereren Stand gehabt hätten.

---

[62] Story (oben N. 5) S. 35.
[63] Story (oben N. 5) S. 29.

Summary
If Wächter met Story

Joseph Story (1779-1845), Justice of the US Supreme Court and Professor at Harvard Law School, was among the very first legal writers who published in English on the conflict of laws. In his treatise of 1834 Story introduced the theories of the European *statutists* to the English speaking world. It was, however, a very special form of the said theory, i.e., the form which the statutist's theory had received under the respective influences of B. d'Argentré, P. Boulenois and, above all, Ulrich Huber. These influences gave Story's variant of the statutist theory a strongly territorialist and rather positivist look. Regarding the application (or the taking into consideration) of foreign laws, Story's position was based on three principles: (1) A state may prohibit the operation of all foreign laws, and the rights arising out of them, within its own territory. It may prohibit the application of some foreign laws and it may admit the operation of others. (2) Where its own Code speaks positively on a subject, it must be obeyed by all persons who are within its reach. When its customary law speaks on the subject, it is equally to be obeyed. (3) When both the written and the customary law are silent, *then and then only*, can the question properly arise of which law is to govern. It was only under this last hypothesis that Story resorted to the theories of Ulrich Huber.

It was almost at the same time, when Carl Friedrich Wächter (1797-1880), Professor at Tübingen and Leipzig, was working on the conflict of laws topic. Like Story, Wächter took, as a starting point, a strong positivist and entirely territorialist position: To the initial question of "what legal rules a judge of our country should apply" when he was to decide on conflict of law problems, Wächter answered: As the first guiding principle, the judge must do what the law of his country specifically provides with regard to the law to be applied. If this law decides upon the question, then every doubt is removed and the judge proceeds in the manner provided for by the legal rule of his country. Wächter's second question was: Which principles should the judge apply when the legal rule of his country lacks a particular rule? Regarding this question, Wächter came to the conclusion that the theory of the statutists did not offer an adequate solution to the problem. Therefore Wächter suggested: If it follows from the sense and spirit of the domestic statutes that it is acceptable (or unacceptable) to apply domestic rules to foreign nationals, to relations created abroad, etc., the judge shall then proceed accordingly and apply (or not apply) domestic rules to them. All in all, the views of Story and Wächter were not that far from one another. What, if they would have had a chance to discuss the topic together? Would the conflict of laws theory have taken a different direction? A joint venture between Story and Wächter might well have been strong enough to temper the influences of Savigny and Mancini.

Überlegungen betreffend die Auslegung fremder Rechtsnormen

Spyridon Vrellis[*]

1. EINFÜHRUNG

1.1 Die herrschende Auffassung und ihre innere Rechtfertigung

Die herrschende Auffassung, man könnte sogar sagen die jetzt in Europa einhellige Meinung auf dem Gebiet des internationalen Privatrechts nimmt an, dass „die fremden Normen (...) auch im Inland aus dem Zusammenhang und Geist der fremden Rechtsordnung ausgelegt werden müssen",[1] mit anderen Worten ist das in einem anderen Staat tatsächlich praktizierte Recht zu ermitteln, so dass unsere Entschei-

---

[*] Professor des Internationalen Privatrechts an der Juristischen Fakultät der Universität Athen.

[1] Kropholler, *Internationales Privatrecht* (Tübingen, Mohr Siebeck 1990) 187; zu dieser Frage siehe weiter Yasseen, „Problèmes relatifs à l'application du droit étranger", *Recueil des Cours* (1962-II) 574ff.

J. Basedow et al., eds., Private Law in the International Arena – Liber Amicorum Kurt Siehr
© 2000, T.M.C.Asser Press, The Hague, The Netherlands

dung im konkreten Fall, „derjenigen so nahe wie möglich kommen" sollte, „die im Lande der lex causae gefällt werden würde, wäre der Prozess dort betrieben worden",[2] fremdes Recht ist also „grundsätzlich so anzuwenden, wie es im Ausland gilt",[3] es ist zu prüfen, wie die konkret anwendbare ausländische Rechtsnorm im Ausland interpretiert und verstanden wird.[4] Unser Richter „verhält sich, wie sich der fremde Richter bei Anwendung seines eigenen Rechts verhalten würde; er handelt, als sässe er an Stelle des fremden Richters".[5]

Die innere Rechtfertigung der soeben dargelegten Ansicht[6] liegt darin, dass die Auslegung der anwendbaren fremden Norm gemäss den Prinzipien der *lex fori* zu einer Deformation der betreffenden Norm – zu einer Veränderung ihres Sinnes – führen könnte. Folglich würden wir eine Norm anwenden, die nicht die tatsächliche ausländische Rechtsnorm (Teil der anwendbaren *lex causae*) ist (weder die Norm eines anderen Staates, noch eine Norm, die irgendwo in der Welt gelten würde), obwohl unsere Kollisionsnorm die Anwendung dieser bestimmten fremden *lex causae* – und nicht die eines anderen Rechts – gebietet. Ein solches Vorgehen aber würde die Anordnungen unserer Kollisionsnorm mißachten.[7]

Den soeben dargelegten Ausführungen ist freilich mit Vorsicht zu begegnen, scheint es doch unmöglich, im Forumstaat die ausländische Norm immer genau so auszulegen und anzuwenden, wie dies im Rahmen ihrer eigenen Rechtsordnung geschieht. Deshalb ist es auch der Kollisionsnorm zu untersagen, die Anwendung eines fremden Rechts als solches – im strikten Sinn – zu gebieten. Folgt man diesen Ausführungen, so ist es denn unmöglich, eine Kollisionsnorm zu verletzen, indem man das (um die Franceskakische Terminologie zu benutzen[8]) *direkt* anzuwendende ausländische Recht im Forumstaat nicht genau so anwendet, wie dieses Recht im Ausland, und zwar im Staat der *lex causae*, angewandt wird. Es gibt Faktoren, die uns anzunehmen zwingen, dass unser Richter bei der Auslegung fremden Rechts in der Regel grundsätzlich wie bei der Auslegung unseres Rechts handeln muss. Vor-

---

[2] V. Bar, *Internationales Privatrecht I* (München 1987) 327.

[3] Raape/ Sturm, *IPR I*, 6. Aufl., (München 1977) 309 in fine; Schnitzer, „L'égalité de la loi étrangère et de la loi interne dans les rapports internationau", *Rev. Hell.* (1969) 37; Kötz, „Allgemeine Rechtsgrundsätze als Ersatzrecht",34 *RabelsZ* (1970) 664.

[4] Keller/ Siehr, *Allgemeine Lehren des internationalen Privatrechts* (Zürich 1986) 505.

[5] Neumayer, „Fremdes Recht und Normenkontrolle", 23 *RabelsZ* (1958) 589; Motulsky, „L'office du juge et la loi étrangère", *Mélanges J. Maury I* (1960) 362-363; Siehr, „Die Zeitschrift für Schweizerisches Recht und das schweizerische Privatrecht in der deutschen Rechtspraxis", *ZSR n.F.* 100 (1981) I 59. Bei einer solchen Tätigkeit „entfalteten die deutschen Gerichte" sehr oft (wie der Jubilar, dem diese Zeilen gewidmet sind (oben S. 57??) zutreffend bemerkt hat („eigene Phantasie, um den Geist des schweizerischen Rechts zu erfassen und zur Geltung zu bringen".

[6] Man hat auch verschiedene andere Gründe vorgeschlagen; siehe z.B. Kropholler (oben N. 1) 187; Kegel, *IPR*, 6. Aufl. (München 1987) 318-319.

[7] Schnitzer (oben N. 3) 45; vgl. Dölle, „De l'application du droit étranger par le juge interne", *Rev. Crit.* (1955) 244.

[8] Siehe Francescakis, *La loi étrangère à la Cour de cassation*, D. 1963 Chron. 7.

ausgesetzt ist jedenfalls, dass das anwendbare fremde Recht, als Recht *ex officio* vom inländischen Richter angewandt wird.[9]

1.2   Zweckmässige Erklärungen

Zwei Vorbemerkungen scheinen zweckmässig: (a) Zuerst müssen wir zwischen der reinen Auslegung des fremden anwendbaren Rechts und der Gültigkeit der fremden Norm unterscheiden. Wenn die Gültigkeit des fremden anwendbaren Rechts in Frage steht, müssen wir der ausländischen Rechtsordnung grundsätzlich folgen und nicht eine fremde Norm als geltend anwenden, die im Ausland nicht (mehr) gilt. Hieraus folgt z. B., dass – bei einer Änderung der ausländischen Gesetzgebung – die anwendbare *lex causae* zu entscheiden hat, ob die alten oder die neuen Rechtsnormen anzuwenden sind.[10] Problematisch bleibt dagegen, wie sich unser Richter bei der Überprüfung der Verfassungsmässigkeit der fremden Norm verhalten soll.[11] Sicher sein dürfte (i) dass unser Richter nicht eine fremde Norm als verfassungswidrig erklären darf, weil dies eine unerlaubte „politische" Maßnahme darstellen würde,[12] und (ii) dass er eine Entscheidung des zuständigen ausländischen Gerichts über die Verfassungswidrigkeit oder -mässigkeit der ausländischen Norm zu respektieren hat, zumindest falls eine solche Entscheidung endgültig ist.

(b)   Es gibt – so erscheint es zumindest – einige Verwirrung im Rahmen der herrschenden Meinung. Man muss unterscheiden und entscheiden: Entweder nimmt man an, dass unser Richter genau so handeln muss, wie der ausländische Richter zu *handeln hat*, oder, dass unser Richter entscheiden muss, so wie der ausländische Richter schon in analogen Fällen *entschieden hat*. Nur im zweiten Fall respektiert man die ausländische Rechtsprechung, indem man nur in diesem Fall das ausländi-

---

[9] Analoge Probleme entstehen auch bei der Auslegung einer ausländischen Kollisionsnorm. Siehe z.B. Kegel (oben N. 5) 249; v. Bar (oben N. 2) 329; Keller/ Siehr (oben N. 4) 503-504; Raape/Sturm (oben N. 3) 169. Siehe auch das englische Urteil *Re the Sixth Duke of Wellington, deceased; Glentanar (the executor)* v. *Wellington*, 15 *RabelsZ* (1949/50) 149f., [betreffend die Stellung des spanischen Rechts zur Frage der Rückverweisung] mit Anm. von Neuhaus 161-165 (164) und Goldschmidt 342ff. Es ist hier nicht möglich auf diese Problematik weiter einzugehen; es sei jedoch angemerkt, dass die Notwendigkeit einer differenzierten Lösung für beide Fälle nicht von vornherein ausgeschlossen werden kann.

[10] So z.B. in Frankreich; siehe Batiffol/ Lagarde, *Droit international privé*, 7 ed. (Paris, Librairie générale de droit et de jurisprudence 1981)391. Zu dieser Frage weiter Yasseen (oben N. 1) 571-573. Anderer Auffassung Raape/ Sturm (oben N. 3) 310.

[11] Zu dieser Frage siehe z.B. Kropholler (oben N. 1) 189; Kegel (oben N. 6) 318; v. Bar (oben N. 2) 327; Raape/Sturm (oben N. 3) 310; Yasseen (oben N. 1) 567ff.; Neumayer, (oben N. 5) 589ff., insb. 596-597. (Problematisch scheint mir auch die Pflicht unseres Richters bei der Prüfung der Völkerrechtswidrigkeit der fremden Norm; siehe darüber Kropholler (oben N. 1) 190; Kegel (oben N. 6) 318, der zwischen Staatsangehörigkeits- und Enteignungsrecht einerseits und Privatrecht andererseits unterscheidet.

[12] Batiffol/Lagarde (oben N. 10) 390; Audit, *Droit international privé* (Paris 1991) 236.

sche Recht anwendet, wie es tatsächlich „en fait" im Ausland gilt. Wer so handelt, handelt zwar gemäss der bisherigen ausländischen Rechtsprechung, aber nicht wie der ausländische Richter handeln würde, wenn er im konkreten Fall gar nicht an die Rechtsprechung seines eigenen Landes gebunden wäre. Es ist sodann fraglich, warum unser Richter geringere rechtsschöpferische Macht haben soll als sein ausländischer Kollege. Es scheint zweifelhaft, dass unsere Kollisionsnorm einen Teil der Freiheit des Richters, die anzuwendende Norm auszulegen, entzieht.

2. DIE NOTWENDIGKEIT DER ANPASSUNG UND IHRE RECHTSSCHÖPFERISCHE ROLLE

2.1 Die Notwendigkeit einer Anpassung der fremden Rechtsnorm

Bei der „direkten" (aufgrund einer Kollisionsnorm) Anwendung fremden Rechts stossen wir auf ein interessantes Phänomen. Wir haben verschiedene Normen anzuwenden, die zu verschiedenen (mindestens zwei, oftmals zu mehreren) Rechtsordnungen gehören, oder die aus verschiedenen Rechtsordnungen entstanden sind. Die anwendbare ausländische Vorschrift genügt freilich nicht, alle Rechtsfragen eines Falles zu regeln.[13] Um den Rechtsstreit zu lösen, ist es notwendig, verschiedene Rechtsnormen aus verschiedenen Teilen des Rechtssystems zu kombinieren. Jeder Teil kann aber (bei internationalen Rechtsfällen) aus verschiedenen Rechtsordnungen genommen werden. Alle diese anwendbaren und zu verschiedenen Rechtssystemen gehörenden Normen müssen eingegliedert und kombiniert angewandt werden, um ein harmonisch konstruiertes und für die Rechtsordnung des Forums erfreuliches Ergebnis zu erreichen. Aber auch wenn wir annnehmen wollen, dass allein das anwendbare ausländische Recht anzuwenden wäre, würde auch in diesem Fall die fremde Rechtsnorm berufen, Folgen in einem anderen Land, d.h. im Forumstaat zu entwickeln.

Diese letzte Notwendigkeit, verschiedene Normen aus verschiedenen Rechtsordnungen zu kombinieren, führt zur Pflicht, eine Anpassung der fremden Normen zu unternehmen,[14] deren Anwendung sonst die harmonische Struktur und die logische Gestaltung des Rechtssystems im Forumstaat stören könnte. Durch eine angemessene Auslegung der am Anfang störenden fremden Norm wäre es oft möglich, diese Norm mit den anderen Regeln unserer Rechtsordnung in Einklang zu bringen. Zu einer solchen passenden Auslegung, die nicht zwangsweise identisch mit der im

---

[13] Manchmal stossen wir auf ausländische Rechtsinstitute und -begriffe, die im Inland ganz unbekannt sind. Vgl. dazu Raape/ Sturm (oben N. 3) 310.

[14] Natürlich könnte man auch an eine Anpassung der inländischen Rechtsordnung denken, bleiben wir aber bei der Anpassung des fremden Rechts, ohne zu prüfen, ob die Anpassung des inländischen Rechts möglich und zweckmässig sei.

Ausland herrschenden Auslegung wäre, sollte unser Richter mit der Hilfe unserer Rechtsordnung fortschreiten. So könnte wahrscheinlich eine Auslegung nach der lex fori ein geeignetes Mittel zur Anpassung bilden. Die Kollisionsnorm gebietet eine abstrakte Anwendung eines (fremden) Rechts; der Richter wird aber der konkreten fremden Norm den Sinn geben, der den Wert der Justiz und die Interessen der Rechtsordnung im Forumstaat *in concreto* vollständiger befriedigt.

2.2   Die richterliche Schaffung einer neuen inländischen Rechtsnorm

Die Anpassung bedeutet häufig eine mehr oder weniger grosse Änderung der Physiognomie der fremden Rechtsnorm, eine Transformation, eine Veränderung der fremden Norm. So ist es nicht die fremde Norm als solche, die wir am Ende im Forumstaat anwenden, sondern eine andere, neue, von jener inspirierte Norm. Und es ist nicht der Gesetzgeber, sondern der Jurist und zwar der Richter, der eine solche Norm schafft, so dass wir wirklich von einem Juristen- oder Richterrecht sprechen müssen. Dieses Juristenrecht ist nicht das Kollisionsrecht; es ist das materielle Recht, das am Ende auf einen „internationalen" Fall im Inland angewandt wird,[15] ein Recht, das natürlich inländisch und nicht ausländisch ist[16] und nicht zwangsweise denselben Inhalt wie die fremde Norm hat.

Demnach scheint die ausländische anwendbare Norm in den Händen des inländischen Richters nicht mehr so fremd. Sie hat insgesamt mit unserem Recht den Sachverhalt in passender Weise zu regeln. Unser Richter wird die fremde Norm benutzen[17] und ihr den passenden Sinn geben. Die ausländische Rechtsnorm ist nicht inflexibel und von aussen als Factum gegeben; sie ist ein lebendiges Material in den Händen unseres Richters. Niemand kann versichern, dass sie zwangsläufig unver-

---

[15] Die rechtsschöpferische Tätigkeit unseres Richters bei der Anwendung fremden Rechts wird mit Recht, obwohl aus anderem Grund, von Keller/ Siehr (oben N. 4) 506, betont.

[16] A.A. z.B. Schnitzer (oben N. 3) 37 („Le droit étranger reste toujours un droit étranger et ce caractère n'est pas changé par le fait que l'organe d'un autre pays l'applique"); Dölle (oben N. 7) 238-239 („Le droit étranger ne devient…ni droit national ni simple fait. Il reste droit, et droit étranger, pour le contenu duquel le législateur décline toute responsabilité". Natürlich hat unser Gesetzgeber keine Verantwortlichkeit betreffend den Inhalt des anwendbaren fremden Rechts. Aber unser Richter ist mitverantwortlich [mit unserem Gesetzgeber] für die passende Regelung des konkreten Falles durch die kombiniert anwendbaren Rechtsregeln mehrerer Rechtsordnungen). Neumayer (oben N. 5) 595, verneinte unserem Richter „jede Macht, mit einer über die Prozessbeteiligten hinausgreifenden Wirkung für die in einem *fremden* Staate organisierte Gemeinschaft verbindliches Recht zu schaffen"; vgl. ebenso Schnitzer (oben N. 3) 37-38. Der Richter des Forumstaats schafft aber keineswegs eine für den fremden Staat verbindliche Norm. Er ist immer nur im Rahmen seiner eigenen Rechtsordnung tätig. In diesem Rahmen benützt er die fremde anwendbare Norm, um ihren Sinn schöpferisch zu konkretisieren, und bietet uns eine Lösung an, die für das Inland gilt. Von der ausländischen Rechtsordnung hängt es ab, ob sie diese Lösung anerkennen würde oder nicht.

[17] Francescakis, D. 1963 Chron. 12: „(…) la loi étrangère interne est *utilisée plutôt qu'appliquée* pour la réglementation satisfaisante des relations internationales".

sehrt angewandt werden kann. Im Gegenteil gibt es immer die Möglichkeit und gelegentlich das Bedürfnis, die fremde Norm transformiert anzuwenden. Die
letztendliche Regelung kann auf jeden Fall weder die unseres Rechtssystems noch
jene der *lex causae* oder irgendeines anderen Rechts sein, sondern eine verschiedene, die *a priori* in keiner eingerichteten Rechtsordnung zu finden ist.[18] Dies, weil –
wie oben dargestellt – in den verschiedenen Teilen des zu regelnden Sachverhalts
verschiedene Rechtssysteme berufen sind.

In Wahrheit sieht die Kollisionsnorm nicht ausdrücklich vor, dass das anwendbare Recht *in globo* anzuwenden ist, sondern nur in einem oder in manchen von seinen Teilen. Dieser Teil wird normalerweise (bei rein inländischen Fällen) mit den
anderen Teilen derselben Rechtsordnung zusammenfügt, und darum hat er dort bestimmte Form und Sinn. Wenn aber dieser Teil der Rechtsordnung A mit den übrigen Teilen einer anderen Rechtsordnung B in Einklang gebracht werden soll, oder
mit anderen Teilen, die zu unterschiedlichen Rechtsordnungen gehören, dann kann
er immer und muss er gelegentlich eine andere Form und einen anderen Sinn be-
kommen. Dieser Sinn wird ihm vom Richter des Forumstaats gegeben werden.[19]

Auf diese Weise haben wir bei internationalen Rechtsfällen besondere Normen
zu schaffen, vom fremden anwendbaren Recht inspirierte, die aber inländische Normen sind. Falls wir diese besondere heimische Norm auszulegen hätten, müssten
wir dies gemäss den Auslegungsmethoden der *lex fori* tun. Die Schaffung einer solchen besonderen inländischen Norm drückt sich in ihrer Anwendung aus. In Wirklichkeit legen wir diese Norm nicht aus und brauchen wir das nicht zu tun. Wir
wenden sie nur einfach an, „telle quelle", d. h. so wie sie von uns (von unserem

---

[18] Somit unterscheiden sich die hier vorgebrachten Ausführungen sowohl von den italienischen
Rezeptions- oder Inkorporationsauffassungen als auch von der amerikanischen local law theory. (Kötz
(oben N. 3) 675, hat uns mit Recht daran erinnert, dass „das IPR gelegentlich nicht vermeiden kann, die
massgeblichen Sachnormen des deutschen oder ausländischen Rechts ,anzupassen', sie also anzuwenden, wie sie weder im Inland noch im Ausland angewendet werden. Zwar stützt sich der Richter (…) in
diesen Fällen auf ein ,fiktives" Recht', doch müssen wir annehmen, dass für Sachverhalte mit ausländischen Merkmalen eine Regelung angemessen sein könne, die nirgendwo für Inlandsfälle gelte".

[19] So geschieht es nicht so wie Dölle (oben N. 7) 239, es darstellt, dass „l'ordre du législateur au
juge national d'appliquer le droit étranger en certains cas concrets veut dire ceci, qu'il peut, à la place
du juge étranger et tout comme celui-ci le ferait, appliquer le droit étranger, parce que les éléments de la
vie sociale qui sont en jeu demandent d'être jugés selon le système étranger". Gemäss Dölle (oben N. 7)
244, „l'ordre impératif de la règle de conflit revient généralement à ceci: juge comme le magistrat
étranger jugerait!" Ein solcher Befehl ist m.E. utopisch und deshalb unmöglich. Unser Richter würde
oft vergeblich versuchen, genauso wie sein ausländischer Kollege zu entscheiden. Der ausländische
Richter würde nur zufällig zu demselben Ergebnis kommen wie der inländische. Denn erstens ist sein
Kollisionsrecht verschieden; zweitens (dies ist hier wichtig) hängt sein Urteil nicht von einer einzigen
Rechtsnorm ab, sondern von einem Ganzen, bestehend aus vielen partiell zu kombinierenden Normen,
was zur Folge hat, dass jede partielle Norm einen bestimmten Sinn annimmt, einen Sinn der nicht derselbe wäre, wenn dieselbe Norm einen Teil eines verschiedenen Ganzen bilden würde. Der Wunsch allein durch die Auslegung und die Anwendung des fremden Rechts zu derselben Lösung zu kommen, zu
der der fremde Richter kommen würde, ist eine Utopie, die nur zufällig realisiert werden könnte.

Richter) geschaffen wurde. In diesem juristischen Gedankenprozess bilden wir die Norm mit dem Sinn, den wir ihr geben wollen, um die Norm mit genau diesem Inhalt – und nicht mit einem anderen – anzuwenden. Die Gestaltung des Sinnes einer solchen Norm realisiert sich, um den konkreten Fall zu erfassen. Bei Inlandsfällen haben wir normalerweise von vornherein eine abstrakte allgemeine Norm, der wir die bestimmten Sachverhalte in jedem konkreten Fall subsumieren. Hier geht es um das Gegenteil. Wir haben den konkreten Sachverhalt, wir betrachten die „anwendbare" fremde Norm und wir schaffen eine andere Norm, mit bestimmtem, von Anfang an bekanntem und demnach nicht auslegungsbedürftigem Inhalt für den konkreten Sachverhalt. Wir subsumieren nicht den Sachverhalt unter die allgemeine Rechtsnorm, sondern wir entscheiden über den Inhalt der zu schaffenden Norm nach Massgabe des konkreten Sachverhalts. Auch wenn diese Norm eine allgemeine Formulierung hat, ist ihr Inhalt von vornherein bekannt und nicht auslegungsbedürftig.[20]

2.3   Die Auslegung der zugrundeliegenden ausländischen Norm

Das wirkliche Auslegungsproblem ist so: Haben wir zuerst den wirklichen Sinn unseres Ausgangspunktes (der ausländischen anwendbaren Norm) durch die Auslegung zu ermitteln, um dann inspiriert zu werden? Aber wie gelangt man zu solch einer Ermittlung? Wäre eine solche Tätigkeit nötig oder aber vermeidbar?

Zuerst darf man bemerken, dass der Richter immer in der Lage ist, ein menschliches intellektuelles Erzeugnis wie die fremde Rechtsnorm (richtig oder falsch) zu verstehen, ihr näher zu kommen, von ihr (wie er sie versteht) inspiriert und beeinflusst zu werden, um weitere intellektuelle Felder zu erforschen, um – begründet auf dieser Norm – andere besondere und konkretere Normen zu schaffen. Demnach ist er in der Lage, mit den Mitteln seiner eigenen Rechtsordnung jene Norm als Sinn, als Bedeutung zu erfassen und weitere Normen zu schaffen. Dann könnte man hinzufügen, dass dieser Weg ausserdem vorzuziehen sei, weil sich die ganze Tätigkeit – wie oben dargestellt – mit dem Zweck entwickelt, eine neue inländische Norm zu schaffen. Bei einer solchen Tätigkeit ist es ganz normal, dass unsere hei-

---

[20]   Die Anpassung der anwendbaren fremden Rechtsnorm ist nicht eine Ausnahme, sondern eine übliche, immanente Tätigkeit in dem kollisionsrechtlichen Bereich, mit der extremen Form der Vorbehaltsklausel. Ausserdem ist sie immer vorhanden, obwohl sie nicht immer sichtbar ist. So gibt es Fälle, bei denen die Störung unbedeutend ist, und so scheint eine Anpassung kaum nötig. Die fremde Rechtsnorm ist von Anfang an „adaptable". Diese Eventualität kann aber weder das Phänomen als solches noch den Denkprozess verändern. Auch in einem solchen Fall haben wir letztlich eine vom inländischen Richter konstruierte und von dem ausländischen anwendbaren Recht inspirierte und beeinflusste Norm anzuwenden, die nur einen Sinn haben kann; den Sinn, den ihr während ihrer Schöpfung unser Richter gibt, um den Einklang unserer heimischen Rechtsordnung zu bewahren; einen Sinn, der nicht zwangsweise identisch ist (das kann nur zufällig geschehen), mit dem im Ausland von der dort herrschenden Ansicht angenommenen.

mische Rechtsordnung eine auf sich ziehende Funktion auf die fremde Norm ausübt. So darf der Richter das fremde Recht frei auslegen, auch wenn im Ausland die
unteren Gerichtsinstanzen an die Auslegung durch deren Kassationshöfe in anderen
Fällen gebunden sind. So dürfen wir den Satz von G. Kegel[21] verstehen: „Wir müssen denkend, nicht blind gehorchen".

2.4   Nachwirkungen auf die Revisionskontrolle

Der Gedanke, dass es sich bei der Anwendung fremden Rechts um die Schaffung
und die Anwendung einer neuen inländischen Rechtsnorm handele, führt zur Folge,
dass die richtige Anwendung dieser Norm (mit anderen Worten „die Auslegung des
anwendbaren fremden Rechts") vom Kassationshof geprüft werden müsse.[22] Diese
logische Folge wird aber nicht in allen Rechtsordnungen angenommen.[23] So wird
die Revisionskontrolle z.B. in Deutschland, wenn auch mit manchen Ausnahmen[24]
und grundsätzlich auch in der französischen Rechtsprechung[25] verneint. Man fürch-
tet die Überlastung der Revisionsinstanz,[26] sowie die Gefährdung ihres Ansehens
durch Irrtümer und man meint, dass die Rolle unseres obersten Gerichtshofs kaum
darin bestehen könne, sich um die Einheit des ausländischen Rechts zu sorgen.[27]

---

[21] Kegel (oben N. 6) 252.

[22] Ausserdem werden auch die fremden Normen von vielen als Rechtsnormen berücksichtigt; so
scheint ihre Überprüfung durch den Kassationshof ganz normal. Siehe Schnitzer (oben N. 3) 48-49; so
auch de lege ferenda Dölle (oben N. 7) 249. Zu der Frage der Revisionskontrolle vgl. weiter Heini, „Zur
Überprüfung des anwendbaren ausländischen Rechts durch das Bundesgericht de lege ferenda", SJZ
(1984) 163-164. Diese Lösung wird heute z.B. in Griechenland angenommen; siehe Areopag 181/1976
in Nomikon Wima 24 710-711; 1557/1986 in Nomikon Wima 35 1042-1043.

[23] Siehe die rechtsvergleichenden Ausführungen von Kerameus, „Revisibilität ausländischen
Rechts", ZZP (1986) 166-184.

[24] V. Bar (oben N. 2) 330ff.; Kegel (oben N. 6) 321; Raape/ Sturm (oben N. 3) 312. Zu dieser Frage
siehe weiter Dölle (oben N. 7) 246-249; Schütze, „Zur Revisibilität ausländischen Rechtes", NJW
(1970) 1584-1586; Fastrich, „Revisibilität der Ermittlung ausländischen Rechts", ZZP (1984) 423ff.;
Frank, „Les problèmes actuels posés par l'application des lois étrangères en droit international privé allemand", in: Les problèmes actuels posés par l'application des lois étrangères (Paris 1988) 104 in fine.

[25] Audit (oben N. 12) 235-236; Batiffol/ Lagarde (oben N. 10) 381-382, 394, 398-399 (die die Stellungnahme der französischen Cour de cassation für einigermassen realistisch halten); Ponsard,
„L'office du juge et l'application du droit étranger", Rev. Crit. (1990) 618-619; Lequette, „L'abandon
de la jurisprudence Bisbal (à propos des arrêts de la Première chambre civile des 11 et 18 octobre
1988)", Rev. Crit. (1989) 331-333. Siehe weiter Loussouarn/ Bourel, Droit international privé, 4e Ed.
(Paris 1993) 258ff.; Mayer, Droit international privé, 4e ed. (Paris 1991) 125ff., 133-135; Motulsky, in
Mélanges J. Maury I 370ff., Francescakis, D. 1963 Chron. 7-14; und zu der „dénaturation" des ausländischen Rechts Loussouarn, „Le contrôle par la Cour de cassation de l'application des lois étrangères",
in Travaux du Comité Français de d.i.p. (1962-1964) 133ff., insb. 139ff.; Batiffol, „La Cour de cassation de France et la dénaturation de la loi étrangère", Dölle-Festschrift II (1963) 209-216. Vgl. aber Cass.
civ. 10.10.1978 (Saccone et consorts Selva c. Soc. Comogav), Rev. Crit. (1979) 775 mit Anm. P. Cour-
be.

[26] V. Bar (oben N. 2) 331; Audit (oben N. 12) 236 N 1.

M.E. muss der inländische Kassationshof die Auslegung des fremden anwendbaren Rechts prüfen. Er wird auch in einem solchen Fall die Einheit der heimischen
Rechtsordnung sichern, weil seine Entscheidung für die unteren Gerichte zukunfts-
weisend sein soll, wenn sie mit der Auslegung desselben fremden Rechts zu tun haben. Ausserdem handelt es sich immer um die Gestaltung unserer eigenen
Rechsordnung, für die unser Kassationshof verantwortlich ist. Man muss nicht partiell sondern im Ganzen die Gestaltung der Rechtsprechung und ihre Rolle berücksichtigen.

3.   FOTOGRAFEN UND ARCHITEKTEN BEI DER AUSLEGUNG UND
      ANWENDUNG VON RECHTSNORMEN

3.1   Der vermeintliche Unterschied zwischen der Auslegung einer inländischen und jener einer ausländischen Norm

Die Vertreter der herrschenden Ansicht meinen, dass bei der Auslegung fremden
Rechts ausländische Rechtsprechung (soweit diese nicht schon Rechtsquelle ist)
und Literatur heranzuziehen und zu berücksichtigen seien, wie die ausländischen
Gerichte es tun,[28] dass unser Richter sich „grundsätzlich…dabei an die methodischen Regeln halten [solle], die in dem fremden Land beachtet werden",[29] und dass
er die Pflicht habe, falls eine Lösung im Ausland existiert, sie zu respektieren. Sie
haben hinzugefügt, dass bei der Anwendung fremden Rechts unser Richter Foto-
graf sei; dagegen sei er bei der Anwendung seines eigenen Rechts Architekt.[30] So
haben sie die Auslegung des inländischen Rechts von jener der ausländischen
Norm differenzieren wollen,[31] indem der Richter nur im ersten Fall wirklich *auslegt*
und der inländischen Norm einen neuen Sinn geben darf, während er im zweiten

---

[27] V. Bar, (oben N. 2) 331; Kegel (oben N. 6) 321; Raape/Sturm (oben N. 3) 312; vgl. in Frankreich
Audit (oben N. 12) 235-236; Batiffol/ Lagarde (oben N. 10) 382, 395. (Argumente für eine *de lege ferenda* entgegengesetzte Lösung siehe in Kegel (oben N. 6) 321; Raape/ Sturm (oben N. 3) 312.

[28] Kegel (oben N. 6) 319; Keller/ Siehr (oben N. 4) 505; Raape/ Sturm (oben N. 3) 309 *in fine*.

[29] Kropholler (oben N. 1) 188-189; Keller/ Siehr (oben N. 4) 505; Mayer (oben N. 25) 132 in fine.
Kegel (oben N. 6) 318, spricht hier über *Rechtsanzeichen*, wo man „*zum Teil gebunden, zum Teil frei*
[sei], d.h. man [habe] *umgrenzten Spielraum*". Diese ausländischen Rechtsanzeichen können freilich
niemals für unseren Richter bindend sein. Sie sind nicht Rechtsregeln; so sind sie nicht in der Lage
durch die Kollisionsnorm als massgebliches Recht bezeichnet werden. Sie sind nützlich nur für die
fremde Rechtsordnung der sie angehören, ohne Teile derselben Rechtsordnung zu bilden. Sie bilden
einfach Mittel für die richtige Auslegung und Anwendung des fremden Rechts durch den ausländischen Richter.

[30] Obwohl diese Metapher das logische Ergebnis der herrschenden Meinung ausdrückt, hat man
versucht, ihren absoluten Umfang zu mildern; siehe Kropholler (oben N. 1) 187-189; Kegel (oben N. 6)
319.

[31] Mayer (oben N. 25) 131-132; Batiffol/ Lagarde (oben N. 10) 387-388.

Fall einfach feststellt, was im Ausland angenommen wird.[32]

Nur für den Fall, daß im Rahmen der ausländischen Rechtsordnung eine solche anerkannte Lösung nicht existiert oder nicht bekannt ist,[33] hat man vorgeschlagen, dass der Richter „auch die ‚frightening task‘ anpacken [müsse], zu einer umstrittenen Frage Stellung zu nehmen" und „sie im Geiste des ausländischen Rechts mit Hilfe des ihm zugänglichen Materials zu entscheiden".[34] Man glaubt, dass der Richter auf dieser Weise „dem Auftrag des Kollisionsrechts besser gerecht [werde] als durch einen Rückgriff auf die lex fori als Ersatzrecht".[35] Das Bedürfnis eines Ersatzrechts, falls der genaue Inhalt der anwendbaren fremden Rechtsnorm nicht klar ermittelt werden kann,[36] hat eine gewisse Diskussion ausgelöst.

Wie soll sich der Richter in einer solchen Situation verhalten? Die auf das fremde Recht gegründete Klage ist nicht allein deshalb abzuweisen, weil keine von den diversen im Ausland bestehenden Auslegungen als herrschend qualifiziert werden kann,[37] soweit die Ermittlung ausländischen Rechts eine Amtspflicht des Richters darstellt. Wenn der Richter eine im Ausland herrschende, festgefügte Auslegung der anwendbaren Rechtsnorm nicht zu ermitteln in der Lage ist, dann muss er nach der herrschenden Meinung so handeln wie der ausländische Richter selbst handeln würde. Viele glauben, dass die direkte Berufung auf ein Ersatzrecht nötig sei und ziehen als solches die *lex fori* vor.[38] Manche ziehen die indirekte Anwendung der *lex fori* durch eine *praesumptio similitudinis* des anwendbaren fremden Rechts mit der *lex fori*[39] (dies war z.B. die von der griechischen Rechtsprechung angenommene Lösung vor dem Inkrafttreten des neuen griechieschen ZGB von 1967/68[40]) vor, was völlig inakzeptabel ist. Viele andere sind nicht bereit, einen vorschnellen

---

[32] Einen solchen Unterschied haltet Yasseen (oben N. 1) 516, für übermässig.

[33] Kropholler (oben N. 1) 188; Mayer (oben N. 25) 132.

[34] Kropholler (oben N. 1) 188; Keller/ Siehr (oben N. 4) 505; Mayer (oben N. 25) 132; Dölle (oben N. 7) 244 *in fine*.

[35] Kropholler (oben N. 1) 188 (Par. 31 I 2).

[36] Von diesen Fällen „ist jener andere zu unterscheiden, dass die Tatbestandsmerkmale, die den *Anknüpfungsgrund* bestimmen nicht feststellbar sind": Raape/ Sturm (oben N. 3) 312.

[37] Vgl. v. Bar (oben N. 2) 325-326. Siehe aber Raape/ Sturm (oben N. 3) 311, die als Ausgangspunkt die Lehre vom fakultativen Kollisionsrecht benützen.

[38] Zu dieser Frage siehe u.a. K. Dilger, „Deutsches Recht als Ersatzrecht?" *StAZ* (1979) 37-38. (Das französische positive Recht ist klar zu der *lex fori* als Ersatzrecht orientiert. Siehe Batiffol/ Lagarde (oben N. 10) 405; weiter Loussouarn/Bourel (oben N. 25) 256-257; Audit (oben N. 12) 232-233; Mayer (oben 25) 133. Vgl. z.B. Cass. civ. 5.11.1991 (*Soc. Masson et autres* c. *Lalanne Bertoudice*), *Rev. Crit.* (1992) 314, 315 („en raison de la vocation subsidiaire de celle-ci"). Aber diese Anwendung des französischen Rechts als *lex fori* muss dem Beweis der *bona fides* des Klägers betreffend die Lieferung der nötigen Merkmale und seine objektive Unmöglichkeit um es zu erreichen, untergeordnet sein. „Faute pour lui de convaincre le juge sur ce point, son allegation serait rejetée au même titre que lorsqu'il ne fait pas la preuve d'une règle particulière qu'il invoque": Audit (oben N. 12) 233.

[39] Siehe Webb/ Auburn, „La ‚présomption‘ d'identité de la loi étrangère et de la loi du for en l'absence de preuve", *JDI* (1978) 272-300.

[40] Vrellis, „La preuve du droit applicable étranger", *Koinodikion* (1996) 259-260.

Rückzug von dem an sich berufenen Recht auf ein Ersatzrecht anzunehmen, und meinen, dass ein Grundsatz der „grössten Wahrscheinlichkeit"[41] gelte oder durch rechtsvergleichende Untersuchungen (mindestens im Rahmen derselben Rechtsfamilie) allgemeine Rechtsgrundsätze zu ermitteln und anzuwenden seien,[42] oder mit Hilfe internationalen Einheitsrechts entschieden werden könne,[43] allerdings, „wollte man allzu früh die lex fori zu Hilfe rufen" stelle das, so meinen sie, „ein unzulässiges Heimwärtsstreben" dar.[44] Man hat auch an kollisionsrechtlichen Hilfs- bzw. Ersatzanknüpfungen gedacht.[45] Man kann leicht verstehen, dass man mit allen diesen Rückgriffsmodalitäten auf Ersatzrechte eine Norm anwenden würde, die wahrscheinlich einen anderen Inhalt hat als die anwendbare Norm.

3.2 Bei der Auslegung irgendeiner Rechtsnorm gibt es nur Architekten

Die oben (unter 2) dargestellten Ausführungen haben dagegen als Folge, dass es zwischen der Auslegung einer ausländischen anwendbaren Norm (in dem Mass, in dem man überhaupt von einer Auslegung einer solchen Norm sprechen kann) und der Auslegung einer Norm unserer eigenen Rechtsordnung keinen Unterschied gibt, in dem Sinne, dass unser Richter in beiden Fällen die Auslegungsmethoden und Rechtsanzeichen seiner eigenen Rechtsordnung benutzen darf und muss, um das bezweckte, dieser Rechtsordnung angemessene Ergebnis zu erreichen; und dass er keinesfalls rechtlich gezwungen ist, die im Ausland herrschende und nicht einmal die höchstrichterliche Auslegung anzunehmen.

So ist es freilich ohne Belang, irgendein Ersatzrecht aufzusuchen,[46] sowie welche Rechtsordnung die Ersatznorm anbieten würde, und wann diese einer anderen Rechtsordnung als der *lex fori* zu entnehmen sind,[47] wie z.B. wenn „der Sachverhalt keine oder nur eine vergleichsweise unbedeutende Verbindung zum Inland aufweist".[48] Unser Richter muss, inspiriert vom fremden anwendbaren Recht, aber zugleich gemäss den Auffassungen seiner eigenen Rechtsordnung, die neue anpas-

---

[41] Kegel (oben N. 6) 323; siehe zu dieser Frage auch Dölle (oben N. 7) 241-243, Luther, „Kollisions- und Fremdrechtsanwendung in der Gerichtspraxis", 37 *RabelsZ* (1973) 665-666.

[42] Kötz (oben N. 3) 663-678.

[43] K. Kreuzer, „Einheitsrecht als Ersatzrecht – Zur Frage der Nichtermittelbarkeit fremden Rechts", *NJW* (1983) 1943-1948.

[44] Keller/ Sier (oben N. 4) 503.

[45] Müller, „Zur Nichtfeststellbarkeit des kollisionsrechtlich berufenen ausländischen Rechts", *NJW* (1981) 481-486; Kreuzer (oben N. 43) 1943ff.

[46] Es muss bemerkt werden, dass es jedenfalls einen Unterschied gibt zwischen der Nichtermittlung des Inhalts des anwendbaren Rechts (dann wird keine grundliegende ausländische Norm angeboten, um die rechtsschöpferische Tätigkeit unseres Richters zu beeinflussen) und der Frage, um die es sich hier allein handelt, d.h. *quid*, wenn im Ausland viele Auslegungen für die anwendbare Rechtsnorm vorgeschlagen worden sind, keine aber als herrschend berücksichtigt werden kann.

[47] V. Bar (oben N. 2) 328.

[48] Kropholler (oben N. 1) 191 *in fine*.

sende heimische Rechtsnorm für den konkreten Sachverhalt schaffen und anwenden, um die für seine Rechtsordnung befriedigendste Lösung zu finden. Er braucht sich aber kaum einem Ersatzrecht als solchem zuzuwenden, während er seine rechtsschöpferische Tätigkeit im oben (unter 2) ausgeführten Sinn ausübt. Die *lex fori* übt hier keine Ersatz- sondern nur eine *Anziehungsfunktion* aus.

Die vorstehenden Gedanken und die oben geschilderte richterliche rechtsschöpferische Tätigkeit machen das Werk unseres Richters schwierig und stellen an ihn besonders hohe Anforderungen. Richter aber zu sein ist von Natur aus immer schwierig und zwar viel schwieriger, als es in Anbetracht des oben Geschilderten erscheint. Jedenfalls bilden diese Überlegungen einfache und zögernde Versuche, das Phänomen der „Anwendung fremden Rechts" zu berücksichtigen und ihm näher zu kommen. Von Zweifeln betreffend deren Richtigkeit kann der Verfasser dieser Zeilen selbst nicht befreit sein. Wenn man über solche Probleme der kollisionsrechtlichen Methode nachdenkt und die verschiedenen vorgeschlagenen Lösungen berücksichtigt, entdeckt man hier und dort richtige Elemente, zugleich aber auch obskure Lücken und dunkle Punkte, so dass mit Sokrates wiederholt werden darf: Wer von uns allen richtiger denkt, weiss niemand, als Gott allein. Trotzdem scheint es nicht völlig ausgeschlossen, dass – wenn wir manche Konfessionen vom Heil. Augustinus zusammenfassend zu umschreiben versuchen[49] – dasselbe Phänomen verschiedene „Wirklichkeiten" enthält und dass jede seiner verschiedenartigen Erklärungen ebenfalls als verhältnismässig richtig berücksichtigt werden kann.

SUMMARY
REFLECTIONS ON THE INTERPRETATION OF FOREIGN LEGAL NORMS

1. A widespread opinion claims that the applicable foreign law rules have to be interpreted in the forum State as they are in the legal order they belong to. In the opinion of the writer it is neither necessary nor correct.

2. A foreign rule often disturbs the harmony and the logical structure of another legal system. So the adaptation, i.e. the modification – more or less – of the meaning of a rule seems necessary, when this rule is applied in another State. In such a case, actually the judge in this other State (the forum State), acts under the influence of the applicable foreign rule and is inspired by it, but always with the aim of respecting the unity and the structure of his own legal order. So in fact he creates a new specific rule in his own system; a substantive domestic rule which does not necessarily have the same content neither as the applicable foreign rule, nor as the

---

[49] Lib. XII, Cap. XV-XXXII; insbes. Lib. XII, Cap. XXVII.

lex fori and which doesn't need to be interpreted. On the other hand, the foreign rule which underlies this new specific internal rule can be approached by our judge with the means offered by our legal order.

3.   Like all other internal rules, the delivered decision is subject to review by the Supreme Court.

4.   Therefore, one has a legitimate reason to believe that a judge exercises the same – if not greater – creativity when he "applies" a foreign rule than when he applies his own law. From this point of view there is no difference between the interpretation of the foreign and the domestic law.

International Set of Rules Concerning Minors in Argentine Legal Literature and Case Law

Inés M. Weinberg de Roca[*]

1. CHOICE OF THE SUBJECT

It is with special joy and some nostalgia that I participate in this tribute to KURT SIEHR, whom I met during my stay at the Max-Planck-Institut für ausländisches und internationales Privatrecht a long time ago and who, since then, and from a distance, as an important authority in the field of family law, has been of great guidance. And it is for this reason that on this occasion I chose a related subject.

This contribution first details the international obligations undertaken by Argentina concerning the protection of minors, and then analyses the cases in which Argentina has applied The Hague Convention of 1980 on Civil Aspects of International Child Abduction.[1]

2. THE LEGAL FRAMEWORK FOR THE PROTECTION OF MINORS IN ARGENTINA

The Hague Convention on Civil Aspects of International Child Abduction establishes that the victim of a case of fraud or violence – i.e., wrongful removal or retention – must, first of all, be returned to his or her habitual residence. This obligation is lifted when the person, institution or organization that opposes the restitution demonstrates that, in the face of an extreme situation and in pursuit of the

---

[*] Professor of Private International Law at the Faculty of Law of the University of Buenos Aires.
[1] Ratified by law 23,857, Boletín Oficial 31.10.90, applicable in Argentina since 1 June 1991.

J. Basedow et al., eds., Private Law in the International Arena – Liber Amicorum Kurt Siehr
© 2000, T.M.C.Asser Press, The Hague, The Netherlands

child's best interests, it is necessary to sacrifice the personal interest of the applicant.[2]

This provision takes into account not only the need to prevent parents from taking matters into their own hands in relation to their children, but also the interest of the child, at present also guaranteed by the Convention on the Rights of the Child,[3] and the international public policy of the participating court, which in matters involving minors finds it difficult to relinquish its own decision-making authority in favor of a foreign colleague.

The conflict of these interests becomes evident in our country, which to this day fears international adoption, and has therefore not ratified The Hague Convention of 1993 referring to the Protection of Children and Co-operation in Respect of Intercountry Adoption.[4] The Argentine adoption law does not contemplate the possibility of an international adoption. The Inter-American Convention on conflicts of laws in the field of adoption of minors), in whose preparation I participated, has not been ratified by Argentina, either.[5]

Argentina ratified the Convention on the Rights of the Child with reservations to four clauses. These refer to the adoption of children by foreign adoptive parents. On recording the reservations, the legislator states that, in his view, in order to apply these clauses, there must previously exist a rigorous mechanism for the protection of the child in the field of international adoption, in order to avoid the trade and sale of minors.[6]

The lack of rulings on international adoption begins with the Civil Code, which nevertheless, in article 4050,[7] recognizes such adoptions carried out before the Code came into force in 1871. In 1948, law 13,252 was passed, which deals only with simple adoption but not with international adoption.[8]

---

[2] Supreme Court of Argentina, Fallos 318-1271. The civil aspects of child abduction differ from the criminal aspects as considered by the V Inter-American Conference on Private International Law held in 1994 in Mexico, in which the Argentine delegation, of which I was a member, had an important participation due, especially, to Alicia Perugini and Gustavo De Paoli. As a result, the Inter-American Convention on International Traffic in Minors was concluded. Argentina ratified this Convention by law 25,179, Boletín Oficial, 26.10.1999. The Inter-American Convention on Child Abduction, done in Montevideo in 1989, has not been ratified by Argentina.

[3] Argentina ratified the Convention on the Rights of the Child with reservations to article 21, b), c), d) and e). Law 23,849, Boletín Oficial 22.10.90.

[4] Rapport explicatif de G. Parra-Aranguren, 31.12.1993 (edité para le Bureau Permanent de la Conférence, La Haye).

[5] CIDIP III, La Paz 1984.

[6] Article 2, law 23,849.

[7] Zulema D. Wilde, *La adopción nacional e internacional* (Buenos Aires 1996) p. 25, explains the evolution and the reservations to the Convention on the Rights of the Child.

[8] Inés M. Weinberg de Roca, *Derecho Internacional Privado* (Buenos Aires, Depalma 1997) pp. 105ff.

On the basis of the ratification by our country, in 1956,[9] of the 1940 Montevideo Treaty on International Civil Law, the courts would have been able to apply this Convention by analogy.[10]

With the adoption and publication of the law on adoption 19,134 in 1971, rulings on this subject appear for the first time in Argentine domestic private international law.[11] Articles 32 and 33 of this law are similar in text to articles 339 and 340 of the present Civil Code, which was amended in the field of international adoption in 1997 by law 24,779.[12] Both the 1971 law and the 1997 law contain specific rulings in relation to the effects of an adoption decreed abroad. They do not contemplate international adoption, echoing the deeply-embedded conviction that it is best to prevent any transfer of minors abroad, even though the State does not assume the social protection of abandoned children within the country's territory. The subsidiary character of adoption was claimed in a statement that the Holy See sent to The Hague Conference, in these terms.[13] "children are not isolated individuals but have been born in and belong to a particular environment. Only if this native environment cannot, in one way or another, provide for a minimum of care and education should adoption be contemplated. The possibility of providing a better material future is certainly not, of itself, a sufficient reason for resorting to adoption". Article 315 of the Civil Code requires from the adopting party five years of residence in the country, excluding all possibility of an international adoption.

3. CONSTITUTIONAL REFORM

The lack of legislation in the field of international adoption is a theoretical and philosophical subject in Argentina, since homeless children are adopted by people residing in the country, without the domestic demand for adoption being thereby satisfied. For this reason, the repeated reticence in legislating on international adoption must be evaluated on the basis of the social and philosophical standing of the institution and not as a response to a factually existing situation.

The link with the foreign element has influenced the discussion regarding the question of the supremacy of international treaties over domestic laws. Under the Argentine constitutional order in force from 1853 until 1994 it seemed clear that in-

---

[9] Articles 23 and 24.

[10] Goldschmidt/ Werner, *Derecho Internacional Privado* (Depalma 1982) no. 292.

[11] Inés M. Weinberg, "La adopción internacional según la ley 19.134", *El Derecho*, 38-1069 and the same author, "Änderungen des argentinischen Gesetzes über die internationale Annahme an Kindes Statt", *Das Standesamt*, October 1972-284.

[12] Published in the Boletín Oficial on April 1, 1997.

[13] Cited by María Susana Najurieta, "La adopción internacional", *El Derecho*, 171-905 and the Parra-Aranguren Report mentioned, p. 553.

ternational law could not prevail, in the domestic sphere, over the Constitution.[14] Article 31 of the Constitution placed laws and treaties on an equal level.[15] Consequently a later law repealed a previous treaty. The Supreme Court, in the 1948 case of *Merck Química Argentina S.A.* v. *Gobierno Nacional*[16] ruled that in peacetime, the supremacy of the Constitution is maintained in the domestic order of Argentina, but that during wartime international law prevails over the Constitution.

Only in 1992, in the case of *Ekmekdjian* v. *Sofovich*[17] and in 1994, in the case of *La Virginia S.A.*,[18] did the Supreme Court declare that "the application by the organs of the Argentine State of a domestic rule that conflicts with a treaty provision, in addition to constituting non-compliance with an international commitment, violates the principle of the supremacy of international treaties over domestic laws. Article 27 of the Vienna Convention on the Law of Treaties[19] commits the organs of the Argentine State, once the constitutional principles of public law have been safeguarded, to ensure the primacy of a treaty, in case of conflict, over a domestic rule, because this priority in rank forms part of the Argentine juridical order and may be invoked on the basis of art. 31 of the Constitution."

Finally, under the constitutional reform of 1994, treaties have a higher hierarchy than laws[20] and the juridical order has been structured in such a way as to confer constitutional rank on some treaties that deal with Human Rights (art. 75 clause 22). A prominent example is the Convention on the Rights of the Child, which, in turn, in its article 11, establishes that Party States shall adopt measures to fight against the illegal removal of children abroad and the illegal retention of children. To this end, Party States shall promote the establishment of bilateral or multilateral agreements or adherence to existing agreements.

4.   RESTITUTION OF MINORS

Argentina ratified The Hague Convention of October 25, 1980, on Civil Aspects of International Child Abduction, approved by law 23,857, and the 1981 Agreement between Argentina and Uruguay on the International Protection of Children, approved by law 22,546.[21]

---

[14] Podestá Costa – Ruda, *Derecho Internacional Público* (Buenos Aires 1994) I-43.

[15] Fallos, 257-299.

[16] Fallos, 211-162, *La Ley*, 51-255/265. This case deals with a claim for restitution of enemy property taken during World War II. The Court decided to postpone the issue of restitution and reparation until peace is re-established.

[17] Fallos, 315-1492.

[18] Fallos, 317-1287ff., translated by the author.

[19] Law 23,782, Boletín Oficial, 7.6.90.

[20] Article 75, clause 22, first part.

[21] Law 23,857, published in Boletín Oficial on 31.10.90 and law 22,546 published in Boletín

The civil aspects of international child abduction must be distinguished from international abuses and illegal activities against children, the latter issue being dealt with in 1994 by the Inter-American Convention on International Traffic in Minors, now ratified by Argentina. The civil aspects of international child abduction were also the subject of the Inter-American Convention on international restitution of minors.[22]

The Hague Convention of October 25, 1980, has been applied by Argentine courts on several occasions.

The Argentine Supreme Court[23] determined that the procedure established by the Hague Convention on the Civil Aspects of Child Abduction is autonomous with regard to the litigation between the parties, because it is set up through the so-called "central authorities" of the contracting States, and is limited to the purpose of re-establishing the prior, juridically protected situation that was breached, by means of the immediate return of the minor who has been removed or is illegally retained in another contracting State. The Court further held that the father's right to obtain the return of the child to his or her habitual place of residence prior to the illegal retention, exists before the legal decision and in no manner requires the intervention of a court. The initiation of the procedure under the Convention before the central authority does not require prior legal action, and there is no case for issuing a ruling on the international jurisdiction to discuss the allocation of the child's custody. The Convention preserves the best interest of the child by means of the interruption of the action undertaken *de facto*, as well as by having this rule set aside when the person, institution or organization, that opposes the restitution demonstrates that, due to an extreme situation and in pursuit of the child's interest, it is necessary to sacrifice the personal interest of the applicant. But the mere general invocation of the benefit of the child, or the change in environment or language, do not suffice to constitute the exceptional situation that would allow restitution to be denied (Art. 13, first paragraph, clause b) of the Convention).[24]

The application of the Convention by the Supreme Court on appeal was excep-

---

Oficial on 4.3.82. See also María Elsa Uzal, "Algunas reflexiones en torno a la Convención de La Haya sobre los aspectos civiles de la sustracción internacional de menores en 1980", *El Derecho*, 169-1253; Eduardo Telechea Bergman, *Restitución internacional de menores, análisis en especial del Convenio sobre protección internacional de menores entre la República Oriental del Uruguay y la República Argentina* (Instituto Interamericano del Niño, Montevideo 1985).

[22] CIDIP IV (Montevideo 1989). A detailed commentary by Gualberto Lucas Sosa, *La Convención Interamericana sobre restitución internacional de menores* (CIDIP IV, Montevideo 1989), Jurisprudencia Argentina, 1990-I-779ff.. The Convention has not been ratified by Argentina.

[23] Case *W.E.* v. *O., M.G.*, 14.6.1995, Fallos 318-1269.

[24] The Court confirmed the decision of the Civil Court of Appeals – sala G, March 1, 1995- published in *El Derecho*, 162-558. A commentary by Soraya Nadia Hidalgo, "Restitución internacional de menores en la República Argentina", in: *La Ley*, 1996-C-1393. The Court of Appeals had ruled that the mother should apply for custody in Canada because the parties were domiciled in Canada at the time of the marriage breakdown.

848

tional, because the ordinary courts have jurisdiction to handle the matter.

The National Civil Court of Appeals in the city of Buenos Aires overruled the decision of a lower court that had authorized restitution. It therefore rejected a petition for the restitution of a minor requested in accordance with The Hague Convention,[25] because the return exposed the child to risks not only of an external and general nature in the requesting country – for example, a civil war – but also to concrete risks that could result from its reinstatement in the situation existing prior to the illegal removal. In this case the life of the father in Great Britain was threatened by an organization of fanatical extremists, and since the minor would live with his father, he too would be placed under threat. Therefore the court accorded priority to the protection of the minor in view of a serious risk to his life.

In another ruling of 1995 the Civil Court of Appeals, overruled a lower court's decision, applying article 3[26] because the mother left the requesting State – Spain – with the minor, although the Spanish court, once the schedule of visits had been established, had required both parents to deposit their passports to prevent them from leaving the national territory with their daughter. The court ruled the return to be effected because it did not consider that the conditions allowing an exception, under articles 12 and 13 of the Convention, had been met. The affidavits in the file did not reveal the date of entry into the country and therefore it was impossible to calculate whether one year had elapsed. Yet the court added that, even if more than a year had elapsed since the removal, it was still necessary to strictly apply the second paragraph of article 12, which provides that if the proceedings begin after the expiry of the period of one year restitution will nevertheless be ordered unless it is demonstrated that the minor has been integrated into his or her new environment.

In another ruling the court found a claim inadmissible since it aimed at validating the illegal conduct of a parent who had abducted the minor from the maternal home when he was only three years old, moved him to a foreign country and caused him to sever all links with his mother for fourteen years. The court further considered the preventive imprisonment decreed against the applicant whose extradition had been requested.[27]

The same court had already in 1989 decided to apply the Convention prior to its entry into force.[28] It held that in the international arena the restitution of minors is appropriate not only when the latter have been "kidnapped" in their country of

---

[25] Cámara Nacional en lo Civil, sala I, September 14, 1995, *El Derecho*, 165-507, with commentaries by Osvaldo Onofre Alvarez, "Pedido de restitución de menores e incumplimiento de la patria potestad" and by A. Ricardo Wetzler Malbrán, "La excepción a un principio y el efecto no querido".

[26] CNCiv., sala H, March 2, 1995, *La Ley*, 1996-B-610 with commentary by Victoria Basz and Sara Lidia Feldstein de Cárdenas, "El derecho internacional privado y la restitución internacional de menores".

[27] CNCiv., sala B, May 24, 1995, *El Derecho*, 163-560ff.

[28] CNCiv., sala B, September 26, 1989, case 57,153, unpublished.

habitual residence, but also in cases in which they unlawfully find themselves in another State and their stay in that State is in violation of the rights of those who exercise parental authority. In that case the centre of the daughter's life was in Chile and the court applied the rulings of the Agreement signed in Montevideo in 1981 by Argentina and Uruguay[29] as a guideline, because The Hague Convention was not yet in force.

A lower court decided to confine its decision to the issues petitioned in the letters rogatory and return a minor to Canada, not allowing the submission of evidence referring the matter to be discussed in Canada,[30] because the jurisdiction to rule is conferred on the court of the last domicile of the married couple, and that court that is called upon to decide the custody and determine the rights of access. In another case a lower court rejected a claim for restitution presented by a mother[31] when the father domiciled in Argentina moved with the child in the United States of America, because of his employment. It considered that there had been no illegal transfer or retention of the minor because the father had obtained custody and the mother had requested restitution without even being in the country. Although, during custody hearings, the parties had agreed that the father would have custody while domiciled in Argentina, and that in the event of leaving the country a new agreement would have to be entered into, the court considered this fact irrelevant to the restitution claim. The judge held that the mother could not compel the father to live permanently in Argentina because at the time of the agreement she herself lived in Germany and her right of access was not hindered by the child being moved to the United States.

This same court rejected another application for restitution[32] because it found that the exception foreseen in Article 13, clause b), of the Convention applied in that case. The mother had left Mexico and returned to her country of origin, Argentina, to avoid physical or psychological peril. The father accompanied his wife and children from Mexico, their place of residence, to Argentina, for a vacation. Upon arrival in Buenos Aires and leaving the airport, the wife explained she had been very unhappy for the last seven years and would not return with the children to Mexico. She insisted on living in Buenos Aires but this was impossible for him. He left for Mexico and expected his family to follow. The wife asked that the claim be dismissed since, as she could also prove in court, the husband had beaten her and the children.

---

[29] Approved by law 22,546, Boletín Oficial 4.3.82.
[30] Juzgado Nacional en lo Civil No. 106, December 7, 1992, case 52,924/92. Unpublished.
[31] Juzgado Nacional en lo Civil No. 10, February 24, 1998, G., B.M.A. c. G.C., unpublished.
[32] Juzgado Nacional en lo Civil.No. 10, November 29, 1995, case 12,443/95, unpublished.

5.   CONCLUSIONS

All the court decisions on restitution of minors take into account the best interest of the minor. It is not the case of restitution of an object owed or disputed among co-owners.[33]

The fact cannot be ignored that all we have are provisional rulings, because The Hague Convention aims at preventing the issue of custody from being solved by force and self-help, taking the case away from the natural judges. It is these judges who will ultimately decide the habitual residence of the minor.

And it is possible that it is this provisional aspect that has marked the success of the Convention and its acceptance by a society that is still debating the question whether, in the field of legislation on minors, it should stay away from applying foreign law.

In the international sphere of private law Argentina has only ratified treaties of a procedural nature. Consequently, it is easy to infer that in the field of substantive private international law Argentina still mistrusts the application of foreign law.

In 1999, the Third Congress of Mercosur Magistrates established the need to unify legislation and harmonize some particular aspects of the legislation on minors, specifically as regards adoption, maintenance, restitution and preventive or protective measures. It proposed to consider general rules on international adoption as a last resort aimed at providing protection for the child when it cannot stay with its biological family and the possibility of its being adopted in its country of origin has been exhausted, giving priority to adoptive parents from Mercosur countries or, failing that, from those countries that have ratified The Hague Convention.[34]

I quote these proposals, made by judges and not by professors of private international law, because they make it clear that international treaties are accepted by non-specialists in matters that require an efficient procedure and rapid decisions but are mistrusted in subjects of substantive law like adoption, where neighboring countries are given priority.

---

[33] Bertrand Ancel, 82 *Rev. Crit.dr.int.privé* (1993) p. 658ff.

[34] Ana María Capolupo de Durañona y Vedia, III Congreso de Magistrados del Mercosur, 2 *Revista de Derecho del Mercosur* (1998) p. 232ff.

Reform of Japanese Private International Law and Public Policy

Jun Yokoyama[*]

1. PRELIMINARY REMARKS

The principal conflicts rules of Japanese private international law are contained in Application of Laws General Act (*Horei*).[1] In 1989, amendments were made to this Act, originally enacted in 1898. The conflicts rules on family were mainly targeted. The aim was twofold: the connecting factors of those rules had to be modified to conform with the principle of gender equality; and the rules themselves had to be adjusted to cope with international situations that had arisen in the last few

---

[*] Professor of Law, Hitotubashi University, Tokyo.

[1] The English, French and German translations of the text are published in: 33 *The Japanese Annual of International Law* (1990) pp. 67-71; 79 *Revue critique de droit international privé* (1990) pp. 844-847; Jan Kropholler, Hilmar Krüger, Wolfgang Riering, Jürgen Samtleben and Kurt Siehr (eds.), *Außereuropäische IPR-Gesetze* (Hamburg/Würzburg, DnotI and Max-Planck-Institut 1999) pp. 308-323. For the reform, see, Monika Schmidt, *Die Reform des japanischen Internationalen Privatrechts* (Köln Heymann 1992).

J. Basedow et al., eds., Private Law in the International Arena – Liber Amicorum Kurt Siehr
© 2000, T.M.C.Asser Press, The Hague, The Netherlands

decades.[2] In order to attain these aims, the legislator used two legislative techniques, namely, having recourse to a range of connecting factors in line with the principle of equality and the adoption of alternative conflicts rules. In making the draft for these reforms, the Advisory Panel to the Minister of Justice was inspired by trends observed in new codifications or reforms of private international law that had taken place in several countries.[3] The survey that the members of academic circles carried out in terms of comparative law obviously helped the advisory panel to adopt the conflicts rules embodying a range of connecting factors, which should be applied either by cascade (*par cascade*, in order of priority) or alternatively. Professor Siehr's observation that academic circles have contributed much to the reforms of private international law, indeed holds true also for Japan.[4]

The comparative survey underlying the legislative work undoubtedly militates in favour of approaching the goal of the international harmony of decisions.[5] However, this was not the sole goal to be pursued by the legislature. The case-law preceding the reform was considered by the advisory panel more important when adopting such conflicts rules. Some cases in which judges had to determine whether public policy should come into operation would illustrate this (Section 2).[6] Certain domestic policies that are linked with some institutions also turned out to be imperative. What we call "Japanese Clauses" embody such policies. During the discussions of the panel, disagreement emerged between the members as to the extent to which a substantive value, enhanced by a series of alternative conflicts rules, should be sacrificed for another value. It was also argued, with respect to a range of connecting factors arranged by cascade, that the general clause expressed by the term of "the closest connection" should be held inconsistent with a pre-existing domestic institution. The "Japanese clauses" represent some compromises reached among the members (Section 3). We may add that a limited span of time did not allow the panel to explore fully repercussions that each new conflicts rule might eventually have on the conflicts rules dealing with the "general problems". The experience

---

[2] Articles 14 to 17 of *Horei* as formulated before the reform provided for the following husband-oriented conflicts rules: personal effects of marriage, matrimonial regime and divorce were governed by the *lex patriae* of the husband. Furthermore, the parent-child relationship was governed by the *lex patriae* of the father, in accordance with Article 20. The constitutionality of these provisions was contested by academic circles and by some members of the Parliament. The Ministry of Justice asserted the neutral character of private international law in principle, but, on the other hand, admitted that those rules had become outdated. Unlike Germany and Italy, there were no Japanese decisions that declared the husband- (or the father-)oriented conflicts rules unconstitutional. See, Junko Torii, 'Revision of Private International Law in Japan', 33 *The Japanese Annual of International Law* (1990) p. 54.

[3] The Advisory Panel for the Minister of Justice began to elaborate a draft in 1984 and finished its work at the end of 1988. Apart from some technical points, the draft as formulated was adopted by the Parliament. The author has been a member of the panel since 1984, but the view expressed here is personal.

[4] Kurt Siehr, 'Rechtsangleichung im IPR durch nationale Kodifikationen', in: *Mélanges d'Alfred E. von Overbeck* (Fribourg, Editions universitaires Fribourg 1990) 210.

gained during the period of ten years following the reforms gives us the opportunity to consider the relationship between public policy and the conflicts rules character-ised by a series of connecting factors arranged by cascade (Section 4).

2.   NECESSITY OF REFORM AND PUBLIC POLICY

Before the reform, judges quite often had recourse to public policy to correct results caused by application of foreign laws, particularly when they were indicated by the husband-oriented connecting factors. While certain foreign law provisions applica-ble in accordance with such rules were shocking to judges, it seems that the true cause that led to such results lay in the imperfection of those conflicts rules rather than the content of the applicable foreign rules as such. They proved to provide weak connecting factors (Section 2.1). On the other hand, there were some cases where even public policy could not correct the results of application of foreign laws, undesirable as they were (Section 2.2).

2.1   **Public Policy as a Mechanism for Correcting the Conflicts Rule**

The first sentence of Article 16 of *Horei* provides that Article 14 on general effects of marriage shall apply *mutatis mutandis* to divorce.[7] Thus, divorce is governed by the law of the common nationality held by the spouses. Failing this, the law of the common habitual residence applies, and failing this, the law of the country with which the spouses are most closely connected. Such connecting factors are obvi-ously explainable in terms of the principle of equality: in the absence of a common nationality, recourse to the national law of either the husband or the wife is not pos-sible. We have to note, at the same time, that the connecting factor of the common habitual residence was welcomed against the background of cases that judges had to face before the reform.

---

[5] See, Pierre Mayer, *Droit international privé*, 6e éd. (Paris, Montchrestien 1998) p. 22.

[6] The public policy clause (Article 33 of *Horei*), along with these rules, were slightly modified to make it explicit that the intervention of public policy is not triggered by the foreign law as such but by the result of its application to a particular case. This modification was introduced to endorse the practice that had prevailed before the reform.

[7] Article 14 of *Horei*:

"The effects of marriage shall be governed by the national law which the spouses have in common; in the absence of such law, the effects shall be governed by the law of the place of their habitual resi-dence if the spouses have such law in common. Otherwise, the effects shall be governed by the law of the place with which the spouses are most closely connected."

Article 16 of *Horei*:

"Article 14 shall apply *mutatis mutandis* to divorces. However, a divorce shall be governed by Japa-nese law if either of the spouses is a Japanese, having his or her habitual residence in Japan."

Article 16, as formulated before the reform, provided that the divorce should be governed by the national law of the husband. This provision frequently induced judges to have recourse to public policy. Particularly when Philippine law was referred to as the law governing the divorce, judges did not hesitate to do so.[8] The elements of the reported cases are almost identical: a Japanese wife living in Japan petitioned for divorce from a Philippine husband also living in Japan. It is true that the content of Philippine law, which prohibits divorce, triggered the application of the public policy clause. This undoubtedly looked extraordinary to judges in Japan, where around 90 percent of marriages are dissolved by agreement. More important, however, is the fact that the great majority of Philippine-Japanese spouses established their matrimonial homes in Japan. Thus, while the nationality of the husband proved to indicate a weak link with the Philippines, the *Inlandsbeziehung* or *Binnenbeziehung* seemed sufficient in most cases. The links with the forum expressed in these terms were found to yield a new connecting factor, namely, the common habitual residence of the spouses. When the advisory panel prepared their draft, they expected the new connecting factor of the common habitual residence to make it as unnecessary as possible for judges to resort to the public policy clause. The experience of the last ten years seems to confirm this expectation. There has been no reported case where the application of Philippine law was excluded on grounds of public policy since the reform came into force.

2.2   Situation beyond Control of Public Policy

Tortuous as Article 18 of *Horei* is in its wording, this provision expresses an alternative conflicts rule for the status of an illegitimate child, in particular the establishment of paternity.[9] In connection with the child's status *vis-à-vis* its father, it lists

---

[8] There is one reported case in which the court rejected the petition for divorce brought by a Japanese wife, applying the Philippine law (Niigata District Court, October 30, 1987, 1292 *Hanrei Jihou* (The Japanese Law Reports) p. 79 (1987)). In this case, the petition seemed unfounded even under Japanese law.

[9] Article 18 of *Horei*:

"1. The parentage of an illegitimate child shall be governed by the national law, at the time of the birth of the child, of the father regarding the paternity, and of the mother regarding the maternity. With respect to establishment of parentage by voluntary acknowledgment, the requirement of the consent by the child or by the third person shall be satisfied if such are required for the acknowledgment under the national law of the child at the time of the acknowledgment.

2. In addition to the laws designated in the first sentence of the preceding paragraph, the establishment of parentage, whether by voluntary acknowledgment or by judicial determination, shall be governed by the national law, either of the parent concerned or of the child, at the time of the establishment. Where the acknowledgment is governed by the national law of the acknowledging parent, the second sentence of the preceding paragraph shall apply *mutatis mutandis*.

3. If the father is dead before the birth of the child, the national law of the father at the time of his death shall be deemed as the national law of the father in the sense of the first paragraph of this Article;

the following three potentially applicable laws: the *lex patriae* of the father at the time of the child's birth; his *lex patriae* at the time of the establishment; and the *lex patriae* of the child at the time of the establishment. It is enough if the paternity is established by one of these *leges patriae*, by the father's voluntary acknowledgment or by judicial determination. The idea behind this provision is, obviously, to facilitate the establishment of the status of an illegitimate child. The advisory panel did not hesitate to adopt this idea, having regard to the trends observed in recent reforms or codifications of private international law. We have to note that, at the same time, they bore in mind the situation where, before the reform, even public policy could not correct the result of the application of the foreign law, however intolerable it had been.

Article 18, as formulated before the reform, contained a distributive conflicts rule. It refers to the *lex patriae* of a parent as regards requirements of establishment on his or her part and to the *lex patriae* of a child as regards those of establishment on its part. This rule did not conflict with the principle of equality. On the other hand, it often created harsh results for illegitimate children who sought the establishment of the paternity, because the possibility of the judicial determination of paternity was interpreted as a bilateral requirement to be answered by the both *leges patriae*. In other words, the rule practically played a role as a cumulative conflicts rule with respect to that issue. A tendency whereby judges avoided the application of the father's *lex patriae* by means of several corrective devices when it led to negation of the establishment could be observed. However, situations arose where even the public policy clause could not correct the result caused by the application of the foreign law.

In one case, Japanese children brought an action seeking the judicial determination of paternity. Their Korean father had been dead. The proceedings were commenced one year after the children had become aware of their father's death. Japanese law, the *lex patriae* of the children, allows a child to bring such an action, within *a period less than three years* following the date on which the alleged father died. On the other hand, Korean law, the *lex patriae* of the father, fixes a different time limit for such an action, namely, *a period of one year after a child had learnt of the parent's death*. Thus, while, according to Japanese law, the children could have successfully brought an action, their action failed to satisfy the condition required by Korean law. The cumulative application of both *leges patriae* led to the impossibility of the judicial determination of paternity in this case. The children invoked the intervention of public policy in order to have the application of Korean law excluded. The Supreme Court of Japan, however, held that the Korean provision was

---

and if the parent referred to in the preceding paragraph is dead before the establishment of the parentage, the national law of the parent at the time of his or her death shall be deemed as the national law of the parent in the sense of the said paragraph."

not contrary to Japanese public policy, and rejected their allegation.[10]

Five years later, the District Court of Kobe dealt with a similar situation. The court invoked public policy to exclude the application of Korean law. Referring to the fact that, apart from the nationality of the deceased, all the elements of the case indicated the links with Japan, the court stated that the eventual application of Korean law would deprive the illegitimate children of all their rights stemming from the determination of paternity.[11] However, the appellate court, the Osaka High Court, following the judgment of the Supreme Court above mentioned, reversed the decision, and stated as follows: "the difference between the statute of limitations of the two laws is merely technical and the Japanese rule in question is not so mandatory as not to allow such a slight derogation from it."[12]

One might agree with the attitude taken by the Supreme Court and the Osaka High Court in the sense that they tried to limit the operation of public policy. The fact remains, however, that, had only Japanese law applied, the children could have obtained all the rights deriving from the establishment of paternity. The result of the case appears to be harsh on them, account being taken of the fact that a close connection existed between the issue and the forum. It seems that this type of case induced the members of the advisory panel to adopt the alternative conflicts rule for the purpose of multiplying the opportunities for establishing paternity.

3.   JAPANESE CLAUSES

The statute named *Horei*, which a French jurist, *Boissonade*, originally drafted, was due to come into force on January 1, 1893. However, the project failed owing to inexplicable reasons. Thereafter, *Horei* was redrafted by Japanese lawyers, mainly modelled upon drafts prepared by a German jurist, *Gebhard* for the Introductory Law to the German Civil Code. *Boissonade*'s aborted project was obviously inspired by the Preliminary Provisions to the Italian Civil Code of 1865 and the project of a Belgian jurist, *Laurent*. It seems natural that it contained a provision, similar to Article 12 of the former and Article 26 of the latter, designed to reserve the application of certain mandatory rules of the forum.[13] On the other hand, the redrafted rule followed the German approach that public policy should play a role of excluding the application of the foreign law otherwise applicable. But the reform of

---

[10] Supreme Court, June 27, 1975, *Katei Saiban Geppou* (Monthly Bulletin on Family Courts), vol.28 no.4 p. 83.

[11] Kobe District Court, March 27, 1980, 417 *Hanrei Times* (The Japanese Law Times), p. 154.

[12] Osaka High Court, September 24, 1980, 425 *Hanrei Times* p. 133.

[13] Article 14 of *Boissonade*'s project reads: "The matters which concern criminal law, other public laws or public policy shall be governed by Japanese law, regardless of place of act, person's nationality or nature of property".

1989 brought into it the two provisions that enable certain domestic rules to come into operation without preliminary reference to the foreign law.

3.1   Formal Validity of Marriage

Article 13 of *Horei* contains an alternative conflicts rule in relation to the formal validity of marriage.[14] As far as the formality is concerned, the combination of Paragraph 2 and Paragraph 3 helps the parties to have their marriage recognized. It is enough that they fulfil the conditions provided by one of the following laws: the *lex loci celebrationis* or one of the *leges patriae* of the parties. Compared with Article 13 as formulated before the reform, which permitted the celebration of marriage only in accordance with the *lex loci celebrationis*, the present provision may be said to show a more liberal attitude towards the formal validity of marriage. A marriage may be validly celebrated in Japan in the form required by one of the *leges patriae* of the parties, whether religious or not. However, this alternative conflicts rule is subject to an exception. If one of the parties is a Japanese national, the couple cannot claim the validity of their marriage celebrated in Japan without registration of their marriage in the Japanese family registry. The form of marriage, which is valid in light of a *lex patriae* of the party, does not suffice to validate the marriage. This exception is explainable by the desire of the Ministry of Justice to have every change of status of Japanese nationals be reflected in the family registry as accurately as possible. Their proposal to the same effect was, indeed, criticised by some members during the panel discussions, because it would go too far in the sense that failure to comply with the requirements of registration affects the validity of the marriage. However, the proposal was finally adopted.

It is true that the necessary inscription is required to facilitate proof of the marriage. Experience tells us, however, that it is likely to create an unexpected result for mixed couples. The marriage which was celebrated in Japan in accordance with the *lex patriae* of the party may turn out to be invalid under Japanese private international law many years later, particularly when the problem of succession arises after the death of a spouse. In fact, before the reform, there was a case in which a Japanese woman could not succeed to the estate of her Taiwanese spouse.[15] The couple openly celebrated their marriage before more than one witness in Tokyo. This mar-

---

[14]   Article 13 of *Horei*:

"1. The substantive requirements of marriage shall be governed for each future spouse by his or her national law.

2. The formal requirements of marriage shall be governed by the law of the place of celebration.

3. Notwithstanding the preceding paragraph, a marriage shall be valid in relation to its form if it complies with the formal requirements under the national law of either future spouse, unless the marriage is celebrated in Japan by the parties one of whom is a Japanese.

[15]   The Tokyo District Court, April 26, 1973, 19 *The Japanese Annual of International Law* (1975) pp. 219-224.

riage was valid under the law of the Republic of China, according to which the open ceremony and the presence of more than one witness are the necessary and sufficient condition of the formal validity of marriage.[16] Many years later, after the death of the Taiwanese spouse, his brother challenged her right of succession to the estate owned by the alleged husband on the ground of the invalidity of their marriage. Under Japanese private international law, the problems of succession are governed by the national law of the *de cujus*, the law of Taiwan in this case. The question was raised before the Tokyo District Court as to whether the alleged wife in question came within the notion of a "spouse" in the sense of the Taiwanese Civil Code.[17] If the court had applied the conflicts rule of the law of Taiwan, the substantive law of which governed the succession (the principal question), the validity of marriage would have been sustained, because the conflicts rule of Taiwan allows a couple to celebrate the marriage according to one of the *leges patriae* of the parties.[18] As a matter of fact, the court applied to this preliminary question Japanese law as a *lex loci celebarationis*, following Article 13 of *Horei* as formulated before the reform, and found the marriage in the case invalid. The couple failed to register their marriage in the registry of Japan. It may be doubted that, account being taken of the surviving partner's expectation, the court should have denied rights of succession to her. It should be noted that the same type of situation is likely to recur after the reform, because the registration in the Japanese registry is still mandatory for a mixed couple as mentioned above. We are of the opinion that the Japanese court should eventually apply to the formal validity of marriage the conflicts rule of the country whose substantive law governs the principal question, taking account of the parties' expectations.

3.2 **Divorce**

Article 16 of *Horei* provides a conflicts rule on divorce. As referred to earlier, the law of the country with which the spouses are most closely connected should govern the divorce of a mixed couple who has no common habitual residence. However, when one of the spouses is Japanese and has his or her habitual residence in Japan, the Japanese authority does not apply to the divorce of such a mixed couple the law indicated by such a general clause but rather applies Japanese law. One might say that this exceptional rule purports to ensure a Japanese spouse living in Japan the divorce available under Japanese law. However, the concern underlying the drafting of this rule is different: it reflects the incompatibility between the general clause and the limited power of the family registrar.

---

[16] Article 982, Paragraph 1 of the Taiwanese Civil Code.
[17] Article 1138 of the Taiwanese Civil Code.
[18] Article 11, Paragraph 1 of the Taiwanese Private International Law.

If Japanese law is applicable, a husband and wife may dissolve their marriage by agreement.[19] This is done by notification in writing of their agreement to the family registrar. The registrar has practically no difficulty in identifying whether a couple, who is going to avail itself of the form of divorce agreement under Japanese law, has Japanese nationality in common. Japanese nationality is easily identifiable. So is the habitual residence in Japan, as far as a mixed couple has lawfully resided in Japan, which the registrar may find only by reference to the relevant public registry. Thus, the connecting factor of the common habitual residence was expected to cause, in principle, little difficulty for the registrar who must accept the notification under Japanese law. Yet, the Ministry of Justice in charge of keeping the family registry book has been perplexed by the open-ended connecting factor mentioned above, because, unlike judges, the family registrar is not empowered to make an inquiry into elements of individual matrimonial life which may eventually indicate that a couple is most closely connected with Japan. Thus, the Ministry found it essential to formulate a rule that enables family registrars to identify easily the situation where Japanese law should be applied, instead of applying the general clause.[20]

It goes without saying that, though applicable on the basis of the combination of a spouse's Japanese nationality with his or her habitual residence in Japan, Japanese law is not necessarily appropriate in terms of proximity. According to the explanation of the Ministry, the rule in question can only be justified in light of the limited power of the family registrar. We have to point out, however, that the rule goes further than compelled by necessity. First, it is not only registrars but also judges that may have recourse to this exceptional rule.[21] Second, the reservation of Japanese law extends to the effects of divorce, in particular, the maintenance obligations between the divorced spouses.[22] One would say that what is unjustifiable in light of ne-

---

[19] As to the divorce by agreement under Japanese law, see, Jun'ici Akiba/Minoru Ishikawa, 'Marriage and Divorce Regulation and Recognition in Japan', 29 *Family Law Quarterly* (1995) p. 593.

[20] If the rule in question is read against this background, it follows that Japanese law is only to be applied after the two preceding connecting factors, namely the common nationality and the common habitual residence, have been found non-existent in a particular case. In other words, a spouse's Japanese nationality combined with his or her habitual residence in Japan do not qualify to override the common nationality or the common habitual residence. This is the prevailing view.

[21] Japanese courts, in principle, do not assume their jurisdiction over divorce on the basis of a spouse's Japanese nationality but of the defendant's domicile (habitual residence) in Japan. It follows that a Japanese spouse is normally not allowed to bring an action for divorce before a Japanese court against a foreign spouse domiciled in a foreign country. However, a Japanese court may have jurisdiction to entertain the divorce proceedings where a defendant enters an appearance before it, or where certain exceptional circumstances exist, such as a defendant's desertion of the plaintiff. These jurisdictional rules were established by the decision of the Supreme Court on March, 25 1964 (8 *The Japanese Annual of International Law* (1964) pp. 175-180).

[22] Japan is a Contracting State of the Hague Convention on the Law Applicable to Maintenance Obligations of 1973. It follows that, pursuant to Article 8 of the Convention, when Japanese law applies to a divorce, it governs the maintenance obligations between the divorced spouses.

cessity or proximity may be explained only by the desire to ensure a Japanese spouse living in Japan a divorce available under Japanese law.[23]

4.   PUBLIC POLICY AND CONNECTING FACTORS ARRANGED BY CASCADE

When the application of a rule of foreign law is excluded by reason of the public policy of the forum, which law is to substitute it? This question seems to deserve a fresh examination in the case of a conflict rule that provides a series of connecting factors by cascade.

4.1   A Japanese Case

In 1990, the Tokyo District Court had to choose which parent would exercise the parental responsibility following the divorce. The father and the children concerned were Korean. The mother was Japanese. All of them had their habitual residence in Japan. Article 21 of *Horei* provides as follows: the legal relationship between parents and child shall be governed by the *lex patriae* of the child, if it is the same as the *lex patriae* of either parent; otherwise, it shall be governed by the law of the country of the habitual residence of the child.[24] Thus, Korean law should have been applied as the *lex patriae* of the children identical with that of the father. Strongly inspired by the paternalistic concepts, the Korean substantive rule (Article 909 of the Civil Code of Korea as it stood at that time) conferred upon the father an automatic parental authority after the divorce regardless of his suitability. The application of this rule was found intolerable in view of the best interests of the children in that case. The court excluded the application of Korean law, and, in its place, searched for another law on the basis of the other connecting factor laid down in Article 21 of *Horei*. Consequently, the court applied Japanese law as the law of the habitual residence of the children and appointed the mother to exercise parental responsibility.

---

[23] The policy according to which the State should open the door widely for its nationals seeking divorce seems to be far from extraordinary. However, the Japanese clause in question is likely to produce divorces not susceptible of recognition by foreign countries, when spouses who have children avail themselves of divorce by agreement under Japanese law. Japanese law allows a couple to determine the parent who will exercise parental responsibility over children after their divorce. The family registrar is not authorised to control their arrangement in terms of the best interests of the child. It may be noted, on this point, that the Tribunal de grande instance de Paris, in its judgment of October 17, 1991, recognised a divorce agreement made under Japanese law on the grounds that the parties had no children (81 *Revue critique de droit international privé* (1992) pp. 508-509).

[24] Article 21 envisages all the legal relationships between parents and child, irrespective of whether the child was born within wedlock or has been adopted. It may be added that, in practical terms, the law of the habitual residence of the child is expected to apply in the situation where the child seriously needs public protection, e.g., when the mother of an illegitimate child is dead.

4.2 Practical Utility of Search for Subsidiary Law

Japanese private international law has no provision such as Article 16, Paragraph 2 of the "Reform of the Italian System of Private International Law", according to which, given the inapplicability of foreign law on the ground of public policy, the law to be applied is that which is referred to by another connecting factor provided for the same situation. The above decision of the Tokyo District Court seems tantamount to the introduction of such a rule into Japanese private international law *de lege lata* in connection with Article of 21 of *Horei*. We doubt that the search for another law on the basis of another connecting factor is practically useful at least in so far as Japanese private international law is concerned.

First, as *Lagarde* rightly states, the requirement of an *Inlandsbeziehung* or *Binnenbezihung* makes recourse to the *lex fori* as subsidiary law less oppressive.[25] As a result of the careful application of the public policy clause, the link with the forum expressed by those terms may even be identical with another connecting factor that the relevant conflicts rule provides for in the same matter. It may safely be said that, in connection with the legal relationships between parents and child, public policy would, in principle, not come into operation without the child's habitual residence in the forum country. Under Japanese private international law, the *lex fori* is likely to be, at the same time, the law of the country of the habitual residence of the child as Article 21 provides and is therefore suitable to fill the vacuum.

Second, the search for a law on the basis of another connecting factor seems to be superfluous in certain situations.[26] For example, when a Japanese court should apply Philippine law as the common national law of the spouses in the divorce proceedings but finds its application intolerable in that case, it is very likely that the court has already come to the conclusion that the spouses should get divorced. This conclusion would remain unchanged, whatever law may be chosen on the basis of another connecting factor. In such a case, to look for a law on the basis of another criterion, *e.g.*, the common habitual residence of the spouses seems to mean nothing more than to seek a law that may endorse the conclusion that the court has reached beforehand.

4.3 Justifiability of Recourse to a Subsidiary Connecting Factor

In the above mentioned case, the Tokyo District Court presumably equated the "primary" connecting factor (the common nationality) with the "best" one and the "sub-

---

[25] Paul Lagarde, "Public Policy", *International Encyclopedia of Comparative Law* (1994) vol. III chap. II p. 57.

[26] Such cases may be identical with the cases where the exclusion of the foreign law implies the positive recognition of a right whose content is specifically determined. Cf., Andreas Bucher, "L'ordre public et le but social des lois en droit international privé", *Recueil des Cours* (1993-II) pp. 31-32.

sidiary" (the habitual residence of the child) with the "second best". If such an equation were possible, it would make the reasoning of the court understandable. It seems only natural that, once the application of the foreign law indicated by the best connecting factor has been rejected because of its incompatibility with public policy, the court was inclined to find another applicable law with recourse to the second best connecting factor. We doubt that such reasoning should be acceptable under Japanese private international law.

First, we are often inclined to talk about the "subsidiary" connecting factor, when its application is triggered by the absence of the "primary" one. For example, the habitual residence of a person is subsidiary to the primary connecting factor of nationality when the personal law should be determined for a stateless person.[27] But, the expression "subsidiary" (or "primary") seems to be somewhat misleading, when such adjectives are put in terms of connecting factors arranged by cascade. It is true that the legislature gave priority to the common nationality in connection with Article 16 of *Horei*: when a married couple of the same nationality has its common habitual residence in a foreign country, the law of the country of the common nationality governs the divorce, regardless of the common habitual residence. In contrast, this is the sole connecting factor for the divorce of a mixed couple. Therefore, we cannot talk about the subsidiary character of this factor in relation to this type of marriage.

Second, should the reasoning in question be followed in the divorce proceedings, the court would apply the law of the country of the common habitual residence as the second best, when they find it intolerable to apply the common national law as a foreign law. Such a general formula as set forth in Article 31 of the 'Reform of the Italian System of Private International Law' would allow the court to use such reasoning. The "country in which the matrimonial life turns out to be preponderantly localised" may be found somewhere not only for a mixed couple but also for a couple of that common nationality whose law has been excluded by the public policy. On the other hand, in the absence of a common nationality, Article 16 of *Horei* on divorce adopts a specific connecting factor, the common habitual residence of the spouses. One might wonder whether this factor, which has been adopted as appropriate for a mixed couple, is adequate just as well for a couple of common nationality, or, put in another way, how a couple sharing the motherland whose law happens to be excluded by the public policy of the forum may be treated as if they were of different nationalities. It does not seem that a provision, containing a series of connecting factors such as Article 16, provides an answer to this question.

---

[27] Article 28, Paragraph 2 of *Horei*.

Legal Culture in the Czech Republic as Challenged by the Perspective of Accession to the European Union

Jiří Zemánek[*]

1.   STRUCTURAL AND SOCIAL TRANSFORMATION

The yearning of the Czech society for the return to "normal conditions", a cultivated organization of public as well as private affairs, in which the citizen could generally rely on the fact that justice and good generally prevail and "what is good and proper" will triumph in the end, has been manifested in the foreign policy of the country after November 1989, by the decision to align itself with the Euro-Atlantic alliance. Full integration in the alliance, however, necessitates a profound transformation of its political, economic, social, institutional and legal organization. Fundamental changes of structural character, confirming the irreversibility of the development trend were introduced – like in other post-communist Central and East European countries – at the very beginning of the 90s with the establishment of democratic institutions, codification of constitutional guarantees of fundamental rights and freedoms and the laying of the foundations to market economy. The necessary stability of the development process, however, can be assured only after the completion of the transformation of the whole society, including also a change of socio-psychological habits and legal consciousness of the people and including the abandonment of deformations burdening legal reasoning and decision-making. Only then can the country become a really reliable and accountable partner which capable of fulfilling its international obligations.

 Central and East European countries (CEEC) are undergoing a – by no means easy – process of completing the restoration of democratic statehood and the full

---

[*] Dr. jur., Jean Monnet Chair, Charles University Prague.

J. Basedow et al., eds., Private Law in the International Arena – Liber Amicorum Kurt Siehr
© 2000, T.M.C.Asser Press, The Hague, The Netherlands

emancipation of citizens as active and responsible members of a civic society. This is accompanied by an ebb of the feeling of triumph, that everything has already been won, which prevailed in the exalted moments of Autumn 1989. This process is all the more difficult because it is taking place in the environment of the fast globalization of the world, personified for the CEECs particularly by the European Union which they wish to join. On the legal level this process may appear as an almost mechanical procedure, a single-sided approximation to standards, in the establishment of which the CEECs cannot take part, as they do not have the right to participate in any decision-making process, as if the emerging world order should be indifferent to values and the lawyers merely a passive instrument of its enforcement whose professional education need not be overburdened with any humanitarian ideals.

Another lopsided aspect which the lawyers have to cope with are the locking tendencies, the adherence to national interest however vaguely formulated with the institutions representing a public authority which finds a nutritive soil in the form of intolerance, aversion to open society and instinctive animosity to the new elements of legal organization arising in a considerable part of the post-communist world. This is due, on the one hand, to a tendency towards the inertia of the past state of society, and, on the other hand, to the reaction to a sudden flood of changes in the settlement of interpersonal conflicts which should have brought about greater stability, but sometimes instead results in making the political and legal conditions uncertain and in producing fear of the future.[1]

The quest for a balanced solution to this situation is an obvious task of every one who has been honoured to engage in one of the traditional centres of European education. Let me emphasize that Professor KURT SIEHR has made a notable contribution in this respect for which I would like to thank him.

2.   JUS COMMUNE

Since its establishment in 1348 the Charles University in Prague has been closely connected with historical developments in Europe. Even in the periods when the country was driven to the margin of political development, Prague University has retained consciousness of European continuity. Moreover, it is also possible to recall the periods when the personalities, to whom Prague University offered education, co-determined this continuity or at least influenced it significantly.

In the High Renaissance period Justinian's *Institutiones* and *Digesta* were taught both in Bologna and Paris as well as in Prague, Heidelberg and Cracow. Consequently, in Continental Europe Charles University contributed to the creation of the

---

[1] The speech by *V. Havel*, President of the Czech Republic, on the occasion of the Open Society award at the Central European University in Budapest on June 24, 1999 (unpublished).

ius commune on the basis of Roman and Canon law. The commentaries, usually written in Latin, such as the German *usus modernus Pandectarum*, were used by judges all over Europe. Where local rules had gaps or suffered from ambiguity, the judges of the period could arrive at a satisfactory solution by the subsidiary application of the *ius commune*. In this way the unifying effect of the *ius commune*, which can be felt vaguely even at present, helped to overcome the existing tendencies towards separatism which served as a permanent source of power conflicts. The spontaneous unification of law, brought about by the necessities of practical needs of everyday life, was based on a common treasury of legal literature contributed to by learned men from various countries. It did not matter much where a young scholar received his legal education.

Following an epoch of great legal codifications which relegated the legal profession to a rather provincial role, Europe has been seeking again, since the 1950s, a common legal basis for its further development under the pressures of globalization. In this process it is using such tools as self-executing rules with direct effect on the individual or the obligatory jurisdiction of international bodies which supervise the uniform application of those rules. The enthusiasm, manifested in this respect by the European Union as a focal point of this endeavour, is motivated by a number of well-known advantages of the unified or harmonized law as compared with the preceding state marked by the differences among individual national regulations. This "unification business", however, has also some internal limits. Where these limits have been reached, a measure of uneasiness has been felt: the "price" for the pragmatic approach to Community harmonization has resulted in the fragmentation of codification. For instance, the harmonization in the field of private law concerns highly specific problems (product liability, package travels, misleading advertising, doorstep selling, unfair terms in consumer contracts, etc.) while the common institutions of contract or torts law have remained codified by national rules only.

Such an approach to legal harmonization represents a shortcoming of the integration process concept. Although Community law enjoys supremacy over national law in EU member states, the system's disharmony is manifested in the interpretation and application of harmonized codification. Therefore, a solution is sought in the draft of a European Civil Code, although it seems that the implementation of this project will only take place in a rather distant future. Another limitation of harmonization is the scope of rigidity of common codification. An amendment of the harmonized codification, required by the need of subsequent adaptation to changed social conditions, is usually much more difficult and lengthy than an amendment of national codification.[2] The "blocking effect" of Community powers connected with it makes it impossible for the individual Member States to mutually compete in the

---

[2] Behrens, "Voraussetzungen und Grenzen der Rechtsfortbildung durch Rechtsvereinheitlichung", 50 *RabelsZ* (1986) pp. 19-34.

"testing" of the legislative response to the problems of contemporary society and new priorities on the scale of value preferences of the population. The irrevocable transfer of national powers to the EU, comprising also the adoption of measures for the unification of national law by its bodies, therefore, ranks among the most controversial subjects of home policy discussions related to EU reforms or referenda organized in newly acceding member states.

3.   THE INTEGRATING ROLE OF THE LAWYERS' PROFESSIONAL
      EDUCATION IN EUROPE

In spite of the different historical, geographic and political context, which makes the drawing of a direct comparison difficult, the experience of the U.S.A. does not confirm the thesis that a far-reaching unification of legislation is the necessary characteristic accompanying a functioning internal market or state organization of a federal type. In contrast to prevalent belief, the legislative power of the U.S. Congress is limited to selected fields, such as foreign policy and defence, currency, federal taxes, matters of citizenship, bankruptcy law, copyright and control of foreign trade in strategic commodities. The remaining part of the commercial law and the whole field of private law fall within the powers of the fifty States of the Union. The scope of nation-wide fully unified regulations is not very large. Even the well known Uniform Commercial Code does not contain the codification of such institutions as contracting capacity or agency, definition of the factual circumstances giving rise to coercion and fraud, grounds of invalidity of legal acts or their potential invalidation, etc. Therefore, the differences among the individual States of the U.S.A. in the field of private law are the rule and the uniformity remains an exception. However, the Americans can tolerate this type of legal diversity since particularly the system of legal education in American universities and the legal literature represent an integrating force of American law in a unitary manner (*"national law school"*). The introduction of the uniform ABA lawyers' examinations has further contributed to the unifying process. Therefore, American lawyers speak "the same legal language" and have no problems with mutual professional communication. As aptly pointed out by Professor *Gray*, "perhaps the biggest obstacle of the unification and harmonization of the law of our States is the simple fact that while it *may be* desirable, it *is not* necessary".[3]

Also in Europe even the most extensive harmonization does not create sufficient incentive for the mutual convergence of national legal systems, in the absence of an adequate system of education of lawyers. If the application of the harmonized

---

[3] Gray, "E Pluribus Unum: A Bicentennial Report on Unification of Law in the United States", 50 *RabelsZ* (1986) p. 155.

legislation in the individual countries is not purposively supported by the education of lawyers on the basis of a *ius commune*, that legislation will yield merely apparent, empty uniformity. And vice versa: if a system of professional education based on the phenomenon of common legal ideas and values is established, then also the maxim *lex multiplex ius unum* will be realized. In this context, it is apt to quote the German historian of law and civil law specialist, Professor *Coing*, who sees the historical lesson primarily "in the enormous role played by academic education in the formation of our common legal heritage, both in the Middle Ages and in the Enlightenment. It was academic education based on European ideas that created a class of lawyers imbued with the same ideals, and it was the European lawyer who heralded the arrival of European law. That is, in my opinion, the moment where our academic responsibility begins. We should struggle for the organization of such academic education in our schools of law in Europe which – instead of dividing the lawyers – would endeavour to enhance their mutual understanding. We must revise the concept which dominated legal education in the 19th century, that legal education must be based on national laws. The curricula of our schools of law must not be limited to national law, possibly seasoned a little with comparative law. What is needed and what we must concentrate on are such curricula in which the basic courses will present national law in the context of those legal ideas which are present in the laws of various countries, i.e. on the background of the principles and institutions common to all nations of Europe."[4]

The universities in the EU member states do not seem to have approached this goal yet. Surveys have shown that Community law – similarly to comparative law and international law – has often been made an elective course in university curricula.[5] Legal education has long been dominated by the attitude emphasizing the formal, dogmatic criteria of the national legal system. This has resulted in the marginalization of attention given to other legal systems, although the European Court of Justice in its case law formulated the well-known principle that Community law is national, not foreign law in the Member States which must be applied therein in a uniform manner.

---

[4] Coing, "European Common Law: Historical Foundations", in: *New Perspectives for a Common Law of Europe* (Cappelletti (ed.)) (1978) p. 44.

[5] E.g. national reports submitted at the symposium "L'enseignement du droit comparé" and published in 40 *Rev. int. droit comp.* (1988) pp. 703-763; Pertek, "New needs for education and training in European Law", 18 *ELRev* (1993) p. 388ff.; Schermers, "Legal education in Europe", 30 *CMLRev* (1993) p. 9ff.; Kötz, "Gemeineuropäisches Zivilrecht", in: *Festschrift für Zweigert* (1981) p. 481ff.; Basedow, "Juristen für den Binnenmarkt: Die Ausbildungsdiskussion im Lichte einer Arbeitsmarktanalyse", *NJW* (1990) p. 959ff.

A certain improvement has taken place as an indirect consequence of the measures adopted by the Community for mutual recognition of diplomas[6] and the facilitation of the free movement of lawyers.[7] This trend has created competition also among the national university education systems. However, these measures were not accompanied by a definition of minimum academic standards regarding content and duration of studies, the compliance with which would be a pre-condition for acquiring adequate education. Nevertheless, they created an important stimulus for the extension of undergraduate education of European law beyond national borders. It has become of the utmost importance "to provide an adequate response to a growing demand by law students to have access to cross-cultural legal experience".[8] A number of universities not only in EU member states but also in other West European countries and a number of countries outside Europe, have introduced special postgraduate programmes in the field of comparative law or European studies, intended for foreign students (*Diplome d' Etudes Européennes Approfondis, M.A. in European Studies, Magister Legum Europae* as an analogy to Anglo-American programmes of L.L.M.).[9] The purpose of these programmes is also to provide an excellent opportunity to acquire experience in more than one educational system. The development of new structures of international university co-operation is supported also by the EU educational programme *Socrates* (*Erasmus*).

The general picture of education in European and Comparative Law is completed by specialized training institutions, such as, in particular, the *Faculté internationale de Droit Comparé* in Strassbourg, the *College of Europe* in Brugges with its branch in Warsaw – Natolin, the *European University Institute* in Florence and the *European Institute of Public Administration* in Maastricht, supplemented by training institutions of a non-university type, catering mostly to the needs of the legal or administrative practice, such as *Europäische Rechtsakademie* in Trier, the *Civil Service College* in Sunningdale and the *Bundesakademie für Verwaltungs-wissenschaften* in Vienna. Although it is not possible to say even under EU conditions that the demand for a transnational basis for legal education has prevailed over the traditional model, the development in this direction is proceeding relatively fast.

---

[6] Council Directive 89/48/EEC on general system for the recognition of higher-education diplomas (OJ [1989] L 19/16); Council Directive 92/51/EEC on a second general system for the recognition of professional education and training (OJ [1992] L 209/25).

[7] Council Directive 77/249/EEC to facilitate the effective exercise by lawyers of freedom to pro-vide services (OJ [1977] L 78/17).

[8] Vranken, *Fundamentals of European Civil Law* (London, Blackstone 1996) p. 223.

[9] Postgraduate Degrees in European Integration, European Commission 1996.

4.   APPROXIMATION OF LAWS AND BEYOND

The ability to adopt the legal norms and fulfil the obligations arising from EU membership – as one of the admission criteria provided by the session of the European Council in Copenhagen in 1993 – is being tested in the course of the negotiations on accession *inter alia* by the ability of the candidate country to fulfil its obligations concerning approximation of laws according to the Europe Agreement on association (Art. 69). Here the Czech Republic undertook "to endeavour to ensure that its legislation will be gradually made compatible with that of the Community". This involves considerable interference with the national legal system in order to enable liberalization of mutual access of commodities and services to the markets, facilitation of the movement of people and achievement of equivalent protection of public interest and creation of prerequisites essential for the subsequent full adoption of *acquis communautaire*. In the field of competition rules and grants of subsidies this effort takes place already in the pre-accession period. The *White Paper* of the European Commission, adopted as a Recommendation by the European Council in Cannes in 1995 for the progress of transposition of current Community secondary legislation relating to the Internal Market, provides also the requirements imposed on the availability of institutional (judicial, administrative) protection of rights and/ or an assurance of enforcement of obligations based on harmonized codification comparable with the measures applied in EU member states. It refers also to the respective jurisdiction of the European Court of Justice (ECJ) as an integral part of Community law.

Although the central executive authorities of the Czech Republic check systematically the compatibility of all legislative drafts with Community law, the European Commission in its assessments has voiced repeated criticism of the present state of public administration and of the insufficient capacity of the judiciary as the weakest points of readiness of the Czech Republic for the accession to the EU.[10] This cannot be attributed merely to the lack of political will to implement more assertively such measures as the Civil Service Act or the strengthening of administrative judiciary *inter alia* by the establishment of the Administrative Supreme Court (envisaged in the Constitution). It is rooted also in the still surviving *stereotypes of legal reasoning* in the application of harmonized codification. If this *signum tempris* should not remain an obstacle to the accession of the Czech Republic to the EU, it is necessary to europeanize not only the legislation. In addition, and perhaps even more important, there is need to europeanize the system of lawyers' education both at the universities and in the framework of the professional training of the judiciary and public administration. A strict requirement of uniform application of

---

[10] Regular Report from the Commission on the Czech Republic's progress towards accession (1999).

Community law and the Community-loyal interpretation of national law will result inevitably in intensive pressure on the appropriation of the *multicultural dimension* of the EU legal area. In the past, the roots of this culture, in the form of common legal principles, were struck in the territory of Bohemia and Moravia. Nowadays, too, the process would partly involve the regeneration of these values. However, the new, Community elements will prevail. In no case should it involve the promotion of degenerated bureaucratic inertia.

5.   SELECTED PROBLEMS

Czech lawyers must get rid of their strong inclination towards legal positivism. Too much emphasis on the wording of the legal rule, overestimation of its normative force and *a priori* mistrust for the ability of the judge to interpret it correctly and to "find" law can be seen everywhere. Moreover, law is often reduced to merely an instrument of governance which can be changed or ignored as required. It is understood merely as a product of the legislator's activity without admitting that it is not a value in itself, but an expression of the values which society wants to respect. This prevalent narrow approach represents yet one more obstacle to the reception of Community law. It is inspired by the plurality of national models and cannot be interpreted correctly without considering the value background represented by these models. It gives a misleading feeling that the successful coping with the process of law approximation is merely a matter of legislation. It is not commonly realized yet that this approach shifts the burden of difficulties connected with the general comprehension of Community law to the shoulders of judges and public servants.

The influence of these residues of the past can be felt in the Czech Republic in the general attitude to e.g. the Community concept of *consumer protection* which might seem to recall the unfortunate experience of the paternalist law of the socialist period. It is considerably difficult to understand that this concept is based on the civil law prohibition on abuse of law (by the producer, seller) and that it is not part of public law upon which the Czech codification of consumer protection is still based. Its indirect economic consequences are stricter requirements (safety, quality, marking of products, etc.) imposed on the manufacturer (seller) and, consequently, improve his competitiveness on other markets. The Czech Republic, in the course of approximating its laws with Community law, has been and will be grappling for some time to come with a certain tension between two aspects of this task: the formal obligation to adopt a certain standard (directive) and its normative content ("normative idea" of the directive). The separation of both aspects is the consequence of a habit developed in those times when the discrepancy between the wording of a legal norm and its declared objective was not exceptional but rather deliberate.

Another manifestation of the overestimated significance of the wording of a legal regulation over its normative substance is e.g., the manner in which the reports on the state of the fulfilment of obligations resulting from the participation of the Czech Republic in international treaties are presented in the framework of monitoring performed by international organizations. This information is usually limited to the implemented modifications of national laws without bothering to mention (i.e., provide prior record of) the changes which have taken place in the judicial and the administrative decisions. Naturally, the informative ability of the decision-making practice of public administration authorities is restricted by the non-public character of individual administrative acts and specific legal treatment. In the implementation of Community directives, therefore, merely changing the existing practice of law application by administrative bodies would not be sufficient.[11] However, a change in the spirit of the judicial interpretation of the law may be sufficient to satisfy the requirement arising from an international obligation.

An insensitive, sometimes even disparaging attitude towards the role of the judiciary is not a *specialité de la maison* of post-communist countries. However, their "speciality" often consists in various shortcomings of the content and formulation of the legal rules themselves, drafted under time pressure or without sufficient knowledge of the matter and, consequently, deprived of the ability of foreseeing the possible stumbling blocks of their application on the one hand, and the missing resolution or will of the judges to make correct use of the possibilities open to them owing to their independence. Much too often prudence is replaced with either a poor sense of proportionality of legal reasoning or merely by over-caution and indolence. The few years of independence were obviously not long enough to change some habits rooted in the past. The situation in the EU is different: while the more abstract primary law requires an often highly exacting deductive interpretation by national courts in co-operation with the European Court of Justice, thus acquiring the significance of *judge-made law*, the secondary legislation, of considerably casuistic wording, leaves very little room for the reasoning of the court. Failure to use it is not due to the lack of the judge's will, but to his low level of inventiveness or excessive routine.

A new task for Czech judges, after the accession to the EU, will consist in their independent decision-making on the possible non-applicability of national law when contrary to Community law (supremacy of Community law), without having to submit this issue for decision to the Constitutional Court. He will also have to assess correctly, whether the time has come for him to turn to the European Court of Justice in the framework of the *preliminary ruling procedure* requesting interpretation of Community law provisions to the extent that such is indispensable for deciding the case at hand (i.e., to know also the relevant ECJ case-law). For the judge to

---

[11] The judgement of the ECJ in case 102/79 *Commission* v. *Belgium* [1980] ECR 1473.

be successful in such "law finding", he will need to undergo some special training, the more so since Czech law is still under a strong influence of legal dualism (national effects of international treaties are still not resolved constitutionally with the exception of treaties on human rights and fundamental freedoms).

Another problem consists in the continued deficit of the procedural instrumentarium of the legal system of the Czech Republic and the ensuing mistrust in its functioning. In the course of democratic development of modern societies, the judicial power has attained considerable emancipation from both the executive and the legislative powers and the number of tools for the exercise of justice have increased. The developments in EU law have resulted in the strengthening of procedural guarantees of the enforcement of rights acquired in the framework of contractual freedom as compared with the extension of substantive law codification of cogent character. Access to justice has been facilitated e.g. by the standardization of the conditions of civil law procedure, acceleration of the procedure by shifting the burden of proof, improvement of legal certainty on the basis of the presumption of legitimate expectations, and the extension of options of alternative – extrajudicial – systems for the settlement of disputes and the enforcement of decisions. Also the basis for the *judicialization of the decisions* of executive authorities and the improvement of the guarantees of counstitutionality of use of legislative powers (state responsibility for the so-called legislative void e.g., for causing detriment to an entity by its inactivity in the implementation of a Community directive). Preference of facultative codification, emphasis laid on the settlement of disputes rather than the assertion of a single, predetermined general codification model, etc. correspond better to the present situation but imposing further new requirements on legal reasoning.

Yet another problem consists in the issue of *legitimacy of decision-making* of lawyers. If the public in the modern, "medialized" European society is expected to accept a law, a judgement or an official decision, it is usually not enough to state that the given decision has been made in conformity with the appropriate provisions of substantive and procedural law or that it is not at variance with them. Arguments based merely on formal legality, "bureaucratic legalism"[12] alone, are not capable of persuading of the fairness of the issued act. The public is not willing to identify with the measure taken by public authorities, if it cannot identify with the material reasons on which that act is based. Otherwise, the public authority will be further alienated from the citizens, one of the civilizational diseases afflicting all developed societies. After the state of justice has really become *res publica* (and not merely the matter of a narrow interest of professionals), the requirements imposed on the ability of lawyers to explain intelligibly the motives for their decisions are

---

[12] Letowska, "The Barriers of Polish Legal Thinking in the Perspective of European Integration", *Yearbook of Polish European Studies* (Warsaw 1997) p. 67.

incomparably higher than previously. *Ars aequi et boni* is one of the universally valid challenges of the human feeling for justice. It always involves *the question of confidence in the legal system as a whole*.

The style of work of Czech courts does not yet measure up to the legal reasoning of European courts. The difference has remained concealed so far, as the judgements of lower courts are not available to the broad public and are known even less abroad. A change for the better, which can be expected in the context of the re-codification of private law in the Czech Republic, however, must take place before Czech courts are obliged to apply Community law against the background of the interpretation rules, procedures and values embodied in European jurisdiction. This jurisdiction should be the object of systematic monitoring and evaluation already at present, so that the interpretation of Community rules (which have stabilized in the meantime), and adopted successively by Czech law, should not ignore it and should not become subsequently an obstacle to the accession of the Czech Republic to the European Union.

As soon as individuals feel depressed by manipulation, even if unintentional, there will be no public *trust* and hence no public support, a *sine qua non* for the functioning of any legal system.

* * *

The number of problems Czech lawyers will have to encounter on the road to accession to the European Union is considerable. In this "multidimensional space" they will not be able to resign to the seemingly Sisyphean task of uniting form and content, the substantive and the procedural aspects, law and justice. Whether as a civil servant or as a private practitioner, the lawyer will remain always a public servant. The European dimension of his readiness, therefore, will corresponds to the deepening of his basic social responsibility arising from the legal profession as such. And that precisely is what the university should impress upon law students first and foremost. The university must also contribute more to the cultivation of the required skills in particular by introducing not only the knowledge of the law in force, but making the students master the *full understanding of law as a social phenomenon*.

Since the past few years Charles University has made a considerable progress in this respect. In spring 1993, the Faculty of Law introduced the course on European Community Law as an obligatory subject, supplemented with optional subjects and further activities, especially in international co-operation (participation in the *moot court* competition, etc.). Another contribution was the opening of three courses introducing the basic principles of German, English and French law, as well as a number of changes in the content of further subjects taught at the Faculty. The course for practicing lawyers and civil servants (at present one-year course under the heading of Europeum, organized in co-operation with the Faculty of Social

Sciences of Charles University) has been running for five years. Further qualitative development of European law studies can be expected from joining the ERASMUS programme. The Faculty is offering the two-semester programme in English for foreign students – *The Czech Legal System in European Contexts (Master of Law)*, too.

Particularities of the Harmonisation and Unification of International Law of Trade and Commerce

Alexander von Ziegler[*]

1. ARE THERE PARTICULARITIES OF THE HARMONISATION AND UNIFICATION OF THE INTERNATIONAL LAW OF TRADE AND COMMERCE?

Umpteen thousand goods are bought and sold, packaged, consolidated, shipped, unloaded, cleared through customs, stored and delivered every day. Umpteen thousand transport documents, packing lists and insurance certificates are processed in the documentation departments of banks every day. Umpteen thousand goods are transported in a never-ending transport flow from one point on the globe to another, placed in the retail trade or processed and then sent back on a journey round the world again in a different shape or form.

This is the world of international trade and commerce. What appears superficially to be chaos turns out to be a cleverly thought-out system. Since the business of trade and commerce extends across the whole world, it needs a uniform standard which must also be embodied in law. How should this be done? What are the particularities of such a standardisation of the law of international trade and commerce?

---

[*] Dr. iur., LL.M., attorney-at-law, associate professor (PD) at the University of Zurich.

J. Basedow et al., eds., Private Law in the International Arena – Liber Amicorum Kurt Siehr
© 2000, T.M.C.Asser Press, The Hague, The Netherlands

In attempting to answer this question, I should like to use the term of "law of trade and commerce" for describing those legal relationships under private law which the parties involved in overseas trade use for the execution of an international export or import transaction. Trade law is not, therefore, an independent field of law in the real sense, but a special and specially developed part of the legal everyday life of international trade. It comprises the phenomenon of international trade in goods under private law.[1]

I will, furthermore, deal with "harmonisation" in the field of trade law. We use the term broadly so as also to cover all instruments aimed at achieving a certain uniformity of law. Thus we are speaking, on the one hand, of uniform law in the form of the international conventions, but also of the alternatives, such as model laws, uniform customs and practice and pre-formulated standard clauses, which are all aimed at the standardisation, alignment or harmonisation of the law.[2]

Every simple trade transaction involves a large number of legal relationships which repeatedly involve international points of contact and continuously interact with one another. Trade law deals with the legal side of such transactions, in particular with the following four legal transactions:

1. the **international sale of goods** and, in particular, the special features of sale in which goods are transported to destination according to the seller's or the buyer's instructions (depending on the agreed delivery system[3] and the trade terms[4] chosen by the parties);

2. the **contracts of carriage** and the legal relationships with the various carriers[5] and intermediaries used for the logistics involved in transportation;

---

[1] This in contrast to the broader term "trade law", which also comprises the legal environment created and governed by national, regional and international trade agreements regulating as a matter of public law, the level of freedom of trade. See, e.g. G. Jiménez, *ICC Guide to Export-Import Basics* (Paris 1997) p.31.

[2] For a more in depth study of the alternatives of harmonising instruments in the field of trade, and in particular maritime law, see: von Ziegler, "The Comité Maritime International (CMI): The Voyage from 1897 into the Next Millennium", *U.L.R.* (1997) pp. 728 et seq.

[3] See e.g. Art. 32 of the United Nations Convention on Contracts for the International Sale of Goods (Vienna Sales Convention) 1980; *UNCITRAL Y.B.* (1974) pp. 210 et seq.

[4] See, e.g. the trade terms FOB (free on board) and CFR (cost and freight) pursuant to *INCOTERMS 2000* (ICC Publication No. 560, Paris 2000).

[5] Sea: International Convention for the Unification of Certain Rules of Law Relating to Bills of Lading, 25 August 1924 (Hague Rules), as amended by the Protocol of 23 February 1968 (Visby-Rules) and the Protocol of 21 December 1979 (SDR Protocol); United Nations Convention on the Carriage of Good by Sea, 31 March 1978 (Hamburg Rules); Charter parties based on the standard contracts prepared by private organisations like BIMCO. Air: Convention for the Unification of Certain Rules Relating to International Carriage by Air, 12 October 1929 (Warshaw Convention), as amended by the Protocol of 28 September 1955 (Hague Protocol) and the Protocols of 8 March 1971 (Guatemala City Protocol), of 25 September 1975 (Montreal Protocols 1. - 4.); Convention for the Unification of Certain

3.   the **financing** of the sale of goods and payment of the price by means of a documentary letter of credit;[6]

and also

4.   the **transport insurance contract,** i.e. insurance against the risks of damage or loss of goods during transport.[7]

Each one of these legal transactions is, naturally, international. This alone suggests that attempts at legal standardisation in the field of trade and commerce law are bound to occupy a very special position.

To create and preserve this legal standardisation and adapt it to the increasingly rapid developments of the economic and technological environment is of vital importance for world trade and, therefore, for the whole global economy. It is important to ensure in standardising this body of law that the harmonising instrument produced lives up to these special standards and particularities and satisfies the special requirements of legal everyday life of all participants in the business of international trade.

2.   PARTICULARITIES OF THE HARMONISATION AND UNIFICATION OF THE INTERNATIONAL LAW OF TRADE AND COMMERCE

2.1   **Starting Point**

Without wishing to lay claim to historical accuracy, it can fairly be said that the regulation of trade and commerce has constituted a transcultural phenomenon since time immemorial.[8] This is in contrast to most of the other fields of law, which have been developed primarily as an internal (tribal and later national) regulatory structure, which largely regulated internal circumstances for a particular political entity.

The law of trade and commerce in ancient times, which is often described as "*lex*

Rules for International Carriage by Air, 28 May 1999 (Montreal Convention). Road: Convention on the Contract for International Carriage of Goods by Road (CMR), Geneva, 19 May 1956. Rail: Uniform Rules Concerning the Contract for International Carriage of Goods by Rail (CIM), 7 February 1970 (CIM), now part of the Convention Concerning International Carriage by Rail, 9 May 1980 (COTIF).

    [6] *Uniform Customs and Practice for Documentary Credits*, 1993 Revision (UCP 500); ICC Publication No. 500, Paris 1993.

    [7] Marine Insurance contracts have been standardised, at least within the national markets, and traditionally follow the principles set out in the terms established by the London market: Institute Cargo Clauses. R. Thomas, *The Modern Law of Marine Insurance*, London 1996, p. 2 and pp. 387 - 507. H.J. Enge, *Transportversicherung*, 2nd ed. (Wiesbaden 1987) p. 34.

    [8] See, e.g. R. Wagner, *Handbuch des Seerechts* (Leipzig 1884) vol. I, pp. 55 et seq.

mercatoria" or, with regard to maritime law, as "*lex maritima*", always concerned trans-national circumstances and naturally developed into separate, independent trans-national separate law largely standardised by trade practice. It left behind traces in Greek and Roman law and in the collections of court rulings of the most important trading centres in the Middle Ages across the Mediterranean and the Atlantic up to the Baltic.[9]

As a separate law independent of national law, trade law also survived various radical changes in the world order. As an autonomous separate law, it further developed quite independently from the various developments in general law within the different legal systems.

A turning point came about with the important national codifications of the 19th century.[10] These comprehensive national legislations achieved a **national** harmonisation of law in the field of domestic law. At the same time, however, they destroyed the autonomous and international development of trade and commerce law as a trans-cultural separate law because the major legislators of the 19th century also included the principles of the so called "*lex mercatoria*" into their national system of law.[11] This nationalistic trend deprived world trade of the chance to satisfy its intrinsic need for **international** harmonisation and unification.

Against this background, it is hardly surprising that a massive movement towards unification law was unleashed precisely in the area of trade law – just at a time when, in the rest of private law, the development of law was regarded as a **purely (internal) governmental** matter and hardly any thought was being given to international harmonisation.[12]

As stated already, the situation was different with trade law, which, with standardisation (or more precisely, the **re**-standardisation) could draw on the familiar, internationally tried, tested and accepted unified substantive law. It is, therefore, not surprising that the unification efforts were able to **concentrate** directly and solely on **substantive law**. This very special starting position explains, why it was not necessary to follow the route of the internationally standardised conflict-of-law rules preferred for the standardisation of the rest of private law.[13] Nor could the uniform conflict-of-law rules have met the special needs of trade and commerce, for it

---

[9] See, e.g. L. Trakman, *The Law Merchant: The Evolution of Commercial Law* (Colorado 1983) pp. 7-21.

[10] In England, harmonisation of the individual, fragmented practices was engendered in order to produce the "common law". R. David, "The International Unification of Private Law", in: *Int. Enc. Comp. L. II/5* (1971) pp. 3 et seq.; R. Goode, "Reflections on the Harmonisation of Commercial Law", *ULR* (1991) pp. 54 et seq.

[11] A paramount example is the astonishing work of J.M. Pardessus in his "*collection de lois maritimes antérieures au XVIII siècle*" (Paris 1828 – 1845), which formed part of the basis for his contribution to the French Code de Commerce.

[12] R. Goode (supra n. 10) p. 54.

[13] R. David (supra n. 10) at p. 141.

is not sufficient for a businessman in a multi-international interlocked transaction to know when which law will be applied. To overstate the argument, for the players of world trade, the application of national laws involved in a particular transaction are mere chance and can only play a subordinate role in the strong need for logistical and legal standards.[14] Only a truly standardised law (i.e. uniform substantive law) will bring about the expected and needed level of predictability in the legal environment in which the transaction will be conducted. Trade law thereby becomes the prototype for an area of law to be unified on an international scale, since trade by definition operates in a truly international (and even multi-international) sphere and occurs frequently using the same pattern[15] while facing the probability of being brought before a variety of national courts.[16]

2.2 Need for Unification and Harmonisation of Commercial and Trade Law

A further important particularity of trade and commerce law is the special need and objectives for harmonisation. The harmonisation and unification of law outside the particular field of trade law starts basically with the need of various countries for improved governmental co-operation, if not co-existence or even political integration. By contrast, the starting point for the harmonisation or unification of trade law[17] is always to be found in the "materialistic" and "pragmatic" yearning of people involved in trade for standardised and efficient rules. Trade presupposes unified rules which make the transaction and any potential problems predictable (i.e. calculable). These standards achieved by the internationally unified rules remain identical, although for each transaction of the same kind, different legal systems are affected on a case by case basis. Despite what one might think, trade law is not created by cosmopolitan minds, but is generally inspired by the naked need and yearning for an efficient unified standard under which the trade transactions can be performed as efficiently (and as profitably) as possible.[18] The stronger and the more relevant a particular obstacle is, the more this issue will form the nucleus for further unification.[19] All too often, artificial "needs" are "created" by those who advocate for a new harmonising instrument for reasons other than pure and pragmatic trade

---

[14] Ibid, p. 11: "National legal systems are ill-fitted to govern international relationships".

[15] Underlying sales contract with various interfaces to separate contracts of carriage, letters of credit and transport insurance.

[16] R. David (supra n. 10) p. 38.

[17] R. Goode (supra n. 10) pp. 54 et seq.

[18] This materialistic approach is quite different from attempts by scholars and international organisation like UNIDROIT to re-gain uniformity in the field of commercial law by re-formulating principles as a "quasi jus commune". R. David (supra n. 10) at p.17. The most recent product of that kind are the "Principles of International Commercial Contracts" prepared by UNIDROIT in 1994.

[19] R. Goode (supra n. 10) p. 56.

efficiency. To embark on such projects is dangerous, since due to the lack of sufficient support by trade and industry, the instrument will probably cause problems of acceptance in all the stages between creation and ratification.[20]

Despite the immense number of transactions, one scarcely resembles another. The ever-decreasing profit margins of world trade necessitate the smooth and efficient execution of not only the logistical, but also the legal processes. Any uncertainty and any loss of smooth coordination affects profit adversely and, therefore, undermines the mechanism of world trade.

2.3 Substance of Uniform Law

Once the particular starting point and need is identified, it is possible to comprehend the particularities as regards the substance of the uniform of law.

The most successful tools in the area of trade and commerce law are not legal masterpieces, but sometimes extremely pragmatic documents. These tools for the standardisation of law solve the practical problems more according to the principle of "functionality" than by trying to find a dogmatically harmonise the different legal traditions.

A good example of this pragmatic procedure can be found in the INCOTERMS[21] (especially the pre-1990[22] versions). The International Chamber of Commerce started to collect different forms of interpretation of the different "trade terms" back in 1930. These have led today to preformulated standard clauses with which the parties to the contract of sale can define the issues involved in an overseas sale. A further example is the seemingly strangely fragmented structure (at least strange to Continental-European eyes) of the Hague Rules of 1924, which merely standardise certain aspects of the law of carriage of goods by sea. In doing so, they have adopted a format of a model bill of lading insofar as the text of the Convention has been written as if it were a standard text of contractual terms for bills of lading.[23]

The interlocking of the different legal relationships of a trade transaction means additionally, that it is not simply harmonisation on an international level that is involved. It is necessary in addition to strive for harmonisation of the interdisciplinary

---

[20] One example is the Hamburg Rules of 1978 which, due to the lack of trade support, have never achieved uniformity.

[21] International Commercial Terms; published by the International Chamber of Commerce (ICC), currently in the version of 2000 (supra n. 4).

[22] The revisions after 1980 (i.e. in 1990 and 2000) were conducted with a great emphasis on creating systematic standard contractual rules, rather than with a view of trying to collect in a pragmatic way and without ambitions for systematic beauty the usages and customs of the trade applied to trade terms used by international commerce.

[23] It is interesting that as a result of protest in particular by delegations of Continental-European countries, a Protocol of Signatures made clear that the Contracting States were free to incorporate the substance of the Hague Rules in an appropriate form into their own national legislation.

interfaces between the individual legal relationships. The **interdisciplinary role of the bill of lading** is mentioned here as an example. The bill of lading is known chiefly as the documentation of the contract of carriage and, in addition, assumes the role of an acknowledgement of a receipt of goods and a certification of claim to delivery of said goods at the place of destination. In addition to its original function, in case of sale (e.g. according to INCOTERMS FOB / CIF) the bill of lading also takes on the function of proof of delivery in accordance with the **law relating to the sale of goods** (with respect to time, quantity and quality). This sort of sales transaction can be repeated countless times with the same bill of lading (i.e. the one and only contract of carriage) in a series of purchases (string sales[24]). In the documentary credit relationship, the same document has the function of triggering payment by the bank and constitutes to a certain extent the collateral security for the trade financing. This interdisciplinary role of the bill of lading explains the special importance of the harmonisation of law in this field.

The necessity for unification and interdisciplinary harmonisation has recently been recognised by UNCITRAL in the context of its work on the Model Law on Electronic Commerce.[25]

A new project of the Comité Maritime International (CMI) is embarking, under the auspices of UNCITRAL, on a harmonising exercise which will attempt to lay down principles for the law on international transportation which could clarify the various interfaces between the sales contract and the contract of carriage of goods by sea.[26]

2.4 Methodology and Process of the Harmonisation and Unification of Law

If these special features are combined, it is hardly surprising that the standardisation of trade law can largely be attributed to **private initiatives**, to **private preparatory work** and to the project management of **private, non-governmental international organisations** (International Chamber of Commerce, Comité Maritime International, International Law Association, IATA)[27]. In contrast, success was not forthcoming where Inter-Governmental Organisations dispensed with this private cooperation. Such attempts led on the contrary to a regrettable dissipation of the previously standardised law. A supreme example of such a failure can be seen in the

---

[24] These "string sales" are found primarily in trade with commodities.

[25] *Report of the United Nations Commission on International Trade Law on the Work of its Twenty-Ninth Session*, 28 May – 14 June 1996, points 210-215, reprinted in *CMI Y.B.* (1997) (Antwerp I, Centenary Conference) pp. 354-355.

[26] *Issues of Transport Law*, Report of the CMI Steering Committee, *CMI Y.B.* (1998) pp. 107-117.

[27] J. Kropholler, *Internationales Einheitsrecht* (Tübingen 1975) pp. 85 et seq., A. von Ziegler (supra n. 2) pp. 728 et seq.

Hamburg Rules of 1978[28], with which UNCITRAL and UNCTAD attempted to create in the area of maritime transportation law a mostly politically motivated rival regime to the Hague Rules which had – in turn – come into being through private initiative and preparation.

The co-operation of non-governmental international organisations is of vital importance even when drawing up Conventions.[29] The Comité Maritime International (CMI) is to be mentioned primarily in this respect. The CMI has been promoting the unification of maritime law for more than 100 years.[30] The organisation has drafted and passed a total 35 maritime conventions or protocols to date at Diplomatic Conferences held by the Belgian government and subsequently by UNCTAD and the International Maritime Organisation.[31]

The interest in trade and commerce in its logistical and legal harmonisation also explains why many fields of international law can be harmonised successfully totally without government participation. There is a large range of alternatives to the Convention, even to the model law[32]. One prominent example is the collection of uniform principles which are applied by the parties as a matter of contract law (Uniform Rules; Standard Clauses/Terms)[33]. Examples are the INCOTERMS of the International Chamber of Commerce[34], which are applied world-wide today and form a recognised collection of standardised trade terms for application in international sales of goods. The same global recognition is enjoyed by the Uniform Customs and Practice for Documentary Credits (UCP 500)[35], also of the International Chamber of Commerce, without which the financing of world trade would be inconceivable today. Another, rather ancient, example for the unification of law by private instrument is to be found in the York Antwerp Rules[36] relating to the principles on general

---

[28] United Nations Convention on the Carriage of Goods by Sea; 31 March 1978.

[29] This fact was clearly confirmed at the ICC/ Unidroit Symposium (18 January 1997) in Rome, where a number of international (non-governmental and inter-governmental) organisations discussed the methods, the co-ordination and the collaboration in the process of harmonisation of commercial law: ICC/UNIDROIT, *The Harmonisation of Commercial Law* (summary record of meeting).

[30] F. Wiswall, *Comité Maritime International, A Brief Structural History of the First Century* (Maine 1997); F. Berlingieri, "The Work of the Comité Maritime International: Past, Present and Future", 57 *Tulane Law Review* (1983) 1260; A. von Ziegler (supra n. 2) pp. 728 et seq.

[31] For a list of the CMI Conventions see e.g. A. von Ziegler (supra n. 2) pp. 742 et seq.

[32] Re the alternative to conventions in form of Model Law see, e.g. S. Lebedev, "Legislative means of unification", in: *Uniform Commercial Law in the Twenty-First Century, New York, 18 - 22 May 1992* (editor, publisher, place, year??); pp. 31 - 33.

[33] See, in general, M.J. Bonell, "Non-legislative means of harmonisation", in: *Uniform Commercial Law in the Twenty-First Century, New York, 18 - 22 May 1992*, ibid., pp. 33-40.

[34] *INCOTERMS 2000* (supra n. 4).

[35] *Uniform Customs and Practice for Documentary Credits, 1993 Revision (UCP 500)* (ICC Publication No. 500, Paris 1993).

[36] Latest Revision dated 8 October 1994.

average, which are universally applied and have sometimes even been introduced 'as is' into national codification.[37]

This harmonisation on a private and completely voluntary basis is explained by the fact that the trade sector of the economy is not only the "initiator" of the harmonising process, but also the "creator" of the standard rules as a result of its direct influence in the non-governmental organisation (ICC / CMI). Even more importantly, the same trade sector is also the "user", who relies on this internationally recognised legal standard when executing various transactions. This personal union of "initiator, creator and user" ensures that the standard rules are followed by the trade and – as a consequence – adapted whenever the trade – as user – is initiating a revision.

As long as it is possible in this process to mobilise the experts and practitioners from the different branches of trade, trade law can be guaranteed to further develop internationally its pragmatic and just standards. Only thus can one ensure that harmonisation will do justice to the special features and particularities of international trade and commerce.[38]

2.5   Further Development by Means of Revision and Protocols

Trade law, on the one hand, is a conservative entity. It is conservative in that it can only either grow at the same pace as there is a (recognised) need for innovation worldwide or develop in line with a internationally recognised development of trading practice. On the other hand, trade law would suffocate without a certain dynamism.

The knack is to ensure that trade law develops more or less consistently worldwide, so that legal harmonisation once successfully achieved, is not lost. It is very important that the revision process not be carried out in the same euphoria of (re)-unification as happened at the beginning of the century. Existing uniformity is a very valuable "commodity" and should not be challenged without real cause and need by adding protocols or by revising the instrument.[39] The great number of under-ratified and under-recognised instruments of "second generation" prove that

---

[37] See, e.g. Art. 122 Section 2 of the Swiss Maritime Code referring – as a matter of national law – to the York Antwerp Rules.

[38] It is interesting to note that the Principles of International Commercial Contracts prepared by UNIDROIT in 1994 are quite distinct from the harmonised commercial law referred to in this article: The need for such "principles" was not defined by trade but by academics; the method did not include a review of the actual pragmatic needs and actual practice of trade and the instrument was drafted without the close involvement of trade. This explains why this body of law, however interesting – and eventually influential – it may be, has not (yet) become part of the commercial law recognised by every day trade practice.

[39] A. von Ziegler, *Alternatives and Methods of Unification or Harmonisation of Maritime Law* (Il Diritto Marittimo 1999) at pp. 235, 238.

the balance of interests (unification – dynamism) has often been misjudged by those entities undertaking the revision.[40]

This explains why there has been an extremely pragmatic approach towards trade law to date, especially as regards revision proceedings. The "protocols" or revisions are thus often reactions to specific "surprises". By this, I mean, for example unforeseen Court decisions or the monetary or technical development of the environment in which trade is conducted.[41] As a result the protocols are quite often "ugly" harmonising instruments which surround the "mother convention" like satellites.

Where the revisions are tackled for political or academic proposes, the process of harmonisation risks coming into conflict with the original need of trade and commerce: the need for efficient and predictable harmonisation of the legal processes in the international and interdisciplinary environment of trade and commerce.

Both the INCOTERMS for the sales contract and the maritime law under the Hague Rules face this challenge today. Both are being revised at the current time, or have just been revised. In both projects, trends can be seen which conflict with this basic need, for motives which until now were alien to trade law.

It is all the more important that any further harmonisation or unification of the law do justice to the special features and particularities of international trade law.

3.   CONCLUSION

The particularities of the harmonisation and unification of the law of trade and commerce can be summarised – as a result of this short overview – **in the following points:**

1.   Trade and commerce is naturally **trans-national**. Since **several legal relationships** are combined in each transaction, which in turn display a large number **of international points of contact**, there is a **definite need for international harmonisation** and for the international unification of law.

2.   This need is strengthened by the fact that the individual legal relationships display interfaces on several occasions which necessitate **interdisciplinary** harmonisation.

---

[40] As the most recent example, I would like to mention the revision of the INCOTERMS 2000, which addressed only minor points, most of which were neither points of great practical importance, nor offered any actual improvement to INCOTERMS 1990, nor solved major problems raised under the application of the INCOTERMS 1990.

[41] See e.g. A. von Ziegler (supra n. 39) pp. 232 - 239.

3.   The history of trade and commerce and the special need for a standard across all national borders explain in the field of trade law the clear pre-eminence of the standardisation of **substantive law** over the standardisation of the conflict-of-law rules.

4.   The **motive** for striving for standardisation does not correspond to the otherwise overriding political goal of an improvement in governmental co-operation or political integration, but fulfils a need – indeed, an essential one – of the private parties involved in trade.

5.   The trading partners' need for efficient and dependable standards means that the substance of the rules must comply primarily with the **principles of "practicability", "calculability" and "efficiency"**. Aims for a comprehensive international legislation or for dogmatic harmonisation of legal traditions are of secondary importance.

6.   **Initiatives** and the **creation** of the standardisation of law are to be left largely to private organisations.

7.   Since the "initiator" and "creator" of the harmonised law is itself also the "user" of the harmonised law, it is possible to take advantage of the **wide range of alternatives** to an international Convention (model law, standard clauses / uniform customs and practices / principles).

Schriftenverzeichnis/ List of Publications

1. SELBSTÄNDIGE SCHRIFTEN/ BOOKS

1. Auswirkungen des Nichtehelichengesetzes auf das Internationale Privat- und Verfahrensrecht (Bielefeld 1972) 159 S.

2. Neubearbeitung: Dölle, Internationales Privatrecht – Eine Einführung in seine Grundlagen (2. Auflage Karlsruhe 1972) XII, 138 S.

3. Mitbearbeitung: Drobnig, American-German Private International Law (Dobbs Ferry/ N.Y. 1972) 510 S.

4. European Private International Law of Obligations, edited by Ole Lando/ Bernd von Hoffmann/ Kurt Siehr (Tübingen 1975) VIII, 352 S.

5. Das gesamte Familienrecht. Das internationale Recht, Christof Böhmer/ Kurt Siehr (Hrsg.) (Neuwied: Luchterhand Verlag. Früher Frankfurt a.M. 1979ff.) Losebl-Ausgabe.

6. Max Keller/ Kurt Siehr, Einführung in die Eigenart des Internationalen Privatrechts (2. Aufl. Zürich 1979) X, 60 S.; (3. Aufl. Zürich 1984) XI, 76 S.

7. Reform des deutschen IPR, vorgelegt von Peter Dopffel, Ulrich Drobnig, Kurt Siehr (Tübingen 1980) 171 S.

8. Münchener Kommentar zum BGB, Bd. 7 Artt. 14-16 EGBGB; drei Haager Uebereinkommen; Gesetz von 1969 über den ehelichen Güterstand von Vertriebenen und Flüchtlingen.
   a) 1. Aufl. (1983) 241 S.; Ergänzungsband
   b) 2. Aufl. (1990) 320 S.; Ergänzungsband
      (1) Lieferung 1 (Stand: Dez. 1990; ersch. 1991) 60 S.
      (2) Lieferung 2 (Stand: September 1991) 13 S.
   c) 3. Aufl. (1998) 384 S.

9. Franz Matscher/ Kurt Siehr/ Jost Delbrück, Multilaterale Staatsverträge erga omnes und deren Inkorporation in nationale IPR-Kodifikationen – Vor- und Nachteile einer solchen Rezeption (Heidelberg 1986): BerDGesVölkR 27 (1986) 45-146.

10. Max Keller/ Kurt Siehr, Allgemeine Lehren des internationalen Privatrechts (Zürich 1986) LXXII, 714 S.

11. Bernard Dutoit/ François Knoepfler/ Philippe Schweizer/ Kurt Siehr, Pollution transfrontière/ Grenzüberschreitende Verschmutzung: Tschernobyl/ Schweizerhalle / Beihefte zur ZSR, Heft 9, (Basel 1989), 55-93.

12. IPRG-Kommentar, hrsg. Von A. Heini/ M. Keller/ K. Siehr/ F. Vischer/ P. Volken (Zürich 1993) 1. Aufl. (1993) S. 492-735; 1598-1629 (2. Aufl. in Bearbeitung).

13. Max Keller/ Kurt Siehr, Kaufrecht (3. Aufl. Zürich 1995) XLVII, 245 S.

14. Kommentar zum schweizerischen Privatrecht. Internationales Privatrecht, hrsg. von H. Honsell/ N.P. Vogt/ A.K. Schnyder (Basel/ Frankfurt a.M. 1996) S. 306-448.

15. Kommentar zum UN-Kaufrecht, hrsg. von H. Honsell, bearbeitet von M. Karollus/ U. Magnus/ W. Melis/ A.K. Schnyder/ H. Schönle/ K. Siehr/ R.M. Straub/ R.H. Weber (Heidelberg u.a. 1996).

16. Neues Schuld- und Sachenrecht im Beitrittsgebiet (München 1997) S. 845-859.

17. Jan Kropholler/ Hilmar Krüger/ Wolfgang Riering/ Jürgen Samtleben/ Kurt Siehr (Hrsg.), Außereuropäische IPR-Gesetze (Hamburg/ Würzburg 1999) XIV, 1126 S.

II. AUFSÄTZE/ ARTICLES

1. Kötz/ Siehr, Brief aus Ann Arbor: RabelsZ 28 (1964) 395-400.

2. Privatscheidungen und Anerkennungsverfahren nach Art. 7 § 1 FamRÄndG: FamRZ 1969, 184-188.

3. Jayme/ Siehr, Schuldausspruch und ausländische Ehescheidungsurteile: FamRZ 1969, 188-192.

4. Die Rechtsstellung von Ausländern im Erbrecht der Vereinigten Staaten von Amerika: RabelsZ 33 (1969)290-314.

5. Auswirkungen des Nichtehelichengesetzes auf das Internationale Privat- und Verfahrensrecht: FamRZ 1970, 457-466.

6. Ehrenzweigs lex-fori-Theorie und ihre Bedeutung für dasamerikanische und deutsche Kollisionsrecht: RabelsZ 34 (1970) 585-635.

7. Der Eigentumsvorbehalt an beweglichen Sachen im Internationalen Privatrecht, insbesondere im deutsch-italienischen Rechtsverkehr: AWD 1971, 10-22.

8. Vaterschaftsfeststellung durch deutsche Gerichte und anwendbares Recht: FamRZ 1971, 292-297.

9. Zweigert/ Siehr, Jhering's Influence on the Development of Comparative Legal Method: Am.J.Comp.L. 19 (1971) 215-231.

10. Die rechtliche Stellung von Kindern aus hinkenden Ehen – Zur alternativen Anknüpfung der Vorfrage in favorem legitimitatis: StAZ 1971, 205-213.

11. Haager Unterhaltsstatutabkommen und gerichtliche Vaterschaftsfeststellung: FamRZ 1971, 398-403.

12. Die Geltendmachung von Unterhaltsansprüchen nichtehelicher Kinder gegenüber ausländischen Vätern: FamRZ 1971, 630f.

13. Internationalprivatrechtliches in der jüngsten Änderung der Dienstanweisung für die Standesbeamten: StAZ 1972, 97-109 = Der hessische Standesbeamte 1972, 37-40, 42-45, 49-55 = Das bayerische Standesamt 1972, 37-42, 61-68.

14. Zur Legitimation eines deutschen Kindes durch nachfolgende Ehe seiner Mutter mit einem Ausländer: StAZ 1972, 181-186 = Leitfaden für die Standesbeamten 1972, 29-34.

15. Grundrecht der Eheschließungsfreiheit und InternationalesPrivatrecht – Zugleich ein Beitrag zur Lehre vom ordre public: RabelsZ 36 (1972) 93-115.

16. Produktenhaftung und Internationales Privatrecht -Zum Entwurf für ein Haager Kollisionsrechtsabkommen: AWD 1972, 373-389.

17. Zur geplanten Revision des englischen Ehegüterrechts und Erbrechts: FamRZ 1972, 419-428.

18. Die Vaterschaftsfeststellung im deutschen Internationalen Privatrecht: DAVorm. 1973, 125-152.

19. Das Haager Minderjährigenschutzabkommen von 1961 in der bisherigen Praxis: DAVorm. 1973, 253-290.

20. Wechselwirkungen zwischen Kollisionsrecht und Sachrecht: RabelsZ 37 (1973) 466-484.

21. Zum Vorentwurf eines EWG – Übereinkommens über das Internationale Schuldrecht: AWD 1973, 569-587.

22. Vom Lesen und Schreiben kollisionsrechtlicher Entscheidungen: RabelsZ 38 (1974) 631-634.

23. Die gerichtliche Vaterschaftsfeststellung und ihre rechtlichen Hindernisse im Nichtehelichenrecht der EWG-Staaten: FamRZ 1974, 401-410; gekürzt in: 5. Internationale Tagung der Gesellschaft für forensische Blutgruppenkunde e.V., Referate (1975) 227-229.

24. Die Reform des deutschen internationalen Privat- und Verfahrensrechts: SchweizJbIntR 29 (1973, ersch. 1974) 171-283.

25. Diritto internazionale privato e diritto costituzionale: Foro italiano 1975, V, 7-16.

26. General Report on Non-Contractual Obligations (Arts. 10-14), General Problems (Arts. 21-23) and the Final Provisions (Arts. 24-36), in: European Private International Law of Obligations, s. oben I 4, 42-79.

27. Kindesentführungen ohne Ende – aber: Il y a des juges à Accra! FamRZ 1976, 255-257.

28. Heilung durch Statutenwechsel, in: Gedächtnisschrift für Albert A. Ehrenzweig (1976) 129-182.

29. Die allgemeine und besondere Geschäftsfähigkeit von Ausländern für eine Vaterschaftsanerkennung im Inland: StAZ 1976, 356-358.

30. Ausländische Unterhaltsentscheidungen und ihre Abänderung im Inland wegen veränderter Verhältnisse, in: Festschrift für Friedrich Wilhelm Bosch (1976) 927-962.

31. Kindesentführungen ins Ausland – Ein deutsch-italienisches Beispiel und eine Initiative des Europarats: DAVorm, 1977, 219-236.

32. Civil Liability of Hospitals and Doctors, in: Drug Monitoring, edited by Gross/ Inman (London, New York, San Francisco 1977) 169-183.

33. Special Courts for Conflicts Cases – A German Experiment: Am.J.Comp.L. 25 (1977) 663-680.

34. Das neue schweizerische Kindschaftsrecht und sein Einfluss auf den deutsch-schweizerischen Rechtsverkehr: DAVorm. 1978, 153-170, 243-260, 331-344 = Internationales Familien- und Kindschaftsrecht (Heidelberg 1981) 17-24 (Auszug).

35. Shapira/ Siehr, The Jundeff Affair – Comparative Remarks on International Child Kidnapping and Judicial Co-operation: Neth.Int.L.Rev. 25 (1978) 3-23.

36. Rownouprawnienie w zachodnioniemieckim miedzynarodowym prawie dotyczacym stosunkow miedzy rodzicami a dziecmi [Gleichberechtigung im westdeutschen Internationalen Privatrecht betreffend die Beziehungen zwischen Eltern und Kindern]: Studia prawnicze 1978, Heft 3 (57), S. 97-122 = Gleichberechtigung im deutschen Internationalen Kindschaftsrecht: ZblJugR 1980, 655-677.

37. Klinische Prüfung von Arzneimitteln – Rechtliche Probleme: Pharma-Recht 1979, 39-43.

38. Kritische Anmerkungen zu den einzelnen Vorschlägen, in: Freiburger Kolloquium über den schweizerischen Entwurf zu einem Bundesgesetz über das internationale Privatrecht (Zürich 1979) 16-24.

39. Zum Entwurf eines schweizerischen Bundesgesetzes über das internationale Privatrecht: RIW/ AWD 1979, 729-737.

40. Drug reactions and the law in the European Economic Community, in: Monitoring for Drug Safety, edited by Inman (Lancaster 1980) 489-509.

41. Thesen zur Reform des Internationalen Privat- und Verfahrensrechts, im Institut bearbeitet von Jürgen Basedow, Peter Dopffel, Ulrich Drobnig, Christa Jessel, Gerhard Luther, Ulrich Magnus, Dieter Martiny, Frank Münzel, Jürgen Samtleben, Kurt Siehr, Jan-Peter Waehler unter Federführung von Peter Dopffel und Kurt Siehr: RabelsZ 44 (1980) 344-366 = Reform des deutschen IPR (Tübingen 1980) 145-152 (nur Text der Thesen) StAZ 1981, 174-176 (nur Text der Thesen).

42. Arzneimittelprüfung am Menschen – Diskussion unter Juristen, zusammen mit Fincke, Granitza, Lewandowski und Samson, in: Arzneimittelprüfung am Menschen, edited by K.D.Bock (Braunschweig, Wiesbaden 1980) 160-185.

43. Internationales Kindschaftsrecht, in: Reform des deutschen internationalen Privatrechts (Tübingen 1980) 53-70.

44. Internationales Namensrecht, in: Reform des deutschen internationalen Privatrechts (Tübingen 1980) 71-73.

45. Protection of the Environment and the Mediterranean Policy of the EEC, in: La politica mediterranea della CEE (Neapel 1981) 159-166.

46. Grenzüberschreitender Umweltschutz – Europäische Erfahrungen mit einem weltweiten Problem: RabelsZ 45 (1981) 377-398 = Foro italiano 1981 V 314-327.

47. Kunstraub und das internationale Recht: Schweizerische Juristen-Zeitung 1981, 189-197, 207-212.

48. Die Zeitschrift für Schweizerisches Recht und das schweizerische Privatrecht in der deutschen Rechtspraxis: Zeitschrift für Schweizerisches Recht n.F. 100 I (1981) 51-64.

49. Der gutgläubige Erwerb beweglicher Sachen – Neue Entwicklungen zu einem alten Problem: ZVglRWiss 80 (1981) 273-292.

50. Schweiz, in: Rechtsvergleichung – Zur neueren Entwicklung des Vertragsrechts in Europa (Gutachten und Vorschläge zur Überarbeitung des Schuldrechts, hrsg. vom Bundesminister der Justiz, Bonn o.D., ca. 1981) 39-45.

51. Domestic Relations in Europe – European Equivalents to American Evolutions (Bericht zum Thema: The Influence of Modern American Conflicts Theories on European Law): Am.J.Comp.L. 30 (1982) 37-71.

52. Die Anerkennung ausländischer, insbesondere schweizerischer Adoptionsdekrete in der Bundesrepublik: StAZ 1982, 61-70.

53. Das Haager Minderjährigenschutzabkommen und seine Anwendung in der neueren Praxis: IPRax 1982, 85-90.

54. Internationales Kindesrecht: Schweizerische Juristen-Zeitung 1982, 173–184.

55. Normen mit eigener Bestimmung ihres räumlich-persönlichen Anwendungsbereichs im Kollisionsrecht der Bundesrepublik Deutschland: RabelsZ 46 (1982) 357-383.

56. Regulatory and Legal Aspects of Causality Assessment, in: Venulet/ Berneker/ Ciucci (eds.), Assessing Causes of Adverse Drug Reactions (London, New York u.a. 1982) 129-141.

57. Eigentumsvorbehalt im deutsch-schweizerischen Rechtsverkehr: IPRax 1982, 207-210.

58. Legitimation eines deutschen Kindes durch einenSchweizer Bürger: StAZ 1982, 237-239.

59. Scherz und Ernst im Internationalen Privatrecht – Gedanken zur Vergangenheit, Gegenwart und Zukunft des Kollisionsrechts, in: Festschrift für Imre Zajtay (Tübingen 1982) 409-437.

60. Internationale Staatsverträge und die Arbeit der Jugendämter: DAVorm. 1982, 1025-1036.

61. Entwurf des schweizerischen Bundesrats zu einem IPR-Gesetz: RabelsZ 47 (1983) 342-348.

62. Legal Research in Legal Education: Tel Aviv University Studies in Law 5 (1980-82) 62-68.

63. Die Rechtsstellung ausländischer natürlicher Personen inder Bundesrepublik Deutschland, bei: Waehler (Hrsg.), Deutsches und sowjetisches Wirtschaftsrecht II (1983)127-154.

64. Billige Flaggen in teuren Häfen, in: Festschrift für Frank Vischer (Zürich 1983) 303-320.

65. Kodifikation des deutschen Internationalen Privatrechts(Mitarbeit): RabelsZ 47 (1983) 595, 612-617, 640-655.

66. Die Anfechtung der Vaterschaftsanerkennung im IPR: IPRax1984, 20-23

67. Das Lösungsrecht des gutgläubigen Käufers im Internationalen Privatrecht: ZVglRWiss 83 (1984) 100-118.

68. Codification of Private International Law in the Federal Republic of Germany: Neth.Int.L.Rev. 31 (1984) 92-97.

69. Kindschaftsrecht, in: Lausanner Kolloquium über den deutschen und den schweizerischen Gesetzentwurf zur Neuregelung des Internationalen Privatrechts (Zürich 1984) 161–196.

70. "Forum Shopping" im internationalen Rechtsverkehr: ZfRV 25 (1984) 124-144.

71. Selbstjustiz durch Kindesentführung ins Inland – Ein höchstrichterlicher Lichtblick mit deprimierendem Nachspiel: IPRax 1984, 309-312.

72. Ökonomische Analyse des Internationalen Privatrechts, in: Festschrift Karl Firsching (München 1985) 269-294.

73. Sachrecht im IPR, transnationales Recht und lex mercatoria, bei: Wolfgang Holl/ Ulrich Klinke, Internationales Privatrecht, internationales Wirtschaftsrecht. Referate eines Symposiums der Alexander von Humboldt-Stiftung, Köln u.a. 1985, 103-126.

74. Die lex-fori-Lehre heute, bei: Rolf Serick/ Hubert Niederländer/ Erik Jayme (Hrsg.), Albert A. Ehrenzweig und das internationale Privatrecht (Heidelberg 1986) 35-136.

75. Drug reactions and the law in the European Economic Community, in: William H.W. Inman (ed.), Monitoring for Drug Safety (2. Aufl. Lancaster, Boston, Den Haag, Dordrecht 1985) 541-563.

76. Codificazione del diritto internazionale privato e convenzioni internazionali, in: Problemi di riforma del diritto internazionale privato italiano (Mailand 1986) 497-507.

77. Die Zivilehe in Griechenland – Ein Requiem auf hinkendeEhen?, in: Festschrift für Wolfram Müller-Freienfels (Baden-Baden 1986) 559-578.

78. Das internationale Erbrecht nach dem Gesetz zur Neuregelung des IPR: IPRax 1987, 4-8.

79. Spezielle Kollisionsnormen für die Heilung einer unwirksamen Eheschließung durch "Statutenwechsel": IPRax 1987, 19-21.

80. Die Anerkennung und Vollstreckung israelischer Zivil-entscheidungen in der Bundesrepublik Deutschland: RabelsZ 50 (1986) 586-609.

81. Gesetzliche Gewaltverhältnisse nach Art. 3 Minderjährigenschutzabkommen und neues deutsches IPR: IPRax 1987, 302-305.

82. Gemeinsame Kollisionsnormen für das Recht der vertraglichen und ausservertraglichen Schuldverhältnisse, in: Beiträge zum neuen IPR des Sachen-, Schuld- und Gesellschaftsrechts, Festschrift für Rudolf Moser (Zürich 1987) 101-118.

83. Die gemischt-nationale Ehe im internationalen Privatrecht, in: Festschrift für Murad Ferid zum 80. Geburtstag (Frankfurt a.M. 1988) 433-446.

84. Internationale Rechtsvereinheitlichung von Innominatverträgen, in: Innominatverträge, Festgabe für Walter R. Schluep (Zürich 1988) 25-43 = Unificazione internazionale del diritto dei contratti innominati: Dir.com.int. 2 (1988) 83-102.

85. Da Livermore a Rabel, Tradizione europea e tradizione americana del diritto internazionale privato: Riv.dir.int.priv.proc. 24 (1988) 17-52; ebenfalls in: Panebianco/ Martino (Hrsg.), La riforma del diritto internazionale privato fra attualita e storia (Italia-Europa-America) (Salerno 1992) 45-92.

86. Maritime Law and Private International Law, in: Miscellanea of Maritime Law 1, Demetrios Markianos in memoriam (Athen 1988) 175-189.

87. Das Urheberrecht in neueren IPR-Kodifikationen: UFITA 108 (1988) 9-25.

88. Questioni in materia di sottrazione internazionale di minori da parte di un genitore, in: Mosconi/ Rinoldi (Hrsg.), La sottrazione internazionale di minori da parte di un genitore. Studi e documenti sul "kidnapping" internazionale (Padua 1988) 1-27.

89. Ausländische Eingriffsnormen im ausländischen Wirtschaftskollisionsrecht: RabelsZ 52 (1988) 41-103.

90. Das forum non conveniens nun auch in Israel: RIW 1988, 909f.

91. Der internationale Anwendungsbereich des UN-Kaufrechts: RabelsZ 52 (1988) 587-616.

92. Vom alten zum neuen IPR. Literaturspiegel der Jahre 1978-1988: ZSR N.F. 107 I (1988) 635-655; 108 I (1989) 107-139.

93. Die Parteiautonomie im Internationalen Privatrecht, in:Festschrift für Max Keller (Zürich 1989) 485-510.

94. Rechtshängigkeit im Ausland und das Verhältnis zwischen staatsvertraglichen sowie autonomen Anerkennungsvorschriften: IPRax 1989, 93-96.

95. Johann Caspar Bluntschli et le droit des conflits de lois dans le Code civil du Canton de Zurich de 1853/ 55, in: Liber Memorialis Francois Laurent 1810-1887 (Brüssel 1989)1017-1038.

96. Verhältnis zwischen Aufenthalts- und Heimatzuständigkeit nach dem MSA: IPRax 1989, 253f.

97. Ausländisches Legitimationshindernis und deutsche Verfassung: IPRax 1989, 283-287.

98. Konfliktvermeidung im Internationalen Privatrecht, bei: Schwind (Hrsg.), Österreichische Stellung heute in Europarecht, IPR und Rechtsvergleichung (Wien 1989) 121-144.

99. Grundrechte und Privatrecht. Einschränkung privatrechtlichen Handelns durch Grundrechte? in: Freiheit und Zwang, Festschrift für Hans Giger (Bern 1989) 627-642.

100. Entführung iranischer Kinder nach Deutschland und ihre Rückführung in den Iran: IPRax 1989, 373f.

101. Rechtsangleichung im IPR durch nationale Kodifikationen, in: Conflits et harmonisation, Kollision und Vereinheitlichung, Conflicts and Harmonization. Mélanges en l'honneur d'Alfred E. von Overbeck (Fribourg 1990) 205-243.

102. Schweiz, bei Dopffel (Hrsg.), Ehelichkeitsanfechtung durch das Kind (Tübingen 1990) 22-31.

103. The Return of Cultural Property Expropriated Abroad, in: Comparative and Private International Law, Essays in Honor of John Henry Merryman (Berlin 1990) 431-441.

104. Die Beerbung von Schweizer Bürgern mit letztem Wohnsitzin der Bundesrepublik Deutschland, in: Mélanges Paul Piotet (Bern 1990) 531-550.

105. Kindesentführung und Minderjährigenschutz. Abgrenzung der Entführungs-Übereinkommen vom Haager Minderjährigenschutzabkommen: StAZ 1990, 330-333.

106. Unmittelbare und mittelbare Wirkungen der Grundrechte im Privatrecht, in: Ergänzungen. Ergebnisse der wissenschaftlichen Tagung anlässlich der Einweihung des Ergänzungsbaus der Hochschule St. Gallen, hrsg. von Matthias Haller, Heinz Hauser, Roger Zäch (Bern und Stuttgart 1990) 539-542.

107. Das Kindschaftsrecht im Einigungsvertrag: IPRax 1991, 20-25; ebenfalls bei: Dieter Schwab, (Hrsg.) Familienrecht und deutsche Einigung (Bielefeld 1991) 105-110.

108. Wer schläft, der sündigt. Die Rückerwerbung von gestohlenem Kulturgut: Vergleich, Rückkauf oder Rechtsstreit?: Frankfurter Allgemeine Zeitung vom 27.2.1991, S. 35.

109. Droit international privé, bei: Fromont/ Rieg (Hrsg.),Introduction au droit allemand, Bd. III (Paris 1991) 583.631.

110. Der Einigungsvertrag und seine internationalen Kollisionsnormen: RabelsZ 55 (1991) 240-267.

111. Zur Anerkennung und Vollstreckung ausländischer Verurteilungen zu "punitive damages": RIW 1991, 705-709

112. Nationaler und Internationaler Kulturgüterschutz. Eingriffsnormen und der internationale Kunsthandel, in: Festschrift fur Werner Lorenz (Tübingen 1991) 525-542.

113. Das urheberrechtliche Folgerecht inländischer Künstler nach Versteigerung ihrer Werke im Ausland: IPRax 1992, 29-33.

114. Manuscript of the Quedlinburg Cathedral back in Germany: Internat. J. Cultural Property 1 (1992) 215-217.

115. Zivilrechtliche Fragen des Kulturgüterschutzes, in: Gerte Reichelt (Hrsg.), Internationaler Kulturgüterschutz (Wien 1992) 41-68.

116. Devletler Özel Hukukunda ve Milletlerarasi Usul Hukukunda Banka Akitleri [Bankrecht und die EG Konventionen zum anwendbaren Vertragsrecht sowie zur Anerkennung und Vollstreckung ausländischer Entscheidungen], in: Avrupa Toplulugunda Banka Hukuku [Bankrecht in der Europäischen Gemeinschaft] (Istanbul 1992) 241-248.

117. Joseph Beuys und das Internationale Folgerecht – Eine Zwischenbilanz: IPRax 1992, 219-221.

118. The UNIDROIT Draft Convention on the International Protection of Cultural Property: Internat. J. Cultural Property 1 (1992) 321-330.

119. Security for Costs: A Valuable Defence or a Burdensome Relic?, in: Law and Reality. Essays on National and International Procedural Law in Honour of Cornelis Carel Albert Voskuil (Dordrecht 1992) 291-300.

120. Recent Developments in Conflict of Laws (Europe): ELSA L.Rev. 3 (1992) 75-86.

121. Rechtsvergleichende Betrachtungen zum Einfluss des Zivilstandsregisters auf das Familienrecht, in: Mélanges en l'honneur de Jacques-Michel Grossen (Basel,Frankfurt a.M. 1992) 231-242.

122. Recent European Developments in Private International Law: ELSA L.Rev. 3 (1993) 311-324

123. The Hague Conference on Private International Law and Germany: Neth.Int.L.Rev. 40(1993) 129-142, and in: T.M.C. Asser Instituut (ed.), The Influence of the Hague Conference on Private International Law (Dordrecht 1993) 129-142.

124. International Protection of Cultural Property in the European Community, in: Etudes de droit international en l'honneur de Pierre Lalive (Basel, Frankfurt a.M. 1993) 763-775.

125. Siehr/ Tejura, Anerkennung ausländischer Adoptionen in der Schweiz: SJZ 1993, 277-281.

126. Handel mit Kulturgütern in der EWG: NJW 1993, 2206-2209.

127. Gutgläubiger Erwerb von Kunstwerken in New-York – DeWeerth v. Baldinger erneut vor Gericht: IPRax 1993, 339f.

128. Recent European Developments in Private International Law: ELSA Law Review 1993, 86-98.

129. Günstigkeits- und Garantieprinzip. Zur Rechtsdurchsetzung im internationalen Rechtsverkehr, in: Recht und Rechtsdurchsetzung. Festschrift fur Hans Ulrich Walder (Zürich 1994) 409-423.

130. Öffentliches Recht und internationales Privatrecht beimgrenzüberschreitenden Kulturgüterschutz, in: R. Dolzer/ E. Jayme/ R. Mussgnug (Hrsg.), Rechtsfragen des internationalen Kulturgüterschutzes (Heidelberg: Müller 1994)83-104.

131. Structure and Method of the "IPR-Schets" Nederlands Internationaal Privaatrecht, Studiedag: Schets van een algemene wet betreffende het Internationaal Privaatrecht, Sonderheft 1994, S. 22-29.

132. Remarks on Transatlantic Product Liability – A Review of Jurisdictional Problems and the 1973 Hague Convention, in: The American Society of International Law/ Nederlandse Vereniging voor Internationaal Recht (ed.), Contemporary International Law Issues – Opportunities at a Time of Momentous Change, Proceedings of the Second Joint Conference held in The Hague 1993 (Dordrecht/ Boston/ London: Nijhoff 1994) 321-324.

133. Rules for Declining to Exercise Jurisdiction in Civil and Commercial Matters – forum non conveniens and lis pendens. Swiss Law, in: Rapports suisses presentés au XIVème Congres international de droit comparé. Athenes, 31 juillet au 6 août 1994, Zürich: Schulthess 1994, 163-181, ebenfalls in: J.J.Fawcett (ed.), Declining Jurisdiction in Private International Law (Oxford: Clarendon 1995) 381-399.

134. Laus lacunae. Rechtsvergleichende Bemerkungen zum Problem derLücke, in: Studi in memoria di Gino Gorla, Bd. 1 (Mailand:Giuffré 1994) 699-711.

135. Nachehelicher Unterhalt im innerdeutschen Kollisions recht: IPRax 1994, 360-362.

136. The UNIDROIT Draft Convention on the International Protection of Cultural Property: Internat.J. Cultural Property 3 (1994) 301-307.

137. Handel mit Kulturgütern in der Europäischen Union und in der Schweiz, in: Aspekte des Wirtschaftsrechts. Festgabe zum Schweizerischen Juristentag 1994 (Zürich: Schulthess 1994) 353-372.

138. Ist ein Carracci ein schlechter Poussin? Zum Irrtum beim Kauf von Kunstwerken. Festschrift fur Hans Hanisch (Köln: Heymanns 1994) 247-255.

139. Mein Kind gehört zu mir! Internationale Kindesentführung und das Recht, in: Comparability and Evaluation. Essays in Honour of D. Kokkini-Iatridou (Dordrecht: Nijhoff 1994) 277-290.

140. Recent European Developments in Private International Law: ELSA L.Rev. 1994, 163-176.

141. International Art Trade and the Law: Recueil des Cours 243 (1993-VI) 9-292.

142. Recent Trends in European Private International Law: Polish Yearbook of International Law 20 (1993) 305-316.

143. Entwicklungen im schweizerischen Internationalen Privatrecht: Schweizerische Juristen-Zeitung 1995, 73-76.

144. Renvoi und wohlerworbene Rechte, in: Rechtskollisionen. Festschrift für Anton Heini (Zürich: Schulthess 1995) 407-428.

145. Rechtsschutz archäologischer Kulturgüter, in: Archäologie, Raubgrabungen und Kunsthandel. Podiumsdiskussionen auf der 23. Mitgliederversammlung des Deutschen Archäologen-Verbandes in Münster, 26.6.1993 (Schrift XIII des Deutschen Archäologen-Verbandes) (Hannover 1995) 49-54.

146. Kulturgüter als res extra commercium im internationalen Rechtsverkehr, in: Lebendiges Recht – Von den Sumerern bis zur Gegenwart. Festschrift fur Reinhold Trinkner (Heidelberg: Verlag Recht und Wirtschaft 1995) 703-722.

147. Vereinheitlichung des Mobiliarsachenrechts in Europa, insbesondere im Hinblick auf Kulturgüter: RabelsZ 59 (1995) 454-468.

148. Zur Anerkennung ausländischer Statusakte, in: Familie und Recht / Famille et Droit, Festgabe für Bernhard Schnyder / Mélanges offerts à Bernhard Schnyder (Fribourg: Universitätsverlag 1995) 697-714.

149. Internationales Recht der Produktehaftung, in: Anton K. Schnyder/ Helmut Heiss/ Bernhard Rudisch (Hrsg.), Internationales Verbraucherschutzrecht. Erfahrungen und Entwicklungen in Deutschland, Liechtenstein, Österreich und der Schweiz (Tübingen: Mohr 1995) 111-129.

150. Entwicklungen im schweizerischen internationalen Privatrecht. Le point sur le droit international privé suisse: SJZ 1996, 65f.

151. Die Schweiz und der Kulturgüterschutz in Europa, in: Fechner/ Oppermann/ Prott (Hrsg.), Prinzipien des Kulturgüterschutzes, Berlin: Duncker & Humblot 1996, 145-157.

152. Private International Law, in: Ebke (ed.), Introduction to German Law (Deventer: Kluwer 1996) 337-356.

153. Editorial: Internat.J.Cultural Property 5 (1996) 7-10.

154. Bibliography of Books [on Cultural Property], Published in 1994 and 1995: Internat.J.Cultural Property 5 (1996) 219-225, 363-370; 6 (1997) 183-189, 427-432; 7 (1998) 291-296, 575-580; 8 (1999) 381-384, 605-611.

155. Art Trade within the European Union: Koinodikion (Private International Law Review) 1 (1995) 169-178.

156. Kulturgüterschutz innerhalb der Europäischen Union: ZVglRWiss 95 (1996) 170-187.

157. The Impact of International Conventions on National Codifications of Private International Law, in: E Pluribus Unum. Liber amicorum Georges A.L. Droz (Den Haag: Nijhoff 1996) 405-413.

158. Vollstreckung ausländischer Unterhaltsurteile, in: Het NIPR geannoteerd. Annotaties opgedragen aan Dr. Mathilde Sumampouw (Den Haag: Asser Instituut 1996) 42-46.

159. Der Verein der Freunde des Instituts, in: Max-Planck-Gesellschaft (Hrsg.), Berichte und Mitteilungen Heft 1/ 96: Max-Planck-Institut für ausländisches und internationales Privatrecht, 3. Aufl. (München 1996) 89f.

160. Jayme/ Siehr/ Kronke, Italienisches Gesetz vom 31.5.1995 über Internationales Privatrecht (Übersetzung): SZIER 6 (1996) 279-298 = StAZ 1996, 250-253 (Auszug) = IPRax 1996, 356 = RabelsZ 61 (1997) 344-362.

161. Traffic Accidents, in: Campbell McLachlan/ Peter Nygh (eds.), Transnational Tort Litigation: Jurisdictional Principles (Oxford: Clarendon 1996) 189-199.

162. Die Rechtslage der Minderjährigen im internationalen Recht und die Entwicklung in diesem Bereich – Zur Revision des Haager Minderjährigenschutzabkommens: FamRZ 1996, 1047-1052.

163. Restitution of Stolen Cultural Objects and Statute of Limitations: Spoils of War No. 2 of 15 July 1996, p. 5-6.

164. Freizügigkeit und Kulturgüterschutz in der Europäischen Union, in: Festschrift für Ernst-Joachim Mestmäcker (Baden-Baden: Nomos 1996) 483-496.

165. Völkerrecht und Internationaler Kulturgüterschutz vor Gericht, in: Rainer Frank (Hrsg.), Recht und Kunst. Symposium aus Anlass des 80. Geburtstages von Wolfram Müller-Freienfels (Heidelberg 1996) 57-71.

166. Recent Developments in Private International Law: ELSA Law Review 1996, 98-112.

167. Der Anwalt und das IPR, in: Collisio legum. Studi di diritto internazionale privato per Gerardo Broggini (Milano 1997) 537-559.

168. Entwicklungen im schweizerischen internationalen Privatrecht/ Le point sur le droit international privé suisse: SJZ 1997, 66-69.

169. Comparative Law as a Yardstick for Academic Legal Education, in: Modern Issues in European Law. Nordic Perspectives. Essays in Honour of Lennart Pålsson (Goteborg 1997) 199-210.

170. Chronicles [on Cultural Property]: Internat. J. Cultural Property 5 (1996) 205-209, 349-356; 6 (1997) 161-167, 401-416; 7 (1998) 272-282, 553-563; 8 (1999) 344-355, 578-598.

171. Comment on the Russian Federal Law of 1997 on Cultural Values: Spoils of War No. 4 1997, 38f.

172. The protection of Cultural Heritage and International Commerce: Internat. J. Cultural Property 6 (1997) 304-325.

173. Die EG-Richtlinie von 1993 über die Rückgabe von Kulturgütern und der Kunsthandel, in: Gerte Reichelt (Hrsg.), Neues Recht zum Schutz von Kulturgut. Internationaler Kulturgüterschutz. EG-Richtlinie, UNIDROIT-Konvention und Folgerecht (Wien 1997) 29-43.

174. Graham-Siegenthaler/ Siehr, Swiss Law of Marriage, Marital relations and Divorce, in: The Marriage (Inchieste di diritto comparato, vol. 11) (Milano: Giuffré 1998) 489-509.

175. Entwicklungen im schweizerischen Internationalen Privatrecht/ Le point sur le droit international privé Suisse: SJZ 1998, 86-88.

176. Europäischer Kulturgüterschutz, in: Fritz Reichert-Facilides (Hrsg.), Recht und Europa. Ringvorlesung am Zentrum für europäisches Recht, Bd. 2 (Wien: Braumüller 1998) 187-194.

177. Private International Law at the End of the Twentieth Century: Progress or Regress?, in: Rapports suisses présentés au XVième Congrès international de droit comparé, Bristol, 27 juillet au 1er août 1998, Zürich 1998, 411-442, sowie in: Symeon C. Symeonides (ed.), Private International Law at the End of the 20th Century: Progress or Regress? (Den Haag 2000) 383-411.

178. Das neue Haager Übereinkommen von 1996 über den Schutz von Kindern: RabelZ 62 (1998) 464-501.

179. Die Rechtslage der Minderjährigen im internationalen Recht und die Entwicklung in diesem Bereich, in: Milletlerarasi Hukuk ve Milletlerarasi Özel Hukuk Bülteni [Public and Private International Law Bulletin] 16 (1996; erschienen 1998) 57-70.

180. The Protection of Cultural Property – the 1995 UNIDROIT Convention and the EEC Instruments of 1992/ 93 Compared: Uniform Law Review N.S. 3 (1998) 671-683 (Uniform Law Studies/ Etudes de droit uniforme. In memory of / A la mémoire de Malcolm Evans).

181. False Conflicts", lois d'application immédiate" und andere "Neuentdeckungen" im IPR. Zu gewissen Eigengesetzlichkeiten kollisionsrechtlicher Systeme, in: Festschrift für Ulrich Drobnig (Tübingen: Mohr 1998) 443-454.

182. A Statute on Private International Law for Israel, in: Alfred G. Kellermann/ Kurt Siehr/ Talia Einhorn (eds.), „Israel Among the Nations" (Den Haag/ Boston/ London: Kluwer 1998) 353-365.

183. International Aspects of Bankruptcy, in: Italo Andolina (Hrsg.), Transnational Aspects of Procedural Law. International Association of Procedural Law. Xth World Congress on Procedural Law, Taormina 17-23 Settembre 1995, General Reports (Università di Catania, Pubblicazioni della Facoltà di Giurisprudenza, N.S. vol. 157/ 2) (Milano: Giuffré 1998) Bd. II S. 783-846.

184. Telemarketing und Internationales Recht des Verbraucherschutzes: Jahrbuch des Schweizerischen Konsumentenrechts 1998, 151-201.

185. Entwicklungen im schweizerischen internationalen Privatrecht/ Le point sur le droit international privé suisse: SJZ 1999, 70-74.

186. Grundfragen des internationalen Konkursrechts: SJZ 1999, 85-94.

187. Drittstaatenklauseln in Europäischen Richtlinien zum Verbraucherschutz und die Schweiz, in: Der Einfluss des Europäischen Rechts auf die Schweiz. Festschrift zum 60. Geburtstag von Roger Zäch (Zürich: Schulthess 1999) 593-605.

188. Kampf gegen Diebstahl und Schmuggel von Kunstwerken. Zur rechtlichen Bewertung des Unidroit-Übereinkommens über gestohlene oder rechtswidrig ausgeführte Kulturgüter: UNESCO heute Nr. 2/ 199, 59f.

189. Die Richtlinie 93/ 7/ EWG des Rates vom 15. März 1993 über die Rückgabe von unrechtmäßig aus dem Hoheitsgebiet eines Mitgliedstaats verbrachten Kulturgütern und das Privatrecht der Mitgliedstaaten der EWG: Kunst und Urheberrecht 1999, 225-236.

190. Europäisches Recht des Kulturgüterschutzes und die Schweiz. Auswirkungen des Rechts unserer Nachbarstaaten auf die Schweiz: Aktuelle Juristische Praxis 1999, 962-970.

191. Protection of Adults in Private International Law under the 1997 Hague Preliminary Draft Convention, bei: Katharina Boele-Woelki/ Ellen Mostermans (Hrsg.), Volwassen maar onselfstandig. Meerderjarigenbeschering in Europees en internationaal privaatrechtelijk perspectief (Groningen: Intersentia 1999) 109-134.

192. Privatrechtliche Probleme der Leihmutterschaft: Deutschland, Österreich, Schweiz, bei: Katharina Boele-Woelki/ Maricke Oderkerk (Hrsg.), (On)geoorloofdheid van het draagmoederschap in rechtsvergelijkend perspectief (Groningen: Intersentia 1999) 69-87.

193. German Jewish Scholars of Private International Law and Comparative Law – Especially Ernst Frankenstein and his Research, in: Mélanges Fritz Sturm (Liège 1999) Bd. II, 1671-1681.

194. Die Zukunft der Vergangenheit – Vergangenheitsbewältigung im IPR und in der Rechtsvergleichung, in: Festgabe Zivilrechtslehrer 1934/1935 (Berlin/ New York 1999) 617-628.

195. Siehr/ Üstün, Antike Grabstelen aus der Türkei bleiben in der Schweiz: IPRax 1999, 489-492.

196. Herausgabe gestohlener Kulturgüter, bei: Schmid/ Ackermann (Hrsg.), Wiedererlangung widerrechtlich entzogener Vermögenswerte mit Instrumenten des Straf-, Zivil-, Vollstreckungs- und internationalen Rechts (Zürich 1999) 1-17.

197. Menschenrechte und internationale IPR-Übereinkommen, in: Wege zur Globalisierung des Rechts. Festschrift für Rolf A. Schütze (München 1999) 821-829.

198. Entwicklungen im schweizerischen internationalen Privatrecht/ Le point sur le droit international privé Suisse: SJZ 2000, 84-88.

III. BERICHTE/ REPORTS

1. von Hoffmann/ Siehr, Kolloquium über den EWG-Vorentwurf eines Übereinkommens über das auf vertragliche und außervertragliche Schuldverhältnisse anwendbare Recht: RabelsZ 38 (1974) 752f.

2. von Hoffmann/ Siehr, Recht des Schwächeren: Rabelsz 39 (1975) 522-532.

3. Siehr/ Thieme, Deutsch-israelisches Symposion in Köln: RabelsZ 39 (1975) 723.

4. Tagung für Rechtsvergleichung 1975: RabelsZ 40 (1976) 128-130.

5. Deutsch-italienische Juristen-Vereinigung: NJW 1977, 994.

6. Jessel/ Siehr, Deutsch-polnische Juristentagung: RabelsZ 41 (1977) 742-746.

7. Der Einfluß moderner amerikanischer IPR-Theorien auf das europäische Kollisionsrecht – Internationales Kolloquium, Bologna, 1. und 2. Juni 1981: RabelsZ 45 (1981) 803f.

8. Kolloquium über die deutschen und schweizerischen Entwürfe für Gesetze über das Internationale Privat- und Prozeßrecht: RabelsZ 47 (1983) 729f.

9. Symposium über Internationales Privatrecht und Wirtschaftsrecht: NJW 1984, 535f.

10. Tagung für Rechtsvergleichung 1983: Unternehmenskonzentration: RabelsZ 48 (1984) 189.

11. Reform des italienischen Internationalen Privatrechts: RabelsZ 48 (1984) 743-745.

12. Europäisches und amerikanisches IPR – Historische Vorbilder und aktuelle Probleme: RabelsZ 50 (1986) 644f.

13. Reform des italienischen IPR. Kongreß in Erinnerung an Edoardo Vitta, Florenz 23.-24.5.1990: RabelsZ 54 (1990) 735-738.

14. Return of Cultural Treasures to Germany: Internat. J. Cultural Property 6 (1997) 134.

15. International Law Association Committee on Cultural Heritage. Helsinki, 12-17 Agusut 1996: Internat.J.Cultural Property (1997) 142f.

16. Paterson/ Siehr, International Association of Legal Science 1996. Conference on the Protection of Cultural Property, Rabat, 11-12 September 1996: Internat. J. Cultural Property 6 (1997) 144-150.

IV. Würdigungen/ laudatory articles

1. Jayme/ Siehr, Paul Heinrich Neuhaus zum 60. Geburtstag: FamRZ 1974, 120f.

2. Zu Leben und Werk von Adolf F. Schnitzer 1889-1989: Anwaltsblatt 1991, 197-199.

V. Veröffentlichte Gutachten/ published legal opinions

1. Internationales und amerikanisches Erbrecht: IPR 1965-66 (1968) Nr. 61, S. 696-710.

2. Internationales und italienisches Kindschaftsrecht: IPR 1972 (1973) Nr. 20, S. 171-181.

3. Internationales und türkisches Kindschaftsrecht: IPG 1973 (1974) Nr. 24, S. 229-234.

4. Haager Minderjährigenschutzabkommen im Verhältnis zur Schweiz: IPG 1974 (1975) Nr. 37, S. 392-395.

5. Internationales und liechtensteinisches Stiftungsrecht: IPG 1975 (1976) Nr. 1, S. 1-9.

6. Anerkennung und Abänderung schweizerischer Unterhaltstitel in Deutschland: IPG 1975 (1976) Nr. 40, S. 338-350.

7. Deutsch-italienisches Kaufrecht und Schweigen auf ein kaufmännisches Bestätigungsschreiben nach italienischem Recht: IPG 1976 (1977) Nr. 16, S. 176-192.

8. Liechtensteinisches Schuld- und Gesellschaftsrecht, insbes. Kauf eines Firmenmantels einer liechtensteinischen Anstalt: IPG 1976 (1977) Nr. 20, S. 246-258.

9. Internationales und niederländisches Erbrecht: IPG 1977 (1979) Nr. 36, S. 343-355.

10. Internationales Vertrags- und Deliktsrecht sowie türkisches Schadensersatzrecht: IPG 1979 (1981) Nr. 7, S. 83-97.

11. Türkisches Schuld- und Familienrecht: IPG 1979 (1981) Nr. 16, S. 162-165.

12. Internationales und schweizerisches Ehegüterrecht: IPG 1979 (1981) Nr. 20, S. 207-210.

13. Anerkennung und Vollstreckung eines schweizerischen Urteils in Deutschland: IPG 1980/81 (1983) Nr. 48, S. 409-414.

14. Lösungsrecht des Art. 934 11 schweiz. ZGB und IPR: IPG 1982 (1984) Nr. 15, S. 157-169.

15. Türkisches Verlöbnisrecht: IPG 1982 (1984) Nr. 17, S. 181-183.

16. Minderjährigenschutz im Verhältnis zur Türkei: IPG 1982 (1984) Nr. 24, S. 244-249.

VI. Entscheidungsanmerkungen/ Case notes

1. Jayme/ Siehr zu AG Hamburg 24.12.1969, StAZ 1970, 129: StAZ 1970, 345f.

2. AG Göttingen 27.10.1970: StAZ 1971, 169f. = Leitfaden für die Standesbeamten 1971, 56-58.

3. Jayme/ Siehr zu OLG Düsseldorf 21.4.1971, FamRZ 1971, 459: FamRZ 1971, 461-463.

4. OLG Düsseldorf 17.5.1971, FamRZ 1971, 463: FamRZ 1971, 464.

5. Kropholler/ Siehr zu OLG München 23.7.1971, FamRZ 1971, 542: FamRZ 1971, 543.

6. LG Mannheim 10.8.1972, FamRZ 1972, 590: FamRZ 1972, 592.

7. AG Duisburg 9.6.1972, StAZ 1972, 351: StAZ 1972, 352-354.

8. OLG Frankfurt/ Main 2.5.1973, FamRZ 1973, 468: FamRZ 1973, 470-472.

9. AG Iserlohn 17.12.1973, FamRZ 1974, 141: FamRZ 1974, 142.

10. OLG ZweibrUcken 27.9.1973, FamRZ 1974, 153: FamRZ 1974, 155.

11. Österr. OGH 17.5.1973, ZfRV 15 (1974) 132: ZfRV 15 (1974) 136-138.

VII. Rezensionen/ Book reviews

1. Gaspar Brown, British Statutes in American Law 1776-1836: RabelsZ 32 (1968) 563-565.

2. Scoles/ Weintraub, Cases and Materials on Conflict of Laws: RabelsZ 33 (1969) 165f.

3. Ehrenzweig, Conflicts in a Nutshell: RabelsZ 33 (1969) 166f.

4. van Hecke, American-Belgian Private International Law: RabelsZ 34 (1970) 372f.

5. Ideologie und Recht: RabelsZ 34 (1970) 386-388.

6. Studien und Materialien zur Rechtssoziologie: RabelsZ 35 (1971) 160f.

904

7. Law and Judicial Systems of Nations: RabelsZ 35 (1971) 165-167.

8. Hotz, Die Rechtswahl im Erbrecht: RabelsZ 35 (1971) 173-175.

9. Paras, Philippine Conflict of Laws: RabelsZ 35 (1971) 176f.

10. Rehbinder, Manfred, Entwicklung und gegenwärtiger Stand der Rechtstatsachenforschung in den USA: RabelsZ 35 (1971) 334.

11. Krause, Illegitimacy – Law and Social Policy: FamRZ 1972, 54f.

12. König, Konsumentenkredit: RabelsZ 35 (1971) 592f.

13. Jayme/ Luther, Das italienische Scheidungsgesetz: RabelsZ 35 (1971) 767f.

14. Jayme, Das nichteheliche Kind im deutsch-italienischen Rechtsverkehr: StAZ 1972, 180.

15. Picone, Norme di diritto internazionale privato e norme materiali del foro: RabelsZ 36 (1972) 209-212.

16. Reithmann, Internationales Vertragsrecht (2. Aufl.): BB 1972, 1147.

17. Grunsky/ Wuppermann, Italienisches Familienrecht: JZ 1972, 669f.

18. Hoyer, Die Anerkennung ausländischer Eheentscheidungen in Österreich: ZZP 86 (1973) 84-87.

19. Röder, Die Anwendung US-amerikanischen internationalen Kindschaftsrechts in Statusfragen durch deutsche Gerichte: FamRZ 1973, 168.

20. Jochem, Das Erbrecht des nichtehelichen Kindes nach deutschem Recht bei Sachverhalten mit Auslandsberührung: FamRZ 1973, 218f.

21. Juristische Beiträge, hrsg. von der Deutsch-Italienischen Vereinigung e.V.: RabelsZ 37 (1973) 167f.

22. Vigoriti, Garanzie costituzionali del processo civile – Due process of law e art. 24 Cost.: RabelsZ 3 7 (19 73) 168-171.

23. Lutter, Das Erbrecht des nichtehelichen Kindes (2. Aufl.): RabelsZ 37 (1973) 193-196.

24. Faraco de Azevedo, Recherches sur la justification de l'application du droit étranger chez les Anglo-américains et leurs antécédents hollandais: RabelsZ 37 (1973) 817f.

25. Finlay/ Bissett-Johnson, Family Law in Australia: FamRZ 1974, 230f.

26. Schulze, Das öffentliche Recht im IPR: FamRZ 1974, 232.

27. Turner, Improving the Lot of Children Born Outside Marriage: FamRZ 1974, 496.

28. Les conflits de lois en matière de filiation en droit international privé français, allemand et suisse: RabelsZ 38 (1974) 777-780.

29. Giger, Systematische Darstellung des Abzahlungsrechts: RabelsZ 38 (1974) 794-796.

30. Ferid, IPR; Firsching, Einführung in das IPR: JA 1975, 66f.

31. Bruppacher, Die aktienrechtlichen Bewertungsvorschriften: AG 1975, 56.

32. Bernet, Rechtsdokumentation: RabelsZ 39 (1975) 191f.

33. Mach, L'entreprise et les groupes de sociétés en droit européen de la concurrence: AG 1975, 112.

34. Colloque international sur le droit international privé des groupes de sociétés: AG 1975, 112.

35. Clive/ Wilson, The Law of Husband and Wife in Scotland: FamRZ 1976, 126.

36. Goldstein/ Solnit/ Freud, Jenseits des Kindeswohls: StAZ 1976, 59f.

37. Ballarino, Costituzione e diritto internazionale privato: Rev. crit. 65 (1976) 235-238.

38. Recht in Japan: FamRZ 1976, 478.

39. Harland, The Law of Minors in Relation to Contracts and Property: FamRZ 1976, 724.

40. Poulter, Family Law and Litigation in Basotho Society: FamRZ 1976, 724.

41. Spaude, Das dänische Rechtswesen: FamRZ 1977, 216.

42. Kellerhals, Die Durchsetzung von Unterhaltsansprüchen in den USA unter besonderer Berücksichtigung des Verhältnisses zwischen der Schweiz und den Vereinigten Staaten von Amerika: ZvglRW 76 (1977) 97-101.

43. Madlener, Das französische Unehelichenrecht: ZvglRW 76 (1977) 122.

44. De Nova, Giorgio, Il tipo contrattuale: RabelsZ 41 (1977) 414f. (zusammen mit G. Procaccia/ Tel Aviv).

45. Majoros, Le droit international privé: RabelsZ 41 (1977) 425f.

46. Festschrift für Walter Wilburg zum 70. Geburtstag (1975): ZblJugR 1977, 313f.

47. Stanzione, Capacità e minore età nella problematica della persona umana: FamRZ 1977, 567f.

48. Opoku, The Law of Marriage in Ghana: FamRZ 1977, 568.

49. Kohler, Das Vaterschaftsanerkenntnis im Islamrecht und seine Bedeutung für das deutsche IPR: NJW 1977, 1578.

50. Raape/ Sturm, IPR, 6. Aufl., Bd. 1 (1977): ZblJugR 1977, 451-452.

51. Le régime matrimonial légal dans les législations contemporaines, 2. Aufl. 1974, hrsg. von Patarin/ Zajtay: RabelsZ 41 (1977) 623-628.

52. Brühl/ Göppinger/ Mutschler, Unterhaltsrecht (3. Aufl. 1973 und 1976): RabelsZ 41 (1977) 628-631.

53. Schweizerisches Zivilgesetzbuch (Berner Kommentar) Bd. 11/2, Sonderband: Die Adoption. Erläutert von Hegnauer (1975): RabelsZ 41 (1977) 631-633.

54. Niedermann, Die ordre public-Klauseln in den Vollstreckungsverträgen des Bundes und den kantonalen Zivilprozeßgesetzen: StAZ 1977, 354.

906

55. Friedmann, Daniel, The Effect of Foreign Law on the Law of Israel: ZvgRW 76 (1977) 202-204.

56. Reichard/ Kühnel/ Wittig/ Grebner, Eigentumsvorbehalt und Sicherungsübertragung im Ausland: AcP 177 (1977) 565-568.

57. Familienrecht im Wandel, Festschrift für Hans Hinderling: RabelsZ 41 (1977) 777-780.

58. Giger, Das Schicksal des Rechts beim Subjektwechsel unter besonderer Berücksichtigung der Erbfolgekonzeption, Bd. I und II: RabelsZ 41 (1977) 783f.

59. Tel Aviv University Studies in Law, Bd. I und II: RabelsZ 41 (1977) 788-790.

60. United States Legislation on Foreign Relations and International Commerce, hrsg. von Kavass/ Blake: RabelsZ 41 (1977) 804.

61. Lewis, Using Law Books: RabelsZ 41 (1977) 805.

62. Neuhaus, Die Grundbegriffe des IPR, 2. Aufl.: BB 1978, 564 = RIW/ AWD 1978, 420.

63. Tommasi di Vignano, La permeabilità intersistematica tra ordinamenti di stati diversi: RabelsZ 42 (1978) 377-379.

64. Wuppermann, Die deutsche Rechtsprechung zum Vorbehalt des ordre public im IPR seit 1945 vornehmlich auf dem Gebiet des Familienrechts: StAZ 1978, 226.

65. Lorenz, Egon, Zur Struktur des IPR: ZvglRW 77 (1978) 234-236.

66. IPR und Rechtsvergleichung im Ausgang des 20. Jahrhunderts. Festschrift für Gerhard Kegel: StAZ 1978, 306.

67. Hegnauer, Grundriß des Kindesrechts: RabelsZ 42 (1978) 583-584.

68. Mélanges Deschenaux: RabelsZ 42 (1978) 584-586.

69. SoÑniak, Précis de droit international privé polonais: RabelsZ 42 (1978) 588-589.

70. Ehrenzweig/ Jayme, Private International Law, Bde II und III: RabelsZ 42 (1978) 760-766.

71. Merz, Ausgewählte Abhandlungen zum Privat- und Kartellrecht: RabelsZ 42 (1978) 771f.

72. Nobel, Entscheide zu den Einleitungsartikeln, Einführung zu Art. 1-10 ZGB: RabelsZ 42 (1978) 772f.

73. Reitz, Spannungen bei der Anwendung portugiesischen Adoptionsrechts durch deutsche Gerichte: StAZ 1979, 78.

74. Wienke, Zur Anknüpfung der Vorfrage bei international-privatrechtlichen Staatsverträgen: StAZ 1979, 79.

75. De Nova, Scritti di diritto internazionale privato: Am.J.Comp.L. 27 (1979) 124-126.

76. Richter, Die Rechtsspaltung im malaysischen Familienrecht, zugleich ein Beitrag zur "gestuften" Unteranknüpfung im internationalen Privatrecht: StAZ 1979, 156f.

77. Volken, Konventionskonflikte im IPR: RabelsZ 43 (1979) 397-400.

78. Ansay/ Wallace, Introduction to Turkish Law, 2. Aufl.: RabelsZ 43 (1979) 598-599.

79. Soyke/ Weser, Bibliographie des deutschen Schrifttums zum internationalen und ausländischen Privatrecht 1945-1970: RabelsZ 43 (1979) 778f.

80. Wähler, Interreligiöses Kollisionsrecht im Bereich privatrechtlicher Rechtsbeziehungen: FamRZ 1980, 524.

81. Beiträge zum deutschen und israelischen Privatrecht -Deutsch- israelisches Juristensymposion Köln 1975:ZVglRWiss 79 (1980) 149-151.

82. Graulich, Introduction à l'étude du droit international privé: RabelsZ 44 (1980) 591**f.**

83. Villiger, Der Auslandschweizer und die schweizerische internationale Zuständigkeit im Personen-, Familien- und Erbrecht: RabelsZ 44 (1980) 599f.

84. Bauermann, Das italienische Adoptionsrecht nach Einführung der Volladoption (adozione speciale): StAZ 1980, 340.

85. Herzfelder, Problèmes relatifs au régime matrimonial en droit international privé français et allemand: FamRZ 1981, 616f.

86. Fadlallah, La famille légitime en droit international privé: FamRZ 1981, 617.

87. Merryman/ Elsen, Law, Ethics and the Visual Arts – Cases and Materials: RabelsZ 46 (1982) 222-224

88. Ottrubay, Die Eintragung des Eigentumsvorbehalts unter Berücksichtigung des internationalen Rechts und der internationalen Harmonisierungsbestrebungen: RabelsZ 46 (1982) 230f.

89. Wohlgemuth, Veränderungen im Bestand des Geltungsgebietes des Vertragsstatuts: RabelsZ 46 (1982) 246-248.

90. Schurig, Kollisionsrecht und Sachrecht. Zu Struktur, Standort und Methode des IPR: RabelsZ 46 (1982) 612-618.

91. Habscheid, Droit judiciaire privé suisse (2. Aufl. 1981): FamRZ 1983, 107f.

92. Hegnauer, Grundriß des Eherechts: RabelsZ 47 (1983) 424f.

93. Vitta & Grementieri, Codice degli atti internazionali sui diritti dell'uomo: Am.J.Comp.L. 31 (1983) 571.

94. Kennedy, The Unmasking of Medicine: RabelsZ 47 (1983) 207f.

95. Mühl, Die Lehre vom "besseren" und "günstigeren" Recht im IPR: RabelsZ 48 (1984) 412-415.

96. Mitzkus, Internationale Zuständigkeit im Vormundschafts-, Pflegschafts- und Sorgerecht: StAZ 1984, 224f.

908

97. Reichelt, Gesamtstatut und Einzelstatut im IPR: StAZ 1986, 182f.

98. Pocar, La convenzione di Bruxelles sulla giurisdizione e l'esecuzione delle sentenze: RabelsZ 50 (1986) 746f.

99. Bucher, Personnes physiques et protection de la personnalité: RabelsZ 51 (1987) 245.

100. Tuor/ Schnyder, Das Schweizerische Zivilgesetzbuch (10. Aufl. 1986): StAZ 1987, 363f.

101. Schweizerisches Zivilgesetzbuch, Textausgabe hrsg. von Schönenberger (36. Aufl. 1986) : StAZ 1987, 364.

102. Anhäusser, Das internationale Obligationenrecht in der höchstrichterlichen Rechtsprechung des 19. Jahrhunderts: ZNR 10 (1988) 96-99.

103. Vom alten zum neuen Eherecht, hrsg. von Hausheer; Hegnauer, Grundriss des Eherechts; M. Näf-Hofmann/ H. Näf-Hofmann, Das neue Ehe- und Erbrecht im Zivilgesetzbuch; Neue Partnerschaft in der Ehe, hrsg. von Schoch: StAZ 1988, 279f.

104. Eichendorfer, Internationales Sozialrecht und internationales Privatrecht: Int.J.Legal Information 16 (1988) 241f.

105. Merz/ Frank/ Librando/ Luzzatto/ Bundschuh, Konkursrecht, Persönlichkeitsschutz, Kapitalverkehr (Jahrbuch für Italienisches Recht, Bd. 1): JZ 1989, 185f.

106. Bianca/ Bonell (eds.), Commentary on the International Sales Law. The 1980 Vienna Sales Convention: JZ 1989, 435f.

107. Völkerrecht, Recht der Internationalen Organisationen, Weltwirtschaftsrecht. Festschrift für Ignaz Seidl-Hohenveldern, hrsg. von Karl-Heinz Böckstiegel u.a., Köln 1988: Int.J.Legal Information 17 (1989) 192f.

108. Czerwenka, Rechtsanwendungsprobleme im internationalen Kaufrecht. Das Kollisionsrecht bei grenzüberschreitenden Kaufverträgen und der Anwendungsbereich der internationalen Kaufrechtsübereinkommen: Int.J.Legal Information 18 (1990) 92f.

109. Wengler, Völkerrechtliche Schranken der Beeinflussung auslandsverknüpften Verhaltens durch Massnahmen des staatlichen Rechts: RabelsZ 54 (1990) 611-614.

110. Henrich, Internationales Familienrecht: JZ 1990, 1018.

111. Deutsche Rechtswissenschaft und Staatslehre im Spiegel der italienischen Rechtskultur während der zweiten Hälfte des 19. Jahrhunderts. Hrsg. von Reiner Schulze: RabelsZ 54 (1990) 759f.

112. Europarecht, Internationales Privatrecht, Rechtsvergleichung. Hrsg. von Fritz Schwind: RabelsZ 54 (1990) 795-798.

113. In memoriam Eduard Wahl. Gedächtnisfeier der Juristischen Fakultät der Universität Heidelberg: RabelsZ 55 (1991) 168.

114. Jayme/ Mansel (Hrsg.), Nation und Staat im Internationalen Privatrecht. Zum kollisionsrechtlichen Staatsangehörigkeitsprinzip in verfassungsrechtlicher und international-privatrechtlicher Sicht: Int.J.Legal Information 18 (1990) 240-242.

115. Pfennig, Die internationale Zustellung in Zivil- und Handelssachen: Int.J.Legal Information 18 (1990) 263.

116. Knott, Der Anspruch auf Herausgabe gestohlenen und illegal exportierten Kulturguts: Int.J.Legal Information 19 (1991) 52f. und NJW 1992, 610f.

117. In memoriam, Max Gutzwiller, Gedächtnisfeier der Juristischen Fakultat Heidelberg am 3. November 1989: RabelsZ 55 (1991) 364f.

118. Madl/ Vékás, The Law of Conflicts and Foreign Trade: RabelsZ 55 (1991) 394f.

119. Spickhoff, Der ordre public im IPR: RabelsZ 56 (1992) 335-339.

120. Platto (ed.), Enforcement of Foreign Judgments Worldwide: RabelsZ 56 (1992) 359f.

121. Blutke, Obskure Geschäfte mit Kunst und Antiquitäten. Ein Kriminalreport: Internat. J. Cultural Property 1 (1992) 429f.

122. Ghandchi, Der Geltungsbereich des Art. 159 IPRG. Haftung für ausländische Gesellschaften: SJZ 1992, 302.

123. Kleeberg/ Eberl, Kulturgülter in Privatbesitz: Internat. J. Cultural Property 2 (1993) 185.

124. Fechner, Rechtlicher Schutz archäologischen Kulturguts: Internat. J. Cultural Property 2 (1993) 410f.

125. Rummel (Hrsg.),Kommentar zum Allgemeinen Bürgerlichen Gesetzbuch, 2. Aufl. ; Schwimann (Hrsg.), Praxiskommentar zum Allgemeinen Bürgerlichen Gesetzbuch: RabelsZ 58 (1994) 752-756.

126. Rinkes/ Samuel, Contractual and non-contractual obligations in English law: ZEuP 3 (1995) 160f.

127. Goepfert, Haftungsprobleme im Kunst- und Auktionshandel: Internat.J. Cultural Property 4 (1995) 187f.

128. Uhl, Der Handel mit Kunstwerken im europäischen Binnenmarkt: NJW 1995, 853.

129. Schmeinck, Internationalprivatrechtliche Aspekte des Kulturgüterschutzes: NJW 1995, 853.

130. Nouveaux itinéraires en droit. Hommage à François Rigaux: ZEuP 3 (1995) 323-325.

131. International Council on Archives (ed.), Archival Legislation 1981-1994, Bde XL und XLI: Internat. J. Cultural Property 6 (1997) 169f.

132. Freier/ Grunert/ Freitag, Reise durch Ägypten; Thomas ScottIII/ Trigger, American Discovery of Ancient Egypt: Internat. J. Cultural Property 6 (1997) 421-423.

133. Benicke, Typenmehrheit im Adoptionsrecht und deutsches IPR: FamRZ 1999, 19.

134. Bleckmann, Die völkerrechtlichen Grundlagen des internationalen Kollisionsrechts: Archiv des Völkerrechts 36 (1998) 481-483.

135. Rabello (ed.), Essays on European Law and Israel: Netherlands International Law Review 46 (1999) 122-125.

136. Funke, Trennung und Scheidung im italienischen Recht – vermögensrechtliche Folgen: Fam RZ 1999, 1643f.